Bialystok
Narew
Bezirk Bialystok
Słonim
Baranowicze
REICH COMMISSARIAT
OSTLAND
Biala
Podlaska
Biała-
Podlaska
Brest
Pińsk
Pripyat Marshes
Parczew
Sobibor
Pripyat
Cholm
Trawniki
Chełm
Kowel
REICH COMMISSARIAT
UKRAINE
Styr
Włodzimierz
Hrubieszow
Sluch
Zamość
Zamosc
Łuck
Równe
Belzec
Dubno
Kamionka-
Strumilowa
Rawa-Ruska
Żółkiew
Bug
Brody
Izyaslav
Horyn
Jaworów
Lwów
Zloczow
Złoczów
Lemberg-Land
GALICIA
Tarnopol
Dniester
Brzeżany
Tarnopol
Bug
Drohobycz
Chodorów
Rohatyn
Skalat
Drohobytsch
Brzezany
Borysław
Stryj
Stryj
Halicz
Czortków
Czortkow
Kalusch
Skała
Stanisławów
Kamenets-
Podilskyi
Stanislau
Horodenka
Kołomyja
Hotin
Kolomea
Dniester
Cernăuți
Prut
Siret
ROMANIA
Sighet
Rădăuți
150 km

The Persecution and Murder of the European Jews by Nazi Germany, 1933–1945

Volume 9

# Poland: General Government August 1941–1945

Executive Editor
Klaus-Peter Friedrich

English-language edition prepared by
Elizabeth Harvey, Russell Alt-Haaker, Johannes Gamm, Georg Felix Harsch, Dorothy A. Mas, and Caroline Pearce

DE GRUYTER
OLDENBOURG

יד ושם
YAD VASHEM
THE WORLD HOLOCAUST REMEMBRANCE CENTER

THE INTERNATIONAL INSTITUTE FOR HOLOCAUST RESEARCH

ISBN 978-3-11-068741-5
e-ISBN (PDF) 978-3-11-068776-7
e-ISBN (EPUB) 978-3-11-068788-0

*Library of Congress Control Number: 2023941385*

*Bibliographical information published by the Deutsche Nationalbibliothek*
The Deutsche Nationalbibliothek lists this publication in the Deutsche Nationalbibliografie; detailed bibliographical information is available at http://dnb.dnb.de.


Typesetting: Meta Systems Publishing & Printservices GmbH, Wustermark
Cover and dust jacket: Frank Ortmann
Cartography: Peter Palm
Printing and binding: Beltz Grafische Betriebe GmbH, Bad Langensalza

www.degruyter.com

# Contents

# Foreword to the English Edition

*The Persecution and Murder of the European Jews by Nazi Germany, 1933–1945* presents a broad range of primary sources in a scholarly edition. A total of sixteen English-language volumes will be published in this series, organized chronologically and according to region. The series places particular focus on the countries which had the highest Jewish populations before the outbreak of the Second World War, above all Poland and the occupied territories of the Soviet Union. The English-language edition (PMJ) reproduces all the materials in the German edition (VEJ) and has been adapted for an English-speaking readership. Apart from those originally written in English, all documents presented here have been translated from the language of the original source. The introduction to the original German version, published in 2014, has been revised, expanded, and updated for this volume to reflect recent developments in research.

This volume, the ninth in the series, covers the persecution and murder of the Jews in the General Government from August 1941 to early 1945. Two other volumes also deal with occupied Poland: volume 4 deals with the period from the German invasion on 1 September 1939 up to the attack on the Soviet Union in summer 1941, covering both the annexed territories of western and northern Poland and the General Government. Volume 10 deals with the annexed territories of Poland in the period from August 1941 to spring 1945. While some documents in Volumes 4, 9, and 10 mention Jews deported from elsewhere in Europe to the formerly Polish territories, the main focus in the three volumes is the fate of the Polish Jews.

The foreword to the first volume of the series details the criteria for the selection of the documents. These criteria can be summarized as follows. First, the sources used are written documents and, occasionally, transcribed audio recordings, dating from the period of Nazi rule between 1933 and 1945. The decision was taken not to include memoirs, reports, and judicial documents produced after 1945; however, the footnotes make extensive reference to such retrospective testimonies and historical accounts. Second, the documents shed light on the actions and reactions of people with differing backgrounds and convictions and in different places, and indicate their intentions as well as the frequently limited options available to them. The volumes include a variety of document types such as official correspondence, private letters, diary entries, legal texts, newspaper articles, and reports by foreign observers.

The documents are ordered chronologically, meaning that the perspective switches frequently in the course of the volume. For example, in a sequence from April 1943 (Docs. 231–234), the focus switches from the text of a broadcast from Moscow on the mass murder taking place in Treblinka, to a police report from Otwock noting the summary execution of eight Jewish men and six Jewish women who had fled the Warsaw ghetto, to a leaflet produced by the Jewish Combat Organization appealing to the Polish population for solidarity with the Warsaw Ghetto Uprising, to a letter from the 30-year-old music teacher Salomea Ochs to her relatives in Tel Aviv describing the murder of Jews in Tarnopol, and, anticipating her own death, calling for future vengeance.

The editors wish to thank the German Research Foundation (DFG) for its generous funding of the German- and English-language projects. The English-language volumes are produced in cooperation with the Yad Vashem International Institute for Holocaust

Research, which provides important assistance in revising the introductions to the volumes and formulating explanatory footnotes regarding Jewish history, culture, and religious practice that appear in the documents. The editors are also indebted to the large number of specialists and private individuals who have provided advice and comments on sources along with information for the annotations, including biographical details for the people featured in the documents.

Kathleen Luft and Martin Pearce translated most of the German documents for this ninth volume in the series; additional translations from German were provided by David Hill, Alissa Jones Nelson, Caroline Pearce, Sarah Pybus, Jessica Spengler, and Isabel Stainsby. The French and Dutch documents were translated by Caroline Pearce. George Szenderowicz translated the documents from Polish, and Zuzanna Kozlowska and Natan Pawłowski assisted with editing them. Isabel Stainsby translated the document from Slovak, with editing assistance from Jennifer Taylor. Yad Vashem provided translations from Yiddish (by Rebecca Wolpe) and from Hebrew (by Naftali Greenwood); Ahuva Weiss edited the Hebrew translations and also contributed to the footnotes. Further editing assistance on the translations from Hebrew was provided by the agency Academic Language Experts. Rona Johnston Gordon, Alissa Jones Nelson, Melanie Newton, Sarah Pybus, and Merle Read provided copy-editing and proofreading services. Peter Palm created and Giles Bennett advised on the map, and Frank Ortmann designed the book jacket. Antonia Franke, Lea von der Hude, Ashley Kirspel, Frederik Körber, Aslihan Özcan, and Charles Perris contributed to this volume, particularly to the production of the index, as student assistants; Leonie Käther also assisted as an intern. The following research associates and assistants contributed to the original German volume: Romina Becker, Giles Bennett, Florian Danecke, Johannes Gamm, Stefanie Haupt, Andrea Löw, Miriam Schelp, Sonja Schilcher, Remigius Stachowiak, Maria Wilke, and Barbara Wünnenberg.

Despite all the care taken, occasional inaccuracies cannot be entirely avoided in a document collection on this scale. We would be grateful for any notifications to this effect. The address of the editorial board is: 'The Persecution and Murder of the European Jews by Nazi Germany, 1933–1945', c/o Leibniz Institute for Contemporary History, Finckensteinallee 85/87, 12 205 Berlin, Germany.

Berlin/Munich/Freiburg/Frankfurt a. M./Klagenfurt/Jerusalem, December 2023

# Editorial Preface

This document collection on the persecution and murder of the European Jews should be cited using the abbreviation PMJ. This citation style is also used in the work itself where there are cross references between the individual volumes. The documents are consecutively numbered, beginning anew with each volume. 'PMJ 1/200' thus refers to document number 200 in the first volume of this series. Within the volume, the individual documents are presented as follows: title (in bold type), header, document, footnotes. Cross references in the footnotes to other PMJ volumes include references to documents in volumes not yet published in English; these documents can be consulted in their German version under the identical document number in the series *Die Verfolgung und Ermordung der europäischen Juden durch das nationalsozialistische Deutschland 1933–1945* (VEJ).

The respective document titles have been formulated by the editors of the volume and provide information on the document's date of origin, its core message, author, and recipient(s). The header underneath the title is part of the document itself. It specifies the type of source (order, letter, regulation, minutes, and so on), the author's name, the source's origin, the file reference (where applicable), remarks indicating confidential or classified status, and other special features of the document. The location of ministries or other central agencies in Berlin at the time, for instance the Reich Security Main Office or the Chancellery of the Führer, is not cited. The header also contains details about the addressee and, where applicable, the date of the receipt stamp, and it concludes with the date of origin and any information regarding its stage of processing, for instance whether it was a 'draft', 'copy', or 'carbon copy'.

The header is followed by the document text. Salutations and valedictions are included, though signatures are only indicated in the header. Instances of emphasis by the author in the original document are retained. Irrespective of the type of emphasis used in the original source (for example, underlined, spaced, bold, capitalized, or italicized), they always appear in italics in the printed version. Where necessary, additional particulars on the document are given in the footnotes. To enhance readability, words which are missing in the original due to obvious mistakes or which are required to clarify the meaning have been added in square brackets.

Abbreviations are explained in the list of abbreviations at the back of the volume. Uncommon abbreviations are spelt out in a footnote upon first mention in a given document. Where the name of an organization appears in English in the footnotes with an accompanying abbreviation, the full foreign name of the organization is given in the list of abbreviations.

Handwritten additions in typewritten originals have been adopted by the editors without further indication insofar as they are formal corrections and most probably inserted by the author. If the additions significantly alter the content – either by mitigating or radicalizing it – this is mentioned in the footnotes, and, if known, the author of the addition(s) is given.

As a rule, the documents are reproduced here in full. They are only abridged in exceptional cases where the original source was overly long, or where, in the case of the written records of meetings, Nazi policies relating to the persecution of Jews were only addressed within a single part of the proceedings. Where the document has been abridged, this is indicated by an ellipsis in square brackets; the contents of the omitted text are outlined in a footnote.

Documents are presented in chronological order according to the date they were produced. There are a few exceptions: descriptive texts written soon after the period covered, but nonetheless retrospectively, are sometimes classified according to the date of the events portrayed rather than the date of writing. The precise dating of documents in the present volume is particularly difficult in the case of the reports collected for the underground archive of the Warsaw ghetto. Where there is any uncertainty regarding the date the documents were written or whether they constitute originals or copies, this is indicated in the footnotes. In the present volume, the sequence of documents in VEJ had to be amended in one instance (transposing Docs. 260 and 261) in order to match more exactly the chronological order in which the two documents were written.

The first footnote for each document, which is linked to the title, contains the location of the source and, insofar as it denotes an archive, the archival reference number, as well as the folio number(s) if available. Reference to copies of archival documents in research institutions and in the German Federal Archives is always made if the original held at the location first mentioned was not consulted there. In the case of printed sources, for instance newspaper articles or legislative texts, this footnote contains standard bibliographical information. The documents in this series have been translated from the original sources. If the source has already been published elsewhere, reference is made to its first publication, alongside the original location of the source. Where a published English-language version of a source or citation is available, reference to this is given. In this volume, all documents previously published in English translation have been newly translated.

The next footnote places the document into context and, where appropriate, mentions related discussions, the specific role of authors and recipients, and activities accompanying or immediately following its genesis. Subsequent footnotes provide additional information related to the document's subject matter and the persons relevant to the content. They refer to other – published or unpublished – sources that can place the document in its historical context.

The footnotes also point out individual features of the documents, for instance handwritten notes in the margin, underlining, or deletions, whether by the author or the recipient(s). Annotations and instructions for submission are referred to in the footnotes where the editors consider them to contain significant information. Where possible, the locations of treaties, laws, and decrees cited in the source text are provided in the footnotes, while other documents are given with their archival reference number. If these details could not be ascertained, this is also stated.

Where biographical information is available on the senders and recipients of the documents, this is provided in the footnotes. The same applies to persons mentioned in the text if they play an active role in the events described. As a general rule, this information is given in the footnote inserted after the first mention of the name in question in the volume. Biographical information on a particular person can thus be retrieved easily via the index.

The short biographies draw on data found in reference works, scholarly literature, or the Central Database of Shoah Victims' Names established and run by Yad Vashem. In many cases, additional information was retrieved by consulting personnel files and registries, municipal and company archives, registry offices, restitution and denazification files, or specialists in the field. Registries and files on persons from the Nazi era held in archives were also used, primarily those of the former Berlin Document Center and the Central Office of the Judicial Authorities of the Federal States for the Investigation of National Socialist Crimes (Zentrale Stelle der Landesjustizverwaltungen zur Aufklärung nationalsozialistischer Verbrechen) in Ludwigsburg, the latter now stored in the German Federal Archives. National archives and special archives on the Second World War and the persecution of the Jews in the respective countries were also consulted. Despite every effort, it has not always been possible to obtain complete biographical information. In such cases, the footnote in question contains only verified facts such as the year of birth. Where a person could not be identified, there is no footnote reference.

As a rule, in the titles, footnotes, and Introduction inverted commas are not placed around terms that were commonplace in Nazi Germany, such as Führer, Jewish Council, or Aryanization, but German-language terms expressing ideological concepts of race, such as *Mischling*, are placed in italics. The terms 'Jew' and 'Jewish' also require some comment. The personal identification of victims as Jews was not the defining factor in someone's persecution. Rather, the terms 'Jew' and 'Jewish' which were used as the basis for persecution were defined by the perpetrators on the basis of racial legislation.

The glossary contains concise descriptions of key terms and concepts that are repeated on multiple occasions. All primary and secondary sources consulted are listed in the footnotes and bibliography.

*Note on the translation*

British English is used in all translations into English. Where a document was originally written in British or American English, the spelling, style, and punctuation of the original have been retained, with silent corrections of minor spelling or grammatical errors and insertions in square brackets to clarify the meaning if necessary.

The spelling, style, and punctuation of the translated documents broadly conform to the guidelines in *New Hart's Rules: The Oxford Style Guide* (2014). Accordingly, the ending -ize rather than -ise is preferred throughout.

SS ranks are given in the original German, as are titles where there is no standard equivalent in English or where there may be confusion with contemporary usage. Police ranks are given in German in most cases, and they indicate the hierarchical difference between members of the police; however, 'police officer', usually with an affiliation to a specific branch of the police (e.g. 'Urban Police officer' and 'gendarmerie officer') has also been used to refer to members of the police without specifying their rank. Wehrmacht ranks are translated into English. Tables showing ranks in the NSDAP, civil service, SS, police, and the Wehrmacht are included as an appendix in order to give an indication of their position in the respective hierarchy. Administrative ranks and other terms have been left in the original language where there is no satisfactory equivalent in English. These terms are either explained in a footnote or, if they appear on multiple occasions, in the glossary.

All laws and institutions are translated into English in the documents. In the Introduction and footnotes, foreign-language terms and expressions are added in brackets after the translation where this is considered important for understanding or context.

The titles of published works not in the English language are not translated unless the title in question is of contextual or substantial relevance, in which case it is given in square brackets.

Where the documents translated from Polish from a specifically Christian perspective contain quotations from the Bible, the New King James Version (NKJV) has been preferred, especially where the context is religious or ecclesiastical. For Bible quotations in documents written specifically from a Jewish perspective, the 1917 Jewish Publication Society (JPS) translation of the *Tanakh* (Hebrew Bible) has been used.

In order to avoid confusion between British and American English, dates are spelt out in the order day, month, and year. Foreign proper names are not italicized. Thus, names of institutions, organizations, and places are written in roman type in the footnotes, but conceptual terms are in italics.

In the titles, footnotes, and translated documents, place names are generally written according to the variant commonly used in scholarly literature on the period. The modern English version of a place name is given where this is widely used, for example Warsaw, Cracow, or Vilna. In other cases, place names in the translated documents are given in either their Polish or their German form according to usage in the original source and the perspective of the writer. Both variants are included in the index. In editorial text and in sources written from a Jewish or Polish perspective, the Polish place names are used in the titles, headers, document text, and footnotes. In the case of Polish cities that were renamed following post-1945 border changes, the Polish place names that applied up to 1945 are used, also in the footnotes (for instance Lwów, Tarnopol). Cities that were German up to 1945 but were then renamed following the border change appear in German, also in the footnotes (for instance Breslau, Königsberg). In the translations of German official documents, newspapers, and letters, German place names are used throughout the document. In the titles of German documents that include a place name, the Polish place name is also given in brackets. In the footnotes to documents translated from German, the Polish place names are used in cases of general references to a town or city, but the German place names are used if they are part of a German title or function. In the case of Belarus/Byelorussia, the older English form Byelorussia has been used rather than that in current usage. In rendering street names in Polish, 'street' is used if the Polish street name included 'ulica'.

On the map at the front of the volume ('General Government, late 1941'), German place names are used for towns, cities, and rivers in the Polish territories that had been annexed to the Reich, and for Bezirk Bialystok. Within the General Government, Polish place names are used for towns, cities, and rivers, but the names of the Kreise are given in their German or Germanized form. For places in the territories that had been part of the Soviet Union, the map uses transliterated Ukrainian or Russian names. For the parts of Poland that were under Soviet occupation from 1939 to 1941, the Polish names are retained.

Diacritical marks in Polish are as a rule retained. However, they are not added if they do not appear in an originally German source. Nor are diacritics included in the names of concentration and extermination camps, where diacritics have been removed in order to emphasize that these camps were established by the German National Socialist regime, hence for instance Sobibor. However, diacritic marks have been retained for place names where camps existed, if the place rather than the camp is meant (e.g. Bełżec). The ghetto in Łódź is referred to as the Lodz ghetto or the Litzmannstadt (Lodz) ghetto. The forms

Lodz and Lodsch are retained where they occur in German documents as Germanized forms of Łódź (renamed Litzmannstadt in 1940). For Chelmno/Kulmhof, the German name is used.

Language-specific characters such as the German ß (*Eszett*) for ss have also been retained.

The YIVO conventions for romanizing words and names written in Yiddish with Hebrew characters are used in this volume. In some cases, the romanized form of a person's name in a text translated from Yiddish may differ in spelling from the same person's name appearing in a text translated from Polish, for example. This is due to the fact that a Jewish person's given name was Polonized one way during the period and region in question, while having been pronounced another way among Yiddish speakers, e.g. Izaak or Icchak vs Yitskhok. In other instances, English-language equivalents of the names in question have also established themselves. Whenever possible, the different spellings and variations are provided in the footnote containing the individual's biographical information. Hebrew and Yiddish terms and relevant cultural and historical references are described in the footnotes or glossary.

A number of specific terminological issues can be noted in relation to this volume. The first relates to administrative divisions imposed by the German occupiers in the General Government. The main administrative subdivisions were the four (from summer 1941: five) districts, below which were the Kreise. Each Kreis in the General Government was headed by a Kreishauptmann (plural: Kreishauptmänner or Kreishauptleute), or, in some larger cities, a Stadthauptmann. At the level below the Kreis in the General Government, Landkommissare and Stadtkommissare were appointed to assist in enacting the orders of the Kreishauptleute. While the German term *Distrikt* has been translated as district (District Radom etc.), the other terms have been left in German to avoid confusion. Polish terms relating to the structures of authority operating under German rule at village or local level in the General Government have generally been left untranslated, as in the case of *wójt* (Polish local administrative official). *Gmina*, meaning a local authority, has been translated as community. The term *powiat*, referring to regions or districts of Poland as they applied up to 1939, is left untranslated in documents translated from Polish. The term is also used in footnotes referring to places in Poland today.

The use of terminology in relation to departments within the civil administration in the General Government (GG) may also be noted. At the level of the government of the GG in Cracow, responsibilities for different policy areas were assigned to Main Departments (Hauptabteilungen). The Hauptabteilungen at the level of the government of the GG had equivalent departments at the level of the districts. In the translated documents, the departments at the level of the GG are as a rule referred to as Main Departments in order to emphasize the distinction between them and district-level departments.

Further specific points about terminology and language use in this volume may also be mentioned. The spelling 'Operation Reinhard' has been used in the Introduction, document titles, and footnotes, following common practice in the English-language literature on the subject. However, where the spelling 'Reinhardt' occurs in the original German document, it is retained in the translation. For the workshops in the Warsaw ghetto where Jews worked as forced labourers, the word *szop* (plural: *szopy*) has been used. With regard to the Wehrmacht's armaments inspectorate, which in German distinguishes between the Rüstungsinspektion (which covered a larger region) and a

Rüstungskommando (at a level below the Rüstungsinspektion, covering a smaller region), the terms used in the translation are GG armaments inspectorate (or armaments inspectorate for the GG) for the Rüstungsinspektion responsible for the General Government as a whole, and 'Warsaw armaments inspectorate', 'Lemberg armaments inspectorate', etc. for Rüstungskommandos at the level of the districts.

A further key issue is the challenge for translation posed by the euphemistic German terms associated with the systematic mass murder of the Jews. In Nazi-occupied Poland between 1939 and 1941, the terms *umsiedeln/Umsiedlung* and *aussiedeln/Aussiedlung* were used to refer to a wide range of diverse operations to evict, displace, and transfer population groups within and to occupied Poland: these included expulsions of Poles from their homes in the annexed territories to the General Government, and the transfer of ethnic Germans from the Baltic states, Soviet-occupied eastern Poland, and Romania to the 'Greater German Reich', including the annexed territories of Poland. These developments are documented in PMJ 4, *Poland: September 1939 – July 1941*. The present volume documents developments from summer 1941 onwards and the onset of systematic mass murder. At this point German officials increasingly used 'resettlement' terminology to refer to the mass murder of Jews, whether they were being removed to killing sites in the immediate vicinity or deported to extermination camps. These euphemistic terms are retained in the translated documents in order to reflect the perpetrators' practice of camouflaging murder, but readers should be alert to their actual meaning. In document titles and footnotes, depending on the events described, the terms forced resettlement, expulsion, or deportation are used.

# Introduction

In August 1941 there were many indications that Nazi Germany would win the war against the Soviet Union and subsequently establish lasting hegemony in Europe. For the Jews in occupied Poland, this was a catastrophic prospect. Many of them had already been living in wretched conditions for some time, confined in one of the countless ghettos established by the German occupiers, but very few suspected that their total extermination – the murder of virtually each and every one of them – was imminent.

At the onset of the systematic murder of the European Jews, the General Government in occupied central and southern Poland was the German-controlled territory with the largest Jewish minority population – more than two million people – and with the densest network of Jewish communities in Europe.

The present volume documents the persecution and murder of the Jews in this territory during the period from 1 August 1941, when Germany incorporated Eastern Galicia – which had been under Soviet occupation since 17 September 1939 – into the General Government, until the beginning of 1945, when the Red Army captured most of the region and liberated the survivors. Almost two million Jews were murdered in the General Government during this period, most of them in the Operation Reinhard (also: Operation Reinhardt) extermination camps (Belzec, Sobibor, and Treblinka), where the victims were asphyxiated with motor-exhaust fumes in stationary facilities specially built for the purpose of mass murder. In addition, tens of thousands of Jews perished in many other camps, including Lublin-Majdanek concentration camp; in the ghettos; or at other sites.[1]

This volume exclusively addresses the developments in the General Government. The persecution of the Jews in the Polish territories annexed by the German Reich (Reichsgau Danzig-West Prussia and Reichsgau Wartheland, the Regierungsbezirke Zichenau and Kattowitz, together with Bezirk Bialystok) during the same period, between summer 1941 and 1945, will be dealt with in volume 10 of the series. Events in both regions during the first two years of the war and occupation are recorded in volume 4.

1 See Artur Eisenbach, *Hitlerowska polityka zagłady Żydów* (Warsaw: Książa i Wiedza, 1961); Tatiana Berenstein et al. (eds.), *Faschismus – Getto – Massenmord: Dokumentation über Ausrottung und Widerstand der Juden in Polen während des 2. Weltkrieges* (Berlin: Rütten & Loening, 1961); Manfred Blank, 'Zum Beispiel: Die Ermordung der Juden im "Generalgouvernement" Polen', in Adalbert Rückerl (ed.), *NS-Prozesse: Nach 25 Jahren Strafverfolgung. Möglichkeiten – Grenzen – Ergebnisse* (Karlsruhe: C. F. Müller, 1971), pp. 35–64; Frank Golczewski, 'Polen', in Wolfgang Benz (ed.), *Dimension des Völkermords: Die Zahl der jüdischen Opfer des Nationalsozialismus* (Munich: Oldenbourg, 1991), pp. 411–497; Christopher R. Browning, 'Mehr als Warschau und Lodz: Der Holocaust in Polen', in *Der Weg zur 'Endlösung': Entscheidungen und Täter* (Bonn: Dietz, 1998), pp. 127–148; Dieter Pohl, 'The Killing of the Jews in the General Government', in Ulrich Herbert (ed.), *National Socialist Extermination Policies: Contemporary German Perspectives and Controversies* (Oxford and New York: Berghahn, 2000), pp. 83–103; Dieter Pohl, 'Die "Aktion Reinhard" im Licht der Historiographie', in Bogdan Musiał (ed.), *Die 'Aktion Reinhardt': Der Völkermord an den Juden im Generalgouvernement 1941–1944* (Osnabrück: fibre, 2004), pp. 15–47; Dariusz Libionka, *Die Ermordung der Juden im Generalgouvernement*, trans. Steffen Hänschen (Berlin: Metropol, 2021 [Polish edn, 2017]).

The crimes committed against the Jews of Eastern Galicia in June/July 1941, during the first few weeks of the war against the Soviet Union and before the incorporation of Eastern Galicia into the General Government, are documented in volume 7.

## Jews in the General Government in autumn 1941[2]

In 1941 most Polish Jews were living in the General Government, the administrative region that the German occupiers had created in central and southern Poland in October 1939. They termed it a *Nebenland*, a sort of colonial borderland of the Reich.[3] By contrast, Eastern Galicia and all of eastern Poland had been occupied by Soviet troops in 1939. After the German attack on the Soviet Union in summer 1941, this territory was seized by the Germans, and Eastern Galicia became part of the General Government, which now consisted of five districts: Cracow, Lublin, Radom, Warsaw, and Galicia. It was headed by Governor General Hans Frank; Frank's state secretary was Josef Bühler, who represented the General Government at the Wannsee Conference in January 1942. Frank reported directly to Adolf Hitler, but over time the SS and police in his area of jurisdiction increasingly extended the scope of their powers and received their instructions directly from Reichsführer-SS Heinrich Himmler in Berlin, rather than from Frank in Cracow. Both the civil administration and the SS and police apparatus in the General Government were responsible for the persecution and murder of the Jews.[4]

Prior to early August 1941 the General Government (GG) had not been the scene of systematic mass murders of the sort carried out in the occupied Soviet Union following the German attack in June 1941. Nonetheless, in the less than two years since the start of the war, the German occupiers had dispossessed and largely isolated the Jewish population of the General Government, stripping the Jews of all civil rights. The ruthless measures employed by the German administration in Poland against Polish Jews – who, like other *Ostjuden* (Eastern European Jews),[5] were treated with particular disdain – were much more brutal than those taken against the Jews in German-occupied Central and

2 In what follows, the terms 'Jews' and 'Poles' are used, notwithstanding the fact that Polish Jews were also Polish citizens, and not all of them considered themselves Jews.

3 See Gerhard Eisenblätter, 'Grundlinien der Politik des Reichs gegenüber dem Generalgouvernement 1939–1945' (doctoral thesis, Johann-Wolfgang-Goethe Universität, Frankfurt am Main, 1969); Czesław Madajczyk, *Polityka III Rzeszy w okupowanej Polsce*, 2 vols. (Warsaw: Państwowe Wydawnictwo Naukowe, 1970) [also abridged German version, 1988]; Martin Winstone, *The Dark Heart of Hitler's Europe: Nazi Rule in Poland under the General Government* (London and New York: I. B. Tauris, 2015); and Libionka, *Die Ermordung der Juden im Generalgouvernement.*

4 Ingo Loose, 'Josef Bühler, State Secretary for the General Government: A Behind-the-Scenes Perpetrator', in Hans-Christian Jasch and Christoph Kreutzmüller (eds.), *The Participants: The Men of the Wannsee Conference*, trans. Charlotte Kreutzmüller-Hughes and Jane Paulick (New York and Oxford: Berghahn, 2017 [German edn, 2017]), pp. 152–170; Bogdan Musiał, *Deutsche Zivilverwaltung und Judenverfolgung im Generalgouvernement: Eine Fallstudie zum Distrikt Lublin 1939–1944* (Wiesbaden: Harrassowitz, 1999); Markus Roth, *Herrenmenschen: Die deutschen Kreishauptleute im besetzten Polen – Karrierewege, Herrschaftspraxis und Nachgeschichte* (Göttingen: Wallstein, 2009).

5 On the history of the term and the associated issues, see Trude Maurer, *Ostjuden in Deutschland 1918–1933* (Hamburg: Christians, 1986), pp. 11–17; and Dan Michman, *The Emergence of Jewish Ghettos during the Holocaust*, trans. from Hebrew Lenn J. Schramm (Cambridge: Cambridge University Press; Jerusalem: Yad Vashem, 2001), pp. 29 and 155.

Western Europe during the initial stages of occupation. While Jews in these latter parts of Europe were not confined to ghettos, the first ghetto in occupied Poland was established in October 1939, in Piotrków Trybunalski in the centre of the country, and was followed by others in a number of large towns in District Warsaw and in the Warthegau in early 1940. From spring 1941 ghettos were set up in larger numbers in the other districts of the General Government as well.[6]

The Warsaw ghetto, the largest in Nazi-occupied Europe, was established in autumn 1940. All Jews living in the western part of District Warsaw were forced to relocate there; as refugees, they encountered even worse conditions than the majority of the ghetto inhabitants, who had previously been residents of the city of Warsaw and its suburbs. The overcrowding in the Warsaw ghetto, which was far too small for the number of residents, and above all the lack of food, fuel, and medicines, led to the death of a great many Jews even before the systematic mass murders started. From spring 1941 thousands perished there every month, particularly children and the elderly as the weakest among the ghetto inhabitants.[7]

The occupiers did not clearly map out the creation of the ghettos in advance; rather, the establishment of ghettos depended on the decisions taken by the regional authorities, such as the mayor or the Kreishauptmann. Often the local occupation administration declared a certain neighbourhood with especially poor infrastructure to be the ghetto, and forced all Poles to leave this area and all Jews from the rest of the town to move into it. Owing to the shortage of building materials and guards, many of these ghettos could not be hermetically sealed off from the outside world, especially not along the town boundaries. However, from mid October 1941 ghetto residents were prohibited under penalty of death from leaving the residential quarter in which they had been forced to live (see Doc. 13).[8]

The news of the German attack on the Soviet Union on 22 June 1941 initially caused many Jews to rejoice and to nurture cautious hopes of liberation following a Soviet victory over Hitler's Germany. In the Cracow ghetto, Halina Nelken noted in her diary: 'A

6 An overview of ghettoization during this first phase of the German occupation is presented in PMJ 4, pp. 53–60; see also Michman, *The Emergence of Jewish Ghettos*, pp. 61–90.

7 See Yisrael Gutman, *The Jews of Warsaw, 1939–1943: Ghetto, Underground, Revolt*, trans. Ina Friedman (Bloomington, IN: Indiana University Press, 1982 [Hebrew edn, 1977]; Ruta Sakowska, *Menschen im Ghetto: Die jüdische Bevölkerung im besetzten Warschau 1939–1943* (Osnabrück: fibre, 1999); Barbara Engelking and Jacek Leociak, *The Warsaw Ghetto: A Guide to the Perished City*, trans. Emma Harris (New Haven, CT: Yale University Press, 2009 [Polish edn, 2001]); Markus Roth and Andrea Löw, *Das Warschauer Getto: Alltag und Widerstand im Angesicht der Vernichtung* (Munich: Beck, 2013); and Lea Prais, *Displaced Persons at Home: Refugees in the Fabric of Jewish Life in Warsaw, September 1939 – July 1942*, trans. from Hebrew Naftali Greenwood (Jerusalem: Yad Vashem, 2015).

8 On the ghettos, see Gustavo Corni, *Hitler's Ghettos: Voices from a Beleaguered Society, 1939–1945*, trans. Nicola Rudge Iannelli (London: Arnold, 2002 [Italian edn, 2001]); Christoph Dieckmann and Babette Quinkert (eds.), *Im Ghetto 1939–1945: Neue Forschungen zu Alltag und Umfeld* (Göttingen: Wallstein, 2009); Guy Miron and Shlomit Shulhani (eds.), *The Yad Vashem Encyclopedia of the Ghettos during the Holocaust* (Jerusalem: Yad Vashem, 2009); Geoffrey P. Megargee (ed.), *The United States Holocaust Memorial Encyclopedia of Camps and Ghettos, 1933–1945*, vol. 2: *Ghettos in German-Occupied Eastern Europe*, ed. Martin Dean (Bloomington, IN: Indiana University Press, 2012); and Michman, *The Emergence of Jewish Ghettos*.

new war, with Russia. Everyone is pleased, even pessimists like our neighbours.'[9] Ghetto residents engaged in heated discussions about the significance of this new development, and rumours of a supposed German defeat soon spread. Yet before long people learned from newspapers smuggled into the ghetto and from foreign radio stations that the seemingly unstoppable German armed forces were continuing their eastward advance, and that there could be no question of liberation in the near future. In addition, the first reports began to trickle out regarding atrocities in the recently occupied territories, where many Jews in the General Government had friends and relatives.[10]

The beginning of the systematic mass murders in the area further to the west – the Warthegau, the region around Poznań and Łódź – did not go unnoticed in the General Government either. In late January 1942, for example, the report by a Jew who had escaped from Kulmhof (Chelmno) extermination camp reached the Oyneg Shabes (also: Oneg Shabbat, Hebrew for 'joy of the Sabbath') underground archive.[11] The archive was run by the historian Emanuel Ringelblum and his colleagues in the Warsaw ghetto.[12] However, only a few of those confined in the ghettos had access to comparable sources of information, and in those weeks and months the reports about mass murders did not yet relate to the General Government itself. Consequently such reports mostly met with a good deal of scepticism, as crimes of such magnitude were utterly inconceivable.[13]

9 Halina Nelken, *And Yet, I Am Here!*, trans. Halina Nelken with Alicia Nitecki (Amherst, MA: University of Massachusetts Press, 1999 [Polish edn, 1987]), p. 83 (entry for 22 June 1941).

10 Emanuel Ringelblum, *Ksovim fun geto*, vol. 1: *Togbukh fun varshever geto, 1939–1942*, ed. Tatiana Berenstein et al. (Warsaw: Yidish bukh, 1961), p. 342 (entry for 26 Feb. 1942) [abridged English edn of the diary: *Notes from the Warsaw Ghetto: The Journal of Emanuel Ringelblum*, ed. and trans. Jacob Sloan (n.p.: Normanby Press, 2015 [1958])]; *The Warsaw Diary of Adam Czerniakow: Prelude to Doom*, ed. Raul Hilberg, Stanislaw Staron, and Joseph Kermish, trans. Stanislaw Staron and the Staff of Yad Vashem (Chicago: Ivan R. Dee, 1999), pp. 334–335 (entry for 13 March 1942).

11 For the report, see PMJ 10/74. See also Ruta Sakowska, *Die zweite Etappe ist der Tod: NS-Ausrottungspolitik gegen die polnischen Juden, gesehen mit den Augen der Opfer. Ein historischer Essay und ausgewählte Dokumente aus dem Ringelblum-Archiv 1941–1943* (Berlin: Edition Hentrich, 1993), pp. 159–185; and Yitzhak Zuckerman, *A Surplus of Memory: Chronicle of the Warsaw Ghetto Uprising*, ed. and trans. Barbara Harshav (Berkeley, CA: University of California Press, 1993 [Hebrew edn, 1990]), pp. 156–158.

12 The contents of the archive are available as a 37-volume document collection: Ruta Sakowska et al. (eds.), *Archiwum Ringelbluma: Konspiracyjne Archiwum Getta Warszawy* (Warsaw: Emanuel Ringelblum Jewish Historical Institute, 1997–2020); published in English translation in *The Ringelblum Archive: Underground Archive of the Warsaw Ghetto* (Warsaw: Emanuel Ringelblum Historical Institute, 2017–), with three vols. available as of 2022: see https://www.jhi.pl/en/oneg-shabbat/projects/english-translations-ringelblum-archive. See also Robert Moses Shapiro and Tadeusz Epsztein, *The Warsaw Ghetto: Oyneg Shabes-Ringelblum Archive. Catalog and Guide*, trans. Robert Moses Shapiro (Bloomington, IN: Indiana University Press, 2009); Samuel D. Kassow, *Who Will Write Our History? Rediscovering a Hidden Archive from the Warsaw Ghetto* (Bloomington, IN: Indiana University Press, 2007); and Israel Gutman (ed.), *Emanuel Ringelblum: The Man and the Historian* (Jerusalem: Yad Vashem, 2006).

13 For other reports about Kulmhof that reached the General Government in early 1942, see PMJ 10/57, 58, 77, and 94. On how the inmates of the Warsaw ghetto responded to rumours about mass killings and death camps in early 1942, see Amos Goldberg, 'Rumor Culture among Warsaw Jews under Nazi Occupation: A World of Catastrophe Reenchanted', *Jewish Social Studies*, vol. 21, no. 3 (2016), pp. 81–125, here pp. 109–110.

In the General Government, violence against Jews was an everyday occurrence. At the end of August 1941, fifty-one inmates at Osowa labour camp were shot in order to contain an epidemic that had broken out there (Doc. 6). The continued expropriation of the Jews was accompanied by great brutality. One example was the *Pelzaktion* ('fur operation') that began at the end of December 1941, when the German occupiers ordered the ghetto residents to surrender all fur items in their possession and confiscated these for the benefit of the German soldiers engaged in the war against the Soviet Union (Doc. 28).[14] Many Jews chose to destroy their furs and down blankets rather than surrender these to the Germans. Jews known to be concealing fur items were severely beaten, and a number of them were shot during this operation, which left the already gravely weakened Jews in the ghetto exposed to the bitter winter. In countless cases, there was no longer the need for even an ostensible reason to kill Jews. German ghetto guards took pleasure in shooting indiscriminately at Jews in the ghettos.

When typhus epidemics broke out in the General Government, the occupation officials repeatedly held the Jews responsible, labelling them 'carriers of epidemic disease'. It is striking that in this situation it was the German medical authorities, who were obviously aware of the connection between persecution and the severe deterioration in the health of the persecuted, that recommended hermetically sealing the ghettos and punishing any escapees with death in order to prevent the spread of epidemics (Doc. 14).[15] On 15 October 1941 the government of the GG in Cracow adopted a corresponding regulation (Doc. 13). Shortly thereafter the German special courts, in summary proceedings, began to impose death sentences on Jews who had been captured after escaping from the ghetto (Doc. 25). However, given the large number of arrests, the German judiciary increasingly complained of being overburdened with the administration of such proceedings. As a result, the Order Police and the Security Police in the General Government issued an order on 21 November 1941 requiring all Jews captured outside their mandatory places of residence to be shot without any legal proceedings (Docs. 17 and 26).

In summer 1941 vast prison camps (*Stammlager*, Stalags) had been created to intern Soviet prisoners of war in the General Government, for example in Chełm, Lwów, and Siedlce; Lublin-Majdanek concentration camp was also initially intended to serve as a prisoner-of-war camp. Epidemics were rife in these camps, and the German occupiers feared they would spread to the population. Between October 1941 and May 1942, approximately 270,000 Red Army soldiers perished of malnutrition and disease in the Stalags of the General Government alone.[16] In addition, certain categories of prisoners,

14 Dieter Pohl, *Nationalsozialistische Judenverfolgung in Ostgalizien 1941–1944: Organisation und Durchführung eines staatlichen Massenverbrechens* (Munich: Oldenbourg, 1996), pp. 164–165.

15 Willi Dreßen and Volker Rieß, 'Ausbeutung und Vernichtung: Gesundheitspolitik im Generalgouvernement', in Norbert Frei (ed.), *Medizin und Gesundheitspolitik in der NS-Zeit* (Munich: Oldenbourg, 1991), pp. 157–171; Christopher R. Browning, 'Genocide and Public Health: German Doctors and Polish Jews, 1939-1941', *Holocaust and Genocide Studies*, vol. 3, no. 1 (1988), pp. 21-36.

16 Wiesław Marczyk, *Jeńcy radzieccy w niewoli Wehrmachtu na ziemiach polskich w latach 1941–1945* (Opole: Centralne Muzeum Jeńców Wojennych w Łambinowicach-Opolu, 1987). On Majdanek, see Tomasz Kranz, 'Between Planning and Implementation: The Lublin District and Majdanek Camp in Nazi Policy', in Larry V. Thompson (ed.), *Lessons and Legacies IV: Reflections on Religion, Justice, Sexuality, and Genocide* (Evanston, IL: Northwestern University Press, 2003), pp. 215–235; and Nikolaus Wachsmann, *KL: A History of the Nazi Concentration Camps* (New York: Farrar, Straus & Giroux, 2016), pp. 277–280.

particularly Jewish Red Army soldiers and political commissars, were separated from other prisoners by Wehrmacht officers before being shot by police units. These shootings were the first instances of mass murder in the General Government on a comparable scale to the crimes committed by the SS and police units in the occupied Soviet Union. Between 21 and 28 September 1941, for example, Police Battalion 306 shot approximately 5,000 Soviet prisoners of war who had been selected by the Security Police in Biala Podlaska main camp.[17]

## Everyday life in the ghettos

Particularly in the ghettos in large towns and cities, which were generally more tightly sealed off than those in smaller towns, the conditions were catastrophic. Several families had to share each small apartment, living alongside one another in extremely cramped conditions, mostly with very poor sanitation.[18] People were also crowded together out in the streets. Roma Ligocka described this in her recollections of the Cracow ghetto – which, with more than 18,000 inhabitants, was crammed with people at the end of 1941:

> They talk, jostle, and push, and they touch me. There are always a lot of people around me: outside in the narrow streets, inside in the small and dirty kitchen where the women fight for a spot at the stove.[19]

While hunger and disease were rampant throughout the General Government, Warsaw arguably had the worst conditions and the highest death rate. The official food rations were so limited that most ghetto residents never had enough to eat. In 1941 the German occupiers in Warsaw stipulated a regular daily intake of 2,310 calories for Germans and 654 calories for Poles, but no more than 184 calories for Jews.[20] Hunger was extreme and dominated everyday life – most first-hand accounts of the period make reference to it. In his memoir, Marcel Reich-Ranicki described what he saw day after day in the Warsaw ghetto:

17 See Jan Piętrzykowski, *Stalag 367: Obóz jeńców radzieckich w Częstochowie* (Katowice: Śląsk, 1976); Edward Kopówka, *Stalag 366 Siedlce* (Siedlce: Stowarzyszenie Kreatorów Unikalnej Niebanalnej Kultury Studenckiej-SKUNKS w Siedlcach, 2004); Tadeusz Mencel (ed.), *Majdanek 1941–1944* (Lublin: Wydawnictwo Lubelskie, 1991); Torsten Schäfer, *'Jedenfalls habe ich auch mitgeschossen': Das NSG-Verfahren gegen Johann Josef Kuhr und andere ehemalige Angehörige des Polizeibataillons 306, der Polizeireiterabteilung 2 und der SD-Dienststelle von Pinsk beim Landgericht Frankfurt am Main 1962–1973. Eine textanalytische Fallstudie zur Mentalitätsgeschichte* (Münster: LIT, 2007).

18 Carlos Alberto Haas, *Das Private im Ghetto: Jüdisches Leben im deutsch besetzten Polen 1939 bis 1944* (Göttingen: Wallstein, 2020).

19 Roma Ligocka, *The Girl in the Red Coat: A Memoir*, trans. Margot Bettauer Dembo (New York: Random House, 2003 [German edn, 2002]), p. 5.

20 Czesław Pilichowski, 'Verbrauch von Nahrungsmitteln durch jüdische Bevölkerung und Häftlinge der Okkupationslager im besetzten Polen', *Studia Historiae Oeconomicae*, vol. 17 (1982), pp. 205–215, here p. 208.

> [I]n the gutter, especially in the early morning, scantily covered with old newspapers, lay the corpses of those who had died of debility or hunger or typhus and whose burial nobody wished to pay for.[21]

The teacher Michał Zylberberg, a colleague and friend of the educator Janusz Korczak in the Warsaw ghetto, wrote in his diary that crowds of German soldiers were always present when the dead were being laid to rest at the Jewish cemetery:

> They gleefully photographed the dead and the accompanying relatives, and even went so far as taking snapshots of the corpses as they were laid out in the mortuary. The Nazis were particularly active in this respect on Sundays, when they would visit the cemetery with their girlfriends. This, rather than a cinema, was a place of amusement for them.[22]

Malnutrition was compounded by cold weather and disease. In winter 1941–1942 the water pipes and waste pipes froze, and the toilets – frequently nothing more than open latrines in the backyards – could no longer be used. Fuel was in short supply, and as a result it was often scarcely any warmer inside the apartments than outside. People walked the streets wrapped in blankets or huddled, shivering, in their beds, wearing all the clothes still in their possession in an attempt to keep warm. The streets were full of beggars, but the general impoverishment and growing indifference to misery meant that passers-by became ever less willing to give them anything. In October 1941 Emanuel Ringelblum noted in his diary:

> There is an evident and terrible slackening of the sentiment of compassion. Walking through the streets, one passes children as emaciated as skeletons, barefoot and naked, stretching out their blue, frozen feet, and nobody takes any notice of them. Human beings have turned to stone.[23]

Shortly after the war, Sophie Leviathan recalled that at times almost one in every three buildings in the Warsaw ghetto was marked with the words 'Typhus, keep out', and that people died 'like flies'.[24] Doctors and nurses attempted to help, but the lack of hospitals and medicines meant there was little they could do.[25] Because the official rations were far too meagre, anyone who wanted to survive was forced to rely on the black market. The food and medicines sold there were mostly smuggled into the ghetto. Ghetto residents who were assigned a place of work outside the ghetto as part of a forced

21 Marcel Reich-Ranicki, *The Author of Himself: The Life of Marcel Reich-Ranicki*, trans. Ewald Osers (London: Phoenix, 2002 [German edn, 1999]), p. 147.

22 Michael Zylberberg, *A Warsaw Diary, 1939–1945* (London: Vallentine Mitchell, 1969), p. 31.

23 Ringelblum, *Ksovim fun geto*, vol. 1, pp. 307–308.

24 Sophie Leviathan, 'Der Krieg von innen', AŻIH, 302/231, fol. 33. Published in English translation in Sophie Goetzel-Leviathan, *The War from Within*, ed. Rebecca Fromer, trans. from German Geoffrey A. M. Block (Berkeley, CA: Judah L. Magnes Museum, 1987), p. 27.

25 See Charles G. Roland, *Courage Under Siege: Disease, Starvation and Death in the Warsaw Ghetto* (New York: Oxford University Press, 1992); Miriam Offer, *White Coats in the Ghetto: Jewish Medicine in Poland during the Holocaust* (Jerusalem: Yad Vashem, 2020).

labour detail sometimes had an opportunity to obtain food through their contact with non-Jews. Others looked for secret ways to leave the ghetto or bribed German and Polish guards at the gates. In the Warsaw ghetto, children who squeezed through gaps in the fencing and the walls to engage in smuggling sometimes became the providers for entire families,[26] though they risked their lives in doing so, as anyone who was caught was shot on the spot. Many smugglers lost their lives in their attempts to bring food or medicine into the ghetto.[27]

Ghetto residents made every effort to obtain work, ideally outside the ghetto. Work allowed them to at least scrape by, either by receiving a pitiful wage or, more importantly, by gaining access to food. Moreover, when the deportations to extermination camps began in 1942, work offered protection from more than hunger, since Jews classified as unfit for work were generally the first who had to board the trains bound for the camps.

In addition to the Jewish councils, which were created at the Germans' behest shortly after the start of the war, the Jewish Social Self-Help (JSS) also operated in the ghettos. This was the only Jewish relief organization in the General Government to be recognized by the Germans. The JSS, which had its headquarters in Cracow and ran numerous branch offices in other towns, was frequently the only point of contact for the Jewish councils, which were otherwise completely on their own.[28] Employees of the JSS and the Jewish councils helped people in the ghetto to organize their lives, to establish self-help structures, and to preserve a remnant of cultural and intellectual life. In soup kitchens and hospitals, they did their utmost to keep the ghetto residents alive. In addition, above all in Warsaw, there were countless private cultural and welfare initiatives. In the Warsaw ghetto, theatre and musical performances continued, and individuals organized reading or music groups, or even set up new orchestras. Tens of thousands of children received schooling or vocational training in the ghettos. The Jewish councils also organized orphanages, homes for the elderly, and soup kitchens for the rapidly growing number of people in need.[29] In addition, an underground press developed in some of the ghettos,[30] and political parties also became active, unless the Jewish councils banned them. People

26 See Maria Hochberg-Mariańska and Noe Grüss (eds.), *The Children Accuse*, trans. Bill Johnston (London and Portland: Vallentine Mitchell, 1996 [Polish edn, 1993]).

27 Engelking and Leociak, *Warsaw Ghetto*, pp. 446–459.

28 On the creation of the Jewish councils and the history of the JSS, see PMJ 4, pp. 47–50. See also Kassow, *Who Will Write Our History?*, pp. 90–143; Marcin Urynowicz, 'Epilogue: Refractions of Jewish Self-Government under German Occupation in the Second World War', in François Guesnet and Jerzy Tomaszewski (eds.), *Sources on Jewish Self-Government in the Polish Lands from Its Inception to the Present* (Leiden: Brill, 2021), pp. 627–680; Melanie Hembera, *Die Shoah im Distrikt Krakau: Jüdisches Leben und deutsche Besatzung in Tarnów 1939–1945* (Darmstadt: WBG, 2016), pp. 123–137; and Annalena Schmidt, '(Selbst-)Hilfe in Zeiten der Hilfslosigkeit? Die "Jüdische Soziale Selbsthilfe" und die "Jüdische Unterstützungsstelle" im Generalgouvernement, 1939–1944/45' (doctoral thesis, Justus-Liebig-Universität Gießen, 2015).

29 See Martyna Grądzka, *Przerwane dzieciństwo: Losy dzieci Żydowskiego Domu Sierot przy ul. Dietla 64 w Krakowie podczas okupacji niemieckiej* (Cracow: Wysoki Zamek, 2012).

30 See Joseph Kermish et al. (eds.), *Ittonut ha-mahteret ha-yedhudit be-Warsha*, 6 vols. (Jerusalem: Yad Vashem, 1979–1997); published in English translation in Tikva Fatal-Knaani (ed.), *The Jewish Underground Press in Warsaw*, trans. from Yiddish, Polish, and Hebrew Shulamit Berman et al., vols. 1–3 (Jerusalem: Yad Vashem, 2017–2021), covering the period from May 1940 to Oct. 1941, with additional volumes forthcoming; and Daniel Blatman (ed.), *Geṭo Ṿarshah – sipur ʿitonaʾi: mivḥar me-ʿitonut ha-maḥteret, 1940–1943* (Jerusalem: Yad Vashem, 2002).

created an alternative world for themselves, which for many was extremely important. At a literary event in the Warsaw ghetto in 1941, an unidentified speaker aptly characterized these efforts as the 'triumph of humanity over all that is inhumane'.[31]

## The path to systematic mass murder

In late June 1941, directly after the attack on the Soviet Union, German SS and police units embarked upon the mass killing of the Jewish population in the territories east of the General Government. Initially almost all of the victims were men. Then, within a few weeks, in the regions east of the former Polish border that were occupied in autumn 1941, the murder squads began killing the entire Jewish population, including women, the elderly, and children. In the Babyn Yar ravine in Kyiv, they shot – according to German reports – 33,771 people in the space of two days at the end of September 1941. In Eastern Galicia, German killing units murdered approximately 10,000 Jewish men in July 1941. Thousands more fell victim to pogroms, which were mainly initiated by the Germans but carried out by ultranationalist Ukrainian militias.[32] The central authorities in Berlin urged on the murder operations targeting Jews, and German officials took note of the mass murders in the other occupied territories as well.

As early as March 1941, in the run-up to the attack on the Soviet Union, Hitler had assured Governor General Frank that the territory Frank controlled would be 'free of Jews' in the foreseeable future. The initial intention was to deport a proportion – or even all – of the Jews under German control to the newly occupied regions.[33] Frank had sought to annex the Pripyat marshes in southern Byelorussia and incorporate them into the General Government in order to oversee personally the expulsion of the Jews into these inhospitable territories. But because this region became part of Reich Commissariat Ukraine after the German invasion, Frank's plans were no longer viable. The occupation administration that was established in the occupied Soviet territories was also eager to reduce the number of Jews in its sphere of control, as quickly as possible and by any means – including mass murder. All the plans made by the occupation officials in Poland to deport Jews to the newly occupied Soviet territories ground to a halt, especially as it was becoming apparent that, contrary to the optimistic predictions of the state and the Wehrmacht leadership, the war against the Soviet Union would not be won within eight to twelve weeks. The Germans were unable to deport the Jews further eastwards from the territories under their control, and at the same time they were preparing for the deportation of additional Jews from the West, as in autumn 1941 there were increasing calls for the Reich to be made 'free of Jews' even while the war was ongoing.[34]

31 Cited in Sakowska, *Die zweite Etappe*, pp. 142–143.
32 See PMJ 7/11.
33 See PMJ 4/260.
34 Götz Aly, *'Final Solution': Nazi Population Policy and the Murder of the European Jews*, trans. Allison Brown and Belinda Cooper (London: Arnold; New York: Oxford University Press, 1999 [German edn, 1995]), pp. 209–230; *Der Dienstkalender Heinrich Himmlers 1941/42*, ed. Peter Witte et al. (Hamburg: Christians, 1999), p. 203 (entry for 2 Sept. 1941). On calls to make the Reich 'free of Jews', see also the Introduction to PMJ 3 and the Introduction to PMJ 6.

In June 1941 there were approximately 540,000 Jews living in Eastern Galicia. After the German attack on the Soviet Union, they endured the same fate as the Jews in the other recently occupied territories. By the end of the month, German SS and police units had already begun murdering the 'Jewish intelligentsia' in Eastern Galicia; these were primarily representatives of the Jewish community, teachers, and other state employees. After Eastern Galicia was annexed to the General Government on 1 August 1941, German forces continued to kill Jews in that region. In early October 1941 the territories bordering on the General Government, which were now under civil administration – the western part of Byelorussia and western Volhynia – also became the scene of large-scale mass murders of Jews. These killing operations, carried out in tandem, were probably directly related to the German assault on Moscow at the beginning of October, which was expected to result in a speedy victory over the Soviet Union and thus achieve a lasting consolidation of occupation rule.

Since August 1941 German officials in Berlin and in occupied Poland had been discussing the future course of action against the Jews in the new District Galicia. Because they could not bank on deporting them to the East, at least not for the time being, they decided to set up ghettos in Galicia too, including one in the town of Stanisławów (German: Stanislau; now Ivano-Frankivsk, Ukraine). The Hungarian authorities had previously begun deporting Jews into this area from Carpatho-Ukraine, which had been annexed by Hungary; most of these Jews were subsequently sent to neighbouring Kamenets-Podilskyi in occupied Ukraine, where they were murdered at the end of August 1941. The violence and murder in District Galicia further escalated in October 1941. On 6 October the Security Police branch in Stanisławów carried out a mass shooting in the nearby small town of Nadworna, which was followed by a large massacre on the outskirts of Stanisławów on 12 October. When the Jewish residents were notified on the morning of 12 October that they had to assemble, they had no idea what awaited them. According to Fryderyk Nadler, 'It was said that this was a resettlement. People took along enough food for several days and whatever else they could carry.'[35] However, they were in fact led to the Jewish cemetery, where mass graves had already been dug. Approximately 10,000–12,000 Jewish men, women, and children were murdered there. Originally the number was intended to be even higher, but the Security Police halted the shootings when darkness fell. During the night, some Jews who had not been fatally injured managed to crawl out of the mass graves and made their way with difficulty to the Jewish hospital, where there were scenes of unimaginable chaos. The 'Bloody Sunday' of Stanisławów, as the massacre came to be known, marked the beginning of the 'final solution' in the General Government. After this operation, the surviving Jews from the Stanisławów area were forced to move into a cramped, run-down part of town that had been turned into a ghetto. Here as many as ten people lived in a single room, in the same disastrous conditions as the Jewish population in the ghettos previously created in the other four districts of the General Government.[36]

35 Statement by Fryderyk Nadler, April 1946: AŻIH, 301/1734, fol. 4.

36 See the statements by Horacy Safrin and Salomon Günsberg: AŻIH, 302/175, fol. 26, and 302/136, fols. 8–10. See also Pohl, *Nationalsozialistische Judenverfolgung in Ostgalizien*, pp. 144–147; and Thomas Sandkühler, *'Endlösung' in Galizien: Der Judenmord in Ostpolen und die Rettungsinitiativen von Berthold Beitz 1941–1944* (Bonn: Dietz, 1996), pp. 149–152.

The German police proceeded in a similar fashion in many places in the southern part of District Galicia, such as Rohatyn (Doc. 50) and, in December 1941, Lwów, where Jews accounted for approximately one third of the population. The German authorities had also started setting up a ghetto in Lwów, and as in Stanisławów, the police took advantage of this development to reduce the number of Jews in advance by organizing a mass shooting. When the Jews were moved out of the other parts of Lwów into the area designated as the ghetto, police sentries screened them at checkpoints, selected those who looked sickly or feeble, took them outside the city, and shot them. However, fearing that the creation of the ghetto would cause the typhus already rampant in the city to spread still further, the authorities put the expansion of the ghetto on hold for the time being. As a result, not all the Jews in Lwów were forced to relocate (Doc. 34). Not until September 1942, in the context of the mass deportations to extermination camps, was an area sealed off and established as the ghetto.[37]

On 13 October 1941, immediately after the Jews of Stanisławów were massacred, Himmler met with the SS and Police Leader in District Lublin, Odilo Globocnik, and Globocnik's superior, Higher SS and Police Leader Friedrich Wilhelm Krüger, at Himmler's field command post in East Prussia. It is thought that at this meeting they decided to create extermination centres in the General Government.[38] After the heads of the Einsatzgruppen of the Security Police and the SD and of the police killing squads had reported that the massacres, which often lasted for many hours over several days, took a heavy psychological toll on the members of the firing squads, it was decided that mass murders of Jews were henceforth to be carried out not only by shooting, but also by asphyxiation with poison gas in extermination camps. However, the instruction to construct such camps was issued not to the leadership of the Security Police of the General Government in Cracow, which was actually in charge of 'combating Jews', but rather to Globocnik.[39] At an early stage, Globocnik – who was a friend and confidant of Himmler – had come forward with deportation and resettlement plans for the area under his authority.[40] In July 1941 Himmler had tasked him with beginning the preparatory work for the construction of SS and police bases in Poland and the Soviet Union, conceived as a chain of fortified frontier settlements,[41] and had also ordered him to expedite the building of a large concentration camp. This was the camp that later became Majdanek.

37 Eliyahu Yones, *Smoke in the Sand: The Jews of Lvov in the War Years, 1939–1944* (Jerusalem and New York: Gefen, 2004); Eliyahu Yones, *Die Straße nach Lemberg: Zwangsarbeit und Widerstand in Ostgalizien 1941–1944*, ed. Susanne Heim (Frankfurt am Main: Fischer, 1999 [Hebrew edn, 1960]).

38 See *Dienstkalender Heinrich Himmlers*, ed. Witte et al., pp. 233–234.

39 Peter R. Black, 'Odilo Globocnik: Himmlers Vorposten im Osten', in Ronald Smelser, Enrico Syring, and Rainer Zitelmann (eds.), *Die Braune Elite II* (Darmstadt: WBG, 1993), pp. 103–115; and Bertrand Perz, 'The Austrian Connection: SS and Police Leader Globocnik and His Staff in the Lublin District', *Holocaust and Genocide Studies*, vol. 29, no. 3 (2015), pp. 400–430.

40 From spring 1941 Hans Frank also developed the idea of 'Germanizing' the General Government in the medium term. Globocnik was responsible for the resettlement of ethnic Germans in the Zamość area, which involved the deportation of thousands of Poles: see Czesław Madajczyk (ed.), *Zamojszczyzna – Sonderlaboratorium SS: Zbiór dokumentów polskich i niemieckich z okresu okupacji hitlerowskiej*, 2 vols. (Warsaw: Ludowa Spółdzielnia, 1977).

41 Jan Erik Schulte, 'Initiative der Peripherie: Globocniks Siedlungsstützpunkte und die Entscheidung zum Bau des Vernichtungslagers Belzec', in Jan Erik Schulte (ed.), *Die SS, Himmler und die Wewelsburg* (Paderborn: Schöningh, 2009), pp. 118–137.

It is unclear whether Himmler had already issued instructions at that point regarding the killing of the Jews in the area controlled by Globocnik.[42] There are many indications that these decisions were taken in September and October 1941.

Globocnik himself depicted the 'Jewish question' as a danger for the district, maintaining that there was a risk of epidemic typhus spreading from the Soviet prisoners of war to the ghettos, but that it was not possible to deport the Jews eastwards. The extermination centres were to employ the 'expert knowledge' of the personnel involved in the murders carried out under the 'euthanasia' programme, in the course of which tens of thousands of sick and disabled people had been murdered in gas chambers in Germany.[43] Although the 'euthanasia' programme continued in other forms, the 'euthanasia' killings by means of poison gas were terminated in summer 1941, meaning that the associated personnel could be used to set up the extermination centres in the General Government.[44] In early November 1941 a German team arrived in the small town of Bełżec, on the railway line between Lublin and Lwów, and began constructing the first extermination facility. Soon afterwards a second centre was planned, near the village of Sobibór on the River Bug, on the eastern border of the General Government.

In the government of the GG too, discussions began at that point about plans for the systematic mass murder of the Jews. After attending Hitler's meeting with the various Gauleiter and senior Party members on 12 December 1941, Hans Frank disclosed these plans to his officials in a speech on 16 December (Doc. 26). A month later, at the Wannsee Conference in Berlin on 20 January 1942, his representative, Josef Bühler, expressed his full agreement with the plans for murder, saying that

> the General Government would welcome it if the final solution of this question were to begin in the General Government, because for one thing the transportation problem was not of overriding importance there, and because issues related to labour deployment would not impede the course of this operation. Jews should be removed from the territory of the General Government as rapidly as possible because it is precisely there that the Jew constitutes an eminent danger as a carrier of epidemics and he also constantly disrupts the economic structure of the region through his continuous illicit trading. Moreover, the majority of the around 2½ million Jews in question are unfit for work. State Secretary Dr Bühler noted further that the Head of Security Police and SD is in charge of the solution of the Jewish question in the

42 Bogdan Musiał, 'The Origins of "Operation Reinhard": The Decision-Making Process for the Mass Murder of the Jews in the *Generalgouvernement*', trans. William Templer, *Yad Vashem Studies*, vol. 28 (2000), pp. 113–153; Dieter Pohl, 'Die Rolle des Distrikts Lublin im Völkermord an den Juden', in Musiał (ed.), *'Aktion Reinhardt'*, pp. 87–107. Plans for the murder of Jews in the Warthegau were also under discussion from summer 1941: see PMJ 4, p. 65, PMJ 4/314, and the Introduction to PMJ 10.

43 Sara Berger, *Experten der Vernichtung: Das T4-Reinhardt-Netzwerk in den Lagern Belzec, Sobibor und Treblinka* (Hamburg: Hamburger Edition, 2013).

44 Günter Morsch and Bertrand Perz (eds.), *Neue Studien zu nationalsozialistischen Massentötungen durch Giftgas: Historische Bedeutung, technische Entwicklung, revisionistische Leugnung* (Berlin: Metropol, 2011); Eugen Kogon, Hermann Langbein, and Adalbert Rückerl (eds.), *Nazi Mass Murder: A Documentary History of the Use of Poison Gas*, trans. Mary Scott and Caroline Lloyd-Morris (New Haven, CT, and London: Yale University Press, 1993 [German edn, 1986]).

General Government, and that the administrative authorities of the General Government would assist him in his work.[45]

## The first phase of the mass murders in the extermination camps, March to June 1942

By early March 1942 the construction of the first extermination camp in the General Government, Belzec, was largely complete. Like the facilities subsequently established at Sobibor and Treblinka, Belzec was built exclusively as a killing site: virtually all the victims were murdered immediately after arrival. Belzec, Sobibor, and Treblinka served as 'camps' over an extended period only for the SS personnel, the guard force made up of '*fremdvölkisch* ('ethnically alien', i.e. foreign, non-German) volunteers', and groups of several hundred Jewish prisoners who were present in each camp for a period of time. These prisoners were selected from among the arriving Jews and were forced to become involved in the process of mass murder; they too were eventually murdered and replaced with deportees from newly arriving transports. The deportations from the ghettos towards certain death in Belzec began shortly after Himmler's visit to the General Government on 13–14 March 1942, with the first transports departing from Lwów on 16 March and from Lublin the following day.

The German occupiers wanted to ensure that the crimes were carried out as efficiently as possible and with few personnel, and for this purpose they forced the local Jewish councils to cooperate. The Jewish Council in Lwów was instructed to provide 30,000 people for the transports (Doc. 49). A sufficient number of people did indeed volunteer for the first transports from Lwów to Belzec. Most of these volunteers, utterly impoverished and without relatives or families of their own, had no inkling of the fate that awaited them. A few days later, however, when people in Lwów became aware that the trains were returning empty after a short period of time (Belzec was only around 70 km from Lwów), rumours about the fate of the deportees spread quickly. From then on, virtually no one came forward voluntarily. As a result, the SS and Police Leader in Lwów, Friedrich Katzmann, intervened and ordered that the Jewish quarter be combed systematically.[46]

45 The German text of the protocol can be found in Norbert Kampe and Peter Klein (eds.), *Die Wannseekonferenz am 20. Januar 1942: Dokumente, Forschungsstand, Kontroversen* (Vienna and Cologne: Böhlau, 2013), pp. 40–54, here pp. 53–54. Published in English translation in Elke Gryglewski, Hans-Christian Jasch, and David Zolldan (eds.), *The Meeting at Wannsee and the Murder of the European Jews: Exhibition Catalogue*, trans. Caroline Pearce (Berlin: House of the Wannsee Conference, 2020 [German edn, 2020]); and in PMJ 6/65. On the Wannsee Conference, see also Kurt Pätzold and Erika Schwarz (eds.), *Tagesordnung, Judenmord: Die Wannsee-Konferenz am 20. Januar 1942. Eine Dokumentation zur Organisation der 'Endlösung'* (Berlin: Metropol, 1992); Mark Roseman, *The Villa, the Lake, the Meeting: Wannsee and the Final Solution* (London: Penguin, 2002); Peter Klein, *Die 'Wannsee-Konferenz' am 20. Januar 1942: Eine Einführung* (Berlin: Metropol, 2017); Peter Longerich, *Wannsee: The Road to the Final Solution*, trans. Lesley Sharpe and Jeremy Noakes (Oxford: Oxford University Press, 2021 [German edn, 2016]); and Jasch and Kreutzmüller (eds.), *The Participants*.

46 See Andrzej Żbikowski (ed.), *Friedrich Katzmann: Rozwiązanie kwestii żydowskiej w dystrykcie Galicja* (Warsaw: Instytut Pamięci Narodowej, 2001), which includes a photomechanical reproduction of the original report.

In Lublin, by contrast, a large police contingent was deployed from the outset, with the ghetto surrounded on the evening of 16 March 1942. The roundups here were conducted with the utmost brutality, and so the victims very soon realized that the operation was by no means part of an effort to recruit workers. In the first week alone, German police forces shot 126 people in the ghetto.[47]

The selection of the deportees also made it obvious that the purpose of the roundups was to find people to murder rather than forced labourers. Of the Jews who were dependant on welfare and considered unfit for work, the Germans aimed to deport as many as possible to their deaths. To segregate the groups earmarked for deportation and make them identifiable at the same time, the employment offices periodically issued new work passes in different colours.[48] In some places the occupation administration divided the ghettos into segregated areas, typically so-called A and B ghettos (fit for work – unfit for work). This segregation itself served as a preselection process to determine the sequence of the deportations. In May 1942 the Labour Main Department in the General Government ordered that statistics be gathered on the number of male and female Jewish skilled workers up to the age of fifty-five who were currently employed in each district, listing their specific skills and indicating whether they were deployed in 'essential war production', in other jobs, or in other sectors, or were unemployed (Doc. 72). Such investigations of Jewish employment were a further step in the preparation for mass murder.

The occupation administration in District Lublin had consented to the plan for Jews to be deported from the Reich, the Protectorate of Bohemia and Moravia, and Slovakia and placed in the local ghettos (Doc. 52). To make room for the new arrivals, the number of local Jews leaving the ghettos was supposed to be approximately equal to the number of new arrivals from the West in each case. As had previously been the case in Riga and Minsk,[49] Polish Jews were also now murdered with reference to the lack of space that had in fact been created by the Germans themselves. In cases in which it was not possible to deport the Polish Jews before the transports arrived from other countries, the transit ghettos were temporarily even more crowded than before. As a result, German or Czech Jews sometimes lived alongside the native Polish Jews for a while.[50] There were as many as twenty people per room, which caused even more hardship as well as inevitable tensions between the victims. While some of the new arrivals found work in the ghettos, many were transported to extermination camps soon after they arrived. Ernst Krombach, a German Jew who was deported to Izbica, wrote to his fiancée in June 1942, in a

47 Halbjahresbericht KdO Lublin [1942], AIPN, CA 156/44, fol. 93. See also Musiał, *Deutsche Zivilverwaltung und Judenverfolgung*; Dieter Pohl, *Von der 'Judenpolitik' zum Judenmord: Der Distrikt Lublin des Generalgouvernements 1939–1944* (Frankfurt am Main: Peter Lang, 1993); Tadeusz Radzik, *Lubelska dzielnica zamknięta* (Lublin: Wydawnictwo Uniwersytetu Marii Curie-Skłodowskiej, 1999); and David Silberklang, *Gates of Tears: The Holocaust in the Lublin District* (Jerusalem: Yad Vashem, 2013).

48 See Stephan Lehnstaedt, 'Die deutsche Arbeitsverwaltung im Generalgouvernement und die Juden', *Vierteljahrshefte für Zeitgeschichte*, vol. 60 (2012), pp. 409–440; and Witold Wojciech Mędykowski, *Macht Arbeit frei? German Economic Policy and Forced Labor of Jews in the General Government, 1939–1943* (Boston: Academic Studies Press, 2018), pp. 221–245.

49 See PMJ 6/22, 42, 60, and 80.

50 Else Rosenfeld and Gertrud Luckner (eds.), *Lebenszeichen aus Piaski: Briefe Deportierter aus dem Distrikt Lublin 1940–1943* (Munich: Biederstein, 1968), pp. 21–22.

letter that was secretly smuggled out of the ghetto: 'In the meantime, many transports have left. Of the approximately 14,000 Jews who arrived, only 2[,000]–3,000 are still here.' Krombach also mentioned the fears of those who remained behind:

> We have heard nothing more of these people [...]. After the last transport, unfortunately, the men who were working outside the village returned to find neither wives, nor children, nor their possessions.[51]

Transports bringing Jews from the Reich also arrived in the disastrously overcrowded Warsaw ghetto (Doc. 65). However, this did not immediately prompt deportations of Polish Jews from Warsaw to the extermination camps. Construction of the extermination camp intended for them, Treblinka II – near Treblinka I, a labour camp in operation from 1941[52] – did not start until the end of May 1942 (Doc. 78).

The systematic nature of the killing operations undertaken from March 1942 is plain to see. In District Lublin and District Galicia, the police squads that organized the deportations swooped on one rural Kreis after another. Sometimes the German occupiers delegated the task of selecting the victims to the Jewish councils, but in most cases the police carried out brutal roundups themselves.

Around 20 April 1942 the deportations ceased temporarily due to necessary construction work at the killing centre in Belzec. The SS had insisted to the civil administration that Belzec could 'admit' 4,000 to 5,000 Jews daily (Doc. 48), but it now halted the deportations and began to build a new, larger building with killing facilities. At the same time, the second extermination centre in Sobibor was under construction. In early May 1942 the first transports from District Lublin arrived in Sobibor, followed soon thereafter by others that came directly from the Reich.[53]

At the end of May 1942 the German occupation administration in District Cracow also began deporting Jews, initially from the district capital. Several days earlier the Security Police had instructed the Jewish Council to draw up lists of people working for German firms and to make preparations for checking the papers of all ghetto residents. Only those who were classified as essential workers and could produce documents with the appropriate stamps were exempt from deportation for the time being. Anyone who could not obtain such a stamp had to report for deportation on 1 June, with a minimum of luggage. The night before, Security Police units and the Jewish Order Service had already begun to take people from their homes and herd them towards an assembly point. A series of dramatic incidents occurred in which many people were beaten or shot on the spot. Michał Weichert, the chairman of the JSS, was grazed by a bullet while on his way to the assembly point to intercede for the poet Mordechai Gebirtig, who had

51 Cited in Mark Roseman, *The Past in Hiding: Memory and Survival in Nazi Germany* (London: Penguin, 2000), p. 191. See also Steffen Hänschen, *Das Transitghetto Izbica im System des Holocaust* (Berlin: Metropol, 2018); and Robert Kuwałek, 'Die Durchgangsghettos im Distrikt Lublin (u. a. Izbica, Piaski, Rejowiec und Trawniki)', in Musiał (ed.), *'Aktion Reinhardt'*, pp. 197–232.

52 Sebastian Różycki, Marek Michalski, and Edward Kopówka, *Obóz pracy Treblinka I: Metodyka integracji danych wieloźródłowych* (Warsaw and Treblinka: Ministerstwo Kultury i Dziedzictwa Narodowego, 2017).

53 Alfred B. Gottwaldt and Diana Schulle, *Die 'Judendeportationen' aus dem Deutschen Reich von 1941–1945: Eine kommentierte Chronologie* (Wiesbaden: Marix, 2005), pp. 180 and 211–212.

not received a stamp. Tadeusz Pankiewicz, a Pole who had received a special permit to continue operating his pharmacy inside the ghetto, recalled the crowded square:

> The sun was beating down mercilessly, parching their throats. Opposite the pharmacy, by the wall of a tenement building, stood a team of doctors in white coats, nurses, hospital matrons and stretcher-bearers. The white of their medical coats stood out strangely against the black and grey of the crowd waiting to be deported. [...] Some sitting, some standing, the crowd waited, frozen by fear and uncertainty.[54]

That day, 1 June 1942, saw the departure of the first train carrying Jews from the Cracow ghetto to Belzec, where the new killing facilities had in the meantime been completed. Additional transports left Cracow in the days that followed, and deportations commenced from other towns in the district as well.[55]

From mid March to mid July 1942, a total of around 180,000 Jews living in the General Government were deported and murdered in the Belzec and Sobibor death camps.[56] Most of them had neither a job nor family members who had work permits: these deportees were thus in the weakest position within ghetto society. In the first days and weeks of the roundups, the Jews incarcerated in the ghetto were still largely unaware of the objective of the deportations. However, people gradually became aware of what the 'Jew trains' actually signified. Jews living near Belzec and Sobibor in particular soon found out about the killing centres and attempted to inform the Jewish communities elsewhere about the mass murders (Doc. 78). Information also reached the other districts through Polish railway workers, though such reports were often only fragmentary.[57]

The Jewish communities in District Lublin and District Galicia, and before long in Cracow as well, were therefore panic-stricken whenever another transport was immi-

54 Tadeusz Pankiewicz, *The Krakow Ghetto Pharmacy*, trans. Garry Malloy (Cracow: Wydawnictwo Literackie, 2013 [Polish edn, 1947]), p. 99.

55 Andrea Löw and Markus Roth, *Juden in Krakau unter deutscher Besatzung 1939–1945* (Göttingen: Wallstein, 2011), pp. 129–145. See also Franciszek Kotula, *Losy Żydów rzeszowskich 1939–1944: Kronika tamtych dni* (Rzeszów: Mitel, 1999); John J. Hartman and Jacek Krochmal (eds.), *Pamiętam każdy dzień ... Losy Żydów przemyskich podczas II wojny światowej* (Przemyśl: Towarzystwa Przyjaciół, 2001); Katarzyna Zimmerer, *Zamordowany świat: Losy Żydów w Krakowie 1939–1945* (Cracow: Wydawnictwo Literackie, 2004); and Elżbieta Rączy and Igor Witowicz (eds.), *Zagłada Żydów na Rzeszowszczyźnie: Album pamięci / Extermination of Jews in the Rzeszów Region: Album of Remembrance*, bilingual Polish-English edn (Rzeszów and Warsaw: Instytut Pamięci Narodowej, 2004).

56 These are the figures for Belzec from mid March to mid June 1942 and for Sobibor from May to mid July 1942; the Sobibor figures also include Jews who did not originate from locations in the General Government: see Yitzhak Arad, *The Operation Reinhard Death Camps: Belzec, Sobibor, Treblinka*, 2nd edn (Bloomington, IN: Indiana University Press; Jerusalem: Yad Vashem, 2018), pp. 73 and 80.

57 On the way information about Treblinka extermination camp spread, see Franciszek Ząbecki, *Wspomnienia dawne i nowe* (Warsaw: Instytut Pax, 1977); Arad, *The Operation Reinhard Death Camps*, pp. 37–43 and 81–99; and Maria Ferenc, *'Każdy pyta, co z nami będzie': Mieszkańcy getta warszawskiego wobec wiadomości o wojnie i Zagładzie* (Warsaw: Żydowski Instytut Historyczny, 2021).

nent. However, there was very little the ghetto inmates could do. Anyone who wanted to avoid deportation but lacked valid proof of employment – and even such proof did not always offer reliable protection in the chaos surrounding a 'resettlement operation' – had to look for a safe hiding place or get out of the ghetto (Doc. 68) and either flee into the forests or go into hiding on the 'Aryan side' (to use a term that was quickly adopted by speakers of Polish and Yiddish). In Lublin at least, many people went into hiding during the two-day pause in the deportation process from 29 to 31 March 1942. From autumn 1942 people started going into hiding on a mass scale. Of those who remained behind, particularly people who had work held on to the hope that they would not be deported. In addition, many ghetto inmates were anxious to avoid being separated from their relatives and friends. Only after they had already lost them did many ghetto inhabitants choose to escape or to resist.

At the time of the deportations to the extermination camps, the Jewish councils' moral dilemma became particularly clear. Most of the councils had cooperated with the German authorities since the onset of the occupation, thereby laying themselves open to criticism from the Jewish population. However, their actions had been motivated by the hope of being able to mitigate the draconian directives of the occupiers and to avert worse measures. Yet it was now increasingly evident that their actions had no influence on the Germans' plans; rather, the Germans forced the councils to compile death lists and to play a part in preparing for the deportations. While many councils did not compile lists, those that did fuelled the aversion many Jews felt towards these compulsory representative bodies. But the Jewish councils were in a hopeless situation: the occupiers replaced the Jews in positions of authority if they failed to carry out German orders unhesitatingly, and in the end the leadership of the Jewish communities was increasingly made up of compliant individuals who merely took orders. Artur Rosenzweig, for example, was made chairman of the Jewish Council in Cracow in autumn 1940, following the arrest of his predecessor, Marek Biberstein.[58] During the deportations in June 1942, the Germans became dissatisfied with Rosenzweig's degree of cooperation: according to the Security Police, the number of Jews forced to gather at the assembly point was too small. Rosenzweig was dragged out of a meeting, assaulted by a member of the SS, and forcibly taken to the assembly point himself. He was deported along with his family and murdered in Belzec – just as the chairman of the Jewish Council in Lublin, Henryk Bekker, had been on 31 March 1942.[59]

Elsewhere in the General Government, the first half of 1942 brought no radical change to everyday life in the ghettos. Mass deportations leading to the annihilation of most Jewish communities had not occurred in District Warsaw or District Radom up to this point. But the use of violence and intimidation against the Jews was on the rise in these districts too, particularly after the order was given for Jewish fugitives found outside the ghetto to

58 Aleksander Biberstein, *Zagłada Żydów w Krakowie* (Cracow: Wydanictwo Literackie, 2001).

59 Aharon Weiss, 'Jewish Leadership in Occupied Poland – Postures and Attitudes', *Yad Vashem Studies*, vol. 12 (1977), pp. 335–365. See also Nachman Blumental (ed.), *Te'udot mi-geto lublin – yudenrat le-lo derekh* [Documents from Lublin Ghetto: Judenrat without Direction] (Jerusalem: Yad Vashem, 1967 [Hebrew, with English preface and introduction]); and Isaiah Trunk, *Judenrat: The Jewish Councils in Eastern Europe under Nazi Occupation* (Lincoln, NE: University of Nebraska Press, 1996 [1972]).

be shot. Moreover, on 17–18 April 1942 Jews throughout the General Government who were deemed politically suspect were murdered (Doc. 70). At the same time, rumours about the 'resettlements' in other parts of the General Government were starting to circulate, as a witness from the Radom ghetto reported:

> Various things were said about the fate of the Lublin Jews, but all the accounts had one detail in common: that they were being resettled from Lublin to the nearby village of Majdanek (at the time, Majdanek was not yet known as a concentration camp). It was also said that the people who had been taken away were being exterminated, but nobody could believe that.[60]

In May 1942 Mary Berg (then: Miriam Wattenberg) wrote in her diary that most people were familiar with the information about mass murders, but many assumed that the events in Lublin could not be repeated in Warsaw because there were simply too many Jews living in the Warsaw ghetto.[61]

At this time, as a first step, the occupiers were focusing on murdering all Jews who were considered unfit for work. However, the German authorities were not yet in agreement as to what should be done with the remaining Jews, particularly those deployed as forced labourers. From the perspective of the occupation authorities, the manpower situation was about to become critical – not only in the Reich, but in occupied Poland as well. Increasing numbers of Poles, particularly young men and women, were being deported to the Reich for forced labour, thereby creating a labour shortage in the General Government. At the same time, by summer 1942 the Wehrmacht had presided over the mass death from starvation and disease of almost two million Soviet prisoners of war – men who could potentially have been used for forced labour. Yet because the General Government was considered relatively safe from Allied air strikes, in contrast to the Reich, the intention was to expand its economy, and many German enterprises had already begun to set up branches in occupied Poland. The civil administration also recognized that the Jews, particularly the craftsmen and skilled workers among them, represented an important labour resource (Doc. 84). In May 1942 the Wehrmacht's Armaments Inspectorate ordered that Jews should be increasingly deployed in war-related economic sectors in the General Government to replace Poles who had been sent to Germany. However, events were about to take a different turn.

## The second phase of the mass murders, July to December 1942

Final decisions were taken in June 1942. On 3 June Globocnik presented Himmler with a number of proposals for additional killing operations. On 9 June Himmler announced that the 'wandering' of the Jews would be over within a year, indicating that Jews across

60 Statement by Chaim Zajda, 5 May 1947, cited in Jacek Andrzej Młynarczyk, *Judenmord in Zentralpolen: Der Distrikt Radom im Generalgouvernement 1939–1945* (Darmstadt: WBG, 2007), p. 288.

61 *The Diary of Mary Berg: Growing Up in the Warsaw Ghetto* (Oxford: Oneworld Publications, 2007), p. 144 (entry for 8 May 1942).

the European continent would be eliminated by summer 1943.[62] On 9 July Globocnik and Himmler met with Higher SS and Police Leader Krüger. Having met Globocnik again on 19 July 1942 in Lublin, Himmler sent Krüger the order to complete the murder of the Jews in the General Government, with the aim of concluding the bulk of this operation by the end of the year (Doc. 96). The civil administration also intensified its efforts to deport the Jews to their deaths; its principal justification for this measure was the food shortage in the General Government. It maintained that most Jews were unemployed in any case and should be murdered for this reason.[63]

At the three extermination centres at Belzec, Sobibor, and Treblinka, the systematic daily mass murders were substantially expanded during the second half of 1942. Internally this was referred to as Operation Reinhard (also: Operation Reinhardt), presumably after Reinhard Heydrich, the chief of the Security Police and the SD, who was among those primarily responsible for the murder of the Jews; he died in Prague on 4 June 1942 of injuries sustained in an assassination attempt.

In mid July 1942 the central phase of the mass murders began, not only in the General Government, but also in many other territories under German control in both Western and Eastern Europe. During this period the liquidation of the last remaining ghettos in General Commissariat White Ruthenia and Reich Commissariat Ukraine began; from mid July a regular succession of transports from Western Europe to Auschwitz-Birkenau extermination camp also took place.[64]

On 22 July 1942 an SS and police unit from Lublin went to the Jewish Council in Warsaw and ordered its chairman, Adam Czerniaków, to henceforth provide 5,000 Jews for deportation every day (Doc. 98). Czerniaków was aware of the import of this demand, and he took his own life the following day (Doc. 99).[65] 'The chairman's death shocked the ghetto. People understood that the Jews' fate was sealed', the physician Ludwik Hirszfeld recalled.[66] Czerniaków 'had evidently hoped', as Meylekh Nayshtadt wrote directly after the war, 'that an alarm signal of this sort would galvanize the world, but his suicide did not become known abroad until a few weeks later, when it was announced in a Reuters cable from Zurich'.[67] Ringelblum's response was more critical: 'The suicide of Czerniaków. Too late – a sign of weakness.'[68] Marek Edelman, one of the leaders of the Ghetto Uprising in April 1943, later commented that, in his opinion, Czerniaków

62 Bradley F. Smith and Agnes F. Peterson (eds.), *Heinrich Himmler: Geheimreden 1933 bis 1945 und andere Ansprachen*, (Frankfurt am Main: Propyläen, 1974), p. 159.

63 Christian Gerlach, 'Die Bedeutung der deutschen Ernährungspolitik für die Beschleunigung des Mordes an den Juden 1942', in *Krieg, Ernährung, Völkermord: Forschungen zur deutschen Vernichtungspolitik im Zweiten Weltkrieg* (Hamburg: Hamburger Edition, 1998), pp. 167–257; see also Christian Gerlach, *The Extermination of the European Jews* (Cambridge: Cambridge University Press, 2016), pp. 215–260.

64 The transports from Western Europe to Auschwitz are documented in PMJ 12.

65 See Marcin Urynowicz, *Adam Czerniaków 1880–1942: Prezes getta Warszawskiego* (Warsaw: Instytut Pamięci Narodowej, 2009).

66 Ludwik Hirszfeld, *Historia jednego życia* (Warsaw: Pax, 2000 [1946]), pp. 388–389.

67 Meylekh Nayshtadt, *Khurbn un oyfshtand fun di yidn in varshe: Eydes-bleter un askores*, vol. 2: *Di gefalene oyf der vakh* (Tel Aviv: Algemeyner yidisher arbeter-organizatsye in erets-yisroel and Yidish-natsionaler arbeter-farband in amerike, 1948), p. 476. See also Urynowicz, *Adam Czerniaków*, pp. 338–340.

68 Written note cited in Kassow, *Who Will Write our History?*, p. 335.

should first have called on the people in the ghetto to fight; only then would he have had the right to die. 'He did not tell the people of the ghetto why he did it and what kind of an ending the Germans had in store for them.'[69]

On 22 July the first transport from Warsaw to the death camps departed for Treblinka, which had just been completed.[70] At first the police in Warsaw employed the strategy of luring ghetto residents to the trains with the promise of a special ration of food. After only a few days, however, word spread that the transports were taking people directly to their deaths. As a result, the Jewish Order Service began to use force to drag people out of the buildings in the ghetto.[71] Soon the German police and their foreign auxiliaries – particularly men from the SS training camp at Trawniki, most of whom were former inmates of prisoner-of-war camps for Soviet Red Army soldiers[72] – began to conduct their own roundups in Warsaw. One residential block after another was cordoned off and then searched; the workshops in the ghetto, the so-called szopy, were also increasingly targeted. Scenes of immense brutality ensued, and between July and September 1942 at least 10,000 people were shot during roundups in the ghetto, of whom approximately 6,000 were shot in a single day, during the 'cauldron' operation on 6 September. Jews designated for deportation were forced to proceed to the so-called Umschlagplatz (literally: 'reloading point'; in practice the holding area for deportees) on the northern edge of the Warsaw ghetto. Soon it made little to no difference whether the individuals targeted by the roundups or selections possessed work papers or not. Instead, the police were primarily interested in assembling a contingent of 5,000 or even 10,000 Jews every day to fill the trains that departed for Treblinka from a siding at Warsaw's Danzig railway station. In the concluding phase of the 'Große Aktion' ('Great Deportation') in the Warsaw ghetto in September 1942 – the term 'Aktion', or 'Aktsiye' in Yiddish, was used by the Jewish population for the roundups that were followed by selections and deportations – the police altered the procedure. From this point on, all ghetto inmates had to assemble at a large crossroads that was cordoned off on all sides, the 'cauldron on Miła Street' (Doc. 131). German employers such as the Walther C. Többens clothing company and Fritz Emil Schultz & Co., a Danzig firm that supplied winter clothing for the Wehrmacht, still had the opportunity to lay claim to their Jewish forced labourers – usually along with their families – and thereby to give them a reprieve from deportation. All the others were herded to the railway station and onto the trains, and taken to their deaths in Treblinka.

69 Witold Bereś and Krzysztof Burnetko, *Marek Edelman: Being on the Right Side*, trans. William R. Brand (Redwood City, CA, and Cracow: Bereś Media, 2016 [Polish edn, 2013]), p. 126.

70 See Havi Dreifuss (Ben-Sasson), *Geto Varsha HaSof* (Jerusalem: Yad Vashem, 2017 [Hebrew]), pp. 143–242, here pp. 143–154.

71 Aldona Podolska, *Służba porządkowa w getcie warszawskim w latach 1940–1943* (Warsaw: Fundacji 'Historia Pro Futuro', 1996); Katarzyna Person, *Warsaw Ghetto Police: The Jewish Order Service during the Nazi Occupation*, trans. Zygmunt Nowak-Soliński (Ithaca and London: Cornell University Press, 2021 [Polish edn, 2018]).

72 These units had been organized since autumn 1941 for the purpose of maintaining security in German settlements in the occupied Soviet territories. From the early spring of 1942, however, they were primarily used to assist with the mass murder of the Jews: see Peter Black, 'Foot Soldiers of the Final Solution: The Trawniki Training Camp and Operation Reinhard', *Holocaust and Genocide Studies*, vol. 25, no. 1 (2011), pp. 1–99.

With a brief respite between late August and early September 1942, the transports to the death camps departed Warsaw over a total of almost fifty days. It is not possible to determine the exact number of victims. Statistics kept by the Jewish Council account for the deportation of 265,000 people.[73] However, the decrease in the number of food ration cards issued suggests that the number of murdered Jews was closer to 300,000. The available statistics also document the age and gender of the victims. More than one third of them were children; virtually all the children and almost everyone over the age of sixty were sent to the gas chambers. Of the women, who had made up approximately two thirds of the ghetto population, only 7 per cent were still alive by November 1942 (Doc. 195, Table III).

The horrific fate of the children from the ghetto is exemplified by the orphanage in Krochmalna Street, which was run by the educator Henryk Goldszmit, known as Janusz Korczak. In summer 1942 there were an estimated 10,000 orphans in the ghetto, children who had lost their parents to epidemics or deportations. On 5 August the order for the children's deportation was issued. Korczak, who would have had a chance to escape, accompanied them on their final journey. The pianist Władysław Szpilman, one of the few inmates of the Warsaw ghetto to survive the war, described the scene in his memoir:

> He [Korczak] had spent long years of his life with children, and now, on this last journey, he would not leave them alone. He wanted to ease things for them. He told the orphans they were going out into the country, so they ought to be cheerful. At last they would be able to exchange the horrible, suffocating city walls for meadows of flowers, streams where they could bathe, woods full of berries and mushrooms. He told them to wear their best clothes, and so they came out into the yard, two by two, nicely dressed and in a happy mood.[74]

Some of the young women working at the orphanage also decided to accompany the children to Treblinka.

When Adina Blady Szwajgier, who worked as a nurse at the children's hospital in the Warsaw ghetto, heard about the order for the deportation of her young patients, she decided to give them morphine and thereby spare them the final journey to the extermination camp: 'And just as, during those two years of real work in the hospital, I had bent over the little beds, so now I poured this last medicine into these tiny mouths.'[75] The vast majority of the children did not survive the 'Great Deportation'. By the end of 1942 only a very few children, whose parents were skilled labourers, were still living in the ghetto.

Almost the entire organizational structure of the Warsaw ghetto collapsed in the wake of the mass deportations. Severe losses were also suffered by the small group of ghetto chroniclers working with the historian Emanuel Ringelblum to collect evidence

73 Gutman, *Jews of Warsaw*, pp. 270–271.

74 Władysław Szpilman, *The Pianist: The Extraordinary Story of One Man's Survival in Warsaw, 1939–45*, trans. Anthea Bell (London: Gollancz, 1999 [Polish edn, 1946]), pp. 93–94.

75 Adina Blady Szwajgier, *I Remember Nothing More: The Warsaw Children's Hospital and the Jewish Resistance*, trans. Tasja Darowska and Danusia Stok (London: Collins Harvill, 1990 [Polish edn, 1988]), p. 57.

secretly for the underground archive, which was set up to record the persecution and document the lives and deaths of the Polish Jews for posterity. Many of Ringelblum's associates fell victim to the roundups and were deported to Treblinka. Among them was Rabbi Shimon Huberband, whose compilation of essays and reports included an account of Jewish religious life under German occupation.[76] In early August 1942 Ringelblum ordered ten crates of materials to be buried. Most of them were recovered after the war, and they proved to contain extremely valuable documents concerning the history of the Polish Jews under German occupation. The approximately 25,000 pages of Ringelblum's Oyneg Shabes archive have been listed in the UNESCO Memory of the World Register since 1999. Ringelblum himself continued to work tirelessly; he even buried additional parts of the archives during the Ghetto Uprising in 1943.[77] In September 1943 he was rescued from Trawniki labour camp by the railway workers Shoshana Emilia Kosower, who was Jewish, and Tadeusz Pilewicz, who was Polish – both members of an underground movement. He returned to Warsaw, where he and his wife and son were among a group of thirty-one people hidden by Żegota (the Council to Aid Jews). He continued to write while in hiding. In March 1944 (Docs. 288 and 289), Ringelblum and his family were betrayed, and they were subsequently shot in Warsaw's Pawiak prison.

Amid the drama of the 'resettlement' operation in summer 1942, in their final texts those associated with the underground archive repeatedly expressed the wish that their names, at least, would live on through their writing. They wanted to remind generations to come that it was individuals rather than anonymous masses who were murdered. Yisroel Likhtenshteyn expressed the hope that people would remember him; his wife, Gele Sekshteyn, an artist who had worked as a teacher after 1939 and who buried some of her art from the ghetto along with the archive;[78] and his young daughter, Margolis (Doc. 106).

Following the 'Great Deportation' in Warsaw, in September 1942 the occupation administration substantially reduced the size of the ghetto and divided it into three separate sections, which were grouped around the workshops. According to official records, of the 400,000 people who originally lived in this ghetto, the largest one established by the Germans, only approximately 30,000 Jewish workers remained. An equal number of 'illegals' were living there in hiding. Those who were still alive had to cope with the loss of their close relatives and friends. At the same time, they could never be certain when another 'Aktion' might threaten their own lives. Emanuel Ringelblum wrote about these fears in his diary in December 1942:

> We are currently going through a tragic time. We, the last remnants of the Warsaw Jews, have no idea what tomorrow will bring. We continuously ask ourselves: What

76 Shimon Huberband, *Kiddush Hashem: Jewish Religious and Cultural Life in Poland during the Holocaust*, ed. Jeffrey Gurock and Robert Hirt, trans. from Yiddish David Fishman (Hoboken: Ktav, 1987).

77 See Ruta Sakowska (ed.), *Archiwum Ringelbluma: Getto warszawskie lipiec 1942 – styczeń 1943* (Warsaw: Państwowe Wydawnictwo Naukowe, 1980); Ruta Sakowska et al. (eds.), *Archiwum Ringelbluma: Konspiracyne Archiwum Getta Warszawy*, esp. vol. 5: *Getto warszawskie: Życie codzienne*, ed. Katarzyna Person (2011), and vol. 6: *Generalne Gubernatorstwo: Relacje i dokumenty*, ed. Aleksandra Bańkowska (2011).

78 Sakowska et al. (eds.), *Archiwum Ringelbluma: Konspiracyne Archiwum Getta Warszawy*, vol. 4: *Życie i twórczość Geli Seksztajn*, ed. Magdalena Tarnowska (2011).

> will become of us? Will the enemy spare us, or are we doomed to destruction, as was the case for the Jews from hundreds of Polish towns and villages as well as from other countries?[79]

Not only in Warsaw, but in the other districts as well, the mass murders reached their peak in the period from July to the end of September 1942. Most of the residents of every ghetto in the General Government were forced to go to assembly points, where some of the workers were separated from the group. The majority of the victims were transported on goods trains to Belzec and Treblinka. Only the rail traffic to Sobibor was interrupted temporarily, because the railway line to that destination was out of service until early October.

While the deportations from Warsaw were still at their height, the Lublin SS and police units went to the eastern part of that district to deport the majority of the ghetto residents.[80] The liquidation of the ghettos also had a devastating impact in District Radom. Around 350,000 Jews were living there in mid 1942, in Kielce, Radom, Tomaszów Mazowiecki, Częstochowa, and other localities. In less than seven weeks in August and September 1942, approximately 300,000 of them were murdered in Treblinka.[81]

In October 1942 the SS and police continued to liquidate the ghettos in many small Polish towns. After the shock of the mass murders in July and August, the survivors made preparations to escape the ghettos while there was still time, or to go into hiding. On 24 December 1942 Emanuel Ringelblum noted in his Warsaw diary that there had been a large increase in the number of hideouts:

> Now, in December 1942, hiding places are very popular. Everyone is making them. Everywhere, in all the shops and elsewhere in the Ghetto, hiding places are being built. Their construction has actually become a flourishing specialized craft. Skilled workers, engineers, etc. are making a living out of it. Hiding places go back many years. People began to hide out in Warsaw when the Germans entered Warsaw, in October, 1939. People hid themselves, hid their goods.[82]

The perpetrators were also aware of this. In late October 1942 Higher SS and Police Leader Krüger issued a regulation listing the towns in which ghettos were still officially permitted to exist (Doc. 168). This meant that all Jews found anywhere else were to be shot. The order to shoot Jews captured outside their mandatory places of residence, which had been in force since late 1941, was thus substantially expanded. Many of the ensuing killing operations that took place between early October and early December 1942 resembled frenzied, chaotic manhunts. In District Lublin, the killing of Jews was considered to be

79 Emanuel Ringelblum, *Ksovim fun geto*, vol. 2, *Notitsn un ophandlungen (1942–1943)*, ed. Tatiana Berenstein et al. (Warsaw: Yidish bukh, 1963), p. 37.

80 Jacek Andrzej Młynarczyk, '"Akcja Reinhard" w gettach prowincjonalnych dystryktu warszawskiego 1942–1943', in Barbara Engelking, Jacek Leociak, and Dariusz Libionka (eds.), *Prowincja noc: Życie i zagłada Żydów w dystrykcie warszawskim* (Warsaw: Instytut Filozofii i Socjologii PAN, 2007), pp. 39–74.

81 Młynarczyk, *Judenmord in Zentralpolen*; Krzysztof Urbański, *Zagłada Żydów w dystrykcie radomskim* (Cracow: Wydawnictwo Naukowe Akademii Pedagogicznej, 2004).

82 Ringelblum, *Ksovim fun geto*, vol. 2, p. 48; Ringelblum, *Notes from the Warsaw Ghetto*, p. 338.

officially concluded as of 9 November 1942, when the residual Lublin ghetto was liquidated.

Only workers still had at least a temporary chance of survival. In spring 1942 the German occupiers had begun to debate whether certain groups of Jews, mostly men between the ages of sixteen and forty, should be kept alive as a workforce. This course of action was advocated particularly by many Wehrmacht officers in the General Government, who used Jewish forced labourers for military contracts and also oversaw the armaments industry. Disputes over the workforce intensified with the start of the mass deportations in July. In one case, a dispute over labour was the occasion for an act of rescue by Wehrmacht officers: by threatening to open fire, personnel from the Ortskommandantur in Przemyśl prevented Jewish workers from being taken away to death camps (Doc. 101). The garrison commander, Max Liedtke, and his deputy, Albert Battel, were later honoured as Righteous Among the Nations by the State of Israel.[83]

The SS leadership now stepped in. Representatives of the Wehrmacht's Armaments Inspectorate and the SS and police leadership in the General Government agreed that, from this point on, Jewish workers were to be housed only in camps supervised by the SS and then 'loaned out' to the Wehrmacht and to other businesses. The SS subsequently established its own labour camps near particular firms or enlarged existing camps. Above all, many ghettos were designated as 'labour ghettos' after most of the residents had been deported. Only Jewish forced labourers were allowed to continue living there, sometimes along with their families.[84] Several large camp complexes were therefore in existence in autumn 1942.[85] The camps along Thoroughfare IV (Durchgangsstraße IV), which was the supply route for Army Group South, and the industrial camps for enterprises in District Radom and District Cracow had been established for some time. The largest of these were in Starachowice, Skarżysko-Kamienna, and Cracow-Płaszów.[86] The number of Jewish inmates in each of these camps reached 10,000 at times. In addition, in District Lublin the SS established a camp system that was intended to help develop

83 Yisrael Gutman (ed.), *Rescuers of Jews during the Holocaust: Europe (Part I) and Other Countries* (Jerusalem: Yad Vashem, 2007), pp. 71–72 (Albert Battel) and 119–120 (Max Liedtke).

84 Jürgen Hensel and Stephan Lehnstaedt (eds.), *Arbeit in den nationalsozialistischen Ghettos* (Osnabrück: fibre, 2013).

85 Józef Marszałek, *Obozy pracy w Generalnym Gubernatorstwie w latach 1939–1945* (Lublin: Państwowe Muzeum na Majdanku, 1998); Yones, *Die Straße nach Lemberg*, pp. 38–104; Mario Wenzel, 'Zwangsarbeitslager für Juden in den besetzten polnischen und sowjetischen Gebieten', in Wolfgang Benz and Barbara Distel (eds.), *Der Ort des Terrors*, vol. 9: *Arbeitserziehungslager, Ghettos, Jugendschutzlager, Polizeihaftlager, Sonderlager, Zigeunerlager, Zwangsarbeiterlager* (Munich: Beck, 2009), pp. 125–154; Mario Wenzel, *Arbeitszwang und Judenmord: Die Arbeitslager für Juden im Distrikt Krakau des Generalgouvernements 1939–1944* (Berlin: Metropol, 2017); Marta Janczewska, 'Obozy pracy przymusowej dla Żydów na terenie dystryktu warszawskiego', in Engelking, Leociak, and Libionka (eds.), *Prowincja noc*, pp. 271–320.

86 On the Skarżysko-Kamienna and Płaszów camps, see Roman Kiełkowski, *Zlikwidować na miejscu: Z dziejów okupacji hitlerowskiej w Krakowie* (Cracow: Wydawnictwo Literackie, 1981); Felicja Karay, *Death Comes in Yellow: Skarzysko-Kamienna Slave Labor Camp*, trans. from Hebrew Sara Kitai (Amsterdam: Harwood, 1996); and Benz and Distel (eds.), *Der Ort des Terrors*, vol. 8: *Riga-Kaiserswald, Warschau, Vaivara, Kauen (Kaunas), Płaszów, Kulmhof/Chelmno, Belzec, Sobibor, Treblinka* (Munich: Beck, 2008), pp. 233–298. On Starachowice, see Christopher R. Browning, *Remembering Survival: Inside a Nazi Slave-Labor Camp* (New York: Norton & Co., 2010).

Ostindustrie, an industrial concern set up by the SS in March 1943.[87] Here too, some camps – such as Poniatowa and Trawniki – held as many as 10,000 prisoners at times.[88]

Over the whole course of the occupation, a total of approximately 300–400 such forced labour camps were set up in the General Government, though some consisted of a single residential barracks and existed for only a short time. While confinement in a labour camp offered temporary protection from deportation, in most cases the living conditions were atrocious. To an even greater extent than in the ghettos, the inmates were subject to the arbitrary actions of their guards, whom they faced day after day. The food supply was entirely inadequate, and murder was an everyday occurrence. Working conditions, however, varied considerably depending on the camp management and the economic sector concerned; for example, the situation in the textile enterprises, which had been relocated from the Warsaw ghetto to Trawniki and Poniatowa, was markedly better than the conditions under which the construction work along Durchgangsstraße IV took place. All in all, however, the circumstances outlined above ruled out any rational 'labour deployment' of Jews, and the economic benefit thus fell far short of what the Germans envisaged.[89]

According to official German reports, in early 1943 only around 300,000 Jews remained in the General Government, most of whom were Jewish forced labourers – both men and women – sometimes with their family members. Only in District Galicia, where persecution had begun later than in the other districts, were nearly one third of the Jewish residents still alive by this point: the official figure for that district was 161,000 Jews.[90]

Deportations to Treblinka from District Radom and District Warsaw continued, while Jews in Cracow were deported to Auschwitz-Birkenau camp, located further to the west. From early 1943 the police in Eastern Galicia again carried out mass shootings, as they had done in 1942. By this point ghettos remained in only a few of the larger towns, and they were all – without exception – liquidated by summer 1943. In July 1943 the German authorities considered the 'final solution' in the General Government to be largely complete.

Only a very few labour camps remained. In October 1943 the SS leadership decided to close the last camps in the southern and eastern parts of the General Government as

87 Jan Erik Schulte, 'Zwangsarbeit für die SS. Juden in der Ostindustrie GmbH', in Norbert Frei et al. (eds.), *Ausbeutung, Vernichtung, Öffentlichkeit: Neue Studien zur nationalsozialistischen Lagerpolitik* (Munich: Saur, 2000), pp. 43–74. Odilo Globocnik was one of Ostindustrie's two managers.

88 Czesław Rajca, 'Lubelska filia Niemieckich Zakładów Zbrojeniowych', *Zeszyty Majdanka*, vol. 4 (1969), pp. 237–299; Ryszard Gicewicz, 'Obóz pracy w Poniatowej (1941–1943)', *Zeszyty Majdanka*, vol. 10 (1980), pp. 88–104; Helge Grabitz and Wolfgang Scheffler, *Letzte Spuren: Ghetto Warschau – SS-Arbeitslager Trawniki – Aktion Erntefest. Fotos und Dokumente über Opfer des Endlösungswahns im Spiegel der historischen Ereignisse* (Berlin: Hentrich, 1988). According to one estimate, a maximum of 14,500 prisoners were held in Poniatowa on the eve of its liquidation: Sam H. Hoffenberg with Patrick Girard, *Le Camp de Poniatowa: la liquidation des derniers Juifs de Varsovie* (Paris: Éditions Bibliophanes, 1988), p. 80. On Ostindustrie, see Jan-Erik Schulte, *Zwangsarbeit und Vernichtung: Das Wirtschaftsimperium der SS. Oswald Pohl und das SS-Wirtschafts-Verwaltungshauptamt 1933–1945* (Paderborn: Schöningh, 2001), pp. 145, 180, 317, 416, and 435; and Wolf Gruner, *Jewish Forced Labor under the Nazis: Economic Needs and Racial Aims, 1938–1944*, trans. from German Kathleen M. Dell'Orto (Cambridge: Cambridge University Press, 2006), pp. 271–272.

89 See Ingo Loose, 'Die Bedeutung der Ghettoarbeit für die nationalsozialistische Kriegswirtschaft', in Hensel and Lehnstaedt (eds.), *Arbeit in den nationalsozialistischen Ghettos*, pp. 71–90.

90 Pohl, *Judenverfolgung in Ostgalizien*, p. 245.

well, and to kill the people confined there. The intention was to pre-empt prisoner rebellions, which they feared in light of the prisoners' desperate situation and the Red Army's advance. In the cynically codenamed Operation Harvest Festival (Aktion Erntefest) on 3 and 4 November 1943, SS and police units surrounded the large forced labour camps at Trawniki and Poniatowa in District Lublin. There, as well as in Lublin-Majdanek camp, the Security Police shot virtually all the prisoners – approximately 43,000 in total (Docs. 276 and 277).[91] This was the last large-scale killing operation in the General Government.

## The liquidation of the ghettos

It is now clearly established that the killing of the Jews in the General Government was not carried out on the basis of detailed orders, but rather followed generally worded instructions from Berlin. The planning and organization of what amounted to far more than a thousand individual operations to liquidate the ghettos and to carry out deportations and shootings, as well as an immense number of other crimes in the ghettos and camps, was largely in the hands of the SS and police apparatus in Cracow and in the districts. At its head was the Higher SS and Police Leader in the General Government, Friedrich-Wilhelm Krüger, though his small department had above all a coordinating function.

The SS and Police Leaders in the districts assigned to these tasks their own officials in charge of Jewish affairs (*Judenreferenten*), who worked closely with the Security Police. When preparing ghetto liquidations, the officials in charge of Jewish affairs and the Security Police cooperated with the civil administration, particularly with the labour administration, and even more so with the Population and Welfare Division within the Interior Administration Department of the General Government, which had played a key role from the outset in determining the policy towards the Jewish population. This collaboration continued in the individual districts and Kreise. As a result, 'Aktionen' generally began with the parties involved holding joint meetings in the areas where the operations were to take place.

Prior to liquidations, the ghettos would usually be encircled by German units consisting mainly of Security Police officials and, in greater numbers, members of the Order Police – that is, the gendarmerie in rural areas and the Urban Police in the cities.[92] Par-

91 On Operation Harvest Festival, see Wojciech Lenarczyk and Dariusz Libionka, *Erntefest 3–4 listopada 1943: zapomniany epizod Zagłady* (Lublin: Państwowe Muzeum na Majdanku, 2009); and Grabitz and Scheffler, *Letzte Spuren*, pp. 262-272 and 328-333. On the liquidation of Trawniki forced labour camp, see Grabitz and Scheffler, *Letzte Spuren*, pp. 328-333. On the murders in Lublin-Majdanek camp, see Wachsmann, *KL*, pp. 330–332.

92 Christopher R. Browning, *Ordinary Men: Reserve Police Battalion 101 and the Final Solution in Poland* (New York: Harper Collins, 1992), pp. 106–113. See also Stefan Klemp, *Freispruch für das 'Mord-Bataillon': Die NS-Ordnungspolizei und die Nachkriegsjustiz* (Münster: LIT, 1998); Thomas Geldmacher, *'Wir als Wiener waren ja bei der Bevölkerung beliebt': Österreichische Schutzpolizisten und die Judenvernichtung in Ostgalizien 1941–1944* (Vienna: Mandelbaum, 2002); and Wolfgang Curilla, *Der Judenmord in Polen und die deutsche Ordnungspolizei 1939–1945* (Paderborn: Schöningh, 2011).

ticularly in District Lublin, but also in Warsaw, these units were reinforced by squads from the SS training camp at Trawniki. Small German police units, often accompanied by Polish police or Ukrainian auxiliary police, Polish volunteer firefighters, and members of the so-called Polish Construction Service (Baudienst), carried out the roundups in the ghettos and forced people out of their homes and into the street.[93] The Jewish Order Service often had to assist with these operations. Older people who could not move quickly enough and small children who had been left behind were mostly shot in their homes by the police. Similarly, the police murdered hospital patients on the spot, not infrequently along with the nursing staff.

In spring 1942, and also in the first few days following the onset of the planned total extermination of the Jews in late July 1942, the unbridled and brutal nature of the violence took the ghetto population largely by surprise. That summer more and more people started to believe the rumours and information that had been circulating and became aware that they themselves might be faced with such a fate. As a result, from August 1942 increasing numbers of Jews began to prepare themselves for the worst by arranging hiding places, planning their escape, and occasionally also by trying to place their children on the 'Aryan side' with non-Jewish friends or acquaintances from before the war, or trying to hide them in orphanages, convents, or monasteries.

Politically active groups increased their efforts to acquire weapons, but this proved to be a very difficult, often impossible endeavour. Above all, however, ghetto residents sought to obtain a certificate from the employment office or a supposedly secure job. Those in possession of the tools of a trade or equipment such as a sewing machine had a chance of a reprieve during a selection process. However, the German authorities repeatedly replaced the work certificates with new ones, issuing fewer each time, and Security Police officials rather than the employment offices were by summer 1942 mostly in charge of these documents. The significance of work certificates in raising the chances of survival therefore dwindled after the end of August 1942.

During the ghetto liquidations residents tried, as fast as they could, to get into residential blocks that were not being surrounded, or into buildings that had already been emptied. Yet only a fraction of the Jews managed to go underground during the roundups; police units fired at anyone who tried to escape. Those arrested were then forcibly taken to assembly points by the guards. There, the police – and often also businessmen or German officials working for the civil administration – decided who would live and who would die.

93 On the Polish 'Blue Police', so called because of their dark blue uniforms, see Jacek Andrzej Młynarczyk et al., 'Eastern Europe: Belarusian Auxiliaries, Ukrainian Waffen-SS Soldiers and the Special Case of the Polish "Blue Police"', in Jochen Böhler and Robert Gerwarth (eds.), *The Waffen-SS: A European History* (Oxford: Oxford University Press, 2017), pp. 169–179; Jan Grabowski, 'Strażacy, wiejska straż nocna i granatowa policja a zagłada Żydów na obszarach wiejskich w dystrykcie krakowskim', in Adam Sitarek, Michał Trębacz, and Ewa Wiatr (eds.), *Zagłada Żydów na polskiej prowincji* (Łódź: Instytut Pamięci Narodowej, 2012), pp. 245–264; and Jan Grabowski, *Na posterunku: Udział polskiej policji granatowej i kryminalnej w zagładzie Żydów* (Wołowiec: Czarne, 2020). The Baudienst was a paramilitary organization for Polish youth established by the Germans in May 1940 and primarily active in District Cracow: see Jan Grabowski, *Hunt for the Jews: Betrayal and Murder in German-Occupied Poland* (Bloomington, IN: Indiana University Press, 2014 [Polish edn, 2011]), pp. 121–129.

Next the guards pushed the victims onto waiting goods trains; at times they reportedly crammed as many as 200 people into a single goods wagon (Doc. 110). In the process, families were often torn apart forever. The Reich Railway or the Eastern Railway (Ostbahn) provided the trains, and their employees very quickly understood the purpose of the transports. The transports did not usually have to cover long distances to reach the extermination camps, but they travelled very slowly, with the result that the people inside endured unbearable torments, suffering from heat and thirst in summer 1942, and from freezing temperatures during the winter months. Some of the deportees perished during the journey, especially the elderly and small children. Only a very few managed to force their way out of the wagons and to escape by jumping from the train. Shots were immediately fired at anyone who did so (Doc. 177). Often the bodies of murdered escapees were left lying on the railway embankments after the deportation trains had passed through. But even those who managed to break out of the sealed goods wagons had only a slim chance of survival. People living near the railway tracks usually refused to help Jews in any way, partly due to their justified fear of German reprisals.[94]

## Extermination camps

Most of the Jews from the towns in the General Government were murdered in the Operation Reinhard extermination centres at Belzec, Sobibor, and Treblinka.[95] Many people from District Lublin, among them Jews who had recently been deported there from Slovakia,[96] met their deaths in Lublin-Majdanek concentration camp (Doc. 79).[97] From 1943 some transports also departed from District Cracow to the nearby Auschwitz-Birkenau concentration camp, which had also begun to operate as a death camp for Jews in 1942.

The Operation Reinhard camps were the main sites at which the systematic mass killing of European Jews was carried out in the period between March 1942 and spring 1943. Tens of thousands of Jews were killed at Auschwitz during this period, but it was not until spring 1943 that this camp, now synonymous with the mass murder, began to

94 On the extent of the escapes, see Grzegorz Berendt, 'Żydzi zbiegli z gett i obozów śmierci', in Sitarek, Trębacz, and Wiatr (eds.), *Zagłada Żydów na polskiej prowincji*, pp. 121–158; on Polish reactions to escaping Jews, see Franziska Bruder, *Das eigene Schicksal selbst bestimmen: Fluchten aus den Deportationszügen in die Vernichtungslager der 'Aktion Reinhardt' in Polen* (Mainz: Unrast, 2019), pp. 53–54.

95 On the Operation Reinhard extermination camps, see Adalbert Rückerl (ed.), *NS-Vernichtungslager im Spiegel deutscher Strafprozesse: Belzec, Sobibor, Treblinka, Chelmno* (Munich: DTV, 1977); Arad, *The Operation Reinhard Death Camps*; and Peter Longerich, *Holocaust: The Nazi Persecution and Murder of the Jews*, trans. Shaun Whiteside (Oxford: Oxford University Press, 2010 [German edn, 1998]), pp. 277–284 and 294–296.

96 See Yehoshua R. Büchler, 'The Deportation of Slovakian Jews to the Lublin District of Poland in 1942', *Holocaust and Genocide Studies*, vol. 6, no. 2 (1991), pp. 151–166; Pohl, *Von der 'Judenpolitik' zum Judenmord*, pp. 107–108 and 119; PMJ 13/94; and the Introduction to PMJ 13.

97 Tomasz Kranz, *Extermination of Jews at the Majdanek Concentration Camp* (Lublin: Państwowe Muzeum na Majdanku, 2010), pp. 20–31. See also Barbara Schwindt, *Das Konzentrations- und Vernichtungslager Majdanek: Funktionswandel im Kontext der 'Endlösung'* (Würzburg: Königshausen & Neumann, 2005).

play a central role as an extermination site. Since the Operation Reinhard documents, like the camp buildings, were almost entirely destroyed by the perpetrators in autumn 1943, reconstructing the history of these camps relies primarily on the accounts of survivors, who recounted their experiences immediately afterwards (Doc. 147) or were questioned after the war. The reports from the Polish underground movement provide an additional source of information (Doc. 136), as do records of German and Soviet trials and pre-trial investigations, as well as archaeological excavations.[98]

All three camps were under the control of SS and Police Leader Globocnik, who was based in Lublin, where he established his own Operation Reinhard department in August 1942. The Operation Reinhard department was headed by Globocnik's chief of staff, Hermann Höfle. The inspector of the three camps was Christian Wirth, formerly a police detective and inspector of the killing centres of the 'euthanasia' operation. Although the murder sites in the General Government were later usually referred to as 'camps', it was not intended that Jewish deportees would stay there for any length of time. The layout of the camps was similar; only Treblinka, the last of the three camps to be built, was spread out over a wide, fenced-off area. They consisted of a relatively simple set of buildings and were equipped with a railway siding as well as a platform for arriving trains. Another part of the camp housed a small number of Jewish forced labourers, temporarily spared from death, while an additional, largely closed-off area contained the building with the gas chambers and the open ground for mass graves.[99]

The German camp personnel usually consisted of only 25–35 Reich Germans, generally low-ranking. Most of them had been recruited from the 'euthanasia' programme.[100] The guard force at each camp, which was responsible for supervising operations inside the camp and for guarding its perimeter, was made up of around 120 non-German auxiliaries from Trawniki camp. Most of these were Ukrainian, but there were also individuals of other nationalities from the Soviet Union (Doc. 92).[101]

98 See, for example, Yoram Haimi and Wojciech Mazurek, 'Uncovering the Remains of a Nazi Death Camp: Archaeological Research in Sobibór', *Yad Vashem Studies*, vol. 41 (2013), pp. 55-94; and Caroline Sturdy Colls, *Holocaust Archaeologies: Approaches and Future Directions* (Heidelberg: Springer, 2015), pp. 20 and 206-208.

99 Eugen Kogon et al. (eds.), *Nazi Mass Murder*, pp. 102–138; Robert Kuwałek, 'Obóz zagłady w Sobiborze w historiografii polskiej i obcej', *Zeszyty Majdanka*, vol. 21 (2001), pp. 115–160; Witold Chrostowski, *Extermination Camp, Treblinka* (London: Vallentine Mitchell, 2004); Benz and Distel (eds.), *Der Ort des Terrors*, vol. 8; Robert Kuwałek, *Das Vernichtungslager Bełżec* (Berlin: Metropol, 2013); Marek Bem, *Sobibor Extermination Camp, 1942–1943*, trans. Tomasz Karpiński and Natalia Sarzyńska-Wójtowicz (Amsterdam: Stichting Sobibor, 2015 [Polish edn, 2011]); Chris Webb and Michal Chocholatý, *The Treblinka Death Camp: History, Biographies, Remembrance* (Stuttgart: *ibidem*, 2014); and Bildungswerk Stanisław Hantz e.V./Forschungsstelle Ludwigsburg der Universität Stuttgart, *Fotos aus Sobibor: Die Niemann-Sammlung zu Holocaust und Nationalsozialismus* (Berlin: Dietz, 2020).

100 Berger, *Experten der Vernichtung.*

101 Dieter Pohl, 'Die Trawniki-Männer im Vernichtungslager Belzec', in Alfred Gottwaldt, Norbert Kampe, and Peter Klein (eds.), *NS-Gewaltherrschaft: Beiträge zur historischen Forschung und juristischen Aufarbeitung*, vol. 11 (Berlin: Edition Hentrich, 2005), pp. 278–289. On the number of people on each camp's guard force, see Black, 'Foot Soldiers of the Final Solution', p. 20; and Angelika Benz, *Handlanger der SS: Die Rolle der Trawniki-Männer im Holocaust* (Berlin: Metropol, 2015), p. 184.

Finally there were the Sonderkommandos, which consisted of between 300 and 1,000 Jewish men: the numbers varied over time. These prisoners were selected from the newly arriving transports, usually on the basis of their physical condition and manual skills (Doc. 151). Their function was primarily to serve the camp officials, but when the transports arrived, they also performed tasks such as collecting and sorting through the deportees' remaining belongings. A special Sonderkommando lived in a sealed-off area within the section of the camp used for killing. The main task of this unit was to remove the bodies from the gas chambers.

The guards used extreme violence to spur on the prisoners in the Sonderkommandos. Prisoners were often beaten so badly that the German camp management then classified them as 'unfit for work' and had them murdered as well. During the first phase of the extermination camps, the camp SS killed the entire Sonderkommando periodically in order to get rid of witnesses; later, from mid 1942, the composition of the Sonderkommandos became somewhat more stable. The prisoners in the Sonderkommandos witnessed unimaginable scenes. As Chaim Hirszman, one of only three known survivors of Belzec, recalled after the war: 'In one of the "transports" taken out of the gas chamber, I found the body of my wife and I had to shave her hair.'[102] Rudolf Reder, another survivor of Belzec, struggled to put the horror into words:

> I don't know how to describe the mood in which we lived, we doomed prisoners, or what we felt hearing those horrible pleas of the people being suffocated each day, and the cries of the children. Three times a day we saw thousands of people on the verge of losing their minds. And we were close to insanity. We moved from one day to the next, not knowing how. We had not a moment of illusion. Each day we died a little along with the whole transports of people who for a short moment still experienced the torment of illusion. Apathetic and resigned, we didn't even feel the hunger or cold. Each waited his turn, knew that he too must die and must suffer inhumanly. Only, when I heard how the children cried out – 'Mama! But I've been good! It's dark! It's dark!' – our hearts were torn to shreds. And then we went back to not feeling anything.[103]

Again and again prisoners tried to escape, and eventually there were even mass escapes from Treblinka and Sobibor.

Once the transports had arrived at one of the three extermination camps, the deported Jews – most of whom were completely exhausted – were forced out of the goods wagons and into a sort of roll-call area. Unlike at Auschwitz, selections for forced labour at Belzec, Treblinka, and Sobibor took place in the ghettos prior to deportation. Upon

102 AŻIH, 301/1476. Cited in Martin Gilbert, *The Holocaust: The Jewish Tragedy* (New York: HarperCollins, 1989), p. 304.

103 Rudolf Reder, 'Testimony of the Camp in Bełżec', in Rudolf Reder, *Bełżec*, trans. from Polish Michael Jacobs (Cracow: Fundacja Judaica, 1999 [1946]), pp. 115–143, here p. 141. For a slightly different translation, see Rudolf Reder, *I Survived a Secret Nazi Extermination Camp*, ed. Mark Forstater, trans. from Polish Feliks Pastusiak (Hove: Psychology News Press, 2015), p. 38. See also Kuwałek, *Vernichtungslager*, pp. 216–217; Jarosław Joniec, *Niemiecki obóz zagłady w Bełżcu: Zarys historii* (Lublin: Państwowe Muzeum na Majdanku, 2016); and Dariusz Libionka (ed.), *Obóz zagłady w Bełżcu w relacjach ocalonych i zeznaniach polskich świadków* (Lublin: Państwowe Muzeum na Majdanku, 2013).

arrival at these camps, only a few individuals – less than 1 per cent of the deportees – were additionally selected for forced labour and left alive for the time being. Those who were unable to move were taken on stretchers to a separate area that was made to look like an infirmary, where they were shot straight away. All the others were taken to a separate part of the camp, where they had to undress. After that, first the men and then the women and children were forced into the building containing the gas chambers, where they were asphyxiated with engine exhaust fumes.

The prisoners in the Sonderkommando had to take the bodies out of the gas chambers, search them for hidden valuables, and then throw them into gigantic pits. In mid December 1942, when the killings at Belzec camp stopped, the graves were reopened and the corpses were burned on huge grids made from railway tracks. A similar process began at Sobibor and Treblinka camps in spring 1943, but there the mass murders continued into the autumn.

According to internal figures compiled by the German occupation administration, by the end of 1942 no fewer than 1,274,166 people had been murdered during Operation Reinhard alone (Doc. 204). This figure included the 24,733 Jews murdered in Lublin-Majdanek: this is an instance of the term Reinhard/Reinhardt (or, as in Doc. 204, 'Reinhart') being used, as it was sporadically in SS documents, to refer to the murder of Jews at Majdanek as well as at Belzec, Sobibor, and Treblinka.[104] It is estimated that by autumn 1943 between 440,000 and 453,000 people had perished in Belzec, approximately 180,000 in Sobibor, and approximately 800,000 in Treblinka, although the figures could be higher. The vast majority were Polish Jews, but the victims also included Jews from the Netherlands, the German Reich, and other countries.[105]

## Reactions

Before the systematic mass murder began, Poles for the most part had distanced themselves from the persecuted Jews. Some of the ghettos were hermetically sealed off, and there were usually few opportunities for contact with those on the other side; as a result, most Poles paid little attention to the fate of the Jews. Many Poles viewed the Jews in general as supporters of communism and held them jointly responsible for the brutal Soviet regime in eastern Poland between September 1939 and mid 1941. After the Wehrmacht had invaded these territories in June 1941, bloody pogroms targeting Jews took place – in the Białystok area, for example – which were often instigated by the German police. The Polish underground movement – still in its infancy at the time – and the Polish government in exile in London also took a rather ambivalent approach to the Jewish minority over the course of 1941 (see Doc. 8).

Up to the present day, controversies continue about the Poles' conduct once the mass murder of the Jews had begun. Some of the reactions of specific Polish institutions and

104 Peter Witte and Stephen Tyas, 'A New Document on the Deportation and Murder of Jews during "Einsatz Reinhardt" 1942', *Holocaust and Genocide Studies*, vol. 15, no. 3 (2001), pp. 468–86; Wachsmann, *KL*, p. 293 and 706, fn. 18. This usage occasionally also extended to include the murder of Jews at Auschwitz.

105 Kuwałek, *Vernichtungslager*, pp. 237–246.

underground resistance organizations in the face of the mass murder are traced in more detail below. However, reaching general conclusions about the reactions of the Polish population more broadly is fraught with difficulty: source materials are fragmentary, and methodologies and interpretations are contested.[106] Poles themselves were in an extraordinarily difficult situation during the war. The German occupiers had murdered sections of the Polish elite and deported almost two million Polish men and women, most of them young, to the Reich for forced labour. Under the occupation, open expressions of support for Jews were possible only among one's closest confidants, because of the risk of being denounced by fellow citizens. Helping Jews, not least giving them places to hide, put individuals in mortal danger: from the end of 1941 at the latest, such actions were punishable by death or other draconian forms of reprisal (Docs. 144, 284, and 287).[107]

Knowledge of the mass murder can be assumed to have spread quickly. Through the black market, the Jewish underground movement, and other channels, most Poles were well informed about what was happening to the Jews, despite the restricted contact between ghetto residents and the outside world.[108] Where Poles were living in geographical proximity to the death camps, they could find out more easily about the occupiers' actions, and this information could then be shared with friends and relatives within Poland, despite the extensive restrictions imposed on the public sphere. In addition, ghetto liquidations took place in almost every Polish town, sometimes in plain sight (see Doc. 59).

There are indications of changes in the Polish population's attitudes towards the Jews from late autumn 1942 onwards. It is possible to trace a range of reactions – including shock, abhorrence, and fear – in response to the extreme violence occurring in the towns and the countryside, as well as the imminent murder of the entire Jewish population. A number of sources written by Polish eyewitnesses at the time express a sense of horror at being at the scene of an unprecedented crime.[109] Other sources suggest that Poles began to ask themselves whether Jews and Poles were to share a common fate: as it became clear that the Germans intended to murder all Jews without exception, more and more Poles wondered what would come after that, and whether they might be the

106 See Andrzej Żbikowski (ed.), *Polacy i Żydzi pod okupacją niemiecką 1939–1945: Studia i materiały* (Warsaw: Instytut Pamięci Narodowej, 2006); Antony Polonsky, Hanna Węgrzynek, and Andrzej Żbikowski (eds.), *New Directions in the History of the Jews in the Polish Lands* (Boston: Academic Studies Press, 2018); Tomasz Majewski and Anna Zeidler-Janiszewska (eds.), *Pamięć Shoah: Kulturowe reprezentacje i praktyki upamiętnienia* (Łódź: Officyna, 2009); Feliks Tych and Monika Adamczyk-Garbowska (eds.), *Jewish Presence in Absence: The Aftermath of the Holocaust in Poland, 1944–2010*, trans. Grzegorz Dąbskowski and Jessica Taylor-Kucia (Jerusalem: Yad Vashem, 2014 [Polish edn, 2011]); Alina Skibińska, 'The Return of Jewish Holocaust Survivors and the Reaction of the Polish Population', ibid., pp. 25–66; Alina Skibińska and Jakub Petelewicz, 'The Participation of Poles in Crimes against Jews', *Yad Vashem Studies*, vol. 35, no. 1 (2007), pp. 5–48; Grabowski, *Hunt for the Jews*, pp. 149-170; and Jan Grabowski and Barbara Engelking (eds.), *Night without End: The Fate of Jews in German-Occupied Poland*, trans. Anna Brzostowska et al. (Bloomington, IN: Indiana University Press; Jerusalem: Yad Vashem, 2022) [Polish exp. edn, 2018], pp. xi, xxvii, and xxix.

107 Grabowski and Engelking (eds.), *Night without End*, p. xxvii.

108 Tomasz Frydel, '"Judenjagd": Reassessing the Role of Ordinary Poles as Perpetrators in the Holocaust', in Timothy Williams and Susanne Buckley-Zistel (eds.), *Perpetrators and Perpetration of Mass Violence: Action, Motivation and Dynamics* (London: Routledge, 2020), pp. 187–203.

109 Feliks Tych, 'Witnessing the Holocaust: Polish Diaries, Memoirs and Reminiscences', in David Bankier and Israel Gutman (eds.), *Nazi Europe and the Final Solution* (Jerusalem: Yad Vashem, 2003), pp. 175–198, here pp. 176–178.

next victims.[110] In addition, following the German defeat at Stalingrad in early 1943, there was for the first time some prospect of an end to German occupation rule. From a mixture of motives, and to differing degrees in different parts of occupied Poland, part of the Polish population took risks to help the persecuted Jews in small ways, or even – at extreme personal risk – to hide them (Docs. 24, 88, and 130).[111] The State of Israel has honoured more than 7,000 Polish men and women as Righteous Among the Nations.[112]

On the other hand, there are also many known cases in which Poles, hoping to receive the rewards advertised by the occupiers, denounced or even murdered Jews who were in hiding or had escaped from the ghettos (Docs. 210 and 247). The persecuted Jews' reactions to such behaviour on the part of the majority population ranged from disappointment to outrage. In Warsaw, Emanuel Ringelblum, while in hiding on the Aryan side in late 1943 and early 1944, wrote an extensive and well-informed essay titled 'Polish–Jewish Relations during the Second World War'. He concluded that Poles could not have prevented the persecution and murder of the Jews or saved most of their Jewish neighbours, and he recognized the risks they had taken in their attempts to hide Jews. At the same time, he was critical of the indifference shown by large sections of the population. This was not only Ringelblum's impression. Diaries, testimonies, and memoirs written by Jews relate their general impression – in more unequivocal terms than Ringelblum's – of a largely hostile Polish (and Ukrainian) hinterland. They mention Poles holding antisemitic attitudes, refusing requests for help, assisting the Germans in detecting Jews in hiding, and committing violent or even murderous acts against Jews who had succeeded in fleeing ghettos and camps.[113]

110 Feliks Tych, 'Witnessing the Holocaust', pp. 178–179.

111 Shmuel Krakowski, 'The Polish Underground and the Jews in the Years of the Second World War', in Bankier and Gutman (eds.), *Nazi Europe and the Final Solution*, pp. 215–230, here pp. 224 and 226.

112 For the most recent number of Poles thus honoured, see the Yad Vashem website: https://www.yadvashem.org/righteous.html.

113 Emanuel Ringelblum, *Polish–Jewish Relations during the Second World War* ed. Joseph Kermish and Shmuel Krakowski, trans. Dafna Allon, Danuta Dabrowska, and Dana Keren (Jerusalem: Yad Vashem, 1992 [1974] [Polish edn, 1958–1959]); on Ringelblum's essay, see also Samuel D. Kassow, 'Polish–Jewish Relations in the Writings of Emmanuel Ringelblum', in Joshua D. Zimmerman (ed.), *Contested Memories: Poles and Jews during the Holocaust and Its Aftermath* (New Brunswick, NJ: Rutgers University Press, 2003), pp. 142–157. On Polish responses more generally, see Grabowski and Engelking (eds.), *Night without End*; Zygmunt Klukowski, *Diary from the Years of Occupation 1939–44*, ed. Andrew Klukowski and Helen Klukowski May, trans. George Klukowski (Urbana: University of Illinois Press, 1993 [Polish edn, 1958]); Barbara Engelking, *'Szanowny panie gistapo': Donosy do władz niemieckich w Warszawie i okolicach w latach 1940–1941* (Warsaw: Instytut Filozofii i Socjologii PAN, 2003); Dariusz Libionka, 'Polska ludność chrześcijańska wobec eksterminacji Żydów – dystrykt lubelski', in Dariusz Libionka (ed.), *Akcja Reinhardt: Zagłada Żydów w Generalnym Gubernatorstwie* (Warsaw: Instytut Pamięci Narodowej, 2004), pp. 306–333; Havi Dreifuss (Ben-Sasson), *Relations between Jews and Poles: The Jewish Perspective*, trans. from Hebrew Ora Cummings (Jerusalem: Yad Vashem, 2017); Marcin Urynowicz, 'Stosunki polsko-żydowskie w Warszawie w okresie okupacji hitlerowskiej', in Żbikowski (ed.), *Polacy i Żydzi pod okupacją niemiecką 1939–1945*, pp. 537–626; Zuzanna Schnepf-Kołacz, 'Pomoc Polaków dla Żydów na wsi w czasie okupacji niemieckiej: Próba opisu na przkładzie Sprawiedliwych wśród Narodów Świata', in Barbara Engelking and Jan Grabowski (eds.), *Zarys krajobrazu: Wieś polska wobec zagłady Żydów 1942–1945* (Warsaw: Stowarzyszenie Centrum Badań nad Zagładą Żydów, 2011), pp. 195–258; and Jan Grabowski, *Rescue for Money: Paid Helpers in Poland, 1939–1945* (Jerusalem: Yad Vashem, 2008).

To date there has been a limited amount of research on the reaction of the Catholic Church, an institution which attained particular importance in Polish life under the conditions of the occupation, and opinions are divided on this topic.[114] Individual examples of assistance, such as the clandestine placement of Jewish children in convents, stand in contrast to the Church's silence in the face of mass murder and even continued antisemitic attitudes among the clergy. At the same time, it was apparent from an early stage that the Church leadership had little scope for action: Prince Adam Stefan Sapieha, the Archbishop of Cracow, who had a record of expressing traditional anti-Jewish views, did not even receive a response to his repeated efforts to intervene with Governor General Frank in support of the Jews in the General Government who had converted to Christianity.[115] However, Sapieha's efforts did not extend to condemning the persecution and murder of the Polish Jews more generally.[116] Meanwhile, in the Ukrainian Greek Catholic Church in Eastern Galicia, Metropolitan Andrei Sheptytskyi was a particular critic of the crimes committed against Jews (Doc. 55), having first welcomed the Germans in the hope that they would help to promote Ukrainian independence.[117] His pastoral letter 'Thou Shalt Not Kill' of 21 November 1942 did not mention Jews specifically, but they were there implicitly: Sheptytskyi reproached Ukrainians for approving or ignoring the killings going on around them.[118] He also actively encouraged the Studite Order to protect Jewish children by hiding them in Studite monasteries and convents.[119]

The underground movement, and through it also the Polish government in exile in London, was relatively well informed about the killing operations. Although the Polish government in exile told the international public very early on about the crimes of the German occupiers in Poland, it was extremely reticent at first to include the specific fate of the Jews in its reports. Not until May 1942, almost nine months after mass shootings in eastern Poland had become widespread, did the government in exile make public reference to these crimes. From then on it attempted to spread news of the mass murders throughout the world.[120]

114 For an overview of different interpretations, see Dariusz Libionka, 'Antisemitism, Anti-Judaism, and the Polish Catholic Clergy during the Second World War, 1939–1945', in Robert Blobaum (ed.), *Antisemitism and Its Opponents in Modern Poland* (Ithaca, NY, and London: Cornell University Press, 2005), pp. 233–264.

115 Zenon Fijałkowski, *Kościół katolicki na ziemiach polskich w latach okupacji hitlerowskiej* (Warsaw: Książka i Wiedza, 1983), pp. 195–203; Bogdan Kroll, *Rada Główna Opiekuńcza 1939–1945* (Warsaw: Książka i Wiedza, 1985), pp. 225–226. See also S. L. Shneiderman, *Between Fear and Hope*, trans. Norbert Guterman (New York: Arco, 1947 [Yiddish edn, 1947]), pp. 323–327; Jerzy Wolny, 'Biogram Kardynała Adama Stefana Sapiehy', in Roman Bogacz (ed.), *Książę Niezłomny: Kardynał Adam Stefan Sapieha* (Cracow: UNUM, 2001), pp. 7–72.

116 Libionka, 'Antisemitism, Anti-Judaism, and the Polish Catholic Clergy', pp. 238–241.

117 Ibid., p. 245; Paul Magocsi (ed.), *Morality and Reality: The Life and Times of Andrei Sheptyts'kyi* (Edmonton: Canadian Institute of Ukrainian Studies, 1989); Kateryna Budz and Andrew Kloes, 'Ethnonationalism as a Theological Crisis: Metropolitan Andrey Sheptytsky and the Greek Catholic Church in Western Ukraine, 1923-1944', in Kevin Spicer and Rebecca Carter-Chand (eds.), *Religion, Ethnonationalism and Antisemitism in the Era of the Two World Wars* (Montreal: McGill-Queen's University Press, 2022), pp. 274-304; and Andrij Mychalejko, *Metropolit Andrey Graf Sheptytskyi und das NS-Regime: Zwischen christlichem Ideal und politischer Realität* (Paderborn: Brill Schöningh, 2020).

118 Budz and Kloes, 'Ethnonationalism as a Theological Crisis', pp. 290-291.

119 Ibid., p. 292.

120 Piotr Długołęcki (ed.), *Confronting the Holocaust. Documents on the Polish Government-in-Exile Concerning Jews 1939–1945* (Warsaw: Polski Instytut Spraw Międzynarodowych, 2022).

Yet the Polish government in exile still did not afford the 'Jewish question' any priority in its policymaking, and it failed to issue a clear statement that would have ensured surviving Jews could remain in a liberated post-war Poland as citizens with equal rights.[121] The fact that reports on the extermination of the Jews nonetheless kept appearing on the radio and in the international press was attributable primarily to the two Jewish members of the Polish parliament in exile, who also made significant efforts to persuade the Allies to intervene. One of them, Szmul Zygielbojm, who represented the Jewish socialist Bund party, took his own life in May 1943, in protest and out of desperation over the fate of the Jews whom he was supposed to represent on the Polish National Council, and in view of the international community's inaction and lack of interest (Doc. 241).

In occupied Poland the government delegation for the Polish government in exile (the Delegatura) operated underground. The government delegation also had a military wing, known from February 1942 as the Home Army (Armia Krajowa). In 1941–1942 the government delegation and the Home Army were still in the process of being established, and they initially paid little attention to the plight of the Jews.[122] Yet they were very much aware of the killing operations, which were documented by representatives of the underground movement in all five districts and in every Kreis. Even at the railway stations near Belzec and Treblinka extermination camps, individual railway workers co-operated with the underground and provided information about the transports to the death camps.[123] In late summer 1941, situation reports by the Polish government delegation and reports sent to the government in exile in London indicate detailed knowledge on the part of the Polish underground both of conditions in the ghettos in the General Government and of mass killings in the newly occupied territories of eastern Poland in the wake of the German invasion.[124] Particularly General Rowecki, the commander of the Home Army, sent reports to the government in exile, including a much-cited radiogram dated 25 September 1941, about crimes committed against Jews in the Polish territories formerly under Soviet rule. Most of the information about the massacres that reached the world at large was derived either from such dispatches by the Polish underground or from Jewish groups such as the one led by Ringelblum, which also supplied news to the underground movement outside the ghettos.[125] However, in terms of

121 David Engel, *In the Shadow of Auschwitz: The Polish Government-in-Exile and the Jews, 1939–1942* (Chapel Hill, NC: University of North Carolina Press, 1987); David Engel, *Facing a Holocaust: The Polish Government-in-Exile and the Jews, 1943–1945* (Chapel Hill, NC: University of North Carolina Press, 1993); Dariusz Stola, *Nadzieja i zagłada: Ignacy Schwarzbart – żydowski przedstawiciel w Radzie Narodowej RP, 1940–1945* (Warsaw: Oficyna Naukowa, 1995); Aleksander Rowiński, *Zygielbojms Reise: Eine Spurensuche*, trans. Agnieszka Karaś (Osnabrück: fibre, 2004 [Polish edn, 2000]); Klaus-Peter Friedrich, 'Die polnische Regierungsdelegatur und ihr "jüdisches Problem" 1940–1945', *Jahrbücher für Geschichte Osteuropas*, vol. 57 (2009), pp. 23–53.

122 Dariusz Libionka, 'ZWZ-AK i Delegatura Rządu RP wobec eksterminacji Żydów polskich', in Żbikowski (ed.), *Polacy i Żydzi pod okupacją niemiecką 1939–1945*, pp. 15–139.

123 See Ząbecki, *Wspomnienia dawne i nowe*, pp. 58–100.

124 Joshua D. Zimmerman, *The Polish Underground and the Jews, 1939–1945* (Cambridge: Cambridge University Press, 2015), pp. 97–102.

125 Adam Puławski, *W obliczu zagłady: Rząd RP na Uchodźstwie, Delegatura Rządu RP na Kraj, ZWZ-AK wobec deportacji Żydow do obozów zagłady (1941–1942)* (Lublin: Instytut Pamięci Narodowej, 2009); Adam Puławski, *Wobec 'niespotykanego w dziejach mordu': Rząd RP na uchodźstwie, Delegatura Rządu RP na Kraj, AK a eksterminacja ludności żydowskiej od wielkiej akcji do powstania w getci warszawskim* (Chełm: Biblioteka Rocznika Chełmskiego, 2018).

practical action, the Polish resistance's response to the mass crimes committed against the Jews was very limited. As a rule, the Home Army sought to avoid armed conflict with the German occupying force, lest this lead to reprisals; moreover, it wanted to be in a position to make preparations for the major confrontation that was planned for the end of the war. For this reason, in contrast to the communist partisans and, east of the General Government, the Soviet partisans, it did not launch a 'rail war' – that is, it did not blow up any railway facilities. Overall, the Home Army and the government delegation did not consider the Jews' situation to be a primary concern. Meanwhile, Jews continued to be viewed as a separate group from Poles.[126] Jewish political parties were not represented in the government delegation, and many Home Army units displayed hostility towards Jews.[127] Indeed, in his dispatch of September 1941, Rowecki declared that antisemitic attitudes among the Polish population were prevalent and warned the government in exile against issuing statements that the Polish underground regarded as overly sympathetic to Jews.[128]

Nonetheless, at the end of 1942 the Polish government in exile supported the establishment of the Council to Aid Jews (Rada Pomocy Żydom), codenamed Żegota – a cross-party organization established by socialists and Catholics, with Jews among its initiators; a precursor organization had been formed in spring 1942, at the urging of Catholic lay groups. Using the limited resources available, Jews in the ghettos were to be given support and the means to improve their chances of escape or of going into hiding, for example through the provision of counterfeit passports (Doc. 295).[129] The Polish government delegation also attempted to prevent Poles, particularly the Polish police and the numerous informers, from participating in the crimes (Doc. 184). In isolated cases, the underground movement executed notorious collaborators and released this information as a deterrent.[130]

The underground press gave expression to the various positions within Poland's resistance movement. Representatives of the political centre certainly voiced horror at the German crimes, but many also seriously debated whether the Jews ought to remain in

126 Puławski, *W obliczu zagłady*, pp. 59–62.

127 On Jews' lack of representation in the Polish government delegation (Delegatura), see Zimmerman, *The Polish Underground and the Jews*, p. 102; Israel Gutman, 'Some Issues in Jewish–Polish Relations during the Second World War', in Zimmerman (ed.), *Contested Memories*, pp. 212–217, here p. 216. On Home Army partisan units and the Jews, see Reuben Ainsztein, *Jewish Resistance in Nazi-occupied Eastern Europe: With a Historical Survey of the Jew as Fighter and Soldier in the Diaspora* (London: Paul Elek, 1974), pp. 454–460; Shmuel Krakowski, 'The Attitude of the Polish Underground to the Jewish Question during the Second World War', in Zimmerman (ed.), *Contested Memories*, pp. 97–106, esp. p. 103.

128 On Rowecki's dispatch and differing interpretations of it, see Zimmerman, *The Polish Underground and the Jews*, pp. 102–106.

129 Marek Arczyński and Wiesław Balcerak, *Kryptonim 'Żegota': Z dziejów pomocy Żydom w Polsce 1939–1945* (Warsaw: Czytelnik, 1979); Teresa Prekerowa, *Konspiracyjna Rada Pomocy Żydom w Warszawie 1942–1945* (Warsaw: Państwowy Instytut Wydawniczy, 1982).

130 Leszek Gondek, *Polska karząca 1939–1945: Polski podziemny wymiar sprawiedliwości w okresie okupacji niemieckiej* (Warsaw: Pax, 1988); Jan Grabowski and Dariusz Libionka (eds.), *Klucze i kasa: O mieniu żydowskim w Polsce pod okupacją niemiecką i we wczesnych latach powojennych 1939–1950* (Warsaw: Stowarzyszenie Centrum Badań nad Zagładą Żydów, 2014).

Poland at all after the war.[131] Speculation about the future of Jews in a post-war Poland among highly placed functionaries of the Polish 'underground state' included suggestions about how to prevent Jews from regaining the economic role they had played in Poland before the war.[132] In any event, the daily mass murder of Jews was not the focus of their political considerations. A much clearer stance was adopted by underground groups that, for political reasons, joined the 'underground state' at a later stage, if at all. The Communist Party, in which many Jews were represented, was only able to reorganize itself after 1942. It was a comparatively weak force which, like socialist and Catholic left-wing groups, lent its support to those being persecuted. By contrast, broad sections of the National Armed Forces (Narodowe Siły Zbrojne, NSZ), which followed the tradition of the Polish right-wing radicalism of the 1930s, were largely antisemitic in outlook. Some individuals were involved in German actions against Jews (Doc. 279). There were admittedly also examples in which members of this group took part in rescue operations.[133] Nonetheless, it is notable that the Polish government delegation as late as March 1942 expressed annoyance at the attention supposedly being given by the Polish government in exile to the fate of the Jews and their future role in Poland (Doc. 59). And a number of groups, such as Konfederacja Narodu, even openly applauded the mass murders committed by the Nazis.[134] Opposition to the murders and efforts to help those being persecuted were therefore to be expected only from part of the Polish underground movement.

At first the Western democracies barely registered the mass murders of Jews which began at the end of June 1941 in the newly occupied territories of eastern Poland and of the Soviet Union. It was not until October 1941 that isolated reports began to appear in the international press.[135] The public was even less aware of the fate of the Jews confined in the ghettos, whether in the General Government or in the annexed Polish territories. In addition, Germany's declaration of war on the USA in December 1941 severed many lines of communication to North America. However, when Poland went on to become

131 Andrzej Friszke, 'Attitudes toward the Jews in the Polish Underground Press', in Bankier and Gutman (eds.), *Nazi Europe and the Final Solution*, pp. 163–174, here pp. 165–166.

132 See Jan Tomasz Gross with Irena Grudzinska Gross, *Golden Harvest: Events at the Periphery of the Holocaust* (New York: Oxford University Press, 2012), p. 106.

133 Krzysztof Kaczmarski, *Podziemie narodowe na Rzeszowszczyźnie 1939–1944* (Rzeszów: Instytut Pamięci Narodowej, 2003).

134 Pawel Szapiro (ed.), *Wojna żydowsko-niemiecka: Polska prasa konspiracyjna 1943–1944 o powstaniu w getcie Warszawy* (London: Aneks, 1992); Klaus-Peter Friedrich, *Der nationalsozialistische Judenmord und das polnisch-jüdische Verhältnis im Diskurs der polnischen Untergrundpresse (1942–1944)* (Marburg: Herder-Institut, 2006), unabridged dissertation version online (http://kups.ub.uni-koeln.de/id/eprint/952).

135 The *Jewish Chronicle*, for example, published a number of articles on the Nazis' mass murder, such as 'Ghastly Pogroms in Ukraine: Thousands of Corpses in Dniester River: 8,000 Slain in Synagogues', which appeared on its front page on 24 Oct. 1941: cited in Michael R. Marrus (ed.), *The Nazi Holocaust*, part 8: *Bystanders to the Holocaust*, vol. 2 (Westport: Meckler, 1989), p. 976. See also Frank Bajohr and Dieter Pohl (eds.), *Der Holocaust als offenes Geheimnis: Die Deutschen, die NS-Führung und die Alliierten* (Munich: Beck, 2006), pp. 56-61 and 86-91; and Joel Zisenwine, 'The Intelligence Community and the Holocaust: Was December 1942 a Turning Point?', in Dina Porat and Dan Michman (eds.), *The End of 1942: A Turning Point in World War II and in the Comprehension of the Final Solution?* (Jerusalem: Yad Vashem, 2017), pp. 45–60, here p. 50.

the scene of the largest-scale murder of Jews during the war, this did not escape the world's attention. But information was very sketchy at first, and a clearer picture only began to emerge in June 1942, following statements made by the Polish government in exile. At the end of May 1942, two reports from the underground archive in the Warsaw ghetto reached Britain, and in June the BBC broadcast the first reports about the killing of Polish Jews (Doc. 87). On 2 July 1942 the *New York Times* published its first reports on gas chambers in occupied Poland (Doc. 89). The first articles about the murder operation targeting the Warsaw ghetto appeared even before the measures had come to an end.[136] In July 1942 a large rally was held in New York to protest against the crimes committed against the Polish Jews. However, in summer and autumn 1942, when the Nazi-occupied territory in Europe was at its greatest extent, the Allies had almost no means of direct intervention. As a result, they limited themselves to the statement they made on 17 December 1942, in which they expressed general condemnation of the German crimes against the Jews.[137] This was preceded by a statement issued by the Jewish Agency in Palestine on 23 November (see below).[138]

Jan Kozielewski, known as Karski, was an underground messenger for the Polish government in exile. Reporting on the Jews in Poland was not originally part of his mission. However, underground groups in the Warsaw ghetto asked to meet him in order to provide information and to send requests to the Polish government and the Western Allies. In 1942 Karski was smuggled into and out of the Warsaw ghetto twice, and he also entered a camp, which he reported to be Bełżec; it may in fact have been the transit ghetto Izbica, although this hypothesis has also been called into question.[139] At the end of the same year, having managed to travel to London, he reported in detail to the Polish government in exile and the British authorities on the horrific conditions he had witnessed, and he issued desperate appeals for help.[140] Karski's report, *Story of a Secret State*, was not published in the USA until 1944. In it, he gave an extensive account of the Warsaw ghetto in summer 1942 and detailed the fate of its residents:

> For us Poles, it was war and occupation. For them, for the suffering Polish Jews, this was the end of the world. [...] In two and a half months, in one district in Poland, the Nazis committed three hundred thousand murders. It was, indeed, the report of an unprecedented species of criminality that I had to bring to the outside world.[141]

136 'Gestapo Plans to Exterminate all Jews in Warsaw Ghetto', *Toronto Globe*, 29 July 1942.

137 Published as 'German Policy of Extermination of the Jewish Race', *Department of State Bulletin*, vol. VII, no. 182, 19 Dec. 1942, p. 1009: see PMJ 6/202.

138 See Michael Fleming, *Auschwitz, the Allies and Censorship of the Holocaust* (Cambridge: Cambridge University Press, 2014), p. 158; Dina Porat, 'The November 23, 1942, Communiqué by the Jewish Agency Executive: A Renewed Examination', in Porat and Michman (eds.), *The End of 1942*, pp. 317–338.

139 Hänschen, *Das Transitghetto Izbica*, p. 167.

140 Puławski, *W obliczu zagłady*, p. 536; on Karski's networks and on his role compared to that of other couriers and sources of information reaching London, see Puławski, *Wobec 'niespotykanego w dziejach mordu'*.

141 A total of 400,000 copies of *Story of a Secret State* were published, and the edition sold out immediately: see Jan Karski, *Story of a Secret State: My Report to the World*, trans. Krystyna Sokołowska (Washington, DC: Georgetown University Press, 2013 [1944]), pp. 323–324.

A small group of Jews was saved through diplomatic channels. The Gestapo sought out Jews who were citizens of neutral countries or had relatives there, potentially in order to exchange them for Germans who had been interned. These Jews were told to assemble at Hotel Polski in Warsaw. However, the German police also used this occasion as a pretext to lure Jews out of hiding. Many of the Jews who turned up were taken to Vittel internment camp in eastern France, but only a very few managed to escape the German sphere of control and survive. Most were deported to Auschwitz, where they were murdered in April and May 1944. Among them was the poet Yitzhak (Itzhak) Katzenelson, who wrote the 'Song of the Massacred Jewish People' – a lament detailing the resistance and killing of the Jews of Warsaw – prior to his deportation to Auschwitz.[142] Additionally, on 13 November 1942, 69 Polish Jews arrived in the port of Haifa as part of a civilian prisoner exchange between the British and the Germans. On the basis of their testimonies, the Jewish Agency for Palestine published a statement on 23 November 1942, which reported on the systematic murder of the Jews.[143] In practice, only the Jewish underground could provide any effective means of assistance. Beyond that, it was primarily small Jewish relief committees in Geneva that continued to gather information and to support the ghettos by sending aid parcels.[144]

## Jewish armed resistance

By the time the murder of the deportees had become a certainty, the Jews in the ghettos were discussing whether armed or other resistance was possible, and if so, in what form (Doc. 150). Unarmed resistance occurred, for example, through the efforts of the Oyneg Shabes underground archive, the activities of which provided the basis for attempts to resist the Germans with force or to organize mass escapes in many localities. From the outset, however, the capacity for mounting physical resistance was limited. The occupation had pushed Polish Jews to the margins of society. In addition, after the collapse of their economic livelihoods, most of them had markedly less contact with Poles, and thus also with the still fledgling Polish underground movement. With the exception of the communists, who were still barely in evidence in 1941–1942, during this period Polish resistance organizations tended to distance themselves even further from the Jewish minority. Many Jews who had been politically active before the war had either fled in 1939 or quickly fallen into the hands of the Gestapo. Therefore it was not easy for the activists in the ghettos to obtain reliable information, let alone weapons. In addition, the Germans made every effort to deceive the victims with respect to the purpose of the deportations. At the same time, they cracked down ruthlessly on any form of resistance, with

142 Yitzhak Katzenelson, *The Song of the Massacred Jewish People*, trans. Jack Hirschmann (Berkeley, CA: Regent Press, 2021 [Yiddish edn, 1945]). On Hotel Polski, see Agnieszka Haska, *'Jestem Żydem, chcę wejść': Hotel Polski w Warszawie, 1943* (Warsaw: Instytut Filozofii i Socjologii PAN, 2006).

143 Porat, 'The November 23, 1942, Communiqué by the Jewish Agency Executive'.

144 Raya Cohen, 'The Lost Honour of Bystanders? The Case of Jewish Emissaries in Switzerland', *Journal of Holocaust Education*, vol. 9, nos. 2/3 (2000), pp. 146–170; Sara Kadosh, *We Think of You as an Angel: Shaul Weingort and the Rescue of Jews during the Holocaust* (Jerusalem: Yad Vashem, 2019), pp. 73-96.

violence directed not only against the resisters, but also indiscriminately against all Jews. Emanuel Ringelblum described the dilemma as follows:

> Jews did not resist anywhere; they passively went to their deaths and they did so in order to let other Jews remain alive. Because each Jew knew that to raise a hand against the Germans meant that he was endangering fellow Jews in another city and perhaps even in another country.[145]

For these reasons, resistance fighters argued at length over the purpose of armed rebellion, as they knew they would potentially be putting lives at risk for the sake of an uprising that would likely have little effect. In spite of this moral dilemma, armed resistance groups did emerge in dozens of ghettos in occupied Poland. The lack of sources makes it impossible to give reliable figures for these groups; most of the information about them is found in the first-hand accounts of surviving partisans and ghetto fighters.[146]

In any event, only a few were able to mount resistance or to escape, especially since entire families seldom succeeded in going into hiding together. The sociologist Barbara Engelking found it understandable

> that in the face of ubiquitous death, bonds with others became the last refuge, that people wanted to be together with their loved ones, offering evidence of love, attachment, loyalty, and courage. This common march toward death reveals many positive feelings, many proofs of magnanimity, faithfulness, and sacrifice. Only the perfunctory glance of a casual onlooker would interpret this as going 'like sheep to the slaughter'.[147]

Consequently, the impetus for resistance came mostly from young men and women, as yet without families of their own, who were already banded together in youth organizations, though not necessarily affiliated with any political faction.[148] Now confined in the ghettos, they discussed how they should respond to persecution. During the early stages of the ghettos' existence, many of them participated in the self-help effort and in cultural life. Once news of the mass murders reached the ghettos, some of these activists began to contemplate armed revolt.

After lengthy discussions, in many places the resistance fighters decided to wait until the complete liquidation of the ghetto was imminent before mounting armed resistance or organizing mass escapes into the forests. With this approach they hoped to ensure that the lives of the remaining population would not be put at risk prematurely. Rebellions occurred in eastern Poland earlier than in the rest of the country – the Warsaw Ghetto Uprising in spring 1943 was therefore not the first incidence of Jewish armed resistance in Poland.[149]

145 Ringelblum, *Ksovim fun geto*, vol. 2, p. 410; cited in Kassow, *Who Will Write Our History?*, p. 350.

146 Shmuel Krakowski, *The War of the Doomed: Jewish Armed Resistance in Poland, 1942–1944* (New York: Holmes & Meier, 1984); Ainsztein, *Jewish Resistance in Nazi-occupied Eastern Europe*.

147 Barbara Engelking, *Such a Beautiful Sunny Day…: Jews Seeking Refuge in the Polish Countryside, 1942–1945*, trans. Jerzy Michalowicz (Jerusalem: Yad Vashem, 2016 [Polish edn, 2011]), p. 32.

148 See Dreifuss, *Geto Varsha*, pp. 281–295.

149 Krakowski, *The War of the Doomed*; on earlier uprisings in eastern Poland, see Ainsztein, *Jewish Resistance in Nazi-occupied Eastern Europe*, pp. 417–454.

At a meeting of the Jewish underground organizations held in Warsaw in March 1942, the members of youth movements in particular spoke out in favour of early, concerted resistance measures. However, both the representatives of the conservative Orthodox Agudas Yisrael movement and the members of the socialist Bund displayed marked reluctance. Accordingly, the appeal for resistance voiced by the left-wing Zionist Anti-Fascist Bloc went largely unheard (Doc. 76).[150]

It was not until summer 1942, when news from Treblinka reached the Warsaw ghetto in the midst of the mass deportation, that the activists agreed on the necessity of armed resistance. Only a very few were still under any illusions about the Germans' plans. Yet they lacked weapons, and their comrades were falling victim to deportation almost every day. As a result, the conditions for resistance, and particularly for armed rebellion, were extremely poor. On 29 July 1942 the Jewish Combat Organization ('Żydowska Organizacja Bojowa' or ŻOB in Polish; 'Yiddishe Kampf Organizatsye' in Yiddish) came into being, composed primarily of members of left-wing Zionist organizations (Hashomer Hatzair, Dror, Gordonia, Akiba, and Poale Zion), the Bund, and the communist Polish Workers' Party. Its first act of resistance was to shoot Józef Szeryński, the head of the Jewish Order Service in the Warsaw ghetto, on 20 August 1942, wounding though not killing him.

After the shock of the 'Great Deportation', which ended in September 1942, the groups – both large and small – in the Warsaw ghetto that had decided to resist began preparations for a response to the next extermination operation. This time, Bund representatives also participated. Under the most difficult circumstances, they managed to get hold of a few weapons. Marek Edelman later identified the rebels' goal:

> The important thing in the ghetto was that someone opened fire. That had to be demonstrated. Not to the Germans. They were always better at that. But because people always regarded firing a gun as the greatest heroism, we had to demonstrate it to that other world, which was not the German world. So we fired our guns.[151]

When German police units moved in to resume the deportations in Warsaw on 18 January 1943, they encountered armed resistance for the first time (Doc. 209). They initially withdrew, and then guerrilla warfare began, with the forces unequally distributed. The battle went on for days. Most of the approximately 1,200–1,400 members of the underground lacked firearms; their only weapons were petrol bombs and the like. Many were dead before the end of the month.

On 16 February 1943, Himmler instructed Krüger to prepare for the evacuation of what remained of the Warsaw ghetto and for its subsequent eradication (Doc. 217). The occupation administration accordingly ordered that a portion of the enterprises and forced labourers be gradually moved to District Lublin. On the morning of 19 April 1943 SS and police units again marched into the Warsaw ghetto (Doc. 227). In what became

150 See Nayshtadt, *Khurbm un oyfshtand fun di yidn in varshe*; Raya Cohen, 'Against the Current: Hashomer Hatzair in the Warsaw Ghetto', *Jewish Social Studies*, vol. 7, no. 1 (2000), pp. 63–80; and Daniel Blatman, *For Our Freedom and Yours: The Jewish Labour Bund in Poland, 1939–1949*, trans. Naftali Greenwood (London: Vallentine Mitchell, 2003 [Hebrew edn, 1996]), pp. 93–95.

151 Bereś and Burnetko, *Marek Edelman: Being on the Right Side*, p. 208.

known as the Warsaw Ghetto Uprising, fighting broke out and lasted for a full four days. Along with the Jewish Combat Organization, the Jewish Military Union (Żydowski Związek Wojskowy or ŻZW)[152] – the fighting unit of the revisionist Zionist youth movement Betar – mounted fierce resistance. The ŻZW was engaged in one of the main battles of the uprising – on Muranowska Square, where it had its main base – and succeeded in blocking the German advance by positioning a machine gun on the square. After the initial fighting, the resisters withdrew to their bunkers and to the sewer network and launched only sporadic attacks, which lasted for about a month (Doc. 235).

The resistance fighters and the rest of the ghetto population had prepared hiding places in attics and cellars in order to elude deportation for as long as possible. Led by the new SS and Police Leader in Warsaw, Jürgen Stroop, armed units began setting the buildings on fire one by one, thereby forcing people out of their shelters. Even prior to being discovered, conditions in the cramped bunkers were appalling, as Halina Birenbaum described in her memoir:

> The place smelled damp and musty, like all cellars, and the air was foul, it was dark and the atmosphere was one of agitation. From the very beginning, more people came than had been bargained for. [...] Anyone who went to the water tap or toilet collided with others or stumbled over their neighbors in the darkness. There was no end to the disputes and squabbling, fights over nothing, insults, name-calling.[153]

Birenbaum's hiding place was ultimately discovered. She was deported to Lublin-Majdanek concentration camp, but survived the war.

Finally, on 8 May 1943, German units stormed the bunker in which many members of the Jewish Combat Organization's command were concealed. Most of the resistance fighters inside – including their leader, Mordechai Anielewicz – took their own lives. Only a very few managed to escape to the 'Aryan side' of Warsaw.[154] Shortly afterwards, Stroop prepared a cynical report on this killing operation. The document, accompanied by numerous photographs, was titled 'Warsaw's Jewish Residential District Is No More!' (Doc. 243).[155]

The Warsaw Ghetto Uprising was an extremely unequal conflict with no prospect of the resisters succeeding or of a sizeable number of lives being saved.[156] Nonetheless, it was of pivotal importance for persecuted Jews across Europe as an act of self-assertion

152 On the ŻZW, see Dariusz Libionka and Laurence Weinbaum, 'Deconstructing Memory and History: The Jewish Military Union (ŻZW) and the Warsaw Ghetto Uprising', *Jewish Political Studies Review*, vol. 18, nos. 1/2 (2006), pp. 86–194; Dariusz Libionka and Laurence Weinbaum, *Bohaterowie, hochsztaplerzy, opisywacze: Wokół Żydowskiego Związku Wojskowego* (Warsaw: Stowarzyszenie Centrum Badań nad Zagładą Żydów, 2011).

153 Halina Birenbaum, *Hope Is the Last to Die: A Coming of Age Under Nazi Terror*, trans. David Welch (London and New York: Routledge, 1996 [Polish edn, 1982]), p. 60.

154 Helge Grabitz and Wolfgang Scheffler, *Der Ghetto-Aufstand Warschau 1943 aus der Sicht der Täter und Opfer in Aussagen vor deutschen Gerichten* (Munich: Goldmann, 1993); Israel Gutman, *Resistance: The Warsaw Ghetto Uprising* (Boston: Houghton Mifflin, 1994).

155 Published in English translation as *The Stroop Report: The Jewish Quarter of Warsaw Is No More! A Facsimile Edition and Translation of the Official Nazi Report on the Destruction of the Warsaw Ghetto*, trans. from German Sybil Milton (New York: Pantheon, 1979).

156 Dreifuss, *Geto Varsha*, pp. 387–517.

and a sign of hope for all those still alive. As late as 23 April 1943 Anielewicz wrote to his deputy, Yitzhak Cukierman, who was then on the 'Aryan side'. He described the desperate situation and surmised that they would never see each another again, but emphasized: 'The dream of my life has risen to become fact. Self-defense in the ghetto will have been a reality. Jewish armed resistance and revenge are facts. I have been a witness to the magnificent, heroic fighting of Jewish men in battle.'[157]

The Warsaw Ghetto Uprising served as a model for many subsequent resistance operations, especially during the ghetto liquidations in June 1943, for example in Lwów and in Częstochowa, but also for the Warsaw Uprising in August 1944 and for other urban armed resistance operations carried out by Poles. In the region around Lublin and Kielce, which was more heavily forested, Jewish refugees joined individual partisan groups. Polish nationalist partisans, however, uniformly refused to accept Jews, and even among communist partisans the Jews sometimes failed to find support. As one example, only a few Jews were allowed to join a Soviet partisan unit after it had reached Eastern Galicia in August 1943 and liberated a forced labour camp there.

Under desperate conditions, prisoner uprisings also took place in two of the Operation Reinhard extermination camps. It was clear to the members of the Sonderkommando that the murders would come to an end, as would the burning of corpses to erase the traces of the crime, and that they therefore had no chance of survival beyond 1943. At Treblinka they managed to get their hands on a number of the weapons that belonged to their guards. On 2 August, when part of the German force stationed at the extermination camp had gone off to enjoy a day's swimming, the prisoners attacked their guards. Approximately 200 prisoners managed to break through the camp barriers and flee into the woods (Docs. 259 and 261). Yet not even one third of them lived to see the end of the war.[158]

Parallel to the plans for an uprising in Treblinka, prisoners at Sobibor also made preparations for a mass escape. A group of Jewish Red Army soldiers from Minsk who had been sent to Sobibor as prisoners of war played a key role in the rebellion, thanks to their military training.[159] The group was led by Aleksandr 'Sasha' Pechersky and Leon Feldhendler. On 14 October 1943 the rebels overpowered some of the guards, and approximately 320 of the 550 prisoners initially succeeded in escaping. As at Treblinka,

157 'The Last Letter from Mordechai Anielewicz, Warsaw Ghetto Revolt Commander, April 23', published in Yitzhak Arad, Israel Gutman, and Abraham Margaliot (eds.), *Documents on the Holocaust: Selected Sources on the Destruction of the Jews of Germany and Austria, Poland, and the Soviet Union*, 8th edn, trans. Lea Ben Dor (Lincoln, NE: University of Nebraska Press; Jerusalem: Yad Vashem, 1999), pp. 315–316.

158 See Samuel Willenberg, *Revolt in Treblinka* (Warsaw: Żydowski Instytut Historyczny, 2008 [Polish edn, 1991]), pp. 176–184 and 267–268; Richard Glazar, *Trap with a Green Fence: Survival in Treblinka*, trans. Roslyn Theobold (Evanston, IL: Northwestern University Press, 1995 [German edn, 1992]); Chil Rajchman, *The Last Jew of Treblinka: A Survivor's Memory, 1942–1943*, trans. Solon Beinfeld (New York: Pegasus, 2011 [German edn, 2009]).

159 See Aleksandr A. Pecherskiy, *Vosstaniye v Sobiburovskom lagere* (Rostov-on-Don: Rostizdat, 1945); Semen S. Vilenskiy, Grigoriy B. Gorbovitskiy, and Leonid A. Terushkin, *Sobibor: Vosstaniye v lagere smerti. Sostaviteli* (Moscow: Vozvrashcheniye, 2008); Selma Leydesdorff, *Sasha Pechersky: Holocaust Hero, Sobibor Resistance Leader, and Hostage of History* (New York: Routledge, 2017); Franziska Bruder, *Hunderte solcher Helden: Der Aufstand jüdischer Gefangener im NS-Vernichtungslager Sobibór. Berichte, Recherchen und Analysen* (Hamburg and Münster: Unrast, 2013); and Kalmen Wewryk, *To Sobibor and Back: An Eyewitness Account*, ed. and trans. from Yiddish Howard Roiter (Montreal: Montreal Institute for Genocide and Human Rights, 1999).

most were recaptured in police roundups or as a result of denunciation and were shot (Doc. 274). Nonetheless, fifty-three Jews who had been held in Sobibor extermination camp went on to survive the war.[160]

## After the large-scale massacres in autumn 1943

Following the Operation Harvest Festival massacres in early November 1943, it was virtually impossible for Jews to stay alive 'legally' – that is, under the conditions set out by the Germans. Only in District Radom were there still a few forced labour camps for Jews who were deemed especially important to the war effort. In the ruins of the Warsaw ghetto, the SS set up a new concentration camp, where prisoners were given the task of clearing away the rubble and sorting it for reuse. However, virtually all the prisoners in Warsaw concentration camp were Jews brought there from other countries. One of them was Max Mannheimer, who had come to the camp via Theresienstadt and Auschwitz, and later recalled his arrival: 'Everything looks so unearthly. Burnt out houses. A great silence. Not a soul to be seen, far and wide.'[161]

While approximately 100,000 Jewish prisoners struggled to survive in the camps in the General Government in autumn 1943, an approximately equal number of people had gone underground. Few were able to hide in the forests over the long term, as it was difficult to obtain food there and there was a high risk of being discovered by German or Polish patrols. Only the young and the strong were in a position to join the partisans. The alternative that was most likely to succeed was to go into hiding in the larger cities, in prearranged hideouts in cellars, bunkers, or attics. Those in hiding, crowded together in the narrowest of spaces, often had to hold out for months in dark, cold, and damp conditions. In Warsaw alone, approximately 15,000–20,000 Jews were in hiding outside the ghetto walls during the final years of the war. Only a few thousand of them survived.[162]

These Jews in hiding were completely reliant on non-Jewish helpers or on Jewish helpers living under an 'Aryan' identity, who supplied them with food and, if necessary, medicine (Doc. 287). The Poles – and in Eastern Galicia, often also Ukrainians – who

160 Arad, *The Operation Reinhard Death Camps*, pp. 270–364; Adam Rutkowski, 'Ruch oporu w hitlerowskim obozie straceń Sobibór', *BŻIH*, nos. 65 and 66 (1968), pp. 3–49. See also Jules Schelvis, *Sobibor: A History of a Nazi Death Camp*, trans. Karin Dixon (London: Bloomsbury, 2014 [Dutch edn, 1993]); Thomas Toivi Blatt, *From the Ashes of Sobibor: A Story of Survival* (Evanston, IL: Northwestern University Press, 1997), p. 232; Bem, *Sobibor Extermination Camp*; Marek Bem (ed.), *Sobibór: Bunt wobec wyroku* (Warsaw: Ośrodek Karta, 2012); and the diary of Selma Engel: Ad van Liempt, *Selma: de vrouw die Sobibor overleefde* (Laren: Verbum, 2010).

161 Max Mannheimer, *A Diary Delayed: Theresienstadt, Auschwitz, Warsaw, Dachau*, trans. Kathryn Woodard (Munich: Oettingen Press, 2017 [German edn, 2010]), p. 80. See also Bogusław Kopka, *Konzentrationslager Warschau: Historia i następstwa* (Warsaw: Instytut Pamięci Narodowej, 2007); and Gabriel Finder, 'Jewish Prisoner Labour in Warsaw after the Ghetto Uprising, 1943–1944', *Polin: Studies in Polish Jewry*, vol. 17 (2004), pp. 325–352.

162 Grabowski and Engelking (eds.), *Night without End*; Havi Dreifuss, 'Changing Perspectives on Polish–Jewish Relations during the Holocaust', *Search and Research*, vol. 18 (2012), pp. 32–69, esp. pp. 42–49, correcting the figures of Gunnar Paulsson, *Secret City: The Hidden Jews of Warsaw, 1940–1945* (New Haven, CT: Yale University Press, 2002).

helped Jews put their own lives at risk. If discovered – often by their Polish neighbours (Doc. 210) – they were either charged with 'harbouring Jews', tried before a special court, and then usually sentenced to death, or they were shot on the spot by police patrols. Entire families frequently fell victim to these murders. To date, we know the names of approximately 1,000 Poles who were killed by the German occupiers for providing assistance to Jews, mostly in the General Government.[163]

Acquiring false documents ('Aryan papers') presented an additional opportunity for survival. To obtain such documents, it was necessary to establish contact with the Polish underground or other individuals who were able to produce them. Additionally, people who went underground in this way had to have an 'Aryan appearance' and, in most cases, to live far from their original places of residence in order to avoid being recognized in the street by chance. Acculturation to Polish customs and Christian religious practices was vital, as was the ability to speak Polish without an accent – the inadvertent use of a Yiddish term could give away an individual's true identity. A good many Jews living under a false identity, particularly women, got themselves recruited for forced labour in the Reich, hoping they could survive in anonymity there.[164]

Even Jewish children who had been placed in the care of Christian family friends or in church institutions were in great danger, and survival was by no means certain. Many of them never saw their parents again and lost all connection to their Jewish origins.

Many of the Jews in hiding had to change their hideouts dozens of times, and on each occasion they were dependent on people to help them.[165] The threat of denunciation was ever-present.[166] German and local police conducted systematic searches for Jews in hiding and murdered those they discovered. The Polish and the Ukrainian police participated in these crimes, as did local village elders and even local forestry management officials, Polish firefighters, and people who worked in other occupations and who were required to provide auxiliary services.[167] In addition, Jews who fled the ghettos and camps were often hunted down by groups of local residents, who denounced or killed them.

***

163 Nechama Tec, *When Light Pierced the Darkness: Christian Rescue of Jews in Nazi-occupied Poland* (New York: Oxford University Press, 1986); Beate Kosmala, 'Ungleiche Opfer in extremer Situation: Die Schwierigkeiten der Solidarität im okkupierten Polen', in Wolfgang Benz and Juliane Wetzel (eds.), *Solidarität und Hilfe für Juden während der NS-Zeit: Regionalstudien I. Polen, Rumänien, Griechenland, Luxemburg, Norwegen, Schweiz* (Berlin: Metropol, 1996), pp. 19–98.

164 Michał Borwicz, *Arishe Papirn* (Buenos Aires: Unión central israelita polaca en la Argentina, 1955); Małgorzata Melchior, *Zagłada a tożsamość: Polscy Żydzi ocaleni 'na aryjskich papierach'. Analiza doświadczenia biograficznego* (Warsaw: Instytut Filozofii i Socjologii PAN, 2004); Halina Zawadzka, *Ucieczka z getta* (Warsaw: Karta, 2001).

165 Feliks Tych estimates that 200,000 Poles helped Jews in Poland: Feliks Tych, 'Polish Society's Attitudes towards the Holocaust', in Beate Kosmala and Feliks Tych (eds.), *Facing the Nazi Genocide: Non-Jews and Jews in Europe* (Berlin: Metropol, 2004), pp. 87–105, here p. 101.

166 Jan Grabowski, *'Ja tego Żyda znam!' Szantażowanie Żydów w Warszawie 1939–1943* (Warsaw: Instytut Filozofii i Socjologii PAN, 2004).

167 Engelking, *Such a Beautiful Sunny Day*; Jan Grabowski, *Hunt for the Jews*; Jan T. Gross (ed.), *The Holocaust in Occupied Poland: New Findings and New Interpretations* (Frankfurt am Main: Peter Lang, 2012).

The Red Army's invasion of the eastern part of the General Government in June and July 1944 came too late for most Jews. The SS deported the few remaining Jewish forced labourers to concentration camps, where most of them perished during the last months of the war. Only those who had gone into hiding and could hold out long enough were liberated in July 1944, during the Warsaw Uprising in August 1944, or during the next Soviet offensive in January 1945. Others were not liberated until later, from the camps in the German Reich. Estimates of the number of Jews who were liberated in Poland as a whole vary; these Jews had survived in hiding among Poles, or in the camps, or among partisans and in the forests. One estimate suggests that 50,000–60,000 Jews were liberated in Poland as a whole, and a further 20,000–40,000 Jews were liberated from concentration camps in the Reich.[168] Jan Grabowski and Barbara Engelking offer a lower estimate and consider the figure of 40,000 Jews liberated in Poland as a whole to be the most generally accepted reckoning.[169] Many Jews – several tens of thousands – who had fled to the Soviet Union in 1939 returned once the war was over (they were called 'repatriants'). However, the complete destruction of their home towns and villages; the border changes, which entailed the incorporation of large parts of eastern Poland into the Soviet Union; and the increasing antisemitism, which culminated in violent attacks, caused most of the surviving Jews to leave Poland soon after the war.[170]

Prior to this, however, the Jewish Historical Commissions that were formed immediately after liberation questioned many survivors and asked them to write accounts of their experiences under the occupation. In addition to the Ringelblum archive, these reports – which number several thousand and are now held at the Jewish Historical Institute in Warsaw[171] – are among the most important sources of information about German occupation rule in Poland, which almost completely annihilated Polish Jewry in an unprecedented campaign of extermination.

168 Teresa Prekerowa, 'Wojna i okupacja', in Jerzy Tomaszewski (ed.), *Najnowsze dzieje Żydów w Polsce w zarysie (do 1950 roku)* (Warsaw: Wydawnictwo Naukowe PWN, 1993), pp. 273–384, here p. 384; Tych, 'Polish Society's Attitudes towards the Holocaust', p. 100.

169 Grabowski and Engelking (eds.), *Night without End*, p. xx.

170 Zofia Wóycicka, *Arrested Mourning: Memory of the Nazi Camps in Poland, 1944–1950*, trans. Jasper Tilbury (Frankfurt am Main: Peter Lang, 2013 [Polish edn, 2009]); Ingo Loose, 'Eastern European Shoah Victims and the Problem of Group Identity', in Randall Hansen et al. (eds.), *Authenticity and Victimhood after the Second World War: Narratives from Europe and East Asia* (Toronto: University of Toronto Press, 2021), pp. 79–93.

171 Frank Beer, Wolfgang Benz, and Barbara Distel (eds.), *Nach dem Untergang: Die ersten Zeugnisse der Shoah in Polen 1944–1947. Berichte der Zentralen Jüdischen Historischen Kommission* (Berlin: Metropol, 2014); Laura Jockusch (ed.), *Khurbn-Forshung: Documents on Early Holocaust Research in Postwar Poland* (Göttingen: Vandenhoeck & Ruprecht, 2021).

# List of Documents

138 *Informacja Bieżąca*, 15 September 1942: report on the murder of Jews in the General Government

139 On 16 September 1942 the Eastern Railway intervenes on behalf of its Jewish forced labourers

140 *Rzeczpospolita Polska*, 16 September 1942: the Polish government's coordinating body for civil resistance issues a declaration condemning the murder of the Jews

141 On 17 September 1942 the Interior Administration Department for Kreis Ostrów Mazowiecka orders the arrest of Moses Seemann and his deportation to Treblinka labour camp

142 On 18 September 1942 the military district commander in the General Government advises against the immediate removal of Jewish workers from armaments factories

143 *Oyf der vakh*, 20 September 1942: article describing Treblinka extermination camp

144 On 21 September 1942 the SS and Police Leader in District Radom states that Poles who help Jews are to be warned they face the death penalty

145 In early autumn 1942 the Home Army reports on events in the Warsaw ghetto

146 On 23 September 1942 Richard Lichtheim sends word of the systematic extermination of Jews in occupied Poland

147 Around 25 September 1942 an escapee from Treblinka extermination camp reports on how the murderers there attempt to deceive their victims

148 On 28 September 1942 Yehoshua Weiss describes a murderous raid on the Jews of Podhajce

149 *WRN*, 28 September 1942: statement on the murder of the Jews of the Warsaw ghetto

150 Emanuel Ringelblum explains why the Warsaw Jews remained passive during the deportations that took place from July to September 1942

151 An escapee from Treblinka reports on his deportation from Częstochowa on 21 September 1942 and on the extermination camp

152 On 1 October 1942 Menakhem Mendel Kon tallies the number of people murdered as part of German extermination efforts targeting the Warsaw ghetto

153 *Biuletyn Informacyjny*, 1 October 1942: article on the murder of the Jewish population in occupied Poland

154 On 2 October 1942 the Bund and the representative of the Polish government in exile report on the situation in the Warsaw ghetto

155 On 2 October 1942 Karol Dresdner, a resident of the Lwów ghetto, describes his loneliness to Aurelia Wyleżyńska in Warsaw

156 *Informacja Bieżąca*, 4 October 1942: report on the murder of Jews in Mszana Dolna

157 *Agencja Prasowa*, 7 October 1942: report criticizing signs of a collapse of moral standards in Polish society

158 On 8 October 1942 the Warsaw Transfer Bureau reports on its forthcoming closure and the transformation of the ghetto into a labour camp

159 On 9 October 1942 Himmler orders that Poles be deployed for forced labour in the General Government instead of Jews

258 On 6 August 1943 a Polish underground organization reports that Jews are being murdered with poison gas at Lublin-Majdanek concentration camp

259 *Głos Warszawy*, 10 August 1943: report on the uprising in Treblinka extermination camp

260 On 13 August 1943 the Polish government's representation in occupied Poland announces that the inmates in Treblinka have destroyed the camp

261 On 14 August 1943 the Wehrmacht reports the murder of 350 people by Wehrmacht and police units during the liquidation of the labour camp for Jews on the Adampol estate

262 On 16 August 1943 members of the Home Army denounce the sołtys of Kurów for participating in the persecution of Jews

263 On 17 August 1943 the Commander of the Security Police and the SD in District Warsaw proposes that the War Merit Cross be awarded for murders committed in the Warsaw ghetto

264 In August 1943 the Polish government's representation in occupied Poland describes the ongoing murder of Jews and the prisoners' uprising in Treblinka

265 *Hechaluc Halochem*, 27 August 1943: the Jewish Pioneer Youth (Halutzim) Combat Organization calls on Jews in the General Government to take up active resistance

266 On 31 August 1943 the Home Army reports on the terror of the German occupation, the hunt for Jews, and the prisoners' uprising at Treblinka

267 In August 1943 the Foreign Affairs Department of the Polish government's representation in occupied Poland advocates a Jewish state

268 On 7 September 1943 the head of the SS Business and Administration Main Office notes that he is taking over the labour camps for Jews from the SS and Police Leaders

269 *Biuletyn Informacyjny*, 7 September 1943: the Directorate of Underground Combat announces that a Pole who blackmailed Jews has been executed

270 On 11 and 12 September 1943 Jerzy Urman, aged eleven, writes about his experiences in Drohobych on the 'Aryan side' and his hatred of Hitler

271 Prior to 28 September 1943 an escapee from Treblinka describes conditions in the camp and how he got out during the prisoners' uprising

272 On 1 October 1943 the Jewish Aid Office reports on supplies for the last labour camps

273 On 19 October 1943 the GG government deems the labour camps for Jews a security threat

274 Around 24 October 1943 an Urban Police officer files a report on the pursuit of escapees from Sobibor by mounted police

275 On 4 November 1943 Globocnik asks Himmler to decorate the SS men who participated in the murder of Jews in the General Government

276 On 14 November 1943 the Home Army reports on the number of victims killed during Operation Harvest Festival in Lublin and Poniatowa

277 On 5 November 1943 the German National [illegible] reports [illegible] the [illegible] in the Łódź ghetto [illegible]

278 Leon Feiner reports in the [illegible] and the situation of the Jews in Poland from July to mid November 1943

279 On 17 December 1943 [illegible] interpreter [illegible] Tarnopol [illegible] asking to [illegible] allegedly [illegible]

280 [illegible] 1943 [illegible] poem about Płaszów camp

281 On 3 January 1944 [illegible] reports on the [illegible] of the possessions taken from murdered Jews

282 On 17 January 1944 the SS and [illegible] administration [illegible] Office inform [illegible] about [illegible] of formerly Jewish owned real estate in the General Government

283 On 3 February 1944 [illegible] reports [illegible] the Harvest Festival murder operation [illegible]

284 On 4 February 1944 Ukrainian police [illegible] family from [illegible] of having sheltered Jews

285 On 9 February 1944 the Security Police report on Jewish inmates who had made preparations to escape from the labour camp in [illegible]

286 On 24 February 1944 the Polish government's representation in occupied Poland submits a detailed report on Treblinka extermination camp

287 From 30 December 1943 to February 1944 [illegible] describes [illegible] in hiding in Warsaw

288 On 5 March 1944 [illegible] took [illegible] the cultural and political work done in the Warsaw ghetto

289 On 2 March 1944 a Polish underground chronicle records the arrest of Jews [illegible] in Warsaw

290 On 28 March 1944 [illegible] notes that the [illegible] family [illegible] because they had helped Jews

291 [illegible] describes an attempt to hand over [illegible]

292 [illegible]

293 On 1 August 1944 [illegible] of the [illegible] in Warsaw [illegible] camp

294 [illegible] the Jewish National Committee [illegible]

295 [illegible] from August to October 1944

296 On [illegible] February 1945 [illegible] writes to [illegible]

# DOCUMENTS

## DOC. 1

## On 2 August 1941, 17-year-old Halina Nelken observes a young German soldier at the ghetto wall in Cracow[1]

Handwritten diary of Halina Nelken,[2] entry for 2 August 1941

I go to Krzemionki[3] with the children. We have been allocated a barren, steep hill and part of the sports field where the wall stands, which, according to Felek, is 'in the style of rabbinic graves'. The wall isn't finished yet, and you can see the 'Aryan side'. I like to sit on the wall and look at the wide, green fields on the one side, and as a contrast, at the row of houses, high church towers, and the Vistula, like a shiny ribbon, on the other side. Germans are housed next door in the barracks. They play football, sunbathe, and look towards the ghetto. Not far from me, one of the soldiers was lying on the dry, sun-drenched grass. The sky was very bright; the setting sun cast a gentle ray on his young, muscular, tanned body. Suddenly he got up and approached the wall. I felt the urge to jump to the ground, but it somehow seemed like a cowardly thing to do, so I remained sitting, even when he lifted himself up and sat next to me on the wall with his feet on the 'Aryan side'. He smiled. He had fair hair and light-coloured eyes and was the epitome of youth, vitality, and health! Although we didn't exchange a single word, we didn't take our eyes off each other. 'Look', I thought, 'I'm young like you, and I'm suffocating here! Why don't you take me by the hand and why don't we run through the fields, to Krakus Mound[4] and back?' He sat right next to me, a complete stranger, and yet so close because he was young and not in uniform. He surely wasn't thinking now about the war, race, religion, and all the walls that people have built between each other. In the end he jumped down nimbly and went off, looking back the entire time. Not for a moment did I think it could be any other way, yet I somehow felt a pang of remorse as his silhouette disappeared among the green fields gently gilded by the setting sun. At home I played the tango 'You pass me by, but don't notice me', and I've composed my own lyrics:

Sitting on a wall, you sadly gaze on by;
In that bright glance, lament and longing lie,
As round this place where you're held captive,
Krzemionki's cliffs loom high –

1 The original document is in the Nelken family's possession. Copy in IfZ-Archives, F 601. Published with revisions made by the author in Halina Nelken, *Pamiętnik z getta w Krakowie*, ed. Stanisław Wcisło (Toronto: Polski Fundusz Wydawniczy w Kanadzie, 1987), pp. 138–139. Published in English (excluding the concluding poem) in *And Yet, I Am Here!*, trans. Halina Nelken with Alicia Nitecki (Amherst, MA: University of Massachussetts Press, 1999), pp. 90–91. This document has been newly translated from Polish.

2 Halina Nelken (1924–2009); attended grammar school in Cracow; lived in the Podgórze district of the Cracow ghetto from March 1941; confined in various camps, 1942–1945; continued her education after the war, went to university, and subsequently worked as an art historian, first in Poland and later in the USA; kept this diary from 1938 to 1942.

3 This was still an undeveloped area of the Podgórze district at the time; one of the hills there is known as the Bare Mountain (Łysa Góra).

4 A 16-metre-high man-made mound in the south of Krzemionki dating from the seventh century and possibly erected as a burial monument.

Your right hand bears a sign – a curse it is;
You sigh – I know exactly what you miss
As you ask, quiet and despairing,
Why it must be like this?

Why does the world have its cinemas, its radios,
Its schools, and trams, and cars, and fields, and glades, and meadows,
While you're here, a captive bird whom bars confine?
Out there is a life for which you pine,
A life that still flows on despite you,
And all thanks to that sign!

Sitting on a wall, you sadly gaze on by;
In that bright glance, lament and longing lie,
As a soldier stands beside you,
A youth with steely eye.

Curled on his brow, some boyish forelocks stray,
But the look he's raised to you is cold and grey.
You speak to him with silent glances
As he takes steps your way.

War and ghetto, why find them concerning,
While you and I – we are both young and yearning?
This world could crumble – if that's how it must fall.
But we desire to live too – damn it all –
And not just clench our teeth with sorrow that makes us want to bawl!

## DOC. 2

## On 16 August 1941 the Kreishauptmann of Grójec forbids the non-Jewish population from taking in Jews or hiring them as workers[1]

Order sent by the Kreishauptmann of Grójec, signed Zimmermann,[2] Grójec,[3] to the mayors in the Kreis, dated 16 August 1941

I ask that the population be urgently informed that it is strictly forbidden to take in Jews or to hire them as workers. Exceptions will only be authorized by the employment office branch in Grojec and its sub-branches. I request that the population be further informed that I will immediately arrest anyone who contravenes this order and have them transferred to a labour camp.[4]

## DOC. 3

## On 19 August 1941 the gendarmerie in Wola Pękoszewska report an organized escape from the Warsaw ghetto[1]

Letter from police officer Schmidt of the Wola Pękoszewska gendarmerie post (log no. 630/41), Wola Pękoszewska, to the gendarmerie platoon in Skierniewice, dated 19 August 1941[2]

Re: illegal transportation of Jews in lorry registration no. Ost 8565 from the ghetto in Warsaw to the Petrikau[3] area
Concerning: directive from the District Governor in Warsaw dated 17 June 1941, regarding restrictions on the movement of Jews,[4] and directive from the Kreishauptmann in Lowicz, dated 7 July 1941[5]

*Enclosures*:
On 18 August 1941 I was instructed to carry out traffic checks on the Mszczonow[6]–Kowiezy[7] road with two Sonderdienst[8] men. This was also intended to combat clandestine trading. On the two preceding evenings our traffic patrols had reported that a lorry

1 AIPN, GK 182/216, fol. 2.
2 Werner Zimmermann (1900–1994), lawyer; worked for the Reich tax authorities in Hamburg in 1925; Regierungsrat in 1929; joined the NSDAP in 1932; Landrat in Meppen, 1934–1939; deputy Landrat in Kattowitz in 1939; Kreishauptmann of Grójec, March 1940 – Jan. 1945; lived in Koblenz after the war.
3 Town located approximately 40 km to the south of Warsaw.
4 The text is followed by a Polish translation of the order, underneath which is a handwritten note in Polish: 'inform the population with a poster – with coloured edges – mayor' (signature illegible).

1 APW, 486/46, fol. 1r–v. This document has been translated from German.
2 The original features handwritten corrections and annotations; receipt stamp of the Skierniewice gendarmerie platoon (date illegible).
3 Piotrków Trybunalski.
4 See Governor Ludwig Fischer's regulation of 17 June 1941, PMJ 4/301.
5 This could not be identified.
6 A small town about 50 km south-west of Warsaw.
7 Correctly: Kowiesy, a village approximately 15 km south-west of Mszczonów.
8 The Sonderdienst ('Special Service') in the General Government was an auxiliary police force made up of ethnic Germans. It was directly subordinate to the government of the GG, in contrast to the police force under the control of the Higher SS and Police Leader.

had failed to respond to the stop signal given by the police (using a red light) on this road and had instead driven off in order to avoid being checked. When darkness fell, the post commander therefore assigned me another two men from the post as reinforcements in order to finally force the vehicle to stop.

At about 9.30 p.m. a vehicle approached from the Mszczonow direction on the road by the Zawady estate. Since only one headlight was on and it was not dipped, I showed my red light in good time as a signal to stop. I had positioned my men on one side of the road in order to open fire on the vehicle if it failed to stop again. I had expressly ordered them to shoot at the lorry's wheels. The driver of the lorry initially obeyed my signal to stop, but then ignored it again immediately by accelerating. This behaviour prompted me to immediately give the order to fire, which appeared to have some effect because the sound of the engine subsequently became irregular. Seven shots were discharged. I noticed a clearly visible trail of petrol along the road in the direction in which the lorry had fled the scene. We then pursued the vehicle and found it approximately 4 km away at Wendrogow. The driver had escaped under cover of complete darkness, and the search for him remained unsuccessful. The covered lorry was carrying Jews who, according to their statements, had been picked up from the ghetto in Warsaw and were due to be taken to the Petrikau area. The Jews were not in possession of any identity documents, but they stated that the driver had told them in Warsaw that he had a permit for this transport. The Jews also explained that they had paid the driver 200 zl. per head for this transport. The detained Jews consisted of seven men, thirteen women, and nine children aged between one and ten. The vehicle has been secured at the Wola Pękoszewska gendarmerie post and is no longer roadworthy on account of the shots that hit it. The Jews were arrested and are being held by the Polish police at Wola Pękoszewska.

After consultation with the Kreishauptmannschaft in Lowicz, orders were given for criminal proceedings to be brought against all the Jews, who were to be forcibly taken to Warsaw by train. The Jews will have to bear the costs incurred, including the provision of policemen.

According to the vehicle registration document found in the lorry, the vehicle is registered in the name of Schmidt, Jan,[9] vegetable business, 79 Gorczewska, Warsaw.[10] The vehicle is licensed, but only until 31 July 1941. Furthermore, it was definitely being driven illegally, since no journey is recorded in the driver's logbook. It has to be assumed that illegal journeys of this kind were also undertaken on 16 and 17 August 1941.

Once all the evidence has been collected, the Jews will be transported to Warsaw under a police guard.[11] The seized vehicle registration document and the driver's logbook will be enclosed with the charges against the unknown driver and/or owner of the vehicle.[12]

9 Correctly: Ludwik Schmidt (b. 1906), gardener; he told the Urban Police that in April 1941 he had taken his lorry, which was no longer licensed, to a garage, where he had left it because he was unable to pay the repair costs. The garage owner, Jan Dudziński (b. 1899), a mechanic, said the lorry had been repaired and was left standing in his yard for six weeks until Stanisław Gąsiorowski, a lorry driver from Warsaw, stole it on 18 August 1941: APW, 486/46, fol. 7r–v.

10 An 'x' is inserted here and on the left margin there is the handwritten note: '79 Forststr.'

11 A total of twenty-eight people, many of whom had escaped from the refugee shelter at 5 Elektoralna Street, were taken back to the Warsaw ghetto by a Polish police officer on 20 August 1941: APW, 486/46, fol. 5; list of detained persons, fol. 4r–v.

12 The police officer in charge of the gendarmerie in Skierniewice reported the incident to the gendarmerie platoon in Skierniewice, the Gendarmerie-Hauptmannschaft, and the Landkommissar in Skierniewice.

## DOC. 4

## *Völkischer Beobachter*, 20 August 1941: article on German orders placed with craftsmen in the Warsaw ghetto[1]

*The Warsaw Transfer Bureau: Jewish labour market in the General Government*[2]

The reorganization of the economy in the General Government has made it necessary for the German administration to address the *Jewish problem* to a degree that is unprecedented when compared with conditions within Germany. After all, about one third of the population of the city of Warsaw are Jews, and it has not been rare to encounter small towns that were almost entirely Jewish domains. However, this has not deterred efforts to eliminate Jewry from Aryan economic life. The necessary restructuring has not infrequently required new methods of handling the Jewish masses. In most cases conditions have made it necessary to gather Jews from widely scattered places of abode together in dedicated residential districts so they can be better supervised. Among other things, this led to the creation of the *closed-off Jewish residential district in Warsaw*, in which there are *about 500,000 Jews.* New by Reich standards and also quite remarkable in this respect is that about 40 per cent of the Jews capable of gainful employment in Warsaw are *craftsmen by profession.* Occupations such as shoe upper maker, tailor, umbrella maker, cabinetmaker, roofer, leather worker, maker of fashion accessories, precision mechanic, etc. were practised on a large scale by Jews. At a time when the German working man has in many cases had to exchange his tools for a gun, the German administration is faced with the task of *deploying* the available *Jewish skilled workers in the service of the German economy appropriately and under supervision.* At the same time, we must not let *those who are nothing but useless mouths to feed place a strain on the entire economy.* With the assistance of interested German firms, it has already been possible to set up a number of large workshops that operate exclusively for German clients under German supervision. The results of their work are satisfactory, even though in many cases the professional equipment provided by the Jewish craftsmen is out of date or incomplete. *There are therefore still manifold opportunities for orders to be shifted to Warsaw from the territories of the German Reich where there is a shortage of workers.*

The Warsaw Transfer Bureau, 23 Königstraße, Warsaw, was recently established as a public institution in order to deal with the economic aspects of the Jewish problem in Warsaw.[3] Its function is to provide German enterprises, in particular those in war production, with advice and support in evaluating Jewish skilled workers and commercial enterprises. These enterprises are organized in associations, which allows for the necessary transparency regarding the type and number of skilled workers available as well as the manufacturing facilities.

1 *Völkischer Beobachter* (Vienna edition), 20 August 1941, p. 6. This document has been translated from German.
2 The wording of this article is almost identical to that of Memorandum no. 1 issued by the Warsaw Transfer Bureau, dated August 1941: ÖGfZ, Archiv, Nl 93, folder 14.
3 The Transfer Bureau was established on 1 Dec. 1940.

## DOC. 5

## Transcription by Emanuel Ringelblum of a poem by Henryka Łazowertówna about the child smugglers of the Warsaw ghetto[1]

Poem by Henryka Łazowertówna,[2] recited publicly in Warsaw prior to 25 August 1941[3] (handwritten copy)

*The Little Smuggler*

By wall and by hole and by sentry,
By wire, by rubble, by slat,
Intrepid, in hunger, intently,
I scurry, I run like a cat.
At noontime, night's falling, day's breaking,
In wind and in rain and in shine,
My life I'm a hundred times staking,
My young neck is right on the line.

My arm holds a canvas sack,
My back wears tattered thread,
My legs are young and nimble,
My heart's in constant dread.
All this I have to suffer,
To this must bend my will,
So that all of you tomorrow,
Have bread to eat your fill.

By wall and by hole and by brickwork,
At night-time, at dawn, and by day,
Intrepid, in hunger, by trickwork,
As silent as shadows I stray.
And if in this game that I'm playing,
I'm seized by the swift hand of fate,
It's merely a trap of life's laying,
For me, Mama, no longer wait.

1 AŻIH, 302/337, fols. 144–145. Published in English translation in Emanuel Ringelblum, *Polish-Jewish Relations during the Second World War*, ed. Joseph Kermish and Shmuel Krakowski, trans. Dafna Allon, Danuta Dabrowska, and Dana Keren (Jerusalem: Yad Vashem, 1992 [1974] [Polish edn, 1958–1959]), p. 148. The poem is part of Ringelblum's essay about Polish-Jewish relations under the German occupation. This document has been newly translated from Polish.

2 Henryka Łazowertówna (1910–1942), poet; studied abroad in Grenoble on a state scholarship from 1930; two volumes of her poetry were published, in 1930 and 1934; active member of the Union of Polish Writers in Warsaw, 1936–1939; lived in the Warsaw ghetto from 1940; worked for the Jewish Social Self-Help (JSS) and the underground archive of the Warsaw ghetto; murdered in Treblinka in August 1942.

3 The date stems from a comment Ringelblum made in his daily chronicle. The poem was recited at public events on numerous occasions.

I will not be returning,
My voice won't faintly sound,
In dirty streets there's no learning,
What fate a lost child found.
There's just a single question,
Lips grimacing, stiffly spread:
Who'll bring to you, my mother,
Tomorrow's portion of bread?

## DOC. 6

## On 9 September 1941 a member of the Jewish Order Service reports on the shooting of fifty-one people at Osowa labour camp on 30 August 1941[1]

Transcript of the statement given by Szmul Siwka, Warsaw, 9 September 1941 (copy)[2]

*Transcript*
Order Service member Siwka Szmul, Ev[idence] no. 747, came to the headquarters of the Order Service, 32 Krochmalna-Straße, Department I, Service and Training Division, and gave the following statement:

On 5 September 1941 I received the order to transport the camp inmates from Krychów labour camp, near Chełm, to Warsaw. This camp had been closed down. Only the people who had been working there remained at the camp, including three Order Service officials and a number of labourers. I set off in the direction of Sobibor with a party of camp inmates numbering around 130 in total. There the camp inmates were to be loaded into railway wagons. Our transport, just like other transports, stopped at Osowa labour camp.[3] This is because the commandant of Osowa labour camp always issues further orders concerning loading and transport and has to be present when this is done. At Osowa labour camp, I found the full complement of Order Service officials, the camp physician, two medical orderlies, the warehouse keeper, one official, and fourteen camp inmates who were on their way back from hospital. When he saw us at the camp, Group Leader Rybojad, the head of the camp guard at Osowa labour camp, told me about the events that had taken place at Osowa on 30 August.

Around midday a number of cars carrying uniformed SS officials had arrived at Osowa labour camp, bringing one machine gun with them. As they entered the camp, they ordered that everyone alive was to get undressed. When everyone had got undressed, they were ordered to go behind a little building approximately 50 m

1 APW, Office of the Governor of District Warsaw, Commissioner for the Jewish Residential District in Warsaw, Transfer Bureau, 482/108, fol. 38r–v. This document has been translated from German.
2 The transcript was translated from Polish and sent on 8 Sept. 1941 by the district head of the Jewish Order Service, head of its Department I, to the head of the Order Service in the Warsaw ghetto, Józef Szeryński: ibid., fol. 41.
3 The labour camp for Jews at Osowa, a village south-west of Sobibor, operated from 1941 to 1943. The number of inmates averaged approximately 1,000; in all, approximately 4,000 people passed through the camp, where they were put to work on draining swampy land. A total of 170 inmates perished and 70 were shot by the German camp guards during the duration of the camp's operation. When the camp was closed, its inmates were deported to Sobibor.

away from the camp in order to dig a grave. At that moment Inspector Holcheimer[4] from the Water Management Board drove up, and when he saw what was happening, he addressed the SS officials with the words: 'Gentlemen, I need the police.'[5] The Order Service functionaries were thereupon allowed to put their clothes back on and step to the side. At the request of Inspector H., they [the SS] also allowed the camp physician, the medical orderlies, and the warehouse keeper to get dressed again. The camp inmates were then lined up in rows of five and, after the first five had been shot, the next five were ordered to throw the corpses into the grave and cover them with soil. In this way fifty-one camp inmates, the warehouse manager, Mośkowicz, and his deputy, Libert, were shot. The Order Service officials who had stayed alive had to bury the last ones. That's what Group Leader Rybojad told me about the incident. When I went to Sobibor with the transport, the commandant of Osowa camp approached me with Group Leader Rybojad, asking whether I knew anything about the shooting of the people at Osowa. After Group Leader Rybojad gave me a sign, I said no and told the camp commandant I didn't know anything about it.

Transcribed: signed K. Goldfeder,[6] deputy district head of the Order Service

## DOC. 7

## On 9 September 1941 the Kreishauptmann of Lublin-Land issues instructions concerning the ghetto in Piaski[1]

Directive issued by the Kreishauptmann of Lublin-Land, signed Ziegenmeyer,[2] Lublin, dated 9 September 1941

*Directive*
concerning the Jewish residential district (ghetto) in Piaski[3]

*Ghetto*
(1) All Jews of the municipality of Piaski shall reside in the Jewish residential district (ghetto).

4 Correctly: Franz Holtzheimer (b. 1908), engineer; water management inspector in District Lublin from July 1940 to Sept. 1943, based in Chełm from spring 1941; lived in West Berlin after the war.
5 A reference to the Jewish Order Service.
6 Kazimierz Goldfeder was a Polish army reserve officer. As a member of the Order Service in the Warsaw ghetto, from March 1941 he was involved in providing workers for forced labour camps.

1 APL, 501/139, fol. 89r–v. This document has been translated from German.
2 Emil Ziegenmeyer (1906–1991), lawyer; joined the NSDAP and the SA in 1931; instructor with the SA and the National Socialist Motor Vehicle Corps; administrative official in Upper Silesia, East Prussia, and Breslau, 1936–1939; Regierungsrat in 1938; Kreishauptmann of Lublin-Land from Oct. 1939 to June 1944; subsequently worked briefly in the Interior Administration Department of the General Government; served in the war, 1944–1945; in 1951 regained his licence to practise law; senior administrator for the City of Duisburg from 1956.
3 Ziegenmeyer had previously ordered the establishment of a ghetto in Piaski, a small town about 30 km east of Lublin, on 2 Dec. 1940: APL, 501/139, fols. 2–4. It was the first sealed ghetto in District Lublin.

(2) The gates to the ghetto are to be kept permanently closed, with the exception of the cases specified in (3).

(3) The gates are to be opened in the following cases: for Germans with *civil servant* status; for transportation of the sick; for physicians, midwives, certain members of the Jewish Council, and certain members of the Jewish Order Service upon presentation of permits issued by the Kreishauptmann of Lublin-Land; and in the event of extreme danger (e.g. fire). Apart from this, the gates at the Lublinerstraße crossing may be opened between 6 and 7 a.m., and between 6 and 7 p.m. for the purpose of fetching water from the ghetto well located there.

(4) Aryans shall be prohibited from entering the ghetto without *written permission* from the Kreishauptmann, with the exception of the cases specified in (3).
The units of the Security Police, the gendarmerie, the police, and other *German* police bodies shall remain unaffected by this.

(5) It is prohibited to leave the ghetto, except with a permit from the Kreishauptmann and for labour deployment.

*Order Service*

(6) The Jewish Order Service shall be deployed to maintain order and cleanliness in the ghetto, in particular to open and close the gates.

(7) The Order Service shall carry out regular patrols in the ghetto, day and night. In particular it shall be responsible for maintaining the ghetto fence; damage is to be reported immediately. Its head shall be responsible to the Kreishauptmann for the proper functioning of the Order Service.

(8) The members of the Order Service shall wear blue caps with a yellow Star of Zion and yellow armbands with the words 'Jewish Order Service Piaski'.

(9) All ghetto residents must obey their orders.

*Penalties*

(10) Contravention of these instructions shall be punished with a fine of up to 1,000 zl. or imprisonment of up to three months, unless a more severe punishment is stipulated.

## DOC. 8

## On 13 September 1941 the Polish underground organization Union of Armed Struggle reports on the activities of communists and national minorities in the area around Warsaw[1]

Report by the Command of the Union of Armed Struggle (ZWZ), Warsaw, dated 13 September 1941[2]

Warsaw area

Situation report for August 1941 on subversive organizations[3] and national minorities.

*I. General situation*

During the period covered by this report, the situation of the subversive organizations and the national minorities was marked by heavy fighting between the Germans and the

1 AAN, 1326/203/X-70, fols. 1–8. This document has been translated from Polish.
2 The original contains handwritten corrections, notes, and underlining.
3 This is a reference to the communist underground.

Allies, especially the Soviet army. It was observed that order among the Germans on the front, behind the lines, and among the occupation authorities is gradually breaking down completely. The loss of weapons (light and heavy machine guns, rifles, grenades, pistols, etc.), equipment (clothing, underwear, bedding, etc.), military equipment (cars, motorcycles, and car as well as motorcycle parts), and supplies is no longer sporadic, but is almost becoming commonplace. Desertion is becoming increasingly common and is taking on bizarre forms, such as [Germans] purchasing the work permits of Polish volunteers being sent for labour in the Reich so that instead of the Poles, they themselves go to the Reich for work and thereby escape their army units. The belief in victory, which was so strong until quite recently, has collapsed and given way to depression. Due to the huge expansion of the occupied territories and the loss of men and armaments on the one hand, and the shortage of raw materials on the other, fewer people are available for work in some sectors. This leads to chaos and confusion where until recently there had been smooth and efficient organization.

On the other hand, the subversive organizations have organized their work better and both in the city and the countryside have been able to penetrate circles where they find support for their work. They receive this support primarily in terms of resisting the Germans, but their ideological demands have also been well received, i.e. agencies acting on behalf of the Third International[4] either taking over or having power transferred to it. The initiators of this operation doubtless include Soviet military service units which, with the help of their operatives, are trying to agitate among all those who sympathize with the Soviet orientation – both staunch supporters and the sympathizers they have influenced. The almost simultaneous mass escape of Bolshevik prisoners of war from the camps is also significant. Many of them have a command of the Polish language and, given their good navigation skills in the field, have quite purposefully sought out places where they can find support, which indicates a planned and organized operation. In particular, the vast majority of the rural population support the refugees and afford them a large measure of goodwill, if not downright sympathy, despite the danger from the Germans. According to our sources, the Germans do not want Bolshevik prisoners of war in their territories and are reluctant to accept any. Therefore they leave the majority of these elements in our territories,[5] which – in connection with the operation described above – has contributed considerably to our difficult supply situation.

Another change in attitude towards the Germans has been observed among the Ukrainians. The Ukrainians have reacted to their mobilization – whether for the police, the army, or the administration – with great reluctance and even outright refusal, and were it not for preventive and repressive measures, this mobilization would have failed. The annexation of the south-eastern voivodeships[6] into the so-called General Govern-

4 This was the designation for the Communist International (Comintern), which was founded in 1919 in Moscow.

5 In 1941 the Wehrmacht held most Soviet prisoners of war in makeshift camps across the occupied territories of the Soviet Union and Poland, particularly in the General Government. These camps were in no way prepared to adequately accommodate such large numbers of people.

6 This refers to the Stanislawów and Tarnopol voivodeships as well as most of Lwów voivodeship, which were annexed to District Galicia.

ment and the German military authorities' persecution of Ukrainian nationalists[7] have decisively contributed to the fact that the [Ukrainians'] hitherto friendly attitude towards the Germans has changed. Many Ukrainians are abandoning their previous stance and their behaviour towards the Poles, if not benevolent, is at least neutral. In any case, the Ukrainians' hostile and negative attitude towards the Poles has softened. Something similar has been observed among the Byelorussians, except that many Byelorussians are trying to curry favour with the Poles because their elite circles are greatly influenced by Poles, and they want to be able to count on support from Poland in future.

No new or unusual activities have been noted among the Russians.

One can speak of a German minority only in the neighbourhoods on the left bank of the Vistula (around Grójec, Łowicz, and Sochaczew, as well as parts of Warsaw) because, with a few exceptions, all the Germans were relocated out of the neighbourhoods on the right bank (around Garwolin, Mińsk Mazowiecki, Siedlce, Sokołów, and parts of Warsaw) in 1940. In view of events on the front and the unfavourable developments,[8] they are revising their attitude towards the Poles. There are incidents of them collecting signatures from the Poles to confirm their [the Germans'] loyalty towards the Polish population (for instance in Grodzisk). More and more complaints can be heard about the Germans, and they are being cursed for the situation they have *created*. This part of the German minority is striving for a good relationship with the Polish population, but they are still outnumbered. The majority still believe in a German victory and try to do business; there are even cases of Poles being mistreated. In general, however, the situation for the German minority is constantly improving.

The Jewish minority still believe in a rapid victory over the Germans and a change in their difficult living conditions. A large majority are counting on the Soviet army and expect it to liberate them. Many Jews even actively participate in the measures against the Germans prepared by the supporters of the Soviet system (communists),[9] even though the goal is to introduce the Soviet system in Poland. The greater part of the Jewish minority is ambivalent towards the Poles, a considerable part is hostile towards them, and only a few are friendly to them.

Among the Jewish political groups, only the communists are actively engaged in organizational-propaganda activity, whereas other groups and organizations are solely concerned with survival and are thus hardly politically active at all. Due to the difficult living conditions in the Warsaw ghetto, the tide of escapees is not abating, but instead intensifying. *The Jews* who have escaped from the ghetto survive mainly by begging. They hide in the adjacent neighbourhoods on the left bank of the Vistula, and from there they go to villages with Jewish populations on the right bank, where they find support.

7 After leading officials in the Bandera wing of the Organization of Ukrainian Nationalists (OUN) proclaimed an autonomous Ukraine on 30 June 1941, the German police began arresting OUN activists.

8 The battle of Smolensk had delayed the German advance.

9 Here and below, the original Polish uses the word *komuna* ('commune') as a designation for communists.

*II. The situation in detail*

Warsaw area

*The communists*

During the period covered by the last report, it was clear that those Communist Party cells in this region which have direct contact with Warsaw – especially Radzymin, with Josek Finkielsztein at their head; Wyszków, with Piotr Tyszkiewicz; and Wołomin, with Bogdan Jeziorański – have become more active. The latter comes from powiat Pułtusk, from where he and others were resettled by the occupiers.

Nothing has been disclosed about the dissemination of the underground press, but agitation has been detected among local workers, especially those with less political experience. Information from Otwock suggests that the communists active there, such as the lawyer Duracz[10] and others, have kept in touch with central Communist Party[11] cells, agents, and Soviet special envoys. In the Warsaw area, on the other hand – according to information from Warsaw – a certain *Werner Rotholc*, a Soviet secret service agent, coordinates political activities in the Polish territories under German occupation. The ghetto is said to be the centre of communist operations in Warsaw. Because of the widespread culture of denunciation among the Jews, the communist press organ *Sierp i Młot*[12] is reportedly printed in the Polish part of the city and then smuggled into the ghetto.

*The national minorities*

*The Jews*

Those who were resettled to the Warsaw ghetto from the neighbourhoods along the left bank of the Vistula and subsequently escaped from the ghetto usually go begging and have dispersed throughout the surrounding villages to work in exchange for room and board. Information obtained from the Warsaw ghetto indicates that the Jews' political work is concentrated entirely in the Jewish-American relief organization the 'Joint' [JDC], which has its offices on Tłomacka Street. The leaders of the individual organizations are said to be employed there and mainly hold managerial positions.

Due to fears that this relief organization might be shut down, especially if America were to enter the war, the Jews endeavoured to rename the 'Jewish Social Self-Help'[13] and thereby create the impression of a solely national organization. In the final days of June this year, the German authorities summoned Laskier[14] and Białobrów,[15] both employees of this institution and well-known functionaries of the revisionist movement. They invited them to take over as editors of a Jewish periodical that the Germans intended to publish in Warsaw.

10 Teodor Franciszek Duracz, lawyer; made a name for himself defending communists at trials prior to Sept. 1939; murdered by the Gestapo in 1943.

11 Here and below, the original Polish uses the word *kompartja* to refer to the Communist Party.

12 Sierp i Młot (Sickle and Hammer) was a communist group that published an eponymous underground newspaper from spring 1941.

13 The Jewish Social Self-Help (JSS) had existed as an officially authorized relief agency for the Jewish population in the General Government since May 1940.

14 Perec Laskier, activist in the revisionist Zionist youth organization Betar (an acronym for Brit Trumpeldor [Covenant of Trumpeldor], founded in 1923).

15 Joel Białobrów, activist in Hatzohar (the Union of Zionist Revisionists, founded in 1925).

Although the revisionist movement has weakened, it nevertheless continues to exist. Most recently the revisionists have published a brochure in Yiddish titled 'A Look Back',[16] which has a photo of Żabotyński[17] and is devoted to his biography and activities. In addition the Bund undertakes a number of other activities, and it publishes two small Yiddish-language periodicals: *Der Morgenshtern* and *Skif*.[18]

All the Jewish people's soup kitchens, clinics, and medical centres remain under its influence.[19] The Bund is clearly pro-Soviet but acts independently of the communists and pursues its own aims among the Jewish masses.

The vast majority of Jews are pro-Soviet, and only a small proportion are favourably disposed towards the Polish state.

*The Ukrainians*

There was no significant activity during the period covered by this report; one merely senses a certain despondency and lack of confidence regarding the occupiers' actions and promises.

*The Russians*

The Russian movement is completely dead here. Its leading functionaries, Yakovlev and Svierdlov from Wołomin, have left for an unknown destination. On 28 August of this year the German authorities ordered the Russian Committee in Warsaw to provide a list of all the Russians registered with the Committee. These lists were sent to Berlin. This order is probably connected with the allocation of various posts in the occupied territories.

*The Byelorussians*

News came from Warsaw that the current secretary general of the Byelorussian Committee in Warsaw, Lastovka, supposedly remained in the service of the investigative branch of the State Police at the government commissariat in the city of Warsaw before the war.

*The Lithuanians*

The Lithuanian organization at 4 Skorupka Street in Warsaw is said to consist mainly of elements who are considered to be of little ideological value.

Some 60 per cent of them are said to be Poles or people of indeterminate national affiliation who are seeking various forms of welfare etc. These allegedly include Dowborczycy,[20] Peowiacy[21] from Lithuania, Polish army volunteers, etc. who previously fled Lithuania due to their pro-Polish activities. Some of them maintain contact with circles

16 This publication appeared in Yiddish in 1940 as the first and only edition of the periodical *Hamedina*.

17 Ze'ev Żabotyńsky (Vladimir Jabotinsky) (1880–1914), lawyer and journalist; founder of Betar; founded Hatzohar in 1925; lived in Palestine from 1928; founded the New Zionist Organization (NZO) in 1935, and its armed wing, Irgun Tzvai Leumi, in 1937.

18 The Sotsyalistisher Kinder Farband (Socialist Children's Association), founded in 1926, was the Bund's children's organization; its tasks included organizing holiday camps for the children of Bund members. Morgnshtern was the name of the Bund's sports organization. There is no record of an underground publication with either title.

19 Such institutions were also maintained by other political groups in the Warsaw ghetto.

20 Followers of the Polish general Józef Dowbor-Muśnicki (1867–1937).

21 Members of the Polish Military Organization (POW), a secret military organization founded by Józef Piłsudski in the Russian-administered part of divided Poland in 1914.

that are striving for Polish independence and they receive underground leaflets, even at the organization's headquarters itself.

The vast majority of the members speak only Polish because they do not know any other language. They explain their membership in the organization as stemming from a desire to save their possessions or their families. There are also a certain number of communist elements among them.

The president of this organization is said to be the priest Daukantas,[22] a refugee from Lithuania. The Germans arrested him for issuing an identity card for a Jew in exchange for 15,000 złoty.

*The Germans*

There have been no significant activities, apart from a few individuals who take part in raids – the general public responds to events in a rather restrained manner.

*Łowicz region – Skierniewice sub-region*

*Subversive agitation*

*The communists*

Although there is a communist cell in the territory of Skierniewice, nothing is known about its activity, nor does the Communist Party have any significant influence. This cell is currently under observation.

*The Jews*

There are no Jews in this region, apart from a few people hiding in the villages and a few in the labour camp on the Kamion estate in the community of Doleck.

*The Ukrainians*

Since the annexation of District Lwów to the General Government and the arrest of the Ukrainian leadership in Lwów, this group's enthusiasm has completely waned. The confiscation of radio sets has also affected the Ukrainians' mood.

*The Russians and Byelorussians*

There are no known signs of any activity on the part of these national groups in this region.

*The Germans*

There is a fairly large German colony in Skierniewice sub-region: 1. In Skierniewice: 80 families, about 400 persons, headed by Werns; 2. In Kochanów, Głuchów community: 118 families – 600 persons, led by the Miller brothers and Aleksander Cymerman, the acting wójt of Głuchów community; 3. In Borowiny, Skierniewice community: 11 families – 44 persons, headed by Jan August. This colony also includes Kreyczi, the forester from Mokra, who is very actively engaged in German life.

*Sochaczew region – Błonie sub-region*

*The communists*

The party has not yet organized itself in this region and has no fixed structure. The existing cells are more like loose associations of individuals who share common views. No distribution of printed matter has been detected, with the exception of underground leaflets from Warsaw that reach parts of the region around Błonie. It is to be expected that these loose cells, groups, and individuals will join together when conditions are right, especially in Grodzisk, Żyrardów, Guzów (sugar factory), and Mszczonów, where

22 Konstanty Daukantas, a Lithuanian who had been held at Pawiak prison, was transferred to Auschwitz concentration camp on 23 July 1941.

there are some indications of Communist Party activity. This issue is currently being treated as a priority. It should be added that many particularly energetic Communist Party leaders left this area for the USSR in September and October 1939.

*The Jews*

There are no Jews in this territory; the individuals who managed to escape from the ghetto beg for alms in the surrounding villages and small towns.

*The Germans*

A – Grodzisk

It has been confirmed that an ethnic German is collecting signatures from Poles to prove his loyalty towards the Poles. The general mood in this group does not seem to be uniform; the greater part does not believe that Hitler will win. The statement of a certain police officer is significant: that after the war, all ethnic Germans will lose their equality with Reich citizens.

B – Żyrardów

In this community the Germans' activities primarily originate with the following families: the Schmidt family, who own the tannery; Fröhlich, who appeared in a novel printed in the *Żyrardowskie Echo*[23] newspaper before the war; Kuhut, who owns a funeral parlour and was recently ousted from the office of deputy mayor by his rival, von Krynicki; and the managers of businesses in Żyrardów, who equate the Protestant faith with Germandom.

C – Błonie

The leader of the local German colony is Blok, who owns a mill and is a reserve officer; at present he is doing good business. This Blok is no different from the others in terms of his approach to the Poles.

*The Ukrainians*

The chairman of the association, Gutko, was arrested for misappropriating butter that was intended for the Ukrainians. This association shows no sign of activity.

*Grójec region*

*The communists*

All communist activity in the territory of Grójec is centred around the former Communist Party official Wojtczak. His work and that of his entourage involves the distribution of underground leaflets and targeted agitation in support of the Soviet Union.

The periodical *Sierp i Młot* is distributed in Gołków, powiat Grójec, but it has not yet been established who distributes it. As a result of agitation among the working-class element, impoverished people, and even among those officials who have no moral qualms, strong pro-Soviet tendencies have been noted, which are aimed at welcoming the Bolsheviks and Bolshevism here.

It is interesting that, after the war began in the East,[24] people believed the rumours spread by subversive agitators that the Bolsheviks would arrive within a week. In general people also believed, as they did in the neighbouring regions, that the Bolsheviks had already taken Dęblin, Mława, Ciechanów, Modlin, Königsberg, etc.

23 Correctly: *Echo Żyrardowskie*; the main newspaper in Żyrardów, published by the writer and translator Paweł Hulka-Laskowski (1881–1946) and his wife from 1921.

24 In other words, as of 22 June 1941.

Soviet aircraft were seen over Góra Kalwaria on the third day of the war; a few bombs were dropped, but no damage was done.

*The Jews*

All the Jews who had escaped from the ghetto were roaming around not only in the countryside, but also in Grójec itself, where they beg insistently. They have even threatened that consequences are to be expected once the Bolsheviks arrive. These Jews would then allegedly be assigned a role by the Communist Party to agitate among escapees from the prisoner-of-war camp and to distribute underground leaflets. The occupiers do not react to these roaming Jews at all and pretend not to notice anything.

In the lives of the other national minorities, there were no conspicuous activities worth discussing.

*The Germans*

When hostilities began, when there were no communiqués from the Eastern Front, the German population in the surrounding colonies met in small groups in Grójec, and because they believed the rumours circulating about the great successes of the Soviet army, which was said to have taken Dęblin, Königsberg, etc., their despair drove them to drink. Only once the first news of German military successes arrived did this part of the population regain its emotional equilibrium.

*Mińsk Mazowiecki region*

*The communists*

There are apparently Communist Party organizations in this region, because in mid August the Gestapo arrested twenty-five Jews and several Poles who were said to be communists or members of the Bund; another indication of the presence of communists is the fact that after the Germans captured the eastern territories in Mińsk,[25] unknown persons appeared from the East, along with the family of Dąbrowski, who worked in Łomża as an NKVD agent. These persons are currently being investigated, and their names and whereabouts established.

*The Jews*

There is no closed Jewish district, and so the Jews move about freely in the Aryan districts and even travel to the countryside. Trade remains in Jewish hands.

The rural population continues to place quite a lot of trust in the Jews, a fact attributable to the occupiers themselves, because individual authorities such as the Kreishauptmannschaft, the tax office, etc. have their own Jewish henchmen who, in return for bribes, settle various matters in these offices and even for the Gestapo. Behind the Aryans' backs, the Jews also supply the occupiers with building materials etc. It is significant that wealthier and poorer Jews denounce each other to the occupiers when they have personal disputes.

Nothing has come to light about the lives of the remaining national minorities in the region that merits special clarification or mention.

*Siedlce region*

*The communists*

The presence of communist activity in this region is illustrated by the fact that Bolshevik soldiers who escaped from the prisoner-of-war camps find support here. Significantly,

25 This is a reference to the territories of the Polish Republic occupied by the Red Army in 1939, which were conquered by the Wehrmacht in early summer 1941.

the escape from the camps took place almost simultaneously and on a large scale. Out of a total of 30,000 prisoners of war in the region, 18,000 are said to have escaped from the camp.[26]

Many of them speak Polish, know their way around the area, and enjoy support.

This may suggest a planned operation and the presence of Soviet agents in the area.

*The Jews*

The Jewish element is not concentrated in the ghetto but lives in freedom and engages in trade and artisan activity as in former times.

*The Byelorussians*

Poles have the most influence among the local Byelorussian authorities. It was noted recently that the native Byelorussians are trying to curry favour with the Poles so they can count on their help and support in future.

*Sokołów region*

*The communists*

As far as the communists are concerned, the situation is similar to that in the Siedlce region.

*The Jews*

The Jews were resettled from the Ostrów Mazowiecki sub-region right at the beginning of the hostilities in 1939.[27]

In some places, such as Długosiodło, many of the Jewish-owned buildings have been completely dismantled and their components sold as fuel or construction material.

[...][28]

In Warsaw's Jewish district, Germans are specifically employed to inform the Jews that the Poles are currently the Jews' greatest enemies. All of their houses, shops, and other properties have currently been taken over by Poles.

[...][29]

In these territories, the occupiers carried out mass arrests of Jews and communists. The occupiers are trying to convince those arrested and their families that the Poles had handed them over. This is inciting hatred for the Polish population among the population of Polesie.[30]

[...][31]

26 Stalag 316 at Siedlce; the number of escapees is greatly exaggerated.

27 On 11 Nov. 1939 German reserve police officers murdered the entire Jewish population of the small town of Ostrów Mazowiecka, in the eastern part of District Warsaw: a total of 159 men and 196 women and children. Members of Reserve Police Battalions 11 and 91 participated in the crimes; the police detail was under the command of Karl Brenner (1895–1954), a senior officer in the Urban Police and SS-Standartenführer.

28 The following section is titled 'Miscellaneous' and contains brief individual news items about the German occupation.

29 This section is followed by reports from the territory occupied by the Red Army until June 1941.

30 Polish: 'Poleszuków'; inhabitants of Polesia who spoke their own dialect and were classified in pre-war Polish nationality statistics as 'locals' (Polish: 'tutejsi', which literally means 'people from here'). Polesia is a historic region mainly located in what is today Belarus; its urban centres include the cities of Brest and Pinsk.

31 This section is followed by further reports of conflicts between Poles and Byelorussians in the territory in question.

## DOC. 9

## On 16 September 1941 the Kreishauptmann of Janów Lubelski reports how many Jews can still be housed in localities within this Kreis[1]

Letter (marked 'secret') from the Kreishauptmann of Janow Lubelski,[2] Interior Administration (Ic), signature illegible, Janów Lubelski, to the chief of staff of District Lublin,[3] dated 16 September 1941

*Re:* designated locations for Jews
*Concerning:* your order of 9 Sept. 1941, log no. 50/41 secret[4]
So far no Jewish ghettos have been created in this Kreis. However, I intend to set up ghettos in the eligible localities. I had already initiated the preliminary work for this, but it was halted again on account of the circular decree of 25 August.[5]

In order to state what decision I would have arrived at concerning the establishment of ghettos (i.e. whether ghettos are to be established or whether, for example, the Jews currently living in all localities should be brought together in certain localities), I would need to address this matter further.

More Jews could, however, be resettled in the following localities:

| Municipality | Currently approx. | Possible further |
|---|---|---|
| Annopol | 1,800 Jews | Approx. 300 Jews |
| Zaklików | 2,200 " | " 300 " |
| Radomyśl | 800 " | " 300 " |
| Ulanów I | 1,300 " | " 1,400 " |
| Zakrzówek | 300 " | " 100 " |
| Batorz | 250 " | " 0 " |
| Urzędów | 400 " | " 100 " |

1 APL, 498/270, fol. 22. Copy in BArch, R 102/II/26, fol. 11. This document has been translated from German.

2 Hans Lenk (1904–1944), municipal official; joined the NSDAP in 1926; became mayor of Falkenstein in 1935; Stadtkommissar in Radomsko in 1939, in Skarżysko-Kamienna and Starachowice-Wierzbnik in 1940, then Landkommissar in Dęblin Irena; from August 1941 Kreishauptmann of Janów Lubelski (later: Kraśnik); killed by Polish resistance fighters in July 1944.

3 Wilhelm Engler (1880–1958), lawyer; active in the pro-republican Reichsbanner organization before 1933; worked for the Baden Buildings Insurance Office from 1930; joined the NSDAP in 1933; Landkommissar in Myślenice, 1939–1940; head of the Interior Administration in District Cracow from Jan. 1940 to August 1941; acting chief of staff in District Lublin until June 1943; subsequently re-employed by the Baden Buildings Insurance Office; classified as a *Mitläufer* ('follower') by a denazification tribunal in 1948.

4 A secret circular decree sent to the Kreishauptmänner in District Lublin had called on them to provide information about existing or planned ghettos in their Kreis by 27 Sept. 1941, and to state how many people could still be housed in 'designated locations for Jews': APL, 498/270, fol. 15.

5 Not in the file.

## DOC. 10

## On 17 September 1941 Jewish religious leaders call on the Jews of Warsaw to observe personal hygiene and religious rules[1]

Circular from the admors,[2] the Rabbinic Aid Council, and the Rabbinic Council of the Warsaw Jewish Community to the building committees in the Warsaw ghetto, dated 17 September 1941

*Circular to the building committees*[3]
*An appeal from the admors and the rabbis to the Jewish population*

On Wednesday, [in the week of] parashah Tavo[4] [5]701,[5] the rebbes and rabbis met to discuss how to combat the frightening spread of the epidemic[6] in the city that has [already] cost thousands of lives. The following was decided unanimously:

a) The sanitary commissions' instructions to wash one's head and entire body daily and to keep clothing, bedding, and the home clean must be strictly followed.
b) The family purity laws[7] from our holy Torah must be strictly observed.
c) The commandment to rest on the Sabbath, not to engage in trade, and not to do any work inside or outside the home must be strictly observed. The Sabbath is the foundation of Judaism; the pillar of its eternal existence; a source of blessing, success, and joy; and thus a remedy for illness and sorrow (may the Merciful One spare us these).
d) As we know, righteousness delivereth from death.[8] That is why we are calling for a large-scale 'ransom' charity drive,[9] whereby every Jew – man or woman, regardless of age – is obliged to donate money.

1 AŻIH, Ring II/314 (171). This document has been translated from Yiddish.
2 An abbreviation of the Hebrew *adoneinu, moreinu, ve-rabbeinu*: 'our master, our teacher, and our rabbi'. Admor is an honorific title exclusively bestowed on rebbes, the Yiddish term for the leader of a Hasidic group.
3 The building committees were established in the ghetto in 1940 as self-governing bodies that performed important tasks for all the residents of the respective building; they looked after the poorest residents in particular.
4 Parashah Ki Tavo is the 50th of the weekly Torah readings, comprising Deuteronomy 26:1–29:8; it is read in late August or September.
5 The Year 5701 is the equivalent of the Gregorian year 1940/41 according to the Hebrew calendar; the Hebrew year begins in September or October of the Gregorian calendar year. In this case, parashah Ki Tavo was read on Saturday, 13 Sept. 1941.
6 Epidemic typhus: see Docs. 12, 14, 37, and 41.
7 According to Jewish law, after menstruation a woman must undergo ritual cleansing in a mikvah before resuming sexual intercourse with her husband.
8 Proverbs 10:2 and 11:4 (quotation from the 1917 JPS translation of the Hebrew bible). The Hebrew word *tzedakah* (the Yiddish equivalent is *tsdoke*), used in the original, means 'righteousness' but often connotes 'charity'. *Tzedakah* represents a religious obligation to do what is right and just. The performance of this mitzvah ('commandment') is therefore crucial to leading a spiritual life and must be done irrespective of one's financial situation. Thus the sense of charity implied by the term *tzedakah* differs from an understanding of charity as a voluntary act of generosity or philanthropy: see Doc. 32.
9 The Hebrew and Yiddish term in the original is *kofer-nefesh-aktsye*, meaning a concerted effort to raise money to 'ransom a soul' or to pay the 'price of a life'.

It is the sacred duty of every Jew to support the charitable institutions, particularly the Jewish Self-Help Society,[10] which runs kosher kitchens. Every Jew is obliged to support the activities of the Jewish Self-Help Society.

The money from expiatory sacrifices[11] must also be used as ransom money.[12]

e) The mezuzahs[13] in every home should be inspected, including those in the gateways and entrances of buildings.

f) Parents are obliged to give their children a religious education and to instil in them – at the very least – the basic principles of Judaism.

g) In every prayer quorum or [even] when one prays alone, five chapters of the Psalms should be recited daily before prayer. Whoever is able to do so should learn four Mishnayot in order.[14] This will be considered public Torah [study].[15]

h) A religious affairs section is to be created within each building committee to ensure the Sabbath is observed and to tend to all religious needs.

i) The rabbis have an obligation to deliver words of encouragement and exhortation in the prayer houses in order to strengthen confidence and faith.

j) It is necessary to strengthen feelings of love and mercy in each individual as regards the sufferings of others and to help as best as one can.

In the firm conviction that by complying with the rules stipulated above we will be helped and we will be written in the Book of Life with a good inscription and seal,[16] we wish all Jews a year of redemption and salvation.

*The admors, the Rabbinic Aid Council, and the Rabbinic Council of the Warsaw Community*

The signed original is held in the office of the Rabbinic Aid Council.

10 This refers to the Jewish Social Self-Help (JSS).

11 *Kapores* in the original: fowl used for ritual purposes on the day before Yom Kippur (the Day of Atonement).

12 *Pidyon nefesh* in the original: literally 'redemption of the soul', meaning to put an end to suffering. The basis for this idea is the teaching that a life in jeopardy can be set free – i.e. redeemed – through a material act of charity.

13 Hebrew: *mezuzah*, plural *mezuzot* (literally: 'doorpost'); the word denotes a piece of parchment with religious texts placed in a case and attached to the doorpost of a Jewish home.

14 A reference to paragraphs from the Mishnah, which is the written collection of Jewish religious laws that had hitherto been passed down orally; these texts constitute the basis of the Talmud.

15 Public Torah study is considered a great *mitzvah* ('commandment'); various rabbis discuss the merits of individual learning vs public learning.

16 *Ksive vekhsime toyve* in the original: Yiddish pronunciation of a phrase used to express good wishes during the Jewish High Holidays.

## DOC. 11

### On 5 October 1941 Doris Seelig contacts the Governor of District Lublin seeking the return of her children, who have been deported from Stettin to Piaski[1]

Letter from Doris Seelig,[2] 32 Dragonerstraße, Berlin N 54, identity card issued at Kolberg, identity card no. A. 000 40, to the Governor of District Lublin[3] (received on 10 October 1941) in Lublin, dated 5 October 1941[4]

To the Governor of District *Lublin*,

I hereby ask you once again to allow my two school-age children, Edith Sara and Ursula Sara Seelig,[5] both in Piaski, near Lublin, who were evacuated from Stettin on 13 February 1940,[6] to enter the Reich. I would have submitted this petition earlier because my husband is of *Aryan descent*, and I wanted to wait for the notification, but as it is taking so long to obtain the documents, I kindly ask you to now approve entry into the Reich for both children. As I previously stated, I will bear all the costs of the return journey.

I look forward to your esteemed decision.

Mrs Doris Sara Seelig
as a mother[7]

1 APL, 498/893, fol. 47. This document has been translated from German.

2 Doris Seelig, née Markus (1890–1943?), originally from Bydgoszcz; on 3 Feb. 1943 she was deported together with her husband, Max Seelig (b. 1886), and their eldest daughter, Margot (b. 1924), from Berlin to Auschwitz, where she and her husband were murdered.

3 Ernst Zörner (1895–1945?), shopkeeper; served with the Border Police in Danzig in 1919; joined the NSDAP in 1925; city councillor and member of the Landtag in Braunschweig, 1928–1933; mayor of Dresden in 1933; Stadthauptmann in Cracow in 1939; governor of District Lublin from Feb. 1940; dismissed at the instigation of the SS in April 1943; subsequently worked for Organization Todt; missing since 1945; declared dead in 1960.

4 The original contains handwritten annotations. The letter was forwarded to the Population and Welfare Division.

5 Edith (b. 1926) and Ursula (Ursel) Seelig (1928–1942), Doris Seelig's two youngest daughters. Ursula perished in Auschwitz; Edith's fate is unknown.

6 Of the between 825 and 842 Jews deported from Regierungsbezirk Stettin to the General Government, 525 were sent to Piaski; see PMJ 3/134 and 4/105.

7 Max Seelig had previously contacted the Gestapo in March 1940 to request the return of his daughters: see PMJ 3/57. Doris Seelig wrote to the District Governor on 11 July 1941 asking him to authorize the girls' return. She explained that she and her husband were German nationals; he had served in the First World War and had been decorated as a combat veteran; he now worked as a senior construction manager with the Reich Railway: APL, 498/893, fol. 44. The Interior Administration of the General Government 'provisionally rejected' her application on 12 August 1941 without stating any grounds: ibid., fol. 46. On 19 Feb. 1942 the Governor of District Lublin (Section II R./We. C 3) again declined to permit the children to leave the General Government: ibid., fol. 48.

## DOC. 12

## On 10 and 11 October 1941 the teacher Chaim Kaplan writes about religious life and the typhus epidemic in the Warsaw ghetto[1]

Diary of Chaim Kaplan,[2] entries for 10 and 11 October 1941

10 October 1941

The opening of our synagogues for worship gave us a glimpse of 'Netsach Yisrael'.[3] On the eve of the festival,[4] our sanctuaries were again illuminated and crowded with celebrating multitudes.[5] Once again the holy and warm Hebrew atmosphere filled our synagogues; once again we communed with our Father in Heaven in His Tent of Meeting;[6] once again the voice of the God of Israel, emanating from our eternal Torah, reached our ears. From the depths of our plight, we poured out our prayers from anguished, agonized hearts. Despite all the deep woes, we experienced some relief from the mere fact that our days have been renewed as of old[7] ('as of old' for us means: before the war!). Three houses of congregation opened their doors for joy and prayer: none other than the Great Synagogue on Tłomackie Street, the synagogue that Nożyk established on Twarda Street,[8] and the Lithuanian Mizrachi–Zionist 'Moriah' Synagogue on Dzielna Street. All of which [was done] officially. But from the standpoint of the Jewish 'Council', which was given discretion for the whole matter under specific conditions that the occupier had imposed on it,[9] there was nothing standing in the way of setting up a minyan[10] in every building, and this opportunity was seized in many courtyards. There is not one

1 Moreshet Archive, D.2.470, fols. 9, 12–14. An incomplete English translation of the diary can be found in *Scroll of Agony: The Warsaw Diary of Chaim A. Kaplan*, ed. and trans. Abraham I. Katsh (New York: Macmillan, 1965). This document has been translated from Hebrew.

2 Chaim Kaplan (1880–1942), Hebrew teacher; trained at the Mir yeshiva (a Jewish school for the study of religious texts); studied pedagogy in Vilna; founder and later head of a Hebrew-language primary school in Warsaw in 1902; murdered in Treblinka. Kaplan kept a diary from 1933, which ended on 4 August 1942. He gave his writings to Władysław Wójciek, who hid them. The section that describes the period from May 1941 to May 1942 is held in the archive at the Moreshet Mordechai Anielevich Memorial Holocaust Study and Research Center in Israel; the sections from August to Dec. 1939 and from June to July 1942 are held at the USHMM in Washington, DC (Collection 2 004 405 and 2 009 212); and the entries from late Dec. 1939 to April 1941 are held at the Jewish Historical Institute in Warsaw (302/218).

3 Hebrew in the original: 'the eternity of Israel'. This is a reference to 1 Samuel 15:29.

4 Isaiah 30:29: 'Ye shall have a song as in the night when a feast is hallowed [...]'

5 Psalms 42:4–5: 'How I passed on with the throng, and led them to the house of God, with the voice of joy and praise, a multitude keeping holyday.'

6 Exodus 33:7: 'Now Moses used to take the tent and to pitch it without the camp, afar off from the camp; and he called it the tent of meeting. And it came to pass, that every one that sought HaShem went out unto the tent of meeting, which was without the camp.'

7 Lamentations 5:21: 'Turn Thou us unto Thee, O HaShem, and we shall be turned; renew our days as of old.'

8 The Nożyk synagogue was built between 1898 and 1902, thanks to private funding from the businessman Zalman Nożyk (1846–1903), and given to the Jewish Community after his death. Following the German occupation the synagogue was converted into stables. With the establishment of the Warsaw ghetto, it was one of three synagogues authorized by the Nazis. After the war the synagogue was again used as a place of prayer until being closed in the 1960s. It subsequently underwent renovation and was reopened in 1983.

courtyard that failed to organize a minyan for those living there and in the adjoining houses. The incessant tribulations have admittedly led to an increase in the number of unbelievers among the Jews; nevertheless, all the 'minyans' were full to capacity. Everyone had longed to come together, for the Hebrew congregation, for the shared religious atmosphere that had eluded them for two years. At home, there is great boredom. Your soul withers if you don't have friends.[11]

But even then, in the midst of our festive days, foreboding clouds filled our skies – the liquidation of the 'Grzybowy ghetto'[12] and additional territorial changes at our expense were imminent. Twarda was to be excised from the ghetto and, with it, the Nożyk Synagogue; even the Tłomackie Synagogue was in grave danger of passing into the oppressor's hands. After all, there is nothing unusual or barbaric that he wouldn't do. But all that fear proved to be a false alarm. For the time being, only the odd numbers on Sienna Street and certain parts of Komitetowa and Wielka Streets have fallen victim to Nazi villainy.

I attended services at 'Moriah', which glowed with the light of the Seven Days[13] on the festival nights. The holy lamps of the ruined Danzig Synagogue, which were moved to 'Moriah', flooded [it] with a sea of light. These are immense bronze lamps, products of astonishing artistic craft.[14] When the Danzig congregation was exiled, so were its lamps, but by good fortune they were privileged once again with spreading their light in the Tent of Jacob[15] and not in some Catholic or Protestant church. It's all a matter of luck![16]

In 1939, on the eve of the war, the 'Moriah' Synagogue underwent major renovation. It wasn't minor maintenance work, such as filling in dents in the walls or a ceiling that needed repair, but a major overhaul involving fundamental structural and architectural renovations that changed the features of the synagogue from top to bottom. A sum of 30,000 złoty was spent on this renovation, which at the time was worth 6,000 dollars (currently 600 dollars). The work was almost finished, but then the war broke out, and so it was never completed. The project came to a sudden halt, and everything was cut off and torn out. A terrible catastrophe fell upon Polish Jewry. The deportations and expulsions of whole communities commenced. Tens of thousands of refugees sought shelter in Warsaw. The gabbais[17] of 'Moriah' said, 'It's time to act for our nation's outcasts – interrupt

9 In Jan. 1940 the German authorities banned religious services in what they called Warsaw's epidemic containment zone (*Seuchensperrgebiet*). This ban was extended to all of Warsaw in Nov. 1940: *Gazeta Żydowska*, 8 Nov. 1940.

10 A prayer quorum.

11 Talmud Bavli; Ta'anit 23a: 'Either friendship or death, as one who has no friends is better off dead.'

12 Meant here is the area around Grzybowski Square in what was known as the small ghetto, south of Chłodna Street.

13 Isaiah 30:26: 'Moreover, the light of the moon shall be as the light of the sun, and the light of the sun shall be sevenfold, as the light of the seven days […].'

14 Exodus 35:33: 'And in cutting of stones for setting, and in carving of wood, to work in all manner of skilful workmanship.'

15 Numbers 24:5: 'How goodly are thy tents, O Jacob, thy dwellings, O Israel!'

16 The writer may be alluding to 'לכיהבש הרות רפס וליפאו לזמב יולת לכה' from certain Kabbalistic sources, meaning 'everything depends on luck, even the Torah scroll in the ark'.

17 A gabbai is a person who assists in the running of synagogue services.

your prayers.'[18] Only a few days later, the [occupation] authorities also issued an edict banning worship altogether. With that, the halls of 'Moriah' were declared assembly points for refugees. Hundreds of expellees and displaced persons, the most unfortunate of the unfortunate, found in 'Moriah' a place of refuge for their wretched bodies. They turned it into a foul place, replacing its sanctity with stench and putrefaction. Misery and suffering turn people into barbarians. In their ignorance and brutishness, they took no heed of the building or its furnishings and sacred objects. Everything was befouled and defaced; everything was broken and destroyed; they left nothing intact[19] behind. But when it came time to restore its days as of old, no heed was paid to all this. Everything was restored and even improved, and for the High Holidays in 5702,[20] 'Moriah' Synagogue stood as it had before in its purity, splendour, and sanctity.

'The adversary stretched forth his hand upon everything precious to [us]'[21] – and the hand came away dry.

11 October 1941

Typhus is wreaking havoc[22] on us! When two of us get together and one tells the other about a third friend's illness, he doesn't call the disease by name, because its name is known anyway; it's presumably 'the' illness and none other. The same happens when a person dies: no one just dies; it's only because of that very illness. It's claiming an enormous toll, and it would be impossible to count the victims. There are households that have lost half of their members. Within our immediate circles, each one of us can count dozens of people who have been sacrificed on the altar of the dreaded typhus. There is no end to the deaths.

Who brought this into our world? Anyone [you ask][23] will give you the answer that the tyrannical occupier gave it to us as a gift. Before he came, we weren't familiar with it, even though we knew its nature. When the deportations, expulsions, discrimination, and vile decrees began, and with them the overcrowding, the stress, the poverty, and the hunger, typhus came along with them, and because it's a contagious disease, it is spreading steadily – even among the affluent. In recent days there have been deaths in wealthy families due to typhus. And such cases have become so prevalent and commonplace that the beggars are rejoicing, expressing their feelings of revenge publicly and loudly.

There are no privileged people before the Holy One, blessed be He! What's more, beggars go on to recover while the high-and-mighty die. A body that has been hardened for survival and isn't pampered can withstand even a dangerous disease, whereas the pampered one – a single glance at him and he is no more.[24]

18 Psalms 119:126 (modified quote): 'It is time for HaShem to work […].'

19 Isaiah 1:6: 'From the sole of the foot even unto the head there is no soundness in it; but wounds, and bruises, and festering sores […].'

20 The year 1941. According to the Hebrew calendar, the holidays of the year 5702 fell in autumn 1941.

21 Lamentations 1:10: 'The adversary hath spread out his hand upon all her treasures […].'

22 The source of this expression is found in Psalms 46:9: 'Come, behold the works of HaShem, who hath made desolations in the earth.'

23 Talmud Bavli; Chagigah 5b. In the original the idiomatic Aramaic expression literally means 'a new student on his first day of learning'. The figurative meaning is that the subject of discussion is so simple that anyone would understand it.

24 An allusion to Proverbs 23:5: 'Wilt thou set thine eyes upon it? It is gone […].'

And here it's worth noting another amazing claim that the Nazi makes about himself, in which he isn't suspected of lying. In his newspaper, he once complained that the Jews were spreading typhus microbes and infecting the Aryans who visit their environs and enter into negotiations with them.[25] Hence the warning to beware of the Jews and keep distance from them! And to demonstrate the Jews' 'guilt' even more powerfully, he also noted that more infected Aryans were dying than were Jews. As he put it, a Jew who develops typhus eventually recovers, whereas Germans and Poles ultimately die. The upshot of the whole thing, therefore, is that typhus-stricken Germans die; Poles follow their lead; and the affluent Jews transgress the injunction against 'following the Gentiles' ways'[26] by also dropping dead. The exceptions to the rule are the Jewish beggars; the disease does not have enough power over them to take their lives. And who is to blame for this situation? The Jews, of course! They don't keep themselves clean; they're by nature dirty and befouled. The overcrowding? That's got nothing to do with it; that's not the reason. The pressure? That's not it either. The high price of soap? Who bothers with such a trivial thing? Hunger? That's not the cause of the disease either. The fatal housing conditions? They're not to blame. What then?

It's [our] racial blood that does it. From blood everything comes and to blood everything returns.[27] Blood is the person![28] The *Stürmer* adds: Even typhus is just a Jewish 'swindle'. It's revenge against the non-Jews! The sanitation laws that the occupier passed in order to staunch the epidemic are, for us, a plague that's not written in the Torah.[29] Here, too, as in other matters, chaos reigns and the strict rules don't bring about the cure that's needed and do not achieve any goal except bribing the sanitation staff, who in their greed deem everything kosher and set all stringencies aside. When the epidemic began, the custom was to impose a two-week quarantine on the courtyard [of those buildings] where any case of typhus occurred. They simply posted a policeman at the gate – sometimes a Gentile, sometimes a Jew – and no one was allowed to come or go.[30] Everyone living adjacent to the courtyard was separated and distanced from the outside world like the impure and lepers. All of this was in theory. In practice, however, you could come and go if you had two or three złoty to spare and stuffed them into the hand of the 'upholder of the law'. Another large source of income for the sanitation staff is the disinfection of all apartments bordering on the tainted courtyard, no exceptions allowed. By spraying Lysol and other disinfectants, they despoil and destroy household implements until they are no longer recognizable. A person's fortune flies out the window. But here, too, bribery comes in handy. Afterwards, everyone living in the courtyard has to march under police supervision to the public bathhouse that's reserved for this purpose. It's a special torture, even if it isn't one of those that a Jew must endure on

25 The life-threatening typhus infection is transmitted through contact with infected lice.

26 Leviticus 18:3: 'After the doings of the land of Egypt, wherein ye dwelt, shall ye not do; and after the doings of the land of Canaan, whither I bring you, shall ye not do; neither shall ye walk in their statutes.'

27 Genesis 3:19: '[…] for dust thou art, and unto dust shalt thou return.'

28 Leviticus 17:11: 'For the life of the flesh is in the blood […].'

29 Deuteronomy 28:61: 'Also every sickness, and every plague, which is not written in the book of this law, them will HaShem bring upon thee, until thou be destroyed.'

30 Joshua 6:1: 'Now Jericho was straitly shut up because of the children of Israel: none went out, and none came in.'

Yom Kippur.[31] A mass bathhouse such as this kills the lice – and the person as well. Its primitive conditions and the dirty, disgusting people around you may bring all sorts of diseases and dire straits upon you. The place of cleanliness – that's where disease lurks. So even here money is the answer for everything.[32] And just as the ghetto was built to enrich the Nazi gendarmes who help the smugglers, so disinfection may enrich the police. What the two have in common is that they serve as sources of evasion, smuggling, bribery, and transgression of the 'law', as well as their corollaries: demoralization and perversion of justice. None of these afflictions was necessary even from a hygienic standpoint, especially since no one was careful about them. Through the power of persuasion, those who had come around to the opinion that the whole thing should be taken less seriously ultimately limited the quarantine to one day. But the disinfection of apartments and having to bathe at the bathhouse remained as at the outset.

The following story illustrates just how pointless all the sanitation rules are: I hosted Dir, a refugee from Białystok, in my apartment. One morning he fell ill with typhus and I promptly reported it to the Health Section. I was sure that a wagon would come from the hospital right away and remove the patient from my home. But a week passed and no wagon showed up. In the meantime, the patient died. Again the Health Section was informed so that the tainted courtyard could be disinfected. Once more a few days passed and no one came. Sometime later, a doctor from the Health Section came by and told us that the apartments bordering on the courtyard wouldn't be disinfected. However, he ordered the tenants of the building where the patient had died, meaning me, my family, and everyone who had been in contact with us, to go to the bathhouse and present bathing cards. I immediately approached a 'makher',[33] paid him 25 złoty for five people, and was exempted from this punishment.[34] As for disinfecting the patient's room, I did it myself and at my own expense.

That's what the Nazi-German order amounts to!

The ghetto rests on three things:[35] bribery, bribery, and bribery!!

31 The 'tortures of Yom Kippur' are the five main prohibitions on the Day of Atonement. They include eating and drinking, wearing leather shoes, bathing or washing, anointing oneself with perfumes or lotions, and sexual relations.

32 Ecclesiastes 10:19: 'A feast is made for laughter, and wine maketh glad the life; and money answereth all things.'

33 Yiddish in the original. A 'makher' ('fixer') is an influential person, usually paid, who mediates in order to bypass procedures, often illegally.

34 An allusion to the blessing 'Blessed be (He) who released me from this punishment'. It is customary for one whose son becomes Bar Mitzvah to say this blessing after the boy has read the Torah portion.

35 An allusion to Pirkei Avot 1:2: 'He used to say: The world stands upon three things: the Torah, worship, and deeds of loving kindness.'

## DOC. 13

## On 15 October 1941 Governor General Hans Frank orders that Jews are to be punished with the death penalty if they leave their ghetto without authorization[1]

*Third Regulation on Restrictions of Movement in the General Government*, 15 October 1941
On the basis of § 5(1) of the Führer's Decree of 12 October 1939 (*Reichsgesetzblatt* I, p. 2077),[2] I hereby decree the following:

Section 1
The following § 4b shall be inserted after § 4a of the Regulation on Restrictions of Movement in the General Government, 13 September 1940 (*VOBl-GG* I, p. 288),[3] as amended by the Second Regulation on Restrictions of Movement in the General Government, 29 April 1941 (*VOBl-GG*, p. 274):[4]

§ 4b
1) Jews who leave their assigned residential district without authorization shall be punished with death. The same penalty shall be imposed on persons who knowingly grant such Jews refuge.
2) Abettors and accomplices who attempt to perpetrate or succeed in perpetrating the offence shall receive the same punishment as the offender. In less serious cases, offenders may be sentenced to penal servitude or prison.
3) Judgement shall be passed by the special courts.

Section 2
This regulation comes into force on the day of its promulgation.
*Warsaw*, 15 October 1941
*Governor General Frank*

1 Dritte Verordnung über Aufenthaltsbeschränkungen im Generalgouvernement, *VOBl-GG*, 1941, no. 99, 25 Oct. 1941, p. 595. This document has been translated from German.
2 The Decree on the Administration of the Occupied Polish Territories named Hans Frank as Governor General. He reported directly to Hitler.
3 *VOBl-GG*, 1940, I, no. 55, 20 Sept. 1940, p. 288.
4 The Second Regulation increased the severity of the penalties imposed: *VOBl-GG*, no. 41, 10 May 1941, pp. 274–275.

## DOC. 14

## In mid October 1941 representatives of the health administration in the General Government discuss epidemic control measures[1]

Minutes of the working meeting of the government of the GG's Health Department at Krynica-Zdrój, 13–16 October 1941 (excerpts)[2]

[…][3]
The Department Head[4] … continued:
Gentlemen,
This brings us to the start of our actual working meeting. On this occasion we have decided to tackle a whole series of topics, which is why several days have been scheduled for the meeting. As the most important item, we have chosen *epidemic control*. I believe this item is of great concern and interest to us all. As work commitments have unfortunately prevented Oberstabsarzt[5] Professor Bieling from attending, there has been a change to the programme, and Public Health Officer *Dr Buurman*[6] will now start by saying a few words to you about this problem and outline Professor Kudicke's proposals in this regard.[7]
Public Health Officer *Dr Buurman*:
Mr Walbaum has asked me to talk to you about 'typhus'. Please be so kind as to make allowances for my remarks since I have had very little time to prepare, having been in Berlin on business until yesterday.

1 AIPN, GK 196/377 (NTN 377), fols. 1–40 (fols. 11–33, 35, 37, 39–40). This document has been translated from German.
2 Many parts of the original have been underlined by hand.
3 The working meeting was opened by Dr Walbaum (see fn. 4), who welcomed the attendees representing the government of the GG; the military commander in the General Government; the Senior Commander of the Order Police (BdO); Luftgau [aerial Gau command] VIII Breslau; the authorities of the districts Cracow, Radom, Lublin, Warsaw, and Galicia; the Higher SS and Police Leader in the General Government; and the Ortskommandantur.
4 The meeting was chaired by Dr Jost (correctly: Josef Anton) Walbaum (1889–1969), physician; joined the NSDAP in 1930 and the SA in 1932; city physician (Stadtarzt) in Berlin from 1933; in 1934 he was also head of the Kreis Public Health Office and a judge at the Hereditary Health Court (Erbgesundheitsgericht); medical officer and senior municipal medical health officer, 1937–1943; Party health leader (Gesundheitsführer) in the General Government from Dec. 1939; head of the Health Department in the Interior Administration of the General Government from April 1941; municipal public health officer in Münster from May 1943; worked as a homeopath in Hanover after the war.
5 Military medical officer with a rank equivalent to major.
6 Dr Otto Buurman (1890–1967), physician; worked for various public health authorities; public health officer, 1927–1939; head of the Health Department in the Office of the Governor of District Cracow from April 1940; deputy head of the Health Department in the Government of the GG, 1941–1943; head of Hamburg-Harburg Health Authority, 1944–1945; head of the Health Department in the Lower Saxony Ministry of Social Affairs, 1946–1954; head of the Health Department within the Federal Ministry of the Interior, 1954–1956.
7 Dr Robert Kudicke (1876–1961), physician; employed at the Government Hospital in Dar es Salaam from 1911; later worked at the University of Guangzhou; head of the State Institute of Hygiene in Warsaw from May 1941; professor of bacteriology in Frankfurt am Main after the war.

The speaker[8] used statistics to demonstrate that there has been no increase in typhus in District Cracow, while typhus is currently on the rise in the other districts, as is to be expected at this time of year. Without exception, the ghettos were identified as the epicentres of the typhus outbreaks, from which the smaller outbreaks in the countryside had emanated. He said the spread of the disease was definitely attributable to the undisciplined behaviour of the Jews, especially their roaming about. For example, the city physician for Warsaw[9] was able to prove that a Jewish woman who had escaped from the ghetto had caused eleven of the cases of infection.

As another example, Dr Buurman referred to a Jewish beggar who – even before the war – was the source of infection for 200 cases of typhus.

With the appointment of the head of the State Hygiene Institute in Warsaw, Professor Kudicke, as 'special commissioner for typhus control in the General Government', Department Head Dr Walbaum, the regional Party health leader, has taken some exceptional measures to prevent the further spread of typhus. To support the special commissioner for typhus control in the GG, district special commissioners will be appointed in all the districts. They will in turn have a team of auxiliary staff at their disposal, primarily disinfection and epidemic control squads. Furthermore, the requisite quantities of petrol, heating fuel, and detergent will be made available, so that everything possible will be done to conduct a large-scale typhus control operation. To support them, the district commissioners will be provided with 44 medical assistants; 65 disinfection squads, each consisting of 5 men; and 65 epidemic control squads, each consisting of 4 male and 4 female auxiliaries. The requisite funds for this operation, 8 million zloty, have been made available by the Governor General.

A regulation recently issued by the Governor General provides for strict checks on the permits of Jews found outside their residential districts, with suitably draconian punishments.[10]

As you will be aware, there has been a significant [infection] curve in Warsaw since week 20 of this year. This is a steep and threatening curve. Even the Landkreise in District Warsaw have seen a general increase in the curve. Kreis Ostrow has remained virtually unaffected: it usually had fewer than 50 new infections a year, with the other Kreise usually between 100 and as many as 400. If one looks at the individual outbreaks on the map, one can see the main epicentres and, emanating from them, scattered outbreaks and clusters. The number of new infections has increased despite stationary and mobile delousing stations being set up. Although some of the delousing stations were used by the Wehrmacht, they were generally sufficient to carry out the delousing procedures until the sharp increase in cases. Unfortunately, the delousing procedures frequently proved to have been conducted too late. In typhus control, it is essential that anyone suspected of having contracted the disease is identified early and that delousing begins

8 The minute-taker changes perspective at this point.

9 Dr Wilhelm Hagen (1893–1982), physician; municipal public health officer in Frankfurt am Main, 1925–1933; then medical practitioner in Augsburg; joined the NSDAP in 1938; medical officer in Warsaw from Feb. 1941 to Feb. 1943; hygienist in the Wehrmacht, 1944–1945; awarded a *Habilitation* (post-doctoral degree) in 1949; adjunct professor in Bonn in 1951; simultaneously a Regierungsrat in the Health Department within the Federal Ministry of the Interior; head of the Federal German Health Authority, 1956–1958.

10 See Doc. 13.

as soon as possible. The sooner delousing procedures are carried out, the more likely the measures are to be successful. It has come to light that delousing procedures have not always been carried out properly, and it could scarcely have been otherwise in view of the insufficient number of auxiliary personnel. However, the necessary measures have now been taken to ensure that lower-ranking healthcare professionals equipped with the requisite expertise are posted to the individual Kreise here. Professor Kudicke, whom we had asked to report on typhus control, informs us of points including the following:[11]

'The spread of typhus in the General Government is not even. While District Cracow, which before the war reported cases almost exclusively brought in from outside, is now experiencing an increase in new infections, conditions there are nonetheless practically normal. Above all, we can observe that the usual reduction in cases during the summer months has been very pronounced in this district. This reduction has been completely absent in the other three districts.

'Recently there have been more reports of people – particularly among the Jewish population – evading the delousing measures, and of such measures being almost completely sabotaged by widespread bribery. This applies particularly to the Warsaw ghetto, but probably to more or less all Jewish settlements, and I do not think I am wrong in assuming that the main cause of the conspicuous increase in the number of new infections during the summer months is to be sought here, i.e. in the lax and irresponsible implementation of disease control measures, above all in Jewish communities.

'A phenomenon such as the increase in vagrant beggars could not have led the typhus curve to rise so steeply if the ground for this had not already been prepared in other parts of the population as well. It is difficult to find an objective scale to measure the degree of lice infestation, which plays a primary role in this respect. *However, from observations already made in 1940 it can be concluded that lice infestation has increased significantly overall. The reasons for this are well known, namely the lack of detergent, the shortage of heating fuel, and the shortage of bed linen and cloth.* All this is likely to be conducive to lice infestation, and as long as resources are not found to remedy these shortages, there will always be a significant risk of lice infestation, and with it the imminent risk of typhus. Only through the rigorous and systematic application of known means of disease control can these risks be reduced or eliminated.

'It is not easy to predict the course of an epidemic and the dimensions it will assume, because the conditions under which it has arisen are of course subject to seasonal fluctuations, quite irrespective of the fact that people will also influence it with the measures they take. Based on a very simple calculation, if all the factors that had an effect on the epidemic during the period from January to August 1941 remain constant, we can expect the number of typhus cases to rise to at least 180,000 in the next eight months. As has been said, there is no proof that this will happen, but there is certainly reason to fear as much.

'From this it is evident that measures have to be taken without delay in order to prevent an increase of this kind, and all available resources must be mobilized.

'To begin with, it is essential to deploy the available disease control instruments in a more targeted and expert manner, and earlier than is probably happening at the mo-

11 Buurman went on to cite the report that follows, which was written by Kudicke.

ment. For this purpose, typhus control must be coordinated under a unified leadership. It is also necessary to appoint a special commissioner, at least for each district, who will be entrusted with the supervision and management of measures in the individual Kreise. I am convinced that these means will make it possible to achieve more than has been achieved so far, albeit only if the special commissioners are made mobile enough to reach every part of their districts at any time. A further precondition is to eliminate the shortcomings in the delivery of heating fuel, and to at least supply existing delousing stations and those that are yet to be set up. Continued efforts are required to combat lice infestation in all segments of the population, including the Jewish one, and more vigorously than has been the case up to now. Given the existing conditions, I believe it would be unrealistic to attempt to achieve the same goal by isolating the smaller and larger Jewish settlements, above all in view of the large number of these settlements and the mentality of both the Aryan and Jewish parts of the population. If we wish to control lice infestation in the population and it is not possible to supply people with soap, we must at least tell them what they can do instead. For this purpose, the population must ideally be given detailed instructions. General orders such as 'beware of lice' are only half measures. For instance, there is no chance of every settlement receiving a proper delousing station, but it is certainly possible to operate temporary facilities in every settlement that likewise serve the purpose, although this is predicated on individual families being checked and instructed. This could be implemented with the assistance of volunteers concentrated around the healthcare hubs.

'Where this has not yet happened, delousing stations of sufficient size must be set up at the main epicentres of typhus outbreaks in each Kreis. An increase in the number of mobile delousing facilities is probably necessary as well, but I cannot assess on what scale at the moment. New facilities of this kind certainly need not be created with undue haste; what is important is that the existing facilities are put to use appropriately and competently.

'What is also important is to create organizations to rapidly detect persons suspected of having contracted typhus (epidemic control squads). Above all, medical students who have not been able to complete their examinations and volunteers with sufficient levels of education could be deployed successfully here. In many instances, known contact cases are quarantined and I have also recommended this practice, but given the current scale of the epidemic, I doubt whether it will be possible. Since people suffering from typhus will not spread the disease if they are free of lice, this measure [quarantine] can be dispensed with if the primary focus is on delousing. Therefore, the most important thing is not to quarantine contact cases but to delouse them, which will probably save not only money, but also a great deal of aggravation.

'People who have contracted typhus must also be put into isolation in hospitals or auxiliary hospitals; schools above all would have to be equipped to serve as auxiliary hospitals. Since isolation is a compulsory measure and many people shy away from the costs of hospital treatment because, ultimately, typhus patients are to be found mainly among the poorest parts of the population, hospital accommodation must be provided at *public expense* in my opinion. This measure alone would certainly have the major advantage that people would report themselves sick earlier than they are doing at present, and that they would not be so inclined to evade detection. The inclusion of all the personnel working in this field in the "A-enterprises" group for the purpose of food rationing would have a significant and favourable influence on typhus control.[12] This measure would probably be much more effective than higher salaries.

'I am still not able to assess the extent of the costs that will be incurred by typhus control because the documentation is lacking.

'A solution will be found for all the individual aspects as soon as a systematic and concerted disease control campaign is under way. It is evident from the preceding remarks that such action is necessary, and past experience has shown that success can also be achieved in the foreseeable future.'

We can only agree, and thus attempts must be made to ensure the measures are implemented appropriately and properly. We have therefore approached the relevant economic bodies, and, as you have requested, Professor Kudicke, sufficient fuel quotas will be made available. As before, a solution is predicated on there being a sufficient number of delousing stations. This requirement, too, is justified, and we have therefore also contacted the Eastern Railway, which has assured us it will deliver sufficient heating fuel. The necessary detergents, soap, etc., which are not entirely easy to procure, will be made available by the goods supply control office as well. Combating typhus must have top priority and we will pursue this objective vigorously. We have already held discussions with the key agencies in the last few weeks, and all parties have pledged us their complete support. As I mentioned at the start of my presentation, the Governor General has made 8 million zloty available for typhus control in response to our proposal.

We hope the measures that are now to be carried out most vigorously will yield the anticipated results in the course of the winter.

(Applause)

Department Head and Regional Party Health Leader *Dr Walbaum* asked those present for their views.

*Professor Kudicke*: Gentlemen, anything that I might add has really already been said. I would just perhaps like to take the liberty of drawing your attention to a few points. At a stage when measures have only just been initiated, it is not possible to formulate a detailed plan stipulating that this will be done this way and that will be done that way. As experience shows, every epidemic teaches us new lessons; conditions are not the same everywhere, even within the General Government, unfortunately. District Cracow is a particularly good example. Here it will be possible to manage with very much simpler and less intrusive measures than in the other districts. I therefore based my proposal on conditions in the districts Warsaw, Lublin, and Radom. Typhus control in the large Warsaw ghetto poses a particular challenge; the conditions there are so challenging that for me it is quite understandable if some parties, even the health authorities, feel there is no point doing anything there at all as they are not being informed anyway, and have to limit themselves to assuming a defensive position. On this point, however, I would like to say that a defensive position is not the best approach to combat an epidemic; rather, the best weapon in this respect is attack. And if this attack costs money, then that can't be helped. Let me

12 A standard food coupon system had been operating in the General Government since 1941. It distinguished between ten groups of consumers with different ration allowances. Non-German employees in 'A-enterprises' (*A-Betriebe*) received the same rations of some products as the best-supplied Germans.

reiterate: I do not believe it is possible to simply cordon off such a large epicentre of an epidemic, let alone one that is located right in the middle of a densely populated city. You can do that with a mine, you simply seal it off and then it continues to burn underground, but with typhus you cannot expect to eradicate the disease simply by cordoning off areas. So the conclusion is that, whatever the circumstances, we must make an effort to tackle things differently, i.e. through a proactive approach. I know perfectly well this will incur a great deal of work, on a scale that may drive some people to distraction. But that is not my intention, since I am certain I will receive the essential support that is needed. In this respect, I am thinking above all of heating fuel for the delousing stations; this is something we cannot do without under any circumstances. That is as much as I can say concerning the epicentre. Dr Hagen, city physician for Warsaw, will talk about this later, and provide a great deal more interesting information than I can give you. The following general points should be mentioned briefly:

Apart from the requisite expertise, epidemic control requires a keen interest on the part of all personnel; furthermore, it requires above all else that personnel go to the epicentres of the epidemic to see things for themselves. It is not possible to control epidemics if one relies solely on reports. As a matter of priority, the operation must be made mobile, which requires unified leadership. I have not put myself forward to lead this operation, but I have been asked to do so. I had suggested potentially bringing in an authority from the Reich for this purpose, but it was felt that I would be up to the job. I will therefore endeavour to justify this confidence in me as best I can; I would like to ask one thing, however, and that is not to put forward too many different opinions. I am quite aware of how to control typhus. This was a tough struggle during the [First] World War, too, but it became evident that control measures can be implemented if they are conducted under a unified leadership. It is equally clear that to tackle such a special task, everyone involved needs to make allowances for one another and avoid friction if possible. My experience in this regard has shown me that such friction can never be avoided completely, but it is avoidable if there is a reasonable amount of goodwill on all sides.

One important issue that I will broach only with great caution is, furthermore, that we cannot achieve any more if we do not eliminate the factors that – I wouldn't say solely, but to a considerable extent – have been conducive to the spread of typhus. One should bear in mind that I am speaking in purely academic terms here, without making any value judgements. The Jewish segment of the population is a segment that has been completely uprooted from its accustomed environment. The Jews formerly subsisted on trading and haggling, and goodness knows what else. That has now been stopped, and they do not know how they are to make a living, and apart from that, it is undoubtedly the case that food shortages have had a quite specific impact, above all among the Jewish segment of the population. If we wish to prevent this, then we would have to seek instruments that are capable of eliminating precisely these factors. I do not wish to do any more than draw attention to this. In my opinion, we could, for example, attempt to utilize the Jews in the work process in another form with the aid of the Jewish labour camps. I am not familiar with the scale of these measures in detail; I only know that I myself am probably inadvertently to blame for these Jewish labour camps being closed again because they became epicentres of the epidemic. The reason for this, however, was that – just like some of the ghettos – we left the labour camps to their own devices and we said, you can do all that, you can organize that yourselves, and it subsequently became evident once again that Jewish physicians are not capable of setting up their own epidemic control organization; that's how it was in the Warsaw ghetto as well. They boasted that they would do it themselves, but not a single one of them bothered to ensure the delousing procedures were carried out.

I am touching on these matters because we need to think about how long we will still have to have the Jews here; as yet we do not know. This is a matter that lies beyond my expertise and beyond my jurisdiction. However, we do need to think about it, since we will have to consider how we want to make sure that these people, who we are now confining together and whose freedom of movement we have taken away, do not harm us. For the time being, this will result in us having to take in hand the things that the Jews are not capable of and, in doing so, to utilize the Jews, as well as the Poles – who in some respects have failed, too – for assistance. One of the issues I mentioned in my report was that the significant food shortages have undoubtedly led to the Jewish population simply breaking out of the ghettos, where there was nothing to eat. We must be aware that if we wish to avoid this in future, then we will have to use the best means to this end, that is to say, we must ensure the Jewish population is more adequately fed. Here, though – I'll be honest here – my strength fails me, everybody's strength fails them. As far as I am concerned, matters are clear, and I also know that the difficulties are so great that it will probably never be possible for these shortcomings to be eliminated. But we have to know this, and we must also be aware that this may potentially be the reason why this whole operation might fail. I will personally do everything in my power to ensure that this operation is not doomed to failure, but as yet I still do not know whether that will be possible. I am not greatly optimistic about the situation, but I do know that, especially in epidemic control, one sometimes actually gets by with certain measures, even if they cannot be implemented 100 per cent, and to ensure that this is done to the greatest possible extent, it is best if all concerned are resolved to work together.

Department Head and Regional Party Health leader *Dr Walbaum* thanked Professor Dr Kudicke for his remarks, which had effectively underlined his proposals. [Dr Walbaum:] To return to your last comments, Professor, I must say that you are completely right. Of course, the best and simplest thing would be to give people sufficient opportunities to feed themselves, but that will not be possible because of the general food situation and war conditions. That is why shooting has now been adopted as a measure when a Jew is encountered outside the ghetto without special authorization. We must – I can say it openly in this company – be aware that there are only two options: either we condemn the Jews to death by starvation in the ghetto or we shoot them. Even if that amounts to the same thing in the end, the second option seems more daunting. But we cannot act any differently, even if we wanted to, because our one and only task is to ensure that the German people are not infected and endangered by this parasite, and any means must be justified for this purpose.

(Applause)

We cannot look at these things from any other perspective.

If anyone else has anything new to say on this topic, please feel free to speak, we are grateful for every suggestion.

*Dr Lambrecht*:[13] Department Head Walbaum; gentlemen. I wish to concur with Professor Kudicke's views, for I too consider it unrealistic to close off the Warsaw ghetto in such a way that not a single Jew afflicted with typhus can get out. We have made truly zealous efforts, we have sent disinfection squads into the ghetto etc., but the men in the Polish disinfection squads are susceptible to bribery, and Jewish money puts paid to people's honesty; for, looking at it another way, it is understandable that it is damned difficult for a man like that to remain honest on monthly earnings of 180 zloty. Of course, we can only condone the decision to put Jews found outside the ghetto without authorization before a summary court, because that would enable us to keep our western Kreise free of typhus.[14] Apart from that, we are using all scientific methods at our disposal to control this epidemic.

There is one difficulty, however. In January I was faced with the question of whether even more Jews should be admitted to the Warsaw ghetto (we were getting 70,000 Poles from the Warthegau). I had made a request to my office to improve the food supply for the Jews in the ghetto because the greater the pressure on the ghetto, the greater the pressure on the perimeter. Unfortunately, I did not receive authorization for the required amount of food because there was nothing there. At any rate, though, it is still better for the Jews to die in the ghetto than for them to be dispersed all over the city and perish there, whereby they only pose an even greater risk than before to other sectors of the population.

(Applause)

We must be consistent here, and it would therefore be appropriate to take a far more rigorous approach vis-à-vis the Jews than to date, and any desire to help the Jews in the ghetto by providing them with medical assistance is condemned to failure in my opinion, in view of the character attributes of the Jews, who will just keep bribing people.

(Applause)

*Dr Lohnsdorf*:[15] Regarding vaccination, a Polish physician approached me, asking how he should conduct himself when people with typhus come to his surgery. People who are already sick are arriving mainly from the northern districts.

The Department Head asked Dr Lohnsdorf to wait with the answer to this question until Public Health Officer Dr Hagen had given his presentation.

Department Head and Regional Party Health Leader *Dr Walbaum* gave the floor to Public Health Officer Dr Hagen:

*Public Health Officer Dr Hagen, City Physician for Warsaw: 'Experience of Epidemic Control in the City of Warsaw'*

[…][16] In conclusion, I can say that, as far as typhoid fever is concerned, the classic disease control measures implemented by my predecessor, Public Health Officer

13 Dr Arnold Lambrecht (b. 1903), physician; joined the NSDAP and the SA in 1931 and the SS in 1933; head of the Health Department in District Warsaw from Aug. 1940; went missing in Jan. 1945; his wife reported him killed in action.

14 The Jews in the western Kreise of the district had been forced to relocate to the Warsaw ghetto at the beginning of 1941: see PMJ 4/236 and 252.

15 Dr Lohnsdorf was the head of St Casimir's Hospital in Radom.

16 Hagen analysed the progress of three infectious diseases – tuberculosis, typhus, and typhoid fever – and the measures taken to control them in Warsaw during the First World War and since 1939; he concluded that typhoid fever had been combatted successfully.

Dr Schrempff,[17] have been a complete and lasting success. In this respect, vaccination has the greatest role to play. This has also been a complete success in the Jewish quarter, even though the attendant circumstances, namely hunger, the dense living conditions, and dirt, have certainly not got any better since then.

Things are different when it comes to typhus. The table illustrates the number of deaths from typhus broken down by month. Up to 18 deaths a month were occurring in Warsaw before the [First] World War. The World War then brought the epidemic of 1917 with a peak of 322 cases; only isolated cases of typhus occurred before the current war. An epidemic only started again in 1939 with a peak of 58 deaths in March 1940. At the end of 1940 the danger appeared to have been eliminated. In spring 1941, however, typhus increased again, reaching 182 deaths in July. These are the official figures. In reality, the conclusion we have now had to reach is probably true for the epidemic during the World War: that the cases reported at the peak of the epidemic only represent a fraction of the new infections.

If for 1941 we look at the daily numbers of people reporting themselves sick with typhus in the period up to mid August, we can see a consistent increase in the Jewish quarter, which represents the epicentre of the epidemic. This increase starts in March, that is, it is initially only apparent in the absence of the reduction in new infections that is to be expected at that time of year.

If the curve from 1916 to 1923 and the curve beginning in 1940 are superimposed, the two curves curiously appear to run parallel. In 1916 too [there was] a pre-epidemic, which increased again somewhat towards the end of the year. A severe outbreak of the disease began to develop during the summer months of 1917, a period which, as experience shows, should have led to a fall in the rate of typhus with the decline in lice infestation. During the present war the 1940 pre-epidemic appeared to have died out at the end of that year. The increase then came in 1941, with 1,800 new infections reported in July. In September we will reach 3,000 new infections, and the number will rise even further in October. This would exceed the peak of the 1917 epidemic. However, I do not believe this to be the case. Our experience suggests that without precise monitoring the reporting is so incomplete that we can assume that in 1917, too, only one third at most of the typhus cases were reported. I will outline later how we have now achieved better reporting.

The first question people will rightly ask is how such a development has been possible. The epicentre of the new typhus infections is, as you will of course be aware, the Jewish quarter. Our picture shows you the location of the Jewish quarter in the centre of the city of Warsaw with an entirely impractical perimeter that it will never be possible to monitor. In January we had about thirty new infections in the Jewish quarter and two new infections among the Poles in the surrounding area. One would think monitoring would be possible with an incidence like this. The incidence for April was certainly more threatening. As it stands there is no room for any more [healthcare] hubs in the Jewish quarter, and the number of hubs in the Polish part of the city has increased significantly. It is hence not the case that classic disease control has come to a halt.

17 Correctly: Dr Kurt Schrempf (1903–1964), physician; medical officer in Landkreis Herford from 1928; member of the NSDAP and the SA; physician for Kreis Lübbecke in 1939; head of the Health Department in the German municipal administration in Warsaw, Oct. 1939 – Feb. 1941; Kreis physician in Halle (Westphalia), 1954–1964.

The curve shows you how delousing and disinfection measures continued, even as the number of new infections fell. The number of buildings sealed by the police naturally went down. The number of buildings disinfested as a precaution increased accordingly, and the number of people bathed and deloused only decreased temporarily around the turn of the year due to a shortage of coal. My predecessor had called for a doubling of the capacity of the delousing stations. That was rejected for financial reasons. The consequence is that today we are not actually in a position to delouse all the people for whom this would be necessary. However, three new bathing facilities are now being built at a cost of 1 million zloty. They are primarily intended to protect the Polish population.

An explanation is required, however, for how epidemic control operations could be so seriously disrupted.

In March this year 40,000 Jews were brought to Warsaw from the west of the district.[18] Our demand for additional new housing to be provided for these Jews in the ghetto was rejected. It was originally planned to quarantine all these Jews in a closed-off district, and only gradually to permit them one by one to have dealings with the rest of the Jewish quarter. This measure, too, had to be dispensed with. On average, 1,000 Jews were arriving every day on transports; they were first deloused and then distributed around the Jewish quarter following a short stay in the quarantine stations. Most of these people were completely destitute. They were put up either with relatives or in refugee camps. It goes without saying that they brought typhus with them. At the same point in time, the Jewish quarter was completely sealed, and the allocation of food almost completely discontinued in order to ensure that any available stocks were used up first. The sealing of the Jewish quarter denied the Jews the opportunity to support themselves through trading, as they were accustomed to do. The organization of workshops did not advance as rapidly as would have been necessary to ensure that this population could make a living. The consequence was increasing impoverishment on a mass scale. Added to this was the fateful illusion that we could leave the Jews to run their own affairs. With regard to healthcare, this certainly appeared quite possible, given the presence of 700 physicians. The medical officer[19] therefore had to refrain from working intensively in the Jewish quarter for several weeks. However, the Jews demonstrated their complete inability to establish and maintain an epidemic control system. The number of typhus cases reported no longer reflected the actual state of affairs. In one case, when the Jewish public health authority itself reported a physician who had brought together typhus [patients] in a dilapidated building and treated them there, the Security Police, to whom the case was assigned, let the man go free after questioning him, and the German Special Court[20] asked why the man was supposed to be punished. It is clear that compliance with the reporting regulations was not to be achieved with such methods. We began working with Polish personnel in the Jewish quarter again in June; the difficulties had increased significantly in the meantime.

The mortality rate in the Jewish residential area was resulting in 1,000 burials a week. The majority of those deaths were purely due to exhaustion. The victims were

18 See PMJ 4/252.

19 Dr Wilhelm Hagen.

20 A reference to the German Special Court in Warsaw, which was headed by public prosecutor Rudolf Naumann.

mainly old people and children, with a predominance of men. However, a study by the State Hygiene Institute carried out on Professor Kudicke's orders came to the striking conclusion that 10 per cent of the people who died had suffered from typhus a short while before. And these people had not been in hospital. If we assume that the mortality rate among the Jews is only around 12 per cent, then a rate of twelve deaths from typhus per day among people who had not been in hospital would indicate that there were approximately 100 unreported new infections a day. And this at a time when the number of new infections reported daily was ranging at around 35. We were therefore only aware of approximately one third of the typhus cases. We attempted to improve our delousing measures straight away. The Jews will go to astonishing lengths in order to avoid having to bathe. Without coercive measures, just under 10 per cent can be persuaded to bathe. By establishing a typhus supervision unit consisting of four groups, each with one German in charge of disinfection, one Polish physician, and one Polish police officer, we were at least able to ensure that between 25 per cent and, in the most favourable case, 50 per cent of the inhabitants of the affected buildings went to bathe. In epidemic control, however, a measure that is [only] 50 per cent effective does not count as a measure at all. Moreover, there were the high number of unreported cases. It turned out to be a fiction that individual buildings could be isolated in the Jewish quarter. The entire Jewish quarter had to be regarded as contaminated.

We undertook a major clean-up operation at one location, on Krochmalnastraße, which was worst affected. At 5 o'clock one Friday morning, 25 buildings on the street were cordoned off by a contingent of 25 German police officers, 60 Polish police officers, and approximately 200 Jewish Order Service men. All the residents had to leave their homes and were assembled outside on a square on this warm summer's day. In this way, it proved possible to send at least 90 per cent of them for delousing, but even then [the other] 10 per cent escaped us. The result was that, instead of the eleven reported cases, we found fifty-seven people with the disease. Things have got better in this quarter since the operation. A total of 4,900 people were deloused by us there in one and a half days. But it would be impossible to apply this method to the whole Jewish quarter. We cannot carry out a hundred such operations. But we did acquire some additional insights into how to continue the epidemic control campaign. We have decided against extending the control measures to entire buildings. By contrast, we have considerably reduced the size of the blocks into which residential areas are divided, so that the block physicians can check each individual apartment twice a week. We monitor these reports physician by physician and block by block. The number of reported cases immediately shot up to almost twice what it had been. After eight days the campaign ran out of steam. However, we were in a position to speak firmly to the individual gentlemen involved, and in this way achieve an improvement in the reporting figures again.

That is the situation in the Jewish quarter. On the Polish side, the number of new infections has risen further in the meantime. It exceeded 300 cases in September. During the summer months people were contracting the disease in the vicinity of the ghetto walls, whereas cases are now distributed across the city. In addition, the disease not only affects people who are infested with lice, but also people who are free of lice, that is, who have at most had the occasional louse. However, the connection with Jews has been demonstrable in every case up until now. All the same, it is conceivable that in these cases the disease was not transmitted by live lice, but rather by Jewish dirt that had been infected by lice, and indeed unfortunately remains infectious for a very long time. Up until now we have been able to assume there is fairly reliable reporting on the Polish side. A fervent appeal to the physicians was made only recently. Despite this, however, some drastic punishments will be necessary.

I am aware that all our disease control measures will remain unsuccessful during the coming winter if the environment remains as conducive to the spread of typhus as it has been until now.

It has spread in the Jewish quarter due to overcrowding, hunger, and dirt. We will see the same thing on the Polish side. I will show you some pictures to demonstrate the nutritional situation. At 600, the number of calories in the food allocated lies far below the norm. Of course, this allocation is supplemented with foods from the free market, and not just potatoes and vegetables that are not subject to controls, but also by clandestine trading in rationed food products. Absolute shortages remain, in particular of fat and protein. While the prices for clandestine goods were barely higher than the regulated prices at the beginning of 1940, and had reached just three times the level of the regulated prices by the beginning of 1941, they rose to twelve to fifteen times the regulated prices in the course of the summer, despite the size of the allocation having been kept approximately the same. This trend has not been reversed following the harvest. This is because of the Wehrmacht's requirements. Unfortunately, there is no prospect at all of the population's demand for potatoes being completely met with plentiful allocations. The consequence has been a rise in the cost-of-living index to 1,600 per cent in June. Although it fell again in August to 1,100 per cent, it has been rising again since then. By contrast, the salaries of employees on fixed pay are currently at 80 per cent and real wages at 6–7 per cent of pre-war income. It is therefore no exaggeration to describe the situation as catastrophic. Inflation, i.e. the flight into tangible assets and the progressive depreciation of the currency, is in full swing. Added to this are the actual absolute shortages of necessary foods. It is time for certain authorities to face these facts without any illusions. The monetary implications are likely to prove incontrovertible at the beginning of next year. For us it is sufficient to note the fact that the population is starving, and that we cannot expect a person who has 6 per cent of his former real income to do his duty selflessly without being susceptible to bribery. Yet this absolutely has to be expected of all those working in epidemic control.

In addition to this, there is the prospect that the civilian population will not receive a single kilo of coal for their domestic fires this winter. On a number of recent occasions, the coal commissioner has been unable to supply me with the coal required for the delousing stations.[21] Private bathing facilities have to be closed. Hospitals cannot be heated. If the shortages of washing products and clothing, the impossibility of changing bedclothes, and the necessity for most people to put clothes on to sleep rather than take them off are factored in, any efforts to organize epidemic control are consequently doomed to failure from the very outset in the face of these overwhelming forces. I do of course recognize the priority afforded to the army whenever requests are made. However, I would like to leave open the question of whether there are dangers here that threaten the army as well. The spread of typhus to railway personnel is not

21 The head of the Coal Supply Control Office in the General Government was Dr Walter Jehne (b. 1910).

such a distant prospect. If the curve continues to rise as it has done so far, then we will have to expect several thousand people outside the Jewish residential district to be suffering from typhus around the turn of the year. They will become a real danger to the Germans who are living in Warsaw, as well as the Wehrmacht units that are working here. I must therefore articulate the standpoint that three things are decisive for the control of typhus at present: bread, coal, and soap. We will certainly do whatever is possible from an organizational perspective. However, with no improvement in the three basic factors I have mentioned, we will be doomed to failure.

[…][22]

If we now compare the [TB] figures for Poles and Jews, the curve for the Jews does not differ fundamentally from the curve for the Poles. This undermines the assumption that, as a consequence of TB infection spreading throughout the Jewish population at an earlier stage, the Jews are in a different phase of the epidemic and the conditions are therefore getting closer to those in Germany, as one might believe if comparing the bare figures. Other aspects appear to be playing a role here. The race's genetic material responds differently, as it does to typhus. In both cases, greater resistance is to be found. Such differences are also known for other diseases of course; for example the Jews are more susceptible to diabetes, and mental illness is more prevalent among them. We are not aware of such differences between Germans and Poles. Above all when it comes to TB, a corresponding reduction in mortality is not found among Germans, in particular among ethnic Germans resident in Poland.

[…][23]

[Reichel:] In June, to be precise in the week after Whitsun[24] – I was on leave at the time – typhus flared up in our area. We discovered that approximately fifty Jews had broken out of the Warsaw ghetto and had been found sick on the streets of Lublin. I don't know how many others had also made their way there; I only know about the fifty Jews we found on the streets. Cases of typhus then went up within a fortnight. In response we set up a Jewish police force with the assistance of the police headquarters.[25] In my opinion, policemen need to be strong people. We had picked out the strongest Jews. Suddenly someone from the employment office turned up and said strong Jews are needed for labour, not as policemen. Quarantine would be a second option. But that is not feasible because of the lack of guards. One day the Jewish Council came to us distraught, saying, 'Help us, our Jewish police have gone, the Jews have left the building, and the SS are tearing it down because they need bricks.' This was true, as we later found

22 Hagen subsequently discussed mortality due to tuberculosis.

23 Hagen went on to describe serial X-ray investigations and other diagnostic measures. There followed another presentation, after which Buurman asked those present for their comments. Among those who contributed to the subsequent discussion were Dr Hans-Joachim Reichel (1901–1988), physician; from 1934 Kreis physician in Jauer; public health officer; joined the NSDAP in 1937; municipal public health officer in Cracow and head of the Health Department in District Cracow, 1939–1940; head of the Health Department in District Lublin from April 1940, and in Cracow again from Dec. 1941; head of Güstrow Public Health Authority in May 1945; had his medical licence revoked during denazification proceedings; lived in Berlin and Munich after the war.

24 In other words, in the first week of June 1941.

25 Mogens von Harbou und von der Hellen (1905–1946) was police chief in Lublin for two months in summer 1941.

out. I learned that this building had been placed at the disposal of the SS in Lublin six months earlier in case they needed bricks. They did not need the building back then, but now they were claiming it.

Public Health Officer *Dr Buurman* asked if there were any other comments; no one requested to speak. He continued: In order to be able to carry out the typhus operation, it is firstly important that the coal does not run out, so that a proper delousing operation can be conducted. However, as has already been said, we are negotiating with the Economic Affairs Department in this regard and have also had the assurance that this problem is to be remedied. As Dr Hellenbrand[26] remarked, this too is obviously one of the most urgent concerns for him, so that delousing procedures do not grind to a halt. Furthermore, Dr Hellenbrand is right when he makes the point that the dense living conditions are partly to blame for the significant spread of typhus. We have to say this over and over again to the agencies responsible within the Interior Administration, and here I come to what Dr Reichel referred to in his comments: there has been repeated interference in the measures taken by the health administration. The medical officers and District physicians have informed us that in some cases the Interior Administration has demanded measures that could not be condoned from a medical point of view. And although the gentlemen pointed this out to the Interior Administration, these measures were demanded without anyone listening to us. Gentlemen, please make sure *we* are informed in all such cases so that we can raise objections. We must insist that, if the control of typhus has been entrusted to us, *our* measures must also be recognized and respected. It is outrageous to unceremoniously disregard our directives.

On the question of quarantine: Dr Hellenbrand is right when he says the question of nutrition is important here. However, this is a matter for the local agencies, and the relevant Kreis physician or medical officer must get his way. However, discipline must prevail in my opinion, otherwise we will not make any progress at all.

[...][27]

26 Dr Josef Hellenbrand (1908–1944), physician; joined the NSDAP in 1940; section head in the Health Department in District Radom in 1941; medical officer in Piotrków Trybunalski in 1943.

27 Buurman then asked for the next presentation. The other topics discussed at the meeting included the control of venereal disease, diarrhoeal diseases, and trachoma; Dr Wiggers talked about the public health system in Eastern Galicia. On the last day of the meeting, the participants inspected the spa facilities at Krynica-Zdrój. Apart from the speakers mentioned, the meeting was attended by the following: Dr Reinhard Busch, Dr Günther Ohrloff, Dr Hoefert, Dr Ruppert, Dr Karl Weber, Fritz Müller, Dr Friedrich (?) Kleber, Dr Schenk, Dr Beck, Dr Giller, Dr Werner Kroll, Dr Lauber, Dr Friedrich Gönnert, Dr Schörcher, Dr Friedrich (?) Schäfer, Dr Kikuth, Hansen, Kroll, Starke, Dr Erich Passauer, Dr Hildegard (?) Reiber, Dr Corwin, Dr Hermann Eyer, Dr Becker, Dr Altheimer, Dr Petters, Dr Walter Oberheide, Dr Maaß, Dr Wurm, Dr Walter Gorgon, Dr Rudolf Makarowski, Dr Zaluznyj, Gebert, Krinner, Dr Eitel-Friedrich Rißmann, Dr Albert Bruns, Dr van Hove, Dr Ludwig Rauenbusch, Dr Alfons Witt, Dr Beck, Dr Günter, Dr Balser, Dr Herbold, Dr Albrecht Puppe, Dr Erwin Motzkus, Dr Guttwein, Dr Erich Waizenegger, Dr Königstein, Dr Richard Krenek, Dr Hünnerscheidt, Dr Schirmer, Dr Spangenberger, Dr Adolf Winkelmann, Dr Lohde, Dr Hans Hoffmann, Dr Friedrich Bünner, Dr Grau, Dr Offe, Dr Hubert Umlauf, Dr Kohmann, Dr Hans Wirtz, Dr Horst Weidenbusch, Dr Scherbel, Dr Jung, Dr Kublinski, Dr Rudolf Wohlrab, Dr Werner Sydow, Dr Carl, Dr Petersohn, Holjewilken, Dr Wilhelm Dopheide, Dr Fanselow, Dr Wladar, Dr Schuhmacher, Dr Konietzko, Dr Herzum, Dr Ernst, Dr Walter Schulz, Dr Plins, Dr Kellner, Dr Fahr, Dr Ruth Johanna Lippold, Dr Weiß, Dr Sältzer, Dr Brinder, Dr Mühlbauer, Dr Bröser, and Mrs Wick-Utecht.

## DOC. 15

## On 15 and 16 October 1941 the government of the GG and leading officials in District Warsaw discuss the Warsaw ghetto[1]

Minutes of the government meeting at Brühl Palace, Warsaw, dated 15 and 16 October 1941

[…][2]

Through the creation of a closed-off residential district the Jews have a special position in Warsaw. Two presentations on this matter will follow. For this reason, I [Governor Fischer] just wish to briefly address the food supply for the Jews.

If the Jewish labour force is to be maintained, workers need to receive sufficient rations to keep them alive. The current allowances amount only to basic rations, which are supplemented with foodstuffs that find their way into the ghetto via illegal channels. Since we intend to seal the ghetto even more tightly from 5 November – we are obliged to do so because of the danger posed by typhus – new ration allowances will then have to be approved by the government. The following rations are proposed:

1,050 g bread per week
300 g sugar per month
1 egg per month
100 g jam per month
50 g fat per month
1 quintal potatoes per year
Fish as available
Vegetables as available[3]

Even these foodstuffs provide too little sustenance. Where possible, the ghetto needs to be provided with special allocations. The mortality figures will undoubtedly rise over the winter. But this war is, after all, a conflict with Jewry in its entirety. The American Jew Kaufmann's publication has shown us what we would have to expect

1 AIPN, GK 95, vol. 16. Copy in IfZ-Archives, Fb 105, vol. 16, fols. 3771–3894, here fols. 3843–3845 (appendix: report by Ludwig Fischer), fols. 3779, 3855–3858 (appendix: report by Fribolin), fols. 3891–3892 (appendix: report by Wigand); ÖGfZ, Archiv, Nl 93, folder 13 (reports by Auerswald and Bischof). This document has been translated from German.

2 On 15 Oct. 1941 Governor Ludwig Fischer began by reporting to Governor General Hans Frank, highlighting Warsaw's significance as the largest industrial city in the General Government, before addressing the question of the food supply. Dr Ludwig Fischer (1905–1947), lawyer; joined the NSDAP in 1926 and the SA in 1929; deputy head of the Legal Department of the NSDAP Reichsleitung in 1931; Regierungsrat and main department head of the Academy for German Law in 1933; chief of staff in the Reich Legal Office in 1938; governor of District Warsaw from Oct. 1939; simultaneously acting governor of District Lublin, April–May 1943; sentenced to death by the People's Supreme Court in Warsaw and executed in 1947.

3 During the afternoon meeting, which was held at Belvedere Palace and attended by Boepple, Emmerich, Fatken [Fattgen?], Fischer, Frank, Hummel, Leist, Spindler, Weh, and Westerkamp, the acting head of the Food and Agriculture Main Department in the General Government, Karl Naumann, expressed reservations about the majority of Fischer's proposals. The Governor General stated 'that further foodstuffs could not be made available for the *Jewish population*': IfZ-Archives, Fb 105, vol. 16, fols. 3771–3782 (fol. 3779).

from the Jews if they were victorious.[4] I believe this can be justified if […][5] of Jewry, from which the whole of world Jewry is constantly being replenished, is dealt a devastating blow by us.

I would, however, like to draw attention to one thing in particular, and that is the provision of supplies for Jews in the Reich, in particular in the Litzmannstadt ghetto. Jews receive the following foodstuffs there:

Per capita per week:

| | |
|---|---|
| Bread | 2.250 kg for working Jews |
| " | 1.523 kg for non-working Jews |
| Grains and cereals | 0.100 kg for working and non-working Jews |
| Meat | 0.250 kg for working Jews |
| " | 0.160 kg for non-working Jews |
| Fat | 0.100 kg for working and non-working Jews |
| Eggs | none |
| Coffee mix | 0.063 kg for working and non-working Jews |
| Vegetables | 3.150 kg for working and non-working Jews |
| Artificial honey | 0.052 ½ kg for working and non-working Jews |
| Sugar | 0.140 kg for working and non-working Jews |
| Potatoes | 5.250 kg for working and non-working Jews |
| Buttermilk and skimmed fresh milk | 2.7 l for children aged 3–6 |
| Full-fat milk | 2.7 l for children aged up to 3 |

Additionally, 100 g of jam per head per week is supplied to sick Jews, along with one egg and 0.011 g[6] of pudding mix each for the same period.

Even if these allowances are not always adhered to, it is evident from the above that the Jews in Litzmannstadt are better fed than the Aryan workers in armaments enterprises in the General Government. This fact must, in my opinion, be made clear to the Reich agencies responsible when they request foodstuffs from the General Government.

In summary, when it comes to the issue of the food supply, I would like to reiterate that here too it largely boils down to a transport problem. I repeat yet again my request for the special allocation of sixty goods wagons for District Warsaw.

Preparations for the procurement of winter quarters for our troops fighting in the East are fully under way here. We have to expect a number of supply channels to be blocked for longer periods again when these military formations return. If we do not succeed by then in ensuring demand is met over the winter months until March, in particular the demand for potatoes, because these obviously cannot be transported in the winter, situations will then arise in Warsaw that could incite even the most patient

4 Correctly: Theodore N[ewman] Kaufman (1910–1980), businessman; at the beginning of 1941 he self-published the pamphlet *Germany Must Perish!* in which he called for German males to be forcibly sterilized following the Allies' victory as a way of preventing future German aggression. The pamphlet went virtually unnoticed in the USA. In late Sept. 1941 the Nazi propaganda authorities published excerpts from it in the pamphlet *Das Kriegsziel der Weltplutokratie* (The War Aim of World Plutocracy), of which millions of copies were printed. Kaufman's bizarre plan was presented as evidence of a Jewish world conspiracy: see PMJ 3, p. 60.

5 Illegible in the original.

6 Correctly: 0.011 kg, i.e. 11 g.

of populations to engage in rash actions. My view is that, if only for political reasons, we should avoid these potential developments if possible.

[…][7]

*The Jews in District Warsaw*

Paper for the government meeting in Warsaw on 15 October 1941, given by the lawyer Auerswald, commissioner for the Jewish residential district in Warsaw[8]

According to findings from September 1941, approximately 116,000 Jews live in the eastern Kreise of District Warsaw, of whom approximately 37,000 live in Kreis Warschau-Land, approximately 26,000 in Kreis Garwolin, approximately 20,000 in Kreis Sokolow-Wengrow, approximately 19,000 in Kreis Siedlce, and approximately 14,000 in Kreis Minsk. The Jewish residential district in Warsaw has approximately 450,000–500,000 residents; a precise figure cannot be given at present. The western Kreise of District Warsaw do not have any permanent Jewish residents.[9]

Accordingly, a total of between 556,000 and 616,000 Jews live in District Warsaw. If it is assumed that approximately 1.8 million Jews live in the whole of the General Government, not including Galicia, about one third of these Jews therefore live in District Warsaw, and one quarter of all the Jews in the General Government live in the city of Warsaw alone.

My intention in this paper is not to deliver an in-depth account of all the issues associated with the presence of the Jews. In particular, I do not intend to present extensive statistical material or other particulars regarding the Jewish residential district in Warsaw. Rather, the purpose of this paper is to address in broad terms the question of what kind of living conditions the Jewish part of the population is to be allowed in general – so long as there are any Jews left in the General Government at all – and, above all, to help answer the question of whether, and to what extent, freedom of movement for Jews should be granted or restricted.

Whether or not they belong to Eastern Jewry, the Jews are particularly asocial. With the egocentricity peculiar to them, their greed for profit, and their unscrupulous methods, they disrupt any orderly administration and any system of economic management that is not built exclusively on the individual's striving for profit. Furthermore, the Jews, at least if we are talking about Ostjuden, are dirty and infested with lice. They therefore pose a great danger as carriers of infectious diseases – they themselves having largely developed immunity.

7 Fischer went on to praise the improvement in housing conditions before briefly discussing the cultural and sporting life of Germans in Warsaw. The commissioner for the Jewish residential district, Heinz Auerswald, then gave a report, which has been inserted here from ÖGfZ, Archiv, Nl 93, folder 13.

8 Heinz Auerswald (1908–1970), lawyer; joined the SS in 1933 and the NSDAP in 1937; legal officer for the SS from 1934 and for the Berlin Court of Justice from 1938; Urban Police officer in Poland in Sept. 1939; subsequently head of the Population and Welfare Division in District Warsaw; commissioner for the Jewish residential district in Warsaw from 15 May 1941 and simultaneously responsible for the Jewish population in District Warsaw; Kreishauptmann of Ostrów Mazowiecka, Nov. 1942 – Jan. 1943; thereafter served in the war; worked as a lawyer in Düsseldorf after the war.

9 Jews in these western Kreise had been forced to relocate to the Warsaw ghetto at the beginning of 1941: see PMJ 4/236 and 252.

The idea of segregating them from the outside world and gathering them together in their own residential and economic communities as far as possible therefore seems obvious.

It is all the more obvious because, unlike the Western Jews, the Ostjuden do not work exclusively in trade or in intellectual fields, but largely as craftsmen and labourers, and it is therefore conceivable for this labour force to be utilized systematically by means of appropriate measures to group together and manage the individuals concerned.

As always when an idea seems particularly obvious, here too it is worth carefully reconsidering whether this is the right approach. Does the creation of Jewish residential districts really represent the expedient solution to the Jewish question as long as we cannot completely remove the Jews from the German area of interest – in this case from the General Government? And, if the answer is yes, what should a Jewish residential district look like?

As I said previously, at first glance three aspects favour the creation of closed-off Jewish residential districts, namely (1) the Jews' asocial disposition, (2) the danger of epidemics associated with Eastern Jewry, and – in a positive sense – (3) their capacity for productive labour. On closer examination, the question cannot easily be answered unambiguously, even in purely theoretical terms.

First of all, as far as the Jew's asocial attributes are concerned, it cannot be expected that these will simply disappear if the Jew is placed in a ghetto. Rather, he can be expected to use all means at his disposal in the attempt to evade the restrictions placed upon him and to render them virtually illusory. For example, the more the Jew is excluded from normal economic dealings, the greater the zeal with which he will endeavour to satisfy his desires through clandestine trading channels. In short, while efforts are made to eliminate the impact of the Jews' asocial attributes on the outside world, the asocial vigour of the Jew will simultaneously be intensified.

Similarly, when it comes to the second aspect, that of reducing the danger of epidemics, we also find effects and counter-effects. If the creation of the Jewish residential district is associated with a reduction in living space – and this will almost always be the case under the current conditions and in places that have been more or less destroyed by the hostilities – the risk of epidemics, and therefore the number of sick people in the Jewish residential districts, will consequently rise. At the same time, if the Jew has the prospect of being able to move about more freely outside the Jewish residential district, he will certainly strive even more than otherwise to leave the Jewish residential district in view of the danger posed by epidemics; having arrived on the outside, he will endeavour to keep himself hidden and will therefore increase the risk of epidemics for the Aryan population as well. If this is not countered with appropriate measures, the creation of Jewish residential districts may therefore to a certain extent even increase the risk of epidemics.

Finally, with regard to the utilization of the Jewish labour force, it is also conceivable that the disadvantages associated with the establishment of a closed-off Jewish residential district would be greater than its advantages. For example, if sealing the Jewish residential district results in Jewish craftsmen not having any employment, not only will the systematic utilization of this labour force not have been achieved, but it will be lost altogether, with the concomitant danger of a welfare burden.

These deliberations lead to the conclusion that the establishment of Jewish residential districts does not in itself represent a straightforward remedy for the difficulties caused by the presence of the Jews. Rather, particular aspects have to be consistently borne in mind in this respect and, above all, we must not be satisfied with taking half measures. More damage could potentially be caused by incorrect ghetto creation measures than if we left the Jews full freedom of movement and accepted the associated disadvantages. At the same time, the establishment of Jewish residential districts will inevitably have the desired effect, i.e. the elimination of the disadvantages associated with the Jews' freedom of movement, if the residential districts are sealed off in a way that is actually effective, and the same basic conditions are created throughout the largest possible territory. In practice, this means that a Jew suffering from typhus will no longer leave the Jewish residential district just like that if there are clear boundaries around the perimeter, and the Jew knows there will be shooting if he approaches these boundaries; he will not even make plans to escape at all if he knows he will not be able to roam freely in the neighbouring Kreis, but rather at best have to reckon with being taken to another sealed residential district straight away. As far as the utilization of Jewish labour is concerned, work must be provided according to a planned system; but in this respect the Jew must also know that his only choice is to undertake the work assigned to him or die.

The practical experience gained in District Warsaw confirms that the conclusions reached by theoretical methods are correct. All imaginable variants can currently be found in District Warsaw: the western Kreise have been freed of Jews and a ban on them residing there has subsequently been imposed. Largely closed-off residential districts have been formed on a large scale in the city of Warsaw and on a small scale in the town of Sokolow. In the town of Siedlce there is a fenced-off, albeit unguarded residential district; in the towns of Wengrow, Minsk, etc., the Jews have been assigned to residential districts which they are forbidden to leave, but there are no surveillance procedures to prevent them from doing so. In a large number of rural localities and smaller towns in the eastern Kreise, there are virtually no restrictions on Jews' freedom of movement.

The experience gained in District Warsaw has led to the absolutely irrefutable conclusion, with respect to epidemic control alone, that the most preferable solution is to have a residential district that is as closed off as possible. At a time when, out of the total number of typhus cases in the city of Warsaw, there were just ten non-Jews to every ninety Jews, in the eastern Kreise there were forty non-Jewish typhus cases to every sixty Jewish cases. This means that, despite the Jewish residential district in Warsaw being in close proximity to the rest of the city, and despite certain shortcomings regarding the sealing off of the Jewish residential district and a series of other factors that are comparatively more favourable in the countryside than in the city of Warsaw, the establishment of the Jewish residential district in Warsaw has ensured that only 10 per cent of the people infected with typhus were Aryans, whereas in the Landkreise 40 per cent of cases occurred in the Aryan population. The ratios have worsened recently, to the detriment of the Aryan population. In the city of Warsaw the ratio of Jewish typhus cases to Aryan cases is now 80:20, while at the same time the ratio in the eastern Kreise in which Jews live has reached 50:50. The closed-off Jewish residential district has therefore again proved to be a convincing measure.

At the same time, the worsening of the ratio in Warsaw from 90:10 to 80:20 demonstrates that sealing off the ghetto alone is still not sufficiently effective. The Governor has therefore instructed me to undertake measures to seal the ghetto more tightly, in consultation with the SS and Police Leader, by making a series of corrections to the perimeter and by routing the dividing line along the perimeter roads themselves. The work required to implement this instruction is already under way and will be concluded in November.

The 50:50 ratio recently seen in the eastern Kreise additionally shows that a more rigorous isolation of the Jews is required there as well. Kreis Ostrow, where there are no Jews, is practically free of typhus. The western districts were also without typhus for a protracted period following the removal of the Jews in March 1941. Only recently have cases of typhus occurred in this territory as well. As the findings reached by the Health Department have indicated, the disease is usually transmitted by Jews who have broken out of the Jewish residential district in Warsaw or come from District Radom. In the eastern Kreise, too, in the vast majority of cases, typhus is transmitted by roaming Jews.

All these observations will compel the German administration to place further restrictions on the Jews' freedom of movement, if it considers its responsibility for the German Wehrmacht and the entire non-Jewish population. Since the necessary surveillance of Jewish residential districts is unlikely to be achieved everywhere, on account of shortages of law enforcement officials, the burden [on these officials] will have to be reduced by imposing more stringent punishments for leaving the Jewish residential district without authorization. District Warsaw presented the government with proposals along these lines some time ago.[10]

Objections could be raised to the views expounded here along the lines suggested at the beginning, namely, that sealing the ghettos more tightly would provoke increased counter-pressure from the Jewish side everywhere and cause economic difficulties. These objections are in some respects unfounded and could in other respects be dispelled by taking appropriate countermeasures.

The experience gained here suggests that the Ostjude may be more aggressive than his West European racial comrade. Despite this, no cases of open rebellion have yet come to light. The Jews will certainly endeavour to exploit the existing loopholes – actual and legal – as much as they are able. But if they realize that a directive is backed up by the unconditional will and power to implement it, they will submit.

The picture is essentially the same in the economic field. Thanks to efforts made in the last few months, in particular the work of the Warsaw Transfer Bureau,[11] the Jews' economic initiative has been reawakened to a certain degree in the Jewish residential district in Warsaw, and successes have already been achieved that give grounds for hope of a satisfactory solution to the economic problems. Nonetheless, the Jew still prefers to engage in clandestine trading rather than to work productively for the relatively low wages that have been set. Insofar as this is the case, the Jews also have to be convinced that, although they have ample opportunities to make the private profits for which they strive within the framework of the economic management of the Jewish residential district, they have no opportunities to make a living outside this economic process.

In addition, the economic difficulties I mentioned at the beginning crop up not only when a rigorous form of isolation is in place, but wherever Jews are prevented in some way from interacting freely with the surrounding Aryan world. If the Jews in the Kreise are to be segregated in a manner that is likely to succeed, sufficient work opportunities

10 No information about such proposals could be identified.

11 The Transfer Bureau in the Warsaw ghetto had started its work on 1 Dec. 1940: see PMJ 4/203.

must be arranged there too from the very beginning. Whether this can be done more expediently through a greater concentration of Jews or by deploying smaller groups will depend on the individual circumstances.

Whatever measures are taken to restrict the Jews' freedom of movement, there is one essential precondition which I must emphasize in particular, namely the need to ensure the minimum level of nutrition required for the working Jewish population. If it is to have any point at all, any form of economic utilization [of the ghetto] must ensure that the minimum needs are met of those who observe the rules concerning economically productive labour either out of obedience or through coercion.

The food rations for the Jewish population were established at a time when Jewish residential districts did not yet exist.[12] They were evidently based on the assumption that the Jews required only an absolute minimum of basic nutrition and, moreover, that they would be able to obtain whatever else they needed to live on in other ways, using the ingenuity for which they are well known. The Jews were, so to speak, directed towards clandestine trading through official channels. This situation has changed fundamentally with the creation of Jewish residential districts. Even though they have not been completely sealed off and this circumstance has been exploited, with clandestine trading taking place on a relatively large scale, the quantities that enter the market in this way are not sufficient to rule out incidences of starvation, especially among the poorer members of the population. The number of deaths per day rose in the Jewish residential district from an average of 29 in January 1941 to an average of 151.5 in September 1941, and even reached a peak of 179 in July and August. This increase is not because the principle of sealing the residential district is wrong, nor is it due to the spread of the typhus epidemic – for typhus is mentioned as a cause of death in just 10 per cent of cases on average.[13] Rather it is because the insufficient food supply has led to debilitation, which makes the organism susceptible and leads to people dying of illnesses that they would have otherwise survived. One piece of evidence to prove this assertion is that the mortality curve, which rose particularly steeply from April to May of the present year, went up less steeply after the number of soup kitchen meals served by the Jewish Social Self-Help increased from 30,000 portions a day to around 110,000. The fact that in September 1941, despite a further increase in the typhus epidemic, the mortality curve fell from a daily average of 179.4 in August to 151.5 in September is also evidence that typhus has not played a significant part in the increase in the mortality curve.

The Food and Agriculture Department in the Office of District Warsaw has undoubtedly made efforts to rectify the situation within the bounds of what is possible. Special [food] allocations were also granted by the Food and Agriculture Main Department for the months May to August, which made it possible to expand the soup kitchen operation. Moreover, the Transfer Bureau Warsaw and my office have done everything

12 Food ration cards were introduced in the General Government at the beginning of 1940; from Feb. of that year Jews were allowed to make purchases only in Jewish shops; later they received cards marked with a Star of David and were excluded from the allocation of certain foods.

13 Since 1940, statistics had shown typhus to be the contagious disease with the highest number of recorded deaths; in 1941 the rate of infection escalated, provoking an epidemic. Physicians and hospitals frequently did not record typhus as the cause of death in order to prevent repressive measures being taken against other residents in the same building.

possible to make some provision for the winter. Nonetheless, the ration quotas defined in the most recent negotiations with the Food and Agriculture Department as the maximum that could be granted are entirely inadequate, even just to ensure provision for working Jews and their family members. While, in line with the arrangements that apply in Reichsgau Wartheland – insofar as documents about this are available here – the Jews there receive more than three times the rations allocated here, it must be expected that all plans for the utilization of Jewish labour in Warsaw will fail because subsistence levels are no longer available. During the deployment of Jewish labourers on land improvement schemes in the summer of the present year[14] it was already apparent that they were in an extraordinarily poor physical condition and extremely susceptible to disease.

A further question that I consider significant in terms of the handling of Jewish residential districts is that of Jewish self-administration. The Governor General's Regulation on the Jewish Residential District in Warsaw, issued on 19 April 1941, enabled the functions and powers of a mayor[15] to be transferred to the chairman of the Jewish Council.[16] Without being able to go into detail on this occasion, I would like to point out that the experience gained so far suggests this principle has proved its worth extraordinarily well. The chairman of the Jewish Council works loyally, and, on the whole, his agencies also perform the functions incumbent upon them. The administration of the Jewish residential district works with its own approximately 2,000-strong Order Service, its own postal administration, its own transport companies, its own financial mechanisms, and similar institutions that are still being established. As a result, even though the usual dissatisfied voices are of course not absent here either, there has so far been no reason for the German side to raise serious objections to or to intervene in the individual aspects of the administration.

In summary, the following can be said: If it is certain that the Jews can be deported from the General Government as early as next year, it would be expedient to essentially leave things as they are at present in order to save unnecessary work and expenditure. However, if it is not certain, the experience gained to date suggests that the principle of the closed-off Jewish residential district should be applied systematically and standardized as far as possible throughout the General Government, and the necessary legislation adopted, but also, and in particular, that tougher penalties should be introduced as quickly as possible. This would also involve the provision of reliable guards. Even if this measure were to necessitate an initial increase in police numbers, it would be justified,

14 In 1941 tens of thousands of Jewish forced labourers were deployed on land improvement and drainage projects across the General Government: see PMJ 4/308 and 321.

15 Governor General Frank's Regulation on the Jewish Residential District in Warsaw (19 April 1941) provided for the appointment of a commissioner: *VOBl-GG*, 1941, no. 35, 28 April 1941, pp. 211–212. The commissioner was appointed by the District Governor on the basis of a directive issued by the latter on 14 May 1941: *Amtsblatt des Chefs des Distrikts Warschau*, no. 5, 20 May 1941, p. 50. The commissioner received his instructions directly from the District Governor and was at the same time responsible for 'general Jewish affairs' in the district. A further directive issued by Fischer that came into force on 15 May 1941 transferred 'the functions and powers of a mayor' in the Jewish residential district to the chairman of the Jewish Council in Warsaw: *Amtsblatt des Chefs des Distrikts Warschau*, no. 5, 20 May 1941, p. 52.

16 Adam Czerniaków.

since the presence of a relatively small number of police officers is of considerable benefit in closed-off Jewish residential districts, whereas, if we let the Jews run around, there would never be enough police available to effectively counter the wheelings and dealings of each individual Jew. Finally, insofar as there is an interest in utilizing the Jewish labour force, [it is] indispensable to ensure sufficient orders for work are procured and people's minimum needs are met.[17]

Paper on economic relations with the Jewish residential district in Warsaw, given [by Max Bischof] at the government meeting in Warsaw on 15 October 1941

When the closed-off Jewish residential district in Warsaw was created in October 1940,[18] economic concerns had to cede to higher demands, and only later was the major economic problem of the 500,000 Jews in Warsaw investigated in order to identify its repercussions and ways of managing it. To deal with these issues, the *Transfer Bureau* was established at the beginning of January 1941 *as a subgroup* of the Resettlement Department in the Office of the District [Governor], and the direction for the Transfer Bureau's further activity *as a public institution*[19] was then laid down by the Regulation on the Jewish Residential District in Warsaw of *19 April 1941* and by the Bureau's statutes, which were adopted on 15 May 1941; changes were made to its management at the same time.[20]

Without anticipating later developments, today it can be taken as read that the inhabitants of the Jewish residential district are to be involved in economic life as extensively as possible and under supervision, *(a)* so that their labour is deployed in line with the needs and opportunities of the war economy, and *(b)* to keep welfare subsidies from public funds as low as possible.

My comments, which will deal with fundamental issues regarding economic life, organizational restructuring, monitoring, and the promotion of economic relations with the Jewish residential district, are to be understood *only in the light of* these currently overriding aspects.

1) *Fundamental issues*

The original attempts to meet the liabilities of the Jewish residential district through the *large-scale deployment of Jews as forced labour* on earthworks and water engineering schemes, as well as by means of compulsory contributions and the search for hidden assets, did not yield the desired results. In order to save public funds, it was also decided

17 Auerswald's presentation was followed by a report by Max Bischof, head of the Transfer Bureau Warsaw and representative of the supervisory authority for public and private banks; his presentation has been inserted here from ÖGfZ, Archiv, Nl 93, folder 13. The original features handwritten annotations and underlining. Max Bischof (1898–1985), banker; member of the Fatherland Front aligned with Engelbert Dollfuß; employed at the Österreichische Länderbank from 1920 and based in Warsaw, 1929–1935; employed at the Länderbank in Vienna, 1935–1945; coordinator of the Polish banks in the General Government from 1939; additionally representative for the supervision of public and private banks in the General Government, 1940–1945; head of the Transfer Bureau, May 1941–1943; head of personnel at the Länderbank in Vienna after the war. Bischof, who was married to a Jewish woman, enjoyed the special protection of Hans Frank. See also PMJ 4/285.

18 See PMJ 4/180, 185, and 188.

19 See fn. 14.

20 Bischof became head of the Transfer Bureau in May 1941.

to refrain from making the residential district a tightly organized *concentration camp.* Consequently, despite all the difficulties caused by the district being closed off, the restructuring of the population, the food situation, and other war-related obstacles, steps had to be taken *to revitalize the economy* in the Jewish quarter. For this purpose, the priority was to create normal *conditions for economic activity* within the Jewish quarter, with the aim of getting Jewish skilled workers in particular, who make up about 40 per cent of the economically active population, into work and enabling them to earn money. *Private initiative* among the higher echelons of [Jewish] society had to be roused from a state of complete paralysis and a certain sense of calm restored following the turmoil surrounding the creation of the ghetto. With these points in mind, the following measures were taken:

a) requisitions and confiscations were largely reined in,
b) the necessary searches for gold, foreign currency, and stocks of goods of importance to the war effort were carried out more efficiently; this was done by excluding untrained agencies and calling in the Customs Investigation Office,
c) further changes to the ghetto perimeter and resettlement operations were deferred,
d) in a move away from collectivist economic mechanisms, it was ensured that every Jew who was willing to work actually received the proceeds of the work he did without any of these being taken by the Jewish Council.
e) Finally, in consultation with the government department responsible, the restrictions on Jewish-owned cash and cash payments to Jews were revoked, and at the same time an amnesty for hidden funds was announced in order to encourage their deployment in the economy (*Amtlicher Anzeiger für das Generalgouvernement*, no. 58, 2 September 1941).

2) *Organizational restructuring*

The *principle* of giving *the Jewish Council* legal and organizational responsibility for all aspects of the life of 500,000 people, which was applied in the first months following the creation of the ghetto, was abandoned as it was a hindrance to the economy. Instead, it was necessary to ensure structure and clarity within the vast pool of Jewish labour. Existing professional bodies, such as the Craftsmen's Association and the Retailers' Association, were therefore endorsed, and their leaders and other business figures brought together in an *Economic Council for the Jewish Residential District*, which provides the Jews with a platform to debate general economic questions and is used by the Transfer Bureau to convey instructions.[21]

For the managers and owners of those *Aryan enterprises* that could not be relocated outside the Jewish quarter for technical reasons, a delegation was formed under the auspices of the Main Trade and Industry Group of the District Chamber of Commerce to consult with the Transfer Bureau on all relevant issues.

Furthermore, various *Jewish Council institutions which engage in commercial activities*, such as the Production Section, the Trade and Industry Section, and the Supply

21 The Economic Council for the Jewish Residential District was established to coordinate economic activities in the ghetto with the German authorities in accordance with instructions from the Transfer Bureau; its members included the chairmen of the Craftsmen's Association and the Retailers' Association. See PMJ 4/312.

Office, were detached from the Jewish bureaucracy and made into legal entities in their own right. For instance, Jüdische Produktionsgesellschaft mbH[22] was founded with capital of 80,000 zł, Liefergesellschaft für das Jüdische Gewerbe mbH[23] with capital of 35,000 zł, and the Supply Office for the Jewish Residential District[24] with capital of 1,000,000 zł.

New funds were paid by the Jews into the first two enterprises mentioned above, while the Supply Office generates its own capital. In these cases at least – further applications to found enterprises are still being processed – evidence has already emerged that if things run smoothly, one could expect the Jews' commercial activities to be *self-financing* to a certain extent.

In addition to this, the *legal and capital foundations for consortia* are of particular importance because they clearly delimit the *responsibilities and interests of Jewish business managers*, while their Aryan partners, who in many cases hand over valuable materials for processing, are consequently protected against negligence or malicious practice. Likewise in the interests of the Aryan partners, the previous prohibition on Jewish businesses being entered in the *Polish commercial register* was also revoked in order to make the legal situation as clear as possible.[25] The trading names of the businesses always indicate that they *have been established by Jews*.

The *operating capacities* at the Jews' disposal are very modest on account of businesses being placed in the hands of trustees, the sale of assets, the relocation [of businesses] outside the Jewish residential district, and the liquidation of hundreds of small businesses by the police when the ghetto was created. The labour force is therefore overwhelmingly utilized in work processes that do not require mechanical equipment and that can therefore be organized in simple workspaces or as domestic outwork.

With regard to *placing Jewish labour under Aryan economic management*, various methods have been used, depending on the practical requirements: Aryan businessmen leasing and managing previously existing Jewish businesses; Aryan businessmen establishing their own business premises with Jewish workers; commissioning Jewish enterprises or workshops to fulfil orders under the supervision of Aryan businessman; concluding simple contracts for the delivery of goods between the Jewish business or agent and the Aryan businessman; and, finally, employing Jewish workers in Aryan businesses or businesses administered by trustees that could not be relocated for technical reasons. In the majority of cases, a direct Aryan *link to the outside world* is required because Jews are understandably not welcomed as partners in the various positions of responsibility in the command economy, in particular when it comes to matters relating to war production.

22 Jewish Production Company; the company was responsible for producing goods and selling them to German and Polish buyers.

23 Supply Company for Jewish Trade and Industry.

24 The Jewish Council's Supply Office was responsible for distributing foodstuffs that were supplied legally to the ghetto.

25 On 17 April 1941 Alexander Palfinger (1894–1961), who was Bischof's predecessor as head of the Transfer Bureau from Dec. 1940 to May 1941, prohibited newly founded Jewish businesses from being entered in the commercial register. This was also consistent with a directive for District Warsaw dated 31 Jan. 1940: see PMJ 4/162. Auerswald revoked Palfinger's directive on 30 July 1941; the first private limited company in the Warsaw ghetto was set up on 15 August 1941, and the last was approved on 16 July 1942.

Just like the Jewish Council, the Transfer Bureau has now *stopped entering into commercial agreements*, and outstanding orders, mostly related to war production, were transferred to German businessmen in August 1941.[26] At the same time, a process of *directly concluding business agreements* between an Aryan and a Jewish partner has been introduced in order to clarify their professional responsibilities, subject to approval by the Transfer Bureau.

Specific organizational measures were required to *introduce cashless transactions* with the Jewish residential district. Such transactions are necessary not just for *security and financial reasons*, but above all as the *precondition for the monitoring and statistical recording* of payments made. The *Jewish Council's Clearing House* was temporarily given limited banking powers and authorized to open a limited access *current account with the Emissionsbank*[27] in Warsaw, and all credits and debits due are gradually being channelled via this account for *centralized cashless processing*. The link to the Aryan banks is provided by a *clearing consortium*, which was established under the auspices of the Emissionsbank and which *the Emissionsbank itself* has joined.

The intention is to convert the Jewish Council's Clearing House into a *cooperative bank*. Interested professional associations and business groups have already submitted an application to found such a bank to the government department responsible. The main purpose of founding this bank is to *collect Jewish-owned invested funds*, which would be used to finance independent Jewish commercial activity. The *legal disparity* with the outside world that has now been created, i.e. the unrestricted availability of credit balances with banks and cash within the Jewish residential district and the restrictions outside the district, provides a conducive environment for the acquisition of deposits. However, these plans are dependent on renewed shocks to economic life in the Jewish quarter being averted. In the meantime, in order to bridge the intervening period, *opportunities to obtain credit* from Aryan banks have been opened up subject to the appropriate collateral being provided, in particular for the storage of winter stocks by the Supply Office.

3) *Monitoring*

The monitoring of economic trade at the level of individual transactions, as initiated by the order issued by the *Stadthauptmann* of Warsaw[28] on 20 March 1941,[29] represents a special case when applied to an enclave of 500,000 people within the built-up urban area of a city of over a million inhabitants, the difficulties of which must not be underestimated. A broad-brush approach is primarily required to tackle problems of this kind, and I believe you will agree with me if I *refrain from registering minor transactions* for monitoring purposes. Above all, it was necessary to prevent the suffocation of the still

26 See also Doc. 4.

27 Central bank created for the General Government in 1941.

28 Ludwig Leist.

29 This order stipulated that goods could only be traded in the ghetto with the permission of the Transfer Bureau; contraventions were to be punished with custodial sentences of three months: Order of the District Governor's Representative for the City of Warsaw Concerning the Trading of Goods with the Jewish Residential District of the City of Warsaw, 20 March 1941, *Mitteilungsblatt der Stadt Warschau*, no. 12, 28 March 1941, pp. 1–2.

*delicate seedling of orderly business transactions* with the Jewish residential district under a suddenly welter of formalities.

In themselves, *transactions can only be monitored individually* if they are declared as requiring approval. However, it is first necessary *to put in place* the *organizational machinery and personnel* in order to manage the anticipated volume of work. In the meantime, the draft of a comprehensive *directive on the mandatory approval* of commercial transactions has been completed and submitted to the commissioner [for the Jewish residential district]. To simplify matters, however, *blanket approval* will be granted where possible when it comes to clearly delineated procedures that can be statistically recorded, particularly with regard to payment transactions.

The following are already being used as tools for *monitoring*:

With regard to passenger traffic: the issuing of permits; with regard to goods traffic: (a) the issuing of goods permits, and (b) the import of goods via the Transfer Bureau's freight transfer depot; with regard to payment transactions: (a) the issuing of approval notifications for the purpose of processing via the banks, and (b) the immediate approval of crossed cheques from the Emissionsbank that are made out to be credited to or debited from the Jewish current account.

The clearance of goods via the Transfer Bureau's *freight transfer depot*, which is located on the perimeter of the residential district and also has a connecting railway line, *is subject to the transaction authorization procedures* and requires the appropriate documentation. A sterilization plant in which vulnerable goods from Jewish businesses – items of uniform for the Wehrmacht, for example – are fumigated prior to their dispatch is also located at the depot.[30]

In connection with current efforts to seal the perimeter more tightly,[31] the *trade in goods* that up until now has been able to evade direct supervision because of the precedence given to *Wehrmacht agencies* and the like is now also gradually *being made subject to the authorization procedure.*

As far as formal questions regarding *the movement of goods* into the Jewish residential district are concerned, it has been agreed with the Economic Affairs Main Department that these can only be prioritized once a sufficient volume of work has been procured. Until then the general principle must apply that the *Aryan partner* is primarily responsible for complying with the provisions governing the movement of goods, in particular with respect to the volume of goods coming out of the Jewish residential district.

On the question of *wages and prices*, it should be mentioned that the war-related difficulties that currently *exist in the overall economy of the General Government* are increasingly becoming apparent in the Jewish residential district as well. In the case of orders subcontracted from the Reich, which are of prime importance, there can of course be *no question of making calculations* on the basis of living conditions here. The tensions must be overcome by increasing the Jews' output in *piece work* and through preferential

30 Fumigation plants used hydrogen cyanide (Zyklon B) gas to kill off insects and insect larvae in textiles. The procedure had been developed during the First World War. From 1941 the SS in Auschwitz used this gas to carry out mass murder.

31 This is presumably a reference to Governor General Frank's regulation of 15 Oct. 1941, according to which Jews were punished with the death penalty if they left their ghettos without authorization: see Doc. 13.

treatment for workers under the *food distribution scheme* run by the Jewish Council. In turn, the *additional freight costs* for the delivery of materials and the return transportation of the completed goods will require corresponding cuts to the rates of pay. *As long as their wages* are paid *without delay*, i.e. without financing difficulties, it can usually be observed that Jewish skilled workers are happy to avail themselves of the work opportunities on offer.

The question of the Jewish residential district's *balance of payments* is *very much coming to the fore* on account of the steps being taken to seal the perimeter more tightly. The economic devastation that characterizes the Jewish quarter today of course means that in the long term it is not in a position to pay off its wide-ranging arrears in *state taxes*, municipal *revenues, social insurance contributions, pre-war commercial liabilities*, etc. in addition to *the costs* for its ongoing maintenance. The depletion of financial resources has now been going on for *almost a year*, so it is urgently necessary to defer further levies. Otherwise the *circulation of legal tender* in the Jewish residential district would inevitably grind to a halt to a degree that would hardly be in the interests of the authorities. The *External Trade Office* alone holds pre-war claims on the General Government from the Old Reich to a value of 5,000,000 zł., the recovery of which has been deferred. The Warsaw Social Insurance Fund is asserting claims to the value of 9,000,000 zł. The prospect of using compulsory contributions and so on to settle these various historic claims, as raised by the Transfer Bureau's *former management* following the creation of the ghetto, cannot be realized at present in view of the absence of funds.

4) *Promotion of the economy*

On the basis of § 2 of its statutes, the Transfer Bureau is obliged to promote economic relations with the Jewish residential district. In general, this is done through the chambers of commerce. However, since any economic activity in the Jewish residential district depends fundamentally on the *food issue*, it was – as previously mentioned – above all necessary to create a certain incentive for the Jews employed in organized labour by providing them with soup and so on. Following protracted negotiations, only in the last few days has it been possible for the Jewish workers involved in production for the war economy to receive assurances about an *across-the-board improvement in their allocations* (B rations), since the volume of the general food allocation for the Jews *is far from sufficient* to sustain the *labour force*.

Furthermore, the Transfer Bureau's fees for the movement of goods and transfer payments have been greatly *reduced* and at the same time a *schedule of fees* has been introduced in order to facilitate commercial agreements.

In order to strengthen entrepreneurial initiative on the Aryan side, early summer 1941 saw the founding of *Deutsche Firmengemeinschaft Warschau GmbH*,[32] the member firms of which are deployed preferentially in the utilization of Jewish skilled workers. However, the *many difficulties* that hinder normal commercial activity still do *not allow* a *proper* development of the Firmengemeinschaft's activities. It would be extremely important to assist the Firmengemeinschaft's efforts also in the *areas where there is demand*

32 A German business consortium founded in March/April 1941 to represent the interests of the ever-greater numbers of German firms that operated in the Warsaw ghetto from 1941.

from the General Government by allocating *quotas* of wood, paper, cardboard, sheet metal, wire, soft iron, etc., which are almost completely lacking.

There are currently *nine* member companies in the Firmengemeinschaft that have already started operating; they have concluded transactions with the Jewish residential district as follows:

| July 1941 | August 1941 | September 1941 |
|---|---|---|
| 961,000 zł | 285,000 zł | 1,411,000 zł |

At the end of September 1941, the value of the orders ready to be placed by the Firmengemeinschaft, including the *follow-up orders* from Wehrmacht agencies passed on to German businessmen *by the Transfer Bureau*, was about 3,000,000 zł.

The workshops established by the Transfer Bureau and Jüdische Produktionsgesellschaft mbH (previously the Jewish Council's Production Section), which are now operated directly by German businessmen, achieved the following turnover:

| | | | |
|---|---|---|---|
| Feb. 1941 | 1,700 zł | June 1941 | 217,600 zł |
| March 1941 | 1,900 zł | July 1941 | 484,700 zł |
| April 1941 | 15,800 zł | Aug. 1941 | 977,800 zł |
| May 1941 | 64,100 zł | Sept. 1941 | 158,100 zł |

The fall in September was due to *increased operational difficulties*, which had to be overcome through organizational intervention. At the end of September, the value of the orders placed was about 2,300,000 zł. The sums paid for employees in this work creation sector developed as follows:

| | | | |
|---|---|---|---|
| Beginning of May 1941 | 220 zł | Beginning of Aug. 1941 | 2,424 zł |
| Beginning of June 1941 | 1,377 zł | Beginning of Sept. 1941 | 3,055 zł |
| Beginning of July 1941 | 2,134 zł | Beginning of Oct. 1941 | 2,316 zł |

The turnover achieved in the *export trading* brokered by the Transfer Bureau was as follows:

| | | | |
|---|---|---|---|
| April 1941 | 31,000 zł | July 1941 | 393,000 zł |
| May 1941 | 67,000 zł | Aug. 1941 | 291,000 zł |
| June 1941 | 84,000 zł | Sept. 1941 | 237,000 zł |

At the end of August 1941, the employment office branch for the Jewish residential district recorded *36,198 persons in employment*. Organized work creation therefore accounts for *only a part of overall employment*, and alongside this there are an estimated *10,000–15,000* Jews engaged in *export* in very small businesses and as domestic outworkers. Jewish craftsmen are very inventive in the reuse of waste and the reworking of second-hand goods, for example the production of *children's shoes and clothes* from garments discarded by adults, tools from *used* iron parts, *bags* from prepared textile waste, etc. These sources generate a considerable volume of unrecorded goods exports, which are overwhelmingly carried out via small-scale smuggling.

While the developments described above are generally to be welcomed, it is nonetheless clear that in absolute terms the figures are a drop in the ocean compared with the mass of 500,000 people [in the ghetto]. At the end of August 1941, the Transfer Bureau therefore launched a *publicity campaign* of its own in the territory of the Reich in order to highlight the opportunities for orders to be moved to the Jewish residential district. For this purpose, a brief article was placed in the Reich German *daily press*, for example, and fifty copies of a *specially printed version* were sent to each of the seventy *chambers of commerce* in the Reich and the *trade groups* for which the placing of such orders would be relevant.[33] There has been an extraordinary response to this initiative, and enquiries arrive daily from interested German parties, many of whom have also made practical suggestions for the manufacture of simple products such as straw shoes, bags, brushes, sheet-metal goods required by the Wehrmacht, mica tapes for the armaments industry, wooden needle-cases, fashion accessories, etc.

The large-scale production for the *Wehrmacht* of shirts, trousers, caps, epaulettes, and shirts along with billeting supplies, buckles, fasteners, etc. has been under way for several months now.

There is a keen interest in utilizing Jewish workers, in particular in the *Berlin and Central Elbe areas, where there are shortages*. These have good transport links, and the deputy head of the Berlin employment office[34] and the managing directors of the *Berlin* and *Magdeburg* Bezirk allocation offices[35] were in Warsaw recently for more detailed discussions on this issue.

Perhaps this is the approach to take if we are to succeed at all in utilizing the Jewish workers of Warsaw to a sufficient extent to serve the needs of the Reich in the final struggle for the future.

[…][36]

[Presentation given by Hermann Fribolin:] Above all, the very acute questions of *epidemic control* and the creation of a Jewish residential quarter are currently affecting the economic and finance sectors in the city of Warsaw, because large volumes of funds that far exceed the amount foreseeable at the beginning of the financial year are being provided for these purposes. The dangerous typhus epidemic, which originally struck the Jewish residential quarter, has been spreading to the Polish parts of the city for months and affects a greater area every day. Since the beginning of June it has caused a total of about 1,000 cases of sickness among the Poles and about 7,500 among the Jews (including about 100 deaths among the Poles and about 500 among the Jews), and redoubled, intensive efforts are therefore required to control it with all available resources. The city of Warsaw has consequently found itself compelled to increase the sum of 3.5 million zloty originally earmarked for general epidemic control, and typhus control in particular, to almost twice that amount in order to counter as effectively as possible the spread of this contagious disease, which will potentially threaten the German population as well, by creating and expanding additional quarantine stations and cleaning stations and by increasing disinfection procedures and the provision of medical assistance.

The *creation of a Jewish residential quarter* and its administrative separation from the administrative apparatus of the city of Warsaw has naturally had an impact on the city's

33 See Doc. 4.

34 During this period the head of the Berlin employment office had two permanent deputies: Regierungsdirektor Dr Walter Heinzel (b. 1896) and Oberregierungsrat Dr Kurt Göttel (b. 1896), who were both lawyers. It is not known which of the two conducted the talks in Warsaw.

35 From the mid 1930s the Bezirk allocation offices (Bezirksausgleichsstellen) were responsible for placing orders and managing deliveries.

36 A presentation was then given by Dr Hermann Fribolin (1886–1944), lawyer; joined the NSDAP in 1933; mayor of Karlsruhe from 1933; head of finance for the German municipal administration in Warsaw from Feb. 1941; later served simultaneously as deputy Stadthauptmann; died during the Warsaw Uprising. In his presentation Fribolin drew attention to the problem of price rises.

budget as well. It is still not yet possible to give a detailed assessment of the financial and economic impact or to establish whether, and to what extent, it will be possible to compensate for the loss of revenue that the city of Warsaw expects to incur through its own tax revenue being paid out to the Jews by cutting costs in other areas, because so little notice was given of this change. The only thing that is certain is that the financial and economic ties between the Polish and Jewish districts of the city will not be severed in the future either under the current conditions. Moreover, the Polish [part of the] city will have to continue to oversee many important matters in the Jewish sector, in particular the maintenance of roads, public places, sewers, and public utility services, as well as the building inspectorate, fire brigade, registration system, etc. in the interests of continuing orderly and expedient administration.

Another problem that will strongly influence the economy as a whole is the question of how to alleviate the severe housing shortage in the city of Warsaw. Since the city has suffered particularly badly from the impact of the war and has lost a large percentage of its housing stock through destruction and damage, there is an acute need to create new residential accommodation. Even though it has been possible to restore some of the damaged buildings in the last two years with the active assistance of the German supervisory authority, there is still a shortage of about 70,000 dwellings today in Warsaw! For this reason the city administration needs to implement generous funding schemes for accelerated housing construction as soon as the general building prohibition is lifted again, although this would be dependent on a reduction in the prices for building materials, which are hugely inflated at present. In general, it should be noted that over the past two years steady and visible progress has been made in eradicating significant war damage, efforts which have gone hand in hand with a considerable *improvement in the city's appearance* and its transport infrastructure. If it has not always been possible for this clean-up operation to be carried out at the desired pace, this is not attributable to the German supervision of the operation, but exclusively to the limited budgetary funds available for such purposes since, as has already been highlighted, such funds had to be made available and used to fulfil urgent, vitally important requirements.

In *one* area, however, financial considerations have to take a back seat to more important concerns, namely the *provision for Germans* deployed in the East, which is to be stepped up in future; this is necessary to ensure that a solid core of German spirit, German energy, and achievement can establish itself in Warsaw, too, with regard to politics, culture, and the economy. In purely spatial terms, the *creation of a German residential quarter*, which is already under way, is an absolute prerequisite in this regard;[37] the necessary local resettlement and exchange of Poles and Germans and the provision of sufficient and suitable housing for Germans is another significant problem facing the German supervisory administration. It should be evident that solving this problem will require great sacrifices, particularly in financial terms, given the many thousands of people affected by this and their very diverse needs. One need only think of the question of rent controls, which poses particular challenges, especially here in Warsaw, in view of

37 In mid Oct. 1940 the Governor of District Warsaw ordered a ghetto to be created for Jews and, at the same time, a 'German quarter' in the prestigious part of Warsaw: see PMJ 4/180. However, the neighbourhood was never exclusively occupied by Germans: see PMJ 4/236.

the high rents. Without state aid and support – general subsidies or tax breaks for land ownership come into consideration here – it will not be possible to accomplish this special task that has been taken on in the interests of strengthening Germandom in the General Government. […][38]

[Remarks by Arpad Wigand:] In addition, German counter-propaganda should also help to ensure that a large proportion of the population, even nationally minded Poles, reject the activities of the resistance movement as inopportune in view of the vast upheavals taking place in Europe. In my opinion, the resistance movement will not be able to spread beyond certain circles and groups of people.

The activities of the Roman Catholic Church should not go unmentioned, although it works very secretively and skilfully. Its key targets are:

a) to ensure the preservation of the national character of the peasants through closer association with the Polish Catholic Church,
b) the patriotic national education of the popular masses along religious lines,
c) the greatest caution in the performance of its national duty; clergymen should never give the Germans cause to attack the Church as a political organization.

Even if it is extremely difficult for the Security Police to combat these resistance forces on account of the specific nature of the circumstances, this does not mean that combatting them is beset with insuperable difficulties. Here, too, it may be said that political opponents do not pose a danger because we know precisely how they operate and by what methods they seek to influence the population.

The Jews have been keeping relatively calm, particularly recently. As they have been kept extremely short of food and earning opportunities, their energy reserves are devoted exclusively to these things. Offences detected by the Security Police have been mainly of a criminal nature, for example clandestine trading, theft, bribery, the forgery of identity documents and passports, etc.

A few statistics may also serve to illustrate the work of the police, in particular the Security Police:

In the last two years approximately 7,000 persons have had to be transferred to concentration camps for political and criminal offences. At present 2,811 prisoners are being held in prisons here, of whom 1,290 men and 268 women have been detained for political offences. The recent rise in crime, in particular aggravated and petty theft, fraud, small-scale theft of food and consumables, manslaughter, and robbery, is in certain respects an indicator of the population's general situation in terms of the availability of food and the economic circumstances. Despite the energetic deployment of the Criminal Police, the offences mentioned have risen slightly from month to month. In the last quarter

38 In the remainder of his presentation, Fribolin drew attention to the fact that it had been possible for the city's budget to be kept 'in order' and called for the 'greatest possible thrift'. When the government meeting resumed on 16 Oct. 1941, it began with a report from Governor Fischer's chief of staff, Herbert Hummel. His remarks were followed by a presentation on the Polish resistance movement by Arpad Wigand (1906–1983), railway operations assistant; joined the NSDAP in 1926 and the SS in 1931; inspector of the Security Police and the SD in Breslau, 1937–1941; SS and Police Leader in Warsaw, July 1941 – May 1942; subsequently served with the Waffen-SS; in British captivity in 1945; later extradited to Poland, where he was sentenced to life imprisonment in 1950; deported to West Germany in 1956; sentenced by Hamburg Regional Court to twelve and a half years in prison in 1981.

alone almost 11,000 people had to be arrested by the Criminal Police, among them 4,000 alone for theft.

[…][39]

## DOC. 16

## On 11 November 1941 the commissioner for the Jewish residential district in Warsaw sums up the Jewish population's situation after two years of German occupation[1]

Report by the commissioner for the Jewish residential district in Warsaw, signed A. [Heinz Auerswald], Warsaw, dated 11 November 1941 (draft)[2]

*Two Years of Development Work in District Warsaw:*
*The Jews in District Warsaw*

I. *The situation when the administration was taken over*
During the years from 1918 to 1933, the Jews in Germany succeeded in a truly monstrous fashion in strengthening the influence they had already acquired in Imperial Germany. Benefiting from the conditions of the Systemzeit,[3] they grabbed one position after another, with the result that they eventually came to hold key roles in all areas of politics, business, and cultural life.

At the same time the 'German' Jews drew fresh supplies of human material from the eastern lands, above all from the Republic of Poland. When these Jews arrived at the Schlesischer Bahnhof [railway station] in Berlin, they were still wearing their kaftans. The streets to the east of Alexanderplatz were crawling with Ostjuden.[4] But only a short time later, having adapted externally to their surroundings, they moved to the western parts of the city, and finally into Berlin's exclusive suburbs.

39 Wigand went on to discuss the functions of the Order Service and demanded the 'toughest penalties' to combat 'political' criminality: AIPN, GK 196/377 (NTN 377), fol. 3893. He was followed by Kreishauptmann Zimmermann, who spoke on behalf of the Kreishauptleute; Naumann then reported on the food situation, Emmerich on economic questions, Frauendorfer on the situation of Polish workers, Schulte-Wissermann on price controls, Watzke on the school system for Germans, Wille on the justice system, and Schönhals on the police, before Frank finished by commenting on what had been said. Apart from the speakers mentioned, the meeting was also attended by the following: Bartsch, Bauder, Bittrich, Blauert, Boepple, Buttkus, Fattgen, Gollert, Gramß, Greiff, Heim, Köhler, Krug, Laumann, Meisinger, Nowakowsky, Ohlenbusch, Ruppert, Schepers, Seifert, Schön, Valentin, Weirauch, Westfal, and others [list partially illegible].

1 APW, Office of the Governor of District Warsaw, Commissioner for the Jewish Residential District, Transfer Bureau 482/1, fols. 25–31. Published in Friedrich Gollert, *Zwei Jahre Aufbau im Distrikt Warschau* (Warsaw: Buchverlag Deutscher Osten, 1941), pp. 68–76. This document has been translated from German.

2 There is a handwritten note at the top left: 'Oct./Nov. 1941'. The date 11 Nov. 1941 is derived from the letter that Auerswald enclosed with the typescript he had corrected.

3 German for 'system era', a term used by the National Socialists to refer disparagingly to the period of the Weimar Republic.

4 The Scheunenviertel, where Jewish immigrants from Eastern Europe had settled, was located close to Alexanderplatz.

Any German coming to the occupied Polish territories in October 1939 was therefore prepared from the outset to encounter the native land of all these Ostjuden. Indeed, even during the September campaign there was no ignoring the large Jewish section of the population. Whenever German troops arrived at a town or village, the usual Jewish types immediately turned up to beg or to sell something to the Germans.

Just like in Germany and other countries of Central and Western Europe, the Jews had managed to gain crucial influence over all areas of life in the Republic of Poland as well. They held positions in the Polish authorities, they played a role in cultural life, and, above all, they were the ones pulling the strings in industry, trade, and commerce.

A key difference from the conditions in Germany was, however, that the Jews here were not primarily active as merchants or as intellectuals; instead there were hordes of Jewish craftsmen and Jewish labourers as well. In short, the German administration not only had the task of breaking the influence the Jews continued to exert on business and cultural life here after the Polish campaign, but rather it found itself primarily faced with the problem of dealing with a Jewish section of the population that was extraordinarily strong in numerical terms.

Conditions in the city of Warsaw were particularly challenging in this respect. Of the roughly 1.2 million inhabitants of Warsaw before the war, approximately one third were Jews. In some city districts the population was 80 or even 90 per cent Jewish. Jewification was manifest in the streets throughout the city.

II. *The need to create Jewish residential districts*

Unless they had already 'made it' and were residing in the Polish parts of the city, these Jews – as mentioned, largely labourers and craftsmen – lived in indescribably unhygienic conditions. The streets in the Jewish quarters of the city were populated by a throng of jostling, haggling, gesticulating Jews reminiscent of the Orient. If you drove past, you were so struck by the stench that you accelerated. The backyards and flats that it was occasionally necessary to enter during police operations presented scenes of dilapidation and filth that would scarcely be found anywhere else.

These quarters of the city were the epicentres of outbreaks of typhus, typhoid fever, dysentery, and other infectious diseases. Efforts to shield German members of the Wehrmacht and officials as well as the Polish population from major epidemics inevitably appeared hopeless from the very outset, as long as it was not possible to isolate the Jewish epicentre of the epidemics to some extent. This was the first, and at the same time the most compelling, consideration pointing to the creation of Jewish residential districts.

In addition to this, there were other, no less serious considerations. Although the legislative measures taken to eliminate the Jews' influence on cultural life and the economy did achieve a certain degree of success in the initial period of German administration, it became increasingly clear that measures of this kind would ultimately not suffice. For these reasons, too, steps therefore had to be taken towards gathering the Jews together in one place.

In the end this was also the only way of realizing the wish to see typically Jewish characteristics disappear from the city's streets. In the long term it seemed intolerable to keep encountering Jews wherever one went in a large city like Warsaw and to put up with all the difficulties that were bound to crop up if Jews enjoyed unrestricted freedom of movement in a territory under German sovereignty.

This is why a Jewish residential district came to be created in the city of Warsaw in 1940 – earlier than in the other districts of the General Government.[5]

III. *The Jewish residential districts in District Warsaw*

Shortly after the occupation of the city of Warsaw, those parts of the city that were overwhelmingly inhabited by Jews were declared an epidemic containment zone. In order to reduce the risk of infection, the zone was off limits to Germans. This measure did not, however, involve any effective population regrouping. Polish and even ethnic German residents were allowed to continue living in the epidemic containment zone, while Jews who lived scattered across the whole urban area did not need to move their places of residence into the containment zone.

Consultations about the creation of one or more Jewish residential districts in the city of Warsaw then began in the spring. The Resettlement Department in the Office of the District Governor was dealing with this question at the time. It initially planned to establish two Jewish residential districts on the outskirts of the city. After the preliminary work had been suspended for a while, it was finally decided in August to establish a Jewish residential district in the part of the city that had already been overwhelmingly inhabited by Jews until then, that is to say, on the site of the former epidemic containment zone.

This plan was implemented in October and November 1940. The resettlement measures affected about 700 ethnic Germans, 113,000 Poles, and 138,000 Jews. About 11,500 non-Jewish dwellings in the Jewish residential district and 13,800 Jewish dwellings in the rest of the city were relinquished.

As can be seen from the enclosed map, the perimeter of this Jewish residential district encloses an area of roughly 400 hectares. Some 450,000 to 500,000 Jews live inside it.[6] The original number of Jews there, just over 400,000, has increased because the Jews living in the western Kreise of District Warsaw were resettled in the Jewish residential district in Warsaw in February and March 1941.[7] The precise number of residents at present cannot be stated; it will only be ascertained once the census planned for the near future has been carried out.

The Jewish residential district in Warsaw is a closed-off district. This means the area in question is closed off from the outside world by walls, fences, and the like, and people and goods are only allowed in and out with special permission. The following can be said about its administrative structure:

A Jewish Council, which in Warsaw consists of twenty four members and is led by a chairman,[8] was created in 1939 as a representative body for the Jews. Based on the au-

5 See PMJ 4/180 and 188.

6 The last two sentences are not included in the published version: Gollert, *Zwei Jahre Aufbau*, p. 72. The published version does not include a map of the ghetto area either.

7 See PMJ 4/236 and 252.

8 Adam Czerniaków (1880–1942), engineer; studied chemistry in Warsaw and engineering in Dresden; taught at a Jewish vocational school in Warsaw; member of Warsaw City Council, 1927–1934; representative for Jewish craftsmen on the Jewish Community Council; appointed head of the Jewish Religious Community of Warsaw by the Stadtpräsident of Warsaw on 23 Sept. 1939; made chairman of the Warsaw Jewish Council by the Gestapo on 4 Oct. 1939; took his own life when the German authorities demanded in summer 1942 that he and the Jewish Council participate in the organization of deportations to Treblinka.

thority granted by the Regulation on the Jewish Residential District in Warsaw of 19 April 1941, the functions and powers of a mayor were transferred to the chairman of the Jewish Council in Warsaw under the directive of 14 May 1941.[9] This signifies that the Jewish residential district in Warsaw is an autonomous municipality, the mayor of which conducts municipal affairs entirely under his own responsibility.

German supervision was initially exercised by the head of the Resettlement Department.[10] The office of a commissioner for the Jewish residential district was then created under the above-mentioned regulation of 19 April 1941. The commissioner, who reports directly to the [District] Governor, oversees the Jewish administration like a Stadthauptmann. The Transfer Bureau Warsaw (mentioned in an earlier chapter of this book) was established to broker economic transactions between the Jewish residential district and the outside world.[11] This body, which is also overseen by the commissioner for the Jewish residential district, has the task of monitoring and promoting economic transactions in the Jewish residential district.

In accordance with its designated functions, the Jewish administration has an administrative apparatus staffed exclusively by Jews, which performs all the functions of a municipal administration. For example, the chairman of the Jewish Council has a Health Section, Billeting Office, Registration Office, a designated Tax and Finance Section, and so on. Not only that, a range of additional institutions have been created in the Jewish residential district in Warsaw in order to ease the burden on German and Polish administrative agencies and reduce the number of Aryans deployed in the Jewish residential district where possible. The 2,000-strong Jewish Order Service should be mentioned in this regard. It is under the supervision of the German and the Polish police and has the task of policing order, trade, and sanitation as well as administering the Jewish postal service. The latter takes delivery of all the post for the Jewish residential district from the German Post Office East and distributes it in the Jewish residential district, as well as collecting outgoing post and forwarding it in consolidated shipments. Jewish transport enterprises and similar facilities complete the profile [of the Jewish administration].

In terms of the economy, a series of measures have been taken to deploy Jewish labour to good effect. In 1941 the Jewish workshops have fulfilled orders placed by the Aryan side of the economy, with a continual increase in the number of employees, and they have above all worked extensively on processing orders from the Wehrmacht. Food and other supplies have been procured by the Supply Office for the Jewish residential

9 Governor General Frank's Regulation on the Jewish Residential District in Warsaw (19 April 1941) provided for the appointment of a commissioner: *VOBl-GG*, 1941, no. 35, 28 April 1941, pp. 211–212. See also Doc. 15, fn. 14.

10 Waldemar Karl Schön (1904–1969), lawyer; joined the SA and the NSDAP in 1930; head of training for Merseburg local NSDAP branch in 1930; Kreis head of training in 1932; held several Party offices including deputy Kreisleiter from 1933 and Reichsredner (Reich orator) from 1938; Reichsamtsleiter with the NSDAP Reichsleitung from 1939; head of the Resettlement Department in District Warsaw from Jan. 1940; head of the Interior Administration in District Warsaw from 1941; clerical worker and later lawyer in Freising (Bavaria) after the war.

11 According to the chapter on the structure of the administration in District Warsaw (Gollert, *Zwei Jahre Aufbau*, pp. 39–51, here p. 50): 'A Transfer Bureau, which is a public institution by law, serves to regulate the Jewish residential district's economic relations with the outside world.'

district,[12] which, under the supervision of the Transfer Bureau Warsaw, purchases the goods required and distributes them within the Jewish residential district in accordance with the commissioner's instructions.

Apart from the Jews found in the Jewish residential district in Warsaw, another approximately 110,000 Jews are living *in the [Warsaw] District's eastern Kreise*. These Jews have been gathered together in a few smaller, closed-off residential districts, for instance at Siedlce and Sokolow, as well as in a larger number of residential districts that are not closed off. In addition to this, a small number of Jews still live in various rural communities.[13]

IV. *Experience and evaluation*

The Jewish residential district in Warsaw has now been in existence for approximately a year. The experience gathered during this year is extremely valuable when it comes to judging whether the measures taken hitherto have been expedient.

In this respect, one thing has been abundantly clear from the start: the creation of a closed-off Jewish residential district in the city of Warsaw was the right way to reduce the spread of typhus to the Aryan population. Despite the close proximity between the Jewish residential district and the rest of the city of Warsaw, despite a range of shortcomings in closing off this district, and despite many other comparatively adverse factors in the city, this measure ensured that for a long time only 10 per cent of all typhus cases were found among the Aryan population [of the city of Warsaw], while during the same period the proportion [of typhus cases] in the Aryan population was 30 per cent or more in the eastern Kreise, where a more radical concentration of Jews had not yet been carried out. This finding alone justifies the establishment of the Jewish residential district at that time.

However, it has also become apparent that the Aryan population cannot be completely protected from typhus if the principle of isolating the Jews is not implemented with the necessary rigour. The existence of a large Jewish residential district in the middle of a city requires clear and comprehensible arrangements for its perimeters, and any misplaced sentimentality must be dispensed with as far as the monitoring of these perimeters is concerned. Moreover, broadly identical conditions need to be established over as large an area as possible, so that Jews have no incentive to leave their Jewish residential district.

In terms of the economy – this too has already been shown by the experience gained to date – satisfactory results can be achieved, even with a construct as undoubtedly difficult as a Jewish residential district of 500,000 inhabitants. However, this depends on the presence of an effective brokering organization of the kind represented by the Transfer Bureau Warsaw. In this respect, the aim must always be to deploy the Jewish labour force

12 The Jewish Council's Supply Office was responsible for distributing foodstuffs that were supplied legally to the ghetto.

13 The last sentence was crossed out and is not included in the published version: Gollert, *Zwei Jahre Aufbau*, p. 74. In a letter to the district's chief of staff, Herbert Hummel, dated 11 Nov. 1941, Auerswald asked for the sentence to be removed because it would 'no longer correspond to the actual situation at the time when the publication comes out': APW, Office of the Governor of District Warsaw, Commissioner for the Jewish Residential District, Transfer Bureau 482/1, fol. 39.

to the maximum possible advantage in line with the requirements of the war. At the very least it should be ensured that their work is productive and that the proceeds from it are sufficient to meet the Jews' basic needs, so that there is no disproportionate recourse to welfare funds.

The experience gained with regard to the Jewish administration allows the conclusion that the Jews' organizational skills do not correspond to their average intelligence. With a host of salaried employees, commissions, and meetings, in short with a vast administrative effort, the Jews only rarely succeed in sorting things out themselves. In their dealings with one another they are crassly egotistical, and their welfare activities cannot conceal the fact that all individuals are ultimately only thinking of their own advantage. They are very far from forming a community.

At the same time, their representatives carry out the German supervisory agency's instructions satisfactorily on the whole. Insofar as this is the case, it has certainly proven to be the right strategy to deploy a relatively small number of German personnel in an exclusively supervisory capacity and to leave the administration itself to the Jews, recruiting the few who have any organizational aptitude.

All in all, one is justified in concluding that the approach taken in District Warsaw was the right one, also in view of the larger political contexts that could not be addressed in this account.[14]

14 In the published version, the final paragraph has been replaced with: 'It goes without saying that all the measures taken in this field are only interim measures until the Jewish question is resolved on a unitary basis for the whole of Europe after the war. Until then, however, the Jewish residential districts will serve their purpose as precursors of the future "Jewish reservations" envisaged by Alfred Rosenberg': Gollert, *Zwei Jahre Aufbau*, p. 76.

## DOC. 17

## On 21 November 1941 the Senior Commander of the Security Police in the General Government gives orders for Jews discovered outside their mandatory place of residence to be shot[1]

Letter (marked 'secret') from the Senior Commander of the Security Police and the SD in the General Government (III A – 627/41g), unsigned,[2] Cracow, to the commanders of the Security Police; SS Obersturmbannführer Großkopf[3] or his representative in office, Cracow; SS Obersturmbannführer Dr Tanzmann[4] or his representative in office, Lemberg; SS Sturmbannführer Müller[5] or his representative in office, Lublin; SS Sturmbannführer Liphardt[6] or his representative in office, Radom; SS Sturmbannführer Dr Hahn[7] or his representative in office, Warsaw; dated 21 November 1941 (copy of a copy)[8]

*Re*: spreading of typhus by vagrant Jews

According to § 4b of the Third Regulation on Restrictions on Movement in the General Government (15 October 1941), Jews who leave their assigned residential district without authorization are to be punished with death.[9] Judgement is to be passed on them by the special courts. The likely result of this regulation is that following their capture Jews will have to spend at least a few days, if not weeks, in prison, where they will spread typhus.

1 AIPN, GK 362/633, fol. 15. This document has been translated from German.

2 Dr Eberhard Schöngarth (1903–1946), lawyer; in 1922 joined the NSDAP for the first time and the SA; rejoined the NSDAP and joined the SS in 1933; worked for the Gestapo in Westphalia from 1935; inspector of the Security Police and the SD in Dresden in 1939; Senior Commander of the Security Police and the SD (BdS) in the General Government, Jan. 1941 – July 1943; commander of the Einsatzgruppe z.b.V. ('for special assignments') in Eastern Galicia in summer 1941; attended the Wannsee Conference in Jan. 1942; BdS in the Netherlands from June 1944; sentenced to death by a British military court and executed for a war crime committed in the Netherlands.

3 Dr Max Großkopf (1892–1945), lawyer and economist; joined the NSDAP and the SA in 1932 and the SS in 1935; served with the Gestapo from 1933; Commander of the Security Police and the SD (KdS) in District Cracow, August 1940 – summer 1943; subsequently head of the Gestapo office in Graz; liaison officer to the collaborationist Russian Liberation Army led by Andrey Vlasov; committed suicide at the end of the war.

4 Dr Hellmut Tanzmann (1907–1946), lawyer; joined the NSDAP and the SA in 1933; worked at the Saxon Ministry of Finance; worked for the Gestapo in Danzig from 1937; simultaneously inspector of the Security Police and the SD in Danzig from Sept. 1940; thereafter head of Section I/II (Law and Administration) of the BdS in the General Government; KdS in District Galicia, Sept. 1941 – March 1943; thereafter served in the south of France; then in Norway, 1944–1945; committed suicide while in British captivity.

5 Johannes Müller (1895–1961), police detective; joined the NSDAP in 1933 and the SS in 1939; worked for the Gestapo in Dresden in 1938 and for the Gestapo in Warsaw in 1940; KdS in District Warsaw, March–July 1941, then KdS in District Lublin until Sept. 1943; deputy head of the Criminal Police in Hessen after the war; member of the Social Democratic Party of Germany (SPD); took early retirement in 1954; arrested in 1960; died in prison in 1961 while awaiting trial.

6 Fritz Liphardt (1905–1947), lawyer; served in the Reichswehr, 1924–1926; joined the NSDAP and the SA in 1933 and the SS in 1936; worked for the Gestapo in Stettin in 1935; head of the Gestapo in Frankfurt an der Oder in 1938; member of an Einsatzkommando in Poland in Sept. 1939; KdS in District Radom and Oberregierungsrat from Nov. 1939; head of the Gestapo Head Office in Stettin from Nov. 1943; died in prison in Poland while awaiting trial.

Since it is well known that Jews only allow themselves to be detained if force is used, and usually mount resistance and exploit every opportunity to escape, in consultation with the Higher SS and Police Leader firearms should be used as far as possible. I therefore order that Jews found roaming in this fashion are to be shot immediately if they put up even the slightest resistance or try to escape. This order is to be applied stringently in order to put an effective stop to the danger of typhus being spread by vagrant Jews who have left the ghetto without authorization.[10]

Reports concerning the effect of this order are to be submitted to me on an ongoing basis.

## DOC. 18

## *Der Mittag*, 21 November 1941: article on Polish and Ukrainian support for the exclusion of the Jews from economic life[1]

*Jewry's Powerful Position in Poland*

*Warsaw, mid November*

The impact of the German measures against Jewry in the General Government, above all the creation of closed-off Jewish residential districts in the towns and cities and all the ensuing consequences, the purging of the Jewish parasites from the countryside, and, above all, the complete elimination of Jewry from the economy, is unfolding in the midst of the Polish and Ukrainian populations, right before their eyes. Since these two largest ethnic groups in the General Government have for centuries had to live closely together with Jewry in its vilest incarnation – Eastern Jewry – it is of the greatest interest to observe how the non-Jewish population has reacted to being liberated from their bloodsuckers by the Germans.

The Polish population has harboured a virulent hatred of the Jews since time immemorial. In the course of Polish history, this hatred has frequently led to the princes and the cities taking stringent combative measures, and to bloody pogroms against the Jews. This hatred by no means abated when the founding of the Versailles Polish state gave the Poles the opportunity to use legislative measures to at least put the Jews who were

7 Dr Ludwig Hahn (1908–1986), lawyer; joined the NSDAP in 1930 and the SS in 1933; worked at the SD Main Office in 1935; head of Einsatzkommando 1 of Einsatzgruppe I in Poland in Sept. 1939; subsequently Stadtkommissar and mayor of Rzeszów; commander of the SD in District Cracow, Jan.–August 1940; then worked at the Reich Security Main Office (RSHA); head of Einsatzgruppe Griechenland in April 1941, then KdS in District Warsaw and Oberregierungsrat from August 1941; went into hiding after the war; worked for an insurance company from 1949; sentenced to life imprisonment in 1975.

8 Under the copy is a handwritten note: 'Received in Breslau by SS-Untersturmführer [name barely legible, probably: Bredehoeft]. B. 18 Sept. 1942 S. II'.

9 See Doc. 13.

10 The Senior Commander of the Order Police (BdO) in the General Government, Gerhard Winkler, subsequently issued his own shoot-to-kill order, authorizing police officers to shoot Jews whom they encountered on public thoroughfares outside the ghetto: see Doc. 26.

1 *Der Mittag*, 21 Nov. 1941, p. 2. *Der Mittag* was a popular illustrated daily that covered politics, transport, sport, and art. It was published by Droste-Verlag in Düsseldorf from 1920 to 1944, and again from 1949 to 1964, with changing subtitles. This document has been translated from German.

flooding all areas of public life in their rightful place. If this did not happen, if, on the contrary, the Jews gained the upper hand in some sectors of the economy after 1918 and more or less monopolized them, this was purely because the Polish upper class, which lived a profligate life, *was heavily in debt to Jewish financiers* and in political terms believed it owed it to the democracies of the West to be a strictly obedient child of the Jewish-liberal plutocracies in its attitude to the Jewish question as well. For its part, world Jewry protected the Polish state all the more because many of its prominent representatives knew their most immediate ancestors had their origins in the Warsaw or Lemberg ghettos. Many generous endowments from Jewish world organizations and millionaire Jews abroad were devoted to the establishment of academic or social institutions in former Poland. Despite this, the natural defensive instinct of the Aryan population, in certain areas with a high concentration of Germanic blood – above all in western and central Poland – was able to keep entirely new occupational groups free of Jewish infiltration. This applied to a certain degree to the judicial administration of the state and to other parts of the civil service, which had only a small percentage of Jews among their ranks. This phenomenon was perhaps attributable only to the Jewish intelligentsia's aversion to occupations that did not appear profitable enough.

*Jewish dominance in all areas of business life had an all the more unbridled impact.* Banks, industry, the wholesale trade, and the lucrative liberal professions became more and more the exclusive domain of Jewry. But even enterprises that were still nominally under non-Jewish management were almost completely subjected to Jewish influence through indirect channels via Jewish capital holdings. In contrast to other European nations, the inundation of Jews in the economy *also extended* to the *artisanal sector.* In certain trades and groups of skilled workers, above all in the shoe and textile industries, a non-Jew's son had virtually no prospect of being taken on as an apprentice any more. As a unique case, it may be mentioned that in Warsaw, for example, even *the roofers' guild consisted of more than 90 per cent Jews.* It seems to go without saying that housing in Polish towns and cities was overwhelmingly owned by Jews (e.g. more than two thirds in Warsaw). Nor can there be any doubt that the retail trade and the market and street trading that have a strong presence in the East would have been completely swallowed up by the Jews in the space of a few years.

Two years ago, when it became known that the German administration was intending to entirely eliminate the Jews from Polish economic life within a short period, Polish business circles as a whole were initially gripped by the fear that this tough intervention would inevitably cause a major new setback to the economy, which had largely collapsed in any case as a consequence of the lost military adventure against the Reich. To their great astonishment, thanks to carefully pre-planned cushioning and transitional measures, *the major operation on the body of the Polish economy was virtually pain-free.* This astonishment gave way to pleasant surprise when some Poles who had been able to salvage a proportion of their assets from the great debacle gained the opportunity to take a Jew's place and become a partner in a business. All of a sudden there were countless job openings for young craftsmen. The German authorities had to rapidly organize the specialized technical college system and the retraining of idle workers in order to secure the new entrants required for the job market. In numerous villages where, in the form of interest on debts and tacitly extorted tributes, the Jews had siphoned off the peasants' meagre yields like parasites, the population breathed a sigh of relief.

For all these reasons, the Polish population, and especially the Ukrainian population, are following the measures taken under the German policy towards Jews in the General Government with enthusiastic or at least approving interest. Frequently it can even be observed that Poles who have to deal with Jewish affairs because they are in the employ of Germans need to be told firmly not to act more harshly than is necessary to achieve the desired purpose. Such cases show the population's centuries of hatred at being plundered by Jewry bubbling up under the surface.

## DOC. 19
## On 23 November 1941 Emanuel Ringelblum describes a Hashomer Hatzair ceremony in the Warsaw ghetto[1]

Handwritten notes by Emanuel Ringelblum,[2] dated 23 November 1941

A young man arrived today from a labour camp. Having nothing to live on, he has decided to try his luck on the Aryan side. He is not afraid of the death sentence[3] because the ghetto is [tantamount to] a death sentence [anyway]. The general opinion is that the death sentences will have little effect on [discouraging people from] going over to the other side because people are so desperate.

I attended a Hashomer Hatzair[4] celebration today. Almost 500 young people of both sexes gathered in the hall for a very diverse programme. One thing that stood out was how they incorporated lots of songs – Yiddish ones, of course, as well as Hebrew, Russian, and Polish. A new group was solemnly inducted into 'Hashomer'. At the end they let out a collective cry of 'chazak ve-ematz',[5] which shook not only the hall, but the whole building as well. In attendance at the celebration was a leading representative of the Polish Scout Association, who had smuggled herself into the ghetto specifically for this day.[6] She had learned by chance that a Reich German, who was in close contact with

1 AŻIH, Ring I/449 (507/1), fol. 195–196. Published in Emanuel Ringelblum, *Ksovim fun geto*, vol. 1: *Togbukh fun varshever geto, 1939–1942*, ed. Tatiana Berenstein et al. (Warsaw: Yidish bukh, 1961), pp. 319–320. This document has been translated from Yiddish.

2 Dr Emanuel Ringelblum (1900–1944), teacher and historian; studied in Warsaw; member of the Poale Zion-Left party; representative of the American Jewish Joint Distribution Committee (JDC) in Zbąszyn (Neu-Bentschen) refugee camp, 1938–1939; took part in the 21st Zionist Congress in Geneva in August 1939; founder and head of the underground archive of the Warsaw ghetto (Oyneg Shabes) in 1940; went into hiding after the Warsaw Ghetto Uprising until March 1944, when he was found and shot dead by the Germans.

3 On 17 Nov. 1941 eight death sentences handed down by the German Special Court in Warsaw for leaving the ghetto without authorization had been carried out: see Docs. 25 and 30.

4 Hebrew: the 'Young Guard'. Founded in 1913 in Galicia, which was then part of the Austro-Hungarian Empire, this secular youth movement embraced the principles of socialism and Zionism. In its early days Hashomer Hatzair was heavily influenced by the scout movement.

5 The movement's motto and a standard scout greeting; Hebrew: 'Be strong and brave'. It occurs on several occasions in the Old Testament: Deuteronomy 31:7, 23; Joshua 1:6, 7, 9.

6 Irena Adamowicz (1910–1963), social worker; leader of the Polish Scouts in the 1930s; courier for the Union of Armed Struggle during the German occupation; transmitted messages between ghettos in German-occupied Poland and Lithuania in 1942; honoured as Righteous Among the Nations by the State of Israel in 1985.

Hashomer before the war as the leader of the Polish Scout Association,[7] had sent greetings from the front near Leningrad to the conference that took place a while ago. In general, the extraordinary boldness that the Hashomer people have demonstrated must be commended. They organize conferences attended by leading representatives from the Reich,[8] who travel there on foot; they do educational work[9] on a large scale; and they publish a paper, which is on a very high […].[10]

Meat is smuggled into the ghetto in two ways: as live animals or as slaughtered livestock. Live horses are brought in as follows: a wagon enters with two horses and leaves with just one. I heard that on Franciszkańska Street people are buying up military saddles and using them to make soles for shoes. It is an altogether interesting phenomenon that soldiers are selling everything.

## DOC. 20
## In or after November 1941 the journalist A. M. Rogowy makes proposals for the improvement of Jewish welfare provision in the Warsaw ghetto[1]

Proposals by A. M. Rogowy,[2] Warsaw, dated November 1941 or later[3]

*'ZOS'*[4] *or 'SOS'?*
With the coming of spring, the Jewish Welfare Service in Warsaw's Jewish district was able to relocate. This happened as a result of the changes to the perimeter of the [Jewish] district.[5] The new, refurbished, and properly renovated premises make a very good impression. Unfortunately the same cannot be said of the work itself, especially during the transition period. The move took place right before the holidays, and although it was foreseen well in advance and there was enough time to make the necessary preparations, the helmsmen[6] lost their grip on the rudder. General confusion erupted before the holidays,[7] which had an impact on the entire holiday campaign.

What happened with regard to our welfare work in the period leading up to the holidays cannot be described in words. Even the strongest criticism casts too flattering a light on the reality, which presents itself in a much harsher light. There was a holiday

7 The Polish Scout Association was active in the underground during the German occupation and carried out small acts of sabotage; many of its members fought in the Warsaw Uprising in summer 1944.
8 Presumably a reference to members of youth associations who came to Warsaw from the territories of western Poland annexed by the Reich.
9 One word is illegible here; the addition is based on Ringelblum, *Ksovim fun geto*, vol. 1, p. 320.
10 The corner of the original document is torn; probably: 'level'. Hashomer Hatzair published a number of underground newspapers in Warsaw.

1 AŻIH, Ring II/321 (115). Published in English translation in Joseph Kermish (ed.), *To Live with Honor and Die with Honor! Selected Documents from the Warsaw Ghetto Underground Archives 'O.S.' ('Oneg Shabbath')*, trans. M.Z. Prives et al. (Jerusalem: Yad Vashem, 1986), pp. 359–361. This document has been newly translated from Polish.
2 A. M. Rogowy (Mordechaj Abram Rogovoj); editor of *Dos Yudishe Togblat*, a daily newspaper published by the Orthodox party Agudas Yisroel prior to Sept. 1939; thereafter head of a welfare centre which distributed aid supplies to Orthodox religious intellectuals; contributed to the *Gazeta Żydowska*, the only legal newspaper for the Jewish population in occupied Poland; murdered in Treblinka in 1942.
3 The original contains handwritten corrections and underlining.

campaign,[8] but it was a mere drop in the ocean in view of the prevailing misery and *sheer need* of the population in the [Jewish] district. The food delivered to the population was barely enough for one day – and certainly not for eight days. So we witnessed the hunger of those under our care and the tragic helplessness of our patrons. The Passover tradition[9] was unscrupulously defiled without those under our care benefiting in any way at all. Thus it came to pass, in the words of a popular Jewish saying: 'He ate rotten fish and was driven out of the city.'[10]

The Jewish Council and its Supply Office[11] followed the voice of faith and tradition. In an announcement made by the chairman of the Council[12] regarding the distribution of food during the holidays, it was made clear that bread would not be baked or distributed during this period. The religious feelings of the population were respected, thereby honouring our time-honoured sacred customs. The population acknowledged this in the appropriate manner. On the other hand, our honourable gentlemen activists 'of the people' scoffed at it all: If the poor were to starve, then let hunger reign everywhere, not only in the belly, but also in the spirit …[13]

And what happened after the holidays, when our activists had already settled into their nicely renovated premises – did the supply situation improve then? In a nutshell: No. Nowadays, few 'gala' events take place at certain food distribution points[14] during the week. An astute and ingenious idea. The easiest solution in the world to the problem. One need only have a head on one's shoulders and a sharp mind. Then a patentable method will be found.

Or perhaps there is no other method? Perhaps there really is no way to increase the resources for welfare provision? [The answer to that is] a definite: No. Those who can look the truth in the face will not say that. On the contrary, we are all convinced that much, much more can be done; only the system of (supposedly) 'voluntary' donations that currently prevails has failed. There are suitable resources. In influential circles it is

4 In Oct. 1940 the Jewish Social Self-Help Coordinating Committee (Żydowska Samopomoc Społeczna-Komisja Koordynacyjna, ŻSS-KK) was renamed the Jewish Social Welfare Association (Żydowski Towarzystwo Opieki Społecznej, ŻTOS) and came under the authority of the Jewish Municipal Aid Committee in Warsaw (Żydowski Komitet Opiekuńczy Miejski w Warszawie, ŻKOM). After the German authorities changed the Jewish Social Self-Help's statutes, ŻTOS was renamed the Jewish Welfare Service (Żydowska Opieka Społeczna, ŻOS) in late Nov. 1941 and it maintained its organizational independence under this name until March 1942, when it was formally incorporated into the ŻKOM.

5 The perimeters of the ghetto were narrowed several times after it had been sealed.

6 This is presumably a reference to those described critically here as the 'honourable general activists' of the ŻOS.

7 The Passover holidays began on 12 April 1941.

8 This is a reference to the collection of donations prior to the holidays; the proceeds were used for charitable purposes.

9 Eating leavened food during the eight days of Passover is prohibited. The author probably means that the amount of unleavened bread (matzo) that had been distributed before Passover was insufficient.

10 The saying relates to the commentary by Mechilta de Rabbi Yishmael on the Beshalah section of the Torah, which relates to the exodus of the Israelites from Egypt.

11 The Jewish Council's Supply Office was responsible for distributing foodstuffs that were supplied legally to the ghetto.

12 Adam Czerniaków.

13 Ellipses here and below as in the original.

14 This is presumably a reference to the ŻTOS/ŻOS public or soup kitchens.

said that a curse hangs over us, so that no one sets about implementing these resources. As soon as people with drive and goodwill take the first step, our proverbial scholasticism immediately comes into play. When someone, speaking 'off the cuff', points out the need to introduce a *compulsory tax* for the benefit of the Welfare Service, spanners are immediately thrown in the works. As a result, everything remains as it was – except of course for the misery, which unfortunately does not stand still.

Yes, there is only one way: to put a radical end to the clumsy system of voluntary donations expressed by the acronym 'ŻOS' [Jewish Welfare Service]. Jokers turn this into 'Jewish Welfare Inertia'.[15] It is necessary to start again with a new system: a system that has a completely different acronym, namely 'SOS' …

Apart from the commonly known meaning of this acronym, in this case it would mean 'Sector for Social Welfare'[16] at the Jewish Council, which in any case accounts for the lion's share of the 'ŻOS' budget (the stomachs of the hungry account for the rest).

Why this hypocrisy? Why the multiple approaches? Why this action according to the motto 'out of the frying pan, into the fire'? This senseless talk, this proverbial 'pouring from empty vessels into empty vessels'? (After all, a few drops are always left in the bottom of every jug …) What is the point of all this?

We clearly have too many institutions dedicated to voluntary welfare work. We must merge all of these institutions, which rest on feet of clay and only increase the chaos and the disorder, and create a robust social welfare sector at the Jewish Council, funds for which would come from the following sources:

1) a compulsory general tax for the benefit of the Welfare Service, calculated according to actual wealth and consumption;
2) a special levy for all types of official services and consumer goods (as suggested by Chairman Gepner);[17]
3) funds that have already been disbursed for charitable purposes by the Jewish Council and its subordinate institutions.

I would just like to add that all the people who have previously been employed in the many different departments of the Welfare Service should be engaged in setting up this apparatus, and that their actual skills and knowledge should be taken into account.

In the new institution, there can be no room for anomalies in which people with higher education waste their time … writing addresses. Such things can be observed at every turn.

If we approach the matter in this way, boldly and courageously, with our goals and our intentions clear in our minds – it will be possible to rescue our Welfare Service from the morass of helplessness and inertia.

Remember, my honourable activists, that the former motto 'ŻOS' has been replaced by the new motto 'SOS'.

15 The acronym ŻOS stands for 'Żydowska Opieka Społeczna' – 'Jewish Welfare Service'; however, it can also be read as 'Żydowska Opieszałość Społeczna' – 'Jewish Welfare Inertia'.

16 Polish: 'Sektor Opieki Społecznej'. Department VI Welfare Services (Wydział VI Opieki Społecznej) was responsible for the provision of welfare services.

17 Abraham Gepner (1872–1943), businessman; member of Warsaw City Council prior to Sept. 1939; chairman of the Jewish Merchants' Association in Poland; head of the Warsaw Jewish Council's Supply Office, 1939–1943; supported the resistance activities of the Jewish youth organizations, 1942–1943; murdered during the Warsaw Ghetto Uprising.

## DOC. 21

## Sometime after November 1941 Stanisław Różycki assesses the relations between Poles and Jews in the Warsaw ghetto[1]

Handwritten copy of excerpts from a longer draft,[2] signed SR,[3] dated sometime after November 1941

*Polish–Jewish relations* (excerpts)

When dealing with this topic I find it difficult to rid myself of a sense of reluctance, because the poison of bitterness threatens to nullify all attempts to justify the Poles' behaviour towards the Jews, even if these attempts are objectively justified, marked by goodwill and a desire to forgive past sins.

It does not matter what happened. We have not forgotten how it was before the war, but we do not want to think about that now. But the Polish nation thinks that – after the Jewish one – it suffers the most out of all nations under the yoke of bondage. For this reason, it should above all have compassion for its fellow sufferers and show solidarity and courage under all circumstances. Unfortunately, this is but a dream. It is difficult today, from the perspective of the sealed ghetto, to grasp the totality of these relations and generalize this sad phenomenon. However, the reality of daily interactions reveals anew how painful and degrading this relationship is and there are no arguments to the contrary.

Nevertheless, let us try to evaluate it anyway to detect any traces of goodwill. So let us begin with the good sides.

The Poles who occasionally (but only rarely) come to the ghetto often give alms to the beggars on the streets. This is a healthy, immediate reflex of human mercy, of compassion for one's neighbour – which is what he is, despite everything. They give even more than generous Jewish citizens because for the first time, with horror, they see the death, hunger, and suffering on the streets, and they react to this first impression with a donation. Later, when they come more often, they become accustomed to the sight and refrain from giving alms. The heart hardens, the mind wins out. One has heard of cases in which starving Jews were given money or large donations in kind, and in Lwów the Poles have also contributed here and there. Many Poles safeguarded and safeguard furniture and Jewish valuables; they loyally look after them – and ensure that they are always available [to the owners] – without touching them or taking advantage of the situation. The same applies to the active, spontaneous, or systematic help given to Jewish acquaintances who are in distress or are living in catastrophic material circumstances. In the end, we know and appreciate that a large number of the enlightened intelligentsia and the educated workers display a commendable attitude towards us and our misfortune, which is expressed in the utmost compassion and in shows of solidarity.

But alas, that is the only good thing that can be said on this subject. Unfortunately the list of sins is much longer, and it is full of unforgivable sins that cry out to heaven

1 AŻIH, Ring I/659 (92), fols. 6–12. Published in English translation in Kermish (ed.), *To Live with Honor*, pp. 615–620. This document has been newly translated from Polish.
2 This has not survived in the underground archive materials.
3 The initials SR most likely stand for Stanisław Różycki; originally from Warsaw; fled to Lwów in 1939; moved to the Warsaw ghetto in autumn 1941; recorded his experiences and wrote several essays for the underground archive of the Warsaw ghetto in late 1941.

for vengeance. This unfortunately applies to the bulk of the population, in other words the so-called lower, uneducated social strata, as well as to all high-ranking officials.

It is enough to look at the faces and expressions of the youth, the hoodlums, the hussies, and the labourers who travel by tram through the Jewish part of town. They are merry, blithely telling each other unseemly and shameless jokes; they clearly display their satisfaction and Schadenfreude,[4] that the Jews have finally got what they had long hoped for. How cheerful, how thoughtless and mean they often appear when they watch the incidents on the bridge at Chłodna Street or at the crossing at Żelazna Street, or observe the mandatory searches at the ghetto entrances of people returning from forced labour. We know that one must not generalize: there is often a pitying silence, a horror in the eyes, a silent expression of solidarity. But it is what the rabble expresses – the youth, the women, the adolescents, the lumpenproletariat, the hooligans, the fringe elements educated in Endek[5] schools – that tips the scales, that hurts the innermost feelings and violates the dignity of those Jews who have no dealings with Poles as friends or comrades, from which they could take some comfort. It is all the sadder that this behaviour is not organized or directed. On the contrary, the Poles are not spurred on by any political calculation, nor is this behaviour even compatible with their own vital interests, their most sincere expectations. Therefore it is not a question of sympathy for parties or particular circles or social groups, but of direct, unvarnished reflexes, of an almost elemental joy that their hopes have finally been fulfilled. And so easily, without any action on their part, because even in their wildest dreams, the Endeks did not go so far as to build ghetto walls – and here all this has been so wonderfully set up for them.

Doing business with Jews? Of course. One can and one must. And to the greatest possible extent. There is equality here, there is no racial or national distinction. It is no sin to swindle a Jew. This is not a one-sided presentation of the problem, for let us state from the outset that the Poles generally do sound and honest business with the Jews, although they have the Jews in their grip, because when there is a dispute, the authorities throw the Jews in prison without much ado. Certainly the Poles make life possible for the Jews in the first place, because if they did not do business with them, if they did not smuggle goods, if they did not bring food, and if they did not take any used goods (clothes, furniture, jewellery), then the Jews would have no money, no food, and would die of hunger. But this is a two-way street.

Nevertheless, it has often happened – and still does – that furniture handed over for safekeeping, clothes, carpets, bed linen, household utensils, and other valuable items have disappeared without a trace. Nothing can be done about this. If the Polish trustee of a house, a business, or a factory is honest, he will pay the Jew his monthly salary. But if he does not want to do so, no one will stand up for the Jew. And there are unfortunately many malicious people. Whether they are the majority is impossible to say – no one can provide any reliable statistics. Some people can provide the names of a few hundred honest Poles, while others give an equal number of dishonest ones; both may be right, but one cannot draw general conclusions from this because I do not know who is in the majority. So, without generalizing, I can say that there are many such cases and that everyone knows about them, which is why it would be ridiculous and pointless to pro-

4 German in the original: 'gloating' or 'taking joy from another's misfortune'.

5 A reference to National Democracy (ND, or Endecja), led by Roman Dmowski (1864–1939).

vide names. It is also quite common for Poles to trick their Jewish business partners, to exploit their situation and not pay them. One has to admit that any Polish customer could do this without taking any risks. Nevertheless, most of them fulfil their obligations honestly. But there have also been cases in which someone has got rid of a Jewish creditor by handing him over to the authorities. In this way more than one human life has been destroyed, and the fault lies with the Polish customers.

We must not preach sermons on commercial ethics and unfair trade practices, because the Jews certainly have a lot to answer for in this respect and engage in fraud, unsound practices, and shoddy workmanship, and are frequently unreliable. But in this case we are concerned with the Poles, and it must be said that they have quickly learned all of these methods from the Jews and are rapidly applying them, including blackmail (which is perhaps the most common) and denunciation. How often they pretend to be Volksdeutsche[6] in order to scare the Jews and gain advantages! This does not apply to those merchants who cooperated with the Jews in their trade before the war and continue to do so now.

Cooperation with such merchants is beneficial for the ghetto. But the fresh-faced landlords, the merchants who naturally exploit circumstances for their short-term gain, the former officials, the opportunists who are loyal to everyone, the nouveaux riches who have found a common language with our smugglers and traffickers – these heroes of our times are not the most honest of people.

It is worst with the officials. Policemen, financial officials, prison staff, employees of the electricity and gas supply services, municipal officials, tram drivers, and all the rest – they are an affliction, a veritable plague. They all have bottomless pockets and voracious appetites; at every opportunity they extort and extract bribes, picking the last penny from a person's pocket. For every little thing, for every trivial occasion, one has to buy one's way free of such officials, because otherwise: denunciation, a report, an arrest, court, and prison, because when a Jew is accused, he must be convicted. For instance, say some tax official comes into a shop and slaps people in the face, regardless of whether they are men or women, if anyone resists him, he'll press charges. You can buy your way out of this with a large bribe. You have to pay for being slapped in the face – if it is to end with slaps in the face. An official enters an apartment, and because he had to knock five times before the door was opened, instead of a 'Good morning', he hits the lady of the house hard and draws blood. Another tax official enters the apartment of a tenant who has not paid on time; he explains that he actually has the right to hit the Jew, but that he will generously refrain from doing so for the time being. The officials and employees of the electricity company, the telephone company, the gas company, the waterworks, etc. simply shut down the relevant equipment repeatedly, demand a bribe, and then switch it back on again. And if one of these officials has money problems or fancies a bit of vodka, he returns a few days later and shuts it down again; or, for decency's sake, he sends another colleague who explains that he does not care what his predecessor did, there is a malfunction, this or that, and it will cost such-and-such an amount. At the same time, it is completely out of the question to discuss things with the official, to persuade him, or to unmask him, because this constitutes libel, an attempt to bribe the

6 German in the original: 'ethnic German'.

official, to insult him, to assault him, etc. Unfortunately, these are not isolated cases, but common everyday practices; every ghetto inhabitant has experienced this.

That they insult Jews without reason, address them as 'ty',[7] demean them, and treat them like dirt, like they are beneath them, is not worth mentioning. The Jews have already grown accustomed to this, which is why remarks such as 'Pay up, you stinking Jew!' or 'Don't hold your head too high!' have no impact on the course of business.

The worst are the policemen, who take the last pennies out of people's pockets at the slightest opportunity, without mercy or compassion. We have never experienced such depravity. If a Jew cannot or will not buy his freedom, they beat him at every opportunity, with a truncheon, with their hands; they kick, spit at, insult, and denounce him without scruple, for every imaginary misdemeanour. There is no point writing about their deeds; they are common knowledge. Even the Poles hate them. They are recruited from among former policemen, informants, or people who are half Polish [...].[8] This is therefore neither the time nor the place to discuss their methods because – to be honest – it sheds no light on Polish-Jewish relations, since even the Polish population rejects and shuns these policemen. On a different note, along with the Jewish policemen, they do excellent business smuggling at the ghetto walls every day. *Ambo meliores.*[9]

In the end, despite all this, it must be said that every merchant or member of the intelligentsia or of any other social group has a Polish benefactor who arranges things for him, helps him and enables him to survive, who takes care of life's necessities, or at least the bare essentials. Sometimes he stores something for him, sometimes he buys or sells something, sometimes he mediates or intervenes, sometimes he organizes protection, sometimes he lends something or provides support, sometimes he facilitates a contact or establishes a link to the world beyond the wall. This mixture of the noblest and the basest characteristics, which the Polish soul paradoxically harbours within itself, creates strange kinds of relationships. They reveal the noblest gestures as well as the bestial cruelty with which slaves are treated. It might be some consolation to think that these two extremes occur in every society. But our response to this has already been that we have no figures to shed light on the feelings and ideas that the majority of Poles associate with the Jews.

And one more thing. When talking about Polish-Jewish relations, then at least a few words must be said about the attitudes of the Jews towards the Poles. Let us leave aside trade relations, because in the here and now, completely different standards of behaviour prevail, which are not subject to the morality of the pre-war period. So first of all, one must say that the Jews remember with great appreciation and gratitude the charity and the helping hand that individual Poles extended to them. They will certainly never forget this, and they will thank them at the next opportunity. Now as for the insults and nastiness – they will not forget those either, but they no longer want to think about them. They have confidence in the Polish people. But there is one unpleasant thing: the explicit feeling of inferiority, this 'Inferioritätskomplex',[10] means that every Jew is still moved whenever someone says he looks like a Pole or praises his acquaintances and contacts with Poles, as if this alone were a great honour for him. Most Jews are subservient to-

7 Informal form of the word 'you' in Polish, used here in a derogatory way.
8 One word is illegible here.
9 Latin: 'both are better'; meaning: 'one is equal to the other'.
10 In German in the original: 'inferiority complex'.

wards Poles; they cajole, flatter, and ingratiate themselves as if they were indeed inferior. A Jewish woman is proud of a fleeting flirtation with a tram driver or mechanic; one bows deeply to a Pole, just as a Jewish tenant farmer once did before a nobleman. This cannot simply be put aside, because it has already become second nature.

## DOC. 22

## On 1 December 1941 Eichmann summarizes the results of a meeting between Heydrich and the Higher SS and Police Leader in Cracow about the 'final solution to the Jewish question'[1]

Note by the Chief of the Security Police and the SD, Section IV B 4–3076/41 g (1180), unsigned,[2] Berlin, dated 1 December 1941[3]

*Re*: final solution to the Jewish question

I. *Note*:

1) On 28 November 1941 SS-Obergruppenführer *Krüger*[4] called on the Chief of the Security Police and the SD[5] in order to discuss matters including the question of the

1 Archiv Ministerstva vnitra České Republiky (AMV), Reich Protector Collection, 114-2-56. Published as a facsimile and in English translation in Yehoshua Büchler, 'A Preparatory Document for the Wannsee "Conference"', *Holocaust and Genocide Studies*, vol. 9, no. 1 (1995), pp. 121–129, here pp. 122–123. This document has been newly translated from German.

2 This section was led by Adolf Eichmann (1906–1962), sales representative; joined the NSDAP and the SS in 1932; worked at the SD Main Office in Berlin between 1934 and 1938; from March 1938 had a leading role at the SD in Vienna in matters pertaining to the Jews; de facto head of Vienna's Central Office for Jewish Emigration from its establishment in 1938, and in a similar role at the Central Office for Jewish Emigration in Prague after the establishment of the Protectorate of Bohemia and Moravia in March 1939; organized the deportation of Jews from the territory of the Reich at the Reich Security Main Office (RSHA) from 1939; head of Section IV D 4 (evacuation affairs and the Reich Central Office for Jewish Emigration) from the start of 1940; head of Section IV B 4 (Jewish affairs and evacuation affairs) by March 1941; attended the Wannsee Conference in 1942; imprisoned, unrecognized, in an American detention camp, 1945–1946, and escaped in 1946; in hiding, first in Germany, 1946–1950, then in Argentina, 1950–1960; kidnapped by the Israeli secret service in 1960 and tried in Jerusalem, 1961–1962; sentenced to death and executed in Israel.

3 The original contains handwritten annotations and corrections, including to the date, where 'November' has been crossed out and replaced with '1 Dec.', above which 'to be filed' has been written; on the left is a handwritten note by Eichmann: 'Letter sent to II 1 and 2 on 1 Dec. [19]41'.

4 Friedrich-Wilhelm Krüger (1894–1945), office clerk; member of the Lützow Freikorps, 1919–1920; joined the NSDAP in 1929 and the SS in 1931; on the staff of the Reichsführer-SS in 1935; worked at the SS Main Office from 1936; Higher SS and Police Leader under the military commander in Łódź in Sept. 1939; Higher SS and Police Leader East for the General Government in Cracow and representative of the Reich Commissioner for the Strengthening of Germandom from Oct. 1939; additionally state secretary for security affairs in the General Government from May 1942; served in the war, Nov. 1943–1945; committed suicide.

5 Reinhard Heydrich (1904–1942), career officer; served in the navy, 1922–1931; joined the NSDAP and the SS in 1931; head of the SD from 1932; head of the Gestapo Central Office (Gestapa) in Berlin (which was initially only in charge of Prussia) from 1934; Chief of the Security Police and the SD, 1936–1942; head of the RSHA, 1939–1942; simultaneously Deputy Reich Protector of Bohemia and Moravia from Sept. 1941; died in Prague on 4 June 1942 following an assassination attempt.

centralized handling of Jewish affairs in the General Government. He said it had become ever more apparent from the recent measures taken in this regard in the General Government that the Governor General was endeavouring to take complete charge of the Jewish problem himself.
2) In the interests of settling and clarifying these matters, during the subsequent discussion the head of Section IV B 4 was instructed to have invitations to the meeting arranged for 9 December 1941 in Berlin[6] sent to State Secretary *Bühler*[7] and SS Obergruppenführer Krüger in addition to the central authorities already invited.
3) The following letters may be suggested:

II. *Letter*: (do not send as secret)
1) To State Secretary *Bühler, Cracow*
Dear Party Comrade Bühler,

On 31 July 1941 the Reich Marshal of the Greater German Reich[8] instructed me[9] to make all necessary preparations from an organizational, practical, and financial perspective for an overall solution to the Jewish question in Europe with the participation of the other relevant central authorities and to present him, in the near future, with an overall draft concerning this matter. I enclose a photocopy of this instruction with my letter.[10]

Given the extraordinary significance pertaining to these questions, and in the interests of reaching a common view among the relevant central authorities with regard to the other tasks connected with this final solution, I propose that these problems be made the subject of a joint discussion, particularly because evacuations of Jews to the East from Reich territory, including the Protectorate of Bohemia and Moravia, have been taking place at regular intervals since 15 October 1941.[11]

I therefore invite you to such a meeting, to be followed by breakfast, on 9 December 1941, 12 noon, at the Office of the International Criminal Police Commission, 16 Am Kleinen Wannsee, Berlin.

I have addressed similar letters to State Secretaries Stuckart, Dr Schlegelberger, Gutterer, and Neumann, and to Gauleiter Dr Meyer, SS-Obergruppenführer Krüger, Reichsamtsleiter Dr Leibbrandt, Undersecretary Luther, SS-Gruppenführer Hoff-

6 The meeting was later rescheduled for 20 Jan. 1942; it was held at the villa at 56–58 Am Großen Wannsee in Berlin. Senior Commander of the Security Police and the SD (BdS) Eberhard Schöngarth represented Higher SS and Police Leader Krüger at this event.
7 Dr Josef Bühler (1904–1948), lawyer; worked in Hans Frank's law firm, 1930–1932; joined the NSDAP in 1933; local court judge in 1933; chief public prosecutor at Munich Higher Regional Court in 1935; head of Frank's ministerial office from 1938; chief of staff, state secretary, and deputy to Frank after the latter's appointment as governor general, 1939/1940–1945; attended the Wannsee Conference in 1942; convicted and executed in Poland in 1948.
8 Hermann Göring.
9 Reinhard Heydrich, who was issuing the invitations to the conference.
10 The photocopy is not in the file; it is published as PMJ 3/196.
11 The systematic mass deportation of German Jews to the German-occupied territories in Eastern Europe had begun on 15 Oct. 1941.

mann, SS-Gruppenführer Greifelt, SS-Oberführer Klopfer, and Undersecretary Kritzinger.[12]

Heil Hitler!

*One enclosure*[13]

## DOC. 23
## On 2 and 9 December 1941 the psychologist Tadeusz Tomaszewski writes in his diary about the persecution and murder of Jews in Lwów[1]

Handwritten diary of Tadeusz Tomaszewski,[2] entries for 2 and 9 December 1941

2 December. The mood remains optimistic, even a little 'upbeat'. Rumours are running rampant, especially those about English successes in Africa. However, people are not generally convinced that the whole thing is already nearing an end. There is frequent talk of 'next autumn'. The Jews still hope that it will be over 'by Christmas'. Mrs Wanda left her shoes with a woman who has taken in many wonderful things from rich Jews for safekeeping. Someone denounced her (a former maid – the Gestapo usually say who the denouncer was), and the house was searched. Everything was taken away. The lady of the house's possessions remained untouched, but Mrs W.'s shoes were taken. They did not fit anyone in the house, so they were deemed to be Jewish. The lady of the house got a terrible fright and told no one about it. She did not want word to get out. (There are many discreet people in Lwów right now: 'Tell no one', not even a family member; not because they fear the family might denounce them, but so as 'not to frighten them and make them worry'.) It was only three days later that Mrs W. found out that her shoes

12 Wilhelm Stuckart (1902–1953), state secretary at the Reich Ministry of the Interior. Dr Franz Schlegelberger (1876–1970), acting Reich minister of justice from 1941 to August 1942. Leopold Gutterer (1902–1996), state secretary at the Reich Ministry of Public Enlightenment and Propaganda. Erich Neumann (1892–1951), state secretary to the Plenipotentiary for the Four-Year Plan. Dr Alfred Meyer (1891–1945), deputy Reich minister for the occupied eastern territories in the Soviet Union. Dr Georg Leibbrandt (1899–1982), head of Main Department I (Politics) at the Reich Ministry for the Occupied Eastern Territories. Martin Luther (1895–1945), head of Department D (Germany) at the Reich Foreign Office; the 'Jewish question' was part of his remit as undersecretary from March 1941. Correctly: Otto Hofmann, head of the Race and Settlement Main Office, 1940–1943. Ulrich Greifelt (1896–1949), chief of staff at the Office of the Reich Commissioner for the Strengthening of Germandom. Dr Gerhard Klopfer (1905–1987), undersecretary at the Party Chancellery. Friedrich Kritzinger (1890–1947), undersecretary at the Reich Chancellery. This penultimate paragraph is missing from the letter to Krüger, the draft of which is the next item in the file; Krüger was not invited to the meeting at Wannsee.

13 Presumably the document referred to in fn. 8.

1 Ośrodek Karta, AW II/3459, fols. 151–154. Published in Tadeusz Tomaszewski, *Lwów: Pejsaż psychologiczny*, ed. Zofia Ratajczak (Warsaw: WIP, 1996), pp. 135–137. The diary covers the period from 5 August 1940 to 15 August 1944. This document has been translated from Polish.

2 Dr Tadeusz Tomaszewski (1910–2000), psychologist; founder of the theory of action; undertook research in Paris, 1938–1939; assistant at the University of Lwów, 1939–1941; hid Aleksander Bloch in his apartment during the second half of 1941; offered psychological consultations, 1941–1942; worked at the Central Food Institute in Lwów, 1943–1944; lived in Lublin, 1945–1950; thereafter worked as a professor in Warsaw until 1980.

had been taken. She has an acquaintance who is a Volksdeutscher[3] and a Gestapo man. She went with him to demand her shoes back. The Polish-speaking officials made excuses for some time, saying the complaint had come too late and that everything was gone. Finally a higher, German-speaking official was called in. He began to question the friend from the Gestapo as to whether he could testify to the fact that the shoes belonged to Mrs W. and how he knew this, whether perhaps he had bought her the shoes himself. In the end the matter was postponed until the next day. Mrs W. protested. Why tomorrow? There was nothing easier than to go down to the storeroom. She would recognize her shoes, take them with her, and be done with it. But her friend the Volksdeutscher calmed her down. He politely offered his thanks and gave assurances they would go back the next day. 'Have you lost your mind?' he asked her later. 'They need time. They have to fetch the shoes from home. Perhaps they have to get them from a cousin or a friend.' In the end, the shoes were not recovered.

Yesterday evening Dzidzia[4] received a visit from a German, her mother's tenant. 'Na, was ist neues?'[5] The German was very concerned. He waved his hand: 'Oh!' He is a chauffeur. He was in a restaurant, and the car was parked in the street. Some tipsy officers, I don't know whether they were his immediate supervisors, ordered him to go home, got in the car themselves, and went off on a late-night jaunt. What was he supposed to do? He went home. But he is responsible for the car. They had already played a trick like this on him once before. He was worried all night. Now he doesn't know what will happen.

The ghetto is taking shape. The majority of the Jews have already moved their furniture there. However, the day before yesterday it was announced that resettlement from some parts of the city would not be completed until 2 February 1942 – and no one knows the deadline for the other areas. The Jews rejoiced. They sit in empty rooms, but still within their own four walls. Many of the intelligentsia are arranging false documents for themselves (fake birth certificates are the easiest) and leaving for 'the other side'. Many go somewhere in the provinces, including those who have been baptized. Kleiner, Loria, and Steinhaus have [already] left.[6] Many young people are leaving. For them it is a kind of adventure. A new name, a journey into the unknown. But most of them go to one of their acquaintances. Of course they do not say where or to whom. Many of them are probably involved in the black market. Once, by chance, I came across 'traders from the other side'. (These are legendary figures in the local black market. The final link in the chain, they take their own money, not someone else's, out of their pockets and end up buying the goods.) These were five Jews with the most impudent Jewish faces, about whose origin there could be no doubt whatsoever. They are not at all interested in the ghetto, neither here nor in Warsaw. They have money and are above it all. 'I can't spend all of my money,' one of them said. 'I need 500 to 1,000 złoty in my pocket for the trip.' Why does he need 500 to 1,000 złoty for the trip, if there is an apartment waiting for him over there just as fine as the one he probably has here in Lwów?

3 Here and below, German in the original: 'ethnic German'.
4 Presumably Elżbieta Lewicka, one of Tomaszewski's work colleagues.
5 German in the original: 'Well, what's new?'
6 The literary historian Juliusz Kleiner (1886–1957), the physicist Stanisław Loria (1883–1958), and the mathematician Hugo Steinhaus (1887–1972) were professors at the University of Lwów.

9 December. For three days – Thursday, Friday, and Saturday – Jews were arrested, and on Sunday they were taken to a sand quarry in motor vehicles.[7] Throughout the morning they were taken away. This was the first time I had seen this spectacle with my own eyes. First I saw a truck driving fast towards the city. Inside were four Gestapo men dressed in black, wearing black coats and black helmets. I was struck by this sight because one seldom sees such things, and at first I didn't understand what was happening. But then a similar vehicle appeared, driving towards the city limits. The vehicle was loaded up, but the cargo was covered with a tarpaulin. Similar figures dressed in black stood at each of the vehicle's four corners. I remembered someone telling me that this was how they would take Jews to the sand quarry. People stopped and turned to watch as the vehicles passed, and no one laughed. At Dzidzia's I met a somewhat agitated dairywoman, who told me she had been held up in Lesienice for an hour and a half because it had taken an hour and a half to shoot the Jews in the sand quarry. On my way home I saw a vehicle driving back. This time there were four Ukrainian militiamen standing in it. Immediately after that another vehicle appeared, racing away from the city. On the truck bed sat two elderly Jewish women, dressed in coats but bareheaded. Three men were guarding them.

All of this made a big impression. Kreutz's wife also saw this vehicle. When she began to tell me about it, her eyes filled with tears. Kreutz[8] wanted to salvage the situation and made some stupid jokes, saying that the people under the tarpaulin should suddenly seize their torturers by the legs and throw them off. They were down there anyway, so it would be easy. Whoops – and the guard is over the side. Ha, ha, ha. But he also spoke of increasing brutality. Everyone is talking like that, including Jaworek.[9] Wesołowski[10] came today with the news that forty such vehicles arrived on Sunday, reportedly carrying not only Jews. He finds life under such conditions nerve-wracking. 'Life under the Bolsheviks was fantastic compared to this.'

By the way, Wesołowski has already had two adventures. The first was when he was caught with cigarettes. The second happened in the cinema. He went to the cinema for Ukrainians.[11] There were few people; the place was almost empty. Suddenly there was a pause, and policemen came in and scoured the audience. 'A shiver ran down my spine. I remembered the roundups.' He had just one thought – to get through the door and away. But it was still light in the streets, and they would catch him. But the policemen passed him by and took some people from the back rows, a man and a woman. W. doesn't know why. In any case, he swore he would never go to the cinema for Ukrainians again.

7 During the operation to relocate Jews to the ghetto, it was primarily elderly people and people who appeared to be impoverished who were selected by the police and later murdered. On 29 Oct. 1941 Tomaszewski had already noted that half-naked people had been shot at the sand quarry near Lesienice railway station to the east of Lwów; he wrote that the Germans had taken the victims' most valuable belongings for themselves and distributed the rest to the local non-Jewish population: Tomaszewski, *Lwów: Pejsaż psychologiczny*, p. 128.

8 Dr Mieczysław Kreutz (1893–1971), psychologist and professor in Lwów; taught Tadeusz Tomaszewski; worked at the University of Wrocław after the war; worked in Warsaw from 1953.

9 Hanka Jaworek (Jaworkówna) taught in the department of education as assistant to Professor Stanisław Łempicki (1886–1947), professor of education at the University of Lwów.

10 Antoni Wesołowski was one of Tadeusz Tomaszewski's school friends.

11 A cinema reserved for Ukrainians.

The Japanese-American war has broken out. On the first day, people were unsettled and did not know whether this was a good or a bad thing. Good because America is finally intervening directly, and bad because this is not directed against the Germans, so the American forces will be tied up elsewhere and supplies to England could be reduced. On the second day, the prevailing opinion was that this was a bad thing after all and could prolong hostilities.

It was announced that workers are entitled to get clothes with ration cards. One has to submit an application stating that one is in urgent need of these items. Then a committee comes to one's home to check whether such a need really exists. Then one receives a Bezugsschein[12] and buys what one needs. But yesterday someone told me that such a committee came to someone's home, opened the cupboard, found a whole pile of undergarments, and instead of giving the applicant a coupon for a jacket, they took away his shirts.

## DOC. 24

## From 29 November to 10 December 1941, a Jewish woman describes her life in hiding in the Delatyn region[1]

Handwritten diary of Mrs Rathauser,[2] Delatyn,[3] entries for 29 November and 10 December 1941

The 21st day in the cellar. This is my chronicle. I've started a new, different life here, and I'm counting the days since Pańczyszynowa[4] brought me here [on] 8 November.

Today is already the 29th. In the neighbouring village the Germans have murdered the Jews they found, and out of fear one landlord killed the three Jews he had been hiding. The matter came to light when blood-stained tools were found. I don't know the details because our landlords are afraid to show any interest in this matter. If you haven't ever seen it, is it possible to imagine that we die such a death? Can you imagine, without seeing it, that we die such a death? All night I sat and listened out, for although I know that our Wasyl won't murder us, I could not shake off the fear the whole night.

What should I do with myself? I am tormented by such thoughts.

12 German in the original: 'coupon'.

1 YVA, O-33/633. The diary entries begin on 8 Nov. and end on 23 Dec. 1941. This document has been translated from Polish.

2 In Sept. 1941 Mrs Rathauser had witnessed a murder operation in Pechenizhyn, and in Oct. 1941 she saw Jews being led out of the town of Delatyn to be executed.

3 A small town at the foot of the Carpathian mountains in the voivodeship of Stanisławów in south-east Poland. On 16 Oct. 1941 staff from the field office of the Commander of the Security Police and the SD (KdS) in Stanisławów and members of the Ukrainian auxiliary police rounded up 1,950 Jews and murdered them outside the town.

4 Aleksa Pańczyszynowa and her husband, Wasyl Pańczyszyn, had previously arranged housing for Mrs Rathauser and (her son?) Igo in Delatyn. Mrs Pańczyszynowa had dressed the two of them in traditional peasant clothing and taken them to a married couple she knew who lived in a remote location, where they went into hiding in the cellar. Pańczyszynowa gave these diary entries to the Jewish Historical Commission in Katowice on 16 March 1946.

*10 December.* I haven't been writing; I was apathetic and discouraged. Pańczyszynowa gave us a German newspaper to read and a prayer book for Igo. I read the newspaper from cover to cover. Unfortunately the situation looks good for the Germans. I'm losing hope, and my spirits are sinking lower and lower.

Igo fervently beseeches God and offers prayers. He's found a certain solace in his suffering. Today he told me that faith in God, who will help us, gives him strength, and that he believes we will survive, that we will live to see the Germans defeated.

We still can't come to terms with the fact that Sal is not here, for where could he be? If he were in hiding nearby, he would have contacted Pańczyszynowa. Apparently in Lwów and elsewhere there are labour camps to which they are taking our Jews, but no one knows anything. Sometimes our landlord goes into town, to Kolomyja, and asks around, but one can't draw any reliable conclusions from what people say. Christmas is upon us, so preparations in the village are under way and the street is bustling with activity. We've already been here a whole month. Late 1941. I never knew much about politics, but now I'm wondering about it. What happens next? Will mighty Russia defeat the Germans? What about America? It's supplying clothes and goods. Oh, it does my soul good whenever I think of [Russia's] victory. The Germans are also occupied with Christmas; they're going to Germany on leave – that's what our landlord said.

## DOC. 25

## On 15 December 1941 the Polish government's representative in occupied Poland reports on death sentences handed down for leaving the Warsaw ghetto without authorization[1]

Report from the government delegation's Press and Information Department, unsigned, Warsaw, dated 15 December 1941

On 15 December 1941, at 8.30 and 9 a.m., further death sentences were carried out. Fifteen people were executed: Rozenbaum, Ałta (b. 1886); Śpiewak, Estera (b. 1920); Kohn, Chana (b. 1923); Elbaum, Masza (b. 1923); Kalksztajn, Itela (aged 27); Rotbard, Moszek (b. 1915); Prowizor, Mindla (b. 1910); Drewnowicz, Srul ([b.] 1925); Kisielewicz, Masza ([b.] 1922); Russ, Rywka ([b.] 1909); Rubin, Chaja (aged 40); Salwe, Hena (b. 1924); Przychocka, Chaja (b. 1917); Mirzanowska, Róża (b. 1913); and Abramowicz, Mejer (aged 21).[2]

Before they were taken from their cells, some scopolamine[3] was added to their morning coffee to stun them, but it didn't help much.

1 AAN, 1325/202/II-27, fol. 32. This document has been translated from Polish.
2 Further information is only available for some of the murdered individuals: Ałta Rozenbaum was a widow from Łuków; Estera Śpiewak was a shop assistant from Biała Podlaska; Chana Kohn came from Putułsk; Rywka Laja Russ and Chaja Rubin were merchants; Hena Salwe was a shop assistant; Mindla (Mendel) Prowizor from Mogielnica and Srul Drewnowicz were labourers; and Mejer Abramowicz was a painter.
3 An alkaloid that has a paralysing effect on the central nervous system.

Present at the execution were: Police Commander Rzeszczyński,[4] Police Deputy Commander Przymusiński,[5] Prosecutor Naumann,[6] a representative of the District, a gendarmerie officer and several gendarmes, several civilians, the head of the Order Service[7] with his adjutant, and the prison authorities.[8]

Two firing squads also arrived.

This execution was even more horrifying than the previous one.[9] The victims were not tied to the stakes properly. They tried to pull themselves free and resisted. The execution was carried out in two rounds, so some of the condemned had to wait until the verdict was carried out on the first group.

The police aimed badly; they fired two salvos the first time around and three the second time. The condemned had to be finished off both times.

Status as of 15 December 1941 at 8 a.m.: 300 men, 340 women, of whom 42 people are in the hospital, 169 minors.[10]

Convicts: 16.

Four people remain with the Criminal Police, Precinct IV: Kopyto, Icek; Lerner; Szlajnberg, Aleksander; and Chaba, Adam.

A total of thirty-two people have been handed over to the Special Court prosecutor.

Forty-one people remain at the police precinct dealing with illicit trade and at the police headquarters.

Twelve people remain with the chairman of R.W.[11]

A hearing on 15 December 1941 handed down three death sentences (Cajtung, Frajda; Rajchman, Ita;[12] and Gotlib, Jochwet); the remaining cases were adjourned.[13]

4 Correctly: Aleksander Reszczyński (1892–1943), police officer; liaison officer to the Polish police under the commander of the gendarmerie in District Lublin from 1939 to mid 1940; thereafter commander of the Polish police in Warsaw; simultaneously clandestinely engaged in intelligence work for the Home Army (ZWZ-AK); killed in an attack carried out by communist resistance fighters in March 1943.

5 Franciszek Przymusiński (1889–1945), police officer; worked for the Prussian police prior to 1920; then with the Polish State Police; powiat commander in Rypin, 1932–1939; deputy commander of the Polish police in Warsaw from 1940, and commander from 1943; simultaneously clandestinely engaged in intelligence work for the Home Army; arrested by the People's Commissariat for Internal Affairs (NKVD); perished in a camp in the Urals.

6 Dr Rudolf (Rudi) Naumann (1901–1978), lawyer; public prosecutor at Dresden Regional Court; public prosecutor at the German Special Court in Warsaw, 1941–1942; public prosecutor in Rzeszów, March 1942 – June 1944; additionally senior public prosecutor in the General Government in 1943; chief public prosecutor in Duisburg after the war.

7 Józef Szeryński was the head of the Jewish Order Service.

8 Leopold Lindenfeld was the head of the central prison in the Warsaw ghetto.

9 Eight people sentenced on the basis of the Third Regulation on Restrictions of Movement in the General Government (15 Oct. 1941) were shot dead on 17 Nov. 1941: see Doc. 30, fn. 10.

10 Taken together, this is the number of people held in the ghetto prison.

11 The meaning of the initials R.W. is unclear.

12 Possibly Ita Rajchman (1900–1942), housewife from Warsaw.

13 These were trials held before the German Special Court in Warsaw.

## DOC. 26

## On 16 December 1941 the government and heads of authorities of the GG discuss the risks posed by typhus and the next steps in the persecution of the Jews[1]

Minutes of the government meeting in Cracow on 16 December 1941

[…][2]

The next speaker, Main Department Head Walbaum, reported on the current incidence of typhus. He said typhus did not peak in the winter months, but in April. No decline in *typhus* had set in this winter. A certain peak had been reached in June. At that time the large-scale deployment of troops had been taking place on the border in the East; as a consequence, the population had been herded together, and the food situation had become most unfavourable. Typhus had not receded in the months that followed, but neither had it spread further thanks to the measures taken. Up to November of this year, the incidence had remained at this level.

The speaker explained the *incidence of typhus* using the typhus tables for the last few months. He said that cases had, however, risen sharply in November. At that point the disease had broken out in the prisoner-of-war camps. Due to the state of hygiene in the camps, once a disease broke out, it inevitably progressed rapidly. In the East, the General Government bordered on Russian territories in which typhus had always been prevalent. When German soldiers advanced into this country, they quite unavoidably came into contact with the local population, and owing to their contacts with the rear, typhus had also spread in the General Government. The Reich Commissioner in Riga[3] had had the same experience. In a telegram, he had stated that typhus was spreading from the north-east to the west of his territory. Furthermore, a number of Ukrainian prisoners of war had been released in Russian Ukraine. The spread of typhus in Galicia had almost exactly followed the retreat route taken by these prisoners of war. Studies had found that typhus even occurred in the buildings in which these prisoners had stayed overnight. Despite the most assiduous countermeasures, the military administration had not been able to avert this development, which was attributable to wartime conditions.

When the incidence of typhus began to rise, he (Main Department Head Walbaum) had appointed Professor *Kudicke* from the Warsaw Research Institute[4] as the special commissioner for typhus control. There was no reason for panic. Successes in disease control could not be achieved overnight. The impact of the measures initiated would

1 AIPN, GK 95, vol. 17. Copy in IfZ-Archives, Fb 105, vol. 18, fols. 4362–4460 (fols. 4398–4406, 4420–4421, 4423–4424, 4426–4427, 4430–4433, 4442–4446 (excerpts)). This document has been translated from German.

2 At the start of the meeting the acting head of the Food and Agriculture Main Department, Karl Naumann, spoke about the supply situation in the General Government; he feared that grain deliveries from the Reich would soon be necessary. The head of the Economic Affairs Main Department, Walter Emmerich, then reported on the general economic situation, above all the problem of supplying heating and vehicle fuels, before the chairman of the Directorate General of the Eastern Railway (Ostbahn), Adolf Gerteis, described the transport difficulties faced by the Eastern Railway.

3 The Reich commissioner for Ostland, Hinrich Lohse.

4 A reference to the State Hygiene Institute in Warsaw.

only become apparent in a few months. However, it could already be stated that they had been crowned with success. The population had shown great understanding for the measures ordered. The mandatory public washdays in individual towns and cities could perhaps be arranged throughout the General Government. Above all, it was necessary to ensure the population changed their undergarments more frequently.

At the last meeting the General Government had pledged to provide substantial support for typhus control. The Health Main Department had launched a programme under which a *delousing station* was being established in every larger town in the General Government. These stations were a key prerequisite for measures to combat typhus and it was therefore necessary to promote their establishment by all possible means. He had commissioned a cost estimate, according to which a sum of 30 million zloty would be required.

The *Governor General* pledged *30 million zloty* for this purpose, but pointed out that cash alone would not be sufficient.

On this topic, Main Department Head *Walbaum* explained that the Reich had given him major assurances of assistance because these measures were clearly needed to protect the Reich as well. The Wehrmacht also needed to have such delousing stations at its disposal. Among the German population, the barracks-based SS and police were particularly at risk of typhus. The SS and Police Leader in Lublin,[5] for instance, had sent him two telegrams reporting cases of the disease among the police in Lublin.

The *Governor General* made the point that typhus posed a threat to the entire population, and asked Main Department Head Walbaum whether *lymph*[6] could be produced in sufficient quantities.

Main Department Head *Walbaum* commented on this as follows: the manufacture of *typhus vaccine* was extremely complicated, and it was therefore only ever possible to have several thousand doses ready for use. (The speaker described the manufacture of lymph at length.) There was a typhus research institute in Cracow under the authority of the Wehrmacht, where work was being carried out using Professor Weigl's procedure.[7] Now that Professor Weigl had principally been deployed by the Wehrmacht, the continued progress of vaccine manufacture had been impeded. For this reason, a request had been made to the Reich Ministry of the Interior to have Professor Weigl placed at the disposal of the General Government as well. There was the prospect of the Wehrmacht giving consideration to this request. In addition, he (Main Department Head Walbaum) had asked several industrial companies to set up *institutes for infectious diseases* in Lemberg, Lublin, and Cracow; industry representatives had also shown willing to accede to this request. As far as the firms were concerned, the manufacture of the vaccine did not represent a risk. It would even earn them large profits because the vaccine could of course only be manufactured by such companies. He would now set about establishing such institutes immediately. The vaccine would only be administered to the groups most at risk. Even if several thousand doses of vaccine were available, this was a mere drop in the ocean for the General Government as a whole. Above all, efforts should

5 Odilo Globocnik.

6 As in the original; the reference is to a vaccine.

7 The Army High Command's Institute for Typhus Research was led by Stabsarzt (military medical officer with the rank of captain) Dr Hermann Eyer from 1939.

be made to vaccinate members of the SS, the police, and above all those officials and salaried employees who have extensive dealings with Jews. This of course applied primarily to physicians and nursing staff.

Main Department Head *Walbaum* went on to mention a letter from the medical officer for District Warsaw, which had included several requests that could probably be taken up. There was little point in looking into the accusations made in this letter that funds had not been approved in good time, although it was necessary to acknowledge that the Kreishauptleute did not in fact have any monetary funds at their disposal. Walbaum said that if the Finance Main Department were to make available a sum of *30 million zloty* for all *typhus control measures*, this was only to be welcomed, but he stressed the importance of issuing the relevant instructions as soon as possible.

The *Governor General* also stated that a sum of 30 million zloty would be made available at the request of the Health Main Department. Secondly, measures for the *production of lymph* needed to be taken immediately. Further, the individual measures were to be discussed with the departments responsible. One of the main risks was the *vagrancy of the population*. Rigorous action needed to be, and indeed would be, taken to prevent *Jews* from leaving the ghetto. The *death penalty* imposed on Jews for this reason needed to be carried out very quickly in future. This regulation stipulating that every Jew found outside the ghetto was to be executed had to be implemented unconditionally.[8] Special court proceedings would have to be simplified if necessary.

Main Department Head Walbaum also pointed out that *transports of labourers* to the Reich had continued to date because the Office of the Four-Year Plan still considered the deployment of Polish workers to be extremely urgent.[9] These transports were bound to include a few people suffering from typhus, but this was unavoidable. He had asked the Reich Ministry of Labour and the Reich Ministry of the Interior to confirm in writing that they agreed that in the event that a person infected with typhus turned up in the Reich, the Reich would bear responsibility for this. He had also expressed concern at the time about the soldiers in Przemysl being deloused, but had been told there was no other option.

In response to a question from the *Governor General*, Main Department Head *Frauendorfer*[10] replied that all workers who were to be deported to the Reich would be deloused at the transit points.

In conclusion, Main Department Head *Walbaum* expressed the wish that the measures taken by the health administration should be supported by the Kreishauptleute where possible. Cleaning products should also be provided as a priority. Moreover, signs should be put up designating locations where there were outbreaks of typhus. He noted

8 See Doc. 13.

9 The Office of the Four-Year Plan led by Hermann Göring was responsible for policy related to the wartime economy. It pressed the General Government to provide increasing numbers of young Poles for forced labour in the Reich.

10 Dr Max Frauendorfer (1909–1989), lawyer; joined the NSDAP and the SS in 1928; administrative official in the NSDAP Reichsleitung in 1931; Reichsschulungsleiter (NSDAP head of training) in 1934; worked in the General Government from Sept. 1939; head of the Labour Department in the government of the GG, Nov. 1939 – Feb. 1943; Ministerialdirigent in 1941; served in the Wehrmacht, 1943–1945; lived under the alias Dr Schreiter in the Allgäu region until 1950; thereafter director of an insurance company in Munich and deputy treasurer of the Christian Social Union party (CSU).

that, given the war-related circumstances, the situation was otherwise serious, but not desperate. Any atmosphere of panic that might arise should be countered at all costs. While the measures initiated by the Health Main Department were yet to have an impact, understanding for them could already be perceived among the population. It would therefore be possible to counter this serious threat during the coming winter. In earlier years, at least 200,000 people had been afflicted by typhus in Poland. Today, thanks to Professor *Kudicke's* procedure, it was possible to diagnose typhus within ten minutes, rather than the twenty-four to forty-eight hours previously required.

The *Governor General* stated that typhus was not endemic in the General Government, but posed an extremely serious problem at present, both in the Old Reich and in all the eastern territories. With soldiers, military units, workers, prisoners of war, etc. all on the move, the problem could no longer be tackled on the basis of individual territories but only within a comprehensive framework. Above all, it was imperative to ensure rigorous delousing.

Following the comments made by Main Department Head Walbaum, Governor *Kundt*[11] gave an overview of the *incidence of typhus* and the measures taken to control the disease in *District Radom*. New infections had reached their lowest level in May, but in October the incidence had risen to twice that in May. Currently, 3,082 typhus cases, including suspected cases, had been recorded across the whole district. The typhus situation in District Radom could therefore in no way be regarded as threatening. Only in Tomaszow was the incidence of typhus very high, its spread having been aggravated by the Organization Todt and Askania[12] camps. However, thanks to the measures taken, a decline could be discerned there as well.

Thirty-two stationary and ten mobile delousing stations were available in the district's ten Kreishauptmannschaften. *Kundt* had restricted *the movement of Jews* to the lowest level possible in his district and given instructions for Jews to be permitted to use the railways only in urgent cases. Furthermore, he had requested that the colour of the identity cards be changed because identity cards were being copied by a forgers' workshop.

Rigorous typhus control measures required ruthless action against Jews who left their assigned residential quarter without authorization, as well as greater discipline by the Germans in their private business dealings with Jews. The behaviour of many Germans in the latter respect was cause for strong criticism. The Party would report to Kundt any German wishing to do business with Jews in his district and he would punish them. In Tomaszow, for example, typhus had been transmitted to an ethnic German village by a Jewish painter and decorator who had been hired to paint a house.

11 Ernst Kundt (1897–1947), lawyer; studied in Prague; co-founded the Sudeten German Party (SdP) in 1935; joined the NSDAP in 1939; Stadtkommandant in Tarnów, Sept.–Dec.1939 and Kreishauptmann there from Jan. 1940; head of the General Government's Interior Administration Department, Sept. 1940 – July 1941; thereafter governor of District Radom until 1945; sentenced to death in Prague and executed in 1947.

12 Under the code name 'Askania Chemische Werke', more than 4,500 labourers worked near Tomaszów Mazowiecki from Dec. 1940 to Sept. 1941, constructing 'Anlage Mitte', one of three sites planned to oversee the campaign against the Soviet Union, consisting of bunkers and a series of concrete tunnels and shelters, including bomb-proof railway shelters for the Führer's train (*Sonderzug*). The project was managed by Organization Todt. Hitler never stayed there; the complex was used in 1944 as a munitions store and workshop for aircraft engines.

The other important point was to shorten the legal proceedings against Jews who left their residential districts without authorization. The *death penalty* now imposed for leaving the ghetto without authorization could be handed down quickly, but only carried out after a long official approval procedure. Kundt therefore proposed curtailing the procedure by empowering the governors to carry out death sentences. The Jews would then realize that the German administration was serious about these measures and that only a short period would elapse between them being captured and their death sentence being carried out. In his district, judges had expressed misgivings, arguing that the regulation was imprecise and referred only to the 'Jewish residential district'. In response to this, Kundt had issued an administrative directive to clarify this term, defining it as meaning any authorized place of residence for Jews.[13] If Jews went from their village onto a public thoroughfare, for example, this in practice constituted leaving their residential district. This meant no Jew was allowed to go onto the thoroughfare without a permit. This would prevent the further spread of typhus by the Jews. Since it was not possible to conduct mass delousing, he had at least ordered the delousing of the Poles who worked for German agencies.

In this connection, the *Governor General* explained that he would transfer the *right of pardon* granted to him by the Führer to the governors in cases where Jews had been sentenced to death by the special courts and summary courts.[14]

[...][15]

[Schöngarth's presentation:] Today the rural population still possessed quite significant *stocks of weapons*. Only very recently the German police had discovered a weapons store with machine guns, carbines, and hand grenades. A store of this kind had also been seized at a cemetery. Another had been raided in District Cracow. All of the weapons were extraordinarily well packed, greased, and ready to use. The number of persons currently in prison for involvement in the resistance movement was extraordinarily high. At the moment more than *7,000 Poles were in detention* for offences against the *Regulation on Violent Crimes.*[16]

Nine Security Police officers had died of *typhus*. He had had ampoules prescribed by the Army Inspectorate Berlin for the individual units; a very large proportion of them had already been delivered; despite this, there was no chance that all policemen would be supplied because the Wehrmacht High Command had blocked the delivery of further typhus ampoules. He would therefore be very grateful if the health authority could intervene. The *security* of the General Government was guaranteed, even if the resistance movement could be expected do everything it could to disrupt the supply lines to the East.

13 The directive could not be found.

14 No such regulation was published in the *VOBl-GG*.

15 Various participants subsequently addressed the provision made for ethnic Germans in District Radom; Frauendorfer reported on the activities of the Labour Main Department; the head of the Finance Main Department, Alfred Spindler, reported on the General Government's financial situation; the head of the Police Affairs Department, Heinrich Schönhals, gave a presentation on the planned registration regulations and obligation to carry identity documents; the Senior Commander of the Security Police and the SD (BdS) in the General Government, Eberhard Schöngarth, then described the activities of the Polish resistance movement.

16 Verordnung zur Bekämpfung von Gewalttaten, *VOBl-GG*, 1939, no. 2, 31 Oct. 1939, p. 10.

[…][17]

[Report by Wächter:] With regard to *typhus*, the situation in Cracow was still tolerable overall. There were as yet no signs of any significant threat from the illness. There were clusters of typhus cases in only two places: firstly, where prisoner-of-war camps had been constructed; and secondly, where Jews were being utilized on a considerable scale. This was the case on the district's eastern border. Some illegal infiltration of Jews into other districts could not be stopped completely, of course. It was imperative to take any measure conducive to the wide-scale elimination of Jewry. He had taken appropriate measures within the district in cooperation with the SS and Police Leader[18] but these measures could help only locally, and could not fundamentally solve the problem. […][19]

Governor *Zörner* reported that District Lublin had been particularly badly affected by *typhus*. The number of cases had risen significantly since the beginning of the year, as had the number of deaths. A total of 700 new infections and 7 deaths had been recorded in the first quarter, 2,150 new infections and 50 deaths in the second quarter, and more than 3,000 new infections in the third quarter. October had seen 1,640 new infections and 80 deaths, and November 3,656 new infections and 157 deaths. This rise was caused by the increasing lice infestation of the lowest strata of the population – not only the Jews, but also the Poles – as well as by the housing shortage and the lack of cleaning products. Vagrant Jews and prisoners of war who had escaped were also typhus carriers. Trade in non-disinfected rags and in garments from prisoners of war who had died of typhus were further possible causes of the epidemic, as were overcrowded trains.

The measures taken by the district's Health Department fell within the spectrum of what had previously been proposed by Main Department Head *Walbaum*. Even though a relatively large number of *delousing stations* were available, they were not sufficient. This was why new delousing stations were being established, for example in Pulawy and Deblin. In addition, schools would be closed where necessary, entire villages closed off, and general washdays ordered for the population. Physicians and medical students would also be deployed in greater numbers.

All the *bathing facilities and delousing stations* were working at full capacity. In addition, disinfection procedures were being carried out. Offices heavily frequented by the public were being given special consideration, and *creosote* was being used in these cases. Appropriate measures had been taken to counter the panic apparent among staff. The welfare of the Criminal Police and the Security Service, who are of course at particular risk, was an ongoing concern. A total of 140 vaccination doses had been made available to the Commander of the Security Police,[20] and he had requested the same number again. The police were evidently acting independently when it came to typhus control.

In order to counteract the threat posed by typhus, he (Governor Zörner) had initiated measures to create a second ghetto to accommodate all the Jews working mainly in the

17 The governor of District Cracow, Otto Wächter, went on to report on the situation there.

18 Julian Scherner.

19 Wächter subsequently warned that the Wehrmacht needed to coordinate its operations better with the district administration, and commented on the situation of the Polish Construction Service (Polnischer Baudienst), a paramilitary organization for Polish youth founded by the Germans in May 1940 and mostly active in District Cracow.

20 Max Großkopf.

German interest, primarily craftsmen.[21] In District Lublin, at any rate, everything possible was being done in the interests of effective typhus control with the crucial involvement of the new head of the Department for Public Health.[22] Fortunately, a slight decline in this contagious disease had recently been noted. Moreover, the percentage of Germans dying from the disease was no longer as high as it had been. [...][23]

In the *healthcare system* the incidence of typhus was constantly rising, caused by prisoners of war. The routes they had marched could clearly be traced, and typhus had broken out in buildings where they had stayed. Control measures had commenced, and the incidence curves were falling. The lack of physicians meant that Jewish physicians had had to be deployed in certain towns and cities. In Lemberg 80 per cent of all the physicians had been Jews. It would be welcomed if the university and the medical institute in Lwów could be opened to allow medical students to finish their studies. [...][24]

Following this, Chief of Staff Dr *Hummel*[25] spoke about the situation in District Warsaw, standing in for Governor Dr Fischer, who was ill. A very good *harvest yield* had been achieved in District Warsaw. It had been possible to harvest 72,000 t of grain for bread and 17,000 t of grain for feed by the end of November. These achievements put Warsaw top out of all the districts. Grain for bread had already reached 65.4 per cent of the target.

Accordingly, the authorities had been able to continue providing the population with the set rations; only with respect to potatoes had they fallen somewhat short because of the poor harvest, and because the district had not received any supplies from other districts. Instead of the 80 kg per capita distributed during the same period the previous year, it had only been possible to distribute 60 kg. He was obliged to point out, however, that the population's *general food situation* was steadily worsening. This was linked to a fall in labour productivity, which was becoming evident in the armaments industry. It went without saying that the so-called tortoise campaign[26] was also playing a role in this respect.

With this, a slackening in the pace of work had also made itself felt. Prices had risen to such an extent that workers were leaving their workplaces for several days in ever larger droves in order to obtain food for themselves and their families from the countryside. An

21 This was probably the ghetto in the suburb of Majdan Tatarski.

22 The name could not be ascertained.

23 After this Zörner discussed the coal supply, the collection of grain contingents, and the increase in attacks. There was then a report on the situation in District Galicia by Dr Karl Lasch (1904–1942), economist and lawyer; joined the NSDAP in 1931; director of the Academy for German Law in 1934; head of the NSDAP's Reich Legal Office in 1936; governor of District Radom, 1939–1941; governor of District Galicia, 1941–1942; arrested for corruption in May 1942; thought to have been shot without trial on Himmler's orders while on remand in prison.

24 Lasch went on to speak about the deportation of forced labourers to the Reich, the training of administrative staff, and the Lwów Theatre; he praised the civil administration's good relationship with the Wehrmacht, SS, and police in the district.

25 Dr Herbert Hummel (1907–1944), lawyer; joined the NSDAP in 1932 and the SA in 1933; public prosecutor in Munich from 1933; chief of staff at the Reich Legal Office from 1935; head of administration at the Office of the Governor of District Warsaw from Dec. 1939; deputy governor of District Warsaw, 1943–1944; killed during the Warsaw Uprising.

26 The Polish resistance called upon workers employed in armaments production to work slowly and used a tortoise symbol to promote this strategy.

ensuing tendency was for people to work only in exchange for supplies of goods. Similar phenomena had also been apparent in the Reich during the period of inflation. […][27]

He [Hummel] said that the threat of *typhus* had increased because of the decline in the population's resistance to the disease, particularly the Jews. The ghetto residents were undernourished. Moreover, cleaning products were in short supply and people were living in cramped conditions. The reported incidence of typhus in the ghetto was currently 2,405 cases, but the actual incidence was much higher. Among the Poles, 503 were known to have contracted typhus in Warsaw and 589 in the Kreishauptmannschaften. In itself, enclosing the Jews in the ghetto was a blessing. What was important now was to seal it off completely. A shoot-to-kill order from the Senior Commander of the Order Police,[28] which allowed Jews to be shot on public thoroughfares, had been gratefully received.

Dr Hummel then reported on the practical impact of the *death penalty* being imposed for illegally *leaving the ghetto*.[29] So far, despite the addition of a third chamber, it had only been possible to hand down forty-five death sentences in Warsaw, and of these only eight had been carried out because the Pardon Commission in Cracow had to take the final decision on each individual case. Another 600 sentencing requests had been submitted. It was impossible to isolate the ghetto effectively by means of special court proceedings. The procedure leading up to liquidation was too protracted; it was burdened with too many formalities and needed simplifying. […][30]

I [Frank] want to tell you this quite openly – an end must be put to the *Jews* one way or another. The Führer once said: if united Jewry succeeds again in unleashing a world war, then the blood sacrifices will be made not only by the peoples hounded into fighting, but the Jew will then have found his end in Europe.[31] I know that many of the measures now being taken against the Jews in the Reich are being criticized. People are deliberately trying again and again – this emerges from the *reports on public opinion* – to speak of cruelty, harshness, etc. I would like to ask you: before I carry on, agree with me first of all on the formula, namely that as a matter of principle, we only want to have compassion for the German people, and for no one else in the world. The others have

27 Hummel subsequently discussed the supply of coal.

28 Gerhard Winkler (1888–1952), police officer; served with the police from 1919; joined the NSDAP in 1933 and the SS in 1939; commander of the gendarmerie in Stettin; inspector of the Order Police in Stuttgart in 1939; Senior Commander of the Order Police (BdO) in the General Government, Sept. 1941 – April 1942; thereafter BdO in Stuttgart; retired in April 1944; last lived at Kleinmachnow, near Berlin; declared dead by Teltow Local Court in 1952. The order has not been found, but it is referred to in Doc. 17.

29 See Doc. 13.

30 Otto Fischer subsequently spoke on behalf of the liaison officers of the three branches of the Wehrmacht and expressed their gratitude for the good cooperation with the civil administration; the acting head of the NSDAP's General Government Section (Arbeitsbereich GG), Adolf Stahl, then reported on his organization, before Frank closed the meeting with a speech in which he discussed matters including relations with the Reich Ministry for the Occupied Eastern Territories and announced tougher action to combat the Polish resistance.

31 This is a reference to Hitler's speech on 30 Jan. 1939, in which he declared: 'if the international Jewish financiers within and outside Europe should succeed in plunging the nations once more into a world war, the outcome will not be the Bolshevization of the earth, and thus the victory of Jewry, but rather the annihilation of the Jewish race in Europe.' See PMJ 2/248.

had no compassion for us either. As a long-standing National Socialist, I must also say this: if the Jewish clan in Europe were to survive the war, while we had sacrificed our best blood for the preservation of Europe, then this war would represent but a partial success. As far as the Jews are concerned, my fundamental expectation is therefore that they will disappear. They have to go. I have commenced negotiations for the purpose of deporting them to the East. In January a major meeting about this question will take place in Berlin, to which I will send State Secretary Dr Bühler. This meeting is to be held at the Reich Security Main Office with SS Obergruppenführer Heydrich.[32] At any rate, a major Jewish migration will commence.

But what is to happen to the Jews? Do you believe we will accommodate them in settlement villages in Ostland? They said to us in Berlin: why are you going to all this effort? They are no use to us in Ostland, nor in the Reich Commissariat either, liquidate them yourselves! Gentlemen, I must ask you to arm yourselves against all considerations of pity. We must exterminate the Jews wherever we encounter them and wherever possible in order to uphold the overall structure of the Reich here. This will of course be done using methods that differ from those which Chief of Staff Dr Hummel has already mentioned. Nor can the judges at the special courts be held responsible for them because this does not fall within the framework of legal procedure. One cannot apply assumptions that have prevailed hitherto to singular events of such enormity. At any rate, we must find a means that achieves the objective, and I am giving this thought.

For us, too, Jews are extraordinarily pernicious eaters. In the General Government, we have an estimated 2.5 million Jews, maybe 3.5 million now if we include the people who have intermarried with Jews as well as all their hangers-on.[33] We cannot shoot these 3.5 million Jews, we cannot poison them, but we will nonetheless be able to take steps that somehow lead to their successful extermination, and we will do so in connection with the major measures to be discussed with the Reich. The General Government must become as free of Jews as the Reich. Where and how this happens is a matter for the authorities that we must deploy and create here; it is also a question of the effectiveness of these authorities, about which I will inform you in good time. […][34]

When it comes to the measures against the *Jews*, we are operating in the context of the Reich as a whole. At the very least, what is happening in the Reich will also have to happen here. In the case of the Poles, we are also operating in the context of the Reich as a whole; the treatment of the Poles in the eastern territories of the German Reich must be coordinated with the way we treat them here. As far as the treatment of the Ukrainians is concerned, we must work in collaboration with the new Reich Commissariat Ukraine. In this respect, there must naturally also be local cooperation between the Reich Commissariat Ukraine and District Galicia.

32 Apart from Frank's deputy, State Secretary Josef Bühler, the General Government was represented at the Wannsee Conference by the BdS in the General Government, Eberhard Schöngarth.

33 These figures are exaggerated. The head of the Population and Welfare Division within the General Government's Interior Administration Department, Lothar Weirauch, estimated the Jewish population in the General Government at 2,092,000 during the period prior to the beginning of Operation Reinhard.

34 Frank went on to talk about the Ukrainians in the General Government.

The following thought must take centre stage: as soon as the process of re-Germanizing the eastern territories of the Reich is complete, this territory, the General Government, will be the next part of Europe to undergo absolute saturation with Germans. We will build the great Reich autobahns to run across our land. Large settlement villages for Germans will be created alongside these Reich autobahns. Large military centres will be created at well-chosen strategic points, around which German life will gradually develop in a broad belt of settlement. Since we will then also have the opportunity here, if need be, to transfer to the East ethnically alien groups that are no longer required, there will be no insurmountable difficulties in letting the German national element put down roots more and more and in increasingly forcing out the ethnically alien element.

This is why you must take to heart the five *theses* I have posited. Beginning with the Germanic settlement of this region and ending with the war in 1941, these set out a succession of legal entitlements to this region that are held by Germandom,[35] for the Führer has granted me powers to make preparations along these lines. Further to the East, the Gotengau[36] will one day take shape, and one day the General Government will become the Vandalengau.[37] As is commonly known, the Vandals were the most vilified Germanic tribe. This was where they resided, this is where they established the first Germanic culture. This Vandalengau will then also help to expunge before the whole world the terrible guilt incurred through the permanent slandering of one of the noblest Germanic tribes, so that its very name has become tantamount to an insult – a masterpiece of anti-German propaganda over two millennia, by the way.

From all this it becomes clear that the *task of the General Government* in the overall framework of the advance to the East is a significant moment in world history. We are the gateway through which one returns to Germany from the East. On our territory stand the scales with their two weighing plates. That is why this area, the 'General Government', has been singled out by the Führer in clear recognition that service in the General Government is a task that can prove one's greatest worth. Of course, all the difficulties that will arise in the East must be considered here. A few days ago I talked to Reich Commissioner Koch[38] about the situation in his Reich Commissariat. Gentlemen, I can tell you: what we took over here in 1939 was child's play by comparison with what is being dished out to the men who are out there now. Because they have nothing to go on there at all. At the moment, in view of the wartime situation and the need to give absolute priority to military operations, there is no chance either of establishing any kind of order, or of setting up an administrative hierarchy, or of getting to a point where things can develop under their own steam.

35 Details could not be identified.

36 'Gothic Gau', a planned purely Germanic settlement encompassing Crimea and the area around Kherson.

37 'Vandal Gau', a reference to Frank's proposal for the territory of the General Government to be expanded and annexed to the Reich after the war.

38 Erich Koch (1896–1986), railway worker; worked for the Reich Railway, 1919–1926; a member of the Von Killinger Freikorps in 1918; joined the NSDAP in 1922; NSDAP Gauleiter of East Prussia, 1928–1945; Oberpräsident of the Province of East Prussia, 1933–1945; Reich commissioner for Ukraine, 1941–1944; extradited in 1950 to Poland, where he was condemned to death in 1959; his sentence was commuted to life imprisonment.

Despite this, the Führer's great words, which he delivered prophetically in his book *Mein Kampf*, shine above this East. The Führer is now in the process of realizing the idea articulated in his book, this great task he has given to the German people. […][39]

## DOC. 27
## On 19 December 1941 the Kreishauptmann of Grójec promises a reward to anyone who reports vagrant Jews and the people who help them[1]

Announcement by the Kreishauptmann of Grójec,[2] dated 19 December 1941

*Announcement*
It has recently come to light that there are still unknown Jews roaming around Grójec.[3] This exposes the population of the Kreis to the risk of typhus spreading more widely. The entire population must play a part in eliminating this risk. I have decided to offer a reward to those inhabitants of the Kreis who make a particular contribution to this defence operation.

For this purpose, I announce the following:
1) Anyone who identifies by name an unauthorized Jew wandering in the Kreis to the responsible police authorities in such a way that the Jew concerned can be punished on the basis of this report *shall receive 1 m*[4] *of bread grain from the Kreishauptmann free of charge.*
2) The same reward will be offered if, instead of a Jew, a person who provides a Jew with accommodation or food is named.[5]

39 Frank subsequently addressed issues relating to wages and food and talked about the position of German officials; he reported on a meeting with Hitler and closed the meeting by thanking the Wehrmacht for its good cooperation with the administration of the General Government. Apart from the speakers mentioned, the meeting was attended by the following: Bühler, Boepple, Krüger, the chiefs of staff of the districts of the General Government (Wolsegger, Engler, Egen, Losacker), Westerkamp, Heuber, Ziehme, Wessel, the district SS and police leaders (Scherner, Globocnik, Oberg, Wigand, Katzmann), Senkowsky, Plodeck, the head of the Foreign Currency and External Economic Affairs Department [Tetzner], Wille, Eißfeldt, Ohlenbusch, Watzke, Bauder, Lauxmann, Paersch, Gutbrod, Weh, Schulte-Wissermann, Schepers, von Medem, Keith, Luxenberg, von Tschammer und Osten, von Dazur, Hinkel, Mühlmann, von Wühlisch, Blum, Heller, Rümelin, Gassner, Stöppler, the Governor General's personal representative for construction projects, the Governor General's Construction Directorate, Blauert, and Hammerle.

1 YVA, O-6/430, fol. 28. Poster in German and Polish. This document has been translated from German.

2 Werner Zimmermann.

3 In Jan. 1941 the authorities concentrated the Jews in this Kreis in confined spaces in six localities: see PMJ 4/225. This caused diseases to spread before the Jews were deported in Feb. 1941, most of them to the Warsaw ghetto.

4 Here a weight measurement equivalent to 100 kg.

5 On 17 Jan. 1942 the head of the Interior Administration in District Warsaw, Waldemar Karl Schön, recommended that the other Stadthauptleute and Kreishauptleute adopt the same procedure as the Kreishauptmann in Grójec: Tatiana Berenstein et al. (eds.), *Faschismus – Getto – Massenmord: Dokumentation über Ausrottung und Widerstand der Juden in Polen während des 2. Weltkrieges* (Berlin: Rütten & Loening, 1961), pp. 130–131.

## DOC. 28

## On 27 December 1941 the Jewish Council in Staszów announces that furs must be surrendered under threat of the death penalty[1]

Announcement made by the Jewish Council in Staszów,[2] issued on 27 December 1941 (poster)

*Final warning!*
The Jewish Council announces that, according to the latest telegram, *failure to immediately surrender all furs* poses grave mortal danger.[3]

As part of special punitive expeditions, the authorities will use the utmost force in carrying out a search for furs that have not yet been surrendered.

Every hour of hesitation endangers the lives of the Jews in our city!

*Think of yourselves, your families, and your brothers, and surrender all of your furs immediately.*

27 December 1941, the Jewish Council in Staszów

*Jews of Staszów!*
Every one of you bears a very great responsibility. The smallest bit of fur that you withhold – God forbid – puts your life and those of the whole town in jeopardy. Do not worry about your insignificant furs, but rather about your lives and the threat of being shot.

Hurry: the deadline is tight.

The Jewish Council

1 YVA, O-6/430, fol. 28. Poster in German and Polish. This document has been translated from German.

2 The small town of Staszów is located 55 km south-east of Kielce. The chairman of the Jewish Council was Efraim (Froym) Zynger (1892–1942), from Staszów; head of the Jewish Community of Staszów prior to Sept. 1939; murdered in Nov. 1942.

3 On Himmler's orders, on 24 Dec. 1941 Senior Commander of the Security Police and the SD (BdS) Eberhard Schöngarth instructed the SS and Police Leaders within the districts of the General Government to confiscate all furs and pelts from the Jewish population immediately: APW, Office of the Governor of District Warsaw, Commissioner for the Jewish Residential District, Transfer Bureau 482/121, fol. 80. The order was communicated to the Jewish councils in Warsaw and Lublin on 25 Dec. 1941 and was only later conveyed to the Jewish councils in smaller towns.

## DOC. 29
## Stefa Szereszewska describes the difficulties involved in providing welfare services at an apartment building in the Warsaw ghetto between April and December 1941[1]

Handwritten report, unsigned,[2] for the underground archive of the Warsaw ghetto, dated 25 April 1942

*19 Gęsia St.*

Report based on a ledger and on conversations with the chairman of the building committee.[3] The ledger covers the period from April to December 1941.[4]

[…][5] front, in a 4-storey […] 45 tenants, 25 subtenants, 20 [?] families, and 38 […]. The house is very poor. Street traders, craftsmen – none of them have workshops or any opportunity to earn money. Twenty refugee families – they either live off what is left of their dwindling possessions or are already completely destitute … and one financial potentate: Blajman[6] the baker, or rather Blajman's bakery, which is in this building.

In general, one can say that 1940 was the heyday of the building committees. In 1941 we were already noting signs of decline, until we eventually reached the final phase this autumn. The house at 19 Gęsia St. experienced its 'golden age' in 1941, like other institutions that are culturally or commercially underdeveloped and oriented towards models that are not suited to them.

[…] 19, although it is not far […] from the western outskirts of the city […], has for the western periphery a [n …][7] commercial and social structure. […] its work in spring 1940, had no major […] with fundraising, did not organize events or card games[8] (the area was unsuitable for this, although the winter of 1940/1941 was exploited all too well in this regard) and carried out its welfare work in the best and truest sense of the term. Each month, some 300–400 złotys' worth of contributions were collected and administered as welfare. For local conditions that is a lot, but compared to the contributions collected by the other building committees it is not much.

1 AŻIH, Ring I/653 (297), fols. 3–16. Published in English translation in Kermish (ed.), *To Live with Honor*, pp. 148–152. The original pages are damaged and illegible in places. This document has been newly translated from Polish.

2 Handwritten note by Hersh Vaser, the secretary of the underground archive, in Yiddish: 'Compiled [by] Stefa Szereszewska'.

3 Shortly after the establishment of the Warsaw ghetto, a network of building committees was established. These autonomous administrative bodies provided support to the residents of individual apartment buildings, particularly those in greatest need. The committees' tasks included the provision of food, clothing, and childcare, and the organization of social activities. The committees were placed under the guidance of the Jewish Social Self-Help (JSS). The chairman of the building committee referred to here was Mr Wajzer.

4 These two sentences were added later.

5 Where ellipses appear here and below, one or several words are missing.

6 Daniel Blajman (Bleiman) (*c.*1895–1942), retailer and businessman; chairman of the Bakers' Association; thought to have been shot in April 1942.

7 Possibly: 'atypical'.

8 In the early days of the Warsaw ghetto, neighbours would meet up, especially on long winter evenings, mostly to play cards; a portion of the stakes would go to the building committee.

In summer 1940 there was a kitchen that provided supplementary food for twenty children. The housewives took turns cooking in their own homes. The work was not organized particularly professionally and appears to have been rather 'amateurish', but great care and consideration were evident in the process, and its value in terms of public funds is suitably appreciated.

In the [...] summary of revenues and expenditure based on the ledger which the building committee kept for 9 months (from April to December 1941), certain features [...] that [...] are typical of this building committee become apparent.

Let us take the first item: the curve of weekly contributions to the building committee shows the development of the work as a whole. The falling curve in June is attributable to the steam bath.[9] This has a gruelling effect because it sucks and squeezes [people] dry like a honey pump; this results in fewer contributions being paid, and the shortfall in contributions causes a deficit, although the building committee, having made up the deficit, almost always manages to retain some surplus.[10]

Payments are gradually dwindling because contributors have become impoverished and their funds are exhausted, or because the treasurer or other members of the building committee have grown weary of the task. The objective deterioration in conditions and the purely psychological aspects, which are not conducive to our operation, are closely connected and, on the whole, paint a sorry picture of how the enthusiasm with which people threw themselves into the work for the sake of the community until [...] is generally waning, and how the contributions are dwindling – only [...] remained, in December he was the only one [...] still paying contributions.[11] After that, the bookkeeping breaks off. One doesn't keep accounts for a single contributor, even if this contributor is Blajman. The illness of the chairman, Mr Wajzer, was another reason why events turned out the way they did, and [this] accelerated both the formal and the actual disintegration of the building committee.

A similar decline was evident with regard to the holiday collections:[12] 330 złoty in donations for Passover, 186 złoty for the autumn festival.[13] This is not only a question of diminished liquidity, but also a sign of increasing indifference, people becoming accustomed to poverty, and – more importantly – helplessness in the face of tremendous need.

The reduced revenues mean reduced benefits and a shrinking budget. The community spirit behind the work is failing, and there is no longer any continuity in the initiatives carried out. Collections for those in need, on the occasion of funerals or in the event of illness, and the payment of fees have taken on the character of a charitable, philanthropic initiative that operates on a very [...] basis. Ultimately [...] the overall work, as in the

9 Polish: 'parówka'. This is a reference to the rigorous disinfection procedures ordered by the Germans and organized by Poles and Jews. The individuals designated for disinfection had to go to a public bathhouse. The residents often suffered considerable material losses as a result of their buildings being cordoned off (quarantined), theft, and the destruction of their vermin-infested belongings.

10 The building committees sought to dissuade the so-called sanitation squads (hygiene units) from carrying out disinfections by paying them bribes. A surplus was presumably left over after the building committee passed on the money collected for these bribes.

11 This is a reference to Blajman.

12 Here in the sense of: 'collections of donations for people in need'.

13 The Jewish Feast of Tabernacles (Sukkot), which was celebrated from 6 to 12 Oct. 1941.

phrase[14] 'not […] typical of this period of work […] that a single tenant […] registers as a person in need and declares that he feels isolated and abandoned because there is no building committee any more. The municipal district[15] is trying everything in its power to organize and revive a building committee in this building, and the building committee will probably resume its work in a slightly different configuration (there are hardly any other candidates). Presumably, however, despite all the goodwill of a few socially minded individuals, the work will not progress without outside help. Such assistance is possible for so-called special houses; this house belongs to that category.

The situation that has arisen in this house is not unique. Rather, it should be considered typical. The building committees are helplessly laying down their arms in the face of tremendous hardship. When the municipal district asked why there are so few activities, the chairmen of the building committees replied: 'We didn't know the war would last so long.' […] 'at the moment there could be a building committee again […], because quite a few of the residents have died.' […] That may sound cynical […] – it is incontrovertible proof that the building committees are overwhelmed by the immense distress, no longer feel up to their task, and believe that the only way out of this paralysis is to dissolve the committees. One must not forget that the advantage of support from the building committee was that it was direct and rapid. The very immediacy of this support has now boomeranged against the institution itself. Even the kindest person is compelled to refuse every request, every petition letter, because he is not in a position to help; but the worst person [too] (as a rule there were no such [people] among the members of this building committee) is also unable to explain indifferently to his fellow residents (with whom he lives every day) that he cannot help them, when he is nevertheless convinced that help is needed. Especially when he […]. The building committee at 19 Gęsia Street was in precisely such a situation, and the chairman, Mr Wajzer, thought it right to dissolve it, i.e. to inform the municipal district that the committee no longer exists and […] of his house to be informed of this as well.

And here we observe an extremely interesting phenomenon. The formal dissolution of the building committee does not mean that it actually ceases to exist. Under the present conditions, a residential building cannot exist without a committee unless the group, which by chance shares a common roof and house number,[16] is represented by a governing body. The building committee, originally an instrument of grassroots charitable work, has gradually developed into an administrative instrument, regulating the collective life of hundreds of people. The most important administrative matters, which had previously been handled centrally, without the tenants having to take any notice of them – in other words, to a certain extent, [things] happened automatically – now fall to the committee. Water, waste disposal, electricity, sanitation – this concerns all the residents and that […] as a collective effort […] are handled by some representative body. The rest of the tenants welcome anyone capable of performing the required action (because they are thereby relieved of this duty).

14 The original has no visible closing quotation mark to end the quotation introduced at this point.

15 This is presumably a reference to the Central Building Committees Commission, which oversaw the building committee at 19 Gęsia Street.

16 The original Polish literally means: 'mortgage number'.

After a short period in which 'significant activity' was recorded, Mr Wajzer (the chairman of the building committee), accompanied by a member of the building committee, came forward once again and explained verbally and in writing that there is no building committee in this building. So I stopped trying to persuade him (which I had done at several of their evening meetings) and calmly replied that I accepted his resignation,[17] but that this would not affect the course of events, 'because [only] your death or the end of the war can bring your committee work to an end'. And the gentlemen know that this is indeed the case and they asked me helplessly [...] what they should do. Ninety per cent are poor [...] and 10 per cent could pay something but do not wish to. They barricaded the entrance to the house in order to collect contributions because a tenant was unable to pay his 90-złoty gas bill, and the gasworks had threatened to cut off the gas supply if the tenants (i.e. the building committee) did not pay this sum. One of the tenants had actually assaulted Mr Wajzer. We looked at the wounds on his hands and face, treated with an iodine tincture, and at his tattered coat. Mr Wajzer really does not want to continue working, he does not want to involve himself in anything any more, he does not want to bear any responsibility. But whenever any action has to be performed, everyone turns to Mr Wajzer, and because he himself has an interest in this (gas, electricity), and also partly because he feels morally responsible despite his resignation, he once again does anything that is particularly urgent.

The situation in this house is currently very serious. [...] 32 families, i.e. 50 per cent of the tenants, are in receipt of welfare from the building committee. Among these families, there are also cases in which every single family member has died in the meantime.

Since spring 1940, seven entire families have died – twenty-five people have died of hunger. Seventeen families are living in extreme poverty and require immediate help. Thirty-five families can barely keep themselves alive; they cannot contribute to the building committee, and in another (richer) house, they would be the first in need of help.

There are twelve to fifteen tenants who could pay small contributions, but most of them refuse to do so.

There are three full orphans and twenty-six half-orphans in the house.

In view of the lack of money, there can be no question of welfare support.

For food we give [...]. We are assembling a new building committee from scratch.

The building committees were created on our initiative, and institutionalization has revived them. If we do not take care of them, they will cease to exist. At first, the economic and social energy was so strong that it only took a spark to set in motion the great possibilities that still existed in 1940, and a multifaceted operation full of the noblest ambitions and aspirations was carried out (everywhere and by everyone) with unprecedented vigour. Under the present conditions (this is not the place to present a detailed [...][18]), the contributions to the building committees are smaller, for good reason.

[...] This is an enormous [...], we should spare no effort to curb it, and no effort [required] to achieve this should be too great for us.[19]

17 Here the author is presumably speaking in her capacity as a representative of the Central Building Committees Commission.

18 Possibly: 'analysis'.

19 This is followed by the place and the date, written in different handwriting: 'Warsaw, 25 April 1942'.

## DOC. 30

## *Za naszą i waszą wolność*, December 1941: a resident of the Warsaw ghetto writes to a Polish comrade about the misery and terror inflicted on the Jews[1]

*Through the ghetto walls … (Letters to a Polish Comrade)*

Comrade,

First, allow me to remind you of myself, not with my name or my surname – that is neither important, nor possible – but with events.

It was more than two years ago. In late September – towards 'the end of the epic'.[2] We were already 'on our way back' from the 'excursion', as it was called at the time; from the mad march behind the army, behind those who were ready and loyal, soldierly, until their last breath … And who had been abandoned by these 'great men', these true leaders … Those who dispersed … As did we … as did everyone … We were left alone …

In a forest near N. It was evening. We were to spend the night in the hay at a farmhouse. But the woman wept, pleaded with bitter tears, and asked us tired, worn-out men over and over again: *My dear, dear gentlemen, will my beloved Stasiek also return? Or has he fallen? Jesus, dear Lord Jesus.*[3] We kept quiet. Until finally you were the first to break the dismal silence. You threw a coin down on the table in front of the woman and bid her farewell. *May God reward you, landlady. For the milk, for your hospitality, for everything.*

But I, standing on the threshold, added: *Your Stasiek will return from the war. He'll be back soon.*

You shot me an angry, aggravated look. And we set off in silence. Into the unknown. *And why, Comrade* – your words resounded through the forest at that time – *tell me why the hell is this happening everywhere? Why doesn't anyone realize that Poland is lost, that we have to start all over again? Why does everybody only ask about their Stasiek, their Janek, their Franek? Why is that, Comrade? Tell me!* you shouted.

I was moved by these strong, wonderful, noble, terrible, and beautiful words. And they were so sad. I shook them off with a shudder and replied: *You are wrong, Comrade. For Poland is these very people – the unfortunate mothers of all these Stasieks, Janeks, and Franeks.*

But you were still sad and remained silent. There was nothing, only the forest and the sound of the tree branches we broke. And the beating of our sad, grim hearts. And nothing, only the poppy-red moon behind the forest, and firelight in the distant north. From Warsaw, which had not yet been defeated …

You already know everything, Comrade. Surely, you remember me now … But for God's sake, don't ask any more where I've been, what I've seen, what I've experienced. Don't hurt me, don't tear open any wounds. They are still too fresh. I will not ask either.

1 *Za naszą i waszą wolność*, no. 9, Dec. 1941, pp. 7–8; AAN, 1583/1196/1, fols. 20–21. *Za naszą i waszą wolność* was a monthly Bund publication that appeared in Polish between 1941 and 1942. This document has been translated from Polish.

2 The Polish armed forces' organized resistance to the German invasion ended in late Sept. 1939.

3 Apart from the title, the passages in the original that are introduced with dashes and represent reported speech are set in italics in this and the three subsequent paragraphs.

I am merely happy that we are still alive, and that there are still so many of us. And that we are together again. Together, despite the walls, despite the ghetto …

Wait. Do not succumb to emotion. I know that your forehead is burning with shame at these very words. Words of disgrace, of humiliation. I know that you often want to tear down the ghetto walls yourself, with your bare hands, and reduce them to rubble. I understand that. But it can't be done. You can't do it yet. Let's leave it for now. For some point in the future. If it becomes necessary, we'll do it together somehow. So that the work isn't in vain.

So greetings, Comrade from the other, 'Aryan', side. I, a 'Jew' from the 'ghetto', greet you with a raised fist. I welcome you to the struggle. To the difficult struggle for a cause that remains the same: 'For our freedom and yours'.[4] For total freedom, the whole, the only one. I would so much like to say, for true – freedom. What a wonderful word.

Red Vienna fought in the name of this freedom.[5] Red Spain[6] shed blood for this freedom, when …

But let's leave these memories behind. After all, dear Comrade, I should write something about myself, about my ghetto, and ask about you, about your health on the 'other' side.

Well, all right. I'll begin. With the ghetto. With our autumn in this ghetto. Autumn in the ghetto. Is there anywhere in the world a pen powerful enough to adequately describe it? Autumn. The third autumn of the war. The second in the Warsaw ghetto. In the past, our Polish autumn was gilded, golden, unique. Would any poet have imagined back then that our golden, sweet autumn would one day knock on the doors of workers' and farmers' huts with its scuffling, worn-out shoes, wet and cold, with filthy paws?

And today … autumn has commenced with a *triumph of Death*, mowing down thousands, tens of thousands of exhausted ghetto prisoners.

Let's leave death aside for now and move on to our life in the ghetto. The so-called life in the so-called Jewish residential district in Warsaw is truly interesting. A 'residential district' that nevertheless has its own autarchic, self-sufficient 'system', about which our 'elders' shamelessly boast.[7] A 'residential district' where the only and central problem is how to escape death from starvation.

Oh, I forgot … Apologies, Comrade, I should not write about death. And indeed, how should I describe it to you? Comrade – the social life in the 'residential district', the hunt for bread, for black and dirty bread, this miserable life on the border between insanity and savagery, the soul of which is typhus? A 'residential district' that kills like the plague, that deprives people of all that is best and most beautiful, where 'self-government' is instituted by the good grace of the executioners, 'social welfare' is run by the stupidest members of the bourgeoisie, who are a miserable reflection of the impotence and apathy of this social stratum, where 'street children' perish in the gutter, begging, whimpering, moaning in the filth and excrement, where, despite everything, hope and

4 'For our freedom and yours' was the rebels' motto in divided Poland during the November Uprising of 1830–1831. The motto was also the title of the Bund's publication *Za naszą i waszą wolność*.
5 This is a reference to the Social Democrats, who governed Vienna between 1918 and 1934.
6 This is a reference to the defenders of the Spanish Republic, governed by the Popular Front, who opposed General Franco's coup during the Spanish Civil War (June 1936 – April 1939).
7 An allusion to the Jewish Council.

faith in tomorrow have not yet been extinguished? Where, on the contrary, the flame of faith burns so high and with such intensity that one day it will ignite the ghetto walls?

But I will mention one more event. It happened recently. I warn you in advance, it will be sad. As sad as my whole ghetto is. As sad as the memory of its hostile creators will some day be.

Well, it happened early on 17 November, at 7.30 a.m. Our ghetto here also has a 'Jewish prison',[8] of course: if there are Jewish 'authorities' and 'police', then there must also be a prison … Well, honourable gentlemen gathered in the prison yard. Honourable representatives of the German authorities. And of the 'Polish' and the 'Jewish' authorities as well. These 'Poles' and 'Jews' – they were 'our' policemen, of course. Well, this honourable company gathered on 17 November 1941 in order to execute 'criminals' in the name of a German court – yes, a court, a 'special' court. There were eight criminals. Six women and two men. Their crime was that they had gone over to your side, Comrade, 'without permission', in order to beg from you or to sell something so they could buy potatoes for their children with ration cards. For such a crime, Polish police officers are to now execute them on the morning of 17 November.

Among the 'criminals' are an 18-year-old girl, an old woman of 60, and a mother of three children, whose youngest child was born in the ghetto barely six months ago. But the law issued by Dr Frank, president of the Academy for German Law,[9] is a 'stringent law'. It is not sentimental. So the sentence was carried out.[10] At 7.30 in the morning precisely. National Socialist 'law' can't take a joke. The 18-year-old girl decided to beg on the Aryan side without 'permission' – a bullet in the head. For the elderly woman – the same. But the other woman is the mother of three children – death for her too. The sentence was carried out. With the help of a squad of 'Polish police'. And the Jewish police, who 'assisted' through the presence of their vile 'commander-in-chief'.[11]

You ask, Comrade, whether the Polish policeman's hand did not tremble for a moment, whether the Jewish commander's throat did not tighten? I don't know. I didn't ask. Perhaps the hand did tremble, perhaps the Jewish commander was moved, but perhaps not even that. I do know that the sentence was carried out. The sentence was handed down by the Germans, by a German court, under Dr Frank's 'new' law. And I also know that the corpses of the eight criminals were buried in a common grave, to the eternal glory of National Socialist law and its blind Polish–Jewish executioners.

But I know something else. At that terrible moment of execution, something boomed in their air above the prison yard. It roared and it crashed down upon the heads of the German men and the Polish and Jewish executioners. It was the mighty, terrible cry of the young mother. Ha, you villains! You will soon die. You will die.

8 A reference to the Jewish Order Service's central prison on Gęsia Street.

9 The Academy for German Law was founded in Munich in 1933. Hans Frank served as its president and oversaw its activities until August 1942.

10 17 Nov. 1941 was the first time that ghetto residents were sentenced and shot on the basis of the Governor General's regulation of 15 Oct. 1941: see Doc. 13. The victims were Mordechai (Motek) Fiszbaum (b. 1903), shoemaker; Luba Gac; Rywka Kligerman (b. 1908 or 1909); Fajga Margules (b. 1903); Sala Pasztejn (b. 1920), tailor; Josek Pajkus (b. 1909), glazier, survived by his wife and two children; Dwojra Rozenberg; and Chana Zajdenwach.

11 Józef Szeryński.

Comrade, I can see your sad face before me, distorted with grief. And I hear your injured heart weeping softly. And although I myself am not made of steel, I beg you to control yourself, to regain composure. After all, we must be tougher than steel and more durable than iron. We must. For the cause. For the fatherland, and for its freedom – for socialist Poland.

I will conclude my letter now, Comrade, and I will go out into the streets and squares of my miserable, narrow ghetto, where even in the daytime it is so dark, so ugly, so sad. I will go to the death zone and stand somewhere there, in a corner of the sad city district. And I will look at the working masses. Poles. Workers. Brothers on this common earth of ours. They are building tombs, laying brick upon brick. I will observe this gruesome, hellish, ghastly work – performed by my Polish brothers – Polish workers. The work of further sealing my ghetto tomb, enclosing it within even tighter walls. I will listen to the sound of their shovels and the rhythm of their work – performed on orders from hell – not without pain, but also without sorrow … Ultimately, I know that infernal forces are building the walls and not Polish workers, for they are themselves prisoners. And I also know that these same workers – these same Poles – will one day tear it down with me, with us, will some day tear down these walls and destroy the ghetto, will create a New Life, a New City – equally happy for all. After all, the common people of Paris also built the Bastille by order of the kings, and the same people reduced it to rubble.

## DOC. 31
## On 3 January 1942 Elsa Binder describes the bleak winter evenings in the Stanisławów ghetto[1]

Handwritten diary of Elsa Binder,[2] entry for 3 January 1942

Stanisławów,[3] 3 January 1942
The evenings are the worst. At 7 o'clock, when we are ordered to put out the lights, the whole family goes to bed. I am the only one to waste a candle, by which I read or write. In the end I enter the unheated room to get into my bed, which has been heated with a hot brick. There I have time to reflect on my life at present.

Life? I very much doubt whether this can be called life.

1 AŻIH, 302/267, fols. 55–158. English translation published in Alexandra Zapruder (ed.), *Salvaged Pages: Young Writers' Diaries of the Holocaust* (New Haven: Yale University Press, 2002), p. 312. This document has been newly translated from Polish.

2 Elsa (Elza, Eliszewa) Binder (b. 1920 or 1921), activist with the Hashomer Hatzair youth organization prior to Sept. 1939; between 23 Dec. 1941 and 18 June 1942, she kept a diary about her life in the Stanisławów ghetto, including her frequent conflicts with her parents and her sister, Dora. Dora was murdered in March 1942; Elsa's subsequent fate is unknown. The ghetto was liquidated in Feb. 1943. The notebook with Eliszewa's name on the cover was found in a ditch beside the road along which the Jews of Stanisławów had been driven to the place where they were shot.

3 More than 25,000 Jews lived in Stanisławów prior to Sept. 1939; their number later increased due to the influx of refugees and expellees. The German police murdered approximately 10,000 people at the Jewish cemetery on 12 Oct. 1941. Approximately 30,000 people were confined in a sealed ghetto in Dec. 1941.

A state of vegetation? Not that either. After all, I think, feel, suffer. Everything in me is a single chord of pain and hope. I dislike the winter. I fear the freezing temperatures. But when I lie in bed at such an early hour, a time when I'd usually get dressed to go into town; when the lifeless face of the moon peeks in through the undraped window; when the sound of sleigh bells passing by eventually reaches me from the streets that I'm not permitted to walk – my entire being, my entire sad, lethargic self yearns for the full moon, the snow, the streets.

And when I think that many of my young comrades will never see or feel this, then, despite everything, rebellion and my survival instinct awaken in me.

Yes! I want to live. I want to eat well (I can only dream of butter, and milk is a distant memory of times past) and to dress well (I haven't done so for ages). I want intellectual pleasures (one last time, something pleasant).

Finally, I want to love and be loved. This is nature's law. Sad, but true. I dream of such trivial things over the fresh graves of my peers. Good God! But I don't want entertainment, parties, flirting. I've never been one for those things. I dream only of things that are as essential to me as oxygen is to plants.

But … milk and butter are but a dream, while the reality is the order to surrender shoes and skis (I could do with the former myself – although I've got elegant shoes and patent leather boots, my wardrobe is not suited to my present work). Art and films are but a dream; instead the reality consists of a letter from Wilk to Zyhawa in which he writes about the typhoid in the camp and the ghetto, and consoles me with the dream that we will soon see each other. And this is how the grey and colourless days, brightened only by dreams, go by – between sad reality and radiant hope.

Today is a very sad day. Tomorrow is unknown.

Announcements appealing to the Ukrainian people have been put up, proclaiming: The Jews will not live to see the red menace engulf Europe. What sad premonitions are these?

The newspapers say: freezing temperatures and snow don't matter, they will pass. God willing, the sun will rise, the snow will melt, we will move on.

But God is way up on high, the sun far away, and the Soviets near.

The heart races with so much crazy hope, and the soul is filled with a fervent plea. Oh God! Where are you? Help! Help!

## DOC. 32
## On 6 January 1942 Rabbi Yitskhok Kats argues for the introduction of a compulsory levy to alleviate hunger and privation in the Warsaw ghetto[1]

Statement by Yitskhok Kats,[2] Warsaw, dated 6 January 1942

What I wanted to say …
(Contribution to the JSS conference held on Monday,[3] 6 January 1942, at which I was a delegate)

Concerning the Talmudic term 'tzedakah'[4] (giving to the poor), a great philosopher and thinker notes that it means justice and duty, and that it should not be understood as some kind of philanthropic matter. And rightly so, because according to the Jewish Torah, giving to the poor is not conditional on the will of men; rather, it is a duty [that has] become a law or a levy. Thus the Torah of Moses obliged the people to give offerings and tithes to the priests from the harvest, from the meat, and from the animals – the shoulder, cheeks, and maw[5] – and to give to the poor the gleanings, the forgotten produce, and the corners of the field;[6] fallen berries and gleanings[7] from the vineyard; the tithes for the poor; as well as alms. Here the Torah of Moses expressly states: 'sufficient for his need',[8] i.e. it is a duty to give the poor man as much as he needs. Yes, it is indeed a duty and a commandment, because the Torah of Moses – unlike other religions that are based on utopias and consider the law superfluous – has given laws, prohibitions, and commandments to [the people of] Israel and to humanity. A great thinker even notes that the aim of the law is its own dissolution, i.e. over time, the law will become psychologically engrained in people's hearts and minds. The Talmud also understands this, although such a state will only occur in the perfect world to come, about which the Talmud says: 'The commandments will be abolished in the hereafter'.[9] This means that in the world to come the law will not be necessary; rather, the duty of the heart will suffice. But in today's world, 'the generations

1 AŻIH, Ring I/423 (251), fol. 2–3. Published in English translation in Kermish (ed.), *To Live with Honor*, pp. 355–357. This document has been newly translated from Yiddish.
2 Yitskhok Kats (Katz) (1905–1942), rabbi and writer; born in Rypin; received a traditional religious education before becoming a rabbi; contributed articles and stories to the Orthodox daily *Dos Yudishe Togblat* in Warsaw; authored a novel and a monograph, among other publications; perished of hunger in the Warsaw ghetto in August 1942.
3 In fact 6 January 1942 was a Tuesday.
4 The Hebrew word for charity, *tsdoke* in Yiddish; in a biblical context the term exclusively means justice before God, but in rabbinic times (between 70 CE and the completion of the Talmud around the sixth century) it was extended to include the obligation to be charitable. Kats's argumentation shifts between the two meanings.
5 Deuteronomy 18:3. All biblical quotations in this document are based on the JPS 1917 edition.
6 This Talmudic designation refers to the three parts of the harvest that a farmer was required to leave for the benefit of the poor and the stranger: Leviticus 19:9–10 refers to *pe'ah* (corners) and *leket* (gleanings), while Deuteronomy 24:19–21 mentions *shikhḥah* (forgotten produce) and *leket*.
7 The term *peret* in the original refers to grapes that fall from their clusters when plucked from the vine, as in Leviticus 19:10; *olelot* are unripe grape clusters: see Leviticus 19:10 and Deuteronomy 24:21.
8 Deuteronomy 15:18.
9 Babylonian Talmud, Niddah 61b.

have not improved [in their morals]'.[10] Laws and their enforcement are necessary. Indeed, according to the Talmud, 'collectors can take a pledge for a charity contribution even on the eve of the Sabbath'.[11] This means that charity can be imposed, and so one of the Talmud scholars forced another to make a donation of 400 złoty. After all, by no means can we rely solely on a person's pious desire, above all when it comes to those things that are the basis for improving the world. No, a thousand times no! We cannot tolerate one person dying of gluttony while another perishes of hunger, one person expiring from overwork and another from sitting idle, etc. Every human being has the right to live in the world, and if that person has the right to live, then that person has the right to food. God, the Lord of the world, created food for the ant as well as for the elephant. Did He not then provide sustenance for people? Who will tolerate evil, wicked people taking everything for themselves and letting others die of hunger?

Jews of Warsaw, you are saddled with a serious charge, namely that you do not fulfil your fundamental duty to show mercy. Walking down the street, one sees people dying of hunger and privation, simply collapsing on the spot, and no one takes pity on these unfortunate souls, who could be saved with a glass of tea and a bit of bread. For heaven's sake, where does such cruelty come from? The Talmud, tractate Baba Metzia,[12] addresses the following problem: two people are walking in a desert with no more than one flask of water. If both drink, then both will die. But if only one drinks, he will remain alive. To this, one tanna[13] says that both should drink and both should die, so that one does not have to watch his companion die. However, Rabbi Akiva[14] says, 'Your life comes first', meaning that one's own life takes precedence. Indeed, the Gaon[15] Rabbi Shneur Zalman of Liadi,[16] of blessed memory, aptly remarks in a responsum[17] he wrote that this only applies when one's life is in danger, but not when it comes to luxuries, such that one person might eat a good tsimmes[18] and another literally die of hunger, or that one might live surrounded by pleasures and another perish as a churl dieth.[19] The Talmud notes that during the destruction of Betar[20] a notable tragedy of this sort occurred: on one side people danced, while [on] the other [side they] shed a sea of blood and tears; neither side knew about the other. Isn't this tragedy repeating itself with us? Those with full bellies

10 Babylonian Talmud, Yebamoth 39b.

11 Babylonian Talmud, Baba Bathra 8b.

12 Babylonian Talmud, Baba Metzia 62a.

13 A tanna ('rehearser' or 'teacher') was the title bestowed on a rabbinic teacher whose views appear in the Mishnah or who taught in Mishnic times (second century CE). The Mishnah is the most important collection of religious legal traditions in rabbinic Judaism and forms the basis of the Talmud.

14 Akiva ben Joseph (c.50/55–135), Jewish scholar; he is regarded as the first person to collect and compile texts for the Jewish exegesis of the Torah (Mishnah) and is one of the most important representatives of rabbinic Judaism.

15 This was originally a title given to the heads of Talmudic academies starting around the sixth century CE. After the gaonic period it came to be used as an honorific title for eminent Jewish intellectuals and Talmudic scholars.

16 Shneur Zalman of Liadi (1745?–1812), rabbi; one of the leaders of Hasidism and the founder of its Lubavitch branch.

17 Responsa are answers to legal questions addressed to Jewish religious authorities.

18 A sweet dish made of stewed fruit or vegetables.

19 2 Samuel 3:33.

20 A fortress in the Judean hills that was destroyed by the Roman emperor Hadrian in 135 CE in the process of quelling the Bar Kokhba revolt.

visit cinemas, theatres, confectioners, etc. and want to turn a completely blind eye to the hungry. On the contrary, this cruelty has become even greater now than [it was] before the war. Man no longer reflects the image of God;[21] he is just like a mouse that snatches a piece of bread and disappears into its hole. That's how it is, Jews of Warsaw! Future historians will not remember you kindly. Why, if the Torah of Moses commanded that the neck of a heifer be broken for one person,[22] then how many such heifers would need to be sacrificed for so many dead? It's as if the eyes that see all of this are closed. There is not even any pity for the little children. At this point, I want to recall a word from the Torah of Moses about the apostate city:[23] 'And show thee mercy, and have compassion upon thee'.[24] In the Tosefta Sanhedrin,[25] Tanna Rabbi Akiva asks how there can be mercy for an apostate city. Only by showing mercy to the little children, he says. This means – as I noted in my book *Kerem Yavne*[26] – that there is mercy and love. And while the latter is a lofty ideal, as the object of humanity and of all of creation, mercy is no more than an instinct. While love can only be felt for a person who is whole and not for a spiritual cripple, there is mercy for every living being in the world. This is precisely what the Torah of Moses says: there can be no love for the apostate city inhabited by cruel idolaters, but there is mercy for such creatures too, and mercy must be shown to the children.

You, Jews of Warsaw, do not even have mercy on the little children who walk around naked in the streets. When they go into shops and beg for a piece of bread, they are cruelly thrown out. At the same time, they have to watch as gluttonous greaseballs come in and ask: Do you have Kagan's rolls?[27] Or are these, God forbid, yesterday's rolls …? And they watch the children die of deprivation and cold. This is a profanation of the Holy Name in the eyes of the other nations who witness it.

Therefore it is my opinion that we must not trifle with delusions of conferences and building committees at this moment – they are nothing more than gimmicks and a waste of time. Rather, we must forcibly collect taxes from the well-to-do to benefit those without means, because if all the thunder and lightning, all the blazing beacons, have still not been enough to show the people the way like a shining torch, then I do not believe that speeches and propaganda will work. That would be nothing more than self-deception. Rather, we must forcibly tax the Jewish population to help the hungry and those in need. And this must happen as soon as possible. It is noteworthy that Tosefta Shabbat, chapter 8, says: 'Know, the people of Sodom were slow', meaning that the people of Sodom were unmoved. They did not hurry to help. We Jews have learned that, when it comes to saving a

21 A reference to that which places man above animals: see Genesis 1:26–28.

22 The ritual of breaking the calf's neck is described at the end of parashah Shoftim (Deuteronomy 21:1–9) and had to be performed when the body of a murder victim was discovered in an unpopulated area within the land of Israel; the closest Jewish city was notified and its inhabitants performed a ceremony which concluded with a prayer of atonement for the crime.

23 A reference to a city that has gone astray, an Israelite city in which the majority of inhabitants have taken up idol worship: see Deuteronomy 13:13–19.

24 Deuteronomy 13:18.

25 Tosefta XIV 3. Aramaic: literally 'extension'; a collection of Jewish oral teachings and traditions from rabbinic times. In many cases the Tosefta supplements the Mishnah and originated alongside or shortly after it.

26 'Vineyard of Yavne'; this publication could not be found.

27 The Kagan bakery, one of Warsaw's largest kosher bakeries, was located in the ghetto at 45 Nalewki Street from 1940.

life,[28] acting quickly is truly praiseworthy.[29] As Rambam,[30] of blessed memory, ruled, one must not ask any questions when it comes to saving lives.[31] A Jewish anecdote tells of a young man who once went to the Gaon Rabbi Yoshe Ber Brisker,[32] of blessed memory, to be trained. The Gaon asks him: What does the law say someone should do if he cuts his finger on the Sabbath? The young man stands there and thinks. The Gaon cries out, 'Human blood is flowing and you stand there thinking?' When blood is flowing like water, one must not think, only act – necessarily as quickly as possible. And whoever fulfils the commandment as quickly as possible will be worthy of Israel's consolation.

## DOC. 33

## On 9 January 1942 the commissioner for the Jewish residential district in Warsaw urges the Kreishauptleute in District Warsaw to shoot Jews who have escaped from their ghetto[1]

Letter from Heinz Auerswald, commissioner for the Jewish residential district in Warsaw (file ref. K-1500, log 1541/41), to the Kreishauptleute of Warschau-Land, Minsk, Siedlce, and Sokolow-Wegrow,[2] dated 9 January 1942

Re: leaving Jewish residential districts without authorization
Below I am forwarding the translation of a letter dated 22 December 1941 from the JSS delegation in Sobienie Jeziory to the Jew Dr Wielikowski,[3] advisor on Jewish welfare matters:[4]

28 A reference to the principle in Jewish law that the obligation to save a life overrides almost all other religious precepts.
29 Babylonian Talmud, Yoma 84b.
30 An acronym for Rabbi Moshe ben Maimon (Moses Maimonides) (1135–1204), a philosopher, physician, and legal scholar from Córdoba.
31 A reference to the principle that it is not necessary to ask permission to violate Sabbath laws in order to save a person's life: see Moses Maimonides, *Mishneh Torah*, Hilkhot Shabbat, ch. 2, Halakha 16.
32 Rabbi Yoshe Ber (also known as Yosef Dov Soloveitchik) (1820–1892), Orthodox rabbi and Talmudist; worked as a teacher in Wołożyń; rabbi in Słuck from 1865; then lived in Warsaw; rabbi in Brest (Yiddish: Brisk), 1877–1892. His collected writings were published as *Beis Halevi* in 1863/64, 1884, and 1891.

1 APW, Office of the Governor of District Warsaw, Commissioner for the Jewish Residential District in Warsaw, Transfer Bureau, 482/40, fol. 24. Published in Berenstein et al. (eds.), *Faschismus – Getto – Massenmord*, pp. 129–130. This document has been translated from German.
2 Kreise in the east of District Warsaw.
3 Dr Gustaw (Gamsej/Gamzej/Gamschei) Wielikowski (1889–1943), lawyer; studied in Munich; active in left-wing Zionist circles until the end of the First World War; member of the executive committee of the Jewish Social Self-Help (JSS), 1940–1942; simultaneously chairman of the Jewish Municipal Welfare Committee in Warsaw (ŻKOM) and head of the Warsaw Jewish Council's Welfare Section from 1941; deputy chairman of Warsaw Jewish Council, 1942–1943; shot in the Warsaw ghetto in April 1943.
4 The original of this letter is headed '*Translation from the Polish*': APW, Office of the Governor of District Warsaw, Commissioner for the Jewish Residential District in Warsaw, Transfer Bureau, 482/40, fol. 25.

Jewish Social Self-Help delegation in Sobienie Jeziory, 22 December 1941, no. 25/41
To Dr Wielikowski in Warsaw

Given that the shootings of Jews who leave the Jewish residential district in Sobienie Jeziory are increasing on a daily basis, we would like to ask you politely whether similar executions are also taking place elsewhere. To our knowledge, this is only the case in Kreis Garwolin.

Is it possible to intervene to ensure that the shooting is not carried out at the place where the Jew is caught, and to inform the Jewish Council in each individual case? We ask this because we know nothing so far about the actual number of people shot or the places where they are buried.

In anticipation of your immediate reply.
Respectfully
The Jewish Social Self-Help delegation in Sobienie Jeziory
Signed A. Frydzon, Sobienie Jeziory

I have notified the Governor[5] of this letter and he wishes the same legal position to be created, if possible, in all the Kreise of [District Warsaw] in which Jews are to be found. The orders issued to the police authorities concerning the use of firearms against Jews[6] who leave the Jewish residential district without authorization enable effective action to be taken in all cases.[7]

## DOC. 34

## On 9 January 1942 leading representatives of the occupation administration in Lemberg (Lwów) discuss the deportation of Jews[1]

Note by the deputy Stadthauptmann of Lemberg, signed Hallbauer,[2] for Stadthauptmann Kujath,[3] dated 10 January 1942

*File note*
*Re*: resettlement of Jews
Dr Ullrich[4] has put forward a directive to be implemented concerning the resettlement of Jews.[5] My previous precautionary submission to the district was rejected outright by

5 Ludwig Fischer.
6 On the Security Police order, see Doc. 17; the order from the Senior Commander of the Order Police (BdO) is mentioned by Herbert Hummel in Doc. 26.
7 On 9 Jan. 1942 Heinz Auerswald sent carbon copies for information to the SS and Police Leader in Warsaw, Arpad Wigand, asking him to inform the gendarmerie commander in District Warsaw, Fritz Göde (b. 1898), and to the Kreishauptmann of Garwolin, Dr Carl Ludwig Freudenthal (1907–1944): APW, Office of the Governor of District Warsaw, Commissioner for the Jewish Residential District in Warsaw, Transfer Bureau, 482/40, fols. 22–23.

1 DALO, R-37/4/140, fols. 57–59. Copy in USHMM, Acc. 1995.A.1086, reel 25. This document has been translated from German.
2 Wilhelm Hallbauer (1889–1969), architect; head of the Urban Expansion Office in Wilhelmshaven in the 1930s; became director of town planning in Łódź in Dec. 1939, and also in Lemberg (Lwów) in Oct. 1941; deputy Stadthauptmann of Lemberg from Feb. 1942; lived in retirement at Bad Nauheim after the war; author of numerous publications on urban development and regional planning.

the Governor's representative, Dr Bauer.[6] Referring to his directive of 8 December 1941, he said the resettlement operation had been halted until further notice and the Cracow directive[7] had in the meantime proven him right.

Dr Bauer has the following requests:

1. Only Jewish skilled workers and specialists who currently remain indispensable for the authorities are to remain in Lemberg until further notice. The police administration should therefore instruct all authorities to provide lists of these individuals. The lists should then be checked by the Labour Department and the required number approved. The Labour Department will also decide how many family members will continue to be granted residence permits for Lemberg so as to enable the continued deployment of the remaining Jews. Jews surplus to requirements are to be transported to those places in the district where the Kreishauptleute have prepared reception facilities in accordance with instructions. Transport arrangements for their resettlement must be secured in advance. Resettlement can only go ahead with an identity card system and under supervision.
2. The residential area north of the railway that has been designated for Jews so far appears unsuitable in terms of its size, boundaries, and type of accommodation. It would appear more expedient to accommodate skilled workers in apartments in the designated sectors II, III, and IV. Parts of the current residential area are only to be added on a scale corresponding to precise lists detailing the number of rooms available in sectors II, III, and IV. In particular, the agricultural land within the current residential area for Jews should remain reserved for Aryans and, where it is already being used, returned to Aryans.
3. Individual operations should only be carried out to the extent required to accommodate German members of the workforce in the German residential area and to establish offices and German firms in the city centre.

3 Hans Kujath (1907–1963), lawyer; joined the NSDAP in 1932 and the SS in 1933; head of the Interior Administration in District Radom from Jan. 1940; additionally Stadthauptmann of Radom from June 1940; Stadthauptmann of Lemberg from August 1941; Kreishauptmann of Czortków, April 1942 – Feb. 1944; served in the Waffen-SS from Sept. 1944; in British captivity, 1945–1947; classed as a *Mitläufer* ('follower') by a denazification tribunal in Lüneburg in 1952; thereafter worked as a lawyer.

4 Correctly: Dr Albert Ulrich (1902–1972), lawyer; taught at Graz Business School; finance officer for the municipal authorities in Graz from 1930; joined the NSDAP in 1938; chief of police in Lemberg from 1941 until at least 1943; responsible for the deportation of Jews; arrested in 1947; tried at Vienna Regional Court; released from prison in Jan. 1950; thereafter worked as an official again in Graz.

5 The directive could not be identified.

6 Otto Bauer (1888–1944), lawyer (without a doctorate); member of the Stahlhelm; joined the NSDAP in 1933 and the SA in 1934; worked at Duisburg Regional Court until Feb. 1940; thereafter president of the German High Court in Cracow; Kreishauptmann of Jasło, Nov. 1940 – Feb. 1941; thereafter senior official in the administration of District Cracow and from August 1941 in the Interior Administration in District Galicia; additionally Kreishauptmann of Lemberg-Land, 1941–1942; chief of staff in District Galicia, 1943–1944; killed by partisans.

7 The directive could not be identified. On 16 Dec. 1941 State Secretary Bühler had instructed the occupation administration to make better preparations for resettlement operations and to coordinate plans with the Interior Administration Main Department if more than fifty individuals were going to be affected: BArch, R 52/II/254, fol. 121.

Systematic resettlement should not be undertaken until the spring, on no account before 1 March, and on no account before precise documents concerning the accommodation options are available.

The undersigned happened to witness a meeting with the Jewish Council at the Housing Office today, the aim of which was to grant a further 20,000 Jews permission to move out of the city and to resettle Jews from the rest of the urban area in the apartments vacated as a result.

The head of the Housing Office appointed by the district, Senior Reich Labour Service Leader Umbeck, explained he was acting in accordance with a directive issued by Dr Bauer on this matter,[8] which had been adopted at a joint meeting with Colonel Bisanz.[9]

Since, at my meeting with him (see above), Dr Bauer had expressly instructed the Stadthauptmann to halt and prevent any continuation of the resettlement operation, and the police administration had received complaints that in their opinion indicated that the Housing Office was continuing the resettlement operation, and indeed without the participation of the police administration mandated by the Governor's directive, I asked Dr Bauer for an explanation and decision. He will provide a record of the detailed discussion with the district authorities arranged in response to this, along with the results of that discussion.[10]

## DOC. 35

## From 11 to 13 January 1942 Dawid Rubinowicz describes in his diary his family's impending deportation from Krajno[1]

Diary of Dawid Rubinowicz,[2] entries for 11 to 13 January 1942

*11 January*: Since early this morning there has been a snowstorm and a biting frost, with temperatures plunging to −20°C. As I watched the wind blow though the fields, I saw the village warden put up an announcement. I immediately went to see what's new on the noticeboard. There was nothing new on the noticeboard, but the guard said he had taken announcements to the sołtys stating that all the Jews from all the villages were to

8 The directive could not be identified.

9 Alfred Bisanz (1890–1951), career officer from Lwów; served in the Austro-Hungarian army, 1906–1918; reached rank of colonel; employed in the Population and Welfare Division within the Interior Administration Department of the General Government as head of the Ukrainian Ethnic Group Section in 1939; joined the NSDAP in 1941; head of the Population and Welfare Division in District Galicia from August 1941; lived in Vienna, 1945–1946; detained by the Soviet authorities in Vienna; died in Moscow.

10 No corresponding document could be identified. Plans to ghettoize the Jews in Lwów were taken up again in spring 1942 after the start of deportations to Belzec. After deportations resumed in mid August 1942, on 21 August SS and Police Leader Katzmann ordered the creation of a closed-off ghetto in Lwów.

1 The original diary was found in Bodzentyn in the Kielce voivodeship in the late 1950s and acquired by the journalist Maria Jarochowska, who first published it in Warsaw in 1960. The original has been missing since then. The diary entries here are published in English translation in *The Diary of Dawid Rubinowicz*, trans. Derek Bowman (Edinburgh: William Blackwood, 1981 [Polish edn, 1960]), pp. 33–34. This document has been newly translated from Polish.

be resettled.[3] When I related this at home, we all became very worried. They will resettle us now in the depths of winter: how and where? Now it's our turn to suffer severe torment. God knows for how long.

*12 January*: First thing this morning, I went out to clear snow. When I came back in to warm up, the deputy sołtys came by and said he had read an announcement at the sołtys's saying that the Jews would be resettled, and they would only be permitted to take with them what they could carry. We were so confused by this news that we didn't know what was happening to us. When Papa[4] returned, we began to pack a few bundles with things that we won't really need, and we took them to the neighbours in case we were unexpectedly resettled, so that at least these items would not be at the house. Papa wanted to sell the wardrobe and other household items, but there was no buyer. Or rather there were buyers, but they only wanted to pay half the price. Papa said he would rather leave things behind than sell them at such a low price. Once we had calmed down a bit, we began to plan who would take which bundle, which undergarments we would wear, and which we should pack. The announcement did not say where and when we would be resettled, only that we would be resettled and nothing else. In the evening a landlord came by and wanted to buy the wardrobe, but he offered only 250 zł. for it and he didn't buy it because the wardrobe should be worth at least 500 zł.

*13 January*: Papa went to Kielce, perhaps to enquire about the resettlement, where we would be resettled and when. We waited impatiently for him, thinking perhaps he would bring better news. When Papa returned, he didn't say anything specific, only that today all the Jewish councils from throughout powiat Kielce would hold a meeting in the starostwo,[5] at which one part of a settlement or a small town is to be designated as a Jewish district. However, Papa did not say where it would be, because he had left before they arrived; they were going to come by but they didn't, because they had probably travelled at night.

2 Dawid Rubinowicz (1927–1942); lived in the village of Krajno, near Kielce; in March 1942 the occupying authorities confined him, his parents, and his siblings to a ghetto in Bodzentyn; six months later the family is thought to have been deported to Treblinka and murdered there.
3 On 11 Dec. 1941 the Interior Administration Department in District Radom issued a circular with directives on the creation of Jewish residential districts in which the Jewish rural population was to be concentrated; these districts were to be established by 1 Jan. 1942: BArch, R 52/II/254, fols. 116–117.
4 Josek Rubinowicz.
5 The Kreishauptmann's office. The Kreishauptmann of Kielce was Hans Drechsel.

## DOC. 36
## Developments in the Warsaw ghetto between 17 and 23 January 1942, as recorded by the chairman of the Jewish Council in Warsaw[1]

Handwritten diary of Adam Czerniaków, entries for 17 to 23 January 1942

*17 January 1942* – In the morning with Szeryński[2] at Mende's[3] and Stabenow's.[4] I asked whether it was true that Lithuanians (Shaulis men) are going to take over ghetto guard duty. They denied it. I asked the commissioner[5] the same question. He replied, 'I am not aware of any such thing.' I said that – as far as I had been told – Shaulis men are already in Książęca Street. He replied that he knew nothing about it.

As for waiving the death penalty for the prisoners, the commissioner said that the Governor[6] (1) has extended the delivery deadline for the 1,500 sheepskins,[7] (2) has accepted the sample delivered, (3) has waived the death penalty for the women, (4) will release children, and (5) has instructed a medical commission (five Jewish physicians and one from the SS) to examine the remaining prisoners, except for the criminals and the smugglers. Those fit for work will be sent to Treblinka camp.[8]

He then discussed the smuggling in Krochmalna Street with Szeryński. Yesterday he confiscated the rickshaws (with soda water etc.). Szeryński explained that the rickshaws are needed to supply the population with coal etc. The Order Service would make sure

1 YVA, O-33/1090. Published in Adam Czerniaków, *Dziennik getta warszawskiego 6 IX 1939–23 VII 1942*, ed. Marian Fuks (Warsaw: Państwowe Wydawnictwo Naukowe, 1983), pp. 241–243. The entire diary has been published in *The Warsaw Diary of Adam Czerniakow: Prelude to Doom*, ed. Raul Hilberg, Stanislaw Staron, and Josef Kermisz, trans. Stanislaw Staron and the Staff of Yad Vashem (Chicago: Ivan R. Dee, 1999), here pp. 316–319. This document has been newly translated from Polish.

2 Józef Szeryński, né Szenkman (1892–1943), police officer; head of the Organizational Affairs Department at the High Command of the Polish State Police; deputy head of the Polish State Police in Lublin voivodeship from 1936; worked in the Warsaw Jewish Council's Transport Section in 1940; head of the Jewish Order Service in the Warsaw ghetto from Oct. 1940; arrested by the Gestapo on 1 May 1942; released on 26 July 1942 so that he could help coordinate the deportations to Treblinka; committed suicide.

3 Gerhard Mende (1911–1944), officer with the Criminal Police; joined the NSDAP and the SS in 1933; responsible for Jewish affairs, along with Karl Georg Brandt, in Department IV B of the Warsaw Gestapo.

4 Dr Gerhard Stabenow (b. 1906), journalist; joined the NSDAP in 1937 and the SS in 1938; worked for the Ethnic German Liaison Office in Eastern Galicia, 1939–1940; head of Department III D (Economic Affairs) for the SD under the Commander of the Security Police and the SD (KdS) in Warsaw, 1940–1943; detained after the war; sentenced to three years in prison in Hamburg in 1948; later worked for the public radio station Deutschlandfunk.

5 Heinz Auerswald.

6 Ludwig Fischer.

7 After the ghetto residents' furs had been confiscated, Czerniaków suggested to Auerswald on 7 Jan. 1942 that approximately 40 condemned prisoners be released from the ghetto prison in return; Governor Fischer agreed to this, provided the Jewish Council supplied him with 1,500 sheepskins within one week: *The Warsaw Diary of Adam Czerniakow*, pp. 312–314.

8 In June 1941 the SS and Police Leader of Warsaw had a labour camp for Poles and Jews (later known as Treblinka I or Treblinka A) constructed next to a gravel pit near the village of Treblinka: see Introduction, p. 29.

that the rickshaws are used only for this purpose. The commissioner ordered the 'Piekiełko' market on Krochmalna Street to be shut down. Before the war, pimps sold women in public at the 'Piekiełko' market.

*18 January 1942* – At the Community in the morning. At 12 [noon] a memorial service in the Nożyk synagogue for the seven deceased Council members.[9] The collection for the sheepskins continues. Frost. The bridge on Żelazna Street[10] is almost complete.

*19 January 1942* – Frost. At the Community in the morning. In connection with the possible release of the prisoners from the Jewish prison,[11] a workshop making sheepskin coats (15 furriers) has been set up in the Community.

Upon the commissioner's request, a medical commission (7 specialists) visited the Jewish detention centre today. They examined the inmates, who have been placed under the jurisdiction of a Sondergericht[12] for leaving the ghetto illegally. The group is estimated to comprise 443 men (including 120 boys) and 213 minors of both sexes (of whom 121 are boys). Auerswald took with him the applications for their release, issued by the detention centre on 213 forms, to submit to the public prosecutor's office.

The [prison] management[13] presented 250 adults to be examined. The commission found 54 of them fit for work. It was ordered that (some of them) should be cured of scabies by the 23rd of this month. They are to be taken away on that day. They must be provided with equipment.[14]

I heard that A[uerswald] has been summoned to Berlin. I constantly harbour the fear that the Jews of Warsaw are at risk of mass resettlement.[15]

*20 January 1942* – At the Community in the morning. There are already more than 500 sheepskins. Given the low revenues, I have decided to ask the wealthier Jews to come to my office in order to encourage them to give more generously. I have inspected four of our elementary schools. From a pedagogical point of view, they are good wherever altruistic people are doing the teaching. By contrast, the classrooms, corridors, and staircases are usually very dirty. I have admonished the office.[16]

*21 January 1942* – At the Community in the morning. The collection (for the sheepskins) is not finished. We are still 500,000 złoty short. The building committees, led by incompetent people, have completely failed. I have summoned their representatives

9 A memorial service for members of the Jewish Council who had died in the ghetto prior to this date.

10 A wooden bridge for pedestrians on Chłodna Street, near the junction with Żelazna Street.

11 The Jewish Order Service's central prison, also known as Gęsiówka, was established on German orders at 22 Gęsia Street in June 1941 and relocated to the Umschlagplatz in late July 1942.

12 German in the original: 'Special Court'.

13 From 1941 the central prison was headed by Dr Leopold Lindenfeld (d. 1942), lawyer; investigating judge in Warsaw; head of the Jewish Order Service's Administration Department in the Warsaw ghetto, 1940–1941; murdered with his family in summer 1942.

14 The Jewish Community was obliged to equip forced labourers with essential items before they left for the camps.

15 The deportations to Treblinka began on 22 July 1942.

16 Presumably the Jewish Council's Schools Section, which was headed by Abram Wolfowicz.

to come to my office today. Another 600 parcels were confiscated at the post office yesterday.[17]

*22 January 1942* – At the Community in the morning. After that, went to the SO[18] to organize fats and sugar for the schoolchildren (2,700 children). I sent Wielikowski to one of the nouveaux riches, who incidentally is quick to give money. He obtained a loan of 200,000 złoty for the sheepskins. I also sent for the first group of citizens and demanded that they add to the money already collected for the sheepskins. Within an hour I received over 20,000 złoty.

The commissioner is back from Cracow and did not go to the office until after lunch. Despite calling him several times, I failed to reach him, so I don't know what he has up his sleeve. Hendel[19] returned from the provinces last night and brought a few dozen sheepskins with him. They are bigger and cheaper. As a result, the price has also dropped in Warsaw, and it looks as if we are going to save over 200,000 złoty.

*23 January 1942* – At the Community in the morning. I went to see Auerswald and asked whether there were any new orders from Berlin. He replied that he had been in B[erlin] on private business.

At 2 p.m. I received a number of Jews who donated little or nothing to the fund for the prisoners' release. Two liars among them pretended to be poverty-stricken, so I had them taken into custody. A certain Obremski, a shoe manufacturer,[20] behaved arrogantly. On top of that, he didn't donate anything at all.

Hendel returned from Węgrów in the evening. He bought a sufficient quantity of sheepskins, [which were] cheaper than in Warsaw.

17 From Feb. 1941 residents of the Warsaw ghetto were forbidden to send parcels by post; they were allowed to receive parcels from the General Government and 'non-hostile foreign countries' until 23 July 1942, when a week-long 'postal blockade' was imposed, but such parcels were repeatedly confiscated by the employees of the police-run Commercial Fraud Unit; 642 parcels were confiscated in Jan. 1942, and 33,160 were delivered to their addressees.

18 The Jewish Council's Supply Office (Zakład Zaopatrzenia, Zakład Zaopatrywania) had the task of distributing food that had been legally supplied to the ghetto.

19 Marian Hendel (Haendel), from Lwów; worked in the film industry prior to Sept. 1939; head of a Jewish labour battalion in 1940; Jewish Order Service inspector in the Warsaw ghetto from 1940, and temporarily the deputy head of the Order Service; had connections with the Gestapo; fled the ghetto in summer 1942; lived in Venezuela after the war.

20 Presumably Henoch Obremski, businessman; owner and, with his three sons, co-proprietor of a firm at 15 Walicców Street in Warsaw prior to Sept. 1939.

## DOC. 37

## At a meeting in Chełm on 25 and 26 January 1942, Jewish Social Self-Help employees discuss the crisis facing their respective branches[1]

Minutes of a Jewish Social Self-Help (JSS) meeting in Chełm, signed Maurycy Drucker, secretary of the JSS committee, and Meier Frenkel,[2] chairman of the JSS committee, Chełm, dated 25 and 26 January 1942[3]

*Minutes*
of the meeting of the branches of the Jewish Social Self-Help (JSS) in powiat Chełm and the JSS Powiat Welfare Committee, held at 8 Kopernik Street in Chełm on 25 and 26 January 1942.
*Start*: 25 January 1942 at 1.30 p.m.
*In attendance*: Dr Tisch, Eliasz,[4] member of the JSS executive committee, Cracow; Frenkel, Meier, chairman of the JSS Powiat Welfare Committee in Chełm, also chairman of the meeting; Drucker, Maurycy, secretary of the JSS Powiat Welfare Committee and of the JSS meeting; Szajn, Józef, member of the JSS committee in Chełm. Other members: Oks, Chaja-Roza; Kac, Nusyn; Dr Goryn, Szymon, absent due to illness, represented by Dr Jeleń, Abram, physician, head of Section VII.1.
The following delegates of the JSS branches in powiat Chełm:

Las, Chaim-Srul, and Gelbard, Estera – Chełm
Kahan, Abraham – Włodawa
Kraft, Calel, and Zynger, Froim – Rejowiec
Lerer, Szulim, and Kruk, Lejba – Siedliszcze
Kriger, Icek; Berger, Fajwel; and Sajkiewicz, Binem – Wojsławice
Perelstein, Mojżesz – Świerże
Fuks, Alter – Sawin
Cyberman, Icek, and Kożuch, Szajndla – Uhrusk
Goroń, Kiwa – Sielec (Nakoł)
Steinwurcel, Kiwa – Żmudź
Bieler, Ewa,[5] and Gerstein, Abram – Cyców
Roter, Pinkus, and Migdal, Icek – Dubeczno
Rosenbaum, Chaim – Pawłów.

The following Jewish Council delegates: Biederman, Anczel; Freiberger, Arie; Rajs, Mordko; Tenenbaum, Szaja

1 YVA, O-6/493, fols. 1–15. Carbon copy of a transcript produced by the Jewish Historical Institute in Warsaw, dated 1 August 1950. This document has been translated from Polish.
2 Meier (Meyer) Frenkel (1892–1942), miller from Warsaw; owned a mill in Chełm prior to Sept. 1939.
3 The original is stamped: 'Jewish Social Self-Help, JSS Jewish Powiat Welfare Committee Chełm'.
4 Dr Eliasz (Elijahu, Eliyahu) Tisch (1889–1956), lawyer and politician; became a Zionist activist in Eastern Galicia in his youth; member of the executive committee of the Jewish Social Self-Help (JSS) and also its managing director, 1940–1942; imprisoned in Plaszów forced labour and concentration camp from 1943; simultaneously active in the Jewish Aid Office (JUS); survived the German occupation (probably thanks to the German industrialist Oskar Schindler, who saved many Jews from Plaszow camp from deportation); later emigrated to Palestine.
5 This name is preceded by Mgr., which denotes a master's level qualification.

Zylberman, Szaja – Chełm
Blatt, Wolf – Rejowiec
Zajd-fuden, Szymon – Pawłów
Kesterman, Aron – Krzywiczki.

The Order Service delegate and property administrator in the Jewish residential district, Szwarcblat, Pinchos – Chełm.

Guests – physicians, representatives of Section VII Sanitation and Hygiene: Dr Oberlander, Natan, and Dr Wolberger, Dawid – Chełm; Dr Szprynger, Abraham – Włodawa; Dr Fürth, Juliusz – Rejowiec; Dr Bieler, Maksymilian – Cyców.

*Agenda*:

1. Opening of the meeting
2. Reading of the minutes of the previous meeting on 16 February 1941[6]
3. Combating the epidemic and improving sanitary conditions
4. Financial and activity reports of all the JSS branches for the year 1941
5. Child welfare provision
6. Welfare provision for resettled people and labourers
7. Food supply issues
8. Obtaining funds
9. Any other business

*Re: agenda item 1*

*The chairman of the Chełm committee, simultaneously chairman of the meeting*, welcomed Dr Eliasz Tisch from the JSS executive committee as well as all the other guests, the delegates of the JSS branches, Jewish councils, and the representatives of the medical profession. He passed on apologies from Dr Alter,[7] the JSS advisor to the District Governor in Lublin, and Dr Siegfried, chairman of the JSS Powiat Welfare Committee in Lublin, the former absent due to important official business and the latter due to illness, and announced their good wishes for a successful meeting.

The chairman remembered Dr Maurycy Kleinhaus, a member of the JSS committee in Chełm and head of the Sanitation and Hygiene Section, who died on 18 September 1941, and declared, among other things: a deserving man of impeccable character has left us, he devoted his life to the welfare of individuals and of society. One of the deceased's last wishes was to be commemorated not with a speech, but with three minutes of silence. The chairman therefore calls for three minutes of silence in memory of the deceased.

Those assembled stood listening reverently to the speech, after which there were three minutes of silence. The chairman then explained that the purpose of the meeting on 16 February 1941 had been to establish Jewish Social Self-Help branches in the powiat. The present meeting was to report on the whole of the previous year. The chairman gave Dr Tisch the floor.

*Dr Tisch, Eliasz* welcomed everyone present both in his own name and on behalf of the JSS executive committee and stated: I have come to you not as a rich uncle, but as a

6 These minutes are not included in the file.

7 Correctly: Dr Marek Alten (1885–1942), lawyer; officer in the Austro-Hungarian army during the First World War; activist in the Zionist Organization in Lublin until 1939; deputy chairman of the Jewish Council in Lublin and head of the JSS in District Lublin, 1939–1942; chairman of the Lublin Jewish Council from late March 1942; shot dead in Nov. 1942.

comrade to a comrade, as a friend to a friend, and as a brother to a brother, to discuss and decide upon the manner of our cooperation. The executive committee recognizes and understands the needs and wishes of the Jewish population in the General Government, gives what it can, and rushes to where help is needed. A circular containing the statement of accounts for the annual activities will be sent out in a few weeks.[8] The executive committee should not stand alone in its activity; rather, this activity should be based on cooperation with the institutions in the General Government, i.e. the JSS committees and branches, and the annual meetings should and will take place on this basis.

The secretary of the meeting announced that on 24 January 1942 the Kreishauptmann,[9] Abteilung Innere Verwaltung, Bevoelkerungswesen und Fürsorge,[10] having been informed of the forthcoming meeting, had sent a letter with the file reference no. III-710-42-Mü-Bo. The text was read aloud: 'General Government, District Lublin. The Kreishauptmann in Chelm, Interior Administration Department, Chelm, 24 January 1942. To the chairman of the Jewish Council, Mr Frenkel, Chelm. At the JSS meeting to be held on the 25th and 26th of this month in Chelm, you will announce: The Jewish councillors and delegates from Kreis Chelm are to strictly adhere to all instructions given by the chairman, Mr Frenkel, who is simultaneously chairman of the JSS in Chelm. I will punish any violations in the strictest manner. The Kreishauptmann, p.p.: Dr Bohrmann.'[11]

*Re: agenda item 2*

The minutes of the meeting of 16 February 1941 were read out.

*Re: agenda item 3*

*Mr Józef Szajn*[12] *presented* the 1941 *financial and activity report* for all the branches in powiat *Chełm*. Powiat Chełm consists of 21 *communities* in which Jews live.

Number of JSS branches – 16
Total number of Jews – 29,942
Number of those in need of assistance – 13,449
Number of soup kitchens – 16
Number of people who use the soup kitchens – 6,014
In the year under review, the kitchens distributed 73,537 meals.[13]
The quantity of produce used mainly for this purpose was 92,912 kg.

In the city of Chełm 385 families received assistance with housing costs over the course of seven months, amounting to 1,925 złoty.

The committee met twenty-three times during the period under review, in addition to numerous meetings of individual sections and commissions.

The members of the committee reviewed the activities of the JSS branches in eighteen locations. A total of 1,646 letters were sent.

In November last year the section for interest-free loans was set up to provide quick and constructive aid to enable people in material need to lift themselves out of poverty by their own efforts. Thanks to the community's generosity, approximately 3,000 złoty

8 Not included in the file.
9 The Kreishauptmann of Chełm was Hans Augustin (1909–1977).
10 German in the original: 'Interior Administration [Department], Population and Welfare Division'.
11 The cited text is in German in the original.
12 Jósef Szajn (1890–1942), retailer.
13 Correctly: 735,375; see the table below.

were collected. More than twenty people have availed themselves of loans of approximately 100 złoty, initially in the city of Chełm. As soon as more funds are available, the section's activities will be extended to the powiat.

A section to help relatives abroad was also set up, serving both the city and the powiat. From the start this section has been very active, and a total of 122 people have benefited from our mediation. We are in constant contact with the German Red Cross via the local Kreishauptmannschaft. In October we ran a special 'esrog' campaign with the 30 'esrog' fruits[14] that the executive committee in Cracow sent us, which brought in approximately 3,000 złoty. In Chełm we distributed 528 items of second-hand clothing to 432 people and 462.5 metres of linen to 263 people – benefiting 695 people altogether. In addition to the more than 100 pairs of donated shoes, the committee bought 300 pairs and distributed them to those in the greatest need. Efforts are under way to obtain Bezugschein[15] for 1,000 pairs of shoes.

*Activity report* for the city and the powiat for 1941

| Place | No. of Jews | No. of people in need of assistance | Kitchens | People using the kitchens | Meals served |
|---|---|---|---|---|---|
| Chełm | 12,500 | 6,928 | 3 | 2,164 | 383,998 |
| Włodawa | 5,586 | 1,710 | 1 | 1,200 | 144,000 |
| Rejowiec | 2,379 | 717 | 1 | 350 | 66,611 |
| Siedliszcze | 2,026 | 1,000 | 1 | 350 | 49,497 |
| Wojsławice | 1,377 | 813 | 1 | 340 | 2,600 |
| Sawin | 840 | 200 | 1 | 100 | 31,068 |
| Sosnowica | 831 | 250 | 1 | 100 | 24,000 |
| Dubeczno | 648 | 200 | 1 | 100 | 5,000 |
| Cyców | 511 | 158 | 1 | 50 | 1,994 |
| Świerże-Ruda | 476 | 240 | 2 | 60 | 16,107 |
| Wereszczyn | 394 | 160 | 1 | 100 | 5,000 |
| Uhrusk | 377 | 270 | 1 | 50 | 3,000 |
| Rakołupy | 398 | 250 | 1 | 50 | 2,500 |
| Turka-Żmudź | 307 | 130 | – | – | – |
| Krzywowierzba | 295 | 100 | – | – | – |
| Olchowiec | 239 | 43 | – | – | – |
| Pawłów | 238 | 86 | – | – | – |
| Żmudź | 182 | 119 | – | – | – |
| Staw | 132 | – | – | – | – |
| Krzywiczki | 56 | 25 | – | – | – |
| Wyryki | 150 | 50 | – | – | – |
| | 29,942 | 13,449 | 16 | 5,014 | 735,375 |

Some of the goods received in kind from the executive committee:

36,000 kg of potatoes
100 litres of cod liver oil

14 Citron, a lemon-like fruit used for ritual purposes during the Feast of Tabernacles.
15 German in the original; correctly: *Bezugsscheine*: 'coupons'.

100 shirts
100 blankets
100 tins of condensed milk
100 kg of peas
75 straw mattresses.
as well as herring, jam, soap, soap powder, pork and other [meats].

Gifts distributed during the year under review:

1 man's coat, 3 women's coats, 1 child's coat, 27 jumpers, 100 pairs of men's shoes, 3 pairs of children's shoes, 3 pairs of rubber boots, 2 pairs of winter boots, 2 scarves, 15 woolly hats, 16 pairs of gloves, 10 girls' jerseys, 10 girls' jerseys, 53 children's jerseys, 12 men's suits, 12 sets of boys' clothing, 2 blouses, 1 jacket, 16 women's dresses, 9 girls' dresses, 6 sets of clothes for infants, 42 children's dresses, 7 pairs of women's stockings, 6 pairs of children's stockings, 1 pair of men's stockings, 101 blankets, 5 bed covers, 2 waistcoats, 49 men's shirts, 11 children's shirts, 462.5 metres of linen.

Of the 101 blankets, 65 were allocated to the powiat branches and 31 to the infirmary in Chełm.

In addition, 100 litres of cod liver oil, 360 metres of potatoes,[16] 150 kg of pork, and 100 shirts were distributed to the city of Chełm and among the powiat branches; jam, herring, and a number of other food items were given exclusively to resettled people.[17] A total of 300 pairs of shoes were bought and distributed with funds from the Powiat Welfare Committee in *Chełm*.

*Activity report for 1941 for the Powiat Welfare Committee, city of Chełm*

Physician visits.

Outpatient clinics: 8,370 people, home visits: 2,271 people.

Hygienists.

Outpatient clinics: 2,910 people, home visits: 1,975 people.

Dental assistance – 581 people.

Physician consultations: adults – 12,518, children – 2,439, consultations free of charge – 3,155.

Medication dispensed: to 8,216 people, in 2,488 cases free of charge.

Immunizations: 5,754 people.

Sanitary patrols inspected 25,943 apartments.

Free haircuts for 1,226 people.

Baths for 18,037 people.

Extra meals: meals were distributed to 7,174 children and the sick, including 691 infants; 1,588 meals were free of charge. 2,116 kg plus 52 decagrams[18] of sugar, 189 kg of rice, 3,223 kg of bread rolls, 72 kg plus 60 decagrams of groats, and 150 kg plus 10 decagrams of crispbreads were distributed.

The kitchens served 383,998 lunches, of which 213,251 were free of charge.

16 Here a measure of weight: one metre is equivalent to 100 kg.

17 In the course of the ghettoization that took place from Oct. 1940 to March 1941, Jews were presumably expelled from the villages in the area around the city of Chełm.

18 A decagram is a unit of weight equivalent to 10 grams.

*Financial report*

Income:

| Place | Local contributions and donations | Subsidies from the JSS and others | Subsidies from the Jewish councils | Payments by those in need | Misc. income | Total |
|---|---|---|---|---|---|---|
| Chełm | 30,739.38 | 26,050.00 | 40,199.32 | 66,288.99 | 4,699.11 | 167,976.80 |
| Włodawa | 1,165.50 | 22,200.00 | 28,329.18 | 15,708.65 | 9,981.88 | 77,385.21 |
| Rejowiec | 1,739.80 | 9,794.10 | 5,638.30 | 1,721.90 | 4,628.30 | 23,522.40 |
| Siedliszcze | 2,474.50 | 10,050.00 | 11,328.18 | 5,461.58 | 3,659.00 | 32,973.26 |
| Wojsławice | 4,933.60 | 7,200.00 | – | 3,792.47 | 6,067.39 | 21,993.46 |
| Sosnowica | 123.05 | 8,200.00 | 830.00 | 254.55 | 168.50 | 9,576.10 |
| Świerże-Ruda | – | – | – | – | 5,629.92 | 5,629.92 |
| Sawin | 6,123.65 | 7,150.00 | 70.00 | 159.30 | – | 13,502.95 |
| Uhrusk | 2,373.00 | 4,300.00 | – | 1,102.00 | 497 | 8,272.00 |
| Rakołupy | 1,132.80 | 1,900.00 | 60.00 | 35.30 | 513.00 | 3,641.10 |
| Turka | – | 500.00 | – | – | 535.00 | 1,035.00 |
| Żmudź | 204.00 | 350.00 | – | – | 320.00 | 874.00 |
| Cyców | – | – | – | 398.80 | 1,785.51 | 2,184.31 |
| Dubeczno | 2,740.50 | 2,300.00 | – | – | 9,202.50 | 14,243.00 |
| Wereszczyn | 1,457.20 | 1,900.00 | 2,059.60 | – | – | 5,416.80 |
| | 55,206.98 | 101,894.10 | 88,514.58 | 94,923.54 | 47,687.11 | 388,226.31 |

Expenditure:

| Place | Extra meals | Products distributed | Financial assistance | Housing assistance | Sanitary and medical assistance | Administrative expenses | Misc. expenses |
|---|---|---|---|---|---|---|---|
| Chełm | 98,172.52 | 16,450.43 | 9,337.00 | 2,291.50 | 16,950.94 | 16,500.82 | 9,257.50 |
| Włodawa | 35,676.19 | – | 12,355.90 | 158.00 | 6,089.40 | 20,732.90 | 3,450.06 |
| Rejowiec | 9,084.40 | 2,892.45 | 897.90 | 418.80 | 6,251.33 | 795.45 | 2,917.32 |
| Siedliszcze | 10,738.94 | 8,129.15 | 3,535.20 | 258.00 | 7,140.94 | 336.00 | 2,828.70 |
| Wojsławice | 13,821.08 | 1,706.90 | 610.70 | 70.40 | 2,697.05 | 1,038.06 | 91.30 |
| Sosnowica | 4,308.88 | – | 2,993.55 | 13.50 | 1,171.32 | 769.67 | 646.00 |
| Świerże-Ruda | – | – | 1,370.50 | 150.00 | 250.00 | – | 3,625.63 |
| Sawin | 10,148.86 | – | 1,648.49 | – | 1,395.80 | 791.10 | – |
| Uhrusk | 1,410.00 | 3,583.00 | 2,661.00 | 125.00 | 596.00 | 397.00 | 416.00 |
| Rakołupy | 243.65 | 831.53 | 1,925.00 | – | 100.00 | 164.50 | |
| Turka | – | 535.00 | 500.00 | – | – | – | – |
| Żmudź | – | – | 400.00 | 55.00 | – | 30.00 | 445.00 |
| Cyców | 1,205.85 | – | 577.00 | – | 127.70 | – | – |
| Dubeczno | 3,894.60 | – | – | – | – | – | 11,127.50 |
| Wereszczyn | – | – | – | – | – | – | 5,498.97 |
| | 188,698.97 | 34,128.46 | 29,568.61 | 3,540.30 | 42,642.78 | 41,725.20 | 39,304.18 |

*Subsidies* from the Lublin District Governor via the Kreishauptmann for 1941: Chełm 2,850 zł, Włodawa 950, Rejowiec 650, Siedliszcze 650, Wojsławice, Sawin 300, Sosnowica 200, Uhrusk 200, Turka-Żmudź 200, Świerże-Ruda 100, Cyców 100, Wereszczyn 100, Rakołupy 100, Dubeczno 100, Krzywowierzba 100; 7,000 zł. in total.

The following issued statements in connection with the financial report:

*Mr Kahan, Abraham*[19] *(Włodawa)*: The figures provided in the reports are not up to date because needs and expenditure are increasing almost daily due to the extensive impoverishment of Włodawa's population, where the number of people in need of assistance, for example, is almost 3,000. The branch does not harbour a grudge towards the JSS executive committee either, despite the fact that it feeds the branch with circulars but does not respond precisely and effectively with information about critical needs and requirements.

*Mr Kraft, Calel*[20] *(Rejowiec)*: I disagree with the criticism raised by the delegate from Włodawa. We are doing everything we can in the face of very difficult conditions. We only reproach the committee in Chełm for favouring the city of Chełm in particular, while it has done nothing for Rejowiec, for example, in terms of fuel for heating. The situation in Rejowiec is deteriorating, poverty is increasing, and those who did not need assistance before are beginning to need it.

*Mr Lerer, Szulim (Siedliszcze)*: There are currently 2,100 souls in Siedliszcze, of whom more than 800 are new arrivals[21] who live in extreme poverty. The place itself is very poor. Every week we distribute three metres of bread among the poor, at the expense of others whose designated ration is being cut little by little. The public soup kitchen is used by 375 people, while hundreds of other impoverished people also ask for help from the kitchen, but in vain.

We know that the committee in Chełm is mustering all of its strength and doing everything in its power, but it is not in a position to achieve anything on its own. I call on the executive committee to provide regular and substantial assistance.

*Mr Kryger, Icek*[22] *(Wojsławice)*: He firstly welcomed the executive committee's delegate and thanked the chairman of the committee, Mr Frenkel, for convening the meeting. [He said:] We are left entirely to our own devices; we do not receive any subsidies from the Jewish Council. We do not share the view of the delegate from Włodawa. This is not the time for criticism. We are interested in finding a way to cooperate and to find funds, especially regarding sanitation and hygiene. In the soup kitchen we supplement everyone's lunch, which consists of one litre of soup, with an additional 10 decagrams of bread every day, and 20 decagrams on Fridays. We ask for any kind of food, especially potatoes at quota prices, or else the soup kitchen will have to close. Sugar and fuel for heating are also essential. The kitchen has been able to keep going thus far because the

19 Abraham Kahan (1878–1942), timber merchant from Sławatycze; lived in Włodawa prior to Sept. 1939; murdered in Sobibor.

20 Calel (Becalel) Kraft (1910–1943), teacher from Rejowiec; perished in Auschwitz.

21 This is a reference to Jewish refugees, primarily from Cracow.

22 Iccak Kryger (Icek Krygier), kosher butcher and meat inspector in Wojsławice; he was murdered.

Verteilungsstelle[23] has been allocating quotas to us, and in addition the JSS also generates income from the quotas.

*Mr Berger, Fajwel*[24] *(Wojsławice)*: He agreed with Mr Icek Krygier's remarks and in addition asked for medicine, flour quotas, and especially potatoes for the soup kitchen. He said that the prices at the local pharmacy are horrendous, even for the simplest items. They are several times higher than for the items in the warehouses in Chełm.

*Mr Perelstein, Mojżesz*[25] *(Świerże)*: Immense poverty reigns in Świerże-Ruda. Only ten families, artisan families, are adequately provided for; all the others are without food and clothing. The local economic conditions make self-sufficiency impossible, and the population is completely dependent on outside help. We can no longer operate the soup kitchens in Świerże or in Ruda due to a lack of potatoes, flour, and heating fuel. We ask for food assistance, clothes, and fuel.

*Mr Fuks, Alter*[26] *(Sawin)*: We ask for food aid, clothing, heating fuel, and for a Jewish physician to settle permanently in Sawin.

*Mr Steinwurcel, Wolf (Żmudź)*: We ask for food aid, clothing, and heating fuel.

*Mrs Bieler, Ewa (Cyców)*: The branch in Cyców commenced its activities on 1 April 1941 and during these nine months has only been able to obtain 600 złoty from various sources, which means we had to be self-sufficient. We run a soup kitchen which is intended primarily for children, because we cannot feed the elderly with what we have. If we do not receive quotas of flour, potatoes, fuel, etc., the soup kitchen will be closed.

*Mr Roter, Pinkus*[27] *(Dubeczno)*: He asked for ration allocations and food aid, clothing, heating fuel, sugar, and soap, as well as financial subsidies. There are 661 Jews living in the territory of the community of Hańsk, to which the Dubeczno branch belongs; 14 of them have ration cards.

*Chairman Frenkel, Meier (Chełm)*: Summing up all the contributions, I conclude that they do not contain any particular accusations against the executive committee or the committee, but merely requests. As far as firewood is concerned, even a quota allocation would make no sense in practice, since the price of a cubic metre of wood is between 10 and 20 złoty, while the transportation costs are more than 80 złoty. As for subsidies, each Jewish Council will be obliged to pay them to the local JSS branch regularly each month, and in the next few days a circular will be sent out to all the Jewish councils in the powiat, instructing them to submit their budget for the previous six months and to provide information on whether the Council has paid any subsidies to the local JSS branch, and in what amount. The Kreishauptmann's letter of 24 January 1942, no. III-710-42 Mü-Bo, will be enclosed with the circular.

*Dr Eliasz Tisch, executive committee delegate*: The executive committee is familiar with the exact statistics and the needs of the JSS branches, as well as the nature and scope of the powiat committees' activities. The committee in Chełm is known for its particularly zealous, energetic, and meticulous work. The executive committee knows

23 Here and below, German in the original: 'distribution centre'.

24 Fajwel Berger (b. 1906), retailer from Wojsławice, where he perished.

25 Mosze Perlsztein (1900–1942); murdered in Sobibor.

26 Alter Fuks (1907–1943), timber merchant from Lublin; lived in Chełm prior to Sept. 1939; subsequently moved to Sawin; murdered in Sobibor.

27 Pinkus Roter (1885–1943), retailer; murdered in Sobibor.

that the committee in Chełm claims nothing for itself at the expense of anther branch. Nevertheless, cooperation of the Jewish councils is absolutely essential. They must recognize the self-sacrificial work of the Jewish Social Self-Help, which relieves them of the burden of their social welfare work to a considerable extent. The soup kitchens alone are a living testament to the good and useful work carried out by the Jewish Social Self-Help. Therefore I call you to mutual understanding, support, and cooperation, as you are both institutions of the Jewish community, and you should complement each other.

*Re: agenda item 4*

*Dr Jeleń, Abram*, spoke on behalf of Dr Goryn, the committee member who was ill.

Combating the epidemic and improving sanitary conditions

1. Combating the epidemic is a struggle for cleanliness and to improve sanitary and hygienic conditions, but combating typhus also represents a struggle against lice as the sole carriers of this disease.
2. In cases in which a physician diagnoses this infectious disease, the infected person must be removed from the home immediately and hospitalized or possibly isolated in a designated building. In locations without a Jewish physician, a Christian physician should be consulted or a Jewish physician summoned from the nearest location.
3. People in the immediate environment of the sick person must be quarantined in a special location for twenty-four hours. In places where there are baths or bathtubs, these individuals should be bathed and given clean undergarments. If no bath or bathtubs are available, they should wash. If their hair is infested with lice, it should be shaved off and burned. The apartment of the sick person should be disinfected with sulphur gas, but if there are several rooms, then all the belongings should be gathered into one room to be disinfected with sulphur gas, while the remaining rooms should undergo a liquid disinfection.[28]
5. The JSS branch and Jewish Council are personally responsible for ensuring that patients are not transferred from one location to another.
6. In order to improve sanitary conditions, the JSS Powiat Welfare Committee will organize a 'Cleanliness Week' in the near future, under the slogan: 'Let's eradicate the lice'. Posters and instructions will be sent out for this purpose. The Jewish distribution centre will provide appropriate quantities of soap and soap powder for distribution among the population.
7. During this 'Cleanliness Week', the JSS branch in each location must raise the sanitary conditions there to a proper standard.
   a) In the apartments, the floors, doors, windows, beds, and other furnishings must be cleaned with a wet cloth.
   b) Bed linen and undergarments must be washed.
   c) The straw in the straw mattresses must be replaced with fresh straw.
   d) Where there are baths, ritual basins, or bathtubs, they should be used so that the entire Jewish population may be bathed during this week, if possible.
   e) Inner courtyards, stairwells, hallways, etc. must be tidied accordingly.

28 The numbering jumps from point 3 to point 5 in the original document.

8. The JSS branch in each locality is responsible for organizing and adhering to the above instructions. The local population must be severely punished should it fail to comply.

*Dr Szprynger, Abraham (physician from Włodawa)*: Infectious diseases, especially typhus, have been brought in to Włodawa and the surrounding areas from the labour camps in Sawin, Krychów, Sajczyce, etc. The lack of soap, soap powder, soda, ethyl alcohol, etc. makes it difficult or even impossible to combat the disease. He requested effective methods and resources with which to combat the disease, and especially the lice. Although there is no typhus epidemic in Włodawa at the moment, there are nine new typhoid patients, for example, and so it is essential to combat the disease and to apply methods to prevent it from spreading. He asked the executive committee and the committee to provide the cleaning agents and hygiene resources discussed above to Włodawa.

*Dr Furth, Juliusz (physician from Rejowiec)*: There is an infirmary in Rejowiec. The medicines in the pharmacy are very expensive. He asked for an allocation of the most important medicines and a quota for the impoverished Jewish population.

*Dr Bieler, Maksymilian (physician from Cyców)*: There is no epidemic typhus among the Jews in Cyców; there have only been a few cases of abdominal typhus. Approximately 500 people in the town have epidemic typhus or abdominal typhus, but there is not a single case among the Jewish population. We are doing everything we can to prevent these diseases from spreading, but we ask for an allocation of soap and soda.

*Dr Eliasz Tisch (Cracow)*: In response to Dr Szprynger, he stated that during the meeting two other physicians had suggested resources and effective control methods, which incidentally should be familiar to every physician. He also recommended consulting Dr Wolberg,[29] an epidemiologist employed by the Jewish Council in Częstochowa, who has very successfully defined and implemented methods and resources including announcements and public appeals. The speaker asked that all the local physicians in the powiat contact the executive committee to place orders for medicine, which will be considered as far as possible

*Chairman Frenkel, Meier (Chełm)*: In consultation with the authorities, the local JSS committee is organizing a Cleanliness Week throughout powiat Chełm, under the slogan 'Let's eradicate the lice'. This campaign will be conducted everywhere simultaneously and supervised by the Jewish Social Self-Help bodies and the Jewish councils. Everything will be aired, rinsed, washed, scrubbed, and people and objects will be cleansed. Soap and detergent will be delivered shortly, one packet per person, at a price of around 1.12 złoty for a bar of soap and washing powder. In addition, the campaign is to be publicized at every opportunity, with the aid of announcements, posters, and verbal notices. The committee will draft the text of the announcements, which will be allotted to each JSS branch, or where there is no JSS branch, to each Jewish Council in appropriate quantities.[30]

Due to the late hour, at 6.30 p.m. the chairman adjourned the meeting until the following day at 9 a.m.

29 Dr Adam Wolberg; murdered by the Gestapo in June 1943 for leading a resistance group in Częstochowa.

30 No such documents are included in the file.

*Continuation of the meeting of the Jewish Social Self-Help branches on 26 January 1942 at 9 a.m.*
*Present*: The same as the previous day, with the exception of the out-of-town physicians, the members of the branch in Cyców, and the out-of-town Jewish councils.
*Re: agenda item 5, presentation by Mrs Oks, Chaja-Roza*
Child welfare should be considered one of the most important tasks of the Jewish Social Self-Help. Children are our hope, our future, our existence. If the young generation does not collapse and manages to persevere through all the turmoil of war and the radically changed social and economic conditions, which the adults comprehend and experience, then we too shall continue to exist. When poverty spread among the Jewish masses before the war, the internal and external consequences were most evident in children, who were the first to be affected by the poor nutritional, sanitary, and hygiene conditions. As a result, attention was focused on the 'TOZ' Society for the Protection of the Health of the Jewish Population, which already existed at that time, and child welfare was recognized as the most important of all tasks. A campaign to provide supplementary meals for schoolchildren commenced, and holiday camps and out-of-school care as well as welfare centres for mothers and infants were set up. During its two years of activity, the JSS provided milk, sugar, and rusks for infants and supplementary meals (bread and soup) for schoolchildren. In the summer, childcare during the school holidays was arranged for 110 schoolchildren in Chełm. They received two meals a day, were looked after from the morning until 4 p.m., and put on an average of two kilograms. The mood was very good because the children were clean, cheerful, and had smiles on their faces. This was also the case because they had been removed from a domestic atmosphere of depression and drudgery, from the damp, cramped, cellars and attics where no ray of sunshine falls, and brought out into the fresh air.

This is why we call for the provision of care for children, comprising measures including the establishment of women's committees. We must distribute supplementary meals to mothers, set up a feeding centre for infants and children, and provide permanent care to meet their sanitation and hygiene needs. Supplementary meals and after-school care must be provided. The children should not only receive supplementary meals and medical care, but also educational supervision in a warm, clean environment. The establishment of summer kindergartens, where children can spend their free time in the fresh air under proper supervision, would not pose any major difficulties. In every location, whether town or village, there is a space, a large, clean, bright room to accommodate those children who are the most impoverished and in need. There the children would be looked after by a responsible person, the child's personal hygiene would be attended to, they would be bathed, have their hair cut, etc.

This care programme envisioned for impoverished children and their mothers is not just a dream: with goodwill, it can be realized in even the smallest locality.

*Mr Kraft, Calel (Rejowiec)*: He agreed with Mrs Oks in every respect, but said that due to the conditions in Rejowiec, it is impossible to implement childcare. There are no premises and no heating fuel. It might be possible to place the children with foster families, but separate premises could only be arranged during the warmer seasons.

*Mr Lerer, Szulim (Siedliszcze)*: He shared Mrs Oks's opinion, because children should take precedence over the elderly. In Siedliszcze there are absolutely no available premises, and it is impossible to spend time with the children. Moreover, there are no potatoes, nor is there any heating fuel, soap, or detergent.

With few exceptions, the inhabitants of Siedliszcze are extremely poor. There are many resettled people. He asked that he be made aware of opportunities to organize and establish childcare.

*Mr Kahan, Abraham (Włodawa)*: There are 700 children between the ages of 8 and 12 in Włodawa. The branch takes care of the children on its own initiative and this is funded by its members rather than by the Jewish Social Self-Help. In principle, supplementary meals are distributed at a designated location and under supervision – food is not taken home – but for the time being the lack of shoes and clothing makes it impossible to provide food at a designated location in winter.

*Mr Berger, Fajwel (Wojsławice)*: In Wojsławice there is a lack of rooms, food quotas, clothing, shoes, money. We ask for an allocation of these items; sugar is the most important.

*Mr Fuks, Alter (Sawin)*: He drew the same conclusions as Fajwel Berger. He also requested a physician for Sawin and medicine.

*Mrs Kożuch, Szajndla (Uhrusk)*: She drew the same conclusions as Fajwel Berger and added that in Uhrusk there are 30 children between the ages of 6 and 8, and 100 children in the community as a whole. Working conditions are very difficult for the branches there, especially because there is absolutely no support from the Jewish Council. In spite of this, the branch is currently setting up childcare facilities and asks the committee for assistance, for the time being in the form of advice, information, and publicity.

*Mrs Oks, Chaja-Roza (Chełm)*: The lack of premises can be remedied, for example, by requisitioning a room. The lack of clothing can be counteracted by a collection, and the women's committee can mend and alter clothing. The sugar intended for the elderly can be given to the children, because the consumption of sugar is beneficial for a child. In extreme cases, coffee with sugar and rusks can serve as a meal for a whole day.

*Chairman Frenkel, Meier (Chełm)*: He considered that the speaker, Mrs Oks, had presented the issue of child welfare very well. He said it was clear from the discussions that there is a shortage of housing and of heating fuel. The committee will approach the Treuhänder[31] so that the Jewish Social Self-Help premises, including those for childcare, can be exempted from rent payments and so that the required space is placed at the JSS's disposal. It will approach the Forstinspekteur[32] for an appropriate quota of wood for the kitchens and for similar requirements to be allocated to the branches. The committee will also endeavour to allocate sugar quotas to benefit children in particular.

*Re: agenda item 6*

*Based on the report by Mr Szajn, Józef (Chełm)*, and the remarks of *Chairman Frenkel, Meier*, it is clear that resettled people and labourers must be given particular material and moral support in all the spheres in which the JSS is active, and that resettled people should be treated on an equal status to the long-established local population in every respect. This principle is indeed being applied in all circumstances. It relates not only to labourers employed by certain local offices, but also to those in the labour camps, most

31 German in the original: 'trustees' .

32 German in the original: 'forest inspector'.

or almost all of whom come from Warsaw. Among other things, we provide sanitary care, in part in the form of food and clothing.

*Re: agenda item 7, presentation by Chairman Frenkel*

Based on the speakers' reports and the delegates' remarks, it is obvious that all the tasks and activities of the Jewish Social Self-Help result from [insufficient] supply – a dominant problem. We must make economies in every area, without exception, because the resources are modest, and moreover, it is possible that the food situation will deteriorate. Throughout the entire duration of the war thus far, the powiat has received no allocations at all for people in need, in other words, the Jewish Social Self-Help has not been taken into account [when allocating quotas]. Moreover, some localities have received nothing at all for their population. If there were any allocations at all, these were minimal. As the statement of accounts for last year shows, the branch in Ruda-Świerże[33] received 2.10 kg of rye flour per person per week, and there was no mention of wheat flour or other products.

[Even] after intensive efforts and numerous interventions with the main people in charge, undertaken with the support of the Verteilungsstelle in Chełm, the population has been allocated 550 grams of flour per person per week, rather than 2.10 kg. In addition, there are special allocations of wheat flour for soup kitchens, people in need, and hospitals.

Independently of the normal quota allocation for the population, people in need, hospitals, and soup kitchens, I have arranged that all locations in powiat Chełm – with the exception of Włodawa, which has already been supplied – will receive an additional 5,000 kg of wheat flour this month; to collect it, the branches should contact the Verteilungsstelle.

I also inform you that, following intensive and multiple efforts, I have succeeded in obtaining an additional 2,500 kg of sugar, solely for people in need in those powiat localities (with the exception of Włodawa) where no sugar has been distributed throughout the duration of the war up to the current month (applause).

I have also arranged a special allocation of noodles and semolina for the hospitals.

There followed questions from the floor as to whether salt can be obtained. Chairman: Of course one can get salt in smaller quantities; our representatives can obtain it at the quota price. I already mentioned yesterday that I had succeeded in obtaining the allocation of a contingent of soap and soap powder, one packet per person at a price of 1.12 złoty. The branches or the Jewish councils should pay this price to the committee's cashier or directly to the Verteilungsstelle. As for sugar, I ask the honourable delegates to distribute it primarily among children, the sick, and those in need. As for potatoes, given the frost a delivery is unfortunately out of the question. Although I have a ration coupon for 2,000 metres of potatoes for the city of Chełm, it cannot be redeemed because of the frost. I hereby announce that of these 2,000 metres, even though they are specifically designated for the city of Chełm, 200 metres will be allocated to Sosnowica.

At this point Chairman Frenkel turned to the representative from Włodawa, Mr Kahan, and called for him to follow his example and to give some of his quota to the neighbouring branches, because it was clear from Mr Kahan's statements that

33 Today the community of Świerże and the village of Ruda are both part of the municipality of Dorohusk.

Włodawa absolutely could not complain about a lack of food quotas, but was coping very well. Besides, he said, we have no way of knowing whether a catastrophic situation may prevail in Dubeczno, Sosnowica, etc. tomorrow.

The chairman then turned to the branch representatives, asking whether they approved the committee's work in this respect. Votes: Yes, yes! Now we are faced with the task of obtaining a certain quantity of wheat flour for matzo. In any case, I fully understand that financial help alone cannot satisfy your needs if you do not get food at quota prices. Even if Cracow,[34] along with America,[35] were to give you a financial subsidy, it would not cover the demand for food. As an example, I have heard that some delegates have declared they are unable to pay 20 złoty for 1 kg of sugar. If you multiply 2,500 kg of sugar by 25, it amounts to 62,500 złoty, whereas the same quantity costs around 4,000 złoty at the Verteilungsstelle. That is equal to a subsidy of more than 58,000 złoty for January. In my conduct and activity I am guided by the principle 'love thy neighbour', and we shall continue our efforts in this direction. I ask that the Jewish councils cooperate with the Jewish Social Self-Help.

*Re: agenda item 8*

*Rapporteur Mr Kac, Nusyn*[36] *(Chełm)*: Based on the delegates' speeches, I got the impression that there is hostility between the Jewish councils and the branches in a relatively large number of locations in the powiat, and there is no need to remind you that this is highly detrimental to the work of the institutions and the interests of the population. In contrast, open, friendly cooperation significantly benefits both sides. I cite the city of Chełm as an example, where the Jewish Council makes every effort to support the Jewish Social Self-Help. Among other things, the Council supports it with a monthly subsidy of several thousand złoty. For their part, the branches should constantly strive to find sources of income fitting to the local conditions, including regular subsidies from the Jewish Council, monthly contributions, voluntary donations, events, festive campaigns, etc. They should introduce and promote all of this in their respective areas.

*Mr Kahan, Abraham (Włodawa)*: As deputy chairman of the Jewish Council in Włodawa, I assure you that the Jewish Council will cooperate with the JSS branch. I request that a copy of the letter from the Kreishauptmann to Mr Frenkel, no. III-710-42 Mü-Bo, dated 24 January, be forwarded to the Jewish Council. Mr Lerer, Szulim (Siedliszcze), and Mr Migdał, Icek[37] (Dubeczno), confirm that the Jewish councils in their localities are making great efforts to support the branches as far as possible, but that the efforts are in vain at the present time due to the lack of resources and the complete impoverishment of the population. Without outside help the situation will deteriorate, and it will be difficult to find a way out.

*Mr Kraft, Calel (Rejowiec)*: He asked for potatoes and firewood for Rejowiec and announced that agricultural training, which continues to be relevant in Rejowiec, will begin soon.

*Chairman Frenkel*: We absolutely require that: (a) all the Jewish councils' income from the quotas be paid to the JSS branches in full; (b) the Jewish councils provide the

34 The JSS's headquarters were located in Cracow.

35 This is a reference to the American Jewish Joint Distribution Committee (JDC).

36 Nusyn Kac (Natan Katz) (1896–1942), retailer; born and died in Chełm.

37 Icek (Icko) Migdał (1900–1942), retailer from Dubeczno (Hańsk); murdered in Sobibor.

JSS branches with monthly subsidies, the amount of which is determined on the basis of the budget over the previous six months; (c) no individual aid in the form of cash is given to people in need, but only dry produce or goods in kind, such as subsidies to pay for rent or heating, etc. In exceptional cases, it is possible to deviate from this stipulation (probably in two localities).

*Dr Tisch, Eliasz (Cracow)*: The task of the meeting was to find a joint solution to the situation and to define guidelines and resources so that the Jewish Social Self-Help can carry out its duties.

At this point I would like to discuss the relationship of the Jewish councils to the JSS. We see no major obstacle that would stand in the way of cooperation between these two Jewish institutions that are still left to us. The Jewish councils should and must recognize the Jewish Social Self-Help's self-sacrificial work, which relieves them of the task of welfare provision to a considerable extent. Excellent examples of the JSS's great and useful work include the soup kitchens, outpatient clinics and hospitals, the institutions for the care and feeding of children, the Drops of Milk[38] for infants, and a multitude of different and beneficial charitable institutions. Therefore I call for harmony, mutual support, and cooperation, as you are both Jewish community institutions and you should complement each other. The 'self-help' slogan was introduced to prevent Jewry from going down the road to ruin, and this slogan has become our institution's mission. What matters is that our support work reaches the poorest masses, wherever the need is greatest and the support is most pressing. With this slogan we turn to the Jewish masses and seek to support them.

However, there is no one solution for all the ills presented by the individual delegates. Everyone should find appropriate methods based on local circumstances and conditions. We are doing everything humanly possible, but our resources are few and insufficient.

In this situation, the most important principle of our welfare work should be child welfare, because children are the foundation and the future of society. With the appropriate efforts, child welfare can be put on the right track, even with the most modest resources.

For the Jews the work of the JSS is also war work. I appeal to everyone to carry it out in such a way that, after the war, we can justifiably claim to have accomplished it.

*Re: agenda item 9 (miscellaneous)*

The following motions were submitted:

*1) Motion by Mr Las, Chaim*[39] *(Chełm branch)*, to introduce uniform, simplified accounting for all JSS branches in powiat Chełm, according to the enclosed template. He justified the motion as follows: During my examination of the monthly accounts of individual branches, I can point to numerous accounting errors relating to income and expenditure, which make it impossible to draw up a proper statement of accounts. Because branch members are not acquainted with the basic rules of accounting, some branches do not submit statements at all. The system I have designed requires no spe-

38 A reference to centres modelled on the French 'Gouttes de lait' dispensaries which provided milk to mothers who were unable to breastfeed. The first such centre in Poland was set up in 1904 in Łódź.

39 Chaim Israel Las (1905–1942), retailer from Chełm.

cialist knowledge or expensive ledgers. It is sufficient to maintain two ledgers: a cash ledger and a general ledger, each with appropriate headings.

The implementation of a uniform accounting system and monthly statements of accounts regarding overall expenditure under the appropriate headings would enable the Powiat Welfare Committee to compile monthly statements from across the powiat.

A trial of this system in powiat Chełm over several months would allow the JSS executive committee to implement its plan for uniform accounting across all branches throughout the General Government.

*2) Motion by Mr Kraft, Calel (Rejowiec),* to intervene with the authorities in order to exempt the premises occupied by the Jewish Social Self-Help from rent payments.

*3) Motion by branch members*: Icek Cyberman[40] (Uhrusk), Szulim Lerer and Lejb Kruk[41] (Siedliszcze), and Alter Fuks (Sawin) to increase the salary of Maurycy Drucker, secretary of the JSS Powiat Committee, to the sum of 500 (five hundred) złoty per month.

It was resolved that the JSS Powiat Welfare Committee in Chełm should decide on these motions.

As there was no further business, Mr M. Frenkel thanked everyone for their cooperation and participation in the meeting; he called for additional intensive work in the field of welfare provision and closed the meeting on 26 January 1942 at 1.30 p.m.[42]

## DOC. 38
## Report dated January 1942 on the expulsion of Jewish farmers from Skryhiczyn[1]

Handwritten report by an anonymous author working for the underground archive of the Warsaw ghetto, dated January 1942

Skryhiczyn

'Today has shaken us all. All the Jews were ordered to leave Skryhiczyn within thirty minutes. You can easily imagine the situation of these unfortunate people.

'They were not allowed to take anything with them apart from household goods. All the Jews of Skryhiczyn had their land taken away as well.

'Who knows what is still in store for us.'

40 Iccak (Icek) Cyberman (1895–1942), retailer from Uhrusk; murdered in Sobibor extermination camp.

41 Lejba (Leibel) Kruk (1902–1942), iron merchant from Siedliszcze.

42 This is followed by the minutes of the Powiat Welfare Committee's business meeting in Chełm on 11 Feb. 1942, which was attended by Frenkel, Szajn, Oks, Kac, and Jeleń. At this meeting they decided to compile the monthly cash report according to the proposed template and to increase Secretary Drucker's salary. Frenkel explained that he had asked the trustee in a memorandum to waive the rent payments for the premises used by individual JSS branches and to allocate them further premises, if possible.

1 AŻIH, Ring I/1006 (913). Published in English translation in Kermish (ed.), *To Live with Honor*, pp. 209–210. This document has been newly translated from Yiddish.

Thus writes a woman from Skryhiczyn who witnessed the expulsion that took place on 22 November 1941.

The village is one of the few in pre-war Poland where Jews were engaged in farming – in the Lublin region, in powiat Hrubieszów, right by the Bug river, near Dubienka.

Jewish farmers owned well-managed farmsteads there and cultivated hundreds of acres of land with their own hands and the help of day labourers.[2]

One could often see the wind playing with the beards of Jewish farmers as they went out to their fields or to sow their plots, and barefoot, healthy Jewish girls and boys setting out with scythes and sickles in the cool of the morning in order to harvest grain in the field or cut the grass in dewy green meadows in the scorching heat of the day.

With the arrival of the occupiers, commissioners were imposed on the larger Jewish landowners, while fixed amounts of crops were taken from the smaller ones.

The mixed peasant population – Ukrainians, Poles, and Jews – enjoyed good, neighbourly relations.

After the Germans arrived, a pogrom took place.

There were victims, and a great deal of Jewish property was looted.

Among those worst affected, I know of the Halpern family, of whom almost all the men were shot.[3]

The old farm was also plundered.

The Jewish sawmill was placed under temporary administration.

But time passed. Jews continued to do farm work, made their living from trade – whatever came along. They even obtained 'permits' to work the fields a day's walk away, right on the Bug.

Of course, they had to pay handsomely for all of this …

When the war broke out,[4] the village endured a great deal, but fortunately the storm did not do any particular damage.

[It was not until] the last arbitrary decree [was issued that] the Jewish farming families that had lived there for generations were ruined, along with a number of larger landowning families, such as:

the Rotenberg family – approximately 150 acres of land and forest;
the Halpern family – approximately 80 acres of land and forest;
the Horovitsh family – approximately 50 acres of land and forest;
the Kaminer family – approximately 50 acres of land and forest;
the Shidlovski family – approximately 50 acres of land and forest;
and others.

There is no further news at present.[5]

January 1942

2 Since the nineteenth century Jews had lived on a rural estate originally purchased by Etta Reyzl Rotenberg. Many members of the Rotenberg family later emigrated. In 1920 the land was divided into smaller parcels and bought up by Jews.

3 Six members of the family were killed in the pogrom.

4 A reference to the war between Germany and the Soviet Union.

5 The mostly Hasidic Jewish population of Skryhiczyn is thought to have been forced to relocate to the Hrubieszów ghetto before the German police deported them to Sobibor in June 1942.

## DOC. 39
## Calek Perechodnik from the Jewish Order Service describes the relationship between Poles and Jews as well as the first reports of mass murders around the turn of the year 1941/1942[1]

Handwritten notes by Calek Perechodnik,[2] Warsaw, written in spring/summer 1943 (excerpt)

*How were relations between the Poles and the Jews in 1941?*
Overall, these relations have *deteriorated* considerably. On the one hand, the Jews are managing their own affairs,[3] so the Poles can profit less from them. In any case, Jewish homes and businesses had already been placed under Polish administration. Anyway, it has turned out that *it is possible to live without Jews.* There are cities without Jews where the Poles are doing very well.

*On the other hand,* the Jews are destroying the Polish apartments in the ghetto, and destitute people cut down the trees at night.

*Would it not be better,* every municipal authority asks, *to expel the Jews from the respective town?* Their furniture, apartments, and 'clothes' would be *left behind* – well then, let them go.

And so the *Kreishauptmannschaften*[4] received one request after another from individual Polish mayors, politely asking that the Jews be removed from their towns because, after all, this town is a health resort, or that one is an industrial city, and typhus, high prices, profiteering, theft, etc. are rampant because of the Jews. How should I know which arguments the mayors or city councillors use?

One ought to ask *Gadomski,* the mayor of Otwock, about it; he has distinguished himself by submitting similar, often repeated requests.

One thing is certain: the *Germans* have certainly sensed that the Poles have nothing against the extermination of the Jews. On the contrary, they will assist them in this – provided they get what's left of the Jewish possessions.

*And the Jews? What are the Jews doing* at a time when such dark clouds are gathering above them?

*They go on about their daily lives calmly,* they are not particularly interested in politics, they find the newspapers rather boring – in any case, who has time for such things?

1 YVA, O-33/426. Published in Calek Perechodnik, *Spowiedź: Dzieje rodziny żydowskiej podczas okupacji hitlerowskiej w Polsce,* ed. David Engel (Warsaw: Ośrodek Karta, 2004), pp. 26–29. An earlier, heavily edited version is available in English translation: Calel Perechodnik, *Am I a Murderer? Testament of a Jewish Ghetto Policeman,* ed. and trans. Frank Fox (Boulder, CO: Westview, 1996), pp. 11–13. This document has been newly translated from Polish.

2 Calek Perechodnik (1916–1944), building contractor; studied in France; employed in the Jewish Order Service from 1941; in August 1942 forced to participate in the liquidation of the Otwock ghetto, during which his wife and daughter were also deported; subsequently imprisoned in a number of camps. After escaping in late 1942, he lived in hiding in Warsaw with several other people, including his parents: wrote his memoir from 7 May to 19 August 1943 at Pańska Street in Warsaw, where a Polish woman (Mrs Hela) hid him, and passed it on to an acquaintance in Otwock. Perechodnik died in unexplained circumstances after the surrender of Warsaw in Oct. 1944, possibly after German troops discovered the bunker he was hiding in.

3 Changes in tense here and below as in the original.

4 German in the original with a Polish ending.

Everyone struggles to earn a living, daily bread, potatoes. And the war? Well, it is clear that things will turn out well and that the Germans will lose sooner or later. Two Jews meet. One says to the other: 'How are things?' The other replies: *'It will be fine.'*

Jewish optimism is truly incorrigible.

Although the Jewish police have unlimited power, they respect the general population. After all, no one wants to be hanged after the war. People threaten each other that *they will settle scores after the war*, but for the time being they all live together in harmony, and everyone is concerned with their daily bread.

*New Year's Eve [1941/]1942.* A cursed year in the history of the world; a *year* that has put an end to the cultural achievements of all mankind; a *year* that has provided the best evidence of wild and sadistic human instincts. This *year* is upon us, and we have *New Year's Eve [1941/]1942.*

Although Jews do not celebrate New Year's Eve, everyone says to his *friend*, the *husband* to his wife, *mothers* to their children, and *children* in turn to their parents: 'May we live to see the coming year, and may the war end this year.'

Unfortunately, the Lord God has not heard the prayers of the Jewish people, *and almost none of these wishes have been fulfilled.*

*At first there* are *vague rumours*, rumours which the Jews believe or disbelieve – it is difficult to believe them in any case; you have to see it with your own eyes to realize that such things are possible – and in the 20th century at that.

In *Słonim* – so it is said – *14,000 people* were herded into a square, and then all of them – women, children, men – were executed indiscriminately with machine guns.[5]

I ask you, people, can one believe such things? *Shooting women and innocent children just like that, in broad daylight?*

Even the worst criminal cannot be sentenced to death if she is pregnant. However, in this case, little children were reportedly killed. *Where* are the men, fathers of children, who would dare to aim their machine guns at defenceless little children? *What* does public opinion in the civilized world have to say about this? *Where* are the scholars, the writers, the professors? *How* can the world remain silent about this?

This just can't be true.

This news is followed by other news, even more horrific. In *Vilna 60,000* people have been killed, and 20,000 in *Baranowicze.*[6] People no longer understand anything. They believe it, but they can't imagine that one day someone can just come and kill their two-year-old daughter, who can hardly talk yet – just because she has a Jew for a mother and a Jew for a father.

Finally *we find an explanation*. The *local* Jews were killed because they were Soviet citizens; they probably fought against the Germans, whereas *we* are citizens of the General Government, and something like that can't happen here. Besides, martial law is in force over there, while here we have a civil administration.

In the eyes of the Jews in Otwock, with their small-town narrow-mindedness, it is an *even greater tragedy* that in January, approximately *200* healthy people – doctors had

5 On 14 Nov. 1941 between 9,000 and 10,000 Jews from a ghetto near Słonim were shot dead: see Docs. 87 and 89.

6 The numbers are exaggerated for the period concerned. In Baranowicze, 400 to 450 Jews were murdered in July 1941, and in Vilna 50,000 had been murdered by Jan. 1942.

weeded out the sick – *were sent to the penal camp at Treblinka*,[7] where apparently only 15 of them are still alive. The rest were cruelly tortured and murdered on the spot.

In this case the Jews of Otwock recognize the full extent of the tragedy: 200 innocent people were taken away and killed. How fortunate that it was the Jewish police who sent [them away] – and that they sent the poorest.

Some are satisfied to have bought their freedom, while others – relatives of those that have been sent away – swear they will take revenge on the Getto-Polizei,[8] but only after the war, of course.

The town is outraged.

*Meanwhile*, not a single day goes by *without several Jews being shot dead for leaving the ghetto*. Without a court verdict, they are killed on the spot and buried in the fields. Hardly anyone leaves the ghetto any more, *as fear has burrowed deep into people's hearts*.

For reasons known only to themselves, the *Germans* are teaching the Jews a vivid lesson: that the penalty for leaving the ghetto is immediate death.[9] And what is the penalty for staying in the ghetto? An intelligent, far-sighted Jew should ask himself that question. What is the penalty? Perhaps also death.

Unfortunately no one has asked himself this question, not even me.

[…][10]

## DOC. 40

## The Jewish Central Association for the Care of Orphans (CENTOS) reports on its activities in the Warsaw ghetto in January 1942[1]

CENTOS activity report (AB/ma) for January 1942, Warsaw, dated 9 February 1942

*Information* on child welfare and on CENTOS's primary activities in January 1942.[2] Child welfare in January 1942 was marked by the establishment of new care centres. The 'Dobra Wola'[3] boarding school at 61 Dzielna Street was established thanks to the 'Miesiąc Dziecka' charitable fund.[4] By late January 150 children had found shelter and protection

7 They were sent to Treblinka labour camp, which the SS had begun to construct in summer 1941.

8 German in the original: 'ghetto police'.

9 See Doc. 13.

10 In the text that follows, Perechodnik discusses the 1942 Easter and Passover celebrations and describes reactions to the news that the Jews have been deported from the Lublin ghetto.

1 AŻIH, Ring I/230 (51), fols. 1–2. English translation published in Kermish (ed.), *To Live with Honor*, pp. 366–368. This document has been newly translated from Polish.

2 The Central Association cared for 4,000 orphaned children at thirty orphanages and boarding schools in the Warsaw ghetto. It also ran more than twenty day schools and day-care homes, which looked after several thousand children whose mothers worked. Almost all the children and educators at the various CENTOS institutions lost their lives.

3 Polish: 'Goodwill'.

4 On 20 Sept. 1941 the Jewish Council, the Jewish Social Self-Help (JSS), and CENTOS launched the Children's Month (Miesiąc Dziecka) fundraising campaign for impoverished children in the ghetto. The campaign raised over a million złoty, 80,000 złoty of which came from donations. The final fundraising event was held on 16 Nov. 1941: *The Warsaw Diary of Adam Czerniaków*, pp. 277, 281, 285, 295, 299, 323, and 347. The boarding school was run by Maria Pinkert, who was married to an officer in the Jewish Order Service; financial support came from Emil Weitz, a Cracow businessman who manufactured brushes for the Wehrmacht at 61 Dzielna Street.

there. The boarding school is intended for about 300–350 children in total. In January an Orphanage for Refugee Children was opened at 29 Ogrodowa Street under the auspices of a group of public patrons set up for this purpose, with the participation of the Committee for Refugee Affairs[5] and CENTOS. Fifty orphans found shelter there.[6]

Over the course of January substantial progress was made in terms of the organization and investment for the large CENTOS building at 14 Zegarmistrowska Street, where CENTOS is setting up a large 'Children's Home'. It will be ready to take in children in February of this year.[7] At the same time, under the auspices of the Bakers' Department of the Association of Jewish Craftsmen, preparatory work was carried out to establish a separate boarding school for orphans from the 'refugee points' [shelters].[8] CENTOS representatives participated in the special committee of the Jewish Council's Social Welfare Section, which has the task of effecting a fundamental reorganization of the Main Shelter at 39 Dzielna Street.[9]

In January the welfare campaign for 'street children' made great strides. On 7 January CENTOS set up the Emergency Care Centre for Homeless and Abandoned Children at 14 Zegarmistrowska Street, where children picked up off the streets can find temporary shelter. In connection with the opening of the Emergency Care Centre, CENTOS carried out a campaign, with the assistance of the Order Service, to bring in children found begging on the streets. This operation, which was carried out systematically by members of the Order Service and CENTOS representatives in all six Order Service precincts, resulted in over 130 child beggars being brought to the Emergency Care Centre. At the Care Centre the children get three meals a day and are cared for by CENTOS educators and nurses. Following anamnesis and a disinfection and delousing procedure, the children receive new clothing and footwear, and following a transitional period, they are transferred to CENTOS boarding or day schools. The Emergency Care Centre has space for 250–300 children. CENTOS will continue this campaign throughout February and will take in more 'street children' found begging.

On 12 January of this year CENTOS opened the first Overnight Shelter for children in a large room at 1 Nowolipie Street. The Overnight Shelter is mainly intended for homeless children from the CENTOS day schools. By late January more than seventy children were spending the night there. At the Overnight Shelter the children receive supper, after which they listen to readings, stories, or sing in a choir, and then they retire to their beds. Each child has their own bed, a plank bed, with its own mattress and bedding. In late January, with support from CENTOS and a special circle of patrons created for this purpose, the Order Service in the second precinct had already commenced work on setting up a third emergency centre for 'street children'. Suitable premises were found on Chłodna Street, which should be ready for use from mid February of this year, following renovations. In January a conference with CENTOS's participation

5 The Central Refugee Committee (Centralna Komisja Uchodźców) provided assistance to resettled people and refugees in the Warsaw ghetto on behalf of the city's Jewish Aid Committee.
6 The orphanage opened on 31 Jan. 1942.
7 Several hundred orphans were housed there from Feb. 1942.
8 These shelters provided emergency accommodation for Jews who had been forcibly relocated from the municipalities in District Warsaw to the Warsaw ghetto.
9 This is a reference to Główny Dom Schronienia. This institution, the largest of its kind, was completely overcrowded with several hundred children and conditions were catastrophic; in the ghetto, the orphanage was known as the 'death home for children'.

was held at the Jewish Council's Health Section on the issue of child beggars. The results of the child welfare campaign to date were discussed, along with plans for the near future. This resulted in the Health Section representatives, led by Dr Hirszfeld[10] and Dr Milejkowski,[11] inspecting a number of CENTOS day schools, the Emergency Care Centre, and one of the reception centres.

By the end of January, thanks to funds from the 'Children's Month' charitable fund, eight new child welfare centres had been founded: two boarding schools, two day schools, two reception centres, the Emergency Care Centre, and the Overnight Shelter. More than 1,000 children found shelter in these facilities.

Some progress was made in January in terms of providing clothing for the children. With the help of donations from the 'Children's Month' fund, CENTOS purchased a certain quantity of used clothing and set up a temporary clothing repair workshop where these clothes (winter coats, children's clothes, etc.) are to be restored so that they can be reused. Nevertheless, the lack of clothing and footwear continues to be one of CENTOS's main problems – especially in connection with establishing a 'Children's Home' for 500–600 abandoned and homeless children – and procuring a larger quantity of bedding and underwear, clothing, and footwear is currently the most pressing issue.

In January CENTOS set up a dedicated Legal Section to deal with the orphaned children's belongings. In addition, CENTOS began to organize a special Vocational Training Section for orphans and children under its care. The newly founded CENTOS Central Education Committee is working hard to expand educational activities across all CENTOS operations and institutions. In this context, a pedagogical review of the work done in all boarding and day schools took place in January, and, on this basis, plans were made to raise the standards of the educational activity carried out. At the same time, the more rigorous inspections of CENTOS kitchens and care homes explicitly noted a significant improvement in both the quality of the food and the organization of the work in the kitchens and food distribution points. The main problem in supplying kitchens, care homes, and distribution points, as well as the boarding and day schools, is the shortage of fats and vitamin-rich foods.

In January a meeting was convened specifically to address the problem of child nutrition. The urgent need to arrange for additional food for children was noted, particularly for the weak and chronically ill, the numbers of whom are increasing extraordinarily rapidly. In January there was also a meeting of CENTOS department and section heads, which was attended by the head of the KOM Statistics Department, on the subject of statistical and financial reports by individual CENTOS departments and sections. This resulted in a decision to introduce uniform financial reporting guidelines for all oper-

10 Dr Ludwik Hirszfeld (1884–1954), physician and immunologist; a Catholic with Jewish origins; studied in Germany; conducted research in Heidelberg and Zurich; one of the founders of the Polish Academy of Sciences; lived in the Warsaw ghetto, Feb. 1941–1943; subsequently escaped, lived under an 'Aryan' identity, and wrote his memoirs; lived in Wrocław after the war; involved in the establishment of the University of Wrocław.

11 Dr Izrael Milejkowski (1884–1943), physician and Zionist activist; department head at the Warsaw Jewish Hospital on Czyste Street prior to Sept. 1939; chairman of the Association of Jewish Physicians; head of the Warsaw Jewish Council's Health Section; secretly trained medical students and, from Feb. 1942, collaborated with other physicians on research into the consequences of starvation; initiated and led the 'Hunger Study' in the Warsaw ghetto which was published in part in Polish in 1946; took his own life while being deported by train to Treblinka.

ational areas and to agree on which issues should be given primary consideration in the monthly and quarterly financial and activity reports of all CENTOS agencies. In January the work of the CENTOS neighbourhood officials was also thoroughly reorganized. The aim was to intensify child welfare work in individual children's homes and neighbourhoods as well as to achieve closer integration across the entire field of child welfare.

## DOC. 41
## Report dated 13 February 1942 on the work of the Jewish Social Self-Help from 1 November 1941 to 31 January 1942[1]

Report by the Jewish Social Self-Help (no. 2180/42 – I.1.Sch., General Affairs and Organizational Department), unsigned,[2] for the Government of the GG, Interior Administration Department, Population and Welfare Division,[3] Cracow, dated 13 February 1942 (carbon copy)[4]

Re: report on the work of the Jewish Social Self-Help in the months November and December 1941 and January 1942
We hereby enclose two copies of the activity report for November 1941 and January 1942.
*Wyciąg*[5]
T.[isch?]/Sch. *Activity report*
by the Jewish Social Self-Help's executive committee concerning the period from 1 November 1941 to 31 January 1942.

*Third Regulation*
The Third Regulation on Restrictions of Movement in the General Government (15 October 1941)[6] had a particularly tragic impact during the period under review. The threat of the death penalty for leaving the Jewish residential districts without authorization placed the Jewish population everywhere in a truly catastrophic situation. Many inhabitants of the Jewish residential districts, though mainly craftsmen and labourers who had previously earned their living from business dealings in the countryside and/or the larger and small towns in the surrounding area, lost all their earning opportunities, as a result of which the number of people in need of aid and support grew beyond measure. In many places, the Jewish population are unable to purchase the most essential medicines at the pharmacies

1 YVA, O-21/19, fols. 22–27. This document has been translated from German.
2 The report may have been compiled by Eliasz (Elijahu, Eliyahu) Tisch, who was in charge of correspondence at the Jewish Social Self-Help (JSS); see also Doc. 37, fn. 2.
3 The Population and Welfare Division was headed by Lothar Weirauch (1908–1983), lawyer; joined the SA in 1930 and the NSDAP in 1932; deputy section leader in the National Socialist German Students' League; head of the National Socialist Association of Legal Professionals' Career Guidance Department for the Gau of Silesia, 1934–1940; deputy head of the Population and Welfare Division within the Interior Administration of the General Government from Sept. 1940 and head of the same division from May 1941; politician for the Free Democratic Party (FDP) after the war; Ministerialdirigent in various West German ministries; at the same time an informant for Eastern Bloc intelligence services.
4 The top line reads: 'Załącznik [Polish for 'enclosure'] no. …'; the document was therefore enclosed with a letter to the authorities.
5 Polish in the original: 'excerpt'.
6 See Doc. 13.

located outside the Jewish residential districts, which makes epidemic control considerably more difficult.

There were reports from some places about cases of Jews being shot without judicial proceedings – even though the Third Regulation provides that they shall be tried by the special courts.

*Jewish residential districts*

The restrictions on the Jews' freedom of movement went hand in hand with the establishment of Jewish residential districts in places where these had not previously existed. This greatly exacerbated the housing shortage among the Jews. Even before this, Jews in smaller towns and villages very often had nowhere to live; they would spend the night in barns and storerooms, and with the onset of winter, which meant they could no longer use these places, they had to move into buildings that were completely empty and did not even have a kitchen stove. However, in many cases, they had to live in temporary wooden shacks and in attics, because it was no longer possible to cram them into other housing. Even where they have dwellings, two or three families are very often crowded together in one room. In Drzewica, Kreis Tomaszów Mazowiecki, a Jewish residential district was established for no fewer than 2,200 Jews in a single narrow street.[7]

The Jewish settlements in the village communities were liquidated and the Jews resettled in the nearest towns. Many Jews who had found paid work with farmers in the villages, whether as craftsmen or as shepherds, labourers, servants, and the like, had to leave their places of work. The number of unemployed and destitute people in the Jewish residential districts has visibly increased as a result of this.

*Resettlements*

Resettlement operations were carried out without interruption throughout the three months – that is to say, even during the cold part of the year. In District Warsaw, orders were issued with the purpose of liquidating small Jewish settlements and resettling the Jews from there in Jewish residential districts in larger localities. For instance, the entire Jewish population of Kreis Mińsk Mazowiecki and Kreis Sokołów was to be confined to seven residential districts, and that of Kreis Siedlce to four residential districts. Similar measures are planned for Kreis Tomaszów Mazowiecki, where implementation was postponed until the end of March 1942. Resettled people from villages have been housed in larger and small towns in the following Kreise: Biała Podlaska, Dębica, Janów Lubelski, Jasło, Końskie, Nowy Sącz, Radom, Sokołów, and Tomaszów Mazowiecki.

*Situation of resettled persons*

Almost all resettled people are living in extremely adverse conditions. They suffer particularly severely from the rigours of winter as they are practically naked and also barefoot. Among them are many families of seven or eight who do not own a single pair of shoes. Conditions are particularly unpleasant in the shelters for resettled people, where there are shortages of undergarments, clothing, footwear, straw sacks, blankets, and bed-

7 After the outbreak of war in 1939, the number of Jews in Drzewica rose from 780 to three times that as a consequence of the influx of refugees. The German authorities deported the ghetto residents to Treblinka in Oct. 1942.

clothes, in other words, of virtually everything. With the best will in the world, the often much smaller number of local Jews are not in a position to put up or feed the resettled persons, who are frequently unable to pay for their ration of bread. Many resettled people lie sick on the ground, in rags, without medical assistance, swollen with hunger and cold. This plight is causing a significant increase in mortality among them. Even in places where resettled persons make up only a relatively small proportion of the population, they account for 90 per cent of the deaths. People in the prime of life suddenly succumb to a fever for no apparent reason and usually perish a few days later. Even people with strong constitutions, whose powerful heart muscles have helped them overcome the fever, and whom it has been possible to get through to the convalescence stage, perish wretchedly for lack of food or anything to help them recover. In many cases, the medical investigation records exhaustion of the organism and atony of the bowels as the cause of death. There are small localities where five, or even eight, burials took place every day. Mortality in the shelters for resettled people in Warsaw, which was already at an annual rate of 51.4 per cent in November 1941, increased further in January.

*Disease*

The housing shortage – which, not infrequently, literally means not having a roof over one's head – the lack of sewers, lavatories, sometimes even any sources from which to fetch water; the shortages of clothing, bedding, and soap; the undernourishment, hunger, and severe cold are fostering the spread of epidemics. Infectious diseases were prevalent in various localities during the period covered by this report. Significantly, the number of such localities fell in the course of the period covered by this report. While the curve of new infections is rising in individual localities (in Białaczów, Kreis Tomaszów Mazowiecki, for example, more than half the Jews fell victim to epidemics), in others – in particular Warsaw and Lublin – the intensity of the epidemic has abated. It has also been increasingly the case of late that while epidemic diseases are virulent among the non-Jewish population, the Jewish residential districts remain spared.

*Epidemic control*

Desperate efforts are being made everywhere to counter the spread of epidemics. New physicians are being sent to individual localities; infectious disease hospitals, sick rooms, isolation rooms, and outpatient clinics, as well as observation wards for people suspected of having typhus, are being set up – sometimes immediately after just a few typhus cases have been identified (twenty such facilities were established during the period under review); disinfection and disinfestation procedures are being carried out, for which disinfection and disinfestation squads and a sanitation inspectorate have been set up – all this is being done even though expenditure on these things almost completely swallows up or far outstrips all revenue. (Not infrequently, the entire share of the revenue from the residents' tax is used for epidemic control.) Despite this, in most cases there are shortages of linen, medicines, and food for the sick, among whom are members of the poorest strata of the local population, but mainly people who have been resettled.

In some places, orders have been given to establish hospitals, under threat of severe punishments such as compulsory contributions, the death penalty, or resettlement. The most severe repressive measures are also being threatened in cases where the cost of caring for Jews in non-Jewish hospitals cannot be met.

Apart from the infectious disease control measures mentioned above, hygiene awareness weeks were organized, during which physicians gave talks in all Jewish institutions on epidemic control; information leaflets were distributed to all Jewish dwellings, and posters on the subject were put up in all streets, shop windows, the offices of the Jewish councils, and at the Jewish Social Self-Help's branch offices and facilities. The talks were followed by the distribution of soap. General washdays were also held for the Jewish population. Despite all of this hard work, however, it has not always been possible to manage the epidemic successfully.

*Mortality*
Hunger and cold are mercilessly decimating the ranks of the impoverished population, in particular those who have been resettled. In Warsaw, the mortality number, which fell somewhat in November and December, rose again sharply in January, namely from 4,801 in November 1941 and 4,366 in December 1941 to 5,123 in January 1942. But mortality rose sharply outside Warsaw as well, in some places by as much as 100 per cent in comparison with the previous months. The mortality rate has in some cases reached an absolutely staggering level. In Opole, for example, 18.8 per cent of the pre-war residents have perished in the course of the past year, along with 21.4 per cent of the people relocated from Vienna, and 24 per cent of the people relocated from the General Government. In the vast majority of cases, even where epidemics are prevalent, starvation, cold, and general exhaustion are established as the cause of death.

*[Food] allocations*
This section leaves a very great deal to be desired. The number of Kreise and/or independent municipalities in which our aid committees were allocated food fell during the period covered by this report. While there were still twenty branch offices that had food allocated to them in November, there were only seventeen in December, and barely twelve in January 1942. This has restricted the provision of food aid in a variety of ways, namely in terms of both the number of portions served and the days on which these could be served, and finally with regard to whether the food could be provided free of charge.

*Residents' tax*
In November 1941 the Jewish Aid Committee in Warsaw City was allocated its share of the revenue from the residents' tax both for the previous financial year and for part of the current financial year – a total of 235,862.03 zloty – and the Jewish Aid Committee in Zamość also received the first sum from this budget item, 2,000 zloty for the first six months of the current financial year. In both cases, the basis for the amount disbursed was not the formula specified in the circular of the Government of the GG, Interior Administration Department, Municipal Administration Subdivision (31 January 1941 IX.-189/40), but the proportion of residents' tax that had actually been paid.[8]

8 The residents' tax was collected in accordance with the Governor General's regulation of 27 June 1940: *VOBl-GG*, no. 44, 6 July 1940. The tax was levied annually and calculated on the basis of individuals' income tax liabilities. Reich Germans employed in public service and their relatives as well as members of the Wehrmacht, the SS, and the German police were exempt. See also Doc. 94.

*Our monetary and non-monetary subventions*
As a consequence of the loss of the subvention from the American [Jewish] Joint Distribution Committee,[9] we were not in a position to finance our branch offices, not even to the previous extent. During the period covered by this report, we received just 820,000 zloty through the Chief Social Welfare Council,[10] with the result that we were forced to take out a loan of 400,000 zloty from it.

The executive committee also distributed donations in kind during the period under review, namely items of clothing and tins of ham. We had only just over 7,000 pieces of clothing available, of which Warsaw (City and District) received 50 per cent; the rest were distributed among places where there are resettled persons and/or restricted capacity welfare institutions for children.

*Food aid*
Including Warsaw, approximately 460 soup kitchens were operating during the period covered by this report, in which the just over 270,000 welfare recipients (that is to say, 30,000 persons more than in the previous months) received soup with a wholly inadequate calorie content. More than twice that number of potential recipients had to remain unprovided for. Should our branch offices not receive substantial allocations of money and food in the immediate future, there is a threat of the soup kitchens closing in many places.

*Winter relief*
Individual branch offices have made attempts to set up winter relief schemes by collecting donations of clothing and cash. Despite the efforts of the aid committees and delegations, as a consequence of the pauperization of the Jewish population, the results have been very modest and could in no way contribute to the alleviation of need. It was not even possible to provide the most essential clothing and footwear to those Jews subject to forced and/or compulsory labour.

*Employment assistance*
On account of the challenging food situation in the General Government and in order to ease the burden on our welfare institutions, we proposed that Jews be employed in agriculture and that vegetables be cultivated in the towns. In response to a circular on this topic, many places have taken the necessary preparatory measures, and we hope to be able to report positive results in the spring.

In many places, our efforts to establish short courses for craftsmen have run into difficulties with the authorities, who regarded the Population and Welfare Division's approval of our resolution[11] on this matter, which was adopted at the meeting on 16 January 1941,

9 Deliveries from the American Jewish Joint Distribution Committee were no longer possible once Hitler had declared war on the USA in Dec. 1941.
10 The Cracow-based Chief Social Welfare Council (NRO) was the main welfare organization for the population in the General Government; it operated from May 1940 to 1944/1945 and was subdivided into three sections: one for the Polish population, one for the Ukrainian population, and one for the Jewish population.
11 YVA, O-21/19, fol. 26.

as insufficient. At present several short courses for craftsmen are being run in Warsaw, as well as in Częstochowa and Rzeszów, while the courses in Radom that had been approved by the Stadthauptmann and started recently are running into difficulties with the Chamber of Craftsmen.[12]

*Sanitary and hygiene provision*
The work of this department mainly encompassed the establishment and upkeep of hospitals, sickbays, isolation units, and outpatient clinics. A total of 87,550 zloty was spent for these purposes during the period covered by this report, while medicines were purchased for the sum of 63,351.67 zloty and distributed to 184 locations, along with the charitable parcels that arrived from abroad via the German Red Cross. Over the same period, 10,000 copies of a brochure about the prevention and control of infectious diseases were also published with the approval of the Department of Public Enlightenment and Propaganda.

*Child welfare*
The Department for Child and Youth Welfare is in close contact with 164 towns and villages. The executive committee has endeavoured to intensify its activities and to increase the number of children cared for, to improve both the quality and quantity of their food, to provide them with education, and to obtain a broader material basis for the individual welfare institutions and/or facilities by enlisting the local population in all kinds of services. The following were set up in Warsaw during the period under review: one boarding school for seventy children, two boarding schools for 800–900 children were at the organizational stage, in addition two day schools for 330 children were set up, as were one children's night shelter for the same number and three reception rooms for 350 street children, who are placed in boarding schools or day schools once investigations and disinfestation procedures have been carried out. Furthermore, institutions with a restricted capacity were created at Międzyrzec Podlaski and Parczew, Kreis Radzyn. Outside Warsaw, the number of childcare facilities grew from twenty-four to forty-five and the number of children they served rose from 4,348 to 8,999. The number of children provided for by the additional food distribution points for children grew during the period under review. Child welfare everywhere includes medical and sanitary provision.

*Expanding the organization*
A Kreis conference of the Jewish Social Self-Help, which was attended by a member of the executive committee, was held in Kreis Cholm on 25 and 26 January 1942.[13]

During the period covered by this report, members of our executive committee visited Lwów, Warsaw, Radom, Krosno, Sanok, Jasło, Gorlice, Koluszki, Tomaszów Mazowiecki, Opoczno, Cholm, Lublin, Rozwadów, and Sandomierz, where they inspected existing facilities and issued instructions to the branch offices.

12 The Population and Welfare Division prohibited further courses in March: see Doc. 45.
13 See Doc. 37.

## DOC. 42

### On 14 February 1942 the temporary administrator of a tannery is accused of having illegally misappropriated furs from the Warsaw ghetto together with Jewish partners[1]

Anonymous letter to the commissioner for the Jewish residential district in Warsaw[2] (log no. 1870/42), Brühl Palace (received on 16 February 1942), Warsaw, dated 14 February 1942

*Re: Mr Arnaud,*[3] *the temporary administrator of the tannery Cytryn & Co., 61 Niskastraße*
The following example demonstrates how Mr Arnaud, the temporary administrator of the tannery Cytryn & Co., respects regulations:

When the directive came into force, in the Jewish district all furs owned by Jews had to be handed in – contraventions are punishable by death[4] – Mr Arnaud together with his Jews, Cytryn,[5] Stein, and two others, bought up the most expensive fine furs at knockdown prices and had them taken to the Aryan side. A sum of approx. 400,000 zloty is said to have been spent on furs that in reality are worth several million zloty.

I would like to take this opportunity to inform you of another affair involving millions of zloty that is happening in this very tannery at 61 Niskastraße and in which the firm's temporary administrator is the protagonist.

After the firm Cytryn & Co. had been seized, the proprietors, the Jews Cytryn and Stein, his [Cytryn's] son-in-law, endeavoured to obtain ownership of the neighbouring tannery located on the same plot, 61 Niskastraße, which belonged to the Weigel company[6] – and to do so under the pretext of wanting to work for the German authorities. Since they were well aware they could not act as the administrators themselves, they got in touch with Mr Arnaud, asking him to make every effort to ensure that he obtained the post of temporary administrator in this factory because they knew Mr Arnaud would go along with and facilitate every one of their schemes. Before the war Mr Arnaud was a business associate of the firm Cytryn & Co. – which can be proven from pre-war correspondence.[7]

Through various intermediaries, Mr Arnaud endeavoured to obtain the post of temporary administrator, and was indeed successful. – Since then, Arnaud, together with a gang – [the] Jews Cytryn, Stein, and comrades – has been earning hundreds of thousands of zloty every month, which are divided up between them.

If the German authorities were to interest themselves in Mr Arnaud's identity, who he was until the outbreak of the war and his financial situation back then, it would be easy to establish what a fortune he has accumulated during his time as temporary

1 APW, Office of the Governor of District Warsaw, Commissioner for the Jewish Residential District, Transfer Bureau 482/39, fols. 2–3. This document has been translated from German.
2 Heinz Auerswald.
3 Boris Arnaud (d. 1942), retailer; ethnic German who lived at 18 Mickiewicz Street (Invalidenstraße) in Warsaw; died in prison.
4 See Doc. 28.
5 Israel Cytryn (d. 1942), tanner and businessman; co-owner of the tannery Cytryn & Co. before Sept. 1939; relocated it to 61 Niska Street in the Warsaw ghetto in 1940.
6 Correctly: Weigle; the Wilhelm Weigle tannery later relocated to 48 Hoża Street, outside the ghetto.
7 Not in the file.

administrator, as well as how many valuables, how much gold, and how many diamonds he currently owns. A thorough search of his home and a rigorous int[...] [...][8] of his family members will convince the relevant agencies about the swindling that has been going on under the pretext that everything is being done for the German authorities.

At the same time I would like to give you a little potted biography of Mr Arnaud. While Poland was in existence, Arnaud was known as a great patriot and an upstanding Pole. When the question of ceding the Polish Corridor to the German Reich was in the news, Arnaud was one of the first to participate in the agitation against Germany and ethnic Germans, and he incited the people against the German population.

After the city of Warsaw had been taken over by the German authorities, Arnaud was himself registered as an 'ethnic German' with the assistance of a very highly respected ethnic German and employed in this capacity as the temporary administrator of the above-mentioned factory where, together with a specific group of Jews, he now engages in illegal tanning on a large scale. Once, sometimes even twice a week, entire lorryloads of hard and soft leather go out to certain Jews, who sell them on at a price of approx. 300 zł. per kg. The revenue that Arnaud and his comrades make from this amounts to tens of thousands of zloty a day, a sum which is in turn converted into various foreign currencies, valuables, diamonds, and gold.

In order to confirm the credibility of the above information, I cite below the words of Mr Arnaud, which he uttered to his acquaintances when in an inebriated state:

> Although I am only an ethnic German, no checks have been carried out at the factory I manage. Checks have been carried out everywhere, whether in Aryan or Jewish enterprises, for instance at Keller's tannery, 58 Okopowastr., Beia Feifer, and so on. But you have to know how to deal with people – when it comes to making money, 10,000 or 20,000 zloty should be neither here nor there. – I have the people at the goods supply control office and other offices in the palm of my hand, so much so that I am at liberty to act just as it suits me, and I'll push those who want to work against me to the point where they have to quit the scene.

I will give you another example that illustrates Commissioner Arnaud's actual mindset and his conduct when he boozes with his Jewish friends after successful deals! The usual toast proposed is: 'I'm with you and I'll protect you now, so that you know how you'll have to protect me when the war is over and I'm no longer an ethnic German.'[9]

8 Illegible (possibly: 'and a rigorous interrogation, also of his family members').

9 According to a letter from the Trade and Industry Subdivision of the Department for Economic Affairs in District Warsaw to Commissioner Auerswald, dated 21 April 1942, Boris Arnaud died of a heart attack on 1 April 1942, 'presumably as a consequence of the investigations instituted as a result of various anonymous reports'; the proceedings against Arnaud at the German Special Court in Warsaw had been terminated on 23 March 1942: APW, Office of the Governor of District Warsaw, Commissioner for the Jewish Residential District, Transfer Bureau 482/39, fol. 7.

## DOC. 43

## *Informacja Bieżąca*, 2 March 1942: report on the mass murder of Jews in Kosów Huculski on 16 October 1941[1]

*The Eastern Territories. Details of Massacres of Jews*

*Kosów Huculski.*[2] On 16 October 1941 a Ukrainian *death battalion*[3] arrived here, in which there were only three Gestapo men. On this day, the Ukrainians dragged 2,400 Jews out of their homes and *one* of the Gestapo men – who, by the way, was clearly insane – killed them with a revolver one by one. The Ukrainians only served as guards and helpers. Once the Jews had been thrown into the giant ditches that they had dug earlier, they [the death battalion] realized that many of them were still alive. They then came up with the fiendish idea of finding those who were still alive and selling them to the Jewish Community. This is how a portion [of the Jews] escaped death.[4]

*Lachowice*, Kreis Baranowicze, Nowogródek voivodeship. [A total of] 10,000 Jews were executed with a machine gun.[5]

Brz.[6]

1 *Informacja Bieżąca*, no. 9 (34), 2 March 1942, p. 3; AAN, 1325/202/III-7/1, fol. 55. *Informacja Bieżąca* was an internal information bulletin with a small circulation, issued by the government delegation's Press and Information Department. It appeared weekly from 1941 to 1944. This document has been translated from Polish.

2 A small town and major spa resort 30 km south of Kolomyja in Eastern Galicia.

3 The Jews in Kosów were shot dead by members of the field office of the Commander of the Security Police and the SD (KdS) in Kolomyja, with the assistance of the Ukrainian auxiliary police.

4 A total of 2,088 people were shot dead, including 149 refugees from Hungary.

5 In Nov. 1941 several hundred Jews were murdered in Lachowice by members of the 707th Infantry Division; several thousand more were murdered throughout the region.

6 Brz[eski] was the code name of Antoni Szymanowski (1914–1985), historian and diplomat; served in the war in Sept. 1939; worked with the Union of Armed Struggle (ZWZ) Information Service from 1940; operated as 'cell' (*komórka*) 1631; active in the Alliance of Democrats (SD) from 1941; later editor of *Nowe Drogi*; in 1944 headed the sub-department that dealt with the German-occupied territories; worked in the Polish Ministry of Foreign Affairs after the war.

## DOC. 44

## On 3 March 1942 State Secretary Josef Bühler instructs the Governor of District Lublin to set up a transit camp for Jews from the Reich[1]

Letter from the state secretary of the government of the GG (file ref. I/23/42), signed Bühler, Cracow, to the Governor of District Lublin, Zörner (received on 6 March 1942), Lublin, dated 3 March 1942[2]

As part of the overall solution to the Jewish problem in Europe, a transit camp needs to be set up in Lublin for Jews who are to be evacuated from certain parts of the Reich.[3]

I have given my agreement for a total of 14,000 Jews[4] to temporarily take up residence in District Lublin in the course of the next month.

## DOC. 45

## On 9 March 1942 the General Government's Population and Welfare Division orders that occupational training courses for Jews are no longer to be approved[1]

Directive issued by the Interior Administration Main Department, Population and Welfare Division, Cracow (file ref. IX 1005–01 c) Ko/S) to the district governors, Interior Administration Department, Population and Welfare Division, Cracow, Lublin, Radom, and Warsaw, signed Heinrich,[2] dated 9 March 1942 (copy)

*Re*: establishment and running of short specialized craftmanship, retraining, and agricultural courses for Jews
*Subject*: n/a
I am writing to inform you that the above-mentioned courses, which have been organized up until now by the individual Jewish aid committees or Jewish councils to train and retrain young Jews, are henceforth no longer to be approved.

Since this matter must be regulated consistently throughout the territory of the General Government, please inform all of the Stadthauptleute and Kreishauptleute in your district of this decision without delay.

1 APL, 498/273, fol. 49. Published as a facsimile in Nachman Blumental (ed.), *Te'udot mi-geto lublin – yudenrat le-lo derekh* [Documents from Lublin Ghetto: Judenrat without Direction] (Jerusalem: Yad Vashem, 1967 [Hebrew, with English preface and introduction]), appendix, doc. V. This document has been translated from German.
2 The original contains handwritten annotations.
3 The ghettos in several small towns in District Lublin were cleared in March 1942 in order to make space for newly arriving Jews from the Reich: see Doc. 52.
4 At least 35,000 Jews were deported from the Reich and Slovakia to District Lublin in the weeks and months that followed.

1 APL, 498/893, fol. 73. Published in Joseph Kermish (ed.), *Dokumenty i materiały do dziejów okupacji niemieckiej*, vol. 2: *'Akcje' i 'wysiedlenia'* (Warsaw: Centralna Żydowska Komisja Historyczna w Polsce, 1946), p. 42. This document has been translated from German.
2 Herbert Heinrich (b. 1915), economist; joined the NSDAP in 1934; posted to Cracow in Jan. 1940; head of the Voluntary Welfare and Jewish Affairs Section in the Population and Welfare Division within the General Government's Interior Administration Department; served in the war from April 1942; head of the Population and Welfare Division in District Warsaw from late 1942 to late 1943; official at the Federal Ministry of Defence in the 1950s.

## DOC. 46

## On 9 March 1942 Thea Huth, a young Viennese woman deported to the General Government, asks relatives for help[1]

Letter from Thea Huth,[2] Opole Lubelskie,[3] to her uncle Ignaz Herschl[4] and her aunt in Vienna, dated 9 March 1942

My dears,

You will be amazed to get post from me. Unfortunately, there is sad news. As you will of course know, my dear mother died in April.[5] Since then I have also been seriously ill and gone to hospital […] already been more […] than here.[6] When, still very weak, I returned to my so-called home, that is to say, to father, he was lying in bed seriously ill. In the end, he had to go to hospital as well, where he died on 17 January of premature calcification of the arteries.[7] Aunt Berta then died two weeks later,[8] and Uncle Otto has been in hospital for two weeks as well. Two cards came back from Aunt Olga[9] with the note 'Addressee has moved house', and I can imagine what that means. Now I find myself completely alone and abandoned and cannot help myself because there are no opportunities of any kind to earn money here. Have pity on me. Mother and father's things are with Miss Weißgram, 6/43F, 2 Taborstraße. Dear aunt, please *you* get in touch with her. Then send me what you can. I am still young, of course, and would dearly like to survive this difficult time, but only you can help me do this. I will be eternally grateful to you. Please write soon.

Best wishes from your niece, Thea[10]

1 The original has not survived. Copy in DÖW, photos 3450/1 and 2. Published in Kurt Schubert and Jonny Moser, *Der gelbe Stern in Österreich: Katalog und Einführung zu einer Dokumentation* (Eisenstadt: Edition Roetzer, 1977), pp. 24–25, with facsimile fig. 178. This document has been translated from German.

2 Thea Huth (1924–1942), originally from Vienna; detained with her parents Fanni and Alois Huth on 15 Feb. 1941 and deported to Opole Lubelskie with another 993 people. The residents of the ghetto there were murdered in Sobibor in May and Oct. 1942. On conditions in Opole Lubelskie, see PMJ 3/151.

3 A small town approximately 40 km south-west of Lublin.

4 Ignaz Herschl (b. 1887) was married to a non-Jew and was therefore not deported.

5 Presumably Fanni Huth (1896–1941). Many of the Jews deported from Vienna died of malnutrition.

6 Ellipses denote several words that are illegible in this line of the original.

7 Presumably Alois Huth (1896–1942).

8 Presumably Berta Herschl (1890–1942); deported to Opole Lubelskie with her husband Otto (b. 1899) on 26 Feb. 1941.

9 Presumably Olga Herschl (b. 1878), originally from Vienna; deported on 2 Nov. 1941 to the Lodz ghetto, where she perished on 10 May 1942.

10 Added in different handwriting: 'Age 15, Opole Kreis Puławy District Lublin'.

## DOC. 47

## *Krakauer Zeitung*, 10 March 1942: article on a speech in Cracow by the NSDAP's senior command leader in the General Government about the Jews' supposed desire to annihilate the German people[1]

*'From Creative Community to Victory'*
*SS-Brigadeführer Schmidt[2] speaks at the SS and Police Theatre in Cracow*

*Cracow, 10 March*
A talk given by the former governor of District Lublin, SS-Brigadeführer *Schmidt* (Berlin), to junior ranks, commanders, and officers of the SS and police at the SS and Police Theatre in Cracow constituted an inspiring avowal of commitment to the historic tasks National Socialist Germany is currently in the process of tackling, and provided an enthralling contrast between those tasks and the state of subversive destruction into which a significant part of humanity had already been led by world Jewry when the largest military conflict in history began. Starting from the fact that the emergence of a truly revolutionary idea is synonymous with the general mobilization of all the forces lying dormant within a nation, SS-Brigadeführer Schmidt made reference to the roots of our current world view – roots that had spread not least in the soil of the experience of the First World War – and explained the concept of the Volk as a new creative community which, out of the sense of belonging felt by all people of German blood, had forged the preconditions for Germany's rise.

Citing the eternally restless wandering of the Jews around the world, in the course of which they are currently gravitating to the country with the greatest racial conflicts, America, the speaker illustrated how it can be that, time and time again, it is the grotesque countenance of the Jew that peers out behind all the subversive phenomena of the day, whether these go under the name of world Marxism, world capitalism of the plutocrats, world Bolshevism of the Soviets, or something else. With the same goal, but applying completely different methods, the Jew avails himself of both the American-style individualist and the Bolshevist who has become a machine among the masses, in whose feral way of life brutality and death have become everyday phenomena. The cosmopolitan Jew pursues only one goal in this respect: the annihilation of Adolf Hitler and the German people. For him it has become an either/or question.

Brigadeführer Schmidt contrasted the abysmal world that – were it to win – would annihilate us all with the clearly and sharply drawn image of the German soldier, with everything that has distinguished him in the campaigns undertaken to date, and particularly in the struggle against the most brutal of all opponents here in the East, with his

1 *Krakauer Zeitung*, 10 March 1942, p. 5. The *Krakauer Zeitung* was the daily newspaper for the German population in the General Government and appeared from Nov. 1939 to Jan. 1945. This document has been translated from German.

2 Friedrich Schmidt (1902–1973), primary school teacher; joined the NSDAP in 1925 and the SS in 1934; deputy Gauleiter of Württemberg, 1933–1937; head of the NSDAP Main Training Office in 1937; district governor in Lublin from Oct. 1939 to the beginning of 1940, when he was recalled to the Reich; NSDAP senior command leader at the headquarters of SS Section East in April 1940; taken prisoner of war by US forces in 1944 and interned in Ludwigsburg; sentenced to 30 months in a labour camp in 1948; thereafter worked as a sales representative in Burghausen.

unwavering will to fight and to achieve victory. At the same time, however, he also discussed the causes that on more than one occasion had helped snatch the laurel of victory from German hands at the last moment in previous centuries. How many examples there are in German history of us failing to achieve certain victory because we believed we had to emulate the defeated. Applied to the territory here in the East, the speaker construed such thoughts as meaning that anyone who sat here in the General Government and was corrupt at heart would make himself guilty of the most contemptible crime because, as a result of his conduct, he too would represent the victory of the defeated over the victor. – However, he gave his listeners the certainty that, as the National Socialist idea had been born of the experience of German combat veterans, the NSDAP and all those who found themselves out at the front or here in this eastern territory would never allow such things to arise again. For this development will culminate in the fulfilment of the idea of the Reich of the Germans, which is not only a geographical necessity, but also a self-evident ideology advancing from a new morality.

At the start of the talk, which was received with resounding applause, the audience, which also included the Senior Commander of the Order Police in the General Government, Police Generalmajor SS-Brigadeführer *Winkler*, were welcomed by the commander of the Cracow Police Regiment, Urban Police Oberstleutnant *Gaßler*,[3] who was representing the SS and Police Leader in District Cracow.[4] An Urban Police military band played before and after the talk.

A. F.[5]

3 Richard Gaßler (1889–1942), police officer; served with the Urban Police from 1919; joined the NSDAP in 1933 and the SS in 1938; Commander of the Urban Police in Augsburg, then in Stuttgart and Cologne; commander of the Cracow Police Regiment from 1941; Commander of the Order Police (KdO) in District Cracow in 1942; died in a reserve base hospital.

4 Julian Scherner.

5 Alfred Finke, Oberleutnant der Reserve in the Urban Police; wrote articles for the General Government's press service and the *Krakauer Zeitung*.

## DOC. 48

## On 17 March 1942 a section head at the Population and Welfare Division in District Lublin makes notes on his preparations for the murder of the Jews[1]

Note by the head of Section V of the Population and Welfare Division, ref. II R./We., Reuter,[2] Lublin, dated 17 March 1942

*Note*

On 4 March 1942 I received a teletype message from the government in Cracow,[3] signed by Department Head Dr Siebert,[4] in which the final sentence reads as follows: 'Please be of assistance to the SS and Police Leader in Lublin[5] with respect to his measures.'

On 7 March there was a call from the government, Major Ragger,[6] regarding the resettlement of Jews from Mielec to District Lublin; I was expressly asked to reach and maintain agreement with the SS and Police Leader and to attach the greatest importance to this. I therefore attempted to get in touch with Stabsführer Nemez straight away.[7] I tried to get through by phone for three days, without success. Only after I managed to speak to the SS personnel office was I told that Stabsführer Nemez was on leave. On 12 March 1942 I was referred to Obersturmführer Pohl,[8] who, however, was not the official dealing with the resettlement of Jews either. He referred me to Hauptsturmführer Höfle,[9] Schreck Barracks, telephone 1570/25 (can be reached on 2004 outside duty

1 APL, 498/273, fol. 53r–v. Published as a facsimile in Blumental (ed.), *Te'udot mi-geto lublin*, appendix, doc. VI. This document has been translated from German.

2 Fritz Reuter (1896–1982), company secretary; employed by an electronics firm in Breslau in the 1930s; worked in the Population and Welfare Division in Lublin from July 1941; briefly posted to the Labour Department in Lublin in autumn 1942; head of Section V (Refugee and Evacuee Welfare) in the General Government's Population and Welfare Division, Jan. 1943 – Jan. 1945; worked as a sales representative in Coburg after the war.

3 The message has not been identified.

4 Dr Friedrich Wilhelm Siebert (1903–1966), lawyer; joined the NSDAP in 1931 and the SS in 1935; mayor of Lindau in 1933; Landrat in Bad Kissingen in 1939; head of the General Government's Interior Administration Main Department from Oct. 1939; became department head in the Bavarian State Ministry of Finance in Sept. 1940; reappointed head of the General Government's Interior Administration Main Department in Feb. 1942; found guilty of war crimes in Cracow in 1948; released from prison in 1956; deputy mayor of Prien am Chiemsee, 1960–1966.

5 Odilo Globocnik.

6 Johann Ragger (1888–1962), career officer; major in the Austro-Hungarian army; worked in the Population and Welfare Division as head of Section V (Resettlement, Evacuee Welfare, and Prisoners of War) from spring 1940; managed a guest house in Velden am Wörthersee (Austria) after the war.

7 Correctly: Josef Nemec.

8 Helmut Ortwin Pohl (1901–1997), bookkeeper; joined the NSDAP and the SS in 1930; detained several times in Austria before 1938 for National Socialist activities; served in the war with the Waffen-SS, 1939–1940; on the staff of the SS and Police Leader in Lublin as an official in charge of Jewish affairs, Feb.–June 1942; manager of a business in Klagenfurt from June 1942; lived in Lienz and Oberlienz (Tyrol) after the war.

9 Hermann Höfle (1911–1962), car mechanic; joined the NSDAP and the SS in 1933; detained in Austria in 1935 for National Socialist activities; Selbstschutz commander in Nowy Sącz, 1939–1940; then on the staff of the SS and Police Leader in Lublin as an official in charge of Jewish affairs, responsible for labour camps and the establishment of Belzec camp; head of the staff of Operation Reinhard in 1942; commander of the protective custody camp within Sachsenhausen concentration camp in 1944; interned, 1945–1947; arrested in Salzburg in 1960; committed suicide while on remand.

hours). I arranged a meeting with Hauptsturmführer Höfle on Monday, 16 March 1942,[10] at 5.30 p.m. In the course of the meeting, the following points were explained by Hauptsturmführer Höfle:

1) It would be expedient if the transports of Jews coming into District Lublin are divided directly at the departure station into Jews who are fit for work and Jews who are unfit for work. If it is not possible to separate them at the departure station, the transport would potentially have to be divided in Lublin instead in accordance with the abovementioned criteria.

2) Jews who are not fit for [labour] deployment will all go to Belzec, the furthest border station in Kreis Zamosz.[11]

3) Hauptsturmführer Höfle is in the process of building a large camp where the Jews fit for [labour] deployment can be registered by occupation in a card index and from where they can be requested [as labour].[12]

4) Piaski will be emptied of Polish Jews and will become an assembly point for the Jews coming from the Reich.[13]

5) Jews will not be sent to Trawniki for the time being.[14]

6) H[öfle] asked where 60,000 Jews could be unloaded on the Dęblin-Trawniki line. Informed about the transports of Jews that are now running from here, H. stated that of the 500 Jews who had arrived in Susiec,[15] the ones who were not fit for work could be separated off from the others and sent to Belzec. According to a teletype message from the government dated 14 March 1942,[16] there was a transport of Jews from the Protectorate bound for Trawniki. These Jews were not unloaded at Trawniki, but taken to Izbiza.[17] A request from the Kreishauptmann of Zamosz[18] for 200 Jews to be brought in from there for work was approved by H.

In conclusion, he stated that he could receive 4 to 5 transports of 1,000 Jews a day bound for Belzec. These Jews would cross the border and never return to the General Government.

10 Incorrect in the original: 16 March 1941.

11 Correctly: Kreis Zamosc (Zamość). On Belzec extermination camp, see Introduction, pp. 33, 42–45.

12 Höfle had young men who were fit for work selected from the transports to Sobibor and Belzec to undertake forced labour in Lublin and Nałęczów; according to witness statements, he participated in the selections and in most cases sent the men to Lublin-Majdanek concentration camp.

13 Approximately 3,500 residents of the Piaski ghetto were deported to Belzec in March 1942; about 1,000 remained behind.

14 Trawniki labour camp was directly adjacent to the SS training camp and operated from June 1942 to Sept. 1943; prisoners had to sort the belongings of murdered Jews before they were sent for repurposing. The first transport to arrive at Trawniki camp left Theresienstadt on 12 June 1942 with 1,000 people. See Introduction, pp. 39–40.

15 The SS and police liquidated the Mielec ghetto in District Cracow on 9 March 1942. Following selections, 3,000–3,500 persons were deported to District Lublin. A transport that left on 15 March 1942 with 2,000 Jews was divided at Zamość: 1,500 Jews were transported to the Hrubieszów ghetto and the remaining 500 were transported onwards to the village of Susiec.

16 This could not be found.

17 The first transport to the Izbica ghetto left Theresienstadt on 11 March 1942 with around 1,000 people; it arrived on 13 March 1942.

18 Correctly: Zamosc (Zamość). The Kreishauptmann was Helmut Weihenmeyer.

## DOC. 49

## On 19 March 1942 the Oberfeldkommandantur of the Wehrmacht in Lemberg reports on the deportation of Jews[1]

Report (marked 'secret') from Oberfeldkommandantur 365 (Ia no. /42 secret), signed Beuttel,[2] to the Military Commander in the General Government[3] (received on 21 March 1942, log no. 1618/1942, secret), St. Qu.,[4] dated 19 March 1942[5]

3 enclosures[6]
*Monthly report*
Period: 16 February – 15 March 1942
[…][7]
VIII *Other matters*
1) *Civilian population*
a) *Morale*

There are not likely to have been any significant changes in the population's morale during the month covered by this report; reference may therefore be made to the more extensive observations on this matter set out in the last few monthly reports.

It is reported that not only the Jews, but certain Polish circles as well have great hopes of a spring offensive by the Russians: some people have apparently not given up on the dream of re-establishing an independent Poland.

A noticeable unease has spread within Lemberg's Jewish population with the start of a resettlement operation in the course of which the approximately 30,000 elderly Jews and other Jews from Lemberg who are not involved in the work process are to be rounded up and, as has been stated, taken to the Lublin area. It remains to be seen how far this evacuation is to be equated to a decimation.[8]

1 BArch, RH 53-23/35, fols. 66–88 (fols. 87–88). This document has been translated from German.
2 Kurt Beuttel (1886–1956), career officer; commander of Nuremberg Ordnance Command from 1937; promoted to lieutenant general in 1941; transferred to the reserve officer pool in Sept. 1941; appointed commandant of Oberfeldkommandantur 365 in Lemberg in mid Jan. 1942; transferred once again to the reserve officer pool in Aug. 1944; discharged from the Wehrmacht in Dec. 1944; prisoner of war, 1945–1947; thereafter lived in Heidelberg.
3 Curt Ludwig Freiherr von Gienanth (1876–1961), career officer; Reichswehr commander, 1920–1933; commander of Border Police Section Command 14 from Sept. 1939; simultaneously commander of Border Section Central in Poland, Feb.–April 1940; military commander in the General Government from May 1940; military district commander in the General Government from 1942; transferred to the reserve officer pool on 1 Oct. 1942.
4 Stabsquartier: 'headquarters'.
5 The original features stamps and one annotation.
6 A list of guard posts and reports from the veterinary officer and chief medical officer is included as an enclosure to the document: BArch, RH 53-23/35, fols. 89–97.
7 The monthly report is twenty-three pages long in total and has nine pages of enclosures. Beuttel firstly discussed organizational changes, then addressed the activities and condition of the troops, their ideological supervision, and further topics of importance to the war effort within the jurisdiction of Oberfeldkommandantur 365.
8 Between 16 March 1942 and 1 April 1942, a total of 15,000 ghetto inmates – mostly women, children, and elderly people – were deported from Lemberg (Lwów) to Belzec.

At any rate it may be described as symptomatic that the Ukrainians participated enthusiastically in the collection of winter clothes and furs, in some places even surprisingly so, while the Poles conducted themselves with great reserve. The collection from the Jews was not voluntary in nature.[9]

b) *Food situation*

This is unlikely to have changed to any significant extent during the period under review; it has certainly not improved. Accordingly, it remains as before with a consistently moderate to very poor supply for the towns and cities, while the rural population, with the exception of the district's southern territories, may be assumed to possess the foodstuffs necessary for subsistence. People in particular need are being fed on a very limited scale by Polish aid committees.

There are plans to create and assign allotments in Drohobych and Boryslav; it would be conceivable for other towns to follow this example.

2) *Particular events*

On Heroes' Remembrance Day,[10] wreath-laying ceremonies were held at the military cemeteries in the places where the Ortskommandanturen are based. This act was given a particularly dignified and ceremonial setting at Lemberg military cemetery; wreaths were laid by the Oberfeldkommandant; by the Italians, Hungarians, and Slovaks; by Governor Dr Wächter[11] for the civilian administration; and by the Party.

IX *Cooperation with the civilian administration*

Cooperation between military and civilian agencies, particularly between Oberfeldkommandantur 365 and the district administration, was also extremely good and comradely during the month under review.

9 This collection had already been carried out around the turn of the year 1941/1942: see Docs. 28 and 42. SS and Police Leader Katzmann later reported that thirty-five railway wagons of furs had been confiscated in the district: see Doc. 251.

10 *Heldengedenktag* was the Nazi name for the day annually commemorating the German war dead. In West Germany after the Second World War, the name *Volkstrauertag* (National Day of Mourning) was restored.

11 Dr Otto Freiherr von Wächter (1901–1949), lawyer; joined the SA in 1923, the NSDAP in 1930, and the SS in 1935; Gau office head in Vienna and head of training with the NSDAP Landesleitung for Austria from 1931; state commissioner under Reichsstatthalter Seyss-Inquart from 1938; governor of District Cracow from 1939; governor of District Galicia from Jan. 1942; head of the military administration in Italy from 1944; lived in hiding in the Austrian mountains and later in the Vatican under an assumed name; died in Rome.

## DOC. 50
## On 20 March 1942 an unidentified author describes the murder of his relatives in Rohatyn to a friend in the Warsaw ghetto[1]

Letter from an unidentified Jew from Rohatyn[2] to his friend Edward in the Warsaw ghetto, dated 20 March 1942

Dear friend,

Unfortunately, there is no longer anyone to buy birthday gifts for. Two days before our ray of sunshine's birthday, we lost our dearest parents, beloved Pepka, and sweetest Imeczek. I am left on my own with Dudek. We are alone in our grief and despair. There is no solace for us.

'We live', but we don't know why or for whom. We've lost four of those most beloved to us. Their death was so terrible – together with 2,000 of our brothers and sisters, in a common grave. There has never been such a 'shechita'[3] anywhere. They didn't spare pregnant women, little children, or the elderly. There were rivers of blood. Genia[4] arrived unexpectedly in the morning, went around the neighbourhood, and gallivanted around with autochtons[5] until the evening. If only they had released Imeczek. That would have been a miracle, and at least we would have had a purpose and something to cling on to. But as things stand, our grief and despair grow from day to day. I just can't come to terms with the fact that they are no more. I see them whenever I close my eyes. I can still hear the sound of Imeczek's laughter.

Edzio, you simply can't imagine what a wonderful child he was, how wonderfully he was developing and how well behaved he was. As you have been with us at such difficult times, you know this and can understand whom we've lost. All children think their mother is the best, but is there a more loving, devoted, dedicated, and understanding mother than my Mama? Whom has she ever harmed? She never even raised her voice. She was always quiet and empathetic, always had a smile on her face, and she lived only for other children.

Or Father. He slaved away all his life, never complained, and he was happy in his children's happiness and joy. He never expressed it in words, but his eyes reflected his unconditional dedication and loyalty.

1 AŻIH, Ring I/988b (559). Published as a facsimile in Ruta Sakowska et al. (eds.), *Archiwum Ringelbluma: Konspiracyjne Archiwum Getta Warszawy*, vol. 1: *Listy o Zagładzie*, ed. Ruta Sakowska (Warsaw: Wydawnictwo Naukowe PWN, 1997), p. 78. The document is a typewritten transcript produced for the underground archive of the Warsaw ghetto. This document has been translated from Polish.

2 In 1931 a total of 3,000 Jews lived in the town of Rohatyn in Eastern Galicia. The numbers later increased significantly due to the arrival of refugees and expellees. On 20 March 1942 staff from the field office of the Commander of the Security Police and the SD (KdS) in Stanislawów and members of the Ukrainian auxiliary police herded approximately 2,000 Jews to pits near the railway station, where they were shot dead. On 2 Sept. 1942 the police deported another 1,000 people, and on 8 Dec. a further 1,500 were deported to Belzec.

3 Hebrew in the original: 'kosher slaughter'.

4 A code word for German police officers.

5 Probably a code word for the Ukrainian auxiliary police.

Or Pepka, endlessly loyal and devoted, happy to be of service to others. In the end, she didn't have a single good day in her life. To her, a child was everything, it was life itself, and she had to witness the death of her little son. Clutching his mother's neck – they both fell into the grave. Is there a greater tragedy, a greater atrocity? I no longer believe in anything. I no longer believe in any fate that could allow such pure and innocent beings to be led like lambs to the slaughter. And what now? We are left to ourselves. What torments me most is this feeling of hopelessness. Man is a beast that has to wash, get dressed, and feed.

No, there is no longer any solace for me. We have no heart, only a stone; otherwise it would have broken a long time ago. Sometimes I convince myself that I have to bear this like a man in order to exact revenge at the right time, but these are just empty words. Everything is empty, nothing will bring back my loved ones.

Keep well, my friend, and don't hold it against me that I'm sharing my pain with you. You knew those dearest to me so well that I have to write to you about them.

Everyone perished […][6] our names on their lips. Their last thoughts, their words, their dying breath […] us. Keep well and remember that it is most critical, indeed essential, that you and your mother prepare yourselves […] a hiding place in the apartment.

I clasp your hand,

## DOC. 51

## Sometime after 20 March 1942 the Polish underground records information about a mass shooting of Jews in Mielec[1]

Reports from resistance cell 1631 [Antoni Szymanowski] to resistance cell 1638 [Henryk Woliński][2] of the government delegation's Press and Information Department, Warsaw, sometime after 20 March 1942[3]

[…][4]

*3. Pogrom of Jews in Mielec*

To this day, Mielec has not had a ghetto because the local Jews paid a ransom every now and then [to buy themselves free].[5] For this reason the matter of the ghetto has been postponed, especially because the town's mayor, Frank, who is from Vienna, was consid-

6 The ellipses here and below indicate several passages in the original that are damaged and illegible.

1 Uniwersytet Warszawski, Biblioteka Uniwersytecka, Zbiór rękopisów, no. 2143, fol. 20. Published in Maria Tyszkowa, 'Eksterminacja Żydów w latach 1941–1943: Dokumenty Biura Informacji i Propagandy Komendy Głównej Armii Krajowej ze zbiorów Oddziału Rękopisów Biblioteki Uniwersytetu Warszawskiego', *BŻIH*, nos. 162 and 163 (1992), pp. 35–61 (part 1), and *BŻIH*, no. 164 (1992), pp. 47–60 (part 2), here part 1, p. 50. The report is part of a collection of materials from the Home Army's Bureau of Information and Propaganda. This document has been translated from Polish.

2 Henryk Woliński, code name Wacław (1901–1986), lawyer; worked in the Warsaw municipal administration in the 1930s; Jewish affairs officer in the Union of Armed Struggle (ZWZ) (later Home Army (ZWZ-AK) Bureau of Information and Propaganda from Feb. 1942; lawyer in Katowice after the war; honoured as Righteous Among the Nations by the State of Israel in 1974.

3 Handwritten notes on the left-hand side of the document: '1631-1638' and 'from 12'.

4 The document has not been preserved in its entirety. It begins with section 2 on the 'intended resettlement' of Polish farmers near Tarnów.

5 In 1941 a ghetto was established in Mielec, District Cracow; 4,500 Jews lived there prior to March 1942.

ered a philosemite. The Jews paid the final ransom at the beginning of March 1942. Shortly thereafter, Frank was removed from his post as mayor and replaced by a certain Mr Zimmermann. This brought about a change in policy towards the Jews and a pogrom occurred as a result.

At 5 a.m. on 9 March 1942, organized patrols and mobs led by the local Germans Weck, Kretschmer, and Daniell began to drag all the Jews from their apartments, whereupon many Jews were shot dead in the streets. The aircraft hangars were the assembly point where they rounded up those who had been arrested.[6] Several hundred of them were taken to Chorzelów (2 km from Mielec), where they were shot dead.[7] The remaining Jewish population was dealt with as follows: approximately 80 Jews were detained at the State Aviation Works as workers, approximately 480 were placed in the prison camp in Pustków,[8] and the rest were taken either to Polesie or to somewhere near Kyiv.[9] In total, approximately 1,300 people were killed.[10]

News from the […],[11] received on 20 March 1942 from a resident of Mielec who came to Warsaw, has not been confirmed.

[…][12]

## DOC. 52

## On 23 March 1942 the head of the Population and Welfare Division in District Lublin makes plans for the deportation of local Jews and the accommodation of Jews arriving from Reich territory[1]

Note by the Population and Welfare Division (T./B.), signed Division Head Türk,[2] Lublin, dated 23 March 1942

*Note*

I gave Obersturmführer *Pohl*, who visited my office today as the representative of Hauptsturmführer *Höfle*, the following information about the resettlement of Jews. Two aspects were crucial for the specifications made:

6 These were the hangars at the Ernst Heinkel Flugzeugwerke, which had taken over the state aviation works at the start of the occupation. From 1939 to 1944 a labour camp for several thousand Polish and Jewish prisoners was located there. In 1942 it was under the control of the SS, who carried out a selection on 9 March 1942.

7 According to estimates, 400–500 people who were deemed unfit for work – the elderly, the sick, and children – were murdered in Chorzelów.

8 Following the selection, 750–1,000 inmates were deported to Pustków, where there had been an SS forced labour camp for Jews since Nov. 1940; the same camp was later used to imprison Soviet prisoners of war and Poles.

9 In fact, approximately 3,000 people were transported to District Lublin.

10 This figure is inflated.

11 The informant's code name is blacked out.

12 Section 4 reports on the closure of the Reichskreditkasse branches in Smolensk, Bryansk, and Bobruisk (branches of the special bank set up to facilitate transactions by the Wehrmacht).

1 APL, 498/273, fols. 39–43[42]. Copy in BArch, R 102/II/29, fols. 11–13. This document has been translated from German.

1) the places in question should be located on the Deblin–Lublin–Belzec railway line if possible, and
2) Reich Jews can be brought in to replace the Jews who are brought out.

In particular, the following places and numbers:

1) *Izbica*, Kreis Krasnystaw, own train stop (number of Jews: approx. 6,500) – two trains out – two Reich trains already arrived,[3] two further Reich trains to be expected, probably from Darmstadt[4] and Gelsenkirchen;[5]
   1a) *Krasniczyn*, Kreis Krasnystaw, east of Izbica, Izbica station – one train out, if not full the remainder from Izbica – one Reich train in.[6]
   1b) *Gorzkow*, Kreis Krasnystaw, Izbica station, west of Izbica – one train out – one Reich train in.[7]
2) *Piaski*, Kreis Lublin-Land, Minkowice station – two trains out – Reich trains in depending on accommodation options.[8]

   Izbica and Piaski are then to continue to be regarded as the main accommodation and transfer points in alternation.[9]
3) *Szczebrzeszyn*, Kreis Bilgoraj, own train stop, 2,100 Jews – one train out – one Reich train in – further inward and outward resettlement in alternation depending on possibilities and requirements.
4) *Krasnobród*, Kreis Zamosc, own train stop, town at a considerable distance and possibilities in the surrounding area – one train out – one Reich train in and potential for further alternation.
5) *Opole*, Kreis Pulawy, narrow gauge railway connection to Naleczow – alternating outward and inward resettlement – several trains.[10]
6) *Rejowiec*, Kreis Chełm, own train stop – alternating outward and inward resettlement – regarded only as a reserve option.[11]

2 Richard Türk (1903–1984), farmer; joined the NSDAP in 1925; mayor of Schreiberhau, 1934–1936; head of the Population and Welfare Division in District Lublin and in charge of coordinating the deportations of Jews from Lublin to Belzec, Jan. 1940 – April 1942; subsequently in charge of Jewish affairs in the General Government's Population and Welfare Division (and deputy head of the division); chief executive of the Rhineland-Palatinate branch of the League of Expellees and Persons Deprived of Rights after the war.

3 Transports had arrived in Izbica from Theresienstadt on 13 and 19 March 1942.

4 A transport from Mainz and Darmstadt that was originally supposed to travel to Piaski arrived in Izbica on 27 March 1942.

5 The Jews from Gelsenkirchen were deported to Warsaw on 1 April 1942.

6 Some of the people who had arrived in Izbica from Theresienstadt were transported onwards to Kraśniczyn. Kraśniczyn took in deportees from Koblenz at the beginning of May 1942.

7 Some of the people who had arrived in Izbica from Theresienstadt were transported onwards to Gorzków; later yet more transports probably went to the area around Izbica in order to reduce the pressure on the extremely overcrowded transit ghetto.

8 A transport from Berlin arrived in Piaski on 30 March, a transport from Munich on 6 April, and two transports from Theresienstadt on 1 and 25 April 1942.

9 A total of sixteen transports were sent to the transit ghetto in Izbica between mid March and the beginning of June 1942; there were no further transports to Piaski.

10 No evidence has been found of the transports from Reich territory mentioned in points 3–5.

11 Rejowiec was the destination for a transport from Theresienstadt on 20 April 1942.

7) *Niedrzwica*, Kreis Lublin-Land, as railway station for Belzyce (3,600 Jews) and Bychawa (2,700 Jews) – also considered a reserve option because 15 km away.[12]
8) Accommodation options in Kreis Cholm and/or alternating outward and inward resettlement potentially possible at Wlodawa;[13] furthermore, occupation of the Water Works Inspectorate camps to be considered; apart from this, Prisoner of War Camp D in Zmudz, south-east of Cholm, which has been released by the Wehrmacht, would be available for at least 6,000 people.[14]

With regard to the preparations for the resettlement of Jews, I brought the following in particular to Obersturmführer Pohl's attention:
1) that he had to briefly communicate his plans to the Kreishauptmann responsible in each case,
2) that his directives concerning the clearance of Jewish buildings, the measures for deportation, and the settlement of newly arrived Jews were to be implemented directly by the relevant Jewish Council on its own responsibility,
3) that Jewish workers would stay behind and, if necessary, he would keep in touch with the sections responsible at the employment office. Obersturmführer Pohl gave assurances that he would comply with the proposals and requests that had been made.

## DOC. 53
## On 23 March 1942 Polish government representatives report on the Warsaw ghetto and the beginning of mass murders of Jews in Chełmno (Kulmhof)[1]

Report by the government delegation's Internal Affairs Department, signed Wacław,[2] Warsaw, dated 23 March 1942[3]

*1638[4] report no. 4, dated 23 March 1942*
*Jews. Warsaw.*
1. The Transferstelle[5] has ordered 100,000 coffins from Jewish joinery workshops.
2. Approximately 20,000 food ration coupons have gone unsold lately: the prices of the coupons, which are fixed by the Jewish Council, continue to rise (2.80 zł. in February, 3.50 zł. in March), and the poor cannot afford such expenditure. The Council collects

12 A transport from Weimar and Leipzig via Niedrzwica arrived in Bełżyce on 12 May 1942; approximately 800 Jews from Stettin, who had been deported there in 1940, were already living there. There is no evidence of a transport to Bychawa.
13 Włodawa was the destination for a transport from Vienna on 29 April 1942.
14 No evidence has been found of transports to this camp. A transport from Würzburg that arrived at Krasnystaw on 28 April 1942, three transports to Zamość from Dortmund and Theresienstadt, and two from Dortmund and Theresienstadt to Lublin in May 1942 are not mentioned here.

1 AAN, 1325/202/II-29, fol. 12. This document has been translated from Polish.
2 Henryk Woliński's code name.
3 The original contains handwritten notes and underlining. Up to item 9, the report is based on handwritten information the Bund provided from the Warsaw ghetto to the Polish resistance on 21 March 1942: see Tyszkowa, 'Eksterminacja Żydów w latach 1941–1943', part 1, doc. 15, pp. 51–52.
4 Resistance Cell 1638 stands for Henryk Woliński: see also Doc. 51.
5 German in the original: 'Transfer Bureau'.

taxes through fees on the coupons, yet does not take into account the different financial situations of individual buyers.

3. Since last year the Council has been offering vocational courses, which approximately 6,000 young people attend. The high fees prevent children from poor families from participating in these courses, as they receive no discounts or grants. The working class is thus excluded from vocational training.
4. In February there were 4,618 funerals. Last year there were 3,603 funerals on average per month.
5. In late 1941 centres operated by CENTOS (Jewish Central Association for the Care of Orphans) accommodated 360 orphans whose fathers had died in labour camps. At present they accommodate 286 [children].[6]
6. In January the Jewish Council paid out 2,050 zł. in welfare to families of 'camp inmates', a few złoty per head.
7. In January there were 9,030 people in 'refugee points',[7] of whom 715 died. The mortality rate at one 'point' with 2,500 occupants amounted to 17.5 per cent in that month.
8. One of the Jewish Council's most recent reports[8] states that the ghetto's more affluent residents have contributed 650,000 zł. to the pelt fund.[9]
9. The bread ration in the ghetto amounts to 2 kg per month. A total of 2,200 policemen, 30,000 workers, 6,000 Jewish Council employees, 8,000 hospital patients, and wards of the state in boarding schools receive a higher ration of 6 kg per month.

*Żychlin* – Nearly the entire Jewish population has been transported to an unknown destination,[10] and four members of the Jewish Council were shot dead in public.[11]
*Krośniewice* – the same.[12]
*Gąbin* – Jews unfit for work were shot dead, and the rest were taken away.[13]

According to the report of an escapee[14] who arrived in Warsaw, a total of 10,000 Jews from Koło and Dąbie, as well as a group sentenced to deportation by the Jewish Council in Łódź, were taken to Chełmno.[15] Transports from smaller towns took place without

6 See Doc. 40.
7 See Doc. 40, fn. 8.
8 This could not be found.
9 On the collections for the compulsory purchase of sheepskins, see Doc. 36.
10 On 3 March 1942 the approximately 3,200 residents of the Żychlin ghetto in Regierungsbezirk Hohensalza, near the border with the General Government, were rounded up and deported to Kulmhof: AAN, 1325/202/III-7/1, fol. 64.
11 The chairman of the Jewish Council, the baker Alter Rosenberg (1900–1942), and the head of the Order Service, Josef Oberman, were publicly hanged in Feb. 1942; subsequently more members of the Jewish Council and Order Service, and members of their families, were publicly hanged.
12 In early March the approximately 900 Jews who remained in Krośniewice in Regierungsbezirk Hohensalza were deported to Kulmhof.
13 The Jews from Gąbin in Regierungsbezirk Hohensalza, between Kutno and Płock near the border with the General Government, were deported in March. The first part of the following sentence has been crossed out: 'The women …'; the Bund's reports (see fn. 3) include the information that women and children were locked up in a church in Gostynin (25 km west of Gąbin).
14 Szlojme Winer: see Doc. 61.
15 Between 16 Jan. and May 1942, a total of 55,000 residents of the Lodz ghetto were deported to Kulmhof. The Jewish Council had to draw up deportation lists for this purpose, and the Order Service had to help round up the people selected for deportation.

any particular mistreatment. In Chełmno a group of the ten strongest men were selected, among whom was the author of this report. The group leader, a German, initially beat them with a truncheon. Each day these people were taken outside the town on vehicles to dig ditches. Once they had dug the ditches, sealed trucks arrived, and the Jews crammed inside were poisoned with gas. After fifteen minutes of shouting, silence set in among the poisoned people, and their bodies were thrown out and searched. Anuses and also women's vaginas were inspected for valuables, which were sometimes hidden there. Then the victims were buried. One time, a vehicle escorting a group of Jewish workers – gravediggers – broke down and stopped. The gravediggers, among them the author of this report, fled. Several are said to have made it to Warsaw.[16]

## DOC. 54

## On 27 March 1942 Joseph Goebbels writes about the systematic mass murder of Jews in the Lublin area[1]

Diary of Joseph Goebbels, entry for 27 March 1942

27 March 1942 (Friday)
[…][2]
General pessimism about the situation in the East now prevails in the enemy camp. They have realized that the hopes and expectations associated with the winter campaign have not been fulfilled in any way. They therefore now have to regroup during the forthcoming German offensive and will have to withstand the severest test of the war. Generally, people in England too are now saying that summer 1942 will probably bring the final decision. God willing, that will be the case!

Apart from that, the thaw has set in along the whole Eastern Front; movements are hardly possible any more. The Bolshevists are therefore no longer in a position to torment us with painful attacks, and when the earth has once again regained its natural dryness, it really will be our turn again and we will be able to have our say.

The Bolshevists seem to have converted Moscow into a vast fortress. All the Moscow women have been used for this purpose in a ruthless deployment of labour. As is well known, the Bolshevists really have no mental inhibitions about this sort of thing. They deploy whatever human labour is available to perform a task and achieve a goal. However, whether this fortress will have the strength to withstand a German assault carried

16 Six people who escaped from Kulmhof are known to have survived the German occupation of Poland: Michał Podchlebnik (1906/1907–1985) and Abram Rój (d. 1985) escaped in Jan. 1942; Jerachmiel Widawski (1913–1986) and Icchak Justmann escaped in Sept. 1942; Szymon Srebrnik (d. 2006) and Mieczysław (Mordechai) Żurawski (d. 1989) escaped in Jan. 1945. Rój and Widawski lived in Berlin for several years after the end of the war; Podchlebnik lived in Zeilsheim displaced persons camp, near Frankfurt am Main, until 1949; along with Srebrnik and Żurawski, he testified at the trials of German war criminals in Poznań (1946), Jerusalem (1961), and Bonn (1963).

1 RGVA, Goebbels's literary estate, Fond 1477. Copy in IfZ-Archives, F 12/8, fols. 804–805. Published in *Die Tagebücher von Joseph Goebbels*, part 2, *Diktate 1941–1945*, vol. 3: *Januar–März 1942*, ed. Elke Fröhlich (Munich: Saur, 1994), pp. 557–563. This document has been translated from German.

2 The entry begins with an account of the military situation on the Eastern Front.

out on an immense scale in good weather conditions, the immediate future will have to reveal.

No reports of any consequence from East Asia. The American and English press are prattling about the fact that the Allies have now started their offensive in Australia. They have become so modest in their ambitions that they actually regard the presence of a better-known general in a particular country as an offensive. These are all manifestations of the degeneracy in the Anglo-Saxon countries that, viewed from a long-term perspective, has to be taken very seriously. The British world empire, above all, finds itself in an ongoing crisis, which makes itself felt now and then in severe, shattering occurrences, but from time to time through seemingly trivial symptoms as well. This state of affairs is one of those symptoms. There is now general concern about Burma again in London. They are also beginning to feel more afraid about India again because the Japanese have now occupied the Andamans. The unease, above all in Indian leadership circles, is growing by the hour. The English are now all the more tempted to reach a compromise mediated by Cripps as quickly as possible.[3] The struggle for India is the most topical issue being debated in London at the moment. It is clear Cripps is doing his utmost to press for a decision; because of course he does not just want to have practical success, an extraordinary amount is riding on this success for him personally as well. He receives journalists and makes stupid, typically English jokes in front of them. Nothing else is to be got out of him. It seems clear the English will attempt to promise the Indians dominion status for after the war, a promise they would certainly not keep if England won the war and were able to rebuild its imperial power. But of course the English will probably not suffer the embarrassment of having to give much thought to whether they will keep such a promise or not after the German victory.

London is telling outrageous lies about the sea battle against the Atlantic convoy. Churchill has sent a pompous telegram of congratulation to the commanding admiral; using such a fact to discredit enemy news reporting is an old trick of which he is mighty fond. But we are defending ourselves with all the forces at our disposal, and he won't succeed in using such a brazen lie in the attempt to wriggle out of the embarrassing shock to the public caused by England's failure. Otherwise, it is possible to detect a slowly, but constantly, growing scepticism all over England, particularly among leadership circles. The most heated criticism of the fall of Singapore is being expressed in the Upper House.[4] The Lords do not mince their words, and even if they fail to ensure that an investigation is conducted into this ignominious affair, they will once again draw a great deal of public attention to the English failure that is apparent there.

Hoare[5] has given a middleman in Madrid the message that he is actually in favour of peace; had he been at the rudder, it would not have come to war at all. This is credible; Hoare was, after all, always among the ranks of those seeking peace. However, these

3 Richard Stafford Cripps (1889–1952), Labour Party politician; British ambassador to the Soviet Union, 1940–1942; a member of Churchill's War Cabinet from 1942; in March 1942 he negotiated an agreement with the Indian politicians Mahatma Gandhi and Mohammed Ali Jinnah that, however, was never signed.

4 The British crown colony of Singapore was captured by Japanese troops on 15 Feb. 1942. This was regarded as the worst defeat in British military history.

5 Samuel Hoare (1880–1959); member of parliament for the Conservative Party, 1910–1944; foreign secretary in 1935; home secretary in 1937; British ambassador to Spain, 1940–1944.

ranks appear to have been outplayed by the Churchill clique during the decisive days in London. Because Hoare represents a rational standpoint, Churchill has sent him to Madrid. He cannot do much harm there.

Incidentally, Churchill himself has spoken in the Lower House.[6] His speech is crammed with obscure expressions. He talks in general terms, declares the situation to have improved dramatically. He is such a shameless liar that one can barely engage in polemics with him. However, he has to admit that England is currently going through the most difficult test in its history. That is really worth something. But in his case the negative is always mixed up in such an impudent fashion with the positive that it is extremely difficult to work out what he is up to.

A speech Mussolini gave before the Party leadership on 3 January has been sent to me by the German embassy in Rome.[7] This speech is extraordinarily hard-hitting and, above all, turns on the defeatist bourgeois circles who are criticizing the conduct of the war. In this confidential address, Mussolini proclaims his unshakeable determination to march on to the end with Germany and the Führer. There are no grounds at all to doubt his loyalty to the alliance. Furthermore, Mussolini declares that the war will potentially last a lot longer; but he says the Italian people are equal to such a test. He attacks war racketeers and profiteers in extraordinarily hard-hitting comments and declares he will drive the rams into the sheep pens to have them sheared there. This speech is of pleasing clarity; one sees that, inside, Mussolini is a true fascist and modern statesman after all. If he does not speak out publicly that often, he may have his good reasons in view of the Italian mentality. Otherwise, though, we can really be extraordinarily satisfied with his policies. He deserves a better people than the one he is currently leading.

The enemy propaganda service is characterized by many reports inciting hatred. They are seeking to come out with the same old story again, to set up conflicts between the Wehrmacht and the Party, and the like.

By contrast, rather more cunning propaganda against the Reich is being put out in the United States. They no longer want to go into battle against the German people, but against Nazism. I see a certain danger in this. Thank God the enemy propaganda is not so consistent as to stick to this propaganda slogan systematically over the years. If that were the case, we would face great difficulties every time we came under severe strain again. If I were on the enemy side, I would have incessantly disseminated the slogan that they were fighting Nazism, but not the German people, right from day one. Of course, that is also how Chamberlain[8] started on the first day of the war; but they have not

6 British Prime Minister Winston Churchill (1874–1965) gave a speech to the Central Council of the Conservative Party at Caxton Hall in London on 26 March 1942 in which he emphasized that Britain's situation in the war against the Axis Powers had improved significantly in the preceding twelve months: see Robert Rhodes James (ed.), *Winston S. Churchill: His Complete Speeches, 1897–1963*, vol. 6: *1935–1942* (New York: Chelsea House, 1983 [1974]), pp. 6604–6607 (here p. 6605). Britain had entered into a military alliance with the Soviet Union in June 1941 and with the USA in Dec. 1941.

7 See *Opera omnia di Benito Mussolini*, ed. Edoardo and Duilio Susmel, vol. 30, *Dall'intervento dell'Italia nella Seconda guerra mondiale al discorso al direttorio nazionale del P.N.F. del 3 gennaio 1942 (11 giugno 1940–3 gennaio 1942)* (Florence: La Fenice, 1960), pp. 152–157.

8 Neville Chamberlain (1869–1940), Conservative Party politician; British prime minister from 1937 to May 1940; sought to avert a war by pursuing a policy of appeasement towards the German Reich; played a crucial role in the negotiation of the Munich Agreement in Sept. 1938; presided over Britain's rearmament drive from March 1939 and gave a security guarantee to Poland in April 1939.

stuck to this slogan, thank God. I prohibit expressions of the kind now increasingly encountered in the American public sphere from being approved for the German press; not even for polemics. We should not speak of these things at all. Even polemicizing against them serves to spread them. The German people must be convinced – which indeed it is – that this war is directed against its life and its opportunities for national development, and that it must therefore defend itself with all its might.

The Wafd Party[9] has achieved a glorious victory, by whatever means, but it has won 216 out of 264 seats. This means Nahas Pasha[10] is in a position to act. However, we cannot expect much from him because he has probably been under the English thumb for a long time.

The Hungarians have announced once again that they wish to maintain a dignified silence concerning the Romanian accusations. And this is indeed the best thing they can do. They have a guilty conscience.[11]

The Jews are now being deported to the East from the General Government, beginning with Lublin. The procedure is a pretty barbaric one and not to be described in any more detail, but there won't be much left of the Jews. By and large, one can say that 60 per cent of them will have to be liquidated, while only 40 per cent can be deployed as labour. The former Gauleiter of Vienna,[12] who is conducting this operation, is doing it fairly circumspectly and using a procedure that does not seem all too conspicuous. A judgement is being meted out to the Jews that may be barbaric, but they completely deserve it. The Führer's prophesy to the Jews of what would occur should they foment a new world war is beginning to come true in the most terrible way.[13] One must not allow any sentimentality to prevail when it comes to these matters. The Jews would annihilate us if we did not resist them. It is a struggle for life and death between the Aryan race and the Jewish bacillus. No other government and no other regime could summon up the strength to find a general solution to this question. Here too, the Führer is the unwavering champion of and spokesman for a radical solution that is necessary in view of how things stand, and therefore appears inevitable. Thank God we now have a whole range of options during the war that would be denied us in peacetime. We must make the most of them. The ghettos that

9 The Wafd Party (literally 'Delegation Party'; Arabic: Ḥizb al-Wafd) was a nationalist liberal party in Egypt active between 1918 and 1952.

10 Mostafa Nahas Pasha (1876–1965), Egyptian politician; leader of the Wafd Party, 1927–1952; prime minister of Egypt several times; King Faruq appointed him to head the Egyptian government in Feb. 1942 in response to British pressure.

11 In the Second Vienna Award of 30 August 1940, Hitler had divided Transylvania between Hungary, which was occupying the north of the region, and Romania. This did not resolve the ethnic tensions between Hungary and Romania, which accused each other of discriminating against the respective minority population on the other's territory and forcing it to flee to the neighbouring country.

12 Odilo Globocnik (1904–1945), qualified engineer and building contractor; joined the NSDAP in Austria in 1931 and the SS in 1934; deputy Gauleiter of Vienna in 1933; Gauleiter of Vienna in 1938; relieved of his duties in Feb. 1939 due to financial irregularities and transferred to the personal staff of the Reichsführer-SS; SS and Police Leader in Lublin, Nov. 1939 – Sept. 1943; head of Operation Reinhard; simultaneously managing director of Ostindustrie GmbH in Lublin in 1943; Higher SS and Police Leader for the Adriatic Coastal Region, 1943–1945; committed suicide after being captured.

13 An allusion to Hitler's speech to the Reichstag on 30 Jan. 1939, in which he openly threatened to annihilate the Jews: see PMJ 2/248.

are being freed up in the cities of the General Government will now be filled with Jews deported from the Reich, and the process is then to be repeated there after a certain interval. The Jews have nothing to laugh about,[14] and their representatives in Europe will have to pay very dearly for the fact that their representatives in England and America are organizing and propagating the war against Germany today, but one has to say this must be seen as justified.

Report about the occupied territories: the situation has not changed significantly. Everyone is waiting in an almost frantic state of tension for the events of the approaching spring.

I have had a lengthy discussion with Esser[15] about private travel. We decided to at least inform the various Gauleiter in a circular about the categories of people authorized to make private journeys. Apart from that, Esser is pleading vigorously for a permit card to be introduced for private journeys, something which the Ministry of Transport has always argued against up until now, however. There is still a whole set of bourgeois elements in the Ministry of Transport who either do not understand the war or are putting up increasing resistance to us.

I spoke to radio representatives responsible for non-entertainment programming. I broadly outlined the tasks that await us, and above all placed emphasis on the presentation of the psychological direction of our news and propaganda policy. I believe this guidance will very soon make itself felt in the scheduling of non-entertainment radio programmes. The military spokesmen were also there in large numbers. There is therefore hope that propaganda about military matters will also improve significantly.

Naval Lieutenant Hartenstein[16] briefed me on a submarine voyage to the Caribbean Sea. Our submarines found rich pickings there. The Americans are in no way prepared and have barely any defence against submarine attacks. In all, the submarines are at sea for approximately sixty days. They shoot away, down to the last torpedo, and, if possible, destroy transport ships they encounter on the return journey with artillery fire. The mood in the submarine arm is marvellous, above all after the considerable successes of late. It is really quite amazing how combat turns young people into truly commanding personalities within a short time. This submarine commander, who has almost schoolboyish looks, is a real man and a commanding personality from head to toe.

The Berlin press is responding to my proposal for Berlin to regain its cultural supremacy with marvellous commentaries. The journalists in Berlin have understood exactly what is at stake and are taking my line. Above all, however, it is important that this propaganda be conducted very unobtrusively, so that it is not possible for it to have an alienating effect anywhere.

14 A reference to Hitler's words in his above-mentioned speech of 30 Jan. 1939.

15 Hermann Esser (1900–1981), journalist; founding member of the NSDAP in 1919 and first editor of the *Völkischer Beobachter;* head of propaganda for the NSDAP in 1923; took part in the Beer Hall Putsch; Bavarian minister of economics, 1933–1934; state secretary in the Reich Ministry of Public Enlightenment and Propaganda from 1939; head of the ministry's Department for Tourism; lived in hiding, 1945–1949; sentenced to five years in prison in 1950; released in 1952. He was the author of *Die Jüdische Weltpest: Kann ein Jude Staatsbürger sein?* (1927).

16 Werner Hartenstein (1908–1943), naval officer; served with the Reich navy from 1928; captained a torpedo boat, Sept. 1939 – March 1941; commander of the submarine U-156 from Sept. 1941; died in the Atlantic, east of Barbados.

I have written an article headlined 'The Great Heart of the German People' in which I examine the differences between the views of the homeland and the front.[17] It is necessary to say something that breaks the tension here because the danger is looming ever more that the thinking at the front will go in an entirely different direction to the thinking at home, that the homeland will overestimate its difficulties and the front will have no sympathy for such attitudes. I have also picked this up from a whole series of letters from the front that have been presented to me. This fear is openly expressed in them as well.

I am hoping for a very great deal from the article against racketeers and profiteers that will appear in the next few days.[18] The Führer has signed a decree addressed to all leading figures in the state, Party, and Wehrmacht, in which he argues quite categorically for the leading men in public life to follow a clean and irreproachable way of life and threatens the severest punishments if anyone should attempt to evade the demands of the war in any way. This decree, which the Führer has proclaimed as the precondition for the success of my propaganda operation, will certainly be of significant help in noticeably easing the dissatisfaction among the people regarding this somewhat delicate topic.[19]

In the evening I received a visit from the Schaumburgs, who were able to tell me a whole range of news from the country. Countess Castell from Nuremberg is also there, and has a great deal to report about Nuremberg, little of it cheering.[20]

We watched the new film by Professor Frölich[21] together: *Hochzeit auf Bärenhof*,[22] in which Heinrich George[23] once again gives a magnificent demonstration of his acting skills. Professor Frölich is an unparalleled master in the depiction of Germany before the World War. He portrays the environment with such profound, intimate knowledge and such fanatical love that its realism is absolutely staggering. This film will undoubtedly enjoy great success.

Thank God the improvement in the weather is holding up. There are hardly any night frosts now. We will hopefully be able to open the potato pits in the next few days. Then

17 Joseph Goebbels, 'Das große Herz unseres Volkes', *Das Reich*, 5 April 1942, pp. 1–2. Goebbels wrote the lead article for the magazine *Das Reich* every week.

18 Joseph Goebbels, 'Offene Aussprache', *Das Reich*, 29 March 1942, pp. 1–2.

19 Hitler had instructed Goebbels to agitate against clandestine trading and bartering, and on 21 March 1942 had issued the Decree Concerning the Conduct of Leading Figures: Martin Moll (ed.), *'Führer-Erlasse' 1939–1945: Edition sämtlicher überlieferter, nicht im Reichsgesetzblatt abgedruckter, von Hitler während des Zweiten Weltkrieges schriftlich erteilter Direktiven aus den Bereichen Staat, Partei, Wirtschaft, Besatzungspolitik und Militärverwaltung* (Stuttgart: Steiner, 1997), pp. 242–243.

20 Prince Friedrich Christian zu Schaumburg-Lippe (1906–1983), lawyer; married Countess Alexandra zu Castell-Rüdenhausen (1904–1961) in 1927; joined the NSDAP in 1929 and the SA in 1932; became Goebbels's aide in 1933; section head in the Foreign Affairs Department of the Reich Ministry of Public Enlightenment and Propaganda from 1934; served in the war in 1943; interned, 1945–1948.

21 Correctly: Carl Froelich (1875–1953), film director; made the first German sound film in 1929; joined the NSDAP in 1933; in 1939 was awarded the National Film Prize and became president of the Reich Chamber of Film; interned in 1945; underwent denazification proceedings in 1948.

22 'Wedding at the Bärenhof'; film directed by Froelich for the German film company Ufa: it was premiered in Germany on 8 June 1942.

23 Heinrich George, correctly Georg August Friedrich Hermann Schulz (1893–1946), actor; starred in numerous Ufa films; artistic director of the Schiller Theatre in Berlin from 1937; perished in Soviet Special Camp 7 at Sachsenhausen.

the potato trains will roll into the big cities first of all. Then there will be food to eat again; and, as is well known, when stomachs are full once again, the world always looks entirely different.

## DOC. 55
## On 28 March 1942 the Metropolitan of the Greek-Catholic Church in Lwów reports to Pope Pius XII on the situation in East Galicia and the mass murders in Ukraine[1]

Letter from the Metropolitan of Lwów[2] in Lwów to Pope Pius XII in Rome, dated 28 March 1942

In Pace[3]
Your Holiness,

We have been living under Hitler's regime for almost ten months now. I have not submitted a report so far, also to avoid burdening Your Holiness with too much correspondence, but I feel obliged to extend my humble thanks to Your Holiness for appointing the apostolic exarchs.[4] They intend to compose a joint letter of thanks, but up to now it has not been possible to contact Exarch Niemancewicz in Albertyn.[5] I would therefore like to thank Your Holiness on their and on my behalf for fulfilling our wishes. I would additionally like to express my deep gratitude for my appointment as envoy to Your Holiness. I pledge to address your concerns as a loyal intermediary and to report to the Sacred Congregation for the Eastern Churches as often as possible.

The victory of the German army and the Red Army's retreat from our country were met with great relief; priests were finally allowed once more to head schools and to teach the catechism.

So far, the new authorities have granted us almost complete freedom – the anti-Catholic legislation in force in the Reich has not been applied to us. We even encounter good Catholics with the best of intentions among the powers that be. However, the majority of the officials who are sent to us, and through whom the central authorities most probably intend to regulate and take charge of everything, are devoid of beliefs and morals, and nothing more than very mediocre administrators. For this reason, the system, which is inadequate in multiple respects, is turning into an unbearable tyranny here in the provinces and, even worse, into a corrupt and opaque system. As the Germans advance to the East, they manifest their boundless national egotism to an ever more wilful and ruthless extent. They regard all Jews as wartime enemies and organize massacres in which thousands of Jews perish, including women and children. In all major Ukrainian towns, for example, they have annihilated all the Jews who did not flee in the face of

1 Tsentralnyi derzhavnyi istorychnyi arkhiv, m. Lviv (TSDIAL, Central State Historical Archives of Ukraine, Lviv), 201/1s/90, fol. 25. This document has been translated from French.
2 Dr Andrei Sheptytskyi (Andrzej Szeptycki), né Roman Maria Aleksander Count Szeptycki (1865–1944), priest and leader of the Greek-Catholic Church; appointed Metropolitan of Galicia by Pope Leo XIII in 1900.
3 Latin: 'in peace'.
4 In Oct. 1939 the Metropolitan had appointed four exarchs (bishops) for the occupied territories of eastern Poland. The Pope confirmed the appointment on 5 Jan. 1942.
5 A community near Słonim.

their army – seemingly credible reports state that almost 130,000 perished in Kyiv, and the figures are comparable for other towns.

When they arrived in our country, they were not yet at the point where they would present the [local] population with such scenes themselves; they appeared to want to place the blame for these murders on the population. They often ordered local militias to kill hundreds of Jews on the spot – Jews who had been condemned without ever standing trial – and they took photos of the executions. According to figures from the Israelite Community,[6] around 15,000 people were executed in this way in Lwów, and municipal officials were forced to attest to the authorities that Ukrainians had committed this massacre of Jews.

Right from the start of the war,[7] hordes of young people joined the local militias, and it seems certain that these people have been deployed to carry out executions. In a letter to Hitler,[8] I naturally voiced my protest at this – evidently to no avail. In the same way, I published a pastoral letter – as was possible at the time – on the crime of murder, and I attempted through the clergy to warn young people against joining militias or organizations which could harm them spiritually. It was not only Jews who were arrested and executed. Hundreds, possibly thousands, of intellectuals were killed without ever standing trial, for the sole reason that they were regarded as enemies. The Ukrainians were called *friends*, and sometime even *allies*, yet within a few weeks we understood that these were but empty words, for on hundreds of occasions we realized that we were being deceived disgracefully – the system required it to be this way. People were played off against one another. But this took place very much according to the principle of divide [and conquer]: they manipulated the good intentions of certain individuals or groups within society with the sole purpose of sowing discord, and they drew benefit from this. The system wanted us to accept all forms of expropriation, the so-called 'nationalization' of private property, as a foregone conclusion; there is always the promise that this property will be returned to its owners, but this has not happened so far. It is common knowledge that the State Police interferes in everything and takes everything into its own hands, and that it causes those it regards as opponents to disappear – and the only thing one can find out is that they are in prison. We therefore presume the worst – and in many parts of the country this regime appears as one of sheer 'Terror'.[9] In districts[10] led by a Catholic, a Protestant, or simply an honest man, we live virtually in peace and despite the rather high levies we cannot complain about the effects of the lengthy war, even though these do pose a burden. Yet if the chief of the district or the chief of police is cruel, mean-spirited, or simply wicked, which is the case in most districts, the population has to endure great suffering. In 1941 the harvest was very poor

6 The term 'Israélite' (in French) as a designation for 'Jew' originated in 1808 in Napoleonic France, based on the notion that Jews should be defined as belonging to a faith – 'Mosaic' – rather than an ethnic entity, and was intended as a means of integrating Jews into West European societies. In contemporary discourse the term 'Jew' often had a negative overtone. It was reintroduced in French official discourse after 1940, though the term 'Israélite' was not entirely abandoned.
7 That is, since the end of June 1941.
8 This letter has not been found.
9 Capitalized for emphasis in the original.
10 A reference to the Kreishauptmannschaften in District Galicia.

throughout our country ([though] extraordinarily good in Greater Ukraine);[11] moreover, God tested the country additionally with floods more severe than any member of the current generation can remember. The whole of Subcarpathia has been affected; the floods have destroyed at least several hundred villages there. We are currently witnessing a veritable famine in these regions, and no less so in the mountain villages that do not produce grain or potatoes.

A rescue operation has begun, but lines of communication are so difficult and it happens so often that the villages suffering from famine send envoys to wealthy villages or to villages that have been spared from the floods in order to purchase food, and that after purchasing the food this is then taken off them by the local authorities or the bogus local authorities, which of course there is no way of punishing. The population's situation is made worse by the fact that lower-ranking officials and policemen beat and whip people often for no reason other than their own enjoyment. These lower-ranking officials are mostly people who are no better than released convicts.

Now that Greater Ukraine has been liberated from the yoke of Bolshevism, or rather has been conquered by the German army, the patriotic ideal is pushing all our youth to work for our dissenting brothers, who have been separated from us for centuries.[12] The people of Greater Ukraine are returning to the Christian faith. We are using the freedom granted to us to renew all institutions of the Christian faith.[13]

## DOC. 56

## On 29 March 1942 a Jew from Lublin writes about the deportations from the ghetto[1]

Letter from Daniel[2] in Lublin to his sister in Warsaw (received by the Jewish post office in Warsaw on 3 April 1942), dated 29 March 1942 (transcription)[3]

Lublin, 29 March 1941, Sunday
Dear Sister,

It is difficult for me to answer your two letters. You must have heard about the Lublin expulsion, which has been going on for fourteen whole days, and no one knows when it will end.[4] Fifteen thousand people have already been sent away – fathers and mothers without [their] children, children without [their] parents. Naked and barefoot. I went out without taking anything, leaving everything behind. No place to stay and nowhere

11 A reference to Soviet Ukraine.
12 A reference to those of the Orthodox faith.
13 The letter has no valediction.

1 AŻIH, Ring I/856 (552/4), fol. 2. Published as a facsimile and in Polish translation in Sakowska (ed.), *Archiwum Ringelbluma: Konspiracyjne Archiwum Getta Warszawy*, vol. 1: *Listy o Zagładzie*, pp. 83–86. This document has been translated from Yiddish.
2 The surname was not noted in the transcript.
3 This is a copy of the original, transcribed for the underground archive of the Warsaw ghetto.
4 The deportations from Lublin to Belzec began during the night of 16 to 17 March 1942 and ended on 14 April 1942. By 28 March 1942, when the deportations were interrupted for two or three days, the number of deportees from Lublin was about 18,000; the ghetto had 15,000–16,000 inhabitants left at the time: see also Doc. 57.

to turn. Around 1,000 people have tragically perished (may it not happen to us).[5] I am still in Lublin, hiding in a dark cellar. I have not seen daylight for fourteen days. Today, Sunday, I went out into the street and to the post office [to see if] perhaps some money had come for me. I have been left without a grosz. In the cellar, my cousin and I lived on bread and water that someone brought to us.

I possess nothing now. No one knows when it will end. Lublin is a complete ghost town. M. Z. and M., all the children, and N. were caught and sent away to who knows where. What has happened in Lublin is indescribable. If they catch me, I don't have 50 złoty on me that I can take along. You must go to P. and, with his help, arrange to have something sent to me as a matter of urgency so that I have a bit of money at the ready to take with me. If only I manage to stay alive. In Lublin they are saying that B–K caused all of this, that he is to blame for the misfortune.[6]

I cannot write any more. I look as though I have already died of hunger. And I will surely lose the little I have managed to preserve, because no one is safe from one day to the next. The sick from the Jewish hospital and the hospital for infectious diseases have been taken away to who knows where, and the hospitals have been closed. Terrible things are happening in Lublin. Consider what is in store for me. It may be that this is the last chance to help me. Because my life is not safe. No one in Lublin is safe. Go straight to P. and show him this letter. Tell him that a fire is devouring the rest of those who remain in Lublin. Help me as long as I am still alive. Until then I will be extremely careful. If only I succeed in this! By the way, I didn't receive the 100 złoty for Lublin, and I certainly won't get it. Because they won't find me. Also I don't know who you sent it through. Send money to this address […].[7]

I send you warm and affectionate regards, and deeply heartfelt kisses too. In the hope of seeing you again and writing to you in future,

5 During the raids, numerous ghetto inhabitants were murdered on the spot, especially people being cared for in institutions.

6 This is probably a reference to Henryk Bekker (1886–1942); studied in Munich to become a civil engineer; active in the Jewish People's Party; city councillor in Lublin from 1929; chairman of the Jewish Community there from 1936; chairman of the Jewish Council, 1939–1942; deported with his wife to Belzec on 31 March 1942; murdered there on 1 April 1942: see Doc. 57. Bekker had no influence on the German authorities' decision concerning the deportations from the Lublin ghetto.

7 The address was omitted during transcription.

## DOC. 57

## On 31 March 1942 SS officers instruct the Jewish Council in Lublin on deportations[1]

Minutes of the meeting of the Jewish Council in Lublin, signed Alten and Hochgemajn,[2] dated 31 March 1942

*Minutes* no. 16/140, General Assembly of the Jewish Council in Lublin

In accordance with an order from the authorities carrying out the resettlement operation,[3] the following Council members convened at 2 p.m: Dr Alten,[4] Bekker, Bursztyn,[5] Cymerman,[6] Dawidson,[7] Goldsobel,[8] Halbersztadt,[9] Hochgemajn, Hufnagel,[10] Kantor,[11] Kerszman,[12] Kerszelnblum,[13] Kelner,[14] Lewi,[15] Lewinson,[16] Lerner,[17] Siegfried,[18] Tenenbaum,[19] Wajselfisz.[20]

1 APL, 891/3. Published as a facsimile in Blumental (ed.), *Te'udot mi-geto lublin*, pp. 247–249. This document has been translated from Polish.

2 Dawid Hochgemajn (Hochgemein) (1905–1942), lawyer from Lublin, where he practised law and was a well-known philanthropist; member of the Jewish Council in Lublin and secretary of its executive committee from 1940.

3 The deportations from Lublin to Belzec were organized by the Commander of the Security Police and the SD (KdS) in Lublin.

4 Dr Marek Alten (1883–1942), lawyer; served in the Austro-Hungarian army in the First World War; member of the executive committee of the Jewish Social Self-Help (JSS) from autumn 1940 and a leading figure in Lublin's Jewish Council.

5 Ajzyk Bursztyn (1892–1942), tailor; member of the Council of the Jewish Community from 1937.

6 Urysz Cymerman (1888–1942), tailor; head of the Jewish Council's Section for Women's Forced Labour; also worked in the Personnel Section and in the section responsible for Jewish craftsmen working in German businesses.

7 Dawid Dawidson (1875–1942), retailer; worked in the Jewish Council's Personnel Section and in the sections responsible for monitoring weights and measures and levying taxes and fees.

8 Abram Goldsobel (1889–1942), retailer; worked in the Jewish Council's sections responsible for housing, welfare provision, and refugee aid.

9 Szloma Halbersztadt (1893–1942), rabbi; chairman of the Jewish Community in Lublin from 1934; secretary of the Jewish Council from 1939; worked in the sections responsible for welfare provision and healthcare.

10 Lejb Jehuda (Leon) Hufnagel (1891–1942), engineer; member of the Jewish Community's executive committee from Sept. 1939; thereafter a member of the Jewish Council and chairman of the Jewish Aid Committee; murdered in Lublin-Majdanek concentration camp in 1942.

11 Aron Jankiel Kantor (1880–1942), teacher and property manager; worked in the Jewish Council's sections responsible for monitoring weights and measures, levying taxes and fees, and collecting contributions.

12 Izaak Kerszman (1892–1942), lawyer; member of the Jewish Council from 1940; head of the Refugee Aid Committee; also worked in the section responsible for levying taxes and fees; murdered in Lublin-Majdanek concentration camp in 1942.

13 Szloma Kerszelnblum, member of the Jewish Council; responsible for economic matters within the Jewish Community.

14 Jakub Kelner (1897–1942), retailer; worked in the Jewish Council's sections responsible for labour deployment, collecting contributions, and refugee aid.

15 Aleksander Lewi, physician; member of the Jewish Council; in charge of the hospital for contagious diseases.

16 Icek Lewinson.

17 Nachman Lerner, member of the Jewish Council; responsible for administering the cemetery.

Absent Council members: Kestenberg, Edelsztajn (imprisoned yesterday),[21] and Rechtman.

In addition, the following individuals, who are not members of the Council, were invited today: Brodt, Ejzyk;[22] Kupferminc, Daniel;[23] Rotrubin, Josef;[24] Tajkef, Szulim;[25] Tenenbaum, Bolesław; and Wiener, Wolf.[26]

After the arrival of representatives of the authorities in the person of SS Obersturmführer[27] Worthoff,[28] SS Untersturmführer Walter, SS Untersturmführer Dr Sturm,[29] and SS Unterscharführer Knitzky,[30] Mr Worthoff and Dr Sturm announced the following:

The resettlement (evacuation) of the Jewish population will continue,[31] with the difference that, in future, the document qualifying its bearer to remain in Lublin will no

18 Dr Josef Siegfried (1898–1942), lawyer; worked in the Jewish Council's Health Section; murdered in Belzec in 1942.
19 Bencjon Tenenbaum (1896–1942), shoe upper maker; from 1940 in charge of the Jewish Council's workshops that produced goods for the Germans; shot dead after being accused of theft in early April 1942.
20 Josef Wajselfisz (1898–1942), accountant; worked in the Jewish Council's section responsible for collecting contributions, and later in the refugee aid and auditing sections.
21 On behalf of the Jewish Council, both of these men had collected money and valuables that had been handed over to the Germans in an attempt to delay the deportations; they were subsequently murdered. Salomon Kestenberg (1891–1942), retailer; second deputy chairman of the Jewish Council from 1940; head of the sections responsible for finance, the civil registry, and the cemeteries. Dawid Edelsztajn (1903–1942), office worker; head of the Jewish Council's Contributions Section from 1939; subsequently head of the Jewish Community's Supply Office.
22 Ejzyk (Mendel) Brodt (1904–1942); murdered in Lublin-Majdanek concentration camp.
23 Daniel Kupferminc is thought to have been murdered in Lublin-Majdanek concentration camp in 1943, following the liquidation of the Majdan Tatarski ghetto in Nov. 1942.
24 Josef Rotrubin (1904–1942), lawyer and teacher; perished in Oct. 1942, prior to the liquidation of the ghetto.
25 Szulim Tajkef was well known in the Lublin ghetto as a Gestapo informant.
26 Wolf Wiener (1898–1942), lawyer; murdered in Lublin-Majdanek concentration camp.
27 Here and below the SS ranks are listed in German in the original.
28 Hermann Worthoff (1910–1982), retailer; joined the SS and the NSDAP in 1933; worked for the Gestapo in Cologne in 1937, and subsequently in Klagenfurt; official in charge of Jewish affairs with the KdS in Lublin (Section IV B 4), May 1941 – August 1944; participated in the deportation of Jews from Lublin and Warsaw in 1942; after the war initially lived under a false name and worked as a sales representative; sentenced to eight years in prison by Wiesbaden Regional Court in 1975.
29 Dr Harry-Georg Sturm (b. 1912), historian; joined the SS in 1939 and the NSDAP in 1940; official in charge of ethnic policy affairs with the SD in Lublin; worked for the Einsatzkommando z.b.V. ('for special assignments') in Polesia, July – Sept. 1941; participated in the deportation of Jews from Lublin and Warsaw in 1942; worked for the KdS in Tallinn in 1943; assigned to the Senior Commander of the Security Police and the SD (BdS) in Belgrade from autumn 1943; subsequently employed in the Reich Security Main Office (RSHA); interned until 1948; subsequently employed as a teacher; sentenced to twelve years in prison by Wiesbaden Regional Court in 1971.
30 Karl Knitzky, né Knicky (1904–1943), engineer; joined the SS in 1932; worked for the illegal national leadership organization of the NSDAP in Austria, 1935–1937; based in Lublin from 1941.
31 The deportations began during the night of 16–17 March 1942 and were temporarily suspended on 28 March 1942. Thereafter the SS deported approximately 8,000 more Jews from Lublin to Belzec in a single transport on 31 March/1 April 1942, and on additional transports from 8 to 14 April 1942. More than 1,500 people were murdered in or near Lublin.

longer be the Arbeitsausweis[32] with the Sipo[33] stamp, but the *J-Ausweis*.[34] Those with a J-Ausweis can and will remain in Lublin; everyone else will be resettled.

The Jewish population is to be informed that everyone who holds a J-Ausweis must ensure that those without a J-Ausweis are not hidden in their apartments in the ghetto, which have been inspected, and will be inspected again in future, because otherwise even those with a J-Ausweis will be resettled. Since only an insignificant percentage of the Jewish population will remain in Lublin, the Jewish Council will be reduced from twenty-four to twelve members.

From among the previous Council members, the authorities have appointed the following: (1) Dr Alten, Marek; (2) Kerszman, Izaak; (3) Hochgemajn, Dawid; (4) Hufnagel, Leon; (5) Kelner, Jakub; (6) Lerner, Nachman; and (7) the Council's former administrative officer, Wiener, Wolf. In addition, the following, who were previously not Council members, were appointed on a provisional basis: (8) Brodt, Ejzyk; (9) Kupferminc, Daniel; (10) Rotrubin, Józef; (11) Tajkef, Szulim; and (12) Tenenbaum, Bolesław.

Previous Council members who have not been appointed to the Council today will be resettled along with their families and will leave Lublin on the first transport.

Those former Council members who live outside the ghetto will be escorted by Sipo officials to their apartments. After they have gathered the items most necessary for resettlement, their apartments will be sealed. At the new places of residence, former Council members Mr Bekker and Dr Siegfried shall assume the leadership functions of the Jewish Council and the JSS, since they already have the relevant experience.[35]

Once the former Council members had left the room, Dr Sturm additionally announced the following:

Dr Alten was appointed chairman of the Council and Kerszman was appointed deputy chairman. Alten, Kerszman, and Kupferminc were appointed to the executive committee. The functions of the various Council members will be divided up as follows, and any suggested changes are to be put forward: Councillor Kupferminc will take charge of provisioning in the ghetto. Councillor Tenenbaum will take charge of the police as well as disinfection, delousing, and keeping the apartment buildings clean. M. Sztokfisz[36] is assigned to assist him. As of today, the Disinfection and Delousing Office is incorporated into the Jewish Council as an integral part thereof. Mendel Goldfarb[37] remains the commander of the Order Service, as the executive authority.

Councillor Brodt will take over employment matters.

Councillor Wiener will take over housing affairs,

Councillor Hochgemajn will take over financial affairs,

Councillor Hufnagel will take over welfare provision,

32 German in the original: 'employment certificate'.

33 German in the original: 'Sipo' is short for Sicherheitspolizei, 'Security Police'.

34 German in the original: 'J[ew] identity document'. These documents were marked with a yellow star featuring a black 'J'; they were issued by the Security Police and the SD.

35 In reality they were deported to Belzec, where they were murdered.

36 Mojżesz Sztokfisz, retailer; owned a clothing accessories and fancy goods shop in Lublin prior to Sept. 1939.

37 Mendel (also known as Henryk) Goldfarb (1898?–1942), retailer; head of the Jewish Order Service; shot dead, along with Dr Alten, during the liquidation of the Majdan Tatarski ghetto in Nov. 1942.

Councillor Rotrubin will take over public health,
Councillor Kelner will take over the civil registry,
Councillor Tajkef will take over tax collection, along with Councillor Hochgemajn.

Dr Alten represents the Council and will act as its representative to governmental agencies, but he is authorized to designate this authority to other section heads.

The Council members are obliged to abide by the instructions of the Council chairman, Dr Alten.

No further applications for issuing J-Ausweise will be considered. The Order Service is to call upon people to volunteer for resettlement; 1,600 people will be voluntarily resettled today.

## DOC. 58

### *Słowo Młodych*, March 1942: a call to avenge the mass murders of Jews[1]

In every generation they rise against us to destroy us[2]
EXORIATUR EX OSSIBUS NOSTRIS UTOR (May an avenger arise from our bones)[3]

The annihilation of the defenceless Jewish population continues. Day by day we receive bad tidings that the Nazi thugs are carrying out mass murders of this population using the most elaborate methods, according to some secret, diabolical plan. Vilna, Słonim, Nowogródek, Koło, Kłodawa, Chełmno, and lately Lublin,[4] Mielec,[5] Lwów[6] – these are just a few of the sites of suffering of our unfortunate brothers. In places where all is 'calm', people await the worst with their hearts in their mouths.

What is the sense of these bestial murders? What benefits do the murderers expect from their deeds?

It is difficult to imagine that this is just madness and sadism, or a desire to deflect the anger of one's own people, or an attempt to win over part of the non-Jewish population, or even all of these things together. This is something new! There is some additional

1 *Słowo Młodych*, no. 9/10 (23/24), Feb./March 1942, pp. 29–30; AŻIH, Ring I/1333 (696), fols. 129–130. Published in French translation in Daniel Blatman, *En direct du ghetto: La presse clandestine juive dans le ghetto de Varsovie 1940–1943*, trans. Nelly Hansson (Paris: Cerf, 2005 [Hebrew edn, 2002]), pp. 500–502. *Słowo Młodych* was a newspaper published by the Gordonia youth organization, which was linked to the reformist Zionist party Hitachdut. The document title has been translated from Hebrew, the rest of the document from Polish.

2 This is a quote from a verse in the Haggadah recited each year on Pesach (Passover).

3 Originally taken from Virgil's *Aeneid*, in which the wording is: 'Exoriare aliquis nostris ex ossibus ultor'. The quotation was inscribed on the gravestones of Polish patriots, such as the insurgents of the November insurrection of 1830–1831.

4 A total of 9,000–10,000 Jews from the Słonim ghetto were shot there on 14 Nov. 1941, and 4,000–5,000 Jews from Nowogródek and the surrounding area were shot on 8 Dec. 1941. The Jews from Koło and Kłodawa were deported to Kulmhof between 8 and 12 Dec. 1941 and were among the first victims to be systematically murdered with gas. The deportations from Lublin to Belzec began on 17 March 1942 and ended on 14 April 1942.

5 See Doc. 51.

6 The deportations from Lwów to Belzec began on 16 March 1942 and ended temporarily on 28 March 1942.

calculation at play here. But what is it? Is the mass killing of the Jewish population undertaken in view of an expected victory? We know that in the 'new order' which the Germans intend to establish after a victorious war, and which is based on enslaving the whole people to the collective German 'lord and master', the Jews have no role to play. Consequently we know that the Jews are to 'disappear from Europe'. But are the methods applied so far, which are to bring about the gradual extinction of the Jewish population, not sufficient for this purpose? After all, there has been some talk of Madagascar, etc.[7]

So why this sudden haste?

No! The current mass murders of the defenceless Jewish population are not part of the programme to establish a 'new order' in the event of victory, rather they are a defensive measure in case of defeat.

*The criminal fears Jewish vengeance*, for he has inflicted such refined suffering on no other population group than the Jews. Therefore he seeks to eliminate the potential avenger. It is true that this fear may be exaggerated. The vengeance of the Czechs, for instance, would undoubtedly be more terrible than that of the Jews. But it is not out of the question that after the Jews, it will be the Czechs' turn, and then perhaps others will be next. It is simply easiest to start with the Jews. This element of the population is not very militant. Moreover, the executions of Jews do not cause much unrest among the non-Jewish population. For non-Jews are accustomed to Jews being treated differently. They draw no disturbing analogy …

We are powerless and at a loss in face of the crushing superiority of the enemy's forces, while we are defenceless. Perhaps we will be saved by a miracle, as has happened so often in the history of our people. Perhaps the criminal's hand, stained with innocent blood, will withdraw. Perhaps … But shall this hand not withdraw, but continue to murder, it will still not achieve its purpose. The criminal shall not escape Jewish vengeance! The murderous weapons will not reach the American or Soviet Jews, nor our brothers in Palestine and in many other countries. Every additional drop of innocent blood shed here strengthens the desire for revenge within every Jew, wherever he may be. The criminal will achieve the very opposite of what he strove for. Young and strong Jews will come here along with the English, Soviet, and American armies, and they will settle scores. These atrocities will not go unpunished. The more crimes are committed, the more severe the punishment will be. Even if the Nazi beasts were to succeed in eliminating the Jewish population whom they now have in their clutches, the avengers – *the Jewish avengers* – shall seek out the criminal in his own lair.
Nun.[8]

7 From mid 1940 the German government briefly pursued a plan to deport the Jewish population of Europe to the island of Madagascar, then a French colony, and to place the island under Reich control: see PMJ 3, pp. 46–47.

8 This is a code name.

## DOC. 59
## Around March 1942 Polish government representatives explain the population's anti-Jewish sentiments[1]

Report (marked 'confidential') from the government delegation (L.dz. 3150/II/42) for the Polish government in exile, unsigned, Warsaw, undated (March 1942 or later)[2]

*The Jewish question in Poland during the war*
*1. Introduction*
The Jewish question is such an extensive topic that I must limit myself to its most current, most obvious aspects, which are currently of burning interest to Polish society in Poland itself. I am writing these remarks without any preparation, and I base them on what I have observed first-hand. My treatment of this issue is therefore somewhat superficial, but for that reason it is direct and honest. It has the advantage of being a popular presentation of the issue as every average Pole currently sees it. The Jewish question remains one of the most burning issues. It is a constant preoccupation, a subject of continuous discussion and contemplation, something that everyone is talking about, and a source of serious concern. To understand this attitude within society, one must be familiar with the behaviour of the Jews during the war. Here I will limit myself to a general description of this.

*2. The behaviour of the Jews during the war*
Here we must distinguish two phases: the period before and the period after the Jews were confined in the ghetto. During the first phase, the Jews were incomparably better off than the Poles. They were neither rounded up in street raids nor shot ... While a Jew was murdered now and then, this was just a drop in the ocean; there was no comparison to the Poles' situation. However, the Jews knew how to exaggerate every single case of this kind and to trumpet about it to the world. In those days the Jewish armband was a sign that one was not to be touched.[3]

At that time the Jews made fun of us: 'Hitler is the Jews' enemy, yet he persecutes the Poles and leaves the Jews alone.' In the first year of the war, there was a strong increase in trade. Those [Poles] who had lost their homes or been expelled sold what was left of their belongings in order to survive. At that time the Jews demonstrated a great entrepreneurial spirit, buying up everything and trading. They preyed on the Poles' poverty, plight, and desperation in unbelievable ways. The Jews' behaviour was the cause of many a tragedy. For example, someone sold a ring that had miraculously been preserved. A Jew paid 1,000 złoty for it. One hour later, the seller found out that he could have got 2,000 złoty for it. There were countless cases like this. Moreover, the Jews were the Germans' eyes and ears as far as theft was concerned. For example, the Germans set up a communal space, an office, or quarters for themselves somewhere.[4] They take over a house or a villa. The furniture does not suit them, so new furniture has to be procured.

1 PISM, PRM, 76/1/21, fols. 345–349. This document has been translated from Polish.
2 This dating derives from the reference to the deportation of Jews from Slovakia to Poland.
3 For a similarly distorted account of the Jews' situation in 1939–1940, see PMJ 4/126.
4 Changes in tense here and below as in the original.

They immediately find a Jew who knows the local context and is willing to help. The Jew accompanies the German soldiers to Mr X's apartment and shows them the valuable furniture, paintings, and carpets. The Germans confiscate everything. I have personally witnessed several such cases, and I have heard a great deal about this subject. Thanks to information from the Jews, the German always knew who had amassed what supplies or quantities of grain and where.

After the Jews had been shut away in the ghetto, their situation changed radically. Now they were actually in a bad way. After an initial period of intense hatred towards the Jews on account of their behaviour, people began to feel sorry for them. After all, they were human beings, and they were being oppressed by our common enemy, the Germans. Yet even then the Jews did everything they could to influence this attitude negatively. Here are a few examples that spring to mind ad hoc. After the ghetto had been established, the news that hunger reigned in the Jewish district spread around Warsaw. Not out of altruism, but in order to earn money, quite a number of people threw themselves into trade with the ghetto. In doing so, however, they also helped the Jews to a certain extent. This was a very dangerous undertaking. Even though the Jewish residential district was cut off from the rest of Warsaw, a hole [in the wall] or a crossing could always be found. A loaf of bread cost 8 złoty in Warsaw at the time, and in the ghetto the price was allegedly 10 złoty. Traders bought bread in the city and took it to the ghetto. But the Jews quickly got wise to this – if someone exposed himself to danger by coming into the ghetto with a sack full of bread, he would certainly not risk leaving the ghetto with a full sack. So they colluded among themselves and paid only 6 złoty for a loaf of bread. The majority of the suppliers had to be content with this transaction and pay 2 złoty per loaf out of their own pockets. There were many cases like this. And here is another example: I was on a tram which passed through the ghetto on the way to Zoliborz.[5] The tram broke down and stopped. From the tram I observed the following scene: the Jewish 'police', i.e. the so-called Jewish Order Service, had seized a Pole with food in the ghetto. They were taking him to the Germans. They beat him up, then they grabbed the first Jew in a caftan they could lay their hands on, told him to drop his trousers and bend over, then ordered the Pole to kiss him. This was met with huge enjoyment by the entire crowd of Jewish onlookers. They applauded, [shouted] bravo, laughed, and made mischievous remarks – that's how they tried to curry favour with the Germans! The entire tram was buzzing. I remember someone saying: 'From this day forward, I will also be an antisemite.' Yet another scene: a Jewish work brigade was marching along Ujazdowskie Avenue. Arrogant young people, with their heads held high, going to work at the Belvedere.[6] On their own initiative they began to sing. I remember more or less how the song began: 'When Marshal Smigly-Rydz[7] still ruled, he gave the Jews nothing. Then came Hitler the Good, and he gave the Jews work.' The tone

5 A neighbourhood in the northern part of Warsaw.

6 Belvedere Palace (Pałac Belwederski) is located on the western edge of Łazienki Park and was Józef Piłsudski's residence from 1926 to 1935; it was then the residence of Warsaw's district governor, Ludwig Fischer, from 1939 to 1944. Jewish forced labourers were deployed to repair war damage and to carry out alterations to the interior.

7 This is a reference to Edward Rydz-Śmigły (1886–1941), Marshal of Poland from 1936, whose political affiliations were with the Camp of National Unity (OZN). He commanded the Polish armed forces during the German invasion in 1939 and after fleeing to Romania was interned there.

in which they sang and the nature of this song were solely intended to please the Germans. It's no wonder that this sort of behaviour on the part of the Jews irritated the Polish population to the utmost degree. The Jews' behaviour during the Bolshevik occupation,[8] though generally known, is [still] particularly noteworthy. They behaved incomparably worse than the Bolsheviks and the Ukrainians, they distinguished themselves by their cruelty, and they sadistically tormented the Polish population whenever and wherever they could. And they had plenty of opportunities to do so.

*3. On the mood of the Polish population*

The Jews' behaviour during the war reminded Polish society, which had itself experienced so many troubles, sorrows, and tragedies, of the Jewish question. It called for vigilance and caution. After the Jews had been confined in ghettos, this question faded into the background to a certain extent. However, our official propaganda – especially Radio London[9] – strove to prevent this question from being forgotten. If they had not constantly talked about the Jews on the radio at every opportunity, then this question would have disappeared from the agenda, at least for the time being. Our propaganda takes up this question again and again, to update it. That is undoubtedly to its credit. But at the same time this propaganda does a great disservice to our government [in exile]. The attitude of our official governing bodies is practically driving the Poles to despair and is causing indignation across the board. Last but not least, the government is constantly under attack on account of its handling of the Jewish question; it is inundated with reproaches, its popularity is undermined, confidence in it is shaken, and its credibility is called into question. Polish society is well aware of the very difficult position in which the government finds itself as far as the Jewish question is concerned. But it is not necessary to speak about it, and if it is, then we can reduce such discussions to a minimum and postpone them until the end of the war. Meanwhile London – despite the people – does not adhere to this, and its declarations[10] fire people up and push them towards fervent antisemitism. It irritates them [the people] that the whole world is up in arms when one Jew is beaten or murdered in Poland, yet when a hundred Poles are shot you hardly hear a thing about it. The Jews in Poland have some extraordinary means at their disposal when it comes to informing [the world] about the persecution they suffer.[11] They actually do this very skilfully. Their life at the moment really is gloomy; they are suffering enormous losses; they are subjected to horrible oppression and are being murdered en masse. But on the other hand their propaganda inflates and vastly exaggerates this persecution. The figures cited are usually three times higher than they actually are.

8 A reference to Soviet rule in eastern Poland between 17 Sept. 1939 and June 1941.

9 Presumably Radio Polskie, the broadcasting arm of the Polish government in exile, based in London.

10 In other words, official comments that, in the eyes of many Poles, made too many concessions to Jews.

11 Employees of foreign organizations and journalists working for foreign news outlets in the General Government – including the US press between 1939 and 1941 – repeatedly reported on the persecution of Jews in German-occupied Poland: see PMJ 4/9, 33, and 80; see also Doc. 197. Additionally, Jewish representatives in Switzerland and Istanbul were making concerted efforts to gather intelligence on events in the General Government: see Docs. 65, 117, and 146. Furthermore, the Jewish National Committee (ŻKN) and the Bund transmitted their reports via the government delegation's communication channels in 1942–1943.

Were it not for the government's current stance towards the Jews, public opinion in Poland would be more or less as follows: 'There is a war on, and we have so many worries of our own that we are not interested in the Jewish question right now. Let's endeavour to persevere. We feel sorry for the Jews as people because they are being persecuted by our common enemy. After the war we will somehow cope with them, because there will be far fewer Jews (though one must not forget that they have been transported to Poland in considerable numbers from Slovakia, Hungary, and allegedly from Romania and Western Europe).[12] Moreover, they have now been pushed out of economic life. In place of Jewish establishments, vast numbers of Polish ones have been set up everywhere. In fact, in the General Government every Pole engages in trade – in everything. This is how the majority of the population survive. It is true that this is not normal, healthy trade – but it is trade, nonetheless. In any case, the Poles are learning to trade. In the end, after the war ends, each Pole will be right where he belongs, in his workshop, his business, or his little corner shop, in every town and village, in every backwater. He will not have to start from scratch, from zero, but will be able to continue his work. Of course this will be difficult due to the lack of capital, but it will work out somehow. Meanwhile the Jews will have to build up their establishments and start all over again. No doubt they will enjoy the huge advantage of having capital, which they will either still have in Poland or will obtain from abroad. But clever laws – not just any Jewish laws, but laws that will encourage the development of purely Polish trade – will also help the Poles.

The general picture is thus as follows: compared to the Jews, our situation will be more favourable than it has been in the past. This will depend to a great extent on us, on our entrepreneurial spirit, on our determination, resilience, and shrewdness, on our courage in the face of international public opinion, and on whether we can solve the Jewish question – or if not, at least substantially reduce its importance.

That would be the opinion, were it not for our propaganda. Because of this propaganda, the mood has changed. Today the Poles think like this: How is this possible? We are the ones who went into battle, we shed our blood, we continue to fight everywhere, we manage the work in the country itself, for Poland alone – and we supposedly have no right to be heads of the household in our own country? It is true that the Germans are murdering the Jews, but are we any better off? Are not our own losses incomparably greater in the grand scheme of things? After all, we are dying for *something*. We know what we are threatened with for this or that activity, we are aware of the consequences of our actions – we want to die for Poland, if necessary. Meanwhile the Jews are dying for nothing, just because they are Jews. Clearly this is unjust. But do they also want to die – and is there something they want to die for? Don't they do everything they can just to preserve their lives?! But all our government can talk about is the Jews: the poor Jews, so and so many of them have perished. But don't worry, after the war you will get everything back – your influence, your capital, your trade, your industry, your press, your cinemas, your theatres, your literature, your art, your radio. Poland will be your home, you will be well off, you will do as you wish. And what is the purpose of all this?

12 In fact, deportations of Jews from Slovakia to occupied Poland were carried out from March to Oct. 1942; non-Hungarian Jews had been deported from Hungary to Eastern Galicia in 1941. Deportations from occupied Western Europe had taken place from Luxembourg from Oct. 1941 onwards, but from France, the Netherlands and Belgium only from 1942 onwards.

For what and for whom? Are we in Poland or in Judaea? And what have the Jews lost? The hotel, which was not theirs, in which they lived; the foreign restaurant in which they ate; the bank in which they invested their capital; the businesses from which they profited. And we – we [Poles] have lost our home. Why this constant talk about what will become of the Jews after the war? No one was wanting to beat them, murder them, or rob them. After the terrible experiences of war, the Polish people have undergone a major transformation. We have matured morally, in a sense; we have become more religious, more ethical. But this constant talk about the Jews' role in the future Poland, at every opportunity, fills us with concern and does not allow us to forget this problem. This undermines confidence in the government and the belief that this government will create a truly great, powerful, and just Poland. Perhaps the government is a tool in the hands of international Jewish politics? If so, then it will indeed hand over the future Poland to the Jews to rule. The government's current stance on the Jewish question leads to the conclusion that these fears and suspicions are well founded. In that case, come what may. We will do everything we can to prevent the Jews from ruling Poland after the war.

Our current propaganda is provoking even such far-reaching thoughts and feelings as these. This must be prevented, and conclusions must be drawn. There is no time to lose; we must act quickly.

## DOC. 60

## On 1 April 1942 the Jewish Aid Committee in Przysucha provides information on the situation of the town's Jewish residents[1]

Questionnaire from the Jewish Aid Committee in Przysucha,[2] signed the secretary (signature illegible) and the presiding physician, [Dr] Dawid Krongold, to the headquarters of the Jewish Social Self-Help, Cracow, dated 1 April 1942[3]

| | |
|---|---|
| Town: | *Przysucha* |
| Powiat: | *Tomaszów Maz.[owiecki]* |
| Region: | *Radom* |
| Population before the war: | *2,007*[4] |
| [Population] on 1 April 1942 | *3,812* |
| of whom refugees: | *1,787* |
| These refugees arrived (from where and when) | *from Litzmannstadt between 15 December 1939 and late 1941, from Mława on 14 December 1940,* |

1 AŻIH, 211/844, fol. 34. This document has been translated from Polish.

2 A small town 35 km west of Radom, a centre of Hasidism since the eighteenth century. Yiddish pronunciation: Pshiskhe.

3 This is a preprinted questionnaire, which the Jewish Social Self-Help (JSS) sent out to numerous communities. The handwritten entries are printed in italics here.

4 This is probably a reference to the number of Jewish residents, but the figure is too low. Prior to Sept. 1939 the town had 4,850 residents, of whom 2,980 were Jews.

| | |
|---|---|
| | *from Płock on 9 March 1941,*[5] *and from Przytyk on 5 March 1941* |
| Is there a Jewish quarter in the town? | *No*[6] |
| Since when? | – |
| Open or sealed? | – |
| Was the Jewish population concentrated in this quarter before the war? | – |
| Number of rooms in the quarter: | – |
| [Number of] houses: | – |
| Average number of residents to a room: | – |
| Does the quarter have a sewage system, and how is it supplied with water? | – |
| Has the town experienced a typhus epidemic, if so, when? | *Since August 1941* |
| Is there a hospital for infectious diseases? | *Yes* |
| Number of typhus patients on 1 April 1942 | *7* |
| Abdominal typhus | – |
| Dysentery | – |
| Tuberculosis | *159* |

## DOC. 61

## On 5 April 1942 Szlojme Winer, an escapee from Kulmhof (Chelmno) extermination camp, informs Hersh Vaser of the murder of the Jews in Belzec[1]

Letter from Szlamek,[2] from Zamość, to Hersh Vaser[3] in Warsaw, undated (5 April 1942)

Dear Mr Wasser,

I can report that I am well, thank God. I hope to hear the same from you, only good news. As for me, I find myself in a precarious situation. I have no idea what to do, as I would like to meet with Mr Kohn.[4] This is my greatest wish. Dear Mr Wasser, the [Jewish] Community doesn't want to help me, and so I ask that you be so kind as to write back to me immediately. I don't have any work or money for now, and I beg you to send me a few złoty so that I can save myself. I have received greetings from my cousin in

5 Thousands of Jews fled to the General Government from Łódź and the Litzmannstadt (Lodz) ghetto before the ghetto was sealed on 30 April 1940. In early Dec. 1940 approximately 3,000 Jews were taken from Mława (Regierungsbezirk Zichenau) to Soldau transit camp, from where they were transported onwards to various destinations in the General Government several days later. Approximately 400 Jews were expelled to Przysucha from Płock (Regierungsbezirk Zichenau).

6 In either 1939 or 1940 the German occupation authorities had appointed a Jewish Council under the chairmanship of Mojżesz First and had set up a Jewish Order Service; they did not establish a ghetto until mid August 1942. The majority of the ghetto residents were deported to Treblinka in late Oct. 1942.

1 AŻIH, Ring I/1481 (596), fols. 1–4. Published as a facsimile in Sakowska (ed.), *Archiwum Ringelbluma: Konspiracyjne Archiwum Getta Warszawy*, vol. 1: *Listy o Zagładzie*, pp. 130–134. This document has been translated from Polish.

Lublin, greetings from my family in Izbica Lub[elska],[5] and others. They write that the whole family has gone to olem emes,[6] the same as in Chełmno. Imagine my despair; I don't even have the strength to weep. This is certainly the last letter I will write you, and I'm certain to go where my parents have gone, and in the same way.[7] Dear Mr Wasser, advise me what I need to do to meet with Mr Kohn, and if [this does] not [happen], I'll never see you again. It's imperative that we meet to discuss my experiences and everything in general. The bajsolem[8] is in Belżyc,[9] the same maise[10] as in Chełmno. My cousin, whom I have not seen for quite some time, also sends me her greetings. She was in Rawa Ruska and has also gone to olem emes.[11] My grandfather has also died recently in Biłgoraj, so that I no longer have any family left. Imagine my grief and suffering. As it seems that I'll see Mr Chaim Ruwen Izbicki[12] again very soon, I'd much rather meet with you. What's new with you? How is your wife,[13] and so on? And what's new with all of my friends? I kiss you all and remain, your Szlamek.

Greetings from all [your] friends. I remain yours, with the greatest respect. Ehr macht kalt of aza ofen wi in Chełmno, es halt bei unz?[14] Das Bajsolem ist in Belżyc. Kalt hat men szojn gemacht die sztetlech, was zenen geszriben in brif.[15] I'll finish here and send kisses to you all.

2 Szlojme (Szlamek) Winer, alias of Jakub Grojnowski (1911–1942) from Izbica Kujawska; in Jan. 1942 deported to Kulmhof, where he had to work as a gravedigger in a Sonderkommando; escaped on 19 Jan. 1942 and reported to the underground archive of the Warsaw ghetto on the mass murder of the Jews in Kulmhof (see AŻIH, Ring I/1115 (412)); subsequently stayed with relatives in Zamość; thought to have been murdered in Belzec in April 1942.

3 Hersh Vaser (Hersz/Hersh Wasser) (1912–1980), economist; member of the Poale Zion-Left party; head of the Central Refugee Committee and secretary of the underground archive in the Warsaw ghetto from 1940; lived in Israel from 1950.

4 Menakhem Mendel Kon (Kohn) was the treasurer of the underground archive and had previously provided Winer with financial support. See also Doc. 114, fn. 2.

5 This is a reference to the deportations from Lublin, which began in mid March 1942, and from Izbica (Lubelska), from where 2,200 Jews were transported to Belzec on 24 March 1942.

6 Hebrew in the original: 'afterlife' (literally: 'the world of truth').

7 On 15 Jan. 1942 his parents, along with other Jews from Izbica Kujawska, were transported to Kulmhof, where they were murdered.

8 Hebrew in the original: 'cemetery'.

9 Correctly: Bełżec.

10 Yiddish in the original: 'story'.

11 In March 1942 approximately 1,000 Jews from Rawa-Ruska were deported to Belzec.

12 Chaim Ruwen Izbicki, one of Jakub Grojnowski's friends; murdered in Kulmhof. 'Szlamek' mentioned this to Wasser in a report he compiled after 19 Jan. 1942: see fn. 2.

13 Bluma Vaser (Wasser) (1912–1990), teacher; contributed to the underground archive.

14 Yiddish in the original: 'He is killing people the same way he did in Chełmno. Do we face the same imminent fate?'

15 German and Yiddish in the original: 'The cemetery is in Belzec. The inhabitants of the shtetls I mentioned in the letter have already been killed.'

## DOC. 62

### On 11 April 1942 a resident of Stanislau (Stanisławów) complains to Reich Foreign Minister Ribbentrop about the mass shootings in Eastern Galicia[1]

Letter from Carl Lehman,[2] Stanislau, to Reich Minister von Ribbentrop,[3] Berlin, dated 11 April 1942[4]

To His Excellency Reich Minister Joachim v. Ribbentrop, Berlin

I venture to address the following letter to you:

I am an *ethnic German*, my name is *Carl Lehman*, forty-one years old, I am patriotically minded to the highest degree, and I am sure that in this struggle our beloved Führer will soon secure us the final victory for thousands of years. –

At the same time I have been moved, Minister von Ribbentrop, to draw your attention to a matter that stains our German people; it is the action taken to *combat our internal enemy, 'the Jew'*. –

This enemy must be defeated, but not in the way that this is being done by the Security Police with H. Krüger[5] at their head. – Are you aware, Minister, that two months ago roughly *4,000 Jews were assembled at the Jewish cemetery in Stanislau? There* they *were chased alive into* a certainly *pre-prepared pit* and then machine-gun fire opened on them, and some of them [were] shot dead, some badly or even just slightly wounded, and then the pit [was] filled in, many people buried alive, eight days ago this was repeated afresh, and *a further 3,000 Jews were executed* in the same way.

Mr Krüger has also used the same tactics at other places in Kreis Stanislau, namely in Tartarów, Delatyn, Kossów, Kolomea, Rohatyn, and many other towns where thousands of Jews have been shot and buried alive. – God in heaven! Are there not many other means, cultural means, to defeat the internal enemy in another way and make life difficult for him? Let the Jew perish under the burden of forced labour; his life will be miserable if the fat-bellied profiteering banker, the big retailer, or the industrialist is engaged in physical labour all day long; at any rate his life will soon be over. – I'm afraid if, after Germany's final victory, we are accused of doing something like this, we will have a stain of this kind on our Volkskörper.[6] – Let us be spared that. –

1 PA AA, Inland II A/B 67/3, fol. 2433r–v. This document has been translated from German.
2 Possibly a pseudonym.
3 Joachim von Ribbentrop (1893–1946), businessman; joined the NSDAP in 1932 and the SS in 1933; Hitler's foreign policy advisor (Bureau Ribbentrop) from 1934; German ambassador to Britain, August 1936 – Feb. 1938; Reich minister of foreign affairs, Feb. 1938 – May 1945; sentenced to death on 1 Oct. 1946 at the International Military Tribunal at Nuremberg and executed.
4 The original features handwritten underlining and annotations.
5 Hans Krüger (1909–1988), agricultural inspector; joined the SA in 1929 and the SS in 1938; worked at Oranienburg concentration camp, 1933–1934; served with the Gestapo from 1938; member of Einsatzkommando z.b.V. ('for special assignments') in Lwów in June/July 1941; involved in a leading capacity in mass murders in Stanisławów (Stanislau) and the surrounding area from August 1941; travelling salesman after the war; sentenced to life imprisonment by Münster Regional Court in 1968.
6 'People's body' or 'body politic': under National Socialism, the notion of a biologically defined collective body of the German people. The concept distinguished between individual bodies deemed to be of (hereditary) 'value' or 'non-value' and provided a framework for policies designed to cultivate certain elements within society and to eradicate others.

I reserve the right, however, if all this is happening with the knowledge of the High Authorities, then I capitulate, for you gentlemen understand it better than me, a common, average person. Minister, see to it that an end is put to these inhumane deeds, or let merely H. Krüger together with his members answer for these deeds, but not the whole German people. – We do not want to have stains of this kind on us. –

Heil Hitler[7]

## DOC. 63

## From 8 to 15 April 1942 the physician Zygmunt Klukowski writes in his diary about the deportation of the Jewish population from Zamość and the mood among the Jews in Szczebrzeszyn[1]

Handwritten diary of Zygmunt Klukowski,[2] entries for 8 to 15 April 1942[3]

8 April

On Saturday, 4 April the new Orthodox church was consecrated. Typical Orthodox chanting could be heard during the night and on the first day of Easter. Through the window on the hospital stairwell, I watched the Eastern Orthodox rites in the formerly Catholic church, and for all my religious indifference, I clenched my fists in indignation at such a violation.[4] On the first day of Easter,[5] at 10 p.m., something unbelievable happened. Two young people came to the municipal prison, threatened the warden with revolvers, forced him to open the door, and freed Kamiński,[6] who had been arrested a few days earlier and was waiting in handcuffs to be taken away. He was so stunned that at first he didn't want to leave the cell. The young men locked the warden and his wife in the cell and led Kamiński out. After a while the warden called out through the window

7 A handwritten note has been added at the bottom of the letter: '(1) A Jew is evidently hiding behind the sender! It can be assumed that the relevant authorities are sufficiently well informed about the measures taken against the Jews in the General Government. (2) To be filed Bln [Berlin], 27 April 1942. [Initialled] W'. To the right alongside this note: *'Party Section* forwarded to Section D III in view of its authority [over the matter]. Bln, 23 April 1942' [initial illegible].

1 Zygmunt Klukowski, Dziennik, notebook 4, fols. 126–133; Biblioteka Uniwersytecka Katolickiego Uniwersytetu Lubelskiego, Dział Rękopisów 813. Published in Zygmunt Klukowski, *Zamojszczyzna*, vol. 1: *1918–1943*, ed. Agnieszka Knyt (Warsaw: Ośrodek Karta, 2007 [1958]), pp. 271–273. A slightly abridged version of the diary entries is published in English translation: Zygmunt Klukowski, *Diary from the Years of Occupation, 1939–44*, ed. Andrew Klukowski and Helen Klukowski May, trans. George Klukowski (Urbana, IL: University of Illinois Press, 1993). This document has been newly translated from Polish.

2 Dr Zygmunt Klukowski (1885–1959), physician; studied medicine in Moscow and Cracow; hospital manager in Szczebrzeszyn, 1920–1946; served in the war in eastern Poland in Sept. 1939; in the Polish underground, 1941–1944; persecuted by the Polish state security service after the war; sentenced to two years in prison in 1951 (released after one year). He kept the diary quoted here between June 1939 and 1945.

3 Words and numbers have been added above the text at certain points, presumably in connection with the printing of the text in 1958.

4 The German authorities had handed over a Catholic place of worship to the Orthodox Church.

5 Easter Sunday fell on 5 April 1942.

6 Mieczysław Kamiński was an official on the Zamojski family estate.

to someone passing through the courtyard of the municipal building and raised the alarm. Gendarmes came rushing in, and frenzied, indiscriminate shooting began. Pressured by the gendarmes, the warden confessed that he recognized the young men and said that they were Wejler and Marczewski from Brody.[7] The gendarmes and the Polish policemen immediately went to the village. They found two revolvers in Wejler's apartment, and when young Wejler tried to escape, police officer Gal[8] of the Polish police shot him dead. Young Marczewski beat it, his father was arrested. Was it really they who abducted Kamiński? No one knows. Right after this incident, the gendarmerie arrested Kamiński's wife, her sister-in-law, and his 12-year-old son, leaving their 4-year-old daughter in the care of the house owners. They never picked up Kamiński's trail.

On the second day of Easter, 6 April, there was a funeral ceremony for the gendarme who had been killed.[9] I was not in town because I had gone to Zwierzyniec, so I did not see the funeral myself, I only heard about it. Apparently there were many gendarmes, German civilians from Biłgoraj, the entire town council, and a lot of people who'd come to gawp. There were several wreaths, for example from Sz[czebrzeszyn] council, the Polish police, and … the Judenrat.[10] Wejler, who had been killed, was buried on the same day, but the Germans did not allow his body to be placed in a coffin, nor were people allowed to attend the funeral. The town was gripped by fear of arrests and reprisals. In the evening, when it was dark, no one ventured into the streets any more. There was terrible despondency among the Jews. We now know for sure that a train arrives in Bełżec from the direction of Lublin and another one from Lwów every day, each with more than 20 carriages. There they let the Jews off, herd them behind the barbed wire fence, and kill them with an electric current, and then burn the corpses. On the way, people – especially railwaymen – witness terrible scenes, because the Jews already know exactly where they are going and why. They are not given anything to eat or drink. At Szczebrzeszyn train station, the railway workers saw and heard for themselves how a Jew exchanged 150 złoty through the window of the train for a kilo of bread, and how a Jewish woman took her gold ring from her finger and offered it in exchange for a glass of water for her dying child. The residents of Lublin have told me unbelievable things about what happens to Jews there. Little children are thrown from windows, sick people are shot on the spot, while healthy people are shot outside the town. They are taken to Bełżec in their thousands.

11 April

The Jews have found out – and they have good intelligence sources – that today the Jews were taken from Chełm and after they were offloaded in Bełżec, the empty train, the so-called 'Judenzug',[11] went on to Zamość.[12] Towards evening the news spread that Zamość is already surrounded. So people are certain that the Jews of Zamość will be rounded up

7 This is a reference to Brody Duże, which at the time was a village near Szczebrzeszyn; today it is part of the city.

8 Klukowski described Jan Gał as 'the cruellest of all' of the German gendarmes and members of the Blue Police who participated in the murder of Jews; Gał was killed by the Polish underground in 1945: Klukowski, *Diary from the Years of Occupation*, p. 222 (entry for 26 Oct. 1942).

9 On 4 April 1942 Klukowski noted that a gendarme called Himler had been killed the previous day in a raid in Zakłodzie: Klukowski, *Diary from the Years of Occupation*, p. 190.

10 German in the original: 'Jewish Council.'

and deported to their deaths. The sense of horror in our small town is indescribable. Some people are completely resigned to it, while others are running through the streets like maniacs – seeking rescue. Everyone is convinced that the same thing will happen in Szcz[ebrzeszyn] at any moment. Many Jews come to me asking to be admitted to hospital. I refuse in order to avoid the suspicion that I am hiding Jews. I will only admit women who are about to give birth and emergency cases, because those are my orders.[13]

12 April
Through various channels, news has reached us from Zamość that – predictably – terrible things have happened there. Apparently they deported some 2,500 Jews and killed several hundred on the spot. They say that some Jews resisted. We do not know the details, and in general we do not know anything for sure.[14] The mood among our Jews is one of panic. Elderly Jewish women spent the night at the Kirkut[15] today. They would rather die here, in their little town, among the graves of their relatives, than somewhere in Bełżec after going through agony. Some are taking a risk and fleeing to the countryside. A great many are preparing hiding places here, while others are sending their children to Warsaw, to be looked after by trustworthy Aryans.

13 April
The night passed without incident, but the Jews are now in an even greater panic. Since morning they have been expecting the gendarmes and the Gestapo to appear at any moment. A considerable number of Jews have disappeared somewhere – they have left town or gone into hiding, no one knows where. Others have been feverishly moving their belongings, taking care of urgent business. The dregs of society are pouring into town, many carts have arrived from the villages, and they have all been waiting almost all day to see when they can start looting. News comes in from various quarters about the scandalous behaviour of the Polish population and the looting of abandoned Jewish apartments. In this regard our town will certainly not lag behind.

The Jews have handed over a lot of things to the townspeople and the farmers for safekeeping. All day long they have been dragging all kinds of bundles, baskets, sewing machines, etc. Huge sums of money were offered to hide children and adults for a few days, but the farmers from neighbouring villages are scared because hiding Jews carries the death penalty, and there are plenty of informants everywhere. I know for a fact that more children are being taken into hiding in distant villages. In the afternoon there were hardly any Jews to be seen. This resulted in a fall in the prices of agricultural products because there were no Jewish buyers. There is also considerable tension among the general population. Many people would like all of this to pass quickly – one way or the other – because the panic among the Jews is affecting everyone.

11 German in the original: 'Jew train' (a deportation transport).

12 The first mass deportation of approximately 4,300 Jews from the Chełm ghetto was carried out from 21 to 23 May 1942; the destination was the nearby Sobibor camp.

13 Presumably a reference to an order issued by the physician for powiat Biłgoraj, Jan Snacki.

14 On 11 April 1942 the Germans deported approximately 3,000 Jews from Zamość to Belzec; 250 people were murdered immediately upon arrival.

15 Term used in Poland to refer to a Jewish cemetery.

15 April
Yesterday towards evening there was a slight feeling of relief among the Jews because no train had yet left for Bełżec, and there had been no bad news from the neighbouring towns and villages. It's the same today, although most people remain in hiding and there are very few Jews to be seen in the streets. On the other hand, the telephone booth at the post office is literally besieged. It is difficult to squeeze through the crowd of Jews waiting to be connected to various towns.

Last night, someone at Szcz[ebrzeszyn] train station tipped off the gendarmes that there were some Jews among the crowd [of passengers]. The gendarmes commandeered the best horses they could lay their hands on – which happened to belong to the hospital – and rushed to the train station. There they arrested eight Jews who were attempting to travel illegally in the direction of Warsaw. Apparently five of them have already been shot today in Zwierzyniec, where executions usually take place.

Yesterday morning the Orthodox priest came to see me, complaining that, for the third day in a row, someone had been throwing stones at the windows of what is now the Orthodox church during the service. He suspected it was someone from the hospital, but it soon became clear that it was some ruffians in the street, shooting stones from a catapult.

## DOC. 64
## Representatives of the Polish government report on the murders in the Warsaw ghetto during the night of 17/18 April 1942[1]

Report from the government delegation's Internal Affairs Department, unsigned, Warsaw, dated 18 April 1942 or later

*All messages from the night of 17 to 18 April 1942*

On 17 April 1942 (Friday) a number of Jews in the Jewish residential district of Warsaw received verbal and even written warnings from Gestapo men with whom they are acquainted that they should be careful on that day and not leave their homes in the evening because it might be dangerous. Around noon the gendarmerie on duty at the exit to the ghetto on the corner of Żelazna and Leszno streets informed the Jewish Order Service that at least 2,000 Jews were to be killed that night. This news spread like wildfire throughout the district, causing general panic, and led to shops and businesses closing en masse, and people hiding in their apartments. By 5 p.m. the streets of the ghetto were completely deserted. A state of mass psychosis set in, as if a pogrom were imminent; this potential pogrom was intended as a reprisal for the murder of a German gendarme and a junak (at the exit to the ghetto on Rymarka Street) during a skirmish between smugglers and junacy.

At 8 p.m. the KSP (Jewish Order Service command)[2] received an order from the German police to provide eighteen German-speaking men from the Order Service, who

1 AAN, 1325/202/II-27, fol. 47. This document has been translated from Polish.
2 The head of the Jewish Order Service was Józef Szeryński.

were ordered to report to the front of the Pawiak prison gates on Dzielna Street at 9 p.m. At 9 p.m. the KSP received an additional order from the German police to prepare a reserve squad of forty men for special duty.

In view of the above events and the prevailing mood on that day, the KSP ordered police across all precincts to be on alert as of 10 p.m.

At 10 p.m., fourteen small cars marked either SS or 'POL'[3] left the prison on Dzielna Street. Each car was manned by one police officer, two non-commissioned officers, a driver, and an SS man armed with a pistol or a light machine gun; each car was assigned a Jewish orderly. Four Jewish orderlies remained at the prison gates.

These cars dispersed throughout the district, following the route maps that each officer carried.

After arriving at a particular building, the squad got out, along with the Jewish orderly, and only the driver remained in the car. The Germans hammered at the gate, and as soon as it was opened, they forced the Jewish orderly to ask the caretaker in Polish whether such-and-such a person, whose name was read out from the German officer's list, was living at that address. In many cases they demanded that the caretaker produce the registration book for the building in question so they could compare the details of the people recorded in the registration books with their own records. This happened most often when the spelling of the name was difficult or when several people with the same name were living in the building.

If the person they were looking for did in fact live at that address, they ordered the caretaker to lead them to the apartment in question. There they asked those who were present for their names, checked them against their list, checked their personal details carefully, asked about their profession, etc. Once they had established the identity of the person they were looking for, they politely asked the person (addressing them as 'Sie' rather than 'Du')[4] to come with them. They waited patiently for the person to get dressed properly, always stressing that the person should take only their identity card with them and leave their money, valuables, watch, keys, etc. behind. If asked where they were being taken, they [the squad] politely replied that they did not know. On the way out, they allowed the person to bid farewell to their family, and in many cases they even reassured the family members who remained behind. Upon leaving the apartment, the commanding officer made the detainee walk in front of him; both were followed by the soldier with the light machine gun. As a rule, the detainee was placed inside the car, which then drove away from the respective building, sometimes a few houses further, or even 2–3 streets away. At a certain moment the officer signalled the driver to stop and told the detainee to get out of the car. In that moment the driver then pointed the headlights at the detainee, and the SS man fired one shot (or sometimes two) at the detainee, usually in the head. Once the murdered person fell to the ground, the car drove to a new address.

In many cases the condemned person was ordered to stand against the wall of a building facing the car, the headlights illuminated their face, and shots were fired in their right eye.

In a few cases the non-commissioned officers searched the apartment during the arrest, but without specifying what they were looking for.

3 Meaning: 'police'.

4 German in the original: 'Du' is the familiar form of 'you', while 'Sie' is the polite form.

The operation described above lasted from 10 p.m. until 4 a.m. After the operation ended, they [the Gestapo] ordered the Jewish Order Service reserve squad to clear away the corpses by morning.

For almost the entire night, the Jewish Order Service went through the streets of the Jewish quarter, collected the dead and the wounded, carried them to the nearest gates, and identified them based on the personal documents found on them.

More than 140 dead and approximately 25 seriously wounded people were recorded. Jewish ambulances brought the wounded to the hospital at 1 Leszno St. They are in a critical condition and not expected to recover (in most cases there are severe bullet wounds to the head, with complications, haemorrhaging, etc.). In addition, around ten people with less serious injuries were taken to private apartments, with the help of the Order Service.

## DOC. 65

## On 20 April 1942 the Jewish head of a deportation train from Berlin reports on its arrival, life in the Warsaw ghetto, and the self-help activities of the Jews from Germany[1]

Report, unsigned, from Warsaw, dated 20 April 1942 (copy)[2]

It is only today that am I getting round to sending you a report briefly outlining the journey of the twelfth Berlin transport and how it fared.[3]

We arrived in Warsaw at about 8 a.m. on 5 April. The journey itself went smoothly, apart from a few minor incidents, and everyone apart from two arrived in good health. The two sick people were immediately taken to hospital. One appeared again eight days later, completely recovered.

All the luggage, including the hand luggage from the compartments, was taken to our accommodation immediately, and arrived there at the same time as we did. Upon our arrival at the railway station, we were greeted by the chairman of the Jewish Council[4] along with some senior gentlemen from various aid committees. We were put up in a former school at 109 Gerichtsstraße[5] that had also been used for a while as an isolation hospital for the military, and we are still living in this building today. The willingness of the various committees to help is tremendous. Unfortunately, their ability to help is not as great because resources are lacking on all fronts. The only support we receive is food. Regrettably, it is not possible for us to be supplied with any other daily necessities. On

1 CZA, C 3/7–14, fols. 92–94. Copy in USHMM, RG-68.045M, reel 2. This is an abridged copy of a report from the Geneva office of the Jewish World Congress. This document has been translated from German.

2 The original of the report is thought to have been addressed to the Jewish Community in Berlin; see below in the document.

3 There were between 645 and 659 Jews from Berlin on the train that left Berlin on 2 April 1942, as well as 57 from Frankfurt an der Oder and an unknown number of Jews from Potsdam and from Radinkendorf labour camp, near Beeskow.

4 Adam Czerniaków.

5 Leszno Street.

the day of our arrival, I was able to get in touch immediately with several gentlemen and talk in detail with them about the options for the future. At that time it was initially said we would only be staying in our temporary accommodation for a few days. We are still living here. No final arrangement seems to have been made for the time being, although I and all reasonable people are very glad about this. Please take note of our address on this occasion: 27 Gartenstraße.[6] We get our post delivered from there. It is not worth sending items direct to our accommodation. The additional forename (Israel) is not required.

Another approximately 1,000 people are living together with us; they are from a transport that arrived three days earlier, which was made up of people from Hanover and Westphalia. I am working closely with the head of the transport from Göttingen. The two of us have complete freedom in leading the people entrusted to us, and as you can imagine, I am completely occupied from dawn till dusk, certainly more so than before. In fact, a fairly large dose not just of good will, but also of iron will, is required to more or less satisfy these people brought together from all strata of society, [and] keep them together in the interests of society and not least in their own interests. Unfortunately, I often have to step in and make a ruthlessly clean sweep in order to bring outbreaks of individual selfishness under control in the interests of the community. I find it truly upsetting to see how many people forget their once impeccable manners in an instant and believe they can give free rein to their own selfishness without consideration for those around them.

We have set up our own Order Police unit in the building, which has had to take drastic action on various occasions in order to put the bad elements in their place. On occasion this could only be achieved with punishment to make an example of them. There is food and drink, both the quality and the quantity of which are as is to be expected under the circumstances. I am obliged to point out to people again and again that they are living in paradise in their current accommodation, and that their lives would inevitably be significantly worse in the Jewish residential district – the official name here for the demarcated Jewish quarter. In the first few days a total of 165 young men aged 17–35 from our two transports were very soon transferred to a labour camp that is approx. two to three hours away.[7] We received news today that they are apparently doing well. There are three teachers with the Hanover transport who have organized lessons for the school-age children from both transports. Some nursery-school teachers look after the pre-school children during regular hours. Our two female physicians and the nursing staff regrettably have enormous amounts of work to do day and night because many people have caught colds, which have proven to be very persistent. Unfortunately, we have the following deaths to record today (eleven names are given).[8] As far as I can tell, they will unfortunately not be the last. The medical staff are devoting themselves heart and soul to the people entrusted to them, and have no rest day or night, especially

6 Ogrodowa Street. Following the establishment of the ghetto, there was initially an emergency shelter there for Polish Jews who had been forcibly relocated to Warsaw.

7 The men were taken to Treblinka on 10 April 1942: see *The Warsaw Diary of Adam Czerniakow*, p. 341 (entries for 9 and 10 April 1942). Their destination was Treblinka labour camp; construction work on the extermination camp (Treblinka II) began later: see Doc. 78.

8 The names were left out in the copy.

since, as a younger person, the male physician from the Hanover transport has also been transferred to the labour camp. Approximately ten people have been asked to go to the ghetto by their relatives.

I very much regret that I have not received a list of the people who came on the journey, and even more so of the stock of foods that was kindly given to us. In the interests of later transports, I would therefore ask you to pass the leader of each transport a list of the people going on his transport and the food to be taken along in the goods wagon. It would have saved us an enormous amount of time and effort if I had been able to present a complete list. For each room, where often up to 140 people sleep, I have appointed responsible spokesmen, who are responsible to me for maintaining cleanliness and order, both in the rooms and in the toilets, etc. All women, irrespective of their age or origin, have to do work of this kind. Anyone who refuses is punished in order to make an example of them. Only in this way has it been possible for me to instil iron discipline in our community.

All the people who came on the journey have asked me to convey their gratitude to you and all your fellow helpers from the Jewish congregation for your unparalleled willingness to make sacrifices while we were being transported. People still like to think back to the support they received in Berlin and are full of praise for the way in which they were looked after, and especially for the food, at Levetzowstraße and in Grunewald.[9]

Immediately after our departure, I had to vigorously draw people's attention to the fact that we needed to economize on the food given to us, and I immediately rationed the drinking water we were allowed to have. I was right to do this because we only had two very brief opportunities to take on a small amount of fresh water on the way.

A new transport arrived here three days ago. The heads of the transport were Mr N. from Radinkendorf (a Jewish agricultural retraining camp) and Dr K. from Magdeburg.[10] I took the opportunity to welcome the new arrivals and help them as far as possible in setting up their new accommodation, along with some ladies and gentlemen from our transport. I have to emphasize again and again that, within the scope of the opportunities granted to them, the gentlemen from the aid committees here do an astonishing amount and have the very best of intentions. However, the resources at their disposal are shockingly meagre.

At our suggestion, the intention is to set up a Landsmannschaft[11] for people from the Old Reich, to which all the people included in this category will automatically belong. I want to push this through, if only due to the mentality of these people, and also hope to have it accepted. The gentlemen on the committee here by no means regard this as a bad idea because it is be founded purely on an economic basis. The committee largely wants to support me in this endeavour. Furthermore, I have negotiated with the gentlemen on the committee about receiving more extensive support than to date. This sup-

9 The synagogue on Levetzowstraße in Berlin had been converted into an assembly camp. Berlin's Grunewald railway station served as a departure point for deportations.

10 The train had travelled from Magdeburg via Potsdam and Berlin between 14 and 16 April 1942: see Doc. 107. Jews from the Mark Brandenburg region were held at Radinkendorf, and some of them were deployed on construction projects before they were taken to the synagogue on Levetzowstraße in Berlin and deported from there via Grunewald railway station.

11 In the Jewish context this term was used from the beginning of the twentieth century to describe mutual aid societies of Jewish immigrants from the same European town or region.

port will hopefully have an impact in the next few days. It is not a matter of support for 'mitzvah'[12] (recipients of alms), but a kind of loan, which we are to organize and arrange completely independently. It is not possible to set out the details of this in the present short report. As a matter of course, all these things will be carried out jointly with the Hanover transport.

On Friday evenings and Saturdays, the three teachers hold religious services as best as they can, and there is a youth service (Oneg Shabbat)[13] for the young people. The teachers and nursery-school teachers receive Polish language lessons every day.

Please, if possible, keep reminding migrants' relatives that they should always enclose a reply card when they send off correspondence, since it is impossible to purchase postcards because no money is yet being earned, and due to its very limited funds the committee is not able to provide postcards for every individual. We still have a number of people who have not yet had the opportunity to write to their relatives. We have therefore introduced a practice whereby anyone fortunate enough to be in possession of a postcard writes to his family members on behalf of several people who came on the transport, and asks them to inform those people's relatives. All the people entrusted to me keep asking me whether it is possible for packets, potentially also cash remittances, to be sent from Germany. Please clarify this question and inform me accordingly.

We have also contacted the employment office here, and one of the senior German gentlemen[14] visited us and promised to arrange [work] as soon as possible. We are in daily contact with this employment office, and it has been possible to place approx. 250 people with German firms here in the meantime.[15]

12 Hebrew: 'commandment' or 'charitable act'.

13 Hebrew: 'Joy of the Sabbath' (Yiddish: Oyneg Shabes); presumably people came together to sing, read biblical texts, and study together. The underground archive of the Warsaw ghetto was also known by this name.

14 Presumably Friedrich Ziegler (1891–1978), administrative official; worked at the Warsaw employment office as head of 'Jewish labour deployment' from 1940, then in the employment office at 77 Leszno Street in the Warsaw ghetto, where he had 300–400 Jewish employees; senior administrative official in 1942; lived in Mannheim after the war.

15 The Jews from the Reich were among the first to be deported to Treblinka at the end of July 1942.

## DOC. 66

## In April 1942 the Home Army reports on the systematic murder of Jews at Belzec extermination camp[1]

Appendix no. 1, unsigned, to the report for the Home Army High Command, from the Home Army's Lublin District Command, on the political situation, in April 1942[2]

Trzcina[3]
*The camp at Belzec*

The Jews have been terrorized for several weeks now. Jews are beaten and shot dead on a daily basis. One sees that they fear being transported to the camp at Bełżec. The camp was fully completed a few days prior to 17 March 1942. The transport of Jews from the direction of Lwów and Warsaw began on that day.[4] On the first day, five transports arrived, and thereafter one from each direction. In Bełżec the transport is redirected to a siding in the vicinity of the camp. After unloading, which lasts thirty minutes, the train returns empty. The train crew is German; the only Pole, the stoker, gets off at the station before the train enters the siding.

Observations made by the population (the camp is within sight and earshot of residents of the railway building) have led everyone to the same conclusion, namely that the Jews are being killed en masse at the camp. The following facts illustrate this:

1. Between 17 March and 13 April, 52 transports arrived at the camp (each transport comprising 18–35 goods wagons, with an average of 1,500 people on board).
2. Jews are not transported back from Bełżec, either by day or by night.
3. No food is delivered to the camp (the Jews who worked in construction were previously given bread and other foodstuffs).[5]
4. Quicklime is delivered to the camp.
5. Transports arrived at the camp at the same time. Jews are not seen at the camp before a train arrives.
6. After every transport, approximately two carriages of clothing are transported from the camp and stored at the railway warehouse (the Selbstschutz[6] steal the clothes).
7. Jews wearing [only] undergarments have been seen at the camp.
8. The camp has [only] three barracks, which could not accommodate even one tenth of the Jews [who arrive there].
9. There is a strong smell from the camp on warmer days.

1 AAN, 1325/202/III-28, fol. 147. Published in Ireneusz Caban and Zygmunt Mańkowski (eds.), *Związek Walki Zbrojnej i Armia Krajowa w Okręgu Lubelskim 1939–1944* (Lublin: Wydawnictwo Lubelskie, 1971), pp. 34–35. This document has been translated from Polish.

2 The report has not survived in its entirety. The parts that have been preserved discuss new regulations issued by the German authorities as well as the political situation, and also include a section titled 'Various', which states that the Germans deported 700 Jews from Lubartów on 7 April 1942; prior to that date, approximately 2,000 Jews, mainly women and children, had arrived from Slovakia. A total of 15 Jews with academic titles were shot dead at Międzyrzec for unknown reasons, and 72 Jews and 2 Poles were shot dead at Wąwolnica in retaliation for an attack on the head of the employment office.

3 Polish: 'Reed'; used here as the code name for the Home Army's Lublin area (Okręg Lubelski).

4 The victims were deported from locations along the railway line in districts Galicia and Lublin.

5 Jews had been deployed in the construction of the extermination camp since late 1941.

10. The Selbstschutz men pay any price for the vodka they drink in copious amounts, even paying with watches and other valuables.
11. […] It is not known how the Jews die in the camp. There are three assumptions: (1) via electricity, (2) via gas, (3) via air extraction by means of suction pumps.

Re: (1) There is no viable electricity source.

Re: (2) No deliveries of gas have been noted, nor any effects from residual gas following the ventilation of gassed premises.

Re: (3) There is nothing to contradict this assumption. However, there is confirmation that during construction, the walls and floor of one of the barracks were lined with thick metal sheeting (presumably intentionally).

Large trenches were dug on the camp premises in the autumn.[7] It was assumed that these would be underground storage spaces. However, the purpose of this work has since been clarified. From the sealed barracks to which undressed Jews are taken, allegedly for disinfection, a narrow-gauge train track leads to these trenches. Jews have been seen transporting their 'disinfected' kinsmen to a common grave along this track.

The term 'Totenlager'[8] has been heard in Bełżec, used in relation to the camp for Jews. The management of the camp is in the hands of twelve SS men (the commandant is Hauptmann Wirth),[9] with forty men from the Selbstschutz to assist them.[10]

## DOC. 67
## In April 1942, 13-year-old Sara Widawska and 10-year-old Hejnoch Jarzębski describe their experiences since the beginning of the war[1]

Handwritten transcripts of oral interviews for the underground archive of the Warsaw ghetto, Warsaw, April 1942 or later

Widawska, Sara, 13 years old, from Konstantynów, near Łódź, was in the fourth year at school. Daughter of Moszek and Frajda, née Mostów. Father: owner of a small grocery store. They lived in their own home, with two rooms and a kitchen. She had four sisters.

6 German in the original, 'self-protection'. This is probably a reference to non-German auxiliary personnel from the SS training camp at Trawniki, who guarded the extermination camp: see Introduction, p. 43.

7 The construction of the killing centre on the site of Belzec labour camp began in November 1941.

8 German in the original: 'camp of the dead'.

9 Christian Wirth (1885–1944), police officer; served with the police from 1910; joined the NSDAP in 1922 and again in 1931, the SA in 1933, and the SS in 1939; office manager at several of the murder facilities operating under the Nazi 'euthanasia' programme, 1940–1941; worked for the SS and Police Leader in Lublin from Sept. 1941; oversaw the construction of Belzec extermination camp and was its first commandant; inspector of the Operation Reinhard camps from August 1942; involved in murder operations in the Trieste area from Sept. 1943; thought to have been shot dead by partisans near Rijeka.

10 The figures here appear to be too low and are more likely to have been around 25 and 120 respectively.

1 AŻIH, Ring I/678 (44), fols. 13 and 11. The file contains reports by eight children between the ages of 10 and 15 years old. Published in Sakowska et al. (eds.), *Archiwum Ringelbluma: Konspiracyjne Archiwum Getta Warszawy*, vol. 2: *Dzieci – tajne nauczanie w getcie warszawskim*, ed. Ruta Sakowska (Warsaw: Żydowski Instytut Historyczny, 2000), pp. 48–49, facsimile p. 56; pp. 51–52, facsimile p. 60. Both documents have been translated from Polish.

They moved us from Konstantynów to Łowicz (she doesn't remember on what date),[2] where we stayed for one year. Papa worked in the soup kitchen there, and we had something to live on. In Konstantynów they gave us one hour to pack our belongings, but you can't do that in an hour, so we got on a cart and left for Łowicz. After a year, the same thing happened again – they expelled us to Warsaw.[3] We went by bus. We lived at the point[4] at 64 Żelazna.

Father couldn't earn any money in Warsaw. He was strong at first, but there was no work. Mother cleaned apartments. That's when the bad times started. In December 1941 things got so bad that Papa swelled up from hunger and had to lie down in bed, and one day when he got up to go and ask acquaintances for help, he collapsed in the street and died. Mama lost her job because she grew weaker and weaker. She died of hunger four weeks after my father's death. We five sisters were left. We lived on whatever the caregivers at the point gave us, but it was too little. In the meantime, two sisters died of ulcers at the point (she does not remember the dates).

2)[5] What were the worst experiences? The hunger at the point and the lice, which tormented us. The sleeping conditions were terrible – seven people on two plank beds. It was stuffy.

3) What were the most pleasant experiences? At home. In the morning we washed ourselves at home; in front of the house we had an orchard; the flowers smelled nice. It was so nice on Friday evenings!

4) What is war? During the war, people starve, 'they beat each other up'. Countries have quarrelled with each other.

5) Plans for the future? (She thinks for a long time.) [To be a] seamstress.

Hejnoch Jarzębski, 10 years old, parents Jankiel and Perle, née Sztejnwasser, was born and lived in Pustelnik.[6] The father was a cobbler, employed two workers, worked at home, died in 1937. The mother worked as a laundress after the father's death.

The siblings – two brothers and two sisters – were maintained by the eldest brother, who was married.

At the beginning of the war, we were doing well. We traded in bread – the brothers baked it, we sold it. Later I also went from village to village and collected bread and groats from the farmers; they were happy to give it to me free of charge. I never knew hunger.

In April 1942 we were expelled from Pustelnik. One day, we didn't suspect anything, gendarmes and policemen came at 5 a.m., surrounded our ghetto, ordered us to bring our belongings to the courtyard, then doused them all with petrol and set fire to all our belongings.

Before that, the gendarmes had gone through the buildings with revolvers and ordered everyone to get dressed and leave their apartment within five minutes. Those who

2 The Jewish residents of Konstantynów were expelled to the General Government on 22 Dec. 1939.

3 From Feb. 1941 a total of 300 Jews were expelled from Łowicz to Warsaw daily.

4 Here and below, 'point' is a reference to shelters providing emergency accommodation for Jews, tens of thousands of whom were expelled to the Warsaw ghetto from the annexed western Polish territories and the small localities in District Warsaw from 1939.

5 Numbering as in the original.

6 Several hundred Jews from the neighbouring villages of Marki and Pustelnik (10 km north of Warsaw) were expelled to the Warsaw ghetto in March 1942.

did not manage to do so were killed. That's how they killed our rabbi and his son, who were [still] half asleep.[7]

We got on the carts provided and left for Warsaw. Many of our people fled to farmers along the way and hid there.

Along with my sister I came to the orphanage at 12 Śliska.[8]

A sad experience? Mother's death.

A pleasant experience? Staying with my married brother; he took great care of me.

What is war? War is when there is nothing to eat, when you are tortured, when they don't allow you to leave the ghetto. I would have liked to go to my goyim;[9] they would have helped me.

Plans for the future? I will become a cobbler, like my father and my brother.

## DOC. 68

## On 3 May 1942 the Jewish Council in Gniewoszów holds a secret meeting to discuss how to save the Jews from an impending murder operation[1]

Minutes of a secret meeting of the Jewish Council in Gniewoszów,[2] Gniewoszów village, dated 3 May 1942 (copy)[3]

Minutes no. 2

The secret meeting of the 'Judenrad'[4] in Gniewoszów, held on 3 May 1942 downstairs in the Jewish synagogue, was attended by the Jewish Council – fifteen people – as well as members of the local council of the community of Sarnów in Gniewoszów: Dr Kiełczyński;[5] Paciorek, Bolesław; Dr Janiszewski, Karol;[6] Dr Kuzior, Franciszek;[7] Skotrupski, Józef; Łęcki, Jan; the chairman of the Jewish Council, Rabbi Lewin; and the secretary, Kuropatwa, Josef; the writer and journalist Tochterman; and Fr[yderyk]

7 On the night before the expulsion, approximately 170 people were murdered in the Pustelnik ghetto.

8 Correctly: 9. The orphanage run by Dr Henryk Goldszmit (Janusz Korczak) was located at this address from late Oct. 1941, after having to relocate from 33 Chłodna Street: see also Doc. 97.

9 Plural of *goy* (Hebrew), 'gentile'.

1 The whereabouts of the original are unknown. The text is taken from a transcript dated 19 May 1977, which is held at the Kozienice Regional Museum (Muzeum Regionalny w Kozienicach) in Gniewoszów. Published in Alina Skibińska, 'Życie codzienne Żydów v Kozienicach pod okupacją niemiecką', *Zagłada Żydów*, vol. 3 (2007), pp. 64–85, here pp. 84–85. This document has been translated from Polish.

2 Prior to Sept. 1939 a total of 1,580 Jews lived in the community of Gniewoszów (on the Vistula river in the eastern part of District Radom), which included the village of Granica. In August 1942 a total of 600 people were sent to labour camps, and the rest were sent to Zwoleń, from where they were deported to Treblinka on 15 Nov. 1942.

3 The stamp of the local council of the community of Gniewoszów has been added at the bottom of the document.

4 German in the original, correctly: 'Judenrat' ('Jewish Council').

5 Presumably Bronisław Kiełczyński (b. 1901), physician.

6 Karoł Janiszewski (b. 1904), physician.

7 Franciszek Kuzior, veterinarian from the Poznań area.

Winnykamień.[8] Agenda points: (1) opening address, (2) acts of sabotage, (3) saving the Jewish population from extermination, (4) motions from the floor, (5) discussion.

Point 1: the opening address was delivered in Polish by Rabbi Lewin, the head of the Jewish Community. He informed those present about the subject of the meeting and asked that it be kept secret. Then he gave the floor to Tochterman, who said regarding point 2: We Jews who feel that we are Polish citizens, together with the existing underground organization B.Ch,[9] have a duty to make life difficult for the German occupiers in all areas of economic life, even under the threat of death. He encouraged the young people, the 'Judenjungen',[10] to join the Jewish 'Sternjungen'[11] of the Orthodox and Zionist underground organization. Point 3: Tochterman went on to say that the Jewish population is threatened with annihilation. To save our lives, he said, we should strive to escape the ghetto. We should hide among the Polish population and earn our living by doing all sorts of agricultural work for free. To avoid being exposed, we must shave off our beards and any other hair, such as sidelocks, and wear the same work clothes as the farmers. False papers must be obtained, if at all possible: birth certificates with Catholic names, kennkarty, and ausweisy,[12] and the gentlemen from the local council of the community can help us with this. Point 5: Kuropatwa,[13] Kiełczyński, Janiszewski, Porębski, Lewin, and others participated in the discussion. Kuropatwa advocated hiding Jews among the Polish population, saying that this would be the best way for people to save themselves. After that Fryderyk Winnykamień spoke, saying it would be best to issue Kennkarty with Polish names to the Jewish population. Tochterman came forward and asked how Winnykamień intended to do this. Winnykamień replied: I will make them with the help of the stamp that is actually used [for the cards], 'Kreishauptmann in Radom-Land',[14] and the forms will be provided for us by Mr Bolesław Paciorek[15] from the community, who has large quantities of them at his disposal; the number of forms is not strictly monitored. Mr Paciorek says he can supply several thousand of these forms because he has a very large number of them. Tochterman said that Winnykamién's idea was very good and asked how he intended to implement it. Winnykamién replied that

8 Fryderyk Winnykamień, later Frederick Weinstein (b. 1922), apprentice; in Nov. 1942 escaped from Łódź to Warsaw, where he was a forced labourer; fled to Gniewoszów in Oct. 1940; lived in the Warsaw ghetto, mid 1942 – Feb. 1943; then went into hiding on the 'Aryan side'; worked under a false identity as an interpreter for German troops, 1944–1945; emigrated to the USA in 1946; author of *Aufzeichnungen aus dem Versteck: Erlebnisse eines polnischen Juden 1939–1946* (Berlin: Lukas Verlag für Kunst- und Geistesgeschichte, 2006).

9 Bataliony Chłopskie (Peasant Battalions), an armed resistance organization originally founded in 1940 by the underground Peasants' Party (Stronnictwo Ludowe, SL); it operated under this name from spring 1941. Franciszek Kamiński (1902–2000) was their commander. Bataliony Chłopskie's first attacks on the German occupiers were carried out in the Zamość region in the second half of 1942.

10 German in the original: 'Jewish boys'.

11 German in the original: 'Star boys'.

12 Here and below, German in the original with a Polish ending. Correctly: *Kennkarten* and *Ausweise*: 'identity cards' and 'identity documents'.

13 Josef Kuropatwa was from Gniewoszów and was secretary of its Jewish Council; he was murdered at the age of 39.

14 German in the original.

15 Bolesław Paciorek, worked for the community of Gniewoszów; helped members of the Winnykamień family by providing them with information and identity documents as well as arranging possible hiding places for them.

he is a student at the technical college for precision engineering in Łódź, and that during the week he can engrave a rubber stamp like the one the Germans use, and then he will issue false Kennkarty to anyone who wants them, and Mr Paciorek will supply the forms. Together we will issue identity cards in the names of Poles who are already deceased or who no longer live here. With this, the meeting ended.

B. Paciorek, Kuropatwa, Lewin, illegible signatures.[16]

## DOC. 69
## On 4 and 7 May 1942 Josef Gelbart describes the miserable conditions in the Warsaw ghetto[1]

Letter from Josef Gelbart,[2] Warsaw, 34/52 Miła Street, to Hans Stockmar,[3] Kaltenkirchen/Holstein, dated 4 and 7 May 1942

My dear, loyal boss, dear Stockmar family,

What must you all think of me, giving you such poor thanks for all your concern and hardly being in touch? Your last postcard and mine crossed in the mail, and I hope mine has reached you. In fact, I have no idea at all what I've written to you in the past few months. These past days I've had a constant fever; even when I was up and about and seemingly in good health. But this past winter has exhausted my strength, and heaven only knows whether my shattered life can ever be mended again. Spring keeps us waiting far too long this year, and we've not had a single balmy day yet – but perhaps, perhaps the sun's first warming rays will succeed in banishing a bit of the gloom and weakness. Today I don't have much to report that would not be very bitter.

Forgive me, please, for talking so much about myself and my misfortune, but it gives me a little relief, you know. When the body is sick, the soul is surely sick too, and you have always been a good therapist to me, dear Mr Stockmar!

It is hard to give a faithful report of what has been happening lately; it is almost impossible, at least for me and at this time. One would have to wield the pen of a Dostoevsky.

16 In this transcript the signatures are simply listed. The statement at the end of the transcript reads: 'I confirm that this transcript is a true copy of the original [illegible signature], Gniewoszów, 19 May 1977'.

1 The original is in the possession of the writer's family in Israel. Copy in YVA, O-75/1126. Published in abridged form in Josef Gelbart, *'Ach, es ist alles ohne Ufer …': Briefe aus dem Warschauer Ghetto*, ed. Konrad Plieninger and Karl-Heinz Rueß, 2nd edn (Göppingen: Jüdisches Museum Göppingen, 2002). This document has been translated from German.

2 Josef 'Jupp' Gelbart (1914–1942), beekeeper's apprentice; was severely hearing-impaired; spent his childhood in Altona and Hamburg, where he attended the Talmud-Tora-School; deported from Germany to Poland with his mother in Oct. 1938; imprisoned in Zbąszyń (Neu-Bentschen) camp, then moved to Otwock; lived in Warsaw from mid 1939, and later in the Warsaw ghetto. His father, Jakob Gelbart (1894–1940), a tailor, perished in 1940 after being deported to Sachsenhausen concentration camp.

3 Hans Stockmar (1890–1961), businessman; adherent of anthroposophy; Josef Gelbart's former employer; lived in New Zealand for a few years, then in 1921 settled in Kaltenkirchen, where he set up honeybee colonies and a candle-making business; honoured as Righteous Among the Nations by the State of Israel in 2001.

Even today I am unable to give a chronological report – only fragments. Maybe a more pleasant day will come soon, and then I'll write again.

It is not inconceivable that my hopelessness is a product of what I have endured, that it is fear of what is to come, but I do think typhus has shattered our lives. Mine and, in turn, my mother's.[4] I am stunned by this, seeing as tens of thousands of people around me are healthy and steady on their feet, although they often lack the bare necessities. And whenever I just can't get the melody of 'Es wird ein Wein sein und ich werd nimmer sein' out of my head[5] (I'm almost sentimental, in accordance with the season!), it raises Job's age-old question, too: 'Why me?' And when I think back and try to get to the bottom of it, I see simply an accumulation of unforeseen events, and this winter this accumulation *had to* turn into a catastrophe for both of us (as well as for my aunt and uncle). And the peculiar thing is that I knew all of it *in advance*. It was all pretty clear – and of course I tried to escape fate (by moving to a different apartment, for example), but I always felt like I was in a game of nine men's morris[6] with two unevenly matched players: the poorer player keeps thinking he is about to make a good move – and then his piece is taken out of the game because his opponent forms a mill.

I had barely recovered from my boil when I came down with a fever and body aches. Later, in hospital, a blood test revealed that I had been suffering from epidemic typhus, probably contracted during my aunt's illness. When the doctor came two weeks later, he advised me to go to hospital, which I did, if only to escape the sanitary shortcomings of our quarters. In addition, my mother did not exactly have any energy to spare (and my long illness then exhausted her completely). By the way, she's really not as old as you think, dear Mr Stockmar; she's only 49. So I went straight to hospital – it's so easy to write, but later on I would like to send you a little record of it. Maybe: 'I Go to Hospital' or 'How I Went to Hospital' or 'Three Weeks in Hospital'. I'll keep it short and sweet today, or better, short and not so sweet: the treatment did not agree with me. I left the hospital only apparently restored to health and got mixed up in the toughest days of the war; no matter which move I made or wanted to make: a mill was formed! The situation today is that we are both on our feet, and all our hopes are pinned on this war being over this summer. I don't believe it will be, but maybe a miracle will occur.

I myself am as debilitated as it is possible to be, and the main things that prevent me from recovering are the severe aches and pains in my body, probably inflammation of the gallbladder, and swollen tonsils. Oh, it really is nauseating to write about; this is an absolutely awful letter I'm jotting down here. My wish has always been to write about things 'as they are', but this inevitably fails, as it is impossible. I would have to report on so many factors: my friends, my landlord (who sold everything he had left over these

4 Frieda Gelbart, née Feigen (Faigin) (1892–1942), housewife; born in Złoczów; settled in Altona with her husband, Jakob, in 1913; deported to Poland in 1938.

5 Correctly: 'Es wird a Wein sein, und mir wer'n nimmer sein' (There will be wine, but we won't be around any more); a popular song in Viennese dialect in the Schrammelmusik tradition, sung by Hans Moser.

6 This board game involves strategically lining up three of one's own pieces in a horizontal or a vertical line to form a 'mill'. A player who forms a mill has the right to remove one of the opponent's pieces from play. A player has won the game once the opponent can no longer form a mill, i.e. has only two pieces left.

past weeks and will nonetheless starve in the coming weeks, along with his family), my aunt and uncle, who are both working in a tailor's workshop! The two of them don't mean a great deal to us, but being ill has brought us a bit closer in the end. They own only the clothes on their backs, and although they are at work almost twelve hours a day (soldiers' uniforms etc.), what they earn doesn't suffice to buy enough dry bread. It's like this: as long as you're healthy and can keep your life in balance, you can get by on the minimum for quite a while. On the day in late autumn when my mother came back from the soup kitchen in the evening and said, 'Josef, I think I'm running a temperature', everything collapsed. The extremely harsh winter, the decaying apartment, and so much more besides wore down our strength and our will to live.

7 May 1942
Several days have now gone by, and I want to finish this letter at last. Today the sun is shining for the first time, and there is a sense of spring. I had focused all my willpower on being stronger by the time this season arrived, so I could work outdoors, but now everything is hopeless. My friends have no way at all to help, and life has become very, very hard here. Admittedly there is hardly anything that could not be obtained in exchange for money, but everything costs twice as much as it did during my mother's illness. Nonetheless, I've had everything I could wish for nowadays, and even now we don't lack the necessities. If I could only get well – I'm such a dreadfully impatient person! Yet I'm not in great pain, only when I have eaten something (of course I can't follow a special diet), I start to feel pressure and spluttering and bloating on the right side of my body, and it makes life hell for me, keeps me from getting up. I also worry about the days to come, as I think they'll determine whether I am to be or not to be. It's possible that part of the population will have to leave Warsaw. We don't yet know anything for sure, but we often hear that this concerns those who came here after the war [started]. (We both registered here two to three months before the war broke out.) Many other things must be decided, and I want to keep you (and also Bernhard[7]) informed as long as it's still possible.

The day my aunt was able to get out of bed again for the first time, she received a Red Cross message from her son in Palestine, saying he was living very happily in a settlement by the Sea of Galilee. Unfortunately there's been no news at all so far from my otherwise very resourceful brother.

You surely remember Fräulein Mast from Mannheim, who once briefly corresponded with you. I also received a Red Cross enquiry from her, from the camp in the south of France. Her mother succumbed to pneumonia right after arriving, and her sister is always ill, but she herself is in engaged in her 'usual activity'. This may be of peripheral interest to you, as you never close your mind to other people's fates.

7 Bernhard Gelbart (later: Dan Gelbart, 1918–2000), Josef's brother; supported his mother and brother in Zbąszyń camp; trained as a graphic artist; active in the Zionist organization Habonim as a young man; accompanied a Youth Aliyah group to Poland in 1938; organized the emigration of Jewish children with documents he forged himself as a member of Hehalutz in Lithuania in 1940; travelled to Iran and then onwards to Palestine with a Zionist group in 1941; thereafter settled on a kibbutz near Haifa.

This past week I received the long-awaited parcel from you, and I was very glad that again everything was in order (trousers, two bars of soap, lecithin, lemons, and glucose). I thank you again with all my heart. There is at least *one* worry we have not had in recent months: we did not lack our daily bread, and every few days my mother sent a little pot of hearty food to the hospital, along with butter and lard. I have you to thank for those, too.

In general, clothing is not as profitable as it used to be, because there are just too many people offering their clothes for sale, but it is the only thing that enables us to hold out. I know, dear Mr Stockmar, that if you could sow the land with trousers for me, even your rock garden would have to make way for this purpose. (Isn't that so?) It grieves me that it had to come to this, and you must forgive me if I can only repay you, once again, with letters full of new bitterness. 'The darkest hour is just before the dawn', you once told me. I thought that hour was already past. I will leave your last letter still unanswered. First I have to see what the man upstairs has planned for me: odd or even.

Thank God, these sheets of paper are full now, so I *must* stop painting my inadequate picture. I may have talked about myself far too much today, and I'd really have preferred to hear a lot of good news about you and all of your loved ones. Whether or not you can continue to hold your protecting hand over us, I never want to lose your friendship and warmth. It is strange that, in the hours of greatest need, there is hardly any path open to me here; my best friends are not within my reach, and nature and the works of man appear to be exhausted.

My regards to you, also from my mother, who joins me in assuring you of our most profound gratitude.

With best wishes,

Jupp

P.S. Should it ever happen to be possible for you to acquire some discarded bedlinen, allow me to note that this is the 'fastest-selling item' at the present time. (My pen is reluctant to write this; if only it would all end.)

## DOC. 70

## On 8 May 1942 Emanuel Ringelblum writes about developments inside and outside the Warsaw ghetto[1]

Handwritten diary of Emanuel Ringelblum, entry dated 8 May 1942

8 May 1942. The mood on the street has improved slightly since the massacre on 18 April (when fifty-two people were shot in the streets).[2] People have calmed down and become a little [more] optimistic. They are once again starting to believe that the war will be over in a few months and that they will be able to go back to normal life. The good mood is also due to the fake communiqués that have been circulating ever since the real ones stopped appearing after the Friday slaughter. Some cunning tricksters (probably unem-

1 AŻIH, Ring I/445 (503/1), fols. 17–22. Published in Ringelblum, *Ksovim fun geto*, vol. 1, pp. 345–351. This document has been translated from Yiddish

2 See Doc. 64.

ployed journalists) have been found who get paid to produce and circulate these communiqués full of lies. What do these communiqués say? First that Smolensk has been taken – thanks to the 60,000 soldiers who landed and joined the Russian army west of Smolensk. This communiqué also states that Kharkov has been taken. Then, according to the communiqué, an entire army arrived in Murmansk on 160 ships, not one of which was sunk. Of course Hitler fainted when he heard about it (this was after his speech on 1 May). Add to this a victory at Lake Ilmen where, according to the communiqué, 43,000 soldiers fell and more than 80,000 were taken prisoner. This is said to have happened to the 19th Army, with two German generals allegedly taken prisoner. As if this were not enough, they killed off Mussolini and fabricated a revolution in Italy. On top of all this is an ultimatum from Roosevelt to the German people with a 15 May deadline. In short, the Jewish population is [not] content with only reciting a chapter of the Psalms,[3] but invents stories that destroy the enemy and achieve peace as quickly as possible.

When will the war really end? The Jews cannot hold out any longer and therefore want to see it end it as quickly as possible, at any price. People are voicing serious opinions that the situation in Germany is reminiscent of 1918, referring to statements made by German acquaintances and news provided by German Jews deported to Warsaw. These Jews report that Germany has recently been inundated with illegal leaflets, so-called circulars, calling on the soldiers, the workers, the intelligentsia, and the masses to stage a revolt against the regime. Further evidence is seen in the four or five illegal radio stations, as well as the poor supply situation. Letters from Germany – encoded, of course – also describe immense discontent. The final argument that the war will end soon is based on a guy called Czerwiec[4] and the fortune teller Madame M. The Jew Czerwiec, who lives on Nalewki Street, predicted the war with Russia in the month of June. When asked what else is going to happen, he predicted that the Germans would be brought to a standstill in November and unable to advance even one step, so people nicknamed him Listopad.[5] Later on they started calling him Luty[6] because he predicted that things would get tough for the Germans in February. Now they're back to calling him Czerwiec again, since he has said that the war with the Germans will end in June.

Madame M., a fortune teller, is a trainee lawyer who lost her husband, a Warsaw lawyer, during the war. She knew about it eleven months in advance, but there is no escaping fate, she says. A few months before the war, she dictated to one of her followers – the wife of a lawyer – details about the outbreak of the war (the exact date) and a description of the bombardment, the destruction of the electricity plant, as well as the lack of gas, electricity, and water. She is said to have predicted other events later on. I know that two or three months prior to November 1941, she predicted that the German army would suffer a defeat in Russia in the second half of November and would not advance any further. Later she predicted very hard times for the Jews. Now she predicts that in June there will be no more [ghetto] walls in Warsaw, but Jews will still live there. [She claims] Jews in Warsaw will not be deported, but very difficult times lie ahead for

3 Psalms are recited at dire moments when people are gravely ill or in danger and fear imminent death.
4 Polish for the month of June.
5 Polish for the month of November.
6 Polish for the month of February.

them. The Germans will incite the Polish population against them. A three-day pogrom will take place, but those who survive will live to see deliverance.

Massacres similar to the one that took place on Friday, 18 April,[7] have occurred in a number of cities throughout the [General] Government. There are reports of such massacres in Cracow, Tarnów, Częstochowa, Radom, Kielce, Ostrowiec, and other places. In each case around 50 people were killed. These murders also took place on the streets at night, although the details differ. In some cities those who came from Russia and were thought to be communists were taken. Everywhere the local authorities stated that they knew nothing about it, had not made any lists, etc. In some cities arrests were made at the same time. Those arrested were deported, and to this day no one knows to where. Among others, Diament,[8] the chairman of the Community in Radom, and his deputy, Merin,[9] were arrested. Based on all of this, it follows that the Community leaders' assertion that the massacre in Warsaw was the result of illegal publications is a lie. Rather, the reason was a general one: during his last visit, Himmler must have issued an order to carry out massacres everywhere in order to strike fear into the hearts of the Jewish population.[10] This was probably also connected to the spring offensive, during which [the Germans] wanted a secure 'rear'. Therefore they needed to dole out a dose of terror to ensure that people would not become overconfident.

The first days of May and the last days of the month of April were marked by fear of deportation. No one knows where the rumour came from. Some say the Polish merchants spread it so that the Jewish population would start selling off their belongings. People even talked about a figure of 150,000 to 200,000 deportees and went so far as to state the direction [of the transports]: Romania. The rumours that unproductive elements would be deported came about due to the orders of the kitchen department at the KOM[11] that only working people would be fed there. People took this as a sign that the unproductive elements were to be eliminated from Warsaw. Community leaders have assured us that the danger of deportation which hovered over our heads has now passed, because there are workshops in the ghetto which provide for the German army's needs. It is a tragic predicament. Jews have a right to live only if they work to supply the German army's needs. This was the case in Vilna, Równe, and dozens of other cities where mass slaughters of the Jewish population occurred. Only those who directly or indirectly worked for

7 18 April 1942 was a Saturday. Presumably Ringelblum means the night of 17 to 18 April.

8 Józef Diament (1894–1942), bookkeeper; came from the assimilated Jewish community in Radom; co-owner of an iron foundry; from late Sept. 1939 chairman of the Jewish Social Self-Help Committee (JSS) in Radom, which was transformed under the German occupation into the 'united' Council of Elders of the Jewish Population in District Radom (Ober-Ältestenrat der jüdischen Bevölkerung des Distrikts Radom). In the other General Government districts, Councils of Elders were to be established in each Jewish community. District Radom was unique in having a 'united' Council of Elders to represent the entire Jewish population within its borders. Diament was arrested and deported to Auschwitz in late April 1942.

9 Aron Merin, deputy chairman of the Jewish Council in Radom; brother of Moshe Merin, who was the head of the Central Office of the Councils of Elders of the Jewish Religious Communities in East Upper Silesia (Zagłębie).

10 Himmler had visited the ghetto on the evening of 17 April 1942, which gave rise to numerous rumours in the ghetto.

11 Komitet Opiekuńczy Miejski; officially the municipal Jewish Aid Committee, but actually the local JSS branch.

the Germans remained alive. In all of history, no nation has experienced such a tragedy before. A people that hates the Germans with all of its 248 limbs[12] can save itself from death only at the price of helping the enemy achieve victory – a victory that spells the Jews' complete annihilation from the face of Europe, and possibly the whole world.

The Warsaw ghetto is indeed hard at work for the Germans: workers here mend and alter dead soldiers' clothes; they are already preparing lined trousers, vests, and men's jackets for winter; they manufacture straw shoes, furniture, etc. The centre of all of this is the Többens firm at 12 Prosta Street, where more than 1,000 workers are employed. As is typical, several riding crops of different sizes and strengths hang on the wall in the reception room belonging to Bauch, the factory manager.[13] Apparently these are implements that no German can do without. They are symbols of the bloodthirsty Hitlerism that one encounters everywhere – in the concentration camp, in the labour camp, in prison, and even at work.

People tell the following typical story, which gives us an idea of the Polish Jews' attitude to charity. Two years ago the rebbe of Radzyń wrote to his Hasidim in Lublin that they should sell their furniture and donate the proceeds to charity. He explained that he knows they have no business any more and therefore have no money, which is why they should sell their furniture. The Hasidim did not obey him and did not sell their furniture. The Germans [subsequently] confiscated the furniture from almost all the homes in Lublin. Then the rebbe wrote to the Hasidim, telling them to sell their furs and donate the proceeds to charity. Again the Hasidim disobeyed him, and the Germans came and confiscated all their furs. Next the rebbe wrote to the Hasidim that they should sell their Sabbath clothes and use the proceeds for charity. The Hasidim did not do that either, and the Jews were expelled from Lublin.

A typical smuggling incident occurred two or three days ago (5–6 May 1942). The corner building at 21 Franciszkańska Street, right at the [ghetto] wall, is a smuggling hub. A ladder is lowered down the wall of the building, and goods are smuggled over on a grand scale all night long. However, the smugglers fought among themselves and denounced each other. Gendarmes came that night and caught them in the thick of it. They opened fire with machine guns, shooting one smuggler dead on the spot and wounding one or two others. Then they searched all the apartments, seized a lot of goods, and arrested forty smugglers. The next day, however, the big shots made peace. For the price of 40,000 złoty, the goods that had been seized were returned and the smugglers were released. The gendarmes demanded this sum as compensation for the losses they suffered due to the fact that the smuggling was conducted over the wall and not through the watch, from which the gendarmes could have taken a cut.

12 Drawing on rabbinic texts, Judaism teaches that the human body consists of 248 limbs, to which the 248 positive commandments to perform specific acts correspond. (The remaining 365 negative commandments to refrain from specific acts are said to correspond to the same number of sinews and ligaments or nerves.) Thus the phrase conveys two meanings: that the hatred is boundless, and that it contains religious overtones.

13 Rudolf Bauch (1888–1976), sales representative; joined the NSDAP in 1937; managed the tailors' workshops for the Többens company in the Warsaw ghetto from Oct. 1941; according to Jewish eyewitness accounts, sent the children of people who worked for him to the Umschlagplatz in July 1942; involved in the murder of inmates in Poniatowa camp in 1943; after the war lived in Hanover, and later in Remscheid.

Most of the smuggling now takes place via the guarded checkpoints. The price is 100 złoty for a haul. The wagoner has to know the password, or he won't get through. There are gendarmes who make up to 2,000 złoty in two hours. However, smuggling still goes on over the walls [of buildings at the ghetto perimeter]. It claims victims – people wounded and killed – almost every day. Even minors and children are often killed. Among the gendarmes there is one who has become famous as a decent German. They call him 'the gentleman'. He takes no bribes and [nonetheless] lets carts with merchandise pass. He also lets through dozens of Jewish children who buy [goods] on the other side, mostly potatoes and other vegetables. Every day people share extraordinary stories of his kindness and decency. He pulls various stunts with the child smugglers. He will line them up in rows, order them to sing, and march them over in a great parade. The inspectors can be bought too. Not long ago an entire wagon of smuggled goods was 'burned' (i.e. seized). However, 200 złoty was enough to persuade the inspector to let the wagon into the ghetto. It is no coincidence that, as the saying goes, there are three things that cannot be defeated: the German army, the island of Britain, and Jewish smuggling.

It is said that Churchill invited the Gerer rebbe[14] to visit him and asked his advice on how to conquer Germany. The rebbe gave the following answer: there are two ways – the natural way and the miraculous way. The natural way: a million angels with flaming swords will descend upon Germany and destroy it. The miraculous way: a million English soldiers will land in Germany and destroy it.

The ghetto is now being filmed. Filming went on for two days at the Jewish prison and in the Community [administrative offices]. On Smocza Street a bunch of Jews were rounded up, and the Jewish policemen were ordered to disperse them. At another location they staged a Jewish policeman who wanted to beat a Jew and a German who came to the assaulted Jew's aid and wouldn't let him be beaten.

There is a German sign at the cemetery, written in large letters, forbidding the Germans to visit the Jewish cemetery. Supposedly the reason has to do with hygiene, but in reality it has to do with something else. Lots of Germans would come to the cemetery to look at the notorious shed where piles of the dead lie every day – skeletons found in the streets or the poorest, those who died of hunger, candidates for the mass graves. During such visits the Germans would get to talking about the Jewish question. There were some who took pleasure in seeing the victims of the Hitlerian extermination policy, while others expressed their outrage, saying 'so that's German culture'. It turns out that these excursions had a devastating effect on the visitors, which is why they have been abolished.

14 Avrom Mordkhe Alter (Abraham Mordechai Alter) (1866–1948); known as the Gerer rebbe; third rabbi of the Hasidic dynasty in Góra Kalwaria (Yiddish: Ger); co-founder of Agudas Yisroel in Poland; visited Palestine in 1924; fled Poland in 1940; died in Jerusalem.

## DOC. 71
## On 9 May 1942 the General Government's Interior Administration Main Department advocates banning Jews from leaving the ghettos[1]

Statement for the GG government, Cracow, from the Department of Police Affairs (Dr Doe[ring][2]/Ci., II S 4/42), dated 9 May 1942[3]

*Explanatory statement*[4]
The prevailing legal situation concerning bans and restrictions on the freedom of movement was no longer satisfactory in practice. Experience showed that it was necessary to tighten the law, and above all to extend its scope. Particular consideration was given to the increasingly frequent cases in which Reich citizens behaved so improperly in the General Government that the reputation of Germandom and the Reich was seriously damaged as a result. Other factors that prompted the revision include political considerations that have made the possibility of a more aggressive use of bans seem desirable. Above all, however, the Jewish question has been the strongest argument in favour of a new version in two respects. First, illicit trade, black-market dealings, etc. have increased again. Second, it has been proven that the Jews specifically, and their begging children in particular, have significantly contributed to the spread of typhus. Over and above the restrictions now in place, it would also be necessary to extend the compulsory visible identification to Jewish children. This point is subject to further negotiations.

In contrast to the first draft,[5] the current wording[6] not only reflects a consideration of all the salient points expressed in the first draft, but also formally includes certain adjustments and alignments that have proven expedient from a legal standpoint.

The current version of the regulation deliberately avoids stating grounds for restrictions and bans on freedom of movement.[7] It leaves [the task of] assessing the overall behaviour of the person concerned to the authority in charge. An exhaustive list of grounds would be impossible to compile – especially today, when things are still in flux and the general state of affairs could give rise to new reasons for such orders at any time. Such a list would incur the risk that deportations, made absolutely necessary based on the relevant circumstances, could not be carried out because the grounds for doing so

1 AIPN, GK 196/335, fols. 146–150 (96–100). Copy in BArch, R 52 II/255, fols. 70–74. This document has been translated from German.
2 Dr Heinz Doering (1894–1972), lawyer; joined the NSDAP in 1933; Regierungsrat in 1926; Landrat in Schrobenhausen in 1938; lived in Mühldorf from 1939; section head in the Police Affairs Division of the General Government's Interior Administration Main Department from May 1942; Kreishauptmann of Opatów, August 1943 – August 1944; thereafter Landrat in Aussig; interned, 1945–1948; member of the Communist Party of Germany (KPD) until around 1952, when he retired.
3 The original contains handwritten corrections.
4 This is a reference to the draft of a regulation on restrictions on freedom of movement in the General Government, which is mentioned in the following paragraph.
5 See the draft Dr Schroth prepared for the General Government's Department of Legislation at State Secretary Bühler's behest, dated 20 Jan. 1942: AIPN, GK 196/335, fol. 107r–v.
6 The second draft of a regulation on restrictions on freedom of movement in the General Government, consisting of ten sections and written by Doering, is part of the file: AIPN, GK 196/335, fols. 141–145.
7 See Doc. 13.

had not been included in the regulation. A list of examples of the most important issues will be included in the planned implementing instructions for the regulation. The appeals option provided for in the draft still offers protection against arbitrary measures.

Jurisdiction has been completely reconfigured. This was primarily motivated by the Führer's recently issued decree on simplifying the administration, which stipulates that authority is to be ceded to lower bodies wherever possible, and that appeals procedures are to be made swifter and simpler.[8] The other decisive factor was the idea that the speed is particularly important, especially in these cases, to ensure that the unwanted persons in question can be removed as quickly as possible and thus prevented from causing more harm with their behaviour. Therefore, as a general rule, the Kreishauptleute and the Stadthauptleute were declared to be the relevant authorities, specifically for all forms of expulsion and restrictions on freedom of movement, even when, for example, the expulsion is intended to encompass the entire territory of the General Government. This arrangement will save a great deal of work, but above all the office that has the closest practical involvement with these matters, that has a direct overview of them, and can therefore best assess them, will be designated as the responsible authority. The concerns of the Security Police are taken into account by the fact that its commanders will also be able to take the planned measures themselves in urgent cases. It is entirely possible that the Security Police will know of activities not yet known to the Kreishauptmann or the Stadthauptmann at the time. If such cases permit no delay, and that will often be the case, then the commanders should also have the authority to take action on their own initiative. The instructions will stipulate that the commanders must inform the responsible Kreishauptleute and Stadthauptleute after the fact of the action taken. For both of the relevant offices, an appeals procedure is envisaged as a counterweight to this arrangement. However, an appeal will not delay the enforcement of the measures ordered, which means that any potential stalling tactics will be prevented. For the same reason, any appeal must be made within a two-week cut-off period. In either case, appeals cannot be taken further than to the next level of authority. The entire arrangement is consistent with the legal situation in the Reich.

When it comes to restrictions and bans on freedom of movement for groups of persons, however, the District Governor had to be put in charge because these cases always concern regional, mainly military, or general political interests, into which the Kreishauptmann or the Stadthauptmann is generally unlikely to have sufficiently in-depth insight – for example, clearing sizeable areas to create space for military training or resettling entire ethnic groups. Of course the legally established rights of the Reich Commissioner for the Strengthening of Germandom will remain unaffected by the regulation, particularly when it comes to resettling Germans. It also goes without saying that the General Government's central offices will still be able to claim jurisdiction over appropriate cases. For example, this could apply to cases in which entire ethnic groups are to be resettled.

The draft regulation also aims to move the Jewish question another step forward by tightening the provisions to the maximum extent possible. The draft is intended to end

8 Streamlining the administration was an effort to free up men for the Wehrmacht and to further the mission of total war: see the Führer's decree on the further simplification of administration, dated 25 Jan. 1942, in Moll (ed.), *'Führer-Erlasse' 1939–1945*, pp. 231–233.

the practice of Jews residing or living permanently outside the ghetto ('assigned residential district') altogether. It should be possible to accomplish this even now, as a fair number of such Jewish residential districts already exist, and new ones will not be difficult to establish, should they be needed. Therefore, in order to gain control over these vermin as effectively as possible, the regulation aims to ensure that all Jews in the General Government, without exception, are housed in such 'residential districts'. The implementing instructions for the regulation will also contain guidelines specifying that such Jewish residential districts are to be set up only in cities and not in rural areas, if at all possible. The regulation also aims to lighten the load for the criminal courts and to create legal clarity, as it considerably alleviates the burden of proof for judges in criminal cases: no proof is needed other than the fact that the Jew was found outside the residential district assigned to him, the boundaries of which are readily discernible. This will eliminate all the standard excuses. While the regulation in general is effective immediately, a period of four weeks in which to establish the residential districts and move [people] into [them] has been granted in order to facilitate the transition for the authorities in charge and to allow for the coercive measures most likely needed in many cases. As a general rule, the Kreishauptleute and the Stadthauptleute should grant exemptions from the obligation to remain in the residential district and permission for non-Jews to enter the residential districts only in exceptional situations. This authorization has the sole purpose of enabling Jewish labour deployment and any other use of Jews outside the residential district. Permission may be granted only in cases in which it serves an urgent public need. Therefore private interests may not be cited as justification for granting such exemptions, either for Jews or for non-Jews.

The punishments established for the Jews and their accomplices are as severe as possible in order to prevent the administration of justice from lapsing in cases that are seen as relatively minor, and to prevent the increased application of prison sentences rather than the death penalty. This approach is intended to counter the nuisance of vagrant Jews, and particularly by Jewish children begging, which has once again become increasingly common. Should the death penalty ever seem too harsh in a rare individual case, the defendant can still be pardoned.

Jurisdiction over these matters has been distributed in such a way as to allow for swift, thorough action, free of all the standard operating procedures, whenever Jews commit an offence. Standard legal procedures are open to non-Jews, except in cases in which they allow the Jews to use them as helpers. In such cases, the non-Jew may deserve an even harsher punishment than the Jew.

With regard to § 1(5), the instructions will additionally clarify that assets should generally be confiscated only if the person concerned has committed serious offences, and that this measure should generally never be used against Germans.[9]

9 § 5 of the same draft regulation states: 'Along with the ban, the person concerned may be obliged to leave their belongings behind, either in whole or to an extent to be specified in the directive, at their previous residence or temporary abode without any compensation': AIPN, GK 196/335, fol. 141. A fourth regulation on restrictions and bans on freedom of movement was discussed for several months but was never issued because the ghettos were being liquidated by means of the mass murder of the residents.

## DOC. 72
## On 9 May 1942 departments of the civil administration in the General Government order a survey of Jewish skilled workers and their current employment status[1]

Letter (marked 'very urgent') from the GG government, Population and Welfare Division, signed Weirauch (telex no. 128), Cracow, to the Governor of District Lublin, Interior Administration Department, Lublin, dated 9 May 1942[2]

A full and detailed list of the Jewish craftsmen and skilled workers in your District must be submitted to me by *16 May* 1942.[3] The list should be organized by Kreis, with the name of the Kreis indicated. Within this breakdown, the number of Jewish craftsmen and skilled workers in the Jewish residential districts is to be presented separately, with the specific ghetto indicated. The total number of craftsmen and skilled workers should be given, subdivided according to the following occupational groups: metalworkers, textile workers, leatherworkers, construction workers, woodworkers, glassworkers, engine mechanics, hairdressers. The numbers for the respective occupational groups are to be subdivided into how many of these craftsmen and skilled workers are involved in work essential to the war effort, and how many are immediately available because they are not deployed in such work or are unemployed. The list should include all Jewish craftsmen and skilled workers in the aforementioned occupational groups who are under the age of 55, with men and women listed separately.

[It][4] has not escaped our notice that producing the required list may involve substantial difficulties in view of the short time period allotted. [However,] it is absolutely essential to the war effort that the deadline is met.

[The] list is to be prepared by the Kreishauptleute and the Stadthauptleute, if necessary by involving the Jewish councils and Jewish relief committees.

1 APL, 498/893, fols. 128–129. This document has been translated from German.

2 The original contains handwritten notes and underlining.

3 This telex was sent in conjunction with a directive from the Labour Main Department in the General Government, which ordered a 'one-time registration of the Jews deployed for labour'. The directive was sent to the employment offices and, for information only, to the labour departments in the districts on 9 May 1942, along with a preprinted reporting form: APL, 498/907, fol. 1; written replies from the Kreise can be found in IfZ-Archives, Fb 96/6.

4 Here and below, illegible words in the left-hand margin of the document have been filled in with the help of a copy: APL, 498/893, fol. 127.

## DOC. 73

## On 11 May 1942 State Secretary Bühler informs General Government officials of plans to liquidate the ghettos and points out the potential risks to the economy[1]

Minutes of the fifth working meeting of the main department heads of the GG government in Cracow, 11 May 1942

[…][2]

Labour deployment

According to State Secretary Dr *Bühler*, new information indicates that there are plans to liquidate the Jewish ghettos, retain the Jews who are fit for work, and deport the others further to the East. The Jews who are fit for work are to be housed in several large concentration camps located at the centres of production. He noted that while these plans may seem very attractive at first, those who are more familiar with the circumstances will unfailingly come to the conclusion that, if these plans are implemented, the harm caused by the destruction of the present forms of organization will be many times worse than any expected benefits of such a measure. At any rate, in his view such a strategy would bring no relief at present. The hope that such a measure would, for example, free up larger numbers of Polish labourers for the Reich will almost certainly not materialize, he believes. A survey of the 27,000 armaments workers has revealed that only forty-two had voluntarily signed up for work in Germany. But if the intention is to use police coercion, then the result would be that many of the workers would simply stop showing up for work out of fear of being taken away to the Reich.

A further proposal from the Reich is to carry out raids in the larger cities to round up people in the street. The hope is to obtain 52,000 workers with such a measure. All such suggestions are utterly absurd,[3] he commented, and if such steps were really taken, they would, with absolute certainty, jeopardize the supplies for the front.

[…][4]

1 AIPN, GK 95, vol. 24. Copy in IfZ-Archives, Fb 105, vol. 22, fols. 5107–5121, here: fol. 5110. This document has been translated from German.

2 The minutes are 14 pages long. First, Karl Naumann, head of the Food and Agriculture Main Department, gave an overview of the new prices for agricultural products; then State Secretary Josef Bühler spoke about the security situation in the General Government; next, Department Head Adolf Gerteis described attacks on railway transports by Polish resistance groups; Bühler added that such attacks were also affecting agriculture and labour deployment.

3 Poles were in fact rounded up in the street, arrested, and deported to Germany for forced labour from 1940.

4 In the following section, Bühler spoke about an administrative reform in the General Government and reminded the attendees to adhere more closely to the rules of confidentiality; then further questions were discussed: improving the food supply for Polish domestic workers in the homes of ethnic Germans, transferring money from the Reich to General Government officials, bringing the families of Eastern Railway officials to the General Government, and the need for a law on expropriating land.

## DOC. 74

## On 11 May 1942 the Bund reports on the systematic mass murder of the Jewish population and calls for measures to end it[1]

Report by the Bund, unsigned,[2] Warsaw, 11 May 1942

Letter from the Bund regarding the persecution of Jews, dated 11 May 1942, sent by post on 21 May 1942[3]

With the outbreak of the Russo-German war, the Germans began the physical extermination of the Jewish population in the Polish territories.[4] They have used Ukrainians and Lithuanian Shaulis men for this purpose. It began in summer 1941, especially in Eastern Galicia. The procedure was the same everywhere: men between the ages of 14 and 60 were rounded up in one place, in a square or a cemetery, where they were slaughtered or gunned down with bullets or grenades. They had to dig their own graves. Children from the orphanages, residents of homes for the elderly, and the sick at the hospitals were also shot; women were killed in the streets. In many towns the Jews were taken away to an unknown destination and murdered in the surrounding forests. In Lwów 30,000 Jews were murdered, 15,000 in Stanisławów, 5,000 in Tarnopol, 2,000 in Złoczów, 4,000 in Brzezany (18,000 Jews used to live in this city, now 1,700). The same thing happened in Zborów, Kołomyja, Stryj, Sambor, Drohobycz, Zbaraż, Przemyślany, Kuty, Sniatyń, Zaleszczyki, Brody, Przemyśl, Rawa Ruska, and other places.

The killing operations were repeated several times in these towns. In many places, such as Lwów, they are still going on.

In October and November the same thing began to happen in Vilna, in the Vilna region, and throughout Kaunas Lithuania.[5] In Vilna 50,000 Jews were murdered in November. There are currently 12,000 Jews in Vilna. According to various estimates, the total number of Jews butchered in the Vilna region and Kaunas Lithuania is 300,000.

1 AAN, 1325/202/XV-2, fol. 30r–v; SPP, Teka 15/26. Facsimile and English translation published in Yehuda Bauer, 'When Did They Know?', *Midstream*, vol. 14, no. 4 (1968), pp. 61–69. This document has been newly translated from Polish.

2 The author is thought to have been Dr Leon Feiner, code name Mikołaj or Berezowski (1885–1945), lawyer; practised law in Cracow; member of the Bund's Central Committee; city councillor from 1937; fled east in Sept. 1939; imprisoned in Lida; escaped during the German attack on the Soviet Union. When the Bund joined the Jewish Combat Organization (ŻOB), Feiner was appointed Bund representative on the 'Aryan side', and together with Abraham Berman formed the coordinating committee for contacts with the Polish underground; he drafted and forwarded most of the Bund's reports and messages on the Jews in Poland to London and the United States. From Jan. 1943 to July 1944, Feiner was deputy chairman of Żegota (the Polish Council to Aid Jews), and he was its chairman from Nov. 1944 to Jan. 1945.

3 The document has no title, and this line is handwritten at the top. Sven Norman, a Swedish employee of the Asea company in Warsaw, received the report in Warsaw on 21 May 1942, took it to Stockholm, and handed it over to Mieczysław Thugutt, an intermediary for the Polish intelligence service, who sent it to London, where it arrived on 31 May 1942.

4 See PMJ 7, for example Docs. 23, 27, 46, 48, 55, and 68.

5 Litwa Kowieńska, term used by Poles who opposed the existence of a Lithuanian national state and considered Vilna to be Polish.

The murder of Jews in the area around Słonim began in September. Almost all the Jews in Zyrowicze, Lachowize, Mira, Kosów, and other places were murdered.[6] The operation in Słonim began on 15 October. More than 9,000 Jews were murdered. In Równe the killing began in the first days of November. Over the course of just three days and nights, more than 15,000 people were shot – men, women, and children. In Hancewicze, near Baranowicze, 6,000 Jews were shot. The operation to murder the Jews took place across all the Polish territories beyond the San and Bug rivers. We have only mentioned a few of the places.

In November and December the murders also began in the areas annexed to the Reich, the so-called Warthegau. Here the murders were carried out with gas, for example in the village of Chełmno, 12 km from Koło (powiat Koło). A special van (a gas chamber) was used for this, into which ninety people were loaded at a time. The victims were buried in special graves in a clearing in the Lubardz forest.[7] In this case as well, Jews dug the graves and buried the gassed victims; at the end of each day, they were shot by SS men with machine guns. An average of 1,000 people were gassed every day. Between November 1941 and March 1942, a total of 5,000 Jews from Koło, Dabie, Bugaj, and Izbica Kujawska were gassed, plus 35,000 Jews from the Łódź ghetto and a certain number of Gypsies.

In February 1942 the extermination of the Jews in the territory of the so-called General Government commenced. It started in Tarnów and Radom, where the Gestapo and SS men visited the Jewish districts daily and killed Jews systematically in the streets, in courtyards, and in apartments. The mass resettlement of Jews from Lublin began in March. Children and the elderly from orphanages and homes for the elderly, as well as the sick in the general hospital and the hospital for infectious diseases, were brutally murdered along with many people in the streets and inside their homes. The total number of victims exceeded 2,000. Approximately 25,000 Jews were taken from Lublin in sealed goods wagons to an 'unknown destination', and no trace of them has been found. Approximately 3,000 Jews were housed in barracks in Majdan Tatarski on the outskirts of Lublin. There is not a single Jew left in Lublin. In the final days of March, more than 50 Jews (according to a list) in Cracow were taken out and shot in front of the city gates.[8] The Gestapo organized a night of bloodshed in the Warsaw ghetto on the night of 17–18 April. Working through a list of names, they dragged more than 50 Jewish men and women out of their apartments and brutally murdered them in front of the entrances.[9] They did not find many of them in their apartments. Since 18 April they have been killing a few Jews each day, now in broad daylight, inside the apartments and in the streets. This operation is carried out on the basis of a list that covers every Jewish neighbourhood in the Warsaw ghetto. There is talk of more bloody nights to come. According to estimates, the Germans have killed 700,000 Polish Jews thus far.

The above facts irrefutably prove that the criminal German government has begun to implement Hitler's announcement that he would murder all the Jews in Europe five min-

6 See Doc. 43.

7 The place where the corpses were buried is known today as Rzuchów Forest (Rzuchowski las).

8 On 19 March 1942 the German police carried out an operation targeting Jewish intellectuals, during which 50 prominent figures were arrested, taken to Auschwitz, and murdered.

9 See Doc. 64.

utes before the end of the war, regardless of its outcome.[10] We firmly believe that Nazi Germany will ultimately be held accountable for its savagery and brutality. This is not much of a consolation for the Jewish population, which is going through an unbelievable ordeal. Millions of Polish citizens of Jewish nationality are threatened with immediate extermination. We therefore call upon the Polish government, as the guardian and representative of the entire population inhabiting Polish territory, to take the necessary steps to prevent the extermination of Polish Jewry immediately. To this end, the Polish government must exert its influence over the governments of the allied states and the powers that be in these countries in order to pursue an immediate policy of retaliation against German citizens and members of the fifth column[11] who live in the territories belonging to the allied states and those in alliance with them. The Polish government and the governments of the allied states should inform the German government about the policy of retaliation. It must know that the Germans living in the USA and other countries are already being held accountable for the brutal extermination of the Jewish population.[12]

We are aware that we are asking the Polish government to take unusual steps. This is the only way to save millions of Jews from inevitable extermination.

## DOC. 75

## On 12 May 1942 the Interior Administration Department in District Galicia asks the SS and Police Leader to deport the family members of Jews taken away for forced labour[1]

Letter (marked 'confidential') from the Interior Administration Department (I/Ha, file ref. A308/700/42), signed Bauer, to the SS and Police Leader for Galicia[2] in Lemberg (received by the Kreishauptmann of Lemberg-Land[3] on 14 May 1942), Lemberg, dated 12 May 1942 (carbon copy)

*Re: resettling* Jews

As a result of concentrating almost 1,100 Jews who are fit for work from the towns of Sadowa-Wisznia, Grodek, Janow, Jaworow, and the surrounding villages [in forced labour camps] a number of Jewish families have lost their breadwinners. Since the Jewish

10 This is probably a reference to Hitler's speech in the Reichstag on 30 Jan. 1939: see PMJ 2/248.

11 This term was coined in 1936, during the Spanish Civil War. In Britain, 'fifth column' was used in 1939–1940 to refer to citizens of hostile foreign countries who were to be interned.

12 In a joint declaration, delivered on 17/18 Dec. 1942 at the instigation of the Polish Ministry of Foreign Affairs, the Allies condemned the German government's 'bestial policy of cold-blooded extermination' but did not announce any concrete measures against the mass murder of Jews: Republic of Poland, Ministry of Foreign Affairs, *The Mass Extermination of Jews in German Occupied Poland: Note Addressed to the Governments of the United Nations on December 10th, 1942, and other Documents* (London: Hutchinson & Co., 1942), p. 12.

1 DALO, R-24/1/123, fol. 98. Copy in USHMM, Acc. 1995.A.1086, reel 20. This document has been translated from German.

2 Friedrich (Fritz) Katzmann (1906–1957), carpenter; joined the SA in 1927, the SS in 1928, and the NSDAP in 1930; member of Duisburg City Council, 1933–1934; full-time SS officer from 1934; member of Berlin City Council from 1936; leader of SS Subdistrict VI in Breslau in 1938; SS and Police Leader in Radom from Nov. 1939 to August 1941, then SS and Police Leader in Galicia; leader of SS District Weichsel in Danzig from April 1943; lived under an assumed name in West Germany, lastly in Darmstadt, after the war.

councils have almost no welfare resources left, the families who have been left behind are now a burden on the welfare programmes provided by the municipalities.

In view of the limited financial resources of the municipal administrations, which are only just being established, I must request that the towns listed above be included, if possible, when the resettlement of Jews resumes. I would also like to request that the Kreishauptmann in Lemberg-Land be informed on what date and at which stations wagons can be made available for deporting the remaining families who have been put forward for resettlement.[4]

## DOC. 76

### *Der Ruf*, 15 May 1942: the Anti-Fascist Bloc calls on the Jewish population to take up the struggle against the German occupiers[1]

*Jewish masses!*

We are standing on the threshold of major events and extremely decisive battles. Throughout the winter the Red Army attacked fiercely, forcing the fascist enemy to retreat from numerous occupied regions, dealing him mighty blows, destroying his plans, and forcing him to dispatch to the front all those forces that were meant to be used for the spring offensive Hitler announced. Huge, well-trained, and well-equipped armies alongside vast reserves from Soviet Russia stand ready for further attack. Soviet industry is working tirelessly, with all of its energy concentrated on the fight, paving the way to victory. Behind the lines of the German army, the partisan movement – which is growing ever larger and stronger – has sprung up and is practising diversion and sabotage.

Hitler was forced to admit that the collapse of the German army was prevented only by summoning the last bit of physical and moral strength.[2] The German soldier sheds his blood at the front only under pressure from the frightful terror of the SS machinery. At the same time the German population, already worn down by the constant air raids, must deal with the further tightening of food rations. Instead of bread, they are fed promises of a swift victory that grows more distant by the day.

Given the setbacks at the front and the feeling of uncertainty in the occupied territories, the fascist beasts have once again tightened the rope they have placed around the necks of the subjugated peoples. A gruesome operation is under way to physically eradicate the

3 The head of District Galicia's Interior Administration Department, Otto Bauer, simultaneously served as Kreishauptmann of Kreis Lemberg-Land; the carbon copy was sent to his deputy, Dr Werner Becker (1905–1991), for information only.

4 The deportations from Kreis Lemberg-Land to Belzec resumed in August 1942.

1 *Der Ruf*, no. 1, 15 May 1942, pp. 1–2; AŻIH, I/1332 (677), fols. 2–3. *Der Ruf* was the official publication of the Anti-Fascist Bloc. Only this one issue has survived. This document has been translated from Yiddish.

2 In his speech at the Berlin Sportpalast on 30 Jan. 1942, Hitler spoke about the difficulties experienced in the first winter after the start of the war against the Soviet Union, and called on the 'homeland' (*Heimat*) to 'do all it can' to support the Wehrmacht: Max Domarus (ed.), *Hitler: Speeches and Proclamations, 1932–1945, and Commentary by a Contemporary. The Chronicle of a Dictatorship*, vol. 4: *The Years 1941 to 1945*, trans. Mary Fran Gilbert (Wauconda, IL: Bolchazy-Carducci, 2004 [German edn, 1965]), p. 2579. In his speech before the members of the Reichstag at the Kroll Opera House in Berlin on 26 April 1942, he took up this theme again: ibid., pp. 2622–2625.

most energetic forces in the occupied countries. In Yugoslavia, Norway, France, Belgium, and Holland, anti-fascist fighters and patriots are being subjected to mass murder.

With animalistic brutality the fascist occupier seeks to wipe out the freedom movement in Poland. The mass expulsions of Poles from the regions of Pomerania and Poznań, the mass murders of Polish peasants, the terrible way people in cities are systematically hunted down, the mass executions in Warsaw, the deportation of thousands upon thousands of victims to the death camp in Oświęcim – these are only [a few] individual episodes in the never-ending succession of the occupiers' violent acts in Poland.

With every day that passes, the bestial extermination campaign that the German occupier wages against the Jewish population also intensifies. Hitler regards the complete annihilation of the Jews of Europe as his historic mission and is now carrying out his bloody plans at an accelerated rate. Rivers of blood flow from the tortured Jewish masses. The bloody trail of Hitler's murderous gangs runs through Vilna, Słonim, Baranowicze, Chełmno, Lemberg, Lublin, and scores of other cities and shtetls. The merciless slaughter of tens of thousands of Jewish people; the mass murder of entire Jewish communities; the gassing of old people and children; and the shooting of women, sick people in hospitals, and children in orphanages – these are the Hitlerian executioners' exploits. They rush to carry out the bloody orders of their Führer so as not to lose any time, God forbid … The death by starvation of tens of thousands of Jews imprisoned behind ghetto walls and the bloody toll taken by typhus and tuberculosis are not enough for the Hitlerian executioners; they have to pick up the pace: murdering tens of thousands of Jews, shooting them, wiping entire Jewish settlements from the face of the earth – that will bring them closer to their goal.

Nevertheless, the Jewish masses must not succumb to feelings of despair and despondence, or passively await whatever fate brings them; rather, they must gather all of their strength and join the anti-fascist struggle waged by all oppressed peoples. Just like these others, they must take up the bloody fight against the enemy, especially behind the front lines. A battle of annihilation and sabotage. Through action, the Jewish masses must assume a worthy place in this very struggle of oppressed peoples against the fascists!

This struggle calls for unity and solidarity. The awareness that such unity is crucial has already taken deep root among wide swathes of the Jewish masses. But there are also those who choose to wait for a miracle. They do not want to believe that fighting is the only path that will lead to freedom and salvation. They still do not understand that now is the time to combine all [of our] forces to fight the bloody occupier, that this moment calls for *establishing a national freedom front by cementing and unifying the people's full strength to take on the enemy!*

Jewish masses! Jewish workers! Jewish intelligentsia! Jewish youth! Join forces and unite in battle! Stand as one, shoulder to shoulder, as a united front in the struggle against fascism!

Only the destruction of Hitler's powerful war machine by anti-fascist armies and the masses of oppressed peoples who have banded with them will finally put an end to our enslavement and create the conditions for the complete social and national liberation of the Jewish masses!

All the robust strength of the Jewish people must now be united [to work] towards a single aim: the fight for freedom and salvation, the fight against the fascist enemy, until ultimate victory [is achieved]!

## DOC. 77

## *Tagespost* (Graz), 15 May 1942: article on the economic output in the Warsaw ghetto[1]

*Warsaw's Jewish district supports itself. It has its own freight transfer depot for the exchange of goods. The exchange is regulated by the Transfer Bureau. From our own correspondent.*

Warsaw office, 14 May
The Jewish residential district in Warsaw also includes a so-called freight transfer depot through which this city of 500,000 Israelites conducts its economic dealings with the outside world. This is where the food deliveries for the Jewish population arrive, and the products from the workshops in the Jewish district also pass through here. From the flow of goods and the lively activity in the area around the station at certain hours, one can surmise that the German administration has achieved what seemed impossible to previous governments, or what these governments never seriously attempted: to engage the masses of Warsaw's Jews, half a million in number, in productive work.

The Jewish residential district in the former Polish capital, where the Jews had clustered densely in recent decades because they had sensed, and indeed found, particularly enticing commercial opportunities there, was first created as part of the effort to combat epidemic diseases, particularly typhus, so that the Jews, as direct carriers of this disease, could be separated from the rest of the population. Its other purpose was to eliminate the noxious economic effect the Jews had on the Poles. The intention was not to paralyse Jewish economic potential and labour power and so turn the Jewish population into paupers. Rather, the objective was to make productive use of these 500,000 Jews.

And to a great extent, this is what the Transfer Bureau, which today directs all economic affairs in the Jewish residential district in accordance with overarching considerations, has managed to achieve. Under the leadership of the commissioner for the Jewish residential district,[2] its task was first to create a sufficient number of workshops to hold the workforce. This was made easier by the fact that many Polish Jews have technical training and have worked in many of the crafts and skilled trades. To give just two examples, more than 80 per cent of all textile craftsmen in the Warsaw Chamber of Crafts district were Jews, while the manufacture of shoe uppers in Warsaw was entirely in Jewish hands. Of course the Jewish craftsman cannot deliver real precision work, but he can certainly be put to use in the garment industry, in dressing and preparing furs, in making fashion accessories, and in the production of basic commodities from remnants and waste materials.

The question of setting up the workshops was not an easy one to resolve; special methods had to be employed in view of the large population in the Jewish residential district. In some instances special-order contracts were used, and in others machinery

1 *Tagespost* (Graz), 15 May 1942, p. 2. The *Tagespost* was published from 1856 to 1945. It then became the official newspaper of the Austrian People's Party, first under the name *Steirerblatt* and then, from 1951 to 1987, as the *Süd-Ost Tagespost*. In 1942 it was published by the NS-Gauverlag und Druckerei Steiermark GmbH under Dr Julius Keil, the publishing director; Alfred Püllmann, the editor-in-chief; or Püllmann's deputy, Dr Hermann Schneider, while Püllmann was serving in the war. This document has been translated from German.
2 Heinz Auerswald.

and buildings were purchased to set up suitable production facilities. This even made it possible to turn small craft workshops into large businesses with a workforce of several thousand. Of course these businesses were only viable if the Jewish workers performed to the requisite level. To ensure this, the individual employee or craftsman was given the opportunity to earn extra money. The piecework system, for example, proved a success in this respect, and a bonus system also proved useful. Moreover, the working Jew is put in a far more favourable position than his idle fellow Jew in terms of both food and welfare benefits, which he receives to a certain extent. The very fact that the Jewish residential district in Warsaw is today able to support itself on the proceeds of its own labour is proof that this course was the correct one.[3]

To give one example: a textile factory with a Jewish workforce of 3,500 people was created in a former school. The staff there work under the direction of three Germans, and their output includes various pieces of equipment [for making] textiles as well as children's clothing. The work is done partly by hand, partly by machine. A physician is in charge of supervising the Jewish workforce's health. A second large enterprise makes fur waistcoats, fur coats, and the like, and simultaneously operates a shoemaking company. This enterprise employs 1,500 Jews as furriers and shoemakers. A smaller Jewish workshop does metalwork. The staff of sixty work in the metal-plating workshop, the punching room, and the welding shop. Another enterprise produces straw shoes. This work is performed almost exclusively by Jewish women. On average, one worker weaves between 80 and 150 metres of straw ribbon per day. This ribbon is then rolled over wooden moulds and sewn to make straw shoes.

The sum total of this work can regularly be seen at the freight transfer depot, when long lines of railway wagons arrive and depart, and many hands are busy loading the goods. This depot, where the Jewish section is marked off by an elongated storage shed with large loading ramps stretching along the lateral sides, is simultaneously the checkpoint for all goods leaving the Jewish district. These goods are completely free of any flaws – also when it comes to hygiene – when they enter the marketplace.

## DOC. 78

## On 1 June 1942 an anonymous author writes a letter in code with information about the extermination camps in Sobibor and Treblinka[1]

Letter by an anonymous author in Włodawa[2] to friends in Warsaw (copy),[3] dated 1 June 1942

A letter from Włodawa[4]

… We are healthy, thank God. We don't know what to do about going to the doctor.[5] We are unable to find a solution on our own. We had decided to go to the doctor, but

3 On the decision regarding the deployment of forced labour in the ghetto, see PMJ 4/263.

1 AŻIH, Ring I/1054 (563). Published as a facsimile and in Polish translation in Sakowska (ed.), *Archiwum Ringelbluma: Konspiracyjne Archiwum Getta Warszawy*, vol. 1: *Listy o Zagładzie*, pp. 152–155. This document has been translated from Yiddish.

[now] Uncle[6] wants to host his children's celebration among you too – God forbid; he is renting an apartment right near you.[7] Perhaps you don't know anything about this.

That is why I am writing to you now, and we are sending [this letter] expressly by messenger so that you know. It's true that you are also meant to rent new apartments outside the city, along with all of our brothers, the children of Israel. And he [Uncle] has already prepared a new dwelling for everyone – the same as the one near us.[8] It's possible you don't know about this. I am writing to you especially so you do know, because Uncle wants to expel Adam[9] and wants you to be united – God forbid – with Shloyme Velvl, may he rest in peace.

We know for certain that Uncle will soon finish [building] the dwelling near you. You need to know that. Perhaps you have an idea [about what to do]. In any case, know that Uncle wants to organize a wedding[10] where you are soon, and he has already prepared housing very close to you.

Remember: remain in your apartments whatever you do, lest you be united with Shloyme Velvl, may he rest in peace. The only good remedy for this illness is dwelling in the covert.[11]

Remember that we are martyrs and that which remains of us until the morning etc.[12]

2 Over 6,000 Jews lived in Włodawa. In April 1940 the Germans ordered the creation of a Jewish Council, and from Jan. 1941 the Jewish population was forced to live in a ghetto. Jewish expellees, including those from Mielec and Vienna, were transported to the Włodawa ghetto. The occupation authorities deported numerous ghetto inhabitants to Sobibor on 23 May 1942.

3 Incomplete copy from the underground archive of the Warsaw ghetto.

4 The heading was added by the person who made a copy of the letter.

5 Code name for the Warsaw ghetto, which was considered safe up to that point.

6 Code name for the German occupiers.

7 Allusion to the construction of Treblinka, which was built around 80 km north-east of Warsaw, not far from the railway line to Białystok in the eastern part of District Warsaw.

8 Allusion to Sobibor, south-east of Włodawa in the eastern part of District Lublin.

9 Quotation from Genesis 3:24. In the original context it refers to God driving Adam out of the Garden of Eden. Here it is a play on words, as the first name Adam also means 'man' or 'human'.

10 Code for mass slaughter.

11 The original draws on a quote from Psalm 91:1 ('O thou that dwellest in the covert of the Most High, and abidest in the shadow of the Almighty') to indicate that the recipients should go into hiding. This biblical quotation is based on the JPS 1917 edition.

12 A slight adaptation of Exodus 12:10, alluding to burning the bodies of murdered people: 'And ye shall let nothing of it remain until the morning; but that which remaineth of it until the morning ye shall burn with fire'.

## DOC. 79

## On 31 May and 3 June 1942 Chaim Kaplan records what he has heard about the murder of the Jews of Lublin[1]

Handwritten diary of Chaim Kaplan, entries for 31 May and 3 June 1942

31 May 1942

We racked our brains over Lublin:[2] Why did the Nazis treat this city with so much greater cruelty and brutality than any of the other cities of the 'Generalgouvernement'? Well, the veil has been lifted a little! Today's *Warschauer Zeitung* newspaper published a letter from Lublin by some literary hooligan.[3] You'll find something of everything in it: reportage full of lies, fallacies, and falsified science. The article is a sword in the heart of Polish Jewry, all of it poison. It's all the nauseating prattle of some hack who doesn't know up from down when it comes to his subject matter. Everything is based on zoological[4] hatred that warps what's straight and falsifies historical facts. The article in question, however, has one merit: it reveals in passing something of the reason for the Lublin deportation.

This moronic Nazi takes Lublin for the spiritual centre of Polish Jewry, from which a web of ideological, Talmudic, and legal ties extends to all of world Jewry. These ties endanger all Aryan peoples and therefore must be severed. And historical facts also help this Nazi to substantiate this view. The Council of Four Lands[5] held its meetings in Lublin; Yeshivat Chachmei Lublin[6] is a Talmudic academy from which thousands of students have scattered all over the world and who now hold the reins of spiritual leadership throughout the Diaspora. They are, in effect, spiritual conduits that carry the pernicious spirit of the Talmud to all Jewish communities. Yeshivat Chachmei Lublin is indeed the fetid, stinking Talmudic well from which its students, the ideological agents of world Jewry, drink. And so it continues in this vein all the way to the end.

Therefore, get rid of this 'stinking' yeshiva! Block the filthy well that quenches the entire world's thirst with its pestilent waters.

1 USHMM, Collection 2 009 212, fols. 21–23. Published in Chaim Kaplan, *Megillat yissurin: Yoman getto varshah* (Tel Aviv: Am Oved, 1966), pp. 505–507. This document has been translated from Hebrew.

2 The Talmudic expression used here in the original for an unresolved problem is *teiku*, a short form of the Aramaic word *tikom*, which means 'will stand'. Because the answer to a question with which Talmudic sages have dealt is not known, the question 'will stand', i.e. will go unresolved. In addition, if read as an acronym קית"ו may also stand for the Hebrew words יבשת ץרתי תוישוק תויעבו, meaning the question will stand and remain unresolved until the day comes when the prophet Eliyahu HaTishbi will provide the answer to the question. (The source of the acronym and its meaning is unknown.)

3 Gustav Andraschko, 'Lehranstalt der Weisen Lublins', *Warschauer Zeitung*, 31 May 1942, p. 5.

4 As in the original. It is a reference to the Nazis' racist description of Jews as 'subhuman'.

5 Kaplan is reflecting here on Lublin's significance in the early modern era. The Council of Four Lands, also known as the Four Lands Sejm and by the Hebrew name Va'ad Arba' Aratzot, was the highest-ranking institution of Jewish self-government in the four parts of Poland–Lithuania between 1580 and 1764.

6 Talmud-Torah Academy of the Sages of Lublin.

And the Nazi has won the prize of being the one who undertakes this handiwork for the good of the world's nations.

And the thousands who were killed, butchered, and incinerated – for what? It's a teiku![7]

By night – slaughter; by day – the hunt!
Two days ago, there was a hunt on the ghetto streets. The Jewish police chased down young Jews and left them like birds ensnared in a trap. No sooner had they been caught than they were put onto a Jewish bus and hauled under the strictest guard to the former military prison building, now the Jewish lock-up.[8] Awaiting their arrival there was Auerswald – the commissioner for ghetto affairs – and three Jewish doctors. Everyone who had been rounded up was examined. Those deemed healthy and strong were taken aside and sent to a labour camp. Where? People are of two minds: some say Germany and others say Estonia.[9] And those deemed weak or ill were released. In the meantime, a new source of bribes – and of subsistence – has opened up for the Jewish police.[10]

Nazism does not recognize the individual Jew, but only the Jewish collective and its agent, the kehilla.[11] When the Nazi authority needs several hundred young Jews for gruelling labour, discharged after some time shattered, frazzled, and dejected, he turns to the commissioner for ghetto affairs, who turns to the 'kehilla'. And the kehilla does a nice business with this. When the Nazi orders it to supply 400 young men, the kehilla goes the extra mile and hunts down 800: 400 for the Nazi, and 400 for bribes. When commotion erupts, everyone wants to flee. So those who are detained are willing to give everything they have to secure their freedom. And the police aren't too particular about it: 'One gives a lot, the other gives a little!'[12] All that matters is 'dawaj!'[13] There have been cases where people were released for ten złoty, a sum that doesn't even suffice to buy a whole loaf of bread. But either way, both sides get something out of it.

Long live the war!!! …

3 June 1942
Polish Jewry is heading for ruin. The 'Führer's' watchword – the total annihilation of Europe's Jews – is steadily becoming a reality. Every day, entire communities are being uprooted from their lands and their people sent to their deaths. For these days are not

7 See fn. 2.
8 This is a reference to what was known as Gęsiówka, the Jewish Order Service's main detention centre.
9 Czerniaków suspected that those arrested were deported to Bobruisk in Byelorussia: *The Warsaw Diary of Adam Czerniakow*, p. 360. Ringelblum also believed Bobruisk was the destination of those who were deported and noted that they would be used as forced labourers by the Organization Todt: Ringelblum, *Ksovim fun geto*, vol. 1, pp. 369–370.
10 This can also mean: for the Jewish regime, i.e. for those who were in the service of the Jewish Council.
11 Hebrew word for 'community'; the term is used here to refer to the Jewish Council.
12 Reference to Berakhot 17a: 'Lest you say: I engage in Torah study a lot, while he only engages in Torah study a little, so I am better than he, it has already been taught: One who brings a substantial sacrifice and one who brings a meagre sacrifice have equal merit, as long as he directs his heart towards Heaven.'
13 Polish: 'give'.

like the first days. The first expulsions[14] were notable for their cruelty and for all the terrible misery and horrible disasters that come with such a categorical decree – but the expellees lived! All those forced into exile were permitted to go wherever their legs would carry them. They were admittedly given little time to leave, but the departure itself was unrestricted; the expellees could even choose where to live as they saw fit.

This is no longer the case: deportees are transported away in sealed and locked [goods] wagons under the watch of Nazi henchmen, and remain in the clutches of the angels of destruction until they reach the site of the gallows where they give up their souls. Many of the deportees – including mothers and their babies – are killed on the way, while the rest are taken to a hidden place that no falcon's eye has seen.[15] There they are escorted out of the world en masse, not individually, but by the thousands and tens of thousands. This is how the Lublin community perished. Some 40,000 Jews of Lublin disappeared and no one knows where they are buried. Aryan agents fanned out across the whole 'General Gouvernement' to search for traces of them and couldn't find a thing, as though they had plunged into mighty waters.[16] However, there is no doubt that they are no longer alive.

Lublin was the first to drink the cup of poison[17] to the bottom, but it is not the last. Since then, not a single day goes by without some Jewish town being wiped off the face of the earth. Włodawa![18] Tłuszcz![19] Both emptied out, down to the last Jew. The deportees were handed over to Nazi gendarmes, who exterminated them along the way. The Tsaddik[20] of Radzyń was put to death.

The beautiful girls and women were all taken aside and shot dead: 'Jews don't need beautiful women!' Mounted gendarmes showed the deportees the way. With premeditation, the horsemen spurred and prodded their horses to speed up as the hundreds of deportees who followed on foot were ordered not to lag behind. The galloping horses disappeared into the distance, trailed by a mass of shopkeepers, mothers with babies,

14 Kaplan is referring to the first expulsions that occurred shortly after the occupation of Poland, namely from the annexed territories to the General Government: see PMJ 4, pp. 38–44.

15 Reference to Job 28:7: 'That path no bird of prey knoweth, neither hath the falcon's eye seen it.'

16 Kaplan uses the biblical expression in the Song of the Sea, which depicts the drowning of the Egyptians in the Red Sea after the Israelites had crossed it when the sea split and left a dry path for them. See Exodus 15:10: 'Thou didst blow with Thy wind, the sea covered them; they sank as lead in the mighty waters.'

17 Reference to Isaiah 51:17 ('That hast drunk at the hand of the LORD, the cup of His fury; thou hast drunken the beaker, even the cup of staggering, and drained it') and 51:22 ('Behold, I have taken out of thy hand, the cup of staggering; the beaker, even the cup of My fury, thou shalt no more drink it again').

18 On 23 and 24 May 1942 the German police deported around 1,300 people from the Włodawa ghetto to nearby Sobibor.

19 The Germans liquidated the ghetto in the small town of Tłuszcz on 27 May 1942. While women and children were transported to Warsaw by train, the men had to walk the approximately 35 km route; over one hundred of them were shot dead during the trek.

20 Title meaning 'righteous one' for a Hasidic spiritual leader and highly respected Jewish religious scholar. This is likely a reference to the Rebbe of Radzyń, Shmuel Shloyme Layner, also known as Shmuel Shlomo Leiner and Szlomo Lajner (1914–1942), the founder of the Sod Yesharim Yeshiva in Radzyń, who urged his followers to rise up against the German occupiers. The Germans captured and executed him in May 1942 in front of the Włodawa synagogue. The Warsaw ghetto underground press reported in June 1942 on Layner's fate. It was then that the poet Yitskhok Katsenelson (Itzhak Katzenelson) composed 'Dos lid vegn radziner' ('Poem about the Radzyń rebbe') in the Warsaw ghetto. On Katsenelson, see Doc. 288, fn. 48.

the elderly with their canes, and all the provincial small-timers who had to make their way on foot and 'not lag behind'. The cruelty of it surpasses anything our history has known thus far!!

These 'communities' have also disappeared, and no one knows whether those deportees are still alive.

Something is going round that's a real joke: Rabbi Stephen Wise[21] ordered the 'El Maleh Rahamim'[22] prayer to be recited! For the ascent of the souls of Polish Jewry. Something inside him foresaw this.

Polish Jewry is facing annihilation!!

## DOC. 80

## On 18 June 1942 leading German occupation officials discuss the deportation of the Jews from the General Government to the extermination camps[1]

Minutes of the police meeting in Cracow, 18 June 1942

[…][2]

[Krüger] said it is very difficult to capture every individual partisan group. Above all the partisan leaders must be flushed out of their hiding places, and the tactics of the police, the gendarmerie, and the Wehrmacht must focus on thwarting the partisans' planned attacks wherever possible.

He noted that he had also spoken with the military commander[3] about the 250,000 *prisoners of war* who are to be moved through General Government territory over the next few weeks; they will be deloused and transported onwards. Naturally this also entails an increased level of danger. But the military commander will ensure the prisoners of war are secured and guarded in such a way during their unloading and reloading, as well as during their march to the camps and their time there, that it is hoped they can be properly transported on to the Reich, where they are to be used as labourers.

[…][4]

21 Stephen Samuel Wise (1874–1949), rabbi; founded the Free Synagogue in New York in 1907 and was a Reform rabbi there; helped draft the Balfour Declaration in 1917; vice president of the Zionist Organization of America, 1918–1920, then its president, 1936–1938; president of the World Jewish Congress, 1936–1949.

22 'God, full of mercy': the opening words of a Jewish prayer that is recited at funerals, on the anniversary of deaths, and when visiting graves or burial sites.

1 AIPN, GK 95, vol. 23. Copy in IfZ-Archives, Fb 105, vol. 22, fols. 5276–5323, here fols. 5288, 5291, 5302, 5305, 5311–5313, 5316, 5318. This document has been translated from German.

2 The original document is 44 pages long. At the start of the meeting, Governor General Frank discussed the agreement made with Himmler on the establishment of a state secretariat for security in the General Government; State Secretary Krüger then reported on the security situation.

3 Curt Ludwig Freiherr von Gienanth (1876–1961).

4 In the following section, Chief of Staff Engler from District Lublin reported that it had proven necessary to withdraw the managers of the Kreis-owned estates due to the partisan threat; Odilo Globocnik opposed such a step, and Governor General Frank also spoke in favour of upholding the 'authority of the state by all means possible'.

Oberregierungsrat Engler[5] then addressed the general situation in District Lublin. The *fields* have been *tilled*, he said. The harvest is expected to turn out better than last year, even though bandits pose a threat to it. The crops must be harvested very quickly, however.

The *administration of District Lublin* is managing with the officials at its disposal. Their performance is also satisfactory overall. The *health situation* has seen considerable improvement, and the typhus epidemic has subsided significantly. *Housing* for the Germans in Lublin is very limited, and it is very difficult to find appropriate accommodation for them. But so far it has always been possible to make the requisite living space available to the German officials and clerks, thanks to the housing office's good work. Theatrical performances, concerts, and film screenings have been arranged to satisfy the cultural needs of the Reich Germans.

When it comes to the *road network*, the situation is partly good, but also partly bad. Some roads are currently being improved, but the work is not proceeding very well.

The *Jewish question* in the city of Lublin has been resolved. The former Jewish quarter has been evacuated, and the Jews who are fit for work have been housed outside the city in a special district.[6] In addition, the Jews in District Lublin have been concentrated in ghettos. The impression is that restricting the Jews' freedom of movement has significantly improved the situation, especially with respect to black market dealings.

[…][7]

SS and Police Leader *Katzmann* elaborated on the *security situation* in District *Galicia* and stated that overall there is no cause for concern. Two police battalions are currently stationed in the district. There are a few trouble spots in the northern part of the district, but they will soon be pacified.

He noted that the Ukrainian police are not yet performing as expected, and the overall conclusion so far has been that the Polish policemen are far more useful. The training carried out in the new Lemberg police academy is beginning to show some results, but there have still been assaults of the kind that should be impermissible in a police officer.

The population is still favourably disposed towards the Germans. He requested that the planned reduction in food rations not be implemented for the time being.

*Jews* have already been evacuated in fairly large numbers. At present, 85,000 Jews are still living in Lemberg, 45,000 of whom have been integrated into the labour process. More Jews will be resettled over the coming weeks.

5 Wilhelm Engler (1880–1958), administrative official; member of Reichsbanner Schwarz-Rot-Gold prior to 1933; joined the NSDAP in 1937; worked for Baden Building Insurance from 1930; Landkommissar in Myślenice, 1939–1940; head of the Interior Administration of District Cracow, Jan. 1940 – August 1941; acting chief of staff in District Lublin until June 1943; thereafter worked in insurance again; classified as a 'follower' (*Mitläufer*) in denazification proceedings in 1948.

6 Most Jews from the Lublin ghetto were deported to Belzec; others who were classified as fit for work were deported to a new ghetto in Majdan Tatarski: see Doc. 74.

7 In the following section, Engler reported on the deportation of Polish workers to the Reich; Frank pressed for stricter measures to get them registered. Then Losacker, chief of staff in District Galicia, talked about reprivatization measures and the food situation in his district, and declared that, first and foremost, the removal of the Jews must be ensured in order to solve the problem of food being traded on the black market: IfZ-Archives, Fb 105, vol. 22, fol. 5296.

[...][8]

In contrast to previous evaluations,[9] the *ghetto* has been successfully spurred to economic activity to such an extent that no government subsidies have been necessary so far. Inside the ghetto, approximately 25,000 Jews are working in production critical to the war effort, while 3,000 Jews are deployed for work outside the ghetto. The second-largest fur business, which produces most of the furs needed by the Wehrmacht, has its production facility in the ghetto.[10] The monthly turnover between the ghetto and the Aryan residential district currently comes to 6 million; in addition, unrecorded turnover may amount to another 2 to 3 million. The ghetto inmates are making a meagre living from this turnover. He said that he hopes the city of Warsaw will be freed from the burden of Jews who are unfit for work in the foreseeable future.[11]

[...][12]

SS and Police Leader *von Sammern*[13] then turned to the *situation in Warsaw*. The police have to comb the city at regular intervals, he said. During an operation several days ago, 2,500 persons were stopped, and forty-four currency smugglers and several hundred idle persons were found and immediately put into the labour market. The use of a motorized patrol along the ghetto wall has proven very successful. In response to State Secretary Dr *Bühler's* question as to whether there is any prospect of reducing the ghetto population more quickly, State Secretary *Krüger* said more would probably be known in the course of August. He noted that a decision on the problem of resettling the Jews must be made urgently. The current measures have shown that the *elimination of Jews* is accompanied by *price cuts* in the black market. In order to achieve the best possible harvest, illicit trade first has to be stamped out, and this, in turn, can only be achieved if the Jews are eliminated. To carry out such an operation, adequate numbers of transport trains must be provided. Although a total freeze on rail traffic has been ordered for the next two weeks,[14] Krüger has successfully negotiated with President

8 In the following section, Katzmann expounded on guarding the border with Reich Commissariat Ukraine. Then Chief of Staff Herbert Hummel from District Warsaw reported on the situation in his district, stating that the food situation had improved; he went on to talk about the economic situation in the Warsaw ghetto.

9 See PMJ 4/263.

10 The company was Schultz & Co., owned by the Danzig businessman Fritz Emil Schultz.

11 The deportations to Treblinka began on 22 July 1942.

12 In the following section, Hummel argued that fluctuations in the number of Polish workers should be limited; then a discussion about using force to register workers ensued; in conclusion, Hummel urged that the Sonderdienst (auxiliary police force made up of ethnic Germans) should increasingly be brought under the control of the Kreishauptleute. Then SS and Police Leader von Sammern reported on the security situation in District Warsaw.

13 Dr Ferdinand von Sammern und Frankenegg (1897–1944), lawyer; member of the Oberland Freikorps and subsequent paramilitary association Bund Oberland, 1920–1926; joined the SS in 1932 and the NSDAP in 1933; practised law in Peuerbach (Upper Austria) from 1929; full-time SS officer after the Anschluss of Austria; head of SS Main District IX in Würzburg from March 1939; SS and Police Leader in District Warsaw, June 1942 – April 1943; killed by partisans in Yugoslavia in 1944.

14 The transport freeze was related to the Wehrmacht's Army Group South offensive in southern Russia.

Gerteis[15] for trains to be provided every now and then to transport Jews. Once the freeze has ended, the operation against the Jews must be carried out with renewed vigour.

[…][16]

Oswald said that the SS and Police Leader [Böttcher] would address the *security situation* in *District Radom*; he merely wanted to point out the following: a major banditry problem persists in Kreis Opatow, at the bend in the Vistula. It has been noted, however, that the Polish population sides with the German administration in the effort to combat these bandits. A *village council* made up of the six wealthiest Poles has been created in every village. They guarantee against their property that every stranger who enters the village is reported at once. This is necessary because the registration system still works extremely poorly in the villages. At the same time, a *night watch* made up of four men has been organized in every village. It is necessary to wait and see what is gained from these arrangements.

Two Reich Germans in the district have contracted *typhus*. The public health officer in Petrikau, Dr Renndorfer, has complained that the so-called Behring serum is highly ineffective. It is therefore paramount to focus on informing persons who have been vaccinated against typhus with this serum to ensure that they do not rely too heavily on the protection afforded by the vaccine.

With respect to the *resettlement of Jews*, District Radom has fallen behind somewhat. Jewish residential districts have been created in this district over the last year, and the intention is now to resettle Radom's 15,000 Jews in these districts. The distribution plan had already been prepared when resettlement to District Lublin became urgent. This resettlement of the Jews now depends solely on the transport problem, and it has been explained in this respect that the district will have to wait another six to eight weeks. However, this would be too late for the operation to collect the harvest.

State Secretary *Krüger* pointed out that the police have prepared the operation against the Jews down to the last detail, and that implementing it is merely a matter of transport. In Radom and Tschenstochau, Jewish workers should be retained for the armaments

15 Adolf Gerteis (1886–1957), railway official; studied road and railway engineering, 1905–1910; joined the Prussian State Railway in 1911, and completed his training followed by the final state examination in 1915; fought in the First World War; served in various positions with the German Reich Railway, including as an auxiliary department head at the Reich Railway directorate in Frankfurt am Main, 1919–1930; head of the Arnstadt (Thuringia) operations office, 1930–1932; department head at the Reich Railway central office in Berlin, 1932–1933; then worked at the Reich Railway directorate in Münster, 1933–1934; subsequently switched to Lübeck-Büchener Eisenbahn (LBE) as a member of the board of directors in 1934; joined the NSDAP in 1936; after the nationalization of LBE returned as operations manager of the Reich Railway directorate in Essen in 1938; appointed vice president of the general directorate of the Eastern Railway in Cracow in 1939, then its president in 1940; continued in railway service after the war, including as deputy president of the German Federal Railway and as permanent deputy to the director general of the German Federal Railway head office, until retirement in 1952, and was awarded the Order of Merit of the Federal Republic of Germany the same year.

16 In the following section, the deputy chief of staff, Alfons Oswald, spoke about the situation in District Radom.

industries. Of course these workers' immediate family members would also have to be left behind; everyone else, however, will be resettled.

[…][17]

SS and Police Leader Dr *Böttcher* then further noted that Governor Kundt has put all resettlement plans in District Radom on hold for the time being. In addition to the regular police officers, the Security Police and the Order Police in District Radom have four companies and five Urban Police units in the respective larger towns. It has been noted that road traffic is not jeopardized, and that there is no other cause for alarm.

[…][18]

SS and Police Leader *Scherner*[19] gave a brief report on the security situation in District Cracow. He noted that security has been ensured overall, and there have been no particular acts of violence, apart from an attack on a bridge in Kreis Nisko.[20] In Cracow 11,000 Jews are working for the Wehrmacht, the GG armaments inspectorate, and various official agencies and companies. In the course of reducing the size of the ghetto, some of the housing previously inhabited by Jews has been made available to Poles. Also, the establishment of a German quarter can now finally be undertaken. Of the 32,000 Jews currently living in Tarnow, 8,000 are now in work. Unfortunately this work must now be stopped, as the Eastern Railway can no longer provide transport. The final liquidation of *Jewish landholdings* is of the utmost importance. There are 300 Jewish properties in Kreis Krakau-Land and 900 in Kreis Przemysl. Families of Jews with fifteen to twenty members live on these properties, and they are able to acquire eggs and butter from the neighbouring farmers.

[…][21]

17 In the following section, Oswald continued his report; SS and Police Leader Böttcher then expressed his satisfaction with the security situation in District Radom.

18 In the following section, District Cracow's chief of staff, Georg Eisenlohr, gave his report.

19 Julian Scherner (1895–1945), career officer; member of the Oberland Freikorps and subsequent paramilitary association Bund Oberland from 1920; took part in the Beer Hall Putsch in 1923; joined the SS and the NSDAP in 1932; head of the SS Leaders' School in Dachau from 1937; commander of the 8th SS Death's Head Regiment in 1940; SS garrison commander in Prague in 1941; SS and Police Leader in District Cracow from August 1941; thereafter found guilty of corruption by an SS court and transferred to the Dirlewanger regiment; died in Bestensee.

20 Nisko was a Polish powiat (administrative unit) that had been incorporated into Kreishauptmannschaft Jaroslau in District Cracow.

21 The following section contains a concluding discussion of individual security questions. In addition to the speakers named here, the following officials attended the meeting: Becker, Bühler, Boepple, Schöngarth, Siebert, and Weh.

## DOC. 81
## On 18 June 1942 Sh. Sheynkinder describes the trade in items from Jewish households on Lubecki Street in the Warsaw ghetto[1]

Treatise by Sh. Sheynkinder[2] for the underground archive of the Warsaw ghetto (transcription),[3] dated 18 June 1942

One of the 'flourishing' branches of trade in Warsaw's Jewish residential district is buying and selling clothing and household items. This trade in movable property, in [the fruits of] one's long years of toil, in [goods created] with one's own blood, sweat, [and tears], is one of the silent and most painful chapters in the great overarching tragedy of the Jewish community in the Warsaw ghetto.

This 'trade' includes the largest and most populous segment of the Jewish population – the so-called middle class – [namely] those who have not managed to exploit the present situation and circumstances, and who are capable neither of risking their own lives nor of living corruptly at the expense of others. At the same time, however, [the members of] this class have not yet given up on life: they still hope to survive these unprecedented times; they do not yet stretch out their hands on the street in any way; and they still make every effort to continue living like normal people.

This group includes people who used to work in trade or industry and have now [...][4] proven to be 'incapable'; owners of immovable goods over which they now have no control; independent professionals who now find themselves independent of any profession; and a host of civil servants, white-collar workers, and non-self-employed people who have lost their means of making a living in the course of the general pauperization. This same group lives yet struggles to subsist, together with a large number of merchants, shopkeepers, craftsmen, and officials who want to live on the honestly earned groszy 'doled out' to them.

They all have to fall back on their movable property with varying degrees of frequency and gradually convert it into cash. Some of them have already used up their reserves long ago and now live exclusively on this 'trade'. Others do it less often, as a way to make up the daily deficit. But all of them are facing dire material impoverishment and are on the verge of complete socio-economic ruin.

The centre of this 'trade' is located on Lubecki, a once quiet side street between Gęsia and Niska streets, given the name 'Gęsiówka'. Every day it is as busy and noisy as a big fair. Throngs of people stand there offering wares – in their hands, on their arms, over their shoulders, on their backs – while throngs of other people pass through as if in a

1 AŻIH, Ring I/630 (55). Published in English translation in Kermish (ed.), *To Live with Honor*, pp. 548–552. This document has been newly translated from Yiddish.

2 Sh. Sheynkinder, journalist; editor of the Yiddish daily newspaper *Der Moment* in Warsaw prior to Sept. 1939; thought to have been murdered during the large-scale liquidation campaign ('Große Aktion') directed against Warsaw ghetto inhabitants from July to Sept. 1942. Excerpts from Sheynkinder's diary have been published in 'The Diary of S. Sheinkinder', *Yad Vashem Studies*, no. 5 (1963), pp. 255–269.

3 This is a typewritten document that was presumably shortened when a copy of the original handwritten version was made, as indicated by the numerous ellipses.

4 A word is missing because the paper has been damaged.

procession, looking, touching, considering, haggling, and buying. The sellers are exclusively Jews; the buyers – mostly Christians from the 'other side' who have recently come into money. Every day now they haul off the few Jewish belongings there [still] are [in the ghetto] and pay for them with paper notes, in return for which it is possible to stuff one's famished belly with dense black bread, with jam, honey, sauerkraut, and preserved beetroot from the Community's Supply Office …[5]

Many sellers part with their possessions with a heavy heart. They have toiled so many years for them … used them for so many years, and now [they have to give them away] for a couple of kilos of bread and potatoes … Yet others put on a brave face while selling: to hell with it! If they survive, they'll buy everything back and start again from scratch … The main thing – to save and to preserve their lives, and to get through these times … Better to outlive the items than the other way around …

Whether this will really help [people] to survive these times is a difficult question. However, it is a fact that the Jewish residential district is growing poorer by the day in terms of clothes and shoes, linens, and other household goods that cannot be bought back again for the time being. A sad fact.

The trade in […][6] and accessories is not only limited to 'Gęsiówka'. Various fellows who sound like hoarse drunkards and look like they once dealt in stolen goods stand in the streets and stop every passer-by who is carrying something with the innocent question: Is it for sale? … These individuals shout in the streets: 'Clothes! Damski, męski!'[7] and usually intercept most of the sellers for whom 'Gęsiówka' is too far away or who are not yet ready to go there.

A larger den of such jackals is located near my building, on the corner of Leszno and Orla. The group [consists] of five to six traders, led by a certain Moritz with a blood-red neck and a prosthesis where his left foot used to be, a pre-war underworld bloke. This group meticulously works over sellers from the area. They sniff out who is in urgent need of money and who they can therefore 'squeeze', i.e. by driving down the price of an item to the bare minimum, and who they can 'bump up', i.e. promise high prices, and then let that person run from one dealer to the next until he gets tired and sells for half the value. They sniff out where they can make hay with someone's poverty and on the back of whose hard labour they can have a nice drink afterwards. These streetwise fellows are masters of their new trade and know how to sweet-talk someone out of their soul.

Later, at home, many sellers dissolve into bitter tears; plenty of them have been left heavy-hearted after dealing with these bloodsuckers. But there is no recourse. It would be pointless to 'appeal' to the better nature of these 'merchants', because they don't actually force anyone [to sell] and don't tear off anyone's clothes. One should ignore them, despise them, avoid them like the plague. But how, when gnawing hunger drives the sellers straight into their arms? …

This trade grew a little sluggish recently. The constant raids and arrests on the other side [of the wall] and the mass expulsions of Jews in District Warsaw had left the traders

5 The Jewish Council's Supply Office was responsible for distributing foodstuffs that were supplied legally to the ghetto.

6 At least one word is illegible here due to the condition of the paper.

7 Polish in the original: 'women's clothing', 'men's clothing'.

on the corner of Leszno and Orla empty-handed, when a new victim was sent to them, as though from the heavens: the refugees from Germany and the Czech lands[8] with yellow 'Jude'[9] badges on the left sides of their chests.

These Jews and half-Jews had led normal, bourgeois lives in the European style until their deportation and were allowed to take considerable portions of their valuable wardrobes with them. They cannot break with their former way of life all at once, and so they sell what they can in order to eat like human beings and not like we do here, i.e. worse than animals did. The refugees from the Czech lands and Germany inhabit the synagogue building on Tłomackie Street, along with the surrounding courtyard. As a matter of course, when they go to sell something, they inevitably fall prey to the cunning and glibness of the traders who stand near my gate. They sniff out their victim like dogs and do not let him continue on his way.

I witness these transactions every day. The sellers are asked into the courtyard so as not to be disturbed. There, in [the entrance to] a building, they do their deals, and the Jews from the Czech lands and Germany, who are accused of having cheated and swindled the Germans, are cheated and swindled … And I truly don't know what the deciding factor is here: the cunning and crafty shrewdness of the traders or the naivety and gullibility (and perhaps hunger) of the sellers. One thing is clear to me, however: the seller certainly profits less from his garment than the trader does, and his lunch is more meagre than the latter's …

Just now I can see through the window how the gang is working over a plump, elderly, neatly dressed gentleman with the yellow 'Jude' badge on his chest. This gentleman takes off his light summer jacket, which is in excellent condition, almost new, and negotiates. I watch as the 'expert' traders turn the practically new garment around to look it over from all sides, examining it like a sick person, and then pronounce their diagnosis. The deportee watches all this, and I have the impression, I feel, that any minute now he will spit on them and hurl one word at their heads: scoundrels!

But he doesn't shout, this hungry deportee. On the contrary, he smiles (as one smiles in pain) and watches as dirty hands touch his clean garment. But what should he do? He is already used to strange hands making decisions about his possessions …

After much haggling he is paid 200 złoty, which seems like a large sum to him. He is pleased and quickly leaves the building. But Red Moritz is pleased too. He beckons to his cronies and they go out too, heading straight to 'Adaś'[10] for a drink. The deportee has certainly not gone out to drink liquor …

In the evening, as I'm standing in the courtyard in the 'fresh air' as usual, I hear a heavy knock at the gate. One of the most loathsome and odious individuals in our sad life enters unexpectedly. He is one of the well-known informers whose den is at 7 Leszno, someone with many Jewish lives and possessions on his unscrupulous conscience. He is

8 *Tshekhye* (Czechia) in the original, both here and below, i.e. from what was then the Protectorate of Bohemia and Moravia.
9 German in the original: 'Jew'.
10 A Polish nickname for the first name Adam; presumably Adam Bojmowicz (b. 1898), confectioner from Warsaw; owned a café at 54 Leszno Street in 1941; lived in Łódź after the war.

known by the name 'Fredek' and is 'Bubi' Nebel's[11] main accomplice. He is followed by Red Moritz, limping along on his prosthesis, and one of his servants, carrying in his hands the jacket they recently bought. They stop in the entrance, and the disgusting deal begins.

'Fredek' strikes a pose and shrewdly examines the jacket from every angle as an expert might (just like Moritz did earlier). The two sellers divvy up the roles between themselves: one praises the merchandise to the skies, and the other – Moritz – retorts: 'No need to talk him into anything. You can see that he knows his stuff, far more than we do …' Fredek enjoys it. 'So,' he says, 'new, not yet washed, no parts turned, my size. Look here, you can't fool me, I'm not just anyone …'

'Of course not!' they both answer in unison. 'We know very well who you are …'

'So, how much did it cost you?' the buyer asks. Now the two salesmen swap roles. Moritz starts thinking about what price he should quote, and his lackey encourages him: 'You don't have to give it much thought. You can rely on him to be fair … He won't fleece you …'

'Do you want to know how much it cost me? For real? As surely as we three live and breathe? It cost me … 380 złoty. And I want to make 200 złoty on it. Fair?'

The buyer doesn't give a toss about that. He puts his hand in his pocket and pulls out a wad of money – blood money stolen and looted from Jews … From the crumpled banknotes he takes out a 500 bill and hands it to Moritz. 'Here, fine.'

'Fine, fine,' they both answer, as though hypnotized. Another sort of fine … They readily help him into the jacket, give him a chummy pat on the shoulder, and leave happy.

And people say that Jews in the ghetto have no way of making money …

## DOC. 82

## On 18 June 1942 Elsa Binder describes being inspected at the entrance to the Stanislawów ghetto[1]

Handwritten diary of Elsa Binder, entry for 18 June 1942

18 June 1942

… We really cannot complain about a lack of excitement. My knees are still trembling. Father sold a beautiful new suit (alas) for 15 kg of provisions and 275 złoty. He sent me to the other side so that I could help the 'shaygets'[2] from the factory to smuggle the stuff over. He couldn't move around so much by himself. For greater security, I took Józia with me, who was supposed to hand me one bag via intermediaries. They gave her two, each weighing 5 kg. I knew I wouldn't be able to pass through with this. She was afraid to help me without a bag, so I asked her to send someone to help me. I walked up and

11 'Bubi' Nebel, thought to have been a boxer from Katowice; considered a collaborator in the Warsaw ghetto; shot dead by members of the Jewish Combat Organization (ŻOB) in 1943.

1 AŻIH, 302/267, fols. 23–24. English translation published in Zapruder (ed.), *Salvaged Pages*, pp. 327–328. This document has been newly translated from Polish.

2 Yiddish in the original: 'non-Jewish boys'.

down in front of our door, which is nailed shut, on our street, which is fenced off by the white stripe of the 'schleuse'[3] and the policemen. Time passed. I broke out in a sweat. It was difficult for me to haul myself around like that in a foreign street – near which I live – so close to my people, and yet so far from them. I was afraid. Should I decide to cross over? Or not? Three Urban Police officers and two Gestapo men who were approaching made me decide, and I found myself between a rock and a hard place. I went! And of course a Ukrainian policeman stopped me. Our people didn't want to have anything to do with it. They didn't know me. And my appearance obviously didn't dazzle them either (I absolutely can't shake off the feeling that if I were prettier, I might have had more luck with them. But perhaps that's only in my imagination.) Meanwhile Father, whom I had managed to notify via Moldauer, came running, and my mother – and they began to scheme. They slipped 20 złoty to the Order Service men, who then took a completely different view of the matter and appealed to the guy to let me through. They were in the midst of this when a Gestapo man approached the schleuse. I froze. At the very last moment they pulled me into the guard booth. It was now that things came to a head. Everyone disappeared into thin air as if touched by a magic wand, and only the two (the Ukrainian and the Jewish policeman) and I were left in the guard booth. My heart beat like a drum. Suddenly bright, cruel eyes fixated on me, the likes of which I have only ever seen on Borys Karloff in Frankenstein.[4] I don't think I'll ever forget that look, which froze the blood in my veins. That's no exaggeration. 'Was macht diese Frau hier?'[5] I'm guessing that the situation wasn't exactly pleasant for this 'OD'[6] man either. 'She was stopped to check where she works.' 'What's this bag?' he asks,[7] and takes a step towards it. 'I am lost' – the thought quickly flashed through my mind and my heart suddenly stopped beating. I have never experienced anything like this before – not the time when my missing armband was pointed out to me, and not the second time either, when four Germans passed me and again I was not wearing an armband. But they were blind to it at the time, and likewise this one apparently also believed there were just odds and ends in the bag and, after a moment's consideration, he walked away. Extraordinary luck. If he had bent down and looked inside, I would have been lost. The policeman did not want to negotiate any more; instead he took me directly to the Wachstube.[8] Father ran behind me all the way there. They took 2.5 kg of cornmeal from us, that is, 100 złoty. This month I earned 17 złoty, but according to Jewish custom I thank God for it, I say and I think that things could have turned out far worse. And perhaps that's why we are doing so badly, because we always say, 'gonzi li toyvy'.[9]

3 German in the original, here 'sluice'.
4 Boris Karloff, pseudonym of William Henry Pratt (1887–1969), actor; appeared in a film adaptation of Mary Shelley's novel *Frankenstein* in 1931. His role as Frankenstein's monster made him world-famous.
5 German in the original: 'What's this woman doing here?'
6 Ordnungsdienst, 'Order Service'
7 Change of tense in the original.
8 German in the original: 'guardroom'.
9 Yiddish in the original: 'This too is for the best', or 'Let's look on the bright side'.

## DOC. 83

## On 21 June 1942 the deputy head of the General Government's Population and Welfare Division writes to his SS comrades about the deportation of Jews[1]

Typewritten letter from the deputy head of the General Government's Population and Welfare Division, Dr Walther Föhl,[2] Cracow, to SS members in Berlin, dated 21 June 1942[3]

Dear Comrade Funke,[4]
Dear comrades,

I felt I wanted to write to you every time I received the latest newsletter[5] – this is how vividly the dear old familiar figures came to life in your notes, greetings, and congratulations, the comrades with whom we served in Berlin year after year at a time when we could scarcely imagine what enormous tasks the future would hold in store for all of us. Today we are all in the thick of things, and for most of us, our heads are spinning so much that any pause to reflect and reminisce is almost a luxury, almost a jolt of delight at the comfortable camaraderie of the old days. Judging by my own reaction and feelings, I believe your newsletter gives enormous pleasure to each and every comrade.

I myself am once again right in the midst of the problems of the territory known as the General Government, a borderland territory of the Reich. If you look for the midpoint of the territory occupied and administered by Germans on a map today, you will end up somewhere around Warsaw, i.e. in the middle of the area where I am now living again. This means that some problems – particularly of course the crucial questions of Ostpolitik, including our food situation – are felt much more keenly here than elsewhere. After all, there are almost sixteen million Poles living here, as well as five million Ukrainians etc., not to mention the Jews. Every day trains with 1,000 Jews each from all over Europe arrive here, and we patch them up and either put them up temporarily or, more often, send them on their way to the Byelorussian marshes, towards the Arctic,[6] where they will all be gathered when the war is over, but not without having built a few roads – if they survive it, that is (and the Jews from the Kurfürstendamm or from Vienna and Bratislava certainly won't). (But we're not supposed to talk about that!)

1 BArch, RS B417, fol. 1494r–v. This document has been translated from German.
2 Dr Walther Föhl (1908–1975), historian; joined the SA in 1933 and the SS in 1935; deputy head of the NSDAP Office for Kinship Research in 1936; deputy head of the General Government's Population and Welfare Division, Dec. 1939 – June 1941, and 1942 – Jan. 1943; served in the war, June–Dec. 1941, and from Jan. 1943; Kreis archivist in the West German town of Kempen after the war; author of numerous historical monographs.
3 Handwritten note at the end: 'NB: thank you very much for the birthday wishes!' Föhl's birthday had been on 1 May.
4 Presumably Ferdinand Funke (b. 1895), hairdresser; joined the NSDAP in 1931 and the SS in 1932; general manager and subdivision head at the Supreme Court of Honour and Discipline of the German Labour Front (DAF) in Berlin; on active duty as a medical NCO, 1939–1940; personnel officer and adjutant in the Waffen-SS in 1943.
5 This was the newsletter of the 2nd Company of the 6th SS Regiment.
6 In summer 1941 German officials briefly considered deporting the Jews from the General Government to the Pripyat region or to the White Sea, but the deportations carried out in 1942 went to the extermination camps instead.

The land here has certainly become more significant to the Reich: alternative sites for industrial production are being established here, countless workers come from here or pass through here, and we can also contribute to the Reich's food supply, thank God, even though we ourselves do not live very well here.

I have become a specialist in Ukrainian questions and have so far been able to duck out of being posted to Berlin, to the Rosenberg Ministry,[7] but it will happen one day. Before that happens, however, I'd really like to take part in the development in the Caucasus,[8] if my leave of absence gets approved, which is somewhat problematic given the personnel shortage of Germans in the administration and their not exactly first-rate quality. You notice at every turn that our best men are at the front – the fourth-rate characters here are no longer under the supervision of the Party etc., and they often behave accordingly. In addition, some think they have to play the lords and masters here, but of course they do it in the wrong quarters and without any political tact. It is clear that the Poles aren't calling the shots any more, but we shouldn't get the Ukrainians riled up against us through bad behaviour, as they will have to do all sorts of things for us yet.

Yes, these are some of the concerns I have to deal with every day. The Party has now made me head of the Racial Policy Office[9] here – and breaking every German swine here would have given me enough to do. But in the end, the other tasks are more pressing. At any rate, one thing is certain: we are fantastic soldiers, but when it comes to foreign nations, we have yet to become politicians as well. As long as this learning process is taking place under the harsh conditions of war, it's still fine.

And in the meantime, let's enjoy [the fact] that things are going well overall. What makes me really happy is that our comrades from 2/6[10] are involved everywhere with such vigour. I grin with delight every time I see the name of one of the old rascals mentioned in your 2/6 newsletter. That's just how it is out here. In the meantime, enjoy yourselves in Berlin. I sincerely hope that I will soon be able to sit down again with the last few stalwarts holding the fort in Berlin – so that when peace is concluded Company 2/6 has not disintegrated into its component parts and the individual men continue to remain out there. Of course the major tasks will really only begin in peacetime, so to speak, and then every one of the men will truly be needed. And that too is a reason to be happy.

I'm sending you my best, all my dear comrades. And do spare a thought for your old training instructor every now and then.

7 Alfred Rosenberg headed the Reich Ministry for the Occupied Eastern Territories from 1941 to 1945.

8 The Wehrmacht's summer offensive in 1942 was directed at the Caucasus. Many German experts were deployed there.

9 Presumably within the Party organization in the General Government (Arbeitsbereich NSDAP).

10 This is a reference to the 2nd Company of the 6th SS Regiment.

## DOC. 84

## On 22 June 1942 German occupation officials argue in favour of keeping Jewish workers involved in production[1]

Record of the 7th meeting of main department heads in the GG government, Cracow, dated 22 June 1942

[...][2]

State Secretary *Krüger* stated that no one will ever be able to prevent workers who cannot support their families from not turning up for work. A radical, total *crackdown on the black market* is therefore necessary if the problem is to be solved. Action must be taken first and foremost against the Jews. After the most recent operations against Jews in Lublin and Cracow,[3] for example, it became apparent that the prices of illicitly traded items immediately dropped by half. He also noted that it will not be possible to bring in the new harvest until the Jewish problem and the issue of black market trading have been resolved. State Secretary Dr Bühler agreed, but pointed out that black market trading will continue as long as there is no guarantee that the Polish population can be fully fed.

Main Department Head Dr Frauendorfer felt that resettling the Jews, who account for a substantial share of the overall population, would have far-reaching ramifications for every aspect of public life. He noted that when it comes to labour, the country has largely been exhausted. The armaments industry is making use of around 100,000 skilled workers, 800,000 workers are in the Reich, and the military commander in the General Government is using another 100,000 workers. Main Department Head Dr Frauendorfer is therefore absolutely dependent on the deployment of Jewish labour at present, and the armaments inspector for the General Government, Lieutenant General Schindler,[4] shared his opinion. Due to the lack of skilled Polish workers, these workers cannot be replaced. The Jews should still be subject to the SS operations, but they should be kept as a source of labour for the duration of the war.

He [Frauendorfer] stated that he has no interest in taking skilled Jewish workers out of the economy or away from industry. This was made very clear in the agreement made with Lieutenant General Schindler on providing Jews to the armaments industry,[5] and he will also be able to satisfy Lieutenant General Schindler's requests in full. Thousands of Jewish workers, both men and women, who will be housed in camps created near the

1 AIPN, GK 95, vol. 24. Copy in IfZ-Archives, Fb 105, vol. 22, fols. 5336–5349, here fols. 5344–5346. This document has been translated from German.

2 The document is 14 pages long (p. 3 is missing). State Secretary Bühler opened the conference in Governor General Frank's absence. The participants first talked about ways to improve the economic situation for ethnic Germans and then discussed the pay increases for non-German railway workers, which had led to a drop in the number of workers who failed to show up to their workplaces, from 20 to 8 per cent.

3 In District Lublin, deportations to Belzec began on 17 March 1942; those from District Cracow began on 1 June 1942.

4 Max-Josef Schindler (1881–1963), career officer; lieutenant general and inspector of the armaments inspectorate for the General Government.

5 In a meeting at the armaments inspectorate for the General Government on 9 May 1942, an agreement had been made to replace a portion of the Polish workers with 100,000 Jews: KTB no.1 MiG/OQu 1.5.41–31.11.43, IfZ-Archives, MA 679/8, fols. 1–510, here fol. 346.

armaments production facilities, will be made available for this purpose, looked after by the SS, fed, and, if necessary, clothed. The Reichsführer-SS, Reich Minister Speer,[6] and the plenipotentiary for labour deployment, Gauleiter Sauckel,[7] went so far as to place increased importance on the *deployment* of Jews who are *fit for work*.

*Main Department Head Naumann*[8] described the great *difficulties in terms of agriculture*. The Ukrainians, deployed for labour primarily in Galicia, are increasingly engaging in sabotage and failing to appear for work, so that tilling the sugar-beet fields has become almost impossible, for example. He suggested that the *Jews* who are volunteering for work at this time due to the operations against Jews should be provided with identity documents and *deployed* in the *agricultural sector*. The point, he said, is to supply approximately 1,800 large-scale farming operations [with labourers], for which 30,000–40,000 Jews would be needed, and these Jews would then be available in the autumn for other purposes. He said the situation is extremely critical, and he asked State Secretary Krüger to place the Jews at his disposal as quickly as possible.

*Main Department Head Dr Frauendorfer* supported this proposal and is prepared to procure the necessary people.

In reply to a related question posed by *state secretaries Dr Bühler* and *Krüger, Main Department Head Naumann* stated that it would be possible to house the Jews immediately and to provide them with meagre food supplies, but the few guards available would not be able to monitor them fully. He must therefore request *police support*.

*State Secretary Krüger* noted that such a measure must be well organized and thoroughly considered. He is *not* able to make police forces available to monitor the Jews. [...][9]

6 Albert Speer (1905–1981), architect; joined the NSDAP and the SA in 1931; planner of monumental National Socialist building projects; general buildings inspector for the Reich capital; Reich minister for armaments and war production from Feb. 1942; tried before the International Military Tribunal in Nuremberg and sentenced to 20 years' imprisonment.

7 Fritz Sauckel (1894–1946), seaman, then unskilled labourer; joined the NSDAP in 1923 and rejoined in 1925; joined the SA in 1925 and the SS in 1934; Gauleiter in Thuringia from 1927; Gauleiter and Reichsstatthalter of Thuringia from 1933; general plenipotentiary for labour deployment from March 1942, responsible for the deportation of millions of forced labourers from occupied European countries to the Reich; tried before the International Military Tribunal in Nuremberg and executed.

8 Karl Naumann (1905–1976), farmer; joined the NSDAP and the SA in 1928, and the SS in 1936; under the Reich Food Estate Kreis farmers' leader in Döbeln, 1933–1939; head of the Department of Food and Agriculture in District Warsaw in 1940, then in District Cracow, and then for the entire General Government from July 1941 to 1945; worked in agriculture after the war; district chairman of the right-wing party League of Expellees and Persons Deprived of Rights (BHE) in 1950; Landrat in Holzminden, 1952–1956; member of state parliament in Lower Saxony, 1955–1963.

9 In the following section, the participants discussed the registration of unemployed people; Siebert made it known that Frank had 'urged that the pseudo-employed or non-employed be put in the worst housing, primarily in the vacated ghettos': IfZ-Archives, Fb 105, vol. 22, fol. 5347. In addition to those named in the text, the participants included Bauder, Bergemann, Eden, Eißfeldt, Fessler, Gerlach, Gerteis, Lauxmann, Senkowsky, Siebert, Watzke, and Weh. There is also a handwritten addition to the list of those in attendance: 'and others'.

## DOC. 85

## *Krakauer Zeitung*, 24 June 1942: article by Gustav Andraschko on the clean-up operations in Lublin's ghetto district[1]

*Lublin's former ghetto is being cleaned up. Pest holes are being eliminated with explosives. The fire brigade is hosing away layers of filth.*

Lublin, 24 June

Once Lublin was free of Jews,[2] the German administration immediately set about making an inventory of the housing that had become available and inspecting whether it was usable in order to alleviate the city's housing shortage. Even for those unfamiliar with Jewish quarters, it should be clear that this is a formidable and strenuous task. The aversion to water is a congenital trait in the Jew, something he will never cast off. This is reflected in his appearance, his abode, and his whole environment. Particularly among the Jews of Poland, the filth is unimaginable and has become a byword for them. In Germany, the poorest of the poor would baulk at keeping their dog in one of the shacks in which the Jew feels comfortable here. There is no trace of sanitary facilities, not even in the most primitive form. The Jewish residential districts, which can be traversed only by wading through filth, teem with vermin of all sorts and have always been the most dangerous centres of epidemic disease, both locally and across the entire country.

As long as Jews have lived in Lublin, they have been carriers and spreaders of disease. The first major epidemic among the Lublin Jews broke out as early as 1648. In that year, the Tatars and the Cossacks overran Poland and arrived in the Lublin region. Under Hetman Khmelnitsky's[3] command, they marched on Lublin. While Lublin's citizens prepared to defend themselves, the rich Jews fled the city with their belongings in the nick of time; only the poorer Jews stayed behind and holed up in their hiding places. An epidemic soon broke out in these filthy dens. It spread quickly and soon killed off around 10,000 people.

The recent inspection of the existing housing has shown that some of the buildings are no longer habitable. The clean-up work, which the police chief[4] assigned to the Stadthauptmann's[5] office is carrying out along with the head of the housing office,[6] began by assembling a number of work details. A kind of 'rag-collecting detail' was the first, and

1 *Krakauer Zeitung*, 24 June 1942, p. 5. A Polish translation was published under the headline 'Porządkowanie byłej dzielnicy żydowskiej w Lublinie' in *Nowy Głos Lubelski*, 8 July 1942, p. 3. This document has been translated from German.

2 Deportations from the ghetto in Lublin's Old Town to Belzec had ended on 14 April 1942. The remaining Jews were forced into Majdan Tatarski, a suburb of Lublin, where they were crowded together and fenced in with barbed wire. On 22 April around 3,000 people were taken to Lublin-Majdanek concentration camp, and approximately 2,000 more were shot in Krępiec Forest.

3 The Cossack hetman Bogdan Khmelnitsky led large peasant revolts in the eastern part of the Polish-Lithuanian Commonwealth in 1648. Many Jews were murdered in the pogroms triggered by these revolts.

4 The police chief assigned to the Stadthauptmann of Lublin's office was Lothar Hoffmann (1905–1992), salesman; head of Dept. IIIA (enemy operations) under the Commander of the Security Police and the SD (KdS) in Lublin; police officer with the State Criminal Investigation Office in Hesse after the war; sentenced to three and a half years in prison by Wiesbaden Regional Court in 1973.

5 Dr Curt Englaender was the Stadthauptmann of Lublin from April 1942 to Jan. 1944.

6 Oberarbeitsführer Umbeck, a high-ranking officer within the Reich Labour Service.

when this group had finished its work, the clean-up detail appeared, taking on what is probably the most difficult and unpleasant part of the job. The quantity of filth and refuse that had to be removed from the dwellings beggars belief. And we should not even mention 'sanitation'. To give just one example: in some toilets, the faecal matter was more than one metre deep. A fire hose first had to be brought in to deal with the mess, and lo and behold, after almost an hour it turned out that underneath it all, there was a decent tiled floor and a normal toilet bowl. The clean-up details were swiftly followed by the joiners and glaziers, who sealed up all the residences in preparation for the fumigation detail's work. Only once all this had been done did the finishing cleaners get to work.

As mentioned earlier, some of the buildings in the ghetto are no longer habitable. Since these pest holes – for that is precisely what they are – must be eliminated, they are blown up and demolished. However, there are also structures of historical value in the ghetto, buildings which the Jews have put in such a dreadful state that no one else can live in them any more either. These buildings will remain and will be restored to the extent possible. The housing office is constantly renovating and renting out apartments. Even though the pace is slow, new usable living space is gradually being added to combat the housing shortage.

Freeing Lublin of the Jews has meant eliminating not only a source of epidemic disease, but also a hotbed of black market dealing. A great deal more effort will be necessary before this part of the city will look new and beautiful. The dirt will disappear along with the dilapidated shacks, and parks or flowerbeds will spring up in their place; there will be nothing left to remind us of the period of decline. Only then can Lublin, once the centre of European Jewry,[7] be rightfully called a city.

G. A.[8]

## DOC. 86
## On 25 June 1942 a businessman demands that the GG government ban the sale of products from the Warsaw ghetto[1]

Letter from Julius Rieche[2] to Captain Behringer,[3] GG government, Cracow, dated 25 June 1942 (copy of a copy)

*Re*: goods from the Warsaw ghetto

Dear Captain Behringer,

To my regret, today I must inform you of events that amount to sabotaging the collection of the harvest and are liable to dangerously affect economic life in general.

Yesterday a representative of a Jewish firm in Warsaw came to me and offered me the following items: women's dresses, aprons, blouses, undergarments, stockings, children's

7 See Doc. 79.

8 Gustav Andraschko (Andraško), journalist and photographer; born in Horní Planá (Oberplan) in Bohemia (Czechoslovakia); Reich citizen from 1938; wrote for the *Krakauer Zeitung* and its local Warsaw edition from 1940 to at least 1942.

1 BArch, NS 19/2664, appendix to Item 3, Trade and Industry, from a 95-page report from the Higher SS and Police Leader in the General Government, dated 9 April 1943, fols. 5–99, here fols. 33–34. This document has been translated from German.

jackets and trousers, children's dresses, caps, overalls, children's sandals, kitchen utensils, etc. All of these items were offered to me without coupons and for resale without such coupons. When I told the salesman that these goods were rationed, as he well knew, and that I would not engage in black market dealings, he told me that these transactions were undertaken with the government of District Warsaw's consent, through the Transfer Bureau, and were intended to make the goods that were still available in the ghetto accessible to the general population.

He quoted me the following purchase prices for the individual items: ladies' blouses, 120 zl.; caps, 27 zl.; children's sandals, 61 zl.; etc. When I asked the salesman whether these prices had been approved, he told me that all I needed to do was send a request to the *Transfer Bureau* in Warsaw, which would then obtain approval from the pricing authority in Warsaw in exchange for a 2 per cent commission. He said authorization had almost always been granted so far.

I explained to the salesman that the sale of these goods without coupons at five to ten times the [officially set] price would substantially disrupt economic life. To which he replied that the population in Warsaw, Lublin, and also in Lemberg would gladly buy the goods and did not baulk at the prices, as the farmers were getting 2 zl. for an egg and ten to twenty times the peacetime price for their other products as well. He said that if I passed up such a chance, then I was not a real businessman, because since my markup was a percentage of the price, I would be able to earn far more than with rationed goods. Also, he added, I would be in good company, as Kaufhaus des Ostens[4] in Lemberg had ordered 300,000 zl. worth of goods from him, for example, and the Promtorg cooperative and Narodna Torhowla[5] had ordered 4,000,000 zl. worth. And after all, I would still be selling below the black-market prices, as a pair of stockings now cost 80 to 100 zl., while I could sell them for around 50 zl.

I declined to buy the goods for both of my firms, in Stanislau and in Tarnow. But I feel that the government should intervene to stop the sale of these ghetto goods. I am convinced that many of these goods were stolen, which would mean we would be buying back goods that are constantly being stolen from us, and at ten times the price. But if we feel we cannot do without the goods from the ghetto, then we should give the Jews food in exchange for them, as that is what they will want to buy on the black market with the money they make. If the Warsaw transaction were to be carried out, then it would mean that the authorities are accepting a devaluation of the zloty, and that the farmers are being given a moral justification for selling their produce at black-market prices.

*Heil Hitler!*

2 Julius Rieche (1903–1966), merchant; joined the NSDAP and the SA in 1925; member of the SS in 1929–1930 and again in 1937; lived in Jamaica, 1930–1933; trade lobbyist in Frankfurt am Main, 1934–1935; with the Reichsbetriebsgruppe Handel within the German Labour Front (DAF) from Dec. 1935; owned the import and export firm Arndt & Cohn in Hamburg from 1937; later a Kreis wholesaler (i.e. a German firm, often from Bremen or Hamburg that had traded in former German colonies or elsewhere overseas and had a kind of monopoly on trade in a given Kreis) in Stanisławów; died in Bad Bramstedt.

3 Adolf Behringer (1894–1963), economic officer for special assignments in the military district commander's office in the General Government in Cracow; captain from 1940; lived in Heidenheim an der Brenz after the war.

4 Literally: 'Department Store of the East'.

5 Ukrainian cooperatives.

DOC. 87

## On 26 June 1942 Emanuel Ringelblum describes the reaction in the Warsaw ghetto to a BBC broadcast about the murder of Jews[1]

Handwritten journal of Emanuel Ringelblum, entries dated 26 and 30 June 1942

Friday, 26 June 1942, has been a day of momentous events for O[yneg] S[habes].[2] This morning Engl[ish] radio broadcast a programme for Polish Jewry.[3] It reported on everything that we are [already] well aware of: Słonim and Vilna,[4] Lemberg and Chełmno, etc.[5] For months we have been distressed by the fact that the world is deaf and dumb to our tragedy, which has no parallel in history. We have reproached the Polish public, the representatives [of the government delegation for Poland][6] who are in contact with the Polish government, for not passing on news about the slaughter of the Polish Jews since the world does not know about it. We have accused the Polish representatives of deliberately keeping silent about our tragedy so their own plight would not pale [in comparison]. Turns out that all [our] interventions have finally succeeded. In recent weeks English radio has been constantly reporting news about the atrocities being committed against the Polish Jews: Chełmno, Vilna, Bełżec, etc. Today the summary of a report about the situation of the Polish Jews was broadcast, which mentioned the number of 700,000 Jews having been massacred in Poland.

At the same time, it was announced that revenge would be taken and those who carried out the violent deeds would be held accountable. The OS group has thus fulfilled a great historical mission: it has alerted the world to our fate and perhaps saved hundreds of thousands of Polish Jews from extermination. Of course, time will soon tell as to the latter. I don't know who from this group will survive – who will live […][7] to work through the gathered materials. However, one thing is […][8] clear to us: our extraordinary efforts, our devotion and living in […][9] fear, have not been in vain. We have dealt a blow to the enemy. It is not […][10] whether the revelation of the unbelievable mass murders of Jews will have the desired effect, whether the further slaughter

1 AŻIH, Ring I/445 (503/1), fols. 50–51, 55–58. Published in Ringelblum, *Ksovim fun geto*, vol. 1, pp. 376–380. This document has been translated from Yiddish.
2 See Introduction, p. 18, 35–36.
3 After Szmul Zygielbojm, a member of the National Council of the Polish government in exile, had received the Bund's report dated 11 May 1942 from Warsaw (see Doc. 74), he summarized it for an article in the *Daily Telegraph*, which appeared under the title 'Germans Murder 700,000 Jews in Poland. Travelling Gas Chambers' (25 June 1942, p. 5). The BBC gave this news the widest possible publicity through its foreign service, including a broadcast on the morning of 26 June 1942 in which Zygielbojm reproduced the essential facts from the article.
4 See Doc. 39.
5 See Doc. 58.
6 During the occupation of Poland in the Second World War, the government delegation for Poland served as an agency for the London-based Polish government in exile. It was the highest authority in the Polish underground state.
7 Word illegible.
8 Word illegible.
9 Word illegible.
10 Word illegible.

of entire J[ewish] communities will stop. But we do know one thing: we have fulfilled our duty. We have overcome all obstacles and pitfalls and succeeded in our [aim] – even our death will not be meaningless, like the deaths of tens of thousands of Jews. We have dealt the enemy a heavy blow and unmasked his diabolical plan to furtively exterminate Polish Jewry. We have put a spoke in his wheel and tipped his hand. And if England now makes good on its threats to take appropriate action, then perhaps we may be saved.

30 June 1942
Over the past few days, the Jew[ish] population has been deeply affected by the London [broadcast]. Learning that the world has been shaken by news of the massacres in Poland has made a profound impact on everyone.[11] For many long months we have endured the most terrible suffering and wondered: does the world know about our suffering? And if it knows, why is it silent? Why did the world not shudder when tens of thousands of Jews were shot in Ponary? Why was the world silent when tens of thousands of Jews were poisoned in *Chełmno*? Why was the world silent when hundreds of thousands of Jews were slaughtered in Galicia and other newly occupied areas? We asked the question and answered it ourselves: why [should] people be shaken by the massacre in Vilna when the Germans slaughtered 180,000 people in Rostov,[12] or when a similar number of Ukrainians and Jews were murdered in Kiev?[13] Why should the world be shaken when torrents of blood are spilled every day on all the battlefields? Is the blood of Jews more precious than that of Russian, Chinese, English, and other soldiers? This was the answer we always gave ourselves, but we felt that this answer was not an answer. Only now do we understand where the reason for the silence lay. London simply did not know about everything that was happening, hence the silence. On the other hand, how is it possible that the Polish government, with its own radio station, didn't know about what was happening here? It raises the baffling question: if in London they knew the next day about the shooting of 100 people in Pawiak,[14] why did it take many months before they knew in London about the murder of hundreds of thousands of Jews? This is indeed a question that demands a straightforward answer.

News that the Polish government's appeal was broadcast on all British stations in all languages of the Allied nations on that festive day[15] [and] several times in German (including by the [BBC's] German Service), along with speeches by the Archbishop of

11 On 29 June 1942 Ignacy Schwarzbart, the Zionist representative on the National Council of the Polish government in exile, read from the Bund's report at a press conference of the British section of the World Jewish Congress, which was reported in the British press the following day.
12 In Dec. 1941 SS Special Detachment 10 murdered approximately 2,000 Jews in Rostov on Don.
13 On 29 and 30 Sept. 1941, 33,771 Jews were murdered by SS and police units in the Babyn Yar ravine near Kyiv.
14 On 2 March 1942 some 100 Pawiak prison inmates, including Labour Party activists and a former member of the Sejm, were executed at Treblinka I labour camp. The names of the murdered victims were printed on the front page of the influential Polish underground publication *Biuletyn Informacyjny* one month later for the issue dated 2 April 1942.
15 This refers to 26 June 1942.

Canterbury,[16] Rabbi Dr Hertz,[17] [and National Council] representative Zygielbojm,[18] had rattled the Jewish public in Warsaw. People rejoiced, but at the same time they feared how the occupier would respond. Most were of the opinion that it is a good thing the world knows about it all, as perhaps now it will find the proper means to force the occupier to stop further mass killings. People quoted passages from Zygielbojm's speech where he talks about reprisals against the Germans in America, [which] will supposedly force [the Germans] to stop the mass killings in Poland. Others believed that the Allies, especially democratic America, would not go so far as to murder Germans because, first, they are American citizens, and second, public opinion wouldn't allow it. However, everyone believes it is very important that the Germans themselves know about what is happening. All those who have had the opportunity to meet with Germans know very well that […][19] the Germans are not aware of the killings and mass murders carried out by special gangs of murderers outside the cities or in […][20] murder sites such as *Bełżec, Chełmno*, etc. The occupier is afraid of the German population, even the German soldiers, knowing about the mass murders of Jews, which is why he tries to have the Jews killed in secret. Even when it comes to burying the murdered victims, Jews are used, who are ultimately murdered as well. If foreign countries limit themselves to speeches and threats, then perhaps the fear of public opinion in Germany itself will save us. A few Germans who had found out about *Chełmno* were outraged, noting that they would have to pay for it with the lives of their wives and children, that bloody revenge would be taken. It is thought […][21] that the commotion [the news has caused] in London and throughout the world will have a certain effect on the attitude of the Pol[ish] population towards the Jews, which is generally bad.

Meanwhile, the German press and radio have taken to keeping their mouths shut and are silent. But what other option do they have? To confirm [the stories] would mean alarming their own people; to deny [the stories] would mean that all the promises about putting an end to the Jews are just empty talk. The public […][22] the reaction of the German government with great interest and is pinning great hopes on this. People believe that from now on the Germans will be afraid of such mass murders being made public […].[23] People are even citing an incident in Ostrowiec, where Jews were freed from the sealed wagons in which they were to be deported.[24] Should this be confirmed, then it would indeed mark the beginning of a new era. Those who are more realistic warn against [indulging in] illusions. No compassion whatsoever can be expected from the Germans. Our life or death depends on how much time they have. If they still have a lot of time, we are lost. If deliverance comes soon, then we are saved.

16 William Temple (1881–1944), Anglican clergyman; Archbishop of Canterbury from early 1942 to 1944.
17 Dr Joseph Herman Hertz (1872–1946), rabbi from Hungary, emigrated from there to New York in 1884; philosophy professor in South Africa, 1898–1911; from 1913 Chief Rabbi in Britain of the United Hebrew Congregations of the British Empire; founded the Council of Christians and Jews with William Temple in 1942.
18 See Doc. 89, fn. 4.
19 Word illegible.
20 Word illegible.
21 Word illegible.
22 Word illegible.
23 Word illegible.
24 No further evidence of this was found.

## DOC. 88

## Dionýz Lenard describes his experiences from April to June 1942 in Lublin-Majdanek concentration camp and during his escape[1]

Report by Dionýz Lenard[2] after his escape from Lublin-Majdanek concentration camp, written in Bratislava, before 26 May 1943 (copy)[3]

My dear friend,

[…][4]

In April 1942 the transports came often enough and of course we were curious as to what would arrive.[5]

Everyone was afraid of seeing the face of an acquaintance or relative again. At first, two transports arrived from the east, I think. From Poprad, from Michalovce, Trebišov,[6] and so on, bringing with them the news that the Bardejov Jews had cleverly got out of being transported. Apparently some doctor [had administered] artificial typhus bacilli,[7] so they couldn't be taken away because typhus would have spread otherwise. To this day I don't know how much of this is true, but that's what I was told. We didn't hear any political news. Nobody could even tell us much about Slovakia. When the transport arrived from Nitra,[8] the one that brought old Gottlieb,[9] whom I mentioned before, we were really shocked to our cores for the first time. Even those who had so far kept their equilibrium felt anxiety and horror. This transport was the first family transport. You

1 Moreshet Archive, A.1564, fols. 26–35. This document has been translated from Slovak.

2 Dionýz (Daniel Dawid Dyonisius) Lenard (Lénard) (1912–1944?); lived with his parents in Žilina in north-western Slovakia, approximately 30 km from the border with the General Government; active in the Zionist youth organization Hashomer Hatzair and in the 1930s travelled to Palestine. On 27 March 1942 Jewish men were deported from Žilina to Lublin. Lenard escaped to Slovakia in July 1942; his final letter, written in German to his sister in Sweden, is dated 11 August 1944: Moreshet Archive, D.1.5562, fols. 1–4. Thereafter all trace of him is lost.

3 This excerpt is taken from an account composed of 35 typed pages and additional ones preserved only as fragments. Lenard likely recorded his account in Bratislava in 1943; on 26 May 1943 he sent one copy to Dr Samuel Hoffmann, a representative of the Jewish Centre (Ústredňa Židov), the Bratislava Jewish Council. In 1968 Hoffmann sent a copy to Lenard's sister, a copy of which is held in the Moreshet Archive.

4 Lenard began by describing his experiences since 1941 in a voluntary labour camp in Svätý Kríž in central Slovakia, the transport to the Jewish labour camp in Nováky in western Slovakia, the subsequent deportation to Lublin-Majdanek concentration camp in early 1942, and his impressions of the living conditions there.

5 The deportations of Slovak Jews to District Lublin began on 27 March 1942. By mid April 1942 a total of 38 deportation trains with some 39,000 people had been dispatched. The first four transports with young men were sent to Lublin-Majdanek concentration camp; the remainder were sent to the ghettos in Chełm, Dęblin, Łuków, Opole, Puławy, Radzyń, and Rejowiec.

6 Jews were deported from western Slovakia in April 1942; transports from eastern Slovakia did not arrive in Majdanek until May 1942.

7 Cases of epidemic typhus in Bardejov, a small town in north-eastern Slovakia, led to delays in the deportation of the Jews, with transports leaving the town only on 17 and 18 May 1942.

8 Two transports carrying 2,086 Jews from Nitra, a small town in western Slovakia, arrived in Lublin-Majdanek concentration camp on 14 and 16 April 1942.

9 Earlier in his report Lenard described how fellow prisoner Gottlieb had asked him to find out whether the transport from Nitra included his father.

can imagine how we felt when they told us that they'd come as far as Lublin with their wives, daughters, and children, and only men came to us. So, in their boundless bestiality they [the Germans] were transporting not just Jewish men but also women and children to Poland. We never found out what happened to them.[10] I only heard from one of them that as far as he was informed, they'd gone to Lubartów. He never told me the source of his news, because he went to work with another group, and on Sunday, when I wanted to talk to him, he'd gone. He'd died.

Then so many transports started to arrive that I entirely lost sight of which one came from where. The people on these transports had already been assigned to Feld 2 and Feld 3,[11] and it was very difficult for me to get to the barracks there. Towards the end of my time, there were 11,000 Slovak Jews, 3,000 from the Protectorate, and 3,000 Lublin Jews.[12] The Czech Jews had previously been held somewhere near Lublin, I don't know how long for, but where they claimed to have been better off by far. They were guarded by the Wehrmacht, which explains why they were treated better. One thing is certain: the members of the Wehrmacht were like babes-in-arms compared to the sadism, cruelty, and perverted proclivities of the SS men, Lithuanians, and Ukrainians.

The Protectorate Jews went to work on the cables, and I saw them when I worked near there. They worked separately from us, and they also got some minimum payment. While we walked distances of 10–12 kilometres to work on foot, they arrived on Wehrmacht trucks. Tibor Schneider[13] told me that he knew one of them, a factory owner from Boskovice in Moravia who had supplied him with sale-or-return clothing. I saw them talking together several times. They didn't know why they'd been sent to Lublin-Majdanek. I also learned that they had come from Terezín, where they had lived with their wives before coming under Wehrmacht supervision. They couldn't say what had then happened to their wives.

Then there were Jews there from the Lublin ghetto, where 50,000 Jews lived.[14] The ghetto was liquidated and 3,000 people were sent to us. They told us that many had been shot and not even half of them remained alive. They were a terrible sight. We'll look like that one day too, I thought, if we stay here for much longer. They were all skin and bone, their skin was an unhealthy colour, and their eyes were sunken. They were all riddled with lice, which directly contradicts what Mr Fiala wrote in the *Grenzbote*,[15] where he praises the order and cleanliness in the camps and ghettos. The Lublin Jews were immediately given clothing from Lublin hospital, which the Germans had emptied of all patients so they could occupy it for the Wehrmacht. Their things were supposed to be

10 Family transports were sent via the transit stops Lublin and Nałęczów to the ghettos in Chełm, Radzyń, and Puławy in April 1942. Starting in June 1942, women, children, and the elderly were sent directly to Sobibor, where they were murdered.

11 German in the original: Feld ('field') was the name given to a camp section (compound) in Majdanek.

12 On 24 June 1942, a few weeks after Lenard's escape, the SS recorded 10,339 male Jewish prisoners.

13 Tibor Schneider (1914–1943?) was from Vrútky, a small town in north-western Slovakia.

14 Lublin ghetto had approximately 36,000 inhabitants in late 1941; of these, 26,000 were deported to Belzec in March and April 1942 and several thousand were shot in the woods at Krępiec.

15 Fritz Fiala (1906–1999), journalist; editor-in-chief of the German-language daily *Grenzbote: Deutsches Tageblatt für die Karpatenländer*, which was published in Bratislava from 1919 to 1945; in 1942 he visited several camps and ghettos in the General Government and compiled propaganda reports on them; later worked as a Gestapo agent in Turkey, then for the American Office of Strategic Services (OSS); journalist in Bonn after the war.

burned, and little by little they were. Various items, such as combs, clothing, toiletries of all sorts, wallets, etc., etc., were all piled up in heaps near our work site and burned. Ignoring the risk of a thrashing, we went there when it was at all possible. We kept circling the bonfire like hyenas and were glad when we managed to save something from the fire.

Two days after the Jewish men had arrived from the Lublin ghetto, 2,000 women arrived, also from the ghetto. They were first housed in the camp, then they were loaded into trucks. By chance I was nearby when they were taken away. What I saw next seemed unbelievable even then. I understand that they beat men up. Men are tougher and can endure more, they don't take it so hard, but kicking defenceless women, hitting them with rifles when they weren't able to clamber onto a truck quickly enough! There was a 5-year-old girl there (at least, she looked that old), pretty as an angel, with long, curly blond hair. Not even Raphael could have painted her prettier. They pushed her into the mud because she was a little bit in the way. When the innocent, uncomprehending child began to cry because someone tried to hurt her for no reason, an SS man boxed her ears. If Politzer[16] from Vrútky hadn't held me back, I would have killed him on the spot. I saw it like this: they weren't human, they weren't even animals, but beings from another world who don't belong on this planet.

Of all the people I knew, Hugo and Emil Mittelmann[17] had the best positions in the camp – they were warehousemen. They distributed tools such as shovels and pickaxes, and they had rails and mine carts in their inventory. Then Dr Szánto[18] and Kohn, the sergeant major's son, both from Žilina, who worked in the office. Even these were only relatively good jobs, because they were thrashed there as well. In fact, most of the SS men spoke a damned impossible dialect, so it was very hard to understand them, and many conflicts erupted as a result. For us Jews, taking over some of the innocent functions in the camp was risky, but even then, Jewish functionaries could help us if they retained some of their humanity, which wasn't always the case.

The first Lagerältester[19] was a tall, likeable young man; I think his name was Weiner[20] (I can't swear to this, but I think he came from Nové Mesto nad Váhom). He and Lagerältester no. 2, Ladislav Goldstücker from Brezno district, also a respectable and likeable youth, were our Jewish direct supervisors, but in theory only. Their duties mostly consisted of assisting the guards as they sent people to work and assigning them to various tasks. They had the advantage of not going to work but being in the camp all day. Less important orders were given to them, and they passed them on to us. In any case, they were respectable men who gave us encouragement, so we didn't lose heart. They also created the illusion that we'd be able to write letters soon, saying they apparently knew

16 Probably Viliam Politzer (1913–1942); originally from Vrútky; deported from Žilina to Lublin on 27 March 1942; perished in Auschwitz.

17 The brothers Hugo (1894–1942) and Emil Mittelmann (1898–1942?) were from Vrútky and lived in Brezno until they were deported; Hugo perished in Auschwitz, and Emil in Lublin.

18 Dr Friedrich (Fritz) Szánto (b. 1913), physician; originally from Žilina; deported to Lublin on the transport on 27 March 1942; murdered.

19 German in the original: 'camp elder'.

20 Bedřich (Fr(i)edrich) Weiner (b. 1909); originally from Nové Mesto nad Váhom; deported from Žilina to Lublin on 27 March 1942; camp elder in Compound I of Majdanek concentration camp; murdered.

this from the best of sources. And when this later turned out to be a false hope, they had meant well and we'd had three weeks of looking forward to something.

In addition, each block had one Blockältester[21] and one Blockschreiber,[22] who were in charge of order and provisions. Nothing good can be said about these people. Most of them were unprincipled gangsters who stole even the little food we were supposed to get. Only occasionally was one of them actually human, a very rare exception.

All the food that was to be divided between us went to them. It wasn't so easy for them to pilfer food from the 'bunkers', so instead they misplaced [our] bread and jam, blood sausage and margarine; they stole from us so much that we didn't even get the minimum allocation of 40 g. They got the bread before lunch and the other things after lunch, but they didn't distribute the bread until evening, so that they had the opportunity to fiddle the portions while we were at work. They stole like magpies and we couldn't speak out against these hyenas. Once, when my good friend Julius Kohn[23] spoke up, asking them to distribute the bread before lunch because we were all hungry and could hardly wait for it, Mr Spitzer from Trnava reported him to the Lagerleitung[24] for rebelling, for which Kohn got 50 lashes on his behind from the strongest of the SS men every week from then on (I hope I will meet this gentleman again, if Kohn himself doesn't kill him first). I have to say that even though from then on Kohn had a lot of bees in his bonnet, I admired him. He didn't make a sound although he was obviously in pain, and I could see the wounds on his body as I lay beside him. The Blockältester from Barrack 5, whose name I don't know, also had the perverted proclivity to thrash people with a belt for absolutely no reason. This stooge hit one of the Barrack 5 men in the eye so hard that he went blind.

What do people like this deserve? Such Jews, healthy or pathological, should be shot without mercy like rabid dogs. However brutally our enemies beat us, we don't expect anything else from them. But our own flesh and blood, our fellow sufferers? You would really have thought you were in a madhouse, and I'm surprised myself that I didn't go mad.

I talked a lot about escaping with Prager[25] from Kremnica,[26] who had arrived with the Žilina transport. As so often, he agreed with me: Yes, you are right – assimilation won't help here; we need to resolve the Jewish question in a different way. Although we generally used the familiar form of address with everyone, every now and then people slipped, and he used the polite form with me here. All the people I talked to were completely agreed on one thing: we had never before experienced anything so brutal, so inhumane. When I was comparing the statement by one of the men from Zvolen,[27] who had been a prisoner in Russia, with what we were experiencing, the difference was beyond words. Some people in Slovakia may think that the young maybe had greater value than the old, and argue that the young are better able to work. That's a fairy tale, nothing

21 German in the original: 'block elder'.
22 German in the original: 'block clerk'.
23 Julius Kohn (1904–1943/1944); originally from Žilina; lived in Púchov; deported from Žilina to Lublin on 27 March 1942; died as a partisan.
24 German in the original: 'camp leadership'.
25 Emil Prager.
26 Small town in central Slovakia.
27 Town in central Slovakia.

more, and a hypothesis with absolutely no basis in fact. You could be young or old, but death was still lying in wait with each step, without the least wrongdoing on your part, under entirely absurd circumstances. I remember this case: A man of around 30 was walking across the yard one evening, maybe at around 7 p.m., sometime in May. He went along the planks that connected the barracks to the latrine. The mud and water were so deep that even the SS-Männer[28] had rubber boots on their feet, even they needed to use the planks so they weren't up to their knees in mud. An SS-Mann was walking about 20 metres ahead of him. The Jew slipped on the plank and fell face down into the mud with his behind sticking out. The SS-Mann seized his revolver and shot him dead. Probably no commentary is necessary. The bare facts suffice.

Tibor Schneider from Vrútky often asked me whether I thought he would ever see his wife again. Will we ever get out of here alive???? What will happen to us??? I told him, 'It's hard for me to give you an answer to these questions, but if things continue at this pace, not one of us will survive, even if they don't shoot us. This can't be endured, either mentally or physically or in terms of nerves. And even if by some miracle we were to get out of this hell, we wouldn't find any of our friends or relatives at home. But even so, it's entirely unrealistic, when you see that of the 50,000 Lublin Jews, only 3,000 remained, so why would they spare us? Despite this, we must keep calm. Maybe at least some of us will make it through and resist, and be living witnesses of the age of the restored, modernized inquisition. Some of us must hold out so we can report on the many crimes of this horde of mass murderers. Would you go with me?' I continued, 'Let's try to make it through in any way we can.' He proposed, 'I must admit, my friend, that I'm not brave enough for such an escape, but try it alone; maybe you'll succeed.' Coming across the yard just then with two buckets of water was Braun from Brezno, who looked terrible. 'You see, I don't want to stay here. Just look at Braun there. I knew him in Brezno, and not long ago I saw him in Slovakia, and what does he look like now? I can't believe that it's him, and I don't want to look like that. I'll get away any way I can.' 'Please, if you succeed,' he begged me, 'go to my wife, explain to her what it's like here. Have her do whatever it takes so she doesn't end up here herself. You advise her what you think is best. Promise me this and go to her.' And this, even though the poor soul already knew that she would no longer be in Slovakia before I could get there. Actually, she was no longer in Slovakia before I got out of the Lublin camp.[29]

Everyone I talked to about the possibility of escaping advised me not to do it, and the closer the decisive day came, the more even my former conspirators Strasser[30] and Schlesinger[31] lost their nerve. Only Prager from Kremnica half-believed it was possible to get away from there, but even he had certain reservations and tried to talk me out of the plan.

People were so intimidated by the way of life [in the camp], constant thrashings, and fear that I regretted even opening up to them about my plan. However, not only did I not

28 German in the original: 'SS men' (below, SS-Mann: 'SS man').
29 Tibor Schneider's wife, Hilda, later Hilda Lebedun, survived several camps and emigrated to the United States in 1948.
30 Heinrich Strasser was from Vrbové, a small town in western Slovakia.
31 Probably Edmund Schlesinger (b. 1907), radio technician; born in Brezno; later lived in Turčiansky Svätý Martin; deported from Žilina to Lublin on 27 March 1942.

give up on my thoughts of escape, but my resolve to carry them out also grew stronger by the day. As I saw more and more transports arriving, more and more new unfortunates with patches on their coats, like oxen driven to the slaughterhouse, women and children being kicked and beaten, 17,000 tragedies,[32] 17,000 personified question marks, worse than slaves from any era – I knew I could not stay there. For some, the best that could happen to you in Lublin was enough – become a latrine cleaner, cleaning up faeces every day and breathing in the stink so as to not have to work in mud and water in winter and frost. But I had to leave because I was afraid I would go mad if I stayed much longer.

I couldn't sleep due to the horrible uncertainty about what had happened to my parents[33] and fiancée. I pondered and perfected various plans for how to get out of there. But sleep wasn't an option, not on the bare wooden planks where we were crammed in like sardines. You had to be careful that those on the bunks above didn't step on your head. Mud from their boots dropped onto you at any time. Initially there were no bedbugs, but they later multiplied to an unbelievable number, which increased from one day to the next. If any sophisticated means of torture exists in the world, it's depriving people of sleep. We couldn't sleep on that wood, however exhausted we were, because we grew thinner every day, we were all skin and bones, and then there were the bedbugs on top of that. We looked like spectres in the morning, when it was impossible to wash unless you wanted to sacrifice your breakfast, and then the nervous tension made it worse. Please don't let them make me work in the Kohlenkolonne[34] (that was what we were most afraid of) or on laying cables. Those and similar worries tortured all of us. No wonder that some began to lose their minds and became like children with all this tension.

Under these conditions my intention to escape at all costs only hardened, no matter how great the risk. Three days before my escape, we were all supposed to get the hospital uniforms, as I learned from a clerk in the office. I knew that as soon I was dressed in such a uniform, any escape would be impossible and I wouldn't even get so far as a metre. Getting hold of boots instead of clogs as well as any clothing and food caused me certain difficulties. I also hadn't yet decided which time of day was best for escaping. I considered Saturday to be the best day. There weren't so many SS men in the camp at dinner time, numbers weren't checked as precisely as at other times, as the SS members, apart from those on guard duty, went to their quarters in town. As the moment of my escape approached, I became more tense and nervous, which is no surprise. A legion of seductive visions ran past my mind's eye. Away, away, away from this hell, only so I could eat a plateful of cooked potatoes (we considered this the height of bliss), away to somewhere where you wouldn't have to be afraid that someone will stop you with a whip from relieving yourself and leave you with a wet behind, where there is no roll call, mud or water, where there are no huts with 17,000 corpses, deader than the dead!

The day before I escaped, I got hold of some size 40 boots, and some clothing. I bartered one suit for a piece of bread and 10 złoty with a Pole. I wouldn't have been able

32 This is a reference to the number of inmates in Lublin-Majdanek concentration camp.

33 Dionýz Lenard's father, Adolf Lenard, was deported from Žilina to Auschwitz-Birkenau on 29 April 1942; it is likely his mother Teresa Lenard also perished in Auschwitz.

34 German in the original: 'coal detail'.

to do any of this so easily if it hadn't been for the Jews from the Lublin ghetto, whose clothes were stored in the storerooms that some of our people had access to. In this way the misery of many led to the deliverance of one. I hid these things among spare parts I found at the construction site. I almost forgot: From the same Pole I also got hold of 200 g of German tobacco, which was a nice colour but tasted like hay, and two packets of cigarette papers in exchange for a pair of shoes. This exchange was later very useful to me. In addition, I also had three old razor blades, soap for washing (approx. 50 g), which I also used for shaving, a razor, and a cap. This was all I was equipped with for making my escape.

On a Saturday in early June,[35] I set out as usual for work with the Facharbeiter.[36] I experienced a very strange moment as I went through the gate and thought that either I would die or I would successfully escape and never see Lublin again. I no longer hoped to find my parents or fiancée in Slovakia, even though I hadn't given up all hope. I was convinced that there were still Jews in Slovakia and that if I couldn't directly help my unfortunate brothers in Lublin, I would instead be able to vividly explain the situation in Poland to any Jews remaining in Slovakia, so they wouldn't wait for slaughter like sheep, submissively, ready with their suitcases, resigned to their fate and God's will. No, this isn't fate; fate does not exist for a man of strong will and an upright backbone! However not even God, if any God exists, wants this, and if any God does exist and does want people to be murdered like cattle, girls to be raped by Ukrainians, and small innocent children to be pushed into the mud, beaten, killed by sadism personified, people to be tortured for being Jews and for daring to be alive, I must cry, with Bialik:[37] 'Where are you, God, if you exist? Show yourself before I destroy your throne!'[38]

I was going to advise the Slovak Jews who remained to hide in the forest, live the life of hermits or live like animals – because life in Lublin is worse than the life of an animal. I thought that I would go from town to town, towns where there are Jews, and tell them the pure truth, so they know that it's not enough to beat their breasts and shout, 'Ashamnu, we have sinned!' It isn't possible to fight violence and brutality with fair methods, because after what I saw in Lublin, I say, 'I can forgive anything, even murder, to save a human life. You cannot live as sheep among wolves, and you need to fight, if not for us, then at least for those who come after us.' If anyone's relative were to be taken away, and that person felt obliged to follow their relative to Poland, they are not being heroic, and I would advise them not to go. Nobody is helped if four people are miserable instead of two, at least not when it comes to Polish camps. It isn't the case that people in reduced circumstances better endure poverty together by sharing the little they have, and in

35 On 6 June 1942.

36 German in the original: 'skilled workers'.

37 Chaim Nachman Bialik (1873–1934); Jewish poet from Russia who wrote in Hebrew and Yiddish; emigrated in 1924 to Palestine, where he became a pivotal activist in Zionist cultural activities. He is considered the modern Jewish 'national poet'.

38 Lenard seems to have misremembered this quotation from Bialik's 'On the Slaughter' (written in 1903, first published in Hebrew in 1904), which begins 'Sky, have mercy on me! / If there be in you a God and to that God a path …' The lines 'And if there is justice – let's see it now! / But if after my 'cleansing' under this sky / justice comes / Let its chair [throne] be cast out for all time!' appear in the third stanza. Taken from Hayim Nahman Bialik, *Songs from Bialik: Selected Poems of Hayim Nahman Bialik*, trans. from Hebrew Atar Hadari (Syracuse, NY: Syracuse University Press, 2000).

Poland it means something entirely different. After all, how will you feel when your loved ones die slowly, right before your eyes, and you are entirely helpless? And how would you feel if you had travelled away with your whole family to, let's say, Lublin, only to be separated from your family, your wife and children sent to Lubartów, and you don't just experience the separation but also maltreatment, and you have to reckon with the fact that your loved ones are experiencing the same? As I feel when women and children are raped by Ukrainians or sell themselves for a piece of bread because they are so hungry! You must think about that. While you still have some opportunity to act, it may benefit both sides, both those in Poland and those who are still free right now.

Alas, many things turned out very differently than I had expected. I had to go to Hungary, so it wasn't possible for me to talk to different people remaining here, but I hope that, even so, my reports reached the right place and they were duly made use of.[39]

At the work site, as soon as it was possible I approached Strasser and Schlesinger, with whom I had agreed to escape, and asked them if they had everything ready for this evening. They answered me very evasively, from which I deduced that they had little desire to escape, or that cowardice had overcome them at the decisive moment. I thought it would pass and that they would still come with me, come evening. Not even in my dreams would it have occurred to me then that despite all the risks, they would abandon the escape. Time passed rapidly, the hours flew by with insane speed. In my mind I combined the possibilities of obtaining food (I wasn't at all informed about the life of Polish Jews; we'd had very little contact with the Lublin Jews, who worked on a different work detail). As a last resort I decided I would break into an apartment or a farmhouse and provide myself with food there. As for sleep, I still didn't have a firm plan, sleeping outside was risky and also unpleasant because of the morning dew, but I hoped that some solution could be found.

Lunchtime came. We went to the barracks, but I didn't have much of an appetite. After lunch I again reminded Strasser and Schlesinger to be ready when I came for them at 5 p.m. and they quietly assured me, fine. At around 4 p.m. I became very nervous. I still had no idea about where we would hide before leaving for the barracks, or about the number and distance of the guards from the work site. I had no information about any of this. However, I was convinced that our escape would be successful. At 4.30 p.m. I waited for Strasser and Schlesinger and told them that it was very nearly time. But they answered that they still hadn't decided, that they didn't have any things or clothing, and they also wanted to talk me out of the plan, citing how dangerous it was. I was very angry, and I think that I even became rude, which was, however, justified, given my situation. Later I was glad that I had set out on this path alone. I told them that they were slaves who deserved to be enslaved. After all, of course, not everyone can get out of the camp, but we are young, courageous, and imaginative, and it is our duty to ourselves and to Jewish society to get away now, even if the likelihood of success is only one in a thousand. They thought that this was hollow talk, that the whole thing was too dangerous, that we would risk certain death if we were caught. That was my opinion

39 Lenard's account was not made known to the Slovakian Jews after his escape. The deportations were temporarily halted in late 1942, by which time 58,000 Jews from Slovakia had been deported to Poland; they resumed in autumn 1944.

too, but at the same time I thought freedom was worth that risk. Then, cautiously, when I saw that they were too afraid to come, I said, fine, I'll change my mind and stay.

At 5 p.m., after carefully collecting all my things, I tried to get underneath one of the front-row barracks on Feld 4 to wait for evening. The barracks all stand on stilts 20 cm above the ground. Unfortunately, I couldn't cram myself underneath despite how skinny I was, and I had to carefully crawl my way out again. In the end I decided to hide among the construction materials. Various components for building barracks were piled up on the work site to a height of three to four metres. There were all sorts of hidden little pathways between them, created by the gradual removal of individual boards and beams. I hid in one of these pathways and, thinking that the mood always improves after eating, I ate my bread and bacon. I finished eating and was soon asleep on the ground with fatigue. When I woke up, it was quite late. The evening was dark. As I looked around me I couldn't see any guards, only the dull light of the floodlights from the inhabited compounds. Fortunately, the floodlights illuminated the centre of the inhabited compounds, primarily the courtyard, so I felt more confident. As far as I knew, the guards were somewhere around, and I had to be very careful. First of all, I removed the clogs from my feet. I was wearing shoes under them. I tore the star and numbers from my jacket and trousers. I also ditched the metal strip from my wrist. It was terribly quiet all around me. I was a bit afraid, that cannot be denied, but as soon as I had discarded those badges and taken off the clogs, I felt a definite relief. I'd also intended to shave, but there was no water anywhere. My beard had grown thick and I was afraid of being conspicuous. So I used saliva instead of water to shave and barely shaved myself at all. With the old razor blade and a beard of two weeks, shaving was torment for my face, and the soap for washing could not make shaving any nicer. Despite this, the more I wiped away the atmosphere of Lublin camp and became a man like before, the freer and lighter I felt. There was still a long and dangerous path before me. I actually wasn't out of reach of the camp or guards yet, and the path was long and full of danger. I crawled out of my hiding place and carefully went westwards. I still didn't have an exact plan for which way I would go, I only knew this much: if I keep going west, I must get to Cracow or Nowy Targ at some point, from where I could then go south to reach Slovakia. After a few metres I spotted the outline of the guards, Lithuanians, maybe 150 metres apart. I dropped to my knees and crawled silently over the still thin grass. It took me about half an hour to get out of the danger zone, and I felt new relief. I had succeeded in this too. Unfortunately, I then suddenly fell prey to fear that I would be discovered. I imagined my absence from the camp and Barrack 6 being discovered, and I pictured the hunt for me that must end with me losing. I hadn't felt so afraid in the entire time I'd spent in the camp, nor afterwards during the entire escape. After a while I pulled myself together and continued on my way. The closer I was to my goal, and the farther from the site of my former enslavement, the more I began to be troubled by practical questions. Should I go along the main road or take country lanes? Where should I get food? How would I sleep? And how would I prove my identity?

The first task was to get away from the camp perimeter. Therefore, although I was very sleepy, I went as fast as my legs could carry me. It was starting to get light, the sun slowly came up, it was maybe around 5 a.m. when near the road to Chełm I passed the last sign with the warning: 'Achtung – Uwaga'.

Now I could breathe a sigh of relief. I was convinced that I had left the worst behind me. I went on westwards, with no exact destination, along country lanes, avoiding people. I walked for two days like this, without seeing anyone from close up. I was afraid that if any Pole said anything to me, he would immediately see I was a foreigner and report me. I also didn't know what I would say if I was questioned by a civilian. I was terribly hungry, and I doubted I could endure this a few more hours. By the end of the first day, my fear was even greater – I slept with my stomach empty. Lying down was also a little comical. Near the railway line I saw thickly planted shrubs. I waited until it got dark and lay down among them. Of course, sleep was out of the question. I dozed off now and then, woke up, fell asleep again for a while, on and on until morning. Meanwhile, the dew fell and getting wet was very unpleasant. The second evening I slept under a tree. At around 6 p.m. I was hit by rain, heavy but not torrential, and I sheltered under a chestnut tree. It was maybe 500 m from the village, standing in a field, and I thought that I could sleep under it, so I did. By the morning of the third day I felt very weak, so I decided to get hold of some food and never mind any risks. I went into the village, where the women and girls were carrying milk in cans. I asked at several houses if I could buy milk. Because I barely knew a word of Polish, I spoke in very broken Slovak. In one place they told me they didn't have any milk because the cow had calved, in another, that they'd already delivered their milk, and so on. I went around maybe 15 houses, but didn't get any food anywhere. This began to seem stupid and, not wishing to attract attention, I left the village. About half an hour out of the village, I saw a pretty little farmhouse, and I couldn't see anyone close by who might harm me, so I went there. Two young men were at home, one of them was about 24 and the other about 20. I repeated my request to buy milk. They then explained milk was in short supply, that in Poland it was mandatory to hand over all milk and eggs, grain, potatoes, etc., but they had coffee and would give me a little. They started talking to me and told me that the farm belonged to their widowed mother, who had gone to Lublin to do some shopping, which was why they were alone at home.

As to myself, I told them that I was Hungarian (I knew that the Poles sympathize with the Hungarians), that I worked at Baťa in Hungary,[40] that the Hungarians had moved me to the Polish border, and that now I was on my way to Slovakia, where I had relatives. As we talked, I saw a green uniform approach on a bicycle. When the bicycle stopped at the house where I was, well, I thought, it looks bad for you now, someone must have been following me when I arrived and reported me. The boys quickly pushed me into the larder, where I waited in fear of what was going to happen. After a while the boys called me out and reassured me. It was only a soldier from Lublin who had come for the eggs.

Although I was very interested in life in Poland, I didn't intend to ask these young men anything, out of caution, in case it compromised me in their eyes in some way. I asked them if I might shave here, and the younger brought me some hot water and I shaved. My hair had also grown a bit long, but I nevertheless worried that a bald head might be more conspicuous. I don't know what they thought of me, but in any case they were very discreet and didn't ask me many questions. (Unlike Jews who, when you ask for something, interrogate you like a detective, so they can finally get rid of you under some pretext or other.) I washed myself properly in the hot water, so despite only sleep-

40 The company founded in 1894 by Czech shoe manufacturer Tomáš Baťa (1876–1932) had numerous branches outside Czechoslovakia. Nowadays the company is known as the Bata Corporation.

ing for a short time, I felt a different man. Meanwhile the coffee had been made, and the older boy offered me a half-litre cup with a big lump of bread. Judging by the colour, the bread was the same as we got in the camp, but it tasted much better. It's interesting that throughout my journey in Poland, I never saw bread the same colour as in Slovakia, except in Tarnów; it was always dark, but there were also plenty of confectionery products made of potato flour. When I had drunk the coffee and eaten the bread, he gave me another such portion of bread and coffee. I forgot to mention that I had brought with me a military water canteen from the camp, which did me great service later too.

Once I had finished my breakfast, they filled the canteen with coffee, gave me three hard-boiled eggs for the journey, as well as 150 g of good pork sausage and a piece of bread. They advised me regarding the direction I should go in, always close to the railway line to Rozwadów. But not too close, because of the railway police who patrol along there. They also taught me to ask the way in Polish: 'Prosze, pana, kde tu drogu do …'[41] I said goodbye, thanked them, and went on my way. After that pleasant intermezzo, I saw everything more rosily, although I was still a very long way from overcoming all obstacles. I went on, staying close to the railway line. When I thought it was time for lunch, I ate from my stocks that the young man had given me for my journey and continued walking. Until the afternoon nothing unusual happened. I walked, tired but cautious. Despite the fact that I was already more or less free, I felt like hunted game, always looking around at all sides, anticipating the possible and the impossible. It was precisely the circumstance that I was out of the camp's reach but still not safe that forced me to be more careful.

Only then did I realize what freedom was, when I saw the difference once I was free. While I was in the camp, I had no yardstick I could use to compare the difference between the periods before and after the camp, to compare those times with each other. When I was drowning in a swamp of brutality and inhumanity, I didn't feel so much or so intensely the value of what I had lost as I did now that I had re-entered human life directly from that disaster. It didn't matter that I slept on the hard, cold ground. It didn't matter that I had no food or hadn't eaten for maybe two days; after all, I was a man again. I was already imagining how happy and surprised my parents and fiancée would be to see me. Oh Hope, if other Jews also see me, they will surely rejoice when I bring them news of their relatives.

It was maybe 3 p.m. when, on a country lane, I met the first Polish Jew whom I talked to. It wasn't me who addressed him, but rather he who stopped me, recognizing me as a Jew immediately. I told him where I'd come from, entirely openly, and expressed my surprise that there were still Jews here. He told me that although the majority of Jews had been taken away and murdered, there were still some Jews in ghettos both open and sealed. I was astonished to hear that a poor Jewish family lived at the end of the village, and that I could try knocking on the door and asking to be put up for the night. In addition, he gave me a white armband with a blue Star of David, the sort that Jews in Poland wear,[42] so I could put it on when I arrived among Jews. I wore that armband on

41 Polish (approximate) for 'Excuse me, how do I get to …'.

42 From 1 Dec. 1939 Jewish residents of the General Government over 11 years old were required to wear a white armband with a six-pointed blue star (the so-called Star of Zion) on the right sleeve of their outer garments.

my left shoulder. Because I was feeling very hungry, I decided to visit that family. I thought all the more that I must inform myself about the rest of my journey, possibly even take a look at a map. I carefully approached the house in which that family lived, and in an unwatched moment I slipped inside. After I knocked, I heard a terrified Polish voice saying 'come in' and entered the room. There were six people in the room, a mother, four children under the age of ten, and a 20-year-old woman. The room was messy and they were cooking.

Later I learned that it was used as kitchen, dining room, and bedroom by eight people. Two families lived here, as well as the 20-year-old woman with her husband. The two men were at work, which is why they weren't present. The furnishings were extremely primitive. This was no surprise. Both families had fled Lublin and further admitted, after I had told them part of my story, that the husband and father of the children had been taken to the Lublin camp at Majdanek. I told them that approximately 3,000 men had come to us from the ghetto, so he was certainly among them.

When I entered the room, a dinner was being cooked, or lunch, of potatoes, borscht, and tea. The borscht wasn't made of beetroot, but of beetroot leaves, and a vegetable of some sort was used to make tea. I'm not sure but I think they might have been strawberry leaves. They also offered me food, although this certainly shrank their household budget, because some extra cooking started as soon as I had eaten my potatoes.[43]

[…]

Equipped with my gifts, I continued on my way again. The sun beat down more and more. I walked along, up and down. I almost instinctively knew the right direction. I must say that in most cases [I went] from village to village gathering information […]. […] [I met] two boys, one 15 and one 22 (the older was deaf), walking with a 20-year-old girl. The four of them lived by begging. They went [to the houses] and were given potatoes or clothing here and there. [They claimed to be] Ukrainians, other times Poles […]. Usually [they sold] what they had begged in the neighbouring village. [I asked them] how things were with travelling, if you regularly had to prove your identity on the train and if an escort passed through the train. By now […] my feet hurt and were red raw. […] got 50 złoty together […], in the morning at 2.30 a.m., before buying a ticket from an Aryan. […]

I went to the usual places, the Judenrat,[44] the Jewish soup kitchen. In this second town I met a Czech Jew who worked in the kitchen as a functionary. I don't know how that happened.

In Tarnów I saw a Jew who couldn't prove his identity shot before my eyes at a distance of four metres. In the Judenrat I met some Shomrim[45] who gave me advice about the path I should take and about how to cross the border. I stayed in Tarnów for one day and then I went on my way on foot to Nowy Sącz. This was now the most difficult part of my journey – getting from Tarnów to Nowy Sącz along the main road, alongside which were armaments buildings guarded by police. I made it through this stretch too, although not with the best of feelings, as I saw many police officers to my right and left. After a while the path led between hills (and starting at Tarnów I walked the whole way along the main road), and the road climbed and zigzagged quite high up. By midday I

43 Here the continuous account stops and is followed by fragments of damaged pages.
44 German in the original: 'Jewish Council'.
45 Members of Hashomer Hatzair.

arrived at Zakliczin or Zaklików[46] and stayed there until the morning of the following day. There they warned me to be careful in Nowy Sącz, because 600 Jews had been shot there, so I should move around the town with caution. The road to Nowy Sącz was very pretty; they are constructing dams. I think the Dunajec river flows there, and all the way I saw Jews and Aryans at work.

Dusk was already beginning to fall when I arrived in Nowy Sącz on the following day. I went to the Judenrat, but they drove me away within five minutes, they were terribly frightened. According to reports, many tragedies had taken place in Nowy Sącz and its surroundings. Jews were hunted like animals in Grybów, old or young, children, invalids, and 600 Jews had been shot there. While I was leaving the town there was a terrible downpour which delayed me there. I ran to one house near the bridge, where the Jewish doctor lived, and ran up the stairs to the attic. Nobody was home at that time. The stairs were wooden and I lay down and slept on the stairs.

During the night I got what Strasser [called] 'Der Drang von Achren'[47] back in the Lublin camp, and had to – forgive me – relieve the pressure on the stairs. I could not go outside as the gate was closed. In the morning, as soon as the gate was[48] [open], I found the road to Stary Sącz, as I didn't want to ask anyone the way. That same day I arrived in Stary Sącz, where my revelation had the same effect on the Jews there as it did in Nowy Sącz. When I asked about some small details about the border crossing where I was to cross, nobody wanted to give them to me. As it was already slowly getting dark, I left the village, having first been shaved by a Jewish barber. I lay down beyond the village behind some barns. I set off early in the morning along the main road towards the village of Pyvnica.[49] I walked for half a day. The closer I came to the decisive step of crossing the border into Slovakia, the more nervous I became. I was already very tired, very drained. At around 1 p.m. I reached a river where I bathed my feet. I was probably very lucky there, because five minutes after I had been soaking my feet in the river, which was lower than the highway, a motorcycle with gendarmes roared by. I went on until around 3 p.m., when I came across some Gypsies who were crushing rocks on the road. One of them, an elderly man, called me into his house, which stood near the highway. I went to him, driven by curiosity about what he wanted from me. Inside, he immediately told me, half in Polish, half in Slovak, that I was a Jew. I agreed, at which he started an entirely companionable conversation. Finally, he told me which direction I should go in, indicated the signposted mountain path across the Tatras to the last Polish village of Nemce, and gave me many useful pieces of advice for the route. When I tried to offer him some of the bread that I had bought in Stary Sącz, he wouldn't hear of it. Ultimately I gave him three Polish cigarettes, a little tobacco and matches, so that I didn't take anything Polish into Slovakia with me. I thanked him for his valuable advice and set off through the forest to Rytičalá.[50] Careful to follow the signs, I had walked for about

46 Lenard probably travelled through Zakliczyn, a small town on the western bank of the Dunajec river.
47 German in the original. Most likely this should read 'Der Drang von Achtern' ('the urge from behind'), a reference to diarrhoea.
48 One or two words missing in the original.
49 Correctly: Piwniczna, a spa town.
50 Presumably Roztoka Ryterska, located in the Beskid Mountains south of Rytro.

three hours when I noticed that I had reached the place I had left from. I set off again, paying close attention. After a while it began to rain harder than I have ever experienced in my life. I was soaked to the skin. The rain stopped as suddenly as it had started and the sky cleared, so I began to walk fast in order to dry out somewhat. Slowly it became time to find myself some sort of shelter. […] only some sort of larger kennel. I lay down in it, having first gathered grass in the clearing, as I didn't want to expose myself to any rain that might surprise me in my sleep.[51]

In the morning I continued on my way, by now extremely hungry, having had nothing to eat other than a piece of bread. I reached some little houses – this was in the border village. I carefully went round it and went on, finding the waymarks beyond it. A few minutes later I arrived at the stone marking the border. If at that moment I had been asked to describe my impressions as I reached the border, I would have found it very difficult to do so. I felt deranged with so many confused, different thoughts and feelings passing through me. Once I was on the Slovak side, I encountered a shepherd, whom I understood only with difficulty. Although he showed me the way to Stará Ľubovňa, I must have taken the wrong path, because after walking for an hour I saw two German 'financiers'.[52] I lay down in the grass, thinking that they would go away, and indeed, a few minutes later they were nowhere to be seen. I went on until behind me I heard a shout, already on Slovak territory, stopping me and asking where I was going. As I already definitively knew that I was in Slovakia, I said that I was from Stará Ľubovňa but had lost my way here when visiting my uncle who has a shepherd's hut in the mountains. One of them probably didn't believe what I was saying, because he asked if I was a Jew. I began to imitate laughter so convincingly that I confused him and they showed me the way, so saying thank you politely, I headed down the hill to the village of Gňazdá.[53] That is how I got back to Slovakia after travelling for 32 days from the Lublin-Majdanek camp, number 2838, from where I proceeded to Hungary.

My dear friend, please inform all your friends and family about what I have written, that I couldn't meet with you in person, as I had to disappear quickly into Hungary and wrote this letter there, the product of twelve days of work. In the hope that my words are not in vain, I send my heartfelt greetings to you and your good […].[54]

Šaňo

51 It is possible that Lenard wanted to stop up holes in the roof with the grass.

52 Presumably a colloquial term for German customs officials who patrolled the border and carried out inspections.

53 A village in north-eastern Slovakia. Since 1948 it has been called Hniezdne.

54 Only the first two letters, 'ma', are legible; it is possible Lenard wrote 'wife' (*manželka*) or 'mama'.

## DOC. 89

### *New York Times*, 2 July 1942: summary of a report that contains figures of murdered Jews with places of executions, and calls for retribution against Germans[1]

*Allies Are Urged to Execute Nazis. Report on Slaughter of Jews in Poland Asks Like Treatment for Germans. Curb on Reich Is Sought. 'Only Way to Save Millions From Certain Destruction,' Says the Appeal.*
Wireless to the New York Times

London, July 1 – The Polish Government in London has been urged in a report[2] on the slaughter of 700,000 Jews in German-occupied territories to call on the Allied governments to adopt a policy of retaliation that will force the Germans to cease their killings.

'We believe,' the report says, 'that Hitler's Germany in time will be punished for all its horrors, crimes and brutality but this is no comfort for the millions menaced with death. We implore the Polish Government, the guardian representative of all the peoples of Poland, to protect them against complete annihilation, to influence the Allied governments to apply similar treatment against Germans and fifth columnists[3] living at present in Allied countries.

'Let all Germans know this, know that punishment will be meted out to Germans in the United States and other countries.

'We realize we ask the Polish Government to do something most difficult and unusual but this is the only way to save millions of Jews from certain destruction.'

The report, describing the Jews' ordeal in occupied Poland and German attempts to exterminate the Jewish population, reached London through underground channels. Szmul Zygelbojm, Jewish Socialist leader and member of the Polish National Council in London, received it and vouched for its trustworthiness. He said the sources were absolutely reliable, although the story seemed too terrible and the atrocities too inhuman to be true.[4]

*700,000 Victims Listed*
The report is supported by information received by other Jewish circles here and also by the Polish Government. Its figure of 700,000 Jews slain by the Germans since the occupation – one-fifth of the entire Jewish population of Poland – probably includes many who died of maltreatment in concentration camps, of starvation in ghettos or unbearable conditions of forced labor.

1 *New York Times*, 2 July 1942, p. 6. The *New York Times* is a daily newspaper that has appeared since 1851.
2 See Doc. 74.
3 See Doc. 74, fn. 11.
4 Szmu(e)l Mordechai Zygielbojm (Zygelbojm), code name Artur (1895–1943), glover; grew up in a Hasidic family; member of the Bund's central committee from 1924; member of Łódź city council in 1938; fled from Poland to France in Jan. 1940, and from France to the USA in Sept. 1940; from March 1942 the Bund's representative on the National Council of the Polish government in exile in London, where he took his own life on 12 May 1943: see Doc. 241.

Here are the main items in the report:

From the first day of the German-Soviet occupation of East Poland the Germans began the extermination of Jews. They started in East Galicia last Summer. Males between 14 and 60 were herded into public squares and cemeteries, forced to dig their own graves and then were machine-gunned and hand-grenaded.

Children in orphanages, old persons in almshouses, the sick in hospitals and women were slain in the streets. In many places Jews were rounded up and deported to unrevealed destinations or massacred in near-by woods.

At Lwow 35,000 were slain, at Stanislawow, 15,000; at Tarnopol, 5,000; at Zloctrow,[5] 2,000; at Brzezany only 1,700 were left of 18,000. The massacre still continues in Lwow.

Last Fall the slaughter of Jews was extended to the Vilna and Kovno districts. By November 50,000 had been murdered in Vilna and only 12,000 were left. In the two districts the victims of the German slaughter numbered 300,000.

Simultaneously a massacre started in the Slonim district in Eastern Poland. Nine thousand were killed in the town of Slonim, 6,000 in Baranowicze. In Volhynia the killing began in November and in three days 15,000 had been massacred in Rovny[6] County.

*Gas Chambers Are Used*

In the early Winter the Germans were methodically proceeding with their campaign to exterminate all Jews. They sent special gas chambers on wheels to Western Poland, territories incorporated in the Reich. In the village of Chelmno near Kolo ninety persons at a time were put in the gas chambers.[7] The victims were buried in graves dug by them in near-by Lubarski forest.[8]

About 1,000 gassed daily from the townships of Kolo, Dabie, Izbica and others between November, 1941, and March, 1942, as well as 35,000 Jews in Lodz between Jan. 2 and Jan. 9. Two thousand 'gypsies' were gassed.[9] They probably were Yugoslav prisoners[10] and terrorists.

In February the murder wave reached the Gouvernement General area in Central Poland, Tarnow, Radom and Lublin. Twenty-five thousand were taken to an unrevealed destination from Lublin. Nothing has been heard of them since. A few were detained in the suburb of Majdanek; the others disappeared. No Jews were left in Lublin.

In Warsaw a 'blood bath' was arranged in the ghetto on the night of April 17. Homes were visited by the Gestapo and Jews of all classes were dragged out and killed.[11]

'This shows,' the report concludes, 'that the criminal German Government is fulfilling Hitler's threat that, whoever wins, all Jews will be murdered.'[12]

5 As in the original. Correctly: Złoczów.
6 As in the original. Correctly: Rovno (Równe).
7 Victims were suffocated by exhaust fumes directed into sealed gas vans.
8 The spot where the bodies were buried is today called Rzuchów Forest (Rzuchowski las).
9 Among the first victims in Chelmno (Kulmhof) were Roma who had been quartered on the periphery of the Lodz ghetto.
10 There is no further evidence of this. The Roma in the Lodz ghetto had been deported from Burgenland.
11 See Docs. 64 and 70.
12 This is a reference to Hitler's speech of 30 Jan. 1939: see PMJ 2/248.

## DOC. 90

### After 6 July 1942 an unidentified author urges Jews to document all crimes[1]

Typewritten record, unsigned,[2] Warsaw, after 6 July 1942

*Preface*

On more than one occasion my friends and comrades have asked me: Why don't you set something down in writing? Why don't you take some aspect from the three years of war and expound on it from your point of view? After all, the bloodbath going on for three years now has caused upheaval in all areas of Jewish life – there is so much material to record. The next generation should read about and know what we had to endure at the hands of the murderous occupier. In truth my friends are right, yet it is very difficult to write at this time when the valley of weeping[3] is overflowing not only with rivers of tears, but also with oceans of blood shed hourly by our brothers and sisters, old and young.

The bloody, bestial hand does not tire. It continues without pause to physically destroy us: to shoot, to burn, to poison with gas tens and hundreds of thousands of our brothers, entire Jewish settlements. The murderous hand has eradicated hundreds of communities. At a time when the murderer is constantly poised with a revolver in his hand and every person sees death before their eyes, it is truly difficult to set something down in writing. It is difficult to focus one's thoughts and take stock of the three years of war in general, and of [the situation of] us Jews in particular. Whenever I pick up the pen and want to start writing about these things, something always happens: beneath my window people are caught, an anguished cry rings out, ended by a shot, with blood flowing from a couple of Jews.

The pen simply falls out of my hand now, following the murderous shooting that has killed 110 Jews. Men and women hastily buried in the previously prepared pit that the executioners forced twenty gravediggers from the Jewish Council's cemetery division to dig 10 km outside Warsaw in Babice. The murderers used trucks to transport one hundred men and women from the prison – mostly members of the intelligentsia, as well as ten Jewish policemen – to the site, where they shot them. And while the warm blood was still pouring out of them, while they were still jerking and wrestling with death, they were thrown into the long, deep pit and quickly buried. Finished with their murderous work, the Nazi sadists released the gravediggers and calmly travelled back to the city to look for new victims. This took place on 2 July 1942.[4] The crimes of the 110 prisoners who were imprisoned in the Jewish prison on Gęsia were (1) searching for a piece of bread [or] a kilo of potatoes on the other side of the [ghetto] wall; (2) forgetting to put

1 AŻIH, Ring I/576 (175), fols. 2–3. Published in English translation in Kermish (ed.), *To Live with Honor*, pp. 22–24. This document has been newly translated from Yiddish.

2 The author probably worked for the underground archive of the Warsaw ghetto, and was possibly Menakhem Mendel Kon: see also Docs. 114 and 152.

3 Hebrew in the original: *emet ha-bakha*, literally 'the valley of Bakha'. It appears in Psalm 84:7 and is often translated as the valley of tears, the vale of tears, or the valley of weeping. It is assumed to be an actual geographical location near Jerusalem referring to a dry, arid valley that posed a challenge for pilgrims to pass through.

4 The shooting took place on 1 July 1942 at 4.30 a.m.

the band of shame, as the murderers call it, on their right arms; (3) improperly crossing from one side of the street to the other in the ghetto itself. Those are the offences for which the one hundred people were imprisoned. On the aforementioned day, at four in the morning, the bloodthirsty beasts violently dragged the martyrs out and shot them. On 5 July the murderers put up posters in the streets of the ghetto, announcing that they had done this as punishment for the following offences: (1) in a fight between Jewish and Christian workers at the eastern train station, a Jew killed a Polish worker;[5] (2) while an Aryan gendarme was shooting at some Jews, one of them knocked the revolver out of his bloody hand; (3) the ten Jewish policemen helped to set up a smuggling operation. The poster states that those are the crimes for which they shot one hundred ordinary Jews and ten Jewish policemen, and warns that they will continue to exact punishment in this way. For what is, in their understanding, the crime of an individual, they will shoot one hundred.

It should be noted here that the lives of the twenty gravediggers were saved due to the official nature of this act of murder. In all other such cases, the gravediggers are shot after they have finished their work. Their bodies are used to cover the people who were shot, and then dirt is thrown over them. The murderers do this to erase every trace of their savage act, so that nobody remains who could reveal how the job is done. In this instance, however, since they themselves announced it openly, they let the gravediggers live.

After this terrible act of murder committed in front of everyone by the vile, savage beasts, I can no longer hold back what has accumulated in my sickened soul. The feeling of self-preservation clamours and compels: *Write!* Write as much as possible about the shocking deeds, about the atrocities that the murderers are committing against us Jews. Like wild bulls, the murderers bellow that they are doing all this to create a better, more beautiful, more cultured Europe. They do it – they say – for the sake of truth and justice. The scoundrels, the executioners, have the shameless gall to tell the peoples whom they oppress that they are the whole world's wellspring of culture and that by hanging, shooting, poisoning, burning, and drowning as many elderly Jews, Jewish women, and Jewish children under the age of ten as possible, Europe will become a better and more cultured place. They feed precisely this vulgar, cynical propaganda to the weary, oppressed peoples. These savage beasts in human form do not want to and cannot understand that they are spitting into their own bloodstained faces with such propaganda.

I consider it a sacred duty that every person, whether or not he [feels that he] can, to record all that he has seen, or heard from those who did see, regarding the murders committed by the barbarians in every Jewish shtetl. Everything must be written down with no detail left out. And when the time comes – which it surely will – the world shall read about and know what the murderers did. It will provide the richest material for the poet [to draw on] when he composes the elegy to lament the present time. It will provide the strongest grounds on which someone will avenge all that has happened. The unyielding avenger is out there, and we are duty-bound to do all we can to support him, to help him, even if we have to pay for it with our own, nowadays very insignificant, lives.

Following this brief preface, I will write about a small slice of our sad social life in Warsaw, where, in defiance of the resolute opposition of our bloodthirsty enemy, there has been the possibility, albeit a limited one, to keep at least a small part of the children

5 See Doc. 102.

of our people alive. By writing about this, I believe I am inserting a bright page into this dark historical chapter. I will present facts, without embellishments […].[6] If I miss something, may the reader forgive me.[7]

### DOC. 91

### *Dziennik Polski*, 9 July 1942: statement by the Polish minister of the interior, Stanisław Mikołajczyk, on the persecution in occupied Poland[1]

*The tragic situation of the Polish people. The country urges the world to awaken its conscience. Minister Mikołajczyk's*[2] *report submitted to the British Ministry of Information.*

We hereby provide information about the state of affairs in Poland that was presented by Minister Mikołajczyk at a press conference for British and foreign journalists at the British Ministry of Information the day before yesterday. This information is an abridged version of the detailed report Minister Mikołajczyk presented to the National Council of the Republic of Poland.[3]

In recent months the Gestapo has once again significantly intensified the [campaign of] terror. The previous oppression, which was to some extent blindly arbitrary in nature, has ceased almost completely. Instead, *all efforts are now placed into tracking down and combating any kind of patriotic activity or work towards liberation in Poland.*

Throughout the entire Country,[4] and especially in Poznań and Warsaw, politically motivated arrests are the order of the day. Virtually no one is released. Almost all the detainees remain in Gestapo or general prisons and concentration camps. In Wielkopolska and Pomerania in particular, the Gestapo executes many detainees shortly after their arrest.

*The torture of innocent people*

Recently the Gestapo has intensified the bestial mistreatment and barbaric torture of prisoners in custody. This manner of interrogating has become the norm, and prisoners are beaten and tortured so severely that deaths are occurring with increasing frequency. Many return to prisons after enduring horrific physical torture under interrogation. This hastens the death of many people in prisons and concentration camps.

6 Several words illegible because the paper has been torn.
7 The text breaks off here.

1 *Dziennik Polski*, 11 July 1942, p. 3. *Dziennik Polski* was the official publication of the Polish government in exile in London and appeared from 12 July 1940 until late 1943; from 1 Jan. 1944 it merged with the newspaper *Dziennik Żołnierza*. This document has been translated from Polish.
2 Stanisław Mikołajczyk (1901–1966), farmer; active in the Polish Peasants' Party (PSL 'Piast') from 1921, and in the Peasants' Party (SL) from 1931; elected to the Sejm in 1933; member of the SL executive committee from 1935; served in the war in Sept. 1939; subsequently fled to Western Europe; minister of the interior and deputy prime minister of the Polish government in exile in 1941; prime minister, July 1943 – Dec. 1944; subsequently deputy prime minister of the Communist-led government in Warsaw; fled to the USA in April 1947.
3 See the full text in *Polish Fortnightly Review*, no. 48, 15 July 1942, pp. 4–8.
4 Capitalized for emphasis in the original.

The Gestapo is particularly brutal in Warsaw and Poznań. The prisoners in custody are mistreated and tortured so that they disclose to the Gestapo information about organizational and personnel connections. The Gestapo can then terrorize new centres of patriotic work and new people all the more easily.

The state of affairs is so difficult and dangerous in this regard that it is imperative to mobilize all forces to at least partially relieve and alleviate the situation.

There is further news on the increased terror in Upper Silesia – gallows have been set up in eighteen Silesian towns. Arrested activists have been hanged. In the Dąbrowa coal basin – in Dąbrowa, Szurlej,[5] Będzin, and Sosnowiec – prisoners have been publicly hanged from gallows and trees. The population, including schoolchildren, were rounded up and forced to watch these atrocities.

In Oświęcim alone, the inmate numbers assigned to the prisoners have soared to 8,000 within the past three months.

In March the German executioner Fischer[6] had his order posted on the walls of Warsaw that 100 Poles would be shot for every German killed or wounded. At the same time many social, economic, and political activists were arrested – not only in Warsaw, but also in Cracow, Lublin, Poznań, and in the provinces. From Pawiak alone, 475 people were transferred to Oświęcim on 17 April, and in May a total of 188 people were shot. The terror has reached the Republic of Poland's eastern regions, such as Vilna, where it was directed particularly against the clergy under Bishop Jałbrzykowski[7] and against the Jews, and in Lwów, where the university professors were deported and have since disappeared without a trace.[8]

Reserve officers are being arrested en masse and Poles are taken from prisoner-of-war camps and put up against the wall for alleged crimes committed before the war. In addition, new atrocities are committed in special concentration camps for farmers who have failed to deliver their agricultural quotas to the Germans, as well as railwaymen, tram conductors, and workers suspected of sabotage.

*Twenty-two concentration camps*

We know of twenty-two concentration camps: *Buchenwald, Ciechanów, Dachau, Dobrzyń, Działdowo, Flossenburg, Groß Rosen, Grudziądz, Hamburg,*[9] *Hohenbrück, Lubawa, Mathausen,*[10] *Nasielsk, Oranienburg, Oświęcim, Płońsk, Ravensbrück, Sierpc, Studhoff,*[11] *Tremblinka,*[12] *Dyle*. In powiat Biłgoraj, a concentration camp was set up for farmers reluctant to deliver the quotas. Other than that, there are also camps in Dziesiąta, near Lublin,[13] and in Bełżec.

5 No place with this name is known.

6 The District Governor of Warsaw, Ludwig Fischer.

7 Romuald Jałbrzykowski (1876–1955), Roman Catholic priest; bishop in the Łomża diocese and secretary general of the Polish Conference of Bishops, 1925–1926; subsequently Archbishop of Vilna.

8 After the city had been taken, the Einsatzkommando z.b.V ('for special assignments') detained Polish professors at Lwów University who had been identified in advance and put on pre-prepared lists; 25 of them were murdered between 3 and 5 July 1941.

9 Neuengamme concentration camp.

10 Correctly: Mauthausen.

11 Correctly: Stutthof.

12 This is probably a reference to Treblinka labour camp.

On 20 March there was a public execution in Zgierz of 100 Polish hostages, including four women, in front of 7,000 people who had been rounded up to watch. Those who survived were finished off with a revolver. The execution took place after a Pole had killed two Germans on 7 March. Prior to this it had been announced that 10 Poles had been shot for every German killed in 1939, but now 50 would be shot.

On 18 March, 140 of the 800 Polish political prisoners brought to the concentration camp past Dziesiąta, near Lublin, were shot. The camp previously held 1,150 Soviet prisoners of war, of whom 950 had been shot. Among them were many farmers who had been arrested for failing to deliver the agricultural quotas.

In Zwoleń, near Radom, 380 people were shot in front of their families, and in Wacławów, near Zwoleń, 160 people for allegedly killing one German. Recently the Gorals in Nowy Sącz were massacred because they didn't want to be part of the 'Góralenvolk'[14] and to participate in festivities to mark the second anniversary of Franck's[15] rule.

So we have 50 Poles shot near Łódź, 100 in Warsaw, 400 near Lublin, and 540 near Radom for one killed German. In Bochnia – 18 people brought from Cracow were shot. In Łańcut, 30. Near Hrubieszów 20 farmers were shot for hiding Soviet prisoners of war. In Rudka Kijańska,[16] near Lubartów, 214 people were murdered in one village alone, shot and killed with hand grenades thrown into their apartments. In Poznań – between 40 and 200 executions in the citadel[17] every month. In Sulmierzyce, Kalisz, Łask, Szczepanów, Radomsko, and Janowiec, near Kozienice – 200 people shot for every two Germans, etc. All these places across Poland have become scenes of executions, murder, and terror.

*The slaughter of the Jews*

The Jews' situation is even worse. The situation in the Warsaw ghetto is well known. The Jewish population is being systematically and continuously decimated by starvation, death, and disease. In Lublin the Jewish population was driven out on the night of 23 to 24 March. The sick and the disabled were killed on the spot.[18] All the children from an orphanage, between 2 and 9 years of age, 108 in total, were taken outside the town along with the nurses and murdered. Altogether 2,500 people were murdered that night; the remaining 26,000 were transported to the camps at Bełżec and Treblinka.[19] In Izbica Kujawska 8,000 people were deported to an unknown destination.[20] In Bełżec and Treblinka the murders are allegedly carried out using poison gas.[21] Mass murders took place

13 This is a reference to Lublin-Majdanek concentration camp, which was built on the city limits, in the village of Dziesiąta.

14 German in the original, 'Gorals people', a term invented by the Nazis to refer to the Gorals (Górale), an ethnically diverse group from the mountainous region of southern Poland. The German occupiers claimed that the *Goralenvolk* was part of the Greater Germanic race. From 1939 they promoted activists who campaigned for autonomy for the Gorals as a distinct ethnic group. The Polish underground regarded such activists as collaborators and put them under pressure, and the Germans in turn responded with reprisals.

15 Correctly: Frank, the governor general.

16 Today the village is part of the community of Ostrów Lubelski.

17 This is a reference to Fort VII camp in Poznań.

18 The deportations from the Lublin ghetto to Belzec began on 17 March 1942.

19 All the transports went to Belzec.

20 They were deported to Kulmhof.

21 All the transports went to Belzec. The mass murder at Treblinka began on 22 July 1942.

in Rawa Ruska and Biłgoraj, where Jewish communities ceased to exist. In Wąwolnica, near Kazimierz, the SS shot 120 people on the market square on 22 March. An unknown number of people were taken to the outskirts of the town and murdered. On 30 March [Jews] from Opole were driven to Nałęczów; 350 of them were killed on the way.[22] The rest were loaded into sealed goods wagons and taken away. On 9 March a total of 1,300 people were killed in Mielec.[23] In Mir 2,000 Jews were murdered, in Nowogródek 2,500, in Wołożyń 1,800, and in Kajdanów 4,000. A total of 30,000 Jews were deported from Hamburg to Minsk, and all of them were shot.[24] The number of Jews murdered in Lwów is estimated at 30,000, in Vilna at 60,000, in Stanisławów at 15,000, in Tarnopol at 5,000, in Złoczów at 2,000, in Brzeżany at 4,000.[25] Murders of Jews are reported in Tarnów, Radom, Zborów, Kołomyja, Sambor, Stryj, Drohobycz, Zbaraż, Brody, Przemyśl, Koło, Dąbie.

The everyday methods used to exterminate the Jewish population include forcing them to dig their own graves, lining them up in rows, and shooting them with machine guns or murdering them with grenades or even poison gas. In addition, the Jewish communities themselves – as in Lwów, for example – had to draw up a list of those sentenced to death.

*A bleak picture in figures*
*The number of Poles executed, murdered, and tortured to death has reached 200,000 people. According to the established data, the number of murdered Jews has exceeded 200,000.*[26]
*This means that approximately 400,000 Polish citizens have been murdered. Add to this*
*1.5 million people deported to Germany for forced labour over the course of the past two and a half years,*
*200,000 prisoners of war in Germany,*
*170,000 Poles from the annexed territories who were drafted into the German army,*
*150,000 who died or went missing in 1939.*
*That gives us a total of some 2.4 million Polish citizens who have been removed from Poland, not counting those who are currently in Soviet Russia.*

This picture becomes even bleaker when we consider that about 1.5 million people have been deported from the areas annexed to the General Government,[27] and that the population has been further decimated by the decline in the birth rate, the increased

22 The ghetto set up in Opole Lubelskie in March 1941 later served as a transit ghetto for Jews. In late March 1942 approximately 1,900 Jews from Wąwolnica passed through it; on 31 March 1942 they were taken from Opole to the railway station at Nałęczów, from where they were deported to Belzec.
23 See Doc. 51.
24 The first transport arrived in Minsk on 10 Nov. 1941 with 1,000 Jews from Hamburg, who were followed in the next few days by another 6,000 Jews from elsewhere in Germany. Many of them were shot during a murder operation on 2 March 1942; 3,000–3,500 German Jews were murdered with gas at Maly Trostenets extermination camp in late July 1942.
25 See Doc. 74.
26 At the same press conference, Szmul Zygielbojm announced that 700,000 Jews had been murdered by that point in time, as reported in *Dziennik Polski* on 10 July 1942, p. 2; see also Doc. 87.
27 This figure is greatly inflated and is not placed into the proper context here: it refers to the resettlement operations that took place within the General Government from 1939 to 1941, and possibly to the murder of Jews during the initial phase of Operation Reinhard.

mortality rate, and the spread of infectious diseases. This is illustrated by the figures from the city of Warsaw.

One of the examples that illustrates the gradual starvation and death of the population is the fact that the mortality rate in the Warsaw ghetto in 1941 increased from 5 to 24.3 [per cent] compared to the same six-month period in 1939,[28] while the birth rate decreased from 10.1 to 3.8 [per cent]. In 1939 there were 131 cases of typhus in Warsaw, in 1940 there were 1,949, and by August 1941 there were already 5,931 cases.

The damage caused by the falling birth rate, the rising mortality rate, the spread of infectious diseases among the exhausted human bodies, and the exploitation of Poland's physical strength and material resources cannot be fully expressed in figures. However, with the prolongation of the war, along with the consequences that will emerge at a later stage, this damage will prove to be far more terrible than the losses caused by violence and terror.

The Germans have pursued and continue to pursue a policy of cleansing the 'Lebensraum'[29] on Polish territory by systematically destroying Poland's population and eradicating all traces of Polishness.

*On the reactions of the Allies and the pope*

People in Poland think that the reaction *of our government, as well as of the pope, and of the Allies to this unparalleled tyranny is too weak.*

One should apply the above-mentioned approach to Germans in the USA and lock up at least a few tens of thousands [of them] in concentration camps and treat them as hostages. *Mere threats of a tribunal will not help.* With regard to the state of affairs mentioned above, a few days ago we received the following demands from Poland made by the respective leaders of the Polish underground to Prime Minister Sikorski:

> *The country urges the world to awaken its conscience.*
> *For two and a half years, the Germans have been conducting an operation, planned well in advance, to systematically exterminate the Polish People,*[30] *who constitute a natural obstacle to their continuous eastward expansion.*
>
> *This insane operation has intensified in the last few weeks to such an extent that the upper stratum of the Polish People is in danger of complete annihilation, and the entire People is threatened with such a loss of strength that we might not be able to fulfil the historic tasks that await us after the war.*
>
> *We are receiving alarming news from all over the country, which makes it clear that the furor teutonicus,*[31] *in a raging fit of murderous greed, is igniting a conflagration and carrying out the mass murder of the innocent Polish population.*
>
> *Examples:*
>
> *(1) For the late delivery of quotas, which are often difficult to meet – torture, disenfranchisement, labour camps, and concentration camps, which usually amount to a death sentence. And recently – as noted in the Lublin area – the destruction and torching of entire farms along with the owners' families, who are locked inside the farm buildings (anyone who tries to save themselves by escaping is killed on the spot).*

28 These are presumably figures for the first six months of the years in question.
29 German in the original: 'living space'.
30 'Polish People' is capitalized for emphasis in the original, both here and below.
31 Latin in the original: 'Teutonic fury'.

*(2) When a German is robbed, when escaped prisoners of war or Bolshevik saboteurs are harboured or helped (even under the threat of violence), and when communications equipment is sabotaged, dozens or hundreds of innocent members of the local Polish population are immediately killed.*
*(3) If a secretly printed document is found or there is the mere suspicion of someone participating in underground activity – torture and the death penalty, or a long stay in a concentration camp – which amounts to death and severe torture.*
*(4) If trade in everyday items is discovered – a labour camp, a concentration camp, the death penalty.*
*(5) Any sign of patriotism or a negative attitude towards the occupiers – concentration camps, with denunciations of any kind, often for personal prejudices, usually accepted as evidence of such 'crimes'.*

*This wave of murders and atrocities has engulfed the whole of Poland, but only fragments of information about this barbarity are trickling through to the civilized world.*

*It has come to the point that today there is not a single Polish family that is not mourning a relative who has been murdered or tortured in a camp.*

*In view of this, the protection of human life in Poland is of fundamental importance for Its[32] future and must inevitably become our Government's chief concern.*

*It is therefore absolutely necessary:*

*(a) to stir up the conscience of the entire civilized world against the barbarians,*

*(b) to apply the most severe retaliatory measures provided for under international law, preceded by a sharply worded diplomatic note to the German government and an appeal with a warning to the German people, that both the diplomatic note and the appeal will be published in all the languages of civilized nations.*

## DOC. 92

## On 10 July 1942 a report by the Polish underground movement describes to the government in exile the extermination process at Belzec[1]

Report by the Home Army, Warsaw, to the Polish government in exile's Ministry of the Interior, London, dated 10 July 1942[2]

*Special report from the site where Jews are executed at Bełżec, dated 10 July 1942*
According to information provided by a German employed at the execution site, it is located in Bełżec, near the station, and is fenced off with barbed wire barriers. Ukrainians stand guard inside and outside the wire. The executions are carried out as follows.

32 The word 'Its' is capitalized for emphasis in the original.

1 Uniwersytet Warszawski, Biblioteka Uniwersytecka, Zbiór rękopisów, no. 2188, fol. 16. Published in Tyszkowa, 'Eksterminacja Żydów w latach 1941–1943', part 2, p. 58. Published in English translation in Chris Webb, *The Belzec Death Camp: History, Biographies, Remembrance* (Stuttgart: ibidem, 2016), pp. 187–188. This document has been newly translated from Polish.

2 This report was enclosed with a letter sent to London under the logbook number K. 4407/42: AIP, PRM 73/4, fol. 205 (384). Published in Tadeusz Pełczyński and Jan Tokarski (eds.), *Armia Krajowa w dokumentach 1939–1945*, vol. 2: *Czerwiec 1941–kwiecień 1943* (London: Studium Polski Podziemnej, 1973), p. 288.

once the train carrying the Jews arrives at the station in Bełżec, it heads along a siding to the wire surrounding the execution site, where the train crew changes. From the wire onwards German operators conduct the train to the unloading ramp, where the track ends. Once unloaded, the men proceed to the barracks on the right and the women to the barracks on the left, where they undress, ostensibly for a shower. After undressing, both groups are led to a third barracks with an electrified plate, where the execution is carried out.[3] The corpses are then transported outside the fence by train, to a trench which is approximately 30 metres deep.[4] Jews dug this trench, and they have all been executed. The Ukrainian guards on duty are to be executed once the operation has been completed. The Ukrainians on guard duty are loaded with money and stolen valuables; they pay 400 złoty for a litre of vodka and 2,000 [złoty] and jewellery for intercourse with a woman.

## DOC. 93

## In October 1943 Emanuel Ringelblum describes the smuggling that took place across the boundaries of the Warsaw ghetto between the end of 1940 and mid July 1942[1]

Handwritten diary of Emanuel Ringelblum, Warsaw, entry for October 1943 (excerpt)

[…][2]
And despite these victims, the smuggling never stopped for a single moment. Even before the pools of blood on the pavement had dried, the next lot of smugglers went to work again – as soon as the lookout gave the signal for 'the coast is clear'. Smuggling over the [ghetto] walls was interrupted only during the resettlement operation,[3] when the walls were manned by a dense throng of new guards whom the smugglers had not yet bribed; but even then, this did not apply to smuggling as a whole. Smuggling took place in the following ways: (1) over the walls, (2) through the gates, (3) through underground tunnels, (4) through sewers, and (5) through houses on the ghetto boundaries.

Smuggling through the ghetto gates was the most important; it took place almost officially and in full view. The 'grajek',[4] as the Jewish 'Order Service man' who bribed the policemen was called, contacted the gendarmerie and the Polish police. He made his arrangements either across the board, for the entire period during which the gendarme in question was on duty, or – and this was more common – specifically for a certain

3 In reality, after undressing, the victims were poisoned with carbon monoxide. Various rumours circulated outside the extermination camps: see Docs. 63, 117, 177, and 234.
4 The bodies were actually buried in trenches inside the barbed wire fence on the relatively small camp grounds, which measured 275 by 265 metres. No other reports substantiate the existence of a siding.

1 AŻIH, 302/337, fols. 71–73. Published in Ringelblum, *Polish–Jewish Relations during the Second World War*, p. 85. This document has been newly translated from Polish.
2 In the previous section, Ringelblum wrote about smugglers who became victims of violence.
3 This is a reference to the deportations from Warsaw to Treblinka, which took place from July to Sept. 1942.
4 This is a colloquial Polish term meaning 'musician' or 'minstrel'.

number of carts[5] to be smuggled in. The carts that entered through the ghetto gate gave the prearranged password. Sometimes it happened, however, that the gendarme was surprised by an unexpected Gestapo or SS inspection; then the cart was busted or, in smugglers' slang, 'burned'. The bulk of the smuggled goods came through the ghetto gates in huge lorries, which then quickly disappeared into a gateway where the goods were transferred to other carts at lightning speed.

Many goods were also smuggled over the walls into the ghetto, usually during the night or at dawn. There were daredevils who smuggled over the walls even during the day. In the initial period after the ghetto was established, food and goods were smuggled through holes in the walls of the houses bordering on the Aryan side. These holes were bricked up daily, but the smugglers hammered them open again every day. The smugglers were organized into Polish–Jewish gangs, which operated on the principle of common 'loot'. The income was quite high, but the risk was also very great, for their lives were in danger. The price differences between the Aryan side and the Jewish side were quite high, even as high as 100 per cent, but there was no other choice, since smuggling was the only way to feed the Jewish population in the ghetto. Smuggling declined sharply after the resettlement operation, and some smugglers began extorting from Jews instead.[6]

To sum up: Polish–Jewish cooperation in smuggling is one of the finest hours in the history of relations between the two peoples during the current war. Such cooperation took place not only in the capital, but in almost all the ghettos across the General Government, which would most certainly have gone under had it not been for the help of Polish smugglers.

[...][7]

## DOC. 94

## On 18 July 1942 the GG government prohibits the Kreishauptleute and the Stadthauptleute from paying fixed allowances to the Jewish relief committees[1]

Letter from the GG government, Interior Administration Main Department, Municipal Administration Department (Dr Pf./Lü.[der] Inn-II-189/40), signed Schmid,[2] to the Interior Administration departments at the district governors' offices in Cracow, Lemberg, Lublin, Radom, and Warsaw, with copies for the Kreishauptleute and the Stadthauptleute, Cracow, dated 18 July 1942

*Re*: residents' tax, use of revenue

Through § 1(9) of the Regulation on the Amendment of the Regulation on Levying a Residents' Tax of 20 October 1941, VOBl. GG, p. 617, the earmarking originally specified

5 Here and below, the Polish word *wóz* in the original can mean cart or car.

6 These extortionists (known in Polish as *zmalcownictwo*) searched near the ghetto walls for Jews who had escaped from the ghetto and then pressured them into handing over money or valuables; they were often organized into groups and succeeded in collecting large sums, particularly in 1942. The government delegation for Poland and the Home Army condemned the activities of these gangs.

7 In the following section, Ringelblum discusses Polish–Jewish cooperation in the sale and purchase of real estate, transactions which were entered into the notary's books with a date prior to 1 Sept. 1939 in order to circumvent the new regulations imposed by the German occupiers.

1 AAN, 540/1, fol. 84. This document has been translated from German.

in § 6 of this regulation no longer applies. As a result, the circular decree of 31 January 1941 – Inn-XI-189/40 – has also lost its legal basis. The circular decree is therefore rendered invalid with immediate effect.[3]

However, I leave it to the discretion of the Kreishauptleute and Stadthauptleute whether or not they will make funds from the residents' tax revenue available to the Jewish relief committees, in accordance with the circumstances and needs in their jurisdiction. Fixed allowances that approximately correspond to the Jews' tax payments will nevertheless be out of the question from now on.

I request that the Kreishauptleute and Stadthauptleute be informed of this immediately.

## DOC. 95

## On 18 July 1942 the head of the Operation Reinhard staff swears the staff members in the extermination camps to secrecy[1]

Printed form issued by the head of the Operation Reinhard staff (log no. /42, secret Reich matter) to be filled out by staff, signed SS-Hauptsturmführer Höfle as department head,[2] Lublin, dated 18 July 1942

*Sworn statement*
concerning the obligations of __________ as someone who has been specially commissioned to perform tasks connected to the resettlement of Jews as part of 'Operation Reinhardt' under the SS and Police Leader in District Lublin.[3]

[Name] __________ hereby declares: I have been fully briefed and instructed by SS-Hauptsturmführer Höfle, the head of the 'Operation Reinhardt' department at the SS and Police Leader's office in District Lublin,

1. that I must not under any circumstances pass on any information to persons outside of the group taking part in 'Operation Reinhardt', either verbally or in writing, about the process and the methods of the resettlement of the Jews, or about any specific incidents connected to it;
2. that the operations to resettle the Jews constitute a 'secret Reich matter' within the meaning of the Classified Information Regulation;

2 Carl Gottlob Schmid (1889–1966), lawyer; joined the NSDAP in 1933; deputy Stadthauptmann of Cracow from Sept. 1939, and acting Stadthauptmann, Feb. 1940 – March 1941; special representative for the reorganization of the municipal administration in Prague, Nov. 1941 – June 1942; thereafter head of the local administration division in the Interior Administration Department of the General Government; civil servant in the states of Württemberg and Baden-Württemberg, 1948–1957.

3 The circular decree from the Municipal Administration Department specified how the revenue collected from the residents' tax was to be distributed: YVA, O-21/19, fol. 25.

1 APMM, II/1. Copy in AIPN, GK, 317/874, t. 10, fol. 1. Published in Berenstein et al. (eds.), *Faschismus – Getto – Massenmord*, p. 300. This document has been translated from German.

2 Hermann Höfle. On Operation Reinhard, see Introduction, pp. 25–40.

3 Odilo Globocnik.

3. about the relevant special provisions in the rules of procedure of the SS and Police Leader in District Lublin,[4] with explicit reference to the fact that these provisions are 'orders concerning official business' and 'commands and prohibitions' within the meaning of § 92b of the Reich Criminal Code;[5]
4. about the explicit ban on photography in the 'Operation Reinhardt' camps;
5. about §§ 88 to 93 of the Reich Criminal Code[6] in the 24 April 1934 version, and about the Regulation against Bribery and Breach of Confidentiality by Persons Not Classified as Civil Servants of 3 May 1917/12 February 1920;[7]
6. about §§ 139[8] (obligation of disclosure) and 353c[9] (breach of official secrecy) of the Reich Criminal Code.

I am familiar with the aforementioned provisions and laws, and am aware of the obligations imposed upon me by the task I have been assigned. I pledge to fulfil them to the best of my ability.

I am aware that my obligation to maintain confidentiality will persist after I have left the service.

Read aloud, approved, and signed: __________ [name].

Ut supra.[10]

4 These could not be found.

5 The paragraph stated that anyone who contravened 'a command or prohibition issued by the Reich government for the purpose of ensuring the defence of the country' in times of war would be punished with imprisonment: Ernst Fuhrmann et al. (eds.), *Strafrecht und Strafverfahren: Eine Sammlung der wichtigsten Gesetze des Strafrechts und des Strafverfahrens mit Erläuterungen*, 33rd edn (Berlin: Schweitzer, 1942), p. 91.

6 These subsections dealt with treason: ibid., pp. 86–93.

7 The Regulation against Bribery and Breach of Confidentiality by Persons Not Classified as Civil Servants threatened anyone who 'accepts, asks for, or is promised gifts or other benefits in return for an action that includes a breach of the obligations entrusted to him' with imprisonment or a fine: *Reichsgesetzblatt*, 1920, pp. 230–231.

8 This subsection threatened with imprisonment anyone who 'obtains credible knowledge' of a plan to commit treason or similar crimes and fails to report this: Fuhrmann et al. (eds.), *Strafrecht und Strafverfahren*, pp. 125–126.

9 This subsection contained the threat of imprisonment for up to ten years for anyone who, 'without authorization, passes on to another person a piece of information which he has been specifically required to keep secret by a competent authority, and as a result jeopardizes important public interests': ibid., pp. 370–371.

10 Latin: 'as above'.

## DOC. 96

### On 19 July 1942 Reichsführer-SS Himmler orders that the killing of the Jewish population in the General Government must be concluded by the end of the year[1]

Directive (marked 'secret') from Himmler (Reichsführer-SS, personal staff, log no. 1285/42), Hegewald,[2] to the Higher SS and Police Leader East, Krüger, Cracow, dated 29 July 1942[3]

I hereby order that the resettlement of the entire Jewish population of the General Government must be carried out and completed by 31 December 1942.

From 31 December 1942 persons of Jewish descent will no longer be allowed in the General Government, unless they are inside the Warsaw, Cracow, Tschenstochau, Radom, or Lublin assembly camps. All other labour projects that make use of Jewish labourers must be completed by then or, if that is not possible, must be moved to one of the assembly camps. These measures are necessary to ensure the required ethnic separation of races and nations in accordance with the New Order in Europe, and for the security and cleanliness of the German Reich and its spheres of interest. Any violation of this order represents a danger to the peace and order of the entire German sphere of interest, a leverage point for the resistance movement, and a source of moral and physical pestilence.

A complete cleansing is necessary for all of these reasons and must therefore be carried out. Any anticipated delays beyond the deadline must be reported to me promptly so that I can take action to remedy the issue in good time. Any requests for changes or exemptions made by other agencies must be submitted to me personally.

1 BArch, NS 9/1757, fols. 1–2. Published in Berenstein et al. (eds.), *Faschismus – Getto – Massenmord*, p. 303. This document has been translated from German.

2 'Hegewald' was Himmler's field command post, near Zhytomyr in Ukraine, from 15 July 1942.

3 On 19 July 1942 Himmler was in Lublin with Odilo Globocnik, who was in charge of Operation Reinhard. The order was not sent out until 29 July 1942, after Himmler had returned from District Lublin.

## DOC. 97

## On 19 July 1942 Janusz Korczak (Henryk Goldszmit) describes an outbreak of food poisoning among his orphans and their last theatre performance[1]

Typewritten diary of Janusz Korczak,[2] entry for 19 July 1942[3]

18 July, night-time
In the first week of what was for us the final stay at the Gocławek summer home,[4] the children and some of the staff suffered a major bout of food poisoning after eating bread of unknown composition and origin.

Diarrhoea – The faeces seethed in the chamber pots; bubbles formed on the surface of the pitch-black brew which, when they burst, gave off a sweet-fetid stench that not only attacked the sense of smell, but also penetrated the throat, eyes, ears, and brain.

[What is happening] now is something similar, only with vomiting and watery stools.

Within a single night the boys lost [a total of] 80 kg in weight, an average of 1 kg per head, and the girls lost 60 kg (a little less).

The children's digestive tracts were under heavy strain. It doesn't take much to trigger a disaster. Perhaps it was the vaccination against dysentery[5] (five days ago), or perhaps the ground pepper which was added to no-longer-quite-fresh eggs to make the Friday 'pâté', according to a French recipe.

The next day, the boys had not regained a single kilo in weight.

Help for those who were vomiting and moaning in pain – which was administered in almost total darkness – consisted of [distributing] limed water (chalk for cleaning teeth) to anyone who wanted it, and as much as they wanted, jug after jug; and also for some a narcotic (to treat headaches); and finally, for the staff – morphine, but sparingly. A caffeine injection to prevent a hysterical new pupil from collapsing. His mother, suffering from furunculosis and intestinal discharge, refused to die until her boy was placed

1 Ośrodek Dokumentacji i Badań Korczakianum, Archiwum Korczakowskie, 278, fols. 56–57. Published in Janusz Korczak, *Pamiętnik* (Poznań: Wydawnictwo Poznańskie, 1984), pp. 35–36. Published in English translation in Janusz Korczak, *Ghetto Diary*, trans. Jerzy Bachrach and Barbara Krzywicka (New York: Holocaust Library, 1978 [Polish edn, 1958]), pp. 167–169. This document has been newly translated from Polish.

2 Janusz Korczak, real name Henryk Goldszmit (1878/1879–1942), paediatrician and educator; spent a year doing advanced training in Berlin; director of the Jewish orphanage at 92 Krochmalna Street in Warsaw from 1912 (from Oct. 1941 the orphanage was located at 16 Sienna Street); divisional medical officer in the Russian army during the First World War; author of numerous children's books and educational texts; on 5 or 6 August 1942, along with the children from his orphanage, deported to Treblinka, where he was murdered.

3 Janusz Korczak kept a diary from May to August 1942. The typed entries were taken to the 'Aryan side' in Jan. 1943 by the educator and actress Barbara Abramow (1908–1973), who later gave the original to the Korczakianum Institute, a department at the Historical Museum of the City of Warsaw (Muzeum Historyczne Miasta Stołecznego Warszawy). On 19 July 1942 Korczak wrote down the events that had occurred during the night of 17–18 July 1942 and on the afternoon of 18 July 1942.

4 In summer 1940 Korczak had visited the summer house at Gocławek (in Wawer, which was then a suburb of Warsaw) for the last time with children from various orphanages.

5 Dysentery is an infectious disease that usually manifests as an epidemic. Symptoms include diarrhoea with blood.

in a boarding school. The boy refused to go to boarding school until his mother had died. In the end, he gave in. The mother died, true to her word; the child has a guilty conscience. Sick, he imitates his mother: he moans, writhes, says it hurts, then he says that he is suffocating, then that it is hot, and finally that he is dying of thirst.

'Water!'

I pace up and down the hall. Will this develop into mass hysteria? It's possible!

But the children's confidence in the management has prevailed. They believed that as long as the doctor was calm, there was no danger.

I wasn't all that calm. But the fact that I yelled at the unruly patient and threatened to throw him out into the stairwell proved that the helmsman was steady. The important thing: he yells, therefore he knows the score.

The next day – that is, yesterday – there was a performance of 'The Post Office' by Tagore.[6] Appreciation from the audience. Handshakes, smiles, attempts to initiate a cordial conversation. (After the performance, Madam Chairman[7] visited the home and found it cramped, but said that the genius Korczak was visibly demonstrating that he can work wonders [even] in a mousehole.)

That is why others have been given palaces.

(I was once again struck by the pomp that accompanied the opening of the kindergarten at the workers' home in Górczewska Street, which was attended by President Mościcki's second wife.[8]) How ridiculous they are!

How would it be if yesterday's actors continued to play their roles today?

Jerzyk would think he was a fakir. Chaimek, he would really be a physician. Adek would be the royal mayor.[9]

(Perhaps the 'illusions' – the performances – would be a useful topic for Wednesday's discussion with the boarders;[10] their role in the life of mankind …)

I'm off to Dzielna [Street] now.[11]

6 The performance was directed by one of Korczak's co-workers, Estera Winogron (d. 1942). The children had already performed the play for Passover in 1942. It tells the story of a boy who is seriously ill and longs to escape to a fantasy land. Written by the Indian author and philosopher Rabindranath Thakur, also known as Tagore (1881–1941), this work was published in 1912 and was banned by the National Socialist censors.

7 Probably the Warsaw Jewish Council chairman's wife, Dr Felicja Czerniaków (1887–1950), educator; headmistress prior to Sept. 1939; worked for the Jewish Central Association for the Care of Orphans (CENTOS); left the ghetto in early August 1942; survived in hiding on the 'Aryan side' of Warsaw.

8 Maria Mościcka, née Dobrzańska (1896–1979), wife of the Polish president, Ignacy Mościcki, from 1933.

9 These are the names of children who acted in 'The Post Office' and the characters they played.

10 Apart from the younger children, between ten and twenty young people who aspired to become educators lived in the orphanage and helped with the day-to-day work. The discussion group was meant to contribute to their educational training.

11 The ghetto's main orphanage was located at 39 Dzielna Street: see also Doc. 40.

## DOC. 98

## On 22 July 1942 the head of the Operation Reinhard staff instructs the Jewish Council in Warsaw to prepare for the deportation of the ghetto's inhabitants[1]

Instructions from the Resettlement Commissioner[2] to the Jewish Council in Warsaw, dated 22 July 1942

*Information and requirements for the Jewish Council*

The Jewish Council is hereby informed of the following:

1. All Jewish persons who reside in Warsaw will be resettled to the East, regardless of age or gender.
2. The following persons are exempt from resettlement:
   (a) all Jewish persons who are employed by German authorities or enterprises and can furnish proof of employment;
   (b) all Jewish persons who are members of the Jewish Council or employees of the Jewish Council (as of the day this directive is issued);
   (c) all Jewish persons who are employed by Reich German companies and can furnish proof of this;
   (d) all Jews fit for work who have not been integrated into the labour process so far; they are to be quartered in the Jewish residential district;
   (e) all Jewish persons who belong to the staff of the Jewish hospitals; also the members of the Jewish disinfection squad;
   (f) all Jewish persons who are members of the Jewish Order Service;
   (g) all Jewish persons who are immediate family members of the persons listed under (a) to (f); family members are exclusively defined as wives and children;
   (h) all Jewish persons who are patients in one of the Jewish hospitals on the first day of the resettlement and are not fit to be discharged; fitness to be discharged shall be determined by a physician to be designated by the Jewish Council.
3. Each Jew being resettled is allowed to take 15 kg of personal possessions as luggage. All valuables can be taken along: cash, gold, jewellery, etc. Food for three days must be taken along.
4. The resettlement will begin at 11 a.m. on 22 July 1942.[3]

I. In the course of the resettlement, the following requirements are imposed on the Jewish Council; the members of the Jewish Council are responsible, on pain of death, to ensure strict compliance with these requirements:

The Jewish Council will take orders related to the resettlement exclusively from the Resettlement Commissioner or his representative.[4] For the period of the resettlement, the Jewish Council can choose a special resettlement committee, the chairman

1 AŻIH, Ring II/25 (190), fols. 2–4, and Ring II/300 (192). Published in Tatiana Brustin-Berenstein, 'Akta i zeznania w drugiej części Archiwum Podziemnego Getta warszawskiego', *BŻIH*, no. 1 (1951), pp. 51–126, here pp. 65–68. This document has been translated from German.

2 The Resettlement Commissioner was Hermann Höfle, who was also head of the SS and Police Leader's staff in Lublin.

3 The original contains an erroneous date: 1943.

4 Höfle's deputy was Georg Michalsen (1906–1993).

of which must be the head of the Jewish Council,[5] whose deputy must be the commander of the Jewish Order Service.[6]

II. The Jewish Council is responsible for delivering the Jews who are due for embarkation each day. To perform this task, the Jewish Council will make use of the Jewish Order Service (1,000 men).

The Jewish Council will ensure that, beginning on 22 July 1942, 6,000 Jews are taken to the assembly point every day, by 4 p.m. at the latest. For the entire period of the evacuation, the assembly point will be the Jewish hospital on Stawkistraße. On 22 July the 6,000 Jews will be taken directly to the embarkation point[7] near the Transfer Bureau. Initially the Jewish Council can draw the required daily contingents of Jews from the general population; later the Jewish Council will receive specific instructions as to which particular streets or blocks are to be cleared.

III. On 22 July 1942 the Jewish Council must empty the Jewish hospital on Stawkistraße and transfer the patients and the inventory to another suitable building in the ghetto, so that on the evening of 23 July 1942 the hospital will be available to receive the daily contingent of Jews for resettlement.

IV. The Jewish Council must also ensure that the objects and valuables left behind by the resettled Jews are gathered at collection sites yet to be determined and are then registered, provided the objects are not contaminated. For this purpose, the Jewish Council will call on the Jewish Order Service and sufficient numbers of Jewish workers. Their work will be supervised by the Security Police, which will issue specific instructions on this matter to the Jewish Council. Any misappropriation of objects or valuables in the course of carrying out this task will be punishable by death.

V. In addition, the Jewish Council will ensure that Jews working in German enterprises or in the German interest continue to go about their work during the resettlement period. To ensure compliance with this order, it will issue a public notice to the Jewish population, announcing the severest penalties for non-compliance.[8] Likewise, the Jewish Council must ensure that enough Jewish food suppliers continue to operate without interruption to ensure that sufficient food is provided, both for the Jews at the assembly point and for those who remain behind.

VI. The Jewish Council is furthermore responsible for ensuring that Jews who die during the resettlement period are buried the same day.

VII. The Jewish Council will immediately make the following announcement to the Jewish population by means of public notices:

5 Adam Czerniaków; after Czerniaków's death on 23 July 1942, Marek Lichtenbaum held this post.

6 The commander of the Jewish Order Service was Jakub Lejkin: see fn. 11.

7 Known as the Umschlagplatz (literally 'reloading point'). This is where the Transfer Bureau was located and where all official movement of goods was handled from late 1940. A train track linked the Umschlagplatz with Warszawa Gdańska (Danzig Station), the main train station in the northern part of Warsaw.

8 The Jewish Council published an announcement the same day: AŻIH, Ring II/52a (186/1); facsimile in Helge Grabitz and Wolfgang Scheffler, *Letzte Spuren: Ghetto Warschau, SS-Arbeitslager Trawniki, Aktion Erntefest. Fotos und Dokumente über Opfer des Endlösungswahns im Spiegel der historischen Ereignisse* (Berlin: Edition Hentrich, 1993), p. 155.

'By order of the German authorities, all Jewish persons, regardless of …' (etc., from items 1 to 4).[9]

VIII. Punishments:

(a) any Jewish person who leaves the ghetto once the resettlement has begun will be shot, unless he or she belongs to the groups of persons listed under 2 (a) or 2 (c), or was previously authorized to leave the ghetto;

(b) any Jewish person who engages in an act likely to circumvent or interfere with the resettlement measures will be shot;

(c) any Jewish person who is complicit in an act likely to circumvent or interfere with the resettlement measures will be shot;

(d) all Jews who are found in Warsaw after the resettlement is completed will be shot, unless they belong to the groups listed under 2 (a) to (h).

The Jewish Council is informed that, if the orders and requirements issued to it are not carried out in full, a certain number of recently arrested hostages will be shot in each case.

Warsaw, 22 July 1942
Dictated by the Resettlement Commissioner

*File note*[10]

1. At the meeting in the Warsaw Jewish Council's main premises on 22 July 1942, Jakob Lejkin,[11] currently the acting head of the Order Service, was appointed head of the Order Service with immediate effect by the Resettlement Commissioner.
2. At the meeting in the Warsaw Jewish Council's main building on 22 July 1942, the Resettlement Commissioner issued an order declaring that all institutions in the Jewish residential district, such as the Supply Office, the Jewish Social Self-Help, the Supply Society,[12] the Cooperative Bank,[13] the Chamber of Public Health,[14] the Craftsmen's Association,[15] etc.[16] answer to the chairman of the Jewish Council in Warsaw. The employees of these institutions are placed on an equal footing with the employees

9 AŻIH, Ring II/52b (186/2); facsimile in Grabitz and Scheffler, *Letzte Spuren*, p. 153.

10 This section, with the exception of the second sentence, was part of Höfle's orders, which were also made public by means of posted notices. Published as a facsimile in Danuta Jackiewicz and Eugeniusz Cezary Król (eds.), *W obiektywie wroga: Niemieccy fotoreporterzy w okupowanej Warszawie (1939–1945)* (Warsaw: Oficyna Wydawnicza RYTM, 2008), p. 326.

11 Jakub Lejkin (1906–1942), lawyer; graduated from a Polish military school in Jarocin; practised law in Warsaw before the war; joined the Jewish Order Service in the Warsaw ghetto and rose through the ranks to become deputy chief; acting chief of the Order Service, May–July 1942; played an important role in the deportation of Jews from the Warsaw ghetto to extermination camps during summer 1942; assassinated by members of the Jewish Combat Organization (ŻOB) on 29 October 1942.

12 Towarzystwo Dostaw Wyrobów Przemysłu Żydowskiego, a society of private entrepreneurs that had taken on the function of an Industry and Commerce Section under the Jewish Council: see Doc. 15.

13 Bank Spółdzielczy, an autonomous credit institution under the Jewish Council. Its director was Edward Kobryner.

14 Presumably the Centralna Rada Zdrowia under the Jewish Council's Health Section, which coordinated the individual institutions working in this field and was headed by Ludwik Hirszfeld.

15 The Związek Rzemieślników-Żydów, the association of authorized craftsmen in the ghetto, was headed by Abram Wolfowicz.

of the Jewish Council in Warsaw. The same applies to the persons employed in the Jewish residential district by the Temporary Administration of Seized Properties in Warsaw.[17]

Warsaw, 22 July 1942

## DOC. 99

## From 18 to 23 July 1942 the chairman of the Jewish Council in Warsaw writes in his diary about the days leading up to the deportations to Treblinka[1]

Handwritten diary of Adam Czerniaków, entries from 18 to 23 July 1942

18 July 1942 – In the morning with Lejkin to Brandt[2] and Mende.[3] A day full of evil foreboding. Rumours that on Monday evening the resettlement (of everyone?!) will begin. I asked the commissioner[4] whether he knew anything about it. He replied that he didn't and he didn't believe it [would happen]. Meanwhile, panic in the residential district: some speak of a resettlement, others of a pogrom. Today and tomorrow we are to clear out the synagogue for foreign Jews to move in. As I was sitting at Mende's, a young Polish girl between 16 and 18 years of age came in and reported that a baptized Jewish woman was living in her house.

19 July 1942 – At the Community in the morning. Unprecedented panic in the city. Kon, Heller, and Ehrlich[5] are spreading wild rumours. This creates the impression of fake propaganda. Let it be so. On the other hand, there is talk of 40 wagons being prepared. It turns out that there are 20, and that the SS has ordered them to be prepared because 720 workers are to leave for the camp tomorrow.

Kon claims that tomorrow, at 8 o'clock in the evening, the resettlement of 3,000 Jews from the small ghetto[6] (Śliska Street?) is to begin, and he himself has decamped to Otwock with his family. Others have done the same.

16 In the public notice (see fn. 10), the refuse collection company 'Müllabfuhrgesellschaft S. Heyman u. Co.' is also listed.

17 Based on the Confiscation Regulation of 24 Jan. 1940, Jewish-owned real estate was placed under the control of a general trustee in July 1940.

1 YVA, O-33/1090. Published in *The Warsaw Diary of Adam Czerniakow*, pp. 381–385. This document has been newly translated from Polish.

2 Karl Georg Brandt (1898–1945), Criminal Police officer; Kriminalsekretär in Bielefeld prior to Sept. 1939; then the official in charge of Jewish affairs for the Gestapo in Warsaw, Dept. IV B; one of the leaders of the Security Police's 'resettlement' special detachment in summer 1942; killed in action in Poznań in Feb. 1945.

3 Gerhard Mende.

4 The commissioner for the Jewish residential district in Warsaw, Heinz Auerswald.

5 Zelig Heller and Moryc Kon (Kohn), merchants and refugees from Łódź; owned the Kohn i Heller company in the Warsaw ghetto; thought to be Gestapo collaborators; shot by German officials in 1942. Józef Ehrlich, nicknamed Josele Kapota, merchant; worked for the Order Service in the Warsaw ghetto from 1940; deputy head of the Order Service from late July 1942; thought to be an informer for the Gestapo and the Criminal Police; went into hiding in late August 1942; murdered in 1943.

6 The smaller part of the ghetto, located south of Chłodna Street.

A certain Czerniaków, supposedly a relative of mine, is a makher[7] at the employment office, where he has worked for a long time. I suggested he be thrown in jail. Due to the panic, I drove around the whole residential district in the car today. I went to three yards. I don't know whether I succeeded in calming the population, but I have done my part. I try to encourage the delegations that come to see me. They don't see what this costs me. Today I took two headache tablets, one Cibalgin and [one] valerian. But I still have a splitting headache. I'm trying to make sure that I keep a smile on my face.

20 July 1942 – At 7.30 in the morning at the Gestapo. I asked Mende how much truth there is in the rumours. He replied that he had not heard anything about it. I then turned to Brandt; he replied that he knew nothing about it. When I asked whether it could happen, he replied that he knew nothing. Uncertain, I left. I turned to his boss, Commissioner Boehm.[8] He replied that it was not his department, and that Hohenmann[9] might be able to tell me something about the rumours. I mentioned that, according to the rumours that had been going around, the resettlement was to begin today at 7.30 p.m. He replied that if this were indeed the case, he would probably know something about it. With no other option, I went to see Scherer,[10] the deputy head of Division III. He was surprised by the rumour and said he also knew nothing about it. Finally I asked whether I could explain to the population that there was no cause for concern. He replied that I could and that everything they are saying is Quatsch and Unsinn.[11] I instructed Lejkin to inform the population via the precincts.[12] I went to see Auerswald. He announced that he had told the SS-Polizeioberführer[13] everything. In the meantime, First[14] had gone to see Jesuiter[15] and Schleterer,[16] who were outraged by the rumours going around and announced an investigation into the matter.

7 Yiddish in the original: 'fixer'.

8 Correctly: Johannes Böhm (1912–1999), Kriminalkommissar; joined the NSDAP in 1932 and the SS in 1933; head of Dept. IV A (Opposition) at the office of the Commander of the Security Police and the SD (KdS) in Warsaw; lived in the Munich area after the war.

9 Correctly: Gottlieb Höhmann (1907–1961), administrator; joined the NSDAP and the SA in 1930, and the SS in 1934; Kriminalkommissar with the Gestapo in Düsseldorf; deputy head of the Gestapo in District Warsaw from 1940; lived in Remscheid after the war.

10 Presumably Rudolf Scheerer (b. 1908), lawyer; joined the SS in 1933 and the NSDAP in 1937; Kriminalrat with the Gestapo in Schneidemühl; later the official in charge of Jewish affairs for the Gestapo in Warsaw (Dept. IV B).

11 German in the original: 'nonsense', 'rubbish'.

12 This is presumably a reference to the Order Service precincts.

13 German in the original. Probably SS and Police Leader von Sammern-Frankenegg.

14 Izrael First (Fürst) (d. 1942); head of the Jewish student dormitory in Warsaw's Praga district prior to Sept. 1939; head of the Jewish Council's Economic Affairs Section and liaison to the German occupation authorities from 1940; sentenced to death by the Jewish Combat Organization (ŻOB) for collaboration and shot dead in Nov. 1942.

15 Max Jesuiter (1897–1972), salesman; joined the SS in 1931 and the NSDAP in 1932; staff aide to the SS and Police Leader in Warsaw from Nov. 1939; head of staff from March 1942; lived in Munich after the war.

16 Correctly: Josef Schlederer (1894–1944), farmer and merchant; joined the SS and the NSDAP in 1932; Obersturmführer on the staff of the SS and Police Leader in Warsaw in 1942; later SS-Hauptsturmführer in Cracow; went missing on 1 August 1944.

I returned to the Community. I found Dr Schmiedt there. We are finalizing the barter of shoes etc. for grain (1,250,000 [kilos]). Today I discussed with the commissioner the issue of the detained children. He ordered me to write him a letter concerning their release, on condition that the children be placed in correctional centres and that they do not run away. I suggested that their education be entrusted to the prisoners' aid society. The commissioner demanded that a person be made responsible for supervising the children. This should be someone from the Order Service. I made an appointment with Kaczka,[17] the administrator of the transit point[18] on Dzika Street, about housing children at this point[19] as well. I plan to set up a home in Ceglana Street (the mikvah) and to house children in this building. It seems that approximately 2,000 children will qualify for the correctional centres.

21 July 1942 – At the Community in the morning. Before noon, officials from the Security Police showed up and ordered that all the councillors present in the building be detained in my office. Shortly thereafter, the councillors were arrested in my office in groups. The S[upply] O[ffice] management, headed by Gepner, was arrested at the same time. I wanted to leave with those who had been arrested. I was told to stay in my office. In the meantime, others drove to my apartment in search of my wife.[20] They were told that she was at the children's home in Wolność Street. They drove off and came back to my apartment with the order that my wife be home by 3 p.m. Some of the councillors were released today. I appealed to Brandt, who said that they would be released tomorrow or the day after. I intervened with Auerswald on behalf of Gepner and his colleagues from the S[upply] O[ffice]. He replied that he would take care of the matter tomorrow. He asked who was actually involved. I got the impression that he was undecided about Gepner, which is why I emphasized that Gepner was the heart and soul of the S[upply] O[ffice].

After bringing my wife to the Community, I stayed there until 6 p.m. The evening was quiet. There were deaths overnight.

22 July 1942 – At the Community at 7.30 in the morning. The borders of the small ghetto were surrounded by a special unit in addition to a regular one.

At 10 o'clock Sturmbannführer Hoefle[21] showed up with escorts. We turned off the telephones. The children from the yard opposite were taken away.

We were told that, with certain exceptions, the Jews are to be resettled to the East regardless of sex or age. By 4 p.m. today, 6,000 people must be provided. And that is how many it will be (at a minimum) every day. We were ordered to clear the house at 103 Żelazna Street for the German officials carrying out the resettlement.[22] The furniture was left behind. Since the Council employees, along with their wives and children, are exempt from deportation, I requested that the JSS officials, the crafts association [members], the rubbish collectors, etc. also be exempted, and this was granted. I requested the

17 Kaczka was head of the Jewish Community's Prisoner Affairs Section for a time.
18 Emergency shelter.
19 See Doc. 40.
20 Felicja Czerniaków.
21 Here and below, correctly: Hermann Höfle, head of staff for the SS and Police Leader in Lublin.
22 Höfle's staff, the so-called command post, was housed here.

release of Gepner, Rozen,[23] Sztolcman,[24] Drybiński,[25] Winter,[26] and Kobryner,[27] which was approved.

By 3.45 everyone is already [back] in the ghetto, with the exception of Rozen. In the afternoon, Lejkin had me informed after lunch that glass had allegedly been thrown at police cars. They have threatened to shoot the hostages should this happen again. The most tragic problem is that of the children in the orphanages, etc. I have raised it – perhaps something can be done.

At 5.30 p.m. one of Forwort's[28] officials drove up and demanded that Józef Ehrlich be made Lejkin's deputy. He already has three stars.[29]

Sturmbannführer Hoefle (Beauftragter[30] for the resettlement) called me into his office and explained that my wife was still free for the time being, but if the resettlement fails, she would be the first hostage to be shot.

23 July 1942 – At the Community in the morning. Wortorf[31] from the resettlement staff showed up, and I discussed several issues with him. He exempted students at the trade schools from resettlement, as well as the husbands of working women. He told me to consult Hoefle on the matter of the orphans. I was to consult him as well with regard to the craftsmen. When I asked how many days a week the operation would be carried out, he replied: seven days a week. Everyone in the city hustles to open szopy. A sewing machine can save a life.[32]

3 o'clock. There are now 4,000 people ready to depart. There have to be 9,000 by 4 o'clock according to the order. Some functionaries showed up at the post office and ordered that incoming letters and parcels be forwarded to Pawiak.[33]

23 Chil Rozen, head of the Jewish Council's Labour Section; shot dead in the ghetto in Sept. 1942.
24 Dr Alfred Abraham Sztolcman, director of the Jewish Aid Committee in Warsaw; responsible on the Jewish Council for trade and commerce; shot dead in the ghetto in April 1943.
25 I. Drybiński, acting head of the Supply Office.
26 Szmuel (Samuel) Winter; worked in the Jewish Council's Supply Office; acted as the Jewish Council's liaison to the JSS; shot during the Warsaw Ghetto Uprising.
27 Edward Kobryner, member of the Jewish Council and its Economic Affairs Section; head of the Cooperative Bank.
28 Correctly probably: Worthoff.
29 This was the appropriate rank insignia for the deputy commander of the Order Service.
30 German in the original: 'commissioner'.
31 Correctly probably: Worthoff.
32 Ghetto inhabitants who owned a sewing machine could be housed in one of the workshops, which primarily fulfilled orders for the Wehrmacht. Nevertheless, some of these people were deported in August and Sept. 1942, while most of the workers in the production facilities were deported to labour camps in District Lublin from Nov. 1942.
33 Czerniaków took his own life on the same day that he wrote this entry.

## DOC. 100

## On 25 July 1942 the Wehrmacht officer Wilm Hosenfeld notes that the Jewish population of Warsaw is being murdered in special killing facilities[1]

Handwritten diary of Wilm Hosenfeld,[2] entry for 25 July 1942

25 July 1942

If there is any truth to what is being said in the city, and by reliable people at that, then it is not an honour to be a German officer, then you can no longer go along with things. But I cannot believe it. Over the course of this week alone, 30,000 Jews are said to have already been taken out of the ghetto to somewhere in the East.[3] And despite all the secrecy, by now what is being done to them has become known. Somewhere, not far from Lublin, buildings have been erected with rooms that have been fitted with electric heating and are heated by a high-voltage current, like a crematorium. The unfortunate people are herded into these heating chambers and then burned alive.[4] In this way, thousands can be killed in a single day. This saves the trouble of shooting them and having to dig the mass graves and cover them up again. The guillotine of the French Revolution certainly can't compete with this, and no such virtuosity in mass murder was ever achieved in the cellars of the Russian GPU either.

But this is all madness; it simply cannot be possible. It makes you wonder why the Jews don't fight back. Many, the vast majority of them, are so debilitated by hunger and misery that they can offer no resistance and surrender numbly to their fate; others, in turn, may be glad to see an end to their torment. One can imagine that horrible scenes of despair take place as well. Supposedly, Ukrainian and Lithuanian policemen are deployed there instead of the German police.[5] I think that is misguided and stupid. After all, everything is supposed to be kept secret, but these people aren't keeping quiet. They are probably helping themselves to the valuables and the like left behind and are being compensated in this way for their service as executioners. I also couldn't imagine that German policemen would be capable of going along with this. At command centre yesterday I met a businessman who informed me that anything and everything can now be had in the ghetto, and very cheaply at that. Watches, rings, gold, dollars, rugs, and whatnot.

1 The original is owned by the Hosenfeld family. Copy in IfZ-Archives, F 601. Published in Wilm Hosenfeld, *'Ich versuche jeden zu retten': Das Leben eines deutschen Offiziers in Briefen und Tagebüchern*, ed. Thomas Vogel (Munich: DVA, 2004), pp. 630–631. This document has been translated from German.

2 Wilm (short for Wilhelm) Hosenfeld (1895–1952), teacher; joined the SA in 1933 and the NSDAP in 1935; served in the war in 1939; with the Oberfeldkommandantur in Warsaw, 1940–1944; head of a Wehrmacht physical training facility from 1941, in which capacity he provided help to Jews and Poles; in Soviet captivity from Jan. 1945; died in Stalingrad prisoner-of-war camp.

3 The Warsaw Jews were deported to Treblinka.

4 The victims were murdered in gas chambers into which carbon monoxide was pumped; in 1942 various rumours concerning the killing methods were in circulation in the General Government: see Doc. 92, fn. 3.

5 The Operation Reinhard extermination camps were run by German and Austrian camp staff and guarded by foreign auxiliary personnel, known as Trawniki men, usually recruited from among the Soviet prisoners of war: see Introduction, p. 43.

Another gentleman I met on the street – that is, we ran into each other, chatted briefly, and parted. Then he came running after me and asked whether I had heard of the business involving Sweden and Turkey.[6] He also talked about the atrocities committed against the Jews and was outraged beyond all measure. For the Führer's birthday, Himmler is said to have reported the liquidation of 50,000 Jews in the General Government.[7] A fine birthday present. All of this is being said. What part of it may be true? In any event, the Jews are disappearing. How they are being killed off is a question of secondary importance.

## DOC. 101

## On 27 July 1942 the SS and Police Leader in Cracow's chief of staff describes a conflict between the Wehrmacht and the police over the deportation of the Jews from Przemyśl[1]

Note by the SS and Police Leader in Cracow's chief of staff, signed Fellenz,[2] Przemyśl, dated 27 July 1942[3]

As ordered, I held a briefing on Wednesday, 22 July 1942, about the resettlement of the Jews from Przemysl, which is scheduled for 27 July 1942. In attendance were persons from all the administrative offices and agencies involved (the Kreishauptmann's office,[4] the Stadtkommissar's office,[5] authorized representatives of the Order Police, the Przemysl branch of the Security Police,[6] and the head of the employment office in Przemysl).[7] During this briefing (see file note dated 23 July 1942),[8] the measures to be taken

6 On 23 July 1942 Hosenfeld had made a note about rumours that Sweden and Turkey, both neutral countries, had declared war on Germany: Hosenfeld, *'Ich versuche jeden zu retten'*, p. 627. In fact, Turkey did not break off diplomatic relations with Germany until 2 August 1944, and the declaration of war came six months later; Sweden remained neutral until the end of the war.

7 No such report by Himmler has been found.

1 BArch, NS 19/1765, fols. 20–24. Published in Peter Longerich and Dieter Pohl (eds.), *Die Ermordung der europäischen Juden: Eine umfassende Dokumentation des Holocaust 1941–1945* (Munich: Piper, 1989), pp. 202–207. This document has been translated from German.

2 Martin Fellenz (1909–2007), bank clerk; joined the NSDAP and the SS in 1932; chief of staff to the SS and Selbstschutz Leader in Cracow from Dec. 1939; adjutant of the SS and Police Leader in Cracow from March 1940, and chief of staff from June 1941 to Oct. 1942; served in the Waffen-SS from Nov. 1942; adjutant of the Higher SS and Police Leader East, Koppe, from 1944; managed a bakery in Schleswig after the war; city councillor for the Free Democratic Party (FDP) in Schleswig from 1955; sentenced to seven years in prison by Kiel Regional Court in 1966.

3 The original contains handwritten corrections.

4 Dr Friedrich Anton Heinisch was Kreishauptmann of Przemyśl, July 1941 to 16 August 1942.

5 Bernhard Gießelmann.

6 The head of the Security Police branch office in Przemyśl from May 1941 to autumn 1942 was Adolf Benthin (b. 1897), police officer; served in the German police from 1920; joined the NSDAP in 1937 and the SS in 1939; served in the Urban Police in Schwerin prior to 1939; imprisoned in a British internment camp after the war; escaped and disappeared; declared dead by Schwerin District Court in 1951. Benthin wrote his own memo about these incidents: BArch, NS 19/1765, fols. 16–19.

7 Günther Neumann.

8 This is not included in the file.

were discussed and established, with due consideration given to the orders that have been issued. In particular, I pointed out the new order issued by the Higher SS and Police Leader East, SS-Obergruppenführer and Police General Krüger, which sets the age range for the Jews remaining in labour deployment at 16–35.[9] I likewise pointed out that the interests of the Eastern Railway and the Wehrmacht must be taken into account as far as possible; this means that Jewish workers who are past the established age limit mentioned above are to be replaced by younger ones wherever possible. I have given permission to keep Jews who are specialized workers (for example, master craftsmen with a speciality) on the job for the time being, even if they are over the age limit, but only in truly exceptional cases. I have stipulated that the women employed by administrative offices and agencies are by no means permitted to stay on the job if their husband does not receive a residence permit, and if the women are not specially trained workers, i.e. if they are employed in ordinary tasks such as housecleaning, other domestic work, and gardening. These women can be replaced by the wives of those Jews who do receive a residence permit, as the existing rules stipulate that a man who is granted a residence permit simultaneously receives such a permit for his wife and children. In this way, the important interests of the Wehrmacht as well as the Eastern Railway, of which we are aware here as well, have been taken into account to the greatest possible extent.

Following a telephone message from SS-Untersturmführer Benthin, head of the Security Police branch office in Przemysl, [informing me that] the local military commander in Przemysl, Major Liedtke,[10] [said] the operation planned for 27 July 1942 was being jeopardized by the closure of the San bridge to police and civilians, I travelled to Przemysl as ordered by the SS and Police Leader in District Cracow, SS-Oberführer Scherner, in order to sort out the matter on site and to take appropriate measures. After talking briefly with SS-Untersturmführer Benthin in the presence of the Kreishauptmann; Hauptmann Schweder from the Urban Police, [who is] also head of Przemysl Police Battalion Company 2/307; Leutnant Hölzner, head of the local Urban Police department; and Oberleutnant Schaller,[11] I got the following picture: SS-Untersturmführer Benthin received a phone call from the local military commander, Major Liedtke, at around 9 a.m. on Sunday, 26 July 1942. Liedtke told him he had learned that approximately 95 per cent of the Jewish workers would be withdrawn from the Wehrmacht agencies due to the impending operation against the Jews. In reply, SS-Untersturmführer Benthin said that he could not tell him how many of the Jews employed at Wehrmacht agencies would be resettled, but one must expect that some of the workers (Jews) employed at Wehrmacht agencies would be subject to the resettlement. However, he said that he could not give him any further details, since the operation was classified. To resolve any questions that might arise, he would have to wait until Monday, 27 July 1942, as the SS and Police Leader's representative would be in Przemysl then. On the same

9 This could not be found.

10 Max Liedtke (1894–1955), journalist; publishing director of the *Greifswalder Zeitung* newspaper, 1929–1937; served as a major in the Wehrmacht; local military commander in Przemyśl in 1942; died in Soviet captivity in 1955; honoured as Righteous Among the Nations by the State of Israel in 1993.

11 Hermann Georg Schaller (1891–1949), police officer; Urban Police Revier-Oberleutnant and head of the Urban Police department in Przemyśl in 1942; lived in Leverkusen after the war. On 11 August 1942 Schaller wrote his own report about the conflict in Przemyśl: BArch, NS 19/1765, fols. 13–14rv.

day, at 10.15 a.m., the local commander's adjutant, First Lieutenant Battel,[12] appeared at the Security Police station and informed him of the contents of a wireless message from the local military commander to the Military Commander in the General Government – enclosure, page 16.[13] Until a decision is taken by the Military Commander in the General Government, the local military commander has ordered the bridge over the San to be closed to all civilians, including the police. The situation created by this step is described in the enclosures.

After familiarizing myself with the circumstances, I went with the gentlemen present to the Ortskommandantur to clarify things there. In accordance with the instructions I received from SS-Oberführer Scherner, I tried to find 'a diplomatic solution' and explained to the local military commander, Major Liedtke, and the approximately 20 officers present that, based on the orders issued by the Reichsführer-SS, a resettlement had to take place and would indeed be carried out. I briefly outlined the provisions and stated that the Wehrmacht's military and armaments interests would be taken into account in this respect as well, of course, but that I was unsympathetic to the Wehrmacht's practice of continuing to keep huge numbers of what have come to be called house and court Jews, whom high-minded NCOs use to clean their quarters and polish their shoes. In addition, I suggested that once some of these working Jews are taken away, the rest should be put to work properly and employed in productive labour. In the course of further negotiations, I arrived at an agreement as per SS-Oberführer Scherner's orders, based on the guidelines in Enclosure 13, Garrison Order No. 30 142, issued by the local military commander in Przemysl.[14] I assured the Wehrmacht that for the time being, all Jewish workers between the ages of 16 and 35 who are employed by the Wehrmacht will remain, regardless of their occupation, along with specialized workers over the age of 35 who cannot be replaced at the moment, and that all Jewish workers who are over 35 and therefore subject to resettlement will be replaced with younger ones wherever possible. To this end, 120 male Jews between the ages of 16 and 35 were kept back as a pool of replacements during the first resettlement on 27 July 1942.

Furthermore, I have issued guidelines for dealing with the working Jews (billeting them in barracks, marching them in closed column formations); see enclosures 13–14.[15]

Since it is hardly likely that all the Jews employed at Wehrmacht agencies and subject to resettlement can be replaced with younger workers, particularly not the skilled labourers, I request instructions as to what is to be done. I have promised the Wehrmacht that all the Jews that it employs will remain in their workplaces until noon on Thursday, and that the Wehrmacht identity document – Enclosure 19[16] – will retain its full validity until then. After noon on Thursday, this document will no longer be valid. The replace-

12 Dr Albert Battel (1891–1952), lawyer; practised law in Breslau from 1925; joined the NSDAP in 1933; served as a Wehrmacht intelligence officer in Przemyśl in 1942; retired from the Wehrmacht due to heart disease in 1944; later in Soviet captivity; classified as a 'follower' (*Mitläufer*) in denazification proceedings in Hochheim am Main; honoured as Righteous Among the Nations by the State of Israel in 1981.

13 This is not included in the file.

14 These are not included in the file.

15 These are not included in the file.

16 This is not included in the file.

ment [of these Jews] with younger workers must also be carried out by this time – as far as is practicable.

In a private talk with Major Liedtke – I asked him to come into an adjacent room for this purpose – I informed him on behalf of the SS and Police Leader that his actions, such as closing the bridge etc., even after consulting with the Oberfeldkommandantur, were neither justified nor authorized. The entire operation is a police matter and does not concern the Wehrmacht. I also asked that he not interfere with the operation again in any way, as appropriate countermeasures would otherwise have to be taken. I made it clear to him that if the SS battalion had come from Debica, it would have crossed over the bridge. To this Major Liedtke replied that he had to represent the Wehrmacht's interests, and that in accordance with some regulation or another, the Wehrmacht takes priority in the event of disputes between the Wehrmacht and civil authorities. He said he did not want to have to answer for the failure to unload a hospital train carrying wounded men, ostensibly because the Jews failed to appear. He continued, noting that he was unable to reach the Kreishauptmann and that SS-Untersturmführer Benthin refused to engage in negotiations. I told Major Liedtke that the Wehrmacht may take priority in other areas, but not when it comes to police operations.

It cannot be the case that he failed to reach the Kreishauptmann or his deputy;[17] see enclosures 11 and 12.[18] It is also not the case that SS-Untersturmführer Benthin failed to negotiate with the Ortskommandantur. SS-Untersturmführer Benthin was completely correct in refusing to discuss the particulars of the operation. Had the local military commander mentioned a transport of wounded men, the correct solution certainly would have been found very quickly. Hauptmann Schweder[19] has told me that in that case he would have been willing to deploy his entire company. Closing and occupying the bridge over the San would then surely have been unnecessary; more specifically, the guards and sentries there would arguably have been put to better use unloading the train.

I also ordered that the edict to the Polish and Ukrainian populations (Enclosure 6),[20] which the local military commander wanted to suppress, should be made public via the Kreishauptmann.

*Execution of the operation on 27 July 1942*

The planned operation began on 27 July 1942, when the first transport got under way. In total, 3,850 Jews were resettled.[21]

The Jews registered for resettlement were sorted, and the following numbers of workers were returned to their workplaces: to the *Eastern Railway*, 150 Jews; to the *Wehrmacht*, 150 Jews; to the W. Fischer company and the commander of the Military

17 Dr Herbert Herbig (1905–1990).

18 These are not included in the file.

19 Carl Schweder (1892–1960), police officer; in 1942 company commander in Police Battalion 308, and later in Police Battalion 307.

20 Presumably the proclamation in which Kreishauptmann Heinisch announced the 'resettlement of the Jews' on 27 July 1942 and threatened that any Ukrainians and Poles who helped the Jews would be shot: see Stanisław Wroński and Maria Zwolakowa (eds.), *Polacy – Żydzi 1939–1945* (Warsaw: Książka i Wiedza, 1971), p. 410.

21 In total, approximately 6,500 people were deemed unfit for work and deported, and several hundred were shot in the streets.

Training Area South in Deba, 80 Jews (as per a letter from the Higher SS and Police Leader East, dated 24 July 1942[22]).

A pool of 120 Jews was kept back as replacements.

The operation was carried out calmly and according to plan. Some Jews who attempted to escape or resist were shot.

The cooperation with the authorities involved was particularly good, especially with the Kreishauptmann, the Stadtkommissar, and the Security Police. Everyone correctly understood the situation and acted firmly and decisively. The support from the Kreishauptmann and the Stadtkommissar for the deployed forces deserves special mention.

The Order Police deployed under Urban Police Major *Binz's* command performed their duties in an exemplary fashion.

The process of establishing the smaller Jewish residential district with a fixed barbed-wire fence is well under way. The first resettlement to the scaled-down ghetto has already been completed.[23]

The process of moving those Jews living in rural areas and concentrating them in Przemysl has begun and will be completed, with the support of the Order Police, by Wednesday evening or Thursday midday.

I have arranged for the SS and Police Leader in Lublin[24] to be informed by wireless message.

The next transport will be carried out on Wednesday, 29 July 1942.

I apologize for submitting a report that is not flawlessly written. This is due to time constraints. In addition, no shorthand typist was available.

## DOC. 102

## *Informacja Bieżąca*, 27 July 1942: reports about mass murders in the Warsaw ghetto, at Belzec extermination camp, and elsewhere[1]

*Jewish matters*

*The Warsaw ghetto*: In the further course of the general liquidation of the Jews throughout the entire area under the German authorities, after Cracow, it was recently Warsaw's turn to be liquidated in the General Government. Ever since the infamous massacre on the night of 18 April,[2] the stream of murders has continued uninterrupted every night,

22 This is not included in the file.

23 On 4 August 1942 a police regulation was issued, ordering a new ghetto to be established solely for registered workers in Przemyśl and defining the boundaries of this new ghetto. Published as a facsimile in Elżbieta Rączy and Igor Witowicz (eds.), *Zagłada Żydów na Rzeszowszczyźnie: Album pamięci / Extermination of Jews in the Rzeszow Region: Album of Remembrance*, bilingual Polish-English edn (Rzeszów and Warsaw: Instytut Pamięci Narodowej, 2004), p. 72.

24 The transports to the extermination camps were coordinated by the staff of the SS and Police Leader in Lublin, Odilo Globocnik.

1 *Informacja Bieżąca*, no. 27 (52), 27 July 1942, pp. 3–4; AAN, 1325/202/III-7/1, fols. 124–128, here fols. 126–127. This document has been translated from Polish.

2 See Doc. 74.

and during the day. This is how, on the night of 17 July, more than forty-one people were killed in the ghetto. Arrests began on a very large scale on 20 July. The people arrested were sent to Pawiak, as well as the prison for Jews on Gęsia, and some were also taken to the prison on Daniłowiczowska. Some of them are seen as hostages in view of the great liquidation operation (more on this below) and are meant to ensure that this operation proceeds smoothly. Foreign Jews, mainly Americans, were also arrested or imprisoned. They were accommodated in Pawiak under exceptionally good conditions, treated with consideration, and in this way they were probably saved from being exterminated 'accidentally in the crowd', which could have resulted in undesirable international reactions and consequences for the Germans.

On 22 July the 'Community Council' posted a notice throughout the ghetto, announcing that all inhabitants would gradually be resettled with the exception of those who worked in German businesses or for Germans, employees of the Community and its subordinate institutions, members of the Jewish Order Police, Housing Commission Board, and building caretakers. Their families (husbands, wives, and children up to 16 years of age) would also be allowed to remain with them. The rest would be sent east in daily transports of 6,000 people.[3] On that day the manhunt began in the ghetto, which was sealed off by the police. In principle the Jewish Order Service is[4] the executive authority in this operation, but Germans and 'junacy' (Ukrainians, Lithuanians, Latvians, etc.) are also taking part. They take people off the streets (the beggars were the first to go), from the poorhouses, the night shelters, and the apartment blocks. Machine guns were set up at the exits to the ghetto, which has been tightly sealed since then, and they have not remained silent. For a few days, a general, unbridled terror reigned with impunity in the ghetto. Shots were fired at passers-by and at houses. Among others, they shoot at Jews from the watchtowers, the so-called 'Pawiak platforms'; they shoot from the windows in the Polish district looking out to the ghetto (e.g. at 11 Rynkowa), etc. Gangs of junacy raid apartments and murder anyone they come across. For example, in the apartment of the well-known antiques dealer Gutmajer,[5] the Polish surgeon Dr Raszeja,[6] a professor at Poznań University, was killed along with his assistant and those who had come to consult him. Raszeja and his assistant had come there with a permit to carry out consultations. Indescribable panic, dejection, and depression reign in the ghetto. It is obvious that the transports lead to death, perhaps to Bełżec (see below),[7] all the more so because the notice grants decidedly cynical permission to take 15 kg of luggage and all kinds of valuables. Those taken for transport were loaded onto goods wagons (exits fitted with barbed wire) standing on a siding at Gdańsk train station near Stawki Street.[8]

3 See Doc. 98.
4 Changes in tense here and below as in the original.
5 Aba (Abe) Gutmajer lived at 26 Chłodna Street.
6 Franciszek Raszeja (1896–1942), physician; head of the Orthopaedic Clinic at Poznań University from 1935; served in the war in 1939; subsequently fled to the east; worked as an orthopaedist in Warsaw from late 1939; involved in providing aid to ghetto inhabitants, for which he was honoured posthumously as Righteous Among the Nations by the State of Israel. According to various reports, SS men or perhaps Gestapo personnel killed Raszeja.
7 The inhabitants of the Warsaw ghetto were deported to Treblinka.
8 In other words, at the so-called Umschlagplatz. Warszawa Gdańska (Danzig station) was a main station in the northern part of Warsaw.

On the first day, 22 July, fifty-five goods wagons departed. The chairman of the Jewish Community, the engineer Czerniaków, committed suicide.[9]

On 12 July, on Waliców Street in the Polish district, the German police detained four people, three sisters and a man, on the charge of smuggling goods to the Jewish district. After being taken to the guard post at 99 Leszno Street, they were all shot. One of the women was pregnant.

On 25 June a row broke out between Polish and Jewish workers at the Eastern Train Station construction site for the following reason: the Poles were dissatisfied because they received the same meals and rations as the Jews, and they refused [the Jews] access to the canteen. One of the Jews struck a Polish worker with a rake and killed him. He was lynched, and in the ensuing brawl twenty-two Jews were killed or seriously injured, and many more were lightly wounded. The German police refused to intervene.[10]

*The death camps*: The two most important camps in the GG are Bełżec and Sobibór in powiat Włodawa.[11] The camp in Bełżec was out of operation for the last ten days of May due to the terrible stench from the decomposing corpses of thousands of murdered people that were barely covered with soil. The camp has been in operation again since 3 June. Two transports arrive every day, one at 6 a.m., the other around 4 p.m. Immediately the torturers commence 'disinfection and bathing', which no one leaves alive. What was probably the first riot in the camp occurred on 13 June. When the Jews were ordered to remove the bodies of the murdered women and children, they found the dead people huddled together inside the chamber, their arms around each other's waists and necks – clearly their final acts before death. Faced with this terrible scene, they fell upon the Wachmannschaft,[12] which alerted the entire personnel and led to a fight in which four to six Germans and almost all the Jews perished; a few managed to escape.[13]

Massacres of Jews are taking place throughout nearly the entire General Government. In mid June approximately 4,000 Jews were deported from Cracow, and more than 150 were shot dead on the spot. In Tarnów, 400; in Nowy Sącz, 500; in Łuków, 50 (on 20 and 21 July); in Szczebrzeszyn, over 70; in Biłgoraj, 60; in Tarnogród, 48; etc., etc. These are merely unsystematic, random figures cited as examples from the past few weeks.

*Otwock*: For a ransom of 20,000 złoty, a certain Kac and two of his sons were released from Treblinka. However, when they returned [home] they were immediately arrested again and shot in front of an invited audience: Ditz,[14] the head of the Arbeitsamt,[15] and

9 See Doc. 99.

10 Various accounts give conflicting versions of the causes and the progression of the confrontation at Warsaw's Eastern train station on 25 June: see *The Warsaw Diary of Adam Czerniakow*, pp. 370–371 (27 June 1942) and pp. 372–373 (1 July 1942); the diary entry by Jechiel Górny (1908?–1943) in Marta Markowska (ed.), *Archiwum Ringelbluma: Dzień po dniu Zagłady* (Warsaw: Karta, 2008), pp. 169–170; and the report by an unknown author in Ruta Sakowska et al. (eds.), *Archiwum Ringelbluma: Konspiracyjne Archiwum Getta Warszawy*, vol. 5: *Getto warszawskie: Życie codzienne*, ed. Katarzyna Person (Warsaw: Żydowski Instytut Historyczny, 2011), pp. 475–476.

11 Treblinka had already been in operation for several days by this point. Most of the Jews from the General Government were murdered there: see Introduction, pp. 29, 34–35.

12 German in the original: 'guard detail'.

13 No other sources mention such a riot.

14 Correctly: Hugo Dietz, head of the employment office in Otwock.

his wife, as well as a certain Kuc, an interpreter for the Kripo. The execution was carried out by the head of the Kripo, Schlicht[16] – the very man who had released them in exchange for the ransom. At the same time he executed two middlemen who had arranged the transaction. The condemned men had to dig a ditch and jump into it, whereupon Schlicht performed an 'Indian dance'[17] around the ditch and fired shots with his revolver until he had killed everyone. The witnesses shook with laughter, the Polish policemen had to form a cordon, and a few of them suffered a nervous collapse.

*Radom*: The Jews in the ghetto had their bicycles, carts, and horses taken away.

*In the eastern territories*: In Wołczyn (Vilna region) 1,400 Jews were brutally murdered between 10 and 15 May. On 29 June the Germans set fire to the Słonim ghetto with hand grenades in many places, allegedly due to support for the partisans. Lithuanians, Byelorussian police, and the SD shot at everyone who tried to escape. In Wołyń, particularly in Kowel, 9,000–10,000 Jews were shot between 3 and 4 June. This massacre was preceded by reprisals of a financial nature, extortion, and the theft of valuables. Today, the possession of a watch, a large amount of cash, etc. involves immediate death. The Jews have had their heads shaved, are not allowed to wear any head covering, and are only allowed to walk in the road. Wearing any kind of head covering or walking on the pavement is punishable by death. In late June the Kowel ghetto commissioner himself walked intoxicated through the streets and shot at pedestrians with a rifle. In early July the entire Jewish police force was shot. Due to mass escapes, searches in the Aryan districts are continuing.

*In the western territories*: All the inhabitants of the Poddębice ghetto (1,800) were taken away and locked up for four days in the parish church, where they were left to starve. Then they were taken to the forest and murdered. Polish women were ordered to clean the filthy, defiled church. During the first half of June there were mass deportations from the Dąbrowa Basin, most likely to Bełżec.[18] A great many of the Jews who remained in the coal basin are now employed in furriers' workshops, where they mainly sew fur gloves for the army.

15 German in the original: 'employment office'.

16 Otto Schlicht (1904–1944?), police officer; SS-Sturmscharführer with the Commander of the Security Police and the SD (KdS) in Warsaw; Kriminalsekretär; head of the Criminal Police (Kripo) in Otwock.

17 This is presumably a reference to Native American traditional dances.

18 There were no known transports to Belzec from the Dąbrowa Basin, a coal-mining area in Upper Silesia.

## DOC. 103

## On 28 July 1942 the state secretary of the Reich Ministry of Transport informs a correspondent that thousands of Jews are being deported from Warsaw to extermination camps every day[1]

Letter (marked 'secret') from the state secretary of the Reich Ministry of Transport and deputy director general of the German Reich Railway, Berlin, signed Ganzenmüller,[2] to the personal staff of the Reichsführer-SS, SS-Obergruppenführer Wolf[3] (file no. AR 10/19/94), Berlin, dated 28 July 1942

Dear Party Comrade Wolf,

With reference to our telephone conversation of 16 July, I am relaying the following message from my Eastern Railway General Directorate (Gedob) in Cracow, for your information:

> Since *22 July one train with 5,000 Jews has been going to Treblinka from Warsaw via Malkinia every day.*[4] In addition, there is a train that takes 5,000 Jews from Przemysl[5] to Belzek[6] twice a week. The Eastern Railway General Directorate is in regular contact with the SD in Cracow. The SD agrees that the transports from Warsaw via Lublin to Sobibor (near Lublin) should be suspended as long as the construction work on this line makes these transports impossible (until approximately October 1942).

The trains were arranged in consultation with the Senior Commander of the Security Police in the General Government.[7] The SS and Police Leader in District Lublin, SS-Brigadeführer Globotschnigg,[8] has been informed.[9]

1 AIPN, GK, Ds 58/69, fol. 24. Copy in BArch, MF 3596, Aufnahme 2 568 629. Published as a facsimile in Raul Hilberg, *Sonderzüge nach Auschwitz* (Frankfurt am Main: Ullstein, 1987), appendix 26, p. 177. This document has been translated from German.

2 Dr Albert Ganzenmüller (1905–1996), engineer; took part in the Beer Hall Putsch in 1923; joined the NSDAP in 1931 and the SA in 1932; worked for the Reich Railway from 1932; head of the Main Railway Directorate for the East in Poltava and state secretary of the Reich Ministry of Transport in 1941; deputy director general of the Reich Railway and commissioner general of the railways in 1942; lived in Argentina after the war, then in West Germany from 1955; worked for the Hoesch AG steel and mining company until 1968.

3 Correctly: Karl Wolff (1900–1984), bank clerk; joined the NSDAP and the SS in 1931; Himmler's personal adjutant from 1933; chief of the Reichsführer-SS's personal staff, 1936–1943; simultaneously the SS's liaison officer with Hitler from 1939; Highest SS and Police Leader in Italy from July 1943; salesman in the West German publishing industry after the war; for his role in the deportations sentenced to 15 years in prison by Munich Regional Court II in 1964.

4 According to the German statistics for the transports, between 5,020 and 7,400 people were deported from the Warsaw ghetto every day during the first week: see also Doc. 111.

5 This probably refers to deportations from District Cracow via Przemyśl to Belzec.

6 Spelled as in the original.

7 Eberhard Schöngarth.

8 Correctly: Globocnik.

9 Wolff sent Ganzenmüller his 'heartfelt thanks' on 13 August 1942: BArch, MF 3596, Aufnahme 2 568 629.

## DOC. 104

### *Biuletyn Radiowy*, end of July 1942: the Polish Workers' Party calls on the Jews to mount active resistance and urges the Polish population to support them[1]

Radio broadcasts published by the Warsaw Committee of the Polish Workers' Party, no. 54, covering the period 27 to 30 July 1942

A few days ago, the mass deportation of the population of the Warsaw ghetto began. The occupiers carried this out with their customary brutality and ruthlessness. They terrorized the inhabitants with whips and gunshots. To make their work easier, the Germans ordered the Jewish Community to provide 6,000 people a day for deportation. The Community took on this shameful task. Those who work in the factories and for the Community are exempt from deportation, as are the Jewish policemen[2] who sold out to the occupiers. But they too will meet the same fate. Extermination inevitably awaits all the deportees. The Germans have already murdered more than 700,000 Jews in Poland. They have used the same method everywhere: they pass off deportation to death as resettlement. Passivity has never saved anyone. It won't save anyone this time either. The Jews have understood this. News has emerged from the ghetto of individual cases of active resistance to deportation and looting. The only chance of salvation is to break out of the ghetto by force. To resist deportation, to organize combat forces, and to resist individually – this is the only correct way to behave at such a dramatic moment. Self-defence must expand into a mass movement. Individuals will perish in the struggle, but thousands will save themselves. The Polish population has a responsibility to help the Jews, who are seeking salvation from the hands of our common enemy, the Nazi occupier.

1 *Biuletyn Radiowy*, no. 54, 27–30 July 1942, p. 1; AAN, 1583/103, p. 19. *Biuletyn Radiowy* appeared from 1941 as one of the underground publications of the Union for the Liberation Struggle (Związek Walki Wyzwoleńczej), a communist group which merged with the Polish Workers' Party (PPR) in Jan. 1942; the publication contained news obtained from Soviet radio broadcasts. This document has been translated from Polish.

2 A reference to the Jewish Order Service (JSS).

## DOC. 105

## On 30 July 1942 the commandant of Treblinka extermination camp apologizes to his wife for not writing to her more often[1]

Typewritten letter from SS-Untersturmführer Dr Irmfried Eberl,[2] SS-Sonderkommando, Treblinka near Malkinia, General Government, to his wife, Ruth,[3] dated 30 July 1942

My dear Ruth,

Many thanks for your nice letter and for the measurements. The letter arrived extremely late, however. I waited for it for days. Now I don't know whether it'll still be possible for me to get the boots. So when I write and ask you to send me this or that as soon as possible, please do so at once, because any delay can mean that I miss a one-time opportunity.

Also, I've not had confirmation of receipt for the packages. One large package and one small parcel – registered post – were sent off to you. I hope you've received everything by now. It is all I was able to send for the time being, as we ourselves are very short of supplies here at the moment.

I know I've not written much recently, but it couldn't be helped, as the last weeks in Warsaw were unimaginably hectic; likewise, the pace here in Treblinka is nothing less than breathtaking.[4] If I could split myself into four parts and there were 100 hours in the day, it would probably still not be enough. That is why I so rarely get around to writing as often as you might like, and as I would gladly do, and probably I will not be able to in future either. Rest assured that I think about you a lot and frequently, but I simply don't have the time and leisure for writing. When one is on one's feet from dawn to dusk and dusk to dawn, as I was last week, when one sleeps perhaps three or four hours a night, snatches the remaining hours of sleep at odd moments during the day, and then the few hours of sleep one does get are made even more delightful by the nuisance of lice, fleas, etc., then you can really and truly believe me when I say that although I might occasionally find a few minutes to write a short message, I don't have the peace of mind for it. You are, after all, my dearest companion, and when I enter into dialogue with you, then I want my thoughts and feelings to be with you fully, I want to be connected to you, but I don't want to burden you with [mention of] dirt and filth.

Over time I have developed nerves of steel. There is no question of my nerves failing. Even less so that I should physically collapse. In recent days I have managed to fulfil my

1 HHStA, GStA Frankfurt 631a/1631, fols. 149–150. This document has been translated from German.

2 Dr Irmfried Eberl (1910–1948), physician; joined the NSDAP in Austria in 1931; worked at the Hygiene Museum in Dresden and as a company physician; worked in the Office of Public Health in the Gau of Magdeburg-Anhalt from 1938; head of the Brandenburg and Bernburg 'euthanasia' killing centres; involved in drafting the Nazis' planned euthanasia law; commandant of Treblinka until August 1942; thereafter returned to Bernburg; committed suicide while in prison on remand.

3 Ruth Eberl, née Rehm (1907–1944); background in home economics; trained as a shorthand typist, 1927–1928; freelance graphologist from 1932; joined the NSDAP in 1932; worked full-time for the German Labour Front (DAF) from 1933; married Eberl in Bregenz in 1938.

4 From 23 July 1942 transports carrying thousands of deportees from the Warsaw ghetto arrived at Treblinka each day; these people were murdered in the gas chambers on the day of their arrival. Enormous mountains of clothing built up in the camp, and operations became chaotic. For this reason Eberl was replaced as commandant in late August.

duty with only half the staff, but at the cost of ruthlessly overexerting myself. However, I have also put my people to work relentlessly wherever necessary, and my people have borne it bravely. And this is an accomplishment I am pleased with and proud of.

All I need now is the necessary understanding on your part. Don't imagine that I don't think of you often and gladly. At night, when the fleas torment me, I often think about my beautiful home in Berlin. And during the day, when I yell until I'm hoarse, I think about the peace and quiet at home. But the task I have been given is being accomplished thoroughly, and that's the main thing.

My dear kitten, don't be angry with me if I'm silent sometimes; I think about you often and a lot, but it's not always possible to sit down and write letters. Because you represent the beautiful side of my life, I don't want you to know anything about all of this.

Warmly, and lots and lots of kisses,
Yours,
Teddy[5]

## DOC. 106

## On 31 July 1942 Yisroel Likhtenshteyn from Warsaw writes his testament[1]

Handwritten note by Yisroel Likhtenshteyn,[2] Warsaw, 31 July 1942

*My testament*

I threw myself with fervour and enthusiasm into the work of helping gather archive materials, which were all entrusted to me to be their final custodian. I have hidden the materials. No one knows where apart from me. I have shared the location only with my comrade Hersh Vaser, who I report to.

It [the cache of materials] is well hidden. If only it survives … It will be the best, most wonderful thing that we have achieved in these cruel times.[3]

I know that we won't make it. It is impossible to live through and survive such horrible murders and massacres. That is why I am writing this testament of mine. Perhaps I am not worthy of being remembered, but my courage to participate in the 'Oyneg Shabes' group is, as well as my being in the greatest danger because I hid all the materials.

5 In the original document, the final words of the valediction are handwritten.

1 AŻIH, Ring I/1450 (1190), fols. 13–14. Published in English translation in Kermish (ed.), *To Live with Honor*, pp. 58–59. This document has been newly translated from Yiddish.

2 Yisroel Likhtenshteyn (Israel Lichtensztejn, Lichtenstein, or Lichtensztajn) (1904–1943), teacher; member of the Poale Zion-Left and editor of the Yiddish weekly *Literarishe Bleter* in the 1930s; head of the soup kitchen for children in the school building at 68 Nowolipki Street in the Warsaw ghetto, member of the Oyneg Shabes group, and archivist of the underground archive; died in 1943 shortly before or during the Warsaw Ghetto Uprising.

3 Likhtenshteyn buried some of the archive's materials in the school building at 68 Nowolipki Street on 3 August 1942. In 1946 Rokhl Oyerbakh and Hersh Vaser arranged for the ten metal containers to be recovered from under the rubble: see Introduction, p. 36.

It would be no great thing to risk my own neck, but I am also risking the life of my dear wife, Gele Sekshteyn, and that of my jewel – my little daughter Margolis.[4]

I do not want any thanks, any monument, or any praise for this. I only want to be remembered so that my brother and sister across the sea will know where my remains came to be.

I want my wife, Gele Sekshteyn, to be remembered – a painter capable of dozens of works, [but who] didn't get to exhibit or see the spotlight. During the three years of the war, she worked with children as an educator and teacher, made decorations and costumes for the children's performances, and received awards. Now, together with me, we are preparing to die.

I want my little daughter to be remembered. Margolis is 20 months old today. Has a perfect command of the Yiddish language. Speaks flawless Yiddish. She began speaking clear Yiddish at nine months. Her intelligence is comparable to that of children who are three or four years old. I don't want to boast about her. The teaching staff at the school at 68 Nowolipki Street – Dr Pole Folman,[5] Mrs Blit-Hertslikh,[6] Mrs Zagan,[7] and others – can attest to it.

I don't lament my own life or that of my wife. I only lament the life of this bright little girl. She too deserves to be remembered.

May we be the redeemers of all other Jews throughout the world. I believe the [Jewish] nation will endure. The Jews will not be eradicated. We, the Jews of Poland, the Czech lands,[8] Slovakia, Lithuania, and Latvia, are the atonement sacrifice for all of Israel in all other countries.

31 July 1942
Eleventh day of the so-called 'resettlement operation'. In reality – extermination operation.

4 Gele Sekshteyn (1907–1943), graphic artist and painter, and Margolis Likhtenshteyn (1941–1943).

5 Dr Pole Folman (b. 1901), physician; member of the Poale Zion-Left party and activist with the Society for the Protection of the Health of the Jewish Population in Poland (TOZ).

6 Fela (Feyge) Blit, née Hertslikh (1902–1943), teacher; member of the Poale Zion party; worked at a Central Yiddish School Organization (CISzO) school before Sept. 1939; perished in Lublin-Majdanek concentration camp.

7 Presumably the wife of Shakhne Froym Zagan (Szachno Efroim Sagan) (1892–1942), Poale Zion-Left politician and underground activist in the Warsaw ghetto.

8 Tshekhye (Czechia) in the original, meaning what was then the Protectorate of Bohemia and Moravia.

## DOC. 107

## A Jewish staff member at the employment office writes about the German Jews in the Warsaw ghetto in the period prior to July 1942[1]

Handwritten memoirs of Stefan Ernest,[2] Warsaw, *c.* early 1943

[…][3]

The Jews of Warsaw, decimated by disease, hunger, frost, and labour camps, had to maintain their numbers as required by the occupier.[4] Of course, under such conditions, the number of births was negligible. The ghetto had already been reduced in size twice, because after death had reaped such a rich harvest, the survivors would have been too well off, they would have had too much space. So groups of people expelled from the surrounding cities and villages in District Warsaw, or from other places, or from the so-called 'Reich' are beginning to stream into the ghetto.[5] The implementation of the 'Judenrein'[6] programme has already begun. Following the establishment of the ghetto, and after [it has been] thinned out repeatedly, part of the population is finished off with machine guns on the spot, while the rest, without their belongings, are herded to concentration points – that is to larger cities, especially to the district capitals, and above all to Warsaw. They are herded in groups of a few hundred, a few thousand to the Warsaw ghetto, where they are accommodated by the Council at so-called assembly points, these collective dens[7] of poverty and disease. Fed only from a meagre public soup kitchen, they quickly develop into the vanguard of absolute destitution and become fodder for the labour camps. And they quickly disappear from the face of the earth.

The fate of those who arrive from abroad is different. They come from the Vaterland ordentlich,[8] with luggage and supplies, well dressed and shaven. This undesirable element, former citizens of the German Reich from various cities – from Berlin, Hanover, Leipzig, Frankfurt am Main, etc.[9] – is being resettled nach Osten.[10] Somewhat favoured by the local German authorities, to whom they gain access thanks to prior contacts, they

1 AŻIH, 302/195, fols. 82–85. Published in Stefan Ernest, *O wojnie wielkich Niemiec z Żydami Warszawy 1939–1943*, ed. Marta Młodkowska (Warsaw: Czytelnik, 2003), pp. 108–111. This document has been translated from Polish.

2 Stefan Ernest, code name of a Jewish staff member of the employment office in the Warsaw ghetto, whose real name is unknown; left the Warsaw ghetto in Jan. 1943 and hid on the 'Aryan side'; wrote his memoirs while in hiding, before all trace of him was lost.

3 Prior to the excerpt reproduced here, Ernest wrote about how the ghetto inhabitants were decimated by successive epidemics in which 200,000 people fell ill and tens of thousands perished.

4 The deceased were replaced by people expelled from the areas around Warsaw, which was why the number of inhabitants in the Warsaw ghetto did not decline significantly prior to July 1942.

5 Changes in tense as in the original.

6 German in the original: 'cleansed of Jews'.

7 One word illegible; possibly: 'breeding grounds'.

8 German in the original: 'Fatherland', 'in an orderly fashion'.

9 The Warsaw ghetto was the destination for transports from Gelsenkirchen, Münster, and Hanover (31 March – 1 April 1942); Berlin (2–5 April 1942); Magdeburg, Potsdam, and Berlin 14–16 April 1942; Terezín (25–27 April 1942); and probably also for three deportation trains that departed on 11 July 1942 carrying Jews from Hamburg and Schwerin, Bielefeld, and Paderborn, as well as from Berlin. There is no record of transports from Leipzig and Frankfurt am Main to the Warsaw ghetto.

10 German in the original: 'to the East'.

somehow manage to adapt to the circumstances during the period of time that separates them from their final journey to Treblinka, finding employment in institutions, offices, even government agencies; after all, they are still fairly well off. Outwardly they are distinguished from the general public by the yellow stars on their chests, and most of them do not want to swap this distinction for the white armbands with the blue star.[11] Moreover, they are housed separately, barracked just beyond the [ghetto] exit in the Great Synagogue and the Judaic Library, and finally they are distinguished from the rest of society by a kind of 'splendid isolation'.[12] As we can see, ties to one's homeland are stronger, and the solidarity of the Jews scattered all over the globe – the nightmare vision of any antisemitism – is weaker than those who believe in the existence of the Elders of Zion would have imagined. It is no surprise that many of them have or used to have this Germanness in their blood, just as it is no surprise that some of us are 'plus catholique que le pape même'[13] when it comes to Polishness. However, that is a level of reflection which has no place in this report. The fact is that, although we are united in our common misfortune and hardship, we have been strangers to each other, more so than was the case with the extremely pleasant Jews from Czechoslovakia, many of whom had already spent time in Theresienstadt.

In any case, isolated and sealed off from the rest behind the walls, they rarely came into contact with us in the city, and the time was too short to get to know each other better. July 1942 was relentlessly approaching.

After the operation, as a member of the clean-up crew, I had the opportunity to see the remnants on Tłomackie left behind by those who were taken away – a tragic battlefield of everyday objects that had been carefully and thoughtfully collected over many years. In those terribly empty halls in the institute, one could still see traces of this Ordentlichkeit,[14] Bequemlichkeit,[15] and even Gemütlichkeit[16] that they managed to cultivate even here, in this prison-like artificial community. Taken by surprise on the first day of the operation, they left just as they stood – in the midst of a meal, some taken from their beds, as the objects they left behind attest. They went just as they were, some with incorrigible confidence in their compatriots, believing they were going to work in the East. Like the vornehme Dame[17] from Magdeburg who came to my office to settle a matter. Doch, ich habe eine Quittung erhalten, behördlicherweise ausgestellt. Selbst der deutsche Kolonnenführer hat mir dies unterschrieben und mit Siegel versorgt.[18] A receipt for the jewellery and valuables she had deposited in the depot before quarantine. She simply could not understand that she would not get them back … German …

11 In contrast to the German Reich, it was compulsory for Jews in the General Government to wear an identifying armband from 1 Dec. 1939: *VOBl-GG*, no. 8, 30 Nov. 1939, p. 61.
12 English in the original.
13 French in the original: 'more Catholic than the Pope himself', here meaning 'more Polish than the Poles'.
14 German in the original: 'orderliness'.
15 German in the original: 'comfort'.
16 German in the original: 'cosiness'.
17 German in the original: 'distinguished lady'.
18 German in the original: 'Yes indeed, I was given a receipt, issued by the authorities. The German Kolonnenführer himself signed it for me and stamped it.' This is possibly a reference to a German official in charge of deportations.

Meanwhile, the final 'de-Jewification' of the cities and towns had begun.

And on the other hand, we received grim news of massacres and pogroms against the Jews in the East, in Słonim, Nowogródek, Baranowicze, Kowel, Brest – news of mass executions, of people digging their own graves, of the drowning of the Jewish residents of children's homes, or of Jewish children being buried alive so as not to waste a bullet. Too bad. That's war. The combat instinct of soldiers in battle. And in a café in the Warsaw ghetto, over a small black coffee and an exquisite piece of cake from Anigstein: 'There is good news … the English have shot down [aeroplanes] … the Germans have lost …'

[…][19]

## DOC. 108

### *Prawda*, late July 1942: the Catholic newspaper warns against Polish society becoming morally damaged by the murder of the Jews[1]

*Prophecies are coming true*

It so happens that we have become passive witnesses to a terrible tragedy: the planned and systematic mass murder of Jews by the Germans on the territory of the Republic of Poland. We receive terrifying news every day. Thousands of people lose their lives every day: men, women, girls, children, infants, the elderly; their only crime is that they were born Jews. Some are buried alive, others are beaten to death with rifle butts, still others are shot with machine guns. Poison gas has recently also been introduced. The executioners kill small children by smashing their heads against walls or trees along the street. The Jews in Lublin, Chełm, Mielec, Kock, Ryki, Baranów, and a number of other cities and small towns were liquidated in a similar way; more recently extermination in the Warsaw ghetto has begun. Witness statements confirm that in all of these places the executions were carried out with unprecedented sadism and savagery.

… 'Daughters of Jerusalem, weep not for me, but weep for yourselves, and your children. For behold, the days are coming in which they shall say: Blessed are the barren, and the wombs that never bore, and breasts that never nursed. Then will they begin to say to the mountains: Fall on us; and to the hills, Cover us …'[2]

… 'In Rama was there a voice heard, lamentation, and weeping, and great mourning, Rachel weeping for her children, and would not be comforted …'.[3] The prophecies are being fulfilled; the curse that was wilfully invoked has become a reality. … 'His blood be upon us and on our children.'[4] The blood of the righteous. 'Daughters of Jerusalem,

19 In the text that follows, Ernest wrote about children who smuggled food into the ghetto for their parents, for which they were mistreated brutally by the German guards at the ghetto walls.

1 *Prawda*, May 1942, pp. 5–6. Biblioteka Narodowa, MF 43 293. *Prawda: Pismo Frontu Odrodzenia Polski* appeared monthly between April 1942 and May 1944 as the underground newspaper of a Catholic lay group, under the editorial supervision of the writer Zofia Kossak (1889–1968). This document has been translated from Polish.

2 Luke 23:28–30 (NKJV).

3 Matthew 2:18, echoing Jeremiah 31:15: 'Rahel weeping for her children refused to be comforted for her children.'

4 Matthew 27:25.

weep not for me'... – With brutal logic, all the Jews' deeds are wreaking vengeance upon them.

No one has impeded Christendom's dominion of the world more than they have, therefore they are the first to perish, because Europe is not Christian. Fuelled by their Talmudic hatred, they recognize no one outside their own race as their neighbour. And they are slain because they have found themselves among a nation that has adopted their slogans and refused to recognize them as neighbours ...

We look on as passive witnesses, gripped by horror. We cannot intervene. There have been heroes who tried to resist, to protect the condemned, and who paid for it with their lives. Any compassionate reflex, any attempt to help, is immediately punished by death. Forced to be passive, we must nevertheless be aware of the scale of the tragedy and take a stand on it, as Catholics and as Poles.

I. As Catholics.

It is not enough to pray for the murdered victims and feel compassion for them; we must search our consciences at the same time. The fate that has befallen Israel is a just punishment, for God does not permit injustice. But to what degree are we Christians to blame for the fact that the Jews have remained the way they are and have therefore earned such a cruel punishment? To what extent are we responsible for neglecting *missionary work* among the Jews, which is the apostolic duty of every Catholic and derives solely from a genuine apostolic Christian love for one's neighbour? Who among us has gone out amid the Jews in the same way as the missionary goes out amid the heathen? ... Was there ever room in our feelings towards the Jews for the sincere, selfless desire for them to change? ... It seems that the answers to all of these questions will tend towards the negative, and therefore our hearts are troubled by the hecatomb[5] of the Jewish children, who have certainly done no wrong. And, in the face of this misfortune, in the face of the prophecy of 'Rachel's weeping', pronounced a few thousand years ago, should there be a person who is capable of saying that it serves the Jews right, and that the Germans are doing the Poles a favour by murdering the Jews – such a person does not deserve to be called a Catholic.

II. As Poles.

It is not worth discussing the mistakes in our policy towards the Jews at a time when the object is ceasing to exist and the nature of the matter is changing. We all know that there have been glaring errors and that our conduct towards the Jews has been haphazard, chaotic, inconsistent, and has fluctuated between two extremes: slavish subservience to the Jews on the one hand, and bludgeoning on the other.

It is to be assumed that these mistakes will not be repeated, and that our society will be able to find decent but at the same time practical standards that are aligned with national interests and comply with Christian ethics. Of course, this is a question for the future ...

However, moral damage and brutalization, which have set in among us as a result of the slaughter of the Jews, have become a burning issue. For it is not only Shaulis men,

5 A large public sacrifice (term originating in ancient Greece and Rome).

Volksdeutsche,[6] and Ukrainians who have been exploited to perform the monstrous executions. In many places (Kolno, Stawiski, Jagodne,[7] Szumów,[8] Dęblin[9]) the local population has participated voluntarily in the massacres. We must combat such disgrace with all the resources available. We must make people aware that they are becoming [like] Herod's henchmen; [they] must be denounced in the underground press; we must call for the boycott of the executioners; we must threaten them, announce that the free Republic of Poland will pronounce harsh judgement on the murderers.

So far no one has taken up this issue; the press[10] shamefully keeps quiet about the issue, while the evil spreads like an epidemic, and the crime becomes habitual.

Under no circumstances must we allow the plague of brutality and sadism to engulf us. God is just, but as for the people who voluntarily serve as the instruments of His punishment, it would be better if they had never been born.

## DOC. 109
## At a Nazi Party rally on 1 August 1942, Governor General Hans Frank mocks the murdered Jews[1]

Speech given by Hans Frank at a large rally of the NSDAP leaders for District Galicia at the Lemberg Opera House on 1 August 1942

[…][2]
I have to say, Party Comrade Wächter:[3] you and your people have done a fine job. Within one year you've made us forget what a hole this was. Lemberg is now once again a proper and proud German city, led by Germans, German in terms of its buildings, and German in the attitude of its leadership.

Indeed, that is the beauty of this war: that once we have taken something, we will never give it up again. (Laughter and applause)

That's the magnificent thing. Of course, it doesn't exactly befit soldiers, nor us administrators, but, my God, it's just the way we talk. It's clear that those of us in the General Government especially, as what you might call the oldest combat unit with experience in setting up a conquered country, know very well what the Führer has given us in District

6 German in the original: 'ethnic Germans'.
7 This is possibly a reference to the small town of Jedwabne in northern Poland, where Polish residents took part in the murder of Jews on 10 July 1941. The first two places mentioned are also located north of Łomża, in the territory that the Soviet Union had occupied until June 1941.
8 This is probably Szumowo, located 40 km south of Łomża.
9 The town of Dęblin is located on the Vistula river between Warsaw and Lublin (and was at that time in District Lublin).
10 This is a reference to the Polish underground press.

1 AIPN, GK 95, vol. 20. Copy in IfZ-Archives, Fb 105, vol. 24, fols. 5670–5688, here fols. 5670–5673, 5678–5679, and 5685–5686. This document has been translated from German.
2 The speech was given on the anniversary of Eastern Galicia's annexation to the General Government and is 19 pages long. Frank began by praising Lemberg's return to the 'sphere of the Greater German Reich'.
3 The governor of District Galicia.

Galicia. And I'm not talking about the Jews we still have here; we will deal with them, too. By the way, I have seen no sign of them today. What's going on? I am told there used to be thousands upon thousands of those flat-footed[4] Indians in this city at one time – but now there are none to be seen. Don't tell me you've treated them badly, in the end? (Loud laughter) Anyway, we National Socialists will also tackle this problem in accordance with our Party programme. And the problem was particularly obvious here.

My God, if I ever write my memoirs and describe how I entered Posen with five men to comply with the Führer's order to establish the General Government – there would be no apt words to capture the kind of Jews teeming there. They were so dreadful that I'm surprised the earth didn't stop spinning (loud laughter), Jews of such shocking hideousness that I believe even the fiercest opponent of the National Socialist movement would have changed his mind if he had seen them. That's what these people kept saying to us during our struggle to get to power: the National Socialists may be really good people, and they mean well too, but they are so barbarous and rough and brutal to the poor Jews. Dear God, they should have been made to march into this city right after the soldiers, and then asked: Now don't you share the view that European civilization cannot be rescued without solving the Jewish question? I think they would all have readily agreed.

We are fortunate that we can treat the Jews here in the same way they treated the German people. I do have to say, when there is all of this complaining, and those compassionate souls pop up here and there, all you can do is make one thing clear: it was the Jews and their descendants from this selfsame Galicia who went to Berlin, Vienna, and everywhere else during the German people's most terrible time of need and drove the German people off their own land and out of their own property. It was the famous Eastern Jew who moved to the democratic republic with his caftan and peyes[5] and cheated thousands of Germans out of house and home, or indeed drove them to suicide. I therefore want to say just one thing on the Jewish question: we are solving this problem, and not one more Jew will go to Germany. (Lively applause) Well, they will take care not to, now that they have to work in Germany. It is also quite a good thing for the Jews to become familiar with practical labour for once, and to be introduced to the more serious side of life in other ways, too. In this land, the Jew is no longer a problem; at most he is apt to be of interest to us as a species.

We are celebrating this anniversary of District Galicia's affiliation with the General Government here in Lemberg at a time when these questions are already in full swing in every part of the General Government. [...][6]

The *General Government* has established itself as a state out of nothing, out of less than nothing. It is self-sufficient and *independent*, both financially and with regard to its food supply. It is a blessing that I am not financially dependent on others. We are so fortunate that we can go our own way here. We work with our own resources, proudly and independently. And everything is in full swing in this land. How proud I have been over the past few days! A year ago there were no roads here, no paths, no railways, no bridges, and

4 Flat feet among Jews was a common antisemitic trope in much of Europe. It was related to the Jews' alleged lack of athleticism and aversion to physical labour.

5 Sidelocks. In the original Frank uses the Yiddish term, presumably as an antisemitic slur.

6 In the following section, Frank spoke about the General Government's future as 'Lebensraum for our people': IfZ-Archives, Fb 105, vol. 24, fol. 5674.

now two thirds of all the destroyed bridges in District Galicia have been completely restored, and the roads have been repaired to the extent that they can be driven on again. That is truly an accomplishment, given that we have only limited personnel available, that we are dependent on non-German labour, and that it takes time to get the Jew to the point where he can use a shovel. And all this has been achieved in one year.

We have other reasons to be satisfied as well. Peace and order largely prevail in this land. The *inhabitants* have come to terms with their fate. We do not torment them; we are reasonable and say that we want to demonstrate loyalty to everyone who is willing to work and is loyal to us. We feed the population to the extent we are able – I can't produce grain if it doesn't grow from the soil. The chickens are doing their duty, and we have enough eggs. The rest will come too, and so I can say: once this harvest has been brought in, I can go home on leave with my mind at ease. The currency is all right; the zloty is not worth much, of course, but at least it's stable. (Laughter) The finances for this land are in order, too. We have no debts, and we declined those we would have had to take on. (More loud laughter) [...][7]

I am particularly pleased that the Germans here in this town and in this district are working with our *soldiers* so wonderfully. It also gives me real joy to greet the wounded men among you. I want them to know and to hear and to see what has become of this region and the countries they risked their health to help conquer. They need to know that those behind them are not middle-class cowards stuffing their bellies, who want to follow the soldier's success with the capitalist's success. No, behind them stands the National Socialist fighter, and behind the National Socialist fighter marches the National Socialist German people. That is the line we are holding. (Lively applause)

Let the Jews around the world unleash their inflammatory allegations of atrocities! Let them say that at least two Poles have been hanged from every lamp post – my only reply to them is this: the Poles did not leave us so many lamp posts; there are not that many lamp posts in this blessed land of culture. But let them go ahead and talk of atrocities; we will get to work. Let them keep saying that German rule is unpopular, too. Well, if the Führer were to come here and say: My dear Poles, do you want my administration to stay or to go? Then some Poles would perhaps say: Please leave. But that's beside the point, anyway. The Poles have brought their fate on themselves. The Führer always wanted to keep peace with this country. He held out his hand to this crew and concluded an agreement with them.[8] And then they themselves brought on what happened to them next. This fate was unavoidable, because sooner or later we would have had to take this Poland. (Laughter) [...][9]

7 Frank went on to describe the special administrative situation in the General Government and emphasized the NSDAP's role as 'the organization representing the German attitude' in the General Government; then he urged his listeners to commit to the 'task in the East', as set by Adolf Hitler: IfZ-Archives, Fb 105, vol. 24, fols. 5683 and 5685.

8 This is a reference to the German–Polish declaration of non-aggression of 26 January 1934. It stipulated that the two countries would engage in bilateral negotiations to resolve any issues and would not engage in armed conflict for ten years.

9 Frank then announced that great work was in store for the Germans in the General Government. In conclusion, he described the NSDAP and the Wehrmacht as 'the pillars upon which the Führer is building the Reich': IfZ-Archives, Fb 105, vol. 24, fol. 5688.

## DOC. 110

## On 1 August 1942 Yisroel Likhtenshteyn reports on the first ten days of the extermination campaign against the Warsaw ghetto[1]

Handwritten record by Yisroel Likhtenshteyn for the underground archive of the Warsaw ghetto, Warsaw, dated 1 August 1942

*Ten days of the 'operation to resettle' the Jews of Warsaw, beginning on the eve of Tisha B'Av[2] 1942*

We have been betrayed!!!

The terrible process of exterminating Warsaw's Jews has been under way for ten days now. Between 5,000 and 10,000 Jews are captured and deported from Warsaw every day. Old people and small children are shot. The rest are deported, surely to be shot or gassed. The Jewish police, who think they will be saved, have been recruited for this operation. But as it turns out, they won't escape death either. The SS want to destroy all of Jewish Warsaw, and they are going about it very cleverly. They have promised that the workers in the szopy producing goods for the military, Community employees, and YHK[3] employees will remain in Warsaw.

Now it turns out that the YHK credentials are worthless – dozens of employees have already been arrested and deported. The same thing will probably happen to the Community employees and later to the tens of thousands of workers from the szopy as well. This is the German system of 'divide and rule'. They enlist one part of the population to hand over a second part; later they will enlist a third part to hand over the second part. It is obvious to see, and this is the error and the betrayal of our Community leaders and the scoundrels commanding the Jewish police.

On the first day that the order from the authorities was made public, the toiling Jewish masses understood that a wave of destruction was about to engulf them and nobody would remain. They clenched their fists against the police, who were carrying out this disgusting dirty work. People said that the Community should not have undertaken the task but left it to the SS men instead. Let them destroy us all. They, the Jewish workers and toiling masses, understood what awaited them. However, the Community leaders wanted to save themselves, even at the price of up to 100,000 Jews being exterminated. They made a mistake. Now the aim of the German extermination process is evident. They made a mistake: the Community leaders, along with the scoundrels from [police] headquarters, the Lejkins, Yosele Kapote (Ehrlich), and the main turncoat – the enemy of Israel and oppressor of the Jews – police commander Szeryński.

1 AŻIH, Ring I/1450 (1190), fols. 3–12. Published in English translation in Kermish (ed.), *To Live with Honor*, pp. 696–700. This document has been newly translated from Yiddish.

2 Tisha B'Av, the ninth day of the month of Av (usually falling during the month of August in the Gregorian calendar), is a Jewish day of fasting and mourning to commemorate the destruction of the first and second Temples in Jerusalem, along with other tragedies that have befallen the Jewish people.

3 This is an abbreviation of Yidisher Hilfs-komitet (Jewish Aid Committee), and probably refers here to Jewish Social Self-Help (JSS) employees.

The operation works as follows: (Jewish) police units march through the Jewish quarter. At a given moment they surround the entrance to a residential building and cordon it off entirely. Everyone has to leave their apartments and go down to the courtyard. The police then conduct rigorous inspections. There is hell to pay for anyone who chooses not to follow orders. Locked apartments are broken open by force, the doors hacked open with an axe, and everything is abandoned. Once all the inhabitants of the building are standing in the courtyard outside, all entrances to the apartments are blocked; these are searched again before the identity checks begin. Everyone must present their identity card. Those who have good credentials, stating that they work in a szop or are employed with the Community or the YHK, are put to the side, while those with unsuitable papers are taken out as they are onto the street, where trucks and buses stand ready. [They are given the order] 'Na wóz'[4] and on they get. All the rest who have no [work] documents are led out – 'Na wóz' – and taken to the Umschlagplatz,[5] which is transformed into a tear-soaked island of Jewish anguish, suffering, sorrow, and death ... Empty goods wagons are waiting there into which 120–200 people are crammed, and off they go. To where?! No one knows. Brest, Bobruisk, Smolensk; that is only one version. However, anyone who knows the accounts from Chełmno or Trawniki knows how these unfortunate people will perish: machine guns, gas, electric current – that's how they are put out of their misery. Then mass graves of 1,000–1,500 people each.

Every day the officers and SS men go to the Umschlagplatz to play their games. Such games cost hundreds of lives. They shoot whoever they feel like, especially old people, the sick, the disabled, and children. They pick out from among all the unfortunate people the old, the sick, the disabled, and children, who are taken in trucks to the Jewish cemetery and – shot.

The police rampage through the streets. Guards grab passers-by and arrest them. Men, women, children, and old people are loaded onto the trucks. Children are torn from their parents, mothers from their children, men from their wives and children. This is what the 'resettlement to the East' of entire families looks like ...[6]

The hunger in the ghetto is frightful. There is either nothing at all to buy, or if there is, you pay 50 złoty for a kilogram of bread, 25 złoty for a kilogram of potatoes, 10 to 12 złoty for a bunch of carrots, and 8 to 10 złoty for a head of cabbage. The need is great; people are starving. Driven by despair and hunger, people are reporting voluntarily to the Umschlagplatz.

The Community has hung signs [announcing] that anyone who reports voluntarily will receive 3 kilograms of bread and 1 kilogram of jam.[7] There are volunteers: better to die from a bullet than of hunger – and so they indeed go to their deaths.

4 Polish in the original: 'Get on board'.
5 The holding area is referred to here and later in the original document by its German name.
6 At the end of its announcement dated 24 July 1942, the Jewish Council in Warsaw declared, on the orders of the German authorities, that families who voluntarily reported for deportation would not be separated: AŻIH, Ring II/54 (187).
7 On 29 July 1942, the head of the Warsaw ghetto's Order Service, Józef Szeryński, promised 3 kg of bread and 1 kg of jam to those who volunteered to leave: AŻIH, Ring II/68 (188), p. 2.

There is intense panic. People are scared to go outside, but it isn't safe at home either, because there could be a raid at any moment – one blockade and you're caught.

There is a vast trade in [work] papers. Thousands of people are besieging the szopy in order to get in there and protect themselves. People pay thousands for a piece of paper that is ultimately of no use. Only the rich merchants, those who trade in foreign currency, and speculators can manage this. The true members of the proletariat who have no money are turned away. The whole 'Jewish underworld' is gathered there, the 'pals' of 'Yosele Kapote' (Ehrlich), the chief Gestapo agent.

From time to time, the gendarmerie and the SS fan out into the streets and then the real rounding up begins. The [work] papers don't help, not even those from the German szopy and workshops. Everyone is bundled [onto trucks] with 'Na wóz'. There are a number of deaths in the process. Killing a person is easier for them than picking up a piece of straw. Every evening, groups of healthy middle-aged men and women are led through the Jewish quarter, singled out by the Germans as healthy and fit for work. They have to be billeted in Warsaw for certain jobs. Until then, they are taken to quarantine at 109 Leszno Street.[8] The streets are empty – no one is allowed on the streets. Violators are immediately shot. The Germans shoot into the windows, shoot at passers-by. As much is known about where these people deemed fit for work are being sent as is known about the destination of those who leave in wagons from the Umschlagplatz. Who knows if the former won't end up later digging the graves for and burying those who are deported. It is possible that these men and women who are fit for work will be sent to dig the graves for the victims of the so-called 'resettlement'.

The moment when it became known why forty-six hostages[9] had been taken – [namely] to ensure that Jews themselves would carry out the resettlement – I understood that death would spare no one. But if indeed we must die, 'then like men and not like lambs'.

I first brought up this thought among my acquaintances and neighbours. At a meeting of the 'CENTOS' executive committee, I proposed the idea, with a detailed plan, to a group of comrades and friends. The friends who listened to my proposals were Oyerbakh and Vaynshteyn from the sixth district of the JSS, Grinkroyt from the Bund, Dr Frenkel from Mizrachi,[10] Tsukerman, [who is] director of the children's soup kitchen at 67 Dzielna,[11] and others. I repeated the same thing to other friends and acquaintances. My opinion was and remains that the Community should refuse to take part in the operation and, at the same time, issue an order, together with the JSS and other social groups, that people should defend themselves and fall upon the gendarmes. In the course of one evening, the [whole] Jewish ghetto should be set on fire. Every building commit-

8 The quarantine building was located outside the ghetto.

9 On 21 July 1942 the Security Police arrested Jewish Council members and staff, who were taken hostage: see Doc. 99.

10 Dr G. Frenkel, educator and teacher; head of a school in the Warsaw ghetto which was run by Yavneh, the school organization of the religious and Zionist movement Mizrachi.

11 This was the site of a boarding school run by the Jewish Central Association for the Care of Orphans (CENTOS) for 400 children.

tee[12] should set its building alight, from attic to cellar, and then take to the streets with knives, axes, sticks, and stones. [People should] storm the walls and offer fierce resistance to the Germans. Even if they shoot us together with our wives and children, we still would have managed to kill some of them too. The ghetto should burn in a great conflagration, it should resound with machine guns, and bombs should fall – who cares? We should go towards death with joy and triumph. If we are to die, then let it be as heroes and not as cowards. Over the ghetto walls! Even if later our neighbours, the Poles, have to bury us.

Surely there would be Poles, the rev[olutionary] element, who would take advantage of the situation to blow up the train stations, military buildings, and bases of our 'protectors'. The fight would certainly spread to the other side of the wall. Our rebellion would perhaps spark an uprising throughout Poland. It would give courage to the partisan brigade in Poland to begin really digging in. And maybe the fight would even spread beyond Poland to all the occupied countries. If the Jews were to burn themselves along with their homes, it would set an undeniable example and model for all oppressed nations to start fighting back. Unfortunately, we have been betrayed. Our ringleaders do not have the courage to die like humans, but rather like fleas, worms, or mice.

We Jews should learn from the Teutons: 'The enemy could not enter the Teuton's hut because the Teuton had set himself and his hut on fire.' We need to muster precisely this same Germanic courage. And the courage exists among the toiling masses, among the Jewish workers. They, the ringleaders, the Community figures, the Jewish scum, they fear for their stinking lives. They are willing to sacrifice others to save themselves. But they too will meet the same end as all of us. The same fate that has befallen the poor, toiling Jewish masses awaits them.

They, the ringleaders, are privileged. Their lives have been extended by another month.

12 See Doc. 29, fn. 3.

## DOC. 111

## On 3 August 1942 the Eastern Railway orders an additional train to run between Warsaw and Treblinka[1]

Scheduling directive no. 548 from the Eastern Railway General Directorate (33 Bfp 15 Bfsv), signed Zahn,[2] Cracow, dated 3 August 1942[3]

*Schedule order* no. 548[4]

From 6 August 1942 until further notice, an additional special daily train carrying those being resettled will run from Danzig Station in Warsaw to Treblinka and back, returning empty, as follows:

1/, P. Kr 9085/30.9/ Warsaw, Danzig Station – Malkinia – Treblinka

| | | | | |
|---|---|---|---|---|
| Warsaw, Danzig Station | | | dep. | 12:25 on schedule Dg 91 335 R |
| Warsaw Marki | arr. | 12:42 | | 12:59 " " " |
| Tluszcz | | 14:00 | | 12:27[5] " " " |
| Malkinia | | 15:54 | | 16:13 on schedule Dg 91 368 |
| Treblinka | | | dep. | 16:20 " " " " |

1 AIPN, GK 196 (NTN 70), fol. 137r–v. Copy in BArch, B 162/21928, fol. 337. Published as a facsimile in Hilberg, *Sonderzüge nach Auschwitz*, appendix 27, pp. 178–179. This document has been translated from German.

2 Albrecht Zahn (1907–1997), engineer; deputy officer in charge of local transport in the Württemberg Ministry of the Interior in the 1930s; worked for the Lublin railway directorate, Jan. 1940 – April 1941; head of Section 31 (main line operations) for the Eastern Railway General Directorate in Cracow until Jan. 1945; promoted to Reichsbahnrat; head of the West German Federal Railway's Stuttgart division after the war.

3 The trains ran from Danzig Station on the Białystok line as far as the village of Małkinia, and from there to Treblinka on the branch line to Siedlce. According to the German statistics for the transports, the number of people deported daily between 28 July and 5 August 1942 ranged from 5,020 to 6,756; on 6 August it reached 10,085, and on 7 August 10,672. The additional train probably ran only on those days, as the number dropped to 7,304 on 8 August and sank below 5,000 in the second half of the month: see Doc. 103.

4 On the abbreviations: '33' refers to the General Directorate's Local Train Scheduling Section, thought to have been headed by Martin Zabel from 1941 to 1942; 'Bfp' refers to the Operations Dept./Scheduling Office; '15' is the number of the administrator in charge of the Special Trains Group, thought to have been Walter Stier, who was responsible for scheduling the trains to the extermination camps; 'Bfsv' refers to the file for the Scheduling Office/Special Trains/Administrative Special Trains. Transports carrying Jews from the General Government were marked 'P Kr', with 'P' signifying passenger transport. 'Dg' stands for goods trains that run directly to their destination without any shunting. 'Lp' is short for empty train. 'Bw' stands for depot. 'Bf' stands for train station. 'C' signifies the two third-class wagons for the guards at the front and back of the train, and '58 G' is the number of goods wagons for Jews, so the deportation train consisted of 60 wagons (120 axles). 'Ga' stands for goods handling. The numbers 30.9 and 30.11 refer to operational statistics for occupied and unoccupied 'passenger trains'. The time for 'Treblinka' was wrongly preceded by 'dep.' instead of 'arr.'

5 As in the original. Presumably this should be 14:27.

2./ Lp Kr 9086/ 30.11/ Treblinka – Malkinia – Warsaw, Danzig Station

| | | | | |
|---|---|---|---|---|
| Treblinka | | | dep. | 19:00 on special schedule |
| Malkinia | arr. | 19:07 | | 19:32 on schedule Dg 9134 |
| Tluszsc | | 20:55 | | 21:38 " " " " |
| Warsaw Marki | | 22:35 | | 23:02 " " " " |
| Warsaw, Danzig Station | arr. | 23:19 | | |

Locomotive provided by: Bw Warsaw Praga/ for both trains/
Train provided by: Bf Warsaw Praga/ for both trains/
Set of wagons consisting of 1C, 58 G, and 1C provided by Bf/Ga Warsaw Danzig Bf

P 1573 runs as follows: Wolka direct[6] 11:45, Treblinka direct 11:52, Malkinia arrival 11:59 (P 1577 does not run)

Correct the notices and timetable documents.
Instruct personnel.

## DOC. 112

## From 17 July to 5 August 1942 Kazimiera Poraj describes her efforts to get her Jewish husband released from Janowska camp in Lwów[1]

Diary of Kazimiera Poraj,[2] entries for 17 July to 5 August 1942

17 July 1942
I was lucky today. Hilda[3] told me that my beloved husband is at a camp, the so-called Janowska camp, across from Kleparowski station. The thought that I've found him has sent me into a mad whirl.

18 July 1942
I brought my husband a parcel to the camp today. Hilda accompanies me.[4] In front of the camp she takes the parcel from me and hands it over to a certain Jakubowicz, the person in charge of the warehouse, who gives it to my husband. I received a letter from my husband in the evening in the same way. My husband writes that people in the camp are dying like flies; during the morning roll call more than 30 people collapsed, and in the evening just as many or even more. What am I, a poor woman, to do? How will I

6 In the original document the abbreviation 'dch' appears here and a few words later. Presumably short for 'durchgängig', meant in the sense of direct travel, no stops scheduled.

1 The whereabouts of the original diary are unknown. The author gave her diary, which covers the period from 30 June 1941 to 24 July 1944 (with occasional gaps of more than six months), to the Jewish Historical Institute in the early 1960s. A typescript of her notes was made and archived there: AŻIH, 302/217, fols. 143–149. Published in Kazimiera Poraj, 'Dziennik Lwowski', *BŻIH*, no. 52 (1964), pp. 79–106, here pp. 86–89. This document has been translated from Polish.
2 Kazimiera Poraj, née Łozińska, a Ukrainian who lived in Lwów.
3 Hilda Goldman worked as a secretary at Janowska camp in summer 1942.
4 The changes in verb tense here and below are consistent with the original.

get him out of the camp? I don't have any money, but they want 15,000 [złoty] for this. I'm tired and nervous; it's already late, 1 a.m., and my heart is beating terribly fast.

19 July 1942
As soon as I returned from the camp today, I went straight to the Jewish Community on Berenstein Street, where I searched for someone with access to the camp. A woman called Filipowa was there, who has access to the Jewish cemetery, where the funeral parlour houses the camp infirmary.

20 July 1942
And so I go to the camp with Hilda every day. Afterwards I make my mother lunch and begin my daily wanderings anew: I look for people. I write to my husband that he shouldn't report himself sick, because sick people are shot dead immediately. I found that out myself. Today I received the address of a female lawyer by the name of Schajewicz with access to the camp, to which she brings bread and soup from the Community every day; the so-called supplementary feeding for the people. When I told her what I had in mind, she made a face as if she were the camp commandant herself. She barely noted down my husband's name and instructed me in an arrogant tone: 'Please return tomorrow'.

21 July 1942
In the morning, as soon as I got back from the camp, I went straight to Mrs Schajewicz and, in tears, begged her to help me get my husband out of the camp faster, because I fear they will kill him. She muttered through clenched teeth that if I gave her 10,000 [złoty], she'd get him out quickly. I knew she wanted to swindle me, so I didn't answer and left with the thought that I'd never go back to her. Perhaps I will still find someone who will help me. But the worst thing is that I'm losing my strength. I'm not eating or sleeping, and that wears me out. I leave home in the morning without eating anything. The camp is 3 km away [and we go] on foot, because Hilda, as a Jew, isn't permitted to travel by tram.

23 July 1942
I receive despairing letters from my husband. It's hard to imagine that I'll get him out, as I have absolutely no money at all. There is nothing to live on. Sometimes I manage to sell something, and thus I torment myself. I always have to give Hilda something because she helps me.

25 July 1942
My husband was badly beaten in the bathhouse last night. He writes that he can't lie down at night, that he has wounds and bruises all over his body; it's a miracle he has survived. I often go to Janowska St. in the hope that I might see my husband, but I never have. Instead I saw how the Janowska camp commandant, lord and master Wilhaus,[5] beat a

5 Correctly: Gustav Willhaus (1910–1945), locksmith; joined the SA in 1924 and the NSDAP and the SS in 1932; worked at the SS Business and Administration Main Office in Berlin from Nov. 1941; assigned to Lwów in March 1942; responsible for Jewish forced labourers at a factory run by Deutsche Ausrüstungswerke; commandant of Janowska camp, July 1942 – June 1943; subsequently served in the war.

man on the street for not doffing his hat as he passed him by. He beat him with the butt of his rifle, from which he never parts. Wilhaus is a handsome man: tall, thin, and athletic, with beautiful, dreamy eyes, a very nicely shaped coral-red mouth, and the face of a Raphaelesque angel – a very nice head. Today I found out that the camp physician is no longer Dr Kurzrok, but Dr Harlig, who lives at 6 Św. Anna St. He is the only one who can have my husband transferred to the infirmary at the Jewish cemetery. Although I've already stopped believing in luck, I'll go and see him tomorrow nevertheless.

26 July 1942
My husband writes that he is sick to his stomach, but he is scared to see the physician, as I keep writing to him not to report himself sick. My husband writes that the camp's deputy commandant, Rokita,[6] has killed twenty-eight sparrows today, i.e. twenty-eight people (not many, given his temperament and the opportunities). I don't know whether I'll ever see my husband again, because I have the feeling I have a heart condition; I feel really ill and have severe arrhythmia attacks all the time. Poor me, what am I to do? Getting my husband out requires a lot of walking and a lot of money, above all. I don't know what I'll do if Dr Harlig doesn't help me tomorrow.

27 July 1942
Today I went to Dr Harlig, but he wasn't at home, despite the fact that it was already late. His wife was quite distraught because Jews aren't permitted to be out after 6 p.m. I left at 8 p.m. and waited in the street for him, but he didn't come.

28 July 1942
On the way back from the camp today I went to see Dr Harlig, but he wasn't there, as he had already left for work at the camp. Last night he was detained against his will. The wife of some Gestapo man was ill, and Wilhaus himself took Dr Harlig to her and drove him home at midnight. Walking along Janowska Street this morning, I saw a group of young women being led away by Germans. One of them was weeping terribly and shouting: 'What kind of friends are you? I'm Ukrainian, our children will avenge us!' When will this finally end?

30 July 1942
I was at Dr Harlig's yesterday. He is a very cultured man, approximately 35 years old. He promised to have my husband transferred to the infirmary at the Jewish cemetery, but he requires a lot from me. He wants me to hide his elderly 70-year-old mother. I found it quite difficult to promise this, because I already have my 85-year-old mother at home and can't put her in danger. After all, I'll be putting myself in even greater danger.[7]

6 Richard Rokita (1894–1976), musician and merchant; joined the SA in 1931 and the NSDAP and the SS in 1932; posted to the SS training camp for non-Germans at Trawniki, 1941–1942; deputy commandant at Janowska camp and official in charge of Jewish affairs under the SS and Police Leader in Lwów; commandant at Tarnopol labour camp, Nov. 1942 – June 1943; subsequently transferred for disciplinary reasons; worked as a porter in Hamburg after the war (under a false name until 1956).

7 This is presumably Kazimiera Poraj's mother-in-law. In early Sept. 1942 she moved with her son to the ghetto, where she soon fell ill with pneumonia and died on 5 Oct. 1942: Poraj, 'Dziennik Lwowski', p. 98.

However, I can offer my life for that of my husband, since without him my life isn't worth anything anyway. Today I forwarded my husband a letter saying he should report sick because he can now. People are being rounded up in the streets all the time. Today I saw two trucks full of young men. I don't know where they were taken.

3 August 1942
My husband only arrived at the cemetery today. No one, no one can imagine what went on in my heart when I saw him. He was thin, even though I had been bringing him food every day; apparently he did not eat it all himself. He has wounds on his face and many festering boils all over his body. He injured himself at work and dirt had got into the wounds, which is why his hands festered. The camp is indescribably filthy. My husband spent twenty-three days at the camp and washed himself only once, on 25 July, and he almost paid for that bath with his life. He can't lie down because of the boils. Whenever one of them bursts, a new one forms immediately. He looks like a hunted animal. He was beaten at the camp many times, hence his fear. I don't have my husband transferred to the so-called infirmary in the funeral parlour, as he could contract various diseases there. He will sleep in the hut that belongs to the gardener, Sommer, whom I will pay 5 złoty per night. I have already brought him a pillow and a blanket. He won't be cold, as the nights are very warm. I visited Dr Harlig on the way back from the cemetery. I wanted to tell him to bring his mother to me, as agreed, but it turned out that she had died of heart failure at 10 a.m. today. Mrs Harlig informed me that her husband was glad that his mother had died a natural death. What horrible times!

5 August 1942
Yesterday I sat with my husband at the cemetery until midnight. People at the cemetery are ill with various odd diseases. Their entire bodies are covered with wounds that have turned black; you can see open wounds and white maggots crawling in them. I ask my husband not to visit the infirmary, even though his acquaintances are there. I feel very sorry whenever I bring my husband food, as no one brings anything for the rest of the poor people. Whenever they see me, they look at me with unflinching eyes [in the hope] that they get something. However, I myself am poor and have nothing with which to feed my husband and my mother. If there were only a few of them, I might be able to think of something, but there are hundreds. I always give something to those who are the sickest. Some of them can no longer eat; they have been lying in the grass for days without bedclothes or covers; they don't even get up any more. Most of them come from villages and small towns in which everyone was killed a long time ago. But there are also people from Przemyśl, Dr Rappaport, the goldsmith Bass, and a secondary school teacher. I don't take my husband home yet. Dr Harlig informed me that a major 'operation' is planned for Lwów soon.[8] I listen to him and pay 5 złoty per day for the hut, in the hope that my husband will be safe there.[9]

8 The deportation from Lwów to Belzec began on 10 August 1942.

9 Kazimiera Poraj secured her husband's release from Janowska camp, then found accommodation for him in the ghetto before taking him with her in Nov. 1942 and hiding him in her own apartment; he survived the German occupation.

## DOC. 113
## On 6 August 1942 the SS and Police Leader in District Galicia informs the civil administration about how the Jews will be killed[1]

Notes (marked 'secret') from the head of the Office of the Governor in District Galicia, initialled N[eumann],[2] on a discussion in Lemberg, dated 6 August 1942[3]

*Notes*
*Regarding*: discussion on the resettlement of Jews
Brigadeführer Katzmann informed us that within six months, there will be no more Jews at liberty in the General Government. Some people will be resettled and some taken to camps.

The few isolated Jews living in rural areas will be killed by individual squads.

The Jews concentrated in the cities will be partly liquidated, partly resettled, and partly concentrated in labour camps in large-scale operations.

The other attendees[4] raised objections in view of the complete absence of trained Jewish workers.

It is completely impossible to bring in the necessary Polish and Ukrainian craftsmen within such a short period of time.

Brigadeführer Katzmann explained that the intention is to remedy this issue by setting up a camp for Jews in each Kreis, where a well-chosen reserve of all the necessary craftsmen is to be kept available.

## DOC. 114
## On 6 August 1942 Menakhem Mendel Kon describes seeking cover from the deportations from the Warsaw ghetto[1]

Handwritten diary of Menakhem Mendel Kon,[2] entry for 6 August 1942[3]

6/8
Day 16 of the bloody deportation of Jews from the Warsaw ghetto. Twelve noon. I am sitting close to the cellar where my hiding place from the Hitlerian murderers is supposed to be; at any moment they will come over from the small ghetto,[4] where they have been

1 DALO, R-35/12/42, fol. 71. Copy in USHMM, Acc. 1995.A.1086, reel 8. This document has been translated from German.
2 Dr Heinzgeorg Neumann (b. 1915); Landkommissar in Limanowa prior to 1941; head of the Governor's Office in District Galicia from 1942; classified as a 'follower' (*Mitläufer*) in denazification proceedings in 1946; thereafter lived in Munich, then in Bonn.
3 Handwritten note in the original: 'PA' (Präsidialabteilung = Governor's Office).
4 Apart from Neumann and Katzmann, the following officials attended the meeting: Chief of Staff Dr Losacker, Department Head Bauer, and Dr Hanns Gareis (1895–1972).

1 AŻIH, Ring II/249 (208), fols. 18–20. Published in English translation in Kermish (ed.), *To Live with Honor*, pp. 80–81. This document has been newly translated from Yiddish.
2 Menakhem Mendel Kon (Kohn) (1882–1943), merchant; Zionist activist, treasurer of the Oyneg Shabes underground archive in the Warsaw ghetto; perished during the Ghetto Uprising.
3 Kon's diary from the period 6 August to 1 Oct. 1942 has survived only in fragments.
4 The smaller section of the ghetto south of Chłodna Street.

on the rampage since 7 a.m. In the span of these few hours of work, the bloodthirsty beasts have chased out thousands of victims from there to the square,[5] from where they will be transported in sealed goods wagons to the extermination site called Treblinka. Already more than 100,000 Jews – men, women, and children – have been gruesomely murdered over the course of the fifteen days that the extermination operation has been under way.

The Hitlerian beasts employ all possible means. They shoot. They kill the elderly and sick immediately on the spot, at the blood-soaked square, or they take them to the cemetery, where they throw them still alive into the prepared pits and then kill them with machine guns.

Just now someone from the Jewish Order Service has come running up to say that the Hitlerian beasts are still on the rampage in the small ghetto. At 5 p.m. they will certainly come over to the large ghetto. Blind panic breaks out in the courtyard. The children are hidden first, as the Hitlerian murderers target them the hardest. I decide not to go into the cellar. I don't want to take a place where a few more children could be hidden. I believe the children must be saved first. So I start running to find another hiding place. I run over to 30 Gęsia, to the carpentry workshop of my friend T. L. There in the square I run into hundreds of people, including many of my friends, who are also seeking refuge there so that the savage Hitlerian beasts don't find them.

No! I see there is no spot for me here. My former friends gaze at me with such unfamiliar, absolutely scathing looks, as though I had forced my way into their territory,[6] where only they have the right to be. It means I must rush to somewhere else. Without thinking twice, I run to 45 Gęsia, where the TOZ society is located. There I meet my best friends and comrades, Dr Blokh[7] and Dr Ringelblum, who inform me of the bad news: the gang is already fanning out in the large ghetto on Leszno and Przejazd Streets – where I left my friends a few hours ago, among them the wives of Dr Ringelblum and Dr Blokh, who are now standing before me in total despair because they don't know what has happened to their wives.

Disregarding the great danger it poses to do so, they run out to discover the fates of their wives. I stay a little longer [because] I realize that it is no longer possible to return to my home. It is already 7.30. Curfew is approaching. Where would it be possible to spend the night? Not actually sleep, but at least sit through the night. With no other choice, I go back to my friend L.'s carpentry workshop at 30 Gęsia. Many of my friends are still there, after all. One of them will probably ask me to join them, I think. I linger there for 10 to 15 minutes and explain to them that it is impossible for me to return to where I live because the savage Nazi gang has already blocked it off, dragging the young and the old alike to the death square. There can be no thought of getting home. Zamenhof [Street] and the low [street address] numbers on Gęsia are surrounded by the SS and SD murderers, who shoot anyone passing by. I notice how my friends and acquaintances begin to draw back from me.

5 This refers to the Umschlagplatz.

6 *Tkhum-hamoyshev* in the original; literally 'Pale of Settlement'.

7 Leyzer Lipa Blokh, also known as Eliezer (sometimes Aleksander) Lipe Bloch, (1889–1944); Zionist activist; one of the Jewish Social Self-Help (JSS) leaders in the Warsaw ghetto and active in underground educational work for the Hehalutz movement; imprisoned in German camps from early 1943; thought to have perished in Mauthausen concentration camp.

Where can I go now? Without much thought, I decide to run to the school kitchen named after Borokhov,[8] which is located at 68 Nowolipki, not far from Gęsia. Surely they will give me a warm welcome there, I think to myself. And so it was. As soon as I arrived, the teacher Comrade Likht[9] and two school graduates, the fine lads Dovid[10] and Nokhem,[11] received me very cordially. They make hot coffee and prepare a place to rest. In mortal fear we lie down. We [try to] work out the plan for 'their operation' today and come to the conclusion that the bloodthirsty Hitlerian sadists won't make it to 68 Nowolipki today. But just in case, we have prepared provisional hiding places. At the crack of dawn I get up, wash myself, and run to see how my close friends, comrades, and acquaintances are doing, if any of them are missing. Already on the way I hear that many of my friends, acquaintances, and others have been captured and taken away to the unknown, 'well-known' destination, where they will all be ruthlessly murdered.
Menakhem

## DOC. 115
## On 7 August 1942 the writer Stanisław Rembek notes what he has heard about the murder of the Warsaw Jews in Treblinka[1]

Diary of Stanisław Rembek,[2] entry for 7 August 1942

Friday, 7 August
Nice weather. I went shopping in Grodzisk with Marysieńka.[3] There was barely anything there. As Lilka[4] said, such is our luck that whenever we get a bit of money, everything becomes more expensive or is no longer available.

This time it's due to the authorities' strict regulations concerning trading in goods and their shooting at people even when they are just carrying milk. Apparently there have already been a few victims: there is talk of a wounded woman, a boy on a bicycle, and a little girl who was killed.

The gendarmes only fire at those who flee. Whoever cooperates is beaten and then sent to the concentration camp in Treblinka. Warsaw Jews are allegedly being eliminated

8 Ber Borokhov (Borochov) (1881–1917); co-founder of the Jewish socialist party Poale Zion in 1900.
9 This is probably a reference to Yisroel Likhtenshteyn.
10 Dovid (Dawid) Graber was 19 years old; he left his testament behind in the documents of the underground archive: AŻIH, Ring I/415 (432).
11 Nokhem (Nakhum) Grzywacz; he left his testament behind in the documents of the underground archive: AŻIH, Ring I/416 (1018).

1 Biblioteka Narodowa, Zakład Rękopisów, akc. 17 418. Published in Stanisław Rembek, *Dziennik okupacyjny* (Warsaw: Agawa, 2000), p. 304. This document has been translated from Polish.
2 Stanisław Rembek (1901–1985), historian, teacher, and novelist; served in the Polish army and fought in the Polish–Soviet War, 1919–1921; teacher in Radom, then in Piotrków, 1924–1938; worked for the underground press as well as both the official and the illegal school systems; worked for the Warsaw-based publishing house PAX after the war.
3 Rembek's wife, Maria, née Dalewska.
4 Rembek's sister-in-law, Janina Nowak.

at this Treblinka.[5] They are taken there, 150 people crammed into a goods wagon, which is strewn with quicklime and chloride. The corpses are dumped into large pits dug by excavators. The pits are then ploughed over. Approximately 100,000 people have allegedly been transported there from Warsaw in this way.

On the way back, near Kwast,[6] Marysieńka and I met Grandmother Dehnelowa[7] with a woman to whom she has rented a room. She has grown old and has lost even more weight, but has not become any more intelligent.

A very friendly letter arrived from Gutek.[8] For the very first time, he sent me an embrace. Not a word about Marysieńka, however.

## DOC. 116

**On 10 August 1942 the Home Army informs readers of its German-language newsletter about the crimes committed against the Jewish population[1]**

*Who is worse – the Jews or you?*

The Germans allege that the Polish nation lacks culture. And this is undoubtedly true, because Poles know the difference between combat and murder. The Poles are not fond of the Jews, and their country was probably the first to see the birth of a scientific anti-semitic movement. But what is happening now, with old people and children being murdered, disgusts them. Here is a brief example to illustrate the situation: On […][2] July, the day on which the National Socialist executioner Himmler paid a visit to Lublin,[3] the German police – with the help of Lithuanians, Latvians, and Ukrainians dressed in the bloodstained uniform of the swastika thugs – locked all the gates to the ghetto, so that 400,000 Jews were left with nothing to eat. The price of bread rose to 50 zl., […] bacon cost 250 zl., potatoes more than 20 zl. Dreadful hunger reigned. To save their lives, the Jews tried everything they could to get food from the other side of the wall … A hail of bullets was the reply. Mothers nursing their babies, pregnant women, and elderly people fell to the ground, dead.

A few days later, mass murder on an unprecedented scale began. The monsters in German uniforms shot at innocent Jewish passers-by in the streets, stormed the apartments, threw the occupants out of the windows, or murdered them in the craftiest ways; there was blood, and wails and cries for help were heard everywhere. Some Jews tried

5 See Introduction, pp. 29, 34–35.
6 A neighbour.
7 The grandmother of Rembek's stepdaughters from his wife's first marriage.
8 August Gustaw Dehnel (1903–1962), zoologist; Maria Dalewska's first husband; imprisoned at Oflag II D prisoner-of-war camp in Groß Born (now Borne Sulinowo), 1939–1945.

1 *Kennst Du die Wahrheit? Mitteilungsblatt für Deutsche in Polen. Ausgabe für Volksdeutsche*, nos. 7/8, 10 August 1942, p. 2: AAN, 1583/366, fol. 2. The Home Army published this newsletter in 1942 as part of its *akcja N[iemcy]* (Operation G[ermans]), targeting the German population; the first issues appeared in German as mimeographed sheets, before the newspaper began publication in print, in Polish, in autumn 1942. This document has been translated from German.
2 In the original document here and below, a few words are missing because the page is damaged.
3 See Doc. 96.

to escape death and fled; they were caught in the streets and savagely murdered or loaded onto railway wagons, 100 per wagon, and then each wagon was sealed. Standing in their own excrement, with no fresh air, the Jews waited for the moment when they would be taken to a new torture site. And so it has gone, day in and day out. The terror does not subside, because the German professors serving the Führer and his ministers have established that the Jew is not a human being; he is merely an animal. But even animals are treated humanely in Europe … In the Warsaw ghetto, they even liquidated the so-called 13 (13 Leszno St.), where there was a cell of Gestapo informants made up of the world's worst scoundrels.[4] One of the murder victims was a Jewish woman called Mrs Judowa; she was Leist's mistress, and he used to visit her frequently in the ghetto.[5] Germans who live in Warsaw: your Kreishauptmann[6] is no exception; there are many such fellows in ruling circles. Not only Mr Leist, but others also had Jewish mistresses, did business with Jews, and earned a great deal of money. But the moment these things became uncomfortable for them, they ruthlessly murdered their accomplices. That is what they're like, your dirty, dishonest leaders. And you put up with it all. You, the so-called 'master race', let yourselves by governed by idiots!

*Do not destroy this sheet after you have read it; give it to another German who, like you, has had enough of Hitler's propaganda and wants to learn the truth.*

## DOC. 117

## On 14 August 1942 an informant reports to the World Jewish Congress in Switzerland on the mass murders of Jews in Warsaw and Belzec, and on the demands made by Jews in Poland[1]

Report for the Geneva office of the World Jewish Congress, unsigned,[2] recorded on 15 August 1942

15 August 1942

A short time ago, a gentleman came directly from Poland and gave an account of pogroms in Lemberg, the incitement of the Polish population, and their unfriendly behaviour towards the Jewish population there.

4 No. 13 Leszno Street was the address of the Office for Combating Illicit Trade and Price Gouging, which was under Gestapo control and was supposed to counterbalance the Jewish Council. Until it was closed on 17 July 1941, it was headed by Abraham Gancwajch and Dawid Szternfeld. Ghetto inhabitants turned to this agency when they sought to make contact with German offices and agencies.

5 Presumably a reference to Regina Judt, who owned a cabaret theatre in the ghetto and had good contacts with the German administration: see *The Warsaw Diary of Adam Czerniakow*, p. 178.

6 Ludwig Leist was the Stadthauptmann of Warsaw from Sept. 1941 to July 1944.

1 CZA, C 3/7–14, fols. 11–12. Copy in USHMM, RG 68 045M, reel 2. This document has been translated from German.

2 The representative of the World Jewish Congress in Geneva was Gerhart Riegner, a lawyer from Germany. The report was recorded by Richard Lichtheim (1885–1963), economist; chairman of the Zionist Association for Germany from 1910; worked for the executive of the Zionist Organization in London from 1921 to 1923, then in Berlin; emigrated to Palestine in 1934; worked in Geneva as representative of the Zionist Organization for the countries occupied by Germany from August 1939; lived in Israel after the war.

Yesterday, Friday 14 August 1942, another person (an Aryan), a very reliable and well-known figure, came directly from Poland and reported the following:

The Warsaw ghetto is in the process of being liquidated. Jews are being taken away from the ghetto in groups and shot, with no regard for age or sex, and *their corpses are being used to produce fat and their bones used as fertilizer*. Corpses are also allegedly being dug up again for these purposes. Of course these mass executions are not taking place in Warsaw itself, but in camps established specifically for this purpose. One such camp is said to be in Belzek.[3] Around 50,000 Jews are said to have been slaughtered on the spot in Lemberg itself over the last four weeks, and 100,000 in Warsaw, according to another report.[4]

Allegedly there are scarcely any Jews to be found any more in the entire region east of Poland, including occupied Russia. As was reported on this occasion as well, the entire non-Jewish population of Sebastopol, for example, has been murdered.[5] The Jewish population in Poland will not be slaughtered all at once, so as not to cause a stir abroad. While Aryans deported from Holland and France are indeed being used for labour in the East,[6] the Jewish deportees from Germany, Belgium, Holland, France, and Slovakia are reportedly taken there to be slaughtered. Since these killings would cause a greater stir in the West, the people have to be deported first, specifically to the East, where it is less likely that the news will reach other countries.

Many of the Jews who were deported to Lithuania and Lublin have already been executed in recent weeks. That may be why the deportees are not allowed to write letters. Most of the German deportees are said to be in Theresienstadt. This camp is only an intermediate stop, however, and the same fate awaits its inmates. Whenever such executions have created more space, new deportations are carried out. One often encounters trains consisting entirely of such deportees, who are shipped in livestock wagons. Approximately forty people are put in each livestock wagon. Of particular interest is the fact that Lithuanian Gentiles are assigned to collect these doomed people from the ghetto in Warsaw.[7]

Tragically, the Germans have managed to incite the Polish population against the Jews to a great extent, and the relationship between the Polish population and the Jews is reaching boiling point. This is true in Lemberg in particular. When I asked what relations were like among the population in Warsaw, the reply was that there were no relations at all, simply because no Pole ever gets to see a Jew in Warsaw. The Jewish population, especially in Lemberg and in the Warsaw ghetto, lives solely in the hope that either

3 The camp's name has been spelled with a K in the original.

4 The SS deported 15,000 Jews from Lwów to Belzec between 14 March and 1 April 1942; additional deportations took place from 10 to 23 August 1942, in which around 50,000 were deported first to Janowska camp, and from there to Belzec. The deportations from the Warsaw ghetto to Treblinka began on 22 July 1942.

5 After the city of Sevastopol on the Crimean Peninsula was conquered, the Jews who lived there were murdered by July 1942. The population had already shrunk to one sixth of its original size as a result of civilian casualties and people fleeing. In June 1941 there had been approximately 65,000 Jews living in Crimea.

6 Almost without exception, non-Jews deported from the Netherlands and France for forced labour were sent to the Reich.

7 The SS used auxiliary personnel from the SS training camp in Trawniki, mostly Ukrainians, to guard deportees from the Warsaw ghetto.

a second front will open up or, by some miracle, the war will come to an end before winter arrives. The Jews in Poland have the following question:

More than 4 million Germans live in America, of whom 2 million subscribe to National Socialism. Why doesn't America undertake any reprisal measures? This is why the Jewish population in Poland is very disappointed in and bitter towards America. People understand that England is doing nothing out of fear for its prisoners of war, but America would have nothing to fear. Poland's Jewish population is now at a point where it knows it has nothing to lose.

Finally, it was pointed out that unoccupied France has promised to hand over 10,000 Jews to Germany.[8] If people, even those in the anti-German French government circles, knew what fate lies in store for those scheduled for deportation, they might be moved to put a stop to this scheme. Only the aforementioned reprisal measures taken by America would be truly effective and valuable. This concludes the report provided by this 'informant'.

Now the following should be considered:

(a) How can we make this plausible in French government circles, so that at least the Jews of France could be saved from being handed over?
(b) How can we make this report known among American Jews – but without revealing the source? Encrypted telegrams to this effect have been sent to London,[9] but reports like this one are published only after a certain time, both on the radio and in black books.[10] But the Jews of America cannot be left in ignorance of the true state of affairs for so long.
(c) As it has been conclusively established several times now that the non-Jewish population of Poland does listen to the Polish-language broadcasts from London, it would be imperative to present to the Polish government in London the idea of using these radio addresses to dissuade the Polish population from taking any part in this horrific operation.[11]

8 The first deportation train from unoccupied France left for Auschwitz on 10 August 1942. In total, approximately 74,000 Jews were deported from across France, one third of whom were French citizens and two thirds of whom were stateless, including 14,400 from Poland.

9 On 30 July 1942, while on a trip to Switzerland, the entrepreneur Eduard Schulte (1891–1966) passed on information about the Reich government's plan to murder all the European Jews. On 8 August 1942 Riegner asked the British and US vice consuls in Geneva to forward this information to their superiors and to use diplomatic channels to send telegrams to Sydney Silverman (1898–1968), chairman of the British Section of the World Jewish Congress, and to Stephen Wise. The State Department did not pass on the message. Silverman received the telegram around 18 August 1942 and then informed Wise in New York.

10 The book *The German New Order in Poland* was published in London in 1941 and included a section on the persecution of the Jews: Polish Ministry of Information, *The German New Order in Poland* (London: Hutchinson, 1941). In 1943 *The Black Book of Polish Jewry: An Account of the Martyrdom of Polish Jewry under the Nazi Occupation* was published by the Roy publishing house in New York (ed. Jacob Apenszlak et al.).

11 In its Instruction No. 2, dated 23 June 1941, the Polish government in exile in London called on the Polish underground to prevent Poles from participating in anti-Jewish violence in the regions of eastern Poland: Pełczyński and Tokarski (eds.), *Armia Krajowa w dokumentach 1939–1945*, vol. 2, pp. 6–8, here p. 8. It was not until a radio address on 4 May 1943 that Prime Minister Sikorski, impressed by the fighting in the Warsaw ghetto, finally asked his fellow Poles to help the Jews in any way they could: see also Doc. 140.

## DOC. 118

## On 18 August 1942 the Ukrainian auxiliary police report attempts at bribery during a mass arrest of Jews in Lemberg[1]

Report from Ukrainian police headquarters, Dept. Ia (log no. 5459/42), signed Ukrainian police major and commander of the Ukrainian police in Stadthauptmannschaft Lemberg, signature illegible,[2] Lemberg, to the Urban Police headquarters in Lemberg, dated 18 August 1942

*Re*: operation against the Jews
*Reference*: none
We hereby report that a total of 3,051 Jews who lacked the required identity documents were arrested and taken to the assembly point during the operation against the Jews on 17 August 1942.

We must also report that the following attempts at bribery occurred during the operation:

1. An unidentified Jewess attempted to bribe Officer Roman *Lyschak* from Police Station No. 3 of the Ukrainian Police in Lemberg by handing him the sum of *700 zl.* and *a wristwatch* (allegedly gold).
2. The Jewess Helene *Kos* attempted to bribe Officer Anton *Ladyk* by handing him a wristwatch (allegedly nickel).
3. The Jew Michael *Semaschkewicz* attempted to bribe Officer Artym *Komanczuk* from Police Station No. 6 of the Ukrainian Police in Lemberg by handing him *a pocket watch* (allegedly silver).
4. The same Jew attempted to bribe Officer Paul *Sydorowicz* with the sum of *400 zl.*
5. The Jew Josef *Liebling* attempted to bribe Officer Wladimir *Pidwirny* from Police Station No. 6 of the Ukrainian Police in Lemberg with the sum of *500 zl.*
6. The same Jew attempted to bribe Officer Orest *Kluczkowski* from Police Station No. 6 of the Ukrainian Police in Lemberg with the sum of *200 zl.*
7. The Jewess Klara *Beer* attempted to bribe Officer Alexander *Korol* from Police Station No. 6 of the Ukrainian Police in Lemberg by handing him three 5-dollar bills and one 10-dollar bill, which has since been destroyed.
8. The Jewess Klara *Beer* attempted to bribe Officer Elijasch […][3] from Police Station No. 6 of the Ukrainian Police in Lemberg by handing him *a ladies' watch* (allegedly gold).
9. The Jewess Anna *Brenzel* attempted to bribe Officer Johann *Pocalujko* from Police Station No. 6 of the Ukrainian Police in Lemberg with the sum of *345 zl.*
10. The Jew Ignatz *Herschoffer* attempted to bribe Officer Alexander *Korol* from Police Station No. 6 of the Ukrainian Police with the sum of *164 zl.*
11. The Jewess Adela *Eichler* attempted to bribe Officer Alexander *Korol* from Police Station No. 6 of the Ukrainian Police in Lemberg with the sum of *500 zl.*

1 DALO, R-12/1/39, fols. 17–18. Copy in USHMM, Acc. 1995.A.1086, reel 3. This document has been translated from German.

2 Volodymyr Pitulej, commander of the Ukrainian auxiliary police in Lemberg; thought to have fled along with the German troops in mid 1944.

3 Name illegible; possibly: Hryojko.

12. The Jewess Anka *Brema* attempted to bribe Officer Alexander *Korol* from Police Station No. 6 of the Ukrainian Police in Lemberg by handing him *a bracelet* (allegedly gold).
13. The Jewess Sara *Weintraub* attempted to bribe Officer Demeter *Schwed* from Police Station No. 6 of the Ukrainian Police in Lemberg by handing him the sum of *110 zl.* and *a wristwatch* (allegedly gold).
14. The Jewess Ame *Tschatschkes* attempted to bribe Officer Johann *Zdobylak* with the sum of *100 zl.*
15. The Jew Simon *Tschatschkes* attempted to bribe Officer Alexander *Korol* from Police Station No. 6 of the Ukrainian Police in Lemberg with the sum of *100 zl.*
16. The Jew Moriz *Waldberg* attempted to bribe Officer Alexander *Korol* from Police Station No. 6 of the Ukrainian Police in Lemberg by handing him the sum of *2,980 zl.* and *a pocket watch* (allegedly silver).

The sums of money and valuables listed under numbers 1 to 16 are being transferred for further processing.

The following attempts at bribery have also been reported; in these cases, German officials seized the money and valuables directly:

17. The Jewess Ewa *Kosebau* attempted to bribe Officer Wasyl *Andruschko* from Police Station No. 3 of the Ukrainian Police in Lemberg by handing him the sum of *500 zl.* and a watch. Officer Erwin Lück from the reserve Urban Police seized the money and valuables and issued a receipt for them.
18. An unidentified Jewess attempted to bribe Officers Wasyl *Andruschko* and Roman *Lyschak* from Police Station No. 3 of the Ukrainian Police in Lemberg by handing them two 10-dollar gold coins, three 1-dollar bills, and one 5-dollar bill, as well as thirteen 1-pound-sterling notes and three Austrian gold coins. These valuables were seized by Oberscharführer Kohr.
19. All the money and valuables handed over to the Ukrainian police officers in the area under the jurisdiction of Police Station No. 5 of the Ukrainian Police in Lemberg have been seized by the head of the assembly point at the National Socialist Motor Corps company.

Thus the following items are being transferred:

Cash in the amount of 6,099 zl.
25 US dollars (the 10-dollar bill was destroyed)
1 wristwatch (allegedly gold)
1 " ( " nickel)
1 pocket watch ( " silver)
1 wristwatch ( " gold)
1 bracelet ( " gold)
1 pocket watch ( " silver)[4]

The items listed, as well as cash in the amount of 6,099 zl., were properly transferred today.[5]

4 One line has been added by hand: '1 wristwatch (allegedly gold)'. Below this line is a stamp reading: 'Ukrainian Police Major and Commander of the Ukrainian Police in Stadthauptmannschaft Lemberg'. This is followed by a signature: 'Pitulej'.

5 Handwritten note: 'Urban Police Officer Pitulej'.

## DOC. 119

## On 19 August 1942 the commander-in-chief of the Home Army reports on the progress of deportations from the Warsaw ghetto[1]

Radio message (no. 734) from Wanda[2] (log book no. 3453), signed Kalina[3] 638, to the leadership of the Polish army in exile, London (received on 25 August 1942, 7.35 a.m., read on 25 August 1942, 2 p.m.), Warsaw, dated 19 August 1942

Since 22 July the German police and Latvian auxiliaries[4] have been in the process of liquidating the Warsaw ghetto (400,000 residents) with great cruelty.

Previously 5,000–6,000 [people] were being deported daily, at present up to 15,000.[5] The majority are allegedly murdered in Bełżec[6] and Treblinka, while a portion seems to be designated for work at the front. Mass murder and plundering accompany the transports. Trained craftsmen working for the army, along with their families – several tens of thousands – are to remain in the ghetto.

More than 150,000 have been deported so far.[7]

## DOC. 120

## Calek Perechodnik describes the Polish police's involvement in preparations for the deportations from Otwock on 19 August 1942[1]

Handwritten notes by Calek Perechodnik, written in spring/summer 1943 (excerpt)[2]

*There was a group of fifty Polish citizens* that day who knew exactly what would happen the following day. At approximately 5 p.m., the Polish police department received a *telegram instructing it to make available fifty goods wagons to transport the Jews from Otwock at 7 p.m. on Wednesday, 19 August, and that at 7 a.m. there would be a roll call of the uniformed and Criminal Police due to take part in the operation to resettle the Jews.*

1 SPP, 3.1.1.13A, fol. 11. This document has been translated from Polish.
2 Code name for a broadcasting station operated by the government delegation.
3 Code name of Stefan Rowecki (1895–1944), career officer, member of Piłsudski's Legions during the First World War; served in the war in Sept. 1939; subsequently active in the underground; general and commandant in the Union of Armed Struggle (ZWZ) (later: Home Army, ZWZ-AK) from 1940, and commander-in-chief from Feb. 1942; arrested by the Gestapo on 30 June 1943; murdered in Sachsenhausen concentration camp.
4 This is probably a reference to non-German auxiliary personnel from the SS training camp in Trawniki.
5 See Docs. 103 and 111.
6 Belzec was not a destination of the deportations from the Warsaw ghetto between July and Sept. 1942.
7 This news was kept confidential and played no role in the assessment of the situation in occupied Poland in the weeks that followed.

1 YVA, O-33/426. Published in Perechodnik, *Spowiedź*, pp. 47–48. This document has been translated from Polish.
2 On the preservation of this text, see Doc. 39.

News that the wagons were being made ready did not spread through the town, but the Jews found out about the police roll call planned for the following day. *However, Polish policemen calmed them down [and assured them] that this was just a normal weekly roll call which just happened to fall on this particular Wednesday.* Other than that, the Polish police only reacted to this news by collecting the items they had left with their tailors and shoemakers, regardless of whether they were ready.

Nothing can excuse the Polish police.

In most towns the police felt obliged to inform the local population of their imminent resettlement. The police in Otwock did not feel obliged to do this and didn't do so.

*Over three years of continuous occupation, the Polish police squeezed the Jews for everything they had.* They regularly collected protection money from butchers, bakers, smugglers, and every wealthy Jew who traded in something or had hidden pre-war goods.

Let us not forget that, after all, all aspects of life were illegal for Jews during the war, as fault could be found with everything: *What* do you live on? *Where* do the potatoes in the ghetto come from? *Where* does the bread come from? *Where* are the fields on which the rye was sown? And even if there are such fields, *how* do you grind the grain? *Where* did you get the meat? This is how the Polish police, who officially had no right to enter the ghetto, nevertheless lived off it – and they lived well, too.

I don't hold that against them. I understand that they couldn't live on their salaries with inflation, but the fact that they didn't do the Jews this last favour by warning them of their imminent resettlement – this shall be to their everlasting shame.

I accuse them of being just as culpable for the deaths of the Jews as the German henchmen.

Of course there have been very sporadic cases of policemen informing their close acquaintances of an imminent resettlement, but they demanded their word [that they would] not tell anyone.

I know, for example, that *Police Sergeant Pietraś* informed the management of the 'Zofiówka'[3] hospital, whereby several people were able to save themselves. However, those who were unable or had no more strength to try took their own lives the same night by swallowing cyanide.[4] Also, to be fair, I exclude *Marchlewicz, the commander of the police department in Otwock*,[5] from this judgement on the police. I cannot accuse him of living off the ghetto during the war, as he virtually never crossed its boundary, either before or after the operation.

*I am strongly convinced* that there is not a single item of Jewish property in his apartment.

*I am strongly convinced* that deep inside, he sympathized with the Jews and had never arrested a Jew himself. Nevertheless I cannot praise his (in principle) noble conduct, his 'splendid isolation'[6] from the Jews. If only all policemen had followed his example; but

3 A psychiatric hospital in Otwock.

4 On 19 August 1942 a Gestapo squad under the command of Karl-Georg Brandt shot dead 108 patients at Zofiówka.

5 Bronisław Marchlewicz (1899–1972), police officer; commander of the Otwock police department from 1937; simultaneously linked with the Home Army during the German occupation and involved in rescuing Jews; honoured as Righteous Among the Nations by the State of Israel in 2005.

6 English in the original.

as far as he is concerned, he should at least have felt a moral duty to warn the Jews directly or, for the sake of his own safety, indirectly. *But he didn't.*

We discovered all of this later.

## DOC. 121
## From 8 to 20 August 1942 the physician Zygmunt Klukowski writes about the deportation of the Jewish population from Szczebrzeszyn[1]

Handwritten diary of Zygmunt Klukowski, entries for the period between 8 and 20 August 1942

*8 August, 11 a.m.*

The Jews in the town are in the throes of tension and despair. It was already clear yesterday evening that something incomprehensible was about to happen to the Jews. Ominous news came from Biłgoraj and Zwierzyniec. Numerous patrols roamed the town in the evening, and pedestrians were asked for identification. At about 1 a.m. we were awakened by a noise in the street opposite the hospital. A Jewish house was being stormed. We could hear screams, wails, and cries in German, Polish, and Yiddish. They were in one apartment for quite a long time; after breaking down the door of a second apartment, they didn't find anyone inside. A Jewish woman had hidden in the attic with four children. Luckily they did not search there. Not a single Jew was to be seen in town all morning. I went out to find out what was really happening. All the Jews, without exception, had been ordered to turn up at the market square near the Judenrat[2] by 8 a.m. They were each allowed to bring along 15 kg of luggage, enough food for five days, and 1,500 złoty. The mayor[3] told me that 2,000 Jews from Szczebrzeszyn were to be taken 'to Ukraine', and the railwaymen said that a train with fifty-five goods wagons had already been prepared and was at the station. None of the Jews had turned up voluntarily, so they [the Germans] began to catch them and bring them to the market hall. I asked a gendarme from the local police force, who spoke fluent Polish, what they would do if the Jews did not turn up of their own accord. He answered briefly, 'Then they'll be gunned down.'[4]

It is almost 7 p.m. All day long, since noon, gendarmes, Gestapo men, Sonderdienst soldiers,[5] members of the Blue Police, bailiffs from the town council, members of the Judenrat, and Jewish policemen[6] have been roaming the city and looking for Jews in

1 Zygmunt Klukowski, Dziennik, notebook 4, fols. 186–192; Biblioteka Uniwersytecka Katolickiego Uniwersytetu Lubelskiego, Dział Rękopisów 813. Published in Klukowski, *Zamojszczyzna*, vol. 1: *1918–1943*, pp. 291–293. Published in a slightly abridged English translation in Klukowski, *Diary from the Years of Occupation, 1939–1944*, pp. 209–211. This document has been newly translated from Polish.

2 Here and below, German in the original: 'Jewish Council'.

3 Andreas Kraus, an ethnic German from Eastern Galicia, was mayor of Szczebrzeszyn from August 1942 to 1944.

4 Change in tense in the subsequent paragraph as in the original.

5 German in the original: an auxiliary police force in the General Government made up of ethnic Germans.

6 This is a reference to the Jewish Order Service.

their homes, dragging them out of various hiding places, and marching them to the market hall. The Jews are a terrible sight – mostly in rags, women with little children in their arms. An almost animalistic fear and utter despair are etched on their faces. They are completely calm; neither weeping nor wailing can be heard. The Jewish houses are deserted; the doors to some apartments are wide open. The bailiffs from the town council transport away the belongings and the hidden goods left behind. I have seen carts fully loaded with bundles and sacks full of a huge variety of objects. Incidentally, most of the Jews have hidden themselves in such a way that they cannot be found. Quite a few Poles, especially the young men, are eagerly helping in the search for Jews. Much commotion in town.

*9 p.m.*
Before 8 p.m. they began to lead the Jews out of the market hall. Some of them tried to flee, upon which frenzied shooting broke out, also in our street. The Poles, who had gathered in large numbers in the streets, were gripped with panic, and everyone who possibly could fled and sought refuge in the houses. Shortly afterwards all the Jews were led, or more precisely forcibly herded, to the train station; a few women and infirm elderly people travelled behind on horse-drawn carts. Anyone who hesitated was beaten with clubs, whips, etc. I saw all of this with my own eyes, as I was standing by the hospital wall, right next to the main road. It was so shocking, so horrifically inhumane, that it is hard to describe. Approximately 1,000 Jews were led out of Biłgoraj and the surrounding towns. They were taken to the train station in Zwierzyniec. No one believes they are being taken to Ukraine; everyone is certain that they will be murdered. It is difficult to recover your senses after such a dreadful day. We have the impression that it is not over yet. A total of thirteen Jews were shot in Szczebrzeszyn today.

*10 August*
Yesterday the Jews did not yet show themselves in the town; only the occasional Jewish figure flitted by. Towards evening, three Jewish women who had emerged from their homes were shot. Of the Jews who were taken away the day before yesterday, all that is known is that they went by train in the direction of Bełżec. Everyone is certain they are no longer alive.

*11 August*
The market is not open at all this Tuesday. The people from the countryside are afraid to come into town. No one is allowed to sell anything to the Jews. The bailiffs from the town council are removing everything from the apartments the Jews abandoned: furniture, bedding, etc. and gathering it all in a single place. Only those Jews who are employed somewhere and [Jewish] craftsmen are to remain in the town. Everyone else is to be 'deported', which means murdered. A 'state of emergency' has been declared. This does not entail any special regulations or restrictions; it merely gives the gendarmes and others the right to shoot people with impunity and for the most stupid reasons. Everything has become much more expensive here because the farmers are not delivering anything to the town. The general living conditions are becoming increasingly difficult.

*12 August*
Last night a Jewish woman with a child and a Jewish man were shot in the street. In the afternoon, the powiat physician Dr Snacki[7] came from Biłgoraj, accompanied by a requisitions official from the powiat. They sealed all the equipment in the practices of the Jewish dentists Sztreicher and Bronszteinowa.[8] They took some of Sztreicher's equipment with them. They made an inventory of all the equipment in Dr Bołotny's practice and issued an order that he was not allowed to sell any of it. So Bołotny is the only one allowed to use his equipment. Mayor Kraus and Dr Snacki declared to me that the Jews here would be liquidated completely.

*20 August*
Hardly a day goes by without at least a few Jews being shot. People have grown so used to this that they are no longer as concerned by it as before. Shootings at night hardly make an impression any more. At least one Pole has also been shot almost every day, young men from the countryside who are considered thieves and robbers and were known for their reprehensible behaviour, even before the war.

Almost everyone arrested after Rytko's[9] murder has been taken from the prison in Lublin to Oświęcim. Their families are reportedly to be subjected to special reprisals. Some of them have already been dispossessed, such as the Taland family. The terror continues to increase and is becoming more and more difficult to bear. We all ask ourselves whether we will hold out until the end of the war. Some people still believe the war will end this year and are not worried about the Germans' alleged successes in the Caucasus. Everyone is waiting for the 'second front' as if for salvation. Yet the winter threatens to be exceptionally severe in every respect. There is a great fear that if there are more failures on the front and the economic situation in Germany deteriorates, then the terror here will be even greater. We live literally from one day to the next and are happy to have pulled through each day.

7 Dr Jan Snacki (b. 1897), physician; ran a practice in Jozefów prior to Sept. 1939.
8 Noemi Bronsztajnowa (Bronstein or Bronsteinowa), née Abramowicz (1901/1902–1942), from Radom; murdered along with her two daughters at Belzec in Oct. 1942.
9 Leopold Rytko, Gestapo informant.

## DOC. 122

## Around 23 August 1942 the soldier Hubert Pfoch describes a scene in which the Jews of Siedlce are loaded onto the deportation train to Treblinka[1]

Handwritten diary of Hubert Pfoch,[2] entry for 23 August 1942 or later

[…][3]
We then continue on via Radom and Lukow to Siedlce, where we arrive in the evening and are given soup. Shots ring out periodically. There we see around 7,000 Jews, and whenever one of them, man or woman, stands up, that person immediately slumps to the ground, shot in the head. We soon go to sleep, and I wake up on the 23rd just as our train is moving past the Jews, very close to them – all Ostjuden, emaciated and ragged. They haven't had any food or water for two days now. A truck carrying Jewish police pulls up now and then and takes the dead away. There are horrific scenes as the livestock wagons are loaded: 180 Jews in a single wagon – the parents in one, the children in another – accompanied all the while by the sound of shots fired by the guards, who are Ukrainian volunteers.[4] Once everyone has been successfully loaded, cries for water ring out from every wagon: 'prosim wody' – please, water [in exchange] for my gold ring, for 5,000 zloty (2,500 Reichsmarks). We are offered watches etc. in exchange for a glass of water. Then, as the first people scramble through the window hatches in the wagons and lie exhausted on the sand, they are shot, which resulted in a massacre that disgusted every one of us; it was a bloodbath like I have never seen before.[5] A mother jumps down [from the wagon] with her child and looks quite calmly into the barrel of the gun, which soon sends a bullet through her head, putting her out of her misery. From the wagons, the cries for water become increasingly hysterical. Women call out to us: 'Please shoot me!' 'Please shoot in this direction!' When the train finally leaves the station, there are at least 50 dead bodies – women, men, children, some completely naked – lying at the train station, which the Jewish police then clear away. Valuables of all sorts disappear into the pockets of those who remove the bodies.[6]

1 The original is in the possession of the author's widow, Leopoldine Pfoch, in Vienna. Copy in IfZ-Archives, F 601. Published in English translation in Gitta Sereny, *Into That Darkness: From Mercy Killing to Mass Murder* (London: Pimlico, 1995 [1974]), pp. 158–159. The diary entries covering 24 Feb. 1941 to August 1944 have survived in four notebooks. This document has been newly translated from German.

2 Hubert Pfoch (1920–2008), joiner; active in illegal Social Democratic youth groups from 1934; served in the war in 1941; deserted in 1945; thereafter worked as a librarian in Vienna; witness at the Treblinka Trial before Düsseldorf Regional Court in 1965; Social Democratic deputy mayor of Vienna, 1973–1978; president of the Documentation Centre of Austrian Resistance (DÖW), 1984–2003.

3 In the entry for 21 August 1942 Pfoch described his departure from Vienna and his journey to the Soviet Union through Moravia and Upper Silesia.

4 These were non-German auxiliary personnel from the SS training camp in Trawniki, near Lublin.

5 Change in tense as in the original.

6 On 21 August 1942 SS men, Ukrainian auxiliaries, and Polish police surrounded the ghetto in Siedlce. The extermination operation lasted from 22 to 24 August 1942. Approximately 10,000 people were deported to Treblinka, and approximately 3,000 were murdered in the city following a selection process. The German occupiers crammed the remaining Jews, approximately 2,000 people, into a smaller ghetto before eventually dispersing them to labour camps in the surrounding area; the last Jews from Siedlce had been killed by March 1943.

When our train takes the same route, there are still quite a few children and others lying along the track. On the journey to Treblinka, where the Jewish 'delousing camp' is located, we overtake the train. The smell of corpses hanging in the air makes us want to vomit. Once again we are right next to the transport of Jews, from which we hear even more piercing cries for water, and the guards are still firing into groups of Jews at random. Three hundred thousand [people] have been amassed here, and every day 10,000 to 15,000 are poisoned with gas and cremated. Any comment on this matter is utterly superfluous. Weapons were found in the ghettos, and this was the countermeasure. [...][7]

## DOC. 123
## On 24 August 1942 the GG government decides to stop supplying food to 1.2 million Jews[1]

Minutes of the government meeting in Cracow on 24 August 1942

*New harvest collection and food plan for the General Government*[2]

The *Governor General* opened the meeting with the following remarks: Gentlemen! I have called you together today in exceptional haste and urgency to inform you of an extraordinarily important measure, one that will be unusually decisive concerning all the coming year's work in the General Government. What I say to you, I say in the strictest confidence. I would like to draw your attention to the fact that any word from today's meeting communicated outside official channels could spell immense harm to our country.

A few days ago a meeting took place at the Reich Marshal's office in Berlin.[3] The Reich Marshal had received reports from all over the Reich about the downright catastrophic development of the *food supply in the German Reich.* According to all confidential reports from both the police and the Gauleiter – confirmed by personal experience, as he put it – the situation is this: unless the food supply in the German Reich improves significantly, we will shortly be facing extremely grave harm to people's health, especially the health of the German working man. Hundreds of thousands of cases of illness already show the shocking effects not only of this dietary constraint, but also and above

7 In the following section, Pfoch described the continuation of his journey through Lithuania and Latvia to Orel.

1 AIPN, GK 95, vol. 24. Copy in IfZ-Archives, Fb 105, vol. 24, fols. 5834–5853, here fols. 5840–5843 and 5848–5851. This document has been translated from German.

2 The document is 23 pages long. The government meeting was preceded by a meeting between Governor General Frank and Karl Naumann the same afternoon, at which Naumann presented 'a new harvest collection and food plan for the General Government', which Frank approved: IfZ-Archives, Fb 105, vol. 24, fol. 5832.

3 Göring's meeting with the heads of the civil and military administrations in the occupied territories had taken place on 6 August 1942. It was preceded by a meeting between Hitler and Göring in early August 1942, in which they decided to exploit the occupied territories to an even greater extent to benefit the Reich's food supply.

all of the deterioration in the quality of the food, which presents a danger to public health. This is especially true of the quality of the bread that has been distributed to the German population in recent weeks: it is causing the severest health complaints.

A serious situation has thus arisen, inasmuch as the German Reich has to provide not just for itself, but also for a large share of the peoples of Europe. The German population must be provided with sufficient food during the months and the winter ahead, so that people can withstand the strain that the coming months will put on their nerves.

Given these circumstances, it will not surprise you to learn that events will now unfold in accordance with the dictum that before the German people experiences a disastrous famine, the occupied territories and their populations will be subjected to hunger. Therefore, we here in the General Government must now also be filled with steely determination to help the great German people – that is to say, our homeland.

[...][4]

This has led to the following outcome for the General Government: the General Government has pledged to send another 500,000 tonnes of bread grains to the Fatherland, in addition to the food we supply from the General Government to ease the burden on the homeland, as well as for the Wehrmacht, police, and SS units stationed here.[5] If you compare this to the amount of our overall contributions from the previous year, then you can extrapolate an approximately sixfold increase in the contributions made by the General Government.

These outcomes will be achieved exclusively at the expense of the *non-German population*. They must be implemented coldly and mercilessly, for this contribution on the part of the General Government is all the more essential this year, as the occupied eastern territories – Ukraine, Ostland, etc. – will not yet be able to contribute anything appreciable to easing the burden on the homeland. Even if one million tonnes of bread grains could be delivered from Ostland and Ukraine, that would be just a drop in the ocean in view of the overall situation in the Reich.

For these reasons, gentlemen, I wanted to let you here in this governmental body know about the resolutions I made today in my meeting with Party Comrade Naumann. They essentially provide for a subsequent *increase in the quota* to be delivered and a *revision in how the population is supplied* [with food], especially the Jews and the Polish population. At the same time, the food supply for the working population, and above all for those people working here on behalf of German interests, is to be maintained at the current level, as far as possible.

The step we are taking together today is one of the most decisive, in that it will most assuredly entail certain repercussions for the internal order of this land in January and February of next year. These repercussions must be accepted, for before the German people starve in any way, it goes without saying that others must bear the burden.

[...][6]

4 The following section contains remarks concerning the grain harvest in Germany.

5 As per Göring's demands at the meeting on 6 August 1942, the General Government was supposed to deliver 500,000 tonnes of bread grains, 100,000 tonnes of feed grain, 25,000 tonnes of meat, 250,000 tonnes of potatoes, and 5,000 tonnes of sugar. These figures had not yet taken into account the requirements of the army and police troops stationed in the General Government.

6 Naumann subsequently reported on the effects of the new food plan.

*1. Grain*

After careful consideration, the grain quota will be increased by 25 per cent, i.e. from 960,000 tonnes to 1.2 million tonnes. The *subsistence farmers' Metze*,[7] which until now has stood at 30 kg per capita per annum, will be raised to 50 kg per capita per annum. This means that the subsistence farmer – that is, a total of 8.8 million people in the General Government who have been permitted to consume 120 kg of bread grains per year thus far – will eat 100 kg per year in future. This step will make it possible to raise the *Metze* contribution from 160,000 tonnes to 264,000 tonnes.

This is the onus we place, and must place, on Polish and Ukrainian farms.

On the other hand, in the food balance sheet from early July, I indicated an overall need for 670,000 tonnes of *bread grains* for the General Government. Reich requirements make it necessary to effect extraordinary savings in the interest of fulfilling all deliveries to the Reich.

Efforts to feed the hitherto-estimated 1.5 million *Jews* will cease, save for an estimated 300,000 Jews who are still working on behalf of German interests as craftsmen or in other capacities. For them the Jewish ration allowances, plus certain special allocations that have proven necessary to safeguard their ability to work, will be retained. The other Jews, 1.2 million in total, will no longer be provided with food.

From 1 January 1943 to 1 March 1943, *ordinary non-German consumers* will receive 2.8 kg instead of 4.2 kg of bread per month; from 1 March 1943 to 30 July 1943, the entire bread ration for these ordinary non-German consumers will be eliminated.

[...][8]

The planned increase in the quota and decrease in the ration allowance must be kept strictly confidential and cannot be made public until such time as the Food and Agriculture Main Department deems proper.

If the decreased ration allowance and increased quota were to be announced earlier, extremely painful disruptions to the collection of the harvest would occur. A great many members of the Polish population would then go out into the countryside and begin to act as additional competitors to our collection agencies.

If the quota increase were to become known prematurely, it would be highly detrimental to the winter sowing and tillage, which is why we have decided to get the winter seed into the ground first and then announce the quota increase.

The General Government has experienced grave, hard times in the food sector over the past three years. However, I believe that the coming year, 1942–1943, will be the toughest one yet in the food sector. Under these circumstances, my colleagues and I will do everything possible to manage the situation.

The *Governor General*: Gentlemen!

You have heard Main Department Head Naumann's very serious remarks. You will also have gathered that any debate about the figures or measures he announced would

7 A reference to an old dry measure for grain; here it stands for the amount of grain subsistence farmers were to be compelled to deliver.

8 In the following section, Naumann defined the group of non-Germans – whom he estimated at more than three million – who were entitled to food because their work benefited the German war economy, and he announced further restrictions on supplies of potatoes and meat. He advocated delaying the planned resettlements in districts Galicia and Lublin to avoid jeopardizing the harvest. Lastly, he called for police supervision of food warehouses and food-processing plants.

be utterly superfluous and in fact completely inappropriate, since any debate would create the impression that another course of action might be possible. I must point out that some sectors of the administration will feel this very keenly. It will affect the *police* above all, since they will have to reckon with the proliferation of illicit trade and what I may call the growing disorder in relation to food supply and consumption. I will gladly grant extraordinary powers to the police so they can deal with these difficulties.

The *economy* will feel it. The decline in productivity will be clearly felt in every area, sector, and line of business. I also assume that our transport system will feel it. The railway workers and the other groups for whom the previous food rations were already insufficient will face extraordinary difficulty in view of the deterioration in their families' living conditions. The monopolies [for spirits] will feel it through the decrease in their income, because the amount of potatoes available for making vodka will be smaller.

But the *Germans* in this territory should not feel it. Despite this new plan, we want to hold tight to the principle that the ration allowances for Germans can be maintained. Nor should the Wehrmacht or the other units quartered in barracks in this territory feel it. We hope that it is possible for us to ensure the full quotas here.

Coinciding with this imperative to help, there is now a move to suspend inspections of people travelling from the General Government to the Reich, above all of military personnel, to check whether they are transporting food out of the General Government. This means that, in addition to all that we must now extract from the land, there is to be a complete suspension of control over that which is doubtlessly being smuggled out of the territory by thousands upon thousands of people, illegally and in violation of our government measures.

So you can see how serious the situation is going to become, but never forget that the Reich's food supply is even less favourable.

In spite of all the difficulties you may observe here in the form of illnesses among your workers, the collapse of your cooperatives, etc., you must always remember that it is still much better for a Pole to collapse than for a German to succumb. Let it be noted in passing that we are sentencing 1.2 million Jews to death by starvation. It goes without saying that should the Jews not starve to death, this will hopefully result in an acceleration of the anti-Jewish measures.

On the other hand, it should also be noted in passing that everyone concerned is now expected to support these government measures. The Reich originally demanded 1 million tonnes from the General Government, but it proved possible to reduce this demand by half.

[…][9]

9 The participants then discussed individual questions and demanded that the Wehrmacht stop purchasing foodstuffs on its own account. State Secretary Boepple closed the meeting with the warning that he would hold accountable anyone who leaked information about the meeting. In addition to the speakers already named, the following individuals also attended the meeting: Bauder, Becker, Behr, Behringer, Bette, Blauert, Breithaupt, von Dazur, Eden, Eißfeldt, Otto Fischer, Gareis, Gerteis, Grafmann, Gschließer, Hermann, Kess, Kobusch, Korff, Krahmer, Krüger, Neumann, Neumann [*sic*], Odenthal, Ohlenbusch, Paersch, Pietschmann, Plodeck, Radtke, Rauber, Reitz, Schöngarth, Schubert, Schulte-Wissermann, Siebert, Tetzner, Topf, Vogel, Watzke, Weh, Wendler, Winkler, Wohlrab, and Zeisner.

## DOC. 124

## On 25 August 1942 the head of the combing-out commission in the General Government provides information on the conflict between the Wehrmacht and the SS in Przemyśl[1]

Report no. 8 (file no. 32/42 secret), signed von Unruh,[2] Przemyśl, 25 August 1942 (copy)[3]

*Report no. 8*
*Przemysl*
Disagreeable incidents occurred here in July.[4] The operation targeting the Jews was supposed to be carried out, but the Wehrmacht did not want to hand over its Jews. As a result, the situation escalated to such a degree that the Wehrmacht, weapons in hand, was deployed against the SS and the police. The bridges were closed to police, whereas the Jews were allowed to pass. The troublemaker in the Wehrmacht was a Captain Dr *Battel* (a lawyer), who assumed the role of the Jews' advocate. He is regarded here as the Jews' great friend and protector. Ultimately the order was issued, apparently by the MiG [Military Commander in the General Government],[5] that the Wehrmacht Jews were to be taken out of the ghetto, barracked, and fed. They were also supposed to receive red Wehrmacht permits[6] and to no longer be subject to police control.

I have straightened out the situation here. It goes without saying that the Jews will live enclosed in the ghetto. Under no circumstances can subordinate authorities be allowed to disrupt the Reichsführer-SS's resettlement work. I have arranged for the Kreishauptmann,[7] the local commander, and the SD[8] to work together to compile a list of the Jews whom we still urgently need for labour for the time being; for other workers to be trained as quickly as possible; and for all other Jews to be released for resettlement at once. Naturally all the Jews will continue to live in the ghetto, and during their working hours they will be under the control of the respective employers, namely the Kreishauptmann and the Wehrmacht. But apart from that, they are unequivocally subject to police oversight. The situation here has been resolved and is now under control. Cooper-

1 BArch, NS 6/794, fol. 32r–v (copy). This document has been translated from German.
2 Walther von Unruh (1877–1956), military general; commander of Rear Army Area 559 from Sept. 1941; the Führer's special representative for reviewing the deployment of military manpower from April 1942; thereafter a US prisoner of war. From 1942 Unruh's Wehrmacht High Command staff, also known as the Heldenklau Commission (the term 'hero-snatching' refers to the practice of commandeering rear-echelon personnel for front line service), was charged with 'combing out' all Wehrmacht agencies and offices to find men who could be sent to the front.
3 The original contains handwritten notes.
4 See Doc. 102.
5 On 15 July 1942 the post of military commander was renamed military district [*Wehrkreis*] commander in the General Government; the position was held by Curt Ludwig, Freiherr von Gienanth.
6 In the original: 'rote Wehrmachtscheine'. It can be assumed that these were a form of certification confirming that the Jews concerned were employed by the Wehrmacht and were permitted to leave the ghetto in order to reach their workplaces.
7 Ernst Peter Paul (1907–1945 or 1948), lawyer; practised law prior to Sept. 1939; later served as police chief in Radom; then deputy Kreishauptmann of Rzeszów; city commissioner in Rzeszów from April 1940; deputy head of the Interior Administration Department in District Cracow in 1941, then department head in 1942; Kreishauptmann of Przemyśl from 16 August 1942 to 1944.
8 The head of the Security Police and the SD in Przemyśl was Adolf Benthin.

ation is assured, so that such incidents will never happen again. However, I request that the MiG be instructed accordingly, because disagreements on this matter seem to have occurred in other places as well. I take the view that the MiG should keep out of this operation, and that the Wehrmacht must understand the necessity for it, and should support the police wherever possible. If our offices and agencies can be certain that the MiG will comply, then there will be no further friction, given the effective cooperation among the individual offices towards which everyone is working. However, the MiG must lift all restrictions. I request further instructions.

Captain *Battel* was the troublemaker here. Even though there is now a capable local commander in place, I consider it necessary to dismiss the *Jew sympathizer* Battel at once.[9]

## DOC. 125

## On 31 August 1942 the NCO Wilhelm Cornides notes what he observed during the deportation of Jews to Belzec[1]

Notes by Wilhelm Cornides,[2] Rawa-Ruska, dated 31 August 1942

*Observations on the 'resettlement' of the Jews in the General Government*
*1. Notes by a German non-commissioned officer, 31 August 1942*[3]
At 12.10 p.m. I saw a transport train arrive at the railway station. Guards with guns were sitting on the roofs and running boards [of the wagons]. You could see from a distance that the wagons were crammed with people. I turned around and walked the entire length of the train: it consisted of thirty-five livestock wagons and one passenger wagon. There were at least sixty Jews in each of the wagons (for transports of military personnel or prisoners, forty men are loaded into [each of] these wagons, but in this case the benches had been removed, and you could see that the people confined in them were standing closely pressed together). Some of the doors were slightly ajar, and the windows were covered with barbed wire. Among the people confined in the wagons, only a few men were to be seen, most of them old; all the others were women, girls, and children. Many children crowded around the windows and the narrow openings. The youngest of them were certainly no more than two years old. As soon as the train stopped, the

9 Himmler learned of Battel's conduct from a report that the Commander of the Security Police and the SD (KdS) in Cracow had prepared for Higher SS and Police Leader Krüger; in a letter to Bormann dated 3 Oct. 1942, Himmler informed him that he intended to have Battel arrested and to initiate Party court proceedings as soon as the war was over: BArch, NS 19/1765, fol. 29.

1 IfZ-Archives, ED 81. Published in Hans Rothfels, 'Zur "Umsiedlung" der Juden im Generalgouvernement', *Vierteljahrshefte für Zeitgeschichte*, vol. 7 no. 3 (1959), pp. 333–336. This document has been translated from German.

2 Wilhelm Cornides (1920–1966), publicist; served in the war from 1939; worked in prisoner-of-war camps as part of a company of interpreters; on sabbatical in Vienna in winter 1942/1943; co-publisher of the journal *Europa-Archiv* from 1946; co-founder of the German Council on Foreign Relations (DGAP) in 1955.

3 Cornides made these observations while on an official trip to Rawa-Ruska and on the train journey past Belzec.

Jews tried to pass bottles or flasks to people outside to get water. But the train was surrounded by SS guards, so no one could get near it. At that moment a train coming from the direction of Jaroslau arrived, and the passengers streamed towards the exit without paying any attention to the transport. A couple of Jews who were busy loading a Wehrmacht truck waved their caps at the people locked in the wagons.

I talked to a policeman who was on duty at the railway station. When I asked where the Jews had come from, he replied, 'Those are probably the last ones from Lemberg.[4] It has been going on like this non-stop for three weeks now. They left just eight people behind in Jaroslau, nobody knows why.' I asked, 'How much further are they going?' Then he said, 'To Belzec.' 'And then?' 'Poison.' 'Gas?' I asked. He shrugged. Then all he said was, 'At the beginning, I think they always shot them.'

Here in the Deutsches Haus,[5] I just spoke with two soldiers from Frontstalag 325. They said that these transports have been coming through every day lately, usually at night. Yesterday one with seventy wagons reportedly passed through.

On the train from Rawa-Ruska to Cholm,[6] 5.30 p.m.:
An empty transport train arrived just as we were boarding at 4.40 p.m. I walked the length of it twice and counted. There were fifty-six wagons. Numbers were chalked on the doors: 60, 70, once 90, sometimes 40 – probably the number of Jews who had been transported in them.

In the train compartment I talked with a railway policeman's wife; she is here visiting her husband. She says[7] that these transports come through every day now, sometimes also with German Jews. She told me that the bodies of six children had been found on the tracks yesterday. The woman thinks the Jews themselves killed these children; they probably perished during the journey. The railway policeman, who is travelling with us as a conductor, came into our compartment. He confirmed the woman's statements about the children's corpses found on the tracks yesterday. I asked, 'Do the Jews know what lies in store for them?' The woman replied, 'The ones who come from farther away probably don't know anything, but those here in the vicinity already know. They try to run away when they realize they are being rounded up. That's what happened recently in Cholm, for instance, where three were shot as they made their way through town.' 'In the railway documents these trains are called resettlement transports,' the railway policeman said. He then added that after Heydrich's assassination, several transports carrying Czechs had passed through.[8] Belzec camp is supposedly situated right next to the railway line; the woman promised to point it out to me when we go past.

4 Between 10 and 23 August 1942, 40,000 to 50,000 Jews were deported from Lwów to Belzec: see Doc. 117.

5 The term Deutsches Haus (literally 'German house') was used to refer to an establishment where the German occupiers could socialize.

6 Chełm.

7 Change in tense as in the original.

8 Heydrich died in Prague on 4 June 1942 as a result of injuries suffered in an assassination attempt. On 12–13 June 1942 two deportation trains from Theresienstadt went to the Lublin area, presumably to Sobibor.

5.40 p.m.:
Short stop. A transport train stops opposite us again. I talk to the policemen riding at the front in the passenger wagon. I ask, 'Are you going back home to the Reich?' With a grin, one of them says, 'You know where we're coming from, don't you? Well, for us the work never ends.' Then the transport train continued on its way. The wagons were empty and swept clean; there were thirty-five of them. In all probability this was the train I had seen at the station in Rawa-Ruska at 1 o'clock.

6.20 p.m.:
We rode past Belzec camp. Up to that point, we had been travelling through tall pine forests for quite a while. When the woman called out, 'It's coming up now', all you could see was a tall hedge of fir trees. A strong, sweetish odour was distinctly noticeable. 'They already stink,' the woman said. 'Oh, nonsense, that's the gas,' the railway policeman said with a laugh. In the meantime – we had travelled approximately 200 metres – the cloying odour had turned into an acrid burnt stench. 'That's from the crematorium,' the policeman said.

Soon after that the fence came to an end. You could see a guardhouse with SS sentries in front. Two railway tracks led into the camp. One was a branch from the main line; the other led out of the camp via a railway turntable to a row of sheds around 250 metres away. A goods wagon was on the turntable just then, and several Jews were busy turning it. SS sentries carrying guns under their arms were standing next to them. One of the sheds was open, and you could clearly see that it was filled to the ceiling with bundles of clothes. When our train moved on, I looked back at the camp. The fence was too high to see anything. The woman said that sometimes you can see smoke rising out of the camp as the train passes by, but I was unable to see anything like that. I estimate the camp is about 800 by 400 metres in size.

2. *Additional eyewitness accounts*
(a) A railway policeman at the marshalling yard in Reichshof[9] had this to say on 30 August 1942:

'A marble plaque with gold lettering will be put up in Reichshof on 1 September because the town will be free of Jews then.[10] The transport trains carrying the Jews pass through the marshalling yard almost every day. They are immediately redirected and usually return the same evening, already swept clean. In Jaroslau 6,000 Jews were recently killed in a single day.'[11]

(b) An engineer recounted the following story at the Deutsches Haus in Rawa-Ruska on the evening of 30 August 1942:

'In addition to Poles and prisoners of war, Jews were also involved in the construction work on the military training grounds being built here; most of them have now been

9 Rzeszów.
10 Kreishauptmann Dr Heinz Ehaus had this plaque mounted on the building in Rzeszów that served as the Kreishauptmann's office.
11 In August 1942 a forced labour camp in Jarosław served as an assembly point and transit station for approximately 10,000 Jews whom the German police deported to Belzec.

deported. The amount of work done by these construction crews (which included women) was around 30 per cent of what German workers would have accomplished on average. Admittedly we only gave them bread; everything else they had to find for themselves. In Lemberg I recently happened to see such a transport train being loaded.[12] The wagons were standing at the foot of an embankment. The way the SS men, some of them wielding truncheons and riding whips, herded the people down the slope and shoved them into the wagons was a sight I will never forget as long as I live.'

The man who gave this account had tears in his eyes. He was around twenty-six years old and was wearing the Party badge. A Sudeten German foreman sitting at the same table commented: 'The other day there was an SS man sitting in our canteen, drunk and crying like a baby. He said he was on duty in Belzec and that if things went on as they had been for another two weeks, he would kill himself because he couldn't stand it any more.'

(c) A policeman at the Ratskeller in Cholm had this to say on 1 September 1942:

The policemen who escort the trains transporting Jews are not allowed to enter the camp. Only the SS and the Ukrainian Sonderdienst (a police force consisting of Ukrainian volunteers) can do that,[13] and they take advantage of this to line their pockets. The other day there was a Ukrainian here who had a wad of cash, watches, gold, and all sorts of things. They find all that when they gather up the clothes and load them.' When asked how the Jews were being killed, the policeman replied, 'First they're told they have to be deloused, and then they have to take off their clothes. After that they go into a room and a blast of heat is released, which already includes a small dose of gas. That's enough to numb them. Then the rest follows. And after that they are cremated right away.'

When asked what had prompted this whole operation, the policeman said, 'Until now the Jews have been used all over as unskilled workers – for the SS, the Wehrmacht, etc. So naturally they overheard all kinds of things, which they passed on to the Russians. That's why they have to go. And then they're also to blame for all the black market dealings and price gouging here. Once the Jews are gone, prices will go back down to reasonable levels again.'

*Note*: Rawa-Ruska is located approximately 80 km north-west of Lemberg. Belzec is situated on the Lemberg–Cholm line, around 40 km north-west of Rawa-Ruska.

12 See Doc. 117. The victims were loaded at Lwów-Kleparów railway station.

13 These were guards from the SS training camp in Trawniki, including Ukrainians and people from other Soviet republics.

## DOC. 126

## On 31 August 1942 Bund member Leon Feiner describes the murder of the Jews in Poland and calls for retaliation against the Germans[1]

Letter, signed L. Berezowski,[2] Warsaw, to National Council delegate Zygielbojm, London, dated 31 August 1942[3]

To National Council Delegate Zygielbojm in London

One of the most shocking and urgent matters with which we in Poland and all the peoples of the world are confronted is the Nazi regime's murder of Europe's entire Jewish population – many millions of souls in total, the majority of whom, approximately 3.5 million, lived in Poland. This problem has moved to the forefront internationally due to both its scale and the manner in which the mass extermination is organized. Therefore it is also the subject of this letter, which, in addition to the news that has been radioed to you several times, also includes conclusions and ensuing demands.

One of the Nazi regime's war aims, as proclaimed on several occasions from the highest Nazi throne, by the Führer himself as well as by Goebbels, is the complete physical extermination of the Jewish population – wherever the bloody, ravenous fist of German fascism reaches. While all its other war aims will ultimately backfire, and the defeat of fascist Germany is inevitable, this aim – the complete extermination of the Jewish population – has already come to fruition. Here the vicious Nazi regime is achieving a complete and easy victory. And even if crushed and defeated, no one will be able to snatch *this* victory from the regime. For by then the Jewish population will have ceased to exist. It will have been 'ausgerottet',[4] just as the Nazis announced. The terrible facts and figures are incontrovertible proof of this; in their monstrosity, they document the mass tragedy of the Jewish population living under Nazi rule, especially in the General Government.

A truly elemental storm has been unleashed over the Jewish community in the General Government and is raging with ever-increasing intensity. One thunderclap after another. This Nazi monster strikes one town after another. The victims are no longer in the hundreds, or thousands, or tens of thousands – but *hundreds of thousands*. The entire community is being exterminated. Children, women, and grown men perish, the flower of the intelligentsia: scholars, writers, lawyers, engineers, physicians. Talent and potential, institutions, work and achievements of every kind are lost. Productive elements such as craftsmen and white-collar workers are also perishing en masse.

The atrocities committed by Nazi criminals in the occupied countries pale in comparison to what these beasts in brown are doing to the Jewish population. The blood curdles in our veins, we stand stunned and petrified in the face of this slaughter – its sheer dimensions and its deliberately vicious forms and methods.

1 AAN, 1325/202/XV-2, fols. 69–74; SPP, 3.1.1.13.5/25, fols. 64–73. Published in Władysław Bartoszewski and Zofia Lewinówna, *Ten jest z ojczyzny mojej: Polacy z pomocą Żydom 1939–1945* (Cracow: Znak, 1969), pp. 963–971. This document has been translated from Polish.
2 Leon Feiner's code name.
3 Handwritten note above the document: 'sent to L[ondon] 26 Nov. [19]42'.
4 German in the original: 'eradicated'.

The blows dealt to the Jewish community from all sides over the course of its centuries-long history pale in comparison. Even the infamous cruelty of the Mongols under Genghis Khan, the Huns under Attila, or the ancient Romans, even the fanaticism of the Middle Ages and other bloody periods of history fade into the background. Even the pogroms against the Jews under tsarist rule, as terrible as they were, seem almost idyllic in comparison. What Nazi fascism is doing to the Jews, in its savagery, its methods, and its dimensions, exceeds even the most bloodthirsty fantasies. In short, for several months now there has been a vast, nightmarish enigma of death, the proportions and reach of which are unprecedented in the history of mankind. An entire people is perishing. And new evil tidings continue to reach us all the time, from this place and that. For the operation continues, here and elsewhere – constant, systematic, and carefully organized.

Even before the German–Soviet war, the situation of the Jewish population under the Nazi yoke was also worse than that of other people oppressed by German fascism. This phase abounded in a variety of utterly inconceivable anti-Jewish regulations. There was extermination on an enormous scale in terms of the food supply, commercial life, cultural life, etc.; concentration camps with dozens or hundreds of victims – this was everyday life at that time for the Jewish people, who were treated far more cruelly in the areas of the Republic of Poland annexed to the Reich, primarily in Łódż. The second phase began after the outbreak of the Soviet–German war. Mass shootings of Jews in the areas vacated by the Soviets – in the Vilna area, in eastern Poland, in Eastern Małopolska,[5] in towns and cities large and small, and in the tiniest settlements – followed one by one in a never-ending stream. Vilna, Stanisławów, Tarnopol, Kołomyja, Stryj, Lwów, and a whole series of smaller localities were the scenes of inconceivable mass murders, the likes of which not even the Nazi gangs had previously committed. And the killing went on and on, systematically, incessantly, with varying degrees of intensity. The lives of hundreds of thousands of victims were claimed during this period.

Finally the third phase came, during which further segments of the already decimated Jewish community were liquidated en masse – including in areas that had already been occupied since the German–Polish war, as well as in the remaining eastern territories. This extermination operation began with the complete liquidation of the Jewish population of Lublin, numbering tens of thousands of people; it is still ongoing and extends ever further.

The most significant link in this monstrous chain of slaughter is the Warsaw ghetto with its 400,000 residents, from which the Nazi executioners have so far snatched about a quarter of a million victims. The 'operation' is still ongoing. The Grim Reaper is working tirelessly. Continuously, uninterrupted, en masse.

Reports have previously been sent with detailed figures illustrating the extent of the massacre of the Jews and the forms it has taken in dozens of towns and cities in Eastern Małopolska and in the area of former Congress Poland.[6] Approximate calculations based on individual data from the most recent period, along with the figures from the preceding phases of the operation, lead to the following tragic totals: of the approximately 3.5 million Jews in the Republic of Poland, the Soviets are said to have deported 0.5 mil-

5 Eastern Galicia.

6 This is a reference to the territory of the Kingdom of Poland which was established by the Congress of Vienna in 1815 and ruled by the Russian tsars until the First World War.

tion to the Russian interior in 1940.[7] Of the remaining approximately 3 million who came under the Nazi yoke (including those who had already fallen into the Nazis' clutches previously), hundreds of thousands of Jews perished of various epidemics, typhus, dysentery, tuberculosis, and starvation (due to the extraordinarily difficult sanitary and hygienic conditions deliberately caused by the Nazi regime when thousands or tens of thousands of people were squeezed into a residential area scaled down to the minimum). *On top of this, approximately 1.25 million Jews perished in the mass murders organized by the Nazi regime. Consequently, between 1 million and 1.25 million Jews are still alive.*

According to descriptions from individual towns and cities, in particular reports on the course of the operation in larger cities, and especially from the *Warsaw ghetto*, the nature of the 'operation' and its methods is as follows:[8]

The operation is carried out by a special destructive unit, the so-called 'Vernichtungskolonne',[9] supposedly independent of the local authorities and receiving orders directly from Berlin;[10] with the help of the SS, the Gestapo, the SD, Shaulis men (Latvians and Lithuanians), and above all the Jewish police.[11] Armed police or military forces surround both the sealed and the still open ghettos, and trucks with armed bandits drive through the ghettos, firing at the inhabitants with rifles and machine guns. The streets are continuously littered with corpses. The operation is referred to as the 'Umsiedlung'[12] of the unproductive population from the ghettos, allegedly to other places, to labour camps, etc. However, this is merely a clever ruse intended to alleviate suspicion and to stifle any emerging active resistance. In reality, in the truest sense of the word, these are transports to death. Productive elements and their families, members and officials of the councils and their families, and the Jewish police and their families are supposed to be spared from the transports, hence from death. The intention is to encourage some to help 'resettle' the others, i.e. to send them to their deaths. But then the 'operation' goes on and on and is also directed against the former helpers, etc. etc., so that ultimately those who are to be kept alive are fewer and fewer. In this way, of the original 400,000 people in the Warsaw ghetto, of whom only 150,000 remained after 4 weeks of the resettlement operation, only 25,000–30,000 Jewish workers are to be kept alive to work in the once huge German factories of Schulz[13] and Tebbens,[14] and for the Wehrmacht. The situation is similar in Lublin, where, out of 60,000–80,000 Jews,[15] only about 4,000 workers without families are left in Majdan,[16] near Lublin. But the same fate – extermination – awaits even this remainder of the elements that are productive for the German authorities.

7 This figure is exaggerated.
8 Changes in tense both here and below as in the original.
9 German in the original: 'extermination unit'.
10 This was a unit controlled by the SS and Police Leader in Lublin.
11 A reference to the Jewish Order Service.
12 German in the original: 'resettlement'.
13 This is a reference to Fritz Emil Schultz's company Schultz & Co.
14 Correctly: 'Többens'.
15 This figure is exaggerated; no more than 40,000 Jews were living in Lublin prior to the deportations.
16 This is a reference to the ghetto located in Majdan Tatarski, a suburb of Lublin, since spring 1942; Lublin-Majdanek concentration camp was on the eastern outskirts of the city.

The orphanages, boarding schools, homes for the elderly, hospitals, and prisons were thus the first to be 'resettled', after which houses and entire streets were blocked off in order to herd the human material destined for slaughter to the assembly point. There the condemned are loaded directly into goods wagons. The extremely cramped conditions, the lack of air, and the stench (people have to relieve themselves in the wagons) are so horrendous that, during unloading at the place of execution, there are always dozens, or even hundreds, of corpses that are tossed out. Initially the old, the sick, the disabled, and children up to twelve years of age were shot at the nearby Jewish cemetery or elsewhere. Later everyone was loaded into goods wagons and liquidated at the destination itself. At one point the Nazi executioners ordered that all the children left in the Warsaw ghetto were to be brought to the assembly point for 'resettlement'. During the process of loading those to be resettled into the wagons, young people of both sexes who are fit for work are picked out and sent to the labour camps, where they live out the remainder of their lives under terrible working conditions, hunger and torture, a situation which quickly results in death. Only a tiny fraction of the total population, amounting to a mere few percentage points, is not sent directly to their deaths. The trains left for the camps at Treblinka, Bełżec, Sobibór (near Włodawa), and elsewhere. On the way, the Ukrainian, Lithuanian, or German guards rob those 'being resettled' of their valuables and other belongings which according to official orders they were allowed to take with them. In the camps, the condemned are made to strip naked and are then executed en masse. This execution takes place by shooting, in gas or vacuum chambers, or by electric shock. The bodies of the murdered are thrown into giant pits, previously dug by the condemned themselves or by bulldozers, which then also fill the pits up again. Often those still alive are also buried in these pits if there is too much [human] material. In many cases the condemned – those being resettled – were loaded into wagons strewn with quicklime, so that they suffocated before reaching their destination, i.e. the place of execution. Their clothes were disinfected and stored for further use by the German authorities. In Sobibór, where the Polish state enterprises for waterproofing railway sleepers were located, the fat is melted out of the corpses of the murdered and flour is ground from their bones for industrial purposes.[17] In some places the authorities order dental technicians to remove gold crowns and teeth from those who have been murdered.

In the ghettos themselves, where hunger reigns due to draconian measures and restrictions on food deliveries, the food prices are many times higher than in other, non-Jewish districts. In the Warsaw ghetto the price of a loaf of bread rose to 80–100 złoty, 1 kg of potatoes went up to 30–40 złoty, and butter up to 250 złoty, while outside the ghetto walls a loaf of bread cost 12–15 złoty, potatoes 3–4 złoty, and butter 120 złoty. In any case, it is impossible to obtain these foodstuffs. The atmosphere in the ghettos is therefore extremely tense, filled with indescribable fear and hopeless despair. There are also widespread cases of insanity and suicide. Parents sometimes poison their children and children poison their parents, so that they do not fall into the hands of the enraged Nazi beasts. There were signs of active resistance here and there. Houses were barricaded. Here and there, armed resistance also occurred, for example in Nieśwież. Naturally these acts of resistance ended in immediate, complete liquidation on the spot

17 These rumours were widespread but cannot be substantiated.

However, these were sporadic phenomena. There has been no active resistance on a mass scale, nor is there, because the condemned cling to the illusion that this is only a resettlement – an illusion which the authorities deliberately, purposefully, and deceitfully uphold in order to stifle any will to resist. It is furthermore a consequence of the interest of other groups (officials, Council members and their families, Jewish police, and persons employed in factories that serve German interests) in ensuring that they are exempt from 'resettlement'. Finally, it is the consequence of the masses being aware that the German thugs proceed according to the principle of *collective responsibility*, on the basis of which everyone would immediately be executed. Those who want to actively resist are faced with the tragic dilemma of whether to put others at risk when they might otherwise still survive. And ultimately there is the awareness that the most important Allies abroad would not react to any active resistance on the part of the Jewish population, and that there is no hope whatsoever for any support from outside the ghetto walls, that they have to drink down to the last drop the bitter cup of their mass departure from this world – without mass resistance. Abused, oppressed, viciously crushed for three years by the most diverse German decrees; imprisoned within the ghetto walls; surrounded by police, military, and gendarmerie; encircled by machine guns; living in an atmosphere of bloody lawlessness, of horror and death, without any hope of help from anywhere – this is the tragic way in which the Jewish population is perishing completely. The politically conscious part of the Jewish working class and the intelligentsia realized that active resistance is necessary, even if such resistance cannot achieve any decisive success on account of the atmosphere and the situation in the ghetto and its surrounding area, which the German authorities have deliberately created. However, conservative Jewish circles have firmly rejected such an idea, citing the immediate, bloody reaction of the German authorities, which would have catastrophic consequences for the entire community.[18] Thus the only potential centres of resistance were paralysed for not wanting to gain the reputation of having caused the immediate slaughter of the entire population by the Nazi gangs. There would be no way of proving that this massacre, albeit in a different form and at a different tempo, would have taken place even without such acts of resistance – as is basically the case now in the Warsaw ghetto and in other cities. I have received news just now from Lwów and from other cities where the 'resettlement' operation is currently in progress – I present it below to give a fuller picture of the current situation.

*Lwów*: After a long period in which approximately 35,000 Jews in Lwów perished during repeated 'operations' carried out by the Nazi bandits (especially in the so-called 'operation under the bridge', in which mainly the elderly were seized[19]), central SS units and the Gestapo began the radical extermination of the Jews three weeks ago. While in previous operations the principle was observed, at least on the surface, that only those considered by the Nazis to be unproductive elements and their families should be seized,

18 When secret exploratory talks were held between political representatives in late July 1942, the Agudas Yisroel representative, Aleksander Frydman, and the former senator and director of Keren Hayesod in Poland, Ignacy Schiper (1884–1943), strongly opposed Jewish self-defence measures.

19 When Jews relocated from Lwów to the future ghetto quarter in late 1941 and Jan. 1942, they had to go through an underpass below a bridge, where German and Ukrainian police officers mistreated and robbed them; several thousand people were taken to Lesienice Forest, where they were shot.

this principle has now been almost completely abandoned. Approximately 55,000–60,000 Jews have been resettled, mainly those employed in various institutions working directly or indirectly for the Wehrmacht. Under pressure from the Wehrmacht, some workers considered indispensable from a military point of view have currently been exempted from the roundup. The so-called municipal workshops, organized according to an American model and operating vigorously, which are directly subordinate to the Stadthauptmann,[20] have lost 2,800 of 3,500 employees, among them the best skilled workers and administrators, including almost the entire medical and healthcare staff. Children were taken away from all the orphanages (these were mostly orphans left behind after people had been murdered in previous operations). The hospitals – three of them – were completely evacuated, including the most seriously ill patients; even patients from the Hospital for Infectious Diseases – suffering from typhus and other contagious diseases, were taken away into the … unknown, along with almost all the physicians, the nurses, the paramedics, the management, etc. The medical staff at both polyclinics, approximately thirty people in all, were also seized (some of the physicians have already been seen in work brigades, performing physical road construction labour). Of course the remainder of the intelligentsia and people in other professions received even harsher treatment. We mention physicians so often in this summary (approximately 200 have been seized so far) mainly because they had been accorded a certain privileged position in previous operations, but now for the first time they have been placed on an equal footing with the rest of the Jews, according to their 'utility value'. As to the fate of those who have been taken away, it can only be established that men in the prime of life are sent to particular forced labour camps, where in conditions of draconian discipline and inhuman torture they perish of starvation and exhaustion or are shot for the slightest offence or for falling ill. In Janowska camp in Lwów, for example (where there are approximately 5,000–6000 people), camp commandants such as Rokita,[21] a certain Wildhaus,[22] or a certain Gebauer[23] shoot between fifteen and thirty people per day. The dentists employed there mostly pull out the gold-crowned teeth of the dead. Some of the more strongly built women are reportedly sent to work in the fields, while everyone else, mainly children, the elderly, and most of the women, is forced to strip naked and is then sent off to be executed (shot with machine guns or poisoned). Apart from the contributions repeatedly paid prior to such operations, at the end of each operation (particularly the last one) the Jews taken away are regularly robbed of their remaining – mostly modest – belongings. Jewish police and even members of the so-called Judenrat[24] have to help with this, which is probably why they are granted a longer 'Galgenfrist'.[25] The approximately 20,000 Jews

20 German in the original. The lawyer Dr Egon Höller was the Stadthauptmann of Lwów from Feb. 1942.
21 Richard Rokita.
22 Correctly: Gustav Willhaus.
23 Gotthard Fritz Gebauer (1906–1979), engineer; joined the SA in 1930 and the NSDAP and the SS in 1931; employed at Siemens; head of the Deutsche Ausrüstungswerke in Lwów, August 1941 – May 1944; worked for the Soviet occupation authorities in Dessau after the war; a member of East Germany's Socialist Unity Party (SED); fled to the West in 1960; sentenced to life imprisonment by Saarbrücken Regional Court in 1971.
24 German in the original: 'Jewish Council'.
25 German in the original: 'stay of execution'.

who remain in Lwów – there were approximately 120,000 when the Germans entered the city – have been allotted a small, neglected area on the outskirts of Lwów, which defies all basic standards of hygiene.[26]

Even more monstrous, even more brutal, were the shootings of the so-called 'Jewish population being resettled' in the street, in courtyards, in apartments (6,000 in Tarnów!), but mostly on market squares or in cemeteries (in Stanisławów, for example, kahal[27] officials were ordered to set up a kiosk in the cemetery with food for the firing squads the day before the mass shootings). Approximately 3,000 Jews were executed.

*Mszana Dolna*:[28] Out of this community numbering approximately 2,000 Jews, 150 are left alive.[29] The rest (including two physicians) were shot after the victims had dug a deep pit. All of this happened within the space of just four to six hours.

Similar bloodbaths took place in *Sambor, Mielec, Rabka, Rohatyn*, and in many other places in Małopolska.

Wieliczka was most recently the site of such scenes.

In *Bochnia* the municipal workshops, the pride of western Małopolska, were burned to the ground just before the operation[30] – even the Nazi press had written about these extensively, just as it had written about the even bigger production plants in Warsaw and other cities in former Congress Poland.

During the 'resettlement operation' from the Warsaw ghetto, the ghettos in Otwock, Falenica, and Miedzeszyn were liquidated in just a few hours, and the famous Medem children's sanatorium, known to educators all over the world, was also completely liquidated. Among the victims were the 250 children and the majority of the medical, nursing, and teaching staff.[31]

Most recently similar 'resettlement operations' – also taking just a few hours – took place in Radom, Mińsk Mazowiecki, Siedlce, etc.

Only a few groups of people have managed to escape this conflagration of mass slaughter, but a tragic fate awaits them too, for the lack of livelihood or opportunities to earn one will drive them into death's embrace sooner or later. While painting this terrible picture of the present realities facing the Jewish population in the General Government, the acts of compassion, support, and assistance on the part of the Polish population must not be passed over in silence.

On the other hand, various forms of blackmail and looting also occurred, along with the theft of the possessions left behind in the homes of 'resettled' people. As a result, the German authorities called upon the population of the surrounding area – as recently took place on the outskirts of Warsaw – to return any stolen Jewish possessions under

26 This area was in Zamarstynów, a neighbourhood in the northern part of the city.

27 Jewish community council.

28 A small town approximately 50 km south of Cracow.

29 See Doc. 156.

30 On 25 August 1942, 4,000 people were deported to Belzec and 500 were shot not far from the town.

31 In 1926 the Bund and the Central Yiddish School Organization (TSYSHO) established a sanatorium in Miedzeszyn, south-east of Warsaw, for children at risk of contracting tuberculosis. It was named after the Bundist leader Vladimir Medem (1879–1923). Prior to 1939 more than 10,000 children had passed through this modern, well-equipped facility, which was run according to the principles of the educational reform movement. The sanatorium was closed down and looted after the German invasion of Poland in Sept. 1939, but the Bund's underground organization reopened it in 1940. The children and most of the staff were deported to Treblinka on 22 August 1942.

threat of the death penalty. They obviously assume that only they – these lords of the Herrenvolk[32] – are authorized to loot other people's property, and especially that of the Jews. Even in the ghetto itself there have been numerous cases of blackmail, mass robbery, and theft, not only by gangs of SS, Gestapo, or Lithuanians, but also by shady Jewish elements, and even by the Jewish police which – apart from a few exceptions – has played and continues to play a very sorry role in this whole monstrous 'resettlement operation'. Although the satanic methods of implementing the 'resettlement plan' were forced upon them by the criminal German authorities, the Jewish police nevertheless carried out this plan to a considerable extent.

However, against this tragic, sad, and negative background, numerous expressions of generosity, mutual help, and quiet heroism shine all the brighter. Mothers torn away from their children followed them to their deaths. Likewise children [followed] their parents. Activists working at orphanages, boarding schools, etc. (such as Janusz Korczak and most of the teaching and medical staff at the Medem sanatorium in Miedzeszyn) sacrificed their lives and went to their deaths along with their children,[33] even though they could have saved themselves.

But this is not the time to go into further detail. The most urgent, pressing, and significant issue is how to save the surviving remnants of the Jewish community from death, a community scattered throughout various towns and cities and targeted daily by the systematic and organized Nazi eradication 'operation'.

*It is about saving the 1 to 1.5 million Jews still alive* – about saving them from certain death. Those dead, murdered, and tortured to death cannot be resurrected. The living must be saved. This is the strongest demand that comes right from the hearts of those still alive. This is also the cry of the hundreds of thousands of Jews from beyond the mass graves, *approximately 1.5 million victims* snatched from the Jewish community by Nazi fascism!

Resolutions and agreements on punishing the Nazi murderers *after* the war are inconsequential and meaningless. For by the time this happens, the part of the Jewish community that is still alive – even if it serves the Wehrmacht's interests as productive and useful Jewish elements – will have been exterminated without a trace, and all that will be left is one gigantic cemetery – the resting place of a Jewish community of several million.

*Immediate and effective action is necessary!*

We are fully aware, and we are firmly and unshakeably convinced, that the Nazi regime and its satellites will be utterly crushed, and that we will build a new world – our world – in its place. The madness with which the Nazi gangs are rampaging throughout all the occupied countries, and especially among the Jews, is most likely one of the unmistakable harbingers of the downfall of warmongering Nazism. These words are not dictated by despair or resignation, but express the desire – apart from purely humanitarian considerations – the strong, unshakable desire that the Jewish community, especially its productive and creative elements, could participate in establishing this new world and new life.

If we touch solely on matters of the extermination of the Jewish population, we do not do so on the basis of some kind of nationalism – which, moreover, is alien to us as

32 German in the original: 'master race'.

33 As in the original, meaning 'the children under their care'.

we indeed recognize the enormity of the world's current sociopolitical and economic problems, and the need to solve them in the context of the interpretations[34] currently imposed upon us. The slaughter of the Jews is without parallel – even against the background of the great atrocities committed in all occupied countries throughout history – and this gives rise to an immediate need to save the hundreds of thousands whom German fascism has condemned to death, but who are still alive.

In view of the mass tragedy of the Jewish community outlined above, which is taking place before our very eyes, we put forward the following *demands*:

1. Retaliatory measures are needed against German citizens living in all Allied territories, with the threat of further immediate reprisals should the slaughter of the Jews continue. This retaliation is to be understood not as a political, but as a strategic act, for what the German authorities are doing to the Jewish population is a war *sui generis* in which the one side – the Nazi gangs armed to the teeth – have cunningly, perfidiously, and deceitfully incapacitated the other side – the Jewish population. Completely defenceless and helpless, the Jewish population has become the target of unparalleled, cruel, and insidious acts of war committed by the knights under Hitler's banner. As a small member of the large Allied family, the Jewish community has the right to demand immediate and effective help from the other Allies in this unequal war.
2. An appeal from the government and the National Council of the Republic of Poland to all free societies of the world, drawing attention to the monstrous Nazi atrocities perpetrated against the Jewish population under the yoke of German fascism. This would also be a call upon the relevant governments to take immediate retaliatory measures (in line with point 1).
3. An appeal from the government and the National Council of the Republic of Poland to Polish society in occupied Poland, urging it render every possible help to the Jewish population.[35]
4. An appeal to the working class (blue-collar and white-collar workers as well as the employed intelligentsia) throughout the world, drawing attention to the Nazi atrocities committed against the Jewish population for what they are and urging them to exert pressure on their governments, in line with the demands in point 1. The main purpose of this is also to address the working class in the Soviet Union, where there are many German prisoners of war and civilian prisoners.
5. Official Authorities[36] must provide significant material relief to the surviving Jewish population, which is utterly impoverished and facing death by starvation.
6. On account of the activities described here and the material relief urgently required, it is necessary to turn to the CKB in New York[37] and to the representatives of the Bund in the Soviet Union[38] and in other countries, insofar as these representatives exist.

34 Possibly an allusion to the Allies' plans to strengthen international cooperation in the post-war period.

35 See Doc. 117, fn. 11.

36 Capitalization for emphasis as in the original. This is probably a reference to the Polish government in London and its agencies.

37 The American delegation of the Polish Bund.

38 In the Soviet Union the Bund was persecuted, its activists were imprisoned, and its leading politicians were murdered.

7. Continuous dialogue with us, prompt information about what has been done and what remains to be done concerning the above issues, as well as information on all other issues of major importance at the national and international levels (sending on any correspondence, documents, etc., as well as significant material relief via the same channels as the correspondence and documents). Everything should be sent for the attention of the CKB member[39] who remains here.

This letter should be forwarded immediately to the CKB in New York, which should confirm receipt.

P.S.: The contents of the interview given to the bearer of this letter[40] must not be shared with Official channels until you and the CKB have read it and returned it to him.

## DOC. 127
## On 2 September 1942 the Jewish Social Self-Help reports on the forced resettlement of 2,000 Jews in the town of Jędrzejów[1]

Letter from the Jewish Aid Committee in Jędrzejów (394/42 I B.), signature illegible, to the Kreishauptmann of Jędrzejów,[2] dated 2 September 1942

*Re*: submission of an activity report for the month of August 1942

On 12 August of this year, the Jewish Aid Committee took over the Jewish hospital for infectious diseases in Jędrzejów,[3] along with its fixtures and equipment, from the Jewish Council in Jędrzejów.

On 28 August of this year, the Jewish populations of Sobków, Małogoszcz, and the communities of Brzegi, Węgleszyn-Oksa, Nagłowice, Prząsław, Mierzwin, and Raków were relocated to Jędrzejów. The number of people relocated is approximately 2,000; they are being looked after by the Jewish Aid Committee and the JS [Jewish Social Self-Help] branch in Jędrzejów. Approximately 1,800 people are being provided with a midday meal at the Jewish soup kitchen, and the relocated people receive medical care in the branch's outpatient clinic. A large number of the relocated people have been given

39 This is a reference to Leon Feiner himself.

40 Jan Kozielewski, code name Karski (1914–2000), lawyer and diplomat; studied law from 1935; thereafter undertook military and diplomatic training; in Soviet captivity in autumn 1939; fled to the General Government and from there to France in 1940; liaison between the Polish government in exile in London and the underground in occupied Poland; conducted talks with Feiner and a Zionist – presumably Menachem Kirszenbaum (1893?–1943), representative of the General Zionists on the Jewish National Committee (ŻKN) – and was accompanied by them when he inspected the Warsaw ghetto in late August 1942; when he returned, he brought with him microfilm containing various documents, including this report; Karski arrived in London on 17 Nov. 1942. Karski reported on the murder of Jews in Poland at meetings with Roosevelt and other figures in July 1943. He was a historian in the USA after the war.

1 AŻIH, 211/489, fol. 2. This document has been translated from German.

2 Dr Friedrich Balluseck (1908–1989), lawyer; joined the NSDAP in 1930 and the SA in 1931; assessor for the government in Liegnitz and Regierungsrat, 1937–1938; Kreishauptmann of Tomaszów Mazowiecki, 1939–1940, then of Jędrzejów until April 1943; religious education teacher from 1949; worked for the Housing Construction Loan Association in Berlin from 1954.

3 A Kreis town in District Radom between Kielce and Cracow.

accommodation. Approximately 600 Jews were relocated to Włoszczowa from some of the neighbouring village communities. They are being looked after by the branch there. The Food and Agriculture Department has allocated food (flour, pearl barley, skimmed milk, and coffee) for the relocated people.

With the evacuation of the entire Jewish population from Sobków and Małogoszcz, the activities of the local JS branches also ceased. The members from those branches are now in Jędrzejów.

The Jewish Aid Committee submitted a request to the Forestry Inspectorate in Włoszczowa regarding the allocation of firewood for the Jewish hospitals in Włoszczowa and Jędrzejów, as well as for the Jewish soup kitchens in the Kreis. The Forestry Inspectorate noted that the respective mayors in charge handle the allocation of firewood.

In July of this year, cash assistance was disbursed in the amount of 9,675 zł. and 55 gr.[4] The relevant reports from Sobków and Małogoszcz are not available.

Enclosed[5] is a monthly balance sheet for July of this year and a budget for September of this year.[6]

## DOC. 128

## On 4 September 1942 the Commander of the Order Police in Eastern Galicia orders that pistol ammunition should be used sparingly during the deportations[1]

Circular decree (marked 'confidential, urgent') from the Commander of the Order Police in District Galicia[2] (Ia-Ib-15 28–42), signed Heitzinger,[3] Lemberg (received by Reserve Police Battalion 133: no. 249/42, 5 September 1942), dated 4 September 1942[4]

*Re*: resettlement of Jews; specifically use of ammunition

Various reports received here concerning the implementation of the plan to resettle the Jews indicate that a conspicuously large amount of pistol ammunition was used in several

4 This is a reference to groszy; 100 groszy = 1 złoty.

5 These enclosures are on the two subsequent pages: AŻIH, 211/489, fols. 3–4.

6 On 15 Sept. 1942 SS men, German policemen, and auxiliary forces surrounded the ghetto and deported approximately 4,500 of its inhabitants to Treblinka.

1 RGVA, R-1323k-2-292b. Copy in BArch, B 162/30095, fol. 66. Published in Longerich and Pohl (eds.), *Die Ermordung der europäischen Juden*, p. 221. This document has been translated from German.

2 Walther von Soosten (1895–1945), policeman; member of the Haase Freikorps in 1919; joined the NSDAP in 1933 and the SS in 1939; commander of Police Battalion 122 from Oct. 1939; worked in the police administration in Dortmund from Nov. 1940, then in Saarbrücken; Commander of the Order Police (KdO) in Lublin from Nov. 1941; KdO in Galicia from early 1942; in Vienna from August 1943; Senior Commander of the Order Police (BdO) in Croatia from May 1944; died in Yugoslavia as a prisoner of war.

3 Franz Heitzinger (1889–1961), policeman; joined the NSDAP in 1941; Ia [operations] officer for the KdO in Galicia; later Oberstleutnant in the Urban Police; in Soviet captivity as a prisoner of war from 1947 to approximately 1955.

4 The decree was sent to the Breslau Guard Battalion, II/Pol.24; the police cavalry squadron; the commander of the gendarmerie; the Urban Police commands in Lwów and Stanisławów; the Urban Police units in Tarnopol, Stryj, Kołomyja, Drohobycz, and Borysław; and Order Police departments Ib and IIIb.

operations involving the German Urban Police and the Ukrainian auxiliary police. The difficult situation in terms of replenishing this ammunition makes it impossible to issue replacement ammunition for the foreseeable future.

If the use of firearms appears necessary in the course of such operations to prevent attempted escapes or to quell resistance, then carbines or rifles should be used, if the situation permits.

## DOC. 129

## On 5 September 1942 the official in charge of deporting the Warsaw Jews to Treblinka orders that the ghetto inhabitants must be registered[1]

Announcement by the Jewish Council in Warsaw,[2] dated 5 September 1942 (handwritten copy)

*Announcement*

By order of the Resettlement Commissioner,[3] the Jewish Council in Warsaw hereby announces the following:

1. *For the purpose of registration*,[4] all Jews in the large ghetto,[5] without exception, must assemble by 10 a.m. on Sunday, 6 September 1942, in the area bounded by the following streets: Smocza, Gęsia, Zamenhofa, Szczęśliwa, and Parysowski Square.
2. The process of assembling the Jews is also authorized to begin during the night of 5 to 6 September.
3. Food for two days and drinking vessels should be taken along.
4. Apartments must be left unlocked.
5. Anyone who does not comply with this order and is found in the ghetto (outside the area specified above) after 10 a.m. on Sunday, 6 September 1942, will be shot.

The Jewish Council in Warsaw.

1 AŻIH, Ring II/54 (187/2), fol. 4. Published in Brustin-Berenstein, 'Akta i zeznania w drugiej części Archiwum Podziemnego Getta warszawskiego', pp. 120–121. The copy for the underground archive of the Warsaw ghetto is based on a poster in German and Polish. This document has been translated from German.

2 The Jewish Council in Warsaw was headed by Marek Lichtenbaum from late July 1942. For more on the subsequent fate of the Council's members, see Doc. 214.

3 Hermann Höfle.

4 The registration operation was part of the last large-scale deportation from the ghetto in 1942. All the ghetto residents who showed up were confined in what was called the 'cauldron' in Miła Street; following selections, many of them were deported to Treblinka.

5 This refers to the larger part of the Warsaw ghetto, north of Chłodna Street.

## DOC. 130
## On 6 September 1942 the sociologist Anna Grasberg asks her daughter's Christian foster mother for help[1]

Letter from Ania[2] in Warsaw to Maria,[3] dated 6 September 1942

Dear Madame Maria,

I'm eternally grateful to finally have at least this opportunity to get in touch with you.

You will understand how I long to talk to you, or at least to exchange a few words about how you and the child are doing,[4] where the little one is now, whether she's still suffering from the skin rash caused by poor nutrition, or from the homesickness and longing that you mentioned during the telephone conversation, which unfortunately took place in my absence.

Only now do I truly understand how Rika's presence filled my life. Nonetheless I'm glad that she's in the countryside, as she'd have had practically no chances of survival in the city.

I have so many questions, but I am so pressed for time and have so little patience, I'll only ask a few. How are you doing financially? How are our friends, the Siennickis, Hulanicka, […][5] doing? I think of you all the time while I'm at work, from 7 a.m. to 5 p.m. Of course I don't find any answers to my questions, and thus no peace. I'm sorry you are in such difficulties, but please believe that I was unable to act differently.

Everything is the same here. Since 2 September the problem with my mother-in-law has been at an end. This pains me very much, as I still hoped I would be able to save her. At the moment I'm doing all I can to make sure that my mother is secure, but realistically I'm not very optimistic. If only Rika, mother, and I were together somewhere in the countryside where I could find any kind of work, even the most difficult. Do you know of any employment opportunities? I know they exist, [that there are] many in fact, but I have no idea where to find them, especially for all three of us.

After all, there are so many country estates, farms, and farmsteads! Isn't it possible to find some kind of work there? Naturally a larger country estate would be ideal, as it would be more secure, but that doesn't matter so much. What matters is that it would be the only chance of survival.

1 AŻIH, Ring II/245 (209). Published in Tatiana Berenstein (ed.), 'Materiały i dokumenty z drugiej części podziemnego archiwum getta warszawskiego, tzw. Archiwum Ringelbluma II', *BŻIH*, nos. 71 and 72 (1969), pp. 137, 140–144, here pp. 143–144. This document has been translated from Polish.

2 Dr Anna (Ania) Grasberg, née Minkowska (1906–1942), sociologist; obtained her doctorate in 1935; married Norbert Grasberg in 1937, then lived in Paris; travelled to Warsaw with her daughter Erika (Rika) shortly before Sept. 1939 and was unable to return; later worked for the Ostdeutsche Bautischlerei-Werkstätte, a carpentry workshop in the Warsaw ghetto.

3 Maria's surname is unknown.

4 On 27 August 1942 Anna Grasberg sent her daughter to live with people she knew on the 'Aryan side': Irena Milewska, née Erika Grasberg (b. 1938); resident of the Warsaw ghetto from 1940; lived with 'Madame Maria' from late August 1942, then with Halina and Tadeusz Paszkowski in the city's Żoliborz district, and finally in a children's home; adopted in 1948; emigrated to France in 1976.

5 One name is illegible.

Dear Madame Maria! I know that I've already overburdened you and shouldn't trouble you any further. However, as I stated before, it is all because of the circumstances. And the desire to live and stay alive even more so! I don't doubt that, because you understand things so well, you will grasp my meaning. It's very urgent. You can't imagine how urgent.[6] My job is rather illusory; in any case, it's very uncertain. Mother has no work at all, which essentially means that she doesn't have a ticket to life. We have nothing more to lose. Can you or one of your closest relatives help me, or rather help us? After all, what will become of a child who lost her mother at such an early age? And one would so like to live a little longer. Please forgive this letter and my renewed request. In this moment, you are my only hope. I am eagerly and anxiously awaiting your reply. The bearer of this letter and the package is supposedly a very respectable young man. This is why, despite the immense costs, I have decided to send both to you. Would you please be so kind as to confirm receipt of these things, according to the enclosed list, and to write something about the matter that is most important to us?

I greet and kiss you with all my heart, dear madam, and for Rika I'm sending all the tenderness I am able to muster.[7]

## DOC. 131

## An unidentified witness describes her experience of being trapped in the 'cauldron' on Miła Street in the Warsaw ghetto on 6 September 1942[1]

Handwritten record, unsigned, for the underground archive of the Warsaw ghetto, Warsaw, written after 6 September 1942

The night of 5 to 6 September. 4 a.m. I am woken up by commotion in the rooms next door, on the stairs, and in the courtyard.[2] The neighbours inform me that by 10 a.m. all Jews must assemble in the streets next to the Umschlagplatz:[3] Gęsia, Smocza, Niska, Nalewki.

It seemed like the finale of a six-week-long game with the Warsaw Jews. Indescribable panic among the people. One can distinguish two groups: those who, as a result of the operation, have got out of the habit of being attached to things such as clothes and bedding. They decide to take only the most necessary items with them. The others still strongly believe that the Jews will be able to settle down in a new ghetto and, more importantly, are unable to leave their belongings to fate, so they pack suitcases, bundles, oh! – even bedding. The extent to which people have lost their minds and don't know what to do is demonstrated by the fact that an old man stops me in the courtyard and asks me in desperation what he should do – a gentleman over 50 years old who, in any

6 The roundups on Miła Street began on 6 Sept. 1942.

7 The letter in the underground archive of the Warsaw ghetto is probably a copy made by the author.

1 AŻIH, Ring II/270 (206). Published in Sakowska (ed.), *Archiwum Ringelbluma: Konspiracyjne Archiwum Getta Warszawy*, vol. 1: *Listy o Zagładzie*, pp. 140–143. This document has been translated from Polish.

2 The use of the present tense throughout most of the document reflects the usage in the original.

3 German here and below in the original.

other circumstances, could have instructed me on account of his greater life experience. In general, throughout the entire operation I observed what a strong influence a calm person can exert on agitated people: they cling to him as if they were seeking his help.

However, the most surprising thing is that the Jewish police – hitherto secure and untouchable – must also leave their block and assemble on Wołyńska. Their families, previously protected, drag their bundles in the direction indicated. Nevertheless, the police are still very self-confident and believe until the last moment that they will escape with their lives.

6 o'clock. The streets, which were deserted until today, are now teeming with people. All in all, there are four hours left. Crowds of people trundle down Smocza, Nowolipie, and Zamenhofa. A terrible sight. The bundles, sacks, bedding, and junk make the most horrible impression on me. People still believe so firmly that perhaps, just maybe, they might survive. And on Smocza – a completely novel sight. On both sides of the street, Jewish policemen regulate traffic and monitor the boundaries, making themselves comfortable on chairs. For weeks these chairs, acting as silent witnesses, marked the Warsaw Jews' way to the so-called large Umschlag[platz].

People mainly go with their szopy. At approximately 8 a.m., the Community announced that some, probably nine szopy and establishments, had been allocated blocks within new boundaries: naturally this affected Tebens,[4] Schultz, and my szop as well. The remaining szopy not mentioned on the list are probably already doomed to destruction. People's despair knows no bounds.

I stand on the balcony on Miła, overlooking Miła, Lubeckiego, and Niska streets. Uncountable masses of people swarm through the streets. A wave of people – reminds me of cattle being driven to the slaughterhouse. Here and there groups have already settled on the roadway, on the pavement, and in the ruins of burned-out houses – veritable campsites. In some places individual szopy have already occupied the buildings 'allocated' to them. The brutality with which the newcomers treat the previous residents is noteworthy. The former feel secure (they do not know what awaits them), while the latter have had the rug pulled out from under them. I saw how, in the house allocated to Röhrich,[5] in which OBW[6] employees had previously lived, the Jewish Werkschutz[7] dealt blows to the heads of old women who had left their previous apartments for a moment and now wanted to return.

My szop is being re-established in the ruins of a burned-out house. The mood among the people fluctuates. Sometimes it's as if in expectation of a blockade,[8] at other times it seems as if it's only a matter of temporary barracking. People look around the new apartments and complain about the lack of water, toilets, and electricity. The day before we had a terrible blockade that decimated our szop. Among those present are many

4 Correctly: Többens.
5 This was one of the largest firms in the Warsaw ghetto; it was owned by Curt Röhrich (1883–1972), businessman; joined the NSDAP in 1940; sack factory owner in Magdeburg; in 1942 ran a factory at 80 Nowolipie Street that produced sacks as well as waterproof covers for carriages and wagons; after the war he lived in Magdeburg until 1951; later lived in Hildesheim.
6 Ostdeutsche Bautischlerei-Werkstätte, a carpentry workshop in the Warsaw ghetto.
7 German in the original, here and below: 'factory security'.
8 During 'ghetto operations' individual apartment blocks or sections of streets were blocked off from the outside so that raids could be carried out.

families torn apart, who suffer the greatest despair. In general, everyone is dead tired above all else; it is terribly hot, there is no water.

The German factory owners arrive around afternoon. A mood of anticipation. People are at the end of their tether. They would put up with several families crammed together in the worst hovels just to survive. Next to me – a woman, who was probably formerly accustomed to greater luxury than I, is downright indignant when I tell her that the new rooms stink unbelievably. 'In Łódź people lived under worse conditions,' she says.

One of the Jewish directors announces happy news: perhaps we will return to our old block in an hour. Indescribable joy. Only here and there a few anxious questions arise as to whether they will let everyone through. People are feverishly tidying up their appearance. Everyone wants to look particularly 'fit to work'. The men put on ties, the women put on headscarves and aprons over their dresses. I remember how I myself succumbed to this general psychosis and went to an acquaintance's apartment to ask them for a headscarf and an apron. I was told to take whatever I want. The most expensive and beautiful objects were lying around on the floor and the furniture. In general, all the apartments looked like after a pogrom; people were feverishly sorting through their belongings to fish out whatever was most valuable.

The directors order us to line up in rows of five. Now that it's all over, I shudder to remember the joy of the people, or their closest relatives, who later went to their deaths. The men threw their hats into the air, parents embraced their children.

Many strangers (the 'wild ones'[9] of today) line up along with the szop. They want to sneak back into their old apartments. The German factory owner states that if a stranger is found in a row of five, all five will be removed. People are seized with fear. Questions are heard: Do you have an Ausweis,[10] who are you, etc. Everyone moves away from the strangers as if they were lepers. In my row of five there was a woman who did not belong to the szop. She was forcibly pulled out of the row, and one of our foremen, Fels, holds forth, declaring that so-called local patriotism is indeed quite justified, for why should 'our people' fall victim to 'strangers'? It's interesting – who is one of us, and who is a stranger, I wonder?

The joyful mood fades. Everyone has misgivings. Green SS uniforms approach from afar, heralding disaster. We are now standing on the corner of Niska and Miła streets. That place still fills me with terror. A group of workers assembles next to us, probably from the Ost-bahn.[11] The men line up in rows and display their strength and vitality as if at a slave market. Most of them have athletic figures and are in sports shirts, flexing their muscles. Germans from the Werkschutz come and inspect their slaves; I am almost waiting for the scene from 'Uncle Tom's Cabin' – that they also check the teeth, as one does with horses, to see whether they are healthy. It is terrible to watch so many grown, strong men line up in rows and cower before a few Germans.

We take a few steps forward. It is difficult to walk; the rucksacks are heavy, small children squirm between our legs as we make our way on foot in the scorching heat.

We stop right on the street corner. The inspection begins. It goes very quickly. I am standing towards the back, so I can hardly see what is happening. The closer I get to the

9 This is a reference to women and men who were not registered as workers.
10 German in the original: 'identity card'.
11 German in the original: Eastern Railway.

checkpoint, the more clearly I see a crowd of people; on the right side it grows larger and larger, women and children, very few men, mainly children. At this point I can already clearly recognize familiar faces. In front, two Ukrainians guard the group that is destined for the wagons. Fresh victims from the rows of five keep heading in that direction. Now it is my row's turn. In front of me is a very young woman with her lovely child in her arms. The SS officer's whip lands on her head. A Jewish policeman quickly pulls her out of the row, the husband follows the woman. A boy pulled out of the row cries out: Mama! The mother has been let through and is afraid to turn around and look at her child. For once, no shots were fired during our selection. We were told that people were dropping like flies elsewhere.

Two SS officers inspect us. With whips in hand, of course. Just one moment: the sentence is handed down. The entire row of five runs in the direction of those who have been released. They order us to kneel. We kneel, one row of five after another. The SS men count us like cattle for the slaughter. The company has been assigned 750 people. Jewish policemen help with the counting. Never in any previous blockade have the Germans treated Jewish policemen in such a way. They beat them at every opportunity. We who are kneeling thought that we had already been through hell, but not at all! Suddenly a German discovers a child hidden among a row of five. He drags the child out, along with the mother. Parallel to the rows of kneeling people are lines of wagons and rickshaws loaded with baggage; porters stand next to the wagons. Suddenly a German kicks a rickshaw. Suitcases fall down, revealing the figure of a little boy, perhaps five years old. A Jewish policeman takes advantage of the German's momentary distraction and pushes the child into a row of five, between two girls laden with rucksacks. The bulky rucksacks conceal the boy, but I can see his little head trembling. One must add that this policeman is the child's uncle.

We no longer look behind us. There is only the sound of screams and weeping. A car stops near us. The driver, also in SS uniform, gets out. His face looks monstrous, as does the face of every SS man to a Jew. He speaks Polish like a Prussian. He walks past us, observes us intently, just for a moment, and then a new kneeling victim is pulled out and runs, driven with a whip, towards the group of condemned people. All women. People hold their breath. The driver searches a coat that someone next to me is holding to see if there is a child hidden in it. He walks on.

Jewish policemen come with the terrible news that a further 30 women are required from the rows of those released. And again there is the renewed torment and fear, that perhaps I … Tired figures rise one after the other and go to their imminent death. Now the Jewish directors intervene. Often it is up to them who remains. A young girl pulled out of the row calls out to the director (Bergazyn):[12] 'Mr Director! You knew my father!' The director raises his arms helplessly. A woman struggles against a policeman. A German comes running, a whip lashes out, the woman runs, she fears a bullet. Lejkin drives up in a rickshaw, checks the efficiency of his little soldiers,[13] strikes a pose in front of the Germans.

12 Eljasz Bergazyn (1892–1942), retailer; originally from Dobrzyń nad Drwęcą in western Poland; managed a joinery workshop in Bernhard Hallmann's business enterprise on Nowolipki Street in 1942; considered a collaborator; shot by a Jewish Combat Organization (ŻOB) squad in the Warsaw ghetto.

13 This is a reference to men from the Jewish Order Service.

The knees hurt, the rucksacks weigh us down, the heart is full of impotent fear.

When will this finally end, when will we finally leave? It is hard to believe when we are ordered to get up. We walk along an empty Smocza Street. The sight of the street comes as a shock. On both sides are the chairs left behind by the policemen; brand new rucksacks, only just sewn, lie in the gutter, stuffed full – left behind by those taken to Treblinka. We walk on. We see our entrance gate from a distance. We all walk on: mothers without children, children without parents, men without wives; once again we have escaped death.

## DOC. 132

## On 6 September 1942 a Jew from Lesko writes a farewell letter to his children[1]

Letter from Yoysef[2] from Lesko[3] to his children, dated 6 September 1942

Dear children,

I'm letting you know that I must pluck up the courage to write about my situation, namely [the Jews of] Istrik[4] were deported yesterday. All of us – men, women, and children – are going today. And just like that [the Jews of] Istrik are gone too. We are not going far, to a village near Linsk.[5] Shmuel Leyb has already been working there the whole time. People say that 3,000 able-bodied men will remain there[6] and the rest will be scrapped.[7] Around 15,000 people are being deported from all of Kreis Sanok.

Now you understand my situation and that of all the Jews here. It seems to me that even the destruction of Jerusalem was not [as bad as] this.

Dear children, it would evidently seem that I am writing you a farewell letter and taking my leave of you and also of this world, because people such as me should expect nothing. Yet it states in our Torah that 'even if a sharp sword rests upon a man's neck, he should not desist from [praying for] mercy'.[8] This means that even if a sharp sword

1 YVA, O-75/540. This document has been translated from Yiddish.
2 Surname unknown.
3 A small town influenced by Hasidic Judaism in District Cracow, Kreis Sanok, approximately 70 km south-west of Przemyśl.
4 The Yiddish place name Istrik is used in the original and refers to the town of Ustrzyki Dolne. The approximately 3,000 Jewish inhabitants were deported to the forced labour camp in Zasław near Sanok.
5 The Yiddish place name Linsk is used in the original and refers to the village of Lesko. The Jewish inhabitants of Lesko were also taken to the forced labour camp in Zasław; from there, two transports with 4,000 to 5,000 people left for Belzec on 9 and 11 September 1942.
6 The forced labour camp in Zasław existed from autumn 1940 to autumn 1943 on the premises of a former cellulose factory and was occupied by 1,200 to 1,800 Jews from Poland and Slovakia. Some 15,000 people in total passed through the camp. Upon its liquidation, the approximately 1,500 remaining inmates were deported to Sobibor.
7 In Hebrew in the original up to the Yiddish expression 'oyf shmelts', which was used for the mass murder of the Jews; *shmelts* literally means scrap or rejects, and designated those who were deemed unfit for work.
8 Babylonian Talmud, Berakhot 10a.

is pressed to your neck, you should not refuse [to ask for] mercy – G-d[9] can still help. G-d can still help me and the Jewish people as a whole. You, children, can still entreat G-d, should the letter reach you and you still have time to ask.

As far as we can tell, all of this has been decreed by heaven. And if it is a decree,[10] then every Jew must accept it with love and go knowing that he is offering Him a sacrifice on earth that shall serve as an atonement for sin – for himself and for all the people of Israel. If the Creator so wills it, there can be no other way.

You children should not think that I have abandoned hope entirely, however. For as long as my eyes remain open, I will continue to hope that the Creator of all worlds will still help. But should G-d save you children and you survive through the Creator's will, do not forget me or that you had a father in this world. And you, Moyshe, are to give a note[11] for me to a tsaddik[12] from the Rizhin dynasty.[13] And if Shloyme, may good health be upon him, survives, you must tell him about it – he will know what to do. I am also sending you the address of our [relative in] Israel: A. Weiss, Tel Aviv, Ben Yehudah 161, Palestine. If, with G-d's help, you survive, get in touch with him immediately. Write to him straight away and he will commemorate me there, at the holy sites. Also [inform] the admor from Leipzig,[14] may he lead a long and good life. And if the admor from Czernowitz, may he lead a long and good life, survives, you should mention me to him in a letter. And you children should cling to faith and trust – G-d will surely help. But who will live to see the good [yet to come]? I hope to G-d that this is granted to you young children. I ask you not to forget me, not to disregard the Creator, and to hold fast to your Jewish faith and ways until the end.

My dear Faydshe, I understand your situation, you poor thing, but what can be done that you were born into such a sinful generation? From the day you were born until now, you have not really lived, you unfortunate soul. However, if G-d helps you to survive, you will still be able to experience life. May G-d guard you from pitfalls. Pray to G-d. You have not sinned yet, so G-d will help you.

Beloved children, I do not have time to write much. Stay healthy and strong and do not forget G-d for as long as you shall live, and don't forget me either. But if G-d helps, we will be able to see each other again in person. With G-d, everything is possible. Do not take your life, for that is heaven sent. I ask only that He aids you children and protects you from every obstacle so that you survive. You will be able to write to Shmuel Leyb in Zasław in Kreis Sanok. I believe that he will remain there working.

9 In the Yiddish original the term used throughout this letter for 'God' translates literally as 'The name, blessed be He' (*hashem yisborekh*). Since the author of the letter was very pious, he always used this phrase to avoid mentioning the name of God.

10 In addition to decree, the term *gzeyre* used here can also mean 'punishment inflicted by God'.

11 This refers to the *kvitel*, which is a note with a petitionary prayer of a Hasidic Jew given to his tsaddik.

12 Leader of a Hasidic community.

13 Rizhin is the name used in the Yiddish original. It refers to the town of Ruzhyn in present-day Ukraine. The dynasty meant here refers to descendants of Hasidic Rabbi Yisroel of Rizhin (1797–1850) in Bukovina.

14 Yisroel Friedman (1878/1879–1951), rabbi; descendant of the Hasidic Rizhin dynasty from Bukovina; settled in Leipzig after his father's death in 1917; travelled to Palestine in 1934, then in Switzerland; active in a synagogue in Tel Aviv from 1939.

Stay healthy and strong. I send you many kisses. May this letter remind you in the future that you once had a father in this world. I wish you *ksive vekhsime toyve*,[15] along with a good and blessed year.[16]

Your father,

Yoysef

## DOC. 133
## On 8 September 1942 the representative of the combing-out commission praises Globocnik for his efforts in murdering Jews[1]

Report by Reichsleiter Bormann's representative on the staff of the Wehrmacht High Command for special assignments,[2] Deputy Gauleiter Albert Hoffmann[3] in Lemberg, to Reichsleiter Bormann at Führer Headquarters (received on 12 September 1942, log no. Dept. II/19287), dated 8 September 1942[4] (excerpt)

*Report no. 5*
*Radom and Lublin*
[…][5]
P.S. For your information I would like to add the following:

1. Several days ago I combed out the industry and trade sector in Cracow, freeing up 500 individuals for the Wehrmacht. Together with the 700 civil servants and public agency employees, the number for Cracow comes to around 1,200 people.
2. I am enclosing a leaflet and a circular with the report.[6] Both items were produced by the Polish resistance movement and show how skilfully the Polish resistance movement operates. Even the envelopes and the stamps are forged.
3. Brigadeführer *Globocnik* is currently carrying out the evacuation of Polish Jews as part of a special mission.

15 The traditional greeting during the High Holidays: 'a good inscription and seal' (in the Book of Life). The Jewish New Year and the ten days beginning with the first New Year's Day until Yom Kippur are considered days of reflection. According to tradition, during this period God judged the behaviour of each individual (inscription) and sealed the judgement on the Day of Atonement.
16 The Jewish New Year Rosh Hashanah 5703 took place on 12 and 13 Sept. 1942.

1 BArch, NS 6/795, fols. 161–185, here fol. 185. This document has been translated from German.
2 For more on General Unruh's Wehrmacht High Command staff, see Doc. 124.
3 Albert Hoffmann (1907–1972), salesman; joined the SA in 1925 and the NSDAP in 1926; department head on the Deputy Führer's staff from 1934; joined the SS in 1936; worked in Austria in 1938, then in the Sudetenland; deputy Gauleiter of Upper Silesia from April 1941; worked on the Unruh Commission as Bormann's representative in 1942; Gauleiter of Westphalia-South from 1943; interned, 1945–1950; subsequently worked as an entrepreneur in Bremen.
4 Handwritten note: 's[een] 18 Sept. Fri[edrichs]'; Helmuth Friedrichs (1899–1945?) was the head of Dept. II (Party affairs) in the Party Chancellery.
5 In the report Hoffmann described his observations during his stay in districts Radom and Lublin (particularly conversations with Governor Kundt of District Radom, the unauthorized appropriation of Jewish property, and the conflict between the civil administration and the SS in District Lublin) and made suggestions on how to combat the Polish underground more effectively.
6 These are not included in the file.

The following valuables have been seized so far:
some 50,000,000 Reichsmarks in banknotes;
approximately 500,000 paper dollars;
and 60,000 gold dollars,
5,000 English pounds,
50,000 gold roubles, and
10,000 gold francs,
as well as many ducats and other coins worth about 10,000 Reichsmarks; approximately 2,000 valuable pieces of jewellery such as rings, pendants, and the like; and some 1,000 wagonloads of textiles, including approximately 300,000 new dresses, an additional 300,000 sets of used garments, and around 5 million kilos of rags.

Commendable work by Party Comrade *Globocnik*, who knows how to do the job, certainly not a pleasant one, with a great deal of discretion and the necessary rigour.

4 enclosures.[7]

## DOC. 134

## A forced labourer in the Warsaw ghetto looks back on his experiences between 11 July and 11 September 1942[1]

Handwritten record by a forced labourer for the Ostdeutsche Bautischlerei GmbH with the first name of Nosn,[2] unsigned, Warsaw, recorded on 10 December 1942

Dedicated to the luminous memory of my beloved only daughter, Ninkele.

Not long ago, on 11 July 1942, we celebrated your birthday. You turned three. Close, good friends – Polie with her Vishke, Felie with Vlodek and Nelushe, Felke Faynlikht with her Rutke – and many others [came]. How many toys – moving, noisy, mechanical, piled up there! How much childish glee, noise, and commotion! And raising a glass of tea, we wished wholeheartedly that you might celebrate your fourth birthday in freer circumstances. And today? No more Ninkele, nor her mother, nor my sister Etl, who so delighted in [Ninkele's] development and cleverness, who so marvelled at her intelligence, initiative, and playfulness. Even the three-year-old knew what a blockade is and what role a Jewish policeman plays as the one who rounds up old people and young children. Even she already knew to hate them.

To my sister in New York, Polin (nicknamed Pesha) Daytshman living at 1468 Leland Avenue in the Bronx: if I don't make it, whoever has the chance to do so shall send this insignificant (because things a thousand times worse have happened) account of our family to you. Your brother, Noske.[3]

7 These are not included in the file.

1 AŻIH, Ring II/255 (201), fols. 2–12. Published in Polish translation in Sakowska (ed.), *Archiwum Ringelbluma: Konspiracyjne Archiwum Getta Warszawy*, vol. 1: *Listy o Zagładzie*, pp. 134–139. This document has been translated from Yiddish.

2 Possibly Nosn Smolar (1898–1943); originally from Zambrów; lived in Warsaw, where he perished in 1943.

3 Diminutive of Nosn (Ashkenazic form of the name Nathan).

The Job-like tale of our family begins with our dear mother, in Zambrów,[4] at the end of July 1941. A week earlier she had decided to risk her life and, using a gold watch (Father's wedding gift), set off on the perilous journey to Białystok to find out if her children were still alive. She took with her for her children a little sack of rusk, a small amount of buckwheat groats, and oil, because the Jews in Białystok were afraid to go out into the street to procure a little food. In Białystok she found only me and Etl, who had fled to Białystok from Zambrów on the second day of the war.[5] Ester left Białystok immediately on the first day and there has been no news of her; Hershl [left] on the second day and has gone missing somewhere among the evil ones. I received greetings from him from somewhere in the Baranowicze area. Mother returned home that same evening – she was with us for one day in total. And a week later, the German murder squads entered Zambrów, assembled the entire shtetl, and chased everyone out into the streets. Some 1,500 old and young people, men and women with small children, were rounded up and taken to a forest around Czyżew, where pits had already been dug. There they were all killed.[6] The news reached us in Białystok three weeks later. We – especially Etl, Mother's anxious, coddled baby – took it very badly.

After a time we made our way from Białystok to Warsaw, first me and later Etl. How happy Etl was when I succeeded in organizing a place for her as an educator in a boarding school for orphans! How heartily she devoted herself to the children! How often she sat for hours humming a suitable song to the children, playing a game with them, loving them like a mother loves her own children. Today the children no longer exist – Etl no longer exists. I have jumped ahead a bit chronologically. Forgive me, sister.

Some time before the 'resettlement' commenced (this was the name the Germans gave to the mass murder of Jews), the prelude or prologue to this tragedy began when shootings started to occur in the streets. Just like that, a car drives by and [the vehicle's occupants] shoot passing Jews from it. Then an organized night-time mass shooting, some 50 Jews taken from their apartments and led a few buildings down. They were told to walk ahead and then were shot from behind.[7] Later, another 100 people were taken from prisons and shot; an announcement was made to the effect that this was a punishment for not following orders from the German authorities or even acting against them. And again dozens, hundreds – individual murders. Rumours circulated, each one bleaker than the next, that [the Jews] were going to be deported from Warsaw to somewhere outside the city. People didn't believe them – how could that be possible, to be expelled from Warsaw, such a truly Jewish city, a city with over 400,000 Jews? While it might happen to the homeless and the newcomers, it would never happen to those born in Warsaw! Until it began. Placards appeared – all Warsaw Jews – with the exception of …[8] The exceptions [were key]. Had there not been any, then perhaps there would not have been so many victims. Then perhaps a self-defence [organization] would have been

4 Small town in Bezirk Bialystok, occupied by the Soviets from 1939 to 1941. The approximately 2,000 Jews who remained after mass shootings were confined in a ghetto in 1941 and used for forced labour.

5 That is, after the Wehrmacht's attack on the Soviet Union, which began on 22 June 1941.

6 In August and Sept. 1941 some of the Jews of Zambrów were murdered, after selections, in nearby wooded areas.

7 See Doc. 64.

8 See Doc. 98.

formed. Then perhaps it would not have reached such shameful proportions, with more than 300,000 Jews, including tens of thousands of young, healthy people, being led like sheep to the slaughter.

'With the exception of' the notices stated: with the exception of all those who work in the szopy, in the institutions of the Community,[9] in the supply offices, for social institutions (Jewish Aid Committee,[10] CENTOS, TOZ), craftsmen's associations, and others. And all these [people who fall under an exception] take their wives and children under their protection (so they do not have to be deported).

A great scramble began. Already 90 per cent had papers stating that they belonged to the privileged categories that were not to be deported, by the time the Jewish police managed to deport all the poorest newcomers from the refugee points [and] the poor people from their homes who did not have the means to buy their way out.

I too, a Community employee, got myself a place in a szop – I became a joiner. After much trouble, my wife and child also came under the protection of the szop, even though she was also a Community employee.

[These steps were taken] because panic had already set in that the YHK (Jewish Aid Committee) IDs would no longer be recognized, that soon even [holders of] the Community IDs would not be tolerated. 'Szopy', on the other hand, became a 100 per cent foolproof amulet. And as if to confirm the rumours, people gave examples: just now someone from the YHK, now someone else from the Community, has been seized, regardless of their papers. When I finally received my registration card with the red SS stamp, I felt safe and reassured. My family, for whom I received a separate confirmation for family members, was also protected. Erring on the side of caution, I took my wife and child with me to the factory, as did hundreds of other szop workers. They waited it out in the courtyard of our factory (at 30 Gęsia).[11] Well hidden, far from any evil eye, they spent their days there, and once the fiends – Jewish police, as well as German SS gangs with their Ukrainian, Lithuanian, and Latvian Nazi servants – had finished their day's work, they would return home to spend the night, often not getting undressed due to the constant night-time shootings and wild rumours about nocturnal pogroms.

Until one day the amulet of the szop [the permit] lost its power. To my misfortune our szop was the first where its protection was breached. This was Friday, 7 August (a total of 17 days after the mass killings began). The women, children, and elderly were sitting in the courtyard, as they did every day, well hidden and not visible from outside, when the SS with the Ukrainians burst in from the back – through a fence from the neighbouring courtyard. The crowd was surprisingly calm. Everyone was ordered to stand up and proceed in orderly fashion to the gate, just to have their papers checked. Everyone had papers, so people were calm and went to the gate: Where are the papers? What papers? Keep going. Anyone who dared to utter a word, to oppose this, received a few blows straight to the face from whips and riding crops, and then everyone kept moving. We, the men, did not even know what was going on because the factory has to run at full speed. Everyone has to be at his place. They didn't even look in the factory then; they took everyone [who had been in the courtyard] and led them to the

9 That is, of the Jewish Council.
10 This refers to the Yidisher Hilfs-Komitet (YHK).
11 Ostdeutsche Bautischlerei GmbH was located here.

Umschlagplatz[12] (the modern-day version of Golgotha, from where they were taken in wagons to the massacre site at Treblinka, where the mass executions were carried out by gas and shooting).

I then raged in vain like a wounded animal in a cage. I ran to the Umschlagplatz and paid to find out whether Ester (my wife) and Ninkele were still there. Afterwards I sent money, a lot of money, to bribe the police through Dr R.[13] Our own factory police[14] were sent. I managed to find out that they had succeeded in avoiding the first transport of 6,000 people, which left at 11 a.m. However, they were driven out of their hiding places with violence and blows when the second transport left the same day. Nothing could help. With the child on her hands it was impossible [for Ester] to avoid [her] bleak fate. I received the message that people had seen her with Ninkele in her little red coat on the way to the wagons. In vain I made further efforts. I phoned someone who had business connections with the camp administration in Treblinka. He said he could do nothing, everything is death there. (He himself was shot later as well.)

And from then on the szop had lost its lustre. The gangs no longer just seized family members, but became indiscriminate, taking anyone they felt like, regardless of whether those people had a szop ID or not. Blockades of the szopy started to occur frequently. [A blockade] went like this: a pair of SS men would come in, immediately followed by the Ukrainians who would fan out over the factory grounds, and then Jewish policemen. Everyone is given the order to go down to the courtyard.[15] Women and children hide. The Ukrainians search. With money, watches, or other jewellery, people buy off [the Ukrainians], but often others come after them and drive [people] out of their hiding places [anyway]. In the courtyard an SS man walks up and down with a riding crop and singles out this person or that person. They are ordered to go to one side – that is, to death. Those who don't step over immediately are hit with the riding crop or, as happened several times at our site, shot on the spot.

Those separated out manoeuvre, trying to switch to the group of those selected to remain. The Jewish policemen serve faithfully and do not allow it, unless you bribe them like the Ukrainians with jewellery or a few hundred złoty. Many manage to save themselves temporarily in this way. Some hide during the blockades in previously prepared hiding places, thanks to which there is still a remnant of women. While the blockade in the 'szop' is being carried out, another blockade is simultaneously under way in the szop's apartment block; from there, too, all those who have not managed to hide well enough or to buy off the Ukrainians are dragged out.

And so by hiding myself at times during the blockades, and by being lucky at other times, I have managed to stay alive until today (10 December).

More bad news came during the night of 5 to 6 September – all szopy, all 'platsuvkes'[16] that work for the Germans on the Aryan side, were going to be shut down. Everyone had to leave their apartments by Sunday, 6 September, at 10 a.m. and go to a handful

12 Here and below, German in the original.
13 Presumably Emanuel Ringelblum.
14 Presumably the factory guard.
15 Change of tense in the original.
16 The term in the Warsaw ghetto for the workplaces of Jewish forced labourers outside the ghetto walls.

of designated streets (Miła, Lubecki, and Stawki). There a further selection of all workers would be made – and those who pass the selection would then be able return to their places.

I live on Miła Street and stood at the window that morning of 6 September watching. No pen, no picture, is capable of capturing the nightmarish scene that morning: tens of thousands of dejected, despairing, and unwashed faces; mothers carrying their children; crying children torn from their mothers; crowds upon crowds walking to and fro, helplessness in their eyes. They walk and walk and keep on walking. The selections are performed; some come back, but the greater part of them, thousands, are taken again to the Umschlagplatz.

A thousand and one stories of misfortune are told by those who remain after those days. Who is able to recount them? Every word means reliving the tragedy. Our selection did not take place until the fourth day – Wednesday. Every day we waited, as though for the Messiah, for our boss – the German Hensel – and finally the good news came that our szop would stay, 500 people may stay. And since there were less than 500 left after so many blockades, apparently everyone would be able to stay. To be on the safe side, some people, women and children, were supposed to hide, while the others boldly present themselves. The entire day was spent waiting for the SS men tasked with carrying out the 'selection', and at 6 p.m. they descended like a violent storm, a swarm of locusts. At the lead was none other than that murderer Brandt himself.[17] With bloodshot eyes and a hoarse bellow – quick, quick – they set about the 'work'. Resourceful businessmen in the factory saw an opportunity to exploit the panic and hammered out numbered brass badges with the inscription O.B.W. – Ostdeutsche Bautischlerei Werkstatt[18] – which they sold for 3 złoty apiece. These badges were called 'dog tags', but still many people bought them as another amulet against whatever misfortune may come. It was not obligatory. To make them appear valuable, the badges were not sold to women. The SS men took these badges for valid documents, and whoever did not have one was doomed. Amid ferocious shouts, with whips, and with riding crops, the people were divided into two groups. The notorious Brandt himself participated, wielding a plank in his hand. Each doomed person was savagely beaten. Twice Brandt broke the planks over the backs and heads of those sentenced to death who did not move fast enough. Blood flowed. And as if to further incite his rage or perhaps to justify his disgusting conduct in the eyes of the civilian German szop owners, with every blow he cried out, '[Too] little, [that is still too] little for you! For three years now we have been shedding blood because of the Jews, because of you the German people are suffering!' Among the hundreds of men and women was Etl – my sister. The children from her boarding school had already been sacrificed on the general altar. I brought her into the factory as my wife. I made an effort to obtain and got a factory ID for her and a registration card with the SS stamp. Everything by the book. She lived with me. She boldly went to the selection. There was no doubt that she would pass. Who, if not her, the young 22-year-old beauty in her prime? Especially since the approved quota for the factory had not been exhausted. Immediately after the SS had separated out those people with the [brass] badges and ordered them to go back to the factory, a rigorous blockade was conducted

17 Karl Georg Brandt.
18 German in the original; this was the name of a carpentry workshop in the ghetto.

in the apartments. People were dragged out of the apartments and some from the hiding places and immediately herded into the wagons. Since then there has been no trace of her. After that there were more blockades, internal selections, and raids. So far I have been left.

I don't know what happened to my sister Khane and her daughter Beltshe. I only know that the same thing happened in November in Zambrów too. There the execution took place in Czerwony Bór.[19] I have no news of them.

## DOC. 135

## On 11 September 1942 the petroleum extraction company Beskiden-Erdöl-Gewinnungsgesellschaft reports on the need to deploy Jewish forced labourers[1]

Letter (marked 'strictly confidential') from Beskiden-Erdöl-Gewinnungsgesellschaft mbH, East Drohobycz Group (BV Jg/Rö A 5), unsigned, from Drohobycz to the Lemberg armaments inspectorate, Hauptmann Westphal,[2] in Lemberg, dated 11 September 1942 (duplicate)

*Deployment of non-Aryan workers*
On 1 November, Beskiden-Erdöl-Gesellschaft operations (extraction and processing) were declared category A operations.[3] Negotiations with the Wehrmacht High Command and Reich Ministry of Economics are nearing completion and will assign our company the priority level of an armaments factory.

In light of the established shortage of workers, particularly workers with specialized skills, we are forced to use a number of non-Aryan workers in our organization. There is unfortunately no way to avoid this if we are to fulfil the demands made of us by the highest authorities.

To avoid significant disruptions to both oil extraction and oil processing (refinery operations), it is important that non-Aryan workers remain able to continue working until suitable replacements can be found. We are constantly striving to obtain skilled workers from the Reich and from friendly nations for our operations, which are critical to the war effort; this will inevitably reduce the number of non-Aryan workers. However, the immediate and total loss of non-Aryan workers would, as noted, cause serious disruptions.

19 A village near Zambrów. On 2 Nov. 1942 German policemen, assisted by Polish firemen, concentrated the ghetto inhabitants, estimated at 14,000 to 17,000 people from the Kreise of Białystok and Bielsk, on the site of a former Soviet military base before deporting them to Treblinka in Jan. 1943.

1 IfZ-Archives, Fa 506/15, fols. 139–140. This document has been translated from German.
2 Kurt Westphal (1897–1963), thought to have been a civil engineer; joined the NSDAP in 1931; Hauptmann in the reserve; in charge of internal affairs at the Lemberg armaments inspectorate; lived in West Berlin after the war.
3 The decision to give enterprises a 'category A' designation was made by the GG government's Economic Affairs Main Department in cooperation with the armaments inspectorate for the GG. The products of category A operations had to be essential to the war effort in terms of armaments. Workers at category A operations were given preferential treatment concerning food rations.

We therefore ask with reference to the imminent Jewish resettlement that you instruct the SD and SS offices to ensure that our operations are not affected by these measures.

The following list shows the number of non-Aryan workers employed at our sites:

| *Oil extraction:* | *Tech./comm[ercial] empl[oyees]* | *Spec[ialist] skilled workers* | *Unsk[illed] workers* |
|---|---|---|---|
| Drohobycz admin. | 14 | 2 | 6 |
| PI[4] Boryslaw | 247 | 321 | 1192 |
| PI Stanislau | 8 | – | – |
| PI Stryj | – | 9 | 19 |
| *Oil processing:* | | | |
| Drohobycz admin. | 5 | 4 | 2 |
| Drohobycz refineries | 19 | 26 | 51 |
| Lemberg refinery | 5 | 4 | 25 |
| Stanislau refinery | 1 | – | – |

We commit to fulfilling the following conditions for the deployment of the Jewish workers in our company:

In Boryslaw all Jews are barracked in a specific residential district. The buildings are watched day and night by our Ukrainian plant guards. We provide their food from a kitchen at the plant, as part of our company catering service. To avoid infectious diseases, a Jewish medical service with Jewish physicians is set up.

The non-Aryan employees and workers in our administrative department and in the refineries in Drohobycz are housed together in four buildings within the Jewish residential district. They are given the prescribed food rations from our company catering service. The same is the case for our non-Aryan workers at our production inspectorates in Stryj and Stanislau and in the Lemberg refinery. We record all Jewish workers using a card index system.

Naturally we will be able to do without the *unskilled* Jewish workers as soon as other workers can be allocated, be they prisoners or other workers from outside Germany. The skilled workers named in the enclosed list[5] can only be replaced by workers with equivalent skills. This will ensure that our operations continue uninterrupted, otherwise a significant loss of production must be expected.

Heil Hitler!

N.B. The workforce ratios given above were in place at the legal predecessors of Beskiden-Erdöl-Gesellschaft in the peacetime economy and had to be retained by Beskiden-Erdöl-Gesellschaft because there were and are not enough replacement workers available, either domestically or within the Reich.

Enclosure

4 Abbreviated as BI (Betriebsinspektion) in the original: 'production inspectorate'.
5 This list is not in the file.

## DOC. 136

## On 12 September 1942 Polish government representatives summarize what they know about Belzec extermination camp[1]

Report by the government delegation for the Polish government in exile, London, dated 12 September 1942[2]

*Part D/3*

*The Camp in Bełżec*

The Jews are taken to Bełżec en masse and in great haste. [In the course of a day], 12,000 to 15,000 Jews arrive on transports (this figure was provided by a Volksdeutscher,[3] who received it from SS men).

They asphyxiate the Jews with gas. When the train arrives [at the camp], the Jews get off, glad that the agony of the journey is over. Then a Jew who belongs to a group of workers employed at the camp appears in front of the newcomers and explains to them that they have nothing to fear because after they have been disinfected, examined, and registered, they will head to the East for work.

Then they undress. Their clothes are searched. After that (all) women are subjected to a cavity search and then led to the barracks with the gas chamber. Once the doors are sealed, a man (perhaps a chemist) appears above the door and from this height looks inside through a spyhole. He releases the gas. The gassing takes up to 15 minutes, after which the doors are opened, and a group of Jews (workers) standing by loads the corpses onto small wagons on a siding and takes them to the prepared pits.

Upon entering the gas chambers to remove the bodies, a lot of blood is seen on the floor, which is the result of haemorrhaging caused by the gas.

The camp presents itself as a well-maintained park: lanes, trees, flowers, lawns, and pathways. There are nice signs everywhere indicating where to go and how to get there.

The Jews, currently numbering 270 people, are divided into two groups: specialists of all trades and the gravediggers – those who remove the [bodies of the] Jews from the gas chamber and dispose of them. This group remains at the camp at all times and is comprised entirely of Jews. Their number hardly diminishes. This is why whoever addresses the newcomers can confirm that he has been in the camp since the very beginning and nothing bad has ever happened to him.

The Jews there are swimming in money. Money no longer makes any impression on them. Vast quantities of gold (under supervision, specialized Jewish dentists remove gold teeth from the bodies) and valuables have fallen into the hands of the SS men.

1 AAN, 1325/202/XV-2, fols. 256–299, here fol. 294. This document has been translated from Polish.

2 The report was sent by the representatives of the Polish government in exile in Feb. 1943 as an appendix to a summary account of the murder of the Jews in Poland, entitled *Second Black Book about the Murder of the Jews in Poland*.

3 German in the original: 'ethnic German'. This is probably a reference to a junior Soviet-German officer from the SS training camp in Trawniki for non-Germans; the men trained there were deployed in Belzec.

There are currently plans to expand the camp. In Bełżec the Jewish houses are being taken down and transferred to the camp. An SS-Sturmführer[4] announced the arrival of a large military contingent.

The following details have been established: (1) based on a conversation with a Jew belonging to the group of specialists, who has already been in the camp for over two months and has buried twenty members of his family there; he is the sole survivor; (2) based on remarks made by a member of the Wachmannschaft[5] and by SS men.

The Jews are exterminated in Bełżec with gas.

Jews carry out all the tasks.

The camp personnel supervise.

The daily influx of Jews is killed immediately upon arrival at the camp. The group of workers remains the same.

## DOC. 137
## On 14 September 1942 a company commander in Police Battalion 133 reports on the deportation of Jews from Kolomea (Kołomyja) to Belzec[1]

Report by Leutnant of the reserve Urban Police and Company Commander Westermann[2] (7th/Pol. 24,[3] log no. 64/42 [g]), Lemberg, for the Commander of the Order Police in District Galicia,[4] Lemberg, dated 14 September 1942

*Re*: Jewish resettlement
*Subject*: order of 31 August 1942 from Comm. OrPol. Gal. Ia-1526–42, log no. 1117/42 (g), dir. of SS and Pol. Leader III, log no. 474/42 (g) of 29 August 1942[5]

Following the Jewish resettlement operations on 3 and 5 September 1942 in Skole, Stryj, and Chodorow, for which Urban Police Hauptmann Kröpelin[6] was in charge of the Order Police forces and has submitted a separate report, the 7th/Pol. 24 entered Kolomea on the evening of 6 September 1942 as ordered. There I immediately made contact with Kriminalkommissar and SS-Obersturmführer Leitmeritz,[7] head of the Security Police

4 German in the original.
5 German in the original: 'guard detail'.

1 RGVA, R-1323-2-292b. Published as a facsimile in Hilberg, *Sonderzüge nach Auschwitz*, pp. 194–197. This document has been translated from German.
2 Albrecht Westermann (1901–1948), police officer; Leutnant in the reserve Urban Police; commander of the 7th Company of Police Regiment 24 in Eastern Galicia; lived in Munich after the war.
3 The 7th Company of Police Regiment 24.
4 Commander of the Order Police (KdO) in District Galicia was Walther von Soosten.
5 There is no record of the order from the KdO in District Galicia and the directive from the SS and Police Leader in Galicia.
6 Kurt Kröpelin (b. 1905), police officer; joined the NSDAP in 1933; Hauptmann in the Urban Police from 1938.
7 Correctly: Peter Leideritz (1911–1948), police officer; joined the SA in 1931, the NSDAP in 1932, and the SS in 1938; with the Gestapo in Darmstadt from 1935; member of the Einsatzkommando z.b.V ('for special assignments') in June 1941; head of the field office of the Commander of the Security Police and the SD (KdS) in Kolomea from Sept. 1941; lived under a false identity in the western German town of Bensheim after the war; extradited to Poland in 1947 and executed in Warsaw.

field office in Kolomea, and precinct Oberleutnant Hertel[8] of the Urban Police department in Kolomea.

Contrary to experiences in Stryj,[9] the operation in Kolomea scheduled for 7 September 1942 was simplified and well prepared for all forces involved. The aforementioned authorities and the Kolomea employment office had instructed the Jews to come to the employment office assembly point for registration at 5.30 a.m. on 7 September. By the specified time, around 5,300 Jews had actually arrived at the assembly point. Using all the men in my company, I cordoned off the Jewish quarter and searched it thoroughly, as a result of which another 600 or so Jews were rounded up.

The loading of the transport train was complete by 7 p.m. In total, 4,769 Jews were resettled, after the Security Police had released around 1,000 of the Jews who were rounded up. Each wagon of this train was loaded with 100 Jews. The extreme heat of the day greatly hampered the entire operation and also made the transport much more difficult. Once all wagons had been boarded up and sealed as required, the transport set off for Belzec at around 9 p.m. accompanied by a 1/9[10] escort. As the pitch-black night descended, several Jews escaped by removing the barbed wire and forcing their way through the air vents. It was possible for the escort to shoot some of them immediately, while the majority of the Jews who had escaped were dispatched during the night or the next day by the Railway Police or other police forces. This transport was delivered to Belzec without major incident, although the length of the train and the extreme darkness meant that the escort was too small, as was reported to me only on 11 September in Stanislau by the head of the transport guard from the 6th/Pol. 24, who had returned directly to Stanislau.

On 7 September around 300 Jews who were old and weak, pest-ridden, frail, and no longer fit for transport were executed. In accordance with the order of 4 September 1942 regarding Jewish resettlement – specifically the use of munitions – which came to my attention only on 6 September, 90 per cent of all those executed were shot with carbines or rifles.[11] Pistols were used only in exceptional cases.

Operations were carried out in Kuty, Kosow, Horodenka, Zaplatow, and Sniatyn (?)[12] on 8 and 10 September 1942. Around 1,500 Jews had to be marched 50 km from Kuty or 35 km from Kosow to Kolomea, where they spent the night in the courtyard of the Security Police prison with other Jews rounded up from the area. Apart from the Jews rounded up in Horodenka and Sniatyn, who had already been loaded into ten wagons at each location by the Security Police, another 30 wagons were loaded in Kolomea. The total number of Jews transported to Belzec on the resettlement train on 10 September 1942 was 8,205.

During the operations in the area around Kolomea on 8, 9, and 10 September 1942, it was necessary to use guns to dispatch around 400 Jews for the reasons previously given.

8 Correctly: Herbert Härtel (b. 1892), bricklayer; joined the NSDAP in 1933 and the SS in 1940; with the police from 1919; worked for the Vienna Security Police; head of the Urban Police in Kolomea.

9 On 3 Sept. 1942 around 5,000 Jews were rounded up in Stryj for deportation to Belzec and 500 were murdered in the ghetto.

10 That is, one officer and nine enlisted men.

11 See Doc. 128.

12 Question mark in the original.

Given the large number of Jews in Kolomea to be resettled by 10 September, the Security Police loaded all the Jews into the thirty wagons provided, despite the concerns I expressed. In view of the extreme heat on those days and the strain placed on the Jews by long marches or days of waiting without being given any food to speak of, the overloading of most of the wagons with 180 to 200 Jews was so catastrophic that the situation proved highly detrimental to the transport.

I do not know how many Jews were loaded by the Security Police into the ten wagons in Horodenka and the ten wagons in Sniatyn. At all events, both transports arrived in Kolomea with entirely inadequate security, which meant that almost all of the barbed wire nailed over the air vents had been removed. I arranged for these transports to be removed from the station in Kolomea as soon as possible and to be coupled to the thirty wagons from Kolomea that were parked at a good distance from the station in the siding. The Jewish Order Service and members of the railway auxiliaries (Eastern Railway track layers) of Kolomea were deployed to properly seal all inadequately sealed wagons before nightfall. A 1/15 unit led by Hauptwachtmeister Witzmann[13] was charged with guarding the parked resettlement train with its fifty goods wagons until its departure and to prevent all escape attempts. As a result of the strain on the Jews already noted, the adverse impact of the heat, and the significant overloading of most of the wagons, the Jews tried again and again to break out of the parked wagons once darkness fell at around 7.30 p.m. The 1/9 escort for the resettlement train arrived at the siding at 7.50 p.m. under the leadership of Zugwachtmeister Jäcklein.[14] It was possible to either prevent attempted escapes from the parked train in the darkness or to shoot the Jews as they fled. The Jews stripped completely naked in all of the wagons due to the heat.

When the train departed Kolomea on schedule at 8.50 p.m., the guard unit returned to their quarters. As I had originally ordered, the escort was posted with five Wachtmeister (SD) in one passenger coach at the head of the train and five Wachtmeister (SD) in one passenger coach at the end of the train. Due to the length of the train and its being tightly packed with 8,205 Jews, this distribution proved unsuitable. At the next stop, Zugwachtmeister J[äcklein] ordered that the guards be spread across the train. The Wachtmeister had to spend the entire journey in the brakesman's cabs, as the most effective means to combat the Jews' attempts to escape. After just a short while, Jews in some wagons attempted to force their way through the sides and even the roofs. One was partially successful in this endeavour, and so five stations before Stanislau, Zugwachtmeister Jäcklein telephoned the station master in Stanislau to ask that nails and boards be made available to temporarily board up the damaged wagons and to order the Railway Police to guard the transport. When the train arrived in Stanislau, workmen from Stanislau station and the Railway Police were waiting to perform the necessary repairs and to guard the train.

13 Correctly: Arno Zitzmann (1908–1992), warehouseman; Hauptwachtmeister; Gruppenführer in the 3rd Company of the 3rd Platoon of Reserve Police Battalion 133, July 1941 – Jan. 1943; with the police in Nuremberg after the war.

14 Josef Jäcklein (1913–1987), police officer; Zugwachtmeister in the Urban Police; with the police in Nuremberg after the war; Kommissar from 1956. He wrote his own report on the transport, see: Ernst Klee, Willi Dreßen, and Volker Rieß (eds.), *'Schöne Zeiten': Judenmord aus der Sicht der Täter und Gaffer* (Frankfurt am Main: Fischer, 1988), pp. 211–216.

The work took one and a half hours. When the train then continued its journey, it was discovered at the next stop a few stations later that the Jews had already created further large holes in several wagons and that most of the barbed wire attached to the outside of the air vents had been torn away. In one wagon the Jews had even used hammers and pliers. When questioned, they explained that they had been given the tools by the Security Police, who had said they would be able to put them to good use at their next place of work. Zugwachtmeister J[äcklein] had the Jews hand over the tools. Throughout the rest of the journey, at every stop the train had to be temporarily nailed shut, as otherwise it would not have been possible to continue the journey.

The train arrived in Lemberg at 11.15 a.m. As no relief for the escort had arrived, the J[äcklein] unit had to continue guarding the train until Belzec. After a short stop at Lemberg station, the train continued to the suburban station of Kleparow, where nine wagons marked with 'L' and bound for the forced labour camp[15] were handed over to SS-Obersturmführer Schulze[16] and unloaded. SS-Obersturmführer Schulze then had around 1,000 Jews loaded again onto the train.[17] The transport continued towards Belzec at 1.30 p.m.

The locomotive hooked up during the engine change in Lemberg was so old that the journey could only continue with constant interruptions. Again and again the slow pace was used by the strongest Jews to force themselves through the openings that had been prised apart and try their luck at escaping, because they barely injured themselves jumping from the slow-moving train. Despite the repeated calls for the train driver to go faster, it was impossible for him to do so, and the frequent stops on open stretches became increasingly unpleasant. The escort had used up its ammunition shortly after Lemberg as well as a further 200 rounds of ammunition provided by members of the Wehrmacht, so for the rest of the journey, they had to make do with stones when the train was moving and with fixed bayonets when the train was stopped.

The ever-increasing panic among the Jews due to the extreme heat, overfilled wagons, and the stench of corpses – around 200 Jews were found dead in the train when the wagons were unloaded – rendered the transport almost impossible. The train arrived at Belzec at 6.45 p.m. and was handed over by Zugwachtmeister Jäcklein to the SS-Obersturmführer and head of the local camp[18] at 7.30 p.m. Jäcklein had to wait in the camp until the entire transport was unloaded at around 10 p.m., while the escort was deployed to guard the wagons parked outside the camp.

Due to the particular conditions described, the number of Jews who escaped from this transport cannot be given. However, we can assume that at least two thirds of the Jews who escaped were shot or rendered harmless by some other method.

15 This is a reference to Lemberg-Janowska camp.

16 Willy Schulze (1894–1984), plumber; joined the NSDAP and the SS in 1931; worked on the staff of the SS and Police Leader in Galicia from July 1942; head of Janowska labour camp in Lwów from Sept. 1942; interned, 1945–1946; thereafter lived in Hamburg.

17 Prisoners from Janowska camp were exchanged for people on the train who had been selected in advance for the camp.

18 Gottlieb Hering (1887–1945), police officer; SPD member in 1920; joined the NSDAP in 1933; worked for the Stuttgart Criminal Police in the 1930s; from 1939 to 1940 based in Gdynia, where he was involved in the resettlement of Germans living abroad, then the 'euthanasia' killing operation; commandant of Belzec from July 1942 and of Poniatowa labour camp in 1943; posted to Trieste in 1944; died from an illness.

No major incidents occurred during the operations themselves in the period from 7 to 10 September 1942. Cooperation between the Order Police and Security Police forces deployed was good and ran smoothly.

## DOC. 138

## *Informacja Bieżąca*, 15 September 1942: report on the murder of Jews in the General Government[1]

*Jewish matters*

*The Warsaw ghetto.* The liquidation is coming to an end. Since 30 August the trains have been departing irregularly, every two to three days. Most of the victims come from the continuously ongoing raids and roundups. They are all taken indiscriminately, a great many from the work details marching to and from work, for example; often the entire work detail without exception. People are still being murdered on the spot, mainly in the Jewish cemetery, but also openly in the streets. A particularly bloody massacre took place on 5 and 6 September, on both days and in the night. This information seems credible because it comes from the Arbeitsamt[2] and Supply Department networks, and states that not more than 30,000–40,000 Warsaw Jews will remain alive and are employed in the 'szopy'. Of course the Order Police[3] now consists of too many members. There have already been the first cases of Order Service men being deported. No more than one hundred are to remain. At present nearly all ghetto entry permits are invalid. Even the disinfection crews that cleaned the vacated quarters (mainly the 'small ghetto'[4]) have been denied access for several days now.

*Death camp in Treblinka.* The place where the Jews are executed is close to a labour camp, which is situated 5 km from Treblinka railway station and 2 km from Poniatowo station.[5] A separate telephone line to Małkinia.[6] There is an old camp (for Poles)[7] and a new one under construction (exclusively for Jews).[8] The camp personnel: 25 SS men and 180 Ukrainians[9] (of whom 12 are Germans and 50 Ukrainians in the old camp). Arms: apart from their own weapons – light machine guns, rifles, and grenades. The inmates mainly load gravel. The Jews are physically punished in every conceivable way. The liquidation of the Jews takes place completely independently of the old camp's operation. A steam locomotive shunts the goods wagons with Jews onto the ramp, one after another. The Ukrainians drag the Jews out of the wagons and lead them to the 'bathhouse'. This

1 *Informacja Bieżąca*, no. 34 (59), 15 Sept. 1942, fols. 5–6. AAN, 1325/202/III-7/1, fols. 152–153. This document has been translated from Polish.
2 German in the original: 'employment office'.
3 This is a reference to the Jewish Order Service.
4 The 'small ghetto' south of Chłodna Street had been liquidated during the deportations in August 1942.
5 This village is today part of the community of Małkinia Górna, as is Treblinka.
6 Today known as Małkinia Górna.
7 Both Poles and Jews were imprisoned in Treblinka I labour camp.
8 See also Docs. 36, 78, and 115.
9 This is a reference to men from the SS training camp for foreign nationals in Trawniki, among whom were also Soviet Germans and men of other nationalities.

building is fenced off with barbed wire. People enter in groups of 300 to 500. Each group is immediately hermetically sealed off and gassed. However, the gas does not really take effect immediately because the Jews still have to get to the ditches, which are several metres away and about 30 metres deep.[10] There they lose consciousness and fall into the ditch, and a bulldozer covers them with a thin layer of soil. The next group follows. There are also cases of Poles being among the Jews. On 28 August a Pole lunged at a Ukrainian, snatched his rifle, and smashed the heads of a German and a Ukrainian. He was immediately shot dead. (The above information comes from Ukrainians on guard duty and needs to be verified. I will shortly present an authentic report from a Jew who managed to escape from Treblinka.[11])

*Radom, Kielce, Sandomierz.* Today 7–8 per cent of the Jewish population is left in Radom. On 4 August the Glinica quarter was liquidated. Approximately 8,000 people were taken to Bełżec; approximately 880 were shot dead on the spot.[12] On 16 and 17 August the other quarter, known as Wały, was liquidated. Fourteen thousand people were taken to Treblinka; 100 were shot dead, leaving behind only a 'labour battalion'.[13] The Waffen-SS, the gendarmerie, and Ukrainians carried out this operation.

German, Ukrainian, and Polish police liquidated the ghetto in Kielce on the night of 19–20 August. Sixteen thousand people were transported to Treblinka: 120–150 people in each goods wagon strewn with quicklime.[14] Approximately 1,000 Jews and dozens of Poles who happened to be in the ghetto were shot dead.[15] At the same time, in the prison, 138 Jewish inmates (all of them) were shot. A work detail of 2,000 Jews was left.

Ten Jews were shot dead in Sandomierz on 2 August. The Jews are being driven from the countryside to the city – this is the prelude to the liquidation.[16] In the process, many children, elderly, and sick people perish, as anyone who is unable to march is killed.

*Biała Podlaska.* Jews have been murdered throughout the entire powiat. On 20 August a squad of Soviet prisoners of war (from Kirgizia)[17] drove the entire Jewish population of Łomazy, 2,000 people, in the direction of Sławatycze and shot them along the way at ditches that had been dug in advance. Those killed as well as those not finished off were

10 All the victims were murdered in the gas chambers, and their bodies were subsequently taken to large pits approximately 6 metres deep.

11 This has not been found.

12 Approximately 5,000 Jews had lived in the ghetto in the Glinica suburb of Radom since 7 April 1941, 4,000 of whom were deported to Treblinka on 4 August 1942, while 1,000 were taken to the larger ghetto to work, and 60 were murdered on the spot.

13 Approximately 27,000 Jews had lived in the larger ghetto in Radom's Old Town since 7 April 1941; 20,000 were deported to Treblinka, 400 were murdered on the spot, and 1,800 were selected for labour. Those who remained were confined to the Glinica ghetto and forced to work in armaments production.

14 A disinfectant.

15 In April 1941 the German authorities established two ghettos in Kielce for more than 25,000 people. The murder operations began on 20 August 1942 and continued for three days: 21,000 people were deported to Treblinka and 3,000 were murdered on the spot; the Germans confined 1,600 to the 'small ghetto'.

16 Change in tense as in the original.

17 The mass shooting in Łomazy was carried out by Police Battalion 101, assisted by a unit from the SS training camp in Trawniki, which consisted mainly of Ukrainians.

thrown into the ditches and covered with clay. The decomposition of the corpses made the mass grave swell, so the farmers were ordered to construct a kurgan.[18]

*Galicia*. Lwów. The operation lasted from 9 to 23 August. Approximately 65,000 people are said to have been taken away. The liquidation of the Jews was used as a pretext to capture and kill a certain number of Aryan elderly and children.

*Sambor*. The operation lasted from 4 to 7 August. On 5 August, 23 goods wagons from the Kreis and the city of Sambor, as well as 25 goods wagons from Turka, Stary Sambor, and the surrounding area, were loaded. On 6 August, 22 goods wagons from Sambor, 24 from Borysław, and 4 from Turka were loaded. Each wagon carried 80 to 100 people. Approximately 40 people were shot.

*Stary Sambor*. The operation lasted from 4 to 6 August. One hundred and ten Jews were shot.

*Drohobycz*. Approximately 1,000 people were deported from 7 to 8 August.

*Stanisławów*. On 11 August the Jews were forbidden to go to work unaccompanied or to make detours, to leave their workplaces during working hours, to use the pavement, to enter Aryan szopy, to speak to Aryans, etc., or to bring food of any kind into the ghetto. On 20 August two members of the Jewish Council (the chairman and one member) and eight members of the Jewish Order Service were hanged for an assassination attempt that a Jew allegedly carried out on a Ukrainian policeman (by pouring hydrochloric acid over him). Everyone in the Jewish hospitals, orphanages, and homeless shelters, regardless of age, was shot dead. On 22 and 23 August, 1,400 Jews were shot dead, including women and children.

*Vilna*. In the final days of July, approximately 200 elderly Jews of both sexes were shot dead in Ponary. Under the pretext of taking precautions for their health, the Germans took them to a municipal holiday centre outside the city, supposedly to a rest home, from where they were transported to the execution site a few days later.

Bor[owski][19]

## DOC. 139
## On 16 September 1942 the Eastern Railway intervenes on behalf of its Jewish forced labourers[1]

Letter from the Head of the Railway Main Department in the GG government (4 P 30g/Pldav), signed Gerteis, Cracow, to the Higher SS and Police Leader in Cracow,[2] dated 16 September 1942 (copy)

*Re*: use of Jewish workers by the Eastern Railway

With reference to my earlier letters on this matter and your recent meeting with the director of the Eastern Railway regional office in Cracow, Oberreichsbahnrat

18 Burial mound of a type found in southern Russia and Ukraine.

19 Borowski was Antoni Szymanowski's code name.

1 BArch, R 5/23128, fols. 43–44 (copy of the original, replaced for restoration). This document has been translated from German.

2 Friedrich-Wilhelm Krüger.

Becker,[3] in the following I again inform you of the deployment and significance of Jewish workers at the Eastern Railway.

The Eastern Railway currently employs 8,568 Jews in its own operations. They are – spread across the entire area – mainly deployed in the Eastern Railway repair workshops, in engine sheds, and at construction inspectorates. Among them are numerous tradesmen, particularly metalworkers, some of whom have been working on the railways for many years and therefore have particularly valuable professional experience. The Jewish element makes up a large part of the tradesmen in Galicia because Jews were strongly represented in its tradespeople class. The unskilled labourers work mainly on the tracks to maintain the railway, shovel coal in the railyards, and provide manual assistance and transport in the repair workshops.

Apart from the Jews working for the Eastern Railway itself, a total of 15,383 Jews work for companies employed as part of the Eastern Railway programme to adapt the capabilities of the Eastern Railway network to meet the increased demands of the Wehrmacht. Here too the number of tradesmen (train drivers for construction work, excavator operators, machine operators, etc.) is not insignificant. These Jewish contract workers are kept in closed-off camps and are therefore a source of particularly reliable help for these companies, because the difficulties that so often occur with free non-German workers – changing jobs without permission, missing work for days at a time to engage in illicit trading, etc. – are almost completely non-existent.

A total of 23,951 Jews are thus currently working for the Eastern Railway. It goes without saying that suddenly removing such a high number of workers would make it impossible to continue the work in which they were involved as planned. At the moment the deadlines for the construction that is to be undertaken by the Eastern Railway require that not a single worker be given up. On the contrary, 10,000 more people are needed to ensure that the programme is completed on schedule. Furthermore, the Eastern Railway needs significantly more workers for its own operations, particularly junior staff for all departments. It can therefore only relinquish workers if they are simultaneously replaced in full.

However, due to the great demands on the GG labour deployment authorities coming from all sides, particularly from the General Plenipotentiary for Labour Deployment[4] on behalf of the Reich, they are not able to suddenly allocate several thousand workers as a group to one single company. It is only for this reason that I have requested that the resettlement of the Jews be postponed until fully adequate replacements, the subject of ongoing efforts by the labour deployment authorities, are available.

If the Jews are nevertheless removed from the Eastern Railway's operations and from contracted companies before this point, it is clear that serious difficulties and stoppages will ensue. For example, removing the Jewish tradesmen employed in the Eastern Railway's Lemberg maintenance depot without replacements would mean that the second locomotive repair shift could no longer be sustained in full. This would result in a loss

3 Kurt Becker (1899–1983), engineer; worked for the Reich Railway from 1924; in Karlsbad, 1938–1939; worked at the Eastern Railway's Warsaw office, 1939 to Feb. 1942 and August 1943 to Oct. 1944; head of the Eastern Railway's Cracow office, March 1942 to July 1943; department head at the railway headquarters in Kassel, 1954–1964.

4 Fritz Sauckel.

per month of thirty locomotives, which would undergo fewer repairs and consequently could not be made available to the company for use in transportation for the Wehrmacht. The situation is similar in other maintenance depots and railway yards. Given the large number of workers, removing the Jews from construction sites in the eastern construction scheme before replacements are allocated would certainly mean that the deadlines set for completion of the work could not be met. As winter approaches, every delay will have incalculable consequences. For example, every day of delay to the large-scale construction around Cracow will mean a daily loss of 200,000 hundredweight of supplies for the front. Similar situations will occur in Lublin, Lemberg, Tarnopol, and other places if the construction work there is not completed on time.

These examples indicate the severity of the situation and why I must continue my emphatic efforts to retain the current Eastern Railway workforce, regardless of who they are. A reduction in the numbers working for the Eastern Railway would harm the front in unjustifiable ways.

The Eastern Railway therefore urges that the workforce currently at its disposal be maintained for as long as required to complete its tasks, and furthermore that its unmet needs be fulfilled as soon as possible. The Jews working for the Eastern Railway can therefore only be resettled if they are replaced with other workers. As soon as these are available, the Eastern Railway will happily forgo all Jewish workers.

The SS and Police Leader assigned to the Governor of District Cracow[5] has received a copy of this letter.

## DOC. 140

## *Rzeczpospolita Polska*, 16 September 1942: the Polish government's coordinating body for civil resistance issues a declaration condemning the murder of the Jews[1]

*From the Field of the Civil Struggle*
*Declaration*

In addition to the tragedy suffered by Polish society decimated by the enemy, a horrific, coordinated massacre of the Jews has been taking place on our soil for almost a year now.

This mass murder is unprecedented in world events. All atrocities known to history pale in comparison. Infants, children, adolescents, adults, the elderly, the disabled, the sick, the healthy, men, women, Catholic Jews, Jews of the Mosaic faith – all are mercilessly murdered, poisoned with gas, buried alive, pushed out of their buildings onto the pavement below, for no other reason than the fact that they belong to the Jewish people.

5 Julian Scherner was the SS and Police Leader in Cracow; Richard Wendler was governor of District Cracow.

1 *Rzeczpospolita Polska*, no. 16 (46), 16 September 1942, p. 5: Biblioteka Narodowa, MF 51 745. *Rzeczpospolita Polska* was the government delegation's official publication and appeared biweekly in Warsaw from March 1941 to July 1945. Its editors-in-chief included Stanisław Kauzik (1891–1959), Teofil Syga (1903–1983), and Franciszek Głowiński (1894–1944). This document has been translated from Polish.

Before they die, they suffer the additional agony of a slow death at the hands of the executioners – a hell of abuse, oppression, and cynical torture.

The number of people murdered in this way exceeds one million and grows with each passing day.

Unable to actively resist this, the Directorate of Civil Combat,[2] on behalf of all Polish society, protests against the crimes perpetrated against the Jews.

All Polish political and civic groups unite in this protest.

As in the case of the Polish victims, the executioners and their accomplices bear the physical responsibility for these crimes.

## DOC. 141
## On 17 September 1942 the Interior Administration Department for Kreis Ostrów Mazowiecka orders the arrest of Moses Seemann and his deportation to Treblinka labour camp[1]

Letter from the Kreishauptmann in Ostrów,[2] head of the Interior Administration Department (II Le/Me.), signature illegible, to the Ostrów gendarmerie platoon, for the attention of Oberleutnant Reiner, Ostrów, dated 17 September 1942

The Jew Moses *Seemann*, who is working here, is involved in criminal activity and is to be arrested immediately.

I therefore ask that you arrange for the Jew to be arrested as soon as possible and to hold him in custody under my orders.

He will be collected by the commandant of Treblinka camp[3] within 48 hours.

Moses Seemann has not been included on the list of Jews working here which was submitted to me.

Presumably someone omitted his name deliberately, or he gave a false name. The arrest must therefore be performed with care.[4]

2 The Directorate of Civil Combat was the central organization that coordinated all aspects of the civil resistance in occupied Poland. It was initially subordinate to the Union of Armed Struggle (ZWZ), and from 15 April 1942 to the government delegation. On 15 July 1943 it merged with the Home Army's Directorate of Covert Combat and reported to the Home Army High Command.

1 APW, 489/70, fol. 48. This document has been translated from German.

2 Karl Valentin (1895–1965), commercial agent; joined the NSDAP in 1931 and the SA in 1933; at the SA administration main department in Munich; chief of staff for the governor of District Warsaw from Nov. 1940; Kreishauptmann in Ostrów Mazowiecka, Jan.–Nov. 1942; in March 1943 sentenced to three years in prison for corruption; in SS-Brigade Dirlewanger from Oct. 1944; held in Soviet captivity as a prisoner of war, 1945–1948; thereafter lived in Wuppertal.

3 This refers to the labour camp in the village of Treblinka: see Introduction, p. 29.

4 The commander of the gendarmerie, Pfüttner, replied to the Kreishauptmann on the same day, stating that Seemann had been 'arrested on 17 Sept. 1942 and handed over to the city for detention'. On 18 Sept. 1942 the recipient wrote the following by hand at the bottom of this letter: 'Mr van Eupen will have the Jew picked up on Friday (18 Sept. 1942) (for Treblinka camp)': APW, 489/70, fol. 48RS. Theodor van Eupen (1907–1944) was the commandant of Treblinka labour camp from summer 1941 until July 1944; killed by partisans.

## DOC. 142

## On 18 September 1942 the military district commander in the General Government advises against the immediate removal of Jewish workers from armaments factories[1]

Letter (marked 'secret') from the military district commander in the General Government[2] to the Wehrmacht High Command, operations staff[3] (received 20 September 1942, O.Qu./Qu.2, ref. SA, log no. 735/42 sec[ret].), H.Qu., dated 18 September 1942

*Re*: replacement of the Jewish workforce with Poles
*Subject*: *OKW/WFSt/(Qu.II/Verw.)* of 5 September 1942, no. 02 553/42 g.[4]

I. To date the orders for the General Government have been as follows:
1) In order to free them up for the Reich, Polish and Ukrainian workers are to be replaced with Jewish workers; to this end camps for Jews are also to be set up for use at the factories.
2) Exclusively Jewish operations or branch operations are to be formed to exploit Jewish labour for the war.

The initiation of the resettlement of the Jews without most Wehrmacht agencies receiving advance notice has seriously impeded supplies and delayed express production for the war economy. SS-level work, with priority level 'Winter', cannot be completed on time.

II. Unskilled workers can be substituted in part if the General Plenipotentiary for Labour Deployment relinquishes the 140,000 Poles who were to be sent to the Reich by the end of the year,[5] and if the police recruitment operation succeeds. Previous experience suggests that this is doubtful.

A small number of students who are currently being trained in government technical colleges can be taken on as semi-skilled workers.

Skilled workers must first be trained. It takes months and up to a year to train such a workforce, most of whom come from agriculture, and even longer in the case of particularly highly qualified workers and tradesmen. I am unable to judge whether this particularly difficult question, on which the continued contribution of the Gen. Gov. to

1 BArch, NS 19/352, fols. 2–4. Also BArch, RH 53-23/v.66 (military log, appendix no. 214). Published in Grabitz and Scheffler, *Letzte Spuren*, pp. 311–312. This document has been translated from German.
2 Curt Ludwig Freiherr von Gienanth.
3 From 1940 the chief of the operations staff in the Wehrmacht High Command was Colonel General Alfred Jodl, né Baumgärtler (1890–1946), career officer; joined the Reichswehr in 1919; head of the National Defence Department in the Wehrmacht Leadership Office from 1935; signed the German Instrument of Surrender in Rheims on 7 May 1945; sentenced to death at the International Military Tribunal at Nuremberg and executed.
4 After the Przemyśl incident (see Doc. 101), Keitel had requested in a letter to the military district commander in the General Government dated 5 Sept. 1942 that Jewish workers immediately be replaced with Poles: BArch, NS 19/2462, fol. 1.
5 On 20 April 1942 the general plenipotentiary for labour deployment, Fritz Sauckel, had ordered from the Nazi-occupied territories of Europe the large-scale mobilization of workers for the war economy.

the war economy primarily depends, could be solved more quickly if skilled workers were provided from the Reich.

III. According to GG government documents – Labour Main Department – the total number of industrial workers is a little over one million, more than 300,000 of whom are Jews. Around 100,000 of these are skilled workers.

In the individual companies working for the Wehrmacht, the number of Jews among the skilled workers fluctuates between 25 per cent and 100 per cent; in companies producing textiles for winter clothing it is 100 per cent. In other companies, for example in the important factories producing Fuhrmann and Pleskau conveyances, the key workers – the wheelwrights – are predominantly Jews. With a few exceptions, the leather workers are all Jewish.

A total of 22,700 workers are currently employed by private companies in the mending of uniforms. Of this number, 22,000 are Jewish (97 per cent), including 16,500 skilled workers (textile and leather workers).

An all-Jewish enterprise with 168 workers manufactures harness fittings, on which the entire production of harnesses in the Gen. Gov., in Ukraine, and to some extent in the Reich depends.

IV. The immediate removal of the Jews would result in the Reich's war potential being significantly reduced and in the stalling of supplies to the front and to Gen. Gov. troops, at least momentarily.

1) There would be serious production losses in the armaments industry of between 25 per cent and 100 per cent.
2) In workshops servicing motor vehicles, performance would drop on average by around 25 per cent, which means that an average of 2,500 fewer vehicles would be repaired each month.
3) Supply units would have to be deployed for provisioning.

V. If the work essential to the war is not to suffer, the Jews cannot be released until replacements are trained, i.e. progressively. This task can only be undertaken locally but must be directed by a *single* office in collaboration with the Higher SS and Police Leader.

It is requested that the special directive be permitted to be carried out in this manner. The policy should be to phase out the Jews as quickly as possible without compromising work essential to the war efforts.

VI. As has now been established, orders essential to the war effort and of the highest priority, above all to cover winter needs, are in progress in the Gen. Gov. from the various Wehrmacht agencies without the knowledge of the GG armaments inspectorate or the military district commander in the General Government. The resettlement of the Jews makes punctual completion of this work impossible.

It will require some time to systematically record all such operations.

It is requested that the resettlement of Jews who are employed in craft and industrial enterprises be suspended until then.[6]

6 On 22 Sept. 1942, at Sauckel's suggestion, Hitler agreed that skilled Jewish workers were to be allowed to remain temporarily in the General Government. Himmler urged that Jewish workers be replaced with Poles: see Doc. 159.

## DOC. 143

## *Oyf der vakh*, 20 September 1942: article describing Treblinka extermination camp[1]

*The Jews of Warsaw are being murdered at Treblinka*[2]

In the first weeks of the 'resettlement operation', Warsaw was brimming with greetings from the deported Jews of Warsaw. The messages supposedly came from Białystok, Brest, Kosów, Małkinia Górna, Pińsk, Smolensk.

These were all lies! All the trains carrying the Warsaw Jews went to Treblinka, where the Jews were murdered in a gruesome fashion!

The letters and messages came from people who managed to escape from the wagons or from the camp itself. It may also be the case that, among the first transports at the beginning of the operation, a handful of the Jews from Warsaw were intentionally sent to Brest or Pińsk so that their messages would fool, mislead, and create false impressions among the Jewish community in Warsaw.

What was in fact the fate of the deported Jews?

We have found out from reports by Poles and those Jews who managed to escape from the wagons and from the camp in Treblinka.[3]

Treblinka is the first station on the Małkinia–Siedlce railway line.

The camp in Treblinka covers an area of half a square kilometre.[4] The camp is enclosed by three barbed wire fences. The innermost and outermost fences are [each] 1.5 metres high, while the middle fence reaches a height of 3 metres. The mesh is very tight, with bushes running through it. A railway siding has been routed behind the first, outermost fence. A modern asphalt train platform has been built there, with big warehouses, a few hundred metres long, next to the platform. Once the living and the dead have been quickly unloaded from the wagons, the Jews are led into the camp. They have to leave all of their baggage by the wagons.

Two long barracks a few dozen metres in length have been constructed inside the camp. On the right side is the barracks for the men, on the left that for women. Apart from the Ukrainians or the Latvians from the convoy [that accompanies the transport], a group of around sixty Jews also helps to unload the train. They are not deportees, but rather young men from Stoczek, near Węgrów, who have been taken as prisoner functionaries to work in the camp. They are armed with clubs. They chase, push, and hit. Where the SS man strikes a single blow, they always give several. They look [to be

1 *Oyf der vakh*, no. 1, 20 Sept. 1942 (title page missing); AŻIH, Varia okupacyjne 230/77, fols. 2–4. A transcript in which some passages contain minor differences from the original is published in *Bleter far geszichte*, no. 28 (1990), pp. 124–131. The Bund's underground paper *Oyf der vakh* appeared in Warsaw in Yiddish in the second half of 1942. Three issues have survived. This document has been translated from Yiddish.

2 The reporter was Zalman (Zygmunt) Frydrych (Friedrich) (1911–1943); came from a Hasidic family in Warsaw; worked as a Bund liaison on the 'Aryan side' in Warsaw, 1940–1942; gathered information on Treblinka in August 1942; fought in the Warsaw Ghetto Uprising and rescued survivors in April 1943; left Warsaw on 10 May 1943; shot dead by German or Polish policemen in the village of Płudy a few days later.

3 Frydrych received his detailed knowledge of the extermination camp from the fugitive Azriel (or Uziel) Wallach, a member of the Bund; he confirmed what was already known from other reports.

4 In fact, the camp covered an area of more than 2 $km^2$.

in] good [physical condition] and are fed well. What's more, they help themselves to the food taken from the deportees.

Even as people get off the train, bullets rain down on stragglers, or shots are fired for no particular reason at all. The dead bodies unloaded from the wagons and those just killed are buried on the spot, between the first and second fences. In pairs, the Jews from earlier transports grab the dead by the hands and feet and throw them into a grave that has already been prepared. However, the Jewish gravediggers, who volunteered for this job, never return to the camp.[5] After completing the work, they are shot on the spot.

One of the gravediggers escaped in the following way: while in the middle of performing the work, instead of going to the platform to pick up more dead bodies, he crawled under the wire fence and hid in the bushes nearby. He met a peasant who, in exchange for a pair of boots, showed him the way to the shtetl. A second gravedigger hid next to the platform, among the baggage that the deportees had to leave behind. At night he managed to hide under a wagon, and in this way he made it out of the camp to freedom.

The deportees' baggage is arranged next to the platform, covering an area several hundred metres long and up to 1.5 metres high. The width of the pile grows continuously as the warehouse workers have not had time to sort the items. Workers are brought in from the camp to put the effects in storage. After finishing the job, they return to the camp. Many of them try to escape. They hide among the belongings and, after the transport has left, attempt to crawl through the first fence, which is relatively easy.

What happens in the camp itself?

The new arrivals almost always encounter people from the previous transports sitting on the ground or in the barracks. Terrible screams and cries for help can be heard. There is constant shooting. Ukrainians with machine guns are perched on the roofs of both barracks and shoot constantly to frighten those Jews who approach the fence.

The incessant noise of a powerful machine excavating the ground can be heard. This excavator is located in the far left corner of the camp, next to the barracks called the 'bath'. There are not many Ukrainians in the camp. The entire camp staff consists of 100 men, including the SS men. Volunteers are immediately selected from each arriving group to fetch water, but none of them have ever returned to the camp. After they leave machine-gun salvos are heard in rapid succession. Then a second party goes to bury the dead.

The newly arrived women and children are put into groups of 200 to go to the 'bath'. They are stripped completely naked and leave their clothes behind while they themselves are led into the little barracks called the 'bath', located next to the excavator. No one returns from the 'bath', and new groups constantly enter. The 'bath' is actually a murder site. The floor in the barracks collapses, and the people fall into a machine. Some escapees believe that the people in the barracks are gassed, while others claim they are killed by electrocution.[6] The excavator works non-stop. The incessant sound of gunshots can

5 This is a reference to the so-called gravediggers inside the death camp area, which was isolated from the other parts of Treblinka camp. They were tasked with retrieving the bodies of the murdered Jewish victims from the gas chambers and burning them in large pits. These men were periodically shot and replaced by others from new transports.

6 False rumours circulated that electricity or hot steam was used to carry out the mass murder.

be heard coming from the turret above the 'bath'. It is said that those who are still on their feet after the gassing are shot dead in the barracks in this manner. The 'bath' accommodates 200 people every 15 minutes, which means up to 20,000 people can be killed in it in a 24-hour period.[7] This explains the continuous arrival of people in the camp, from which no one ever returns, apart from a few hundred over the entire period [of the camp's operation] who have managed to escape.

For a time two trains from Warsaw would arrive each day, with 12,000 people on each one. Whenever only one train arrived from Warsaw, a second one would come from another city.

Around 20 August four trains arrived in the camp: from Warsaw, Kielce, Skarżysko-Kamienna, and one from Polesia.[8] On certain days trains also arrived from Germany and from the Czech lands.[9]

By day the women and children are liquidated in the camp, by night the men.

Among the escapees are people who were in the camp for seven days. They repeatedly joined the newly arrived transports. One woman who was wearing trousers hid for nine days in the group of men. Escaping from the camp itself is difficult and risky, but there are people who try, despite the fact that the camp grounds are brightly lit at night and even the smallest movement is met with machine-gun fire. One of the escapees was already set to go into the 'bath', [i.e.] he was naked, [but then] he smeared himself with mud and thus managed to crawl past the guards and through the fences unnoticed. One of the escapees tells the story of a Jew who suddenly rushed a Ukrainian and grabbed his rifle. He returned the weapon to the Ukrainian in exchange for the Ukrainian enabling his escape. The Ukrainian hid the man in a wagon and got him out of the camp that way.

The Jews from Stoczek, the prisoner functionaries, circulate among the Jews in the camp, calling for them to surrender their money and valuables. The Ukrainians have pockets full of gold, diamonds, and watches. Many people do not want to give their possessions to the murderers, so they tear up the money and bury the valuables [instead]. In the camp there is a brisk trade in a drink made from human urine and sweetened with saccharin. One of these beverages costs 100 zł.

Why is there no mass outbreak?

Rumours circulate that the area all around the camp is heavily guarded and that the fences are charged with high-voltage electricity. The people have also been broken by the terrible experiences at the Umschlag[platz], during the journey, and in the camp. The general dejection affects even those who are more active by nature. One guy, a butcher, had his knife with him and wanted to do 'something' with it, but the Jews around him stopped him.

The younger, stronger, and more active men are weeded out immediately upon arrival, because they usually volunteer to fetch water or to bury the dead. None of them return to the camp. They are all shot.

7 This figure is inflated. The trains from Warsaw brought approximately 6,000 people to the extermination camp daily: see also Doc. 111, fn. 3. In addition, it took longer than 15 minutes to murder the victims with poison gas and to subsequently empty and clean the gas chambers.
8 A historical region in Byelorussia; between the world wars it was a voivodeship in eastern Poland.
9 Referred to in the original as *tshekhye* (Czechia), i.e. what was then the Protectorate of Bohemia and Moravia.

When the wind blows in the direction of Małkinia, the smell of corpses from Treblinka is distinctly discernible at the Małkinia train station.

The Jews in the surrounding shtetls know very well the fate of the Jews in Treblinka, which is why they did not allow themselves to be loaded onto the wagons. Many of them were shot on the spot; anyone who could hide or flee did so. That is what happened in Węgrów and in other shtetls.

Three such camps exist: one near Minsk for the eastern territories,[10] one in the Lublin region in Bełżec, and the third, the biggest, in Treblinka, near Małkinia.

An SS man gives a speech to every arriving transport, providing assurances that everyone will be taken for work in Smolensk or Kyiv.

On the night of 29 to 30 August, during the bombing of Warsaw,[11] Treblinka camp went dark for the first time. An SS man gave a speech to the Jews, saying that the German government and Roosevelt had reached an agreement on sending the European Jews to Madagascar, and that the first transport would deport from Treblinka the next day. The Jews were elated by this news. As soon as the all-clear was given, the killing machines resumed their 'normal' work again.

Even in the camp itself, the Hitlerites seek to fool the Jews until the very last moment. Not only the speeches, but also the inscriptions and the 'way of life' there are meant to create the impression that Treblinka is a stop on the way to somewhere else: to another journey or to work, but to life ahead at any rate. The SS is afraid of an attempted rebellion or revolt, which is why misleading the Jews plays such a large part in their operations targeting Jews.

There were voices in Jewish society during the initial days of the operation warning the community what the operation really entails.

Today every Jew must know what fate awaits the deportees.

The same fate awaits the handful [of Jews] who still remain in Warsaw.[12]

The conclusion to be drawn here is this: Don't get caught! Hide! Do not let yourselves […].[13] Do not be deceived by any registrations, selections, numbers, or inspections.

*Jews, help one another, take care of the children!* Help the 'illegals'![14] The shameful traitors and accomplices – the Jewish policemen – must be boycotted! Do not believe them. Beware of them. Resist them!

We are all soldiers [fighting] on a terrible front!

We must endure in order to settle scores for our tormented brothers and sisters, children and parents, who have perished at the hands of murderers on the battlefield for freedom and humanity!

10 A reference to Maly Trostenets, near Minsk; there the deportees were shot or murdered in gas vans.

11 The Soviet air force carried out a major attack on Warsaw during the night of 1 to 2 Sept. 1942.

12 After the deportations that took place from 22 July to 21 Sept. 1942, several tens of thousands of people remained in the Warsaw ghetto.

13 One line in the original is illegible.

14 A reference to Jews who were hiding in the Warsaw ghetto but were not registered as workers.

## DOC. 144

### On 21 September 1942 the SS and Police Leader in District Radom states that Poles who help Jews are to be warned they face the death penalty[1]

Letter from the SS and Police Leader in District Radom, Radom (log no. 1560/42/Dr Bö./Lg.), signed Dr Böttcher,[2] to the offices of the civil administration in District Radom, dated 21 September 1942

*Distribution list IIIa* from the Governor of District Radom, Governor's office, 21 January 1942
*Re*: the harbouring of escaped Jews by Poles
The experiences of recent weeks have shown that Jews are fleeing from the small Jewish residential districts in the countryside in order to avoid the evacuation. These Jews must have been taken in by Poles. I request that all mayors and wójts be immediately instructed to make it absolutely clear to the residents of their villages that any Pole who harbours a Jew is in breach of the Third Regulation on Restrictions of Movement in the General Government of 15 October 1941, *VOBl-GG*, p. 595.[3] Likewise, Poles who do not give fleeing Jews shelter but feed them or sell them food will also be considered accessories. In all cases, these Poles face the death penalty.

I further request that the Jewish residential district be officially cleared in all places where the evacuation of Jews has already taken place. Exception is made for those towns where residual ghettos remain.

## DOC. 145

### In early autumn 1942 the Home Army reports on events in the Warsaw ghetto[1]

Report by the Information Department, Home Army High Command Bureau of Information and Propaganda, unsigned, sometime after mid September 1942

*The liquidation of the Jews in Warsaw*
The year 1942 will be remembered as that of the bloody mass liquidation of the Jews in Poland, which is the last phase in the National Socialists' strategy for solving the Jewish question.

The methods have changed in a number of ways over the course of the German occupation of Poland. They began with anti-Jewish propaganda, which continued to

1 AIPN, Rd 108/273, fol. 11. Copy in BArch, R 102/I/1, fol. 61. Published as a facsimile in Adam Rutkowski, *Męczeństwo, walka, zagłada Żydów w Polsce 1939–1945* (Warsaw: Wydawnictwo Ministerstwa Obrony Narodowej, 1960), fig. 248. This document has been translated from German.
2 Dr Herbert Böttcher (1907–1950), lawyer; joined the SS in 1939; acting chief of police in Memel, 1939–1940; served in the war, August–Dec. 1940; chief of police in Kassel; SS and Police Leader in District Radom from April 1942; in 1949 stood trial in Radom, and was executed there in 1950.
3 See Doc. 13.

1 Uniwersytet Warszawski, Biblioteka Uniwersytecka, Zbiór Rękopisów, 2188, fols. 18–22. Published in Tyszkowa, 'Eksterminacja Żydów w latach 1941–1943', part 2, pp. 52–57. This document has been translated from Polish.

escalate and was accompanied by the gradual isolation of Jews and by them being harassed, above all when they were undertaking forced labour.

Initially rather improvised in nature, over time they assumed the character of a planned operation (compulsory forced labour in camps for the entire Jewish population, men and women, from the ages of 16 to 60[2]) which was intended to affect large swathes of the population. In practice, however, this operation remained comparatively limited (of the 150,000 people in Warsaw in autumn 1940 who could have been taken to the forced labour camps, only around 5,000 in total were transported there). Those affected were mainly the poorest members of the proletariat, as the wealthier people bought their freedom. Soon thereafter, in mid 1941, the camps (in which, just as in other similar cases, torture and inhuman treatment occurred) were liquidated. A much more rigorous approach was taken to isolating the Jewish population, a process which began in 1940 with the establishment of ghettos – some more strictly closed off than others – in the cities and larger towns. But even this operation did not achieve its intended goal: the gradual eradication of the Jewish element. There was a huge spike in the mortality rate, especially in larger areas; in Warsaw, for example, it was 10 per cent in 1941 and 15 per cent in the first quarter of 1942 on a year-on-year basis. However, the intention to starve the Jewish population confined in the ghetto failed, despite an extremely low supply quota (in Warsaw, approximately half a kilo of bread per capita per week, and virtually nothing else) and strict bans on food imports. Due to the extremely brisk trade in smuggled goods, which was supported by official German agencies and yielded very high profits for those involved, the city's Jewish population was barely worse off than its Aryan population. Despite walls and barbed wire, the differences in food prices were minimal. Nor could the Jewish population be completely prevented from earning a living, because the Germans themselves exploited those fit for work, especially the skilled workers, on a large scale, particularly for war-related work in the so-called 'szopy'. Moreover, various production departments were again created in which the Jewish population worked on illegal exports: making cigarettes (bypassing the tobacco monopoly), illegal saccharin, quality vodka (despite the fixed quotas), decorative items, watches, imitation jewellery, and the like. The official exchange of goods between the Warsaw ghetto and the rest of the city, which was officially overseen by the *Transferstelle*,[3] amounted to only 13 groszy per capita in spring 1942, and communication with the ghetto was made very difficult – nevertheless, the bartering trade flourished. Nalewki was the main shopping point, just as it had been before the war, with wholesale supplies from the pre war period to fall back on.

In the second half of 1941, the penalty for Jews leaving the ghetto became more severe and the regulations on the death penalty were introduced[4] – the manifestation of the Germans' peculiar revenge for the unfavourable course of the war on the Bolshevik front. Since the outbreak of war with the United States, further restrictions and harassment have been introduced (furs were confiscated last winter and the system of sealed Jewish residential districts was extended across almost the entire territory of the General

2 According to the Second Implementing Regulation to the Regulation of 26 October 1939 on the Introduction of Forced Labour for the Jewish Population in the General Government (12 Dec. 1939), Jewish people between the ages of 14 and 60 were subject to forced labour: see PMJ 4/58.

3 German in the original: 'Transfer Bureau'.

4 See Doc. 13.

Government), but it was not until 1942 that the situation escalated to become mass murder. The situation was foreshadowed in the Führer's speech at the beginning of that year, which cited the radical solution to the Jewish question as one of the aims for 1942.[5] Indications of what this solution would look like in practice had been pouring in from the East since autumn 1941 and escalated over the course of that winter and from the spring of 1942: this was mass murder. In Vilna, for example, 60,000 Jews were murdered, and only 12,000 were left alive; Lublin's population of 30,000 Jews was liquidated and reduced to 2,500 people; in Lwów, 50 per cent of the population were murdered, and it was a similar situation in towns across Malopolska and Volhynia. The operation intensified after Himmler's tour of the General Government in March.[6] In addition to Belzec camp in Malopolska, in which 80,000 people were executed by electrocution[7] over the course of a single month (March–April 1942), two additional execution sites were established in the spring: in Czerwony Bór, near Małkinia ('Treblinka no. 2'),[8] and in Sobibór, in powiat Włodawa. In sum, it can be said that of the 2.5 million Jewish people in the territory of the General Government (if we take into account not only Polish Jews, but also the Jews brought en masse from Germany, Czechoslovakia, Vienna, etc.), nearly half a million perished due to the rise in mortality, and approximately 1.5 million (if not more) were 'liquidated' between autumn 1941 and summer 1942. By now there are probably no more than half a million still alive. The climax of this bloody operation was the liquidation of the Warsaw ghetto in summer 1942, after which only 40,000 of the original 370,000 Jews (the official figure of 435,000 people was inflated, as it was based on the number of ration cards issued, a large number of which people had claimed under false names) were still alive in October.

The Warsaw ghetto, established in October 1940 and sealed that November, became increasingly isolated from the Aryan residential district; its boundaries were moved more than ten times and it became smaller and smaller, also because more Jews were brought in from outside Warsaw. Despite the acts of terror increasing, people were able to adapt to the harsh living conditions. This spring the news of the murder of Jews in the East and the establishment of new camps in the General Government intensified concerns, though these quickly subsided: even the pessimists did not reckon with the surprise turn in events that was to occur so soon.

The signal for this was another visit that Himmler paid to the General Government in mid July. His orders must have been quite categorical, because the liquidation operation began immediately.[9] It began on 17 July, with the registration of foreign Jews who were brought to Pawiak and thereby eliminated.[10] Three days later, the task of guarding

5 Presumably a reference to Hitler's New Year's message of 1 Jan. 1942, in which he announced: 'The Jew will not exterminate the European people, he will instead become the victim of his own plot.' In his speeches on 30 Jan. and 24 Feb. 1942, Hitler spoke about the fact that the war would result in the annihilation of Jewry: Domarus (ed.), *Hitler*, pp. 2564, 2574, 2591.

6 Himmler was in Cracow on 13 March 1942 and in Lublin on 14 March 1942.

7 The victims were in fact murdered with carbon monoxide in gas chambers.

8 A reference to the extermination camp which was constructed from April 1942.

9 See Doc. 96.

10 Several hundred British and US nationals and people with identity documents issued by neutral states, including Central and South American countries, were detained on 17 July 1942 in Pawiak prison in Warsaw, which was run by the Security Police.

the ghetto boundaries (which had been carried out by the Polish police up until then) was transferred to the 'junacy'– that is, security battalions specially trained for this purpose and composed of Ukrainians, Lithuanians, Latvians, and Bolshevik prisoners of war. They formed dense cordons [around the ghetto], thereby cutting off the smuggling trade, which had already been very difficult because the smugglers were frequently shot. The 'junacy' went on a shooting spree, targeting Jewish houses located on the ghetto boundaries; at the ghetto exits (which had been reduced from a dozen in the spring of last year to two, if one does not count the third one – via the cemetery) the German police posts were reinforced and armed with machine guns. Moreover, German policemen on motorcycles patrolled the ghetto boundaries non-stop 24 hours a day.

The next day (21 July) at 11 a.m., German police cars drove up to the Jewish Council's headquarters: orders had been issued to arrest the members of the Jewish Council, and those who turned up were taken to Pawiak. At the same time, numerous police cars carrying uniformed Germans appeared in the ghetto, conducting street raids and primarily targeting those who were better dressed (just like the members of the Jewish Council who had been arrested, these individuals were to serve as hostages in order to ensure that the liquidation operation went smoothly). They also raided the buildings, where they mainly searched for the intelligentsia and killed the apartment residents without checking their personal details. This is how, on that day, the late Professor Raszeja, who had come to the ghetto with a pass for a medical consultation, was killed.

On the following day (22 July) at 10 a.m., German police cars again drove up to the Jewish Council's headquarters. They dictated to the Council members who were still at liberty a detailed order for the 'resettlement' of the Jewish population from Warsaw, the most important provisions of which were immediately posted as a public announcement (see Appendix 1).[11] At the same time, they also dictated the technical details which were not included in the announcement: the number of people to be resettled was set at 6,000 per day and they were to be assembled in the hospital building on Stawki, from where they would be taken to the neighbouring reloading point,[12] the railroad siding that had previously served to facilitate the exchange of goods with the ghetto. The Jewish Order Police were to bring the people designated for resettlement to this place every day by 4 p.m., whereby the first transport – consisting of prisoners, the homeless, and the like – was to be made available that very day. The members of the Jewish Council and the hostages interned in Pawiak had to ensure these instructions were strictly observed, at the risk of their own lives.

One day later (23 July), two uniformed Germans again came to the Jewish Council premises and held a meeting with Council President Czerniaków.[13] Shortly after they left, Czerniaków committed suicide. Since he did not speak to anyone before his death, the specifics of that conversation remain unknown. However, based on the note he left behind and a letter to his wife, it appears that they demanded that a contingent of

11 See Doc. 98.

12 Here and below, 'reloading point' is presumably a reference to the so-called Umschlagplatz, the holding area for deportees.

13 See Doc. 99.

10,000 people be taken away on 24 July, and over the following days the contingent was set at 7,000.[14] Czerniaków's successor, Mr Lichtenbaum, fulfilled these conditions.

The quotas were met by picking up people in their homes and in street roundups. In order to motivate the Jewish policemen, the Germans issued special certificates affording protection from resettlement – not only for their wives and children (they were already exempt, according to the order), but also for other relatives. Since the order also exempted the employees of large German companies and their families, there ensued a veritable race in the ghetto to obtain certificates providing proof of such employment. People paid sums running into the thousands for this privilege. Later, however, it turned out that the certificates issued by the German companies were worthless, as were the special certificates issued to the Jewish police, because the Germans did not abide by them and simply took everyone away without considering the documents. Indeed, after a few days, the Germans grew dissatisfied with the Jewish police (although they continued to work assiduously) and began to round up the contingents themselves, with the help of the 'junacy'. In the process, they completely sealed off entire apartment blocks and they went into the courtyards and started to shoot: this was a signal to leave the apartments and gather in the courtyards. Anyone who tried to hide or who could not get out quickly enough was killed in their apartment; senile, elderly, and disabled people were also killed in their apartments. Families destined for resettlement were separated while being driven to the reloading point: women from their husbands, children – even little ones – from their parents. Upon arriving at the square, amidst the constant shooting, the Germans segregated the elderly and the disabled from the transport and took them (60–100 people per day) to the cemetery, where they were killed immediately. The rest were loaded into goods wagons, 100–120 people per wagon; these were then sealed, and the train set off. The people were squeezed so tightly together that they could not breathe, and the situation was made even worse by the quicklime spread on the wagon floors, which caused the suffocation of those trapped inside when it was slaked. This is also why the railway tracks along the route were littered with numerous corpses.

The transports were directed to the three camps already mentioned above: Treblinka, Sobibor, and Belzec.[15] A report dated 10 July 1942[16] given by a German employed at the execution site in Belzec provides information about the fate of the 'resettled' people, and the fact that in Treblinka, the main execution site, large excavators were procured to bury those who were killed, and these were in use non-stop. The stench of the decomposing corpses made the peasants in the 5-kilometre radius surrounding the camp vomit and forced them to flee. Apart from two small transports carrying a total of 4,000 young, particularly physically fit people, which were taken to a section of the front (in the direction of Brześć and Małachowicze),[17] we are not aware of any instance of those who were 'resettled' escaping death – which was reportedly mainly brought about using gas in so-called 'baths'.

14 An extract from Czerniaków's letter to his wife, Felicja, is reproduced in Czerniaków, *Im Warschauer Getto*, p. 285.

15 The deportees from the Warsaw ghetto were transported to Treblinka.

16 See Doc. 92.

17 The transports on 28 and 31 July 1942 went to Bobruisk and Minsk in Byelorussia.

The people who were exterminated were mainly the elderly, the disabled, and children, while young, physically healthy people were exempted in principle as a valuable labour force. In contrast, the residents of the children's homes and after-school care centres were all taken away, including those at the orphanage run by Janusz Korczak, who, despite being offered the chance to stay in the ghetto, went to the reloading point, along with the head of the boarding school.[18] Evidence of the unbelievably fast pace of the liquidation operation is provided by the fact that, by late August, about a quarter of a million people had been taken from Warsaw, and this despite a five-day break from 20 to 24 August, when they were busy murdering the Jews in the ghettos in the suburbs of Warsaw: in Otwock, Falenica, Rembertów, Nowy Dwór, Kałuszyn, and Mińsk Maz[owiecki], and other places. This took place in full view of the Polish population, who were deeply shocked to witness the mass shootings at the forced marches of deportees, as well as the hunt for fugitives, and to see the hundreds of corpses lying in the streets, on the roads, and along the railway tracks. The fact that only 120,000 ration cards had been provided in advance for the month of September, and 40,000 for October, is proof that the operation was carried out according to a precise plan. After the 'resettlement' ended, around mid September,[19] only 40,000 people remained in the ghetto as workers for the Germans; their families were taken away despite the promises made.

The atrocities committed in the course of the resettlement are shocking: for example, a pregnant Jewish woman managed to escape from the ghetto to Grochów,[20] where she was taken in by a Polish family and gave birth. However, a German gendarme tracked her down, shot her dead on the spot, and trampled the infant to death. In general, however, the terrorized Jewish population, driven to despair, passively surrendered to their fate. The one thing was that the suicide rate, of both individuals and entire families, increased to the point that the Germans closed all the pharmacies in the ghetto to prevent suicide by poisoning. There were also a huge number of cases of people becoming mentally deranged. There were also instances when Jews who, no longer able to bear waiting for death, asked the 'junacy' to shoot them. However, as nothing is free nowadays, the fulfilment of such a request cost 100 złoty …

Excerpts from eyewitness accounts will add further details to this overview.

A woman who managed to escape to the other side with the help of Polish friends reports:

'Some time before the mass resettlement from the Warsaw ghetto began, news began to arrive about liquidations of the ghettos in other cities, such as Łódź, Cracow, and especially Lublin. Not everyone believed this news, and even if they did, most of them were of the opinion that the Germans would not dare to use such methods in a city as big as Warsaw, in full view of the whole world … On Sunday, 19 July, the news spread that the resettlement would happen. Indescribable panic arose in the city. The next day, the news was officially denied, and the spreading of false reports was forbidden under penalty of death …'.

18 This is probably a reference to the deputy director of the orphanage, Stefania Wilczyńska (1886–1942).
19 The deportations came to a temporary halt on 21 Sept. 1942 and resumed in Nov. 1942.
20 An area on the 'Aryan side' of Warsaw.

'The blockading of apartment buildings began … In addition to these blockades, raids took place on the streets throughout the entire day. The Jewish police distinguished themselves in this operation by their immense brutality. I witnessed how women were grabbed by their hands, legs, and hair. Theoretically you were allowed to take up to fifteen kilos of luggage with you, but people were usually picked up on the spot and the Germans took parcels off those who did have any before the people were loaded on to the train … In theory, children were protected from resettlement if their mothers and fathers were in work. In practice, however, the Germans surrounded the apartment buildings that served as workers' barracks (employees who worked for the Germans were barracked with their families in separate apartment buildings when there was no room for them in the factories) while the parents or the husbands were at work, dragged the women and children out, and took them away. I was in the fortunate position of being unmarried and having work, but day after day I had to deal with desperate mothers and fathers whose children had been taken during working hours, or sons and daughters whose parents had been taken. At a certain point, blockades began to take place in the factories. The elderly and often young people were removed from their places of work and taken away. The Germans came and said that so and so many people from the respective workshop had to be taken away, and they even dragged skilled workers out without checking their documents. During one of these blockades, I also ended up at the reloading point, along with the others …

'Even though everything I had been experiencing for weeks was absolutely horrendous (not enough food or sleep, eleven hours of hard labour every day, the constant fear of death), the hell at the reloading point surpassed everything. There a man ceases to be a man; there he is no longer even an animal – he is nothing more than rubbish, destined to burn. The Germans and the Jewish police beat the crowd incessantly; children, the ill, and the elderly are trampled to death; one is up to one's ankles in human excrement … I made it out of that hell thanks to the help of my friends.'

Another refugee reports:

'Since this spring, rumours had been circulating that special SS detachments for the extermination of Jews, so-called Judenvernichtungskommandos,[21] would be set up in Germany. Hitler's speeches and Goebbels's threats in the *Reich*[22] increased concern for the future … Some illegal workers' organizations came up with the idea of preparing resistance operations in case of a pogrom, but such plans did not resonate with the vast majority of the already terrorized population. In late June, rumours about the planned extermination of Warsaw's Jewish population began to circulate once more. Panic broke out every few days. By the second half of July, everyone was talking about resettlement. Concerned for the fate of the residential district, Mr Czerniaków turned

21 German in the original: 'Jew-extermination squads'.

22 *Das Reich* was a weekly magazine published by Deutscher Verlag – part of the Franz Eher publishing house – from May 1930 until 1945, with a circulation of up to 1.4 million copies. Goebbels was an editorial writer for the magazine, and Dr Eugen Mündler (b. 1889) was its editor-in-chief from 1940 until Dec. 1942.

to ghetto commissioner Auerswald on 20 July to ask whether the rumours about the resettlement of the Jews had any basis in fact. He received a firm denial in reply …

'The Germans entrusted the resettlement operation to the Jewish Order Service, under the leadership of J. Szeryński, who had previously held an important post in the Polish police force and had been the head of the local Jewish police since the Warsaw ghetto was established. In winter 1942 he had been imprisoned on charges of smuggling his furs into the Polish district, but on the eve of the resettlement the Germans released him, no doubt on the condition that he would lead the operation as they wished.[23] Szeryński did not disappoint them …

'Total panic reigned in the ghetto. People ran with their suitcases from one street to another in order to escape the resettlement. This horrible situation was aggravated by hunger, because smuggling from the Polish part of the city had collapsed … There were days when approximately 15,000 people were resettled. The operation increasingly intensified. The desperate population tried to save themselves by registering en masse at the 'szopy' of Többens, Schultz, Döring,[24] and others. They paid enormous bribes, handed over their sewing machines, and pleaded for admission. The population expected the Germans to leave the workers and their families alone. Many sought to save themselves by fleeing the ghetto. Completely desperate and driven by hunger, some volunteered to go to the "Umschlagplatz".[25] They believed the Germans' promise that the families of volunteers would not be separated; specifically the news that children and wives would be split up from their husbands had caused awful terror. Many were under the illusion that they would be taken away to work. But most tried to hide. Hunts and blockades continued to rage. To exacerbate the chaos, the Germans ordered the simultaneous evacuation of certain streets, first in the "small" and later in the "large" ghetto. Under the threat of being shot, the population had to vacate their apartments within a few hours. Of course this intensified the confusion and chaos …

'Gangs of SS men began to invade the "szopy"; they removed the workers and then took their families from the neighbouring apartments. One had the impression that some of the factory management deliberately cooperated with the Vernichtungskommando[26] in order to get rid of the surplus workers – and especially their families – for a variety of reasons. From 13 to 15 August many women and children fell victim to the attacks on the Többens, Döring, and Schultz "szopy". The majority of the employees lost their next of kin … Around 28 August the attack on Szeryński failed.[27] The resettlement operation is ongoing. We expect that in the autumn, when the factories have completed their orders for the winter, some of the workers will be dismissed and then resettled.'[28]

23 The Gestapo arrested Szeryński on 1 May 1942 and released him on 26 July 1942.

24 Wilhelm Döring Apparatebau GmbH, an armaments factory, was located at 26 Grzybowska Street and remained there after the liquidation of the 'small ghetto'.

25 German in the original.

26 German in the original: 'extermination squad'.

27 On 20 August 1942 Szeryński was wounded in an attack carried out by a member of the Jewish Combat Organization (ŻOB).

28 On 10 Nov. 1942 deportations from the Warsaw ghetto resumed for a few days.

Excerpts from another eyewitness account of the liquidation of the ghetto, by a Christian, describing a series of cases of cruelty and savagery, are provided in Appendix 3.[29]

And finally – several excerpts from a report by a Polish policeman with official access to the ghetto.[30]

'The "hunt" in the streets significantly contributes to the accelerated liquidation of the Jews. Gestapo men and the "White Guard" (i.e., Bolshevik prisoners of war who have gone into German service)[31] drive through the streets using rickshaws driven by Jews among other vehicles, and open fire with their light machine guns as soon as they see a bigger crowd. Often thirty to forty Jewish corpses lie on a single street over the course of one day … The Jewish Community determines which Jews are to be transported, while the Jewish police, who carry out this heinous operation with great zeal (and who have no weapons except for a rubber truncheon), hand over this "contingent" to the Germans. There is a documented case of a Jewish policeman who led his own mother away, explaining to her that the quota had to be filled; if she did not go, he would have to report for transport himself, and she would be better off, since death would claim her sooner …

'The total, almost pathological passivity of the Jews is striking; there are no desperate responses at all. This psychological breakdown is so extensive that many Jews who were still in hiding in the beginning are now volunteering for transport and wish to die as quickly as possible. No Jew doubts the fact that they are being taken away to be murdered. There are many instances of suicide among the Jews. For example, in one of the "cleared" buildings, the door to an apartment is closed, and you can smell the gas leaking from inside. Inside – the corpses of people who have taken their own lives. In one of the apartments, a dead Jewish woman lies on the bed, and next to her a vial of Veronal.'[32]

29 Not published here.

30 The entire testimony is published in 'The Liquidation of the Warsaw Ghetto' (Likwidacja getta warszawskiego), appendix 6, which the government delegation sent to London on 7 Oct. 1942: see AAN, 1325/202/XV-2, pp. 61 f., and PISM, PRM, 73/4/205, pp. 382 f. (appendix B to Diary no. 4407/42).

31 This is a reference to auxiliary personnel from the SS training camp in Trawniki; most of the recruits were Soviet prisoners of war.

32 Veronal was a sleeping pill containing the active ingredient barbital, which, if taken in large doses, quickly resulted in death.

## DOC. 146
## On 23 September 1942 Richard Lichtheim sends word of the systematic extermination of Jews in occupied Poland[1]

Letter from Richard Lichtheim,[2] Geneva, to L. Leder,[3] Hotel Bristol, Istanbul, dated 23 September 1942 (carbon copy)[4]

*The Executive of the Zionist Organization*[5]*/The Jewish Agency for Palestine Geneva Office*[6]

Dear Mr Leder,

Supplementary to my letter of 19 September,[7] I can also inform you of the following: I wrote to Mr Grünbaum[8] a good number of weeks ago at his request on the matter of Mr Czerniakow, stating that there is absolutely no reliable news to be had. Correspondence with the Jews in Warsaw has not functioned for quite some time now, although one can still write to other places in Poland.

The news of Czerniakow's suicide that appeared in the British press certainly seems highly probable, as the events that led to the suicide according to these reports have been confirmed for me by a range of sources. Through various channels, which I do not wish to give details of here, I received verbal and written messages that all concur that mass deportations from Warsaw have taken place in recent weeks and months, and we must unfortunately assume that those deported are no longer alive. Similar events have transpired in other places where larger centres of Jewish life existed, particularly in Eastern Galicia.

I have actually been writing continually to Dr Lauterbach[9] about all these things. Ultimately, with respect to the aid sent to Poland from neutral countries such as Switzer-

1 CZA, WJC Collection, series C, subseries 3, box C159/9 (Institute of Jewish Affairs Archives). This document has been translated from German.

2 Richard Lichtheim (1885–1963), economist, journalist, and politician; editor-in-chief of *Die Welt*, the main publication of the Zionist movement in Germany, 1911–1913; representative of the World Zionist Organization (WZO) in Constantinople, 1913–1916; president of the Zionist Federation of Germany, 1917–1920; emigrated to Palestine in 1934; head of the WZO office in Geneva, 1938–1946; later lived in Israel; author of *Die Geschichte des deutschen Zionismus* (Jerusalem: Rubin Mass, 1954).

3 L. (Leyzer or Eliezer) Leder was an envoy for the Committee of Four appointed by the Jewish Agency for Palestine in Istanbul in 1939: see also fn. 8.

4 The original contains handwritten underlining and annotations.

5 The Zionist Organization was founded by the First Zionist Congress, held in Basel in 1897, on the initiative of Theodor Herzl.

6 The Executive of the Zionist Organization and the Jewish Agency for Palestine in Geneva stayed in contact with the Jewish communities in occupied Europe, provided the offices in Palestine with news, and initiated or supported measures to aid and rescue persecuted Jews.

7 Not in the file.

8 Izaak (Yitskhok, Yitzhak) Grünbaum (Grinboym) (1879–1970), lawyer, politician, and Zionist; member of the Sejm, 1919–1932; editor-in-chief of the *Haynt* newspaper from 1920; chairman of the Zionist Organization in Poland, 1930–1932, then emigrated to Palestine; head of the Immigration Department and from 1935 to 1948 head of the Labour Department at the Jewish Agency for Palestine; chairman of the Jewish Agency's Committee of Four from 1939; chairman of the Jewish Agency's Rescue Committee, 1943–1944; Israel's minister of internal affairs, 1948–1949.

9 Dr Leo Lauterbach (1886–1968), practising lawyer; head of the Organizational Department of the Zionist Organization.

land, Sweden, and Portugal, the most recent news is that it is no longer permitted to send money or food to individuals or to the Jewish councils that still exist; the approval of the Cracow foreign exchange control office is required and is practically impossible to obtain. Aid can therefore only be sent via the Red Cross now, and it seems that shipments sent recently via the German Red Cross have indeed arrived in some areas and have been distributed.

One cannot gain a truly precise overview of the situation in individual cities and provinces because circumstances differ from district to district, and reports by mail are not possible. As mentioned, reliable information can only be obtained through special channels. However, the events outlined above have been confirmed by reliable reports of this kind, and one must conclude from this that a systematic policy of extermination against the larger centres of Jewish life is under way at various points. Nevertheless, there are still many Jews in the various ghettos and spread throughout the entire General Government in smaller places, including many deported from Germany.

This is pretty much all I can tell you at the moment, but in my letters to Dr Lauterbach, I have already expressed my fear that the extermination process will be conducted at an ever-increasing pace in the coming months. I assume that Dr Silberschein[10] has already written to you, but I do not believe he would have been able to tell you anything significantly different. For your information, I would like to point out that the offices of the World Jewish Congress and RELICO are in the same building as my office, and that we are collaborating constantly. However, Dr Silberschein opened his own small office many months ago because certain disagreements had occurred between him and the World Congress office.[11] Letters addressed to him that are sent to the World Congress or to RELICO continue to reach him.

I have enclosed a photocopy of a postcard that a local man received from the mayor of Lodz (Litzmannstadt).[12] You will see that in Lodz, too, the Jews can receive neither letters nor packages, which is sure to be connected to the measures mentioned above. I assume that you will pass on all of this news to Jerusalem in a suitable manner.

Best regards,

10 Dr Abraham (Adolf Henryk) Silberschein (also known as Avrom Zilbershayn) (1882–1951), lawyer; one of the leaders of the Zionist workers' party Poale Zion-Hitachdut in Eastern Galicia in the 1920s; member of the Sejm, 1922–1927; delegate at the 21st Zionist Congress, held in August 1939; afterwards founder and director of the RELICO aid organization and co-founder of the World Jewish Congress in Geneva; published a documentary record with the title *Die Judenausrottung in Polen* (The Extermination of the Jews in Poland) in 1944.

11 The work of RELICO (Relief Committee), which was largely funded by the World Jewish Congress, intended to help Jews leave Germany and countries occupied by Germany or threatened by German occupation. From 1942 Silberschein focused on helping refugees leave Eastern Europe, while another branch of RELICO tracked down missing people, protected Jewish children in Western Europe from deportation, and sent food parcels to Theresienstadt.

12 Not in the file. The mayor of Litzmannstadt was Werner Ventzki (1906–2004), lawyer; joined the NSDAP in 1931; Gauamtsleiter of the National Socialist People's Welfare Organization (NSV) in Pomerania, 1934–1939; simultaneously member of the municipal government in Stettin until 1936, then head of the Welfare Department for the Oberpräsident of Pomerania; head of welfare for the ethnic German population in Posen, 1939–1940; mayor of Litzmannstadt, April 1941 to mid 1943, then served in the Waffen-SS; representative of the Ministry for Expellees in West Berlin after the war; later Oberregierungsrat in Bonn.

## DOC. 147

## Around 25 September 1942 an escapee from Treblinka extermination camp reports on how the murderers there attempt to deceive their victims[1]

Handwritten report, unsigned,[2] for the underground archive of the Warsaw ghetto, Warsaw, written on or around 25 September 1942[3]

The wagons are parked at the ramp, which is located at the edge of a relatively small square surrounded on three sides by a barbed wire fence. On the fourth side is a large wooden barracks. The Germans herd the selected women with their children into the barracks and order them to take off their shoes first. On one side of the square there is a tall pole with a board bearing a large sign: 'Achtung Warschauer![4] You are being resettled for work. Before you are assigned work, you must take a bath. Everyone must strip naked. Valuables and money must be left behind. You are to take documents and soap with you.' A Ukrainian armed with a light machine gun stands on a platform on the right side of the square; next to him is a searchlight.

As soon as the Jews appear on the square, they are greeted by the so-called Kapos – well-dressed and well-fed young Jews who have triangular yellow patches sewn onto their trousers just above the knee. They quickly shout one order after another: 'Line up in rows of ten!' 'Take off your shoes!' Whenever the Jews ask what will happen to them, the Kapos respond with blows and tell them to obey orders quickly. Once everyone has lined up in rows, a German inspects the human material. He weeds out the short, the emaciated, and the weak. It seems as if he were selecting them for labour. After the selection […][5]

To illustrate German perfidy and systematic deception, the following is a further example of an incident in Treblinka in the second half of August. Soviet bombers conducted heavy night-time raids over the General Government. As already mentioned, strong searchlights light the whole square at night, due to the fear that the Jews might escape before they are killed. One night, the lights were switched off during an impending air raid.[6] The camp commandant[7] feared that the Jews might take advantage of the night and try to escape their place of execution. To prevent this, he ordered all the Jews to assemble on the square before the lights were switched off. He delivered a speech and,

1 AŻIH, Ring II/381 (298), fols. 1–2. Published in Sakowska (ed.), *Archiwum Ringelbluma: Konspiracyjne Archiwum Getta Warszawy*, vol. 1: *Listy o Zagładzie*, pp. 122–123. This document has been translated from Polish.

2 Jakub Rabinowicz wrote the report.

3 Rabinowicz returned to Warsaw between 21 and 25 Sept. 1942.

4 German in the original: 'Attention Varsovians!'

5 The text breaks off here, after which follows the further account in the same handwriting.

6 This was probably during the night of 1–2 Sept. 1942, when Soviet bombers raided Warsaw.

7 From Sept. 1942 the camp commandant was SS-Obersturmführer Franz Stangl (1908–1971), weaver and member of the Criminal Police; joined the NSDAP and the SS in 1938; worked in the section for Jewish affairs at the Gestapo in Linz; administrative director of the 'euthanasia' killing centre in Hartheim, 1940–1941, then at the killing centre in Bernburg; participated in the construction of Sobibor from March 1942, and served as the camp's first commandant; interned, 1945–1947; escaped from custody in Linz in 1948; subsequently lived in Italy, Syria, and Brazil; following his extradition, he was sentenced to life imprisonment by Düsseldorf Regional Court in 1970.

with a very serious expression, explained that Hitler and Roosevelt had agreed that Polish Jews would be sent to Madagascar, and that the first transports would leave Treblinka the very next morning. The lights were turned off, and the diesel motor was switched off until the bombers had flown over. Afterwards everything returned to the previous state of affairs, and the relentless murder continued.[8]

## DOC. 148
## On 28 September 1942 Yehoshua Weiss describes a murderous raid on the Jews of Podhajce[1]

Letter from Yehoshua Ben Berl Weiss[2] from Podhajce to his brother Abraham Weiss[3] in New York, dated 28 September 1942

First day of Chol Hamoed Sukkot, 28 September 1942
From Thursday morning, 24 September 1942, the day before the beginning of Sukkot, until now I was in no condition to collect my thoughts enough to consider the kind of situation in which we find ourselves following the great calamity of Yom Kippur.[4] Even now I am not capable of assessing the scope of what happened. Only because I now see that the 1,100–1,200 victims of Yom Kippur – among whom I also lost two people, namely my parents, Father and Mother[5] – have not completely mollified God's anger, and black clouds are gathering again, the thought suddenly occurred to me that I should put the bitterness of my heart, my feelings, on paper. Perhaps this letter will reach the people for whom it is meant.

For several weeks the cloud of a [looming] 'pogrom' had also been darkening our skies, so we all took care to find somewhere to hide ourselves and our families – perhaps we would manage to save ourselves. I took these steps too, of course. At that time I brought Father over to my place, which cost me enough effort and mortal fear. Mother, on the other hand, remained at home; she was still sufficiently capable of holing up in her hiding place at a moment's notice. I also wanted us to be spread out, because it is

8 See Doc. 143.

1 The original is in the possession of the Weiss family in Israel. Yehoshua Weiss wrote the letter immediately after the raid and gave it to a Ukrainian friend to send to Yehoshua's brother Abraham in the United States. Copy in YVA, O-33/1108. Published in Meir Shimon Geshuri (ed.), *Sefer Podhaytse* (Tel Aviv: Farlag fun der podhaytser landsmanshaft in yisroel, 1972), pp. 231–232. This document has been translated from Yiddish.

2 Yehoshua Ben Berl Weiss (1893–1943), merchant from Podhajce; probably killed on 6 June 1943 in the final liquidation in Podhajce.

3 Dr Abraham Weiss (1895–1970), rabbi and Talmud scholar from Podhajce; studied in Vienna, 1917–1921; lecturer in Warsaw from 1928; deputy chairman of the religious Zionist party Mizrachi in Poland, 1935–1940; became a member of the Jewish Citizens' Committee in Warsaw on 12 Sept. 1939; member of the Jewish Council from Oct. 1939; emigrated to the United States in 1940; professor at Yeshiva University in New York until 1967; thereafter lived in Israel.

4 On 21 Sept. 1942 the German police and their Ukrainian auxiliaries rounded up the Jewish inhabitants of Podhajce; approximately 1,000 people were deported to Belzec extermination camp.

5 Dov (also known as Berl) Weiss (1865–1942), merchant; Sara Weiss, née Geller (1870–1942), housewife; both were from Podhajce.

impossible to know where would make a good hiding place and whether there would be enough time for them to make it over to my place. That I in fact assessed the situation correctly is proven by the following: after a few days, that is on Yom Kippur, it became apparent that they had lulled us into a false sense of security, [because] everyone came out of hiding after two days. Father was also no longer in a condition to remain with me in hiding and went home. His health deteriorated, so much so that he became completely bedridden and could no longer get up. The eve of Yom Kippur arrived, and things were completely calm. I went to see him a few times. On the last visit I sufficiently impressed upon him that he should not fast, not even for a minute, and he gave me his word. At 7 a.m. on Monday morning, on Yom Kippur, [the news] struck like lightning. I was still in bed – for some time already, we had been spending the nights in hiding and would go to sleep at daybreak. Word had it that the city was surrounded and the 'pogrom' was already raging, which meant we had only a few seconds to get to the hiding place and I couldn't think about [helping our] parents. Even if I had wanted to sacrifice myself, I would certainly have fallen into [the pogromists'] hands as soon as I left my hiding place without achieving my aim. My hunches regarding [what happened to] our parents proved to be correct, according to the woman who lived with them. She says she was still in bed when she suddenly heard the […][6] murderers' savage shouting. She jumped out of bed, looked out the window, and saw the victims being led away. At that very moment she went into our parents' room, and they were already praying because it was Yom Kippur. Mother and the woman quickly ran to the hiding place. Mother was already in the attic when she suddenly changed her mind and went back, to her great misfortune. The murderers entered soon after, shot Father, who was lying in bed, dressed in his prayer shawl, and his soul immediately departed.[7] Mother was lined up with the victims to be taken away. The woman who lived with them remained in hiding for two days and two nights and was saved. I also sat in hiding for two days in mortal fear. Only on the second day, in the afternoon, did I by chance find out about the terrible misfortunes, which had befallen Mother as well.

At the same time, I was told that the Jewish Council, which was spared this time and could move about freely, was preparing a mass grave and gathering the [bodies of the] martyrs, which included my holy father. Still at the risk of my life, I ran to the cemetery and searched for the holy martyr among the others, some of whom were mangled, and pulled him out with my own hands. I personally helped the non-Jew dig the grave, then climbed down there myself, and with my own hands laid the martyr to his eternal 'rest'. I also backfilled the grave myself, because the non-Jew did not want to lift a finger. Mania[8] was also there to bid a final farewell to the martyr. I did not say Kaddish because there were only two Jewish Council members present.[9] For Mincha[10] there were scarcely nine adult men. I arbitrarily included my barely nine-year-old son[11] in the count and

6 One word in the original is illegible.
7 The final part of this sentence is in Hebrew in the original.
8 Mania Weiss, née Shulwolf (1900–1943), Yehoshua Weiss's wife.
9 Kaddish – the mourner's prayer or the Jewish prayer for the dead – may only be said if there is a minyan, i.e. ten adult male Jews, present.
10 The afternoon prayer.
11 Mordechai Weiss perished in 1943.

said the first Kaddish, but there is no telling how long I will be able to keep it up.[12] This is how I dealt with our holy father. Things with Mother were much worse, as stated above.

While our holy father gave up his sacred soul, Mother had to join the rest of those who were able to walk and was taken to the assembly point, where she and all the rest, facing their dark fate, languished outside in the sun all day. Only in the evening were they herded on foot to the train station, like sheep. Elderly people, children, and those unable to walk [were taken] in vehicles and loaded up for Bełżec, which is allegedly the place where the martyrs are exterminated and their remains, it is rumoured, used to produce artificial fertilizer. The victims were mistreated prior to the transport – many were badly beaten and treated like vile scum. Perhaps 1 per cent managed to escape, some of whom also fell victim. Imagine my mental state, knowing that Mother would have been happy had she had the privilege of dying on the spot as well. There are even worse incidents of parents losing grown-up children, being left completely childless, and yet they live on …[13]

Whole tribes[14] have been uprooted as well. However, one sorrow does not heal another. Only one thing occupies those who remain alive: how long they will continue to live, the abysmal situation, the moral degradation, the extreme constraints, the constant, terrible hunger; for those with fewer means […][15] even further. The organized and brazen theft of the least scrap of worthless Jewish possessions that still remain is technically punishable by death but [in reality] exceeds the limits of the imagination. On top of this, there is the constant threat to one's life. At this point I must add a few words about the Jewish Council.[16] While it is indeed an institution invented by the evil, vengeful spirit thirsting for Jewish blood, the Jewish Council itself far oversteps its bounds, such that it has many victims – and not just from Yom Kippur, but stretching back over the entire period [since the Council was formed] – on its conscience, not to mention Jewish tears and indescribable sorrows. Should anyone survive this, the Jewish Council will be a 'bekhya ledorot',[17] a frightful epithet not found in any language in the world. When someone speaks of 'Jewish Council members', they will mean Jewish criminals and Jewish tormentors. When someone hears about a Jewish institution or a Jewish home with Jewish administrative bodies, they will want to flee to the 'Sahara' desert, where they will not encounter a living soul, because the concept of man is the most horrible thing in the world. Better to be among the wildest animals of the desert instead. I would have described everything in even darker terms, but sadly I lack more forceful expressions.

12 The Kaddish is to be recited daily for one year from the time of burial, and thereafter on each anniversary of the father's or mother's death.

13 In early autumn the Germans set up a ghetto where they concentrated the Jews from the town and the surrounding area. On 30 Oct. 1942 approximately 1,000 of the ghetto residents were deported to Belzec. Many subsequently perished of hunger and disease. The remaining residents were murdered in June, with the exception of some who managed to escape.

14 This term is meant here in the sense of extended families.

15 One word in the original is illegible.

16 The Jewish Council was headed by L. Lilienfeld.

17 Hebrew in the original: 'cause for eternal lament'. This phrase is typically used in connection with Tisha B'Av: see Doc. 110, fn. 2.

I have discovered that the aforementioned aspects apply not only with regard to the Jewish Council here, but also to others, as far as I have heard. Nothing positive has reached my ears yet. Since it isn't possible to travel anywhere, you have to rely on hearsay. The Jewish Council can move around a little in the local voivodeship, however.[18]

With the very brief characterization presented above, I aim only potentially to leave behind at least a 'tipa min [ha]yam habakha'[19] for posterity, because as a writer I am completely unsuited to describing everything in detail, as is evident from the style of writing found above. Moreover, one human lifetime would be too short to put down on paper all of the individual cases in general and of the *Jewish Council* in particular. Perhaps God will still intervene and we will be able to tell the rest of the world about it. Amen.

Ben Nun[20]

## DOC. 149

## *WRN*, 28 September 1942: statement on the murder of the Jews of the Warsaw ghetto[1]

*There has never been such an atrocity*

With the murder of approximately 350,000 Jews and people of Jewish origin sealed in the Warsaw ghetto, Hitler has brought the extermination of the Jews to its intended conclusion. When he assured the German people that the Jews would cease to exist regardless of the war's outcome,[2] surely no one believed that this promise would be fulfilled so quickly in the twentieth century and that the murder of the Jewish people organized on a gigantic scale would compensate for the failure to achieve victory. Who could have imagined that anyone – even Hitler himself – would be capable of murdering tens of thousands of defenceless elderly, children, and women every day? Who would have imagined that an apparatus would be found to carry out such a mass atrocity in full view and that so many people would be willing to commit mass murder? Yet such Germans and human scum were found and taken from the Ukrainian steppes and the alleys of Latvian and Lithuanian cities. A special 'Vernichtungskommando'[3] apparatus, with the support of SS men and gendarmes, was set in motion. It realized these bestial

18 Podhajce was part of Tarnopol voivodeship under the Second Polish Republic.

19 Hebrew in the original: 'drop in the sea of tears'.

20 This pseudonym presumably refers to Yehoshua Ben Nun, who was Moses' successor and led the Israelites in the war against the Amalekites.

1 *WRN*, no. 18 (100), 28 Sept. 1942, pp. 1–3. Biblioteka Narodowa, P. 537 konsp. arch. During the first weeks of the occupation, leading Polish Socialist Party (PPS) politicians created an underground organization called the Central Directorate of the Movement of the Polish Working Masses – Freedom, Equality, Independence (Centralne Kierownictwo Ruchu Mas Pracujących Polski – Wolność, Równość, Niepodległość, WRN). Its underground publication, *WRN*, appeared fortnightly from May 1940 to June 1944, had a circulation of 4,000–8,000, and was edited by Zygmunt Zaremba (1895–1967) and Stanisław Niemyski (1904–1962). This document has been translated from Polish.

2 This is a reference to Hitler's public threat of extermination in his speech to the Reichstag on 30 Jan. 1939: see PMJ 2/248.

3 German in the original: 'extermination squad'.

intentions within two months, in broad daylight, in the heart of Europe – on the streets of our capital and on the roads leading to all our larger cities. There are only approximately 40,000 Jews left in Warsaw today. They were left alive so that the last bit of strength can be squeezed out of them for German industry before they die. Such small groups still exist in many Polish cities where, just like in Warsaw, the overwhelming majority of the Jews has been exterminated.

What an incredible variety of ways to dispense death the Germans have developed here! First of all, the selection: anyone unable to run fast enough to keep pace with this procession of death of the 'resettled' was killed with bullets on the spot. Mainly the elderly, the disabled, and the sick were weeded out in this way. In Warsaw hundreds of them were taken from their homes straight to the cemetery, where they were killed with a shot to the back of the head. After that, individuals who had somehow attracted the perpetrators' attention were next: a mother had hidden her child – the child was killed before her eyes, hit against the pavement and its little head crushed under a heel; after the child it was the mother's turn. During a search for someone who hid from the perpetrators,[4] an old man is found in his apartment and is thrown out of the window onto the pavement, still in his chair, and becomes a target at which the perpetrators shoot from above and then assess their shooting with satisfaction. Better-dressed apartment owners, from whom greater booty could be expected, perished one by one. Day after day the rest trekked in groups of 7,000, 10,000, or even more to Stawki,[5] where they were loaded into livestock wagons, 100–120 people to a wagon that would normally hold 40. The wagons were sealed shut; the floors were strewn with quicklime 'for the sake of hygiene'. Absolutely no one could leave the wagon. Biological needs had to be satisfied on the spot. The quicklime is slaked and the gas fills the wagon; it suffocates, it kills. A few hours later, when the train arrives at Treblinka or another destination, there is no one left alive in the wagons.[6] For this reason there is no accommodation waiting for them, save for the final resting place: ditches dug by large mechanized excavators, mass graves for several hundred people each. They are filled just as quickly and just as mechanically. But the earth cannot take in such an excess of victims. There is a suffocating stench of decay in the entire area surrounding Treblinka. Inhabitants have to flee some of the villages, and on the trains passing through Treblinka,[7] local passengers close all the windows and doors long before the train reaches the site of the mass graves, just to get through this contaminated zone.

German ingenuity has devised dozens of other methods of murder. Those who survived the quicklime in the wagons on their final journey met their end in gas chambers, by electric shock, or with an ordinary revolver bullet.

The world has never witnessed such a monstrous atrocity, both in terms of its scale and method of execution. And the world is slow to realize that it has actually taken place.

4 Changes in tense both here and below as in the original.
5 In other words, they went to the so-called Umschlagplatz in the northern part of the Warsaw ghetto. The Umschlagplatz was on Stawki Street.
6 Some of the deportees did in fact die of exhaustion in the wagons, but the overwhelming majority were murdered in the extermination camp.
7 The extermination camp was located in the immediate vicinity of the railway line from Małkinia to Siedlce.

Meanwhile approximately 1.5 million Jews have already been murdered. There are no words that could express people's reactions to Nazi bestiality. There is no punishment severe enough for the perpetrators of this atrocity.

All of Polish society is full of indignation and contempt for the murderers and has strongly condemned the mass murder of the Jews. The Directorate of Civil Combat has published a vehement protest on behalf of all the organizations in Poland that shape public opinion.[8] The Catholic 'Front for Poland's Rebirth' has published a similar protest independently.[9] The Germans have made help given to the Jews, who have escaped the torturers in vanishingly small numbers, punishable by death. Every decent person regards these threats with contempt, because he knows that offering help in the face of misfortune, rescuing a neighbour threatened with death, is an obligation stronger than death. It is the duty of every Pole to help the victims of German bestiality.

## DOC. 150
## Emanuel Ringelblum explains why the Warsaw Jews remained passive during the deportations that took place from July to September 1942[1]

Handwritten notes by Emanuel Ringelblum, written in or around October 1943 (excerpt)

The main reason for the Jews' passivity in 1942 was the excellent strategy pursued by the Germans, whereby they deceived the Jewish population as to the actual purpose of the resettlement. The Jews had so thoroughly embraced the tall tale of resettlement to the East, perpetuated by the Jewish Council [and] by a pack of Gestapo agents from Lublin, that thousands of people – starving because of the permanent blockades and because smuggling had come to a complete standstill – voluntarily reported to the Umschlagplatz[2] to go to work in the East. I saw with my own eyes how several 'weaklings' from the Jewish Order Service, without the assistance of Ukrainians or SS men, led a group of porters, each sturdy as an oak, with broad shoulders and muscles of steel, to the Umschlag[platz]. If it had occurred to these people that they were going to their deaths, all they would have had to do is lift a finger – and the 'brotherhood' of the Jewish Order Service would have vanished into thin air. It is regrettable that the government agencies[3] did not warn the Jewish population, for surely they must have been informed about the fate of the Lublin Jews who had been deported to unknown destinations several months before the Warsaw Jews, and they were surely aware of what the SS had planned for the capital's Jews. It may be that private individuals and Jewish organizations did not know

8 See Doc. 140.

9 This is a reference to the leaflet entitled *Protest!* (with a print run of 5,000), issued by the Front for Poland's Rebirth (FOP) group and dated August 1942. Published as a facsimile in Teresa Prekerowa, *Konspiracyjna Rada Pomocy Żydom w Warszawie 1942–1945* (Warsaw: Państwowy Instytut Wydawniczy, 1982), facing p. 112.

1 AŻIH, 302/337, fols. 158–161. Published in Ringelblum, *Polish–Jewish Relations during the Second World War*, pp. 159–167. This document has been newly translated from Polish.

2 German in the original.

3 This is a reference to the government delegation for Poland.

what was to happen to the Warsaw Jews deported to the East, but the government's representative in the territory[4] had agencies throughout the country from which he could have obtained information about Treblinki.[5] Why wasn't the Jewish population warned that the so-called resettlement was in fact a large-scale, monstrous mass murder? This was the cardinal error that sealed the fate of 400,000 people – the largest Jewish community in Europe. Only after a few people had escaped from Treblinki, the destination of all the transports from Warsaw, did the Jews realize the true purpose of these journeys. In August 1942 the Jewish Combat Organization, which came into being when the Warsaw Jews faced their greatest defeat, published several appeals clarifying the meaning of Treblinki and calling for resistance.[6] The German campaign of terror, the exhaustion caused by the constant blockades, and the resignation and complete paralysis of the Jewish population in general were so great that no credence was given to the unconfirmed news from Treblinki. Anyone with a normal state of mind found it difficult to accept the idea that there could exist on earth a government that considers itself European and yet murders millions of innocent people just because they are Jews. A healthy common sense could not conceive of the morbid, apocalyptic ravings of degenerates, sadists, and born murderers from Düsseldorf.[7] Therefore it was no wonder that the Jewish Combat Organization's calls for resistance were thought to be a provocation on the part of the Germans, who wanted to provoke resistance as a pretext for destroying the rest of Warsaw's Jewry. Without weapons, at times without any resonance in the community, with heavy hearts and full of despair, the Jewish Combat Organization had to stand idly by while hundreds of thousands of working people, professionals, social, cultural, and political activists, the best of the young people, innocent women and children, etc. were led to the slaughter. It is not our aim here to absolve the political and social activism of the Warsaw Jews for failing to live up to its task, for allowing itself to be terrorized by the SS, and for allowing this mass murder of Warsaw's Jewry to be carried out without German or Haydamakian[8] blood being shed. It is our firm conviction that had influential Polish circles provided moral support and assistance in the form of weapons, the Germans would have had to pay for the sea of Jewish blood they caused to be shed in July, August, and September 1942. Let me stress that I have not examined the question of resistance from all sides or exhaustively here, but have limited myself to the attitude among Polish circles.

A terrible disillusionment set in only once the blockades were lifted in September 1942 and numerous eyewitness reports on the bloodbath in Treblinki began to pour in.

4 This is a reference to occupied Poland. Until 5 August 1942 the representative (Delegat Rządu na Kraj) of the London-based government in exile was Cyryl Ratajski (1875–1942); Jan Piekałkiewicz was his successor.

5 Correctly, here and below: Treblinka.

6 The Jewish Combat Organization (ŻOB) was founded on 28 July 1942. In August 1942 it warned the ghetto residents that the deportations were destined for Treblinka and would mean death, instructing women and children to go into hiding and men to mount violent resistance. The ŻOB also imposed a death sentence on the head of the Jewish Order Service, Józef Szeryński.

7 This is a reference to the serial killer Peter Kürten (1883–1931), who had committed a number of sexual assaults and murders in Düsseldorf in 1929.

8 The Haydamaks were peasants and Cossacks from the area east of the Dnipro river in Ukraine, who had massacred Jews and Poles during the so-called 'Haydamak Uprising' of 1768.

The Jewish population realized that it had been a terrible mistake not to resist the SS. It became clear that if everyone had revolted on the day the resettlement operation was announced in Warsaw; if one had lunged at the Germans with knives, crowbars, shovels, and cleavers; if one had poured hydrochloric acid, liquid tar, hot water, etc. over the Germans, Ukrainians, Latvians, and the Jewish Order Service; in short, if men, women, and children, young and old, had launched a general attack, then 350,000 people would not have been murdered in Treblinki, and instead only 50,000 shot in the streets of the capital. Husbands tore out their hair because they had allowed their wives and children, their dearest ones, to be taken away with impunity; children vociferously reproached themselves because they had allowed their parents to be taken away. They swore: Never again will the Germans take us away with impunity – we will perish, but the vicious occupier will pay for our blood with his. It is said that our fate is sealed. Every Jew has in his pocket a death sentence handed down by the greatest murderer of all time. We must not focus so much on saving our lives, which seems like a very doubtful endeavour anyway. Instead we must focus on an honourable death, a death with a gun in our hands. We kept this oath, sworn in memory of the victims dearest to us. The ghetto began to arm itself and prepare for new attacks, which were expected at any moment. Underground 'bunkers' were dug so that we could seek shelter when the situation became dangerous. The ghetto was cleansed of its own traitors, the Jewish Gestapo men.[9] Intending to nip any thought of resistance in the bud, they had circulated baseless rumours during the resettlement operation about the end of the operation and fairy tales about the journey to the East, alleging that the children are given fresh milk. They were shot like dogs for spreading tall tales about camps for the Warsaw Jews in various places, about camps for the children of Warsaw, etc. in order to disarm the Jewish population. The Jewish Combat Organization has finished off in particular the people who carried out the resettlement operation.

## DOC. 151
## An escapee from Treblinka reports on his deportation from Częstochowa on 21 September 1942 and on the extermination camp[1]

Handwritten report for the underground archive of the Warsaw ghetto, Warsaw, written after Sept. 1942

A man from Częstochowa, born in 1922, with seven years of school [reports]: On Yom Kippur,[2] at 7 o'clock in the morning, Ukrainians (about ten) and gendarmes came to Dreszer Street.[3] They ordered everyone to come out, then they searched the houses thoroughly and forced everyone to proceed to the wagons, beating them along the way. Many did not want to board the wagons because they knew the wagons would be sealed – they

9 The ŻOB carried out targeted killings of a number of Jewish Order Service men and Gestapo informants.

1 AŻIH, Ring II/380 (297), fols. 2–14. Published in 'Relacje dwóch zbiegów z Treblinki II', *BŻIH*, no. 40 (1961), pp. 78–88, here pp. 85–88. This document has been translated from Polish.

2 21 Sept. 1942.

3 Today: Ogrodowa Street.

were violently forced into them. On the same day, the author's sister, who was ill in hospital with dysentery, was shot dead. All of the seriously ill people who could not get up were similarly shot. The trains travelled for two days and two nights. There was no water. The farmers charged 100–200 złoty for a bottle of water. Such purchases took place on sidings during night stops that lasted 10–15 minutes. The farmers knew about these continual transports and were already waiting for the train. There were 80 people in the wagon. Each person had been carefully counted. When the author wanted to escape, the others would not let him. There were mainly young people in the wagon. The gendarmerie guarded the train, keeping to the first and last wagons.

In Małkinia the transport (approximately 5,000 people) was divided into three groups, each of which was taken to Treblinka separately. This was carried out by a locomotive that came specially from Treblinka. The author was in the second group and waited about half an hour for the transport to Treblinka. Many, almost everyone, knew that they were going to their deaths. Even before Małkinia, the farmers had asked them: 'Why do you need water when you're going to your deaths anyway?' They also described what the place looked like.

Upon arrival, the Jews were driven out of the wagons and beaten. Jews opened the wagons, but they did not carry out the beatings. Upon leaving the wagons, they were informed that anyone who did not leave their bundles in the wagon would be shot. Then they were taken to a square surrounded by barbed wire, where there were two barracks. Right at the entrance, the women[4] were ordered to go into one of the barracks, and the women and children into the other. Skilled craftsmen were selected right at the entrance to the barracks, at the whim of the SS men. After the stipulated quota had been met, everyone was ordered to undress. The so-called 'Kapos' stood next to them with truncheons. They wore yellow armbands with the word Kapo in black letters. In exchange for gold and cigarettes, they helped individuals join the group of those selected for work. The Kapos only carried out beatings in the presence of SS men, or when someone did not undress quickly enough. As soon as everyone had undressed, they were led into the death chamber. The entrance to the clothes-sorting room was on the way. Everyone was made to turn around to take their clothes there. The author saved himself by putting on clothes when the order was given to hand them in. He pretended to be one of the Kapos and urged the others to hurry up. One Kapo wanted him to undress again, but another defended him. The men also handed in the clothes belonging to the women, who had been led away first. Then they themselves were led to the execution site.

Upon exiting the wagons, it became clear that a certain number of people were no longer able to get out: the weak, the sick, the elderly, the injured. Jewish workers led them away or carried them, wrapped in blankets, to a grave in which some of the workers had also been buried. There these people knelt down at the grave and a Ukrainian standing alongside shot them. Next to the Ukrainian stood an SS man, who often snatched the rifle from the Ukrainian and, with deep satisfaction, carried out the shooting himself. Pine branches were burning continuously in the grave; Jewish workers accompanied by an SS man brought these in specially from the forest outside the camp. Three Jewish paramedics, approximately 50–60 years old, wearing Red Cross armbands stood at the

4 The context suggests that this should read 'men'.

grave. It was unclear what their task was. They were seen positioning the children at the graveside in such a way that they fell straight into the grave after being shot.

The author was assigned to the group that sorted clothes. The group consists of between 15 and 25 men and a Vorarbeiter.[5] They sorted the clothes by separating them into suits, jackets, trousers, linen, silk, and wool. Gold and valuables were put into the prepared suitcases. Tailors were involved in this work, as they knew where to look for things that had been sewn in [to the lining]. The SS man on duty gave the order to search every item of clothing thoroughly, regardless of the time it took. When the camp commandant[6] arrived at the square (he came by bicycle), he picked out one or two people he didn't like the look of, ordered them to undress, led them to the burning grave, and shot them. This procedure took place twice a day, after breakfast and after lunch. If someone tried to ask for anything before being shot, the commandant would hit that person in the face with his whip for as long as the person was speaking, and then he would shoot him. There is no known case of him ever reprieving anyone he had selected to die. In rare cases, other SS men reprieved someone who was due to be shot if the Kapos interceded on their behalf. No Kapos were shot while the author was in the camp. The Vorarbeiter wore a green armband with the word Vorarbeiter printed on it in black.

Lunch was from 12 to 1 p.m. They were given rice with meat and other delicacies. They could eat as much as they wanted. In the morning they were given coffee and dry bread, and in the evening it was similar. While they worked, they could eat as much as they wanted, but out of the SS men's sight.

New transports arrived at the execution site every fifteen to thirty minutes throughout the day. As the naked victims carry their clothes to the sorting room, the SS men posted along the way amuse themselves by holding sticks in front of the legs of those who are running.[7] Then they have to jump over the sticks and whoever cannot is beaten. Sometimes the men sorting the clothes, mainly young men, would see their own fathers running naked with their clothes, shouting greetings to them as they ran. Muffled screams would come from the execution site for three to four minutes, especially when women were there.

When the Ukrainians went to the barracks in the evening, they aimed machine guns and searchlights at the barracks. The workers slept only in the men's barracks, on the square where they had arrived directly after exiting the wagons. On the first day the commandant came to the barracks and gave a speech in German, while a so-called Lagerältester[8] – a Jew, approximately 36 years old, tall, handsome, and energetic[9] – translated

5 German in the original, here and below: 'foreman'.

6 This is probably not a reference to Franz Stangl, whom the workers hardly ever saw, but to the deputy commandant Kurt Franz (1914–1998), cook; joined the SS in 1937; served with the guard detail at Buchenwald concentration camp; worked as a cook at the killing centres of the T4 'euthanasia' programme from autumn 1940; posted to Belzec from spring 1942; in summer 1942 transferred to Treblinka, where he was deputy commandant, then commandant from August 1943; construction worker and cook after the war; sentenced to life imprisonment by Düsseldorf Regional Court in 1965. See also Doc. 169.

7 Change of tense here and below as in the original.

8 German in the original: 'camp elder'.

9 The precise identity of the camp elder, an engineer called Galewski, is unclear. Various sources provide conflicting information about his first name and his biography.

his words into Polish. The author describes him as 'one of the better people' – he spoke Polish. He wore a dark armband with white lettering. He received better treatment and was not beaten. The commandant said to them: 'This is not a hotel, but a labour camp. As an SS man I assure you that you will be treated well, you will eat and sleep well. I went to school with Jews, played football with them, I had Jewish acquaintances. Work, for I too am only human.' At the same time he ordered everyone to work and to obey.

The wake-up call was around 5 a.m., there was breakfast, and then work. Jews arrived from Vienna on the second day. They left notes bearing their names and a message for anyone who found them. They knew they were going to their deaths.

On the sixth day, seeing that the work was coming to an end, the author made an effort to get himself assigned to a group of upholsterers who were draughtproofing the SS barracks with straw. The upholsterers went into the forest outside the camp to fetch branches, while an SS man and a Ukrainian guarded them. On that day the Ukrainian was the only one guarding them, because he was such a brute that the SS man trusted him and only five Jews went. In the forest, approximately 1 to 1.5 [km] outside the camp, the Ukrainian bought some vodka from shepherds, and while he was drinking, the author managed to escape.[10]

Many workers escaped by sorting the clothes near a pile of sand heaped up by a bulldozer and hiding behind them in these clothes. During the night they scrambled out of the graves onto the piles of sand, which were as high as the fence, and jumped across to the other side.[11]

## DOC. 152

## On 1 October 1942 Menakhem Mendel Kon tallies the number of people murdered as part of German extermination efforts targeting the Warsaw ghetto[1]

Handwritten diary of Menakhem Mendel Kon, entry for 1 October 1942[2]

1 October 1942

Now that the Hitlerian beasts' mass extermination campaign in Warsaw is over, it is time for a reckoning of their murderous actions over two months, of the devastation they have wrought here.

Prior to 22 July, that is one day before the Hitlerian murderers commenced the campaign to eradicate the Jews of Warsaw in Treblinka death camp, there were 390,000 Jews in Warsaw. Today, after two months of extermination efforts, around 40,000 Jewish people remain in Warsaw. In the course of two months, the Hitlerian murderers slaughtered 350,000 Jews. It is estimated that the murderers shot 50,000 people in Warsaw itself and killed 300,000 Jewish men, women, and children with gas in the now infamous Treblinka camp. The figure includes only the city of Warsaw.

10 This is followed by a simple sketch of the extermination camp.

11 This is followed by three further sketches of the camp and a detailed key in which 41 items are labelled.

1 AŻIH, Ring II/249 (208), fols. 2–5. Published in English translation in Kermish (ed.), *To Live With Honor*, pp. 85–86. This document has been newly translated from Yiddish.

2 This is the final diary entry: see also Doc. 114.

In Treblinka they gassed 6,000–8,000 Jews every day and tossed them into 30-metre-deep pits excavated by machines. Anyone still living [after being gassed] is thrown alive into the pits, which are covered with lime.[3] The dead are thrown into the pits by Jewish gravediggers, who are then shot once the day's 'Arbeit'[4] is finished. The following day 'fresh' gravediggers are put to work. That is how it's done in the pits – day in, day out. The Hitlerian exterminators do this to get rid of the traces of their murderous deeds. However, the beasts did not succeed, because a few of the gravediggers managed to escape. How they managed to do so is another story. Those who survived for the time being have told us in detail how the 'Arbeit' is done. There in the camp, where everyone is already facing death, uniformed Hitlerian murderers make soothing speeches, explaining to the wretched throngs that they are going to be sent to the East to perform agricultural work. They will have a good life there. The women will take care of the children, and the men will work. But they must hand over everything they have on them – gold, jewellery, money. Everything will be returned to them once they arrive at their destination. But seeing as how they are dirty, they must first undress and bathe. After bathing they will get new clothes. With cynical talk of this nature, they manage to get 6,000–8,000 Jews into the gas chambers every day. From there [the victims] are tossed into the pits, dead and swollen, after only five or six minutes. The world cannot begin to imagine even a fraction of the murderous deeds that the Hitlerian executioners are inflicting upon us Jews in Poland. In their despicable newspapers the wild Hitlerian beasts present 'the resettlement of the Jews of Warsaw', as they call it, to the world in a very different light.

In the end, however, the whole world will learn the bitter truth. A new form of revenge must and will be created for the Hitlerian murderers. If we Polish Jews do not live to see this (as they claim [we will not]), then our brothers from the other side of the ocean must do it for us. And we are more than certain that they will. Knowing this, our millions of victims fall at the bloodstained hands of the Hitlerian gang. Know this, Jews of the whole world! Over the course of 60 days, the frenzied Hitlerian murderers killed 350,000 Warsaw Jews and more than 150,000 Jews from around Warsaw: Radom, Kielce, Częstochowa, Będzin, Piotrków, Otwock, Węgrów, etc.[5]

The Hitlerian murderers dispatched 500,000 Jewish lives in the most heinous manner. The small surviving remnant of Jews in Warsaw live in fear. They do not know what will happen to them tomorrow. Like rabid dogs, the murderers bark that by 1 December they intend to cleanse Warsaw of Jews entirely.[6] Our only hope is that the long-awaited miracle happens before 1 December.

May it be so![7]

3 The change in tense in this section is as in the original.
4 German in the original, here and below: 'work'.
5 Some of these cities and towns in the General Government and in East Upper Silesia were located quite far from Warsaw.
6 In Lublin on 19 July 1942, Himmler had ordered that the 'resettlement' (i.e. deportation and murder) of the Jewish population in the General Government should be largely completed by 31 Dec. 1942: see Doc. 96. After 21 Sept. 1942, further deportations from Warsaw took place on 10 Nov. 1942, in mid Jan. 1943, in March 1943, and during the Warsaw Ghetto Uprising in late April 1943.
7 Hebrew in the original.

## DOC. 153

## *Biuletyn Informacyjny*, 1 October 1942: article on the murder of the Jewish population in occupied Poland[1]

*The liquidation of the Jews*

The campaign of murdering the Jews on Polish territory continues. Although it has become somewhat less intense in the last two or three weeks due to the 'requisitioning of the harvest' and the rounding up of Poles for forced labour in Germany, there is no doubt that the occupier has resolved to complete his murderous work.

Thus far the Germans have spared only the few who are assigned to work details (they account for less than 10 per cent of the Jewish population); their numbers are, moreover, constantly depleted by summary executions. News from German sources, for instance, confirms that no more than 30,000 Jews remain alive in Warsaw.

The camps at Bełżec, Treblinka, and Sobibór (the so-called Vernichtungslager[2]) are operating day and night. In Radom approximately 7 per cent of the [former] Jewish population remains to date. Approximately 1,000 people were shot on the spot, and approximately 22,000 Jews were taken to Treblinka and Bełżec.[3] In Kielce the ghetto was liquidated in the course of a single night (19 August), with 16,000 people deported and about 1,200 killed on the spot. A labour contingent of approximately 2,000 people was left behind.

In powiat Biała Podlaska all the Jews have already been murdered.[4]

The situation is similar in District 'Galicia'. Between 9 and 23 August, 65,000 Jews were deported from Lwów.

In Sambor twenty-three wagons were loaded with Jews from Sambor and powiat Sambor, and twenty-nine wagons with Jews from Turka and the surrounding area.

In Borysław twenty-four wagons were loaded; many people were murdered on the spot.

On average, 100 people were loaded into a single wagon.

On 7 August more than 1,000 Jews were deported from Drohobycz.

Mass executions of Jews have taken place in Vilna.

The aforementioned information is merely fragmentary and it is incomplete, but it illustrates the scale of the crimes being committed by the Germans.

1 *Biuletyn Informacyjny*, 1 Oct. 1942, p. 7; Biblioteka Narodowa, MF 45 817. This document has been translated from Polish.
2 German in the original: 'extermination camps'.
3 All the deportations from Radom are thought to have gone to Treblinka.
4 Approximately 3,000 Jews whom the German occupiers considered unfit for work were deported from Biała Podlaska to Sobibor on 11 June 1942. See also Docs. 160 and 171.

## DOC. 154

## On 2 October 1942 the Bund and the representative of the Polish government in exile report on the situation in the Warsaw ghetto[1]

Radio messages from the government delegation in Warsaw to the Polish government in exile in London, dated 2 October 1942

*No. 124*. STEM.[2] I am sending a dispatch from the Bund to Zygelboim.[3] WER.[4] 1 October 1942.
Approximately 300,000 Jews have been slain in Warsaw from 22 July until today. The same fate awaits the approximately 60,000[5] that are left. A handful of our family members[6] saved themselves.

A similar operation is taking place throughout the entire [General] Government.

The sanatorium in Miedzeszyn has been destroyed.[7] Maria [and] Artek survived.[8] We have sent three radio messages on this matter. No response from you.

The fact that England, America, and other countries remain silent about this unbelievable massacre of the Jews in Poland is an even worse blow to us than Hitler's crimes themselves. We have no help. We have no money at all. Deposit 5,000 emanuelki[9] with the government immediately, so that it can be wired to us. We will be lost without your help.

Confirm receipt and money transfer by radio.

C.K.R. of the Jew[ish] work[ing] masses. JANCZYN.[10]

2 October 1942–269 grup.[11]

1 AAN, 1325/202/I-6, fol. 26, reports no. 124 and no. 125. This document has been translated from Polish.
2 The code name of the addressee, Stanisław Mikołajczyk.
3 Szmul Zygielbojm.
4 The sender; Wer[nic] was one of the code names of Dr Jan Piekałkiewicz (1892–1943), economist; professor in Warsaw from 1924; active in the Peasants' Party (SL) from 1931; led the party when it went underground from 1940; deputy representative of the government in exile from 1941, and its representative from August/Sept. 1942; arrested by the Gestapo in Feb. 1943 and murdered that June. Piekałkiewicz forwarded the Bund's report to London because the Jewish underground had no communication channels of its own.
5 The decoded version of this report, which was received in London on 19 Dec. 1942 (L. dz [log no.] K. 4927/42, no. 124), incorrectly reads: 'Half a million remain'; SPP, 3.1.1.13.5/30, Teka 74/221, fol. 88.
6 Meaning: 'of the members of the Bund'.
7 See Doc. 126.
8 Mania Zygielbojm, stage name Maria Rozen (d. 1943), actor; Szmul Zygielbojm's second wife; in 1942 worked at the Medem Sanatorium in Miedzeszyn, near Warsaw, where her son Artur (Artek), a minor, was also staying; both perished during the Warsaw Ghetto Uprising.
9 A code word for US dollars.
10 The code name of Maurycy Orzech (1891–1942/1943), trade unionist; joined the Bund around 1907; member of the Party Council from 1919; later city councillor and councillor for the Jewish Community in Warsaw; chairman of the Union of Craftsmen; deputy chairman of the Bund in the Warsaw ghetto, 1940–1941; from July 1942 lived on the 'Aryan side', where he either perished or was murdered in August 1943.
11 As in the original; this may be the key to deciphering the message.

*No. 125*. STEM. On 12 September the German authorities announced that the expulsion of the Jews from the Warsaw ghetto had been completed. The 33,000 Jews of both sexes who remained in the ghetto have received 'life numbers'. They already include the work details deployed outside the ghetto. In addition, a few thousand have remained in hiding in cellars and sewers, and face death by starvation or being shot.

The liquidation of the Jews in Lwów began by hanging all the Jewish Community councillors from the balcony of the Community building. The corpses hung there for 24 hours. The massacres and deportations followed and reduced the number of Jews to 20 per cent of the number prior to 10 August 1942. A sealed ghetto was established for the rest.

WER.

2 October 1942–236 grup.

## DOC. 155

## On 2 October 1942 Karol Dresdner, a resident of the Lwów ghetto, describes his loneliness to Aurelia Wyleżyńska in Warsaw[1]

Postcard from Karol Dresdner,[2] Lwów, to Aurelia Wyleżyńska,[3] Warsaw, dated 2 October 1942 (copy)

Dear Madam,

Once again I find it hard to bring myself to write a few words. Even from a purely technical point of view, writing a card involves indescribable difficulties. In any case, the things one should write about cannot be expressed in words. The tongue belies all sound, and sound all thought.[4] One must inwardly prepare to depart [this world], but it is another thing when you go around with the cruel verdict in your pocket. In such cases, death takes on hundreds of different forms. A double-faced Janus.

I apologize for this sad and painful candour.

Unfortunately, I am no longer capable of conducting trivial, purely social correspondence. Please understand me correctly … St. Z promised to write, and he was even going to take up my case seriously, but so far I have not heard anything from him. I am so lonely and desolate that even a remotely kind word means a lot to me. Could you give me Mrs Konstancja's exact address? Perhaps it would be possible to get in touch with

1 AAN, 1349/231/I, t. 4, fols. 236–237. Only the typewritten copy of this postcard has survived, along with six other cards sent between 4 June and Sept. 1942. Published in Aurelia Wyleżyńska, 'Z notatek pamiętnikarskich (1942–1943)', *BŻIH*, nos. 45 and 46 (1963), pp. 212–231, here p. 230. This document has been translated from Polish.

2 Dr Karol Dresdner (1908–1943), poet, translator, and critic; contributed to publications including the Lwów daily newspaper *Chwila* and the Polish Jewish journal *Miesięcznik Żydowski*; produced school textbooks in Polish in 1940; lived in the Lwów ghetto from 1942; posted his postcards from the 'Aryan side', which he was still able to visit during the day; murdered at Janowska Street camp.

3 Aurelia Wyleżyńska (1889–1944), writer and journalist; lived in Paris for several years; supported Jews in many ways after 1939; lived in Lwów in 1941, then in Warsaw; worked for the underground press; published a moving tribute to the memory of the defenders of the Warsaw ghetto in *Nowy Dzień* on 14 May 1943 under the title 'Gloria victis!' (Glory to the Vanquished); perished during the Warsaw Uprising in 1944.

4 A quotation from Adam Mickiewicz's play *Forefathers' Eve* (1820–1832).

someone on the other side before the coffin lid is finally closed … I reiterate the words with which I concluded my previous card. Any further correspondence will be only a farewell.

I send you warm greetings and kiss your hand,

## DOC. 156

## *Informacja Bieżąca*, 4 October 1942: report on the murder of Jews in Mszana Dolna[1]

*Report from Mszana Dolna*[2] *– liquidation of the Jews*[3]

In mid August a Gestapo unit led by Hamann[4] set out from Nowy Sącz for Mszana Dolna, where 958 Jews of both sexes, including children, were shot,[5] leaving only 80 [people] (capable of physical labour) alive. Prior to the execution the Jews were ordered to pay a ransom of 50,000 złoty. After this sum was received, the day when the Jews were to be taken away was fixed. Each person was allowed up to 10 kilos of baggage. When the Jews arrived at the designated place on the morning of the set day, the Gestapo demanded another ransom of 25,000 złoty. The sum was received within two hours, after which the Jews were led to the nearby hills, where two long trenches, supposedly drainage ditches, had been dug. There they were ordered to put down their baggage and to place money and jewellery in suitcases prepared for this purpose. Those who do not comply – will be shot.[6] The Jews surrendered more than 100,000 złoty and a considerable amount of jewellery. After this new ransom had been collected, Hamann ordered the Jews to undress and to line up in rows along the trenches. Two Gestapo men came up close to them and began shooting at them. After a dozen shots, one of them appeared to suffer a nervous collapse, because he stopped shooting and moved off to the side, while the other continued shooting until the end. In one case he missed a woman with the first shot, causing her to just fall into the ditch, and it took eight shots for him to finish her off. The eighty Jews left alive were placed under guard until the evening, and they were ordered to watch the execution.

After this massacre, on Hamann's orders, Sobieski, the mayor of Mszana,[7] held a festive reception for the Gestapo unit. The local choir sang Polish songs. Hamann and Sobieski

1 *Informacja Bieżąca*, no. 37 (62), 5 Oct. 1942, supplement 2; AAN, 1325/202/III-7/1, fol. 165. This document has been translated from Polish.

2 A small town between Cracow and Zakopane. There were approximately 800 Jewish residents in Mszana Dolna before 1 Sept. 1939; their number increased by 100–200 people as refugees and expellees arrived.

3 Underlined by hand in the original.

4 Heinrich Hamann (1908–1993), retailer; joined the NSDAP and the SS in 1931; worked at the SD Main Office in Munich from 1934, then in Berlin; trained as a Kriminalkommissar from 1938; from Sept. 1939 served in Nowy Sącz, where he was appointed head of the Border Police Commissariat in 1940; assigned to the Security Police in Cracow from autumn 1943; worked as a floor layer in the Ruhr region of Germany after the war; sentenced to life imprisonment by Bochum Regional Court in 1966; released from prison in the mid 1980s.

5 According to other sources, 881 people were murdered.

6 The change of tense here is as in the original.

7 The mayor of Mszana Dolna from Nov. 1939 to Nov. 1943 was Władysław Gelb.

gave speeches. Hamann stressed the significance of the execution, thanks to which Mszana had been saved from the threat of being inundated by the Jewish race. Sobieski thanked Hamann and his unit for liberating the town from the 'Jewish invasion' and officially declared that 'if the Polish government had not fled the country and the victorious German army had not arrived, Mszana Dolna would never have been able to free itself from the Jews'. He stressed that he himself, like all the residents of Mszana, was very grateful to the Germans. After the reception, which lasted several hours, Mayor Sobieski bid Hamann's unit a warm farewell, and they left for the next executions in Grybów.[8]

Reported by Bor.[9]

## DOC. 157

## *Agencja Prasowa*, 7 October 1942: report criticizing signs of a collapse of moral standards in Polish society[1]

*The internal danger*

This most terrible of all wars has not spared our nation from immeasurable damage, which includes not only the many thousands of lives lost, the cities laid waste, and the total economic collapse, but also the damage caused to the psyche of the general population and the erosion of the basic values of human decency and dignity.

Under the watchful eye of the despicable occupier, this epidemic is spreading at an alarming rate. Even though every war creates conditions that weaken ethical norms to a greater or lesser extent, the present war is truly unparalleled in this respect. The last few weeks in particular have provided us with more than enough shocking evidence of this.

For it is difficult to come to terms with the thought that the tragedy of the Jews, whose shameful persecution is unfolding before our eyes, will give them [the Germans] an opportunity to arouse and to lay bare the vilest instincts that seek to steal the property that the Jews have left behind.

No sooner had the houses in the Warsaw ghetto been deserted than the jackals set out in droves – behind those ghostly walls – to blindly steal the blood-soaked belongings permeated with the stench of dead flesh. The police – of whatever stripe – were the first to stretch out their filthy, greedy paws for these pitiful scraps, and they look on with approval as the dregs of society follow them down this path – looting and stealing for all they're worth.

8 The Jews from Grybów had in fact been expelled on 16 August 1942 to Nowy Sącz, 20 km to the east, where they were murdered.

9 This was the code name of Antoni Szymanowski.

1 *Agencja Prasowa*, 7 Oct. 1942, p. 1; AAN, 1583/7/2, fols. 331–332. *Agencja Prasowa* was published in Warsaw from 1940 to 1945 as the press service of the Union of Armed Struggle (ZWZ) (later Home Army (ZWZ-AK)) High Command Bureau of Information and Propaganda. It had a circulation of 200 copies. The Latin teacher Roman Goldman (d. 1958) was its editor-in-chief from Dec. 1941 to early 1944. This document has been translated from Polish.

Ultimately, one must assume that the occupation authorities are deliberately displaying such a 'tolerant' attitude, fuelling the basest of instincts in order to weaken the morals of our society, which nowadays are our only weapon against them.

The results are truly frightening. Groups of adolescents, even 12-to-14-year-olds, now prowl the streets and shamelessly trade in stolen goods. Particularly disturbing is the fact that the general public remains impassive in the face of this repugnant practice, and all sorts of fine gentlemen and ladies are eagerly purchasing any measly clothes, plates, paintings, etc. 'dirt cheap'.

Full of shame, we must admit that it is not only the ordinary people, those of low intelligence, who taint themselves by stealing Jewish goods, but also individuals from an intellectual background and those who consider themselves part of the intelligentsia. These include all manner of caretakers of Jewish houses who 'secure' valuables, as well as people who hold 'permits' to enter the ghetto and do not miss the unique opportunity ... to taint themselves for the rest of their lives.

Reports of similar cases of a collective lack or loss of decency and humanity are reaching us from various parts of the country. Among the information we have received are reports from the area around Cracow where, during the resettlement of the Jews from small localities within a powiat to the main town, the rural population rushed to the abandoned apartments from even the remotest areas in order to steal even such things as stove doors, doorknobs, etc.

When writing about this, we do not only mean the looting of the Jewish property left behind. The matter is actually even more dangerous. The appetite for theft and robbery has recently increased to such an extent that it really threatens to destabilize the lives of the Polish population in the near and distant future.

For instance, theft has become a common occurrence on the railway. During night-time air raid alerts, the looting of abandoned apartments has assumed alarming proportions. It is said that even the victims' immediate neighbours sometimes participate in this. Spontaneously formed gangs of thieves focus all their energy on carrying out increasingly brazen robberies. We also know that such 'partisans' are waiting impatiently for the occupation to end, because they have already set their sights on the private or state property the Germans will leave behind.

We describe this alarming picture of degeneration because we want to make clear the danger to internal security, which may jeopardize our future if there is no sufficient counterweight and resistance to it among the healthy and respectable strata of society. Since today we have no executive authority of our own and no proper leadership, we consider it our duty in this case to engage public opinion in the fight against evil. Under these enormously difficult combat conditions, we must brand thieves of all kinds as saboteurs and vermin, equal to the hated enemy. We must denounce and curb their destructive actions. We must not shy away from vigilante justice, if necessary.

In addition, we must not allow these brazen thieves to become convinced that the goods left behind by the Germans will not belong to 'anyone' and that they can then later plunder them with impunity. The formerly German goods will become the property of the entire nation and will somewhat compensate for the losses suffered since September 1939. They will undoubtedly be the foundation for rebuilding our national economy as we emerge from the rubble and ashes.

We cannot allow our Poland to be completely plundered and robbed by dregs and scum

## DOC. 158

## On 8 October 1942 the Warsaw Transfer Bureau reports on its forthcoming closure and the transformation of the ghetto into a labour camp[1]

Report by Bischof (log no. 13 487 Oe.), head of the Warsaw Transfer Bureau, 23 Königstraße, Warsaw, to the commissioner for the Jewish residential district in Warsaw,[2] Palais Brühl, Warsaw (received on 8 October 1942), dated 8 October 1942[3]

*Re: report for September 1942*

The basic principles for transforming the Jewish residential district into a labour camp under police command became clear in repeated sweeps to which the remaining inhabitants of the residential district were subjected by the SS and Police Leader[4] during this reporting month. Of particular importance in this regard was the order given by the SS and Police Leader on 14 September of this year, reference: I a 32.15.02, log no. 3600/42. In accordance therewith, as of 1 September of this year, those business operators still authorized to make use of Jewish labourers are to pay a fee of 5 zl., minus the costs of board, to the SS and Police Leader. However, no further wages are to be paid to the Jews themselves.[5] As a result, the Transfer Bureau – the activities of which, under the regulation of 19 April 1941,[6] relate to the 'economic' affairs of the Jewish residential district – is also formally relieved of the obligation to regulate and oversee such services and to collect permit fees. The SS and Police Leader has allowed various war production and public firms (a total of thirty-three, including the Jewish Council) to retain approximately 35,000 Jewish workers.[7] These workers are to receive standardized food rations in accordance with the improved allocation rates. By order of the SS and Police Leader, the residential district was further reduced in size towards the end of the reporting month, in line with the reduced population. The cleared streets will remain cordoned off, as before, until the collection of assets has been completed.

The SS and Police Leader, with the agreement of the local office, set 31 December of this year as the final day of the Transfer Bureau's external operations.

With the approval of the SS and Police Leader, old *goods and services* transactions were settled to the following extent in the month under review:

1 APW, Amt des Gouverneurs des Distrikts Warschau, Der Kommissar für den jüdischen Wohnbezirk, Transferstelle 482/12, fol. 31–33. This document has been translated from German.
2 Heinz Auerswald.
3 The original contains handwritten annotations.
4 The SS and Police Leader in Warsaw from June 1942 to April 1943 was Ferdinand von Sammern-Frankenegg.
5 The SS and Police Leader in Warsaw had forbidden wage payments to Jews on 14 September 1942 and ordered that companies must pay 'a flat rate of 5 zl. per day for each Jewish labourer' to the SS and Police Leader: Staatsanwaltschaft Hamburg, Staatsanwaltschaft LG – NSG, StA 213–12, 0070–102, fol. 7048. Published as a facsimile in Grabitz and Scheffler, *Letzte Spuren*, p. 172. See also Doc. 162.
6 Regulation on the Jewish Residential District in Warsaw (19 April 1941), *VOBl-GG*, no. 35, 28 April 1941, pp. 211–212.
7 The overall number of people in the ghetto at that time was, however, much higher.

In zloty:

| | August: | September: |
|---|---|---|
| Members of the Deutsche Firmengemeinschaft:[8] | 209,000 | 79,700 |
| Waste collection: | 42,000 | 11,000 |
| Other exports: | 1,731,000 | 1,048,000 |
| | 1,982,000 | 1,138,700 |

Negotiations with the office of the SS and Police Leader were conducted in a number of cases in order to protect the justified interests of Aryan export partners. The steps that the Trade and Industry Main Group has taken to continue the furniture operation (to supply the needs of the Reich Germans working in the private sector) have so far been unsuccessful. As an alternative, some finished furniture stock was sent to companies that had registered for the operation.

In the month under review, due to the allocation slips, *food was procured and distributed separately* by large companies, and otherwise by the organizations of the Supply Office for the Jewish residential district.

| | |
|---|---|
| The value of the imported food amounted to | 2,724,000 zl. |
| along with everyday staples in the amount of | 68,000 zl. |
| Total | 2,792,000 zl. |

The turnover figures for the Emissionsbank's clearing office, given below, show the continuing *decline in payment transactions,* which have decreased from 8,150,000 zl. in August to 4,498,000 zl. in September.

The applications submitted to the previous management[9] under the '*settlement of claims operation*' (2,232 in total) were sorted by subject and origin, and based on the results thus obtained, proposals for formally winding up this operation were submitted to the local office.

In the month under review, 283 *goods permits* were issued.

There were 127 applications for *personal passes* forwarded to the local office for processing, with positive outcomes.

The first step towards *reducing staff numbers* in the Transfer Bureau involved dismissing forty staff members, particularly those with notice periods of more than three months.

8 See Doc. 15, fn. 31.

9 Bischof's predecessor as head of the Transfer Bureau from late 1940 to May 1941 was Alexander Palfinger (1894–1961).

## DOC. 159

## On 9 October 1942 Himmler orders that Poles be deployed for forced labour in the General Government instead of Jews[1]

Letter (marked 'secret') from Reichsführer-SS Himmler (log no. AR/31/22/42, RF/V.) to SS-Obergruppenführer Pohl, Krüger, and Globocnik, Reich Security Main Office, and Wolff (with copies for Army Quartermaster General Wagner[2] and Lieutenant Colonel Tippelskirch[3]), dated 9 October 1942[4]

Regarding the letter from the military district commander in the General Government to the Wehrmacht High Command on replacing Jewish labourers with Poles,[5] I have the following comments:

1. I have ordered[6] that SS-Obergruppenführer *Krüger* and SS-Obergruppenführer *Pohl*[7] must place all the so-called armaments workers who only work in tailors', furriers', and shoemakers' workshops together in concentration camps where they are currently located, that is, in Warsaw [and] Lublin.[8] The Wehrmacht should place its orders with us, and we guarantee that we will continue to supply the articles of clothing it requests. However, I have given instructions to crack down ruthlessly on those who may be inclined to speak out against this measure, ostensibly on the basis of armaments requirements, but who actually only want to support Jews and their dealings.
2. The Jews actually placed in armaments firms, e.g. munitions workshops, automotive workshops, etc., are to be removed gradually. As a first step, they are to be put into segregated sections in the factories. The second step in this development is to swap out and pool the workers from these separate sections in enclosed factories, thus creating a limited number of sealed-off concentration-camp factories in the General Government.

1 BArch, NS 19/352, fol. 11, 16. Published as a facsimile in Grabitz and Scheffler, *Letzte Spuren*, p. 179. This document has been translated from German.

2 Eduard Wagner (1894–1944), career officer; member of the Epp Freikorps; general of the artillery; army quartermaster general from Oct. 1940; committed suicide after the attempted assassination of Hitler on 20 July 1944.

3 Werner von Tippelskirch (1900–1967), career officer; served in the war, 1939–1940; lieutenant colonel and head of the Quartermaster's Department in the Wehrmacht Operations Staff from 1941; colonel from July 1942; wounded in Oct. 1943; head of the Attaché Department in the Wehrmacht High Command, 1944–1945; detained as a US prisoner of war; thereafter worked as a sales representative in Stuttgart.

4 Date stamp in the original.

5 See Doc. 142 and, in response, the circular OKW/WFSt./Qu (II) of 6 October 1942: BArch, NS 19/1766.

6 This could not be found.

7 Oswald Pohl (1892–1951), ship's officer; joined the NSDAP and the SA in 1926, and the SS in 1934; head of administration in the SS Main Office; in charge of SS businesses and chair of the administrative board of the German Red Cross from 1938; from 1942 head of the SS Business and Administration Main Office, where he was responsible for the intensified exploitation of forced labourers in concentration camps; founded the industrial concern Ostindustrie GmbH in Lublin in early 1943; in 1947 tried before and convicted by a US military tribunal as part of the Subsequent Nuremberg Proceedings ('Pohl trial') and executed.

8 At that time only one concentration camp, Lublin-Majdanek, existed in the General Government; Warsaw concentration camp was not established until 1943, after the suppression of the Ghetto Uprising.

3. We will then make every effort to replace these Jewish labourers with Poles and to merge most of these Jewish concentration-camp factories into a handful of large Jewish concentration-camp production sites, where possible in the eastern part of the General Government. However, in line with the Führer's wishes, Jews should one day disappear from there as well.

## DOC. 160

## In October 1942 Polish government representatives report on the murder of the Jews[1]

Situation report from the government delegation (d[epartment] I.),[2] unsigned,[3] for the period from 26 August to 10 October 1942, Warsaw, compiled after 10 October 1942[4]

[…][5]

*VIII. The cruel liquidation of the Jews continues*

*In the Warsaw ghetto.* The Germans cruelly and conclusively settled scores with the Warsaw ghetto during the period covered by this report. The mass murder and deportation of the Jews, which resumed in late August following a break of several days, went on for approximately 14 days, and it continues on a smaller scale to this day. Between 23 August and 12 September, several trains loaded with Jews left the ghetto every day. Meanwhile, cruel manhunts began in the Warsaw ghetto on 6 September. On that day, all the Jews were required to assemble in front of the Jewish Community headquarters on Zamenhof Street at 10 a.m. Here 'life numbers' (the official German term) were given to those who were to remain in the ghetto. These are yellow slips of paper with handwritten numbers, stamped and signed by the Jewish Community. The numbers contain no names. All those who were not given a number were taken to Stawki,[6] where Jews are continuously being loaded onto trains and deported from Warsaw. After this fateful Sunday, on 6 September, house searches began for Jews in hiding and without numbers; they lasted around a week. A bloody massacre accompanied the searches. On 8 September, the German authorities announced that the operation of 'resettling' the Jews from the Warsaw ghetto had ended.

Those who had received a 'life number', 33,000 people of both sexes who had thus been granted the right to live, remained in the ghetto. This number also includes the work details outside the ghetto. In addition, according to estimates from mid September,

1 AAN, 1325/202/I-31, fols. 72–88 (fols. 87–88). This document has been translated from Polish.
2 Department I was the government delegation's executive office.
3 This report is probably largely based on information supplied by Henryk Woliński.
4 Handwritten above the document: '24 Oct. [1942]'.
5 The following section is found at the end of a 17-page report on the terror the German occupiers inflicted on the Polish population: in prisons, penal camps, and concentration camps; through resettlement operations, deportation to the Reich for work, economic plunder, and the 'ethnic struggle' (*Volkstumskampf*); through acts of sabotage carried out by Soviet groups and acts of repression by the occupiers in eastern Poland. The report noted that terminally ill people had been murdered at Auschwitz concentration camp since June 1941 and that in the Birkenau gas chambers, which were built later, mainly Soviet prisoners of war and Jews had been murdered with gas: AAN, 1325/202/I-31, fols. 72–88 (fol. 77).
6 A reference to the Umschlagplatz on Stawki Street.

approximately 4,000 people are said to be in hiding in cellars, sewers, and the ghetto's various nooks and crannies. These people face death at any moment, by starvation or by being shot, if they encounter a representative of the occupation authorities. Of the former 370,000 ghetto inhabitants, approximately one in ten remain. The area of the ghetto has been reduced several times, but the new boundaries have not yet been finalized, although the construction of the new walls has already begun. The number of work details that go to work outside the ghetto every day has been greatly reduced. However, since they are the only ones who can bring food from outside [the ghetto], the already poor supply situation has deteriorated even more. The survivors in the ghetto are in the throes of great hunger. The streets of the ghetto from which the Jews have been removed – with their abandoned houses and apartments, and the traces of violence and massacres – make a shocking impression. According to information circulated by the Germans, the ghetto is intended to remain in its present form for approximately six months, after which it will be liquidated for good.

*Outside the ghetto.* A few Jews managed to escape from the ghetto during the bloody liquidation phase and to hide among the Christian population in Warsaw and the surrounding area. The Germans have therefore intensified their search for these Jews in hiding. In rare cases that they are found, they are usually brutally tortured and murdered on the spot. The German torturers shoot at them inside the apartments, on the staircases, and in the courtyards; they are not disturbed in the least that there are often numerous eyewitnesses to these crimes. The following incident demonstrates the extent to which the Germans lose themselves in their savagery. A pregnant Jewish woman hid in the attic of a building in Grochów where she gave birth to a child. A German gendarme discovered her there a few days after she had given birth. The German shot the sick, unfortunate woman on the spot and trampled the infant to death. Given that the Christian population is willingly and selflessly helping the hounded Jews in hiding, on 8 September the German occupiers in Warsaw announced the death penalty for anyone who hides Jews, gives them accommodation or food, transports them by any means, or buys goods from them.[7] At the same time, the announcement assured that any Christians who reported the whereabouts of Jews in hiding to the German police by the following day would not be punished. In Warsaw there has not been nor is there currently any indication that the Poles are complying with this instruction. On the contrary, we know of many cases of people having been arrested for helping the Jews.

*In Treblinka, Bełżec, and other camps.* During the period covered by this report, the Jews from the Warsaw ghetto and from ghettos in the surrounding area continued to be transported primarily to the camps in Treblinka and Bełżec, where they were brutally executed en masse in gas chambers.[8] According to information from Treblinka, 300–500 people die by gas in this death camp every day.[9] Jews are taken to Treblinka camp not only from Warsaw and the surrounding areas, but also from further regions. When

7 Announcement by the SS and Police Leader in Warsaw, Ferdinand von Sammern-Frankenegg, 5 Sept. 1942: APW, 204/290; see also Doc. 144.
8 Those deported from Warsaw and the surrounding area were murdered exclusively in Treblinka.
9 The number of people murdered in Treblinka every day was much higher: see Docs. 103 and 111.

each train arrives, its overcrowded wagons strewn with chlorine and quicklime, 20 to 30 per cent of the Jews inside are usually dead. Rumour has it that in addition to the camps in Treblinka and Bełżec, the Germans have put into operation other camps for the execution of Jews in the General Government. Some of the deported Jews, the healthiest and the strongest, are taken to special camps in the East for particularly hard and often dangerous work

*The bloody extermination of Jews across Poland.* During the period covered by this report, new information kept coming in from all over the country about the Germans' mass extermination of the Jewish population. In the western regions, the ghettos in Kalisz, Zduńska Wola, and Turek were completely liquidated. In powiat Łask, the Jews in Lutomierz, Zelów, and Bełchatów were murdered. In Radom only 7–8 per cent of the former Jews survived the liquidation of the local ghetto, which took place during the period covered by the last report. In Siedlce the Germans dealt with the Jews after transporting them there en masse from the small towns nearby, including Mordy. The bloody liquidation of the Jews in Siedlce lasted several days; many were killed on the spot, but the majority of the crowd, numbering several thousand people, were shot with machine guns on the way to the remote loading station. The farmers in the surrounding area had to transport thousands of corpses to mass graves in their own carts. The rest were crammed into wagons strewn with chlorine and quicklime, and transported away. Prior to being loaded, many groups were doused with water. After the condemned had been loaded into the wagons, inhuman screams and wails were immediately heard.[10] In Biała Podlaska and powiat Biała Podlaska all the local Jews were murdered. According to reports by several eyewitnesses, in late August an execution squad, consisting of former Soviet prisoners of war[11] and commanded by the Germans, led 2,000 people – the entire Jewish population that had been resettled from Łomazy, which was located in this powiat – out of town on dirt roads. At a certain point along the road, where ditches had already been prepared, all the Jews were shot with machine guns.[12] Whether dead or not yet finished off – they were all thrown into the ditches. They were all covered with dry clay soil. The decomposing bodies caused this monstrous mass grave to swell. As a result, the farmers from the surrounding area were herded there and ordered to build a kurgan[13] over it. Moreover, as to central Poland, it must be noted that during the period covered by this report the Germans liquidated the Jews in a number of small towns located both near and farther away from Warsaw. In western Małopolska 13,000 Jews from Bochnia were murdered or deported, 7,000 from Wieliczka, and 1,000 from Mszana Dolna. The Jewish communities in Jasło, Nowy Sącz, Nowy Targ, and Rabka were also completely liquidated. In Lwów the massacre of the Jews during the expulsion continued throughout the entire second half of August.[14] It began one day when the German gendarmerie appeared at the Jewish Community

10 See Doc. 122.

11 These were non-German auxiliary personnel from the SS training camp in Trawniki, who had been recruited from among Soviet prisoners of war.

12 Members of Reserve Police Battalion 101 carried out the shootings at Łomazy.

13 Burial mound of a type found in southern Russia and Ukraine.

14 Between 10 and 23 August 1942, approximately 40,000–50,000 Jews were deported to Belzec.

building, where the complete Jewish Council had just assembled. The Germans demanded a large quantity of rope. A few Council members were sent to buy some. When the rope was brought in, all the Council members were hanged from the balconies of the Community building. The corpses hung for twenty-four hours. Then the deportation of Jews from the city began.[15] This operation lasted a few weeks, after which about 25 per cent of the former inhabitants were left, and a completely sealed ghetto was set up. In Przemyśl approximately 12,000 Jews have been murdered or deported (but mostly murdered) so far. Massacres and mass deportations also took place in Stanisławów, Borysław, and Sambor. In the Vilna region the complete liquidation of the Jews is coming to an end. All that is happening there is simply the wholesale murder of the Jews. Recently the Byelorussian militia murdered all the Jews in Druja. The Jews in most of the towns and small cities in the Nowogródek region were liquidated in a similar way.[16] Only in a few places did specialist workers, mainly skilled craftsmen, survive. In a few places, the Jews put up active resistance. As a result of the serious fighting in Nieśwież and Słonim, the latter was burned to the ground. In Polesia[17] the Germans are gradually exterminating the Jews in every larger and smaller town, one after the other. In Volhynia the remaining Jews in Równe, Kiwerce, and Klewań were exterminated during the period covered by this report.

## DOC. 161

## *Rzeczpospolita Polska*, 14 October 1942: report on reactions to the mass murder of Jews[1]

*In the face of the German crimes against the Jews*

The liquidation of the Warsaw ghetto is coming to an end. The 33,000 Jews (less than 10 per cent of the former population) who have survived have received 'life numbers' which allow them to exist. The guard posts of the Shaulis men have been dismantled. The situation is similar in other cities and towns across Poland. Everywhere 70–90 per cent of the Jews have been murdered. This 'liquidation' usually took place on the spot. From some places the victims were transported to Treblinka and to Sobibór, near Włodawa. Trains full of the condemned travelled along a newly laid siding to newly erected buildings that no one knew about, and from there they returned empty. It has never happened that anyone has come back alive along this siding. The human transports have disappeared as if the earth had swallowed them up just behind the gate.

The Polish Jews knew what was in store for them, and a deadly cry full of terror and despair rose to the heavens from the wagons standing on the track. Occasionally,

15 The members of the Jewish Council were murdered after the deportations on 1 Sept. 1942: see Doc. 154.

16 The murders in General Commissariat White Ruthenia were committed by the German Security Police and the gendarmerie, with the support of local auxiliary police.

17 Polesia is a historic region mainly located in what is today Belarus; its urban centres include the cities of Brest and Pinsk.

1 *Rzeczpospolita Polska*, 14 Oct. 1942, pp. 5–7. Biblioteka Narodowa, MF 51 725. This document has been translated from Polish.

however, transports of German, Czech, and French Jews also arrived. The wagons were not sealed, but the guards closely guarded them. These people did not anticipate their imminent end. They stood at the wagon doors, looked around, and talked casually. And they too disappeared behind the gate of the 'Sobibór Industrial Plant' as if the abyss had swallowed them up.

The Jewish tragedy on Polish soil has come to an end. Rumour has it that Gestapo-led gangs of Ukrainian, Lithuanian, and Latvian thugs will soon begin a similar operation against the Polish population. That tragedy would take a different course – because we will defend ourselves. But that is a different matter. Let us in the meantime take another look at the Jewish matter, at what is most important – the reaction to this atrocity which is unparalleled in history.

Ukrainians, Lithuanians, and Latvians accepted the role of executioners forced upon them by the Germans without hesitation. They fulfilled it zealously, with all due haste, and with unprecedented sadism. As far as we know, not a single representative of these three nations protested; there was not one sign of humanity. We must not forget this fact.

Right up to the end, Jews all over the world have remained mysteriously silent about the martyrdom of their brothers in Poland. They still do not acknowledge it. Certainly not for lack of information. At the time, accurate reports were sent out and received. However, they generated no echo, no protest, no cry of indignation. Why not?

Two possible explanations present themselves:

1. They simply do not believe it. They simply cannot imagine that such things could actually happen. The descriptions of the terrible agony suffered by thousands of women, children, elderly people, and young people are so far removed from a normal person's sensibility that they believe they are dealing with a fanciful invention of Polish propaganda permeated by hatred of the Germans.
2. The stubborn silence on Jewish martyrdom obviously plays into the plans for a great political manoeuvre on the part of certain Jewish circles. They foresee the return of good Jewish–German relations sooner or later, and [intend to] burden the Poles with the responsibility for the crimes committed by the Germans.

Either explanation is possible, and perhaps both are correct.

Let us consider the other reactions.

The German population has been stupefied; it is innately obtuse, deprived of any independent judgement or critical thought. It has completely succumbed to the influence of its own propaganda and believes that the Poles, together with the Lithuanians and the Ukrainians, murdered the Jews. Like international Jewry, the other European peoples do not believe that the crime has taken place.

We know nothing about the moods and prevailing opinions on this subject in Russia. Statements made by members of gangs that commit acts of sabotage cannot be taken into consideration. In any case, these expressions are antisemitic – in a Ukrainian or a Lithuanian way.

And the Polish population?

Despite encouragement from the occupiers, cases of Polish involvement in German crimes were rare and sporadic, and the general public has strongly condemned them.

Polish society provided such extensive and spontaneous assistance to the Jews that the German authorities found it necessary to issue an order threatening with the death penalty anyone who helped, sheltered, transported, or hid a Jew. At the same time, the order promised that anyone who voluntarily handed over fugitives who were in hiding or disclosed their hiding place by 7 September would not be punished.[2] This shameful call for denunciation failed. The reports the Germans expected never came. At the same time, a number of Polish underground publications carried articles about the Jewish martyrdom. A Catholic group protested vehemently by publishing a leaflet. Influential circles[3] publicly condemned the crime committed against the Jews in terse and decisive terms.[4]

There were no differing opinions. In Poland there is no shortage of people and parties who consider the Jews as our main and dangerous enemies. However, none of them praised Hitler's crimes.

Whether a farmer, a labourer, or an intellectual, whether conservative or left-wing – every Pole reacted in the same way: *These are people* …

… These are people. These are people who are exposed to the heat without water, who are dragged out of their homes, hunted down in the forests like wild animals, poisoned with gas like rats, buried alive, and forced into minefields … These are people. Terrible vengeance must be wrought upon the executioners for the crimes committed against these people.

The unanimity with which this position is held in society serves as wonderful proof of the fundamental *decency* of Polish society, the fact that it has been so deeply and permanently imbued with Christian ethics that any collective reflexes contrary to these ethics are unthinkable.

That is an important and significant observation.

The Ukrainians, Latvians, and Lithuanians have *failed* the test life has set for them. We have proven our spiritual maturity for the umpteenth time in our history.

*From the editors*: We have been asked to announce publicly that, on the initiative of a range of social organizations from Catholic and democratic circles, a commission is being set up for the Jewish population[5] affected by the bestial persecution of Jews by the Germans. The commission will endeavour to render assistance to the victims of Nazi acts of violence, to the best of its ability under the prevailing living conditions in occupied territory, and according to its means and opportunities.

2 Announcement by the SS and Police Leader in Warsaw, Ferdinand von Sammern-Frankenegg, 5 Sept. 1942: APW, 204/290; see also Doc. 144.

3 This is a reference to the Polish government's representation in occupied Poland.

4 See Doc. 140.

5 This is a reference to the Council to Aid Jews.

## DOC. 162
## On 15 October 1942 the Governor of District Warsaw reflects on the economic consequences of deporting 400,000 of the Warsaw ghetto's inhabitants[1]

Activity report for August and September 1942 (marked 'confidential') by the Governor of District Warsaw,[2] signed Hummel, for the government of the GG, dated 15 October 1942 (extract)[3]

Bimonthly report by the Governor of District Warsaw, dated 15 October 1942, for the months of August and September 1942
[…][4]
The evacuation of the Jews, who apart from a small remainder were resettled from District Warsaw during the period covered by this report, has had an immense economic impact. The illegal activities[5] described in the last report have consequently come to an end with surprising rapidity. The undesirable transfer of orders to the Jewish residential districts, the illegal production of goods, and sales at black-market prices, as well as miscellaneous irregularities that have been particularly prominent in the Jewish residential district in Warsaw until now, have all ceased. The Jewish residential district is essentially empty. The Jewish population now only works in a few enterprises, and only for armaments purposes. However, these Jews are monitored so strictly that no further illegal activities can be undertaken. This means that the wellspring and source of countless price-distorting economic transactions have been blocked. However, the quantity of used furnishings and clothing in circulation is a clear indication that numerous thefts are currently being committed in the abandoned areas of the Jewish residential districts.

At the moment, it is still impossible to gauge what the economic consequences of reducing the city of Warsaw's population by approximately 400,000[6] people will be. Doubtless the food shortage in the district will now be alleviated, just as the deportation of the Jews has led to a sharp drop in prices in the majority of the Kreishauptmannschaften. On the other hand, we are now short of approximately 100,000 workers, who can only gradually be replaced by the Aryan working population.

Furthermore, it should not be overlooked that numerous enterprises and properties have suffered extraordinary damage. Losses amounting to 155.9 million zloty have been

1 AIZ, doc. I-10, fols. 70–86, quoted passages fols. 70v–72v, 73–74, 75, 76r–v, 84r–v. Published in Polish translation in Krzysztof Dunin-Wąsowicz et al. (eds.), *Raporty Ludwiga Fischera gubernatora Dystryktu Warszawskiego 1939–1944* (Warsaw: Książka i Wiedza, 1987), pp. 566–599. This document has been translated from German.
2 Ludwig Fischer.
3 Many lines in the original have been underlined by hand.
4 In the previous sections of the report, Fischer first discussed the political situation and Polish resistance activities in the district, then turned his attention to the economic situation.
5 In the report for June and July 1942, dated 15 August 1942, Fischer had complained that large quantities of raw materials and semi-finished products 'important for the war' were being smuggled into the ghetto and turned into consumer goods; these, he alleged, were then being sent out of the ghetto and sold at extortionate prices: Dunin-Wąsowicz et al. (eds.), *Raporty Ludwiga Fischera*, p. 544.
6 The actual number of deportees was lower: see Doc. 243.

calculated for the Jewish residential district according to a conservative estimate of the costs of pest control, defaults on outstanding rent arrears, the loss of rent payments, depreciation as a result of poor maintenance, and destruction of the buildings. These economic disadvantages must be endured, however, as the eradication of the Jews is absolutely necessary for political reasons.

III. *The food situation*

The principal task of the food policy was to secure the grain quotas. In the context of the emergency currently affecting the harvest, comprehensive measures have been taken to ensure that 100 per cent of the quota is brought in this year.

The extraordinarily favourable results of grain procurement are already evident, and therefore it is expected that the entire quota will be secured.

Harvesting has been substantially impeded by the fact that the large-scale operation to deport Jews and recruit workers[7] ran in parallel with the harvest. [...][8]

IV. *The labour situation*

[...][9]

The loss of Jewish labour due to the evacuation of the Jews has ultimately had a drastic effect. The Jews constituted a cheap reserve of labour available for periods of peak activity and tasks at short notice, e.g. loading and unloading at all the railway stations. Applications for Polish replacements are naturally now flooding in from all the firms and agencies who have lost their Jewish workers. [...][10]

V. *The situation in the Jewish residential district*

Resettlement in the city of Warsaw's Jewish residential district came to an end for the time being in late September. Approximately 35,000 Jews have remained in Warsaw's Jewish residential district. They are almost exclusively workers in those armaments factories that are still authorized.[11]

A total of approximately 400,000 Jews have been evacuated from Warsaw.[12] As there were previously over 540,000 Jews in the city of Warsaw at times, the population has consequently been reduced by around half a million.

The evacuation of the Jews caused a great stir among the public. However, it can be observed that the evacuation of the Jews was ultimately welcomed by the Polish population as well.

The food and economic situation in Warsaw's Jewish residential district now rests on entirely new foundations. The SS and Police Leader responsible for implementing

7 A reference to Poles who were deported to the Reich as forced labourers.

8 The following section contained information on crop yields.

9 In the passage omitted here, Fischer referred to the labour shortage, which meant that the goal of recruiting 35,000 forced labourers by the end of the year would encounter 'the greatest of difficulties': AIZ, doc. I-10, fol. 72.

10 Fischer subsequently called for 'greater severity' in recruiting Polish labourers for the German war economy: ibid., fol. 72v.

11 See Doc. 158, fn. 5.

12 This number is an overestimate. Current estimates indicate that 250,000–300,000 people were deported to Treblinka from the Umschlagplatz in the ghetto in summer 1942.

the entire Jew operation[13] has required the enterprises to pay a daily rate of 5 zl. for those Jewish labourers who remain as of 1 September 1942. Of this amount, 3 zl. is to be paid to the SS and Police Leader, while the remaining 2 zl. goes to feed the Jewish workers.[14] All foodstuffs are to be uniformly purchased by the Jewish Supply Office.

Now that the Jewish residential district has been reconfigured, it no longer has a distinct economic life. While exports reached more than 15 million zloty in July, this amount fell to 1.9 million in August and to 1.1 million in September, the latter figures based on previous transactions for goods and services.

The number of funerals was 4,516 in August and 4,244 in September. The number of suicides was 155 in August and 69 in September.

The remaining Jews are in a good state of health. No further typhus infections have been confirmed. There are only 45 people in the sole hospital remaining in the Jewish residential district, although this hospital has a capacity of approximately 350 beds.

VI. *The situation in the Kreise*

[…][15]

Jews were also evacuated from the Kreishauptmannschaften during the period covered by this report. This has likewise led to profound changes everywhere. Numerous Kreishauptmannschaften are now free of Jews, except for a small remainder. With the exception of the city of Warsaw and the Kreishauptmannschaft Warschau-Land, evacuating the Jews from the Kreishauptmannschaften has had an extraordinarily favourable impact in terms of food and pricing policies, as henceforth no Jews can buy food on the black market to sell on at inflated prices.

[…][16]

B. *Particular areas of activity*

Regarding individual areas of activity, the following can be reported:

*I. Economic Affairs Department*

*a) Subdepartment I: Industry*

[…][17]

*3) Individual branches of industry*

[…][18]

The resettlement of the Jews has greatly affected the *Warsaw textile industry*. With few exceptions, this industry was in Jewish hands until late 1939, and the majority of the workforce was also Jewish.

The Jews did not train any Aryans, meaning there were almost no skilled Aryan workers. Of the 3,500 people formerly working in the knitwear industry, at least 3,000

13 Ferdinand von Sammern-Frankenegg.

14 See Doc. 158.

15 In the passage omitted here, Fischer discussed the increase in partisan activity.

16 In the passage omitted here, Fischer commented that the Kreishauptmannschaften had managed to complete their 'substantial […] tasks' despite 'staff shortages': see AIZ, doc. I-10, fol. 74.

17 The passage omitted here dealt with issuing permits for new businesses and the fuel supply.

18 In the passage omitted here, Fischer complained that it had been impossible to bring mothballed companies back into operation due to the lack of fuel and combustibles.

were Jewish. The resettlement of the Jews has consequently resulted in a noticeable decline in production.

In August, production slumped from 4.4 million zloty to 3.3 million zloty, or by 25 per cent. However, production actually fell by 50 per cent, as the companies offered more goods than they had in stock.

Normal production can only resume once a sufficient number of skilled Aryan workers have been trained.

[…][19]

*Subdepartment II: Trustee management*

1. *Trustee enterprises*

During the reporting period, four enterprises were requisitioned, meaning that 899 companies are now under trustee management.

2. *Resettlement of Jews*

The resettlement of the Jews has caused great difficulties, as countless enterprises and properties have suffered considerable damage, and it is currently impossible to compensate for this damage using routine management methods.

Furthermore, since the deportations began, rental income in the Jewish residential district has collapsed. The figures for the months of July and August 1942 can be broken down as follows:

In the Aryan residential district, 4,542,100 zl. was spent on rent in July and 4,343,200 zl. in August. In relation to target rent, this amounts to 96 per cent in July and 91.8 per cent in August.

Total expenditure in August 1942 was 4,253,891.38 zl.

By contrast, rental income in the Jewish residential district has come to an almost complete standstill.

The loss of 155.9 million zl., already quoted in the main part of this report, can be broken down into the following individual sums:

| | |
|---|---|
| Loss of rental income over three months | 8,267,000 zl. |
| Depreciation due to inadequate maintenance and destruction of buildings (100,000 zl. per building) | 105,100,000 |
| Pest control costs (5,000 zl. per building) | 5,245,000 |
| Loss due to debts in arrears | 37,348,000 |
| | 155,960,000 |

In addition, the burden of short-term debt increased by 5,249,000 zl. It goes without saying that the real estate management department cannot make up for these losses on its own.

[…][20]

19 This was followed by statements on other enterprises and branches of industry.

20 In the passage omitted here, Fischer reported on air-raid damage with which the real estate management department had to contend, and price-control activities; he then went on to report on the activities of other departments.

## DOC. 163

## On 15 October 1942 the Kreishauptmann in Kreis Warschau-Land orders that the assets of deported Jews be recorded[1]

Letter from the Kreishauptmann of Kreis Warschau-Land (file reference Wi 505 A), signed Dr Rupprecht,[2] Warsaw, to the mayors and village officials of Kreis Warschau-Land, dated 15 October 1942

*Re*: abandoned Jewish assets

Now that all Jewish residential districts in Kreis Warschau-Land have been liquidated and the Jews resettled, we must precisely establish the extent of abandoned Jewish assets (movable and immovable) so they can be seized and confiscated. I hereby instruct the mayors and village officials to establish immediately what *Jewish* assets still exist within their communities. Separate lists of movable and immovable assets are to be submitted to me.

A register of abandoned real estate (immovable assets) is to be submitted with the following information:

1) Surname
2) First name
3) Type of real estate (garden plot, building plot, villa grounds, etc.)
4) Mortgage status
5) Size of real estate in hectares.

For abandoned *movable* assets, only the surname, first name, and type of abandoned asset should be stated.

*Deadline*: 15 November 1942

## DOC. 164

## *Pressedienst des Generalgouvernements*, 20 October 1942: report on three years of anti-Jewish policies in trade and industry in the General Government[1]

*General Government Economic News Service. Business restructuring in the General Government*

Pressedienst des Generalgouvernements, Cracow, 20 October 1942

Trade and industry in the former Polish state were concentrated in Jewish hands. In the drive to establish viable economic governance in the General Government following the

1 The original has been lost. Copy in BArch, R 102/I/1, fol. 68. This document has been translated from German.

2 Hermann Rupprecht (1905–1985), lawyer; Regierungsrat with the Alzenau Landratsamt, 1933–1939; joined the NSDAP in 1937; Kreishauptmann of Warschau-Land, Oct. 1939 – Jan. 1945; in US captivity, 1945–1946; in Nov. 1946 extradited to Poland, where he was sentenced to life imprisonment; released to West Germany in 1956; high-ranking official within regional administration in Bavaria from 1958.

1 *Pressedienst des Generalgouvernements*, 20 Oct. 1942, pp. 4–5. The *Pressedienst des Generalgouvernements* appeared twice weekly in Cracow between 31 August 1940 and 10 Dec. 1943 as a typed, duplicated news digest. This document has been translated from German.

establishment of the German administration, it was not possible to eliminate Jewish workers altogether straight away, due to the shortage of suitably skilled Polish workers.

Over the three years of German administration, Polish and Ukrainian workers have received specialist training as part of a systematic programme of training and retraining courses. They are steadily being brought in to replace the Jewish workforce. One example of this is the garment-industry town of Tarnow, which was a markedly Jewish city when it was still Polish;[2] crafts, industry, business – in a word, all economic life there was Judaized. Tarnow's clothing workshops, which are renowned well beyond its borders, employed male and female Jewish workers until quite recently. As the result of a special measure on the part of the German school administration in the General Government, the creation of ongoing short-term training courses in tailoring, and the deployment of vocational school students in their final year of schooling, the Jewish workforce has now vanished from Tarnow's clothing manufacture entirely. Tarnow is free of Jews.[3] Of course, the significance of de-Jewification in the General Government lies primarily in eliminating the risk of epidemics, which – as has been officially proven – were spread above all by Jewry. By concentrating all the Jews together in their own living spaces, the rest of the population is spared this terrible danger.

In the course of de-Jewification, trade in the General Government is being restructured. Small Jewish enterprises are being closed, and a few vital businesses taken over by Poles. Large Jewish enterprises are handed over to Germans who have been wounded in action.

The restructuring of Polish trade also goes hand in hand with de-Jewification. The large number of small shops is being reduced to a smaller number of viable distributors. Almost every small shop used to be run as a 'general store', which was a particular phenomenon in former Poland. Fancy goods, textiles, ready-to-wear clothing, and even pictures were sold alongside food, confectionery, and fruit. In 1939 a number of these shops had to be closed, or their sales methods had to be regulated. This was necessary for reasons of hygiene: given the wide variety of goods for sale, the dirt and disorder that prevailed in these shops were enough to pose a real danger to public health.

2 Prior to Sept. 1939 approximately 25,000 Jews lived in Tarnów, a number which corresponded to half the population; after the war started, refugees arrived and increased the Jewish population to approximately 40,000.

3 In June 1942 employees at the field office of the Commander of the Security Police and the SD (KdS), along with German and Polish police officers, conducted initial deportations to Belzec, while members of the Waffen-SS carried out mass shootings; of the approximately 20,000 ghetto residents who remained, the German police deported 8,000 Jews to Belzec in Sept. 1942 and a further 2,500 in mid Nov. 1942. In early Sept. 1943 the approximately 10,000 Jews still living in the Tarnów ghetto were transported to Auschwitz or to the Plaszow and Szebnie camps. A few hundred Jews remained behind in *Aufräumkommandos* ('clean-up details' charged with sorting through Jewish belongings) or in hiding. On 9 February 1944 German authorities declared Tarnów officially 'free of Jews'.

## DOC. 165

## On 25 October 1942 a police company commander makes observations on the arrest and deportation of escaped Jews from the Drohobycz area[1]

Letter (marked 'secret') from the 24th Police Regiment, 5th Company,[2] signed Lederer,[3] Hauptmann of the Urban Police and company commander (log no. 177/42 [g]) in Drohobycz, to the Commander of the Order Police in District Galicia, Oberstleutnant Soosten of the Urban Police, or his official deputy in Lemberg (received by 2nd Battalion/24th Police Regiment on 28 October 1942), dated 25 October 1942[4]

Re: resettlement of Jews
Reference: Vfg. SSuPolF. XIII, log no. 658/42 (s[ecret]), dated 14 October 1942[5] (n[ot] p[ublished])
The operation began on 21 October 1942 at 10 a.m. and continued until 24 October 1942, after the platoon had arrived from Breslau Police Guard Battalion.

The platoon assigned by Breslau Guard Battalion was given marching orders and set off for Lemberg on 23 October at 15:30.

| | |
|---|---|
| Resettled from Drohobycz | 1,179 Jews |
| from Sambor | 460 Jews |
| from Boryslaw | 1,020 Jews |
| from Stryj | 800 Jews, |
| Total | 3,459 Jews |

The Jews in Drohobycz and Boryslaw had already fled days before the operation, which meant that the operation was very difficult and not as successful as expected. In my view, ongoing local operations to arrest Jews who return will be more successful. This process has already been implemented in Stryj and Sambor.

1 RGVA, R-1323k/2/292b, fol. 28. Copy in IfZ-Archives, Fb 101/07, fol. 502. Published in Polish translation in Aleksander Krugłow, 'Deportacja ludności żydowskiej z dystryktu Galicja do obozu zagłady w Bełżcu w 1942 r.', *BŻIH*, no. 151 (1989), pp. 101–118, here pp. 117–118. This document has been translated from German.

2 The 5th Company was formed from Police Battalion 133.

3 Ernst Lederer (1913–1944), police officer; joined the SS in 1933 and the NSDAP in 1937; served with the SS-Verfügungstruppe, 1933–1935; served in the Gestapo Central Office (Gestapa) in 1938; served with the head of the civil administration in the Army Command 3 area in 1939; worked for the Order Police from 1940; commander of the 5th Company of the 24th Police Regiment in Security District North in Drohobycz (District Galicia); went missing in action in the Soviet Union in mid 1944; legally declared dead in Jan. 1964.

4 Distribution list: Kdr. d. Orpo, II./Pol.24, Kdr., 5./Pol.24 [Commander of the Order Police, 2nd Battalion/24th Police Regiment, commander, 5th Company/24th Police Regiment].

5 No details of this order could be found.

## DOC. 166

## On 25 October 1942 Abram Borowski asks his brother in the Warsaw ghetto to send clothing and money to him at a labour camp in Lublin[1]

Letter from Abram Borowski,[2] Lublin, 7 Lipowa Street,[3] kom.[4] 19, to his brother D. Borowski,[5] Ostdeutsche Bautischlerei [carpentry] workshop, 30 Gęstrase,[6] Warsaw, dated 25 October 1942[7]

Lublin, 25 October
Beloved brother, I received your letter of 10 October one day before the postcard dated 28 September. Dear brother, just imagine, I'm standing at roll call and receive a letter from you.[8] Imagine my joy, but when I read that Szlamek[9] is also gone, I was full of despair and pain.

Beloved brother, I received a postcard from a woman who had read my letter and asked about a Mrs Tympulper. I can only report that no women came with us from Lublin.

Beloved brother, Heniek came with me to Lublin, but I don't know where he is. Pyńy Borowski is with me.

Dear brother, I ask you to find out something about Berek Mangut, because he deserves it, because Moszek shares [everything] with me like a brother.

Dear brother, tell me what things are left in our apartment on Parysowska Street,[10] whether everything is there, because we did not take anything with us. And I beg you, please send me something warm to wear, especially a pair of long johns, because I'm still wearing the ones I had on when we arrived. I got a pair of shoes with uppers here, so send me some puttees, and above all, a few złoty, because I'm completely broke.

Goodbye.

Your brother, Abram Borowski

1 AŻIH, Ring II/377 (274), fols. 2–5. Published as a facsimile in Sakowska (ed.), *Archiwum Ringelbluma: Konspiracyjne Archiwum Getta Warszawy*, vol. 1: *Listy o Zagładzie*, pp. 268–271. This document has been translated from Polish.

2 The Borowski family came from the village of Okuniew, to the east of Warsaw. Abram Borowski (1918–1943?), metalworker; lived in Miłosna prior to Sept. 1939, then in Warsaw, and finally in Lublin.

3 The camp for Jewish forced labourers on Lipowa Street in Lublin.

4 The Polish abbreviation probably stands for '[work] detail'.

5 Presumably Dawid Borowski (b. 1918) from Warsaw, who survived the war.

6 This is presumably a reference to Gęsia Street, which was renamed Gänse-Straße under the German occupation.

7 Stamp: 'Camp mail checked'. The post office in the Warsaw ghetto changed the street name to 'Gęsia Street', and the following note was written on the back of the envelope: 'no building at 30 Gęsia Street, addressee unknown, 29/10[/1942]'.

8 Jewish prisoners in the labour camps were allowed to receive post. The Security Police had suspended all postal deliveries in the Warsaw ghetto with a week-long 'postal blockade' from 23 July 1942. This was partially loosened thereafter. Postcards could still be sent from the Warsaw ghetto until mid Nov. 1942.

9 Presumably the author's brother Szlomo Borowski, who lived in Miłosna prior to Sept. 1939 and later perished in the Warsaw ghetto.

10 Parysowska Street was located outside the ghetto.

Beloved brother, send me a scarf and some old gloves.

Beloved brother, what I wrote to you in my second letter about myself to Mr Lande is the return address, *so this is the address they should write to.*[11]

Dear brother, my comrade will now write on my behalf, because I have to go to work. So I beg you to take care of this.

Your brother, Abram Borowski

Write to tell me what Warsaw looks like and whether you're living in the apartment on Miła Street, and what you've done with our apartment on Parysowska Street.[12]

Dear brother!!! Do me a big favour. There's a friend here with me from Warsaw, he left his wife in Warsaw. He has already sent twenty letters and can't get in touch with her, so I will send you the address here. Will you go and find out what's going on? Here's the address: Fela Borodowska, that's the woman, or her cousin, Bronka Borer. The address of the szop is: Curt Rörych,[13] no. 80 Nowolipie Street, Doitsche[14] Textil-Fabrik.

My friend's name is Szmul Zeldman, and he works with me.

Attend to this matter as soon as you can, before I have to ask you again. In case nothing comes of it, he also has a brother: Aron Zeldman,[15] 49/6 Miła Street, front building, third floor.

I am awaiting a quick reply!!!

## DOC. 167

## On 27 October 1942 the Polish government's representation in occupied Poland describes the search for Jews in Ostrowiec Świętokrzyski, Ćmielów, Otwock, and Piotrków[1]

Communications for the government delegation's Internal Affairs Department, signed Krystyna,[2] dated 27 October 1942[3]

Jewish matters.

On 2 October 1942 they deported Jews from *Wiślica*[4] – Kielce region. They tie up those they pick up in the woods with barbed wire and then kill them.

On 10 October a so-called punitive squad composed of Latvians, Lithuanians, and Gestapo men came to *Ostrowiec Kielecki.*[5] There were approximately 9,000 Jews in the city. On 11 October they were rounded up in the market square. Some of them were taken away

11 The following one and a half lines have been crossed out and are illegible.
12 The handwriting in the original is different from this point on.
13 Correctly: Röhrich.
14 Spelling as in the original. Correctly: 'Deutsche' ('German textile factory').
15 Presumably Aron Zeldman (d. 1942), a retailer from Warsaw.

1 AAN, 1325/202/II-29, fol. 54. This document has been translated from Polish.
2 Code name of Zofia Wawrzyńska, military liaison for the Home Army High Command Bureau of Information and Propaganda; arrested on 5 Jan. 1944 and shot shortly thereafter.
3 The original contains handwritten notes and underlining.
4 A town approximately 40 km south of Kielce.
5 Known today as Ostrowiec Świętokrzyski.

immediately, and some remained outside in the market square until Friday, 16 October. The informant does not know how long they remained there because she herself left for the nearest town on that day. In Ostrowiec the identity documents of everyone on the street were checked. One of my informant's acquaintances had her documents checked seven times in one day, after which people held off going to this town.

On the night of 14 to 15 October they drove the Jews from the area around Ćmielów[6] into Ćmielów and brought them to the market square. They were not allowed to stand, but had to lie in the mud. It was a cold night, windy and rainy. On 15 October the Jews from Ćmielów were also taken away, with the exception of several dozen people, perhaps 100, who worked in the porcelain factory and the iron ore mine. In addition, a few weeks earlier, about 100 Jews had been taken to the factories in Skarżysko.[7] The families of those taken to the factories were deported. At midday on 15 October the Jews from the surrounding area, followed by those from Ćmielów, were first to go to the railway station located 1.5 km away. In town they had to surrender all the cash that they had on them, valuables, and luggage, which were stored under guard. They left them with only 20 złoty [each]. An eyewitness saw that before they were loaded into the wagons, they all had to take off their shoes and hand them over, tied together. These shoes were taken to Ćmielów. The furniture from the Jewish apartments was auctioned off. Only two Jews were killed on the way to the station.

The informant knew about a dozen Jewish families in Ćmielów. These people had no idea what fate awaited them. They prepared the things they wanted to take with them. One woman from Vienna even took her cork bathtub, because she could not imagine not being able to bathe every day.

Having liquidated the ghetto in Otwock,[8] the germans[9] set out on a hunt for Jews hiding in the local forests. One hunt led to approximately 300 people being captured who were guarded by German soldiers and the Polish police until their execution. A young 17-year-old girl stood out among these wretched and unfortunate people. She sang loudly the entire time. Finally, a german asked her why she was so cheerful. Did she not know she was going to die soon? She replied: 'Why shouldn't I be cheerful? I'm young and the world is so beautiful, it is smiling at me. Poland [already] existed when I was not yet in the world, and it will continue to exist once I'm gone.' And she kept singing. She was among the first to be sent to her death. In the Warsaw ghetto 35,000 food ration cards were issued. According to someone who recently arrived from there, 70,000 people remained in the ghetto, while according to someone else – 55,000. In any case, all the people in excess of the 35,000 are there illegally.

Excerpts from a letter from Piotrków:[10] … we are currently unable to work. Absolutely nothing is going smoothly. This is the mood. Imagine, people have allegedly hidden Jews on account of the intended liquidation of the ghetto. Well, of course there are arrests,

6 A town 10 km south-east of Ostrowiec Świętokrzyski.
7 The SS had established a forced labour camp for Jews in Skarżysko-Kamienna in August 1942.
8 The ghetto was liquidated on 20 August 1942: see Doc. 120.
9 In the original this term is deliberately written in lower case here and below as an expression of contempt.
10 Approximately 25,000 people lived in the Piotrków Trybunalski ghetto in early Oct. 1942.

because this is forbidden, after all. The city is gripped by intense fear. Moreover, roundups have been resumed, in the buildings and on the streets. My landlady walks around in a daze. Prices have shot up here again, and you can't get anything. I don't know when I'll be back. Apparently it's dangerous on the trains. People stare at dark-haired people as if they were Jews. On the street everyone gawks at everyone else to see whether they're Jewish. It's all a farce. Everyone is suspicious of everything! At the railway ticket office they check identity documents. H. can't use the express train because you need to get a permit from the gendarmerie to travel by express train. As far as the liquidation of the ghetto is concerned,[11] our people are behaving scandalously. They loot, steal, break into empty houses, and take with them whatever they can.

## DOC. 168

## On 28 October 1942 the Higher SS and Police Leader in the General Government specifies which ghettos in District Warsaw and District Lublin may continue to exist for the time being[1]

*Police Regulation on the Establishment of Jewish Residential Districts in District Warsaw and District Lublin*, 28 October 1942

On the basis of § 3 of the Regulation on Security and Order in the General Government of 26 October 1939 (*VOBl-GG*, p. 5),[2] I hereby order as follows:

§ 1

(1) In District Warsaw and District Lublin, Jewish residential districts are to be established in the following towns and communities:[3]

- (a) in *District Warsaw* in the city of Warsaw (ghetto), Kałuszyn (Kreishauptmannschaft Minsk), Sobolew (Kreishauptmannschaft Garwolin), Kossów[4] (Kreishauptmannschaft Sokolow), Rembertów (Kreishauptmannschaft Warschau-Land), Siedlce (Kreishauptmannschaft Siedlce);
- (b) in *District Lublin* in Luków, Parczew, and Miedzyrzec (Kreishauptmannschaft Radzyń), Włodawa (Kreishauptmannschaft Cholm), Końskowola (Kreishauptmannschaft Pulawy), Piaski (Kreishauptmannschaft Lublin-Land), Zaklików (Kreishauptmannschaft Kraśnik), Izbica (Kreishauptmannschaft Krasnystaw).

(2) These localities are the residential districts assigned to the Jews on the basis of § 4(b) of the Third Regulation on Restrictions of Movement in the General Government of 15 October 1941 (*VOBl-GG*, p. 595).[5]

11 Units controlled by the SS and Police Leader in Radom liquidated the ghetto between 13 and 21 Oct. 1942; more than 80 per cent of the ghetto's inhabitants were deported to Treblinka.

1 *VOBl-GG* 1942, no. 94, 1 Nov. 1942, pp. 665–666. This document has been translated from German.
2 The Regulation on Security and Order in the General Government empowered the Higher SS and Police Leader to issue police regulations: *VOBl-GG*, no. 1, 26 October 1939, p. 5.
3 Almost all of these ghettos were already established. The purpose of the police regulation was actually to specify the ghettos in which Jews were still permitted to stay.
4 Kosów Lacki.
5 See Doc. 13.

§ 2

(1) On the basis of the Regulation on the Definition of the Term 'Jew' in the General Government of 24 July 1940 (*VOBl-GG* I, p. 231), all Jews in District Warsaw and District Lublin have until 30 November 1942 to take up residence in one of the Jewish residential areas specified in § 1 for District Warsaw or District Lublin. All other persons are to leave the Jewish residential districts by this deadline, unless the police have given them a residential permit. The responsible District Governor (SS and Police Leader) will settle the specifics by issuing a directive.

(2) As of 1 December 1942, no Jew in District Warsaw or District Lublin may reside outside or leave a Jewish residential district without a police permit. As of 1 December 1942, other persons may reside in or enter a Jewish residential district only with a police permit. Permits for the Jewish residential district will be granted by the responsible Kreishauptmann or, for the Warsaw ghetto, by the commissioner for the Jewish residential district.

(3) Jews who are employed in factories pertaining to war production or armaments and are being held in closed-off camps are exempt from the obligation to seek a Jewish residential district.

§ 3

(1) Jews who violate the provisions of § 2 will be punished by death under the existing regulations.

(2) Any individual who knowingly harbours such a Jew, i.e. anyone who specifically shelters, feeds, or hides a Jew outside the Jewish residential district, will be punished in the same way.

(3) The Security Police will take action against anyone who obtains knowledge that a Jew is residing outside the Jewish residential district without authorization and does not report this to the police.

(4) Non-Jewish persons who, contrary to the provisions of § 2, do not leave the Jewish residential district by the stipulated deadline, or who enter it without a police permit, will be punished in administrative proceedings with a fine of up to 1,000 zloty, or alternatively with up to three months in prison. The Kreishauptmann (Stadthauptmann) will issue the penalty for the offence.

§ 4

(1) The Jewish residential districts are to be administered separately.

(2) A Jewish Council will be in charge of each Jewish residential district. The provisions of the Regulation on the Appointment of Jewish Councils of 28 November 1939 (*VOBl-GG*, p. 72)[6] are applicable here. The Jewish Council is responsible for housing the Jews in the Jewish residential districts and for the fair and proper distribution of the food allocated by the Kreis authorities.

(3) The responsible District Governor (SS and Police Leader) will settle the specifics by issuing a directive.

6 See PMJ 4/46.

§ 5
The Senior Commander of the Security Police in the General Government[7] will issue implementing regulations[8] pertaining to this police regulation.
§ 6
This Police Regulation will come into force on 1 November 1942.
*Cracow*, 28 October 1942
The Higher SS and Police Leader in the General Government. The State Secretary for Security
*Krüger*[9]

## DOC. 169
## In October 1942 an escapee from Treblinka describes his time in the extermination camp and his escape[1]

Report by an unidentified Jew from Warsaw[2] for the underground archive of the Warsaw ghetto, prepared in October 1942[3]

During the resettlement period, I worked in the 'Palma' artificial honey factory as a night watchman. Since I deluded myself into thinking that working in the factory would protect me from resettlement, I moved out of my apartment in Nowolipie Street and spent all my time in the factory.

On 25 August the factory yard was surrounded and cordoned off. In our yard there was a szop that produced goods made of straw and bore the name 'Waldemar Schmidt'. We continued working. Suddenly an SS man, accompanied by Ukrainians, stormed into our factory. 'Alle heraus,'[4] he shouted.

The employees of the Waldemar Schmidt szop were already grouped outside in the yard. We joined them and were escorted to the Umschlagplatz[5] by the Ukrainians.

I tried to escape from the ranks before entering the square. A Jewish policeman noticed this and forced me back violently.

Our group was immediately herded towards the wagons. There was no selection of any kind. Everyone was loaded. The train left after a few minutes.

7 Eberhard Schöngarth.
8 No information on these has been found.
9 Krüger issued similar regulations for District Radom (4 localities), District Cracow (5 localities), and District Galicia (32 localities) on 10 November 1942: *VOBl-GG*, no. 98, 14 Nov. 1942, pp. 683–686.

1 AŻIH, Ring II/378 (295), fols. 1–14. Published in 'Relacje dwóch zbiegów z Treblinki II', pp. 78–88, here pp. 78–85. Published in English translation in Kermish (ed.), *To Live with Honor*, pp. 710–716. This document has been newly translated from Polish.
2 Probably Jakub Krzepicki (1915–1943); originally from powiat Wieluń; later lived in Danzig, then in Poland; served in the war in Sept. 1939; member of the Noar Zioni (Zionist Youth) group in the Warsaw ghetto; died during the Warsaw Ghetto Uprising. A detailed account given by Krzepicki of his experiences in Treblinka extermination camp and subsequent escape from there, which was recorded in Yiddish by Rokhl Oyerbakh beginning in Dec. 1942, was published in *Bleter far geszichte*, no. 11 (1956), pp. 71–141 (AŻIH, Ring II/382 [299]).
3 The report is untitled and is written in two alternating styles of handwriting.
4 German in the original: 'Everybody out'.
5 German in the original.

The wagon I was in was crammed with people. It was terribly stuffy, and it was getting worse by the minute.

As the train began to move, profound despondency spread through the wagon. The thought of imminent death consumed us all and it filled us with dread.

The Mourner's 'Kaddish' rang out from all sides of the wagon. Two hours later the train stopped. It remained standing the entire night. At about midnight a Latvian entered the wagon with a revolver in his hand. He grouped us all on one side of the wagon, threatened us with the revolver, and demanded money and valuables. After the raid the Latvian left the wagon and carefully closed the door behind him.

The train remained stationary. Two men pushed their way to the little open window and jumped out onto the tracks. Almost simultaneously, several shots rang out.

I thought about escaping the same way, but the unbearable heat robbed me of the strength and energy needed to force my way to the window.

People in the wagon fainted and became weak due to thirst and the lack of air.

The half-naked bodies were covered in sweat.

Towards morning the train started to move. We travelled for a long time. We didn't know where we were heading.

A few hours later an SS man entered the wagon. He assured us politely and convincingly that we were being taken to the village called Treblinka where we would briefly stop and, after the selection, would then be taken on to our workplace. He asked us to be obedient and hard-working. He finished by announcing that we were close to our final destination.

The German left the wagon. The mood lifted. Worn out and thirsty, we awaited the end of the journey.

At last.

The train stopped. The door opened abruptly, and we found ourselves in a square surrounded on all sides by barbed wire. Buildings and barracks of various sizes could be seen nearby. An SS man appeared and divided us into two groups. In one were women and children, in the other only men. We walked a short distance and came to a yard surrounded by barbed wire. Barracks stretched along both sides of the yard. Next to them were two signs with the inscription: 'Achtung Warschauer'.[6] Camp regulations hung below.

Despite our incessant pleas, we were not given anything to drink. The women were led to the barracks on the left side of the yard, and the men were instructed to line up in the centre of the square.

On the square we noticed corpses and vast quantities of rags and clothing. Everyone was gripped with horror. A sense of death hung in the air, but no one did anything. We were paralysed with fear, exhaustion, and hunger.

Then an SS man appeared. He gave a speech. He announced that everyone would be given work and food, and that we had nothing to fear.

Those there – he said, pointing to the corpses – had perished because they were rebels.

He chose 10 people for work and left. Everyone else was ordered to wait. A few minutes later another SS man appeared and explained that he needed 60 people for work.

6 German in the original: 'Attention Varsovians'.

Despite their exhaustion, everyone volunteered. Seeing this, the German then began his selection. I was among those selected. We were led out of the yard to a square behind the buildings. There lay heaps of corpses with horribly contorted faces. They had suffocated in the wagons.

Our job was to carry the corpses to the ditches nearby. This was terrible work. The mask-like faces of the corpses were blue-black and bloated, the eyes had a wild expression, the bodies were intertwined and heavy. We staggered with exhaustion. Even so we were not allowed to rest, not even for a moment. When a German noticed that someone had slowed his working pace, a shot rang out and another corpse fell to the ground.

The number of people working began to decrease. I felt worse and worse. Suddenly I felt as if I was about to faint. I looked for rescue.

I took advantage of a German's momentary inattention and hid behind the nearest barracks, next to which lay huge piles of clothing. I hid myself among them. I heard the German shouting and the echo of gunshots. Then silence descended again. An hour passed. Something was happening nearby. I lifted the rags a little and looked out. There was a group of several dozen people on the square. Not one of the people I had worked with was among them. I carefully wriggled out of the rags and approached them.

As it turned out, this was a new group that had been selected from a new transport. No one knew anything about the people who had worked there earlier. Our conversation was interrupted by the arrival of an SS man and a few Ukrainians. They ordered us to move. We were led to a siding. A train with large Russian wagons stood on the track. The transport was from Międzyrzec.[7] The wagons were full of bodies of the people who had suffocated – corpses with their tongues hanging out, bloodless lips, bulging eyes.

We were ordered to empty the wagons. There was a small child in one of them.

'Drink!' it begged in a terrified voice, but no one had any water. We were all terribly thirsty. The Germans had promised us water and soup when the work was finished. Long hours full of agony and thirst went by. With an enormous effort of will, I forced myself to work. My back ached terribly with every slight bend; my mouth and my insides were one big wound thirsting for a drop of cool liquid.

At last, we finished. We get in line.[8] Buckets of water arrive. Everyone receives a cup of water. I feel life awakening in me. I slowly become aware again that I am a human being, that I live, feel, and think.

For a short while, relief pushes the horrific reality into the background, but then it seeps back into our consciousness. We all knew that the group of workers in question – as soon as they finish their work – would go to their deaths, would become scrap,[9] as the tragic end of hundreds of thousands of people was described. After a while, a new group of workers was indeed formed. Feverishly I thought about how I could escape my group, which was already destined for death. I tried to join the workers who had come from the 'Treblinki One' penal camp, which is different from the death camp 'Treblinki

7 On 25 and 26 August 1942 SS and police units rounded up approximately 11,000 Jews in Międzyrzec Podlaski and deported them to Treblinka; several thousand were murdered on the spot.

8 Changes in tense here and below are as in the original.

9 Polish: 'na szmelc'; derived from the Yiddish phrase 'oyf shmelts', which was used to refer to the mass murder of the Jews; 'shmelts' literally means 'scrap' or 'waste', and was used as a term for people who were unfit for work.

Two'. But they objected. They were so afraid for themselves that they mercilessly pushed me out of the ranks. As I returned to the square, I saw a golden twenty-dollar coin on the ground. I picked it up and approached a Ukrainian guard. In return for the gold, he let me go to a nearby privy. There I sat, hour after hour.

Meanwhile a selection took place on the square, as a result of which some of the people were immediately shot, and the rest were led to the bathhouse.[10] I heard gunshot echoes, the curses of the Ukrainians, the terrible screams of those who were being murdered. My whole body trembled feverishly, although I had already become less sensitive to the sight of blood and corpses. When you hear shots, you could not help but feel glad that you yourself are still alive, that this bullet was meant for someone else.

The execution on the square ended. I waited a while longer and then stepped out. The bodies lay on the ground in their own blood. Those destined for the bathhouse were awaiting their turn. Most of them were frozen in total physical and mental apathy in the face of this inhuman horror, which was beyond their strength. Another group of workers from a transport that had just arrived was waiting to be assigned to work. Unnoticed, I approached them. A Jew from Vienna was in charge of the group.[11] I spoke to him in German. His feeling of compassion and solidarity with all of us who were in the same situation had not yet given way to panic. He let me join his group. But in that moment, a German recognized me. He grabbed me by the collar, kicked me, and wanted to take me to the group condemned to death. But I was saved by my knowledge of the German language, and by the Viennese Jew's intervention. I had miraculously escaped death once again.

We were assigned to work in the storage barracks. We had to sort through an enormous amount of clothing and separate any valuables we found. This took us eight days, during which no transports of people arrived at the camp. Our working life at the camp stabilized for a while. During this time I got to know the camp and learned details that I had not known before.

On the giant square surrounded by barbed wire, there are warehouses for clothing, barracks for the camp personnel and the workers, an empty space where people can be rounded up, and several sites earmarked for executions. But most of the space seems to be taken up by the ditches. Before people were transported here day and night, excavators churned up the earth to create graves for millions of people.

A path from the square in the centre leads through the forest to the bathhouse. It is a small building hidden in the bushes, camouflaged with a green net on the roof. People herded to the bathhouse undress along the way and hand over their pieces of clothing to the workers who are posted along the path especially for this purpose. If they are careless or imprecise in folding the clothes, for example, the guards beat them cruelly, and in certain cases – at a sign from a German – *the Ukrainians* shoot [them]. The workers quickly remove the corpses lining the path to the execution site. Incidentally, such cases are rare – the people who are herded here are already so resigned to their fate, stunned and terrorized, that they put up virtually no resistance.

At any given time, 800–1,000 people are let into the bathhouse. None of us workers knew exactly how they were killed. Nevertheless, it seemed to us that there was a faint

10 A term for the gas chambers used in the camp.

11 This may have been Karl Blau (1892–1943), a Kapo at Treblinka.

smell of chlorine in the air around the bathhouse.[12] Emptying the chamber of bodies was never one of my tasks, but I knew that they were taken to the ditches nearby, where they were subsequently burned along with the camp waste. Before that, however, the corpses' gold teeth are pulled out in a small hut next to the bathhouse. The gravediggers – particularly privileged workers – perform this work. Incidentally, they are destined for the same death at which they assist. We all knew that the work to which we clung like a lifeline merely prolonged the agony of waiting for death in this camp full of monstrous horror. Hopes of rescue or escape were negligible.

There are workers in the camp who are marked with yellow or red patches. They receive better food, have better barracks, and have given in to the vain hope of being allowed to live longer. The women employed in the barracks for personnel have been working there ever since the camp was established. In general, Jews do all the work on the camp premises. The camp guard detail consists of a few dozen Germans and more than one hundred Ukrainians.

We were a group of ordinary workers. In the barracks we slept on the bare earth and received three meagre portions of soup per day. We had the opportunity to collect huge amounts of money and valuables, which were hidden in the murdered victims' clothes. I myself buried about a kilo of gold in the camp so it would not fall into German hands. But it was no use hoarding treasures. We knew that the moment would come when we [too] would leave our clothes behind on the way through the green grove, on the way to execution.

Eight days passed. A new transport of deportees from Warsaw arrived. On the square, a new selection from among the group took place: along with others, two of my comrades, who had been standing to my right and my left, were pulled out of the ranks. Once again I was left. I cheated death again.

In the new group, the work consisted of collecting pieces of clothing. I collected the shoes of the women who were led straight to the bathhouse after arrival. While working, I was beaten whenever I accepted shoes that had not been tied together. The women who had not tied them were beaten. A German beat them – sadistically and long.

Another selection was to take place shortly thereafter. I was convinced that this would be the end, that this time I could not trust the blind fate and chance that had spared me so far. On the evening before the anticipated execution, it took a long time for any of us condemned to fall asleep, even though we were exhausted from work. I cried. I had miraculously escaped death so many times that I could not bring myself to surrender. I had not become resigned and was not apathetic, but was full of intense, impotent despair. One of the comrades calmed me down. He had resigned himself to death as one among the masses of millions of the condemned. I couldn't. I didn't want to.

The next day we lined up for selection on the camp's central square. But at the very moment when the first group of those destined for death had moved to the side, something extraordinary happened. One of my comrades (an Argentinian citizen who had been illegally picked up, along with his entire family)[13] broke away from the group, quickly approached the German who was carrying out the selection, and with a single

12 In the gas chambers at Treblinka, the victims were murdered with carbon monoxide, which was generated by internal combustion engines.

thrust, plunged a knife into his back.[14] The German fell to the ground, *but the enraged Ukrainians beat our comrade to a bloody pulp with their shovels.* What followed was terrible. The horrified Germans hid in the barracks *and ordered the inhuman Ukrainians* to carry out a pogrom. The slaughter began. Groups of workers were shot every evening. Blood flowed in rivers.

Immediately after this incident, I took advantage of the tremendous confusion and hid in a pile of clothes. Later I managed to join a group of workers who were loading clothes into wagons. However, I already knew that there was no more time to think, that the final days or even hours of those who had survived in the camp had dawned, and I was determined to try to escape at all costs. I planned to hide among the clothes in the wagon. The task was not easy. Workers at the wagons had been counted, and if anyone went missing, all the rest would be held responsible. In the end I managed to persuade my comrades to help me hide under the incredible amount of clothes in the wagon. Two other men, a father and son, hid along with me. In our place, we managed to sneak into the group of men who were led out of the square.

Buried under the pile of clothes, I waited in unusual tension to see what would happen. Shortly afterwards the doors swung open. We felt a hand rummaging through the clothes, looking for people hiding; we noticed bright searchlights. We waited with frozen hearts, ready for anything.

The slamming door heralded the end of our torture. After a while, a shot rang out; obviously the search in the next wagon had achieved the desired result. The train remained standing for a while, and shots rang out.

At last, there was a violent jolt: the train started moving. Relief – we were saved. But what next?

We did not know in which direction the train was headed, but we knew that we could not go all the way to its destination. I waited until the train slowed down and jumped out the window into the unknown. The fresh night air overwhelmed me. For a moment I revelled in the feeling of freedom. The nightmare of recent days disappeared, but how quickly it was to return, along with the nightmares of the days to come.

A long, strenuous journey began. We received no help from anyone along the way. The farmers not only refused us accommodation and food, they even refused to give us directions. We walked at night and slept in the open air in roadside ditches in daytime. Parting from my two comrades was a sad affair. The farmer with whom we had wanted to spend the night realized that we had money and was sneaky enough to separate us from one another. He claimed that he was afraid and therefore had to lead us to the hut one by one. I was the first to go. In the forest he robbed me, and I lost about 50,000 złoty that I had taken from the camp. He left me the securities, the value of which he did not

13 Meir Berliner (*c.*1898–1942), Argentinian citizen. The occupation authorities generally exempted citizens of neutral and hostile third-party states resident in Warsaw from the mass murders; they were held at Hotel Polski in 1943 and later deported to Bergen-Belsen concentration camp or to Vittel internment camp: see Doc. 277, fn. 33, and Doc. 278. In Oct. 1943 many of those taken to Bergen-Belsen were deported to Auschwitz via Bergau camp near Dresden. On Hotel Polski, see Docs. 248 and 277.

14 On 11 Sept. 1942 Berliner stabbed SS-Rottenführer Max Biala (1905–1942), who died shortly thereafter in the field hospital at Ostrów Mazowiecka.

understand (I also saved some precious stones I had hidden in a matchbox), and released me into the unknown.

I reached the small town of Stoczek,[15] where I lived for a month by selling the valuables. When rumours about an imminent resettlement grew loud in Stoczek, I left the town one evening and went into the forest.

In the morning I was awoken by gunshots, which indicated that the town was surrounded.[16] In the forest I met many refugees from the surrounding small towns. We lived in the forest, and whenever there was a raid we hid in camouflaged foxholes, which we dug, and we paid dearly for the food delivered to us. But we remained in one place only as long as the local residents, especially the wójtowie and the sołtysi, remained unaware of our presence. We led a nomadic life. However, once the situation became hopeless, I decided to return to Warsaw. I owe my happy return, this time without incident, to one of the farmers and his family. It was the only time I experienced a farmer helping a Jew.

After arriving in Warsaw, I stayed for a while in an apartment on Złota Street with that man's relatives, but since I did not want to overstay my welcome with complete strangers, I bid them farewell and […][17]

## DOC. 170

## Around October 1942 the Warsaw employment office issues house rules for its Jewish staff in what is left of the Warsaw ghetto[1]

House rules for employment office staff,[2] undated (around October 1942)

*I. General schedule*

| | |
|---|---|
| 1. 6 a.m. | Wake-up call |
| 2. 6.15–6.45 a.m | Morning exercise |
| 3. 6.45–8 a.m. | Wash, tidy up, breakfast |
| 4. 8 a.m. – 4 p.m. | Administrative work; lunch break 12.30–1.30 p.m. On Saturdays work ends at 1 p.m. Sunday is a day off. |
| 5. 10 p.m. | Lights out (curfew) |

*II. Rules for the rooms and adjoining corridors*

1. Beds must be made and rooms must be tidied by 8 a.m.
2. Lights may be switched on between dusk and 10 p.m.

15 The community of Stoczek, 70 km north-east of Warsaw.

16 On 22 Sept. 1942, the day of Yom Kippur, approximately 2,000 Jews were deported from Stoczek to Treblinka, which was roughly 15 km away. Approximately one hundred elderly and ill people were shot on the spot during this operation.

17 The report breaks off at this point. The author evidently returned to the Warsaw ghetto in early Oct. 1942, before he handed over his report to the underground archive.

1 AŻIH, Ring II/27 (265). Published in Sakowska (ed.), *Archiwum Ringelbluma: Konspiracyjne Archiwum Getta Warszawy*, vol. 1: *Listy o Zagładzie*, pp. 65–66. This document has been translated from Polish.

2 The employment office had a branch in the Warsaw ghetto: see Doc. 107.

3. The use of electricity for heating, ironing, and cooking is prohibited.
4. Windows must be blacked out in compliance with general air-raid defence and anti-aircraft regulations.
5. A notice with the surnames of the room's occupants must be posted on the entrance doors.
6. Each employee is obliged to clean the section of the corridor adjacent to his room on a daily basis and to keep it clean.

*III. Dispensing hot water, cooking, ironing, laundry, haircuts*

1. Hot water (e.g. for making coffee) will be dispensed in the kitchen from 7 to 7.30 a.m. and from 7.30 to 8 p.m. The use of heaters is prohibited; otherwise, the electricity will be switched off completely.
2. Warm water for washing will be dispensed from 6.45 to 7 a.m.
3. Undergarments will be washed on Mondays and Tuesdays, and ironing done on Thursdays and Fridays.

   Undergarments in need of washing will be collected by the administrative office on Sundays and returned on the following Saturday.
4. Undergarments handed over for washing must be marked with the employee's number.

4a. Hanging up undergarments or bed linen in public spaces is prohibited.

5. A barber will be available for employees once a week, on Saturdays from 1 to 5 p.m.

*IV. Healthcare*

1. Employees must undergo regular medical examinations.
2. In the event of illness, a doctor may be called or visited between 8 a.m. and 4 p.m.

*V. Common room*

1. The common room is open from 5 to 10 p.m.
2. Two duty officers are responsible for maintaining order in the common room.

*VI. Guard duty*

1. Guard duty lasts from 7 a.m. until the end of office hours.
2. Guards are prohibited from leaving their posts.
3. Employees may receive visitors only during the lunch break.
4. Leaving the building without a special pass is prohibited.

*VII. Inspection duty*

1. Inspection duty lasts from 6 to 10.30 a.m.
2. While on duty, the inspection officer is discharged from all other duties, with the exception of administrative tasks.
3. The inspection officer is responsible for checking that the guard detail is carrying out its duties correctly, ensuring that wake-up times, lights out, quiet hours, and mealtimes are adhered to, that the windows are blacked out, and that general order is maintained.
4. In cases of emergency the inspection officer may issue orders, which he must then report to the office manager as soon as possible.

## DOC. 171

## An unidentified author describes the ghettoization and murder of Jews in Biała Podlaska, Międzyrzec, Siedlce, and Łomazy in the period up to October 1942[1]

Handwritten report, signed Ewa, after October 1942[2]

In the first year of the war, there were about 3,000 Jews living in Biała Podlaska. In January of that winter, this number doubled, because Jews from Suwałki and Serock were brought here.[3] The latter arrived completely robbed of everything, without clothes or money. Since the town's Jewish population was being evicted at that time from dwellings on the main streets, a severe housing shortage soon emerged, which also made it considerably more difficult to give support to those people who had been resettled [from Suwałki and Serock]. Even at that point two families often had to share one room. Straight away, with the permission of the Landrat's office,[4] an 'aid committee' was formed to set up a soup kitchen that would provide food for the poorest, and especially for children. The Landwirtschaft[samt][5] provided some of the food at official prices; the kitchen administration purchased the remainder with the money from membership contributions. Things got increasingly worse as time went by. More and more people frequented the soup kitchen, and it became increasingly difficult to procure food, as the Landwirtschaft[samt] had stopped supporting the committee. Everything had to be obtained on the black market, which became impossible due to the ever-increasing prices. At this time a branch office of the ŻTSS[6] was established in the town – its headquarters were in Warsaw or Cracow. Thanks to their subsidies, it was possible to continue providing aid. That summer the Jewish hospital in town received better equipment, and an outpatient clinic was set up. The doctors, a surgeon and a specialist in internal medicine, were brought in from Warsaw. In view of various illnesses, medical assistance was essential.

The establishment of a Jewish quarter began in earnest that summer. Almost all Jews were squeezed into an area covering only a few streets. The lack of space was unbearable, and diseases of all kinds began to spread. Mortality in the quarter increased tremendously during this period. Bodies were removed every single day, sometimes a few, sometimes a dozen. Because the inhabitants were not allowed to leave the quarter, their material situation also deteriorated. The Aryans were also affected by these restrictions, because they no longer had access to the ghetto. Only the workers employed at Wehrmacht facilities outside the town could move freely. They were also the ones who han-

1 AŻIH, 230/121, fols. 23–26. The original is held in the Varia okupacyjne collection, and was presumably produced for the Polish underground organizations' intelligence service. This document has been translated from Polish.

2 The original contains handwritten deletions and insertions. The upper left edge of the original is damaged, meaning one or two words are missing on each page.

3 In late 1939 the German occupation administration expelled Jews to Biała Podlaska from Suwałki, which had been annexed to East Prussia, and from Serock in District Warsaw.

4 This is a reference to the Biała Podlaska Kreishauptmann's office. From Nov. 1939 to Dec. 1942 it was headed by Hubert Kühl (1903–1942), editor; joined the NSDAP in 1930 and the SA in 1931; official in the Reich Ministry of Public Enlightenment and Propaganda in the second half of the 1930s.

5 German in the original: 'agriculture office'.

6 This is a reference to the Jewish Social Self-Help (Polish: ŻSS; German: JSS).

lled all the illegal trade. Over time, people grew accustomed to the official directives and circumvented them in all sorts of ways. The winter of that year brought no changes, but already in spring 1942 punishments were made more severe. The penalty for leaving the quarter was death.[7] Workers were allowed to move freely only during working hours. Those who dared to break the law and got caught very often paid for it with their lives. Night-time robberies by German soldiers became increasingly frequent inside the quarter.

The ghetto was supposed to be walled in during this period, but this was prevented by the payment of a considerable ransom. In May the germans[8] demanded a quota of 2,000 people who had no employment. The [Jewish] Community[9] complied very efficiently, even transporting the victims to the railway station. It was predominantly elderly people, children, and women who were taken away. The Germans hauled out with their own hands healthy young men who had wanted to accompany their families on the transports. The deported people were taken via Lublin to Sobibór. There, all trace of them was lost.[10]

Soon afterwards, the starosta's office[11] issued a new order to provide a further 2,000 people, but for reasons unknown it was withdrawn until further notice.[12] In early June, Shaulis men arrived in Biała [Podlaska] and began a manhunt for the male population. Some 400 young men were captured and, together with the recently formed Jewish police, taken away to Lublin to repair railway tracks. A few days later, by order of the head of the starosta's office, the leaders of the Jewish Community, the ŻTSS committee, and the doctors were deported to Majdanek near Lublin.[13] Those who disregarded the order to turn up were the only ones to survive. At the request of the authorities, these people formed the new leadership for the Community. Those who had been taken away to perform the railway work returned one month later.

Shortly thereafter, the Jews from surrounding small towns, such as Janów Podlaski and Wisznice, were moved to Biała. Resettlement became a widely discussed issue. Resettlement to Międzyrzec occurred that same month.[14] Remaining in Biała were about 1,000 men employed at Wehrmacht facilities, where they were barracked. All the Jews were taken away, even from small villages and farms surrounding Międzyrzec, where a few were still working. Two days later Shaulis men and the local military units rounded up everyone without exception in the centre of Międzyrzec. A mass execution took

7 See Doc. 13.
8 In the original this term is written in lower case here and below as an expression of contempt.
9 This is a reference to the Jewish Council, here and below.
10 According to other sources, the Jewish Council had to hand over 3,000 people who did not hold certificates of employment, which it did with the assistance of the Order Service; these people were deported to Sobibor on 11 June 1942.
11 This is a reference to the Kreishauptmann's office.
12 The killing at Sobibor was temporarily suspended in summer 1942, when track work was carried out on the railway lines to Sobibor, and new gas chambers were constructed.
13 According to other sources, German police officers carried out these deportations in mid August 1942 with the assistance of Ukrainian units – presumably auxiliary personnel from the SS training camp in Trawniki.
14 Between 26 Sept. and 1 Oct. 1942 approximately 4,800 Jews were deported from Biała Podlaska to the Międzyrzec ghetto, which had only been established in late August or early Sept. 1942.

place. More than 1,000 people died. The rest were deported in sealed wagons in the direction of Treblinka.

The same fate befell the workers remaining in […][15] – the only difference was that they were murdered on the spot.[16] A very few people, supposedly about 200, hid in the surrounding woods. No one remained in the town itself.

P.S. The residents of Międzyrzec had already experienced two resettlements. During the first one, elderly people and children were taken away, and there was also a massacre at the square where they were gathered.[17] The second time, anyone not employed was taken away.[18] The third time, the Jews from Biała, Wisznice, and Janów were taken away.[19]

In 1942 the Germans shut the Jews together with the Gypsies in a ghetto in Siedlce. The Gypsies threw their weight around in an impossible manner. The German authorities set them against the remaining residents and gave them special treatment, so the Gypsies felt they were the masters. Violent attacks and robberies were a daily occurrence. Resettlement took place two months before the one from Biała.[20] Some of the Gypsies were also deported with the Jews. The few remaining Jewish workers were later finished off on the spot.

In Łomazy, in June, all the inhabitants were rounded up in the town square, where the German police mowed down everyone – without exception – with machine guns.[21] Only two young boys escaped and ran away to Biała during the night.

## DOC. 172
## On 6 November 1942 the SS and Police Leader in Lemberg orders that Jewish forced labourers be moved into closed-off camps[1]

Draft circular (marked 'secret') from the SS and Police Leader in District Galicia (XIIIa, log no. 735 42 (g) – Ch/Fr.), signed Katzmann, Lemberg, to the distribution list, dated 6 November 1942[2]

*Re*: deployment of Jewish labour
*Subject*: agreements between *Krüger*, state secretary for security, SS-Obergruppenführer and police general; General *Hänecke*,[3] military district commander in the General Government; and the General Government armaments inspectorate

15 Based on context this should read 'Biała Podlaska'.
16 According to other sources, the Germans transported 1,200 Jewish forced labourers from the area around Biała Podlaska to the Międzyrzec ghetto on 6 Oct. 1942; they were later deported to Treblinka as well.
17 This took place on 25 and 26 August 1942.
18 Approximately 7,000 Jews were deported to Treblinka between 6 and 9 Oct. 1942.
19 The Germans deported a further number of Jews, approximately 9,000, to Treblinka between 27 and 29 Oct. 1942.
20 See Doc. 122.
21 Following the flight and expulsion of Jews from the surrounding municipalities to Łomazy, the Jewish population there increased to 1,700 in May 1942. Reserve Police Battalion 101 murdered these Jews in a nearby forest on 17 August 1942; only one survivor from this locality is known.

1 IfZ-Archives, Fa 506/15, fols. 192–198. This document has been translated from German.
2 The original contains handwritten notes and underlining.

On the basis of the instructions issued by the Reichsführer-SS and Chief of German Police on the *provisional retention* of Jewish workers[4] for the GG armaments inspectorate, military agencies, and firms working for the military district commander in the General Government (Wehrkreisbefehlshaber im Generalgouvernement, or WiG), referred to below as WiG firms, special directives and guidelines have been issued.

The armaments firms led and managed by the armaments inspectorate for the General Government are to be differentiated from the firms that work for the Wehrmacht and receive their commissions from the military district commander or from an agency under the Army High Command. The latter are to be regarded as 'WiG armaments firms'.[5] A special badge will be distributed to identify the Jews who work for the GG armaments inspectorate, for the WiG Wehrmacht agencies, and for WiG firms. The Jews working for the GG armaments inspectorate will receive a badge bearing a machine-embroidered black 'R'[6] on a white background with the SS and Police Leader's red seal of office, *to be sewn onto the outermost garment on the left side of the chest at pocket level.* The Jews employed by the Wehrmacht agencies and WiG firms will receive the same badge, but with a 'W', and which is to be affixed in the same manner. These badges will be distributed centrally by the SS and Police Leader to the Lemberg armaments inspectorate and Oberfeldkommandantur 365, and from there to the individual recipients. The recipients are responsible for ensuring that their Jewish workers *wear these badges as soon as they are received.* The recipients are to charge the Jews 20 groszy for each badge and transfer the sum collected to the SS and Police Leader's factory cash account at the Emissionsbank in Lemberg. By order of the Reichsführer-SS and Chief of German Police, all Jews employed by the [Lemberg] armaments inspectorate or by the WiG are to be housed in *strictly closed-off* quarters (barracks). In their camps and lodging, Jewish workers are to be placed under the control and supervision of the SS and Police Leader or the police authorities appointed by him.

In particular, the following agreements have been reached:

1. *Lodging*

Camps for Jews established by WiG Wehrmacht agencies and armaments firms are to be relinquished to the SS and Police Leader, subject to the agreements reached by the Oberfeldkommandantur or the [Lemberg] armaments inspectorate with the SS and Police Leader. These camps or barracks are to be merged locally where possible, so that the Jewish labour from the camps thus created may be made available to individual agencies or firms. However, care must be taken to ensure that the individual agencies or firms retain *their own* core workforce, especially skilled workers. That means

3 Correctly: Haenicke.

4 See Doc. 159. On 11 October 1942 the military district commander forwarded Himmler's letter of 9 October 1942 to the agencies under his authority: BArch, RH 53-23/70.

5 During a meeting between the military district commander and Higher SS and Police Leader Krüger on 13 October 1942 in Spala, it was agreed that Wehrmacht agencies would hand their Jewish labourers over to the SS; that factories under the supervision of the Wehrmacht's armaments inspectorate were to be dealt with separately; and that Jews were to be isolated in the remaining armaments factories working on behalf of the military district commander and the Army High Command, prior to the creation of 'closed-off Jewish factories': BArch, RH 53-23/70.

6 'R' is short for Rüstung (German for armaments).

that no unauthorized change in the workforce is permitted. Where possible, care must be taken to ensure that the camps are located no farther than 3 km away from the deployment sites. As the Wehrmacht and the police have not yet set up their own camps everywhere, immediate steps must be taken to house the Jewish workforce in closed-off barracks. If closed-off lodging cannot be provided at the firms or agencies concerned, then the Jewish workers are to be housed in specific *closed-off* apartment blocks in the existing or former Jewish residential districts. Factory managers and Wehrmacht agencies are to communicate with the Security Police field offices regarding this accommodation (I refer the commanders of the Security Police and the Order Police to my order of 23 October 1942, log no. XIII 688/42-g, and I request appropriate action in this case as well).[7] Care must be taken to ensure that no relatives of Jewish workers use this lodging as a bolthole under any circumstances. *Only those Jews who are identified as 'W' or 'R' Jews may be accommodated.* Before being transferred to the camps or to closed-off accommodation, the Jewish workers are generally to be permitted to take with them plenty of clothing, particularly winter clothes, blankets, quilts, etc. At least one Jewish physician with appropriate support staff is to be placed in each closed-off lodging facility.

The equipment necessary to furnish the camps and lodgings, as well as the instruments and medicines required by the physicians, may be taken from the stocks gathered during resettlement. In order to obtain such supplies, there is no requirement to submit a special application to the SS and Police Leader according to the customary procedures. Instead, the Security Police field offices should merely provide a receipt for their requisitions to the relevant warehouse manager and subsequently submit a list of items taken to the SS and Police Leader. Up to 5 per cent more staff may be recruited to clean the lodgings etc. Food will be provided for this extra 5 per cent as it is for the remaining Jews who work for the firms and agencies. (See item 3 in the penultimate paragraph on payment.)

II. *Food*

The Wehrmacht agencies and firms concerned bear overall responsibility for providing the Jewish workers with food. Food may be provided only at the factory or the agency concerned. *Even in the event of illness, full food rations are to be provided.* Firms will request and receive food in accordance with the rates set by the Market Regulation Department in the Food and Agriculture Main Department in the GG government [log no.] IIIa 1a/100 of 18 August 1942. For Wehrmacht agencies, the provision of food for workers in barracks is based on the generally applicable provisions made by the Oberfeldkommandantur or on special orders of the military district commander. For essential hygiene, one piece of standard soap per month is to be issued to each worker. In addition, one piece of shaving soap is to be issued to male workers once every four months. Additional detergents are to be provided when the work is particularly dirty. Likewise the necessary detergents for laundering underclothes and household items are to be supplied.

7 On 23 October 1942 the SS and Police Leader issued directives and instructions on employing Jewish forced labourers in armaments factories: see Doc. 251.

III. *Payment*
Once the Jewish workers are accommodated in barracks or other closed-off facilities, they will no longer receive cash wages. This rule will come into force for the [Lemberg] armaments inspectorate on 1 November 1942, and for WiG agencies and firms on 15 November 1942. For each Jewish worker, the agencies or firms will pay the SS and Police Leader in Galicia 5 zl. per calendar day or per shift for each male worker and 4 zloty for each female worker. *Wage tax and social security contributions are to be discontinued.* The costs of food and management (administrative expenses) are to be deducted from the aforementioned amounts of 5 and 4 zl. The amount to be deducted from the daily rate may not exceed 1.60 zl. *The amounts payable are to be transferred to the SS and Police Leader in Galicia's factory cash account at the Emissionsbank in Lemberg.* Transfers for the preceding month must always be received by the third of the current month. Transcripts of daily wage lists (in summary form; the workers are not to be named) with the same effective date are to be sent to the administrative office of the SS and Police Leader in Galicia, 75 Siegfriedstraße, Lemberg, as a record of the amounts transferred. The firms and agencies are to provide food for the 5 per cent additional staff employed to clean the camps and do the laundry, by virtue of the fact that taxes and social security contributions will no longer be deducted. *There will be no additional payment or settlement for this purpose.* The SS and Police Leader's administrative office is authorized to carry out inspections in the factories to review the wage lists.

If a Jew (Jewess) is temporarily unable to work due to illness, food will continue to be provided for no longer than a full calendar month, provided this worker cannot be permanently dispensed with. *Cash payments and compensation will be suspended for the duration of the illness.*

Insofar as Jewish agricultural workers are deployed on Wehrmacht estates or properties, for reasons of equity, there will be no obligation to remit wage payments, as is the case for other workers. However, the employers are liable for the full costs of housing, food, clothing, and supervision.

IV. *Clothing*
If replacement clothing is necessary in order for workers to remain or once more become fit for labour deployment, a request can be submitted to the SS and Police Leader.

V. *General*
The SS and Police Leader in Galicia, Oberfeldkommandantur 365, and the [Lemberg] armaments inspectorate agree on the need to ensure that Jewish workers remain fit for work. This requires appropriate lodging, clothing, nutrition, and medical care. Employers are responsible for implementing the required epidemiological measures (delousing etc.).

The agencies and firms are asked to resolve any problems with local Security Police offices or the camp management already installed by the SS and Police Leader. If problems cannot be remedied locally, the relevant requests are to be referred to the SS and Police Leader as quickly as possible, and also communicated to the Oberfeldkommandantur or the [Lemberg] armaments inspectorate. *Despite these agreements, the overriding principle is and remains the swiftest possible withdrawal of even this Jewish labour force from the work process without any disruption to supplies for the front or to the operation of war production. For this reason, the agencies and firms must continue their efforts to find Aryan replacement staff.* As far as possible, the SS and Police Leader will provide any necessary assistance. The offices of the Security Police and the inspector of the forced labour camps[8] must constantly monitor the required elimination measures. Sporadically employed Jews should be replaced as swiftly as possible.

Appropriate notice of any planned dismissals should be given to the Security Police field offices or to the camp leaders appointed by the SS and Police Leader at least one week in advance. *As a rule, any workers who are dismissed should be handed over to Security Police field offices.* The field offices will receive special instructions on how to deal with dismissed Jews.

The list of all the firms managed by the Lemberg armaments inspectorate as well as of Wehrmacht agencies and WiG firms is appended for the offices of the SS and Police Leader. The Security Police field offices will report continually on camps being taken over and on housing in closed-off apartment blocks. A list of established Wehrmacht camps and those in preparation will be submitted separately.

*In future resettlement operations, extreme care must be taken to ensure that Jews who work for the firms and agencies listed here are not evacuated.*[9]

## DOC. 173

## In a report written after 6 November 1942 Henryk Woliński calls for the Home Army to support the Jewish National Committee in its preparations for armed resistance[1]

Report from Cell 163A-9[2] in the intelligence/counter-intelligence department of the Home Army High Command Bureau of Information and Propaganda, signed Wacław,[3] Warsaw, written after 6 Nov. 1942

The Jewish National Committee[4] (the name is still subject to change) has been formed in the Warsaw ghetto as a representation of the Jews still remaining on Polish territory. The Committee primarily represents the largest group that was able to escape extermination – young people, who are recruited from Jewish nationalist scouts and other youth organizations ('Hashomer' and 'Hehalutz'), as well as from a small group of scouts that

8 Friedrich (Fritz) Hildebrand was the inspector of the forced labour camps from July 1942.

9 This letter was sent to Oberfeldkommandantur 365, the Lemberg armaments inspectorate, the Commander of the Security Police and the SD (KdS), and the Commander of the Order Police (KdO), in some cases in multiple copies to be forwarded to offices and firms under their authority, with copies for the gendarmerie Kreis commanders; to SS-Obersturmführer Bolten, the official responsible for the administration of forced labour camps on behalf of the SS and Police Leader; to Inspector Hildebrand; to SS-Untersturmführer Löhnert, the official who dealt with Jewish and forced labour camp affairs; to SS-Obersturmführer Lohr, the representative of the Reich Commissioner for the Strengthening of Germandom; and to Krüger, the Higher SS and Police Leader East in Cracow: IfZ-Archives, Fa 506/15, fol. 191.

1 AAN, 1325/202/XV-2, fol. 78. This document has been translated from Polish.

2 This stands for the Jewish Section.

3 Handwritten at the end of the document: Henryk Woliński's code name.

4 Polish: Żydowski Komitet Narodowy (ŻKN).

support assimilation. The Committee is composed of representatives of Poale Zion (Left and Right factions), revisionists, and various unaffiliated groups.[5] The Polish Bund has still not reached a final decision on whether to participate in the Committee.[6] A representative of this Committee, with whom I have initiated contact at his invitation, explained to me that at the beginning of August, when the liquidation of the Warsaw ghetto was in its initial phase, the Jews contacted official Polish decision-makers (probably from the [Home Army's] Warsaw area?[7]) and asked for weapons so they could engage in armed resistance against the crimes being perpetrated against them. At that time the Polish decision-makers refused this request.

The ŻKN views the Jews' current situation pessimistically. That is undoubtedly a valid assessment which (without going into the acts known today of the bestial extermination of the Jews on Polish territory) is grounded in the events of the last three weeks alone: the total liquidation of the ghetto in Piotrków, in Ostrowiec Kielecki (1,500 people out of 15,000 survived), in Końskie – the last ghetto in District Radom (between 3 and 6 November) – as well as in Hrubieszów, Białystok, Cracow (8,000 people deported to Bełżec), and Tarnów. There is no doubt that the 'resettlement' operation's objective is the complete elimination of the Jews. In view of this situation, the ŻKN wishes to wage, as part of the Polish struggle for freedom, a worthy campaign of active resistance against the German extermination operation in the most expedient and useful way. The Committee's representative[8] assured me of the following: (1) the complete subordination to Polish civil and military authorities in the country; (2) the launch of a struggle against the occupiers within Jewish [residential] districts on Polish territory; (3) the launch of this struggle in partisan units outside the ghettos. To be able to put these plans into action, the ŻKN representative requested instructions and weapons; he pledged that he would be able to call upon thousands of healthy, young, and most importantly resolute people from all over Poland to spring into action at any time. Notwithstanding this oral declaration, I demanded written requests. Yet, given the scale of the ongoing extermination, the matter is of the utmost urgency and, for this reason, I am requesting an immediate resolution and, for my part, I present the following assessments.

1. A positive response from the Polish authorities to the ŻKN declaration will make it possible to prove, in a clear and unambiguous manner, Poland's stance towards the German extermination of the Jews, that is to say, citizens of the *Polish state*. The approval of the declaration, providing the Jews with aid, and taking command over the operation planned by the ŻKN – all this is of far-reaching political significance that will surely become even more evident in the war's final phase (German propaganda is among other things blaming the Poles for the murder of the Jews).
2. According to the ŻKN declaration, the Jewish forces are placing themselves at the disposal of the Polish command; as a result, it may be possible to deploy them in the name of the Polish *raison d'état* and detach them from the influence of the Polish

5 At this time the ŻKN was the political body that represented the groups who had formed the Jewish Combat Organization (ŻOB) in late July 1942.
6 The Bund, which had a long tradition of resistance, initially did not wish to place itself under the leadership of Hashomer Hatzair. See also Doc. 186.
7 Question mark as in the original.
8 Probably Arie Wilner: see Doc. 186.

Workers' Party. Because the core of the forces belonging to the ŻKN consists of nationalistically disposed elements, the separation of Jewish society from the influence of the Polish Workers' Party should be considered a realistic aim, given their inherently negative attitude towards the Polish Workers' Party (the Bolshevik persecution measures in the Vilna area targeted Jewish nationalists).[9]

3. A positive response to the ŻKN declaration does not and will not impose any particular obligations on the Polish authorities, only such obligations that the Polish government has already accepted. The ŻKN presents no conditions for the deployment of its forces in the fight against the occupier.

## DOC. 174
## *Dziennik Polski*, 7 November 1942: article on the partial liquidation of the Cracow ghetto[1]

*Local news*

During the night of 19 to 20 October, the Cracow ghetto was partially liquidated. The Schutzpolizei[2] and the Sonderdienst, assisted by the Blue Police and the Jewish police, herded all the Jews to Zgoda Square, regardless of their sex or age. There they were ordered to sit upright on the ground – until the morning – and if they in any way tried to support themselves with their hands, the torturers responded immediately with blows and kicks.

Around thirty police trucks arrived in the morning. People were crammed into the trucks and driven to Płaszów, where specially prepared goods trains were already standing by. They were loaded into the wagons without a prior selection – [they seized] whoever was nearest. That led to sharp disputes between the Wehrmacht authorities and the SS, which was carrying out the liquidation of the ghetto, because many skilled Jewish workers who were employed at German armaments companies were also loaded onto the trains. Consequently, four armaments companies in Cracow ceased operations. Among others, the large Hanomag firm lost 300 Jewish employees, and the Park Garage approximately thirty. Intervention from the military authorities came too late; the trains had already left.

The deportees were packed into the trains so tightly that they literally stood squeezed in next to each other. The wagons were covered with a thick layer of unslaked quicklime inside, and from the outside they were disinfected with carbolic acid. Thus filled, the wagons were carefully sealed, and then these ghost trains departed for an unknown des-

9 A reference to the harsh treatment of the Jewish population by the Soviet secret police in Lithuania, which was under Soviet occupation from June 1940 to June 1941: see PMJ 4/275.

1 *Dziennik Polski*, 7 Nov. 1942, p. 4. Biblioteka Narodowa, Mf 55 886. *Dziennik Polski: Organ Demokratyczny* was an underground newspaper published under the auspices of the Alliance of Democrats (SD) in Cracow from Jan. 1940 to Oct. 1943, then under the left-wing splinter group Polish Democracy Party (SPD) until 1945. It was edited by Ferdynand Arczyński. This document has been translated from Polish.

2 German in the original: 'Urban Police'.

tination. The trains are left standing on sidings in desolate areas, and once everyone on the transport has died, the bodies are unloaded and buried.[3] Approximately 6,000 Jews were transported away on the last train.

In the meantime, the perpetrators who remained in the ghetto were busy liquidating those 'unfit for transport'. The sick in the Jewish hospital and in the home for the elderly were all shot in their beds; small children and babies were thrown into laundry baskets and loaded onto trucks by literally being poured out of the baskets like goods. The trucks left for an unknown destination.

In the afternoon older children up to the age of sixteen were led to the nearby Krzemionki forest, where they were to be shot. The number of people murdered is unknown.

Approximately 10,000 Jews remain in the Cracow ghetto – awaiting their turn. According to the information we've received, the Cracow ghetto is to be liquidated in four weeks' time. The Jewish population's despondency reached new depths; it was so profound that there was no reaction, not even signs of desperation, in the course of this entire operation.

## DOC. 175
## On 10 November 1942 the Kreishauptmann in Sokolow (Sokołów) bans the employment of Jews[1]

Announcement no. 226 by the Kreishauptmann in Sokolow,[2] Gramß,[3] Sokolow, dated 10 November 1942

*Announcement*

With reference to my announcement no. 225 concerning the establishment of a Jewish residential district in Kossow,[4] I draw attention to the following:

From 1 December 1942 no office, no agricultural or other operation, no labour camp, and no private individual may still employ a Jew.

All permissions issued by me or by branches of the employment office expire at that moment.

Employment of Jews after 30 November 1942 will be possible only with my express permission, given only in highly exceptional cases.

3 Change in tense as in the original. The people who were deported were all taken to Belzec.

1 It is not known where the original announcement appeared. Published as a facsimile in Gerszon Taffet (ed.), *Extermination of Polish Jews: Album of Pictures* (Łódź: Wydawnictwa Centralnej Żydowskiej Komisji Historycznej przy C. K. Żydów Polskich, 1945), p. 10. This document has been translated from German.

2 A Kreis seat in the eastern part of District Warsaw.

3 Ernst Gramß (1899–1946?), agronomist; took part in the Beer Hall Putsch in 1923, and joined the NSDAP the same year; rejoined after the ban on the NSDAP was lifted in 1928; joined the SA in 1928 and the SS in 1934; held various posts in the Reich Food Estate (Reichsnährstand), the Nazi organization that oversaw the production, distribution, and pricing of food, 1933–1938; head of the Food and Agriculture Department in District Warsaw, 1939–1940; Kreishauptmann in Sokolow, June 1940–1944; subsequently served in the war; officially declared dead in 1956.

4 Correctly: Kosów Lacki, a town located some 89 kilometres north-east of Warsaw.

*Anyone who continues to employ Jews after 1 December 1942* will be dealt with according to paragraph 3, section 2, of the police regulation of 28 October 1942,[5] and *can* therefore in particularly severe cases even *be punished with death*.

*All offices and operations* are *accountable* to me for ensuring that the Jews they employed *have been resettled* to the Jewish residential district in Kossow by 30 November 1942.

Applications for permission to continue to employ Jews are to be submitted to my office, room 23.

*The Kreishauptmann in Sokolow*
*Gramß*
Sokolow, 10 November 1942[6]

## DOC. 176
## The Finkelshteyn siblings describe the destruction of the Jewish community of Łuków in October 1942 and their escape[1]

Report by the Finkelshteyn siblings for the underground archive of the Warsaw ghetto, end of November 1942 or later

*The destruction[2] of Łuków[3]*

The informants …[4] Finkelshteyn, 18 years old, and his sister … Finkelshteyn, … years old, report the following:

On 5 October 1942 (when the destruction began), there were around 10,000 Jews in the city of Łuków. Of these up to 2,000 had been deported from Slovakia. At first there was no ghetto. Jews and Poles lived together. The first tremor occurred about six weeks before the actual disaster struck. Although entreaties made at that time succeeded in getting the evil order repealed, afterwards the peace and equilibrium were completely shattered.[5]

5 See Doc 168.

6 With the exception of a few tradesmen, the entire Jewish population of Kosów Lacki was murdered in late Sept. 1942 in nearby Treblinka. Between 50 and 100 Jews who had been able to save themselves from being deported subsequently returned to the town; several of them were murdered by the SS. The survivors were taken to Treblinka (I) labour camp by the German police in Feb. 1943.

1 AŻIH, Ring II/352 (306), fols. 1–5. Published in English translation in Kermish (ed.), *To Live with Honor*, pp. 210–213. This document has been newly translated from Yiddish.

2 Rendered as *khurbm* in the Yiddish original, which actually refers to the destruction of the First and Second Temples in Jerusalem. As early as 1939 the term – usually written as *khurbn* – was often used to indicate the destructive anti-Jewish policies in Poland. In post-war Yiddish publications, it became the leading term to refer to the systematic mass murder of the Jews under German occupation during the Second World War, which destroyed entire Jewish communities.

3 In 1942 Łuków was located in Kreis Radzin, in the north-western part of District Lublin.

4 Ellipses in the original, here and below.

5 This is possibly a reference to the railway wagons sent to Łuków in late August 1942 for the purpose of deporting Jews to Treblinka. The camp was unable to 'handle' another transport at that time, so the wagons left empty.

Faced with the prospect of being annihilated, there was no work or way to earn a living, all the more so as news about Treblinka began trickling in. At first Treblinka was not taken to mean extermination, only deportation. People thought the place was located on the other side of the Bug river.[6] Slowly the real, murderous nature of Treblinka became clear to everyone, especially from accounts given by eyewitnesses who had miraculously escaped from there.

The Gestapo. Jews often conflate the terms Gestapo, SS, and SD. The Gestapo are all those who wear the death's head insignia on their uniforms.[7]

The post in Radzin[8] promised [us] protection and supervision, ordered the creation of a residential ghetto (incidentally very loosely guarded), and instructed the Jewish Council to phone at once in case of an unwanted visit by armed Germans or Ukrainians so it could protect the Jews from any evil or harm.

Apart from this, the Jewish Council instituted a compulsory labour requirement for Jews. Whereas about 75 per cent of the Jewish men had been employed either by the railway or as illegal workers for the Reckmann construction company[9] and the Dietz poultry company before the first tremor, which ended well, later on certainly 80 per cent of the entire Jewish population went to work, both men and women, from 12-year-old boys and girls to the elderly. For the price of working for starvation wages, the Jews thought they had bought the right to bare physical existence. The officials indicated clearly and unambiguously that they were happy with the situation and that nothing bad would happen to the Jews. Every day in the early morning hours, literally everyone would leave the ghetto, only to return to the crowded confines of their [residential] area after work. A life of slavery for a helpless, defenceless mass.

People kept watch in the Jewish Council building day and night. They scouted for the enemy as though from an observation tower.

During the evening hours of Saturday, 3 October 1942, a rumour spread through town that around 60 goods wagons were waiting on the railway tracks. The news was soon confirmed and created an immense panic. People consoled themselves by saying that no operation would take place on a Sunday, and that by Monday it might perhaps be possible to avert the terrible danger facing the community. The situation struck mortal fear into everyone's hearts. People prepared hiding places in haste, as everyone realized that the only way to escape the merciless murderer was to burrow deep underground – and to remain hidden there until the deadly storm had passed.

Fleeing to the surrounding villages was practically out of the question. For one thing, draconian regulations threatened any Pole who hid Jews with the death penalty. For another, the Poles' attitude towards the Jews' misfortune was marked, if not by hatred, then at the very least by ill will. Still fresh in the memory of the Jewish population was

6 Treblinka was actually located on the near side of the Bug river, in the eastern part of District Warsaw.

7 These were presumably members of the SS-Totenkopfverbände (Death's Head Units) that carried out deportations in the General Government; in the occupied territories Gestapo members usually wore grey uniforms without the death's head insignia.

8 Possibly a Polish police station.

9 Presumably the company belonging to Richard Reckmann (b. 1905), engineer and contractor; joined the NSDAP in 1937; lived in Eichenrode in the Soviet occupation zone after the war, and then in Oberhausen in West Germany.

a certain incident that had occurred a few weeks earlier. One day Poles entered the Jewish residential district intent on pillage. Had the Germans not intervened, a pogrom would have ensued. In connection with this incident, a few dozen Poles were sent to a penal camp in Majdanek, near Lublin. The Germans did not want to concede the right to rob Jews of their property to anyone else. A sense of hopelessness gripped the Jews of Łuków with all its might and held their nerves in thrall.

Only on Monday, 5 October, did it become evident that all the Jews were trapped. The ghetto was hemmed in by groups of gendarmes, Schupos,[10] Ukrainians, SD, and Polish police. Incidentally it should be noted that the extermination squad was already in town as of Sunday afternoon. In general the Jewish ghetto police did not take part in the operation.

The Germans surrounding [the ghetto] were all armed to the teeth.[11] Some of them were equipped with hand grenades.

As previously mentioned, many people had hidden themselves in any cranny they could find. The younger men and women who had jobs outside the ghetto set off for work, albeit glumly. The guards did not let them pass, however, and instead assembled them at a square not far from the railway. At 10 a.m. the selection began. Women, children, and elderly people all went to their deaths, as did the Slovakian deportees. Only 10 per cent of the male work brigades were left behind. By 4 p.m. the disaster had already ended. The number of victims on the first day stood at 5,000 (five thousand) souls. All of them were deported to Treblinka, a fact that was verified by a number of young men and women who jumped off the wagons. On Thursday, 8 October, the Germans announced to the remaining population via the Jewish Council that everyone, whether still in hiding or not, had to report to the Jewish Council, where they would be assigned one of the existing jobs. Some 2,000 men and women showed up. In the afternoon Germans and Ukrainians[12] surrounded the assembly point, and all the Jews were taken away and loaded into wagons, also going to Treblinka. That day ...-year-old ... Finkelshteyn was seized as well, who [then] managed to jump out of the moving train in the middle of the night. Without being at all accustomed to the darkness or having any knowledge of the terrain, she went where her eyes led her. In the pitch-black darkness she walked through meadows, fields, and groves, trudging aimlessly through the mud, carried onwards by her nerves, frayed to the point of being raw. When she finally reached a village, she pretended to be a Christian girl who had fled from the Germans who were rounding up people for forced labour in Prussia. Thanks to her Aryan looks she managed not to arouse any suspicions. The next morning a farmer took her back to Łuków on his wagon, without the slightest inkling that he had saved a Jewish girl.

After the second roundup and deportation, six more followed – always the same. Using deceit and ruthlessness, cruelty and murder, they sent Jews to their deaths. Only quantity mattered, not quality.[13] The murderers didn't care at all who their victims were, although as a rule the killing began with women, children, and the elderly.

10 German abbreviation in the original for Schutzpolizei: uniformed 'Urban Police'.

11 These were mainly members of Reserve Police Battalion 101.

12 This is a reference to non-German auxiliary personnel from the SS training camp in Trawniki.

13 That is to say, it did not matter to the perpetrators whether the victim could still potentially be of use to them, for example as a forced labourer.

On Saturday, 8 November 1942,[14] I was arrested, along with hundreds of other Jewish workers, at the water main.[15] It happened at 4 a.m., so no one could think of escape. [We were] loaded into wagons [heading in the] direction of Treblinka. The young people in our wagon broke open the door and jumped out one at a time. Although people talk a lot about jumping from wagons, they know very little about the mortal danger and the thousands of difficulties involved. For the hundreds of lucky ones who managed to jump unharmed, there were hundreds of others who suffered injuries, were killed, ended up with cracked skulls or broken hands and feet, and for whom there was no hospital, no medical care, but only death to redeem them all. No fewer dangers awaited the lucky jumpers.

Finkelshteyn jumped out (while the train was in motion, of course) by the village of *Krynka*.[16] He lost consciousness for a moment but quickly came to, and with the impulse of a hunted animal started running along the railway track. A gang of around forty local peasants between the ages of 20 and 40 years old, wielding clubs and iron bars, caught each one of those who had escaped, beat them to death, and stole their clothes and money. Around 250 Jews – bloodied and beaten – were taken [alive]. The Christians removed the informant's boots and jacket, and they also combed the neighbouring woods, intent on stealing. Later they phoned the railway police in Łuków, who came immediately.

All the captured Jews were escorted to Łuków by the Christians and the railway police. Those who had been most severely beaten were shot on the spot. In Łuków everyone was put in jail at the police station. Until Tuesday, 11 November,[17] groups of people were continuously led out and shot dead in the police station yard. Those captured in Łuków informed … Finkelshteyn that hundreds of Jews had been caught there and shot dead in the local cemetery. They were all indifferent to death – the effort of jumping had completely drained them all.

On Tuesday, 11 November 1942, the remainder of the people who had been caught, 200 in total, were taken to the Jewish cemetery. There hundreds of Jewish men, women, and children who had not yet been buried lay in a heap. The cemetery was surrounded by gendarmes, and all the prisoners were divided into groups of twenty persons each. On the sergeant's order the first twenty Jews lay down on the ground after first stripping down to their shirts. A Schupo (policeman) stood next to each victim. The victims lay with their faces to the ground, covering their eyes with their hands. Each Schupo stood between the legs of the prostrate victim, pointed his rifle at the victim's head, and then, after the sergeant gave the signal – 'aufpassen', 'fertig'[18] – pulled the trigger. Bang.

The informant was in the second group. He got undressed, lay down, and simply waited for death. Indifferent to everything, he only wanted it to be over as quickly as possible. He doesn't know how, but the shot only grazed his head. He continued lying there. After that came eight more groups. At the end of the entire execution, the Schupos

14 This date actually fell on a Sunday, not a Saturday.

15 Finkelshteyn's report switches to the first person here. The arrests probably took place during the morning wash.

16 Krynka is located approximately 5 km north of Łuków, on the train line to Siedlce.

17 This date actually fell on a Wednesday, not a Tuesday.

18 German in the original: 'ready', 'fire'.

checked whether all the victims were dead. The informant was shot again, in the arm and the neck.

As soon as the executioners had left, many Poles descended [on the cemetery] to steal clothes and shoes. Finkelshteyn got up, put on someone else's trousers and shoes, and dragged himself to a Christian acquaintance. Two weeks later he arrived in Warsaw at his brother's place, at 36 Muranowska, where his two younger sisters also were.

## DOC. 177

## Sometime after 11 November 1942 Eugenia Szajn Lewin describes the situation in the Warsaw ghetto and the experiences of an escapee from Treblinka who has vowed to take revenge on the Germans[1]

Journal of Eugenia Szajn Lewin,[2] Warsaw ghetto, entry recorded sometime after 11 November 1942[3] (excerpt)

Eda[4] fought to save the lives of her mother and her sister. She did not succeed. Both have been taken to the train. Eda is lying on the bed in her coat. She covers her ears with her hands: 'Don't talk to me. Don't speak. Leave me alone.' The last hope that work would save them is gone. Now they will no longer believe in any German promises.[5] Nearly all the Jewish managers at the K. G. Schultz[6] company have fled. Only Konar[7] and Line[8] remain.

1 YVA, O-33/2445, fols. 61–66. The excerpt here is based on a typescript by Maria Line; she gave the original to Eugenia Szajn Lewin's daughter, who later lost it. Published in Eugenia Szajn Lewin, *W getcie warszawskim: Lipiec 1942 – kwiecień 1943*, ed. Maria Line and Anna Grupińska (Poznań: a5, 1989), pp. 44–47. This document has been translated from Polish.

2 Eugenia Szajn Lewin, née Szajn (1909–1944), journalist; married to Artur Lewin, engineer; lived in Łódź; published the novel *Życie na nowo* under the pseudonym Giza Szen in 1938; moved to Warsaw with her family in Nov. 1939; lived in the Warsaw ghetto until early April 1943; thereafter hid with family members in Puławska Street; perished in the Warsaw Uprising in 1944; her twin sister, Maria Line, recovered her journals in Jan. 1945.

3 The journal begins with the first day of the deportations to Treblinka on 22 July 1942 and breaks off after the deportations resumed in Jan. 1943. The author primarily describes the period when she worked at the K. G. Schultz factory at 29 Ogrodowa Street, outside the ghetto.

4 Eda Salomon was married to a lawyer from Warsaw; her mother was arrested while visiting her; her sister Łaja Perla Szulman's name was on a list of 20 people who were to be taken from the Schultz factory to workshops in camps near Lublin: Szajn-Lewin, *W getcie warszawskim*, pp. 73–75. See also fn. 10.

5 This is a reference to the K. G. Schultz factory's Jewish employees, with whom Eugenia Szajn Lewin worked and whose experiences she describes here.

6 Karl Georg Schultz, salesman; ethnic German from Aleksandrów, near Łódź; worked as a pedlar and lived in poverty until 1939; thought to have taken over the Braun & Rowiński textile factory in Warsaw in 1940.

7 Aleksander (Olek) Konar (Konarski), Eugenia Szajn Lewin's cousin; originally from Łódź; department manager at the K. G. Schultz factory in 1942; murdered by the SS in the Warsaw ghetto in 1943.

8 Michał Line (d. 1975), engineer; officer in the Polish-Soviet War in 1920; department manager at the K. G. Schultz factory in 1942; went into hiding with his daughter on the 'Aryan side' in April 1943; lived in Israel after the war.

In the morning, when they leave Leszno Street, where they are quartered, and proceed as a group to Ogrodowa Street, they are joined by people carrying bundles. They are on the run. Michael, the German manager and SS man, kept his word – he brought these people back from the Umschlagplatz.[9] Bitterness and concern among the workers. The Jewish managers have left the factory. Only Konar and Line remain. They try to reassure the workers – we are with you. But the workers are not working. They sit at their machines and their tables: the irons turned off, their hands idle.

What happened yesterday is the topic of endless conversations.[10] They took away old Szapiro, the whole Radziejewski family – their nephew went with them voluntarily. Ginger's[11] wife quietly went along with her husband, as if they were going for a walk. But now they are back at the factory. They were in the group that did not leave on time. Ginger is preparing a hiding place next to his workplace.

The smartest ones were those who hid. The conductor hid in the toilet as soon as Michael entered the factory. Bigan sat under the table the whole time. The Chinese man crawled under the bench. One of the women who was singled out simply sat down at a different table. In the courtyard, a Polish manager released half-mad Rebova, from whom he had personally taken money so that she would get into K. G. Schultz. He also released Nowicka, whose husband was an officer in the Polish army, and Stanisław the mould-maker's sister, because of her pretty face.

Elster's brother and Poket[12] are at the factory. They were taken off the list,[13] but have nowhere to go. Those whom Michael brought back from the Umschlag[platz] yesterday have got their work permits back. But no one continues to believe that the factory will save them all. The central ghetto is silent. The illegals[14] have their hiding places, and one can still earn something there. A rush to the central ghetto sets in.

But some think that perhaps 11 November was just a glitch.[15] Michael ultimately brought the people back from the Umschlagplatz, and perhaps now they can work in peace. What else can they do but believe [this]? It is impossible to live in constant fear. Only now they know that the Jews are being taken to their deaths. They flee the columns under a hail of German bullets, they jump from the trains … Maybe they will get lucky? What does it matter that they fall under the wheels, that they can get injured, that a

9 German in the original, here and below.

10 Between 9 and 12 November 1942 the SS resumed deportations from the ghetto. The businesses in the ghetto were instructed to hand over a fixed quota of workers to be transported to factories in the camps at Trawniki, Poniatowa, and Budzyń, all near Lublin. On 11 November 1942 the SS in Lublin took 20 workers from the K. G. Schultz factory to the Umschlagplatz; since the deportation train had already left by that point, they spent the night and the next morning there, after which an SS officer with the surname Michael escorted them back to the factory: Szajn-Lewin, *W getcie warszawskim*, pp. 94, 113.

11 The Polish original has Rudy, which means ginger- or red-haired.

12 Poket worked in the K. G. Schultz factory from Sept. 1942; he fled to the 'Aryan side' towards the end of 1942 and was arrested during a house search the next day.

13 See fn. 4 and fn. 10.

14 This is a reference to unregistered ghetto inhabitants who were not employed in any of the businesses there, and were therefore in the ghetto illegally.

15 See fn. 10.

German gendarme, a Polish policemen, or an extortionist[16] is lying in wait for them on the Polish side? That is no real risk. Death in Treblinka is the worst thing. Now everyone already knows about Treblinka.[17] There they boil people alive. They already know that Bigan[18] was in Treblinka and escaped.

On one occasion, he [Bigan] told Tadeusz[19] everything. He broke down and could no longer carry the nightmarish memories with him. He didn't know that Tadeusz's family had been taken away, or maybe he no longer remembered. Now Tadeusz walks around as if in a daze. He is sure that he will also perish. He repeats this constantly. Perhaps he is comforted by the thought that he will also suffer all the torture that those dearest to him had to endure. In the evening, black-haired Bigan[20] and Tadeusz sit together, and Bigan blurts out: 'No, I want to live. I want to survive the war. I want to experience their defeat. And then, when the moment comes, I will take my revenge, my revenge.' He pronounces these words clearly; he is intoxicated by them. He clasps his hands together as if in a stranglehold. He will build barracks like those in Treblinka. Everything will be modern: electric boilers containing steam – gas, a sloping and movable floor. 'I will herd the Germans inside, all of them naked. Many, many Germans, so that every corner, every centimetre is filled. And from the boilers the gas is conducted through the pipes, the boilers burn red, and the steam … a hellish, boiling bath. Four minutes will suffice, and then one can automatically lower the trapdoor, and the slimy mass of red, crumpled, contorted corpses will be emptied into the pits. And that's that, simply pour chlorine into the pits, and there will be no trace of that which was once alive. It all takes just seven minutes, you see?' And then Bigan bursts out laughing: 'If you'd only seen how the first ones arrived, not knowing what to expect, with loads of parcels, suitcases. They were politely ordered to undress. Men were separated from the women and the children. An SS officer gave a beautiful speech. They were to deposit their money and valuables calmly, in exchange for a receipt, and hand in their clothes for disinfection. They themselves would go into the bathhouse so that they could be clean for their journey to the labour camps in the East. This was merely a bath as a precaution against epidemics, so they would not carry typhus from the ghetto to their new place of residence. As they entered the bathhouse, lively music was played for them, the best Warsaw jazz. The musicians had been selected from among those destined for execution. They had gone into exile with their instruments. Do you want to hear more?' Bigan bellows. 'I myself led my wife and daughter to their

16 In the Polish original, the word is *szmalcownicy*. This is a term for Polish extortionists who ambushed Jews in the streets outside the Warsaw ghetto and demanded that they hand over 'money for lard' (as in greasing someone's palm).

17 The German authorities had spread the word that the deportees were being taken to labour camps 'in the East'.

18 Bigan lived in the Warsaw ghetto until the end of July 1942, when he was deported to Treblinka; in August or early Sept. he encountered his wife and daughter there following their deportation to the camp. After his escape he returned to the ghetto and worked for K. G. Schultz from Sept. 1942; the circumstances of his death are unknown.

19 Tadeusz Prywer (d. 1944), the first husband of Eugenia Szajn Lewin's sister, Maria; in the Warsaw ghetto he took care of his parents, who were there illegally, as well as other family members; perished in the Warsaw Uprising.

20 The original has 'black Bigan'.

deaths.' And then he starts from the beginning, when they took him from the Warsaw ghetto in the first days of the operation. In Treblinka, behind the barbed wire, people were sorted into groups. They selected him and a few others for the auxiliary service. Their work consisted of sorting thousands, hundreds of thousands, huge mountains of the murdered people's clothes and belongings, and loading them on to trains. The clothes were cleaned and the belongings sorted in Lublin, and then they were sent to the Reich for the Germans. Goebbels personally distributed the murdered Jews' clothes to air-raid victims. After a few days of such work, which he [Bigan] carried out as if in a daze because the items of clothing continually increased in number, he saw his wife and daughter on a transport that arrived one morning. He threw himself at a German's feet. This German knew him, he was quite decent to the auxiliaries. Bigan wallowed at his feet and begged him. The German gave him a kick. When he [Bigan] returned to them [his wife and daughter], powerless, they were already undressing. And there his daughter put her arms around his neck, kissed him, and said quietly, 'It's no use, Papa.' She knew she was going to die. He did not say farewell to his wife. She said something to him, but he did not understand her. He walked behind them as if hypnotized. He accompanied them to death's door. 'Do you want to know what happened next? After that I had only a single thought: escape from here, escape. I felt I was losing my mind, that I could no longer fathom anything. As we were loading the clothes into the wagons, I got in, underneath the clothes. I jumped off once the train was moving.'

The Jews already know about Treblinka. But not everyone believes it. Old Szapiro says that Bigan is mentally ill, that he is hallucinating. The Radziejewskis believe that their beautiful fifteen-year-old daughter is working in the barracks in the East, and Małamedowa is sure that her little daughter will survive the war somewhere in Russia, in a children's home, even on just a single bowl of soup a day.

A letter from a worker from Lublin has arrived. He was one of those resettled on 11 November. He doesn't mention his wife. So in order to keep from giving in to despair, they believe that not everyone has been murdered. Poket received a letter from his son-in-law in France. His wife had gone to Poland, to the Treblinka estate, and he was planning to follow her voluntarily. Poket is mad with despair. So even in France, there is resettlement.[21]

On the premises of another factory is someone else who escaped from Treblinka. The workers are already talking about it. Jews from Belgium and the Netherlands have arrived at Treblinka.[22] They were so trusting. They brought their beloved dogs, their little birds in cages, with them on the journey. The Germans have 'their' Jews, who do their bidding. They are aware that the Jews know the truth, so now they are spreading the rumour that Treblinka has been liquidated. There are labour camps in Lublin,[23] Trawniki, and Poniatowa. There are escapees from Lublin, which is worse than

21 There were no known deportations from France to Treblinka, but transports from France to Sobibor took place in March 1943.

22 Tens of thousands of Jews were deported from the Netherlands to Sobibor in March 1943; there were no known transports from Belgium or the Netherlands to Treblinka.

23 Several thousand Warsaw Jews were deported to Lublin-Majdanek concentration camp.

Treblinka. Treblinka means immediate death, while the labour camps mean a slow death. They are not even penal camps, but places where they kill people off. You live there amidst hunger and filth, and you die as a result of torture and bullets.

They are back at work.[24] There is of course no alternative. The German company managers bring in new workers. There are approximately 800 of them. This is the quota that was fixed during the selection in Miła.[25] Of those who were taken on 11 November, some have returned from the Umschlag[platz]. Not everyone. Some went to Lublin. There are still some people at the Umschlag[platz] who are waiting to be taken away. But no trains are arriving. There will be no more trains, the Germans explain, because there was no resettlement on 11 November. They say that the people have to be released, and the Umschlag[platz] liquidated.[26]

## DOC. 178

### On 15 November 1942 a resistance organization in the Warsaw ghetto describes Treblinka extermination camp and the murders taking place there[1]

Enclosure no. 17 to the report by the United Anti-Fascist Organization[2] for the government delegation for Poland, Warsaw, dated 15 November 1942[3]

*Treblinka. A monument to the German people's everlasting shame.*

'Since the establishment of the Geneva Convention, which was signed in 1864 by representatives of thirty-five states, but ratified by only twenty-one, Germany has been most scrupulous in complying with its provisions, which are intended to guarantee that a certain current of humanitarianism prevails even under conditions of the most bitter warfare. The protection of the wounded adversary, the humane and dignified treatment of the captured enemy, the respect for medical facilities, and the humanitarian provisions prohibiting attack against the civilian population – especially women and children – all these have always been fundamental and inviolable matters of honour for the German soldiers fighting on the front and in occupied territory, as well as for the German military command. This is an undeniable fact which even the adversary in his hatred has

24 This is a reference to the K. G. Schultz factory's Jewish employees.

25 See Doc. 131.

26 Deportations from the Warsaw ghetto were only suspended temporarily and resumed in mid Jan. 1943.

1 This document is included with the report 'The Liquidation of Jewish Warsaw' ('Likwidacja żydowskiej Warszawy') as enclosure no. 17: AAN, 1325/202/XV-2, fols. 208–252 (fols. 244–249). Published in Krystyna Marczewska and Władysław Ważniewski, 'Treblinka w świetle akt Delegatury Rzadu RP na Kraj', in *Biuletyn Głównej Komisji Badania Zbrodni Hitlerowskich w Polsce*, 19 (1968), pp. 129–164 (here pp. 139–143). This document has been translated from Polish.

2 A joint designation for the Jewish National Committee (ŻKN) and the Jewish Combat Organization (ŻOB).

3 Handwritten addition at the top of the document: 'sent to L[ondon], 6 Jan. 1943': AAN, 1325/202/XV-2, fol. 208.

acknowledged in black and white, albeit against his will.' Max Gröters,[4] 'Ein Fetzen Papier – Genfer Konvention und "Soldaten Christi"', *Warschauer Zeitung*, no. 255, 28 October 1942[5] (see enclosure no. 10).[6]

The village of Treblinka lies near to the Warsaw–Białystok railway line, a few kilometres from Małkinia, in a wooded and sandy area. The Polish population of the village comprises farmers and forestry workers. In 1940, on a sandy plot near this village, the Germans established the penal concentration camp 'Treblinka A' for Poles who had been convicted of certain misdemeanours against the occupiers – whether failing to deliver the right quotas of agricultural products, or having been caught smuggling. The discipline in this camp is very strict – prisoners are shot for trivial reasons. The camp is already as notorious as the penal camp in Oświęcim.

In March 1942 the Germans began constructing a new camp, Treblinka B, near Treblinka A. This camp was designated as an execution site for the Jews of Poland and other European countries. Poles from the neighbouring camp were deployed to prepare and level the site, as were Jews who had been rounded up in the nearby towns. This work lasted until late April, during which time the central feature of this camp was built: the House of Death No. 1 (14).[7] The new camp, Treblinka B, is situated on sandy hills between groves of trees. The camp grounds are relatively small, covering about five hectares.[8] The entire site is surrounded by a hedge, densely interlaced with a barbed wire fence (3). Part of the fence runs through a young forest on the northern side (25). Observation posts for the Lagerschutz[9] are located at all four corners of the site. The Lagerschutz consists mainly of Ukrainians armed with light machine guns. The observation posts are equipped with powerful searchlights to illuminate the entire area at night. There are also observation posts in the middle of the site itself, on the hills next to the groves of trees. The western boundary of Treblinka B is formed by a railway embankment, atop which there is a siding that connects the camp to the main line (1). The siding (2) was laid in recent months so that the wagons with the transports can proceed directly to the execution site. The northern boundary of the camp consists of a young forest, while the eastern and southern boundaries run between the sandy hills. A long belt of undergrowth stretches through the camp grounds, beginning at the northern boundary and running parallel to the railway line (25).

4 Max Gröters (1900?–1989), journalist; worked for the *Kieler Zeitung*, 1930–1934, for some of this period as its editor-in-chief; joined the NSDAP in 1931; worked for the Dortmund Gau newspaper *Westfälische Landeszeitung – Rote Erde* in 1937; appointed political editor of the *Krakauer Zeitung* in 1942; member of the All-German People's Party (GVP) after the war.

5 German in the original: 'A Scrap of Paper? The Geneva Convention and "Soldiers of Christ"'. This editorial appeared on the front page of the newspaper.

6 A reference for the quotation given above. The original German-language editorial was reproduced as enclosure no. 10: AAN, 1325/202/XV-2, fol. 241.

7 Note in the original: 'The figures included in brackets in the text refer to the corresponding points marked on the site plan of Treblinka B': see Marczewska and Ważniewski, 'Treblinka w świetle akt Delegatury Rzadu RP na Kraj', p. 141.

8 In fact, the camp grounds extended over approximately 17 hectares.

9 German in the original, here and below: 'camp guard'.

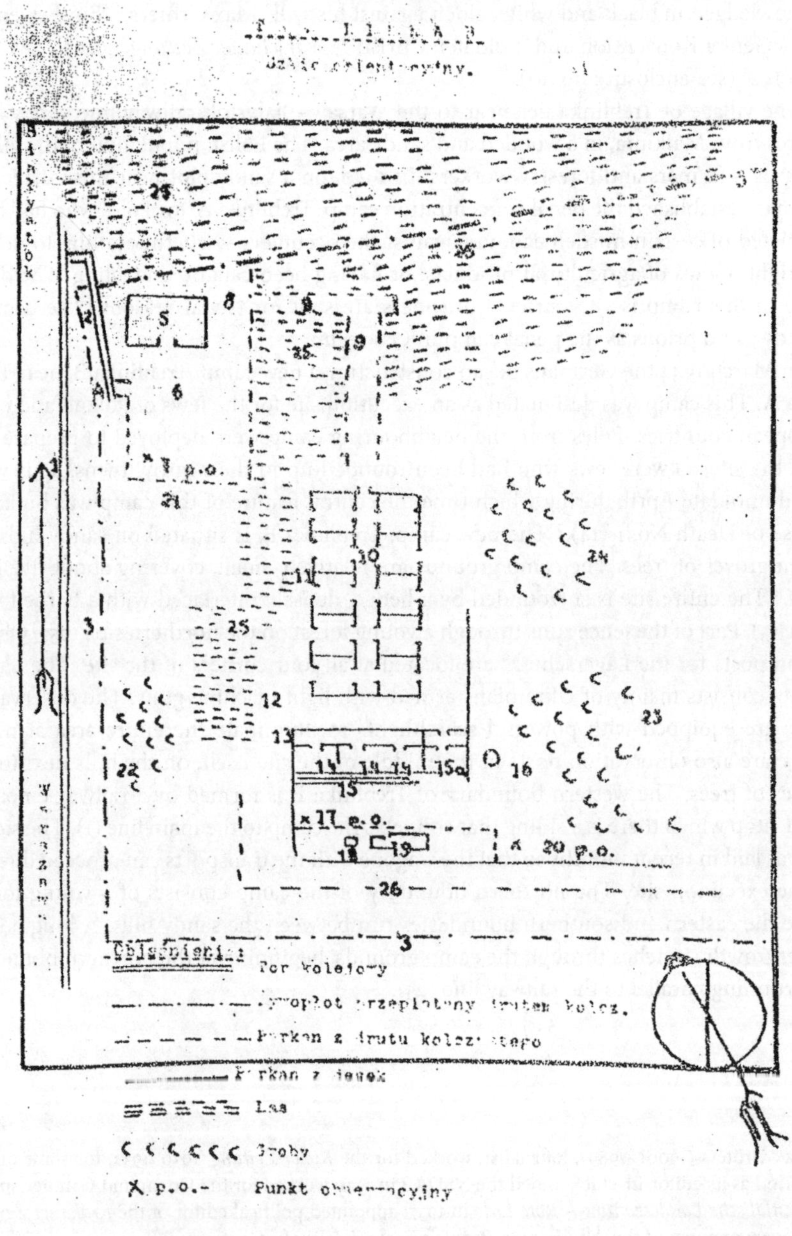


The plan has the heading 'Treblinka B: map'. Captions (from top to bottom): railway line; hedge interlaced with barbed wire; barbed wire fence; fence made of wooden planks; forest; graves; observation point.

The ramp (4) is located at the siding, where the trains arrive with the transports. This ramp leads onto a square that can hold two to three thousand people (6). This square is surrounded by a separate barbed wire fence. There is a large wooden barracks on the square, near the northern boundary. At the south-western corner is a watchtower, which is manned around the clock by a military guard (7). On the southern side of this square, beyond the fence, is the so-called clothes-sorting yard (Lumpensortierungsplatz)[10] (21), and further south are the camp commandant's execution site and the graves of the victims he has murdered (22). The arrivals area (6), which we mentioned earlier, is connected to the rest of the site by a gate at the north-eastern corner of the fence (8). From there, a forest path leads eastwards, approximately 200 metres long (9), then turns south at a right angle and follows the little grove, parallel to the western boundary of the arrivals area. This path ends at a large, odd-looking building (10): it is the shell of an unfinished, single-storey brick building approximately 40 metres long and 15 metres wide. In the first half of September, when we received news of Treblinka B, the building was nearing completion. The Germans had begun constructing this brick building at an early stage of the operation, probably in mid August; Jewish craftsmen selected from the death transports brought to Treblinka were used to assist with construction. Interestingly, the bricks were delivered from Warsaw, in wagons coupled to the transports. Jewish workers loaded the bricks at the Umschlagplatz[11] in Warsaw. According to an eyewitness report, the inside of the building looks as follows: a corridor approximately 3 metres wide runs down the centre, and on each side are five rooms or chambers; each chamber is approximately 2 metres high and 35 square metres in size.

The execution chambers have no windows, but they have a door to the corridor and a kind of flap on the outer walls. Next to these flaps are ramps with a slightly concave surface, similar to large baking troughs. The workers installed pipes through which steam could be admitted. This is meant to be the House of Death No. 2.

The forest path (9) leads between trees, passes the western wall of the building, and ends at the next building (12), House of Death No. 1 (14); this building stands at right angles to House of Death No. 2. It is a stone building, much smaller than the first. It consists of only three chambers and a boiler room. Along the northern wall of this building runs a corridor via which one can reach the chambers through a door. On the outer wall of the chambers is a flap (until recently a door, which was replaced by a flap for convenience). Here too, at the level of the flap, there is a ramp in the shape of a baking trough (15). A boiler house adjoins this building (15a). Inside the boiler house is a large boiler to produce steam. The heated steam enters the chambers through pipes that run through the death chambers and are fitted with a suitable number of openings.[12] While this death machinery is in operation, the doors and flaps are hermetically sealed. The floors in the chambers are made of terracotta and become very slippery when water is poured onto them. Next to the boiler house is a well – the only one on the entire Treblinka B site. Not far from the House of Death, on the southern side, outside the barbed-wire fence and the wooden screening, is the gravediggers' camp. They stay in a barracks (19); next to the barracks are the kitchen buildings. On either side of this camp are two watchtowers (17, 20). The remaining area of Treblinka B is intended for the graves of the murdered victims. Part of the site is already a large cemetery (22, 23, 24). At first, the

10 German in the original, here and below; the term literally means 'rag sorting yard'.
11 German in the original.
12 Murders in the gas chambers were carried out by introducing carbon monoxide produced by internal combustion engines into the chambers.

Poles employed in the camp prepared the graves, but later, when the murder operation escalated, more and more pits were needed. Special machines, excavators, were brought in to dig graves day and night. They are powered by diesel engines, and the thrumming of these engines is a characteristic sound in Treblinka B death camp.

The personnel who supervise and carry out the executions consist of only a few people. At the head of the murder machinery is an SS man with the rank of gendarmerie captain (name: Sauer).[13] The German service personnel comprise SS men who are terrified of their 'boss'. As soon as they see him from a distance, they herd the worker Jews and the victims to their deaths even more energetically. There are ten Germans altogether. By contrast, there are thirty Ukrainians.[14] The German personnel change from time to time. Sometimes SS men come to the camp from various parts of the so-called GG, where they are engaged in the 'resettlement'.

In addition to the German-Ukrainian Lagerschutz, there is also a Jewish auxiliary service, part of which is assigned to sort the murdered victims' clothes (Lumpensortierungsplatz), while others work as gravediggers to clear out the execution chambers and bury the dead, and the rest are deployed in the arrivals area. Group leaders, whom the Germans refer to as Kapos, head the individual groups that make up this Jewish auxiliary service. They are comparatively well fed and they have triangular yellow patches sewn onto the knees of their trousers to distinguish them from the others. The composition of the Jewish auxiliary service changes almost daily. Cases in which a Jew in this service lasts more than two weeks are seldom, due to the inhumane treatment from the Germans. They are constantly tortured and beaten with whips, and there are frequent corporal punishments (twenty-five lashes) as well as shootings of those who are too weak and have lost the ability to work. The 'boss' usually deals with this himself.[15] Every day after lunch there is a roll call for those unfit to work. When the German asks who does not feel strong enough to continue working, some of them step forward, report themselves to the boss as unfit for work, and ask – as if for mercy – to be shot. The execution takes place in a specially designated area. The victim positions himself next to the grave, standing upright, and the boss shoots him in the back of the head with a revolver. The next victim must come and throw the body of the murdered person into the pit, only to then share his predecessor's fate a moment later. These young Jews are so exhausted that any desire to resist is extinguished, and the terror inflicted by the Germans is so horrific that they want to end their lives as quickly as possible, so as not to have to endure the inhumane torture any longer. In the first few days of September, the 'boss' at Treblinka murdered 500 young Jews in a single day, killing them with a rifle, one after the other; what is most remarkable is that, out of this group of several hundred people, not one of them attacked the Germans to defend himself against death. The execution lasted from 7.30 a.m. until 3 p.m. Comparatively, the easiest work in the death camp is sorting the clothes of those who have been murdered. One can eat one's fill at will, because the 'resettled' Jews brought a lot of food supplies with them: bread, jam, fats, sugar. But the

13 Franz Stangl.

14 The 25–30 German and Austrian camp staff members were supported by 100–120 former prisoners of war from the Soviet Union, who had been trained at the SS training camp in Trawniki.

15 In contrast to Stangl, whom the victims hardly ever saw, the deputy camp commandant, Kurt Franz, often appeared in the camp, where he committed numerous murders.

boss does not let the Jews work there long; after a few days, he assigns them to the gravediggers.

The Jewish auxiliary service is replenished from the transports arriving in Treblinka. Normally two transports arrive at Treblinka every day, in the morning and towards evening; but at the height of the operation, several transports arrived every day. Each train consists of several dozen goods wagons. Some of the wagons stop on the siding right in the arrivals area, and the rest are shunted to the side and wait there until the first wagons have been dealt with. The wagons are emptied quickly. The mistreated and utterly exhausted crowd of people breathe a sigh of relief upon entering the arrivals area. They are immediately welcomed by the Jewish auxiliary service, with the Kapos in front. They are given orders in Yiddish. The women and children are told to go to the barracks immediately, while the men remain on the square. Looking around, they see a notice hanging on a pole with the huge inscription: Achtung Warschauer,[16] although mass transports of Jews arrive in Treblinka from many other towns in the so-called [General] Government, Germany, and Western European countries as well. 'Do not worry about your fate', the sign further instructs: 'You are all going to work in the East. You will work, and your wives will take care of the household. But before you leave, you must take a bath, and you must hand in your clothes for delousing. You must deposit your valuables and money at the cash office here. You will receive receipts for them, and after the bath and the delousing you will get everything back intact.'

In the initial phase of the murders in Treblinka, an SS officer with an angelic expression on his face[17] would appear in the arrivals area. He inspired complete trust and delivered a speech with more or less the same content to the assembled groups. However, as the operation proceeded and more and more transports arrived from different directions, and the vast numbers of new arrivals had to be liquidated more quickly, the Germans did away with the speech as it was considered redundant. To get the Jews to trust the Germans and to believe that the selections on the arrivals square are genuinely based on occupation and that people will be sent to work in different occupational groups, signs are posted in parts of the arrivals square with inscriptions such as tailors, shoemakers, joiners, etc. But of course such a selection never took place.

However, the Kapos quickly line up the men in rows of ten[18] and order them to take off their shoes, strip naked, and prepare for the bath. Everyone is allowed to take a bar of soap and their documents. Meanwhile the sorting service collects the gathered clothes and brings them to the appropriate place. The women must also strip naked, along with the children. And then comes the final act of the Treblinka tragedy: the terrorized mass of men, women, and children sets out on the final road to death. In front, the group of women with children hurries along, escorted by Germans who, with whips in their hands, urge them along with lashes and blows. They drive this group forwards faster and faster, and increasingly violent blows rain down upon the heads of the women, who are crazed with fear and pain. The women's screaming and wailing, the Germans' curses and shouts break the silence of the forest. At last, the people have understood that they are going to their deaths. At the entrance to House of Death No. 1 stands the boss himself,

16 German in the original: 'Attention Varsovians'.
17 Irmfried Eberl or Franz Stangl.
18 Changes in tense here and below as in the original.

mercilessly forcing the women inside with lashes from the whip in his hand. The floor in the chambers is slippery. The people slip and fall, and they can no longer get up because new masses of victims are forced in, piling on top of them. The boss throws little children into the chambers over the women's heads. Thus the execution chambers are filled up to the brim and then the doors are hermetically sealed and the people who are [still] alive are slowly suffocated with steam from the numerous openings in the pipes. At first muffled screams come from the inside, which gradually become weaker, and after fifteen minutes the execution is over.

Now it is the gravediggers' turn. With shouts and curses, the German guards force the gravediggers to start work. They have to remove the corpses from the execution chambers. The gravediggers stand on the ramp directly in front of the flaps. The flaps open, but not a single corpse falls out. The effect of the steam has turned all the corpses into a homogenous mass, so to speak, glued together with the murdered victims' sweat. In their final agonies – before they give up the ghost – their hands, legs, and torsos became intertwined to form a giant, macabre clump. In order for the gravediggers to remove the bodies one by one, the mass is doused with buckets of cold water from the nearby well. Then the individual corpses come unstuck, and it is easier to get them out. In general, the bodies appear unchanged – as far as outer appearance is concerned – only their heads and buttocks are violet in colour. Urged on and continuously beaten by the Germans, the gravediggers pile the corpses on the ramp until the chambers are empty. They all lie there like meat in a slaughterhouse, and then they are buried. Until recently (the first half of August), the Jewish gravediggers had handcarts with which they took the bodies to the pits – this had to be done at an insane pace. But the boss recently abolished this convenience. Ein Mann – zwei Leichen.[19] This means that every gravedigger has two corpses to bury. He binds the corpse's arms or legs with a belt, and drags it at a run from the ramp to the pits, throws it in, and has to run back for the next load. Previously the graves were right next to the House of Death, so the burial of those who had been murdered could be done faster. But as more and more victims kept arriving, the graves shifted further and further east, and it is taking longer and longer to drag the corpses to their final resting place. When a grave is full, the gravediggers quickly cover the dead with earth while the excavator is already preparing the next grave nearby.

The execution of men proceeds in an identical way. They too are herded to their deaths along the forest path. People react differently as they are herded to the House of Death: some loudly recite penitential psalms and confess their sins, while others curse God – but a German's sudden shout and blows falling upon the backs of the morituri[20] immediately silence the whole crowd. Sometimes not all the victims can fit in the overcrowded chambers, in which case the Germans detain the others in the grove next to the execution site. These people see and hear everything, but they lack any instinct of self-preservation. This fact is irrefutable proof of the ghastly terror the Germans inflict on their victims.

The new House of Death is designed to finish off 8,000–10,000 victims. If we consider that 2,000,000 (two million) Jews, in other words the lion's share of Poland's Jews,

19 German in the original: 'One man – two corpses'.
20 Latin: 'those about to die'.

have already been buried on the grounds of Treblinka,[21] then the disturbing question arises: For whom have the SS men planned the new House of Death? Who is condemned to draw his last breath in this execution site? In all probability this death machinery, once set in motion, will not be limited to killing Jews alone. It is the Polish people who now face the spectre of death in the steam chambers; certain signs of this have already appeared. According to an eyewitness report, in the second half of August the Germans executed a group of Poles in House of Death No. 1.[22]

## DOC. 179

## On 17 November 1942 Himmler orders that insufficiently secure camps for Jewish forced labourers be closed down and the inmates deported to better-guarded concentration camps[1]

Telex message (marked 'secret') from Himmler to SS-Obergruppenführer Krüger in Cracow, dated 17 November 1942[2]

I see from reports that the attacks in the General Government are markedly increasing. *Bandit activity* is escalating. This cannot continue. I am particularly struck by the fact that prisons are being attacked methodically, the guards assaulted, and the prisoners freed.[3]

For reasons of security, I am ordering that all individual vulnerable labour camps for Jews and all poorly guarded prisons not secure against attack be closed down and the inmates transferred to central concentration camps and prison camps.[4]

Please contact the judiciary immediately and examine the situation within the judicial system as regards security.

21 Approximately 700,000 people had been murdered in Treblinka by late 1942.
22 There is no known evidence for this.

1 BArch, NS 19/1433, fol. 32, also BArch, R 19/321, fol. 2. This document has been translated from German.
2 Stamp with dispatch note; the initials Br [Rudolf Brandt] appear at the end.
3 For example, in mid Nov. 1942 a combat squad from the communist People's Guard, led by Grzegorz Korczyński, attacked the waterworks administration camp in Janiszów, Kreis Krasnik, and killed the camp's commandant, Peter Ignar. The partisans declared the 900 Jewish prisoners liberated and took 15 of them into their unit.
4 By the end of the year, 38 of the 42 waterworks administration camps in District Lublin had been closed down, along with other forced labour camps; such camps were also closed down in District Radom.

## DOC. 180

## On 18 November 1942 the Security Police instruct the GG government in Cracow to hand over responsibility for Jewish welfare to the SS and the police[1]

Letter (marked 'secret') from Heim,[2] Deputy Senior Commander of the Security Police in the General Government, to Weirauch, head of the Population and Welfare Division in the GG government's Interior Administration Department, Cracow, dated 18 November 1942

According to the additional instructions since given by the Reichsführer-SS for accelerating the evacuation of the Jews, which indicate in particular that, from the appointed date, Jews and Jewesses who are fit for work are effectively available only for war production and the GG armaments inspectorate, and then only if they are housed in sealed camps under SS and police supervision, the Jewish Aid Office's work is no longer required.

By this date all Jews, except those mentioned above who are fit for work and housed in labour camps, will have vanished from the General Government, so that any further welfare measure for the remaining Jews will effectively be in the hands of the SS and the police.

Any fundraising on the part of the Jews is superfluous and must be refused.

Given the efforts to bring the entire operation against the Jews to a rapid conclusion, foreign policy considerations in relation to the Jewish Aid Office's activities should no longer be regarded as an important factor. It is irrelevant whether foreign aid for Jews from international intermediary organizations is still being received. If there will soon be no more Jews in the GG who require international assistance, then foreign countries cannot be prevented from finding out about this.

Based on these considerations, I request that you withdraw your decree to the district governors of 20 October 1942[3] and refrain from further welfare measures in this area.[4]

1 The location of the original is unknown. Copy in BArch, Ost-Dok 13/246. Published in German in Tatiana Berenstein, Artur Eisenbach, and Adam Rutkowski (eds.), *Eksterminacja Żydów na ziemiach polskich w okresie okupacji hitlerowskiej: Zbiór dokumentów* (Warsaw: Żydowski Instytut Historyczny, 1957), p. 319. This document has been translated from German.

2 Franz Heim (1907–1944), pharmacist; joined the NSDAP and the SA in 1930; worked for the SD in 1935; leader of an Einsatzkommando in Poland, 1939; Deputy Senior Commander of the Security Police and the SD (BdS) in the GG, Sept. 1941 – August 1943; died of an illness.

3 This could not be found. Richard Türk, the official in charge of Jewish affairs in the GG government's Population and Welfare Division and deputy head of the same division, had ordered on 16 Oct. 1942 that a Jewish Aid Office be established: see Berenstein, Eisenbach, and Rutkowski (eds.), *Eksterminacja Żydów*, pp. 317–318.

4 In response to this letter, on 1 Dec. 1942 Türk informed Weichert, the director of the Jewish Aid Office, that from then on 'all further welfare measures for Jews are in the hands of the SS and the police': see ibid., p. 319, fn. 1.

## DOC. 181

## On 20 November 1942 the racial researcher Elfriede Fliethmann writes about her anthropological studies on Jews in the General Government[1]

Typewritten letter from the Race and Ethnicity Section of the Institute for German Eastern Research, signed Fl.,[2] to Dora Maria Kahlich,[3] 6/10 Van Swietengasse, Vienna 72/IX, dated 20 November 1942 (carbon copy)

Dear Dr Kahlich,

It has taken me some time to get back to you with definite information on the matter.[4] As the gentlemen from the Security Service told me, there is no prospect whatsoever of getting any information on deported Jews. Their names are not recorded, so it is impossible to find out anything about their subsequent whereabouts. In this case the only thing to do is to let fate run its course.[5]

As far as the publication of the photographs is concerned, I am sorry to say that the *Mitteilungen*[6] are [only] able to publish two pages of photographs, or thirty-two photographs, in the format [I use] for my Jews.[7] For an anthropological study that is, of course, not nearly enough.

So what will happen with regard to the Jews? I am getting Dr Jasicki[8] to make calculations on the proportional figures, and I will soon need your diagnoses for purposes of comparison and for the final version.

1 Archiwum Uniwersytetu Jagiellońskiego, IDO 70. This document has been translated from German.

2 Dr Elfriede Fliethmann, married name Henseling (1915–1987), anthropologist; originally from Vienna; worked in the Race and Ethnicity Section of the Institute for German Eastern Research's Racial Research Unit, July 1941 – Dec. 1943; served as its de facto head, 1942–1943; worked as an educator in West Berlin after the war.

3 Dr Dorothea (Dora) Maria Kahlich, née Könner (1905–1970), anthropologist; worked at the University of Vienna's Anthropological Institute in 1934; provided expert opinions on ancestry and conducted research on Viennese Jews from 1938; assistant to Prof. Leopold Breitenecker (forensic medicine, University of Vienna) from 1959.

4 On 29 Oct. 1942 Kahlich had provided an expert opinion in court in favour of Emil Blau and, on the same day, asked Fliethmann to ascertain whether Blau – who had been deported from Vienna with his nine children on 12 March 1941 and later sent to the Łagów ghetto, 35 km east of Kielce – was still alive.

5 The Łagów ghetto was surrounded by a barbed wire fence in March 1942; assisted by Ukrainian and Polish police, the SS rounded up the Jews and shot the sick, the elderly, and many of the children on 7 Oct. 1942. The remaining 2,000 Jews were deported to Treblinka on 27 Oct. 1942.

6 This probably refers to the journal *Deutsche Forschung im Osten: Mitteilungen des Instituts für deutsche Ostarbeit Krakau*.

7 No such article ever appeared in *Deutsche Forschung im Osten*.

8 Dr Bronisław Jasicki (1907–1992), anthropologist; researcher at the University of Cracow; research assistant at the Institute for German Eastern Research from 1940; completed his post-doctoral degree at the University of Cracow in 1946; became assistant professor in 1963 and full professor in 1972; head of the Institute of Anthropology, 1965–1976. His field of research both before and after the war was anthropometric studies.

The new head of the section[9] started the day before yesterday. Dr Plügel[10] will very likely come here on leave at the beginning of December to discuss the details with the relevant gentlemen personally. I am naturally curious about working with the new man, but I think it will be good.

Warmest regards, and I hope to see you again in Vienna very soon; I will be coming home for Christmas after all.

Heil Hitler

## DOC. 182

## On 26 November 1942 the gendarmerie station in Ostrowiec Świętokrzyski lists the proceeds obtained from the auction of Jewish property[1]

Report by Bezirksleutnant Sommer (log no. 2641/42), Ostrowiec gendarmerie station, Kreis Opatow, District Radom, dated 26 November 1942 (carbon copy)

A complete list of the sums obtained for Jewish inventory sold at auction during the resettlement of Jews from *Denkow*,[2] *Kunow*, *Cmielow*, *Ozarow*, and *Zawichost*.

| | |
|---|---|
| Denkow | 11,412 zl. |
| Kunow | 9,494 zl. |
| Cmielow | 19,992 zl. |
| Ozarow | 115,665 zl. |
| Zawichost | 58,771 zl. |
| Total | 212,334 zl.[3] |
| Money secured in cash: | 216,135.41 zl. |
| Total | 428,469.41 zl. |

In words: 'four hundred and twenty-eight thousand four hundred and sixty-nine zloty and 41 groschy.'[4]

9 Dr Erhard Riemann (1907–1984), Germanist and folklorist; joined the NSDAP in 1933; head of the Race and Ethnicity Section of the Institute for German Eastern Research from 1942; classed as *entlastet* ('exonerated') during denazification proceedings; thereafter professor at the University of Kiel.

10 Dr Anton Plügel (1910–1945), anthropologist; joined the NSDAP in 1930 and the SA in 1932; worked for the Hitler Youth in Vienna and Munich, 1932–1935; worked in the GG government's Science and Education Department from 1940; head of the Racial Research Unit at the Institute for German Eastern Research from April 1941; served in the war from May 1942; went missing in action at Königsberg.

1 AIPN, GK 675/1 (CA MSW 372/1), fol. 500. This document has been translated from German.

2 Today part of the town of Ostrowiec Świętokrzyski.

3 Correctly: 215,334 zł.; the correct final total is therefore 431,469.41 zł.

4 This is a reference to groszy; 100 groszy = 1 złoty.

## DOC. 183
## In late November 1942 Franciszka Reizer describes the hunt for Jews in the area around Albigowa[1]

Diary of Franciszka Reizer,[2] entries for 20–30 November 1942

*20 November*
The Germans mustered a large number of farmers – members of the village fire brigade, and with their help organized a hunt for Jews. In a line formation, they combed the fields with dogs and guns, ready to shoot. Then they surrounded the Albigowa and Honie[3] forests. The Germans rode motorcycles along the paths and the broad strips on the edge of the fields. They captured seven Jews in this operation – old people, teenagers, and children. Then they locked them up for the night in the shed of the fire brigade next to the 'Kółko' (a shop). Designated farmers from the village fire brigade guard the shed in two-hour shifts.[4] They stand guard in pairs and are liable for those locked in the shed at the risk of their own lives. Władysław Bartman, one of the guards, told me that it was the worst night of his life. He heard people wailing non-stop: 'Mr Bartman, let us out, let me out, if you have God in your heart, by the wounds of Jesus, your God, let us out. God of Abraham, have mercy on us.' The wailing and moaning lasted all night, until the early morning. In the morning the executioners arrived. They ordered the Jews to be let out. They led them to 'Jaroszówka',[5] put shovels in their hands, ordered them to dig. The people dug their own pits, larger and smaller ones, according to their strength. The farmers mustered by the Germans looked on. And then the machine guns barked and the bodies rolled down into the pits. On orders, the farmers took up the shovels and had to cover the bodies with soil. The fresh soil convulsed. A few days later the farmers exhumed the bodies, laid them on a hay cart covered with straw, and took them to the Jewish cemetery in Łańcut. I saw the head of an old Jew hanging over the edge of the cart. His white beard bounced up and down as the cart went over the potholes on the road.

A strange connection. A year ago, two bells were taken away on two carts. The clapper in one of them bounced around over the potholes in a similar way, sounding the alarm. The sołtys commissioned Stanisław Sobek, 'Szanio', to transport the Jews. He had also transported the bells.

*21 November*
The Jews were flushed out – a drive hunt. In 'na Równe' forest[6] they found a hut in which seven Jews had taken shelter. The gendarmes were furious with Augustyn Bator,

1 The whereabouts of the original are unknown. Published in Franciszka Reizer, *Dzienniki 1939–1944* (Warsaw: Ludowa Spółdzielnia Wydawnicza, 1984), pp. 71–73. The text reproduced here possibly consists of edited excerpts from longer entries. This document has been translated from Polish.

2 Franciszka Reizer, née Dudzińska, a Polish teacher from Upper Silesia; taught in Albigowa, near Łańcut; worked in the clandestine school system during the German occupation.

3 A hamlet near Albigowa.

4 Change in tense as in the original.

5 An uncultivated field where Jews had made a number of dugouts.

6 A forested area near Albigowa.

who lived right next to the forest, because he had not reported to the Gestapo that Jews had a hiding place there in the field near the forest. They beat him up terribly. They kicked him and wanted to shoot him. He fell unconscious, as if lifeless. They drove off without shooting him. But Bator survived. He is being looked after.[7]

The Jews had made a dugout in Augustyn Bator's field. The smoke rising from the mound betrayed them. Gendarmes who were out hunting for Jews saw it. There were seven of them there. The gendarmes shot them all and ordered that they be buried on the spot.

*25 November*

It was pitch-dark outside. We were sitting down to dinner. A small flame was burning in the carbide lamp. We heard scratching at the door. The cat wanted to be let in, as always. 'Shoo! Go away!' cried Grandma Tereska Reizerowa. But the scratching stubbornly persisted. I went to the door and opened it wide enough for the cat to slip through. It wasn't the cat, but a trembling hand that slipped through the door: 'Have mercy, give me a piece of bread.' I cut a slice of bread and pressed it into the hand. And after a while: 'God bless you.' The visitor departed, or rather ran off, as quietly as a cat. Then he scurried unnoticed across the road and disappeared into Józef Kluz's orchard. After that he again flitted behind Zofia Kluz's barn and was gone. We all recalled the order from the Germans which the sołtys had emphatically read out in front of the church after mass: 'Anyone who hides Jews or helps them in any way will be punished under martial law.' The Jew disappeared into the darkness of the cold November night.

*30 November*

I was rinsing the laundry by the well. It was nice outside. I heard muffled shouting. I saw Mrs Ulmanowa, the sołtys's wife, having an argument with someone. She was gently pushing an old woman off the porch and telling her quietly: 'For God's sake, woman, run away!' And again: 'Go, you silly thing. Get out of here. Do you want to hand yourself over to them?' The Jewish woman wailed in despair: 'Oh! Oh! I'm so miserable. Give me a horse and cart [to get] to Łańcut! I should meet my end, too!' She tore out her hair and moaned with sorrow: 'My husband, my daughter, my grandson. They're all gone, gone!' Again the sołtys's wife tried to plead with the unhappy woman: 'There is no cart. Go on, get out, here's some bread, don't let anyone see you. Go on, straight through the field.'

The old Jewish woman put the bread down on the stone steps. Moaning with sorrow and grief, she scuttled off in the direction of Łańcut. Before her the road to Golgotha, to crucifixion.

7 After this incident Augustyn Bator was unable to work and was ill for several years; he died in 1948.

## DOC. 184
## In November 1942 Polish government representatives report on the murder of Jews in District Radom[1]

Communications for the government delegation's Internal Affairs Department, signed Sabina,[2] recorded at the end of November 1942 or later (excerpt)

*Lublin Land.* News from *Zamość,* November 1942
[...][3]
*New earning opportunities for the German military*
Through an intermediary, German military personnel approached a Jewish family considered wealthy and influential, and suggested that they flee abroad in a German bomber plane. This was in August. The trip (to Sweden) was to cost 60,000 złoty per person. The intermediary related that rather a lot of people had already escaped in this way. The bomber would descend over Sweden to a low altitude and signal with a white flag. There were cases in which the bombers had been forced to land and the German military personnel had been interned, but civilians were always released. Sometimes, however, a bomber managed to land at a prearranged spot in a sparsely populated area. There the bomber would be repainted in a matter of hours, and then the Germans would bring the passengers all the way to England. The family to whom this proposal was made did not have that much money and did not believe that such a journey could possibly succeed. Then, out of curiosity, one of the relatives met with the intermediary, who renewed the offer, with the difference that this time the trip would cost 100,000 złoty per person. This story has been definitively confirmed.

*Jewish affairs*
In and around Busko[4] the liquidation of the Jews did not occur until mid October this year. Jews from the area of Pińczów, Nowy Korczyn, and the surrounding area were herded to Busko and loaded onto a train, which departed in the direction of Jędrzejów. They were probably taken to Oświęcim.[5] In Busko the local population did not loot the Jewish apartments because the German and Polish police did not allow it: of course they themselves took the most valuable things and auctioned off the rest. Complete liquidation of the Jews in Busko; *two craftsmen were left.* Since there were no Polish craftsmen there at all (not a single tailor or shoemaker), things are now at a complete standstill, and the population does not receive any of these services. The ghetto in Busko was an open ghetto.

In Radzymin the Jews were liquidated in early October, in a particularly bloody and bestial manner. It began at around 1 a.m. and lasted the entire day. A great many Jews

1 AAN, 1325/202/III-28, vol. 3, fols. 417–420, here fols. 419–420. This document has been translated from Polish.
2 This is presumably a code name for Halina Krahelska, née Śleszyńska (1892–1945), journalist, writer, and social policy activist; member of the Polish Socialist Party (PPS) from 1908; active in the underground movement from 1939; worked with the Alliance of Democrats (SD); wrote a daily chronicle for the High Command of the Union of Armed Struggle (ZWZ) from April 1940; arrested in July 1944; perished in Ravensbrück concentration camp.
3 The first two pages contain information about the Polish population.
4 Today: Busko-Zdrój; a small town halfway between Kielce and Tarnów.
5 They were in fact deported to Treblinka.

were killed on the spot, in their homes, and in the streets. The Germans shot at women and children as if they were dogs. In the evening, several thousand people were loaded into wagons – 200 people in each wagon; and they were stationary on the tracks for 24 hours, crammed in together and hermetically sealed in like this. It is likely that hardly anyone survived, because first there was terrible wailing, screaming, and lamenting, but then everything went quiet.

Inside, the wagons were strewn with quicklime. When the so-called 'operation' began, the lamentations and cries of despair from the ghetto shocked the whole of Radzymin. Later, during the day, the Poles witnessed the terrible exodus of the expelled Jews. Our informant saw a German shoot a Jewish woman who could not keep up (she was staggering); he ordered a Pole standing by the roadside to bury her in the ditch. Someone else saw a German in a deserted apartment shoot a paralysed boy in his bed; his mother had not been allowed to take him with her. After the Jews had been driven from their apartments in Radzymin, these were first looted by the Germans (they came out wearing several rings on each finger), and then by the Polish police. The local policemen's wives were more uncomfortable, but the policemen's wives from Wołomin and other nearby places arrived and loaded themselves up with Jewish women's furs and clothes. After these 'privileged' looters it was the turn of the local population, some of whom looted the apartments in an unprecedented manner. Of course most of them were very poor, haggard, starving people who took various items in order to sell them. But others including the wife of a sołtys from the area and the wife of a farmer who owned 40 acres of land were also seen among the looters. The latter arrived with a cart, and when she found nothing of value, she cursed and raved. Then she took an old, worn-out washbowl with her on the cart. The sight of these Poles looting was sickening.

A few Jews managed to escape; a few hid in generous Polish households. In one case a Polish woman denounced a Jewish woman who was being hidden by a Polish family. The Jewish woman was killed on the spot and the Polish family were taken away somewhere.

*News from Rzeszów* (from someone who was in Warsaw in late September this year). In Rzeszów there were about several thousand Jews,[6] and until September of this year it had a (sealed) ghetto.[7] In September the Jews were ordered to pay all of their taxes, not only for the current year (1942), but also in advance for 1943. Then the liquidation of the Jews began.[8] Some of them (a few thousand) were led to a square in Rzeszów, and the (completely drunk) Gestapo men herded them towards the railway station, which is in the city centre. Anyone who so much as stumbled or did not run fast enough was shot. The street was littered with corpses. This procession passed through the German district of the city and aroused protests and signs of indignation even among the Germans. A delegation even visited the Landrat[9] on account of this matter. The remaining Jews were

6 The original uses a vague formulation that suggests a number between 11,000 and 15,000. According to various sources, 12,000–15,000 Jews lived in Rzeszów prior to Sept. 1939.

7 The ghetto was fenced in with barbed wire in Dec. 1941; at the outset 12,500 people lived in the ghetto.

8 The deportations to Belzec took place between 7 July and 7 August 1942. Between 10,000 and 12,000 Jews had previously been expelled to Rzeszów from the surrounding localities. Approximately 20,000 ghetto inhabitants were murdered.

9 German in the original. This refers to the Kreishauptmann, Dr Heinz Ehaus (1906–1945).

removed in a completely different way, with truly unparalleled sadism: the sick were put on carts and driven along streets that had been specially cleaned beforehand. This procession was led by the Landrat himself, who kept calling, 'slower, slower' (thus demonstrating his 'humanity'). A plane flew over this procession and took photographs. The Jews were loaded into the railway wagons most elegantly and taken to … Bełżec. A small number of craftsmen were left behind.

The Polish population's reaction was downright hostile towards the Germans: almost everyone was outraged – regardless of their views.

News from *Bereza Kartuska* (from a person who came directly from there).
The Jews here resisted the Germans when they began to liquidate the ghetto. They put up armed resistance for a few hours, after which some of them joined the Soviet partisans in the woods. This was in September of this year.[10]

## DOC. 185

## In early December 1942 police officers in Radom report Jews being arrested and shot[1]

Report by Radom Reserve Urban Police Oberwachtmeister Baumann[2] (precinct station, log no. 756/42), Radom, dated 1 December 1942; report by Urban Police Revier-Oberwachtmeister Jaensch,[3] Radom, dated 3 December 1942

*Report*
*Re*: Jews encountered without an escort, armbands, or identity documents in Nowa-Wola-Golembiowska[4]
Around 2.15 p.m. on 1 December 1942, the Jews Zimuch *Hofman*, aged 45, and Schmerek *Wertman*, aged 26, both formerly resident in Magnussew,[5] were handed over to the precinct station by Woycech[6] *Duda*, a Pole, b. 7 April 1897, resident in Wolwa-Wola-Golembiowska.[7] The two Jews were roaming around the aforementioned village without an escort, armbands, or identity documents.

The Jews were taken to Polish Police Station 1.

10 When the ghetto was sealed on 15 Oct. 1942, the ghetto inhabitants set fire to their belongings, machinery, and tools; the majority of the Jewish Council members took their own lives. Young people had prepared for armed resistance under the leadership of individuals named as Mojsze Tuchman, Bekler, and Apelbojm, and they called for ghetto inhabitants to flee into the forests. During the extermination operation, Tuchman escaped along with other young people, and they joined the Soviet partisans.

1 AIPN, GK 675/1 (CA MSW 372/1), fol. 484r–v. This document has been translated from German.
2 Erich Baumann was an Oberwachtmeister with the reserve Urban Police in Radom from Nov. 1941.
3 Correctly: Willy Jentsch (b. 1894), police officer; Hauptwachtmeister in the Urban Police; served on the Urban Police force in Radom, Nov. 1942 – Jan. 1945; lived in Wilhelmshaven after the war.
4 Correctly: Nowa Wola Gołębiowska, today part of the city of Radom.
5 Correctly: Magnuszew, a village in Kreis Kozienice, 60 km south-east of Warsaw.
6 Correctly: Wojciech.
7 Correctly: Nowa Wola Gołębiowska.

*Report*
*Re*: shooting of Jews
*Concerning*: Order of the SS and Police Leader in Radom of 3 September 1942, and Order of the Commander of the Order Police in District Radom – 15 28/– no. 486/42 (s[ecret]), of 4 September 1942.[8]

The Jews Zimuch *Hofman*, aged 45, and Cmerek *Wertman*, aged 26, were shot dead today because they were present outside the ghetto without an escort, identity papers or armbands.

They were buried on the spot.

## DOC. 186

## On 3 December 1942 Henryk Woliński summarizes talks with representatives of the Jewish Combat Organization about preparations for armed resistance[1]

Report, signed Wacław,[2] Warsaw, dated 3 December 1942[3]

On 2 December 1942 I contacted Mikołaj,[4] representative of the Bund, and Jurek,[5] representative of the Jewish National Committee (ŻKN). During the meeting Jurek gave me the enclosed statute of the Coordinating Committee[6] and the Combat Organization, which represent all the Jews in Warsaw. The statute was adopted in the ghetto by the Coordinating Committee on the night of 1 to 2 December 1942. All previous doubts raised by Mikołaj about the ŻKN's authority to represent the Jews with respect to the Polish authorities were cleared up, and since then both representatives of the Jews, Mikołaj and Jurek, have been jointly representing the Coordinating Committee according to the powers specified in the statute.

On the initiative of the ŻKN, organizational work among Jews in the countryside is still being carried out.

Both representatives of the Coordinating Committee (Jurek and Mikołaj) stressed the need to immediately supply the Jewish Combat Organization with weapons, as they have no doubt that the operation to liquidate the Jews in Warsaw is by no means finished and may start again at any moment (lately there have been large-scale shootings in the streets and in the szopy). The liquidation of various szopy and the recent complete separation of the Többens szopy from the remainder of the ghetto show that the extermination operation is essentially continuing unabated. The assumption that this operation will intensify is based on the fact that there are a large number of beggars. (The work in the

8 These orders have not been found.

1 AAN, 1325/202/XV-2, fols. 81–83. This document has been translated from Polish.
2 Code name of Henryk Woliński.
3 Handwritten note above the document: 'Return'.
4 Code name of Leon Feiner.
5 Code name of Izrael Chaim (Arie) Wilner (1917–1943), member of the Hashomer Hatzair youth organization prior to 1939; escaped to Vilna in Sept. 1939; returned to Warsaw in 1941; co-founded the Jewish Combat Organization (ŻOB) on 28 July 1942; arrested on the 'Aryan side' in March 1943 freed from a concentration camp with Polish assistance; among the leaders of the Warsaw Ghetto Uprising who took their own lives in the besieged bunker on 8 May 1943.
6 The Jewish Coordinating Committee.

szopy is unpaid, and only 10–20 decagrams[7] of bread and soup are supplied to keep workers alive; so anyone who has nothing left to sell 'disappears' from the szopy for a few hours and goes begging.)

In view of these circumstances, Mikołaj and Jurek are asking for:
1) a larger quantity of weapons, as the ten pieces they have received are not enough to organize armed resistance or any other collective, as opposed to individual, action;
2) the possibility to purchase weapons; for their part, they will look into the possibility of mobilizing the funds for this (my opinion on this: to enable monitoring, it should be us that carries out the purchasing);
3) training and instructors. Some members of the combat groups received their training during their Polish military service before the war. There is a shortage of instructors, because those with the appropriate qualifications hold various positions in the police[8] and the Combat Organization does not trust them.

Regarding point 1, I would like the delivery of weapons to amount to at least the 'dozens' of pieces that have been already mentioned several times.

Please make your decisions swiftly.

*Enclosed: Statute*

In order to defend the Jewish population of Warsaw against the occupier's extermination campaign and to protect them from traitors and agents who collaborate with the occupier, a Coordinating Committee is hereby established, consisting of the Bund and the Jewish National Committee, and the following constituent parties of the National Committee: the Zionist Organization, Poale Zion-Right, Poale Zion-Left, Revisionist Party, Hehalutz, Hashomer Hatzair, and Dror.

The work of the Coordinating Committee is based on the following statutes:

*Coordinating Committee*
1) On the basis of an agreement reached between the Jewish National Committee and the Bund, a Coordinating Committee shall be formed in Warsaw.
2) The purpose of the Coordinating Committee is to:
   a. organize the ghetto's defence in the event of a further resettlement operation,
   b. protect the Jewish masses against the occupier's collaborators and stooges.
3) The Coordinating Committee shall establish the Combat Organization, determine the guidelines for its activity, and control it.[9]

7 100–200 grams.
8 The Jewish Order Service.
9 The Jewish Combat Organization (ŻOB) was established in the Warsaw ghetto in July 1942. The reference here is to an aspiration for a united Jewish armed resistance organization including members of important factions from all across the political spectrum (e.g. left-wing Zionists, the Bund, and right-wing revisionists). Conflicts between the revisionists and ŻOB leaders ultimately could not be resolved. As a result, two armed resistance groups – the ŻOB and the Jewish Military Union (ŻZW) – coexisted in early 1943.

4) The Coordinating Committee shall be composed of a duly authorized representative of each political party.

*Combat Organization*

*I. Composition*

1) The basic unit is a combat unit composed of six people (hereinafter: 'group of six'), commanded by a leader.
2) The 'groups of six' shall be organized according to szopy. At the head of each szop is the command, composed of a commander and two deputies.
3) At the head of the Combat Organization is the commander-in-chief and a five-man High Command.
4) The 'groups of six' shall be formed according to organizational affiliation. Where this is not possible, mixed 'groups of six' shall be formed, and persons not belonging to any organization will also be admitted to such groups as the operation develops.
5) The selection of leaders shall be based solely on the candidates' qualifications.

*II. Weaponry*

1) The following are recognized as weapons: firearms, axes, knives, knuckle rings, corrosive substances, combustibles, and others.
2) Each member of a 'group of six' shall be armed.
3) Each site[10] shall be equipped with weapons and the resources required for a comprehensive operation.

*III. General guidelines governing combat operations*

1) Resistance against any further resettlement operation will be conducted under the motto: 'We shall not give up a single Jew'.
2) Acts of terror will be carried out against the Jewish police, the Jewish Community,[11] and the Werkschutz.[12]
3) Active combat will be carried out against the leaders of the szopy, against group leaders, and overt and covert Gestapo officers in order to protect the Jewish masses.

*IV. Immediate tasks*

1) Formation of 'groups of six' and selection of leaders.
2) Arming the 'groups of six' and szopy.
3) Obtaining funds.
4) The commands of the szopy will:
   a. prepare an accurate plan of the site (storerooms, financial office, Werkschutz, management),
   b. draw up a list of harmful elements,
   c. produce a precise plan of action on the site of the respective szop.
5) The High Command shall prepare a plan for the central sabotage and terror campaign.
6) Propaganda for resistance among society.

10 The ŻOB subdivided the ghetto into various sectors.
11 This is a reference to the Jewish Council and its employees.
12 German here and below in the original: 'factory security'.

*Nomenclature*

1) The Combat Organization shall bear the name: Jewish Combat Organization.
2) To maintain close contact between both bodies, i.e. between the Combat Organization and the Coordinating Committee, the commander of the Combat Organization[13] shall attend Coordinating Committee meetings.

The Coordinating Committee shall be represented vis-à-vis the [Polish] military authorities by a member of the Jewish National Committee with the pseudonym Jurek and by a member of the Bund with the pseudonym Mikołaj.

## DOC. 187
## *Wiadomości*, early December 1942: report on the deportations to Treblinka and the threat to the rest of the Warsaw ghetto[1]

22 November – 5 December 1942. ARG.[2]

Contrary to circulating rumours that the liquidation in Treblinka has come to an end, it must be strongly emphasized that the killing in Treblinka is in fact continuing at full speed. Entire transports of Jews from eastern Małopolska,[3] and most recently apparently also from Romania,[4] continue to fill the graves of our brothers in Treblinka.

*Terror in the Warsaw ghetto.* The last days of November this year were marked by an intensified campaign of terror in the Warsaw ghetto. On 25 November, 26 Jews – men and women – were shot on the streets of the ghetto, and 9 [were shot] the next day, on 26 November. The circumstances surrounding the executions indicate that this operation was neither random nor arbitrary on the murderers' part, but was in fact planned by the Umsiedlungsamt.[5] The victims were shot because they had allegedly been out and about in the ghetto during working hours. In Warsaw the Jews are forced to live and work in a climate of constant, unadulterated fear. In early December, too, several people still fall victim to the Nazi murderers' bullets every day.

13 Mordechai Anielewicz (1919–1943), Hashomer Hatzair activist from Warsaw; lived in Vilna for a time in late 1939; editor on the underground publication *Neged Hazerem* and trainer at the kibbutz at 23 Nalewki Street in the Warsaw ghetto, 1941–1942; travelled to the Będzin and Sosnowiec ghettos in mid 1942; commander of the ŻOB from Nov. 1942; commanded a group during the fighting in the Warsaw ghetto on 18 Jan. 1943; involved in the street fighting with the main group of fighters on 19 April 1943, and later with his unit in the bunker at 18 Miła Street, where he took his own life on 8 May 1943 when the Germans stormed the bunker. A Hashomer Hatzair kibbutz in Israel was named after him: Yad Mordechai.

1 *Wiadomości*, no. 2, 22 Nov. – 5 Dec. 1942; AŻIH, Ring II/423 (388). Published in Szymon Datner, '"Wiadomości": Podziemny organ prasowy w getcie warszawskim z okresu po wielkim "wysiedleniu"', *BŻIH*, no. 76 (1970), pp. 49–79, here pp. 54–55. *Wiadomości* was an information bulletin compiled by the contributors to the underground archive of the Warsaw ghetto and issued by the Jewish Coordinating Committee (ŻKK). Five issues were published between 21 Nov. 1942 and 15 Jan. 1943. This document has been translated from Polish.

2 These initials were code for Archiwum Getta ('ghetto archive'), which was a reference to the underground archive of the Warsaw ghetto, also known as the Ringelblum archive.

3 Eastern Galicia.

4 There are no known instances of deportation from Romania to Treblinka.

5 German in the original: 'Resettlement Office'.

*The Killing of Fürst.* On Sunday evening, 29 November, the head of the Jewish Council's Economic Affairs Section in Warsaw, Izrael Fürst, was assassinated. The assassination was politically motivated.

*Resettlement?* The ghetto is in a state of agitation following rumours that a further partial liquidation of Warsaw's Jews is planned for the period of 7 to 15 December. This is said to involve those employed in smaller establishments on the Aryan side and in a few unspecified factories – szopy. It is said that 10,000 of the approximately 40,000 Jews remaining in the ghetto will be transported to Treblinka to their deaths.

*Relocation.* As of 1 December, Jews from the camps in the area around Warsaw are being relocated to the Warsaw ghetto. They have come from the camps at Karczew,[6] Kuflów,[7] Wilanów,[8] and Klimontów,[9] approximately 300 people in total. The camp inmates were subjected to torture and physical torment at their places of work. Starved, emaciated, and haggard, in rags and covered in boils, these new ghetto residents are the epitome of misery and despair.

*A wall around the ghetto.* The wall around the ghetto and the Jewish szopy in the area of the former ghetto is nearly complete. At most, these walled-in factories will become the scene of a race between work and death.

*Domestic news.* News is still coming in concerning the liquidation of Jewish towns in Poland.

On 19 August of this year, 7,000 Jews from Otwock were 'resettled' in Treblinka. An SS officer delivered a speech to the Jews loaded into the wagons for 'resettlement', assuring them that they would be sent to the East, via Warsaw. Over the next few days, 3,000 Jews who had been in hiding were shot. This operation was carried out by the gendarmerie from Rembertów, under the command of Wachtmeister Lüppschau,[10] on the initiative of the Polish mayor of Otwock, Gadomski.[11]

On 20 August the entire Jewish population of Falenica, 8,000 souls, was 'resettled' in Treblinka, leaving only 100 Jewish workers employed by the local sawmill behind. The desperate Jews killed two junacy.

Towards the end of August, the Jewish populations of Mińsk Maz[owiecki], 5,000 souls, and Kałuszyn, 5,000 people, were liquidated. The destination of the 'resettlement' – Treblinka.

6 From July 1941 to August 1942 the Specht construction company in Karczew ran a labour camp on the Jagodzianka river.

7 Correctly: Kuflew, a village in Mrozy municipality, near Mińsk Mazowiecki.

8 There was a labour camp in the Warsaw suburb of Wilanów from April to Dec. 1942. It held approximately 400 Jews from Poland and Germany who were required to undertake forced labour, building roads and dykes. Many perished as a result of epidemics.

9 Correctly: Klimonty, a labour camp east of Siedlce. Approximately 1,000 people were held there in 1942; roughly one fifth of them perished of typhus.

10 Presumably: Lipscher, Leutnant of the gendarmerie in Otwock in March 1943.

11 Jan Gadomski, mayor of Otwock from early 1939 to May 1943.

On 27 September the entire Jewish populations of Kołobiel, 2,000 souls, and Sobin,[12] 6,000 souls, were driven to Piława, where they were loaded into wagons – destination Treblinka. The local Blue Police participated in the operation, using truncheons and rifles.

On 28 September the Jewish population of Parysów, 10,000 souls, was liquidated and transported to Treblinka.

On 30 September the Jewish centre of Żelechów, 14,000 people, was liquidated and transported to Treblinka.

On 5 October the majority of the population of Łuków, 7,000 Jews, was 'resettled' in Treblinka.

In the first few days of December of this year, 900 Jews from Radom were sent to Treblinka (following the last operation, only 4,000 of the former Jewish population of 40,000 remain).

## DOC. 188

## On 5 December 1942 the Higher SS and Police Leader in the General Government asks Himmler to intervene personally so that deportations can continue[1]

Telegram (marked 'secret') from the Higher SS and Police Leader East (file ref.: Kr/Fi.1240/42 sec[ret]), signed SS-Obergruppenführer and Police General Krüger, Cracow, to Reichsführer-SS and Chief of the German Police Himmler, Hochwald,[2] dated 5 December 1942[3]

SS and police leaders have reported to me unanimously today that the transport shutdown[4] will preclude all transport options for the resettlement of Jews from 15 December 1942 until at least 15 January 1943.

This measure is putting the overall plans for resettling Jews in extreme jeopardy. I beg you most respectfully to conduct negotiations with the central Reich offices of the Wehrmacht High Command and the Reich Ministry of Transport to ensure that at least three trains running to their destination and back are made available for this top-priority task.

The transport of any and all consignments of textiles, clothing, etc. requested by Wehrmacht authorities is also impossible.

Since yesterday I have had a request from the Reich Minister of Aviation[5] for the urgent delivery of complete sets of equipment for aid organizations.

12 Correctly: Kołbiel and Sobienie Jeziory.

1 BArch, NS 19/2655, fol. 70. Published in Longerich and Pohl (eds.), *Die Ermordung der europäischen Juden*, pp. 221–222. This document has been translated from German.

2 Himmler's field command post near the village of Possessern (renamed Großgarten in 1938, known in Polish as Pozezdrze) in Kreis Angerburg, East Prussia.

3 The original contains the stamps 'Reichsführer-SS's personal staff', 'Records management', 'File no.', and 'Secret'; it also contains two illegible stamps, as well as handwritten annotations.

4 The transport shutdown was likely connected with the encirclement of the Sixth Army in the vicinity of Stalingrad.

5 Hermann Göring.

## DOC. 189

## On 9 December 1942 Governor General Hans Frank expresses cautious criticism of the murder of Jewish forced labourers[1]

Address given by Governor General Frank to the members of the GG government, the district governors, and the Kreis- and Stadthauptleute at the government meeting in Cracow on 9 December 1942

[…][2] I would also like to make an impassioned appeal from this standpoint to the Kreishauptleute, to whom I have now essentially delegated labour recruitment at the governors' request: empty for me those villages where the people are sitting idle! Try to rustle up workers wherever possible! Out of a population of more than 14 million, we can find again the same number of workers we have already.[3] I have high expectations of your resourcefulness and ask you not to use ambiguous points in economic plans as excuses. You are clearly instructed to bring in workers wherever possible.

We have had workers in our long-standing Jewish communities who are not unimportant taken from us. It is clear that operations are made more difficult if, in the midst of this wartime labour programme, the order is given that all Jews are to be exterminated. The responsibility for this does not lie with the government of the GG. The order to exterminate the Jews has come from a higher authority. We simply have to deal with the ramifications to the best of our ability and can only inform the Reich authorities that the decision to take away the Jews has caused immense difficulties in terms of labour. I was recently able to demonstrate to State Secretary Ganzenmüller, who had complained that a major construction project in the General Government had ground to a halt, that this would not have happened if the many thousands of Jews put to work there had not been hauled off.[4] Now the order is that the Jews are to be taken out of armaments [production].[5] I hope this order will be rescinded, if that has not already occurred; otherwise the situation will look even worse.

You have already stated in your reports that some of the methods used to recruit labourers must be condemned. It is impossible to achieve satisfactory results with such methods. Having cinemas surrounded and bundling the men off in sealed wagons are not actions that strengthen our Reich's authority. Chatter about constant violence and brutal-

1 AIPN, GK 95, vol. 24. Copy in IfZ-Archives, Fb 105, vol. 26, fols. 6251–6304, here fols. 6282–6283. Published in Werner Präg and Wolfgang Jacobmeyer (eds.), *Das Diensttagebuch des deutschen Generalgouverneurs in Polen 1939–1945* (Stuttgart: DVA, 1975), p. 588. This document has been translated from German.

2 Frank's 'end-of-year address' was 47 pages long. He first talked about the creation of the General Government in 1939 and its development into a *Nebenland* of the Reich (a sort of colonial borderland) in 1940, as well as how its function as a link between Germany and the 'East' (*Ostraum*) was necessary for a global German empire. He then discussed how the General Government and its population had contributed to the German war economy.

3 Frank had previously stated that 960,000 workers had been sent from the General Government to the Reich since Dec. 1939, and that almost 1.5 million Polish prisoners of war were also working there: Präg and Jacobmeyer (eds.), *Das Diensttagebuch des deutschen Generalgouverneurs*, p. 587.

4 The complaint cited by Frank is not included in the minutes of his meeting with Ganzenmüller on 25 Nov. 1942: IfZ-Archives, Fb 105, vol. 26, fols. 6196–6201.

5 See the teletype message from Wehrmacht High Command to Military District Commander in the General Government Siegfried Haenicke (1878–1946): BArch, NS 19/1766, fol. 1.

ity will soon cease. This is a key talking point impressed upon us in the Reich, the impossibility of which becomes evident, however, if you think of our Kreishauptleute with perhaps thirty gendarmes and ten Sonderdienst men to cover a territory of 3,000 square kilometres. He [the Kreishauptmann] has to find sound footing so he can get to grips with his population.

[…][6]

## DOC. 190

## On 15 December 1942 the Reich Commissioner for the Strengthening of Germandom decides on the use of Jewish immovable property in the General Government[1]

Directive (marked 'secret') of the Reich Commissioner for the Strengthening of Germandom (0-6/10/19.9.42, log no. 38/42 g), signed Himmler, Field Command Post,[2] dated 15 December 1942

*General Directive no. 18/C*

of the Reichsführer-SS and Chief of the German Police, Reich Commissioner for the Strengthening of Germandom, concerning the treatment of Jewish property in the General Government

Based on the Decree of the Führer and Reich Chancellor on the Strengthening of Germandom of 7 October 1939,[3] and on the powers vested in me as Chief of the German Police, I hereby decree the following:

1. All immovable property of Jews in the General Government is to be made available for use with immediate effect for purposes of strengthening Germandom (in particular for accommodating resettlers and other preferential applicants).[4] The property shall be turned to account for the benefit of the General Government exclusively by the Higher SS and Police Leader in the General Government, State Secretary for Security,[5] as my representative in my capacity as Reich Commissioner for the Strengthening of Germandom.

6 Frank went on to describe the deteriorating food supply and the situation facing the ethnic Germans and Reich Germans in the General Government. He also argued for a more flexible policy towards the Poles in order to gain their loyalty. He paid tribute to the work of the Polish Baudienst ('Construction Service'), a paramilitary organization for Polish youth.

1 IfZ-Archives, Nürnberg Dokument NO-1943; also AIPN, GK 196/332 (NTN 332), fols. 215–216 (copy). Published in Berenstein et al. (eds.), *Faschismus – Getto – Massenmord*, p. 411. This document has been translated from German.

2 On 15 Dec. 1942 Himmler met with Ulrich Greifelt, chief of staff at the Office of the Reich Commissioner for the Strengthening of Germandom, in Friedrichsruh manor at his field command post Hochwald, near the village of Possessern in Kreis Angerburg, East Prussia.

3 With this decree Hitler gave Himmler responsibility for settlement projects undertaken in pursuit of racial policy goals: see PMJ 3/18.

4 In March 1942 the General Government administration still intended to take over what was regarded as ownerless real estate and real estate confiscated from Jewish owners, and to transfer such property to a centralized property company: 'Lagebericht des Gouverneurs im Distrikt Warschau für März 1942', in *Raporty Fischera*, ed. Dunin-Wąsowicz, p. 497.

5 Friedrich-Wilhelm Krüger.

2. The offices and persons hitherto appointed to administer [Jewish assets] shall continue to administer [such property] under the supervision, and in accordance with the instructions, of my representative, unless he stipulates otherwise in individual cases.
3. Immovable property within the meaning of Item 1 above includes urban and rural residential properties and landholdings of any kind, as well as going commercial enterprises with all the associated facilities, stock, shares, holdings, rights, and interests of any kind.
4. My representative in the General Government is authorized to take all measures and issue all directives necessary for the performance of this task.[6]

## DOC. 191

## On 15 December 1942 the Kreishauptmann of Grojec (Grójec) threatens Jews who escape from the ghetto, and those who aid them, with the death penalty[1]

*Activities in support of Jews in District Warsaw*

Six Jewish residential districts have been established in District Warsaw by the Police Regulation of 28 October 1942 on the Establishment of Jewish Residential Districts in District Warsaw and District Lublin (*Verordnungsblatt für das Generalgouvernement*, p. 665).[2]

The Jews of Kreis Grojec must be placed in the city of Warsaw's Jewish residential district (ghetto) by 30 November 1942. From 1 December 1942 no Jew in District Warsaw may be present outside a Jewish residential district or leave a Jewish residential district without a police permit. Other persons may only enter or be present in a Jewish residential district with a police permit.

Jews who contravene the provisions outlined above shall be punished by death, in accordance with the current regulations.[3] Any person who knowingly provides shelter to such a Jew, i.e. specifically houses, feeds, or conceals a Jew outside the Jewish residential district, shall also be punished.[4]

Security Police measures (e.g. internment in a concentration camp) shall be taken against any person who becomes aware that a Jew is present outside a Jewish residential district without authorization and fails to report this to the police.

Non-Jews who enter a Jewish residential district without a police permit shall be punished in administrative criminal proceedings with a fine of up to 1,000 zloty, or alternatively with imprisonment for up to three months.

6 On 26 Jan. 1943 Governor General Frank declared Himmler's decree of 15 Dec. 1942 null and void; only in 1944 did Frank and Himmler agree on the exploitation of the real estate and the use of Jewish movable property: see Doc. 282.

1 *Amtliches Mitteilungsblatt des Kreishauptmanns von Grojec*, no. 4, 15 Dec. 1942, p. 39, [no.] 51; Biblioteka Narodowa, P. 77 180 A. This document has been translated from German.

2 See Doc. 168.

3 See Doc. 13.

4 Announcement by the SS and Police Leader in Warsaw, von Sammern-Frankenegg, 5 Sept. 1942: APW, 204/290.

The gendarmerie and the police, as well as the mayors and wójts,[5] are hereby instructed to pay special attention to compliance with the preceding police order, which has been announced on public notices in the Kreis.

## DOC. 192

## *Informacja Bieżąca*, 17 December 1942: report on the deportations from Częstochowa, the role of the Polish police, and a mass shooting in Miechów[1]

*Jewish matters*

*Warsaw.* The area partly inhabited by Jews between the sections of the ghetto was thoroughly cleansed last week, between 14 and 21 November. During this SS operation, in which all the belongings that the Jews had left behind were collected, 400 men from the Urban Police cleared the apartment blocks of their remaining inhabitants.[2]

Several dozen German police officers, armed with truncheons, hatchets, and crowbars, meticulously search[3] building after building; those that have been searched were marked with chalk. Urban Police sentries stand guard in front of the buildings that had been searched. During the week of 8–14 November, the Jewish Council's Labour Section issued two notices, according to which all unemployed men and women between the ages of 16 and 60 were required to report to the 'Werterfassung'[4] office.

*Częstochowa.* On the night of 23 to 24 September, early in the morning, the liquidation of the Częstochowa ghetto began. An Urban Police unit, a Russian unit,[5] and 80 Polish policemen took part in the operation. SS units were also deployed on other days. Approximately 5,000 people were deported every day. All in all, 33,280 people were deported within seven days, 600[6] were beaten to death or shot to death, and 100 people died [in another way]. At present there are approximately 4,500 Jewish men and women left in the Częstochowa ghetto. In some cases Jews were taken out of the ghetto in official German vehicles after paying a mind-boggling sum. Almost the entire Jewish intelligentsia, mainly lawyers, were deported; on the other hand, almost all the doctors remained behind. The Jewish Council has been reduced to fifteen people; the remaining members have been taken away and shot.

*Kozienice.*[7] The German police are hunting down Jews in hiding. Twelve people have been shot dead.

5 Polish in the original.

1 *Informacja Bieżąca*, no. 47 (71), 17 Dec. 1942, pp. 4–5; AAN, 1325/202/III-7/1, fols. 186–187. This document has been translated from Polish.

2 This is a reference to the streets from which the ghetto inhabitants had been deported in summer 1942, and which were now to be reincorporated into the rest of the city. There were still a few Jews hiding there who had hoped to escape to the 'Aryan side' in this way.

3 Change in tense as in the original.

4 German in the original: 'asset registration'.

5 This is a reference to non-German auxiliary personnel from the SS training camp in Trawniki.

6 Corrected in the original from 6,000.

7 A small town in the north-eastern part of District Radom.

*Zawichost*. The Jews here were deported in November. Approximately 6,000 Jews were resettled. Zawichost is an assembly point for [Jews from] the surrounding area and from smaller towns.[8]

*Lublin area*. In October the entire Jewish population was resettled from Annopol and Ćmielów. In both of these small towns, the Jews were employed in the chemical industry, but they were shipped to Treblinka nonetheless.

*Blue Police and firemen at the executioners' service*. In powiat Łuków, with significant assistance from the Blue Police, the Germans nabbed Jews in hiding. In some places in the Lublin region, including powiat Kraśnik, the Germans used the fire brigade to capture groups of Jews in the forests. The majority of the firemen accepted this task without protest.

*Miechów*. During an execution of the Jews on 18 November, one gendarme refused to shoot children. Mayor Schmidt drove to the execution site and personally carried out the execution.[9] When it was the turn of the children standing next to their father, the latter threw himself on the mayor and cut his throat with a penknife. The mayor died.[10] There were no reprisals.

*In the areas around Grodno and Białystok*, they have been murdering Jews since 1 November. The execution site is Czerwony Bór.

*Brześć*. They have been liquidating the Jews since 15 October. Approximately 12,000 people have been shot dead in the first three days. The execution site is Bronna Góra. The last ones who are in hiding are currently being liquidated. A mobile SD task force and the local police organized the liquidation. At present it is only the local police, *a high percentage of whom are Poles*, who are engaged in 'finishing the job'. *They often demonstrate greater zeal than the Germans*. Some of the Jews' belongings are used to furnish German apartments and offices, and some have been auctioned off. Although large quantities of weapons were found during the liquidation, the Jews remained passive.

*Mir*. On 13 August all the Jews were shot dead, with the exception of 150 who managed to escape. They are currently being tracked down and shot.

*Bezirk Zichenau*. During the period of 8–14 November, the Jews from Płońsk, Mława, and Ciechanów,[11] the only places in the Pomerania voivodeship that still had a Jewish population, were brought here.[12]

8 On 29 Oct. 1942 approximately 5,000 people were deported from the small town of Zawichost in the south-eastern part of District Radom to Belzec. Zawichost was not one of the towns where Jews were allowed to stay until further notice under the terms of the Police Regulation of 10 Nov. 1942: see Doc. 168.

9 Several hundred Jews from the Miechów ghetto were shot in the forest near the village of Zagorzyce.

10 In fact, he was merely injured: Dr Friedrich Schmidt (1901–1977), economist and lawyer; joined the NSDAP in 1931; became Stadtkommissar in Borek Fałęcki in 1939; Stadtkommissar in Neu Sandez, 1940–1941; appointed deputy Kreishauptmann of Dembitza in early 1942; deputy Kreishauptmann of Miechów from August 1942; Stadthauptmann of Tschenstochau from March 1943; thereafter served in the war; worked as a night watchman in Schleswig in 1945; practised law from 1950.

11 The context suggests that the Jews from Płońsk, Mława, and Ciechanów were in fact not brought into but taken out of this Bezirk, because Płońsk, Mława, and Ciechanów were towns in Bezirk Zichenau. The last transports from these ghettos went to Auschwitz.

12 These three towns were not in fact located in the Pomerania voivodeship, but in the Warsaw voivodeship.

## DOC. 193

## In autumn 1942 members of the Jewish Pioneer Youth Combat Organization in Cracow vow to fight the Nazis and their allies to the bitter end[1]

Handwritten document, unsigned, Cracow, autumn 1942

Text of the oath taken by the Jewish Pioneer Youth Combat Organization[2]

I hereby join the Jewish Pioneer Youth Combat Organization and agree to participate actively in the struggle.

I swear by all I hold dear, and especially by the honour of Polish Jewry, which is in the process of perishing, that I shall fight the greatest enemy of the Jewish people and of all humanity – the German National Socialists and their allies – with every weapon at my disposal, until my final breath. I pledge to avenge the innocent deaths of millions of Jewish children, mothers, fathers, and the elderly.

At the risk of my own life, I pledge to proudly raise the banner of freedom and of the Jewish spirit in order to secure a bright and independent future for the Jewish people. I pledge to fight for justice in the world and for the right to live in freedom for all those who strive for liberty and who seek to achieve it by standing alongside us in combat.

I swear to serve the cause loyally, to submit to discipline without reservation, and to subordinate all of my personal desires and goals to the common good.

I swear that he who stands arm in arm with me against the enemy shall be a brother to me, and that any traitor who betrays our common ideals will be punished with death.

I swear to persevere until the very end and not to shy away from any challenge, nor even from death.

1 MHK, R. 1135. Published as a facsimile in Yael Peled (Margolin), *Krakov ha-yehudit 1939–1943: Amidah, Mahteret, Ma'avak* (Tel Aviv: Hakibbutz Hame'uhad, 1993), p. 277. This document has been translated from Polish.

2 The Jewish Pioneer Youth Combat Organization in Cracow, also known as Hehalutz Halohem, was founded in summer 1942, when the Cracow branch of the Akiva youth movement – led by Adolf Libeskind, Szymon Draenger (1917–1943), and his wife, Gusta Dawidsohn-Draengerowa (1917?–1943) – merged with a resistance group led by Hersz Bauminger, which was made up of communists and members of the left-wing Zionist organization Hashomer Hatzair. The organization's name was made public only towards the end of the year, although negotiations had already begun earlier, before the start of the deportations to the death camps in June. From autumn 1942 members were engaged in various underground activities, including forging identity cards and papers. From late October that year they also carried out acts of sabotage against the Germans. See also Doc. 265.

## DOC. 194

## On 21 December 1942 the Polish ambassador to the Holy See demands that the Vatican condemn the crimes committed by the Germans in Poland[1]

Memorandum (marked 'top secret') by the Polish ambassador to the Vatican,[2] signed K. Papée, for the Polish government in exile in London, dated 21 December 1942

Upon submitting the note about the persecution of the Jews in Poland (see enclosure),[3] I expressed my conviction that the Holy See would clearly condemn these and other German crimes which, in their magnitude and extent, surpass anything known to history.

Monsignor Tardini[4] replied that one should at the same time condemn the Soviet atrocities committed against the Poles.

In my response, I made it clear that I personally would have nothing against matters being presented in this way. The most important thing is a condemnation in itself, [one that is] public and unequivocal.[5] I indicated that we have been waiting a long time for it. I also noted that one might even question whether our presence – that is, the presence of diplomats from the non-Axis countries – in the Vatican has any use at all, whether it is becoming redundant, to say nothing of the violation of our status by Italy. It may be recalled that our notes are ever more frequently remaining unanswered (admittedly these are not formal responses[6]), and there have been rumours lately that the courier service between our governments may be discontinued. And these are matters of fundamental significance for everyone in the embassies here.

Monsignor Tardini replied that he knows nothing of any change to the existing courier service. There are merely certain concerns for the safety of the courier, who crosses occupied France. As for the air connection with Lisbon, he notes that it is very difficult to obtain a seat on the Italian aircraft.

I replied that, in my opinion, the Holy See should not only have seats available on the Italian aircraft, but also have aircraft of its own. I continued that unfortunately, however, this matter once again shows how heavily dependent the Vatican is on the Italian state. One would conclude that not all the problems between the Holy See and Italy have

1 AIP, A.11.122/28. Published in Dariusz Libionka, 'Głową w mur: Interwencje Kazimierza Papée, polskiego ambasadora przy Stolicy Apostolskiej, w sprawie zbrodni niemieckich w Polsce, listopad 1942–styczeń 1943', *Zagłada Żydów*, vol. 2 (2006), pp. 307–308. This document has been translated from Polish.

2 Dr Kazimierz Papée (1889–1979), lawyer; Polish high commissioner for the Free City of Danzig; relocated to Prague as Polish envoy to Czechoslovakia in 1938; Polish ambassador to the Holy See, 1939–1958.

3 In his note (no. 122/SA/283) of 19 Dec. 1942, Papée had written that Poland's entire Jewish population was in danger of death, and more than a million Jews had already been murdered. The note additionally stated that in the Warsaw ghetto, where 400,000 Jews had been living, provisions had been made to issue food coupons to just 40,000 people for Oct. 1942, while the liquidation of the population in other towns and cities was advancing at the same pace.

4 Domenico Tardini (1888–1961), secretary of the Congregation for Extraordinary Ecclesiastical Affairs and deputy secretary of state of Vatican City; cardinal secretary of state, 1958–1961.

5 The last three words of the sentence in the original are in French.

6 The words in brackets in the original are in French.

been solved.[7] Regarding general ecclesiastical affairs, the Vatican must be under constant pressure from the Italian state. That the Holy See has not yet spoken out against so many atrocities committed by the Germans can only be explained by its dependence on Italy. 'We are not free.'[8]

Monsignor Tardini, greatly annoyed, replied that not everything people say is true.

I replied that I was not the only one who had drawn these conclusions and that all this was taking place at a time when the war had already taken a dangerous turn – when the Allies' victory was drawing nearer, when Italy should consider how to salvage from the calamity what was still left to salvage, when Italy needed the Vatican much more than the Vatican needed Italy.

'I am saying all this,' I finished, 'not just in the interests of the country I represent, but also in the interests of the Holy See. And the future will surely prove me right.'

## DOC. 195

## *Wiadomości*, 22 December 1942: report summarizing the conditions in the labour camps and the number of men, women, and children murdered at various locations[1]

ARG.[2] 22 December 1942
*From the Warsaw ghetto*
To supplement the news in *Wiadomości* no. 2,[3] we are providing a list of the liquidated labour camps in District Warsaw. Over the course of the past month, groups of Jews arrived in the ghetto from the liquidated camps in Tarchomin, Kołbiel, Słomczyn near Grójec, Karbów, and Częstoniew. On 10 December, 83 Jewish workers from the disbanded post for agricultural deployment in Czerniaków (a suburb of Warsaw) arrived.[4]

All of these people, still in their prime and until recently full of energy, present a picture of misery and despair. Dishevelled, dressed in rags, in torn shoes or wooden clogs, with sunken cheeks and a vacant look in their eyes, they move through the streets of the deserted urban district, presenting a suitable [...][5] for the city destroyed by pogroms. Quartered in various labour camps, infamous torture sites, they performed a series of public and military jobs that demanded superhuman physical effort, all while enduring starvation and bestial treatment. The practice at Oświęcim – humiliation, the

7 The latter part of this sentence in the original is in French.
8 This sentence in the original is in Italian.

1 *Wiadomości*, no. 3, 22 Dec. 1942, pp. 1–4; AŻIH, Ring II/423 (388/1), fols. 35–38. Published in Datner, '"Wiadomości"', pp. 58–62. This document has been translated from Polish.
2 These initials were code for Archiwum Getta ('ghetto archive'), which was a reference to the underground archive of the Warsaw ghetto, also known as the Ringelblum archive.
3 See Doc. 187.
4 There were labour camps for Polish Jews in the Warsaw suburb of Tarchomin and in Częstoniew, near Grójec. The Kołbiel ghetto south of Mińsk Mazowiecki was liquidated on 27 Nov. 1942, and most of its residents were deported to Treblinka. The construction of an airfield in Słomczyn began in 1940, and a labour camp was constructed there for Jews from the Grójec ghetto. It has not been possible to identify the place referred to as Karbów.
5 One word is missing in the original.

elimination of any positive instincts, branding the workers with the shame of slavery, and the cruel mistreatment of defenceless people at the mercy of the Germans – is typical of almost every labour camp for Jews in Poland. As a way of providing a more detailed description of the camp conditions, we hereby offer a few examples of the Germans' blatant dehumanization.

And so: in mid November, 32 (thirty-two) Jewish workers employed at the Modlin shipyard were tortured to death because they were five minutes late for work. German soldiers (not the SS!) used truncheons to beat to death those guilty of this 'crime'. It is enough to say that within less than an hour, the bodies of these 32 'criminals', beaten to a pulp, lay in pools of their own blood at the execution site: arms and legs severed from their bodies, faces frozen in horror and agony before death, sunken eye sockets, covered in blood and bits of brain matter, intestines kicked out – and all this in full view of all the Jewish camp inmates and the German personnel, who were clearly satisfied with the deed.

In Siedlce there was an incident that can only truly be understood by people familiar with the 'ways of the Herrenvolk'.[6] The German construction company Reckmann, which 'normally' liquidated on a daily basis those Jews who were no longer fit for work, allowed itself the following novelty: in one of the newly constructed buildings, three Jewish workers were buried alive behind concrete walls. The screams of the suffocating victims made the torturers break into a veritable frenzy of joy. We stress that this deed was perpetrated by German civilians (so neither the SS nor the Wehrmacht).

The third incident took place in the camp in Karczew: the notorious gendarmerie commandant in Rembertów, Lüppschau,[7] executed one of the Jewish camp inmates. What is significant about this case is not the fact that a Jewish worker was murdered, but rather the accompanying circumstances. Before the execution the henchman delivered a speech full of hatred for the Jews. The accused victim had to undress on his own and stand in a way that was comfortable for the executioner. All the Jewish workers had to assist in carrying out the execution, whereupon they had to march around the corpse of the murdered man and spit on it. During this spectacle Lüppschau stood with one foot on his victim's battered head.

Fresh human wrecks arrive in Warsaw every day – the Jewish labour force at the service of the bloodiest murderers of all time – the 'victorious' German army.

Jews caught on the Aryan side of Warsaw are 'resettled' to the ghetto almost daily. Hence, on 6 December approximately 200 of these 'criminals' were taken to the 'Befehlsstelle'[8] at 103 Żelazna Street (the SS headquarters for the Warsaw ghetto), and subsequently delivered to the Jewish residential district. On 12 December, 36 Jews were delivered to the ghetto. The settlement operation is under way.[9] Police agents continue to catch Jews or persons of Jewish descent outside the ghetto. Under the threat of being shot immediately, they are forced to leave their homes and are then herded into the ghetto without clothing or bedding.

6 German in the original: 'master race'.
7 Presumably: Lipscher.
8 German in the original: 'command post'.
9 See Doc. 187.

In contrast to the 'liberal' policy of the SS towards these criminals, we must stress that these practices have taken on truly tragic forms in the outskirts of the so-called General Government. This is especially true in District Cracow, where hunts for 'illegal' Jews in the countryside take place with the use of dogs. The 'prey', mainly women and children, is taken under guard to the nearest town and publicly executed at the local Jewish cemetery. The following incident serves as an example of this German practice. On 5 December of this year, an execution took place at the cemetery in Wolbrom. A group of 29 people, surrounded by members of the Blue Police and a crowd of local gawkers, was led to the cemetery. Each of the condemned had to strip naked and lie down on the hard earth covered in ice and snow. A shot to the head ended the victims' suffering. The executioner was a German gendarme. In this way 29 boys, girls, women, men, and children were killed. The laughter, mockery, insults, and loud swearing of the local rabble accompanied the victims' senseless and tragic deaths. Similar executions also took place in Pilica, Miechów, and a number of other locations. It is worth mentioning that ever since the tragedy of Treblinka was revealed, the German authorities say they will murder every Jew they come across, regardless of age or sex – under the pretext of eliminating future avengers of German crimes.

*Echoes of Fürst's assassination.* During his visit to the chairman of the Jewish Council, Mr Lichtenbaum, to express his condolences over the shooting of Fürst, SS-Oberscharführer Mende expressed his regret at the loss of 'such an excellent employee as Fürst'. Mende said he knew that Poles had committed the murder with the help of Jewish hitmen; of course, he knows the names of the murderers, and the guilty will not escape punishment. The matter died down after that.

*A good deed with the mark of Cain.* According to a directive issued by the German authorities, all sums of money that reach the Warsaw ghetto from abroad – in cases where the addressee is no longer there – are to be paid to their relatives up to the third degree. This procedure exposes German perfidy. On the one hand, the Germans want to maintain the illusion of a supposedly normal life in the ghetto vis-à-vis foreign countries, but on the other hand they admit that the 'resettled' addressees are no longer alive, as otherwise the money would surely be forwarded to their new places of residence.

*German gratitude.* In the early days of December this year, the Germans brought a German soldier who had been severely wounded on the Eastern Front to the Jewish hospital on Gęsia Street. They explained to the physician on duty that the soldier was not German, but Jewish, and therefore he cannot be placed together with German patients. The soldier comes from a godforsaken village in Austria. He is probably of Jewish descent, but he has no connection to Judaism. The soldier was raised a Catholic, and in the Jewish hospital he regrets that there is no Catholic church in the ghetto where he might pray.

*Miscellaneous.* At present there are 240 serving ghetto police officers in the Warsaw ghetto.

In November of this year, nine distribution centres were in operation in the Jewish residential district, serving about 7,000 customers.

In November of this year, 55 wagons arrived via the reloading point (Umschlagplatz[10]) with goods such as potatoes, beets, and peat for various 'Rüstungsbetriebe'.[11]

10 German in the original.

11 German in the original: 'armaments factories'.

In November of this year, 5,094 letters were sent, 387 postcards [went] abroad, and telegrams were not accepted. Some 8,403 letters and 18 telegrams were received.[12]

*Mortality.* In the month of November there were 414 deaths (1.2 per cent of the Jewish population), of which 241 were men and 173 were women. In total, 124 people were shot, of whom 81 were men and 43 were women.

Below we present three tables that clearly illustrate the full extent of the extermination of Warsaw's Jewish population by means of so-called resettlement.

Table I. Breakdown of the population of the Jewish residential district in Warsaw, according to sex and age (as of late October 1942)

| Age group | Male | Female | Ratio of women to men (men = 100) |
|---|---|---|---|
| 0–9 | 255 | 243 | 95.3 |
| 10–19 | 2,183 | 2,263 | 103.7 |
| 20–29 | 3,851 | 4,581 | 119.0 |
| 30–39 | 6,748 | 4,791 | 71.0 |
| 40–49 | 4,319 | 2,564 | 59.4 |
| 50–59 | 2,019 | 948 | 47.0 |
| 60–69 | 353 | 143 | 40.5 |
| 70–79 | 30 | 15 | 50.0 |
| Unknown | 179 | 48 | – |
| Total | 19,937 | 15,696 | 78.7 |
| 15–24 | 3,626 | 4,244 | 117.0[13] |

Table II. Percentage breakdown of the population of the Jewish residential district in Warsaw, according to sex and age (as of late October 1942)

| Age group | Male | Female |
|---|---|---|
| 0–9 | 1.3 | 1.6 |
| 10–19 | 11.1 | 14.5 |
| 20–29 | 19.5 | 29.5 |
| 30–39 | 34.1 | 30.8 |
| 40–49 | 21.9 | 16.5 |
| 50–59 | 16.2 | 6.1 |
| 60–69 | 1.8 | 0.9 |
| 70–79 | 0.1 | 0.1 |
| Total | 100.0 | 100.0 |

12 A week-long 'postal blockade' was imposed on the Warsaw ghetto from 23 July 1942. It was partially loosened thereafter: see Doc. 166. The Jewish post office continued in operation until the Warsaw Ghetto Uprising in April 1943.

13 Final line of this table (15–24 age group) placed as in original.

Table III. Resettlement rate of the population of the Jewish residential district in Warsaw

| Age group | Male population | | | Female population | | |
|---|---|---|---|---|---|---|
| | Late Oct. 1942 | Early 1942 | Resettle-ment rate | Late Oct. 1942 | Early 1942 | Resettle-ment rate |
| 0–9 | 255 | 25,759 | 99.0 | 243 | 25,699 | 99.1 |
| 10–19 | 2,183 | 35,283 | 93.8 | 2,263 | 39,790 | 94.3 |
| 20–29 | 3,851 | 19,747 | 89.3 | 4,581 | 36,041 | 87.3 |
| 30–39 | 6,748 | 29,155 | 76.9 | 4,791 | 40,892 | 88.3 |
| 40–49 | 4,319 | 21,128 | 79.6 | 2,564 | 30,652 | 91.6 |
| 50–59 | 2,019 | 14,758 | 86.3 | 948 | 20,812 | 95.4 |
| 60–69 | 353 | 8,881 | 96.0 | 143 | 12,335 | 98.8 |
| 70–79 | 30 | 2,553 | 98.8 | 15 | 4,361 | 99.7 |
| Over 80 | – | 287 | 100.0 | – | 603 | 100.0 |
| Unknown | 179 | 59 | – | 148 | 107 | – |
| Total | 19,937 | 157,610 | 87.4 | 15,696 | 211,292 | 92.6 |

*Hospital.* The ghetto hospital is becoming completely overcrowded because various labour camps have been liquidated and the workers, many of them sick, have returned to Warsaw.

*Health.* In November of this year, twenty cases of epidemic typhus and forty cases of typhoid fever were recorded. There were ninety-four cases of epidemic typhus in the first half of December. Despite the apparent calm in the Warsaw ghetto at the moment, tension has not subsided, and nerves are still frayed. The Jewish population is being subjected to all kinds of credible and unbelievable rumours, which rob them of their sleep. Everyone clearly feels that the current phase of relative stability is merely temporary. The danger that Warsaw's Jews will be eliminated once and for all has not diminished.

*Domestic news.* Reports from those who managed to save themselves from execution in Treblinka clearly and irrefutably confirm the following: (1) Probably due to the still insufficient technical set-up of the death machinery in Treblinka, the Germans murdered their victims at the start of the so-called resettlement operation in Warsaw and the surrounding area in a simple way: they opened deadly machine-gun fire on the masses of people – men, women, and children – who arrived in Treblinka and everyone was gunned down without exception.[14] The team of gravediggers threw everyone – the bodies of the dead, the seriously or lightly wounded – in previously prepared ditches, where those who were still alive died in inhuman agony. (2) When in August and the following months the 're-settlement operation' intensified to the extent that it exceeded the capacity of Treblinka's steam chambers,[15] the Germans loaded the people from the places included in this operation into wagons that had been strewn with a layer of quicklime and chlorine. Upon arrival at the destination in Treblinka, the corpses – most of them bloated and of a characteristic violet-blue hue – were thrown out of the wagons; everyone had died in horrible agony, suffocated in the death wagons. For these human transports – for example, a group from

14 In fact, the victims were murdered with carbon monoxide in gas chambers.

15 This translation with 'steam' reflects the Polish original; the gas chambers are meant.

Międzyrzec Podlaski, from Kielce – Treblinka was merely a cemetery. From this one can conclude that the Germans were concerned with implementing a premeditated plan punctually and precisely. The methods of mass murder described above were considered helpful when the efficiency of the death machinery in Treblinka failed for one reason or another.

*The desecration of the corpses.* Nor were the corpses removed from the steam chambers in Treblinka spared the 'scientific' methodology of exploitation applied to the Jews condemned to extermination. Before throwing the corpses into the ditches, the Germans examined their dentition and removed all the gold teeth and gold bridges with the aid of dental instruments.[16] The desecration of the corpses is complete and total. According to reliable reports, approximately 500 Poles were executed in Treblinka on 8 September of this year. The executions always took place in the early morning and afternoon hours. All the condemned – men as well as women – were led out to the execution site near the prepared graves and – lined up naked along the ditches – shot with machine guns. The bodies of the victims were blue, probably as a result of torture and beatings.[17]

*Table.* Figures from some of the places in the so-called General Government where the 'resettlement operation' took place in September, October, and November of this year.

| Town/City | No. of Jews prior to 'resettlement' | No. of Jews remaining |
|---|---|---|
| Siedlce | 5,000 | 500 |
| Radom | 30,000 | 2,000 |
| Parczew | 4,000 | – |
| Pilica | 2,700 | 30 |
| Piotrków | 23,000 | 1,500 |
| Opoczno (conc.)[18] | 10,000 | 180 |
| Skarżysko | 4,000 | 200 |
| Opatów | 10,000 | Operation in progress |
| Sandomierz (conc.) | 10,000 | 300 |
| Bodzentyn | 4,000 | – |
| Kielce | 27,000 | 1,580 |
| Suchedniów-Bliżyn | 3,000 | – |
| Częstochowa | 40,000 | 4,500 |
| Tomaszów Maz. | 10,000 | 1,000 |
| Końskie (conc.) | 1,000[19] | 300 |
| Szydłowiec | 4,000 | 150 |
| Ostrowiec (conc.) | 15,000 | Operation in progress |

16 This was carried out by members of a Jewish forced labour detail.

17 No further evidence of this has been found.

18 This abbreviation is used here and below to indicate that Jews from various places had been assembled in a town or a city before the deportation began.

19 Corrected from: '10,000'.

## DOC. 196

## On 25 December 1942 Gestapo chief Heinrich Müller reports that Jewish resistance fighters in Cracow have been shot[1]

Teletype message from the Reich Security Main Office, Office IV, signed SS-Gruppenführer Müller,[2] to SS-Obergruppenführer Wolff, Führer's Headquarters Wolf's Lair,[3] dated 25 December 1942[4]

When a terrorist hideout that had been discovered as a result of the sustained interrogation of the Jew Abraham Leibowicz was raided in Cracow on the evening of 24 December 1942, the Jews found in the hideout – Adolf *Liebeskind*, b. 3 October 1912 in Zabierzow, Kreis Cracow, resident in the Cracow ghetto at 9/18 Limanowskiego, and Juda *Tennenbaum*, b. 16 August 1920 in Cracow, unmarried, resident in the Cracow ghetto at 20/17 Krakusa – were shot dead after a heavy exchange of fire. The hideout was located in the cellar of a building inhabited only by Reich Railway officials. The Jews, who were disguised as Poles with fake identity cards, had been smuggled into the building by the Polish caretaker in exchange for a large payment and kept hidden there in the comfortably furnished hideout. The following items were seized in the hiding place:

1 Mauser pistol, serial no. 182 890, 7.65 mm calibre;
1 FN pistol, orig. serial no. 201 999, 7.65 mm calibre;
1 VIS Polish army pistol, serial no. 19 063, 9 mm calibre;
43 pistol cartridges, 7.65 mm calibre;
radio set;
1 typewriter;
1 duplicating machine, flatbed press, [manufactured by] Greif;
200 dollars;
10,540 zloty;
2 uniforms, each consisting of a cap and a coat, for a Polish police officer and a Reich Railway official, respectively.

1 BArch, NS 19/1813, fols. 1–3. Published as a facsimile in Jochen Kast, Bernd Ziegler, and Peter Zinke (eds.), *Das Tagebuch der Partisanin Justyna: Jüdischer Widerstand in Krakau*, trans. Victor Mika (Berlin: Elefanten Press, 1999), pp. 238–239. This document has been translated from German.

2 Heinrich Müller (1900–1945), aircraft mechanic; employed at Munich police headquarters from 1919; joined the SS in 1934; transferred to the Gestapo Central Office in Berlin; became deputy head of the Political Police Section in the Security Police Main Office in 1936; joined the NSDAP in 1938; director of the Reich Central Office for Jewish Emigration and head of Office IV (Gestapo) in the Reich Security Main Office from 1939; participated in the Wannsee Conference in 1942.

3 Wolfsschanze (Wolf's Lair): code name for one of Hitler's headquarters. Organization Todt began constructing it in a forest near Rastenburg (now Kętrzyn) in East Prussia in 1940. The Wolf's Lair was Hitler's main base from 1941.

4 Two resistance groups – to which members of Akiba, Dror, the Polish Workers' Party, and Hashomer Hatzair belonged – carried out attacks on occupation officials in Cracow from summer 1942. In July 1942 they united to form the Jewish Combat Organization (ŻOB). On 22 Dec. 1942 ŻOB members attacked the Ringkasino restaurant and the packed theatre café (Café Cyganeria), killing or injuring more than 20 Germans. Abraham (Laban) Lejbowicz (1917–1943); member of Dror; arrested on 23 Dec. 1942; shot dead in late April 1943. Adolf (Dolek) Aron Libeskind (1912–1942), law student; part of the Akiba movement's leadership; simultaneously an employee of Jewish Social Self-Help (JSS) in Cracow, 1940–1942. Juda (Idek, Czesiek) Tenenbaum (1920–1942); supported the ŻOB through his contacts with German officials and police officers. The exchange of fire is thought to have taken place on Żuławska Street, where Libeskind lived.

The Polish caretaker and his wife were arrested. Investigations into this matter are being vigorously pursued. I will report any additional developments immediately.

For the purpose of giving a complete account of the Security Police's successful work, I also report that officers from my station managed to catch a local sabotage group off guard on the evening of 21 December 1942. The leader of this sabotage group, the Pole Henryk *Janiszewski*, alias Henryk Psiorz, originally from Litzmannstadt, was arrested after a brisk exchange of fire and fierce resistance. At the time of his arrest, he was in possession of three ready-to-fire pistols and another sixty-five spare cartridges. This arrest prevented an attack with explosives on the Cracow–Lemberg railway line, which this sabotage group had planned to carry out during the night of 22–23 December 1942, some 15 km east of Cracow.

## DOC. 197

## *Neue Zürcher Zeitung*, 28 December 1942: article on the Warsaw ghetto[1]

*The Warsaw ghetto*
*Stockholm*, 28 December 1942 (United Press)

The Swedish newspaper *Dagens Nyheter* has now published detailed reports on the systematic *depopulation* of the Warsaw ghetto, which come from both Jewish and Polish sources.[2] According to these reports, the Warsaw ghetto was established in October 1940, and all Jews had to move to their assigned neighbourhood by 1 November 1940. After 15 November, Jews were no longer allowed to leave the ghetto. Non-Jews still had the right to enter the ghetto without a permit until 23 November, but from that date the ghetto was completely *sealed off*. The whole area around what is known as the 'small ghetto' – the historic Jewish quarter with 40,000 residents – was surrounded by a three-metre-high wall.[3] Official dealings with the non-Jewish part of the city were handled by the so-called Transfer Bureau, a German authority that also arranged the *supply of food* to the ghetto.[4] Since the rations issued to the Jews were far below subsistence level, the ghetto residents were forced to rely on smuggling from the outset, which entailed systematically selling off their belongings. The difference in prices between the ghetto and the rest of Warsaw was immense. A kilogram of bread cost 60–85 zloty in the ghetto, and 8–12 zloty outside the ghetto; a kilogram of sugar cost 400–500 zloty in the ghetto, and 35–70 zloty in the rest of Warsaw; for potatoes

1 *Neue Zürcher Zeitung*, no. 2139, 28 Dec. 1942, evening edition, p. 2. The *Neue Zürcher Zeitung* is a German-language Swiss newspaper founded in 1780. This document has been translated from German.

2 Among other sources the newspaper cites an article published in *Dagens Nyheter* on 21 Dec. 1942. News of the mass murder spread to Stockholm in 1942 via employees of the Warsaw branch of the Swedish company ASEA, who were in contact with the Polish underground.

3 In order to isolate the residents, a wall of this kind was constructed not only around the 'small ghetto', but also around the entire ghetto area. In some cases extant dividing walls were used as part of this structure.

4 See Docs. 4 and 158.

the Jews in the ghetto had to pay 16–30 zloty per kilogram, while non-Jews paid 3–5 zloty on the Warsaw market.

The *mortality rate* in the Warsaw ghetto rose markedly; in 1941 it stood at 13 per cent, whereas in the first six months of 1942 it had already exceeded 15 per cent. The number of births was tantamount to zero. The number of ghetto inhabitants nevertheless remained constant, due to the arrival of deported Jews from elsewhere in Poland, as well as from Germany and Holland.[5] The actual number of inhabitants was approximately 370,000, while the official number was given as 450,000. This difference can be explained by the fact that the 'Jewish Council' – the ghetto's Jewish administrative authorities – deliberately provided false information in order to obtain more food.

On 21 July 1942 the German authorities informed the Jewish Council that the [population of the] Warsaw ghetto was going to be '*resettled*'; the Council was ordered to expel all ghetto inhabitants who were not employed in enterprises working for Germany. The number of Jews to be prepared for deportation each day was initially set at 6,000, later at 7,000. On 23 July, Jewish Council Chairman Czernikow[6] committed suicide shortly after receiving a visit from two uniformed German police officers. It is presumed that they presented him with Himmler's demands during that meeting.[7] In the meantime the resettlement has advanced to the point that only a vanishingly small number of Jews are left in the Warsaw ghetto.[8] The Germans have neither officially announced the resettlement nor given any indication as to the deported Jews' fate.

5 The German authorities concentrated the Jewish population from the towns and villages of District Warsaw in the Warsaw ghetto. As a result the number of ghetto residents rose by several tens of thousands of people: see PMJ 4/236 and 252. From 31 March 1942 the German authorities also deported Jews from the Ruhr region, Westphalia, Hanover and its environs, Magdeburg, Berlin and its environs, and – on 11 July 1942 – from Hamburg to Warsaw. There is no known evidence for deportations from the Netherlands to the Warsaw ghetto.

6 Correctly: Czerniaków.

7 See Doc. 99.

8 Approximately 60,000 people remained until mid Jan. 1943.

## DOC. 198

### On 29 December 1942 a public health officer in Radomsko enquires about guidelines for determining whether abandoned children are of Jewish descent[1]

Letter from the public health officer assigned to the Kreishauptmann of Kreis Radomsko[2] (Dr Ho/Fr., file ref.: I – 8–9/42), signed Dr Hoffmann,[3] Radomsko, to the Governor of District Radom, Interior Administration Department, Public Health, Radom, dated 29 December 1942[4]

During the deportation of the Jews,[5] abandoned children between the ages of a few months and two years were repeatedly found on the street. I have been instructed to examine the children to determine whether they are potentially of Jewish descent. I kindly request guidelines for performing these examinations.[6]

## DOC. 199

### In December 1942 Dovid Briner, aged eighteen, describes his life in the Warsaw ghetto[1]

Handwritten report by a ghetto inhabitant for the underground archive of the Warsaw ghetto, Warsaw, December 1942

*Looters*

Outwardly ragged, worn, wrinkled, and tattered, [but] always on the go – it's a shame to be wasting time that could otherwise be used for *shabreven*,[2] that is, breaking into the abandoned buildings. Here you have a few of these characters.

*Dovid Briner*: a tall, big-boned teenager, with a full face, black eyes, and coal-black hands, wearing an olive-coloured cap, short military boots, and a torn, dirty overcoat. Eighteen years old.

His life story: Before the war his father owned a large carpentry workshop at 11 Skaryszewska Street, which worked for the military. During the bombing of Warsaw the

1 Historical Archive at the Max Planck Institute of Psychiatry, GDA-14. This document has been translated from German.
2 From Dec. 1939 to Jan. 1945 the Kreishauptmann of Radomsko was Kurt Drießen (1906–1974).
3 Presumably Dr Hans Hoffmann (b. 1899), physician; joined the SS in 1933.
4 Stamp (illegible). A carbon copy was sent to the German Society for Racial Hygiene, 2 Kräpelinstraße, Munich.
5 Between 6 and 12 Oct. 1942 approximately 16,000 Jews were deported from Kreis Radomsko to Treblinka and murdered there.
6 In a reply dated 14 Jan. 1943 the physician was informed that his request could not be granted because, 'based on the findings of current scientific research', it was impossible at that time to determine whether children up to two years old were of Jewish descent. Moreover, even if one knew who the parents were, 'a biological heredity examination of children under two years old' had been 'rejected by most experts in the Reich': Historical Archive at the Max Planck Institute of Psychiatry, GDA-14.

1 AŻIH, Ring II/242 (170), fol. 2–3. This document has been translated from Yiddish.
2 'Shabreven' (also 'shabern'): term used in the parlance of the Warsaw ghetto for taking or stealing abandoned property.

workshop burned down, so he found work at two other workshops instead: one at 7 Miła Street, manufacturing toothbrushes, where the young Dovid worked with another four labourers, and the other at 19 Smocza Street. During the deportation Dovid left for a worksite[3] in Okęcie.[4] When he came back two weeks later, his mother was no longer there. For three days he sat and wept. After the third day he went back to the worksite and returned five weeks later to find no one left from his family (five sisters, four brothers-in-law, three cousins, a brother, and his father). They were all taken during the selection on Miła Street.[5] With no money and no family, he began going to a worksite in Praga every day,[6] where he made a bit of money, 4,000–5,000 złoty. He invested his talents in becoming a master at finding for himself the best food, and above all drink: a bottle, or at least half of one, every day. After the period of his work assignment had ended, he began looting, along with another crony (called Malina,[7] the son of a rich [but] simple dairy owner).

He now describes his new profession: We chose the area between Pawia and Dzielna Streets as our territory. Why this area in particular? Because it is too dangerous on Leszno, Solna, and Orla. Too many Germans wandering around there, but it's relatively quiet here. Every day the two of us walk around and search all the nooks and crannies. We have developed our own system: first cellars, then attics. Just last week we got hold of a Persian rug (I spotted it) in a cellar at 24 Pawia Street, then a kilim[8] in an attic on the corner of 15 Dzielna Street. After that, window parapets. We know from experience that furs are often hidden there. Yes indeed, we packed two paws[9] in a quilt cover. When we have a successful venture, we stash the loot at a friend's place and head out to eat something. 'Something' means spending up to 1,000–1,500 złoty and drinking three or four bottles of vodka. Imagine the kind of fear we endure, he says. Gendarmes often walk down the street near us while we're working. We [then have to] crawl on all fours, listening to see whether they have noticed us, and then go, run a bit, then hit the ground again, and so on.

Take a look at me and you would think I have always been like this: a looter, a lout. But I was a quiet, respectable boy growing up. What I want to see is revenge. Because whatever happens to me, I cannot forget my five beloved sisters – especially the youngest, Perl, such a tall, beautiful, nice young woman – or my father. Sometimes I long to hear him shout, to see the angry look on his face, and even to receive the blows he often gave me when I botched my work. *Mensch*! (An expression of the Germans.)[10] Is it possible to forget all that? What am I doing? Just eating and drinking. Should I save

3 'Platsuvke' (from Polish: 'placówka') is used here and below in the original text; the term was used in ghetto parlance for the sites where Jewish forced labourers worked beyond the ghetto walls.

4 The Luftwaffe maintained a camp for Jewish forced labourers in Okęcie.

5 The ghetto inhabitants were assembled for about a week from 6 Sept. 1942 in what was known as the 'cauldron' on Miła Street, where approximately 30,000 workers were separated from the remaining Jews, more than 50,000 people, who were deported to Treblinka: see Doc. 131.

6 An urban district of Warsaw east of the Vistula river.

7 Either a surname or a nickname (Polish: 'raspberry'). This was also the term used in ghetto parlance for a hiding place.

8 A kind of handwoven rug or covering also made in Iran and other nearby areas.

9 This is presumably a reference to coats made from the fur of animals' paws.

10 This explanation appears in the original. The German interjection translates as 'man!' or 'damn!'

money? Money is shit. Should I take it with me to Treblinka? Just yesterday my lunch cost 220 złoty (chicken, broth, apples, and a schnaps). I don't think about what tomorrow will bring, and I don't want to know. You ask me if girls interest me. No way! Why do I need the bother? What can a girl give me? Can she be a substitute for my loved ones? Not at all.

Do you know what worries me? That the looting will come to an end. It's been four days already since I last went looting. This past Monday my friend and I suffered a serious setback. A former merchant from Nalewki Street tipped us off that two of his furs were [hidden] on Pawia Street. We had agreed to split the profits three ways. Sure enough, we found the furs in the window parapet, but as we were walking down Pawia with the parcels, two gendarmes came towards us, stopped us, and searched the parcels. As they performed the search, my friend and I fled, putting our lives on the line. Since then we haven't dared to go looting. I am considering maybe finding a different job now and going to the other side on my own. I am even already trying.

When I ask him why he is wearing a soldier's hat and military boots, and not boots with a modern cut, he says: You see, man, this is what's left of my older brother. He served in the Polish army, survived the battle with Bortnowski[11] at Kutno,[12] then defended Warsaw with a light machine gun.[13] They took him during the deportations. If I still have some respect for anything at all, it's for those who picked up weapons, first and foremost for my unforgettable, dearly beloved brother.

## DOC. 200

## In late 1942 Władysław Szlengel writes a poem about Treblinka[1]

*The small Treblinki[2] train station*
On the Tłuszcz–Warsaw route
From Warschau-Ost station,[3]
The train leaves along the track,
And goes straight ahead.
Sometimes the journey takes
Five and three-quarter hours,
But sometimes the journey lasts

11 Władysław Bortnowski (1891–1966), career officer; general in the Polish armed forces; commander of the 'Pomorze' (Pomerelia) army; prisoner of war in Germany, 1939–1945; thereafter emigrated first to Britain, then to the United States.

12 The battle of Kutno (also known as the battle of the Bzura) was the largest battle during the German invasion of Poland. It began during the night of 8 to 9 Sept. 1939 as the result of a Polish counter-attack, and lasted nine days.

13 The original uses the Polish abbreviation: RKM (ręczny karabin maszynowy).

1 AŻIH, Ring II/400 (353/1), fol. 2. Published in Sakowska (ed.), *Archiwum Ringelbluma: Konspiracyjne Archiwum Getta Warszawy*, vol. 1: *Listy o Zagładzie*, pp. 228–229. This poem has been translated from Polish.

2 The extermination camp's name was sometimes rendered incorrectly in Warsaw in 1942.

3 German in the original: 'Warsaw East' (Warszawa Wschodnia), a railway station in the city's Praga district, east of the Vistula.

A lifetime, until death.
The station is tiny;
Three pine trees grow there
And a simple inscription reads:
This is Treblinki station.
There is no refreshment here,
No chocolates or tangerines,
No books or newspapers;
There is nothing – only Treblinki.
Not even a ticket booth,
Not even a porter,
Not even a million will get you
A return ticket.
No one waits at the station,
No one waves a handkerchief;
Only utter silence hangs in the air
A desolate greeting welcomes you.
The signal mast is silent too;
The pine trees stand silent,
The black inscription is silent:
*Treblinki* train station.
Only a rusty old sign from former times
(Surely an advertisement)
Still imparts its message:
Cook with gas.[4]

4 Władysław Szlengel (1914–1943), poet and satirist; graduated from Warsaw Business School in the 1920s; wrote texts including scripts for cabaret performances; became known for his poems about the Warsaw ghetto; thought to have fought with the Jewish Military Union (ŻZW) during the Warsaw Ghetto Uprising; perished in the bunker at 36 Świętojerska Street.

## DOC. 201

## In or around December 1942 rabbis in the Warsaw ghetto compose a prayer for those deported to their deaths in summer 1942[1]

Prayer composed by rabbis in the Warsaw ghetto, Warsaw, late 1942

*Prayer specially composed for the present time*[2]
*This prayer was composed on the basis of a proposal of the Great Sages of Israel*[3] *and should be recited every day by every Jew. Psalms 94, 102, and 142 should be recited before the prayer.*

*Reboyne shel oylem!*[4] Lord of the world! Hear our weeping and the groaning of our hearts, see our pain and sorrow, and give us succour in our great need.

We, the children of Abraham, Isaac, and Jacob, are being hunted down, tormented, and led like sheep to the slaughter. May it be Your will, O G-d,[5] to protect us from all evil, and may You do away with all *evil decrees* against us.

Our nearest and dearest, wives and children, fathers and mothers, brothers and sisters, and all of our other fellow Jews have been taken from us, led into captivity, and no one knows where their bones lie.

May You – *Almighty G-d* – be the guardian of all those led into captivity. Protect them from hardship and pain. Give them the strength to endure and to survive the torments inflicted by the captors. May they live to return safe and sound to their families. And may the little *children*, who have been torn from the bosoms of their *parents*, return to them, as once during the deliverance from Egypt.

I shall give *charity* for hungry people in need and, by virtue of this, may You *protect and help* the person …[6] (people …) – (say the person's name and their mother's name) – who has been taken into captivity and bring him (her/them) back alive and healthy to his (her/their) family.

*Eyl rakhum vekhanun!*[7] You are gracious and merciful to all those who call on You with all their hearts. Have mercy on the remaining survivors of Your people, Israel. Say that we have already suffered enough *sorrows*, and protect us – the small remnant of

1 AŻIH, Ring II/413 (371), fol. 2. Published in Sakowska (ed.), *Archiwum Ringelbluma: Konspiracyjne Archiwum Getta Warszawy*, vol. 1: *Listy o Zagładzie*, pp. 332–333, 378. This document has been translated from Yiddish.

2 In Orthodox Judaism it was customary to use Hebrew to compose special prayers, even though the majority of Jews were not very familiar with this language. The use of Yiddish for this prayer indicates that the aim was for the masses to really understand what they were praying for and to identify with the message.

3 This is presumably a reference to the rabbis in the ghetto.

4 Hebrew in the original: 'Lord of the world'. Repeated in Yiddish immediately afterwards.

5 Spelling here as in the original, in which the middle vowel of the word 'God' has been omitted here and below. This is taken as a sign of respect for the name of God, which observant Jews and Jews who follow Talmudic tradition avoid pronouncing in its form as the Tetragrammaton. It also relates to an interpretation of the commandment in Deuteronomy 12:3–4 that God's name, when written, should not be erased or destroyed.

6 The name of the individual being prayed for was to be inserted here.

7 Hebrew in the original: 'Forgiving and merciful God'. Repeated in Yiddish immediately afterwards.

Jews left – as You protected our father Abraham from the hand of Nimrod; our father Jacob from the hands of Esau and Laban; our teacher Moses from Pharaoh; King David from Goliath, the Philistine; and Hananiah, Mishael, and Azariah from Nebuchadnezzar; as You saved Daniel from the lions' den; and as You saved Mordechai and Esther from the hand of Haman the Evil One, so may You protect Your people Israel from all its enemies and send the Redeemer to deliver us from bitter *exile, soon and in our days. Amen.*

## DOC. 202

## In early January 1943 the Jewish Military Union calls on residents of the Warsaw ghetto to fight the German occupiers[1]

Flyer issued by the Jewish Military Union,[2] Warsaw, early January 1943

*Prepare for action! Be alert!!!*

We rise up to fight!

It is we who have resolved to rouse the people. We want to call on our community:

*Wake up and fight!*

Do not abandon hope of salvation!

Be certain that salvation is not to be found in proceeding meekly to our deaths like a flock of sheep.

It is found in something much greater – *in fighting!*

He who fights for his own life stands a chance of saving himself! He who refrains from self-defence from the outset has lost immediately! All that awaits him is a shameful death in the suffocation machine at Treblinki.[3]

*Wake up, nation, and fight!*

Muster the courage to commit audacious deeds!

Enough of the dishonourably submissive assumption that we are all condemned to death!

*It's not true!!!*

We too are predestined for life! We too are entitled to it!

You only need to know how to fight for it!

There's no virtue in living if life *has been granted to you graciously!* It's a virtue to live when they want to tear your life away.

*Wake up, nation, and fight for your life!*

May every mother become a lioness who defends her cubs!

1 AŻIH, Ring II/426c (333/3), fol. 5. Published as a facsimile in Wroński and Zwolakowa, *Polacy – Żydzi*. p. 163. This document has been translated from Polish.

2 The Jewish Military Union (ŻZW) was formed in 1942 by representatives of the revisionist Zionist youth movement Betar, among them Jews who had formerly served in the Polish army; its headquarters were at 7/9 Muranowska in the Warsaw ghetto. In April 1943 the group participated in the Warsaw Ghetto Uprising under the command of Paweł Frenkel (1920–1943), supplying 200–250 fighters: see Doc. 233. Of the few who managed to escape from the ghetto, most perished before the end of the war.

3 Correctly: Treblinka.

May no father look on calmly as his children perish!
May the shame of the first act of our extermination[4] never be repeated!
Down with resignation and disbelief!
Down with our slave mentality!
May the enemy pay for each Jewish life with his own blood!
May each of our houses become a fortress![5]
*Wake up, nation, and fight!*
Your salvation lies in fighting!
If you fight for your life, you can save yourself.
We rise up on behalf of the fight for the lives of these helpless masses whom we want to save, and whom we must incite to act! It is not just our own lives we want to fight for. We may think of our own salvation only when we have fulfilled our duty!
*As long as the life of just one Jew is in danger, we must be alert and fight!!!*
*This is our call:*
Not a single one more Jew shall die in Treblinki!
Down with the traitors of the nation!
A relentless fight against the occupier to the last drop of our blood!
*Prepare for action!*
*Be alert!!!*

## DOC. 203

## On 8 January 1943 the Higher SS and Police Leader East reports that the gendarmerie has killed a group of Jewish refugees near Wola Michowa[1]

Telegram from the Higher SS and Police Leader East[2] (no. 259, 8.1.43, 19:00 [hours], file ref.: I ab Ke(?)/Kue. – 1345–164/43), signed SS-Sturmbannführer Specht,[3] Cracow, to the command staff of the Reichsführer-SS, SS-Gruppenführer and Waffen-SS Generalleutnant Knoblauch,[4] Hochwald,[5] dated 8 January 1943[6]

Re: elimination of bandits
Concerning: report from the Senior Commander of the Security Police and the SD, dated 5 January 1943[7]

4 This is a reference to the deportations from the Warsaw ghetto between 22 July and 21 Sept. 1942.
5 This is possibly a reference to a line – 'May every house's threshold be our fortress!' – in the poem 'Rota' ('The Oath') by Maria Konopnicka (1842–1910), which was set to music by Feliks Nowowiejski (1877–1946) in Cracow in 1910 and immediately became one of the most popular songs in the Poles' struggle for national self-determination.

1 BArch, R 19/321, fol. 15. This document has been translated from German.
2 Friedrich-Wilhelm Krüger.
3 Harry Specht (b. 1900), farmer; joined the SA in 1930, the NSDAP in 1931, and the SS in 1933; chief of staff to the SS and Police Leader of Radom, 1939–1940; then head of Department Ia on the staff of the Higher SS and Police Leader East; on the executive staff of the SS Personnel Main Office in Berlin, 1944–1945; went missing.
4 Kurt Knoblauch (1885–1952), career officer; member of a Freikorps in 1919; joined the NSDAP and the SS in 1933; served in the Reichswehr, 1920–1933; subsequently worked at the SS Main Office; chief of the Command Staff of the Reichsführer-SS, 1941–1943; head of Office Group B (Waffen-SS) in the SS operations headquarters in 1944; lived in Munich after the war.

On 3 January 1943 near Wola-Miechowa,[8] easting [...], northing 52,000,[9] sheet 414, Kreis Sanok, District Cracow, the Einsatzkommando commanded by Gendarmerie Officer *Baum*[10] succeeded in tracking down and eliminating a gang of twenty-five men consisting of escaped Jewish bandits, who were looting in the vicinity of Wola-Miechowa.

## DOC. 204
## On 11 January 1943 British intelligence intercepts radio transmissions in which the head of the Operation Reinhard staff reports the number of Jews murdered in the extermination camps[1]

Radio transmission (marked 'secret Reich matter') from Hermann Höfle to Adolf Eichmann and Deputy Senior Commander of the Security Police in Cracow Heim, dated 11 January 1943[2]

GPDD[3] 355a 2
12. OMX de OMQ[4] 1000[5] 89 ??
Secret Reich matter! To the Reich Security Main Office, for the attention of SS-Obersturmbannführer *Eichmann, Berlin* ... rest missed ...

13/15. OLQ[6] de OMQ1005[7] 83 234 250
Secret Reich matter! To the Senior Commander of the Security Police, for the attention of SS-Obersturmbannführer *Heim, Cracow.*

5 Himmler's field command post Hochwald in Kreis Angerburg, East Prussia.
6 The original contains a stamp with postal service instructions.
7 It is not clear what document is referred to here.
8 Correctly: Wola Michowa; today the village is part of Komańcza municipality, powiat Sanok, in south-eastern Poland.
9 Easting and northing are terms used in the Gauß-Krüger coordinate system, which makes it possible to pinpoint precise areas with metric coordinates.
10 Albert Baum (1895–1969), gendarmerie officer in Sanok; lived in St Wendel in the West German state of Saarland after the war.

1 The National Archives (Kew), HW 16/23, decode GPDD 355a. Printed as a facsimile in Peter Witte and Stephen Tyas, 'A New Document on the Deportation and Murder of Jews during "Einsatz Reinhardt" 1942', *Holocaust and Genocide Studies*, vol. 15, no. 3 (2001), pp. 468–486, here p. 469. This document has been newly translated from German.
2 The radio messages were intercepted and decoded by British intelligence at the Government Code and Cypher School.
3 This acronym stands for: German police decrypt; also: German police decode; the Government Code and Cypher School used this abbreviation for German police radio transmissions that had been decoded.
4 These are transmitter and receiver call signs – OMX: SS Business and Administration Main Office (WVHA) radio station; de: from; OMQ: transmitter of the SS and Police Leader in Lublin. It is not clear why the radio message addressed to Eichmann was sent to the WVHA, but it may have been intended as a copy for information purposes or to be forwarded to Eichmann.
5 This is the time of transmission: 10.00 a.m.
6 This is the receiver call sign – OLQ: probably the radio station of the Senior Commander of the Security Police and the SD (BdS) in Cracow.
7 This is the time of transmission: 10:05 hours.

Re: 14-day report on Operation *Reinhart*. Concerning: there[8]
Registered intake up to 31/12/42, L 12 761, B 0, S 515, T 10 335, altogether 23 611. As at … 31/12/42, L 24 733, B 434 508, S 101 370, T 71 355, altogether 1 274 166.[9]
SS and Police Leader in *Lublin*, *Hoefle*, Sturmbannführer.

## DOC. 205

## On 12 January 1943 Colonel Freter of the Warsaw armaments inspectorate summarizes a meeting with Himmler[1]

Memorandum (marked 'confidential') from the Warsaw armaments inspectorate of the Reich Minister for Armaments and Munitions, Warsaw, signed Freter,[2] to the armaments inspector for the General Government,[3] Cracow, dated 12 January 1943 (copy)

On Saturday, 9 January 1943, at 2.15 p.m., Reichsführer-SS and Chief of Police *Himmler* telephoned with instructions to attend a meeting at the SS Officers' Club in Warsaw. The meeting was attended by the Reichsführer, a Waffen-SS general,[4] SS-Oberführer Dr v. Sammern, and Colonel Freter.

The Reichsführer stated he had come to Warsaw to ascertain whether it was true that a direct order from the Führer to liquidate the ghetto in Warsaw by the end of 1942[5] had not in fact been complied with, as had been reported to him. He had seen for himself that in fact the ghetto still existed, with approximately 35,000 Jews [living there], the majority of whom – approximately 20,000 Jews – are employed in works overseen by the armaments offices. I drew the Reichsführer's attention to the fact that all the directives concerning the continued employment of Jews in Warsaw had been issued in agreement with SS-Obergruppenführer and Police General State Secretary Krüger and the GG armaments inspectorate.[6] The Reichsführer thereupon ordered SS-Oberführer Dr v. Sammern to carry out the liquidation of the Warsaw ghetto and to transfer the Jews to the concentration camp prepared by the SS in District Lublin by 15 February 1943.[7] He asked me to make the GG armaments inspector aware of this order for the police and, at the same time, to note that the transfer would be carried out in cooperation with Field Mar-

8 This indicates that Höfle was replying to a request from the BdS in Cracow.

9 The abbreviations stand for the following: L: Lublin-Majdanek; B: Belzec; S: Sobibor; and T: Treblinka. The figure of 71,355 victims at Treblinka is either a typographical or a transmission error. If the figures for the other camps are subtracted from the total, the correct number is 713,555 victims. The total figure of 1,274,166 murdered Jews appears again in a report by the SS statistician Richard Korherr, 'Die Endlösung der europäischen Judenfrage', 23 March 1943: BArch, NS 19/1570.

1 BArch, RW 23/20, fol. 15r–v. This is the first of four appendices to the military log. Published in Grabitz and Scheffler, *Letzte Spuren*, pp. 315–316. This document has been translated from German.

2 Wilhelm Freter (1887–1955), career officer; joined the NSDAP in 1933; colonel in the Luftwaffe; head of the Warsaw armaments inspectorate, 1942–1943; dismissed from his post, demoted, and assigned to a penal battalion in 1944; lived in Hamburg after the war.

3 The armaments inspector for the General Government was Max-Josef Schindler.

4 Karl Wolff.

5 See Doc. 96.

6 See Doc. 172.

shal Keitel.[8] [He explained] that the SS would take over and process orders placed with the companies such that, although consignments for the Wehrmacht units would not be delivered for a time during the relocation period, increased production at the concentration camp over the course of the ensuing weeks would make up for it. The SS has taken responsibility for the commitment to the Wehrmacht to adhere to the delivery period and the delivery dates. The Reichsführer commented that, for reasons of security, he intended to concentrate all the Jews in just two camps, in Auschwitz and Lublin. He does not think it is a good idea to maintain a small camp in Starachowice and a camp in Skarzysko-Kamienna, for example, alongside these large camps. He will leave it to his agencies to consider setting up a centrally located Jew camp for both enterprises.[9]

## DOC. 206
## On 13 January 1943 the Polish police in Stanin report on the arrest and shooting of Jews in Tuchowicz[1]

Handwritten report by the commander of the Polish police post in Stanin,[2] signed Platoon Leader Marus, to the area commander in Łuków, dated 13 January 1943 (copy)

I hereby report that on the evening of 11 January 1943, the sołtys of Konuchówka village assembly apprehended six Jews who were loitering in the village and brought them to the local police station. The sołtys of the Jonnik village assembly, Stanin community, brought three male Jews and one female Jew. The sołtys of Sarnów, Tuchowicz community,[3] brought three Jews. The residents apprehended Jews on their own initiative and took them to the Tuchowicz community administration to be detained, which resulted in a total of twenty-three people being detained, two of them female Jews. One of the Jews died in detention, twenty-two were left. Of these, eleven were shot on 12 January 1943, leaving eleven. Because of the poor quality of the ammunition, i.e. a large number of duds, the police refrained from further shootings.

7 See Doc. 159. During his trip to Warsaw, Himmler ordered Higher SS and Police Leader Krüger to deport 8,000 ghetto inhabitants over the following days; the private companies still active in the ghetto were to continue their operations elsewhere in the General Government, while the 'guarding and isolation' of the Jewish workers were to be 'enforced most rigorously'; the Többens group's financial statements were to be examined by auditors and the workshops, with their 16,000 forced labourers, relocated to a concentration camp in District Lublin: BArch, NS 19/352, fols. 20–21. Well over 10,000 ghetto inhabitants had been transported to the Trawniki and Poniatowa camps by April 1943.

8 Making reference to the conflict in Przemyśl (see Doc. 101), the chief of the Wehrmacht High Command, Keitel, had already ordered on 5 Sept. 1942 that the military district commander in the General Government must 'immediately replace' the Jews employed by the Wehrmacht 'with Poles (non-Jews)': BArch, NS 19/2462, fol. 1.

9 The forced labour camp for Jews in Starachowice was in operation until July 1944, when the approximately 3,000 inmates were relocated to Auschwitz. The forced labour camp at a munitions factory run by HASAG in Skarżysko-Kamienna was also closed down in July 1944, and some of the approximately 8,000 inmates were sent to HASAG factories in Częstochowa and Leipzig, while others were deported to Buchenwald concentration camp.

1 APL, 1035/13, fols. 1–2v. This document has been translated from Polish.

2 A small town approximately 80 km south-east of Warsaw.

3 Today this village is part of the Stanin municipality.

On 12 January 1943, at 11 a.m., together with Platoon Leader Wagner, I went to Łuków to collect some rifles, and I encountered a Jew who disobeyed my order to stop and ran off. He was shot on the run near the village of Jozefów, Tuchowicz community.

The Jews that were apprehended and taken to the police station had escaped from a train transport taking them from Dęblin to Łuków.

Five dead Jews were found next to the railway tracks near Sarnów station in Tuchowicz community. They were buried on the spot.

The following items were found next to the Jews who had been killed: 86 (eighty-six) zł. in cash, 10 (ten) Reichsmarks, one damaged pocket watch, 13 wedding rings and 34 stone-set rings, as well as 1 cigarette lighter – I enclose the collected items for you to make a decision.

List of the objects taken from the Jews who were killed in Tuchowicz.

These Jews had already been wounded by the German guards during the departure from Garwolin to Łuków. The most important items still of use were taken from them, as follows:

1 light-coloured jacket
1 padded jerkin
1 black jacket
1 striped grey jacket
1 grey jacket
1 chequered jacket
1 light-coloured padded jacket
1 pair of dark grey trousers
1 pair of dark blue trousers
1 light brown jacket
1 striped light brown waistcoat
1 drill shirt
1 black children's jacket
1 striped light-coloured jacket
1 brown Jewish kaftan
1 winter shirt
1 red pullover
1 chequered pink pullover
1 striped shirt
1 white shirt
1 violet pullover
1 grey cap (bicycle racing cap)
5 pairs of shoes with uppers
1 grey-coloured cap (bicycle racing cap)
1 large pocket watch
86 złoty in cash
10 Reichsmarks
1 cigarette lighter
34 stone-set rings
13 wedding rings

## DOC. 207

### *Wiadomości*, mid January 1943: report on the murder of three million Jews in Poland[1]

9 January – 15 January 1943 ARG[2]

During the period covered by this report, the Warsaw ghetto again experienced critical, restless days filled with nervous anticipation and fear bordering on insanity. Sleepless nights spent standing watch, days spent constantly on our guard. It is no exaggeration to compare the ghetto to a bundle of nerves, on edge, worn out from the emotion and therefore overreacting to the slightest shock from the outside. News of continuing deportations of Jews to Treblinka or to other execution sites, or of massacres carried out locally, is arriving from all over: from Vilna, Białystok, Sandomierz, Lwów, Opoczno, Radom, Częstochowa, intensifying the sheer horror and primal fear in the eyes of every ghetto resident.

Aside from these ghetto 'news items', or, to be more exact, in parallel with them, the Warsaw ghetto is witnessing a tragedy rooted, on the one hand, in the conviction that the German criminals will not leave the ghetto and its surviving inhabitants unharmed and, on the other hand, in the hopelessness expressed in desperate acts of heroism. Without wishing to make comparisons with periods of history marked by savagery and barbarism, we would like to draw attention to a highly typical and prominent aspect that is discernible in the Jewish residential district in Warsaw. Before proceeding to the main topic which, *as we have already indicated, concerns a new German propaganda campaign against the Jews* that has been stepped up this week and is being conducted extensively but discreetly, we shall allow ourselves a small digression.

According to the law of the jungle, the primeval code of the forests and jungles, the consumption of a victim to satisfy physical hunger [and] the fight for existence and for life, even in its most dramatic manifestation, involving the use of teeth, fangs, and claws, are natural phenomena and as such are not things that are concealed or covered up with lies. When fighting for everything, in other words for life, the utmost ferocity and ruthlessness come into play. But the law of the jungle does not recognize death purely for the sake of death. On the contrary, this law is imbued with a strong instinct for life. Not even the most bloodthirsty beast kills unnecessarily. When it has satisfied its hunger, it gives up the hunt for further victims. And one more thing: no animal erases the traces of its struggle, defeat, and victory – it acts in accordance with the requirements of the law of the jungle.

The above digression should help us better understand the German 'idea' of struggle against other nations. Compared to this, the law of the jungle appears as the whimpering of an infant against the thunder of sea waves, as a soft breeze against a wild storm. What set it [the German 'idea'] apart are the unrestrained thought processes, raging insanity, refined sadism, depths of immorality, and mastery of technical resources. Furor teutonicus[3] in its devilish form.

1 *Wiadomości*, no. 6, 9–15 Jan. 1943; AŻIH, Ring II/423 (338/1), fols. 76–82. Published in Datner, '"Wiadomości"', pp. 71–79. This document has been translated from Polish.

2 These initials were code for Archiwum getta, the underground archive of the Warsaw ghetto.

3 Latin: 'Teutonic fury'.

Having reduced the Jewish population to 10 per cent of its original size, the criminals have not ceased their process of extermination. On the contrary: everything suggests that the tragic fate of the tortured and devastated Jewish population is to be fulfilled. Hence the need for even greater suspicion and caution towards the new German propaganda-based manipulation, which is aimed at generating a certain mood among the Jewish masses.

Germany's predilection for presenting the world with faits accomplis is well known. The faits accomplis successfully used in the policy of conquest to date are now also being widely applied in the struggle against the Jewish 'enemy'. One of these faits accomplis was Chełmno, another was the monstrous mass murder in Lublin and the hellish 'operation' to liquidate the Warsaw ghetto. For certain reasons, it has not suited and does not suit Hitler and his followers to inform their own people and countries outside Germany of the atrocities committed against the Jews and other peoples. They correctly conclude that atrocities on this scale can only be committed under specific, suitable conditions and cloaked in secrecy. It would be uncomfortable and inconvenient to make known the achievements in the struggle against the Jews – although from the point of view of militant antisemitism, Treblinka and Bełżec were a major success. It would be inconvenient for the following three reasons: (1) The reaction from the Jewish masses, who would be aware of their fate and determine that they no longer have anything to lose, (2) The objections from the conquered and allied nations, who consider such a 'solution' to national problems utterly unthinkable, and (3) the reaction of the united [Allied] nations against their citizens of German nationality.

For the reasons stated above, a crime unprecedented in the history of warfare, migration, and epidemics in terms of its scale and tragic dimensions has been committed in total seclusion and isolation. The murder of three million Jews in Poland has undermined the entire framework of German propaganda. The remaining Jews suddenly became aware of the unheard-of massacre to which their loved ones had fallen victim. Their eyes were opened. Consequently, news about the execution sites and the entire complex of German deeds, described collectively as the extermination of the Jews, has come to permeate Polish and German society, and later foreign societies. The declaration of the twelve *Allied states* regarding the punishment of those guilty of this atrocity, while inadequate and following the path of least resistance (postponing justice until after the war), was inconvenient for the Germans.[4] The German government responded with an official declaration,[5] the main purport of which was that the removal of the Jews from German territory had been one of the main tasks of German policy and would remain so. Society at home and abroad was led to believe that this meant merely the removal of *living* Jews from the territories occupied by the Germans. The intention was clear.

Greater awareness of the 'German deed' could have had undesirable consequences for the occupiers. Something had to be done to counter this. And suddenly a number of 'confirmed' reports on 'resettlers' appeared, especially in the Warsaw ghetto. During the period covered by this report, letters have 'arrived' in Warsaw from a women's camp near Smolensk, as well as news that 40,000 Jews are living and working in Treblinka,

4 This is a reference to the joint declaration issued by the Allies on 17/18 Dec. 1942 on the German programme to exterminate the Jewish population of Europe. The declaration demanded retribution for these crimes: see Doc. 74, fn. 12.

5 See fn. 7.

and that there is a camp near Równe in which 120,000 Polish Jews are living. This news is spreading in the ghetto and, suitably edited, kindles fresh hopes in the hearts of the despairing people. The purpose of this propaganda campaign is clear. The Germans do not want the Jewish masses to react; they are afraid of the behaviour of the Jews and of their possible reaction. This explains the obvious efforts of the occupiers to use this 'reassuring' propaganda campaign to create a certain mood in the ghetto. The sources of these rumours are the offices of the SS and the Gestapo. Their intention is not to tell the truth or even half the truth, but merely to create the semblance of authenticity.

What has been said above illustrates just one of the 'achievements' of the Nazi criminals. We now wish to concentrate on a different aspect of the 'resettlement problem'. Nowadays, no one is any longer under the illusion that the Germans' actions will be limited to the Jews. The reality of the recent past clearly shows that this is neither theory nor fantasy, but fact. The Poles have woken up; the underground press is reporting the crimes of the perverted Germans. For its part, German propaganda is attempting to counteract this by various means and, last [but] not least,[6] with the aid of allegedly authentic news reports from the ghetto. We are familiar with the refined, amoral methods of German propaganda. We have no doubt that German propaganda relating to the 'resettlement' will use any means at its disposal to finally 'solve' the Polish problem. The Germans are fully aware of the importance and significance of the news reaching the 'Aryan side' from the ghetto. They insist that no elimination of the Jews has taken place, rather that they have been sent eastwards as a labour force (which the Jews themselves 'confirm'), let alone of the Poles, Aryans whom the Germans have no intention of liquidating but at most plan to 'resettle' in other areas. We are all too aware of the real meaning of resettlement or relocation. But the Germans do not really care. They are acting according to the well-established principle that a lie repeated several times and in various ways creates the impression of truth. Accordingly, the Germans are allowing a veritable deluge of the most varied kinds of news into the ghetto, in order to kill two birds with one stone: to 'prepare' the Jews for further 'resettlements', and to use the reaction to this on the Aryan side to sow disorientation and confusion there.

We find ourselves on the edge of the abyss; there is no help, no rescue in sight. But even at this point we wish to stress once again how closely the fate of the Jews is linked to that of the Poles and how much it is subject to the same laws. The continued rule of the German occupiers no longer means only the extermination of the remaining Polish Jews, but also the physical destruction of the Polish nation.

*Warthegau.* We have recently been receiving a series of letters from our Polish friends in Koło, Dąbie, Grabów, Kłodawa, Izbica Kujawska, and Krośniewice, from which it is clear how similar the fate of the Poles is to that of the Jews. The difference might be that the campaign against the Jews is more intense, but the policy of extermination is basically the same. Our correspondents report that in the above-mentioned towns only working-age Poles, *employed in workshops operating for the benefit of the German army*, are left. The remainder, mainly the elderly and minors, have been deported *to an unknown destination*. The German operations so far are too fresh in our minds for us not to fully grasp the Polish reality in the Warthegau.

6 'Last not least' is in English in the original.

To complete the picture, one must add that the atmosphere in which the Poles in Koło and nearby eke out their existence as slaves is similar to that experienced by us Jews.

This is also apparent in the situation in the towns around Ciechanów, that is, in Nowy Dwór, near Modlin; Płońsk; Czerwińsk; Nowe Miasto, near Płońsk; Ciechanów; and Mława. In their reports the refugees from these areas lament the fate of the Polish population.

That is what the 'new order in Europe' looks like.

*An official note from Germany about the Jewish question (Corriere della Sera)*[7]
Berlin, 19 December 1942

Germany's official note concerning a joint declaration on the Jewish question drawn up recently and issued by the English, American, and Soviet governments and various governments in exile[8] states among other things that for Germany the Jewish question basically ceased to exist on 30 January 1933.

The expulsion of Jews from German territory was already a central tenet of the National Socialist agenda ten years before they came to power. This aspect has been unchanged ever since. If the Jews believed that National Socialism would amend its programme or abandon that part of it relating to the Jewish question, it was all the worse for them.

In any case, one must stress that the German Jews have had ten years to draw consequences from the National Socialist programme and leave the country.

The Jews in other European countries have had even more time, and many of them still had an opportunity to emigrate one or two years ago. For the Jews in a few European countries, the opportunity still exists.

Finally, it is also worthwhile recalling the Führer's stern warning shortly before the conflict erupted: 'If the Jews cause a new world war, they will be the first to feel the consequences of this crime.'[9]

*Częstochowa.* Following the liquidation of the ghetto in Częstochowa at the end of last year, about 5,600[10] people remained, housed in various local factories and small streets. Officially, the ghetto no longer exists; instead the entire Jewish community is called a labour camp – Arbeitslager.[11]

Nevertheless, the remainder of the Jewish community were not permitted to live relatively undisturbed. Since the beginning of January, there have been various rumours in the town about a further 'resettlement' of the Jews, including dates. This time, the victims were meant to be only women and elderly people. According to the statement by the local gendarmerie commander, Degenhardt,[12] these two categories of the Jewish population, classified as being unfit for work, were not allowed to exist at all within Częstochowa labour camp. A total of 800 people were due to be resettled, but Degenhardt 'magnanimously' declared that he was prepared to hide 500 of these 800 'illegals'.

7 'Una nota ufficiosa tedesca sul problema ebraico', *Corriere della Sera*, 20 Dec. 1942, p. 4.
8 This is a reference to the declaration described in fn. 4.
9 Hitler used similar wording in his speech to the Reichstag on 30 Jan. 1939: see PMJ 2/248.
10 The first numeral has been typed over, so the number can also be read as '4,600'.
11 'Labour camp' in Polish and German in the original.

He also said that the resettlement was essential for the welfare of the workers because the 'illegals' deprive them of their food.

On Monday, 4 January, the 'resettlement'[13] began. At 10 a.m., after the people set out to reach their workplaces, the ghetto police gathered together a large number of Jews – men, women, and children – on the so-called *Ryneczek*,[14] where six (!) gendarmes made the selection in the absence of Degenhardt, who was represented by the gendarme Rohn. They let many of them go, but the old people and children were taken away.

Something that happened during the selection is clear evidence of a change of attitude among young Jews, who have started to engage more actively in a hopeless struggle with the Nazi criminals in order to protect their honour and their lives.

Because a certain group of young people arrived late at the square where the selection was taking place, Rohn, the leader of the 'operation', ordered all of them to go straight to the wagons. At that moment Mendel Fiszlewicz,[15] aged twenty, threw himself at him with a revolver. The revolver jammed after the first shot, but he took out a knife and attacked Rohn with it, slashing his coat and wounding him. In the struggle, Rohn was unable to draw his revolver, but another gendarme, a certain Sapport, came to his aid and gave him his own revolver. Rohn shot Fiszlewicz three times, seriously injuring him, but Fiszlewicz, lying on the ground bleeding, continued to defend himself by kicking his assailant.

Fiszlewicz was helped by his friend Ajzyk Fajner, aged nineteen, who launched himself at Sapport with a revolver. He fired twice at the gendarme, but when he saw the gendarme was unhurt, he attacked him with his fists. During the scuffle the gendarme broke his arm, but he managed to shoot his victim prior to that.

It is remarkable that the remaining gendarmes stood by while all this was happening, without helping their colleagues, even though Rohn shouted: 'Habt keine Angst, euch wird nichts passieren, schiesst!'[16] Only a fresh platoon of gendarmes could bring the situation under control. Twenty-five people were subsequently shot for resistance against the authorities.[17]

Understandably, this event caused a major stir throughout the city and aroused a sense of satisfaction and justice. Even the Germans acknowledged the Jewish resistance and defence ('Die Juden haben einen Aufstand gemacht').[18]

A group of 'resettlers' was led to the wagons, accompanied by a large escort of gendarmes and Blue Police. It turned out that the resistance by the despairing young Jews,

12 Paul Degenhardt (b. 1895), police officer; joined the NSDAP and the SA in 1932, and the SS in 1940; worked for the Security Police from 1919; stationed at Sosnowiec from April 1941; head of the Urban Police command at Częstochowa, early 1942 – late 1943; sentenced to life imprisonment by Lüneberg Regional Court in 1966.

13 Approximately 35,000 Jews were deported from Częstochowa to Treblinka between 22 Sept. and 7 Oct. 1942; by the end of the year the number of ghetto residents who remained rose to more than 5,000 on account of refugees arriving from the surrounding areas.

14 Ryneczek means 'small market'; today it is called ulica Bohaterów Getta (Heroes of the Ghetto Street).

15 Resistance cells were set up in the Częstochowa ghetto in Oct. 1942; in late Dec. 1942 a Jewish combat organization was formed out of several resistance groups. Mendel Fiszlewicz had joined a combat group after escaping from Treblinka.

16 German in the original: 'Don't be scared, nothing will happen to you, shoot!'

17 During the murder operation 350 people – mostly women and children – were deported to the Radomsko ghetto and from there to Treblinka; 200 Jews were shot on Kawia Street.

18 German in the original: 'The Jews have rebelled.'

although resulting in a relatively low number of victims, had aroused such interest that the criminals were compelled to deploy a relatively large number of gendarmes, over sixty, to guard the Jewish 'resettlers'. They were taken to an assembly point in Radomsko.

*Radomsko.* The official Jewish ghettos in District Radom[19] are being completely liquidated. During the first ten days of January, almost all the Jews were 'resettled' from the following ghettos: Sandomierz, Szydłowiec, Radomsko, and Ujazd.

The 'resettlement' in Radomsko took place on 6 January. The operation affected over 8,000 (eight thousand) people, who had been concentrated there following resettlements from surrounding towns and from Częstochowa.[20] Some 30 (thirty) Jews are said to be left in Radomsko.

The Germans forced them all to leave behind their coats, pullovers, and other warm clothing before boarding the wagons. Many fled the wagons, not caring about the continuous fire from the Ukrainian escorts. Only a few succeeded in returning to the Jewish districts.

*Liquidation of further Jewish centres.* On Thursday, 8 January,[21] a locomotive with forty wagons passed through Warsaw, carrying the remainder of the Jewish population, some 6,000 people, from Końskie, Skarżysko, Opoczno, Tomaszów Mazowiecki, and Ujazd, to Treblinka.

*Szydłowiec.* All of the Jews in Szydłowiec were 'resettled'[22] towards the end of last week.

*Vilna.* In the first few days of January, a train full of Jews from Vilna was seen at Warsaw East railway station. They told the Jews working there that they were being taken to Upper Silesia where, according to the Germans, they were going to be assigned work involving assisting with executions in Auschwitz or Szczawnica.[23]

*Treblinka.* From a series of macabre German ideas: Music in Treblinka.
The following is a further indication of German cynicism at the death camp in Treblinka: The procession of naked men and women being led to the steam chambers[24] is often accompanied by music from a Jewish band playing merry Jewish melodies and jolly

19 On 10 Nov. 1942 Higher SS and Police Leader Friedrich-Wilhelm Krüger specified in a police regulation which ghettos in District Radom were to be allowed to remain in place for the time being: *VOBl-GG*, 98, 14 Nov. 1942, pp. 683–686.

20 From mid Nov. 1942 there were about 4,500 Jews living in the Radomsko ghetto who had previously been staying in surrounding settlements or concealed in hiding places; they were required to undertake forced labour. In late 1942 the Germans registered them, supposedly in preparation for a prisoner exchange with the Allies; in fact, most of them were deported to Treblinka, 260 were shot at Radomsko, and 250 were taken to a forced labour camp run by the munitions concern HASAG.

21 8 Jan. was a Friday.

22 In Dec. 1942 the Germans concentrated several thousand Jews who had been in hiding or had come to Szydłowiec from the surrounding area at a former factory site in the town; they were deported to Treblinka on 13 Jan. 1943.

23 There was no camp at the spa town of Szczawnica, which is located in the Beskid mountains south of Nowy Sącz, on the border with Slovakia.

24 A reference to the gas chambers.

marches. Salwe,[25] an artist and orator well known in the Warsaw ghetto, performed at the house of the German camp personnel recently.

*German perfidy in Radom and Opoczno.* Yet another 'resettlement operation' was carried out in Radom last week. Over 1,000 people were 'transported': 1,200 Jews were allowed to remain behind – those who had applied to emigrate to Palestine a week before.[26] At the same time there was a 'resettlement' from Opoczno, where the SS men assured the victims that they were going to Palestine, and even helped them load their baggage on to the trains.[27]

*Mińsk Mazowiecki.* To 'celebrate' Christmas Eve, the Germans in Mińsk Mazowiecki massacred the Jewish camp inmates. Following a large number of extensive 'resettlements', only one work detail with over 300 Jewish employees is left in Mińsk Maz. On 24 December 1942 the Germans took 218 Jews and shot all of them at the Jewish cemetery there. The gravediggers were fifteen Jews from Fort Wola[28] in Warsaw, who had been brought to Mińsk by car expressly for this purpose. Some of the Jews hid in the surrounding forests.

We have just found out that a second crime against the remaining 100 Jews was committed early this week.[29] They were all burned alive, without exception. This is nothing new given the anti-Jewish actions resulting from the Germans' frenzied rage. The example of Chełm Lubelski and a camp in Lublin, where hundreds of Jews were burned alive,[30] shows that this is a standard procedure of rabid Nazism.

*Sandomierz.* On Saturday, 9 January this year, 8,000 (eight thousand) Jews from Sandomierz were 'resettled' to Treblinka.[31] One should note that Sandomierz was one of the officially sanctioned Jewish ghettos.[32] Most of the victims – not just the young, but also the elderly – jumped from the railway wagons under the worst of conditions – in freezing temperatures of minus 15 degrees, at risk of receiving a bullet from the first German they encountered, and frequently encountering the unfriendly attitude of the terrorized and intimidated Polish population.

*Staszów.* We have been informed that the final act of the tragedy of the Jews in Staszów has been played out. On Saturday, 9 January, the remaining Jews, 300 in number, were 'resettled'. There is not a single Jewish resident left in Staszów.[33]

25 Izaak Salwe was a popular actor who had worked at Yiddish theatres in Warsaw and performed at the Nowy Azazel Theatre in the Warsaw ghetto; he is thought to have perished in August 1943 during the prisoners' uprising at Treblinka.
26 This group was deported to Treblinka on 13 Jan. 1943.
27 This group was initially deported to the Ujazd ghetto, and from there to Treblinka on 6 Jan. 1943.
28 Fort Wola was a neighbourhood in Warsaw.
29 The Germans murdered approximately 300 Jews on 10 Jan. 1943. A total of 104 Jewish forced labourers remained. They were murdered on 5 June 1943.
30 It is not clear what incident is being referred to here.
31 Approximately 6,000 Jews were deported to Treblinka on 10 Jan. 1943.
32 See fn. 19.
33 In late 1942 Staszów was one of the ghettos in District Radom that were officially allowed to remain for a while longer; the ghetto inhabitants were deported to Treblinka on 10 Jan. 1943.

*Conference in Cracow.* On Monday, 11 January, there was a conference in Cracow convened by the central SS leadership and devoted to the Jewish question. The results of the conference are not yet known.[34]

*Himmler in the Warsaw ghetto.* On Saturday afternoon, on the 9th of this month, there was a visit to the Warsaw ghetto by Reichsführer-SS Himmler, the leader of the Nazi bandits, whose hands are stained with the blood of the exterminated Jewish people. The sight of His Excellency, the murderer of Europe, made a macabre impression. Ahead of him drove two combat-ready armoured cars, and at the rear were another two armoured cars bristling with rifle barrels. Himmler was in a civilian car surrounded by armed SS officers. The motorcade raced through the dead, empty streets. He was observed only by the open windows of ransacked formerly Jewish homes, which had been robbed of anything of any value and emptied of their rightful residents. The motorcade seemed to be following its inseparable companions – the horsemen of the Apocalypse: War, Death, Conflagration, and Famine.[35]

In the ghetto Himmler inspected the warehouses of the Werterfassung[36] at 35 and 69 Dzielna Street (not the only locations where looted Jewish property is stored). He showed no interest in the Jews' szopy, factories, and workshops, but only in his own work – Werterfassung. The ghetto inhabitants regard the visit by their executioner as the worst possible warning of a 'resettlement' à la Treblinka, or a similar operation.

Both the departure from and arrival in the ghetto were marked by a nightmarish calm and were devoid of any pomp and ceremony. This is what the visit was like in the European capital that had been the first to be captured and that had endured the worst suffering in the war.

*Miscellaneous.* The influx of Jews into the Jewish district in Warsaw in December of last year was as follows:

1 December 109 people
2 December 122 people
3 December 42 people

And on the following days fewer than forty people in each case.

Turnout for work at the Werterfassung:
Beginning of December – approximately 3,200 people daily,
Second half of December – approximately 3,700 people daily.

*Construction work.* In December about 340,000 bricks were delivered, of which 320,000 were to build walls around the szopy.

*Health.* Last month, 205 cases of typhus and 12 cases of typhoid fever were recorded. The 205 cases of typhus included 171 arrivals from camps who had arrived in the ghetto from closed work sitess.[37]

34 Nothing is known about a conference of this kind.

35 This is a reference to the Four Horsemen of the Apocalypse, which conventionally represent war, pestilence, famine, and death. In this text, the Polish word for 'pestilence' does not appear, but instead *pożoga*, meaning 'conflagration'.

36 German here and below in the original, a reference to the Asset Registration Office.

*Deaths*. The total number of deaths in December of last year was 334:

| | |
|---|---|
| Men | 218 |
| Women | 116 |
| | |
| People shot | 65 |
| Men | 52 |
| Women | 13 |

## DOC. 208
## On 15 January 1943 Himmler urges the utilization of objects stolen from murdered Jews[1]

Letter from the Reichsführer-SS and Reich Commissioner for the Strengthening of Germandom (file no. sec[ret]/181/5, log no. I 110/43/Ad[?] (g), RF/V.), signed Himmler, Field Command Post,[2] to the Higher SS and Police Leader in the General Government, Krüger, and the head of the SS Business and Administration Main Office, Pohl, dated 15 January 1943[3]

During my visit to Warsaw[4] I also inspected the warehouses containing the materials and goods taken from the Jews or during their emigration.[5]

I ask SS-Obergruppenführer Pohl once again to make written arrangements with the economics minister[6] for all individual categories: whether glass coverings from watch faces, lying there in their hundreds of thousands – maybe even in their millions – which could probably be conveniently allocated to German watch shops; or lathes we need for our workshops, and which the economics minister can either legally give to us or which we can buy from him; or sewing machines, for which the same is true; or utility furs or fine ladies' furs. The degree of precision we need to apply here cannot be overestimated.

I also noticed that no real administrative officers have been seconded. SS-Obergruppenführer Pohl has made the Higher SS and Police Leaders his representatives, and under them the SS and Police Leaders. I personally do not believe that the individual Higher SS and Police Leader and [individual] SS and Police Leader can cope with these matters on their own.

I would like both the assigned commander and an assigned administrative officer to sign off on all reports and all deliveries to the Ethnic German Liaison Office.

37 Work sites at which exclusively Jewish forced labourers were working.

1 The whereabouts of the original are unknown. IfZ-Archives, Nürnberger Dokument NO-1257. Copy in AIPN, GK, 912/DC/409, fols. 1–2. Published in Berenstein et al. (eds.), *Faschismus – Getto – Massenmord*, p. 412. This document has been translated from German.
2 Himmler's field command post, Hochwald, in Kreis Angerburg, East Prussia.
3 A carbon copy went to SS-Obergruppenführer Karl Wolff for his information. The document contains handwritten annotations and underlining.
4 Himmler was in Warsaw on 9 Jan. 1943: see Docs. 205 and 207.
5 The SS Registration Office for Jewish Assets, also known as the Asset Registration Office, was located in the ghetto at 20 Niska Street; one of its warehouses was in St Augustine's Church on Leszno Street; it employed 3,700 workers in late 1942.
6 Walther Funk (1890–1960).

A very nice administrative officer from the Cavalry Brigade, who made an excellent impression, was very helpful in putting things in order in Warsaw.[7] His deployment, however, had not come about in a properly regulated fashion; rather, SS-Oberführer von Sammern had very sensibly brought him in to help.

I request that SS-Obergruppenführer Pohl clarify and arrange these matters down to the last detail, because the greatest precision now will save us a great deal of trouble later.

Heil Hitler!

## DOC. 209
## Sometime prior to 18 January 1943, the Jewish Combat Organization calls on the residents of the Warsaw ghetto to engage in resistance[1]

Jewish Combat Organization leaflet,[2] Warsaw, January 1943

*Number 1 – Warsaw ghetto – January 1943*

*To the Jewish masses in the ghetto*

22 January 1943 will mark six months since the deportations began in Warsaw.

We all clearly recall the terrible days during which 300,000 of our brothers and sisters were sent away and brutally murdered in Treblinka death camp. Since then, we have lived in constant fear of death for six months, never knowing what the next day will bring. News has reached us from all over about the extermination of the Jews in the GG, in Germany, and in the occupied territories. Hearing this sad news, we have awaited the moment [of our death] every hour of every day. Today we must understand that the Hitlerian murderers have kept us alive only because they want to exploit the labour we provide, right down to our last drops of blood and sweat, down to our last breath. We are slaves. And when the slaves no longer yield a profit, they are killed off. Each one of us must understand this and always bear this in mind.

In recent weeks certain people have been spreading news about letters supposedly arriving from the deported Jews of Warsaw. According to these sources, they are in labour camps near Pińsk or in Bobruisk.[3]

7 Probably Franz Konrad (1906–1951), salesman; joined the NSDAP and the SS in 1932; interned in Austria after taking part in the July Putsch of 1934; fled to Germany in July 1935; full-time SS-Führer from April 1938; served in Warsaw from 1939; head of the SS Registration Office for Jewish Assets in the Warsaw ghetto, June 1942–1943; took part in the fighting at the start of the Warsaw Ghetto Uprising on 19 April 1943; executed in Warsaw in 1951.

1 AŻIH, Ring II/426d (333/4), fol. 6. Published as a facsimile and in Polish translation in Sakowska (ed.), *Archiwum Ringelbluma: Konspiracyjne Archiwum Getta Warszawy*, vol. 1: *Listy o Zagładzie*, pp. 336–337 and 379. This document has been translated from Yiddish.

2 On 29 July 1942 representatives of the left-wing Zionist organizations Hashomer Hatzair, Dror, and Akiba founded the Jewish Combat Organization (ŻOB) in Warsaw; Gordonia and Noar Zioni joined later, followed by the Bund, Poale Zion, and the Polish Workers' Party (PPR) in the autumn. From that point on it was possible, with the help of contacts in the Polish underground, to obtain more weapons, which were used in the fighting on 18 Jan. 1943. The ŻOB was the most important force involved in the Warsaw Ghetto Uprising in April and May 1943.

Jewish masses, you must *not believe* these stories. *They are spread by Jews who are in the Gestapo's service.*

The bloodthirsty murderers are pursuing a specific aim with this strategy: to calm the Jewish population in order [to carry out] the upcoming deportations without difficulties, with minimal manpower, and without the Germans suffering any losses. They want to ensure that the Jews do not prepare hiding places or engage in resistance. Jews, do not pass on these lies!

Do not help the agents! The criminal servants of the Gestapo will get what's coming to them. *Jewish masses*, the hour is approaching when you must be ready to resist and refuse to be slaughtered like sheep. *Not a single Jew should get into a wagon. Those who have no chance to actively resist should engage in passive resistance, i.e. hide.*

We have just received news from Lemberg that the Jewish police *themselves carried out* a deportation of 3,000 Jews there. This will not happen in Warsaw. Lejkin's assassination[4] proves it.

Our motto now must be:

*Everyone should be prepared to die like human beings.*

## DOC. 210

## On 22 January 1943 *Gazeta Lwowska* receives a neighbour's denunciation of Wiktoria Dziedzic for sheltering Jews[1]

Anonymous letter to the *Gazeta Lwowska*,[2] Lwów, unsigned (received on 22 January 1943),[3] undated

Dear Editors,[4]

A few Jews are hiding in the apartment of my neighbour, Wiktoria Dziedzic.[5] During the day she locks them in and goes off to work. She does all this for money. Please could you kindly forward this letter to the appropriate authorities.

*Address: 8 Kleparowska St.*
Neighbour

3 The first transport, carrying 960 Jewish men, was sent from Warsaw to Bobruisk on 30 May 1942, and a further transport followed on 28 July 1942.

4 The first attacks that the ŻOB carried out targeted Jews who had collaborated with the Germans. On 29 Oct. 1942 Eliahu Różański killed Jakub Lejkin, the deputy chief of the Jewish Order Service, who had supervised the deportations from the ghetto in summer 1942.

1 Zakład Narodowy im. Ossolińskich, Rękopis 14 757/II, fol. 185. This document has been translated from Polish.

2 *Gazeta Lwowska* was a Polish-language newspaper run by the German propaganda authorities. It appeared in Lwów from 1941 to 1944; its circulation peaked at 90,000 copies in 1943.

3 Receipt stamp of the publishing house Zeitungsverlag Krakau-Warschau (ZKW), Lwów.

4 The letter was preserved in the correspondence of the *Gazeta Lwowska*'s cultural affairs editor, Dr Stanisław Wasylewski (1885–1953).

5 Wiktoria Dziedzic, married name Skrzypiec (1916?–2005); helped Jews escape from the Lwów ghetto and supported them on the 'Aryan side'; honoured as Righteous Among the Nations by the State of Israel in 1965.

## DOC. 211

## On 26 January 1943 the Landkommissar in Chodorów presses for action to be taken against Jews still living in his territory[1]

Letter from the Landkommissar in Chodorów (Ho/Kö, 56/Kö), Chodorów, signed Hohlmann,[2] to the Kreishauptmann in Stryj[3] (received on 29 January 1943), dated 26 January 1943[4]

*Re*: the Jewish question
*Concerning*: n/a
I feel duty-bound to briefly submit the following concerning the aforementioned matter:

There are still a great many Jews in my area[5] without badges. Jews are now once again present in any number of communities in my area. No one cares if the Jews are able to run around freely and do whatever they want. The sugar factory – and this is very revealing – actually used to employ few Jews, only 18 at times, but now they cannot make do without 200 Jews. They are certainly not all needed, especially as the campaign is slowly coming to an end. I have the distinct impression that the Polish director is keeping a back door open here, in a manner of speaking, and treating the Jews well, perhaps in order to enjoy certain advantages. The Jewish rag-and-bone men are still running around here in large numbers.

The danger posed by the further spread of false news that is unfavourable to the Germans is exceptionally great – such findings have been made a number of times. The way in which sentiment has turned against us is partly due to this fact. In addition, we have found that a great many Ukrainians and Poles are together in some form.

Furthermore, it is a fact that a great many Jews have become Ukrainians or Poles. Incidentally, it may be noted here in passing that Jews have also been taken along on the transports to Germany.

I regard clearing up this question as one of our most urgent tasks.[6]

1 DALO, R-1952/1/172, fol. 41. Copy in USHMM, Acc. 1995 A 1086, reel 32. This document has been translated from German.

2 Karl Hohlmann (1899–1982), farmer; joined the NSDAP in 1933; Stadtkommissar in Kołomyja in 1942; became Landkommissar in Chodorów in Jan. 1943; later a prisoner of war in Soviet captivity; released in 1949; then worked in the advertising department of the *Westdeutsche Allgemeine Zeitung*; full-time general manager of the sports club ETB Schwarz-Weiß Essen, 1956–1976; established the Stiftung Rüttenscheid für behinderte Kinder, a foundation for disabled children, in 1970.

3 Dr Viktor von Dewitz (1905–1994), lawyer; joined the NSDAP and the SA in 1933; junior lawyer in Frankfurt an der Oder; completed probationary civil service as a legal officer in Saarbrücken; Kreishauptmann in Nowy Targ from Sept. 1939; Kreishauptmann in Stryj, August 1941 – mid July 1944; worked for the Regierungspräsident in Cologne from Nov. 1944; classed as *entlastet* ('exonerated') during denazification proceedings in 1950; later Kreis director at the Cologne Landrat's Office.

4 The original contains handwritten annotations.

5 Hohlmann uses the term Bezirk to refer to the territory (a subdivision of Kreis Stryj) under his authority as a Landkommissar.

6 The Jews who remained in Chodorów were shot dead near the sugar factory in Feb. or March 1943.

## DOC. 212

## On 31 January 1943 the General Government's Military District Command reports on attacks by partisans and on action taken to combat the armed resistance[1]

Report (marked 'secret') from the chief of the general staff at the General Government's Military District Command (Dept. Ic/Ia no. 415/43 sec[ret]), signed v. Wedel,[2] dated 31 January 1943[3]

*Situation in the General Government* in January 1943

I. *Enemy action*

a) Two enemy incursions by air [took place] on 25 and 26 January. A bomb was dropped near Zamosc railway station; a parachute was found in District Warsaw.

b) Seven sabotage balloons with incendiary devices were launched. No damage was sustained.

II. *Bandits*

a) *Raids*

Bandits carried out 1,097 raids and larger gangs 28 raids, which is a month-on-month decrease of 259 raids. As before, they were mainly concentrated in District Lublin. The raids focused primarily on the theft of food and other necessities. In 21 cases Polish police stations and police officers were attacked. Fourteen attacks were directed against community administration offices. One raid was carried out on a prison and a prisoner assembly camp. A large quantity of explosives was stolen from an explosives depot near Krosno. A Polish mechanic was forced to repair a transmitter in a bandits' hideout.

*Attack on members of the Wehrmacht*

Six soldiers in Warsaw and one soldier in Siedlce were knocked down and had their weapons stolen.

One Kriegsverwaltungsrat,[4] one corporal, and two soldiers were shot dead in broad daylight in Warsaw.

Three soldiers were shot at in Zloczow, and one was injured by a pistol round in Demblin.

b) *Attacks on telephone lines*

[Telephone] poles were destroyed at three locations, cables at five locations. Telephone lines and equipment were destroyed during attacks at another 13 locations.

c) *Attacks on railway lines and railway properties*

| | | |
|---|---|---|
| Track blown up | on the | Warsaw–Brest line. |
| " | in the | tunnel between Warsaw central and Warsaw East stations. |
| " | on the | Skierniewice–Warsaw line. |
| " | " | Warsaw–Lomianki line. |
| " | " | Lublin–Rozwadow line. |

1 BArch, RH 53-23/65–67. This document has been translated from German.

2 Presumably Hasso von Wedel, major; chief of the general staff in the General Government military district, July 1942 – March 1943.

3 The original contains handwritten annotations and underlining. The report was sent via a special distribution list not specified in the document.

4 Senior rank in the military administration with responsibility for a range of key areas of occupation policy.

" " Lublin–Lubartow line.
" " Rawa-Ruska–Uhnow line.

One attempt to blow up a bridge on the Wyszkow–Dalekie line was prevented.

One passenger train on the Lukow–Biala Podlaska line ran over a mine and was shot at.

One " " on the Zwierziniec line and one freight train on the Lukow–Deblin line were shot at.

Coal train derailed and shot at near Miedzyrzec.

Postal wagon robbed on a light railway near Opatow.

Water tower in Susiec blown up.

Attempts to blow up tracks on the Warsaw–Kutno line near Lowicz, the Skole-Lemberg line near Tuchla, and at Radzywillow railway station were prevented.

Equipment was destroyed at the Bialaszow and Petrykozy railway stations, and at the Sitowa signal box.

Five train collisions occurred as a result of incorrect switch setting and signal crossings due to negligence on the part of railway personnel.

d) *Acts of terrorism*

Twenty-one murders of Poles in German service.

Three attacks with time bombs at two cinemas and in the waiting room at Warsaw central railway station. One attack with bottles of acid at a cinema in Warsaw.

One incendiary device at the Organization Todt petrol station in Warsaw, fire extinguished.

Forty-three ampoules with various poisons were found on detained Poles.

Road signs in Warsaw were defaced with black paint.

III. *Fires*

There were eleven cases of arson in the Zamosc resettlement area.

IV. *Enemy propaganda*

Inflammatory writings with subversive and communist content were found and seized in large quantities in Warsaw and Miechow.

V. *Action to combat bandits*

Action to combat bandits was taken by the police and the gendarmerie, in six cases supported by the Wehrmacht; 2,170 bandits were shot dead, and 589 bandits were arrested.

*Activities of the resistance movement*

The activities of the Polish–Russian terrorists and the Young Zionists (Halutzim) have increased, as has the presence of Jews within the gangs. These terrorist groups directed by Moscow have already carried out numerous attacks on railways and telephone lines. The illegal combat groups led by General Sikorski are biding their time. The extraordinary measures taken by the police to round up workers and the resettlement operation being carried out in Kreis Zamosc[5] have caused enormous agitation among the Polish population. The various political groups have joined forces.

*Assessment*

Our military situation on the Eastern Front is strengthening the Poles' notions of regaining independence. Moscow is endeavouring to increase unrest among the people and to nurture the idea of an uprising. The situation is tense and demands the greatest vigilance.

5 A reference to the deportation of the Polish population from the Zamość region, which began in Nov. 1942. A German 'settlement area' was in the process of being created there.

## DOC. 213

## Klara Szwarc describes how she survived in hiding in Żółkiew from November 1942 to January 1943[1]

Handwritten diary of Klara Szwarc,[2] entry from around mid 1943[3]

Then comes the 22nd November, that memorable day. We spent the night at Mehlman's[4] because on Saturday, i.e. one day earlier, panic had broken out: people thought that the town was surrounded by the Gestapo. It's[5] 5 a.m, we are all still in bed, only Patrontasch[6] goes out on patrol, as always. Shortly afterwards he comes back and tells us to make preparations [to go into hiding] because two cars with Gestapo and Jewish militia (members of the Lwów Order Service) are on the way to the market square. He goes out again but soon comes running back. Raid! He's seen people being led away, we can hear shots, Gestapo men are running around in front of the windows. It's too late to run to the oil mill, only Mr Mehlman runs across the yard to inform Brytwitz,[7] the neighbour. What takes place there is nothing short of a miracle. When Mehlman rushes in, he finds them [the neighbours] calmly having breakfast, completely unaware. Hardly have they opened up the hiding place when one of the Gestapo men knocks on the door. Mehlman escapes through the rear entrance, and Brytwitz holds the door until the hiding place is secured; then he lets go of the door and runs off in order to distract the Gestapo man, and the Gestapo man runs after him. The father had to sacrifice himself for the family (we found all this out later from Brytwitz himself, because he jumped from the deportation train

1 USHMM, Acc. 1994.95, fols. 2–5. This document features in abridged form in Gerszon Taffet, *The Holocaust of the Jews of Zolkiew*, trans. Piotr J. Drozdowski (Łódź: Centralnej Żydowskiej Komisji Historycznej, 1996 [Polish edn, 1946]), pp. 45–47. English translation of the diary adapted by the author published in Clara Kramer (with Stephen Glantz), *Clara's War: A Miraculous Story of One Girl's Survival under the Nazis* (London: Ebury Press, 2009). This document has been newly translated from Polish.

2 Klara Szwarc (later Clara Schwarz, married name Clara Kramer) (1927–2018), born in Żółkiew, a town north of Lwów; in 1941 she and her family were among a group of eighteen who went into hiding in an underground bunker at the home of Valentine Beck, an ethnic German; she and her parents survived; her sister was captured and killed by the Germans. Klara and her family spent the first four years after the war in displaced persons camps in Germany and Austria, where she married. She emigrated to Israel in 1949 and in 1957 to the USA, where she dedicated her life to speaking about her experiences in the Holocaust. Klara kept a diary during the twenty months she was in hiding. Beck, his wife, and his daughter were honoured as Righteous Among the Nations by the State of Israel in 1995.

3 The original diary, begun in mid 1943, starts with this look back to 22 Nov. 1942 and the subsequent weeks in Żółkiew; it contains daily entries for the period from 31 August 1943 to 26 July 1944.

4 Mehlman (Melman) had been an employee at the oil mill run by Klara Szwarc's father, the engineer Meir Szwarc (1886–1959); before 1939 the mill was owned by Klara Szwarc's maternal grandfather, Szymon Reitzfeld (d. 1941).

5 Changes of tense here and below as in the original.

6 Presumably Leon Patrontasch (1904–1943), businessman; worked for Klara Szwarc's father in 1942; came from Żółkiew, where he perished in 1943. A mill at 43 Lwowska had been owned by the Patrontasch family prior to Sept. 1939.

7 Presumably Szyja Britwic (1898–1943), timber merchant; came from Żółkiew, where he perished in 1943.

and came back). Meanwhile we, i.e. my parents, my sister,[8] and me, Mehlman with his wife and child, and Patrontasch with his wife and child,[9] go down into the hiding place under the floor.

We spend one or two days in the dark; the candle refuses to burn for lack of oxygen (we answer the call of nature on the spot). Towards evening on the second day, Patrontasch and Mehlman dare to go and take a look at what is happening. After a few minutes, which seems like an eternity, they return. The operation is still going on. At that exact moment, they shot Lockman[10] (one of our neighbours) as he was trying to escape. We stay down below for another night. We are inside the hiding place and Patrontasch under the floor close to the ventilation hatch. Towards morning, Patrontasch's brother Lajbek[11] comes up close to the ventilation hatch (he didn't know exactly where the hiding place was, therefore he had to search). Lajbek was a member of the Order Service. Patrontasch calls him over and finds out that the operation is over and the train is departing. To be on the safe side, we stay hidden for another hour and then we come out. Inside the house we meet Aunt Ućka[12] with her children and the first people who jumped [from the train], along with Kohn and Trachtenberk (two of Ućka's cousins).[13] So Ućka's hiding place in the barn of an Aryan (Skibicki) proved its worth. A friend with her child had also stayed there overnight; Ućka had invited them because they were wandering helplessly in the streets. This woman's child was crying; it was given a sedative that was intended for Zosia,[14] but Zosia was quiet. Uncle Josek and his wife hid in the oil mill. On the previous day they had handed their child, a one-year-old boy, to an Aryan.

In town there is devastation, weeping and wailing. They are taking away in carts the bodies of the people who were shot on the spot (because either they attempted to flee or they stood up when the Gestapo men in the market square had ordered them to kneel) and of those who died when jumping off the train, had perished of cold and hunger, or who had been handed over by farmers in the vicinity and then shot.[15] Rela's (Josek's wife's)[16] mother, brother, and sister-in-law were taken away. The sister-in-law came back, but not the others. The Patrontaschs lost their sister Pepka[17] and her child (Pepka had run to a prearranged place at the home of a Catholic woman, but at the last minute the woman refused to let her in). Taube reported that he had seen Pepka lying

8 Klara's mother was Salka Szwarc (1904–1996), housewife; Mania Szwarc (1928–1943) was Klara Szwarc's younger sister.

9 Presumably Mr Mehlman with his wife Batia and son Igo, as well as Leon Patrontasch with his wife and his daughter Klara.

10 Josef Lockman (Lukman) (1895–1942), trader from Belz; later lived in Żółkiew, where he was married to Szpryncа Patrontasch (1896–1943).

11 Leib (Lajbek) Patrontasch was murdered.

12 Rachel (Ućka) Orlender, née Reitzfeld (1914–1943), housewife; the youngest sister of Klara Szwarc's mother; she was murdered.

13 They were cousins of Rachel Orlender's deceased husband.

14 The daughter of Rachel Orlender and her husband Hersz (Herman) Leib Orlender, who had been recruited into the Red Army in June 1941 and later perished in Tarnopol.

15 A total of 2,000 Jews were rounded up in Żółkiew on 22 and 23 Nov. 1942; 300 were murdered on the spot, and approximately 1,700 were deported to Belzec.

16 Rela Reitzfeld, née Schrenkenhammer (1924–1943), and Josef (Josek) Reitzfeld (1911–1943); Rela and her one-year-old son were murdered.

17 Pepi (Pepka) Lichter, née Patrontasch (1910–1942), housewife.

in her own blood on the railway track. He tried to lift her up but she fell back down again. The child was not with her. On the following day, a farmer came from Wola with a message from Pepka, but when they [the Patrontaschs] drove there, she had gone. The farmer must have killed her or handed her over to the Gestapo. They also took my friend Letzterówna[18] and her parents. She and her mother jumped from the train, but the father has not returned.

One week later, they tell us to move to the ghetto.[19] Father resolves not to go to the ghetto, but to go into hiding with some Aryan. The political situation is favourable; we expect the end [of the war] in a few weeks' time. Mr Mehlman arranges with a Volksdeutscher,[20] Mr Beck, a tenant in Mehlman's building, that he will take us and the Patrontaschs into hiding. In town we spread the news that Mr Mehlman's brother, who has influence in Janowska camp in Lwów, has hidden us, and we disappear. We enlarge the hiding place directly under the floor in the room where the hatch is; electric light is installed, two electric hot plates and places to sleep are prepared, and then we go in. Apart from us there is Mrs Klara, Patrontasch's sister. The days pass by monotonously; one day is like the next. Above, the women cook together, below, we only make breakfast and supper. Everyone washes in the kitchen above once a week, for it is too cold in the hiding place. One rarely meets people like Mr and Mrs Beck. They are very nice to us. Their family comprises Mr and Mrs Beck, their daughter Ala, and Mania, Mrs Beck's sister. On Christmas Eve we were invited to supper above. It was wonderful; we sang carols and forgot our woes. We had to hide once because someone knocked, but it didn't matter, we were used to it. On Christmas Day, Mr Beck's brother, sister-in-law, and nephew came to visit. Over a drink, Mr Beck confided to them that he had Jews in his apartment. There's nothing we can do about that; if Mr Beck trusts them, so must we.

Meanwhile, there is no happy news for us from the ghetto. The brothers of Mehlman and Patrontasch, who snuck out and reached us in the evening, report that typhus is raging in the ghetto. An average of ten to fifteen people are dying every day, mainly young people. The time passes in this way until 12 January, when Herman (Mehlman's brother) came to see us in the afternoon and said that a certain Lewicki had found out about us. We decide to move to the ghetto. Mum goes with Patrontasch that same evening; Dad goes with the Mehlmans, in a temperature of minus 20 degrees, to the hiding place in the yard of the oil mill, and in the meantime, Uncle Josek brings everyone else into the ghetto (uncle was in the militia and pretended he was escorting us to work). Dad resolved to find somewhere else to hide and get us out of the ghetto. The ghetto made a ghastly impression on me. Most of all, the barbed wire around it makes it feel like a kind of cage. Inside, the ghetto is teeming with life. People are out and about all the time, all the cake shops are full. The bakers are doing a roaring trade. Everyone tries to eat and drink as much as he can. No one wants to think about tomorrow. Everyone merely wants to eat his fill before he dies, for an operation is expected any day. Older

18 Klara Letzter.

19 On 1 Dec. 1942 the Germans established a ghetto under constant guard in Żółkiew, which was liquidated in March and April 1943; this was not one of the thirty-two ghettos in District Galicia where Jews were allowed to remain temporarily under the police regulation of 10 Nov. 1942: *VOBl-GG*, no. 98, 14 Nov. 1942, pp. 683–686, here p. 684.

20 German in the original: 'ethnic German'.

people describe this as 'szajdym chasyny' – wesele duchów.[21] After two days in the ghetto, we return to Mr Beck's (the matter was resolved favourably in the meantime) but Mama stays behind in order to sell a few things. The next day I learn that Aunt Ućka has caught typhus. I wait until evening and go with Miss Ala to fetch Mama. But Mama doesn't want to leave until she has found a nurse, and not until Rela and Josek assured her they would look after my aunt and find a nurse did she come back, but only after three days. Those three days were an eternity for me. I fear that Mama has been infected, in which case we will all have to leave the hiding place; Ućka is healthy, but with her asthma Mama would certainly not withstand typhus. The day after Mama's return, Josek brought Rela to us because panic was spreading in the ghetto in the face of a forthcoming operation. The operation never took place, it was just panic, but Aunt Rela remains with us, whereas Uncle has hidden the child with a worker he knows and has himself stayed behind in the ghetto. There are again eleven of us, for Mrs Klara has remained in the ghetto, where she has to care for her mother, two brothers, her sister, her brother-in-law, and Mrs Patrontasch's sister, who are all sick with typhus. Only after her mother has died and the others have recovered does she return.

## DOC. 214

## In January 1943 the Polish government's representation in occupied Poland reports on deportations from the Warsaw ghetto and Lublin-Majdanek concentration camp[1]

Situation report for January 1943 from the government delegation in Warsaw, unsigned,[2] to the Polish government in exile in London, dated January 1943[3]

*Report from the Jewish sector,*[4] January 1943

The situation of the Jewish population at the beginning of 1943 is above all characterized by the continued physical extermination of the remnants of this community who have managed to save themselves up to now. The problem of rationally employing the Jewish population no longer exists, there is no longer even any tendency to isolate the semitic element: all that remains is the murder of those who have not yet been finished off, a hunt for the remainder of those left alive, the total and final extermination.

21 Hebrew and Polish in the original: 'ghost wedding'. This is a reference to the 1910 play 'Wesele' (The Wedding) by Stanisław Wyspiański (1869–1907), which is about a wedding during which guests are visited by a range of spirits. The term can also refer to a ceremony for someone who has died or is awaiting death.

1 AAN, 1325/202/XV-2, fols. 253–254. This document has been translated from Polish.
2 The author is probably Witold Bieńkowski (1906–1965), journalist; Catholic activist and journalist prior to Sept. 1939; active in the resistance from 1940; in summer 1941 co-founded the Front for Poland's Rebirth (FOP) and was editor of the underground newspaper *Prawda*; later served simultaneously as head of the Section for Jewish Affairs and the Department of Prisoner Welfare within the government delegation's Internal Affairs Department; one of the founders of the Council to Aid Jews.
3 Handwritten note above the document: 'sent to L.[ondon], 26 Feb. [19]43'.
4 Original title crossed out: 'Żydci' ('the Jews').

The official announcement by the Germans in December 1942 of the creation of 55 points to concentrate the Jewish population in GG territory (District Warsaw – 6, District Lublin – 8, District Radom – 4, District Cracow – 5, District Lwów – 32),[5] which might have created the impression that they wanted to assign the Jewish population a final home and give them the chance of a livelihood, or tolerate their existence, at least for some time, has proved to be pure fiction. These very small ghettos (the largest one, Warsaw, had approximately 35,000 people at the end of 1942) offer no guarantee of survival for the unfortunate Jews; instead they are merely assembly points and staging posts, through which the Jewish masses flow in a rapidly dwindling stream on their way to extermination in Treblinka, Bełżec, Majdanek near Lublin, and other death camps. The ghettos stipulated in these regulations are places where German bestiality manifests itself continuously: it is here that scattered Jews are gathered together – Jews from liquidated forced labour camps or from other towns (for example in the territories incorporated into the Reich) – and, after being starved, robbed, and physically and mentally tortured, anyone who has not yet been finished off is sent to the death camps to be executed. Incidentally, these ghettos are being completely dismantled: although ghettos were created in Siedlce and Kałuszyn not even two months ago, all the Jews from these places have already been sent to Treblinka to be executed.

A clear example of these methods is the course of events during the latest massacre in the Warsaw ghetto on 18–21 January 1943. The particular reasons for this massacre are not known: it is said among German circles in Warsaw that it was a reprisal for attacks allegedly carried out by Jews (time bombs in German cinemas), but this appears to be entirely fabricated. Because there are no concrete or obvious reasons for this massacre, it was undoubtedly yet another everyday outbreak of the German destructive insanity that most easily targets those who are totally defenceless.

This latest show of violence proceeded as follows: after the German police had cordoned off the ghetto at night, on the morning of 18 January 1943 an extensive resettlement operation began, targeting mainly the so-called illegal housing blocks (i.e. people not billeted in connection with forced labour for German firms), but billeted Jews and even Jewish Community institutions such as the supply, health, and construction sections were also affected. Even the Community Council together with its chairman and office staff were targeted and sent to Kawki,[6] where the train wagons are loaded (however, the chairman[7] and the members of the executive committee[8] were saved on this

5 The Higher SS and Police Leader in the General Government, Friedrich-Wilhelm Krüger, had issued police regulations on 28 Oct. 1942 and 10 Nov. 1942 that specified which ghettos in the General Government were to be allowed to remain in place for the time being: see Doc. 168.

6 Presumably: 'to Stawki [Street]', the location of the so-called Umschlagplatz.

7 Marek Lichtenbaum (1876–1943), engineer; on the Council of the Jewish Community in Warsaw prior to Sept. 1939; member of the Jewish Citizens' Committee founded in Sept. 1939; deputy chairman of the Jewish Council, Oct. 1939 – July 1942, and its chairman after Adam Czerniaków's death; shot and killed by the Germans in the ghetto on 23 April 1943.

8 This was only true for some of the executive committee's members. Nine of them did not survive the murder operation: journalist Ber Ajzyk Ekerman (b. 1891), one of the leaders of Agudas Yisroel; engineer Dr Rachmil Henryk Glücksberg (b. 1883); lawyer Natan Grodzieński; Zygmunt Hurwicz; Józef Jaszuński; and Bernard Zundelewicz (b. 1886) were murdered on 18 Jan. 1943. Tadeusz Bart (b. 1873), Dr Izrael Milejkowski, and Bolesław Rozensztat (b. 1887) were deported to Treblinka in Jan. 1943.

occasion). It should be noted that this operation took place at almost the same time as a roundup of the Polish population in the streets of Warsaw, which lasted several days, from 15 to 19 January, and which incited unrest in Warsaw.

This time the ghetto population mounted resistance against the German acts of violence. Passive resistance involved escaping and hiding, ignoring German demands to gather in the streets. It was generally effective. There was also active resistance, but because of the element of surprise and a lack of weapons, it did not assume any significant proportions. Nonetheless, there was shooting and street fighting, buildings were besieged, and there were bloodied casualties on both sides. The Germans were compelled to deploy heavy weapons such as machine guns, apparently also artillery and armoured cars, hand grenades, and so on. They operated in units in full field equipment, and in fairly large numbers (up to 600 men). On the Jewish side it became apparent that there was an active and operational combat organization that deployed a number of specific, targeted street-fighting tactics and demonstrated a certain will to fight, which generally came as a surprise.[9] Of course, this resistance yielded no direct results as the deportations continued regardless, reportedly involving 5,000 to 6,000 people. The quashing of the resistance entailed bloody reprisals from the Germans (over 200 Jews killed during the fighting and during subsequent house searches). The overall situation in the ghetto has not improved, for example in regard to nutrition, health, and the risk to life and property. The German losses are estimated – perhaps excessively – at around 20 killed and 10–20 wounded. After 21 January calm prevailed again in the Warsaw ghetto; in other words, there was some life in the streets, groups of workers from the outside reappeared in the streets, and the gendarmerie cordons at the ghetto walls were scaled back or even removed entirely. The above events made a considerable impact on Warsaw, particularly in view of the fact that the Polish population was attacked at the same time: the view is that the reflex of Jewish self-defence, even if late and purposeless, redeems the honour of the Jewish people and serves as an ominous warning for the thuggish occupiers.

In other news about the Jewish community, there are snippets of information from Majdanek, near Lublin, brought by Poles released from there. These pieces of information are significant because they provide a more accurate picture of the fate of the Jews confined in the resettlement camps, for example in Treblinka. In mid January this year, there were several thousand Jews in Majdanek who had been brought there from various parts of the GG, especially the Lublin region. They are in a terrible state: clothed only in 'suits' made of washable paper, lice-ridden, starving, completely weakened – they are perishing in their hundreds every day, mainly from cold. In the barracks and squares Jewish stooges stand guard, never letting their whips and clubs out of their hands. The mistreated Jews are beaten and broken. Horrible punishments and reprisals for even the slightest misdemeanour are the order of the day: whipping until the victim loses consciousness or dies, and shooting people dead; there is even talk of hanging as a punishment, where the Jews themselves assume the role of executioners. However, no one in this camp has reported any mass murders with a view to extermination of the kind

9 A reference to the Jewish Combat Organization (ŻOB).

that have made Treblinka and Bełżec so infamous (gas chambers, mass death baths,[10] shootings of entire groups with machine guns, etc.).[11] Nevertheless, in the Jewish barracks at Majdanek, the mortality rate is extremely high. On the other hand, the Jews in Majdanek trade in vodka, cigarettes, sweets, etc. Most of the mass of imprisoned Jews have a passive attitude towards the imprisoned Poles, but on the other hand, the behaviour of the Jewish camp auxiliary service towards the Poles is terrible: they threaten them with whips, knock them about, demand signs of respect and obedience, announce mistreatment, etc.

An example of the attitude of the Germans towards the Jewish population is the use of the Great Synagogue in Warsaw (Tłomackie Street) to store furniture robbed from the Jews, and as an auction house, where there is a brisk trade at all times.

## DOC. 215
## On 7 February 1943 the Polish police station in Chęciny reports that Szraga Najfeld has been shot dead[1]

Handwritten letter from the Polish police station in Chęciny (log no. 95/43), signed by Polish police officer and group station commander Mańka, to the gendarmerie platoon commander in Kielce, dated 7 February 1943

I report that at 8.00 p.m. on 4 February 1943 the Pole Przezdzik Zygmunt, resident in Chęciny, stopped the Jew Najfeld Szraga,[2] 28 years old, in Chęciny and brought him to the station here.

Najfeld stated that he was staying in the forest and that he had come to Chęciny to get food.

Najfeld was shot dead by Officer Pułap on my orders.

Najfeld had 849.55 gr.[3] on his person, enclosed as evidence.[4]

10 The sick and those considered unfit for work were subjected to ice-cold 'baths' during which they were blasted with jets of water. Many perished from circulatory collapse or drowned. This practice had previously been introduced in the concentration camps and labour camps.

11 Mass murders using poison gas were also committed at Lublin-Majdanek concentration camp from Sept. 1942 to Sept. 1943.

1 AIPN, GK 675/1 (CA MSW 372/1), fol. 510. This document has been translated from German.

2 Jair Szraga Najfeld, also Neufeld (1921–1943); originally from Jedlińsk; student at a yeshiva (Jewish religious school) prior to Sept. 1939.

3 Here: groszy. Correctly: 849.55 złoty.

4 At the bottom of the letter is a typewritten note by the Bezirks-Oberleutnant of the gendarmerie platoon in Kielce dated 7 Feb. 1943: 'Original submitted to the SS and Police Leader in District Radom with the 849.55 zloty in cash enclosed' (signature illegible).

## DOC. 216

## On 11 February 1943 a Home Army counter-intelligence officer advises against supplying the Warsaw ghetto with weapons[1]

Reports from the Home Army's intelligence/counter-intelligence department, signed 'Mandaryn',[2] Warsaw, dated 11 February 1943

On site, 11 February 1943
Murders, assaults, looting.
On 1 February 1943 at 11 p.m., the bodies of two people were found – shot. Names unknown. Medical Forensic Institute.

On 2 February 1943 at 7 p.m., three unknown individuals (one of them in a German uniform) broke into a certain Rab Anna's apartment at 5 Krakowskie Przedmieście Street. They took with them: four furs and three fox furs. They were not apprehended.

On the same day at 7.15 p.m., Officer Banaszczyk of the 23rd police precinct at 24 Szczęśliwicka Street was disarmed. A Vis pistol and ammunition were taken from him.

On the same day at 7.40 p.m., three people (one of them in a German uniform) stormed into a certain Mrs Obozimska's apartment at 22 Świętojerska Street. They took clothing with them.

On 3 February 1943 at 6 p.m., four people stormed into Arbuz Teodor's apartment at 11 Nabielak Street. They took 4,000 złoty, jewellery, and clothes.

On 6 February 1943 at 2 p.m., shots were fired in Długa Street (two Germans were killed). During a search on Długa Street, two people were encountered by chance; a trail led from them to the *Szaniec* printing house. A struggle ensued, in which two Germans as well as two Poles employed at the printing house were killed. The editorial staff escaped. Orders and instructions were being printed at the time. It was not possible to destroy these.

On 6 February 1943 at 7 p.m., shots were fired in Filtrowa Street; one German was killed.

On 6 February 1943 at 7 p.m., shots were fired in the Italia Passage; there were no recorded victims.

On 9 February 1943 at 2 p.m., an alleged Jew was killed in 39 Wspólna Street. He had put up fierce resistance by shooting back.

On 10 February 1943 at 7 a.m., during a house search at 8 Salezy Street, Officer Boszko from the Criminal Police was killed. Jews are said to have lived in this building.

On the same day at 2 p.m., shots were fired at 29 Królewska Street.

1 AAN, 1326/203/X-57, fol. 34. Published in Dariusz Libionka, 'ZWZ-AK i Delegatura Rządu RP wobec eksterminacji Żydów polskich', in Andrzej Żbikowski (ed.), *Polacy i Żydzi pod okupacją niemiecką 1939–1945: Studia i materiały* (Warsaw: Instytut Pamięci Narodowej, 2006), pp. 15–207, here p. 158. This document is part of a file named 'Komenda Obszaru Warszawskiego – Meldunki 1942–43'. This document has been translated from Polish.

2 Code name of Bolesław Nanowski (1912–1975), career officer in the Polish army with the rank of lieutenant; head of the Counter-intelligence Section of the Police Division in the Home Army's Warsaw Area Command from autumn 1942; fought in the Warsaw Uprising; lived in Britain after the war.

The ghetto. It seems that the rest of the Jews in the ghetto intend to organize resistance should the liquidation operation resume. For this purpose money is being collected to purchase weapons. Such contributions are often mandatory. Additionally, a few raids have been carried out in order to increase the stocks of weapons, namely on the Jewish Supply Office, from which over 40,000 złoty were taken (office manager Marynower),[3] and on the Jewish elder's office, from which approximately 120,000 złoty were stolen.

In my opinion, this operation may result in a certain number of quality weapons being taken beyond the ghetto walls and thus indirectly falling into German hands. One cannot expect the Jewish resistance to be so significant as to justify supplying it with weapons. German losses would not compensate for the value of these weapons, and the Jewish resistance will not merit even a mention in relation to the 'honour of the Polish Jews'.

Work is being carried out at the former military prison in the ghetto area.[4] A camp is to be set up there, probably also for Poles. Five Criminal Police officials have been assigned to it.

Warning: *Kostrzewa Stanisław*, at 43 Królewska Street, an official at the Coal Office. In conversation, he occasionally emphasizes that he is ashamed to be a Pole. He has friends in the Gestapo who have often helped him get out of various shady affairs. He is known to take bribes.

[…][5]

## DOC. 217

## On 16 February 1943 Himmler orders the complete demolition of the remaining part of the Warsaw ghetto[1]

Letter (marked 'secret') from the Reichsführer-SS (log no. 38/33/43g.), signed Himmler, Field Command Post,[2] to the Higher SS and Police Leader East, Krüger, Cracow, dated 16 February 1943

For reasons of security, I give the order to demolish the Warsaw ghetto following the relocation of the concentration camp.[3] Any parts of the buildings and materials of any kind that can be used in some way should be salvaged beforehand.

It is necessary to demolish the ghetto and move the concentration camp,[4] as we will most likely never bring Warsaw to heel or be able to eradicate criminal activities if the ghetto remains.

3 Probably Jerzy Marynower, head of the fuel division of the Warsaw Jewish Council's Supply Office.
4 This was the Order Service's former prison.
5 Two further reports follow.

1 BArch, NS 19/1740, fol. 9. Published as a facsimile in Léon Poliakov and Joseph Wulf, *Das Dritte Reich und die Juden* (Berlin: arani, 1955), p. 171. This document has been translated from German.
2 Himmler's field command post Hochwald in Kreis Angerburg, East Prussia.
3 This is a reference to the so-called residual ghetto (*Restgetto*), in which approximately 30,000 forced labourers lived and worked for the German war economy. The SS did not establish the concentration camp in Warsaw until mid 1943, after the Ghetto Uprising: see Doc. 256.
4 In Feb. 1943 some of the enterprises in the Warsaw ghetto, along with the people working for them, were relocated to the Trawniki and Poniatowa camps. There were plans for the other enterprises to follow suit shortly thereafter.

A master plan for the ghetto's demolition must be presented to me. It must absolutely succeed in wiping off the map all the housing hitherto available for 500,000[5] subhumans, which will never be suitable for Germans, and in reducing the size of the million-strong city of Warsaw, which has always been a dangerous hotbed of subversion and rebellion.

## DOC. 218

### On 25 February 1943 a Polish underground organization's intelligence service reports that exhumed corpses are being burned in the extermination camps[1]

Reports from the National Armed Forces Intelligence Service[2] for the National Armed Forces High Command, dated 25 February 1943[3]

*Dept. II.*[4]
*To the High Command*
Special report dated 25 February 1943[5]

I. […][6]
II. We are receiving information from various sources that in the extermination camps (Treblinka, Sobibór, Bełżec, and others) and in other places where mass exterminations took place (such as the Warsaw ghetto), the Germans have recently started to exhume corpses from the mass graves and burn them. Most of the information speaks of the exhumation of *Jewish* corpses. The presumed purpose of this operation: the destruction of material 'evidence' of the crimes committed. This indicates that the Germans reckon with a rapid collapse, or at least with withdrawing from these areas.
III. We have received (absolutely reliable) news that new financial aid for the Jews in Warsaw has arrived in the last few days.[7] The group engaged in distributing these funds consists mainly of people who are affiliated with Sanacja. Some of them are now with

5 In fact, far fewer people were living in the ghetto.

1 AAN, 1329/207/6, fols. 30–31. This document has been translated from Polish.

2 The National Armed Forces (NSZ) was an underground military organization linked to the National Democracy (ND) movement; with tens of thousands of members, it constituted the second-largest armed group in occupied Poland after the Home Army, which part of the NSZ joined in 1944. In Jan. 1945 a brigade of approximately 1,500 NSZ soldiers under German supervision retreated ahead of the Red Army into the Protectorate of Bohemia and Moravia.

3 Additional copies were sent to the National Armed Forces' (political) leadership and to the archives.

4 The Intelligence Department.

5 A handwritten notation is inserted next to this: 'No. 3 – K 30'.

6 The first section discussed how the German police intended to completely annihilate the Polish underground by 15 March 1943. In response, the Intelligence Service recommended that a series of precautionary measures be taken.

7 This is presumably a reference to financial support provided by the recently formed Council to Aid Jews.

Zuzanna.[8] According to the information received thus far, the money for the Jews comes via Zuzanna. Personal and other details are being processed.
[…][9]

## DOC. 219
## *Biuletyn Informacyjny*, 25 February 1943: article expressing admiration for the Jewish resistance[1]

*The Jews are putting up resistance*

The shots and explosions that echoed throughout the Warsaw ghetto in mid January have reverberated across Poland. Polish society has reacted with admiration to this evidence of determination and brave resistance. The Germans are not hiding their surprise and still cannot believe it. Meanwhile, alongside sad reports of atrocities committed by the occupiers against the Jewish population, which is in the process of being liquidated, news of frequent cases of resistance is reaching us from other parts of Poland.

In the first half of January, the liquidation of the ghetto in Lwów continued. Some 8,000 Jews were taken away. In response to armed resistance and their own losses, the Germans locked up women and children in a number of buildings, which were then set on fire.[2]

The liquidation of the ghettos in Sandomierz and in Mińsk Mazowiecki was also met with active resistance.[3]

In Krynki, near Białystok, twelve gendarmes were killed under similar circumstances.[4] Everyone escaped from one of the transports carrying the Jews from the Białystok ghetto – only the elderly and the children reached their destination.

8 Code name for the government delegation used within the NSZ.
9 Sections IV–VI reported on various matters, including the German military's ideas about building up a 'Polish Wehrmacht' to be deployed against the Soviet Union; the NSDAP had spoken out against this.

1 *Biuletyn Informacyjny*, no. 8, 25 Feb. 1943, p. 6; Biblioteka Narodowa, MF 45 818. Published as a facsimile in Wroński and Zwolakova (eds.), *Polacy – Żydzi 1939–1945*, p. 207. *Biuletyn Informacyjny* was the underground weekly of the Union of Armed Struggle (ZWZ), which later reorganized into the Home Army (ZWZ-AK). The bulletin appeared in Warsaw from late 1939 and became the most influential underground publication, with the highest circulation (over 40,000 copies in 1944). The final issue appeared in Jan. 1945. This document has been translated from Polish.
2 From 5 to 7 Jan. 1943 the Gestapo murdered approximately 10,000 Jews on the edge of Janowska camp in Lwów. During the preceding murder operation on 5 Dec. 1942, police units had set fire to buildings in the ghetto in order to force out people hiding inside.
3 The deportations of about 3,200 people from Sandomierz to Belzec began on 29 Oct. 1942. The attempt by a Jewish resistance organization to work jointly with the Home Army came to nothing. A total of 300 Jews from the Mińsk Mazowiecki ghetto who had been taken to a labour camp were murdered on 10 Jan. 1943 after actively resisting an evacuation order.
4 No further details of this incident are known. There had been a ghetto at Krynki since Dec. 1941, the residents of which underwent a selection procedure on 2 Nov. 1942. The Germans deported approximately 5,000 ghetto residents to Kiełbasin transit camp, and from there to Treblinka on 14 Nov. 1942. The ghetto was liquidated in Jan. 1943, and the remaining Jews were transported to Treblinka – according to other sources they were taken to the Sokółka ghetto and later to Auschwitz.

Throughout the last few days, the liquidation of Jews in the Dąbrówa Basin has continued. The operation is said to have included Sosnowiec, Chrzanów, and other places. So far, no further details are available.

In the ghetto in the capital [Warsaw], the Germans have proceeded to shut down the so-called szopy, i.e. the workshops, calling upon the workers to report voluntarily for work in the Lublin area. This operation was unsuccessful. There were no volunteers. Forced deportations then began. A fitting response from the Jewish workers was the first major act of sabotage carried out in the ghetto. On the night of 18th–19th of this month, a warehouse filled with several million zlotys' worth of furniture produced in the ghetto and ready to be shipped to the Reich burned to the ground.

All the above cases demonstrate that Jewish society has reached a turning point and that a brave determination to resist, the will to fight the German criminals, has come to the fore.

## DOC. 220

## On 3 March 1943 Odilo Globocnik accounts for the assets stolen from murdered Jews[1]

Letter from the SS and Police Leader in District Lublin (Gl/T, log no. 16/43/gRs), Lublin, to the personal staff of the Reichsführer-SS, for the attention of SS-Hauptsturmführer Grothmann,[2] Berlin, dated 3 March 1943[3]

Dear Grothmann,

As you will recall, on his most recent visit[4] the Reichsführer-SS requested several documents from me, which I am now forwarding to you enclosed with this letter.

They are as follows:

1. Assets delivered from Operation Reinhard,
2. Promotion recommendations,
3. Lists of nominees to receive the War Merit Cross,
4. Statement concerning the tower on the road to Kulm (Cholm),
5. Newsletter for settlers,
6. Activities of the BDM[5] leader Ilse Wilhelm,
7. Findings from the resettlement operation,
8. People screened for German ancestry,

1 BArch, NS 19/2234, fols. 1–3. This document has been translated from German.
2 Werner Grothmann (1915–2003), banker; trained as an officer at the SS-Junkerschule in Braunschweig, 1933–1935; served in the war, 1939–1940; served on Himmler's personal staff as a military adjutant from August 1940, and as chief adjutant of the Waffen-SS from April 1942; lived in various places in West Germany after the war, latterly in Krailing, near Munich.
3 The same handwritten note appears repeatedly next to the log number: 'secret Reich matter!'
4 Himmler had visited Lublin in Jan. 1943.
5 Acronym for Bund Deutscher Mädel (League of German Girls). The BDM dispatched a number of its leaders to the General Government to assist with Germanization, typically by means of propaganda, education, and welfare targeted at ethnic German resettlers.

9. Resettlement of Germanic populations,[6]
10. Figures on resettlers and Germans placed [on farms],
11. Measures for further resettlement.

*Assets delivered from Operation Reinhard*

The following assets from Operation Reinhard have been delivered to the SS Business and Administration Main Office, Berlin, for forwarding to the Reichsbank or the Reich Ministry of Economics:

| | | |
|---|---|---|
| a) sums in Reichsmarks with a total value of | RM | 53,013,133.51 |
| b) foreign currency in banknotes from all the principal countries of the world (among which half a million dollars is particularly noteworthy) with a total value of | » | 1,452,904.65 |
| c) foreign currency in gold coins with a total value of | » | 843,803.75 |
| d) precious metals (some 1,800 kg of gold and approximately 10,000 kg of silver ingots) with a total value of | » | 5,353,943 |
| e) other valuables, such as jewellery, watches, spectacles, etc. (of which the number of watches is particularly noteworthy, with approximately 16,000 in working order and around 51,000 in need of repair, which have been made available to the troops) | » | 26,089,800 |
| f) approximately 1,000 wagonloads of spun textiles with a total value of | » | 13,294,400 |
| Altogether: | RM | 100,047,983.91 |

There are roughly 1,000 more wagonloads of spun textiles, as well as other assets worth approximately 50 per cent of those listed above – which are still being counted and valued – in storage here. It should be emphasized at this juncture that the figures cited above have been calculated based on the officially set rates and prices, although the market value is significantly higher, for example when precious stones or precious metals are sold abroad, because the rush for hard assets is greater there than in Germany. Moreover, foreign sales will bring us foreign currency.

These prices were taken as the basis for the valuations here in order to provide a picture of the assets delivered; in general, this calculation is not especially important. The value of what has been received lies principally in the fact that it was possible to obtain such large quantities of urgently needed raw materials, and that it is possible to acquire foreign currency based on the assets collected – thanks to which Reich agencies will in turn be able to purchase raw materials again.

One detailed list is enclosed.[7]

6 Among the Germanization measures envisaged for District Lublin were plans to bring in 'Germanic' (e.g. Dutch) settlers, similar to measures implemented in some other parts of Nazi-occupied Eastern Europe.

7 This list of the value of Jewish belongings handed over by 3 Feb. 1943, dated 27 Feb. 1943, is not published here: BArch, NS 19/2234, fols. 4–7. See also Doc. 281.

## DOC. 221

## On 3 March 1943 the Jewish Combat Organization in Warsaw calls for active resistance and threatens to exact retribution on those who help the Germans[1]

Message, signed Wac[ław][2]/9, for 'Mr Grab'[3] and 'Mr Sob.',[4] Warsaw, dated 14 March 1943

I am passing on this message from the Jewish Combat Organization.[5]

*Warning*

The passive and active resistance of the Jewish masses during the memorable days of 18 to 22 January 1943 took the Nazi bandits by surprise and convinced them that the Jews will no longer go like lambs to the slaughter. The German bandits had no other option but to interrupt the forced resettlement operation. The blood-stained occupiers realized that the methods used so far will not destroy the remnants of Warsaw Jewry.

Unfortunately, the most despicable scum of Jewish society came to their aid!

With the support of this scum, the occupiers want to trace and destroy the cells of armed resistance. The informers pass on details about hideouts, and their degenerate brains inspire the [German] beasts to make plans to exterminate Warsaw's Jews according to the system applied in Poniatowa[6] or Lublin.[7]

The Gestapo collaborator *Arek Wajntraub*, shot on 21 February, was found to have a document confirming that he and his accomplices had suggested to the Germans a plan to resettle the Jews to Poniatowa 'voluntarily' and 'using peaceful means'.

The Gestapo collaborator *Nosik*,[8] shot on 22 December, supplied the Germans with information on Jewish 'bunkers'[9] located in attics and cellars.

The chief loader on the Umschlagplatz,[10] *Brzeziński*, shot on 26 February, reacted aggressively to the demands of the Combat Organization and set snitches to spy on its representatives.[11]

The known Gestapo collaborator *Bobi Nebel*,[12] shot on 28 February, spied on centres of Jewish political life.

1 AAN, 1325/202/XV-2, fol. 255. This document has been translated from Polish.
2 Henryk Woliński's code name.
3 Stefan Rowecki, one of whose code names was Grabica.
4 Jan Stanisław Jankowski, one of whose code names was Sobol or Sobolewski.
5 Added by hand next to this: '[to] Mr Grab > Mr Sob.'
6 There was a labour camp for Jews in Poniatowa (District Lublin). See Docs. 264, 276, 277, 278, 281, 285, and 288.
7 This is possibly a reference to the deportations from Lublin to Belzec a year earlier. The ghetto in the Lublin suburb of Majdan Tatarski was liquidated on 9 Nov. 1942, and all but a few of its residents were murdered.
8 Correctly: Dr Alfred Nossig.
9 A reference to shelters in which large numbers of people were able to hide during deportations.
10 German in the original.
11 Mieczysław Brzeziński was an officer in the Jewish Order Service and worked closely with its deputy chief, Jakub Lejkin; during the deportations in summer 1942 he was in charge of the workers who had to round up ghetto residents at the Umschlagplatz. He refused to support the Jewish Combat Organization financially.
12 Correctly: Bubi Nebel.

*Adaś Szajn*,[13] the editor of the despicable Gestapo magazine *Żagiew*,[14] shot on 28 February, had been involved in denunciations and in demoralizing Jewish political life.

The Combat Organization has a full, exhaustive list of *all those* who, still in the service of the Germans, *have forgotten that they are Jews and human beings!*

*The Combat Organization warns all these scoundrels that they will be shot if they do not put an immediate stop to their despicable acts!*

All Order Service officers and functionaries are warned not to interfere with the work of the Combat Organization cells. They too should remember that neither Oberbandit[15] Brand,[16] nor any hideout, nor escape to the so-called 'Aryan side', will save them from a bullet delivered by the fighters.

All managers of the szopy inside and outside the ghetto are warned not to promote voluntary resettlement or to encourage their employees to participate in this.

*Jews!*
The German bandits will not leave us in peace for long. We therefore urge you to rally around the banners of combat and resistance. Hide your wives and children and stand up and fight the Nazi criminals with everything you have. The Jewish Combat Organization is counting on your complete moral and material support.
*The Command of the Jewish Combat Organization*
Warsaw ghetto, 3 March 1943

## DOC. 222

## Between 25 January and 18 March 1943, Edith Jacoby writes from the Warsaw ghetto to her sister in New York to say she does not believe she will survive[1]

Typewritten letter from Edith Jacoby,[2] Warsaw, to her sister Ida[3] and her family, New York, dated 25 January – 18 March 1943

Dear little Ida, dear Erich, dear Inge,

When you receive this letter, I will no longer be alive. I have tried so hard to pull through, but I have not succeeded. For three years – that is, ever since I got here – I have

13 Adam (Adaś) Szajn was employed at a brush-making factory in the Warsaw ghetto.
14 Żagiew (Torch) was a group made up of members of the Office for Combating Illicit Trade and Price Gouging (Urząd do Walki z Lichwą i Spekulacją) at 13 Leszno Street. The group was set up in late 1940 by the Gestapo's Section for Jewish Affairs with the aim of infiltrating the Jewish underground. It published an eponymous underground bulletin in Polish.
15 In German in the original: 'top gangster'.
16 Correctly: Karl Georg Brandt.

1 USHMM, RG 05 003*0. This document has been translated from German.
2 Edith Jacoby, née Aron (1900–1943), housewife; married Kurt Jacoby (b. 1900), who owned a porcelain shop, in Danzig in 1927; moved to Poland, from where they sent their two children Klaus (b. 1927) and Irene (b. 1931 or 1932) to Britain on a Kindertransport; Kurt Jacoby died shortly thereafter; Edith Jacoby was relocated to Trawniki with Schultz & Co. in late April 1943; she was murdered during Operation Harvest Festival in Nov. 1943.
3 Ida Joston, previously Josephsohn, née Aron (1895–1985), Edith Jacoby's sister; married Erich Josephsohn in Danzig in 1921; the couple emigrated to New York in 1938 with their daughter, Inge.

had nothing but worries, a lot of emotional turmoil, and great financial concerns. I have endured everything in the hope of seeing you and the children again. But what we have gone through here for the past half a year has been so unbearable that we are almost out of our minds with fear. Everyone is trying to save themselves, and I will do all I can too, but it is almost impossible without money. – A day after my birthday my best friend was taken away from me, so now I am left here all alone. He was a noble, distinguished man. Fate did not grant him the pleasure of seeing his wife and children again; they are living in the same country as Klaus and Reni. We lived together, with me looking after him and us sharing our last little bit of bread. L. Gersten from Leipzig.[4] – Since August I have been working at a large factory, in the office of the furriers' workshop.[5] The work seems to be stopping, and our end is drawing near. Most of my friends and acquaintances are no longer here, and Egon and [his] parents are no more. The Goldsteins put an end to their lives in August. Like all of us, their greatest desire was to see their children again; when they realized they would no longer be able to manage it, they did the wisest thing they could do. They have been spared a great deal of suffering. We took our leave of each other; I knew perfectly well that I would not be seeing them again the next day. Due to the terrible times, it was unfortunately no longer possible for us to bury them in a single grave. Mrs Cohn, who I lived with for a year and a half, is also said to have been gone for a few days now. The last people I have left are the Hirschls.[6] Through them I hope to save myself, but I don't know whether he will take me on and help me. It is a plan of mine – I want to give it a try. We all have enough on our plates.

There is not much to report about me. Time has left its mark – I weigh just 55 kilos, my hair is grey, and my face has aged! No wonder, after all the horrible things we experienced. Don't ever forget what we suffered here! How often I think of Kurt, who would never have been able to bear all of this, but it doesn't matter now anyway; we are all feeling absolutely desperate because we cannot see a way out. The tiny remnant of people still left is dwindling, and one's number grows ever closer to being up! It is pure chance that I have been able to save myself so far. God has protected me, and perhaps he will continue to do so. – I have only one wish: that the children grow up to be honest, decent people who do not lie or cheat. I have seen it over and over again, that a person gets ahead in life by being honest and upright. Giving away the children back then was the wisest thing I ever did in my life! The foster parents on both sides have performed superhuman feats. We have completely forgotten that there are such good and noble people in the world.

4 Chaim Lazar Gersten (1893–1943), retailer from Łańcut; lived in Germany from 1910; served in the Austro-Hungarian army, 1914–1918; owned a ready-to-wear fur shop in Leipzig from 1923; emigrated to Poland with his family in June 1939, with the intention of going from there to London. His wife, Rosa, née Künstlinger (b. 1895), their daughter, Hadassa (b. 1925), and possibly also their son, Abraham (b. 1923), had fled to Britain.

5 Edith Jacoby worked in the administrative department of Schultz & Co. Fritz Emil Schultz was an entrepreneur from Danzig and owned large tailors' and furriers' workshops in the Warsaw ghetto from 1941. In autumn 1942 his company still had 8,000 workers; some of them were transported to Trawniki between Feb. and April 1943; they were murdered when the forced labour camp for Jews was liquidated on 3 Nov. 1943 as part of Operation Harvest Festival.

6 Correctly: Hirschels. The sales representative Jakob Hirschel (1889–1943) and his wife, Bianka Hirschel, née Kasper (1892–1943), had lived in Danzig in the 1930s; Jakob Hirschel managed Bernhard Hallmann's enterprise from 1942 to 1943.

The last message from our dear, sweet mama was from July. She too has gone through the ordeal, like so many before her and after her![7] How is one to bear so much suffering and grief?!

I will close, [although] there could be infinitely more to say in such a 'final' letter. Franz knows which banks (two) our money is in. There is also a small amount at Amsterdamsche Bank in A'dam. Freeze the account with Anglo Bank by sending a telegraph message immediately after you receive this letter. I have written various cheques here to be drawn on that bank. Those who hold these cheques must be negotiated with on a new basis due to the extortionate rate, which I only accepted in my greatest need. The sums as they are stated [on the cheques] must not be paid out under any circumstances; my distress was exploited most shamefully. If I wanted to live, I had no choice but to accept this extortionate rate. Mr Loria is to be paid 1,500 [zloty] and Mr Hirschl 1,250 zloty so far. It is necessary to agree upon a new exchange rate with these two gentlemen.

This letter lay around for several days. In the meantime I have been to see H[irschl], approximately five minutes away from our residential district. He is the manager of a carpentry enterprise. He will probably not be able to take me on, since it is very difficult to place women there. People at all the enterprises are now talking about relocation (as opposed to resettlement),[8] but we fear it amounts to exactly the same thing. Everyone is in a constant state of terrible nervous tension, and in the evening you fall into bed completely exhausted. Understandably, however, no rest is to be found even then, because the fear keeps sleep at bay. What else can I tell you, of all the endless things I could say? How I live? In an awful building, six buildings away from my workplace. That is my only walk during the day (and has been for months). I have a dreary, bare room, which contains four beds, a table, chairs, and that's it. I have to go to my suitcase every time I need a handkerchief. The room is missing three of its windowpanes, which means the wind enters unimpeded. The door has no latch, so it is always open. My washing water is frozen in the mornings, my toothbrush turned to ice. When I moved in, four men were living in the room – one has stayed, but the others have been taken away! What else? My work is perfectly agreeable, [since] we aren't worked to death. The pay consists of one eighth of a loaf of bread with jam and, at lunchtime, soup – no more! We work eleven hours a day, from 7 o'clock in the morning until 6 o'clock in the evening. We are staying alive, and we all want to keep it that way; [the main thing is to] just survive the war. As far as my 'living situation' is concerned, I also have to report that there is neither lighting nor gas, the water is frozen, and I have to fetch it in jugs from the neighbouring building. Almost all of us have a little stove in our rooms, on which it is possible to cook, but for that you need wood, and that costs money, and money is something I simply do not have. I sometimes go for weeks on end with 1–2 zloty, until someone turns up who will give me something.

Quite the pleasant letter full of chitchat this 'final' one has become! You will certainly want to know a bit about Mr Gersten as well! Forty-eight years old, a Polish citizen, went to Leipzig at the age of 18. He owned what was probably the biggest fur shop there, [and] a branch in Königsberg. He was a highly knowledgeable Talmudist, and I learned an

7 Helene Aron, née Altschüler (1872–1942); wife of Jakob Aron (1856–1927) from Worms; mother of Edith Jacoby and Ida Josephsohn (Joston); lived in Danzig from 1928; perished in Theresienstadt.

8 A reference to the enterprise's relocation to Trawniki.

immeasurable amount from him on that subject. He was a very rich man, but lost his whole fortune here. He was so charitable, more so than I ever knew a person could be. An eccentric but strong individual.

So now I will close. As I write, I still harbour a glimmer of hope that I will be able to send you this letter personally after all. We have inadvertently become contestants in a race! Sometimes even an underdog wins.

Farewell, and may life be kinder to you and my children than it has been to me!

Yours,

18 March

Another month has passed now after all, a month full of agitation and fear. The whole furriers' workshop has had to leave for Trawniki, Kreis Lublin. I work in the office of the fur[riers' workshop][9] and have stayed behind for another couple of days, but I'm sure it is only a matter of days. We did not know [whether] it is the same there as in Tremblinken,[10] or [whether] it might be our salvation. They promise us all sorts of good things there: work, food, and employment until after the war. People have grown numb and, because there is no other way out, are resigned to their fate. – I do not know how or whether I will be able to write again from there. The woman who passes on this letter will be informed about me for the time being, and she will tell you everything you wish to know later.[11]

All my love!

Yours, Edith

## DOC. 223

### On 25 March 1943 Dutch resistance fighter Cornelis van der Hooft records SS officer Kurt Gerstein's account of mass killings in the extermination camps[1]

Report by Cor 'Snor',[2] dated 25 March 1943[3]

Tötungsanstalten[4] in Poland

The following report, with all its horror, astonishing brutality, and callousness, has reached us from Poland with an urgent appeal to inform mankind of its contents. A senior German SS officer vouches for the accuracy of the report. He made the following statement under oath, with the request that it be published:

9 The German original uses the short form Kur, which presumably stands for Kürschner ('furrier').

10 A reference to Treblinka.

11 Maria Kadłubowska, who corresponded with Ida Josephsohn (Joston) in 1946, forwarded this letter to her and informed her about the last months of Edith Jacoby's life. Kadłubowska recounted that she had sent food packages to Jacoby.

1 Herinnerungscentrum Kamp Westerbork, RA 1581. Copy in Landeskirchliches Archiv der Evangelischen Kirche von Westfalen, 5.2/684. This document has been translated from Dutch.

2 Cornelius van der Hooft, code name 'Snor' (1909–1945), official; worked with the Landelijke Organisatie voor Hulp aan Onderduikers, a Dutch organization that arranged hiding places and support for people going into hiding; wrote for the Dutch underground newspaper *Trouw*; arrested by the Germans in April 1944; perished in Germany.

In conversations with German officers serving in Poland and Russia, I heard the most unbelievably horrific accounts, and when I received sudden news of the death of my mentally ill sister-in-law,[5] I decided not to rest until I had established the truth about these horrific accounts and the killing of the mentally ill. I now invested all my energies into establishing contact with leading members of the SS in Poland and gaining their absolute trust.

Months later I thus managed to secure permission to visit two so-called Tötungsanstalten. The first one that I visited is in Belsjek,[6] on the route between Lemberg and Lublin; the second is in Treblinka, around 80 km north of Warsaw. There are two more in Poland, but I have not yet succeeded in gaining access to these. The two Anstalten[7] mentioned above are located in remote forest and heathland settings. From the outside they look no different to normal concentration camps. There is a wooden gate with some inscription or other on it, ending in 'Heim',[8] so anyone passing by would not suspect that this is a murder site.

The trains arrive there carrying victims from all parts of occupied Europe. They are made up of livestock wagons with barbed wire across the window openings. There are 120 people in each wagon. Under normal weather conditions around 90 per cent of them are alive when they arrive, although there was one occasion last summer when 50 per cent were dead on arrival due to a lack of water. Once the wagons have arrived at the camp, whips are used to force the people out and they are then herded into the surrounding barracks, where they are locked up. Either the next day or a few days later, depending on the size of the contingent, between 700 and 800 people are forced to assemble in an internal yard. They are then ordered to strip naked; their clothes have to be put in a neat pile, and their shoes placed side by side. Completely naked, the men, women, and children are now forced to proceed along a long passageway that is secured with barbed wire. Ukrainian criminals now begin to cut off and shave off the hair of the women and men. The hair is carefully collected and later used as 'Dichtungen'[9] for submarines. The unfortunates are made to stand for hours on end in the freezing cold or the blazing sun.

3 The report was based on an account given to Johan Herman Ubbink (1909–1990), engineer; owned an iron-smelting works in Doesburg (Netherlands); hid Jews in his home during the occupation; later emigrated to Canada; honoured as Righteous Among the Nations by the State of Israel in 1972. Ubbink received the information verbally from his friend Kurt Gerstein (see fn. 4), who visited Ubbink in Berlin in Feb. 1943 and told him what he had witnessed at Belzec and Treblinka. Ubbink relayed Gerstein's account to van der Hooft, who initially intended to publish it in *Trouw* but had doubts about its accuracy and decided not to do so.

4 Here and below, German in the original: 'killing centres'. The term was probably used in the original account given by Kurt Gerstein (1905–1945), engineer; joined the NSDAP in 1933, the SA in 1934, and the SS in 1940; member of the Confessing Church; from Jan. 1942 at the Waffen-SS Hygiene Institute; was tasked with increasing the efficiency of mass murder techniques in the extermination camps; while in French captivity after April 1945 wrote several reports on these activities and what he had witnessed at the camps; thought to have committed suicide in July 1945.

5 Bertha Ebeling, the sister of Gerstein's wife, Elfriede, was murdered at Hadamar psychiatric hospital, one of the killing centres in the Nazi 'euthanasia' programme.

6 Correctly: Belzec.

7 German in the original: 'centres'.

8 German in the original: 'home', often a reference to a residential institution.

9 German in the original: 'sealing'.

As soon as someone collapses from exhaustion due to the bitter cold or the searing heat, the executioners lash the naked body with their whips. Indescribable misery and suffering occurs in these passageways. Mothers attempt to warm their naked infants against their own naked bodies. There is barely any talking; the eyes of the unfortunates alone tell of their utter sorrow and numb resignation. The corridor goes as far as the iron door of a brick building. The door is opened and whips are used to force inside the 700 to 800 people condemned to death; they are packed in like sardines until they are no longer able to move. A little three-year-old boy who ran out was caught and lashed with a whip to force him back inside.[10] Then the door was hermetically sealed. Outside, to the front of the building, a large tractor is started up; the exhaust fumes are conducted into the building. I was now permitted to observe the effect on the victims through a glass pane on the outside. Crammed together, the unfortunates stood awaiting their last moments. There was no panic, no screaming, but a faint murmur permeated outside, as if a joint prayer was being sent up to heaven. Within the hour, they were all dead. The sliding windows were now opened from the outside to release the carbon monoxide. After half an hour, a number of Jews arrived – the horrendous task that now commenced is the reason they are alive. They open a rear door and now have to pull out the corpses of those gassed to death. Before these are brought to the prepared chalk pits, they have to remove the rings from the fingers, open the mouths and smash out any gold teeth.

In each Anstalt statistics are kept on the number of Tötungen.[11] Every day, i.e. every twenty-four hours, three to four Tötungen are carried out. In the four centres together, this amounts to 8,000 to 9,000 deaths per day. A total of 6.5 million people have already been killed in this way, of whom 4 million were Jews and 2.5 million mentally ill and so-called Deutschfeindliche.[12] The programme affects 16.5 million people, that is, all Jews in the occupied territories and all Polish and Czech intellectuals. The higher powers are currently pushing for the killings to be speeded up and for a more efficient method of killing to be found. Hydrogen cyanide[13] has been proposed; however, it appears that it is not yet usable for this purpose and so the aforementioned cynical method of killing continues to be the one employed.

25 March 1943.[14]

10 Changes of tense here and below as in the original.

11 German here and below: 'killings' (here in the sense of 'killing operations'). For a numerical account of killings in the Operation Reinhard extermination camps, see Doc. 204.

12 German in the original: 'enemies of the Germans'. The figures are overestimated: see Doc. 204 and Introduction, p. 45.

13 An element of the Zyklon B gas produced by the chemical company Degesch for use at Auschwitz-Birkenau.

14 An abridged version of the report had reached the Dutch government in exile in London by early May 1943. The report was never made public; the original was hidden on a farm near Doesburg. After Gerstein had been to Belzec and Treblinka, he also revealed what he had seen to the Swedish diplomat Göran van Otter and made efforts to inform the Swiss diplomat Paul Hochstrasser, the Vatican, the Confessing Church, and members of the German resistance. Details were never communicated to the Allied governments, however.

## DOC. 224

## *Walka Młodych*, 5 April 1943: Jewish fighters declare their solidarity with communist youth[1]

*Letter from the Jewish youth. To the comrades beyond the walls*

We, the fighters from the Warsaw ghetto, also get *Walka Młodych*. Separated for over two years by the walls erected by the occupiers,[2] we gladly welcome every fraternal thought about the fight against the Germans. Two months ago, the first 'machine'[3] we captured replaced the axe and the acid bottle. Now we are better armed. The fascist criminals and their Jewish henchmen have felt this first-hand. We are constantly in battle. Each day we gain valuable experience. The German knows that upon entering the ghetto a fighter's bullet awaits him from every crack in the wall, from every abandoned apartment. We shall never forsake our arms. Only death will part us from our weapons.

In the difficult January days, when criminals from the SS and the SD carried out mass murders of the defenceless population, every evening we drew strength for our struggle from the news that we were not alone, that bombs were exploding in Warsaw's cafe-clubs,[4] that the Yugoslav partisans are fighting successfully, and that acts of sabotage are on the rise in France. Our hearts beat faster when we heard about the Red Army's victories in the fight for freedom of all the oppressed.

Friends! We are with you!

With revolvers in hand, we await the moment when together we will blow up the walls and go forth together for the decisive battle for a Free Poland. A fraternal handshake to all the fighters in the forests, the villages, and the cities.

1 *Walka Młodych*, 5 April 1943, pp. 7–8: AAN, 1583/1040/1, fols. 15–16. The letter was presumably written in Feb. or March 1943. *Walka Młodych* was published in Warsaw in 1943–1944 as the underground newspaper of the Union of Fighting Youth (Związek Walki Młodych), the communist Polish Workers' Party's youth organization, founded on 3 Feb. 1943. The editor-in-chief was first Hanna Szapiro, code name Sawicka (1917–1943), then Jan Krasicki (1919–1943). This document has been translated from Polish.

2 The construction of the walls around the Jewish quarter began in April 1940.

3 This is presumably a reference to a small firearm.

4 On 24 Oct. 1942 a People's Guard squad had carried out an attack on Café Club, a bar in Warsaw which was located at the corner of Jerozolimskie Avenue and Nowy Świat and only admitted Germans; three police officers were seriously injured in the attack and other individuals sustained minor injuries.

## DOC. 225

## On 13 April 1943 Globocnik argues that a number of men under his command should be promoted[1]

Letter from SS-Obergruppenführer and Police Generalleutnant Globocnik, Lublin, to the head of the SS Personnel Main Office, von Herff,[2] Berlin, dated 13 April 1943[3]

Dear Gruppenführer von Herff,

SS-Obersturmbannführer Dr Brandt informed me that I should once again send you the nominations for promotion. I did have some slight hope that your announced visit would take place. As this is not the case, however – and since 20 April, the next date for promotions, is looming – I am sending the nominations to you by courier and request that you take them into consideration.

1. On the occasion of his visit in March, the Reichsführer-SS visited Operation Reinhard facilities[4] and, as I have already informed you verbally, approved promotion for the best men and SS-Führer[5] taking part in this operation.

I have already sent him the enclosed promotion list, a copy of which I am enclosing for you again. Major SS-Hauptsturmführer Christian *Wirth* will be promoted to SS-Sturmbannführer, about which […][6] corresponding certification is still pending. The […][7] camp commandant – Police Hauptmann Reichleitner[8] […] become SS-Hauptsturmführer. […] the greatest share […] 13 mentioned in the list […] SS-Hauptsturmführer […]. Among the SS-Unterführer […] the question.

Here I take the liberty of drawing special attention to *SS-Oberscharführer Schnur*,[9] mentioned third.[10] Not only has he been in charge of running the entire sickbay here for years, but he has also played an essential role in this operation by keeping our men healthy. I have therefore included him here, as already discussed with you, as an SS-Untersturmführer on the promotion list.

1 BArch, BDC, SSO 251B (Christian Wirth personnel file). The original document has been damaged by fire, and parts of it are illegible along the lower margin. This document has been translated from German.

2 Maximilian von Herff (1893–1945), career officer; member of a Freikorps; accepted into the SS in 1941, with effect from 1 Oct. 1939; joined the NSDAP in 1942; became commandant of the Herff Combat Group and the Africa Corps in 1941; acting head of the SS Personnel Main Office from April 1942, and its permanent head from Oct. 1942; died in British captivity.

3 The original contains handwritten annotations ('II A', '21/6'), underlining, and an illegible note dated 15 April 1943.

4 Himmler was in Lublin on 12 Feb. 1943.

5 SS leaders (of different ranks).

6 At least one word is illegible here; possibly: 'a'.

7 This and the six subsequent ellipses represent illegible parts of the text.

8 Franz Reichleitner (1906–1944), officer of the Criminal Police; joined the NSDAP in 1935 and the SS in 1937; Kriminalsekretär with the Gestapo in Linz; deputy head of the T4 'euthanasia' programme killing centre in the Hartheim psychiatric hospital, 1940–1942; commandant of Sobibor from Sept. 1942; sent to Istria to fight partisans in Oct. 1943; shot dead by partisans near Rijeka.

9 Mauritius Schnur (1905–1953), medical orderly; joined the NSDAP in 1933 and the SS in 1935; medical orderly for the Sonderkommandos in District Lublin; lived in the Saar region after the war.

10 This probably refers to the aforementioned promotion list, in which Schnur is listed third.

2. I am sending you the documents for SS-Sturmmann Dr Franz *Stanglica*,[11] whom I have already discussed with you. As you will recall from our meeting, I request that he now be granted the rank of SS-Führer on account of his outstanding academic work. Stanglica, who has been serving here in the most selfless manner for almost three years now, and has been overlooked time and again, truly deserves this promotion.

Requesting that you approve my submitted nominations by 20 April, I remain with best regards and the hope that your announced visit will take place soon.

Yours,

*PS*

The nominees (1) SS-Sturmmann Erwin Fichtner[12] and (2) [...][13] Fritz Jirmann[14] on the promotion list for members of the Operation Reinhardt Sonderkommando have recently been killed in action taken against armed bandits.

*SS-Führer and men involved in Operation Reinhard nominated for promotion*

After his inspection of Sobibor camp, the Reichsführer-SS agreed in principle to the promotion of the most deserving SS-Führer and men.

The enclosed list[15] gives an overview of the best men from all three camps.[16]

*Police Major Christian Wirth* is the responsible inspector. He was promoted to major on 30 January 1943.[17] My request is that Wirth be promoted to SS-Sturmbannführer at the same time.

In accordance with their functions as members of the police, *SS-Obersturmbannführer Gottlieb Hering* and *Police Hauptmann Franz Reichleitner*, who are listed second and seventh on the enclosed list, would have to be promoted to SS-Hauptsturmführer. *Police Oberleutnant Franz Stangl*, listed thirteenth, is nominated to become a Hauptmann and an SS-Hauptsturmführer.

11 Dr Franz Stanglica (1907–1946), historian; joined the SS and the NSDAP in 1941; worked at the Aulic Chamber Archive (Hofkammerarchiv) in Vienna from 1932; employed in the Department for the Jewish Question of the Reich Institute for History of the New Germany in 1937; then head of the Jewish Question Research Centre at the Vienna Court Archive (Hofarchiv); worked on settlement projects for Globocnik from 1940; served with the Higher SS and Police Leader East, 1943–1944; latterly active in the Operational Zone Adriatic Coast.

12 Erwin Fichtner (1912–1943), distiller; joined the SS in 1933 and the NSDAP in 1937; involved in the T4 programme in Bernburg from 1939; later served on the guard detail at Belzec.

13 At least two words are illegible here.

14 Fritz Jirmann (1914–1943), labourer; joined the Sudeten German Party (SdP) in 1934, and the NSDAP and the SS in 1938; initially served at Buchenwald concentration camp in 1939; then assigned to the T4 'euthanasia' programme; posted to the Grafeneck killing centre in 1940; later served on the guard detail at Belzec; accidentally shot dead by Heinrich Gley.

15 Two different versions of this promotion list follow in fols. 328–329: the first contains 28 names, the second 27 (leaving out SS-Unterscharführer Alois Rzepa).

16 This is a reference to the Operation Reinhard extermination camps: Belzec, Sobibor, and Treblinka.

17 In response to an enquiry from the SS Personnel Office to the Reich Security Main Office (RSHA), Department I A 5, Department I A 5 noted that Wirth was merely an Obersturmführer and had been a Kriminalrat since 30 Jan. 1943, not a major; promoting him was therefore out of the question until 30 Jan. 1946: BArch, BDC, SSO 251B (Christian Wirth personnel file), fol. 333. Wirth was nevertheless promoted directly to Sturmbannführer in August 1943, bypassing the rank of Hauptsturmführer.

The last three men mentioned are camp commandants, of whom Stangl is the oldest and the best, a man who was previously active in the SS illegally as a member of the police in the Ostmark.[18]

All the other SS-Unterführer nominated on the list have been involved in Operation Reinhard [from] the beginning and have proven their worth.

My request is that the Reichsführer-SS announce […].[19] The requisite papers [and] […][20] then from here to the Personnel Main Office […][21] with the Personnel Main Office about it […][22] [Gruppen]führer v. Herff is with […].[23]

*Promotion list*[24]

## DOC. 226

## On 13 April 1943 Hulda Pohoryles describes the persecution of Jews in Lwów and Brzeżany to her relatives and foresees her own death[1]

Letter from Hulda Pohoryles,[2] Brzeżany, to an aunt[3] and other relatives, dated 13 April 1943

13 April 1943

My dearest ones,

We've all become obsessed with writing farewell letters before we die. Each one of us who has someone living abroad is writing, in the firm belief that one day our murderers will receive the punishment they deserve. But you won't understand it; this letter, the words and images it contains, will not penetrate your consciousness. This doesn't surprise me at all, by the way, because not even I, though aware of it all, am able to comprehend such abject barbarity.

I don't know if I can convey even one hundredth of all the things we've been through over the last two years. I'll do my best, even though it may be ineptly at times, to relay to you what the infamous 'ausrotten'[4] was like. On 1 July 1941 the Germans entered Lwów, where I was living with Mama and Papa.[5] I won't describe my memories of that time in detail, as although they were terrifying, they have already started to fade. I'll simply mention the worst ones: the Ukrainian pogrom where each month thousands of people died

18 The name used for Austria following its annexation to the German Reich in 1938.
19 At least one word is illegible here; possibly: 'these promotions'.
20 At least two words are illegible here.
21 At least two words are illegible here.
22 At least one word is illegible here; possibly: 'spoken'.
23 At least two words are illegible here.
24 See fn. 15; this list is not published here.

1 YVA, O-3/3307, fols. 1–9. The handwritten original has not survived; a typewritten copy has been preserved. This document has been translated from Polish.
2 Hulda Pohoryles (Pohorilles) (1920–1943); from Lwów.
3 Klara Schwager in Tel Aviv.
4 German in the original: 'eradication'.
5 Roza Pohoryles, née Freudenthal (1896?–1943), and Emanuel Pohoryles (1896–1943), farmer; both were from Husyatyn.

as martyrs; SS units passing through the town and leaving behind a memento in the form of several hundred corpses with the SS mark branded on their foreheads; and other such incidents, which the three of us have by some miracle survived. On 1 September we came to Brzeżany, where my Igo[6] was, and we were full of hope that in a small town it might be easier to endure this hell. They did not let us enjoy being with one another for long. In October, on Yom Kippur,[7] all men aged between 18 and 60 were taken away to be registered. Seven hundred of them were imprisoned. Among them were my Igo and his brother. No one knew why they had been imprisoned. There was general talk of a camp. When, on the third day, I went to see a friendly doctor at seven in the morning to get a medical certificate for Igo (because at the time I still believed in such nonsense as medical commissions etc.), I witnessed something that froze the blood in my veins. The street was blocked off on all sides by Gestapo men, and people were being led out of the prison and into trucks, beaten and mistreated on the way, guilty of nothing other than being Jews. There were four such trucks, in each of which there were eight Gestapo men and about fifty Jews. I stood there and waited because I still wanted to see Igo (I was not wearing an armband, for a Jewish woman would have been shot for doing something like that). Thirty minutes later the trucks returned to collect the next load – and the process was repeated four times. I was unable to spot Igo in that crowd, but I did see the despair of others. Auntie, I will never be able to find the words to describe the look in people's eyes when they realize they can't escape death. The next day, some farmers came to us and said that all of them had been shot. None of us believed them, because the Germans insisted, 'man hat sie zur Arbeit genommen'.[8] For almost six months I kept kidding myself that my Igo would come back to me. Later, the continuous stream of transports made me realize that the farmers were to be believed.[9] On 18 December, Hanukkah, the Judenrat[10] was told to hand over 1,000 people, each with a 10 kilogram bundle. They were to be taken to Podhajce.[11] The city was beset with terrible despair, but ultimately it's not so tragic if you have to change your place of residence, especially if the starosta[12] personally telephones the authorities in Podhajce and tells them to prepare accommodation and lunch for 1,000 people. But the records fail to mention that these people never reached Podhajce but instead were all shot in the woods past Brzeżany,[13] along with the militia[14] escorting

6 Hulda Pohoryles's husband, whom she had recently married; his surname is not known.
7 The festival fell on 1 Oct. 1941.
8 German in the original: 'They have been taken for work.'
9 Between 500 and 700 Jews were murdered outside the town; they were buried at a former quarry.
10 Here and below, German in the original: 'Jewish Council'.
11 Podhajce is approximately 25 km from Brzeżany.
12 Here a reference to the Kreishauptmann Hans-Adolf Asbach (1904–1976), lawyer; joined the NSDAP in 1932; worked in the Gau administration of the German Labour Front (DAF) and headed its social welfare office in Stettin, 1934–1939; group leader in the General Government's Interior Administration Department from Jan. 1940; Kreishauptmann in Janów Lubelski, Oct. 1940 – August 1941, and later in Brzeżany; served in the war from Feb. 1943; taken prisoner by US forces in 1945; co-founder of the League of Expellees and Persons Deprived of Rights (BHE) in 1950; member of the Landtag and minister for social affairs, labour, and expellees in Schleswig-Holstein, 1950–1957.
13 It was overwhelmingly elderly people, women, and children who were shot halfway between Brzeżany and Podhajce.
14 Presumably a reference to men from the Jewish Order Service.

them. This operation was labelled a resettlement to Podhajce. Then there were various other roundups in which people were arrested and taken away to a camp. They resisted with their last ounce of strength. No doubt you think that a camp means only work. No, my dears, a camp means a period of heavy labour that exceeds human capabilities, a period of terrible hunger, misery, and typhus, ending with death by firing squad or hanging when one's reserves of strength have been utterly exhausted. In June, when the pre-harvest period became too difficult for us to bear, I decided to travel, without an armband, to Medowa[15] in the company of the gentleman with whom I am leaving this letter.[16] I was apprehended and handed over to the Ukrainian militia, who locked me up again. I sat in prison for three days and three nights, my mind full of extremely unhappy thoughts, until finally, thanks to several miracles, I could again behold the light of day. A few days later Mama broke her leg – and the resettlement operations resumed. They began in Warsaw, where there had been 500,000 people and only 60,000 were left, and continued in Lwów, where out of 80,000 people 16,000 remained, as well as in Tarnopol and other small towns. On 21 September (another fine day), a raid occurred where we were.[17] We spent three days and two nights inside a shelter made out of boards, a small wooden structure 1.20 m long, 50 cm wide and 1.30 m high, and looked death in the eye twice, when the Germans came in, as all they would have had to do was lift just one board. The owner of the house saved our lives, someone whom we least expected to do such a thing; he said the shelter didn't belong to the Jews.

On 15 October we were ordered to move to the [Jewish] residential district.[18] We felt like a fox that has been caught in a trap. For one and a half months, we lived in constant fear of this operation. We would get up at 5 a.m.; every single vehicle made our hearts race. On 5 December, again at Hanukkah, we were woken by the word 'raid!'[19] We went down to the shelter, where we were discovered at 6 in the evening. We were certain we would be sent to the square from where people were taken away, when we suddenly heard the words, 'Machen wir Geschäft.'[20] We began to gather the gold and silver, and what we didn't hand over they took themselves. For a full two hours they kept us in uncertainty and in fear of death, acting out a scene from a gangster film: 'Ich bin doch ein SS Mann, ein Teufel im Zivil, und Ihr seid Juden.'[21] It was like in the cinema, except that we were playing the starring roles. Then one of them took me upstairs and tried to test my courage by holding his gun against my head and telling me to count to three. I had no choice, so I counted and for this I received the accolade 'mutiges Mädel'.[22] I forgot to tell you that

15 Community halfway between Brzeżany and Tarnopol.

16 Stanisław Czerwiński; head of the highways authority in the Żagań community in 1946. He sent this letter together with several letters from Hulda Pohoryles's parents to their relatives in Tel Aviv after the end of the war.

17 Yom Kippur fell on 21 Sept. in 1942. Between 1,000 and 1,550 people were deported to Belzec, and several hundred were shot on the spot.

18 The creation of Brzeżany ghetto began in Sept. 1941; from Jan. 1942 Jews were no longer permitted to leave it without special permission. It was sealed in Oct. 1942.

19 Approximately 1,000 people were rounded up and deported to Belzec on 4 and 5 Dec. 1942.

20 German in the original: 'Let's do business.'

21 German in the original: 'I'm an SS man, a devil in civilian clothes, and you're Jews.'

22 German in the original: 'brave girl'.

from June this operation was called a resettlement to Polesie.[23] People travelled in goods wagons, 100 people on each one, without bread or water, [treated] worse than cattle. A few days later they arrived in Bełżec (if you have a map of Poland, you'll find it above Rawa-Ruska), where they were killed with an electric shock, to then be processed into soap (!) and synthetic fertilizer.[24] I'm sure you can't believe what I'm writing, you must be convinced there's something wrong with my head, but no, it's all true. During such an operation, posters were put up saying that a resettlement of Jews would take place on such and such a day and that any Aryan offering them shelter would face punishment. So you can imagine that not many Aryans were inclined to hide anyone. After the December operation, we were promised peace until 15 March. But none of us believed this, and we were right not to do so, because even though there were no raids during this period, several hundred people were killed for various reasons. Most of them were shot because they were sick with typhus or because they had committed various offences such as leaving the district, hiding their children with Aryans, Schleichhandel[25] (for buying two litres of milk and ten eggs), trade in general, and sometimes for no reason at all, simply for drawing attention to themselves. Oh yes, and because a mother refused to reveal where her husband and children were hidden, all of them were fit for a camp. So as you can see, there is no shortage of reasons.

On 30 March and on 1 and 2 April, after Purim, we experienced the final operation, which was now called Aussiedlung.[26] Three hundred people – men, women, and children – were thrown into jail, and after two days the women and children were taken to the cemetery and shot. The men were taken to the camp.[27] The scenes that were played out there are indescribable, and you'll find it hard to believe me when I write that as they were being led through the streets to the cemetery, the crowd were shot at incessantly and people kept falling to the ground.

Now we ourselves are on the threshold of death, we ourselves face a death worse than anyone before us, because we are fully aware of what to expect. And there is no escape, no reprieve. We would so like to live now – to survive this terrible time and to continue to live, to laugh [out] to the sun and to the entire world, and to live, to live.

I'm twenty-three years old, and for eighteen months I've had a deep, constant pain in my heart, but still I want to survive and to avenge the death and suffering of my Igo. But it's not possible – so I'm writing to you so that at least you can avenge our terrible death. So many people have poison, but still they allow themselves to be herded to the cemetery like sheep because they believe in some kind of miracle, something that will save them from the hands of the executioners at the very last minute. We don't have any poison because it's difficult to get hold of these days, therefore we have no choice but to proceed to our own funeral, take off our clothes, stand with our faces towards the grave, and receive a bullet in the back of the head. I shall certainly go alone because Mama can't walk, so they'll finish her off at home, and Papa still has a camp ahead of

23 Polesia is a historic region mainly located in what is today Belarus; its urban centres include the cities of Brest and Pinsk.
24 This rumour was untrue.
25 German in the original: 'black marketeering'.
26 German in the original: 'resettlement'.
27 Kamionka labour camp.

him. We expect this to happen at Easter – and presumably this will then be a liquidation operation.[28] So you see that when wine flowed in your home during the holiday, hot red human blood flowed here.

In the beginning the Judenrat and a militia, the Order Service, were formed. Back then no one could have imagined what they were going to be used for. No one could have imagined that the militia would first be used to work with the Germans to force people to the operations and then bury them in the cemetery. How many people have received gunshot wounds – not severe enough for them to die, but too severe for them to survive. And now those militiamen who still have a bit of heart are bedridden, lamenting what they have seen: human wrecks. I'm writing and writing, but I am still unable to render in the slightest what we've been through all this time. For I can't count all the times my heart suddenly contracted at the thought of an oncoming operation. I'm unable to convey the sheer animalistic terror that gripped us when the Germans broke into the cell or when they destroyed our shelter. And I'm unable to describe to you the scenes in the shelter when they simply ridiculed our men, saying that not a single one of them was able to save his wife and children from the injustice. I haven't described all the interludes between the operations, all the raids which they called inspections, when they took everything they could and said, 'Wirst doch sowieso sterben, Mensch.'[29] And, most of all, I can't describe to you our terrible, immense fear of the death that awaits us, such a death. But nevertheless we live, we are not going mad, we are not crying and screaming. We live as if everything that is happening doesn't affect us. We laugh and sing until the very last moment of our life. Only sometimes, when the voice of reality becomes too loud, do we forget to laugh. Uncle,[30] a few days ago I read your letter to us in which you write about the Russkies[31] and say that not even Hitler, the embodiment of what is despicable, evil, and malicious, has attacked any villages so far (you meant air raids.) Well, what do you think of him now? Has he not attacked villages because he thinks it unethical or because he thought it to be a waste of bombs? Wiwuśka,[32] you're twenty-one now, I bet you're pretty, with a nice figure, and your biggest worries are probably that your friend has a prettier dress or that your boyfriend cheated on you once. Believe me, compared to what we're living through now, all those worries can be left behind, like the skin shed by a chameleon. Nothing remains today, only naked life and naked death.

Well, I've written you a really long letter and can say farewell. Believe me, when this letter reaches you, I would much rather greet you myself. Everything I've written is a brief chronicle of Brzeżany. In other places it's been different, better or worse. In Stani-

28 The approximately 1,700 Jews who still remained in the ghetto and had been housed in a building near the Brzeżany ghetto so they would be available for forced labour were murdered on 12 June 1943. Emanuel Pohoryles, the letter writer's father, shot at the police officers who were rounding up Jews in Brzeżany during the murder operation, and he used his last bullets to kill his wife, his daughter, and himself: letter from Stanisław Czerwiński, Żagań, to Rubin Schwager, lawyer, Tel Aviv, 16 July 1946: YVA, O-3/3307, fols. 13–14.

29 German in the original: 'Come on, you're going to die anyway.'

30 Rubin Schwager.

31 The original has 'Moskali': a disparaging term for Russians.

32 Familiar form of the forename Wiktoria, presumably the letter writer's cousin, the daughter of Klara and Rubin Schwager.

sławów, for example, there was not a single day without a raid for twenty-two whole months, until the day when it was declared 'judenrein'.[33] In Bolszowce,[34] when clearing the town (people were hiding in shelters), grenades, incendiary bombs, and other toys were used. One could write so much more on this subject, but I have no more patience. I hope that what I've written so far has given you a more or less accurate picture of what we went through until our death. But even so, I'm sure that you won't be able to understand what we're experiencing and that after a few days you'll forget it like a bad dream, and I'd so like to prevent that. I'd like you to publish our letters at the right moment (there will be more of them), so that the vengeance is no less terrible than our suffering. I enclose a newspaper clipping.[35] Look at the barbarity: 124 people shot, most of them women and children. Is such hypocrisy possible?

Keep well, have fun, and don't waste your lives with trivialities. Today, I would be able to view life differently, but I resolved to do so too late. Now I know that everything is 'Scheiss'.[36] And the spring is as beautiful as our death will be terrible.

My love and kisses to you all,
Hulda.

I forgot to write one more thing. There are some Jews who enjoy certain privileges, mainly specialists who are identified by the letter W (wichtig)[37] on their armbands. During the liquidation period, barracks are being built for them, into which they have to move without their families. At some stage, these barracks will no doubt be presented as evidence of the favour which working Jews enjoy, for they have bathrooms. But the Germans will definitely not show you the food that is served, nor how terrible these barracks are, surrounded by a barbed wire fence two metres high. And they will certainly not tell you that eventually, when these people are no longer needed, they will all be shot like the rest of us. There are still idiots who go to camp voluntarily just to prolong their lives for the time being. But these are hopeless idiots. If something else comes to my mind, I will write.

My love and kisses to you all,
Huldzia.

33 German in the original: 'cleansed of Jews'.
34 Community near Stanisławów.
35 Not enclosed with this copy of the letter.
36 German in the original: 'shit' (correctly: 'Scheiße').
37 German in the original: 'important'. In fact, the 'W' on their armbands indicated that they were working for the Wehrmacht.

## DOC. 227
## On 19 April 1943 the command of the Jewish Combat Organization reports on the start of the Warsaw Ghetto Uprising[1]

Report by the Jewish Combat Organization, Warsaw, after 19 April 1943 (copy)

[…][2] [After][3] a few days, the patrols we had sent out encountered patrols from our other groups. We established contact. The Combat Organization command gathered in full and deliberated on the situation. Communication with the world outside the ghetto took place via telephone. Not everything could be discussed. By Good Friday[4] the telephones had already been taken from us and when we tried to connect our own telephone to the socket in the courtyard, we established that the electricity had been turned off. According to the group leaders, the combat operation inside the ghetto proceeded as follows: [At][5] 5.35, when the first SS unit marched into the ghetto via Nalewki Street, from the front of number 33, they were attacked with bombs, grenades, and incendiary bottles. Several shots were fired. The Germans quickly gathered the wounded and the dead and withdrew from the ghetto. A few shots were fired from this building towards the guardhouse on Nalewki and Świętojerska Street; two of the shots were on target. This unit had clearly been given the objective of securing Miła Street, which the Germans for a long time had considered the centre of the rebellion. At around 7 o'clock an SS unit was repulsed in the same way and in the same section. To secure our line of retreat, we used a few bottles to set fire to the building on the corner of 2/4 Gęsia Street and 37-31[6] Nalewki Street, which was full of flammable materials – in the courtyard, there were gathered […],[7] ma[ttresses], and sofa b[eds].[8] The groups withdrew after using up all the bombs, grenades, and incendiary bottles. However, the revolvers were not used in the operation.

1 AŻIH, Varia okupacyjne 230/121, fols. 7 and 9. Published in Berenstein et al. (eds.), *Faschismus – Getto – Massenmord*, p. 516, here titled 'Combat Reports Dossier', no. 2. The report is written in pencil on badly damaged paper; it was first found in a cellar in 1956, after which the copy reproduced here was archived. This document has been translated from Polish.
2 The first sentences are missing.
3 Part of the page was torn off here in the original; 'After' was added to the copy.
4 23 April 1943.
5 Part of the page was torn off in the original; 'At' was added to the copy.
6 There are question marks on the copy behind these numbers. The number 37 has been written over the top of another number, so it is possible that the original figure was different.
7 One word is missing here in the original.
8 The additions in the last two sets of brackets were inserted in the copy.

## DOC. 228

## On 19 April 1943 the Jewish National Committee and the Bund announce that fighting has started in the Warsaw ghetto and demand an international investigation[1]

Telegram from the Bund representatives and the Jewish National Committee, signed M[ikołai][2] and B[orowski],[3] Warsaw, to the Polish government in exile's Ministry of the Interior, London, dated 19 April 1943[4]

19 April 1943. Today, a few hours ago, armed SS units began to completely destroy the remnants of the Warsaw ghetto with tanks and artillery. The ghetto is putting up fierce, heroic armed resistance. The Jewish Combat Organization, which encompasses almost all groups,[5] is leading the defence. Artillery fire and loud explosions can be heard constantly from the direction of the ghetto. The glow of fire [can be seen] above the district. Aircraft are circling the scene of the massacre. Of course, the outcome of the fighting is a foregone conclusion. There is agitation throughout the city. This evening the defenders hoisted a flag bearing the message: We shall fight to the last man! The people of Warsaw are following this unequal struggle with admiration and pronounced sympathy for the ghetto resistance. Once again, we call for immediate reprisals. Demand immediately that the International Red Cross visit the ghetto as well as the internment camps in Oświęcim, Treblinka, Bełżec, Sobibór, Majdanek, and other concentration camps in Poland.[6]

1 The original could not be found. Copy in AŻIH, 230/124, fol. 10. This document has been translated from Polish.

2 Leon Feiner's code name.

3 Code name of Adolf Abraham Berman (1906–1978), psychologist and editor; member of Poale Zion-Left from 1926; after Sept. 1939 a key employee at CENTOS and co-editor of the underground Yiddish-language publication *Der Ruf*; secretary of the Council to Aid Jews on the 'Aryan side' from 1943; head of the Jewish Section of the National Council of Poland from Jan. 1944; deputy chairman of the Central Committee of Polish Jews (CKŻP), 1945–1949; in 1950 emigrated to Israel, where he was a Knesset delegate, first for the socialist party Mapam (from 1951), then for the Israeli Communist Party (from 1954).

4 Probably addressed to Schwarzbart and Zygielbojm in London.

5 Along with the left-leaning Jewish Combat Organization (ŻOB), the right-leaning Zionist Jewish Military Union (ŻZW) was also involved in the fighting. There were non-aligned resistance fighters as well.

6 After the German news reported on 13 April 1943 that mass graves with thousands of Polish victims of the Soviet secret police had been discovered in Katyń, the Polish government in exile demanded that the International Committee of the Red Cross investigate. This investigation did not materialize because the Soviet Union vetoed it, but the commission of international experts that examined the findings in late April 1943 included representatives of the Polish Red Cross (PCK) from the General Government.

## DOC. 229

## On 21 April 1943 the businessman Walther Többens issues orders for enterprises to be relocated outside the Warsaw ghetto with immediate effect[1]

Plenipotentiary for the Relocation of Enterprises in the Jewish Residential District of Warsaw Walther C. Többens,[2] 14 Prosta-Straße, Warsaw, to the management of the companies Schultz & Co. GmbH, Karl Georg Schultz & Co., Bernhard Hallmann & Co. KG, and Oskar Schilling & Co.; the Army Base Administration;[3] the enterprises W. v. Schöne, W. Leszczyński, E. Welk, Juljan Kudasiewicz, W. C. Többens, W. Hoffmann, Oxaco AG, Curt Röhrich GmbH, Hermann Brauer, Ostdeutsche Bautischlerei GmbH,[4] and G. Gerlach; Warsaw, dated 21 April 1943

Based on the plenipotentiary powers granted to me by the SS and Police Leader in District Lublin, SS-Gruppenführer and Police Generalleutnant *Globocnik*, in accordance with his letter of 12 March 1943, reg. 5423/43Mi/Oll.,[5] and in agreement with the SS and Police Leader in District Warsaw, Brigadeführer and Police Generalmajor *Stropp*,[6] I hereby inform you of the following:

1) All Jewish workers will be relocated on 21 April 1943. Departure at 6 o'clock in the morning.[7]
2) Materials and machines will be shipped according to my specific instructions.
3) As in the past, Jewish workers will be able to take personal belongings with them. Maximum weight per person: 15 kg.
4) Rations for two days are to be provided by the enterprise.
5) Some police officers are standing by. I will assign them to the [respective] enterprise starting this evening at 6 p.m. They must be catered for by the enterprise.
6) Equipped with a special ID issued by me, to be stamped by the SD, a small percentage of Jewish workers will remain in Warsaw to secure and dispatch the materials and machines.

1 AŻIH, Kolekcja B. Marka, S 333/622. Published in Tyszkowa, 'Eksterminacja Żydów w latach 1941–1943', pp. 250–251. This document has been translated from German.

2 Walther Caspar Többens (1909–1954), businessman; joined the NSDAP in 1937; from 1932 acquired seven shops that had previously been owned by Jews; worked at a coffee roastery in Bremen until 1934, worked as a wholesaler in Kreis Tomaszow in 1939; entrepreneur in the Warsaw ghetto, 1941–1944; arrested in Bremen in 1945; escaped from prison in 1946; gave himself up to the authorities in April 1951, classed as a *Mitläufer* ('follower') in denazification proceedings in 1952.

3 Heeresstandortverwaltung; also Army Billeting Administration (Heeresunterkunftsverwaltung): a reference to the brush-making factories at 34 Świętojerska Street, which had 3,600 workers in Nov. 1942.

4 The Ostdeutsche Bautischlerei carpentry workshop at 30 Gęsia Street had 200 workers in Nov. 1942; their housing blocks were located on Miła Street.

5 This has not been found.

6 Correctly: [Jürgen] Stroop.

7 These factories and workshops were moved to labour and concentration camps in District Lublin. Többens's operations and the Jewish forced labourers involved in them were relocated to Poniatowa camp, for example, while Fritz Schultz moved his manufacturing operations and forced labourers to Trawniki camp. SS-Sturmbannführer Georg Michalsen later testified that he personally supervised the Többens transfer to Poniatowa on 20 or 21 April 1943.

a) The workers at the W. C. Többens (Gerichtsstraße block) and Karl Georg Schultz enterprises will assemble for departure on the side of the street in the restricted area.[8]
b) The workers at the Schultz & Co. GmbH, Bernhard Hallmann & Co. KG, Oskar Schilling & Co., W. Hoffmann, and Curt Röhrich GmbH companies will assemble on Nowolipie Straße for departure.[9]
c) The workers at the Hermann Brauer enterprise will assemble in the enterprise's factory yard, at 38 Nalewki.
d) The workers at the Army Base Administration, E. Welk, G. Gerlach, and Juljan Judasiewicz enterprises will assemble in the courtyard at 32 Sto. Jerska.[10]
e) The workers at the W. v. Schöne enterprise will assemble in the Hühnerstraße factory yard.

I expressly point out to the management of these enterprises the fact that any workers found in the restricted area following departure who do not hold the aforementioned special ID will be summarily shot.

f) Finally, I hereby call upon the management of the individual enterprises to make every effort to ensure the smooth departure [of the workers], while at the same time safeguarding the materials and machines on hand.
g) The preceding directive has been issued because the difficulties that were becoming greater by the day no longer permitted any other solution.

8 With up to 25,000 workers, the Többens factories constituted the largest enterprise in the Warsaw ghetto; they produced textiles for the German war economy. At this point the company had 8,000 workers (all the figures given here and below pertain to Nov. 1942). Karl Georg Schultz & Co. (800 workers) produced socks for the Wehrmacht; its headquarters were located at 78 Leszno Street.

9 The Hallmann carpentry factory at 59 Nowolipki Street had 700 workers; the Schilling enterprise at 54 Nowolipki Street had 500 workers; the Hoffmann enterprise at 51a Nowolipki Street had 1,000 workers; the Röhrich enterprise had 500 workers.

10 32 Świętojerska Street; presumably the premises of the G[ustaw] Gerlach enterprise, which manufactured precision optical equipment.

## DOC. 230

### On 21 April 1943 the Polish government's representative and the Home Army's commander-in-chief provide information on fighting in the Warsaw ghetto[1]

Radiogram (marked 'secret') from the representative of the Polish government in exile and the commander-in-chief of the Home Army (log no. O.VI,[2] L.dz. 1994/tjn/43), signed Sobolewski[3] and Kalina[4] 639, Warsaw, to the supreme commander[5] and the deputy prime minister,[6] London (received on 26 April 1943, decoded on 27 April 1943), dated 21 April 1943

From: Wanda 1[7]
[To the] *supreme commander and* [to] *Stem.*[8] *No. 14a 43*

The liquidation of the main ghetto in Warsaw began at 4 a.m. on the 19th of this month. The ghetto was cordoned off by numerous German police and Blue Police, and substantial contingents of gendarmerie and SS drove into ghetto territory. Armoured cars and a few small tanks were even used for this operation. The Jewish Combat Organization is putting up fierce resistance. There has been continuous fighting in the streets for three days. Huge explosions are shaking the whole of Warsaw and clouds of smoke are hanging over the ghetto because numerous fires have broken out. Today, the 21st, the fighting continues. The Jewish enclaves that had previously been excluded from the ghetto, for example the Goebbels factory[9] in Prosta Street, were not included in the liquidation.

## DOC. 231

### On 21 April 1943 Radio Moscow quotes from an article in *Pravda* about mass executions of Poles in Treblinka[1]

Report (marked 'secret') from the Sonderdienst Seehaus,[2] dated 21 April 1943

Radio station: Moscow; language: Russian; time: 11:45–12:00 SW[3]
Ref: URu 93Sch; report: M
Text:
Announcement. And now the press review of the capital's newspapers:
[...][4]

1 SPP, 3.1.1.13.4/11, fol. 67. Published in Pełczyński and Tokarski (eds.), *Armia Krajowa w dokumentach 1939–1945*, vol. 2, p. 500. This document has been translated from Polish.
2 Department O.VI. refers to the armed forces' intelligence service, which reported to the Polish government in exile.
3 Stanisław Jankowski's code name.
4 Stefan Rowecki's code name.
5 Władysław Sikorski.
6 Stanisław Mikołajczyk.
7 The name of one of the transmitting stations.
8 Stanisław Mikołajczyk's code name.
9 Correctly: 'Többens Works'.

1 BArch, R 6/684, fols. 235–237, here fols. 236–237. This document has been translated from German.

Subject: concentration camps for Poles
6. An article by Comrade Sergeyev[a] has been published in *Pravda* with the headline 'Poland is the Hitlerian House of Death':[5]

'It is well known that, with the assistance of Hitler's Polish collaborators, the Hitlerian propaganda now seeks to use sham reports to conceal and wipe away the traces of the atrocities committed by the Germans in Poland.[6] However, the Polish people will forget nothing and forgive nothing. The article in *Pravda* uncovers the Hitlerian atrocities in Poland, and paints a shocking picture of the Hitlerites' systematic and deliberate extermination of several thousand people.

'Located between Warsaw and Białystok is the camp *Krelin-Tabeck*[7] (ph),[8] among other concentration camps for Poles. This camp is referred to as the headquarters of death. Mass executions take place there daily. People are killed with fumes, which are pumped into hermetically sealed chambers. Many people are taken to the headquarters of death every day. The people who arrive are lined up in rows. They are given the order to undress, and then the terrible procession begins. On the way, the people gradually realize they are being led to their deaths. The women and children begin to scream. But none of this lasts long. The German machinery runs just like clockwork. There is no hesitation. A German officer stands at the entrance to the chamber. The children are thrown over the women's heads. The floors in the cell are slippery. People usually fall and can no longer stand up again.[9] Once they have all been herded into the chamber, the door is shut and fumes are pumped into the chamber. The groans of the dying can be heard at first, but then it falls completely silent.

'The Hitlerites have exterminated nearly two and a half million people in Poland; a vast river of blood is overflowing there. No provocations on the part of the Hitlerian bandits will be able to wipe away the traces of their crimes there, which they have committed and continue to commit.'[10]

[…][11]

2 Sonderdienst Seehaus (named after the building in which it was located) was an agency that gathered and evaluated intelligence by monitoring foreign radio stations. Its approximately 500 employees were based at 28–30 Am Großen Wannsee in Berlin.
3 This abbreviation stands for 'short wave'.
4 The preceding portion of the broadcast contains reports on *Pravda* articles dealing with subjects including the mistreatment of Soviet forced labourers in Germany and the fighting in the Kuban region. *Pravda* was the official publication of the Central Committee of the Communist Party of the Soviet Union (Bolshevik) from 1918 to 1991.
5 *Pravda*, 21 April 1943, p. 4.
6 According to the official Soviet version of events, the Soviet mass murder of Polish officers in Katyń had been committed by the Germans. When the Polish government called this account into question, the Soviet government accused it of collaborating with Germany.
7 The *Pravda* article describes Treblinka A labour camp, constructed in 1941, as a concentration camp for Poles; the article also reports that Treblinka B, centred on ten gas chambers, had been constructed over an area of 5,000 square metres in 1942. This information was not included in the Radio Moscow broadcast.
8 The precise meaning of this abbreviation in German is unclear; potentially: 'phonetisch' ('phonetic'). The name of the camp in question – Treblinka B – was transcribed incorrectly by the Seehaus Sonderdienst: see previous footnote.
9 See Doc. 178, which contains similar wording.
10 On 13 April 1943 German propaganda stated that the mass murder of Polish officers at Katyń had been committed under the Soviet occupation; Soviet propaganda dismissed this claim as a 'provocation'.
11 The subsequent portion of the broadcast contains reports on further articles in the Soviet press.

DOC. 232

## On 23 April 1943 the Warsaw gendarmerie platoon reports from Otwock on the murder of refugees from the Warsaw ghetto[1]

Report from a gendarmerie officer in the Warsaw gendarmerie platoon, signature illegible, to the Warsaw gendarmerie headquarters, dated 23 April 1943 (copy)[2]

*Re*: daily dispatch

At 6 a.m. on 22 April 1943, fourteen Jews, eight male and six female, were apprehended as the gendarmerie carried out a major patrol in Otwock, Kreis Warsaw (24 km south-east of Warsaw). Action was immediately taken, based on the current measures.[3]

Some of these Jews exhibited minor injuries, which they had sustained on the night of 20 to 21 April 1943 during the events [that took place] in the Warsaw ghetto. The Jews left the Warsaw ghetto through underground passages and sewers.[4]

At 2.30 a.m. on 22 April 1943, six unknown bandits armed with pistols and hand grenades stole 270 zloty in cash, [as well as] clothes and linens worth 4,000 zloty in Mladz, Wiazowna municipality, Kreis Warsaw (22 km east-south-east of Warsaw).

No firearms were used.

The local guard post did not notice the raid.

Search: Rembertow gendarmerie station. Investigation: Otwock Criminal Police.

Action taken based on the current measures:

22 April 1943 – Rembertow – 2 Jews: 1 male, 1 female

22 April 1943 – Otwock – 14 Jews: 8 male, 6 female

Rembertow gendarmerie station

A. B.

1 AIZ, doc. I-42, fol. 297. Copy in AŻIH, 233/116, fol. 1. This document has been translated from German.

2 This is a copy, made on 29 April 1950, of a document from the Warsaw gendarmerie platoon's daily dispatches file, 12 Feb. 1943–2 Jan. 1944.

3 This is a reference to the directives to shoot all Jews found outside their mandatory place of residence.

4 The persons murdered were members of the Jewish Military Union (ŻZW) who had probably left the Warsaw ghetto via the tunnel between 7 Muranowska Street in the ghetto and 6 Muranowska Street on the 'Aryan side'.

## DOC. 233

## On 23 April 1943 the Jewish Combat Organization explains the purpose of the Warsaw Ghetto Uprising to the Polish population[1]

Leaflet issued by the Jewish Combat Organization, Warsaw, dated 23 April 1943[2]

*Poles, citizens, freedom fighters!*

Amid the thunder of the guns with which the German army bombards our homes – the homes of our mothers, children, and wives; amid the rattle of the machine guns which we seize in the fight against the cowardly gendarmes and SS men; amid the smoke of the fires and the dust left behind by the bloody massacre of the Warsaw ghetto – we, the ghetto prisoners – send you our fraternal and heartfelt greetings.

We know that you have been following our war against the *cruel occupier* for many days with profound pain, tears of compassion, admiration, and concern for the outcome of this fight.

So you should also know that, as before, every threshold in the ghetto will continue to be a fortress;[3] that we may all die in battle, but we shall never surrender; that, just like you, we seek vengeance and punishment for all the crimes committed by *our common enemy!*

*This is a battle for your and our Freedom!*[4]

*For your and our honour and dignity as people, as a society, and as a nation!*

We shall avenge the crimes of Oświęcim, Treblinki,[5] Bełżec, and Majdanek!

Long live the brotherhood of arms and blood of Poland's resistance!

Long live Freedom!

Death to the executioners and the torturers!

Long live the fight to the death against the occupier!

1 AAN, 1325/202/II-31, fol. 1. Published in *Na oczach świata* (Zamość [Warsaw]: Wydawnictwo 'GLOB' [Wydawnictwo K.O.P.R.], 1932 [1943]), pp. 37–38. This document has been translated from Polish.

2 This leaflet was reprinted in a pamphlet about the destruction of the Warsaw ghetto which was published in the underground press with a print run of 2,100. The pamphlet was written by Maria Kann (1916–1995), writer and educator; involved in the Polish Scout movement; active in the underground from 1940 to 1944 as editor of the underground publication *Wzlot* and on the Council to Aid Jews.

3 See Doc. 202, fn. 5.

4 See Doc. 30.

5 Correctly: 'Treblinka'. The name of the extermination camp was sometimes misspelled in Warsaw in 1942–1943.

## DOC. 234

## On 7 and 26 April 1943 the music teacher Salomea Ochs describes the persecution of the Jews in Tarnopol since summer 1941 and urges her relatives to avenge her[1]

Letter from Salomea Ochs,[2] Tarnopol, to Anselm, Dora, and Sigfried Lichtblau,[3] 3 Geulah, Tel Aviv, dated 7 and 26 April 1943

My dearest ones,

Before I depart from this world, I want to leave behind a few lines for you, my nearest and dearest. Once this letter reaches you, I – and all of us – will no longer be here. Our end is drawing nigh. We can feel it, we just know it. We are all condemned to death, just like the innocent, defenceless Jews who have already been executed. The small remnant left behind since the mass murders will have their turn in the very near future (days or weeks). Dreadful, but true. Unfortunately there is no way for us to escape this horrible, terrible death.

I have so much to tell you, but how am I to describe all of these horrors and torments? It is impossible. No pen is capable of capturing the tragedy of our people on this blood-soaked ground – the sufferings, the unspeakably sophisticated [yet] brutal way that people have been harassed, hounded, hunted, humiliated, and finally murdered. First we were squeezed like lemons and sucked dry, down to the last drop, and only then thrown into the sewer. First our hearts were cut out and we were deprived of all human feelings, of all human instincts; only then, after we had become mere mechanical drudges, were we killed en masse.

No, you will never understand, never know what it feels like to go through what we have experienced. No sane individual would believe that it is possible to bear such tortures, that people would experience such atrocities in the twentieth century.

I will attempt to tell you very briefly about our fate in July 1941.

Right at the outset, in July 1941, approximately 5,000 (five thousand) men were killed, including my husband. David[4] left home on *7 July 1941* (12 Tammuz 5701) and never returned. He volunteered for the 'Jewish Council' that was supposed to be organized. Despite my objection, he regarded it as his duty as a future spiritual leader to sign up and go there. He was meant to speak on behalf of the people. Six weeks later, after five days of moving corpses that were being taken from the brickworks (where they had been executed) to the cemetery, I found his among the many others. My life stopped that day, and it has had no purpose ever since.

Long ago, in my girlish dreams, I could not have wished for a better or more faithful partner in life. Just two years and two months of genuine happiness were granted to me.

1 YVA, O-75/346, fols. 1–12. An English translation is published in B. F. Sabrin (ed.), *Alliance for Murder: The Nazi-Ukrainian Nationalist Partnership in Genocide* (New York: Sarpedon, in association with Shapolsky, 1991), pp. 76–83. This document has been newly translated from German.

2 Salomea Ochs, née Luft (1912/1913–1943), music teacher; lived in Tarnopol prior to Sept. 1939; married David Ochs in Tarnopol in May 1939; murdered in Piotrków on 20 July 1943.

3 Dr Anselm Lichtblau was Salomea Ochs's uncle; Dora Lichtblau was her aunt, her mother Hana Luft's sister; Sigfried Lichtblau was Anselm and Dora Lichtblau's son.

4 Dr David Ochs (1911–1941), grammar school teacher and rabbinical candidate; prior to the war lived in Tarnopol where he perished.

How peculiar – we lived together exactly two years and two months to the day (7 May 1939 wedding day – 7 July 1941 parting). There is no point in regaling you with tales of my anguish. Oh this bloody, aching heart! Burying this person with my own hands, the one who was dearest and most precious to me, whom I loved so dearly, who understood me so well, and who was so loyal and kind. How do I describe how all the searching among dead bodies leaves you so weary that you are actually 'glad' to find 'yours' among the many decaying corpses? Is it possible to put such scenes, these inner agonies, into words? Here a woman who has lost her husband, another her only child, and a third both husband and children. So much suffering and so much pain – is it possible to describe this? This is what it was like for thousands [of people].

But David is dead and gone. Oh, how good he has it. It is all behind him. He has not had to witness these approximately two years of atrocities. The *coup de grâce* is all that awaits us now.

At first I was convinced that I wouldn't get over his death. I believed I would no longer be able to carry on without him. O humans, what resilient creatures we are! I have carried on living. Of course it is difficult to say how. This deep, bleeding wound was never to heal. It was awful, oh, it was so very sad to remain so alone, precisely because I had been so spoiled by my loyal spouse and had been used to such a peaceful, contented, and quiet home. But I kept on living.

We were sent to the ghetto in September 1941. Imagine, we were fenced in and were only allowed to enter the Aryan quarter with passes that were only issued to workers. A big gate, guarded by German or Ukrainian police, was the 'boundary'. Food was smuggled into the ghetto amid great fear and much looking over shoulders.

In September 1941 I got a job typing as a secretary at a German company. It was strange [because] the office was in what had once been our apartment. The dining room was converted into the office space. My desk was where the piano once stood, but instead of playing the piano, I started 'playing' (typing on) the typewriter. I really cannot complain; I had a very good job. My boss and the whole staff were very good, very nice to me. I was treated like a *human being*, not like a Jew.

Papa[5] and Bubi[6] then found work as labourers in this construction business.

The ghetto was very depressing at first, but you gradually get used to this way of life too.

The winter of 1941–1942 was very severe and cold; it was really hard to get through. Masses of people died of starvation or froze to death. But you carried on living, despite the 'raids' and the inspections, despite the frequent hunger and cold. You carried on living. You sold something different every time – clothes, linen, etc. – and scraped by in this way. Until March 1942, when it began again. It was a downright Bartholomew's Day massacre (23 March 1942).[7] The Jewish Council received the demand to provide a 'quota'

5 Szmuel (Shalom) Luft (1889/90–1943), merchant; lived in Tarnopol prior to Sept. 1939; then in the Tarnopol ghetto.

6 Possibly Salomea Ochs's younger and only brother, Szmuel Luft (b. 1919); he later lived in Israel.

7 The reference is to the night of 23 August 1572, when the wars of religion in France escalated: Catherine de' Medici (1519–1589) ordered the killing of thousands of Huguenots who had gathered in Paris for the wedding of Henry of Navarre, the later Henry IV (1553–1610), and Margaret of Valois (1553–1615).

of '700 head' of people to be murdered.[8] What, you don't want to believe it, do you? But that's how it was. *Our own brothers*, our *own* police officers led the people to their deaths. The assembly point for the victims was in the former synagogue. It was made nice and warm there, so that the 'poor people' did not freeze before they died; they were given bread and jam as well.

Then they were loaded into motor vehicles and taken to Janówka.[9] Everything was conveniently prepared. The graves were ready and waiting, a machine gun, and that was it.[10]

Oh, that night was so horrible, but again that was just the beginning. Then there was 'quiet' for a while, or whatever passes for quiet. The constant fear of forced labour camps, the constant fear of tomorrow, but you carried on living in terror and distress.

Cyla[11] went to the labour camp in Jagielnica in July 1942 because she wasn't working.[12] She didn't fare badly.

In August, on *the 31st*, the really 'big operation' began. Approximately 3,000 (three thousand) victims were needed. Exactly how many departed this world at that time is unknown – 2,500 people or more.[13]

That was when we lost our beloved, sweet, self-sacrificing mother.[14]

There was a new trick again at that time. People who were working, along with their families, got special stamps from the police on their work documents and were purportedly exempt from this operation. Again (as in March) it was supposed to affect only children and people who were not capable of working. Our own Jewish Order Service men once again searched the apartments and hiding places for the victims slated for death.

Bubi and I went to work. Mama and Papa stayed at home, since they also had the 'life stamp'.[15] At the perimeter gate, we were not allowed through. Bubi and I were taken to the victims' assembly point and were convinced we would not get out alive this time.

We were not at the assembly point for long, because we fled. And we succeeded, since many people were shot on the spot. I made it to the office, feeling fortunate. I had a great deal of work at that time. I sat down in the office, while outside thousands were waiting to die. Oh, how to describe it all to you. In the afternoon I learned that Mama and Papa had been seen at the assembly point. I had to continue working. I could not help. I believed I was going mad, but not at all; you do not go mad. In the evening our German

8 The Jewish Council was called upon to compile a list of 500 ghetto residents, supposedly for resettlement. The directive was issued by Hermann Müller (1909–1988), head of the Tarnopol Border Police Department.

9 A rural community near Tarnopol.

10 The operation was led by Friedrich Lex (b. 1902), deputy head of the Security Police in Tarnopol.

11 Cyla (Zilla) Luft (1921–1943), Salomea Ochs's sister; born in Vienna; died in Tarnopol.

12 The labour camp in Jagielnica was in operation from August 1941 to March 1944; the inmates there carried out agricultural work for the German war economy.

13 On 31 August 1943 German personnel carried out a selection on the orders of Hermann Müller, with the assistance of the Ukrainian police and the Order Service, during which they murdered a number of children on the spot; approximately 5,000 people, mostly elderly and sick, were loaded into railway wagons and deported to Belzec two days later.

14 Hana Luft, née Ochs (1887–1942), from Tarnopol; Szmuel (Shalom) Luft's wife.

15 This is a reference to the special police stamps for workers and their families temporarily exempting them from deportation.

colleague arrived; he had saved forty people from our firm, including my father. He couldn't get Mama out. You couldn't get women out, particularly if they were not working, mere housewives. I didn't know whether to grieve, to weep that I had lost my mother, or to be 'glad' that at least I had my rescued father. Is it possible to grasp this, to understand this? It shouldn't normally be possible, or else the brain and the heart would burst. But no, nothing happened to the ones left behind. The victims, again only the victims perished.

That 31 August was horrible. Thousands were crammed into sealed livestock wagons – women, children, men, old and young – they were all loaded into wagons and taken to the specially built human slaughterhouse at Belzec. The victims [were] supposedly poisoned there with gas; others thought an electric current was used. No one knows for certain exactly how the people were executed. I also want to tell you that, at that point, David's whole family was no longer alive and hadn't been for a long time. Of course it was exactly the same everywhere, in the big cities, the smallest hamlets, it made no difference. 'Orders' were orders, […][16] everywhere.

After that we went on living without Mother. That kind, faithful soul, that maternal heart – oh how we missed her, whatever we were doing.

Cyla returned from the labour camp in Jagielnica in October. In the meantime there were the daily worries to deal with and the continuing arduous struggle for this stupid existence. We had to move again, and the ghetto was once more reduced in size, as the homes of the people who had been murdered were vacant, after all.

We moved, this time to 22 Szeptyckich; just three buildings (20, 22, and 24) were still part of the ghetto. We carried on living. The 'operations' began again on 3 and 5 November 1942. People were pulled from every conceivable hiding place, from specially built underground 'bunkers', and taken to their deaths. So many precious young people were pulled out for the scrapheap[17] again by our own Order Service men; whole families, whole buildings with all their residents were wiped out.

On 5 November, which was a Sunday,[18] people were moving house again. Quite unexpectedly, the ghetto was surrounded at 11 o'clock in the morning, and the dance began anew.[19]

I was particularly lucky that time as well. Without having heard anything about an operation, I went out, believe it or not, ten minutes before the ghetto was surrounded. Destined to go on the last transport.

Afterwards we moved house again. Once more streets had to be vacated, and people were crammed even more tightly together.

Over time you got so used to the conditions, you grew so numb that when you lost someone close to you, you hardly reacted any more. You didn't cry. You were no longer a human being, just a stone, completely without feeling. No news made an impression any longer. People even went calmly to their deaths, those at the assembly point; the victims were completely composed and calm.

16 One word is illegible here.

17 'Auf Schmelz'; from the Yiddish expression 'oyf shmelts': see Doc. 169, fn. 8.

18 In fact, 5 Nov. 1942 fell on a Thursday.

19 In early Nov. 1942, 2,500 Jews from Tarnopol and the surrounding area were murdered in two killing operations under orders from Hermann Müller.

In January 1943 we went from the company to the labour camp. We were put in barracks. Women and men separately. We were no longer allowed to be on the streets by ourselves; only isolated labour detachments, accompanied by an Order Service man, were permitted in the Aryan quarter. We became labour prisoners.[20]

Papa and Bubi lived in the men's block, Cyla and I in the women's block. I dragged Papa into the camp with a severe kidney infection. I wanted us to be together and to go to our deaths together. And so we carried on living in the camp as well.

Many of the people we knew escaped to other towns with 'Aryan documents'. Many were caught, but perhaps there were individual people who managed to smuggle their way through.

Things were calm from January to April 1943. Again we carried on living and put up with all the discomforts, all the scary roll calls in the camp, etc.

Activity picked up again in April. A small number of people were taken from the ghetto and murdered. Twenty people one day, 50 on another day, etc.[21]

26 April 1943

I am still alive and want to give you an account of everything that has occurred from the 7th to today. It is generally said that 'everyone' will get their turn. Galicia is to remain completely 'free of Jews'. Above all, the ghetto is to be liquidated by 1 May. There are just 700 people left in the ghetto.

Thousands have been shot again in recent days. Now a new method is being applied, whereby people are 'officially' taken to their deaths. It used to be called 'relocation, resettlement'. Not any more. The most recent events were once again horrific. The assembly point was in our camp, where the human sacrifices dragged from their hiding places by the Jewish Order Service men were sorted and taken to their deaths. Those of us in the camp were able to 'observe' everything from our living quarters. Oh, those scenes, those images – how to describe them? None of us are people any more – we are animals; we have lost all sense of humanity.

Sons took their own parents to their deaths, fathers their own children. Mothers left their children behind at the assembly point and tried to escape. In another case children see their parents at the assembly point and go with them to their deaths, although they would be able to save themselves for a short while by coming into the camp.[22] You see how the assembly point fills with ever more people going to their deaths. This time the mass graves were prepared in Petrikow.[23]

The victims had to leave their coats in the camp at the assembly point. The men were even undressed down to their shirts and led to their deaths like that, 'on foot', like a herd. It was close by, after all. Why use petrol for motor vehicles, why make use of the railway? That would be a pity. After all, it is much simpler to dispose of this harmful

20 Following the killing operations in Nov. 1942, a so-called Julag, or Jew camp, was set up as a sub-camp of Janowska Street camp. Up to 5,000 prisoners were being held there in spring 1943.

21 Individual groups of Jews were murdered from mid March 1943, including 150 Jewish Council and Order Service employees.

22 Change in tense as in the original.

23 Polish spelling Piotrków, located just south of Tarnopol. In 1943 it became the site of repeated murders of Jews from the Tarnopol ghetto and the forced labour camp.

element on the spot. Besides, when people were sent away on trains, individuals managed to escape from the wagons, but this was no longer a possibility either. In my opinion, though, this death is easier. Because travelling for two or three days with the knowledge that you are going to your death must be something truly terrible. At least it happens faster here.

So this is what happens in Petrikow. Standing in front of the grave, people are stripped completely naked, forced to kneel, and then they wait for the shot. The victims stand lined up and wait their turn. While this is happening, those who are waiting have to arrange the people who have been shot in the graves so the space is well utilized and there is 'order'. The whole procedure does not take long. The clothes belonging to the thousands of people who have been shot are back at the camp again in half an hour.

It is too much, really. My nerves can no longer bear it.

If someone had once told me that I would witness so much horror, I would never have been able to fathom it. Where does a person find the strength to endure it, and for what, for what, when you know that everything is in vain? There is no salvation. It would be a waste of time to imagine escaping from these terrible mass murders.

We have no hope at all any more. We live from day to day, or rather, from hour to hour.

On 9 April, 1,500 people were killed, followed by two or three days of quiet, before it all began again.[24] Without end, in other words. Now there are just 700 (seven hundred) Jews left in the ghetto.

I also want to tell you that after the operations, the Jewish Council received a bill for 30,000 (thirty thousand) zloty for 'spent bullets', which were to be paid for. Interesting, isn't it?

After our working hours those of us in the camp have to go into the apartments of the people who have been shot and loot all of their belongings. Oh, it is so horrible, so terrible. These heaps of rubble, these vestiges of an entire people. These empty dwellings, these deserted alleys, this 'dead city'. Oh, how it hurts! Why, oh, why does it have to be this way? Why can't we scream? Why can't we get weapons and fight back? How can we watch so much innocent blood flowing and say nothing, do nothing, and just wait for the same death ourselves, until we are taken away one fine day? Oh, it is so ghastly. You think you are going to burst, but you don't. You carry on living. If it can actually still be called 'living'. And the whole world knows we are dying like this, and nothing happens. No one wants to help us, no one wants to save us. We have to perish so miserably, so mercilessly.

Do you think we want to end like this, die like this? No! No! We don't want to. Despite everything we have experienced. Quite the contrary.

The drive for self-preservation is often greater now, the will to live stronger the more closely death approaches. How dearly we would like to live, would like to see vengeance for so many millions of victims, for so much innocent blood, so much immeasurable suffering.

Alas, we will not live to see vengeance taken.

24 Müller and Lex supervised a selection on 8 and 9 April 1943, after which 1,000 people were shot dead near Piotrków and the remainder sent to a camp.

My dearest ones! You must take vengeance. You must do something to avenge so many injustices, such inhumane barbarities.

In reality there will be no vengeance at all. Whatever happens will be far too little, *nothing* compared to our fate. What has been done to us is unfathomable.

Oh, I can't go on any longer, I can't write any more. I could fill many more sheets with my scribbles, but you wouldn't understand anyway. I want to close.

My dears! David is buried in the Jewish cemetery, and my mother I don't know where; she was taken away to Belzec. I don't know where I will be buried, whether in Petrikow or Zagrobek, Zarodzin,[25] I just don't know. Maybe if you come here after the war, then you will find out from acquaintances where the transports from the camp were executed.

It is not easy to say goodbye forever, but we will face death bravely.

Farewell, be well, and if you can, take vengeance one day.

## DOC. 235
## On 27 April 1943 a resident of the Warsaw ghetto describes her emotions and observations in an underground shelter[1]

Handwritten diary of Maryla,[2] entry for 27 April 1943

27 April. My entries are no longer regular as I only write when I have light – because I presently live mainly in the darkness of the cellar – and when I can somehow gather my scattered thoughts.

On Wednesday, 21 April, we received the order to depart, and the retaliatory operation began the same afternoon. This time, in reaction to our negative response, they decided to exterminate us, using the most radical methods.

From that afternoon, noises that sounded more and more clearly like fighting reached us in our place in the cellar, where we were at risk of suffocating due to the lack of air. Since we had no connection with the outside world – because no one dared to take a look outside – we had to try to piece together the madness that was occurring there by means of the symphony of sounds that was reaching us. First I heard above me the coordinated marching of hundreds of soldiers, which appeared and then quickly died away. The noise of the steps struck frantic fear into our already half-crazed minds, where only one thought reverberated: Will they succeed? Will they find our bunker?

25 This is a play on words in Polish: the name Zagrobek literally means 'beyond the grave', that is, in the hereafter; Zarodzin means 'beyond birth'.

1 APMM, V-2, v. 22, fols. 326–334. Published as a facsimile in Piotr Weiser (ed.), *Patrzyłam na usta… Dziennik z warszawskiego getta* (Cracow: Homini, 2008), pp. 121–137. All that remains of the author's diary is a fire-damaged notebook; it was found on the grounds of Lublin-Majdanek concentration camp. The surviving entries cover the period from late March to 27 April 1943. This document has been translated from Polish.

2 Maryla, whose surname is unknown, was a Polish-speaking Jewish woman from Warsaw who worked as a forced labourer in the Többens factories in 1943; sometime after 27 April 1943 she was probably deported to Lublin-Majdanek concentration camp, where she is thought to have perished.

After that we could hear unidentifiable sounds and noises, which were most likely preparations for the fighting that would take place. And then, one after another, we hear[3] gunshots, the reverberations of exploding grenades, the rattle of a machine gun, and incessant, strange echoing sounds like thunder during a summer storm, which drift away, only to return with remarkable speed. There is no longer any doubt that the operation is taking place in our area, and that this time the Germans literally want to wipe us off the face of the earth, so that every trace of us disappears. We are absorbed in listening to the ever-increasing sounds of fighting, and we are paralysed with fear. We cease to be human beings and become jittering bundles of nerves, almost to the point of losing our minds. We bury ourselves in silence, and even the smallest rustle from inside, a whisper or a cough, seems like a hurricane that could lead the enemy right to us at any moment.

Suddenly a child crying breaks the silence. Sweat breaks out all over me. From all sides curses rain down on the unfortunate creature, who is completely unaware. Someone says: 'We have to suffocate it, or it'll betray us all.' A moment later, a cough splits the air. Insults and accusations fly in the direction from which it came: 'Cough. How dare you cough at a time like this? And an adult at that!' For a moment it seems as if the storm of war raging outside will tear our house apart. A strange noise, like a wall collapsing, comes nearer and nearer. The shelter commandant loses his nerve, babbles that someone has pushed the cart away, that he heard footsteps over the trapdoor, that we are all doomed. That's all it takes. The panic does the rest; one's agitated imagination conjures up images of the thugs marching in, fear constricts the throat and turns the heart into a racing, spinning motor. I am completely drenched in sweat, first hot, then cold. I notice it is becoming increasingly difficult for me to gasp for air, I feel my nerves are going to snap, and I reach for my Luminal.[4] I take out a few tablets, until someone knocks them out of my hand. I become furious and let out some crude expletives. Damn you! I'd rather die than go mad. This hysterical state of waiting for death lasts ten hours. For ten whole hours the outside noises seeped through to us, drilling like nails into our shattered brains. The whole time, every carelessly spoken word increases the hostility among everyone gathered; anger at the mothers grows with every child's cry, and the mutual hostility intensifies with everyone's increasing nervous tension.

Sadly, to [our] general misfortune, during these crucial, perhaps even final moments of our lives, we were crammed in among a crowd of people made up of the worst boors, mainly carters. We therefore experienced our tragedy much more intensely, because we were at the mercy of their vulgar, malicious tongues and habits day and night. That is why my worst fears were realized from the very start of living among such a disparate hotchpotch of people – hostility increases with every moment and finally gives way to blind, unbridled hatred.

The carters went for us, and we went for the carters; they in turn began to argue among themselves, and gradually each one's tiniest weaknesses were magnified by our frayed nerves, further increasing our irritation. I felt I was slowly beginning to drown and had nothing to cling to. I will return to these matters again, if I have enough time.

3 Changes in tense here and below as in the original.

4 A sleeping pill that was widely used at that time.

After ten hours of bombarding us with artillery, silence suddenly fell. Of course, no one dared to look out of the hole, and so we had to rely on our own assumptions and make more or less educated guesses. We knocked on the wall separating us from the shelter next door but received no reply. We came to the right conclusion, as we later discovered. The shelter had been burned out; some of the occupants were killed on the spot, while the rest were taken away.

The next day, two friends of ours, who to their misfortune had visited us on Sunday[5] and were then unable to return to their szop, resolve to get out at all costs. They want to ask around, to sound out the situation and to find a way to get back to their place. The deliberations and assurances that they would rather die than betray the bunker last a long time. After much persuasion, they finally succeed in getting out. One of us volunteers to go with them, but he turns back after only a few steps because he is so shocked by the sight of the rubble and the corpses of children before him.

In the meantime, the storm of war that threatened to engulf every living thing yesterday has gradually quietened down somewhat. In the depths of our hiding place, we can hear the sound of human footsteps now and then, groups of people passing by, and in our blessed naivety, based on past experience, we begin to believe that Werterfassung[6] works.

## DOC. 236

## On 28 April 1943 Leon Feiner and Adolf Berman describe the resistance on the ninth day of the Warsaw Ghetto Uprising and call on the Allies to intervene[1]

Radiogram from the government delegation (Sobol),[2] Warsaw, to Stem,[3] London (received on 19 May 1943), dated 28 April 1943

*No. 81*
*Stem, I'm sending you a telegram and ask that you pass it on – Sobol*
*For Zygelbojm[4] and Szwarcbard[5]*
The Warsaw ghetto is fighting heroically for the ninth day. The SS and the Wehrmacht are besieging it. They bombard it incessantly. Against 40,000 Jews they are using artillery, flamethrowers, and incendiary bombs dropped from aircraft. They use mines to blow up housing blocks where there is resistance. The ghetto is in flames. Clouds of

5 25 April 1943 was Easter Sunday.
6 German in the original: 'asset requisitioning'; a reference to the Asset Requisitioning Office (Werterfassungsstelle), an SS office in the Warsaw ghetto responsible for expropriating the possessions of Jews from Warsaw who were murdered in Treblinka.

1 AAN, 1325/202/I-7, fol. 21, no. 81. Also in SPP, L.dz K. 2517/43 and 2518/43. Published in Pełczyński and Tokarski (eds.), *Armia Krajowa w dokumentach 1939–1945*, vol. 2, pp. 506–507. This document has been translated from Polish.
2 Jan Stanisław Jankowski's code name.
3 Stanisław Mikołajczyk's code name.
4 Also spelled: Zygielbojm.
5 Also spelled: Schwarzbart.

smoke hang over the city. Women and children perish on the spot. The enemy is committing murder on a mass scale. The sewer outlets have been blocked, and German guards have been posted there. The insurgents are fighting doggedly. They are inflicting heavy losses on the enemy. They set fire to the factories and warehouses of the German armaments industry. German losses – approximately 1,000 dead and wounded.[6] The defenders' attitude arouses admiration among the country's population, and among the Germans there is shame and anger. The Jewish Combat Organization issued an appeal to the population of the capital.[7] In response, the Polish workers' parties pay their respects to the ghetto fighters.[8]

Now, [only] the power of the Allies can provide immediate and effective help. In the name of the millions of Jews who have already been murdered, in the name of those who are currently being burned and massacred, in the name of the heroic fighters and all of us who have been condemned to death, we call upon the whole world:

Let the Allies retaliate with force against the bloodthirsty enemy now, rather than sometime in a murky future – and in a manner that is commonly understood as revenge.

Our closest allies must finally realize the extent of their historic responsibility, which they have assumed as a result of their inaction in the face of the unprecedented National Socialist crimes perpetrated against an entire people, the tragic epilogue of which is currently unfolding. Let the heroic and historically unique uprising of those condemned to death in the ghetto finally move the world to action on this matter; action that corresponds to the magnitude of the moment.

For the CKRŻMP[9] in Poland – Berezowski.[10] For the ŻKN – Borowski.[11]

6 This figure is heavily inflated, though the exact number of German casualties is disputed. According to the summary given in the first five pages of Jürgen Stroop's final report, including guards from the SS training camp in Trawniki, the German losses amounted to 16 dead (including one Polish police officer) and 85 wounded; foreign auxiliaries are not included in these statistics. See Docs. 243 and 245.

7 See Doc. 233.

8 This is presumably a specific reference to a leaflet dated April 1943, issued by the Central Directorate of the Movement of the Polish Working Masses – Freedom, Equality, Independence (WRN) – a code name for the Polish Socialist Party (PPS), which had gone underground. The leaflet described the fighting in the ghetto as part of the Polish liberation struggle and called upon the world to provide help quickly and to rescue the Jewish fighters: see Wroński and Zwolakova (eds.), *Polacy – Żydzi 1939–1945*, p. 191.

9 The Central Directorate of the Jewish Working Masses in Poland (CKRŻMP) was a code name for the Bund's underground organization.

10 Leon Feiner's code name.

11 Adolf Abraham Berman's code name.

## DOC. 237

## *Rzeczpospolita Polska*, 30 April 1943: the Polish government's representative denounces the hypocrisy of German propaganda and begs his compatriots to help the Jews[1]

*Notices and Communiqués*

*Notice*

At a point in time dictated by their propaganda, the Germans announced to the world that the Bolsheviks had viciously murdered Polish officers in Katyń.[2] The purpose of disclosing this fact was to promote and advance a major German propaganda offensive across Europe, and especially in Poland, in order to persuade the peoples of Europe, including the Poles, to support Germany with arms, labour, and material resources. The calls for a crusade against Bolshevism are intended to serve this purpose – to multiply German forces.

In view of these German propaganda efforts, one should note that they are undertaken by the very same Germans who, while they have much to say about Soviet barbarism, have themselves provided the world with an example of their unparalleled barbarism and cruelty over almost four years in Poland. There are millions of Poles whom these alleged defenders of culture have murdered and starved to death, expelled from the places where their ancestors have lived since time immemorial, and deported for forced labour. To this day, the same Germans who are so hypocritically outraged by the crime in Katyń are torturing thousands of Poles to death in the camps at Oświęcim, Majdan,[3] Ravensbrück, Oranienburg,[4] Mathausen,[5] Treblinka, and others, and in prisons and Gestapo torture chambers all over Poland. The same Germans who apply the principle of collective responsibility throughout Poland are murdering hundreds of innocent Polish peasants to this very day.

Further proof of the Germans' hypocrisy and barbarism is provided by their crimes against the Jews. It has now been over a year since the Germans began to murder the Jewish population en masse throughout Poland, following years of severe persecution, and they continue to do so. Just in the last few weeks, the Polish capital became the scene of bloody incidents in which the German police and Latvian mercenaries liquidated the remnants of the Warsaw ghetto. At present they are engaged in tracking down and mercilessly driving out the Jews who are hiding in the ruins of the ghetto and outside its walls. The Polish nation, imbued with the spirit of Christianity, knows no double standards, and abhors the Germans' anti-Jewish bestiality. When the unequal struggle broke out after 19 April, it viewed the brave Jewish fighters with respect and compassion, and their Ger-

1 *Rzeczpospolita Polska*, 6 May 1943, pp. 1–2; Biblioteka Narodowa, MF 51 746. Published as a facsimile in Halina Czarnocka and Józef Żmigrodzki (eds.), *Armia Krajowa w dokumentach: 1939–1945*, vol. 3: *Kwiecień 1943–lipiec 1944* (London: Studium Polski Podziemnej, 1976), facing p. 17. This document has been translated from Polish.

2 In April 1943 the Wehrmacht discovered the bodies of approximately 4,000 Polish officers who had been shot in 1940 by the Soviet secret police (NKVD) in Katyń, near Smolensk. The Nazi regime exploited this discovery for its propaganda against the Soviet Union and saw it as an opportunity to weaken the anti-Hitler coalition. The USSR, on the other hand, claimed the massacre had been committed by German troops. It adhered to this version of events until 1990. German radio announced the discovery of the mass graves on 13 April 1943.

3 Correctly: Majdanek.

4 This is a reference to Sachsenhausen concentration camp in Oranienburg.

5 Correctly: Mauthausen.

man murderers with contempt. The country's political leadership[6] has already strongly condemned the Germans' bestial treatment of the Jews[7] and would like to stress this condemnation even more strongly today. Polish society is right to feel compassion for the hunted and persecuted Jews and to help them. They should continue to help them.

I condemn the hypocrisy of the Germans, who are constantly committing terrible crimes, and who are trying to present themselves through their deceitful propaganda as the guardians of civilization and of Christianity, and to win over Polish society in order to exploit it for their own purposes. I call upon all those who are aware of the nature and aims of the German political machinations to expose them and to combat them with all the necessary determination.

Warsaw, 30 April 1943

*The representative of the government of the Republic of Poland, for the country*[8]

## DOC. 238

## *Polska Informacja Prasowa*, 7 May 1943: the radical right-wing Szaniec Group interprets the Warsaw Ghetto Uprising as a communist-led operation[1]

*In the territory of the Republic of Poland*

*The ghetto resistance in the correct light.* Contrary to claims circulated in sections of the underground press, the resistance put up during the final liquidation of the Warsaw ghetto was not a collective resistance that would testify to a certain shift in the attitudes of the remaining Jews. Since the overwhelming majority of European Jewry have been completely passive in the face of their annihilation, the remaining Jews, with the materialism embedded in their race, were even less likely to resist. Only a tiny portion, approximately 10 per cent of the tens of thousands of Jews who remained in Warsaw, took up the fight, and that only at the communists' instigation. Unregistered Jews, the 'illegal' ghetto inhabitants, resisted, whereas the registered Jews, who were employed, did not take part in the operation and surrendered en masse to the Germans, who, true to form, took them to the new execution site in Majdanek.[2]

The Bund and the communists were behind the arming and resistance of several thousand Jews. These very elements have been extremely hostile to the Poles throughout the occupation and, within the framework of the communist organizations, prepared to

6 This is a reference to the government delegation, which was headed by the representative of the Polish government in exile.

7 See Doc. 140.

8 Jan Stanisław Jankowski.

1 *Polska Informacja Prasowa*, no. 18, 7 May 1943, p. 29. AAN, 1583/713/4, t. 1, fols. 182–211, here fol. 210. Published in Wroński and Zwolakova (eds.), *Polacy – Żydzi 1939–1945*, pp. 262–263. *Polska Informacja Prasowa* was an underground newsletter published from 1940 to 1944 by the Szaniec Group, whose main publication was *Szaniec*, one of the most influential underground publications in the General Government. This document has been translated from Polish.

2 The Jewish combat groups were in fact organized by the young forced labourers in the Warsaw ghetto's German factories; non-registered ghetto inhabitants were significantly restricted in terms of their freedom of movement.

seek a bloody showdown with the Poles during the transitional phase.[3] According to the communists' plans, the ghetto was to play a decisive role in the premature uprising that the PPR[4] wanted to instigate.[5] Communist printing presses were operating in the ghetto for a long time. There were also arms depots and communist cells from which Soviet officers directed the subversive activities.

In this light, the Jewish resistance should be considered a positive development, as it has led to the emptying of one of the arsenals of the communist movement and has in the process caused the Germans severe difficulties, losses, and disgrace.[6]

*Oświęcim*. The inmates in Oświęcim are gradually being transported to the Reich, to the camps in Dachau, Gross-Rosen near Wrocław, and Hamburg-Neuengamme.[7]

*Treblinka*. In Treblinka, the disposal of the corpses of the murdered Jews has been perfected. A corrosive mixture is sprinkled on the corpses, which burns the bodies along with the bones.[8] Not only is this method applied to those who are currently being exterminated, but old mass graves are now being dug up to burn the bodies of last year's murder victims.

[…][9]

## DOC. 239
## On 9 May 1943 an unidentified Jew reports on his deportation from Warsaw, his time at Poniatowa camp, and his escape[1]

Report by an unidentified individual, unsigned, for the government delegation's Internal Affairs Department, Warsaw, dated 9 May 1943[2]

*Poniatowo*[3]

On the morning of 12 April, Brandt[4] came into our cell,[5] and after inspecting us all carefully, ordered that we should all be taken to the barber. This meant that we would indeed be sent who knows where. Once our heads had been shaved, we were all brought

3 This is a reference to the internal power struggles that were expected to take place after the Germans' departure, for which the armed associations set up by Szaniec and other right-wing groups were preparing.
4 The communist Polish Workers' Party.
5 The Polish right wing was convinced that the Warsaw ghetto served as a centre of communist subversion and that any premature uprising in the ghetto would diminish the prospects of success for a planned Polish national uprising.
6 The Polish original uses the word 'komuna' (commune) as a designation for communists.
7 In spring 1943 several thousand Polish prisoners were transferred from Auschwitz to concentration camps in the Old Reich to perform slave labour there. The transports went to a number of different destinations, including Gross-Rosen, Sachsenhausen, Buchenwald, and Flossenbürg.
8 This is not accurate. In reality, the German camp officials had the corpses stacked on special scaffolding and burned.
9 The following section contains reports on crimes committed by the German occupiers against non-Jews in a number of rural Polish communities.

1 AAN, 1325/202/II-29, fols. 66–69. This document has been translated from Polish.
2 The date has been added by hand at the top of the document. The original also contains additional handwritten notes and underlining.
3 Correctly, here and below: Poniatowa.

to the prison yard, and one by one we were called to collect the belongings we had deposited. To our amazement, everything was returned, even the valuables.

We waited very nervously in the yard for about an hour, until finally a couple of Germans drove up in a car. One of them – as one of my companions informed us – was von Schultz – supposedly one of the partners at Toebens.[6] He gave a short speech and said that we should kiss Mr Toebens's hands in gratitude, since he had put in a request for us [as labour], and that we were all going to Poniatowo. We had been met with 'mehr als Glück',[7] as he put it. Then we were all put inside a vehicle escorted by six gendarmes and taken to the Umschlagplatz.[8] There the wagons had already been partly loaded with Toebens's people, who were travelling with us voluntarily and were allowed to move around freely. Only one wagon, bearing the inscription 'Warsaw–Treblinka', was completely empty. We were loaded into this wagon, and the doors were sealed. Gripped with panic, we rushed to the tiny window to find out where we were actually going. But all the Jews who were moving around freely in the square full of gendarmes assured us that we were going to Poniatowo along with the rest of the transport, and that the inscription on the wagon was merely a coincidence. We did not believe this, and we asked a Jewish policeman with whom we were speaking to get us a file and a saw. He assured us that this was completely unnecessary because the gendarmes had been bribed and would open our wagon at Gdańsk railway station.[9] In any case, he advised us against an escape and told us that Poniatowo was one of the best labour camps, and that we would certainly survive the war there. Other Jews who managed to approach our wagon window said the same. In general, my companions felt reassured, but in my opinion this was obviously propaganda and I did not stop thinking about an escape. At approximately 4 o'clock our wagon was opened, a gendarme came in and counted us, and a pot of soup was brought in. Although the soup was excellent, we barely touched it, because everyone was thinking [only] of notifying their families. One of the managers at Toebens, a Jew, made this easier for us and handed us a pencil and paper through the window. Everyone wrote down their surname and telephone number, and he promised that he would take care of everything (he did indeed keep his promise).

About an hour later the wagon was opened again, and each of us received a package of food: bread, four hard-boiled eggs, and about ten decagrams of margarine. Then everyone searched out a place for himself. I settled down next to the door with one of my companions. There was quite a lot of room in the wagon, since there were [only] forty of us. At about 8 o'clock the train set off. We travelled very slowly and stopped frequently. The Germans escorting us turned out to be very friendly. They opened the wagon at each station and let us get out two at a time. They brought us 200 cigarettes and as much water as we wanted. One of them even offered us a litre of vodka for 150 złoty. Of course we bought it, and he had a drink with us. Then we asked him to open the

4 Presumably Karl Georg Brandt from the Gestapo's Jewish Affairs section in Warsaw.
5 At Pawiak prison in Warsaw.
6 Correctly: Többens. On the Schultz and Többens companies, see Doc. 229; the man in question was presumably Rudolf Bauch, the deputy manager of the Többens works.
7 German in the original: 'more than good fortune'.
8 German in the original.
9 Also known as Danzig station, in the northern part of Warsaw. The goods depot of this station served as the Umschlagplatz prior to deportation.

wagon at Gdańsk station. But he refused, explaining that he could not take the responsibility for that. He advised us against escaping by raving about the wonders of Poniatowo. We negotiated with him at some length, by which time we had already passed Otwock. After that conversation, I noticed that we were being guarded more closely. Jumping out of the window was out of the question, because we were too near to Dęblin.

Resigned, we went to sleep. Some of the fellows amused themselves by singing various songs. This is how we travelled until we reached Nałęczów at about 1 p.m. Here a gendarme entered our wagon. He said that from then on we were considered free men (oh the irony!) and could join the rest of the transport. We were instructed to get out and line up in rows of five. We waited about half an hour until the narrow-gauge railway wagons were ready. The railway journey took four hours. We passed through a beautiful area surrounded by forests. I tried to memorize the direction of travel, but it was impossible due to the winding track.

Our party was in excellent spirits. Everyone praised Toebens for showing so much interest in the Jews and for offering them such excellent living conditions. The majority were happy about having left Warsaw. At about 6 o'clock we arrived at our destination. The first thing I noticed was the triple barbed wire fence surrounding a large site. Along the fence, two-storey small [watch]towers stand[10] quite close together. Behind the fence was a crowd of people: they were Jews who had come to wait for us, but they were immediately dispersed. Our transport, approximately 700 people, was lined up in rows of three. A German came. As someone told me, it was Hantke.[11] He instructed us to take off our armbands and distributed food vouchers to everyone. As it turned out, they were for the next day's rations. Then we were led to a large square – already on the camp grounds – and instructed to settle into the small, single-storey wooden huts – barracks that had not yet been completed. Here we were to wait until it was time for our bath – the bathing hours began at 11 o' clock and went on until 5 in the morning. In the meantime, Jews from earlier transports joined us, and we began to look for people we knew. I myself did not find anyone, and I noticed that intellectuals accounted for less than 1 per cent. The rest consisted of very bad elements. Everyone in high spirits, suntanned, happy to be here. Everyone states that they will certainly survive the war here, because Toebens has huge plans for the future and the camp is constantly being expanded. Talking with these people, I learned that the camp is not guarded particularly well. Just 10–12 Ukrainians[12] stand guard around the camp. The watchtowers are not being used at present. It turns out that Bolshevik prisoners had been here in the past, but all of them – about 15,000 – were murdered a year ago in the dungeons surrounding the camp.[13]

10 Changes in tense here and below as in the original.

11 Otto Hantke (1907–1986), retailer; joined the SS in 1933 and the NSDAP in 1937; worked on the staff of the SS and Police Leader in Lublin; posted to the camp on Lipowa Street, which was in the Kraśnik ghetto at that time; served in the Waffen-SS from Feb. 1942; camp commander at Budzyń and Poniatowa; temporarily assigned to Warsaw during the Ghetto Uprising; transferred to Stutthof concentration camp in late 1944; sentenced to life imprisonment by Hamburg Regional Court in 1974.

12 Here and below, 'Ukrainians' refers to guards from the SS training camp for non-German auxiliary personnel at Trawniki.

13 A main camp for Soviet prisoners of war had been located on the camp grounds in 1941–1942. Most of the inmates died of malnutrition.

While we were waiting for our bath, my companions and I set off to inspect the whole camp grounds. One can walk around the grounds unhindered because there are no Germans to be seen anywhere. They all live in a hotel several hundred metres outside the fence. The Jewish workers live in the main barracks. This is an enormous hall in which, strictly speaking, there are [only] huge bunk frames, arranged four on top of each other. Every few metres there is a ladder one can use to reach the higher bunks. Approximately 4,000 people, men and women, live together in these barracks. Those in senior positions, such as managers, foremen, and physicians (approximately 1,000 people), live in the so-called settlement. This settlement is outside the fence and is completely unguarded. It is said they live in fabulous conditions, four or five to an apartment. There are two-storey villas surrounded by a beautiful garden. All the apartments are connected to the sewage system and apparently even have bathrooms. One can only get there with a permit. I found all of this quite odd, as I realized that the Jews here enjoy many freedoms and the rations are good. The people who came here on the last two large transports that arrived more than two weeks ago still have no work, yet they receive the same rations as the workers. In short: Toebens has opened a boarding house for Jews. I discovered this over the next few days of my stay there.

After we had had a wash (incidentally, there are only five showers in what is pretentiously referred to as the bathhouse), we were given permits granting access to the communal barracks. There, after a lot of arguing, each of us was given a quilt and a straw mattress for two people. The sleeping quarters were even quite comfortable, but the hygiene conditions could not have been worse. At the slightest movement from a neighbour in the bunk above, clouds of dust trickle down on one's head. That's why people don't use bed linen, even if they have it, because it's black after a single night. The next day I began to closely observe the lives of the workers. At 5 a.m. a wake-up call from the Werkschutz.[14] Jews walk around in the hall and whistle. An indescribable noise erupts. Everyone rushes to take a place in the queue for the washrooms. They are right next to the barracks. Everyone gets dressed sitting on their bunk or gets down and does it in front of everyone. It's a sight to behold. I wanted to compare it to something I have seen before, but I couldn't. At 6.30 all those employed go off to work. The factories are on the camp grounds, and there the workers get coffee and a quarter of a loaf of bread for breakfast. Everyone who does not work – and there were considerably more of them at that time – gets their breakfast in the kitchen next to the barracks. Everyone rushes to get in the queue with their pot. Shouting, bickering, even fights. In the barracks the Werkschutz personnel drag people down from the bunks and take them to work for a few hours. So everyone who can flees to the meadow behind the barracks. To my surprise, people there lie in the grass sunbathing. Masses of children play and make a terrible racket. This is how the time passes until lunch. Lunch is at 12, but by 11, crowds of people are already queuing up. Again there are arguments, shouting, people bartering vouchers for lunch (soup costs 3 złoty). The Werkschutz personnel cannot cope and threaten to fetch the Germans to help. It calms down for a few minutes, but then it continues as before. Everyone prefers to jostle around for an hour without queuing than to form an orderly queue for half an hour. After the food has been distributed,

14 German in the original, here and below: 'factory security'.

bartering begins in the barracks. Here one can get anything, the prices are relatively low: bread […],[15] an egg 5 złoty, butter 350, and so on. At 12, it turns out, the work details return from the surrounding villages, bringing contraband with them. At 4 o'clock they start handing out supper. We get sweetened coffee and bread with jam or an egg. Once the workers are back, the barracks become intolerable: screaming, shouting, laughter, singing. Everyone goes to the meadow. There some play volleyball, others sing. You forget that you're in a camp. They say there will be a concert in the evening. And indeed there is. It's really interesting to see. Musicians who are known from the ghetto play and sing on one of the stacked-up bunks. Crowds of spectators all around. Some Werkschutz personnel listen, while others disperse the crowd. Chaos reigns, no one knows what to do, and in the end everyone goes back to the meadow and enjoys themselves there. Some make a campfire and put potatoes in it, others drink vodka. Meanwhile it is quiet in the barracks, because everyone has to go to bed at 9. The curfew applies only in the barracks, while one can move freely around the entire camp grounds, even all night long. In the evening, all those who had previously been in Pawiak gathered around, and we shared our impressions. We alone could assess the conditions here objectively, because everyone else had come here more or less voluntarily.

The conditions here gave us a lot to think about. It's too good here. All this is obviously Toebens propaganda to recruit as many people as possible. It was clear to us that the Germans would not tolerate such a large number of children and elderly people here who were unfit for any kind of work.

The Easter holidays came. Everyone received half a kilo of matzo and twenty cigarettes. In their hopeless naivety, the Jews praised Toebens, saying that things had changed. On the first day of the holiday, a day off work, the Germans gave their permission for a football match with the Ukrainians. Relations were genuinely warm. After the match, the Ukrainians amused themselves by chatting with Jewish women. It must be said that on the morning of the same day, these very Ukrainians had killed two Jews whom they had found in possession of large quantities of smuggled goods.

Under these conditions, I concluded that one had to split while it was still possible. Because it would get worse – that was clear to me. But there is still time, because there are several thousand [more] people who are supposed to arrive in due course.

The next transport was announced for 20 April. And people did indeed arrive, but their arrival was a little different to ours. Above all, they were guarded by Ukrainians and Latvians. For two days we were not allowed to approach them. There were merely rumours that a veritable war had broken out in the ghetto. The Jews had defended themselves to the last man. We were very worried by this news, because contact with the outside world came only via the ghetto.

After two days the guards were withdrawn, and we were allowed to approach these people. There were about 3,000 of them. Again we looked for acquaintances and inquired about those who had remained in the ghetto. The news from the ghetto is worse than ever. Apparently all the houses are burning.

That evening, it was like a scene from Dante's inferno during the distribution of blankets and the search for places to sleep. Places were being reorganized all night long.

15 One number is illegible here.

There were supposed to be four people to a bunk. Again shouting, bickering, fights. Conditions are becoming unbearable in every respect. The kitchens are not equipped to cater for such a large number of people. The next day, a new transport arrives, all men. They are treated terribly. They are kept in the meadow for a few days. They wait for a bath. There is no water in the whole of Poniatowo. Prices skyrocket. A loaf of bread 250, an egg 20, cigarettes 2 złoty each. Hunger, no one is able to buy anything, and the food is getting worse and worse. They promise that this is only temporary and that everything will return to normal.

Meanwhile new transports arrive every day, with 500 or 1,000 people, all of them in a terrible state. There is nowhere to sleep and nothing to eat. The water shortage is devastating. I and a few of my companions are determined to escape. We find out that partisans raided the settlement the day before. They took money and some food. They also wanted to take a few people with them, but no one wanted to go because they feared these were bandits. We decided to wait for a favourable opportunity and join them.

A coincidence facilitated our escape. When I was in the meadow one evening, the Ukrainians on guard at the barbed wire fence approached me and asked for a light. Then we had a very friendly conversation, during which they complained that they would so much like to flirt with the Jewish women, but they always run away from them. I said I would bring two girls who would be happy to talk to them. At the same time, I informed my companions that our moment had come. We took advantage of the time during which the Ukrainians were talking to our female friends and built a kind of bridge over the barbed wire fence with boards. In the dark, we managed to reach a very thick forest. Here we spent almost four days roaming around without being able to find any trace of the partisans. Hunger and exhaustion forced us to return to the camp by joining a work detail. Life in the camp had become unbearable. So one day I put together a very simple plan, almost frightening in its simplicity: get to the settlement, from there walk to the first narrow-gauge railway station in Rozalin, take the narrow-gauge railway to Nałęczów, and continue by train to Warsaw. A risky plan because I have no papers and the route is swarming with Germans. But so what, I have to risk it. Once I had got hold of a few hundred złoty, which was difficult, I managed to get into the settlement. The guards were in a good mood and did not check the permits. Life in the settlement took me completely by surprise. Beautiful one- and two-room apartments with kitchens, quite primitively furnished, but with a beautifully kept garden. Here people live in civilized conditions, and with adequate financial resources, they run a normal household. The prices are much lower than inside the grounds.

At 4 a.m. I set off and walked along the edge of the forest, which runs parallel to the main road to Rozalin. At 7 o'clock I arrived safely at Rozalin station, without having encountered anyone along the way. The narrow-gauge railway service does not depart until 11. The passengers are mainly peasants. By 2 I was already in Nałęczów, but there is no train to Warsaw until 7 in the evening. I wait at the station. Incredibly tense during the train journey. Dęblin. A baggage check. And at last, almost a miracle, the arrival in Warsaw.

## DOC. 240

## On 10 May 1943 Himmler plans the reinforcement of police units in the General Government in order to have the remaining Jews murdered as quickly as possible[1]

File note (marked 'secret Reich matter') by the Reichsführer-SS, signed Himmler, for 12 May 1943, Berlin, dated 10 May 1943.

*File note on combating bandits*

I. SS and police forces currently available
1) General Government
   Order Police 11,400 men
   Security Police 2,200 men
   13,600 men

Non-German police forces (Polish and Ukrainian) 15,000 men
[…][2]

IV. *Situation in the General Government*
a) I request that the Griese[3] Police Regiment, currently in Marseilles, be made available immediately.
b) For my part, I will transfer three more police battalions that are in the process of being newly formed to the General Government until the situation has been resolved.
c) Of the police battalions I have with the army security divisions, I will assign three battalions to the General Government as soon as I get them. I will immediately replenish these battalions once they have been transferred. I will only be able to arrange the other police battalions, some of which consist solely of cadres,[4] a few weeks later.
d) I will likewise reinforce the Security Police in the General Government with an additional 250 men.

The police forces would then increase in number as follows:

| | |
|---|---|
| 1) Griese Regiment | 2,000 men |
| 2) Three home battalions | 1,800 men |
| 3) Three battalions from security divisions | 1,800 men |
| 4) Security Police | 250 men |
| | 5,850 men |

The German police forces would consequently increase to some 19,500 men.

I should also mention that I have 17,000 men on the ground in the General Government in SS formations, although these are replacement units. These formations have been and are being deployed on shorter operations, such as street fighting in the Warsaw ghetto.

1 AIPN, GK, 912/DC/849, fols. 1–5. This document has been translated from German.
2 Himmler subsequently listed the German and foreign police forces in the occupied territories of the Soviet Union and added notes on 'combating bandits'.
3 Bernhard Griese (1887–1964); commander of Police Regiment 14.
4 These were reserve forces consisting of men who had been deployed for only a short while and lacked experience.

e) I will not stop the evacuations of the roughly 300,000 Jews who remain in the General Government, but will carry them out with the greatest haste. Just as the evacuation of Jews causes unrest at the moment it occurs, in the same way it will be key to the territory's fundamental pacification after it has been concluded.[5]

## DOC. 241

## On 11 May 1943 Szmul Zygielbojm informs the Polish government in exile that he is taking his own life in protest against its inaction in the face of mass murder[1]

Letter from Szmul M. Zygielbojm, member of the National Council of the Republic of Poland, 12 Porchester Square, London W2, to the president of the Republic of Poland, Władysław Raczkiewicz,[2] and the chairman of the Council of Ministers, General Władysław Sikorski, dated 11 May 1943

Mr President,
Prime Minister,

I take the liberty of addressing my final words to you – and through you, to the Polish government and its population, to the *governments* and *nations* of the Allied states, and to the conscience of the world:

The latest news from the *country*[3] leaves no doubt that the Germans, with all their ruthless cruelty, are already murdering the rest of the Jews in Poland. The final act of a tragedy unparalleled in history is currently playing out behind the ghetto walls.

The responsibility for this crime – the murder of the entire Jewish population in Poland – lies first and foremost with the criminals themselves. However, it is also indirectly attributed to the whole of humanity, to the nations and the governments of the *Allied countries*, who to this day have been unable to bring themselves to take concrete measures to put an end to this crime. They have become complicit by idly standing by and watching as millions of tortured and defenceless children, women, and men are murdered.

I must also state that while the *Polish government* has done a great deal to influence public opinion around the world, it has not done nearly enough. It has not come up with anything sufficiently extraordinary to equal the magnitude of the drama that is unfolding in the country.

According to the underground Bund leadership's official reports sent to us by the government representative, of the nearly 3.5 million Polish Jews and the approximately 700,000 Jews deported to Poland from other countries, approximately 300,000 were still alive as of April this year. And the murder continues without interruption.

5 On 12 May 1943 the head of the Office of the Reich Commissioner for the Strengthening of Germandom, Ulrich Greifelt, noted a directive from Himmler as Reich Commissioner for the Strengthening of Germandom to 'remove the 300,000–400,000 Jews who are still present' in the General Government: BArch, NS 19/2648, fol. 135.

1 AIP, PRM.E, 158. Published as a facsimile in Czarnocka and Żmigrodzki (eds.), *Armia Krajowa w dokumentach: 1939–1945*, vol. 3, facing p. 17. This document has been translated from Polish.
2 Władysław Raczkiewicz (1885–1947), Polish president in exile, 1939–1947.
3 Poland.

I cannot remain silent and I cannot continue to live while the remnants of the Jewish people in Poland, whom I represent, are being killed.

In a final, heroic surge, my comrades in the Warsaw ghetto fell with weapons in their hands.

I was not destined to die like them and alongside them. But I belong with them, in their mass graves.

With my death I wish to express my strongest protest at the inaction with which the world is watching the extermination of the Jewish people and allowing it to happen. I know how little a human life is worth, especially nowadays. But since I haven't succeeded at this during my life, it is perhaps with my death that I can contribute to rousing from their indifference those who can and must act immediately to save this handful of surviving *Polish* Jews from inevitable annihilation, perhaps at the last possible moment.

My life belongs to the Jewish people in Poland, and so I give it to them. May this handful that remains of the millions of Polish Jews experience liberation along with the Polish masses, so they may breathe a sigh of relief in a country and a world of socialist freedom and receive justice for all their inhuman torment and suffering. I firmly believe that such a Poland shall arise and that such a world shall come.

I trust that you, Mr President, and you, Prime Minister, will convey these words of mine to all those for whom they are intended, and that the Polish government will immediately take the appropriate steps in the field of diplomacy and propaganda in order to save this handful of surviving Polish Jews from extermination.

I bid farewell to everyone and everything that once was beloved and dear to me.

## DOC. 242

## On 14 May 1943 the Polish government's representation in occupied Poland reports that the Gestapo has carried out a massacre at the Karl Georg Schultz factory in the Warsaw ghetto[1]

Reports for the government delegation's Internal Affairs Department, signed Sabina,[2] Warsaw, dated 14 May 1943

*Jewish issues.* Warsaw ghetto. April–May 1943.[3]
News from the Schultz[4] garment factory (the so-called 'little' Schultz: he employed 1,800 people, including 800 Jews, at the beginning of this year).

Between 1 and 5 May nearly all the Jews in this factory were deported. Women constituted the majority in this 'szop'. They were taken to Poniatowa (near Nałęczów, which is accessed by a narrow-gauge railway), and it seems certain that they were needed there for some kind of work. Only 29 Jews of both sexes remained in the factory. They were

1 AAN, 1325/202/II-28, fol. 95. This document has been translated from Polish.
2 Thought to be one of Halina Krahelska's code names.
3 The location and the date have been added to the original by hand.
4 This is a reference to the firm operated by Karl Georg Schultz; the term was used to distinguish it from 'Big Schultz', a larger factory run by Fritz Emil Schultz which produced winter clothing for the German army.

put on a special list, approved by the Germans, and were thus saved from deportation by Schultz personally. (I remember how he went from house to house in Łódź selling hosiery and knew all the 'big shots' in this and related industries.) Included in this list were Braun,[5] the former owner of Schultz's factory; the entire Rowiński family;[6] a certain lawyer 'in the textile industry' in Vienna, along with his wife; one of Schultz's acquaintances; and others. As the fighting raged in the ghetto, the Polish employees of the factory had no access to it, except for no more than twenty people who were ordered to report for 'standby duty'.

This week the Gestapo turned up at the factory office out of the blue and demanded that Schultz hand over the Jews who were in hiding. Schultz explained that there were no Jews in hiding; there were only twenty-nine Jewish skilled workers who had been allowed to remain, with the German authorities' consent. The Gestapo men began to beat one of the Jewish women. She could not withstand the blows and divulged that there were 'bunkers' under the factory and the neighbouring property in the direction of Leszno Street where many Jews were sheltering. (This did not save her, as she was killed afterwards.) The Germans asked for large quantities of vodka to be brought in, helped themselves to copious amounts, and then began to search out and destroy the bunkers. After destroying the bunkers, they did indeed bring out a huge crowd, approximately 150 people, but these were mostly women and children. The massacre of these unfortunates took place on the spot, in the factory yard. It was a horrible sight; the blood of those murdered literally flooded the yard. Afterwards the executioners appeared intoxicated by the bloodbath. They took leave of their senses to such an extent that they attacked Schultz himself and wanted to beat him up as well, but they refrained from doing so and instead mistreated the twenty-nine Jews whose lives had previously been spared. Only three of the Jews from this group were spared, thanks to a German woman, the manager of one of the factory halls, whom we wrote about in our previous report on these premises.[7] This German woman hid these three people beneath some wares and brought them out later. The rest were beaten to death in a barbaric manner in the hall where they had been found. The Poles who witnessed these terrible events were forced to watch. It took them a long time to kill one woman (the lawyer's wife from Vienna), because she clung to life so stubbornly; she kept raising herself up to embrace her husband's corpse.

Shocked by this scene, Schultz feared (certainly not without reason) that the Germans, barely in their right minds after murdering so many Jews, would pounce on the no more than twenty Poles who were on standby at the factory that day and kill them. He hit upon the idea of alerting the police. And indeed, a police car came and collected the Poles – except for two, whom the Germans ordered first to guard the factory and then to set to robbing the murdered Jews of all their valuables. They had to comply, and thus a small pile of wristwatches, rings, and money accumulated.

5 Pinkus Braun (Broun) (1878–1943), businessman from Ukraine; co-owned the Braun & Rowiński textile factory at 78 Leszno Street in Warsaw prior to Sept. 1939, before it was taken over by K. G. Schultz.

6 Josef (Josel, Józef) Rowiński (b. 1877), businessman; co-owner of the Braun & Rowiński textile factory; lived in Konstancin (today Konstancin-Jeziorna, a suburb south of Warsaw) after 1944.

7 In a previous report on the Warsaw ghetto, dated Feb. 1943, Sabina had written about a 'young, pretty' German woman who had been sent from the Reich to work as a manager and had made efforts to increase productivity: AAN, 1325/202/II-28, fols. 88–89.

The Germans took everything and gave the Poles 100 złoty each. As they were leaving, they explained that the army would soon arrive to take over the 'purged' premises. When an officer arrived, he turned to the Poles with the following words: 'So these bandits were here, murdered people, and robbed the corpses, and now we, the army, have to cover it up.'

## DOC. 243
## On 16 May 1943 SS and Police Leader Jürgen Stroop describes the creation and destruction of the Warsaw ghetto[1]

Report by the SS and Police Leader in District Warsaw, signed SS-Brigadeführer and Police Generalmajor Stroop,[2] Warsaw, dated 16 May 1943

*Warsaw's Jewish residential district is no more!*
[…][3]
I.[4]
The creation of Jewish residential districts and the imposition of residence and economic restrictions on Jews are nothing new in the history of the East. Their origins stretch as far back as the Middle Ages, and such restrictions have also been observed repeatedly throughout the centuries. These restrictions were put in place with a view to protecting the Aryan population from the Jews.

On account of the same considerations, the idea of establishing a Jewish residential district in Warsaw was taken up as early as February 1940. Plans initially called for making the part of Warsaw bounded to the east by the Vistula a Jewish residential district.[5] Given the special circumstances in the city of Warsaw, this idea did not at first seem feasible. Various parties, especially the city administration, also raised objections to this plan. In particular, it was argued that the establishment of a Jewish residential district would cause significant disruption to industry and business, and that it would not be possible to feed the Jews concentrated in such a sealed residential district.

1 AIPN, GK 166/202 (NTN 2022), pp. 1–12. Published as a facsimile in Andrzej Wirth (ed.), *'Es gibt keinen jüdischen Wohnbezirk in Warschau mehr': Stroop-Bericht* (Neuwied: H. Luchterhand, 1960). This document has been translated from German.
2 Jürgen Stroop (1895–1952), surveyor; joined the NSDAP and the SS in 1932; Selbstschutz leader in Poland in 1939; posted to the staff of the Higher SS and Police Leader Rußland-Süd in 1942; posted to the staff of the SS and Police Leader in Lemberg in Feb. 1943; from 17 April 1943 SS and Police Leader Warsaw, in command of the suppression of the Warsaw Ghetto Uprising and the destruction of the ghetto; from Sept. 1943 Higher SS and Police Leader in Greece; from Nov. 1943 Higher SS and Police Leader in Rhein-Westmark. He was sentenced to death by a US military court in 1947; the sentence was not carried out and he was extradited to Poland, where he was sentenced to death in 1951 and executed in Warsaw.
3 The document comprises a total of 126 pages. The 12-page report published here is preceded by five pages listing members of the SS and auxiliary forces who were killed or wounded in the fighting between 19 April and 15 May 1943 and providing information about the number of forces deployed and the units to which they belonged.
4 The first section repeats information from a report by Waldemar Schön, head of the Resettlement Department in the Governor of District Warsaw's office, dated 20 Jan. 1941: AIPN, GK 317/894, t. 9, fols. 72–96.
5 The governor of District Warsaw, Ludwig Fischer, had initially argued that the ghetto should be established in the city's Praga district.

As a result of a meeting held in March 1940, the plan to create a ghetto was shelved for the time being, in view of the misgivings that had been voiced.[6] At the same time consideration was given to the idea of declaring District Lublin the gathering place for all the Jews in the General Government, particularly Jewish refugees and the evacuated Jews arriving from the Reich.[7] However, as early as April 1940 the Higher SS and Police Leader East[8] in Cracow announced that there were no plans to concentrate the Jews in District Lublin.[9]

In the meantime, Jews were making unauthorized and unwarranted border crossings more frequently, as was evident particularly at the border of the Kreishauptmannschaften Lowitsch and Skierniewice.[10] Due to this illegal influx of Jews, conditions in the town of Lowitsch were becoming dangerous, both in terms of hygiene and from the point of view of the Security Police. In order to ward off these dangers, the Kreishauptmann in Lowitsch therefore started forming Jewish residential districts in his Kreis.[11]

The experience gained from establishing Jewish residential districts in Kreis Lowitsch revealed that these were the only appropriate methods to avert the dangers repeatedly posed by the Jews.

In summer 1940 it became all the more urgent to create a Jewish residential district in the city of Warsaw as well, as more and more troops were being marshalled in the territory of District Warsaw following the conclusion of the French campaign. At that time the Public Health Department described the establishment of a Jewish residential district as particularly urgent in the interest of safeguarding the health of the German troops, and of the population as well. The creation of a Jewish residential district in the suburb of Praga, which was originally planned for February 1940, would have taken at least four to five months, in view of the relocation of almost 600,000 people.[12] However, since experience had shown that a major outbreak of contagious diseases was to be expected in the winter months, and for this reason the resettlement operation had to be carried out by 15 November 1940 at the latest according to the District physician,[13] the plan for a ghetto in Praga on the outskirts of the city was dropped. The city's existing epidemic containment zone was selected instead as the area for the Jewish residential district that was to be created. In October 1940 the Governor instructed the District Governor's representative for the city of Warsaw to conduct the resettlement operations necessary to create the Jewish residential district in the city of Warsaw by 15 November 1940.[14]

6 This decision was taken at a meeting on 8 March 1940.
7 Thousands of Jews from the Reich had been deported to District Lublin between late Oct. 1939 and Feb. 1940, before Hitler turned against the idea of a reservation again in March 1940: see PMJ 4, pp. 39–40.
8 Friedrich-Wilhelm Krüger.
9 This could not be found.
10 These Kreise were located in the western part of District Warsaw; thousands of Jews fled there from the western Polish territories that had been annexed by the Reich.
11 In May 1940 Heinz Werner Schwender arranged for a ghetto to be established in the Kreis seat of Łowicz; this ghetto was isolated from the rest of the town by walls and fences. In addition to this, Jews were concentrated in four other municipalities.
12 This figure includes Jews as well as Poles.
13 Arnold Lambrecht.
14 See the Second Directive on the Establishment of the Jewish Residential District of 31 Oct. 1940: *Amtsblatt des Chefs des Distrikts Warschau*, 1940, no. 10, 11 Nov. 1940, pp. 147–148. The governor of District Warsaw was Ludwig Fischer; the District Governor's representative was Ludwig Leist.

The Jewish residential district thus created in the city of Warsaw was inhabited by approximately 400,000 Jews. It contained 27,000 apartments with an average of two and a half rooms. It was separated from the rest of the urban area by firewalls and barrier walls, and by walling up streets, windows, doors, and gaps between buildings.

The administration of the newly created Jewish residential district lay in the hands of the Jewish Council of Elders, which received its instructions from the commissioner for the Jewish residential district,[15] who reported directly to the Governor. The Jews had a self-administration, in which German supervisory authorities took an interest only to the extent that German concerns were involved. A Jewish Order Service, identified by special armbands and caps and equipped with rubber truncheons, was set up so that the measures taken by the Jewish Council of Elders would be enforced effectively. This Jewish Order Service was tasked with ensuring order and security within the Jewish residential district and was under the control of the German and Polish police.

II.

It soon became apparent that not all the dangers had been averted, despite this concentration of the Jews. The security situation made it necessary to remove the Jews from the city of Warsaw altogether. The first large-scale resettlement took place from 22 July to 3 October 1942,[16] during which 310,322 Jews were resettled.[17] In January 1943 another resettlement operation took place,[18] in which a total of 6,500 Jews were rounded up.

During his visit to Warsaw in January 1943, the Reichsführer-SS gave the SS and Police Leader in District Warsaw the order *to relocate to Lublin those factories and enterprises in the ghetto that were producing armaments and goods for the war effort, along with their workers and machines.*[19] Carrying out this order turned out to be rather difficult, since the managers of the enterprises as well as the Jews resisted this relocation in every conceivable way. The SS and Police Leader therefore decided to relocate these enterprises forcibly, in a large-scale operation scheduled to last three days. My predecessor[20] had made the preparations for this large-scale operation and issued the final order. I myself arrived in Warsaw on 17 April 1943 and took command of the large-scale operation at 8 a.m. on 19 April 1943, after the operation itself had already begun at 6 a.m. that day. Before this large-scale operation began, the perimeters of the former Jewish residential district were sealed off by an outer cordon in order to prevent the Jews from escaping. This cordon was in place at all times, from the beginning to the end of the operation, and was also particularly reinforced at night.

15 Heinz Auerswald.

16 The deportations were temporarily halted on 21 Sept. 1942.

17 According to statistics compiled by the Jewish Council, approximately 254,000 Jews were deported to Treblinka; the actual number is thought to be higher.

18 On 10 and 11 Nov. 1942 the German authorities deported possibly several hundred Jewish workers, primarily tailors, to District Lublin; the deportations to Treblinka resumed between 18 and 21 Jan. 1943.

19 Himmler was in Warsaw on 9 Jan. 1943, visiting SS and Police Leader Ferdinand von Sammern-Frankenegg: see Doc. 205.

20 Ferdinand von Sammern-Frankenegg.

During the initial advance into the ghetto, the Jews and Polish bandits[21] succeeded in beating back the deployed forces, including armoured cars and armoured personnel carriers, by means of a planned ambush.[22] During the second assault at approximately 8 a.m., I deployed the forces, which had already been divided into combat patrols, separately in squad-like formations to sweep the whole ghetto. Despite being under continued fire, they were then able to comb the building complexes systematically. The enemy was forced to retreat from the rooftops and elevated defensive positions into the cellars, bunkers, and sewers. In order to prevent people from escaping into the sewer system, the sewer network under the Jewish residential district was immediately flooded with water, although the Jews rendered this ineffective for the most part by blowing up the slide valves. Greater resistance was encountered on the evening of the first day, but it was quelled swiftly by a combat group deployed especially [for that purpose]. As the operation continued, it proved possible to drive the Jews out of the defensive positions, foxholes, etc. that they had set up, and over the course of 20 and 21 April to gain sufficient control of the greater part of the residual ghetto, as it was known, so that it was no longer possible to speak of major significant resistance within those building complexes.

The Jews' main combat group, mixed with Polish bandits, had already retreated in the course of the first or the second day to what is known as Muranowskiplatz.[23] There it was reinforced by a larger number of Polish bandits. Their plan was to use all possible means to entrench themselves in the ghetto in order to prevent us from penetrating it. The Jewish and Polish flags were hoisted on a concrete building as a call to fight against us.[24] However, a special combat group was able to capture these two flags on the second day of the operation. SS-Untersturmführer *Dehmke* was killed during this firefight with the bandits, when enemy fire detonated a grenade he was holding in his hand and fatally wounded him.

After the first few days I soon realized that the original plan could not be executed unless the armaments factories and enterprises producing goods for the war effort, which were scattered throughout the ghetto, were closed down. It was therefore necessary to call upon these enterprises to clear their premises and relocate immediately, while setting an appropriate deadline.[25] One enterprise after another was dealt with in this way. As a result, within an extremely short period of time, it was possible to ensure that the Jews and the bandits were denied the opportunity they had previously had to transfer over and over again to those enterprises supervised by the Wehrmacht. Thorough inspections were necessary to decide how long it would take to clear these enterprises. The state of affairs uncovered during these inspections is indescribable. I cannot imagine there could be worse chaos anywhere than was seen in the Warsaw ghetto. The Jews had

21 Poles from outside the ghetto did not participate in this fighting.

22 The forces entering the ghetto were attacked at the intersection of Nalewki and Gęsia Streets by two ŻOB units under the command of Zachariasz Artsztejn, a member of Dror, and Lutek (Leib) Rotblat (b. 1918). Another German unit was attacked shortly afterwards by four more ŻOB units at the intersection of Zamenhofa and Miła Streets; these units were commanded by Ber Braudo (Berl Brojde) (1920–1943), a student from Słonim and a Dror member; Lewi Icchak Gruzalc (1920–1943), a student from Warsaw; Aron Bryskin; and Mordechaj Growas.

23 Jewish Military Union (ŻZW) members armed with a machine gun had entrenched themselves on Muranowski Square and Muranowska Street.

24 The Polish and Zionist flags were raised on the building at 7 Muranowska Street.

25 See Doc. 229.

everything in their clutches, from chemical agents for manufacturing explosives to pieces of Wehrmacht clothing and equipment. The managers had so little idea what was going on in their enterprises that the Jews were able to produce all kinds of weapons within these factories, in particular grenades, Molotov cocktails, etc.

Furthermore, the Jews succeeded in setting up defensive positions in these enterprises. One such defensive position in an Army Billeting Administration enterprise had to be combatted on the second day by deploying a platoon of sappers with flamethrowers as well as artillery fire. The Jews had entrenched themselves in this enterprise in such a way that it was impossible to persuade them to leave the premises voluntarily, which was why I decided to burn down the factory the next day.

In almost all cases the managers of these enterprises, which were usually supervised by a Wehrmacht officer as well, were unable to provide concrete information about their stocks and the locations where these were stored. In no case was the information they provided about the number of Jews working for them correct. We discovered time and again that, under the guise of being armaments workers, rich Jews and their families had found accommodation in these labyrinths of buildings that belonged to the armaments enterprises as apartment blocks and were living very comfortably there. Despite all the orders issued to tell the Jews to leave the enterprises, on several occasions it was found that managers had locked in Jews with the expectation that the operation would only last a few days, in order to then carry on working with the Jews they had left. According to statements given by captured Jews, the owners of these firms held drinking parties with Jews. Women are also said to have played a major role on these occasions. The Jews reportedly sought to maintain good relations with the Wehrmacht officers and men. Drinking sessions took place frequently, in the course of which mutual deals were struck between Germans and Jews.

The number of Jews rounded up and removed from the buildings in the first few days [of the operation] was relatively small. It became apparent that the Jews were hiding in the sewers and in specially prepared bunkers. Whereas it had been assumed during the first few days that there were only a few bunkers, it became apparent over the course of the large-scale operation that the whole ghetto was systematically lined with cellars, bunkers, and passages. In all cases these passages and bunkers had access points to the sewer system, which allowed for undisturbed underground communication between the Jews. The Jews also used this network of sewers to escape underground to the Aryan part of the city of Warsaw. There was a constant stream of reports that Jews were attempting to escape through manholes. The bunkers had been constructed in this former Jewish residential district beginning in late autumn 1942, under the pretext of building air-raid shelters. They were intended to accommodate all the Jews when the new resettlement operation, which had been anticipated for a long time, was carried out, and as places from which to organize the resistance against the forces deployed. The communist resistance movement in the former Jewish residential district had also used placards, leaflets, and word of mouth to ensure the bunkers were occupied immediately when the new large-scale operation began. The Jews' far-sighted approach to the work [of building the bunkers] is demonstrated by the bunkers' clever layout in many cases, with living quarters for whole families, washing and bathing facilities, toilets, weapons and ammunition stores, and large stocks of food sufficient for several months. There were special bunkers for poor and rich Jews. The forces we deployed had an extremely difficult time finding the individual bunkers because of how they were camouflaged; in many cases finding the bunkers was only possible if Jews gave away the location.

After the first few days it was already clear that the Jews were on no account considering voluntary resettlement any longer, but were determined to put up a fight with all the means and weapons at their disposal. So-called combat groups had been set up under Polish–Bolshevist leadership. They were armed, and paid any price that was asked for the weapons they were able to get their hands on.[26]

During the large-scale operation we managed to catch Jews who had already [been] relocated to Lublin or Treblinka, had escaped from there, and had returned to the ghetto equipped with weapons and ammunition. Polish bandits used the ghetto time and again as a hideout and were all but left in peace there because there were no forces available to penetrate the chaos. While it was initially possible to capture the intrinsically cowardly Jews in larger numbers, during the second half of the large-scale operation it became increasingly difficult to catch the bandits and Jews. Again and again, renewed resistance was sparked by combat groups of 20–30 or more young Jewish men between the ages of 18 and 25, who had similar numbers of females with them. These combat groups had orders to defend themselves to the death with armed force, and if necessary to evade capture by committing suicide. One such combat group succeeded in climbing out of the sewer system through a manhole in what is known as Prosta [Street] and onto a truck, and making their escape with it (approximately 30–35 bandits). A bandit who had arrived on this truck detonated two hand grenades, which served as the signal for the bandits waiting in the sewer to clamber out of the manhole.[27] The bandits and Jews – there were often Polish bandits among them, armed with carbines, handguns, and one light machine gun – got into the truck and then drove away in an unknown direction. The last man in this gang, who had kept watch in the sewer and whose job it was to close the manhole cover, was captured. The information provided above comes from him.[28] The organized search for the truck was unfortunately fruitless.[29]

26 Of the 22 ŻOB units, 14 were recruited from Zionist youth organizations and 4 from the Bund and its sub-organizations; communists were a minority in the ŻOB, just as they were among the members of the revisionist ŻZW.

27 This rescue operation was led by Szymon (Symcha) Ratajzer, later Rotem (1924–2018), member of the Akiva youth organization; acted as the ŻOB's liaison on the 'Aryan side', 1942–1943; took 34 survivors to Łomianki on 10 May 1943; participated in the Warsaw Uprising in 1944; from 1945 worked for the Bricha movement, a post-war underground movement organizing Jewish emigration from Eastern Europe; emigrated to Palestine in late 1946; wrote his memoirs, published as Kazik (Simha Rotem), *Memoirs of a Warsaw Ghetto Fighter*, ed. and trans. from Hebrew Barbara Harshav (New Haven, CT, and London: Yale University Press, 1994). The rescue was organized by Władysław Gaik, code name Krzaczek (1914–1944), member of the Polish Workers' Party (PPR); lieutenant in the People's Guard (Gwardia Ludowa); deployed near Wyszków in spring 1943; killed by the People's Guard in Jan. 1944, after several Jews in Warsaw and near Częstochowa were betrayed and he was suspected of collaborating with the Polish police. According to other accounts he was killed by German police officers in autumn 1943 or on 28 Feb. 1944: see also Doc. 248.

28 Between 10 and 20 people who were waiting a certain distance from the manhole and were unable to climb out in time were left behind; they were supposed to be picked up in another rescue operation, but the Germans discovered and murdered them before such an operation could be organized.

29 The refugees were taken to Łomianki, near Warsaw: see Doc. 248.

The women who belonged to the combat groups of the armed resistance were armed in the same way as the men, and some of them were members of the Halutz movement.[30] It was not uncommon for these women to shoot with pistols in both hands. They frequently kept pistols and hand grenades (Polish egg-shaped hand grenades) hidden in their knickers until the last moment, in order to use them against the Waffen-SS men, the police, and the Wehrmacht men.

The resistance that the Jews and bandits put up could only be overcome by the aggressive and tireless deployment of assault forces, day and night. *On 23 April 1943 the Reichsführer-SS gave the order via the Higher SS and Police Leader East in Cracow to sweep the ghetto in Warsaw with the greatest severity and unrelenting rigour.*[31] I therefore decided to undertake the total destruction of the Jewish residential district by burning down all the apartment blocks, including those at the armaments factories. One enterprise after another was systematically evacuated and subsequently destroyed by fire. Consequently the Jews almost always came out of their hiding places and bunkers. It was not uncommon for the Jews to stay in the burning buildings until the heat and the fear of being burned to death became so great that they preferred to jump from the upper storeys, having first thrown mattresses and other cushioned objects from the burning buildings onto the street. With broken bones, they then still attempted to crawl across the street into blocks of buildings that were not yet or only partly in flames. The Jews often switched hiding places during the night by moving into burned-out ruins and taking shelter there until the individual assault forces found them. Staying in the sewers was also no longer pleasant after the first eight days. Loud voices could frequently be heard in the street coming through shafts from the sewers. Waffen-SS men, police, or Wehrmacht sappers then bravely climbed down the shafts in order to bring out the Jews. Not infrequently they stumbled over Jews who had already died or found themselves under fire. Smoke grenades were always necessary to drive the Jews out. On a single day 183 manholes were opened and smoke grenades were lowered into them at a prearranged time, with the result that the bandits – fleeing from what they supposed was gas – converged in the centre of the former Jewish residential district and could be brought out via the manholes located there. Numerous Jews, so many it was impossible to count them, were finished off by blasts in the sewers and the bunkers.

The longer the resistance went on, the tougher the Waffen-SS men, the police, and the Wehrmacht men became. Here too they tirelessly set about the performance of their tasks as part of a loyal brotherhood in arms, always standing their ground in an exemplary fashion. They were often in action from early in the morning until late at night. Night patrols with rags wrapped around their feet stayed on the Jews' heels and kept up the incessant pressure on them. Jews who used the cover of night to replenish their food supplies from abandoned bunkers or to make contact or exchange news with neighbouring groups were frequently caught and finished off.

If one considers the fact that, for the most part, the Waffen-SS men had only three to four weeks of training prior to their deployment, then one must particularly recognize the grit, courage, and dedication they displayed. It should be noted that the Wehr-

30 This is a reference to members of Zionist youth organizations (*halutzim*).

31 This order has not been found.

macht sappers also worked tirelessly and enthusiastically as they carried out the blasts used to destroy bunkers, sewers, and concrete buildings. The police officers, many of whom already had experience on the front, proved themselves once again with exemplary dauntlessness.

Only through the incessant and indefatigable efforts of all forces was it possible to capture or verifiably exterminate a total of 56,065 Jews.[32] The Jews who perished as a result of blasts, fires, etc., the numbers of whom could not be recorded, must also be added to this figure.

While the large-scale operation was still under way, posters were used to inform the Aryan population that entering the former Jewish residential district was strictly forbidden,[33] and that anyone found in the former Jewish residential district without a valid identity card would be shot. At the same time these posters warned the Aryan population once again that anyone who knowingly harbours a Jew, and in particular provides lodging for, feeds, or hides the Jew outside the Jewish residential district, would be punished by death.

In cases in which a Jew was arrested in the Aryan part of the city of Warsaw, the Polish police were authorized to give one third of this Jew's cash to the Polish police officer who made the arrest.[34] This measure has already been demonstrably successful.

By and large, the Polish population welcomed the actions taken against the Jews. Towards the end of the large-scale operation, the Governor addressed a special appeal to the Polish population, which was presented to the undersigned for approval prior to its publication. The appeal informed the population of the reasons for the destruction of the former Jewish residential district, with reference to the assassinations recently committed in the city of Warsaw's territory and to the mass graves in Katyn, and urged them to fight against communist agents and Jews (see the enclosed poster).[35]

The large-scale operation was concluded on 16 May 1943 at 20:15, when the Warsaw Synagogue[36] was blown up. There are no longer any enterprises located in the former Jewish residential district. All assets, raw materials, and machines have been removed and relocated. Everything that was there, whether buildings or otherwise, has been destroyed. The only exception is the Security Police's Dzielna prison,[37] as it is known, which was exempted from destruction.

III.

Since it is to be expected that isolated Jews will still be living under the rubble of the former Jewish residential district, even after the large-scale operation, this area must be tightly sealed off from the Aryan residential area and guarded in the short term. Police

32 In fact, the number of Jews killed in the ghetto is estimated at approximately 12,000.

33 On 23 April 1943 Stroop imposed a ban on entering 'the former Jewish residential district': poster published in Taffet (ed.), *Extermination of Polish Jews*, p. 85.

34 The order has not been found.

35 Governor Fischer's appeal is not enclosed with the report. It can be found in AIPN, GK 141/76, t. 45; copy in BArch, R 102/I/3, fol. 30 (599).

36 This is a reference to Warsaw's Great Synagogue on Tłomackie Street, which had been built in 1878.

37 The prison at 24/26 Dzielna Street was known to the people of Warsaw as 'Pawiak'.

Battalion III/23 has been deployed for this purpose.[38] This police battalion has orders to monitor the former Jewish residential district, in particular to ensure that no one enters the former ghetto, and to immediately shoot anyone who is present there without authorization. The commander of the police battalion[39] will receive further instructions directly from the SS and Police Leader on an ongoing basis. This will ensure that any small remnant of Jews who may still be present is kept under constant pressure and exterminated. Any chance to carry on existing must be denied the Jews and bandits who still remain by destroying all buildings and hideouts, and by cutting off the water. It is proposed that the Dzielna prison be turned into a concentration camp,[40] and that the millions of bricks, the scrap iron, and other materials be removed, collected, and sent [there] for the prisoners to put to use.[41]

## DOC. 244
## On 20 May 1943 the Security Police accuse a gendarmerie officer of raping two Jewish women in the Zloczow (Złoczów) ghetto[1]

Report (draft) from the gendarmerie commander in District Galicia (B-33 14 Schla., log no. 2179/43), signed Gendarmerie Oberstleutnant (signature illegible),[2] Lemberg, to the judicial authority for Cracow SS and Police Court VI – Lemberg Branch Court – Lemberg, dated 20 May 1943

The accused was provisionally detained on Saturday, 29 May 1943, and is being held in the SS and Police Court prison in *Lemberg*.

*Crime report*
Against *Schlamilch*, Walter,[3] gendarmerie officer, Zloczow gendarmerie station
Placed under oath on: (date unspecified)

38 Battalion III of SS Police Regiment 23.
39 Urban Police Major Otto Bundke (b. 1897).
40 See Doc. 256.
41 The report is followed by copies of Stroop's daily teletype messages to Higher SS and Police Leader Krüger and captioned photographs taken during the fighting. According to Stroop, three copies of the report were made; two have survived. One is the bound version, from which the text used here as the basis for translation was taken, which Stroop sent to Higher SS and Police Leader Krüger, and which Krüger forwarded to Himmler on 2 June 1943. The US Army secured this copy for the Supreme Headquarters Allied Expeditionary Forces Document Section in 1945; it was handed over to the Polish judicial authorities in 1947. A different, unbound version can be found in NARA, IMT Documents, RG 238/10611 PS, box 21–22. It contains an additional fourth section, which essentially repeats final figures from another teletype message that Stroop sent to Krüger on 24 May 1943. According to these figures, of the 56,065 Jews who were 'caught', some 7,000 were murdered on the spot in the ghetto, 6,929 were deported to Treblinka and murdered there, and 5,000–6,000 were killed in blasts and by fire; additionally 631 bunkers were destroyed, and weapons, valuables, and money were also seized.
1 AAN, 119/5, fols. 33–35. This document has been translated from German.
2 Alois Schertler (b. 1899), police officer; gendarmerie Oberstleutnant; commander of the gendarmerie in Cracow from Jan. 1940; served in Galicia, July 1941 – August 1943; gendarmerie general in the Austrian police after the war.

Born: 1 October 1900, in Braunschweig
Party member since 1 May 1937; Party no.: 4 497 733; local branch: Olbersdorf
General SS member since —, SS no.: —, SS Company: —
Other organizational affiliation: — since — unit: —
Civilian occupation: commercial employee; permanent place of residence: Olbersdorf, Saxony
Father's surname and first name: Friedrich Schlamilch
Mother's maiden name and first name: Auguste, née Jahn
Marital status: married; number of children: one, out of wedlock
On suspicion of the crime of race defilement (§§ 2 and 5(2) of the Law for the Protection of German Blood and German Honour of 15 September 1935).[4]

*1. Facts of the case*

Gendarmerie Officer Schlamilch of Zloczow gendarmerie station, Kreis Zloczow, Tarnopol Gendarmerie Headquarters, District Galicia, is accused by the Jewesses Tonie Wienitzer[5] and Regina Rotenberg,[6] both resident in the Jewish ghetto in Zloczow, of having had sexual intercourse with them in April 1943. The accused denies having done so. He admits only to having performed lewd acts on the Jewesses.

Given the circumstances of the case, sexual intercourse with the Jewesses is probable.

According to § 2 and § 5 of the Law for the Protection of German Blood and German Honour of 15 September 1935 (*Reichsgesetzblatt* I, p. 1146), extramarital intercourse between Jews and citizens of German or racially related blood constitutes an offence or crime.

Based on the interpretation of this law (see Lehnert and Schäfer's book on the criminal code[7]), any act intended to achieve sexual gratification equivalent to normal coitus is to be understood as sexual intercourse.[8]

It is therefore likely that Gendarmerie Officer Schlamilch's act falls within the statutory definition of §§ 2 and 5 of the Law for the Protection of German Blood and German Honour of 15 September 1935.

3 Walter Schlamilch (b. 1900), commercial employee; joined the NSDAP in 1937; career soldier, 1918–1930; served with the Urban Police in Ober-Ramstadt, 1934–1939; in the gendarmerie from Nov. 1939; based in Horodenka, August–Sept. 1941; then in Turka until Jan. 1943; in Złoczów from Feb. 1943; went missing in action.

4 § 2 of this law prohibited 'extramarital relations between Jews and subjects of the state of German or kindred blood'; § 5(2) stated that men who contravened this prohibition were to be 'punished with a prison term or penal servitude': see PMJ 1/199.

5 The statement by Tonie Wienitzer (b. 1922), an unmarried seamstress from Złoczów whose parents had 'both been resettled', is included in the file: AAN, 119/5, fol. 18r–v.

6 Two statements by Regina Rotenberg (Rottenberg) (b. 1920), an unmarried seamstress from Złoczów, are included in the file. While in her first statement on 14 May she had denied having sexual intercourse, she stated on 17 May 1943 that she had given this testimony because she was afraid: AAN, 119/5, fols. 30 and 32.

7 Reinhold Lehnert and Karl Schäfer, *Kleines Strafrechts-Lehrbuch (Strafrecht und Strafprozeß) für Polizei und Gendarmerie: Mit einer Übersicht über die Grundgedanken des kommenden Deutschen Strafrechts*, 28th edn (Berlin: Kameradschaft Verlagsgesellschaft Gersbach & Co., 1941), p. 134.

8 This paragraph and the preceding one are crossed out in the original.

*II. Grounds for suspicion*

Based on the charge sheet drawn up by Kriminalsekretär Zigmund[9] and Gendarmerie Officer Schlamilch's partial confession, it is to be assumed that he committed the racial defilement with which he is charged.[10]

*III. Evidence*

1) Charge sheet of the Criminal Police Office in Zloczow;
2) Partial confession by Gendarmerie Officer Schlamilch (see sheets 5–7 of the dossier);
3) Testimony of the Jewess Tonie Wienitzer (sheet 2 of the dossier);
4) " " " Regina Rotenberg (sheet 3 and back of sheet 4 of the dossier)
5) " of the Jew Manie Pasternak (back of sheet 2 of the dossier).

*IV. Enclosures*

(The interrogation transcripts and other evidence, as well as a detailed service record, an excerpt from the personnel roster, an excerpt from the disciplinary action log, and a photograph of the accused are to be enclosed.)

1 dossier

To be signed[11]

9 Correctly: Otto Zikmunt (b. 1903), police officer; served with the Vienna Criminal Police, then in Złoczów; taken to the Soviet Union in 1949; declared dead in 1959. The Kriminalsekretär at the Złoczów Criminal Police office under the Commander of the Security Police and the SD (KdS) in Galicia initially drew up the charge sheet 'on the basis of interrogations and rumours that have reached me' before handing the matter over to the gendarmerie platoon commander in Złoczów on 19 May 1943. In his undated final report, Gendarmerie Hauptmann Dorsch also came to the conclusion that Schlamilch had committed 'racial defilement': AAN, 119/5, fols. 27 and 38.

10 Schlamilch was ultimately sentenced to two years' imprisonment on 27 Oct. 1943: AAN, 119/5, fol. 72.

11 The dossier enclosed with the criminal report contains Schlamilch's curriculum vitae; the final report by the investigating gendarmerie Hauptmann, Dorsch; Schlamilch's service record; a (blank) excerpt from the personnel disciplinary action log; documents from the remand prison; and three interrogation transcripts. In addition to the two Jewish women involved, the Order Service man Manie Pasternak (b. 1920) was questioned about the rape of Tonie Wienitzer; he incriminated Schlamilch.

## DOC. 245

## On 31 May 1943 leading representatives of German authorities in the General Government discuss the resistance against the German occupation and the consequences of the deportations[1]

Minutes of the GG government's working meeting on the security situation, Cracow, dated 31 May 1943

[…][2]

Main Department Head Dr *Losacker*[3] noted that in recent months the problem of security has grown acuter than ever before. He explained that latent signs of a certain amount of unrest had always been discernible in the General Government, but that the population had been so subdued following the rapid conclusion of the Polish campaign that such unrest was merely local in nature and had not affected administrative work in any way. Following that, in 1941, when the General Government was filled with German troops as a result of marshalling forces for the beginning of hostilities with the Soviet Union, there was hardly any sign of unrest or bandit activity. But after the first hard winter of the war in the East in 1941–1942, i.e. in the spring of 1942, a stronger increase in bandit activity began to make itself generally felt in connection with the events of the war. However, even this increase in bandit activity did not change the fact that the services required by the Reich in terms of bringing in the harvest, obtaining labourers,[4] the armaments industry, the petroleum industry, transport management, and supplies could be undertaken without disruption.

According to Main Department Head Dr *Losacker*, the situation has really come to a head in recent months, as the following figures reveal. From 1 January to 24 May of this year, 1,512 attacks were carried out in District Warsaw. The city of Warsaw recorded 93 attacks in January, 89 in February, 75 in March, 226 in April, and 163 up to 29 May. In the rest of the district, there were 1,312 attacks during the same period. In the city of Warsaw alone, 6 Germans were killed in February, 14 in March, 11 in April, and 29 in May, which makes 60 altogether. Across the rest of District Warsaw, 26 Germans were killed. In addition to this, there were 92 non-German fatalities in District Warsaw. Fifty-seven Germans were injured in the city of Warsaw, of whom 30 were members of the

1 AIPN, GK 95, vol. 33. Copy in IfZ-Archives, Fb 105, vol. 29, fols. 7289–7325, here fols. 7300–7304, 7308–7309. Published in Präg and Jacobmeyer (eds.), *Das Diensttagebuch des deutschen Generalgouverneurs*, pp. 678–684. This document has been translated from German.

2 Frank began by addressing the 'state of emergency' in the General Government and called for a 'change of course with regard to the entire political and economic treatment of the local population'; State Secretary Bühler explained that the administrative machinery's effectiveness had been impaired: AIPN, GK 95, vol. 33; copy in IfZ-Archives, Fb 105, vol. 29, fols. 7295–7296, 7298.

3 Dr Ludwig Losacker (1907–1994), lawyer; joined the NSDAP in 1931 and the SS in 1933; worked in the SD, 1936–1937; subsequently held posts in the Reich Ministry of the Interior and various companies; Kreishauptmann in Jasło, 1939–1940; chief of staff in District Lublin, Jan.–July 1941; then in Galicia; head of the General Government's Interior Administration Department from Jan. 1943; governor of District Cracow, May–Oct. 1943; subsequently served in the Waffen-SS; representative of the Chemical Industry Employers' Association and director of the German Industrial Institute in Cologne after the war.

4 The General Government had to provide the Reich with forced labourers.

Wehrmacht, 13 were members of the police, and 17 were civilians. The number of Germans in the rest of the district who sustained injuries came to 23. There have also been numerous attacks in District Lublin in recent months on German administration facilities, businesses, and the Wehrmacht. From 1 January to 19 May, 98 Germans were shot and killed in District Lublin, with police officers comprising a very high share. In particular, men from the Security Police and the SD are having to perform absolutely unheard-of feats. Only 42 per cent of posts in the Security Police are filled at the moment. Apart from the 98 Germans who were shot and killed in District Lublin, 60 Polish mayors and local officials and 84 Polish police officers were also shot dead. In the period from 1 January to 19 May, there were 95 attacks on municipal and local officials' offices; 35 attacks on railway trains, railway premises, and railway stations; 46 attacks on dairies, distilleries, etc.; and 23 attacks on sawmills and forestry infrastructure.

District Radom reportedly saw a sharp rise in the rate of attacks as well. While the number of monthly attacks was [less than] 100 up to March 1942, 105 attacks were recorded for the first time in April 1942. This figure rose to 206 in June, 365 in November, 493 in February 1943, 705 in March 1943, 965 in April, and it will likely exceed 1,000 in May.

In District Lublin[5] 14 Germans were murdered during the first quarter of 1943, 36 in April, and 6 so far in May. The number of Poles murdered came to 37 in April and 57 in May. In District Radom 102 attacks were carried out on municipalities and municipal institutions in the month of May. The number of murdered police officers in District Radom amounted to 20 in 1942, 7 in the first quarter of 1943, and 14 already in May.

A comprehensive overview of attacks in the General Government, broken down by districts, shows a total of just eight attacks in District Lemberg[6] from January to 15 May, none of which were particularly serious in nature. During the same period there were 28 attacks in District Cracow, 28 in District Warsaw, 95 in District Lublin, and 216 in District Radom.

Main Department Head Dr *Losacker* explained that the bandits have become more and more methodical of late in their operations. The size and strength of the groups of bandits have not yet reached alarming levels, although there have already been instances of smaller groups of bandits being absorbed into larger ones. That said, hardly any groups with more than 100 men have been active to date. The groups are well equipped. They are led by Bolsheviks. With the Soviet air fleet becoming more active, commissars have been air-dropped into the General Government. In addition to this, prisoners of war have joined these groups, along with Jews who escaped into the forests during the course of the resettlement of Jews. In view of communist propaganda, a number of Poles from the Polish Peasants' Party[7] and other desperate people are being driven into the forests by some measure or other and are also joining the bandits. The bandits are becoming increasingly systematic in their approach, as they have now begun to systematically destroy German administration facilities, to steal money, to obtain typewriters and duplicating machines,

5 As in the original. Logically it should read: 'Radom'.

6 This is a reference to District Galicia.

7 Stronnictwo Ludowe, known during the Second World War as Stronnictwo Ludowe 'Roch'. However, this is probably a reference to the partisan organization known as the Bataliony Chłopskie (Peasants' Battalions).

to destroy quota lists and lists of labourers in the municipal offices, and to remove or burn disciplinary action logs and tax lists. Attacks on key German production sites in rural areas; on sawmills, dairies, and distilleries; on bridges, railway facilities, and post offices have also increased. The bandits already have a very pronounced military setup. They are using women and children as informers. Another difficulty in combating them is the fact that the groups of bandits do not stay together in the lands[8] and bivouac there, but rather largely comprise peasants and labourers who go about their business during the day and then, based on call-up orders, assemble outdoors, where they first learn the purpose of their mission. The bandits work with raiding parties. The police are often misled by bogus informers. If the police then set out, municipal offices or production sites will be destroyed. During the most recent attacks, particularly in District Lublin, the bandits displayed a certain uniformity in their attire, wearing caps and red-and-white armbands. The military uniform plays a major role among the bandits, especially in District Radom. Polish police uniforms are highly sought after by the bandits.

Various reasons for this growing insecurity can be cited, according to Main Department Head Dr *Losacker*. The main reason is the aggravated situation with regard to the war, as well as the intensification of enemy propaganda, which is extremely effective in the General Government. Another factor is the support provided by the Soviet air force, which is dropping men, commissars, weapons, uniforms, ammunition, and communications equipment.

Main Department Head Dr *Losacker* noted that for some time now the government of the GG has been aware that the amount of food rations given to non-Germans could under no circumstances be maintained for any length of time without the population resorting to helping themselves or being driven to revolt. For this reason it is particularly important that rations that are just sufficient be allocated starting in September of this year. The difficulties with regard to the food situation, which naturally have a negative impact on attitudes among the population; the marked increase in prices; and the sometimes extreme and tight-fisted salary and wage policies have resulted in segments of the Polish population being driven to despair. The weakened positions in the field, the withdrawal of police stations to larger towns, and the consolidation of individual commands into platoons have had a particularly unfavourable effect. It is evident that the resettlement in District Lublin[9] has also had particularly unfortunate consequences. These factors have impacted District Warsaw as well. The fact that it was necessary to put up with this resettlement due to considerations of overriding importance in no way changed the fact that it initially resulted in very unfavourable consequences. The effect of the resettlement of the Jews was such that Jews were able to join forces with the bandits. In addition to this, some operations in the General Government had an extremely unfavourable effect on the mood of the population, particularly the large-scale operation to round up labourers in January 1943, in the course of which people were taken from the streets, churches, and their homes at random.[10]

8 As in the original. Presumably this should read: 'forests'.

9 From Nov. 1942 the German police had deported tens of thousands of Poles from the Zamość region in order to create an area in which ethnic Germans were to be settled.

10 In Jan. 1943 the police arrested tens of thousands of people in the General Government who were then deported to the Reich to perform forced labour.

Furthermore, police forces have been withdrawn from the General Government in large numbers, as have Wehrmacht forces. Trained police officers were replaced with untrained ones. The fact that battalions and units were withdrawn before their replacements had even arrived also had an unfavourable effect. In many cases there was no clarity concerning the chain of command between the police, the Wehrmacht, and other formations in the Kreishauptmannschaften and in smaller towns. During the government's tour in recent days, those authorities taking part expressed the desire for a very clear system of command to be put in place, right down to the smallest villages, through an agreement between the Wehrmacht and the police.

[...][11]

De-Jewification [said Krüger] has undoubtedly had the effect of calming [the situation] as well. It was one of the most difficult and unpleasant tasks for the police, but it had to be carried out on the Führer's orders because it was vital to Europe's interests. De-Jewification has also had a positive impact in terms of illicit trade, and there was no other way in which orderly conditions could ever be achieved. The murder of Germans in Cracow was undoubtedly the work of the Young Zionist movement, a Jewish organization.[12] The police rooted out this organization. Based on what the police found, the group consisted of Jews who had escaped from the ghetto and had acquired fake identity cards with the aid of the counterfeiting centre. He had only just received the order to carry out further de-Jewification within a very short period.[13] It was also necessary to pull the Jews out of the armaments industry and the enterprises involved in war production, unless they are deployed exclusively for work that is of the greatest importance for the war effort. In such cases the Jews are concentrated in large camps, from where they are deployed as day labour in these armaments factories. However, the Reichsführer-SS has expressed his wish that the use of these Jews should also cease. He [Krüger] has spoken about this matter at length with Lieutenant General Schindler and believes that, in the final analysis, it will probably not be possible to accommodate the Reichsführer-SS's wish. There are specialists, precision engineers, and other skilled craftsmen among the Jewish workers who could not easily be replaced with Poles at present. He has therefore asked SS-Obergruppenführer Dr Kaltenbrunner[14] to explain this situation to the Reichsführer-SS and to request that he refrain from removing these Jewish workers.

Those Jews who are physically the best workers have been left in place – the Maccabees,[15] as they are known, who are excellent workers – as well as female workers, who

11 In this section Losacker expressed his appreciation for the police forces and proposed that the Germans in the General Government should be better armed and concentrated in their residential quarters. Higher SS and Police Leader Krüger expressed the view that adequate food for the Polish population was a necessary measure to gain their loyalty and advocated providing the families of forced labourers working in the Reich with more food. Krüger then turned to the treatment of the Jews.

12 See Doc. 196.

13 See Doc. 240.

14 Dr Ernst Kaltenbrunner (1903–1946), lawyer; qualified to practise law in 1929; joined the NSDAP in 1930 and the SS in 1931; detained in Austria, 1934–1935; head of the SS in Austria from 1936; Higher SS and Police Leader Danube in Vienna from 1938; simultaneously chief of police in Vienna, 1940–1941; head of the Reich Security Main Office and chief of the Security Police from Jan. 1943; sentenced at the trials before the International Military Tribunal at Nuremberg and executed.

15 The Maccabees were Jewish freedom fighters who rose up against the Seleucid dynasty in the second century BCE.

have been found to be physically much stronger than male Jews. Incidentally, the same phenomenon was also observed when the ghetto in Warsaw was cleared, which was a very difficult task. Police casualties included 15 dead and 88 wounded.[16] There, too, it was observed that Jewesses with weapons in their hands had fought to the last against the Waffen-SS men and the police.

One should really [said Krüger] no longer bother oneself with the question of de-Jewification; it has already been exploited far too much in foreign propaganda. Irrespective of this, attempts have to be made to somehow capture the Jewish elements that have evaded resettlement and are running about everywhere in disguise. He has received a report from the Security Police that attacks and murders in the city of Warsaw are repeatedly carried out by Jews.

[…][17]

## DOC. 246

## On 4 June 1943 Szymon Günsberg writes from Czystyłów labour camp about the death of his relatives in Belzec and asks that his daughter be cared for[1]

Letter from Szymon Günsberg, Czystyłów, to his brother Henryk and others, Haifa,[2] dated 4 June 1943 (copy)

Czystyłów village, near Tarnopol, 4 June 1943
My dearest ones,
Dear Żaneczka, sweet Giniuś, faithful Haneczek,[3]

I am writing you this letter in a difficult and trying situation, and one so inhumanely tragic that I can hardly describe it. I'm (still) 'living' in an area that is under Hitler's authority, and no one is capable of describing this to you. I don't know whether this

16 Stroop's final report lists 16 dead, among them one Polish policeman, and 85 wounded. Other sources estimate that the number of German victims was far higher: see Doc. 250 and *Informacja Bieżąca*, no. 16 (89), 20 April 1943, pp. 4–5; AAN, 1325/202/III-7, t. 2, fols. 251–255, here fols. 254–255.

17 In the following section, Krüger explained that the resettlement operations in the Zamość area would be discontinued with Himmler's consent, and that he wanted to combat the Polish resistance, which had been growing stronger there, with additional police forces and with the assistance of the Wehrmacht; Frank concluded the meeting by stating that a state of emergency would not be declared in the General Government. There were 32 people in attendance at this meeting: Albert, Boepple, Bühler, Otto Fischer, Frank, Friderici, Gerteis, von der Goltz, Haenicke, Haseloff, Hummel, Kaltenbrunner, Kobe, Kobold, Krüger, Kundt, Losacker, Paersch, Plodeck, Roedenbeck, Max-Josef Schindler, Sommé, von Stutterheim, Wächter, Weh, Wendler, Winkelmann, Zippert, and four other participants.

1 The handwritten original has not survived; a typewritten copy has been preserved: YVA, M.1.E 29/9. Published in Dr J[ózef] Kermisz (ed.), *Dokumenty i materiały do dziejów okupacji niemieckiej*, vol. 2: *Akcje i wysiedlenia* (Warsaw: CZHK, 1946), pp. 402–405. This document has been translated from Polish.

2 According to the copy, a confidential addendum was posted with the original letter: 'Send to the address: Günsberg Henryk or Żenia Parnass or Gizela (Gizia) Schützer, Hadar Hakarmel, Haifa, Palestine'.

3 Żenia Parnass, Gizela Schützer, and Henryk Günsberg.

letter will ever reach you, but I expect it will, because the person to whom I am giving it is worthy of trust, respect, high regard, devotion, esteem, admiration, adoration, and love. Everything this person has done for me proves it! But more [on that] later, perhaps. If there is a merciful God in this world, of whom I was once told, whom I was once taught to love, and whose existence I now doubt, then this person shall live, and you will receive this letter – of this I am sure! And I wish that for this person! We have been through so much: the war! … The Germans! Our life – the life of the Jews – under German rule is a never-ending succession of torture, suffering, tears, the most sophisticated persecution and mistreatment – it is one big pogrom. It is impossible to describe how this plays out, and it plays out in different ways: sometimes chaotic, sometimes organized, but always inhumane. Everything that history has told us about our martyrdom, about the suffering of the Jews in Egypt, in Spain, and in former Russia, is nothing compared to what we have experienced and are still experiencing. I can't really write at length and go into detail, because everything is about the details: the fact that Maks is gone as I write this! He was tortured to death! Our parents – you'll remember our lovely Mama and our father – they were deported to Bełżec and killed there. (In Bełżec, near Rawa-Ruska, a mass execution site for Jews has been established. Rumour has it that the Jews are being made into soap[4]). Iko, Berta, Pola, and the Suchman family perished during the pogrom in Zbaraż. At present I am left with Erna and Heko. Erna is in the ghetto in Tarnopol, Heko in Kozowa, and I'm in the Lager[5] at Czystyłów. The mass extermination of the Jews is beginning as I write this; soon we will all be no more![6]

I'm very happy that at least you will remain [alive], and that we will live on in your hearts. I would like to write to you about everything in detail, but I can't. I only ask you to look after my little daughter as you would an innocent angel. You don't even know that I got married under German rule. I met and married Zofia Distelfeld, a pharmacist from Jarosław who had fled from there. She was a true friend and a pillar of strength for me in the most difficult times, and on 17 April 1943 she bore me a daughter. Earlier I wrote about a person worthy of respect. Unfortunately, for the sake of this person's safety, I cannot write about this person or mention them by name. I very much regret this, but I hope you will meet this angel in human form! It is a Pole, an engineer, the head of the office where I worked. It is thanks to this person that my wife and I are still alive today, and that our little daughter is alive and will continue to live. One day you will learn the truth from him. At two days old, our little daughter went 'out into the world' to meet her destiny. Should anyone ever approach you [and say that] Gizela Anna Zofia Darmont (for this is the name she was given at her baptism – let me stress that she was even baptized), of the female sex, is my daughter, then take her in and recognize her before God and humankind as the heiress to all my rights, the moral as well as the material. I beg this of you – as someone with one foot in the grave. I beg you with the voice of my heart and the hearts of our parents: look for the little one and give her all that I could not give her – be her parents. I know you will do it!

4 This rumour was untrue.

5 German in the original: 'camp'.

6 Czystyłów labour camp was shut down in July 1943. The last 500 inhabitants of the Tarnopol ghetto were murdered on 20 June 1943, and the 1,000 remaining residents of the Kozowa ghetto (powiat Brzeżany) were murdered on 12 June 1943.

I very much regret this, and it grieves me that things must be this way. The world is so big, there is so much room on earth, but there is no room for us.

Our tragedy is all the greater because we know that the world will change, that this bestial hydra will perish – but, unfortunately, we shall perish before it does.

We are the last of the Mohicans, and we wish you, the free people, the people of the future, happiness and peace – things we have been denied. We live as if in a closed chicken coop, and they are slowly finishing us off. Our death is nigh; it comes to us in such different ways, but it is always cruel!

It is the Jews' dream to die a natural death because the road to life is closed to them! The law grants the condemned, even the worst criminal or bandit, a last wish. We have been deprived of even this pleasure. The world cannot imagine this and even if it knew all about it, no one could imagine that our experiences are real!

Believe, my children, believe in the very worst, because the worst is almost trivial compared to the sad reality! Stay healthy. I bid you farewell forever on behalf of myself, on behalf of my Zofia, on behalf of Erna and Leni, and the Heks family. Stay healthy, I wish you this from the bottom of my heart, and remember my last wish: look after my poor, beloved little daughter, whom I loved like no one else in the world and to whom I could give nothing but her unfortunate life.

From your slowly dying, though healthy and strong and so thirsty for life, dying with the death of each person close to us, resigned to awaiting his own terrible death, and thinking of you,

brother Szymek, and your sister-in-law Zofia

## DOC. 247

## On 6 June 1943 Moshe and Binyamin Wald describe their survival in the western part of District Radom[1]

Two letters from Moshe Wald[2] and Binyamin Wald[3] to their relatives, dated 6 June 1943

My dears,

Whoever receives this letter, please read it and pass it on to my remaining family, i.e. my brother Shlomo Wald[4] in Belgium, in Brussels; [my] sister Freyde Wald-Binenshtok[5]

1 YVA, O-75/184, fol. 1–2. The first letter has been translated from Yiddish and the second from Hebrew.

2 Moshe Wald (1899–1985), businessman; lived in Łódź prior to Sept. 1939; fled with his family first to Tomaszów Mazowiecki, and then in late 1942 to Szydłowiec; imprisoned in 1942; in Nov. 1943 avoided deportation along with his son Binyamin; thereafter hid in various locations and served with the Home Army; emigrated to Sweden in 1947; lived in Israel, 1950–1952; thereafter lived in the USA.

3 Binyamin Wald, later Benjamin Yaari (1925–2006); member of the Akiva youth association; lived in Łódź prior to Sept. 1939, then in Szydłowiec; imprisoned along with his mother, brother, and father in 1942; escaped with his father; lived under an 'Aryan' identity in Częstochowa, then served in the Home Army; emigrated to Palestine in 1945.

4 Shlomo Wald (1896–1943?), labourer; originally from Tomaszów Mazowiecki; lived in Brussels prior to Sept. 1939; perished in Auschwitz.

5 In an enclosed third letter from Moshe Wald and his son written in Polish, she is called Aliza Binensztok; she was the sister of Moshe and Shlomo Wald.

in Eretz Yisrael; my nephew Shlomo Wald in Eretz Yisrael, in Haifa, Beit-Yehoshua, on behalf of [me], Moshe Wald, and my son, Binyamin Wald, born in Tomaszów Maz[owiecki]. Up until the war [we] lived in Łódź, at 21 Południowa Street. After three years of shuffling from one ghetto to the next, I ended up in the small town of Szydłowiec. Very early on the morning of 23 September 1942 we were surrounded by German Gestapo, Mongols,[6] Polish police, and the fire brigade. All the Jews, 15,000 of them, were rounded up in one place. Half of them were immediately loaded into goods wagons, 150 people per wagon. The wagons were sealed and took the people to the slaughterhouse at Treblinka. The other half were held in an old castle without bread or water. On 25 September they too were deported. When we were deported, the Poles stood by and rejoiced, and later helped to drag the Jews who had been in hiding out [of their hiding places].

But after we had overpowered the guard, we managed to jump out of the second floor: twenty men, one woman, and one girl.

Four weeks later, however, eighteen [of these escaped] men were killed, thanks to the help of the ethnic German Albert Meisner; his wife, Maria Meisner, née Wolski, from Tomaszów Maz[owiecki]; and his Polish helpers. Hundreds of other Jews were later tracked down in the forests and in their hideouts, and exterminated. Finally, in Sulejów, near Piotrków, a woman and a child were handed over to the German authorities in the Sulejów town hall by the Poles Edek Pichota; his mother, Zygmunt Serafin; and his family, his sister, and Capala Wasna and were killed. The woman's name was Estera Beyle Flantsboym, née Gliksman, from 21 Południowa Street in Łódź.

The Poles are very pleased that Hitler is exterminating the Jews for them. Individual Poles were willing to help us hide, but only in exchange for a lot of money. But now one Pole denounces another, and the few who are better don't want to help us any more either. We live day and night in the fields and forests, without sleeping or eating. We are looking to join up with the partisans. We expect to encounter them at any moment. Death does not frighten us. We only want to live so that we can take revenge. We want to get our hands on a gun as soon as possible. We are ready to fight to the death.

Now we ask you, my remaining family, and all remaining Jews, to avenge the millions of Jewish victims. You should form your own nation of people who live in their own land. We salute the Jewish people and wish them a different and better life, a different life than before.

Moshe Wald

Binyamin Wald

We are now called Skalski.

We are currently staying amid bushes and undergrowth near Mokra, a village near Piotrków.

Dear Aliza and Shlomo Wald,[7]

Today is 6 June 1943. I, Binyamin, and my father, Moshe Wald, are the only ones of the whole family still alive. Already nine months ago our relatives were sent to Treb-

6 Presumably a non-German unit under the command of the SS.

7 Aliza and Shlomo Wald were Binyamin Wald's aunt and cousin, who had emigrated to Palestine before the war.

linka – my mother[8] and my brother Jakob[9] from Szydłowiec, and the rest of the family members from Tomaszów [Mazowiecki].

Chana and Estera (Shlomo's mother)[10] were visiting us five months ago. They were with us in Szydłowiec for two months and then were sent to perform [forced] labour in Pionki.[11] Fate accompanies my father and me from town to town, from village to village. There are some good people who hide us, but most are very bitter and they are happy about our people's fate. Our lives are very bitter, but we want to survive the war to take vengeance on the Germans and on most of the Poles for the fate of [our] people. And now we have no place to live with [the Polish] people, so we are forced to go to the forest and live there by the sword.[12]

Perhaps we will live to see you once again, and if not, may peace be upon you.

But remember: revenge against our enemies is permitted and must be extreme.

And the people of Israel, if they want to live and prevent what happened to those in Poland from happening again – which I am unable to write about, because it was much worse than death – must live like other nations, a people apart, with [their own] territory, with [their own] army. To think only about what is good for the homeland, on behalf of the murdered people, I appeal to my brothers to work tirelessly for our homeland, because Eretz Yisrael was our hope until the final moment. And in the final moment we saw how wrong our path [in the Diaspora] was.

There would be much more to write, but our hearts and souls are sick, and there is not much to write about us, for we are but the few who have remained of the many.

I send greetings to my land [Eretz Yisrael] and to my Israeli brothers and all of my relatives.

One of the last,
Binyamin Wald

Today our names are Stanisław and Tadeusz Skalski.

We have enclosed two pictures of ourselves as keepsakes.[13]

8 Chana Wald, née Ayzenberg (1889–1943), housewife; originally from Działoszyce; lived in Łódź prior to Sept. 1939; murdered in Treblinka.

9 Jakob Wald (1928–1943), younger son of Moshe Wald; murdered in Treblinka.

10 Estera Wald, née Bornshteyn (1892–1944), housewife; originally from Łódź; lived in Tomaszów Mazowiecki prior to Sept. 1939; lived in the Tomaszów ghetto during the war; perished in Auschwitz.

11 A forced labour camp was located in Pionki, in which approximately 1,000 inmates produced armaments.

12 This expression is taken from Genesis 27:40, in which Isaac blesses Esau: 'And by thy sword shalt thou live, and thou shalt serve thy brother; and it shall come to pass when thou shalt break loose, that thou shalt shake his yoke from off thy neck.'

13 Not included in the file.

## DOC. 248

## From 19 May to 15 June 1943 Tuvia Borzykowski describes how resistance groups in Warsaw organize the survival of Jews in hiding[1]

Diary of Tuvia Borzykowski,[2] entries for 19 May to 15 June 1943

19 May 1943

Our Marrano[3] family became larger today.[4] *Cywia Lubetkin*[5] arrived from Łomianki.[6] Apart from the three 'official Aryans', there are now already five of us who are actually in hiding.[7] Cywia's arrival means that a member of a Halutzim[8] group has again begun to operate within this community of hidden people, some with official and some with unofficial status. The [Halutzim] espouse a kind of conduct and approach to personal relationships which differ greatly from that of the others in the 'maline'.[9] For example, they cannot believe that Cywia is not my sister and that we are not related in some way, apart from through our Halutzim connection, for how would it otherwise be possible

1 The original has been lost. Published in Tuvye Bozhikovski, *Tsvishn falndike vent* (Warsaw: Merkaz Hehalutz, 1949), pp. 170–191. The diary entries span the period from 17 May 1943 to 27 Jan. 1944. Published in English translation in Tuvia Borzykowski, *Between Tumbling Walls*, trans. from Yiddish Mendel Kohansky (Tel Aviv: Ghetto Fighters' House, 1972). This document has been newly translated from Yiddish.

2 Tuvia Borzykowski (Tuvye Bozhikovski) (1911–1959), social activist; member of Dror and the Poale Zion party; lived in Warsaw from mid 1940; editor for the underground press; instructor at a Zionist agricultural training facility in the Warsaw suburb of Czerniaków until late 1942; then lived in the Warsaw ghetto; fought with the Jewish Combat Organization (ŻOB) in 1943; emigrated to Israel in 1949; founding member of the Ghetto Fighters' House Museum (Beit Lohamei Hagetaot).

3 A term for Iberian Jews who were forced to convert to Christianity.

4 The first entries concerned Borzykowski's stay in an apartment belonging to a Jewish woman and her daughter, who called themselves Stanisława and Zosia Kopik as per their adopted Polish identities.

5 People's names, both here and below, often appear in italics in the published Yiddish version of the diary. Cywia (Zivia/Tzivia) Lubetkin (1914–1976); executive board member of Dror from 1938; initially in Soviet-occupied Poland from 1939; founding member of the Jewish Combat Organization (ŻOB) in 1942; member of the Jewish National Committee (ŻKN); took part in the Warsaw Ghetto Uprising in 1943; active in the Bricha movement in 1945; lived in Palestine from 1946; founding member of the Ghetto Fighters' House Museum. Her memoirs have been published in English translation in Zivia Lubetkin, *In the Days of Destruction and Revolt*, ed. Yehiel Yanay, trans. Ishai Tabbai (Tel Aviv: Hakibbutz Hameuchad, 1981 [based on the 3rd Hebrew edn, 1980]).

6 A community located north-west of Warsaw, near which the surviving members of Jewish combat units who had escaped the Warsaw ghetto through the sewer system on 10 May 1943 initially found refuge: see also Doc. 243.

7 According to Borzykowski there were three official 'Aryan' residents in the apartment: Mrs Kopik, her daughter, and Icchak Cukierman (Yitskhok Tsukerman, see fn. 11), who was pretending to be the daughter's fiancé: Borzykowski, *Between Tumbling Walls*, p. 119. The parties involved made varying statements regarding the number and identities of the other residents, whose appearance was not considered 'Aryan'. Apart from Borzykowski and Cywia Lubetkin, some of the Kopiks' relatives who were not registered with the authorities also lived there: see also the entry for 15 June 1943 below.

8 Hebrew: 'pioneers'; a Jewish youth movement that trained young people for agricultural settlement in the land of Israel.

9 'Maline' (also spelled 'malina', from the Polish for 'raspberry') was the term used in ghetto parlance for a hiding place created to help a Jew survive. It appears in quotation marks every time it is used in the published Yiddish version, and this punctuation has been retained in this translation.

for her to tend a sick person[10] who isn't kin, as she does, and to be as devoted to him as she would to a brother? For people with a completely different worldview and way of relating to others, it is nevertheless difficult to grasp the Halutzim way of life, even when they are the last survivors in a 'maline' on the 'Aryan side'.

Although we are in hiding here, we are in close contact with the entire Jewish underground on the 'Aryan side'. Our 'maline' at 4 Komitetowa is one of the few places to which the couriers directly funnel all news about the lives and hardships of the thousands of Jews in hiding on the 'Aryan side'. A large share of the relief work is organized here, in this place, and is led by the [Jewish] National Committee and the [Jewish] Coordination [Agency], in which *Yitskhok Tsukerman*[11] (Hehalutz Dror), *Dr Adolf Berman* (P. Z.-Left),[12] and *Leon Feiner* ('*Mikołaj*' – Bund) are active. The file with the names of the Jews who are receiving support is kept in our hiding place.[13] From here connections branch out to the various hiding places – wherever Jews are to be found. The couriers reach the hidden Jews in every corner of Warsaw. A few of them come to us to report on their work. Others meet with Yitskhok at the various meeting points in the city. Every evening when Yitskhok comes home, he gives us all the news that the couriers have brought him.

And there is plenty to hear. Not a day goes by without a few dozen Jews falling into German hands, which happens in various ways. Many are recognized on the street. They are stopped by a 'shmaltsovnik'[14] who demands a large sum of money. Those who are unable to pay the sum demanded of them are handed over to the Germans, never again to see the light of day. There are cases when someone has only enough to pay part of the sum, so they are taken into a building and stripped of their clothes. Quite a few 'malines' are surrounded by the Gestapo at night. The Jews are dragged out and taken in vehicles to 'Pawiak' to their deaths. Poles also face harsh consequences for hiding Jews. Various factors contribute to the discovery of apartments involved in the conspiracy: 'shmaltsovniks' spy on 'malines'. They extort as much money as possible from their victims and later report to the Germans the addresses where the Jews can be found. If two Polish neighbours quarrel and one of them has the slightest suspicion that the other is hiding Jews, he immediately informs the Gestapo and the Jews pay with their lives for these quarrels between neighbours. It takes no more than a simple visit from a friendly neighbour who notices something strange in the place and later, without thinking anything of it, whispers the secret to another neighbour, a relative, or any old acquaintance.

10 After his escape from the Warsaw ghetto, Borzykowski temporarily stayed with the ŻOB in the forest near Łomianki, where he was ill with typhus.

11 Yitskhok Tsukerman (Yitzhak Zuckerman, Icchak Cukierman), also known under his nom de guerre, 'Antek' (1915–1981); lived in Soviet-occupied Poland, 1939–1940; Dror leader from early 1940; ŻOB second-in-command and liaison to the Home Army and the People's Guard in 1942; active on the 'Aryan side' in rescuing survivors of the Warsaw Ghetto Uprising in 1943; fought in the Warsaw Uprising in 1944; active in the Bricha movement in 1945; founding member of the Ghetto Fighters' House Museum; married Cywia Lubetkin.

12 Poale Zion.

13 This is a reference to the aid provided by the ŻKN; at this time its work was integrated into the Council to Aid Jews.

14 Yiddish: a person who blackmailed Jews in hiding on the 'Aryan side'; the author derives the term from the blackmailer's demand, 'Dawaj na szmalec' (Polish: 'Hand over your money'): Bozhikovski, *Tsvishn falndike vent*, p. 155.

Then at night the Gestapo pulls up to the gate in a vehicle and rings the building caretaker's doorbell. In the best-case scenario 'shmaltsovniks' come, and the matter can be settled with money. But the apartment is then 'burned'. After such a visit, those in hiding are afraid to stay in the 'maline' even a moment longer, because they are not safe from future visits.

'Aryan' papers are only good for calming your nerves. But they absolutely cannot save your life if you have to show them to verify your racial extraction when confronted by a German or a Polish blackmailer. Jewish women with an especially 'fine' ['Aryan'] appearance somehow manage to wriggle out of difficult situations, whereas men who are stopped on the slightest suspicion are not even asked to show an ID or a work pass. Instead, they are first subjected to a physical examination. In such cases the best documents, the best 'Aryan' looks, and an excellent command of Polish don't help. An 'Aryan' appearance does indeed fool all the big bad wolves lying in wait to claim Jewish lives on the streets and in the buildings. Only rarely is a Jew who looks like this caught on the street because he is suspected of being a Jew. However, no small number of such Jews fall into the trap during a 'lapanke',[15] in which Poles are rounded up for forced labour. The medical examination that all those who are caught must undergo often reveals the Jewish heritage of those who are sadly not lucky enough to be only as unlucky as those sent to Germany for forced labour …

According to the news that the couriers are constantly bringing about the lives of Jews in hiding, the situation of the Jewish children on the 'Aryan side' is particularly sad. Before the ghetto was liquidated, many parents jettisoned their little Moyshes and Sores[16] and left them with Polish friends on the 'Aryan side' so that the children would remain as a trace of the wiped-out families, of the decimated generation. The children have already forgotten what their names used to be. They no longer remember their parents. They have already grown accustomed to a new 'mame' and a different 'tate'.[17]

But even in their 'Aryan' families, they feel every minute of every hour that they are forbidden to live. Their guardians never let them go out into the street to play with all of the other children because people might recognize them. They must sit confined in the house all day long, often in a dark hiding place where they almost never see the sky. The Jewish children are not permitted to sing or to cry whenever they feel the need to do so, because the neighbours might hear a child's voice in a home where they know there is no child.

In places where the Jewish children live with the other children of the household, the former have bonded with their 'little sisters' and 'little brothers', but every time a stranger knocks on the door, the children are confronted with a riddle. before the person enters, why do their parents push one child into a cubbyhole or a cellar, but not the others? The hidden child grows up feeling like a persecuted person, oppressed by an inferiority complex. The household's unencumbered child, at liberty to indulge every one of its basic whims without constraint, feels superior and privileged, and this shapes its relationship with the Jewish child.

15 From the Polish word 'łapanka': 'raid' or 'roundup'.
16 These are the Yiddish forms of the names Moses and Sara with an English plural ending for this translation.
17 Yiddish: 'mother' and 'father'.

Just like their elders, Jewish children are not exempt from having to wander from one place to another. Sometimes it becomes necessary to take a child out of a place because an outsider has recognized the child. Not having anywhere to put the child just then, the head of the household foists the child on an acquaintance or a relative until the courier from the Jewish underground comes and arranges a 'maline'. But the child is unable to let go of the people who were its 'parents' up to that point and feels strange with its new 'parents' and in the entire[ly new] surroundings. So the child cries and screams until it gets used to its new home.

Such are the terrible tidings and problems involved in the struggle for survival, as the couriers have relayed them to us. They bring such news to a place where none of these woes is unfamiliar, where everyone has experienced them all first hand. The worries and suffering concentrated within the four walls of our 'maline' multiply exponentially every day, in keeping with the suffering of thousands of Jews. We sense the bitterness emanating from the Jews' hidden lives accumulating in this room, where we spend our days and nights, and condensing into a mass that piles up in thick layers. After each new update and distressing piece of news, the thick air becomes truly palpable – the air from which we neither can nor want to free ourselves, but which is impossible to breathe.

While the Polish underground movement is busy undermining the occupying power's foundations every day – by blowing up bridges, destroying railway lines, sabotaging factory work, and attempting to assassinate distinguished Gestapo members and SS leaders – while it is carrying out this strenuous work to foil Hitler, Jewish anti-fascist activity of a completely different stripe is under way. Namely, to save every Jew's life, to ensure every Jewish child's continued existence, to support all those in their gloomy hiding places who have been condemned to death by keeping their spirits up and giving them a feeling of courage and strength, letting them know that they are not completely alone, that the pulse of an organized societal collective is still beating, that there is still someone out there to look after Jewish children.

The coordinated work of the Jewish National Committee and the 'Bund' is manifold. Of the approximately 20,000 Jews in hiding in Warsaw, 12,000 are under the care of the national authority,[18] which distributes financial aid every month – practically the sole source of income for those in hiding, because under such conditions it is completely out of the question for Jews to work or conduct trade. The relief efforts are also focused on creating 'malines' for all the Jews who come to Warsaw having escaped from the camps or from the ghettos in other towns, or who come here from the forests. All those who have to flee their 'burned' apartments are provided with other housing. If anyone has to relocate from one place to another, our couriers watch over that person while they move, so that in case something happens, they can immediately pay the ransom money. In general, after receiving news that a Jew has fallen into a trap somewhere, they rush to help. If it is possible to ransom [the Jew] with money, then no one has ever perished in such a case, even if the sum in question is large.

The Jewish underground movement also furnishes everyone with documents, which are produced under the auspices of the Council to Aid Jews' legalization cell.[19] There

18 This is probably a reference to the ŻKN.

19 See also Doc. 295.

are two types of such documents. The first are 'lipove' (false),[20] which the cell members manufacture themselves, with forged stamps and 'Stadtkommandanten'[21] signatures, with names taken from the 'Haftoyre'.[22] Then there are good identity cards, which bear the real names of people who appear in city registers but who have died or been killed. Whoever possesses such a document can be certain that, in the event he is caught and enquiries are made at town hall, the reply will be that such a person indeed appears in the records. Genuine documents of this nature are obtained from town hall officials, building managers, and others. In reality, however, there is no good identity card or work ID, because the Germans and the Polish police presume that the best identity cards are fake, and their first question is: 'How much did it cost you?'

Aid is not limited to the Jews of Warsaw. Couriers from the Jewish underground movement carry aid to the forests. They also take money and weapons for self-defence to the Jews in the camps in Trawniki, Poniatowa, Skarżysko[-Kamienna], Częstochowa, Płaszów, etc. The Jews in camps are furnished with documents so they can flee. Those who have no chance of escaping from the camps are called upon to put up resistance and not to let the Germans kill them.

The Jewish underground movement feels strengthened in its daunting and dangerous task through contact with the outside Jewish world, with Eretz Yisrael. The illegal post, which brings letters and news from abroad by various circuitous routes, has an extraordinarily uplifting effect on the spirit. The money sent by foreign Jewish organizations is more than mere material support; it is an expression of a deep fraternal bond. The letters that arrive from time to time from *Eng. Reiss*,[23] *Dr Schwarzbart*, and others are sources from which we draw strength. When you read the letters, every sentence makes its way deep into your soul, never to be forgotten. The very scant news from Eretz Yisrael and the wider world, with which [these letters] enrich us, falls like the thinnest rays of light through narrow cracks in a dark, locked prison.

To a certain extent, the Polish underground movement is also involved in the aid efforts on behalf of the Jews in hiding. It has created a *'Council to Aid Jews' (Rada Pomocy Żydom)*.[24] This council includes the finest members of Polish society, intellectuals, social activists, and true democrats. The council is one of the most active underground organizations. Its members have a compassionate, humanitarian attitude towards the persecuted Jews. The 'council' provides a framework that enables the Jewish aid organizations to function properly.

20 From the Polish word 'lipa': 'fraud' or 'swindle'.

21 German in the original, 'city commanders'; a reference to heads of the military administration for a city.

22 A chapter from the books of the Prophets, which is read in the synagogue after the weekly or holiday reading from the Torah. In Yiddish and Hebrew the expression 'from the Haftoyreh/Haftarah' can mean invented, far-fetched, or very uncommon, which is apparently the intended meaning here.

23 Anzelm (Ansh(e)l) Reiss (1886–1984), engineer and socialist; president of the Central Palestine Office in Warsaw until August 1939; later a World Jewish Congress representative in London; chairman of the board of the World Federation of Polish Jews after the war; died in Tel Aviv.

24 Members of the ŻKN and the Jewish Coordinating Committee (ŻKK) worked with the Council to Aid Jews.

Since only a small, socially active segment of the population is working to preserve every single Jewish life, and given that all the Jews are in hiding on the 'Aryan side', every day is invariably accompanied by great disappointments and emotional shocks. Each new piece of news about recently discovered 'malines', Jews caught on the street, and similar sorrows increases the doubt that gnaws at everyone: Are we not wasting our energy? Isn't it futile to torment ourselves, because in the end we will all be caught like fish in a net? Only some primal instinct whispers that, as long as we are still alive, we must do everything we can to keep on living.

24 May 1943
The beautiful, summery day will soon draw to a close. The sun, which has flooded the room with an abundance of light and warmth all day, moves incessantly on its westward course. Its last golden rays pass over the household furniture and the walls, and only one luminous corner near the ceiling remains in the otherwise already nearly darkened apartment. The twilight casts its shadows on the soul, and it is impossible not to wonder how this day may have ended for the Jews in hiding in Warsaw.

Yitskhok shuffled into the apartment, gloomy and dejected.[25] He had returned from the city without his usual humour and remained silent for a long time. It took quite a while until Cywia managed to find out what was bothering him. He held back from me, fearing the bad news might worsen my health. But then I pestered Cywia until, in a trembling voice and with halting speech, she revealed the secret to me: the group that was in hiding at no. 10 on 11 Listopada Street[26] is no more. The words hit me like an electric shock. Instantly I felt dizzy. In my mind's eye I saw images of the comrades who had perished. Only after a few minutes had passed did the whole tragedy become clear to me in all its particulars. A fire broke out when a match was lit in the factory building at no. 10 on 11 Listopada Street, where *Tosia Altman*,[27] *Eliezer Geler*,[28] *Marek Majerowicz*,[29]

25 Change in tense as in the original.

26 The street name refers to 11 November (Polish: 11 listopada), the Polish national holiday. ŻOB members had hidden in the attic of the decommissioned celluloid factory at that address in the Praga neighbourhood for a few days after escaping from the ghetto when it was destroyed.

27 Tosia Altman (1918–1943); originally from Włocławek; leading member of the Hashomer Hatzair youth movement from 1938; organized resistance groups in the Vilna ghetto in 1941; visited the ghettos in Grodno, Białystok, and Upper Silesia in 1942; ŻOB representative on the 'Aryan side'; took part in the Warsaw Ghetto Uprising.

28 Eliezer Geler (Geller) (1918–1943/1944), merchant; member of the Gordonia youth movement; lived in the Warsaw ghetto after he was released from captivity as a prisoner of war; chief editor of the underground publication *Słowo Młodych*; organized resistance groups in Upper Silesia, 1941–1942; joined the ŻOB and fought in the Warsaw Ghetto Uprising; registered at Hotel Polski in May 1943; sent from there to Bergen-Belsen in summer 1943; then sent to Bergau camp, near Dresden; in October 1943 deported to Auschwitz, where he was murdered.

29 Marek Majerowicz (1911–1943), member of the Poale Zion party; editor of a Polish underground newspaper in the Warsaw ghetto; commanded a Poale Zion combat group during the Warsaw Ghetto Uprising. A German patrol ambushed them, and in the ensuing battle, all the fighters fell except Majerowicz and one other young fighter. When the uprising was suppressed, Majerowicz was among those who escaped through the sewers to Warsaw's 'Aryan side'. As described in this document, he and other fighters took refuge in the attic of the celluloid factory at no. 10 on 11 Listopada Street. Majerowicz perished in the fire that broke out in the factory on 24 May 1943.

*Moyshe Sharfshteyn*,[30] *Zigi Kirshner*,[31] *Yitskhok Morgnlender*,[32] *Shifra*,[33] and *Manye Grayek*[34] were hiding.[35] The celluloid stored there instantly began to burn, and a few minutes later the entire building was engulfed in flames. Most of the comrades burned to death. Eliezer Geler escaped with burns. Tosia Altman and Shifra also ran out, having sustained severe burns, but were caught by the Polish police and handed over to the Germans. They were taken to a German hospital, where they received no medical care and perished from their injuries.

News of people dying is nothing new. Every day entails another stab to the heart. But we had never before experienced such a shock as we did following the news of what happened on 11 Listopada Street. These were not just some unknown Jews, whose death [also] causes deep pain and makes us agonizingly aware that a few more people have once again been thinned from our ranks. This time the pain was even deeper and keener, because people close to us, friends, comrades have left this world. I went through the whole chapter of organizing the fight, the uprising, and escaping through the sewers with some of them. In my mind's eye I see every one of them in the various situations we got into. That's why it is so difficult to come to terms with the sad fact [of their deaths], even more so because a carelessly lit match was the cause.

A glimmer of hope has suddenly spread through the Jews' hiding places on the 'Aryan side', thanks to an encouraging piece of information that offers people the prospect of survival and has recently been passed on by word of mouth: in exchange for money, you can buy a passport that will get you out of Poland as a foreign citizen. These are the magic words holding all the Jews hiding in cellars, dugouts, and behind false walls in thrall. All of the everyday problems caused by life on the 'Aryan side' are suddenly of secondary importance. Everyone's sole aspiration is to have the good fortune to become a citizen of a foreign, neutral nation.

The rich Jews who still have gold and dollars are going to great lengths to get in contact with the source of the life-giving papers, sparing no expense, paying various 'makhers',[36] and often achieving their aim via the second or third middleman. The poor Jews, who have barely enough to pay the Polish landlord for their room, and often not

30 Moyshe (Moszek) Sharfshteyn (1919/1920–1943); originally from Warsaw; member of Hashomer, then of Dror; active at the Zionist agricultural training facility in the Warsaw suburb of Czerniaków in 1942; joined the ŻOB after he was forcibly relocated to the ghetto; took part in the Warsaw Ghetto Uprising; left the ghetto in early May 1943; went into hiding in the Praga neighbourhood.

31 Zigi Kirshner (Kirshnboym) (1914/1915–1943); forcibly expelled from Germany to Poland in 1938; lived in the Dror kibbutz at 34 Dzielna Street in the Warsaw ghetto; took part in the Warsaw Ghetto Uprising; left the ghetto in late April 1943; hid in a bunker at 29 Ogrodowa Street, then at the disused factory in Warsaw's Praga neighbourhood after the bunker was discovered.

32 Yitskhok Morgnlender (Icek Morgenlender); originally from Ostrowiec Świętokrzyski; activist in the Hashomer Hatzair youth movement; lived in the Warsaw ghetto from Feb. 1943; took part in the Warsaw Ghetto Uprising as part of the group in the workshop area led by Binyamin Wald; escaped from the ghetto through the sewer system.

33 Shifra/Szyfra (Stenia) Sokółka (1920/1921–1943); Hashomer Hatzair member; probably hid on the 'Aryan side' with a Polish family from Jan. 1943, until she was forced to leave her hiding place.

34 Manye Grayek (d. 1943); managed to escape the ghetto as it burned; initially hid along with Shifra Sokółka in a Polish family's apartment, then in the factory in Warsaw's Praga neighbourhood, where she was badly injured in the fire; was handed over to the Germans by Polish police, along with Tosia Altman.

35 On 24 May 1943.

even that, can do no more than envy the rich and lament their own fate, that they are left with such little chance of survival due to their poverty.

News of these opportunities came from the Gestapo, which started a rumour that the Gestapo has a large number of foreign visas for citizens of neutral countries which foreign consulates have sent. Because most of the people for whom these visas have been issued are no longer alive, the Gestapo is prepared – for great sums of money – to transfer the visas to other people and to call them by the names of those who are no longer alive.

The Jewish Gestapo personnel – Kenig,[37] Adam,[38] and others – register everyone who pays tens of thousands of złoty for a visa in order to be sent abroad.[39] (According to information from the Gestapo, people are temporarily taken to special camps for foreign citizens in Vittel.[40]) All those who are registered are put up in 'Hotel Polski' at 29 Długa Street. The influx of Jews there is immense, and the hotel is overflowing. From time to time, groups of Jews are transported from 'Hotel Polski' to the foreigners' transit camp in 'Pawiak', and from there transports leave for Vittel. All 'foreigners' are allowed to take an unlimited amount of baggage and valuables with them.

Whenever a group of Jews is taken from 'Hotel Polski', the vacated places are immediately occupied by others. There are always more applicants than places. Since 'Hotel Polski' has become the only island where Jews can officially reside with the Gestapo's knowledge, it has also become a place of refuge for Jews with no foreign papers. There are always Jews who have no 'maline', or those who have had to leave their discovered 'maline' and wander the streets in extreme danger until they get a new one, not knowing by day where they will sleep that night, and at night having no idea where they will spend the next day. They all go to 'Hotel Polski', where they commingle with the 'foreigners'. It is hard to determine who has a right to be there and who does not. In this way people buy themselves a bit of time during which they can find themselves a place to stay.

However, the Gestapo got wind of the fact that a certain number of unregistered Jews (those who did not have enough money to pay the large sums) were hiding at 'Hotel Polski' and recently carried out a thorough check. The Germans took all those who were not registered as foreigners to Pawiak, where they were shot.

Generally speaking, 'Hotel Polski' is not such a straightforward matter, even for those who have large amounts of money. Poor people, who cannot hope to save themselves in this way in any case, do not have to worry about the actual value of becoming a 'foreigner'. They can do nothing more than lament their bitter fate. It seems to them that they are doomed simply because they do not have enough money. All of these embittered,

36 Yiddish in the original. A 'makher' is a 'fixer', namely an influential person, usually paid, who mediates in order to bypass procedures, often illegally.

37 According to other sources his name was Kenigel or Kenigeld.

38 This is a reference to Adam Żurawin (d. 1992); originally from Łódź; had connections with the Gestapo from 1940; lived on the 'Aryan side' in Warsaw; sentenced to death by the ŻOB due to his involvement in the visa scheme described here; in possession of Honduran passports in Vittel internment and transit camp from mid 1943; jumped from a train headed to Auschwitz in 1944; businessman in New York after the war.

39 The head of the group was Leon (Lolek) Skosowski.

40 The internment and transit camp, located in the spa town of Vittel in Lorraine, was established in April 1941 to concentrate citizens of all nationalities; it was in operation until May 1944.

impoverished Jews are incapable of recognizing the great dangers, the many downsides, and the uncertainty linked with going to 'Hotel Polski'.

However, those who can become 'foreigners' or have already done so face a very deep internal struggle. Their doubts give them no peace. They are tormented by the question of why the same murderers who leave no stone unturned in their search for every single [adult] Jew and Jewish child have suddenly become so benevolent that they are prepared to save some of the Jews. The situation in which they find themselves seems strange to them. They know that while German military units are still busy blowing up the last bunkers in the ghetto and ploughing up every place where a Jew could possibly be in hiding, and while the small number of Jews who escaped from the ghetto are still being persecuted in the streets on the 'Aryan side', at the same time Jews are sitting free and unmolested at 29 Długa Street. Germans go in and out of that building and do not bother anyone. Isn't this a sign that the Germans want to entrap all those Jews in hiding whom they have difficulty finding, and that they intend to do so using 'foreign passports' as a means of deception, to get the Jews to voluntarily hand themselves over along with all of their possessions?

The more they are tormented by this feeling of distrusting the Germans, the more the memories of German deception tactics begin to surface. During the 'operations' in the ghetto as well, the Germans always created illusions among a certain segment of the Jewish population. With work cards, 'szopy', etc., they gave some Jews a feeling of security, and it was precisely the ones who felt 'safe' and did not go into hiding whom they took without the slightest difficulty whenever they felt like it. So perhaps the foreign papers are nothing more than another trick? The fact that letters to relatives have arrived from the foreigners' camp in Vittel, in which those who have taken foreign citizenship write that they are doing well, that they live freely, and that the 'Red Cross' is taking care of them, has done nothing to reassure them either. After all, letters also arrived in the Warsaw ghetto from Treblinka in July and August 1942, in which those who had been deported wrote that they were living 'quietly and happily', as the Germans had dictated.[41]

In the internal struggle over whether to register at 'Hotel Polski', *yes* or *no*, arguments nevertheless arise in favour of doing so: The war is going to continue still for a long time, and it will be impossible to keep oneself safe for such a long period and not fall into the Gestapo's clutches. The nerves are already too weak to be able to endure the fear caused by every rustle coming from outside or from the neighbouring apartments, to constantly wonder whether *this person* noticed something or whether *that person* harbours some kind of suspicion. Thus the conviction grows that whoever is hiding on the 'Aryan side' and manages to avoid misfortune ten times will ultimately run out of luck the eleventh time around. As a result, the reasoning goes that it is better to try one's luck at 'Hotel Polski', where there are indeed serious dangers, but also a little hope: maybe the Germans won't engage in deception this one time, maybe they will leave a few Jews [alive]

41 Some of these letters were probably written by people who had escaped from the transports to Treblinka but were afraid to write openly about their experience, while others were probably written by Poles claiming to be the deportees, many of whom were likely no longer alive, and asking for money and valuables. The Gestapo also spread false rumours in order to create the impression that Treblinka was a labour or transit camp.

to show the world they are not the murderers they are thought to be, or maybe they will simply do it for reasons of historical preservation?

No one can make a wise decision when it comes to the path that determines life or death. No one can give advice to another person about whether to continue the fight in the daily war of nerves on the 'Aryan side' or to become a foreign citizen. Everyone must rely on their own intuition. Even serious social activists, in particular the director of the 'Joint' [JDC], *D. Guzik*,[42] are helping a number of Jews to obtain such passports with money from the 'Joint', believing that this may indeed offer salvation.

The German intention to catch a few Jews in this pułapka[43] and kill them is all too transparent, however. Sadly, many cannot see this, because remaining in their hiding places in Warsaw no longer offers any prospect of survival.

12 June 1943
Our landlady[44] keeps good tabs on the Jewish holidays. Two weeks ago she calculated when Shavuot would fall this year. She impatiently awaits the Sabbath or a holiday so she can light candles or make a good meal to express her connection with Jews and simultaneously remind us of the same. In truth she does not have a solid traditional education, but she expresses it all in her own way. She constantly reassures us that no Jew will fall into German hands in her home, because she prays to God, and doing so will have an effect …

Yesterday morning our landlady announced to us that today is the eve of Shavuot. We tried to work out whether she was mistaken. One of us thought we had slept through the holiday, and that Shavuot had already come last week. According to another calculation, Shavuot will not be for another week yet. However, the landlady's calculation won out, even though she didn't keep track of the Counting of the Sfire.[45]

The first night of Shavuot sticks in my mind, not because of the holiday food, but because of a noisy vehicle.

Around 11 p.m. the beds – which are tucked away all day, along with the bedding – were already laid out side by side, as in a hospital, prepared for the night. Some of us were already lying in bed, one was in the process of fastidiously undressing, and another was still loafing about in the narrow gaps between the beds. Suddenly the sound of a vehicle made everyone freeze. Rigid and unmoving, like statues, we all stayed exactly where we were, pricking up our ears to determine whether the sound of the engine was moving closer to our building …

When we heard it getting closer and closer, and the vehicle began to slow down, we cut the lights and in the greatest haste dismantled the beds, packed the bedding, and

42 Daniel Dawid Guzik, nom de guerre 'Kaftor' (Hebrew: 'button') (1889/1890–1946), head of the American Jewish Joint Distribution Committee (JDC) in Warsaw and on the board of the Jewish Social Welfare Association (ŻTOS); imprisoned for nine months in 1941; supported the ŻOB, 1942–1943; lived on the 'Aryan side' in 1943, including for a time at Hotel Polski; escaped following his arrest and internment in Pawiak prison; survived in a bunker after the Warsaw Uprising until Jan. 1945; died in a plane crash.

43 Polish in the original: 'trap'.

44 Stanisława Kopik.

45 *Sefirat ha-Omer*, or the Counting of the Omer, is the verbal counting of the 49 days between Passover and Shavuot.

carried everything to the hiding place in utter silence, literally on tiptoes, so that nobody in the vicinity would hear any suspicious commotion from [our flurry of activity]. In the midst of our concentrated work, we heard the vehicle stop at the gate. A few people got out, and through the windows facing the street we could hear them talking. No one had any doubt at that point that the Gestapo had got wise to our 'maline'. We continued to remove any traces [of our presence], thinking we still might be able to fool them. At the same time we readied our only two revolvers to shoot if there were no other choice.

We could already hear people ringing and knocking at the gate. We used the time it took for the building caretaker to open the gate to get dressed. Just then we heard people walking up the stairs. We were already completely sure that they were here for us. They climbed ever higher, up to the fourth floor, where we are, and the sound of their footsteps grew ever louder. The next minute would determine whether we lived or died.

Then they stopped. The first knock. In a flash we realized that they were knocking on a neighbouring door next to ours. [Thoughts flashed through our minds:] Do they not know our exact address and therefore have to ask the neighbour? Or are there Jews hiding in the neighbour's apartment too, and they have come to take them away? Our nerves were stretched to breaking point as we waited for the end.

They were in the neighbour's apartment for a few minutes. During this time each one of us stood rooted to the spot and didn't make a peep. It was dark in the apartment, and we could barely see one another. The light from the gas lantern across the street shone through one window. Only those standing in the corner lit up by the gas streetlight were able to communicate with each other by means of glances. Each one of us was occupied with various thoughts while those minutes passed. We all interpreted it as a good sign that they were spending a long time in the neighbour's apartment, because if they had intended to come for us, then they would have come straight in. But this did little to calm us, for as long as they were still in the building, right next to us, we had not yet escaped disaster.

The most critical moment was when we heard them leaving the neighbouring apartment. We thought that then, right then, they were going to come over to our place. The first steps we heard going down the stairs eased our hearts a little. With each floor they descended, we felt better. Only when we heard their footsteps far away did we begin to stir and quietly talk about what had just happened.

But our relief was short-lived. Again we heard them coming up the stairs, and again we began to tremble. The same waiting, the same fear that at any moment they would be knocking on our door. But they went into the neighbouring apartment this time too. They went up and down like that many more times, and we could not understand what was going on.

We gradually got used to the commotion on the stairs, but we did not know a moment's peace until we heard the vehicle leaving. The sound of an engine, which always gives us a fright, was music to our ears this time. For a long time we listened attentively to the sound as it grew ever more distant, and we felt as if we had been reborn.

The next morning our landlady innocently asked the neighbour who had 'disturbed her sleep' during the night. She learned that the neighbour had received a delivery of goods by vehicle. The merchandise was unloaded and then the vehicle left.

Of course the neighbour has no idea how much his goods strained our health and our nerves.

15 June 1943
Yesterday *Marek Edelman*[46] came to live with us. His arrival has brought our 'maline' to the point of overflowing. There are now nine of us in all, apart from Marek Folman,[47] who is staying here temporarily until he leaves on a 'Dror' mission for the combat organization in Będzin.

In order to make more space at 4 Komitetowa Street, today I moved to another 'hideout' at 31 Twarda Street, where *Szloma Grayek (Stefan)*[48] is located. This 'maline' was built by Grayek's Polish friend *Felek Rajszczak*,[49] who purchased a dilapidated apartment especially for this purpose many weeks ago, renovated it himself, and created a well-disguised hiding place.

Upon entering the apartment at 31 Twarda, I met a tall man with a thick head of hair and a pair of intelligent and expressive black eyes. My escort – Kazhik[50] – introduced me. It was Felek Rajszczak. He is over 40 and a long-standing communist activist from before the war. Because of his communist activities he served several years in prison under the Sanacja regime. Rajszczak is someone with deeply held ideological convictions, a strong political temperament, and an ingrained sense of internationalism, and he is completely free of even the slightest prejudice against Jews, which one often encounters even among more progressive Polish citizens. His willingness to help Jews is largely due to his ideological stance.

Felek led me into another room and told me to look for Grayek, who was in the hiding place. He wanted to test whether a stranger could find the disguised hiding place that had taken so much effort to create. I probed literally every corner and every section of the walls and the floor, and it was impossible to find an opening leading into the hiding place. After half an hour, when I had grown tired of searching and given up on any further attempts to find the hiding place, Felek revealed the secret to me.

I could not believe my eyes when I saw that the entire secret is situated inside a stove. It is a tall tiled stove standing in a corner next to the double wall, and it looks quite

46 Marek Edelman (1919–2009), physician; member of the Bund's children's and youth organizations; joined the ŻOB's Bundists in Nov. 1942; ŻOB deputy commander during the fighting in the Warsaw ghetto in April 1943; escaped to the 'Aryan side' on 10 May 1943; took part in the Warsaw Uprising in 1944; worked as a physician in Łódź after the war; supported the opposition to communism from the 1970s; member of the Sejm, 1989–1993; author of *The Ghetto Fights* (New York: American Representation of the General Jewish Workers' Union of Poland, 1946 [Polish edn, 1945]).

47 Marek Folman (1925/1926–1943), engineer; member of Dror; sent to Upper Silesia to organize resistance groups in 1941 or 1942; lived in the Warsaw ghetto from Dec. 1942; arrested in Jan. 1943; escaped from a transport to Treblinka; then active as a partisan for a time; led ŻOB members out of the ghetto to Wyszków in May 1943; murdered thereafter.

48 Stefan (Szloma, Sholem, Shalom) Grayek (Grajek) (1916–2008), social activist; Poale Zion member; head of the hachsharah training programme in Grochów; active in the Poale Zion party's underground leadership in the Warsaw ghetto; founding member of the ŻOB and the ŻKK; worked on the Schultz and Többens factory premises, 1942–1943; took part in the Warsaw Uprising in 1944; member of the Central Committee of Jews in Poland in 1945; emigrated to Israel in 1950.

49 Feliks (Felek) Rajszczak (1902–1977), construction worker; member of the Communist Party of Poland (KPP); helped ŻOB members escape to the 'Aryan side' in spring 1943; he and his family hid several Jews from May 1943; denounced and arrested in Jan. 1944, but the ŻOB organized his release; honoured along with his wife and two children as Righteous Among the Nations by the State of Israel in 1978.

50 Szymon Ratajzer's nom de guerre.

normal. Like all stoves, it is set against the two walls that meet in the corner of a four-sided room. The stove has double doors. When you open the first two half-doors, which are covered by a lattice you can see through, there are two more doors that can be screwed shut. The stove is heated through them. You only have to open these doors when you want to heat the stove; you don't have to open them to enter the hiding place. Rather you push up the whole case containing the doors, the grate, and the ashpan. Doing so reveals a large opening through which you wriggle horizontally into the hiding place located between the double walls. Once inside you lower the case again, which hangs on an iron cable and moves on wheels. Immediately the stove looks normal again, and no one would think that it serves as the passage to a hiding place.

I looked at this stove construction and came to the conclusion that this is the best-disguised hiding place of all the 'malines' in Warsaw. Felek Rajszczak built it with such a flair for subterfuge that only an architect could possibly ferret out any trace of the hiding place, after first measuring all the other rooms on the lower floor and noticing that this room is smaller by a few dozen centimetres. But even then, it would not occur to him that the entrance to the hiding place is through the stove.

However impressively disguised this hiding place may be, the way the work was carried out is no less impressive. Normally the renovation of a dilapidated apartment consisting of nothing more than four walls requires a few craftsmen plus ordinary labourers. For reasons of secrecy this was not possible. The extraordinary skill and innate technical knowledge with which Felek Rajszczak is blessed were put to the utmost use in the 'maline's' creation. He carried out the work of a mason, a painter, a carpenter, an electrician, a plumber, a glazier, a locksmith, and a stove fitter. And not only does he have a good theoretical and practical command of all these trades, which were necessary in building the 'maline', but he also keeps up with the experts in other areas. He can repair watches and is a good hairdresser as well. He can cook any dish and bakes the best pastries.

Felek has probably never had a better opportunity to put all of his skills to use than in this dark period for the Jews. Indeed, he has put these talents at our disposal with great moral integrity, responsibility, and a deep sense of humanity.

## DOC. 249

## On 21 June 1943 Globocnik provides information about Jews performing forced labour for the SS enterprises in District Lublin and expects further operations to be set up there[1]

Memorandum from SS-Gruppenführer and Generalleutnant of the police, SS and Police Leader Lublin Globocnik, Lublin, dated 21 June 1943 (carbon copy)[2]

*Memorandum*

The establishment of SS labour camps with Jews performing forced labour has so far yielded the following results:

1 BArch, R 9361-III/526483. Published as a facsimile in Grabitz and Scheffler, *Letzte Spuren*, pp. 324–327. This document has been translated from German.

1. There are currently 45,000 Jews in the camps. They are employed in the following ways:

*SS labour camp Poniatowa*
with a weekly production capacity of:

| | |
|---|---|
| Blouses, trousers, and coats | 38,000 |
| Shirts or items of underwear | 18,000 |
| Caps | 6,000 |
| Pairs of socks | 7,200 |
| Knapsacks | 6,000 |
| Haversacks | 4,200 |
| Shoulder harnesses | 2,400 |

The camp currently has work sufficient to last three months.

In view of the camp's construction, 60 per cent of its production capacity is being utilized at present.

*SS labour camp Trawniki*
Current order backlog for 3/4 of a year, specifically:

| | |
|---|---|
| Fur coats | 20,000 |
| Rabbit-fur waistcoats | 116,000 |
| Fur caps | 100,000 |
| Fur gloves | 150,000 |

Approximately 300 wagonloads of furs for repair are expected.

Utilization of production capacity currently at 90 per cent.

*SS camp Budzyn*
The Heinkel aircraft factory is being set up.

*Deutsche Ausrüstungswerke*[3]
Utilization of wood processing capacity at 100 per cent – among other things, conversion of trucks and shovel shaft production, tar paper, crate production for the Wehrmacht, furniture for settlers, manufacture of wooden clogs (50,000 pairs per month), repairs of boots brought from the front.

*Clothing works*
Processing and sorting of items from Reinhardt[4] (1,800 wagonloads of textiles delivered to date).

Incoming items are sorted, inspected, cleaned, and shipped.

2 The version printed here is the second copy. Globocnik sent this memorandum to Himmler's adjutant, Rudolf Brandt, on 21 June 1943: Grabitz and Scheffler, *Letzte Spuren*, pp. 322–323.
3 The Deutsche Ausrüstungswerke (DAW) was an SS enterprise during the Second World War which exploited the forced labour of prisoners from Nazi concentration camps and Jewish ghettos in German-occupied Poland to provide the German military with equipment and clothing, to repair railway lines and goods trains, etc.
4 A reference to Operation Reinhard.

Bristle and brush factory with an order backlog of 3.5 million brushes for the Wehrmacht, and one peat works due to supply 10,000 tonnes in 1943.

Capacity utilization at 100 per cent.

*Lublin concentration camp*
Camp construction, supply of labourers to various production enterprises important to the war effort, bristle-sorting works, and willow and straw-shoe weaving shop. Capacity utilization currently at 50 per cent.

The remainder constitutes a reserve labour pool for factories that have yet to be incorporated into the concentration camp, e.g. for aircraft fittings and aircraft instruments, which will be introduced in the very near future. Approximately 10 per cent will also be resettled after jobs are ultimately assigned.

An explosives factory will also be brought in, as will a scrapyard for vehicles damaged at the front.

2. Increases in output, currently confirmed at 20 per cent compared to the previous level, have already been recorded.

3. The plan is to relocate Bialystok here as well; Litzmannstadt is still under discussion.[5] With regard to Litzmannstadt, I propose that highly trained workers and machines be assigned to Poniatowa labour camp, that this camp be enlarged accordingly, and that the entire production then be relocated from Litzmannstadt to Poniatowa. This would mean Litzmannstadt could be liquidated, because of the 78,000 Jews currently living there, only some of them are working in war production.

4. The difficulty that has now cropped up is that the Wehrmacht agencies are holding back from placing orders with the well-functioning SS labour camps. They are not refusing to place orders, but we are being told 'that orders have just been placed, and we will be taken into consideration next time' or 'that there is no work at all in this or that sector' etc.

Moreover, the economic agencies within the Reich that are responsible for the distribution of work are disinclined to assign orders to these production sites.

Litzmannstadt was recently flooded with orders to prevent resettlement, whereas the same orders could have been transferred here, thus causing an automatic shutdown [in Litzmannstadt].

The labour camps were established here in order:

a) to ease the burden on Reich industry,
b) to thereby free up people in the Reich,
c) to establish fallback locations for factories destroyed by bombing, and
d) not only to increase production by means of concerted action and appropriate oversight, but also to guarantee that deliveries are made on time.

In addition, there are no profit-seeking motives, since all net earnings go to the Reich.

5 A reference to the ghetto factories in Białystok and Łódź. Only forced labourers from Białystok ended up in Lublin-Majdanek concentration camp.

These reasons are probably not to the liking of the German industries either, because they see this as a loss of profit.

I therefore request that a central authority issue corresponding instructions that current orders should be placed with the camps that have been made ready here, and that further industries likewise be relocated here. Transferring Bialystok and potentially Litzmannstadt would free up so much manpower that a significant increase in the labour force could be expected at the end of this year.

It is easily possible to comply with the Reichsführer's wish that places formerly inhabited by Jews be used for industrial premises,[6] but if there are no orders, and if no operations are relocated, then there is no point in setting up any new camps.

Moreover, I am of the opinion that developments in the war could still put such strains on us in terms of production that we will not be able to prepare enough fallback locations.

## DOC. 250

### On 22 June 1943 Leon Feiner informs the Bund's representation in London about the fighting in the Warsaw ghetto and the situation of the survivors in hiding[1]

Report from the CKRŻMP, signed Berezowski,[2] Warsaw, for the Bund representation in London, dated 22 June 1943[3]

To the Bund representation in London
My dear, esteemed comrades,

I have the opportunity to send you a letter, which is unfortunately very limited in scope. I'm taking advantage of this to send a report (with reference to the last communication from 31 August last year[4]) for the period from 1 September 1942 until today. Due to space constraints, I shall limit myself to the subject of the Jews.

A comprehensive, intensified campaign of extermination is under way; those members of the Jewish population who are still alive are being liquidated as quickly as possible. Mass 'roundups' are taking place, during which people are deported to work in the Reich, or taken to camps or prisons, and mass arrests and shootings are carried out incessantly; entire towns, villages, and regions are being depopulated. By 31 August of last year, the occupiers had killed off about 1.5 million Jews – since that date, the same number again have been killed. This leaves approximately 250,000 alive, with the numbers dwindling further every day. The period covered by this report was marked by two liquidation phases. The first was a continuation of the previous liquidation phase and involved killing the vast majority of Jews on the spot, in death camps: women, children, the elderly, and the sick. The so-called productive elements were left in the ghettos, barracked in the so-called szopy, i.e. in large German factories that operate completely

6 No evidence of this has been found. See Doc. 253.

1 AAN, 1325/202/XV-2, fols. 372–377. This document has been translated from Polish.
2 Leon Feiner's code name.
3 Handwritten note at the top of the document: 'Sent to L[ondon] 29 Nov. [1943]'.
4 See Doc. 126.

independently of one another. A tiny portion were deported to the East, to penal and labour camps, where they have to undertake heavy labour of various kinds. The living and working conditions in the szopy and on the work sites outside the ghettos and camps are terrible. Hunger and cold, whippings and rifle bullets, sophisticated methods of torture and humiliation – that is the daily bread that the Nazis serve their slaves. As a result, a series of greatly reduced ghettos remain, which more closely resemble the szopy. So-called illegals have sought refuge there and gone into hiding. These are Jews who managed to escape the so-called resettlement but failed to find a place in the szopy. In the Warsaw ghetto, for instance, approximately 35,000 remained in the szopy during the period covered by the previous report, while 10,000–20,000 were in hiding; in the Cracow ghetto 10,000 remained, in the Lwów ghetto about 20,000, and in the Częstochowa ghetto between 10,000 and 20,000. Many towns and cities, which had previously been spared, have now experienced such operations, carried out swiftly and thoroughly, though sometimes with certain deviations from the usual pattern. Moreover, during the period covered by this report, fresh mass transports from Western and Southern Europe[5] have continued to pour into the death, penal, and labour camps.

The greater the military setbacks encountered by the Germans, the more brutal, cruel, and rapid the liquidation.

The second phase during the period covered by this report involved the liquidation of the already reduced ghettos on account of the so-called resettlement and the relocation of the szopy to the camps. It was now all about the complete de-Jewification of the cities. The ghettos are vanishing, and the remaining Jews are being placed in camps in Poniatowa; in Trawniki (approximately 25,000 from the Warsaw ghetto); in Płaszów; in Bieżanów, near Cracow; in Janowska Street camp (Lwów); and in the camps in Skarżysko, Ostrowiec, Starachowice, Piotrków, Częstochowa, and a number of other towns, mainly in Eastern Małopolska[6] or in the Kielce region.

Active armed resistance is a characteristic feature of the current liquidation phase. Whereas there were only sporadic incidents [of this kind] during the period covered by the previous report (individual cases of resistance were reported in some of the small towns and larger cities), the situation has now changed fundamentally. The Warsaw ghetto deserves special mention in this respect. The first battles in the Warsaw ghetto took place from 19 to 23 January 1943.[7] The battles fought there between the armed German gendarmerie and the SS, on the one side, and the Jewish Combat Organization (ŻOB) which was fighting for the first time, on the other side, raised hopes that greater things were to be expected in the future, and they were an embarrassing surprise for the Germans – a prelude to the later fighting.

Unfortunately, due to limited space, I am not able to describe these events to the appropriate extent and in as much detail as befits their significance. This must and will be done at some point. Here follow just a few fleeting remarks. What took place in Warsaw in April and May of this year was a Jewish-German war, christened the Battle of Ghettograd or of Judengrad[8] against the Reich. This war eclipses all similar events in

5 This is probably a reference to South-East Europe.
6 Eastern Galicia.
7 The first battle had taken place on 18 Jan. 1943.
8 An allusion to the Sixth Army's defeat at Stalingrad.

the history of our own and other peoples – so different were the phases of this war, its forms and methods, the acts of aggression, defence, and partisanship dictated by the special circumstances and carried out under these very circumstances. Unforgettable, shocking images of the ghetto – illuminated by sheets of flame and shrouded in thick clouds of smoke – the rattle of machine guns, the thunder of artillery, the explosions of shells and mines, the crash of collapsing houses – and our people, who lived under these conditions. No master of pen, brush, or clay can capture the vividness of the extraordinary events that unfolded before our very eyes, all that we experienced during these dangerous, tragic, yet so moving and magnificent days.

The main fighting began on 19 April and lasted about a month. But even afterwards there were active pockets of resistance for a time, even up until the end of May. The defence operation was led and largely executed by the Jewish Combat Organization [ŻOB], the armed wing of the joint Coordinating Committee of the Bund and the Jewish National Committee. The revisionists and the Agudas[9] did not take part. The revisionists formed their own little 'Retaliation Organization', which gave up the fight after two days.[10] The ŻOB members were mainly workers and young people. The youngest was 13-year-old Lusiek[11] from the Young League;[12] the oldest was 40 years old. They all represented different currents. The brotherhood in arms (of Bund members, Halutzim,[13] Hashomer,[14] etc.) was exemplary. The population's general attitude is currently diametrically opposed to that of the previous year. It would be extremely unfair and inaccurate to attribute the heroism and determination of those days to pure desperation. Quite a few fighters would have had the opportunity to escape from the ghetto, but they did not take advantage of it – on account of a staunch determination to fulfil a high moral obligation and to carry out a mission: to wreak vengeance on the enemy and to take up the struggle for dignity and honour, the struggle against fascism – the enemy of humanity and of their own people. On the German side – caution, bordering on cowardice. The longer the heroic battle continued to play out, the more the aura of German military invincibility faded, and the Polish population was made to realize that in the struggle against the occupiers lies great opportunity and hope. This German-Jewish war strengthened the Polish underground's spirit and resolve in fighting the Germans. In return, the Germans gave free rein to their fury and frenzied behaviour by reducing the entire ghetto to rubble. On the fifth day of fighting, we published a fine appeal from the ŻOB, in which the fighters conveyed their greetings from the battlefront to the Polish underground and to the capital [Warsaw].[15] In response, parts of the Polish workers' movement expressed their solidarity and admiration. In general, the entire Polish underground movement – depending on the attitudes of individual

9 Agudas Yisroel was an Orthodox, conservative Jewish party active in Poland.

10 This is a reference to the Jewish Military Union (ŻZW). Numerous ŻZW members were engaged in the fighting for more than a week.

11 Eliezer (Lusiek) Błones (1930–1943); member of the Socialist Children's Association (Skif) prior to Sept. 1939; fought with the Bund in April 1943; acted as a liaison between the combat groups in the Warsaw ghetto; escaped to Łomianki, near Warsaw, on 10 May 1943, and subsequently to Wysków. He and his group were denounced and shot by Germans at Płudy.

12 Polish: 'Młody Bund'; presumably a reference to the Bund's youth organization Tsukunft.

13 Hebrew: 'pioneers'.

14 Members of the left-wing Zionist organization Hashomer Hatzair.

15 See Doc. 233.

groups towards the Jewish problem – expressed respect and admiration for the defenders [of the ghetto] in light of their struggle. The events had an electrifying impact on both the capital and the entire country. On behalf of the joint committee of the Bund and the ŻKN [Jewish National Committee], we published reports from the scene of the fighting at regular intervals, often on a daily basis. They appeared in the current issues of the bulletin,[16] secretly printed by official civilian bodies, and were broadcast by the radio station 'Świt'.[17] The results of the fighting: on the Jewish side, several thousand people were killed, burned alive, shot, gassed – approximately 25,000 were deported to the camps at Trawniki, Poniatowa, and Majdanek, and to the concentration camp in Lublin[18] – they met their deaths as a result of mines, artillery shells, or fire, or in the ruins and the burned-out buildings. The Warsaw ghetto is one big graveyard. Hundreds or even thousands of survivors are still wandering around below ground, slowly expiring. Two days ago a 13-year-old boy turned up with a note dated 10 June, a witness to the 'life' in that world, in the catacombs of our time. The bombing of Warsaw in 1939 destroyed 75,000 dwellings, while the war in the ghetto resulted in the destruction of over 100,000 dwellings. The losses on the German side – more than 1,000 dead and wounded,[19] plus enormous damage to the property of enterprises supporting the German armaments industry, which the ŻOB destroyed or set on fire. The ŻOB's losses were comparatively low, although brave individual fighters met their deaths, led by their commanders (M. Ordshe,[20] a Hashomer); Klepfisz,[21] who procured most of the armaments for the ŻOB; Berek,[22] a member of our Central Committee;[23] and many others. When the various ŻOB groups – which, incidentally, operated independently – were no longer able to fight for reasons including the fact that they had run out of ammunition, they made every effort to escape this hell. Approximately 200 ŻOB people were left. The first messenger to bring news from the scene where the ŻOB was engaged in combat was Frydrych from the Bund (a 'Jutrznia'[24] activist), a long-serving soldier in the Polish army and an exceptionally brave and bold man. He was arrested along with a group of fighters outside the ghetto and shot by the enemy shortly thereafter. In dramatic circumstances, he had reached us via underground passages and so carried out his mission. Under extraordinary conditions, so terrifying and dangerous that they almost beggar belief, the surviving ŻOB members escaped the

16 Possibly a reference to *Biuletyn Informacyjny*, which appeared weekly.

17 Radio Świt: a radio station run by the government in exile in London.

18 This is a reference either to the Lipowa Street camp or the aforementioned Lublin-Majdanek concentration camp.

19 SS and Police Leader Stroop's official report states that 15 Germans died and 85 were wounded, but it does not include all the fatalities among non-German auxiliary troops: see Doc. 243.

20 This is a reference to Mordechai Anielewicz.

21 Michał Klepfisz (1913–1943), engineer; member of the Bund's children's and youth organizations, then of the movement's political party; fled to the Soviet Union in 1939; thereafter active in the Jewish resistance in Warsaw; escaped from a transport to Treblinka in 1942 and returned to the ghetto; began military training in Dec. 1942 as a result of his links to the Home Army; thereafter armourer for the Jewish Combat Organization (ŻOB); killed during the Warsaw Ghetto Uprising.

22 Berek (Abraham Szmul) Sznajdmil (1904–1943), accountant; member of the Bund; escaped to Vilna in 1939; thereafter lived in Warsaw; Bund representative in the ŻOB High Command, and from Nov. 1942 on the Jewish Coordinating Committee (ŻKK); killed in early May during the Warsaw Ghetto Uprising.

23 A reference to the Bund's Central Committee.

24 The Polish name of the Bund's sports organization, Morgnshtern.

hell of the ghetto through the underground sewers. Two larger groups of about seventy people each managed to reach the forests; others fell with weapons in their hands, some at the sewer outlets, others outside [the ghetto]. The rest, approximately sixty in total, must have been killed by the German troops who had surrounded the sewers.

The Warsaw ghetto – just like many other ghettos – thus officially no longer exists. An announcement threatening Jews and anyone who hides them with the death penalty already mentions the 'former' residential district.[25] In this current, second phase – during the liquidation of the ghettos – there have been loud calls for weapons from various quarters. But there are very few weapons or, to be more precise, none at all, and so elsewhere there is no other fighting comparable to what took place in Warsaw. Nevertheless, there are pockets of resistance in several places, more numerous than during the period covered by the previous report. The example of Warsaw has stirred people. Unfortunately, conditions have not allowed them to prepare themselves for such a battle.

There are currently four settings in which the Jews who are still alive in Poland are located: the ghettos, the labour and concentration camps, the forests, [and] the Aryan urban districts and the villages. Only a few of the larger ghettos remain (in the Dąbrowa Basin, in Łódź, Białystok, Vilna, and Radom, and certainly a few smaller ones as well). Sooner or later they will all meet the same fate: liquidation. So in fact only three spheres of Jewish life remain, each with their own specific appearance and way of life. The smallest in terms of numbers is the forests, where groups of partisans are hiding, some of which consist solely of Jews, but some of which are mixed. The labour and penal camps are the largest in terms of numbers. The living and working conditions there are well known: the inmates exist under the constant threat of being shot and are subject to whippings, torture, and starvation. The Aryan residential districts, where isolated Jews live as Aryans, constitute the final sphere of Jewish life. This is an entirely conspiratorial sphere. Jews are not allowed to stay in the Aryan residential districts and in the localities that have already been de-Jewified. Simply for being Jewish or descended from Jews, every Jew is considered a criminal who must be punished by death on the spot if he is discovered. The Jews who survive in the cities must therefore blend in with their surroundings completely and cannot stand out in any way. Hence the tragedy of their double life, especially because the housing problem is exceedingly difficult: apartments are scarce, very expensive, and very hard to get; the most one can find is a sublet. The problem is aggravated by the fact that the authorities are increasing the pressure on anyone who hides Jews or helps them in other ways. As a result, a psychosis is setting in among the population, which is deliberately induced and nurtured by the occupiers: the Jew-related psychosis. The pressure exerted by the Germans is increasing; the persecution and liquidation of the Jews is intensifying. Scores of informants and various police units – both in and out of uniform – are snooping around, and day after day they avidly track down new victims in the streets, in public places, and in apartments. This creates excellent opportunities for extortion, which has reached catastrophic proportions. Some people are blackmailed repeatedly. The extortionists not only demand money and valuables, but completely plunder their victims' apartments; on the streets they take their clothes and shoes. The struggle against extortion is already under way; this is in the interest of the entire Polish underground movement.

25 See also Doc. 243.

The Jews in the Aryan districts are forced to live under such conditions; in a state of constant tension, fearing every moment that their appearance, a coincidence, or a particular conduct might betray them and that catastrophe will befall them; not to mention the overall pressure of the cruel German reign of terror directed against the entire population. All four, or rather three, of the above spheres of Jewish life will be completely liquidated, one sooner, the others later. This liquidation is already under way; its final phase has begun. So far the only victory Hitler has achieved is nevertheless a total victory, despite his humiliating setbacks – the victory over millions of defenceless Jews, whom he has murdered with impunity. Without a doubt, the most important task right now is the direct rescue [of the Jews], which must be accomplished as quickly as possible. The surest way would be to end the war, but until that happens, we should retaliate and threaten to take further steps, especially because the number of German prisoners of war is considerable. But if this is not considered an appropriate remedy – in view of the well-known passivity of our powerful Allies – then only one route to rescue remains: an international exchange agreement. All other measures – financial aid, liberating people from prisons and camps, obtaining documents, and paying ransom in cases of extortion – are indeed necessary, and we are undertaking them even though they are difficult and nerve-wracking, and involve considerable expense. But these are emergency remedies, and moreover they address individual problems, not the overall picture: the social activism of the surviving Jews, all of whom will ultimately perish, without exception. Perhaps only white ravens[26] will remain. The predictions I made ten months ago, on 31 August last year,[27] have already come true. The rest will also all come true if we now – at the last moment – fail to immediately carry out this major operation that I have just proposed.

Under such conditions and circumstances, which are historically unprecedented, and in such an atmosphere, we must now carry out our organizational work. In such decisive times, every socialist workers' organization faces monumental tasks. In the current phase, we have had to fight to save people from physical extermination and focus on preparations for the ongoing armed struggle. This has been the core of our organizational work and has determined almost all the steps we have taken. Circumstances have made it necessary to have two active organizational centres – one in the ghetto, the other outside. Of course, both have concentrated their efforts on the most important task. The centres have worked in different ways and followed different paths, as dictated by their respective living conditions.

While we were in the process of preparing for active armed resistance, we decided to coordinate our struggle against the occupiers with the activities of other Jewish, primarily Zionist organizations, and their youth groups, which are amalgamated in the Jewish National Committee. The result was the joint Coordinating Committee of the Bund and the ŻKN. The ŻOB emerged out of this, and its task was limited to active resistance in and around the city of Warsaw. With respect to clandestine military organizations outside the ghetto, two people represented the Coordinating Committee, one from the Bund and one from the ŻKN.[28] Their task was to procure weapons – in the event of a

26 In Polish, reference to a white raven signifies something particularly rare.

27 See Doc. 126.

28 Namely Feiner and Berman.

new liquidation operation in the ghetto, possibly from the outside – and to set up the planned partisan units with Jewish participation. One of our significant contributions was to supply the ŻOB with explosives and to produce ammunition for the armed resistance, both here and inside the ghetto. In this respect Klepfisz, who lost his life in the final battle, carried out invaluable work for us. In addition, we filled the [...][29] coffers of the ŻKN and the ŻOB with our money. The centre outside the ghetto maintained contact with the civilian and military representatives of the Polish underground, as well as with its organizations, i.e. with the WRN, the PS[30] with the provinces, and with you. It was also heavily involved in supporting the active resistance and took on important duties in the ghetto during the battle with the Germans. The centre outside the ghetto sent you dispatches but received significantly fewer from you; there was only one report sent to you, dated 6 March,[31] and there were no publications. Even before the final battle, we suggested including self-help activities in the coordination work and extending this across all Polish territory. Our proposal was accepted, but it was never implemented because the final armed combat operations against the Germans were just beginning at that time. Nevertheless, during this period we did settle a few matters together. Among other things, three joint dispatches were sent to you, joint statements were addressed to the Polish government's representative[32] and to the clandestine military organizations,[33] and reports from the scene of the fighting were collected and submitted.

The centre outside the ghetto also participated in the work of the Council to Aid Jews, in which two people represent the Jews – one from the Bund and one from the ŻKN.[34] The Council is composed of: the PPS-WRN (the chairman),[35] the Peasants' Party (vice chairman),[36] the Bund (vice chairman),[37] the Alliance of Democrats (treasurer),[38] the Polish Democratic Organization (Housing Section),[39] the ŻKN (secretary),[40] and a

29 One word is illegible here.

30 A reference to the Polish Socialists (Polscy Socjaliści), a left-wing faction that broke away from the underground Polish Socialist Party (PPS-WRN).

31 This could not be found.

32 Jan Stanisław Jankowski was the Polish government's representative in occupied Poland from Feb. 1943: see Docs. 186, 228, and 236. Further dispatches were sent on 4 May 1943 (see Czarnocka and Żmigrodzki (eds.), *Armia Krajowa w dokumentach: 1939–1945*, vol. 3, p. 4) and on 11 May 1943 (AAN, 1325/202/I-7, fol. 24).

33 The Home Army.

34 Namely Feiner and Berman.

35 Julian Grobelny (1893–1944), official; member of the Polish Socialist Party (PPS) from 1915; first chairman of the Council to Aid Jews, Jan. 1943 – Feb. 1944; arrested in March 1944, but then released; served as starosta of Mińsk Mazowiecki following the Soviet advance into Poland; died of tuberculosis.

36 Tadeusz Rek (1906–1968), lawyer; on the executive committee of the Peasants' Party (SL) from 1935; imprisoned in various concentration camps, 1940–1941; active on the Council to Aid Jews, 1943–1944; chairman of the pro-communist Polish Peasants' Party (PSL) after the war; deputy minister of justice and judge at the Supreme Court of the People's Republic of Poland.

37 Leon Feiner.

38 Ferdynand Arczyński.

39 The Polish Democratic Organization had close ties with the Alliance of Democrats (SD); the two merged to form the Polish Democracy Party (SPD) in July 1943. The head of the Housing Section was Emilia Hiżowa (1895–1970), architect; worked for the Medical Section from Oct. 1943; participated in the Warsaw Uprising in 1944; involved in the reconstruction of Warsaw after the war; member of the Polish National Council and the Sejm.

40 Adolf Berman.

deputy of the government's representative.[41] As long as we have our own funds, we receive no additional funds from the Council. The Council's budget rose from an initial amount of 50,000 złoty to 550,000 in June, of which 150,000 is spent on the provinces. The Warsaw Council is the central office; the councils in Cracow and Lwów are branch offices and are financed from funds provided by the central office. In Warsaw approximately 1,000 people are receiving welfare payments. The average amount is between 300 and 400 zł. [per person], which of course is not enough to sustain even the most modest existence. In addition to financial assistance, every Jew obtains documents free of charge – an extremely beneficial form of assistance which is of the utmost importance. The Council has issued appeals for assistance and to combat extortion.

During last summer's operation, the organization[42] inside the ghetto published an issue of the periodical *Szturm* in which it called upon the masses to put up resistance.[43] Two further issues appeared in November/December, and in April, before the most recent events, the last issue of our periodical was published in the Warsaw ghetto – all in Yiddish. Unfortunately, the centre outside the ghetto has so far been unable to issue a periodical, mainly due to technical difficulties. We will probably soon be able to publish the reports that have piled up, as well as a newsletter, once the aforementioned difficulties have been overcome. Apart from these general matters, organizational work probably takes up the most time and effort, and places the greatest strain on the nerves. It consists of providing our people with financial aid and supporting them in their search for accommodation or after their identity has been uncovered. At this point, it is important to note that if clandestine activity under tsarist rule was almost idyllically straightforward compared to the conditions under which the whole of Poland is operating [today] – our clandestine activity is one hundred times more difficult. Outsiders can barely imagine what it is like. Our clandestine activity is in fact twofold: we are Jews, and we also represent a Polish underground political organization. And this explains everything. We live under the pressure of terror. People are being killed every day. The engineer Kwiatek[44] (a member of our Central Committee) and Rozowski[45] (the brave commander of part of the front line in the ghetto), who had managed to escape from the ghetto after the fierce fighting, recently died after becoming victims of extortion. It is simply impossible to name all those who have perished. Our organization was hit particularly hard by the fact that our covert activities were compromised even before the official liquidation of the ghettos as the result of an incident that occurred during the distribution of our underground publications throughout the provinces. In Cracow, Lublin, Tomaszów, Częstochowa, Radom, and Piotrków, many of our best comrades who were

41 Witold Bieńkowski.

42 This is a reference to the Bund.

43 Possibly a reference to the underground publication *Oyf der vakh*: see Doc. 143.

44 Code name for Abram (Abrasza) Blum (1904–1943), engineer; one of the founders of the Bund's Central Committee in the underground after Sept. 1939; lived in the Warsaw ghetto, 1940–1943; director of schools for the Central Jewish School Organization (CISzO); Bund representative on the ŻKK; escaped from the ghetto through the sewer system on 10 May 1943; denounced; probably murdered at the Gestapo prison on Aleja Szucha on 20 May 1943.

45 Welwel (Włodek) Rozowski (d. 1943), a member of the Bund and its youth organization, Tsukunft; escaped from a transport to Treblinka in 1942; thereafter led a resistance group at the Röhrich factory in the Warsaw ghetto, and a ŻOB combat group in 1943; after the Warsaw Ghetto Uprising escaped to the 'Aryan side', where he was shot and killed after being blackmailed and denounced.

active in those places at the time were taken to Oświęcim, where they were murdered. Only a few managed to escape. Dr Fensterblau[46] escaped from Radom and hid from the Gestapo in the Warsaw ghetto. From there he and his entire family were deported to Treblinki[47] during the operation. Samson escaped from Piotrków, where the best activists died before and during the operation (his family perished); Kimelman[48] also escaped from Piotrków; he was deported from here to Treblinki. In Lwów, Comrade Lejb Landau died as a result of a denunciation.[49] You already heard about Sonia Nowogródzka in the dispatch – she was deported in one of the wagons last August[50] – in her we lost an active member of our Central Committee. I will not list all the others. I will mention the names of my comrades in arms who are either actively working or under our protection, and who are important to you. From Cracow: Papier,[51] with his wife; Dr Lifszyc, with his wife and son;[52] Dr Glasner,[53] with his family; Fiszgrund,[54] with his family (but without

46 Dr Szyja Fensterblau (1881–1942), lawyer; studied in Vienna; officer in the Austro-Hungarian army during the First World War; member of the Bund from 1919; practised law in Radom; lived in Cracow from 1922; active in the underground in Cracow from 1939, then in Piotrków and Radom; lived in the Warsaw ghetto from late 1941; member of the Bund's Central Committee; murdered in Treblinka in July 1942.

47 Correctly, here and below: Treblinka.

48 Lejb (Leon) Kimelman (d. 1942), bookkeeper; murdered in Treblinka.

49 Dr Lejb Landau (1879–1943), lawyer; fled from Przemyśl to Lwów in 1939; worked as an advisor on Jewish welfare to the governor of District Galicia in 1941; became head of the Jewish Social Self-Help (JSS) in 1942; briefly served on the Lwów Jewish Council; denounced on the 'Aryan side' and murdered in Jan. 1943.

50 Sonia Nowogródzka, née Sheyne Gitl Czemelińska (1883/1884–1942), seamstress; joined the Bund prior to 1914; held as a political prisoner several times, 1917–1919; married Emanuel Nowogródzki in 1919; trained as a teacher; active on the Bund's Central Committee in the underground from 1939; head of CISzO in the Warsaw ghetto, where she also worked with the Organization for Yiddish Culture (IKOR) and with the Jewish Central Association for the Care of Orphans (CENTOS); murdered in Treblinka in August or Sept. 1942.

51 Mojsze (Maurycy) Papier (1882–1952), painter and trade unionist; member of the Jewish Social Democratic Party (ŻPS) in Western Galicia and editor of the party publication *Sotsial-Demokrat*; member of the Bund's Central Committee for some time after 1919; active in the underground in Cracow and Warsaw after 1939; fought and was wounded in the Warsaw Uprising in 1944; after the war lived in Sweden, and later in London.

52 Correctly: Dr Stanisław (Samson) Liwszyc (1893–1957), physician; member of the Bund and the PPS; completed further training in Vienna in 1928; then worked for the Polish Health and Social Insurance Institution (ZUS) in Cracow; lived in Lwów, 1939–1941; later undertook clandestine activities for the Bund and the Council to Aid Jews in the area around Warsaw; physician with the High Command of the Workers' Militias during the Warsaw Uprising in 1944; professor at Cracow Medical Academy after the war. Dr Elżbieta Salomea Liwszyc, née Grossbart (1895–1957), physician; headed the chemical-bacteriological department at the Social Insurance Office of the City and Voivodeship of Cracow. Ryszard Liwszyc was killed during the Warsaw Uprising in 1944.

53 Presumably Dr Rubin (Roman) Glassner (1877–1943/1944), veterinarian; practised in Cracow-Podgórze, 1909–1939; murdered in Skarżysko.

54 Salo (Henryk) Fiszgrund (Fischgrund) (1893–1971); involved in Jewish socialist organizations in Cracow from 1907; active in the underground on the 'Aryan side' of Warsaw after Sept. 1939; involved in the ŻOB's preparations for the Ghetto Uprising, 1942–1943; member of the executive committee of the Social and Cultural Society of Jews in Poland (TSKŻ) from 1950; official representative of the American Jewish Joint Distribution Committee (JDC) in Poland until 1968; emigrated to Israel in 1969.

his wife); Hanka Aleksandrowiczówna, Dr Ignacy's daughter;[55] Dr Nemer[56] and Dr Goldfinger (both are presently in a camp near Cracow). From Warsaw: Zdzisław, with Mrs Polakowa[57] and her son, Bernard Samsonowicz;[58] Mrs Orzech, with Marek's daughter (he himself is in prison);[59] Celemeński;[60] Mrs Hodes, with her daughter;[61] Mrs Szefner, with her sister;[62] Mrs Morgelis from Łódź, with her daughter;[63] Zybert's son;[64] Lucjan's children;[65] Kwiatek's wife and children;[66] Klepfisz's wife, with her daughter;[67]

55 Hanka Aleksandrowicz (1927–1944); escaped from Cracow to Skawina, near Cracow, with her mother, Sala, and sister, Ewa, in 1941; later deported to Belzec; Hanka jumped from the train, then lived under a false name on the 'Aryan side' in Warsaw; she was killed in 1944. Her father was Dr Izak Mendel (Ignacy) Alexandrowicz (1891–1964), lawyer; fled in 1939 via Lwów, Vilna, the Soviet Union, and Japan to New York, where he worked for the Bund and the representation of the Polish government in exile; taught economics at a college in Geneva, New York, from 1946.

56 This can also be read as 'Nener'.

57 Zdzisław Muszkat, code name Zygmunt Dobrowolski (1878–1960), engineer and economist; member of the Bund's Central Committee; one of Poland's leading trade unionists prior to Sept. 1939; worked in the Warsaw municipal administration after the war; his second wife was Dr Jadwiga Wołczyk-Polakowa, dentist.

58 Probably Ignacy Samsonowicz, code names Samson and Tadeusz Leszczyński, journalist; represented the Bund on the ŻKK, 1942–1943; member of the Communist Party of Poland (KPP), and active in the Social and Cultural Society of Jews in Poland after the war.

59 Janina Orzech, née Awin, came from Lwów; some sources state that she was murdered along with her daughter and her husband, Maurycy Orzech, in August 1943.

60 Jakub (Jankiel) Celemeński (1904–1986), tailor; courier for the Bund in the underground, 1941–1944; lived near Wysków after the Warsaw Ghetto Uprising; held in Auschwitz as an 'Aryan' prisoner following the Warsaw Uprising, then in Mauthausen concentration camp; settled in New York after the war; author of *Elegy for my People: Memoirs of an Underground Courier of the Jewish Labor Bund in Nazi-occupied Poland, 1939–1945*, ed. Sandra Goldblum Zerbo, trans. Gershon Freidlin (Melbourne: Jacob Celemenski Memorial Trust, 2000 [Yiddish edn, 1963]).

61 Rose (Róża) Hodes, nurse; survived along with her daughter, Chevka (Joanna), and worked as an administrator for the Jewish Children's Home at Otwock in 1945; thereafter emigrated via Sweden to New York to join her husband, Lejvik Hodes, and their younger daughter.

62 Helena Szefner (Shefner) (1898–1962), teacher; worked at the Schultz factory in 1942; emigrated to the USA after the war; completed a doctorate at Columbia University. Her sister Regina (?) Margules is thought to have perished in a camp.

63 Anna Margolisowa (Margulies or Morgelis), née Markson (1892–1987), paediatrician; studied medicine in Bonn; went to Warsaw after her husband was murdered in Łódź in 1939; then lived in the ghetto; lived on the 'Aryan side' from the beginning of 1943; director of a sanatorium for children with tuberculosis in Łódź from 1945. Her daughter was Alina Margolis-Edelman (1922–2008); attended the nursing college in the Warsaw ghetto; participated in the Ghetto Uprising; worked as a paediatrician after the war; married Marek Edelman; emigrated to France in 1968; worked with Médecins sans Frontières; author of the autobiography *Ala z elementarza* (London: Aneks, 1994). Published in English as 'Ala from the Primer', *Polin: Studies in Polish Jewry*, vol. 11, *Focusing on Aspects and Experiences of Religion*, ed. Antony Polonsky (Liverpool: Liverpool University Press; London: Littmann Library of Jewish Civilization, 1998), pp. 94–111.

64 Selim Zybert (b. 1919), son of the Polish teacher, journalist, and Warsaw city councillor Gershon Zybert (1888–1946); thought to have been shot dead in Pawiak prison in 1943.

65 This is presumably a reference to Lucjan Blit (1904–1978), journalist; secretary general of the Bund's youth organization, Tsukunft, prior to Sept. 1939; fled to Vilna in 1939; worked for Zygielbojm in London, Jan.–May 1943. His twin daughters Neli and Włodzimiera (b. 1931) survived, having lived separately on the 'Aryan side'.

66 Code name for Abram Blum; his relatives lived separately from him on the 'Aryan side'. His wife was Luba Blum-Bielicka (1905–1973), nurse; principal of the nursing college at the Jewish Hospital in Warsaw from August 1939; escaped from the ghetto to the 'Aryan side' in early 1943; head of a

Felicja, Józef's wife, with her daughter Irka and her grandson;[68] Rachela Auerbach;[69] Ewa Kirszenbaum[70] from Kutno; Falk (in the concentration camp in Budzyń); Mrs Falk, with her son;[71] Dr Kalsonówna[72] ([previously] in Pawiak prison, now in Oświęcim); Gałka Leszczyńska[73] (in the camp for foreigners, where she had gone without our knowledge); Mrs Zelman from Łódż; Mrs Mermelsztajn and her son from Łódż (he [her husband] perished during the last operation).[74] Artur's wife was still living with her son[75] in the ghetto until 12 May. I must note that a few of our best people may yet escape from the underground in the ghetto, if they are still alive (Kaufman[76] and Wirowski[77] were still in the ghetto bunkers after the operation – they must have died). In the camps in

children's home in Otwock after the war; principal of a nursing college from 1949; emigrated to the USA, then worked at New York Hospital. The Blums had two children. Wiktoria (later Aviva) Blum, married name Wachs (b. 1932); lived in the Warsaw ghetto from 1940; escaped with her mother to the 'Aryan side' in early 1943; liberated at Radość, near Warsaw, in autumn 1944. Wiktoria's brother Aleksander Blum (b. 1936) survived with a Polish family. Both children lived in the orphanage their mother ran in Otwock from 1945. Wiktoria Blum emigrated to Israel in 1949; Aleksander Blum emigrated to the USA in 1980.

67 Rose (Róża or Lodzia) Klepfisz, née Perczyków; active in the Polish Teachers' Union (ZNP) and the Central Committee of Trade Unions (CKZZ); also active in the underground movement after 1939. Her daughter, Irena, survived in an orphanage on the 'Aryan side'; both emigrated to the USA after the war, where Dr Irena Klepfisz (b. 1941) became a poet, a translator from Yiddish, and a professor at Columbia University.

68 Felicja Goldberg, née Barbanel (1872–1959), dentist and oral surgeon; married Stanisław Goldberg in 1898; after his death, married Jekutiel Portnoj; died in Warsaw. Jósef was the code name for Jekutiel Portnoj, correctly Portnej (1872–1941), teacher; chairman of the Bund's Central Committee from the 1920s; fled to New York via Vilna and the Soviet Union in 1939. Felicja's daughter was Irena Krzywicka, née Goldberg (1899–1994), writer, translator, and feminist; worked for the Home Army, 1943–1944; cultural attaché at the Polish embassy in Paris, 1945–1946; city councillor in Warsaw from 1954; cultural attaché at the embassy in Bern, 1957–1958; lived in Geneva from 1963, and later in Paris. Irena's son was Dr Andrzej Krzywicki (b. 1937), physicist; survived the German occupation of Poland under a false name; later worked as a professor at Paris-Sud University.

69 Rokhl Oyerbakh (also known as Rachel[a] Auerbach) (1901–1976), journalist and author who wrote in Yiddish; managed the writers' canteen at 40 Leszno Street and contributed to the underground archive of the Warsaw ghetto, 1940–1942; in 1950 emigrated to Israel, where she founded the department that collected survivors' testimonies at Yad Vashem.

70 Correctly: Ewa Kirszbaum, née Landau (c. 1897–1945), teacher; founded a girls' school; lived in Warsaw after 1939; active in underground work for the Bund in the ghetto.

71 Izrael (Ignacy) Falk (1904–1996), bookkeeper; lived in hiding in Warsaw after Sept. 1939; escaped from a transport to Treblinka in Sept. 1942; fought in the Warsaw Ghetto Uprising in 1943; imprisoned in various camps; worked at Oskar Schindler's factory in Brněnec in 1945. His wife Laye (Leonia) Falk (1898–2005), teacher, and their son Michał (b. 1931) lived in hiding from March 1943 – Jan. 1945 after escaping from the ghetto; the family emigrated to Canada in 1949.

72 Correctly: Kelsonówna.

73 Gala (Gałka) Leszczyńska, Bund activist; daughter of the journalist and left-wing Bundist theoretician Józef Leszczyński.

74 Mrs Mermelsztajn, née Tański, widow of the Bundist and trade unionist Majer Mermelsztajn; lived in hiding with her son, the composer Stefan Mermelstein, on the 'Aryan side' in Warsaw, 1943–1944.

75 Mania Zygielbojm, Szmul Zygielbojm's wife; his code name was Artur, which was also their son's first name.

76 Mojżesz (Mojsze) Kaufman (1908–1943), trade unionist; member of the Bund's Central Committee; worked for the Jewish resistance at the Röhrich factory in the Warsaw ghetto in 1942; later escaped from a transport to Treblinka and returned to the ghetto.

77 Beniamin Wirowski (1900–1943), Polish teacher; member of Poale Zion, initially in Kryńsk and Białystok; subsequently active in local politics for the Bund and director of the Culture League in Łódź; senior manager for IKOR in the Warsaw ghetto.

Poniatowo and Trawniki, in Cracow, Częstochowa, and Piotrków, there are numerous groups of party members engaged in self-help activities and organization in preparation for the struggle; many of our comrades are also in Skarżysko, in Starachowice, and in Eastern Małopolska,[78] and we are in contact with them.

When we learned the details of the horrible execution of Henryk Erlich and Wiktor Alter,[79] we drafted a solemn protest during the conference on organizational issues which we held at the time, addressing the perpetrators of this unprecedented crime and expressing our indignation. We sent this resolution to the Polish socialist press, and it appeared in the periodical of the PPS-WRN. Finally, we took Zygielbojm's[80] death, which had shaken us all, as an opportunity to send a dispatch to the chairman of the National Council in L[ondon], as you know.[81] As far as financial matters are concerned, we recently informed you that certain misunderstandings had arisen because we did not receive all the sums which Zygielbojm had told us about. A telegram on this matter was sent via the government's honourable representative.

I am concluding this report that broadly outlines the period from 1 September 1942 to 22 June 1943. I have not touched upon many subjects. I may come to them next time.

I cannot end this report without the following remarks. We have faced great challenges, the greatest any people has ever faced. But when I analyse and reflect on this subject, I cannot but emphasize that the thunderbolts we have been struck by are the result of the military operations of fascism, a highly reactionary and counter-revolutionary movement. The sad reality that has so tragically befallen us therefore confirms our previous position and our world view. Even if our situation compels us to deal almost exclusively with the subject of the Jews – which we do from the point of view of the entire Jewish population and in accordance with our political position – we nevertheless bear in mind the whole of Poland and the *freedom of the struggling peoples*. It is clear to us what the war is about, all over the world, and what it is intended to achieve. But at the same time, we – who are actively involved here in our party – know that we will most likely no longer be able to help shape the basis for a new world of peace and social justice along with our fraternal organizations. And this we deeply regret. However, we realize that Jewish society, and we along with it, has made the most tremendous sacrifice – and not just in terms of numbers – for the emergence of that world, and therefore we shall continue to fulfil our duty until our very last breath.

78 Eastern Galicia.

79 Wiktor Alter (1893–1943) and Henryk Ehrlich (1882–1941/1942), leading Bund politicians; arrested by the Soviet secret police in eastern Poland in 1940; released from prison in Oct. 1941 as a result of the Polish–Soviet Agreement of July 1941; arrested again on 4 Dec. 1941. Alter was shot without trial in Feb. 1943; Ehrlich died in custody. See also PMJ 4/275.

80 Spelled 'Zygelbaum' in this document: see Doc. 241.

81 The government delegation's executive office sent this dispatch to London on 8 June 1943: AAN, 1325/202/I-7, fol. 28.

## DOC. 251

## On 30 June 1943 the SS and Police Leader in Galicia prepares his final report on the murder of Jews in the district[1]

Report (marked 'secret Reich matter') by the SS and Police Leader in Galicia (log no. 42/43 g.R.-Ch/Fr.), Katzmann, Lemberg, to the Higher SS and Police Leader East, Krüger, Cracow, dated 30 June 1943

*Two copies*
Copy 1
Re: solution to the Jewish question in Galicia
Concerning: the enclosed report
Enclosures: one report (three copies)
Copy 1 (bound)
Enclosed I submit copy 1 of the final report on the solution to the Jewish question in District Galicia, for your attention.

*Solution to the Jewish question in District Galicia*[2]
Due to the term 'Galician Jew', Galicia was probably the one place on earth best known and most talked about in connection with Jewry. They lived here in huge, dense hordes, forming a world of their own that repeatedly supplied the next generation for the rest of world Jewry. Jews were encountered by the hundreds of thousands in all parts of Galicia.

According to old statistics dating from the year 1931, the count stood at about 502,000 Jews. This figure is certainly unlikely to have decreased between 1931 and summer 1941, [although] it is not possible to provide exact data on the number of Jews present in Galicia when German troops invaded. The Galician Jewish councils merely gave the figure of 350,000 at the end of 1941. As is evident from the resettlement figure cited at the end [of this report], this number is not correct.[3] The city of Lemberg alone was home to some 160,000 Jews in July–August 1941.

This Galician Jewry's influence, which was already significant under the Austrian and Polish governments, rose to a scarcely credible level when this region was occupied by the Soviet Russians in 1939.

They held all the positions of power here, so it only stood to reason that in July 1941, after this region was occupied by German troops, Jews were found everywhere. Therefore our most urgent task was necessarily to ensure that this problem was resolved as quickly as possible.

The first step was to visibly identify all Jews with a blue Star of David on a white armband. According to a regulation issued by the Governor General, responsibility for the visible identification and registration of Jews, as well as for the creation of Jewish

1 AIPN, GK, Zbiór 'Z'/203. Copy in BArch, R 58/9386. Published in *Trial of the Major War Criminals before the International Military Tribunal*, vol. 37 (Nuremberg: Secretariat of the Tribunal, 1949), pp. 391–431. This document has been translated from German.
2 The document is 64 pages long and includes numerous enclosures and photographs.
3 On p. 14 of the original document, the number of Jews said to have 'received special treatment' is given as 434,329, and the number of those still alive as 21,156.

councils, lay in the hands of the Interior Administration [Department].[4] As police, our task was first and foremost to combat as effectively as possible the rampant illicit trade throughout the land that was conducted by the Jews. In particular, the most vigorous action had to be taken against all the loafing idlers and layabouts.

The best way to do this was for the SS and Police Leader to establish forced labour camps. There were opportunities for work, primarily thanks to the extremely important upgrading of Thoroughfare IV,[5] which was necessary for the entire southern section of the front, and which was in a disastrous state. The construction of the camps on the main supply route[6] began on 15 October 1941, and despite considerable difficulties, after only a few weeks seven camps had been set up, housing 4,000 Jews. These first camps were soon followed by others, so that it was possible to report 15 such camps to the Higher SS and Police Leader within a very short period. Over time some 20,000 Jewish workers passed through these camps. Despite all the conceivable difficulties that cropped up in relation to this problem, today it can be reported that around 160 km of road has been completed.

At the same time all the other Jews who were fit for work were registered with the employment offices and assigned to productive tasks. It was in connection with both the visible identification of the Jews and the registration by the employment offices that it first became evident that the Jews were attempting to evade the orders of the authorities. The controls implemented in response to this led to thousands of arrests. It became increasingly apparent that the civil administration was not in a position to find anything remotely like a satisfactory solution to the Jewish problem. Since the Lemberg city administration had failed in its repeated attempts, for example to house the Jews in a sealed Jewish residential district,[7] the SS and Police Leader and his agencies also resolved this matter without further ado. This step became all the more urgent as major outbreaks of epidemic typhus occurred throughout the metropolitan area in the winter months of 1941, endangering not only the local population, but also and to a greater extent the troops stationed here as well as those passing through. When this resettlement of the Jews to a particular quarter of the city was carried out, several checkpoints were set up where all the work-shy and asocial Jewish rabble were rounded up and given special treatment from the very beginning when they were processed on arrival.[8]

Due to the fact that almost 90 per cent of those in craft trades in Galicia were Jewish, the task at hand could only be carried out step by step, since [their] immediate removal would not have been in the interest of the war economy. Nevertheless, the Jews deployed

4 See the Regulation on the Visible Identification of Jews and Jewesses in the General Government, 23 Nov. 1939: *VOBl-GG* 1939, no. 8, 30 Nov. 1939. The Second Regulation on the Introduction of Provisions of the General Administration in District Galicia of 6 Sept. 1941 extended the compulsory visible identification of Jews to District Galicia with effect from 15 Sept. 1941: *VOBl-GG* 1941, no. 83, 13 Sept. 1941, pp. 522–523.

5 Thoroughfare IV (Durchgangsstraße IV), an important supply route for the German Eastern Front, was supposed to run from Berlin to the Caucasus. More than 25,000 Jewish forced labourers perished during the road's construction in Eastern Galicia between 1942 and 1944.

6 Thoroughfare IV was also known as Main Supply Route South (Rollbahn Süd).

7 See Docs. 34 and 49.

8 When the first ghetto was being established in Dec. 1941 and Jan. 1942, several thousand Jews were 'selected' at the checkpoints and shot in Lesienice forest, near Lwów.

in the work process did not display a notable level of productivity. In many cases their jobs were merely a means to an end, first in order to evade the stricter measures taken against Jews, and second to be able to pursue their racketeering with less interference. Only continual police interventions were able prevent things from getting out of hand. After ever more cases were discovered in which the Jews had contrived to make themselves indispensable to their employers by obtaining goods that were in short supply etc., we were forced to introduce utterly draconian measures. Unfortunately we reached the unavoidable and extremely regrettable conclusion that the Germans assigned here, in particular [those at] so-called deployment firms[9] or the 'notorious trustees', were engaging in the most outrageous racketeering with the Jews. Cases came to light in which, for the purpose of obtaining a work pass, not only did Jews not insist on receiving wages, they even paid money on an ongoing basis. In addition, the 'organizing' the Jews did for their 'employers' reached such disastrous proportions that the most vigorous action had to be taken in the interest of [protecting] the reputation of Germandom.

Since the administration proved too weak and unable to deal with this chaos, the SS and Police Leader summarily took over the entire labour deployment of Jews. The existing employment offices for Jewish labour, which were staffed with hundreds of Jews, were closed down, all work documents issued by firms and agencies were declared invalid, and the cards the employment offices had given to the Jews were revalidated with stamps received at the police stations.

In the course of this operation, thousands of Jews who possessed forged identity cards or had obtained work passes under all manner of pretexts were once again rounded up. These Jews were also subjected to special treatment. In particular, Wehrmacht agencies had encouraged Jewish parasitism by issuing special identity cards in an unregulated manner. Out of the multitude of identity cards seized, only three have been appended, based on which it is possible to ascertain the methods used in the attempts to sabotage the SS's measures: …[10] There were cases in which detained Jews were in possession of ten to twenty such identity cards.

If Jews were then arrested in the course of these additional checks, most employers felt obliged to intervene on behalf of their Jews. This often happened in a manner that can only be described as profoundly shameful.

A great example of this was a wholesale butcher working for the Wehrmacht in Lemberg, a certain *Schmalz*, who sent the following telegram from Berlin to the office of the SS and Police Leader:

> Urgent – SS-Untersturmführer Löhnert[11] at the SS and Police Leader Lemberg District Building. The two cards submitted [belong to] skilled professionals, watchmakers. [They] live in my more recent factory as watchmen [and are] watchmakers by day. [I] would not like to be responsible for their demise. [You] can have them both

9 'Einsatzfirmen': German companies at which Jews were deployed.

10 The official documents enclosed at this point in the original, all of which had been issued by Wehrmacht agencies, are not published here.

11 Anton Adolf Löhnert (b. 1906), businessman and company secretary; joined the NSDAP and the SS in 1938; served with the Waffen-SS, Nov. 1939 – Nov. 1941; wounded; thereafter official in charge of Jewish affairs and forced labour camps for the SS and Police Leader in District Galicia; sentenced to seven years in prison by Stuttgart Regional Court in 1968.

after my return. [They] will not run away of course. [I] beg [you] most sincerely.
Yours – Rich. Smzaidz[12]

When this wholesale butcher's conduct was subsequently scrutinized more closely, it turned out that the fellow had engaged in the most unbelievable racketeering with the Jews. Schmalz was arrested and handed over to the public prosecutor's office.

Despite all of these measures to regulate the labour deployment of Jews, their resettlement outside District Galicia began in April 1942 and was conducted on an ongoing basis.[13] By the time the Higher SS and Police Leader once again intervened in the Jewish question generally with his Police Regulation on the Establishment of Jewish Residential Districts[14] of 10 November 1942, 254,989 *Jews* had already been relocated or resettled.

Upon further instruction from the Higher SS and Police Leader to accelerate the complete resettlement of the Jews,[15] extensive efforts were once again necessary to round up the Jews who were to be allowed to stay behind in the armaments enterprises for the time being. These remaining Jews were declared the Higher SS and Police Leader's labour prisoners and were barracked either in the factories or in camps specially built for this purpose. A large camp for Lemberg itself was set up on the outskirts of the city, in which 8,000 Jewish labour prisoners are currently being held.[16] The agreement reached with the Wehrmacht on the deployment and treatment of these labour prisoners was put in writing. The decree on which the directives that have now been issued are based is included below.

The SS and Police Leader in District Galicia
Lemberg, 23 October 1942
XIII – log no. 688/42 (g)
Re: deployment of Jewish workers
Concerning: letter from the GG armaments inspectorate dated 21 September 1942, 11 b 16 24 ZA/Ia no. 15/317/42 sec[ret], and letter from the Lemberg armaments inspectorate dated 19 October 1942, file ref.: 103 St/Fr.Br.Nr. 613/42 sec[ret][17]
Secret[18]
To the *Lemberg* armaments inspectorate [and] *distribution list*[19]

12 The telegram was sent on 10 August 1942.
13 The deportations to Belzec began in mid March 1942.
14 With this police regulation of 10 Nov. 1942, Higher SS and Police Leader Krüger stipulated which ghettos in districts Radom, Cracow, and Galicia were to be allowed to continue to exist for the time being: *VOBl-GG*, no. 98, 14 Nov. 1942, pp. 683–686; see also Doc. 168.
15 Krüger spoke with Himmler on 25 Oct. 1942 and presumably received the 'further instructions issued meanwhile by the Reichsführer-SS that the evacuation of the Jews should be carried out more swiftly': BArch, Ost-Dok 13/246, Senior Commander of the Security Police (BdS) to the General Government/Population and Welfare Division, 18 Nov. 1942. He evidently forwarded this order to Katzmann immediately afterwards.
16 This is a reference to the camp located on Janowska Street.
17 See the Lemberg armaments inspectorate circular of 19 Oct. 1942: IfZ-Archives, Fa 506/15, fols. 125–126.
18 This is a stamp in the original.

Special directives and guidelines have been issued by the armaments inspectorate for the General Government and the Higher SS and Police Leader East, State Secretary for Security in the General Government, concerning the uniform treatment of the Jewish workers deployed in the armaments factories. Following a meeting between the commander of the Lemberg armaments inspectorate and the SS and Police Leader in District Galicia, the following agreements were reached on 17 October 1942:

I. *Lodging*

In general, Jewish workers are to be billeted in barracks. In the camps they will be under the control of the SS and Police Leader in District Galicia or the police stations he has authorized [for this purpose]. Since camps run by the police have not yet been established everywhere, the management at the enterprises is responsible for arranging temporary lodging for the Jewish workers. If secured lodging at the factories is not possible, then the Jewish workers employed must be quartered securely in specific apartment blocks in the remaining Jewish residential districts. Management at the enterprises must contact the local Security Police stations about this lodging. Care must be taken to ensure that relatives of the Jewish labourers under no circumstances find lodging with them in these apartment blocks. Special provisions will be enacted for the Jewish workers employed in the Lemberg factories. They will also be billeted in secured quarters in the Jewish residential district for the time being. (This will be arranged by the SS and Police Leader.)

II. *Food*

The factories will assume responsibility for providing the Jewish workers with food, which must occur exclusively at the factories themselves. Apart from the main meal, breakfast and supper are also to be served. Full rations are to be provided even in the event of illness. The enterprises will request and receive food according to the rates set by the GG government, Food and Agriculture Main Department, Market Regulation Department III a 1 a/100 of 18 August 1942.[20]

III. *Payment*

As of 1 November 1942 Jewish labourers will not receive cash wages. For each Jewish worker, management at the enterprises will pay the SS and Police Leader in District Galicia 5 zloty per calendar day and shift for a man and 4 zloty for a woman. Wage tax and social security contributions will not be payable. Costs for food and administration are to be deducted from the aforementioned sums of 5 and 4 zloty, respectively. The amount to be deducted from the daily rate cannot exceed 1.60 zloty. The SS and Police Leader's administration is entitled to carry out checks.

*The amounts to be paid are to be transferred to the SS and Police Leader in District Galicia's factories' cash account at the Emissionsbank in Lemberg.*

19 The enterprises Schwarz & Co., Textilia, Metrawat A.G., the Ausrüstungswerke training workshops, and Hobag-Holzbau A.G., all in Lwów; the barrel stave factory and furniture factory in Bolechów; and Karpathen-Öl A.G. were to be informed by the Lemberg armaments inspectorate. The following agencies were also to be informed: the Commander of the District Galicia (Lemberg) Security Police, with copies for the local police stations; the Commander of the District Galicia (Lemberg) Order Police, with copies for the Kreis gendarmerie commanders; and SS-Untersturmführer Fichtner, Löhnert, and Friedrich Hildebrand, who were on Katzmann's staff.

20 No details could be found.

In all cases, the transfers for the previous month must be made by the 3rd of each month. As receipts for the amounts transferred, copies of daily payrolls with the same reference date are to be sent to the SS and Police Leader in District Galicia's administration, 102 Siegfriedstraße, Lemberg.

IV. *Clothing*

Before they are transferred to the camp, the Jewish workers will receive permission to take plenty of clothing with them, especially winter clothing. The local police stations have been specifically informed of this fact. To supplement and replace workwear, enterprises may request replacement clothing through the SS and Police Leader in genuinely justified cases.

V. *General matters*

The SS and Police Leader in District Galicia and the Lemberg armaments inspectorate agree that it is necessary to keep the Jewish workers fit for work; this requires appropriate lodging, clothing, and medical care.

The management teams at the enterprises are requested to resolve any issues that arise with the local Security Police stations. The SS and Police Leader in District Galicia and the Lemberg armaments inspectorate are to be informed in each case. Should it prove impossible to resolve issues locally, relevant requests are to be sent to the SS and Police Leader in District Galicia as quickly as possible.[21]

In the meantime, continued resettlement efforts were vigorously pursued, which made it possible to liquidate all Jewish residential districts with effect from 23 June 1943. District Galicia is thus Jew-free, with the exception of those Jews in the camps under the SS and Police Leader's control.

The Jews who are still occasionally picked up receive special treatment from the respective Order Police and gendarmerie stations.

A total of *434,329 Jews* had been relocated by 27 June 1943.

There are still camps for Jews located in:

| | | |
|---|---|---|
| Lemberg | Kosaki | Drohobycz |
| Weinbergen | Zborow | Boryslaw |
| Ostrow | Jezierna | Stryj |
| Kurowice | Tarnopol | Skole |
| Jaktorow | Hluboczek | Bolechow |
| Lackie | Borki-Wielki | Broschniow |
| Pluhow | Kamionki | Njebielow |

with a total labour force of 21,156 Jews. These are being further reduced on an ongoing basis.

The seizure of Jewish assets was conducted at the same time as the resettlement operations. Extraordinary [amounts of] assets were secured and placed at the 'Reinhard' task force's disposal.[22] Apart from the seized furniture, large quantities of textiles, etc., the following assets were seized and handed over to the Reinhard task force, specifically:

21 In the original document this is followed by SS-Brigadeführer and Police Generalmajor Katzmann's signature.

22 The SS and Police Leader Lublin's Operation Reinhard Department.

*As of 30 June 1943*:

| | | |
|---|---|---|
| 25.580 | kg | copper coins |
| 53.190 | kg | nickel coins |
| 97.581 | kg | gold coins |
| 82.600 | kg | necklaces – silver |
| 6.640 | kg | necklaces – gold |
| 4,326.780 | kg | scrap silver |
| 167.740 | kg | silver coins |
| 18.490 | kg | iron coins |
| 20.050 | kg | brass coins |
| 20.952 | kg | wedding rings – gold |
| 22.740 | kg | pearls |
| 11.730 | kg | dental gold – false teeth |
| 28.200 | kg | powder boxes – silver or metal |
| 44.655 | kg | scrap gold |
| 482.900 | kg | silver cutlery |
| 343.100 | kg | cigarette cases – silver and metal |
| 20.880 | kg | rings – gold with stones |
| 39.917 | kg | brooches, drop earrings, etc. |
| 18.020 | kg | silver rings |
| 6.166 | kg | various pocket watches |
| 3.133 | kg | pocket watches – silver |
| 3.425 | kg | wrist watches – silver |
| 1.256 | kg | wrist watches – gold |
| 2.892 | kg | pocket watches – gold |
| 68 | | cameras |
| 98 | | pairs of binoculars |
| 7 | | stamp collections, complete |
| 5 | | travel cases of loose stamps |
| 100.550 | kg | three sacks of costume jewellery rings |
| 3.290 | kg | one case of corals |
| 0.460 | kg | one box of corals |
| 0.280 | kg | one box of corals |
| 7.495 | kg | one suitcase with fountain pens and mechanical pencils |
| | | one travel case with " " " |
| | | one suitcase with fire tongs |
| | | one suitcase with pocketknives |
| | | one suitcase with watch parts |

*Banknotes*: paper – metal

| | |
|---|---|
| 261,589.75 | US dollars – paper |
| | Gold dollars: 3 x 5 [dollar coins], 18 x 10 [dollar coins], 28 x 20 [dollar coins] |
| 2,515.75 | Canadian dollars |
| 124 | Argentinian pesos |
| 18,766.64 | Hungarian pengő |

| | |
|---|---|
| 231,789 | roubles – paper |
| | roubles – gold 1 x 7.5 [rouble coins], 11 x 10 [rouble coins], 29 x 5 [rouble coins] |
| 4,318 | roubles – paper |
| 513 | French francs |
| 2,460 | Swedish[23] francs |
| 52 | Austrian ducats – gold |
| | Austrian crowns: 36 x 10 [crown coins], 25 x 20 [crown coins], 8 x 100 [crown coins] |
| 2,229.18.60[24] | English pounds |
| 23 | African pounds |
| 13,490 | Romanian lei |
| 25,671 | Russian chervontsi |
| 4,600.70 | Czech crowns – paper |
| 185 | Dutch florins |
| 5,277 | Palestinian pounds |
| 9,300 | " mils |
| 160 | Lithuanian öre[25] |
| 360 | English shillings |
| 1 | Irish pound |
| 1 | Hungarian[26] peso |
| 2 | Mexican pesos |
| 10 | Norwegian crowns |
| 3,817.70 | Slovakian crowns |
| 435 | karbovantsi |
| 16,795,000 | zloty |

Thirty-five wagonloads of furs were delivered during the fur operation[27] conducted in December 1941.

*Funds generated from forced labour camps as well as Wehrmacht and armaments enterprises*

*As of 25 June 1943*

1. *Forced labour camps*:

a) *Revenues*:

| | | |
|---|---|---|
| Wages | 11,511,606.98 zl. | |
| Money found hidden in clothing | 1,232,143.71 " | |
| Proceeds from unusable tools | 807.93 " | 12,744,558.62 zl. |

b) *Expenditure*: (inmate maintenance)

| | |
|---|---|
| 1) Food, clothing, medicine | 3,108,866.62 " |
| 2) Wages, Ukrainian police guards | 47,358.51 " |

23 Correctly, presumably: 'Swiss'.
24 This refers to the breakdown into pounds (2,229), shillings (18), and pence (60).
25 Either Swedish öre or Lithuanian centų.
26 Correctly, presumably: 'Uruguayan'.
27 On the 'fur operation', see Introduction, p. 19.

| | | |
|---|---|---|
| 3) Camp maintenance, building repairs, rent | 118,063.15 " | |
| 4) Draught horses | 1,448,863.57 " | |
| Motor vehicles | 83,324.14 " | |
| Equipment | 3,037.10 " | |
| 5) inventory procurement | 2,410.15 " | |
| Portis telephone | 5,678.44 " | |
| Office supplies | 29,005.59 " | |
| 6) Authorization for buildings | *220,000.00* " | 5,066,607.27 zl. |
| 2. *Wehrmacht and armaments enterprises* | | |
| Revenues | 7,711,428.92 " | 7,711,428.92 zl. |
| 3. Sum transferred *to the SS business officer*: | | |
| a) Camps | 6,867,251.00 " | |
| b) *Wehrmacht and armaments enterprises* | 6,556,513.69 " | 13,423,764.69 zl. |

Further transfers to the SS *business officer*[28] will be made on a regular monthly basis.

In view of the large number of Jews and the geographical extent of the area to be combed, the operations were conducted as numerous individual actions, with assistance from the Security Police, the Order Police, the gendarmerie, the SD, and the Ukrainian police. Sheet 19 contains an overview map that shows how the Jews used to live scattered throughout the whole district before the Jewish residential districts were created.[29]

The task forces were continually subjected to considerable physical and mental strain. It took constant effort to overcome the reflexive disgust and to enter the Jews' dirt- and disease-ridden dens. During the searches leaflets in Hebrew were also found that advocated breeding lice infected with epidemic typhus, which was meant to bring about the police forces' demise. Indeed, various glass vials containing lice were also found. Downright catastrophic conditions were encountered in the Jewish residential districts in Rawa-Ruska and in Rohatyn. Fearing resettlement, the Jews in Rawa-Ruska had kept quiet about their typhus patients and concealed them in holes in the ground. When the resettlement operation was supposed to begin, it was discovered that 3,000 Jews suffering from typhus were lying all around this residential district. All the police officers who had been vaccinated against typhus had to be called in immediately to eradicate the site of this outbreak. Then it was actually possible to destroy this pestilence bubo with the loss of just one man. Virtually the same conditions were encountered in Rohatyn. In addition, our forces repeatedly came across smaller or larger outbreaks in all the towns and villages. Despite all precautionary measures, a total of 120 men contracted typhus, out of whom only eighteen fatalities were recorded, thanks to the protective measures implemented.

Some photographs of these filthy dens give an idea of the disgust that had to be overcome just to enter these sordid places.

28 The SS business officer in the office of the Higher SS and Police Leader in the General Government was Erich Schellin.

29 A map of District Galicia is inserted at this point in the report, with the caption: 'This map shows how the Jews used to live scattered throughout the whole district before the Jewish residential districts were created. The large dots on the map represent [one or two words missing; possibly: places] formerly inhabited by more than 1,000 Jews; the smaller dots represent places formerly inhabited by fewer than 1,000 Jews.'

The following pictures document the kinds of live pestilential buboes that had to be pulled out of these sordid places: […][30]

After being 'unmasked', this Jewish woman, who was found lying in bed during one of the operations, turned out to be an utterly vile Jewish urchin. […][31]

The 'Tateleben'[32] and his offspring!! […][33]

Three rabbis from Brody! […][34]

A Jewish cemetery near Lemberg, from which 2,000 cubic metres of road construction materials were obtained. […][35]

Further immense difficulties arose during these operations, since the Jews endeavoured to evade resettlement at all costs. They not only attempted to escape, but they also hid in the most unimaginable nooks and crannies, in sewer drains, in fireplaces, even in cesspools, etc. They barricaded themselves in catacomb passages, in cellars converted into bunkers, in holes in the ground, in ingenious hiding places in attics and barns, inside furniture, etc.

The smaller the number of remaining Jews became, the stiffer the resistance grew. Weapons of all kinds, including those of Italian origin in particular, were used for defence. The Jews bought these Italian weapons from the Italian soldiers stationed in the district for large sums in zloty.

The pictures below depict a small sample of the range of weapons seized. The sawn-off carbines of all varieties were particularly dangerous. […][36]

Underground bunkers with masterfully camouflaged entrances were found, some of them in dwellings, some outdoors. In most cases the entrances to the bunkers were just large enough for a single person to slip through. The entries to the bunkers were so well concealed that they could not be found without prior knowledge of the site. Time and again, the only thing that helped in this regard was assistance from a Jew, to whom who knows what was promised. The following photographs with explanatory notes show how the bunkers were laid out: […][37]

*Large bunker*:
The Jews had built three large underground bunkers in the Rohatyn ghetto and given them the following names: 'Stalingrad Bunker', 'Sebastopol Bunker', and 'Leningrad Bunker'.

30 In the original document this sentence is followed by portrait photographs of Jews and photographs of street scenes that evidently dated from the period prior to the systematic mass murders (individually numbered from 22 337 to 22 349); the armbands Jews had to wear from mid 1941 are only visible on some of the people photographed.

31 In the original document this sentence is followed by four photographs of a young man who had disguised himself.

32 Yiddish in the original: nickname for the father of a family.

33 In the original document this sentence is followed by photographs of Orthodox Jews, two young women, and a young man in work clothing.

34 This photograph shows three bearded men with armbands in an interior setting.

35 This photograph shows gravestones at a Jewish cemetery.

36 In the original document this section is followed by four photographs of small arms and ammunition.

37 In the original document this section is followed by 17 photographs of entrances to shelters and the surrounding structures, each one captioned; the locations and dates of the photographs are not provided.

The pictures below are of the 'Stalingrad Bunker'. This bunker was approximately 30 metres long and was built into a knoll in a garden. Side passages led off from the main passage and opened into chambers of approximately 2.5 square metres. The approximately 10-metre-long access passage led from a [nearby] building and was approximately 1 metre high. However, the entrance to this tunnel was so small that it was necessary to crawl through it.

The subsequent passage and the chambers were 2.5 metres high. The layer of soil over the bunker was 1.8 metres [deep] or more. The bunker contained an approximately 3-metre-deep water well neatly lined with boards, as well as a toilet constructed in the same way. There was also electric light and a radio. The antenna was located in the chimney of a [nearby] building that was also used for ventilation during the day and as the flue for a small cooking stove at night. Sheet-metal pipes were also installed for ventilation. These pipes emerged under berry bushes and were not visible, especially as nothing of the kind was suspected to exist there. This bunker was found because [someone] betrayed [its location], but the informant did not know where the entrance was located. During a thorough search of the area, a ventilation system was found, and when dug out, the bunker's ceiling was at a depth of approximately 2.5 metres. The tunnel and the bunker were *expertly* shored up and lined with boards. The bunker was equipped with two- and three-level bunk beds made up with good bedding. There were tables and benches, as well as kitchenware. The food stores would have sustained the approximately 60 Jews in the bunker for a long time. [...][38]

After the ventilation pipe had been exposed and the bunker's ceiling had consequently been reached, and the bunker had finally been breached, the officers who climbed in came under fire. Since the Jews did not come out despite being called upon to do so, several holes were dug into the bunker. When none of the Jews came out even then, a fire was set and the bunker was smoked out.

In the course of the resettlement operations, we also noticed that the Jews were increasingly attempting to flee abroad. These were Jews who possessed significant amounts of money, jewellery, and forged papers. They tried any and all means to manage their escape, and in many cases approached German servicemen or foreign allies, asking to be transported to or over the border in military motor vehicles. They offered disproportionately large sums for this, in many cases up to 5,000 zloty or more per person. Although in individual cases members of foreign armed forces – particularly Hungarians – placed themselves at the Jews' disposal and carried out the transports, in the majority of cases go-betweens notified the Security Police in time, which allowed the requisite countermeasures to be taken, the Jews rounded up, and their assets seized. A few cases are related below to illustrate this point:

In September 1942 an Italian soldier (an ethnic German from Switzerland) informed the SS and Police Leader's office that Jews were staying in the Italian accommodation in Lemberg. In the next few days members of the Italian Armed Forces were to smuggle

38 In the original document this section is followed by photographs of the excavation, the ground above the shelter, and the shelter's interior; then there is a photograph of the 'architect of the aforementioned bunker'; this is followed by another nine pages of photographs of large shelters and smaller hiding places, each one captioned; the locations and dates of the photographs are not provided.

them across the border to Hungary. Shortly before the time of their departure, two officers in plain clothes entered the barracks and actually succeeded in arresting a group of seven people, seizing 3,200 gold dollars and a large number of diamonds and pieces of jewellery in the process. In this respect, it was interesting to discover that 970 gold dollars had already been shared out among four members of the Italian Armed Forces as bribes. It also proved possible to seize this money. The Italian soldiers were subsequently deported to their homeland.

On 13 May 1943 two Reich German drivers with the Charkow Air District Command reported that a Jew had approached them and asked them to take approximately 20–30 Jews from the camp for Jews in Lemberg to Brody. Some of the Jews were said to be in possession of weapons. Forged movement and marching orders, issued in the driver's name, would be brought along. The drivers were offered the sum of 20,000 zloty to transport the group. The two drivers were instructed to accept this offer. It was agreed that the Jews would be loaded onto the Luftwaffe truck at 5 a.m. on 15 May, and that the drivers would set off in the direction of Brody and then suddenly turn in at the Lemberg National Socialist Motor Vehicle Corps headquarters, which is located on the road to Brody, and drive into the courtyard of the accommodation block. In fact, the truck, which was carrying 20 Jews and one Pole, drove into the courtyard of the accommodation block at 5.30 a.m. The Jews, some of whom were armed with loaded pistols and sawn-off carbines with their safeties off, were overpowered and disarmed by a squad that had been positioned there. The following weapons were seized:

1) 1 P. Beretta pistol, 9 mm calibre, serial no. 725 508,
2) 1 P. Beretta pistol, 9 mm calibre, serial no. 627 565,
3) 1 Polish revolver, 9 mm calibre, 7.65 mm, FB Radom, Ng. 30-1931r,
4) 1 F.N. 'Baby', 6.35 mm calibre, serial no. 36 148,
   1 F.N. 'Baby', 6.35 mm calibre, serial no. 39 788,
5) 1 Walter pistol, 6.35 mm calibre, serial no. 56 679,
6) 1 Steyer pistol, 6.35 mm calibre, serial no. 119 187 A,
7) 1 M.A.B. pistol, 6.35 mm calibre, serial no. 55 286,
8) 1 Russian automatic rifle, model 40 – serial no. 4481 (dismantled),
9) 2 Polish carbines (sawn-off).

The first two pistols on this list had been sold to the Jews by members of the Italian Armed Forces for the sum of 2,000 zloty each. The names of the soldiers were not discovered.

After a careful investigation, a considerable number of valuables were also seized. A thorough interrogation of the detained Jews revealed that a certain Jew, Horowicz, who was living in the woods near Brody with an even larger group, had organized these transports. The interrogation also led to the arrest of the Jews who had produced the forged identity papers for those fleeing. During his interrogation, the Pole, who had been likewise arrested, admitted to belonging to the 'PPR' Polish resistance movement. Furthermore, he described the Jew Horowicz as the main 'PPR' official in Lemberg.

Since the interrogations revealed that the contact point was in the woods near Brody, the gendarmerie, the Ukrainian police, and two Wehrmacht companies surrounded and swept that entire wooded area the very same day. In the course of this [operation] they came across smaller armed groups of bandits in various places that had set themselves up in bunkers and dugouts dating back to the Russian period. In all of these instances the bandits made use of their firearms, but it was possible to disarm them all. Thirty-three Jewish bandits were shot dead. Several sawn-off carbines were seized, as well as Russian automatic rifles and pistols. The bandits fatally wounded a Polish gamekeeper who took part in the sweep. During the arrest in Lemberg one SS man was wounded by a bullet that lodged in his lower left leg. The two Reich German drivers were each paid a reward of 2,000 zloty for their exemplary conduct. See the movement orders and travel order documents forged by the Jews below: […][39]

On 21 May 1943, near Rawa-Ruska, it also proved possible to exterminate a Jewish group of bandits that was once again equipped with 0.8 pistols of Italian origin.[40] (All Italian soldiers have since left the Galician region.)

A few days later, specifically on 31 May 1943, it once again proved possible to destroy six large underground bunkers holding 139 Jewish bandits during a repeated sweep of the woods near Busk.

On 2 June 1943 more Jews who had intended to flee to Hungary in a Hungarian army truck were arrested and were shot when they put up resistance. A considerable number of valuables were also seized from them. The Hungarian soldiers involved were paid a commensurate reward.

Now that the resettlement has ended, tracking down disguised and concealed Jews will require a considerable amount of painstaking work, as is proven by the fact that people with all kinds of forged identity papers and transit permits are encountered every day. Several forged identity cards, transit permits, marching orders, and leave permits are enclosed as evidence: […][41]

Since ever more alarming news was coming in about the increasing extent to which the Jews were armed, action was taken simultaneously in all parts of District Galicia during the second half of June 1943, using the toughest means to exterminate Jewish banditry. Special measures were necessary in the liquidation of the Jewish residential district in Lemberg, where the bunkers already illustrated above had been constructed. In order to avoid losses to our own forces, it was necessary to take brutal action there from the beginning, with several buildings having to be blown up or destroyed by fire. Once this was done, the astounding fact came to light that, instead of the reported 12,000 Jews, a total of 20,000 Jews had been rounded up. At least 3,000 corpses of Jews who had committed suicide by ingesting poison had to be retrieved from all manner of hiding places during the clean-up work.

Losses suffered by the German forces during these operations:

| | | |
|---|---|---|
| Died of typhus: | 18 men | 120 men taken ill |
| Shot dead by Jews: | 7 men | 12 men wounded |
| Stabbed to death by Jews : | 1 man | |

Lost due to accidents during the resettlement of Jews:

| | | |
|---|---|---|
| Dead: | 2 men | 5 men wounded |

39 These two enclosures are not published here.

40 This could be a reference to the Beretta M1923, which was a service pistol used by the Italian army until 1945. It weighed 800 g.

41 These nine enclosures, five photographs of 'Arrested criminals in the Lemberg ghetto with their housebreaking tools' and four photographs captioned 'Some atmospheric scenes from the former Jewish market in the Lemberg ghetto', are not published here.

Despite the extraordinary strain that every single SS member and police officer had to endure during these operations, the men's spirits and morale were exceptionally good and commendable from the first day to the last.

Only thanks to the personal sense of duty on the part of each officer and man was it possible to get this *plague* under control within an extremely short period of time.

## DOC. 252

## On 3 July 1943 a gendarmerie officer requests a transfer out of the General Government because of the psychological strain of his deportation assignment[1]

Letter from gendarmerie officer Otto Schart,[2] Zloczow gendarmerie station, Zloczow, to the commander of the gendarmerie in Lemberg,[3] through official channels (received on 13 July 1943), dated 3 July 1943

*Re*: transfer home from the General Government

The most recent resettlement of Jews in Brody[4] has left my nerves so shattered that I cannot sleep at night, and I constantly have dreams about the resettlement of Jews.

I see ghosts in my dreams who want to attack me. I feel I have had a mental breakdown, and no longer consider myself fit for duty.

For this reason I ask to be recalled to my former base in Langenfelde, Kreis Schloßberg (East Prussia), Regierungsbezirk Gumbinnen.[5]

1 AAN, 119/4, fol. 32. This document has been translated from German.

2 Otto Schart (b. 1897), bricklayer; served with the regional police from 1920; member of the gendarmerie from 1931; joined the NSDAP in 1937; became a police Oberwachtmeister in 1940; stationed in the General Government from Dec. 1940; assigned to the gendarmerie station in Złoczów, Oct. 1941 – Sept. 1943.

3 Alois Schertler.

4 The SS and police liquidated the ghetto in Brody (Eastern Galicia) and closed down the labour camp there in April and May 1943. In the process, buildings were set on fire, 3,500 people were deported to Lublin-Majdanek concentration camp, and countless individuals were murdered on the spot.

5 Schart's superior supported the request, particularly as Schart had played an active role in previous deportations: AAN, 119/4, fols. 32–33.

## DOC. 253
## On 5 July 1943 Himmler orders Sobibor extermination camp to be converted into a concentration camp for the repurposing of captured ammunition[1]

Directive (marked 'secret Reich matter') from the Reichsführer-SS, signed Br[andt], Field Command Post,[2] to the SS Business and Administration Main Office, the SS operations headquarters,[3] the Higher SS and Police Leaders for the East (in the General Government),[4] for the Ostland,[5] for Russia-Central,[6] and for Ukraine,[7] the SS and Police Leader in District Lublin,[8] and the chief of the Anti-Bandit Units (RF/Bn 1674/43), dated 5 July 1943[9]

*Directive*

1. Sobibor transit camp in District Lublin is to be converted into a concentration camp. A facility for the disassembly of captured munitions is to be established at the concentration camp.
2. All Higher SS and Police Leaders are required to deliver all captured munitions to this facility, unless they are needed as ammunition for captured guns that are in use.
3. Metal and especially gunpowder must be used with care.
4. At the same time a production site for our multiple rocket launchers[10] or for other munitions is to be established at this concentration camp.[11]

1 BArch, NS 19/1571, fol. 1. Published in Adalbert Rückerl (ed.), *NS-Vernichtungslager im Spiegel deutscher Strafprozesse: Belzec, Sobibor, Treblinka, Chelmno* (Munich: DTV, 1977), p. 176. This document has been translated from German.
2 'Hegewald', Himmler's field command post near Zhytomyr in Ukraine.
3 In the original: SS-Führungsamt; correctly: SS-Führungshauptamt. It was under the command of Hans Jüttner (1894–1965).
4 Friedrich-Wilhelm Krüger.
5 Friedrich Jeckeln (1895–1946).
6 Erich von dem Bach, né von Zelewski (1899–1972); also head of the Anti-Bandit Units (Bandenkampfverbände, effectively SS anti-partisan units) from June 1943.
7 Hans-Adolf Prützmann (1901–1945).
8 Odilo Globocnik.
9 Carbon copy for information sent to the head of the Security Police and the SD.
10 The *Vielfachwerfer* was a mobile rocket launcher used by the Waffen-SS; its design was based on the militarily very effective Soviet Katyusha rocket launcher.
11 After a discussion with Globocnik on 15 July 1943, Oswald Pohl, head of the SS Business and Administration Main Office (WVHA), objected that Himmler's objective was being 'attained even without this conversion', i.e. without formally turning Sobibor into a concentration camp; Himmler agreed on 24 July 1943: see BArch, NS 19/1571, fols. 2–3.

## DOC. 254

## On 14 July 1943 the People's Guard reports on Jewish partisan groups in the area around Wyszków[1]

Report by the commander of the People's Guard[2] in Sector I Warsaw, Area III Warsaw Periphery Right [Bank of the Vistula], signed Tadek,[3] dated 14 July 1943

*Report no. 4*

*Wyszków*

As of 8 July there were four combat groups with three squads each. At present there are only two groups in the area, each with two squads, one of which is armed with nine handguns. There is a shortage of ammunition (usually 7–8 cartridges per weapon). The operational commander has disarmed part of the second group due to the suspicion that this group intends to break away from us.

Group strength:

1st group: 12 guardsmen.

2nd group: 13 guardsmen, of whom 8 are armed.

The rest have either been killed or have broken away from us with their weapons.

The reasons for the current state of affairs are as follows:

The groups in this area were Jewish groups. Only one group was composed of former Soviet prisoners of war: the so-called Mikołaj group.

In the area where the groups were active there are no forests, only sparse groves averaging 500 x 100 metres in size and hemmed in by forest paths. These conditions led to numerous encounters with the local population (who were picking berries, grazing livestock, etc.). As a result, news spread through the surrounding villages that there were partisan groups in the forests, and Jewish ones at that. No one had yet seen Polish groups in this area, and Mikołaj's group consists of Russians and is moreover thought to be a band of robbers. So it is no wonder that the locals – with their antisemitic attitudes – told the German authorities that there were Jews in the forests and provided precise information on the units' locations. The gendarmerie searched all of these locations and burned the hideouts. In the village of Udrzynek, one informer was sentenced to death.[4] In view of this situation, the operational command will submit a plan for further action in this area.

The gendarmerie and the army have carried out numerous raids in the area. The occupier's basic approach is to lie in ambush and carry out night-time inspections on

1 AAN, 1315/191/XXI-6, fol. 5. Published in Marek Jan Chodakiewicz, Piotr Gontarczyk, and Leszek Żebrowski (eds.), *Tajne oblicze GL-AL i PPR: Dokumenty*, vol. 2 (Warsaw: Burchard Edition, 1997), pp. 82–83. This document has been translated from Polish.

2 The People's Guard (Gwardia Ludowa) was established in late 1942 as the combat organization of the communist Polish Workers' Party (PPR), under the command of Marian Spychalski (1906–1980).

3 Code name of Tadeusz Maciejewski (1919–1943), partisan leader; former member of the Communist Union of Polish Youth (KZMP); member of the PPR from Feb. 1942; in April 1943 withdrew to the Wyszków area, where he was initially deputy commander then commander of a partisan unit from July 1943; the members of this unit were killed by the Germans on 2 Sept. 1943.

4 Presumably by the People's Guard.

all the roads, on forest paths and trails, and at crossroads. The enemy units are well informed about the whereabouts of our units. During one of these raids, Comrade Mikołaj lost his life when he was shot in an ambush. He was in a bunker along with a partisan named Michał. The Germans got quite close to them. Mikołąj managed to escape and died 3 km further away. Michał threw a grenade from the bunker and killed three gendarmes. He was wounded but managed to escape. Comrade Cygan from Mikołaj's group was also killed, along with many other comrades from the other groups. Comrade Ignac[5] took the machine gun and absconded with six other men. Many others did the same. Part of Merdek's group[6] defected to Sikorski's people.[7] We are trying to maintain order and discipline among those who remain in the area.

## DOC. 255

## In mid July 1943 a German woman in Warsaw describes numerous attacks on the German occupiers and claims that the operation to liquidate the ghetto has been betrayed[1]

Anonymous handwritten letter from a Reich German woman in Warsaw, written after 15 July 1943[2]

*Experiences and insights of a Reich German woman in Warsaw over approximately eight months!*[3]

I. General conditions:
Great uncertainty in Warsaw since December 1942 after the first setbacks on the Eastern Front; daily attacks (shootings) on Wehrmacht soldiers and members of the civil administration. Letter bombs in parcels to authorities,[4] many threatening letters, attacks on

5 Probably Ignac Gajowy (a code name).
6 Mordechaj (Merdek) Growas (1921–1943), Hashomer Hatzair activist in the Warsaw ghetto; commander of a Jewish Combat Organization unit in Jan. 1943 and during the Ghetto Uprising; later commander of a partisan unit in Wyszków that cooperated with the Home Army; killed along with his group in summer 1943, probably by members of the National Armed Forces (NSZ) or the Home Army.
7 This is a reference to Home Army units that were ultimately under General Sikorski's command. Sikorski died in a plane crash on 4 July 1943.

1 BArch, NS 19/1740, handwritten fols. 26–32, typewritten fols. 34–35. Published in Polish translation in Tatiana Berenstein, 'Dokument o ruchu oporu w Warszawie', *BŻIH*, nos. 19 and 20 (1956), pp. 162–168. This document has been translated from German.
2 The letter was contained in a report that the Potsdam police chief, Heinrich von Kozierowski (1889–1967), sent on around 20 July 1943 to SS-Obersturmbannführer Paul Baumert (1904–1961) on Himmler's staff. From there the report was forwarded as a 'secret Reich matter' to SS-Sturmbannführer Dr Achim Ploetz (1911–1944) at the Reich Security Main Office (RSHA): see BArch, NS 19/1740, fol. 33.
3 The typed copy is titled 'Report on Warsaw (submitted by SS-Standartenführer v. Korzowski [correctly: Kozierowski])'.
4 In March 1943 the Home Army's Directorate of Sabotage sent parcel bombs built by Zbigniew Lewandowski to German authorities. Several Germans were injured in the explosions and two were killed.

banks,[5] the state printing office, shooting of the only two German managers of the state printing office on 3 March (after disarming the guard, three men lured the managers out of their apartment in the building next door, one in the uniform of a Party leader, the second in an SD uniform, the third in civilian clothing, speaking very good German. Killed in the guardroom of the state printing office by a shot in the back of the neck after the attempt to get the keys to the safe had failed.[6]) The head of the employment office shot during working hours in his office,[7] his successor shot in the street,[8] the *third* head of the employment office was buried on 15 March.[9] On the way back from the funeral service, the SA marching band was pelted with hand grenades and fifteen men were injured.[10]

The ghetto operation, which was carried out by the SS and had been prepared in strict secrecy the previous day, was betrayed. Upon entering the ghetto with trucks, the SS was fired upon from all sides. The evacuation of the ghetto, which by all accounts was scheduled to take three to four days, took almost five weeks. Underneath the buildings of the ghetto was a scarcely penetrable labyrinth of underground tunnels and extremely well-camouflaged bunkers, running from building to building and including exits through the sewer system that led to the Vistula and into the Polish quarter.[11] In the end, to complete the operation the buildings were set on fire one by one by incendiary squads, and vast assets were destroyed in the process. After the ghetto operation, intensified attacks by Jews and bandits continued, including an armed attack on a cabaret (Adria)[12] and hand grenades repeatedly exploding in the Café Club[13] and the waiting room at the main railway station.[14] Numerous attacks recently on all the dairies in the immediate environment of Warsaw, Polish farms subjected to extortion.

II. Economic conditions

German shops (Julius Meinl) sell the most inferior vegetables and fruit (the latter only very rarely), while in Polish shops and at markets the choicest fruit and vegetables are

5 On 30 Nov. 1942 members of the People's Guard, led by Jan Strzeszewski (1894–1943), carried out an attack on the Municipal Savings Bank in Warsaw, at 5 Traugutt Street, and carried off more than 1 million złoty. On 15 Jan. 1943 they stole half a million złoty in an attack on the social insurance system's finance office.

6 A group of People's Guard members attacked the State Printing Office for Securities on 28 Feb. 1943. The German police detectives Benzin and Blobelt were shot after the operation failed in its actual objective of obtaining a large quantity of newly printed banknotes.

7 Kurt Hoffmann worked in the General Government from early 1940. In 1943 he was the head of the Warsaw Employment Office and the Labour Department in District Warsaw; on 30 March 1943 he was shot and killed in his office at 38/40 Długa Street by a tactical unit of the Home Army.

8 Two weeks later, Hoffmann's successor, Hugo Dietz (1905–1943), was also shot and killed.

9 The newly appointed head of the Warsaw Employment Office, Werner, was killed in an attack.

10 The attack took place on Ujazdowskie Avenue; according to the underground press, members of the People's Guard killed four Germans and injured twenty.

11 This refers to the city districts outside the ghetto.

12 On the evening of 22 May 1943, three Gestapo officers were shot and killed at Adria, a restaurant on Moniuszko Street; the assassin, 21-year-old Jan Kryst, was killed on the spot by the Germans.

13 On a previous attack on the Café Club, see Doc. 224, fn. 4. On 11 July 1943 members of the People's Guard or the Union of Fighting Youth attacked the Café Club again with hand grenades, causing deaths and injuries. In addition, a People's Guard detachment had carried out an attack on Bar Podlaski, at 15 Nowogrodzka Street on 10 May 1943, injuring several German soldiers.

14 On 24 Oct. 1942 and 17 Jan. 1943, members of the People's Guard carried out attacks on the Mitropa restaurant at Warsaw's main railway station: see also Doc. 212.

openly displayed and available at many times the price; the same is true for meats and sausages. *Anything* else is also to be had in Warsaw at insane prices.

In Polish restaurants, all the fancy foods, wine, liqueur, and sparkling wines are available. The Germans became aware of the special ration of lemons and oranges when, around two weeks before the allocation, these items began to be sold at unbelievable prices (1 orange for 20–30 zloty) in the street.

III. Special privileging of ethnic Germans
In many cases Poles with distant relatives of German descent declare themselves part of Germandom simply to obtain food ration coupons. Only ethnic Germans are employed in the so-called German shops, and they treat the Reich Germans, who are made to wait to be served, rudely and impudently. The misappropriation and illicit trading of special rations is probably the result of embezzlement that the ethnic Germans engage in.

IV. Summary
At all events Warsaw and the surrounding area have been declared bandit territory, and the circumstances described above demonstrate that the civil administration installed in Warsaw is by no means in control of the situation. While the honest German can afford nothing, dishonest elements are making a fortune for themselves and, just like the rich Pole, can afford everything!

## DOC. 256

## On 23 July 1943 the SS Business and Administration Main Office informs Himmler that a concentration camp has been established on the site of the Warsaw ghetto[1]

Letter from SS-Obergruppenführer and General of the Waffen-SS Pohl (D II/1 29a/27 Ma./Hü.), Berlin, to the Reichsführer-SS (received on 27 July 1943, log no. 38/32/43g), Berlin, dated 23 July 1943

*Re*: establishment of a concentration camp in the former ghetto in Warsaw
*Reference*: order of 11 June 1943[2]
Reichsführer,

I report that the concentration camp in the Warsaw ghetto has been established and that it was filled with the first 300 prisoners on 19 July 1943.[3]

1 BArch, NS 19/1740, fol. 22. Published as a facsimile in Berenstein et al. (eds.), *Faschismus – Getto – Massenmord*, p. 452. This document has been translated from German.
2 The suggestion that Pawiak prison, which was located between Dzielna Street and Pawia Street and run by the Security Police, might be converted into a concentration camp came from the SS and Police Leader in Warsaw, Jürgen Stroop: see Doc. 243. Himmler gave Pohl instructions to this effect on 11 June 1943: BArch, NS 19/1740, fol. 7. Warsaw concentration camp was established in a complex of buildings on Gęsia Street which had been used by the Polish army as a warehouse and prison until 1939 and by the Jewish Order Service as the central detention centre for the Jewish residential district from 1941 to 1943.
3 The transport, carrying non-Jewish, mostly Reich German prisoners, came from Buchenwald concentration camp.

I have appointed as commandant SS-Obersturmbannführer Goecke,[4] who has gained experience over the past few months at Mauthausen concentration camp.

As ordered, the prisoners are deployed for retrieving and collecting salvaged material. As additional housing is built, the number of prisoners will be increased on an ongoing basis in order to carry out the work as quickly as possible.

The work in the former ghetto is being undertaken in closest consultation with the SS and Police Leader in District Warsaw, SS-Brigadeführer Stroop.

## DOC. 257
## On 31 July 1943 Artur Norman writes from Janowska camp in Lwów to say that he does not have long to live[1]

Letter from Artur Norman[2] to his aunt, Gizela Flig,[3] and her daughter[4] in Lwów, dated 31 July 1943[5]

Saturday, 31 July 1943

My dearest,

Thank you so much for sending me the shirt, thread, and needles, which will come in very handy. But you really don't have to go out of your way to help me, because unfortunately it won't make any difference. My dearest, you ask what happened to the pharmacist. He has been gone since May. Fate dealt us an even harsher blow last Thursday. We lost our beloved Luduś[6] when the brigades employed by the Wehrmacht were dissolved. It is difficult to describe what is going on in my heart and what I went through during the night of Thursday to Friday. In any case, the same thing awaits me soon as well, I'm quite aware of that. It may take another day or two, or perhaps even longer. Unfortunately there's nothing I can do about it. I have nowhere to go and nothing to live on. Only early last week I received a beret from Ludek,[7] and on Wednesday 100 złoty, and on Thursday evening, instead of going back to his bunk, he and the entire brigade were

4 Wilhelm Göcke (1898–1944), career soldier; joined the NSDAP in 1930 and the SS in 1931; in 1942 he was commandant of the Narvik labour camp; then at Mauthausen as camp compound leader and from Dec. 1942 as commandant of Steyr-Münichholz, a subcamp of Mauthausen; commandant of Warsaw concentration camp from July 1943, and of Kauen concentration camp from Sept. 1943 to June 1944; killed by partisans in the Operational Zone Adriatic Coast.

1 YVA, O-75/410, unnumbered (four fols.). This document has been translated from Polish.
2 Artur Norman (1913–1943), lawyer; lived in Cracow prior to Sept. 1939, and thereafter in Lwów, where he perished in Janowska camp.
3 Gizela Flig (Flieg); lived in Israel after the war.
4 Since the Polish second-person plural is used several times, the letter is possibly also addressed to Gizela Flig's daughter Paulina (1919–1942); lived in Cracow prior to Sept. 1939, and thereafter in Lwów.
5 Dr T. Cytron presented the letter to the Yad Vashem Archives. It is written on paper forms with the word 'Complaints' printed on them.
6 A familiar form of the Polish first name Ludwik; this is presumably a reference to one of Artur Norman's cousins, Ludwik Brand (b. 1919).
7 This is another familiar form of the Polish first name Ludwik.

taken down Pilichowska Street to the sand … The stench of burned bodies and bones still hung in the air the next day …[8]

I am prepared for my final journey. I have neither debts nor obligations. I have nothing, and I'll leave nothing behind, just a faint smell of something burned. And some day soon, in a better future, you will find a trace of me in the form of my documents, kept by the Gusz gentlemen[9] in Brzuchowice. It is hard to defy fate. The last letter from my beloved mother[10] is also there.

God willing, we might perhaps continue our correspondence (Wednesdays and Saturdays), perhaps it shall be granted that we meet again and survive this cataclysm, but I bid farewell already now, aware of my future, which I can't change. May you soon get all that you've been longing for.

Thank you so much, my dearest, for the motherly care you've given me since I came to Lwów. You shall remain the sole representative of our entire family.

All of the others went in rank and file, and I shall have to end this procession by joining the ranks and bravely treading the path to eternity.

Just as my beloved mother did, I am now writing this farewell letter. I offer no advice and guidance, as I don't consider myself qualified to do so.

As it stands, I will live for a few more days (I presume). I will reply if you write to me. Uncle is doing very well. He's coming back on the 5th and will be sleeping over here again.[11] He even offered to lend me money. I refused.

I no longer need anything, except a miracle, perhaps. I await your news. I send you a kiss and warm greetings,

Your cousin

I am not writing any verses;
I'm simply bidding you farewell and wishing[12]
you lots and lots of luck.

8 There was an execution site in a sandy area behind the camp, where inmates were shot. From early June 1943 corpses were systematically dug up and burned there.

9 The abbreviation 'p.' used in the Polish original can mean 'Mr', 'Mrs', or 'gentlemen'.

10 Eleonora Norman, née Fränkel (1880–1942), merchant; murdered in Tarnów in 1942.

11 This is presumably a coded message. Artur Norman's uncle, the addressee's husband, was Ferdynand Flig (Flieg) (1879–1941), merchant from Gorlice; lived in Cracow prior to Sept. 1939; murdered in Lwów. Another of Artur Norman's uncles was Ludwik Brand's father, Samuel Brand (b. 1900–1942), merchant; perished in Tarnów.

12 Rhymes in the original.

## DOC. 258

### On 6 August 1943 a Polish underground organization reports that Jews are being murdered with poison gas at Lublin-Majdanek concentration camp[1]

Handwritten report,[2] signed Elżbieta,[3] Lublin, dated 6 August 1943

Details of the camp in Majdanek, 6 August 1943

[The inmates] in numbers:

Men: 6,100 Ruthenians,[4] 5,000 Jews, 5,000 Poles.[5]

Women and children: 7,200 Poles, 2,000 Ruthenians, 1,000 Jews.

Correspondence: They may receive letters in any quantity. Sending letters is prohibited.

Rations: Prisoners of war who perform heavy labour receive an additional half litre of soup from the PCK and 10–12 decagrams[6] of bread from the camp kitchen.

Treatment: As a rule – brutal. Jews and Poles are treated differently, the latter [are treated] better. The treatment of women is less harsh.

Deportations (not counting those resettled from the pacified territories): On 15 July 500 women were deported to the Reich. On 31 July they deported 500 men to the Reich.

On 13 July I received the following message from 'our man' in Compound III:[7] 'About 8,000 new people have arrived here. All of them farmers, mainly from powiat Biłgoraj and Chełm. Women, men, children. They are divided into transports of several hundred people and sent to work. Where to, no one knows.

'Several thousand Jews were also sent to work, and about 2,000 were gassed in the Gaskammer.[8] Mainly women, the elderly, and children. The gassing is carried out with CO[9] for ten minutes. The corpses are taken to the forest and burned. The Poles are treated somewhat better than the Jews, but both groups are beaten.'[10]

1 APMM, XII-9, fols. 1–2. Published as a facsimile in *Listy z Majdanka: KL Lublin w świetle grypsów – katalog wystawy* (Lublin: Państwowe Muzeum na Majdanku, 2008), no page numbers. This document has been translated from Polish.

2 The report comes from the Central Underground Welfare (OPUS) organization, under the Home Army's Lublin District Command. The organization supported Home Army members who had been imprisoned in 1943–1944 and used their reports to find out what was happening in Lublin-Majdanek concentration camp.

3 Wanda Szupenko, code names Sahara and Elżbieta (d. 1986), teacher; worked for OPUS; sentenced to ten years in prison for her activities in the anti-communist underground movement after the war; subsequently pardoned. In late 1944 she gave the OPUS archive to a Home Army agent, who hid it; the archive was recovered in 1971 and presented to the State Museum in Majdanek.

4 Polish: 'Rusini'; these were prisoners from the region whom the camp administration categorized as neither Poles nor Russians (Ukrainians, Byelorussians, and 'locals').

5 There is a question mark in the right-hand margin next to this figure.

6 A decagram is a unit of weight equivalent to 10 grams.

7 The camp was subdivided into separately fenced-in sections (compounds); the gas chambers were located in Compound III.

8 German in the original, with a Polish grammatical ending: 'gas chamber'.

9 The gas used was probably Zyklon B.

10 This quotation is taken from a report by an informant for the Polish resistance movement, dated 13 July 1943: APMM, XII-10, part 1, fol. 3.

Mood: One should not misjudge the people from Majdanek. Sometimes they are holding up better than many of us who live in freedom. These are words from a letter:[11] 'Don't think that everything here is sad. There are many friendly people here, and sometimes we spend time in a nice atmosphere.' – 'I am holding up well. With God's help. I have the best living conditions that are possible here: [fresh] air, sun, a pleasant job, peace of mind, as far as it is possible. I don't go hungry. We live like one [big] family and run a common household. All in all, the devil is not as black as he is painted. We'll get through it.'

Everyone is yearning for news of what is happening in the world.

No news has come in yet from the main source.[12]

## DOC. 259
## *Głos Warszawy*, 10 August 1943: report on the uprising in Treblinka extermination camp[1]

*From Poland.*

*News from Treblinka.* Over the course of last week news about the events in the well-known death factory – the camp in Treblinka – began to reach the capital. According to fragmentary reports from various sources, the events unfolded as follows: there were still approximately 3,000 Jews[2] in Treblinka, who were engaged in burying the bodies of the victims who had been murdered by the thousands, or – under the threat of the Gestapo's revolvers – operating the gas chambers, etc. These unfortunate victims, who were also killed at certain intervals – once they'd 'had their day' – and replaced with new ones, finally revolted. Driven by hopelessness and despair, the Jews killed about a dozen Gestapo men, seized control of the local arsenal, armed themselves, and fled into the surrounding forests, having first set a few buildings on fire. Approximately 2,800 people, most of them armed, escaped into the forests. They took up partisan warfare and inflicted heavy losses on the units pursuing them.

11 From a letter by a Polish female prisoner.
12 This sentence was added subsequently.

1 *Głos Warszawy*, no. 49 (58), 10 Aug. 1943, p. 2; AAN, 1583/269/2, fol. 216. *Głos Warszawy* was an underground publication produced by the Warsaw Committee of the Polish Workers' Party (PPR) and appeared in Warsaw from late Nov. 1942 to 1944. Władysław Bieńkowski (1906–1991) was its editor from May 1943. This document has been translated from Polish.
2 This figure is a considerable overestimate. According to eyewitness estimates, there were 850 Jews in the camp on that day; approximately 400 managed to initially escape.

## DOC. 260

## On 13 August 1943 the Polish government's representation in occupied Poland announces that the inmates in Treblinka have destroyed the camp[1]

Report from the government delegation's intelligence service, Warsaw, dated 13 August 1943

*Overview of the most important events in the country.* Weekly report, 13 August 1943
30/43
[…][2]
*A stop to pacification in the Lublin region*:
On Frank's orders, the pacification operation was halted.[3] Gendarmerie, police, and Kalmuck[4] units are only deployed in larger centres of population to ensure that requisitioning quotas are met. It has been confirmed that children and the elderly who had been deported to Majdanek[5] were gassed en masse in gas chambers and [their corpses] were incinerated in Kazimierzówka, near Lublin, on 5, 7, and 9 July.[6]

*Treblinka set on fire*:
In addition to the SS unit and the Ukrainians[7] (160 people), there was a special group of Jewish helpers – numbering 600 [people] – in Treblinka No. 2[8] who helped execute the Jews.[9] On the 3rd of this month[10] this group attacked the guards, disarmed them, captured the weapons arsenal, set buildings on fire, and made its way into the forest.

1 AAN, 1325/202/I-42, fols. 65–66, here fol. 65. Published in Krystyna Marczewska and Władysław Ważniewski, 'Treblinka w świetle akt Delegatury Rzadu RP na Kraj', *Biuletyn Głównej Komisji Badania Zbrodni Hitlerowskich w Polsce*, vol. 19 (1968), pp. 129–164, here pp. 155–156. This document has been translated from Polish.
2 The first paragraph contains reports of sadistic crimes committed by members of the German police in reprisals against the rural Polish population.
3 Governor General Frank and Governor of District Lublin Ernst Zörner had criticized the settlement programme. Globocnik put a stop to the resettlement and the intensified anti-partisan resistance efforts on 15 August 1943.
4 This is presumably a reference to the so-called Caucasian Company, which had been set up by Einsatzgruppe D in the North Caucasus and transferred to the General Government.
5 The children and the elderly deported to Majdanek are thought to have been Polish villagers expelled from their homes in the Zamość region in the course of Globocnik's resettlement campaign. In summer 1943 a number of transports of Polish villagers were sent to Majdanek; most of these prisoners were sent on to the Reich as forced labourers and others were released. Contrary to rumours at the time, it is not thought that any of these non-Jewish Polish prisoners were murdered by gas. Somewhat earlier, in May 1943, a number of transports of Jews had been sent to Majdanek, including from Białystok. It is thought that children from these transports were murdered by gas in Majdanek.
6 The reference to the burning of corpses is to the Krępiec forest, which had been a site where Poles had been executed in 1940 and which was again a site of mass murder from 1942, this time of Jews. In summer 1943 the bodies of thousands of murdered prisoners from Lublin-Majdanek concentration camp were burned there.
7 Non-German auxiliary troops from the SS training camp in Trawniki.
8 Treblinka extermination camp.
9 Only German camp officials and guards from Trawniki carried out killings directly.
10 The uprising began on 2 August 1943.

Approximately 200 Jews died in the fighting. Approximately fifty Germans and Ukrainians were wounded or killed.
[…][11]

## DOC. 261
## On 14 August 1943 the Wehrmacht reports the murder of 350 people by Wehrmacht and police units during the liquidation of the labour camp for Jews on the Adampol estate[1]

Daily report (by telex) from the Military District Command for the General Government (Department Ia,[2] no. 3389/43 secret), headquarters,[3] to the Army High Command, Chief of Army Equipment and Staff of the Commander of the replacement army,[4] dated 14 August 1943[5]

*Daily report*

*Report from OFK 365 Lemberg*
14.8. Kolpak bandit group[6] with weak forces in the woods south of Buczacz. Clean-up operation is being carried out in this area.
*Area of OFK 603 Kielce*
12.8. Patrol of Volga Tatar Legion[7] fired upon by bandits at railway station in Kamienna.[8] One legion fighter wounded.
*Area of OFK 372 Lublin*
13.8. Clean-up of Adampol estate (9 km west of Wlodawa)[9] by Wehrmacht and police units. 350 Jews and bandits arrested, who were exterminated during an escape attempt.[10]

11 The following section contains further news concerning the Polish population.

1 BArch, RH 53-23/42. This document has been translated from German.
2 Department Ia of the Military District Command for the General Government was responsible for operational planning.
3 The headquarters were located in Spała, near Łódź.
4 The commander of the replacement army was General Friedrich Fromm (1888–1945).
5 Additional copies were sent to the distribution list for daily reports.
6 The troops under the command of Soviet Major General Sydir Kovpak (1887–1967) formed one of the largest partisan armies, several thousand strong; they operated primarily in Ukraine.
7 The Volga Tatar Legion, established in 1942, was composed of members of Muslim Turkic peoples in the Soviet Union and comprised up to 12,550 men.
8 This is a reference to the town of Skarżysko-Kamienna, approximately 140 km south of Warsaw.
9 The estate was located on the eastern border of the General Government; today it is part of the community of Wyryki in powiat Włodawski.
10 An average of around 600 prisoners from the Włodawa ghetto were held at the labour camp; 475 prisoners were shot when the camp was liquidated.

## DOC. 262
## On 16 August 1943 members of the Home Army denounce the sołtys of Kurów for participating in the persecution of Jews[1]

Handwritten report by Kula and Turoń[2] detailing accusations against Stanisław Djupero, addressed to the Directorate of Underground Combat (KWP),[3] dated 16 August 1943

Denunciation of *Djupero Stanisław*, approximately 50 years old, residing in Kurów, powiat Puławy, former sołtys of the rural community of Kurów.

Djupero Stanisław, sołtys since the germans[4] invaded Poland, has harmed the Polish Nation[5] by overzealously performing his duties, whether enforcing quota deliveries, aiding 'recruitment' for work in Germany, spreading defeatism among the local population, quelling the spirit of resistance, or cooperating with the occupier in the destruction of the Jews.

In response to a German order according to which every sołtys is held personally liable for any Jews found in his community,[6] he initiated a raid in autumn 1942 during which between ten and twenty Jews were picked up and then shot.[7]

## DOC. 263
## On 17 August 1943 the Commander of the Security Police and the SD in District Warsaw proposes that the War Merit Cross be awarded for murders committed in the Warsaw ghetto[1]

List of nominations by the Commander of the Security Police in District Warsaw, signed Hahn,[2] for the SS and Police Leader in Warsaw, Stroop, Warsaw, dated 17 August 1943

*Nominations list no.*[3] *for the War Merit Cross 2nd Class (with Swords)*
Warsaw, 17 August 1943
signed Hahn, SS-Obersturmbannführer, Oberregierungsrat

1 AAN, 1326/203/XIII-3, fol. 39. This document has been translated from Polish.
2 Kula and Turoń are code names.
3 The Directorate of Underground Combat (KWP) was established on 15 July 1943 through the amalgamation of the Directorate of Civil Combat (KWC) and the Home Army's Directorate of Covert Combat (KWK); it reported to the Home Army High Command. This announcement also appeared in other underground publications.
4 This term is written in lower case in the original as an expression of contempt.
5 This term is capitalized in the original.
6 See *Amtliches Mitteilungsblatt des Kreishauptmanns in Grojec*, no. 3, 28 Oct. 1942, p. 20: '(29) Accommodation of transient itinerants and beggars': Biblioteka Narodowa, P.77180 A.
7 At the bottom of the document is a note of the charges recommended by Stefan Mika, a Home Army second lieutenant, dated 22 Oct. 1943. These call for Djupero to be punished for his role 'in collecting agricultural quotas [and] recruiting Poles to work in Germany' with a reprimand and a warning. This sentence was imposed by the Judicial Commission in its verdict of 23 August 1943: AAN, 1326/203/XIII-3, fol. 37.

1 AIPN, GK 317/874, t. 10, fols. 3–5. Published in Josef Wulf, *Vom Leben, Kampf und Tod im Ghetto Warschau* (Bonn: Bundeszentrale für Heimatdienst, 1958), pp. 92–93. This document has been translated from German.

signature of the representative of the highest relevant Reich authority: read and approved: the SS and Police Leader in District Warsaw
Stroop, SS-Brigadeführer and Police Generalmajor
[…][4]

*Short rationale and opinion from the intermediate superiors*
*Blösche*[5] has been involved in carrying out the resettlement[6] of the Jews in the ghetto for several months. After the resettlement was completed, he primarily undertook patrol duty and guarded the Jews in the ghetto. Before the beginning of the operation on 19 April 1943, Blösche had repeatedly succeeded in capturing armed Jews or finding and raiding smaller bunkers in which Jews had been hiding for some time. When the operation began on 19 April 1943, he was assigned as someone particularly familiar with the area, and he repeatedly and fearlessly overcame armed resistance. His achievements and his constant readiness for action must be particularly emphasized.[7]

## DOC. 264

## In August 1943 the Polish government's representation in occupied Poland describes the ongoing murder of Jews and the prisoners' uprising in Treblinka[1]

Report by the government delegation for the period from 26 July to 26 August 1943 (excerpt)[2]

[…][3]
*V. Continued extermination of the Jews*
*The Warsaw ghetto.* In Warsaw the Jewish ghetto remains sealed and is monitored by German guard posts – the German police – because thousands of Jews are still hiding

2 Dr Ludwig Hahn (1908–1986), lawyer; joined the NSDAP in 1930 and the SS in 1933; head of Einsatzkommando 1 of Einsatzgruppe 1 in Poland in Sept. 1939; Commander of the Security Police and the SD (KdS) in Cracow from Jan. to August 1940, then at the Reich Security Main Office; from August 1941 KdS in Warsaw and Oberregierungsrat; in hiding after the war; director of an insurance firm from 1949; sentenced to life imprisonment by Hamburg Regional Court in 1975.
3 No number is given.
4 Fol. 4 contains personal details about SS-Rottenführer Josef Blösche from Friedland, who lived at 16/21 Straße der Polizei and who served in the office of the KdS for District Warsaw.
5 Josef Blösche (1912–1969), waiter; joined the Sudeten German Party (SdP) in 1935 and the NSDAP in 1938; worked for the SD in Warsaw from March 1940; worked at Department IV (Gestapo) with the KdS in Warsaw from Oct. 1941; from summer 1942 at the SD outpost in the Warsaw ghetto, where he was known to the inmates as 'Frankenstein' because of his many murders; after the war lived in the Soviet occupation zone and then East Germany, where he stood trial; sentenced to death and executed in 1969.
6 The deportation of the ghetto inmates to Treblinka between 22 July and 21 Sept. 1942.
7 Hahn awarded Blösche the decoration in summer 1943.

1 AAN, 1325/202/I-34, fols. 162–187 (fols. 170–171). This document has been translated from Polish.
2 There is a handwritten insertion at the top of the document: 'sent to L[ondon] 8 Sept. [1943]'.
3 The report from the government delegation's executive office is 26 pages long. It starts off by addressing the German occupiers' policies towards the Polish population in the General Government, then discusses communist activities, living conditions under the terror of the German occupation, and the deportation of young Poles for forced labour in the Reich.

within the territory of the ghetto in bunkers, specially extended cellars, and sewers. They are supplied with food by Polish smugglers who reach this territory through the sewers. Police patrols go around the ghetto on rubber soles, with listening devices, hunt down Jews and smugglers, and drag them out of the various nooks and crannies in which they are hiding. Those who are caught are transported to Pawiak, where they are executed soon afterwards. Executions of entire groups of 10–20 Jews each – men, women, and children – take place in Pawiak and nearby every day.

*Echoes of the liquidation of the Lwów ghetto.* Exhaustive reports on the liquidation of the Jewish ghetto in Lwów have recently reached Warsaw. It began with the Jews being taken en masse – 140 people loaded into each wagon – to the death camp in Bełżec.[4] In this way more than 30,000 Jews were transported from Lwów to their deaths. Bestial scenes unfolded as the Germans and Ukrainians brutally murdered those who tried to save themselves by escaping. Nonetheless, numerous Jews hid in various nooks and crannies in the ghetto. The Germans and Ukrainians proceeded to track down and seize these Jews in an operation that lasted several weeks. In Lwów they estimate that approximately 12,000 of the Jews in hiding were tracked down. They were all murdered on the spot. At present only about 3,000 Jewish craftsmen remain in Lwów; they are kept alive as long as they continue to undertake the work assigned to them.

*Jews in the camps.* During the period covered by this report, the Germans executed a large number of Jews – several thousand – in Majdan.[5] According to information recently received from Oświęcim, 468,000 Jews had been executed in gas chambers there by the end of 1942,[6] and in the first half of 1943 approximately 180,000 Jews. A certain number of particularly strong and healthy Jewish women in Oświęcim were earmarked for experiments in artificial insemination, sterilization, and castration.[7] There is a large camp for Jews in Trawniki, initially intended for Bolshevik prisoners of war and used for Jews since the second half of 1942. At present there are approximately 8,000 Jews there on average; they are employed in the Schultz factories, which have been relocated from the Warsaw ghetto. These factories produce fur coats, hats, uniforms, and undergarments for the German army. The living and working conditions in the camp are extremely harsh, and therefore the mortality rate is very high. Moreover, every 2–3 weeks large transports of people are taken to Sobibór for execution. They are replaced with healthier workers who arrive on new transports in Trawniki and remain there. A large number of Jews brought from the Netherlands passed through Trawniki recently. In addition, there is a penal camp next to Trawniki camp: the peat-mining camp in Dorohucz,[8] 6 km from Trawniki. The inmates are sent for the slightest misdemeanour to Dorohucz, where they soon perish in horrible conditions, or else after a time they are taken to Sobibór to their deaths. There is a second large labour camp for Jews in Poniatowa (in the Lublin region), where 14,000 Jews are held. They work in the Többens[9] factories, which

4 By the start of 1943 no further deportation transports went to Belzec. These deportation trains are thought to have gone to Sobibor.

5 Correctly: Majdanek.

6 This figure is greatly overestimated; approximately 200,000 Jews had been deported to Auschwitz by late 1942.

7 'Castration' used here as in the original.

8 Correctly: Dorohucza.

9 Correctly: Többens.

were also relocated from the Warsaw ghetto. The living conditions in Poniatowa are better than in Trawniki.

*Bloody revolt in Treblinka.* Several hundred Jews remained in Jewish Treblinka[10] – craftsmen employed by the Germans in various work projects and labourers used for work in the camp. Recently they were engaged in digging up large mass graves of Jews executed in Treblinka and burning the excavated corpses. Some of the Jews still alive in Treblinka formed a secret combat organization. One day, in early August, they chose an opportune moment to act: some of the German-Ukrainian camp guards had gone swimming [in the Bug river]. The Jews attacked the remaining staff, disarmed them, murdered about fifty Germans and Ukrainians, and then set fire to the barracks. All the Jews who were in the camp fled into the forests around Treblinka. The Germans organized large-scale manhunts in these forests. Some of the Jews were captured and murdered, and some managed to escape.

*The search for Jews in hiding.* All over the country, the Germans continue to conduct a meticulous search for Jews who are still in hiding among or being sheltered by the Aryan population. Such Jews are discovered very frequently. The Jews that are caught are usually severely tortured and then executed immediately afterwards. If they are kept alive for a time, it is only to force them to testify as to who among the Aryan population had helped them. As a result of such testimonies, Poles who harboured Jews are subjected to harsh reprisals, and very often they are even shot.

*Number and concentration of Jews in Poland.* According to calculations made by prominent representatives of Jewish social and political life, the number of Jews left alive in Polish territories is as follows: Vilna – 15,000; Eastern Małopolska[11] – 20,000; Cracow (the camp in Płaszów) – 7,000; Łódź – 80,000 (of these, 35,000 are from the local area, and the rest come from abroad); Warsaw – 15,000 (very few in the ghetto, most in the Aryan part of the city); Białystok and Białystok region – 20,000; Tarnów – 4,000; Częstochowa – 1,000; the Dąbrowa Coal Basin – 30,000; Trawniki – 8,000; Poniatowa – 14,000; Lublin (in the camps) – 4,000; Oświęcim – 12,000; scattered across various areas – 50,000. From the above list it appears that, taking into account possible fluctuations and misinformation, only approximately 300,000 Jews are currently living in the territory of the Republic of Poland.

[…][12]

10 This is a reference to the extermination camp; the majority of the prisoners in Treblinka labour camp were Poles.

11 Eastern Galicia.

12 The sections that follow describe the Ukrainians' anti-Polish reign of terror and the Poles' flight from Eastern Galicia and Volhynia; the Germans' use of political terror campaigns against the Polish population; the Majdanek, Auschwitz, and Ravensbrück concentration camps; German 'pacification operations' in the areas around Lublin and Cracow; murders and violent operations in central Poland and Bezirk Bialystok; Polish resistance and counter-terror in the General Government; and the activities of partisan groups.

## DOC. 265

## *Hechaluc Halochem*, 27 August 1943: the Jewish Pioneer Youth (Halutzim) Combat Organization calls on Jews in the General Government to take up active resistance[1]

*Combat order to all Jewish groups in the General Government*

The final extermination is near. The enemy is mobilizing its forces against the remaining Polish Jews. Let's not wait idly for death! Let's not count on a sudden end to the war and a rapid liberation!

We must take the fight for our lives into our own hands.

*Young people* – only with a weapon in your hands can you weather this storm. Join the ranks of the fighting youth! Join the general combat operation! Let everyone take their place in the ranks of the active resistance. Don't let the events of the day take you by surprise.

*Jews* – if you have no strength to fight, if you are no longer able to take up arms, then save your own life. Today, every escape from the clutches of the executioners is a militant act. We must make their destructive work more difficult. Don't put your own neck in the noose!

We must not hesitate. Don't let the real danger be obscured by a misguided avoidance of inconvenience and a fear of the consequences. Flee through every crevice – over walls, fences, barbed wire. Blend into the anonymous urban crowd to deceive the enemy. Go into the forests and the hills. Use every escape route! Once and for all – cast off the shackles with which the enemy and your own subservience have bound you.

Rise, so that you are ready at the decisive moment.

*The High Command of the Jewish Pioneer Youth Combat Organization*

## DOC. 266

## On 31 August 1943 the Home Army reports on the terror of the German occupation, the hunt for Jews, and the prisoners' uprising at Treblinka[1]

Report, signed Rylski,[2] from the Home Army's Węgrów area, dated 31 August 1943

*Wilga VI.*[3] On site, 31 August 1943
*Report*
*Economic issues*
Quota deliveries are proceeding calmly and with no obstacles from any quarter. Overall, the farmers are determined to deliver half of the established quotas 'for the sake of peace'. The rest depends on the circumstances and on demand. Thanks to the good

1 *Hechaluc Halochem*, no. 31, 27 August 1943, p. 1; Muzeum w Bochni, Depozyt Stowarzyszenia Bochniakówi i Miłośników Ziemi Bocheńskiej, teka 52. *Hechaluc Halochem: Pismo Bojowej Organizacji Żydowskiej Młodzieży Chalucowej* was an underground periodical published from May 1942 to Nov. 1943 by Szymon Draenger and his wife, Gusta Dawidsohn-Draengerowa, first in Cracow, then in Bochnia. This document has been translated from Polish. See also Doc. 193, fn. 2.

1 AAN, 1326/203/X-69, fols. 214–215. This document has been translated from Polish.

harvest, despite this year's considerable increase in quotas, farms are not being driven to ruin, and there have not been any particular complaints.

Cattle and pig stocks are on the way to being almost entirely eliminated. The livestock inventory had already been drastically reduced previously on account of the stipulated monthly meat quotas as well as the extraordinary quotas for the military. At present, according to the current regulations, whatever is left does not need to be surrendered; for example, each farm may retain one cow. The occupier knows how to help himself by other means. Under any pretext whatsoever, a village is surrounded and a punitive operation carried out, for example, for not delivering the egg quota, or for hiding Jews, or for something similar. In the course of such an operation, as well as everyone in the village having to identify themselves and approximately ten or twenty people being taken to Treblinka,[4] above all the cows and pigs are taken away. It makes no difference whether they have markings, or whether they are dairy cows or heifers: everything depends on the whims and appetites of those who take them, and of course on the instructions. Such operations have already been carried out in a few localities in our territory. Approximately 100 cows and more than 100 pigs were taken each time. All the pigs weighing more than 80 kg were taken. The cattle are loaded directly on to vehicles and driven to the railway station.

*Sabotage*

There are virtually no acts of sabotage. One dairy has been destroyed. In addition, unknown perpetrators destroyed the traction engine of a threshing machine on a farm in the north (Miednik). Piles of grain have been set alight on farms on several occasions. Otherwise there have been quite a few robberies in the area, especially in the north. There must be 2–3 groups active there, each with several members. They are well armed, speak Polish, claim to be activists from the organization,[5] and always demand money for the Polish army. These gangs are probably made up of the riffraff from the surrounding villages, so they are difficult to root out. They raid mills and rob wealthier farmers, especially in the settlements. They always raid several neighbouring farms in a single night. They take money, jewellery, and clothing. During one raid they shot a farmer's son when he tried to escape. There is no reaction from the germans.[6]

*Minorities*

There are still cases of Jews being discovered, usually by the population and the gendarmerie; obviously on the basis of someone having betrayed their whereabouts. The Jews are shot on the spot in every case. After a large group of Jews had escaped from Treblinka, many of them came to the area.[7] They are well clothed and quite well fed (most of them had been assigned to special tasks in the camp for a long time).[8] Many of them carry weapons (pistols) and large sums of money or valuables; incidentally, this spells their demise because it makes them targets for the hunts carried out by the riffraff

2 A code name for Stefan Walczyna (b. 1914), official; member of the Home Army; editor of the underground publication *Informator*; worked in the Ministry of Finance in Warsaw after the war.

3 This is a code name for the Home Army's Węgrów area.

4 This is a reference to the labour camp for Poles and Jews at Treblinka (also known as Treblinka I).

5 In other words: from the Home Army, or more broadly, the Polish underground.

6 This term is written in lower case in the original as an expression of contempt.

7 After the prisoners' uprising of 2 August 1943: see Doc. 259.

8 See Doc. 143.

from the villages and cities. These days, one no longer encounters vagabond Jews. Almost all of them have already found some kind of permanent shelter, often sitting in some cramped hole in the ground for several months.

*The occupier*

During this month's reporting, a whole series of special punitive and inspection operations took place in the area. These operations were directed against six larger localities in the area, but the town itself has not yet been affected. These operations proceeded as follows each time: at dawn, the selected locality was surrounded by a special military unit (about battalion strength) and by gendarmerie units, in a pretty large radius of about 6 km. All the inhabitants were rounded up in one place, and houses and outbuildings were searched – albeit relatively perfunctorily. Then the Gestapo and people from the employment office arrived, and another inspection of the assembled people began. First, they had to approach (one by one) a table that the Gestapo used for their business. There the Gestapo examined the kennkarte[9] and checked whether a given surname appears in their files. The Gestapo had two card indexes: one was printed, like a telephone directory (probably a registration and search record), and the second one was typed and contained only the surnames [of residents] in the powiat. The Gestapo rarely took anyone away during these operations. As a rule, reserve officers who had been registered during the last registration process in early August were taken away. In our area none of them have been taken yet, because only those who were in the town and were already widely known to have been officers before the war registered. No such operation has been conducted in the town so far. During these operations, the Gestapo always asked whether 'there are any officers here among you'.

After the Gestapo inspection, there was an inspection by the employment office, during which employment cards were checked. Anyone without a card was detained on the spot. During each of these operations, the employment office took a few dozen people for work, usually young men, of course. They were immediately loaded on to prepared trucks and were almost always taken directly to Skaryszewska in Warsaw.[10] Their stay in Skaryszewska was very short, as they were promptly transported to the Reich. Only a few managed to return. Such operations lasted from sunrise almost until evening. In some localities the cattle and pigs were also taken away.

*The labour camp*[11] *in Treblinka*

On 8 August a big group of Jews escaped from Treblinka.[12] This escape was planned not just by the 'patients'[13] in Treblinka death camp, but also by those who had been there almost from the very beginning and held various permanent posts. They organized themselves into two combat groups. On 8 August they took advantage of the fact that fifteen Ukrainian guards had gone swimming in the Bug river, and they began to put their plan into action. At a prearranged signal, one group attacked the barracks with weapons and murdered several Ukrainians. Having destroyed the barracks, they began

9 German in the original (correctly: 'Kennkarte'): 'identity card'.

10 From 1942 to 1944 there was a transit camp at 8 Skaryszewska Street in Warsaw for Poles who were being sent to the Reich for forced labour.

11 This is a reference to the extermination camp (also known as Treblinka II).

12 The prisoners' uprising took place on 2 August 1943.

13 This is a reference to the Jews who were to be murdered immediately upon arrival at the camp.

to destroy the camp installations by setting fire to the barracks. The few Ukrainians who were in the Jew camp at the time put up no resistance. Only the guards manning the machine guns on the watchtowers opened fire. The group that escaped numbered approximately 1,500 Jews.[14] Many of them perished during their escape from the camp, and the rest dispersed throughout the surrounding area.

That same day large gendarmerie units were called in, and they organized a major manhunt in the vicinity of Treblinka, during which approximately 120 Jews were shot.

*Miscellaneous*

The police in the area have been instructed to keep an eye out for aircraft and hot-air balloons. These instructions clearly mention the possibility that the British and American air forces might drop [bombs].

Troops are being stationed in larger localities in the area: in Grębków, 70; in Korytnica, 60; in Stoczek, 20; and in the town, 52 – all SS. They act calmly. The purpose of the deployment is unknown. They are barely interested in the quota deliveries.

## DOC. 267
## In August 1943 the Foreign Affairs Department of the Polish government's representation in occupied Poland advocates a Jewish state[1]

Memorandum from the government delegation's Foreign Affairs Department, unsigned,[2] dated August 1943

*Remarks on our international policy, no. 1*

[…][3]

Jewish matters

Our questions regarding nationality also include the Jewish question. We have seemingly treated this as merely a domestic matter. In reality, it has always been connected to international affairs and has influenced Poland's position internationally. We are aware that this will be even more the case after the end of this war, in which world Jewry is officially part of one of the warring factions. The mass murders of Jews in Poland, perpetrated by the Germans, are diminishing the Jewish problem here, but they will not eliminate it completely. Many Jews will certainly survive, and if they emigrate back after the war, then it may mean having to reckon with a Jewish population of 1–2 million. However, in view of the appalling persecutions to which the Jews in Europe have been subjected,

14 This figure is an overestimate.

1 AAN, 1325/202/XIV-9, fols. 127–136, here fols. 134–135. An abridged version is published in Libionka, 'ZWZ-AK i Delegatura Rządu RP', pp. 173–174. This document has been translated from Polish.

2 The author was the head of the department, Roman Knoll (1888–1946), diplomat; ambassador to Moscow, then Ankara, then Rome, and finally Berlin, 1921–1931; went underground in 1939; appointed foreign policy advisor to the representative of the Polish government in 1940; head of the government delegation's Foreign Affairs Department, March 1943 – May 1945.

3 Knoll began by commenting on Poland's relations with its Western allies, Britain and the USA, as well as with Germany and the Soviet Union, and then formulated the central demands of Polish foreign policy before proceeding to comment on Poland's national minorities (Lithuanians, Byelorussians, and Ukrainians).

global public opinion will be much more sensitive to their fate and will pay greater attention to their interests. Christian compassion for the tormented Jews largely predominates in the country at present, but beyond that, the mood in the eastern part of the country towards Jews is one of great irritability, which still stems from the time of the Bolshevik occupation. Regardless of these psychological factors, however, the situation throughout the entire country is such that the Jews' return to their workplaces and workshops is completely out of the question, even in much smaller numbers. The non-Jewish population has taken the Jews' places in the cities and small towns, and this is a fundamental and irrevocable change across large swathes of Poland. The population would perceive the mass return of the Jews not as restitution, but rather as an invasion, against which they would defend themselves even by means of physical force. It would be fatal to our political objective if Poland were to be pilloried before the global public as a country of militant antisemitism at the very time when our borders are being defined, loans are being obtained, and alliances or federations are being formed. All those hostile to us would take advantage of this moment to devastate us and to deprive us of the fruits of the victory we bought at so dear a price. The government is doing well to assure the global public that there will be no antisemitism in Poland, but this will be the case only if the Jews who survive the pogrom do not try to return en masse to Polish cities and towns. The country sees only one way out of this difficult situation, namely that the Polish government must take the initiative soon, if possible immediately, to create a national homeland for the Jews in Eastern Europe. This programme must be implemented in communication with Zionist-oriented Jewish circles. A region in Eastern Europe should be earmarked as the territory of a future Jewish state, instead of Palestine, which is too cramped and too exotic for this and would cause conflicts with the Arab world, or even tropical colonies[4] to which the Jewish masses will not want to relocate. It is perhaps too soon to provide precise details of where this territory might be. Our stance on this issue must not be anti-Jewish, but pro-Jewish. The Jews are a nation and have a right to their own territory where they can establish all the social strata and classes. For Jewry the diaspora is a curse, and it is entitled to compensation for its current monstrous persecution, which should be ensured above all by those nations who have hosted Jews for centuries and who, after this peaceful separation, are prepared to participate in economic and military aid for the new state. We do not know to what extent an initiative in this direction would be easy to accomplish, but we consider it essential to work towards it with the greatest effort, via both diplomacy and propaganda. The programme itself seems much more realistic to us at a time when borders are generally being revised and new constellations of states are being created than at a time of lasting peace.
[…][5]

4 This is a reference to plans to settle Jews on Madagascar or in British Guiana.

5 In the last section of the memorandum (AIP, A-9.Ie/15, doc. 55/13, fols. 1–10), which was classified as top secret in London, Knoll addressed the failure of the plans for an East-Central European federation. After the memorandum was leaked to the outside world, the government in exile distanced itself from it, declaring that it was a piece of private correspondence from Knoll to the foreign minister, Tadeusz Romer (1894–1978).

## DOC. 268

## On 7 September 1943 the head of the SS Business and Administration Main Office notes that he is taking over the labour camps for Jews from the SS and Police Leaders[1]

File note (marked 'secret') by the head of the SS Business and Administration Main Office (D II/1, file ref.: 29 Ma./F, log no. 407/43 sec[ret]), signed Pohl, Berlin, dated 7 September 1943

*File note*

Following the meeting with SS-Obergruppenführer Krüger on 3 September, a meeting took place at the SS Business and Administration Main Office on 7 September. The attendees were SS-Obergruppenführer *Pohl*, SS-Gruppenführer *Globocnik*, SS-Brigadeführer *Glücks*, SS-Brigadeführer *Lörner*, SS-Obersturmbannführer *Schellin*, SS-Obersturmbannführer *Maurer*, SS-Sturmbannführer *Florstedt*, and SS-Obersturmführer Dr *Horn*.

The following was decided:

1) The approximately ten existing labour camps under the authority of the SS and Police Leader in District Lublin will be transferred to the SS Business and Administration Main Office as subcamps of Lublin concentration camp. Upon their transfer, they will come under the responsibility and administrative supervision of the SS Business and Administration Main Office and will be under the direct authority of SS-Sturmbannführer Florstedt,[2] who will be in charge of security and their proper management.
2) Upon transfer to the SS Business and Administration Main Office (Office Group D), the inmates of these labour camps will become concentration camp prisoners.

   These prisoners will be assigned to the workshops in these camps currently operated or yet to be established by Osti[3] in return for payment of a prisoner fee, which will go to the Reich treasury.

   The expenses for the prisoners will be paid by the Reich.
3) Independent of these approximately ten labour camps in District Lublin, all existing labour camps in the General Government will be transferred to the SS Business and

1 BArch, BDC, SSO 387A (personnel file of Oswald Pohl), fols./fr. 1010–1011. Published as a facsimile in Henry Friedlander and Sybil Milton (eds.), *Archives of the Holocaust: An International Collection of Selected Documents*, vol. 11/2: *Berlin Document Center* (New York: Garland, 1992), pp. 171–172. This document has been translated from German.

2 Hermann Florstedt (1895–1945?), career soldier; joined the NSDAP and the SS in 1931; commanded an SS regiment in Ansbach in 1934, and in Kassel in 1937; posted to Buchenwald concentration camp in 1939; at Sachsenhausen concentration camp from July 1940; commandant of Lublin-Majdanek concentration camp, Nov. 1942 – Sept. 1943; arrested in Oct. 1943 by the SS for embezzlement; detained in a police jail in Weimar until spring 1945; his subsequent fate is unclear.

3 In March 1943 Oswald Pohl used the movable property of murdered Jews to found Ostindustrie GmbH (Osti), which set up SS-owned armaments factories in the General Government or took over existing enterprises; the exploitation of the approximately 10,000 Jewish forced labourers in eight plants proved profitable, but the company was dissolved eight months later, after the prisoners had been murdered.

Administration Main Office in the interest of a general corrective adjustment.[4] SS-Sturmbannführer Florstedt will be responsible for the transfer of these camps to the remit of Office Group D at the SS Business and Administration Main Office. He will discuss the details with SS-Obersturmbannführer Schellin,[5] SS-Obersturmbannführer Maurer,[6] and SS-Obersturmführer Dr Horn.[7] He will first establish the number, location, and strength of the inmates as well as the guard forces and the type of production as quickly as possible, and will then make contact with the aforementioned SS officers.

The goal is to close down camps with low occupancy and those where the production is not important to the war effort or critical to winning the war.

4) Those involved are aware that it will only be possible for the SS Business and Administration Main Office (Office Group D) to take over all of these labour camps if the guard forces (police and Askaris[8]) currently deployed at these camps remain there; if said guards are placed under the authority of the SS Business and Administration Main Office for as long as these camps exist; and if they are officially transferred, insofar as they are members of the SS or can be admitted to the SS.

SS-Gruppenführer Globocnik stated in this regard that this would be a matter of course and that SS-Obergruppenführer Krüger would readily agree to it.

4 On 22 Oct. 1943 Pohl ordered Group D of the SS Business and Administration Main Office to take over the labour camps in Trawniki, Radom, Budzyń, Cracow-Płaszów, Alter Flugplatz ('Old Airfield'), and the Deutsche Ausrüstungswerke (DAW) plant in Lublin, as well as the Janowska camp in Lwów: IfZ-Archives, Nürnberger Dokument NO-60. The camps in Trawniki, Radom, and Budzyń later became subcamps of Lublin-Majdanek camp. Meanwhile, Płaszów was turned into a main concentration camp – the last to be established by the SS in the occupied east.

5 Erich Schellin (1892–1978), businessman; joined the NSDAP and the SS in 1931; SS business officer with the Higher SS and Police Leader East, and thus representative of the SS Business and Administration Main Office in the GG in charge of labour camps with Jewish inmates from August 1942; in charge of the concentration camps in the GG from 1943; member of Osti's supervisory board; businessman in Celle after the war.

6 Gerhard Maurer (1907–1953), businessman; joined the NSDAP in 1930 and the SS in 1931; worked full time for the SS from 1934; director of DAW from 1939; head of Department D II (labour deployment of prisoners) at the SS Business and Administration Main Office from March 1942; deputy inspector of the concentration camps from Nov. 1943; extradited to Poland in 1947; sentenced to death in Warsaw in 1951 and executed in 1953.

7 Dr Max Horn (1904–1989), accountant; joined the NSDAP and the SS in 1933; tax advisor in Hamburg from 1937; served in the war from 1939; worked for the SS Business and Administration Main Office from 1942; with Odilo Globocnik co-director of Osti from Feb. to Nov. 1943; in Soviet captivity, 1945–1950; classified as a *Mitläufer* ('follower') during denazification proceedings; thereafter self-employed accountant and tax advisor; author of numerous publications.

8 The term 'Askaris' was first used for local forces serving with colonial troops in German East Africa. Here it refers to non-German auxiliary personnel from the SS training camp in Trawniki.

## DOC. 269

## *Biuletyn Informacyjny*, 7 September 1943: the Directorate of Underground Combat announces that a Pole who blackmailed Jews has been executed[1]

*Notice*

By verdict of the Special Court[2] in Warsaw, dated 7 July 1943, the following person has been sentenced to *death* and to the loss of his political and civic rights: Borys, alias Bogusław, alias Bogusław,[3] Jan *Pilnik*, born on 5 May 1912, son of Aleksander [Pilnik] and Felicja, [née] Szołkowska, resident in Warsaw at 17 Pierackiego Street – for handing over Polish citizens of Jewish nationality to the German authorities from whom they had been hiding;[4] for extorting large sums of money from his victims for his own benefit, under the pretext that he needed it to protect those in hiding, and then handing them over to the German authorities; for thereafter extorting various valuables from their families, allegedly to give them to the detained, but which he then used for his own benefit – while he cooperated with the German occupation authorities as an informant, to the detriment of Polish society, during the German occupation of Poland.

The sentence was carried out by shooting on 25 August 1943.

7 September 1943. Directorate of Underground Combat.[5]

1 *Biuletyn Informacyjny*, no. 37 (122), 16 Sept. 1943, p. 1; Biblioteka Narodowa, MF 45 818. This document has been translated from Polish.

2 The Special Court (Sąd Specjalny) was one of the Polish underground's judicial organs. These types of court mostly dealt with cases of collaboration.

3 Repetition as in the original.

4 Pilnik posed as a Russian, was in contact with the German Criminal Police, and hired numerous informants to observe comings and goings in the streets. They supplied him with the addresses of Jews in hiding, Jewish-Christian married couples, and their helpers, who were then coerced into making payments.

5 See Doc. 262, fn. 3.

## DOC. 270

## On 11 and 12 September 1943 Jerzy Urman, aged eleven, writes about his experiences in Drohobych on the 'Aryan side' and his hatred of Hitler[1]

Diary of Jerzy Urman,[2] entries for 11 and 12 September 1943

Saturday, 11 September 1943

*Marysia*[3] told *Hela*,[4] who had gone to see her, that in *Borysław* a few people had been arrested and taken away in a truck. Grandmother[5] immediately began to worry whether Uncle *Emil*[6] was among them. We reassured her as much as we could but – just like all old people in such circumstances – she believed we[7] were to blame for this event, which in her mind was a raid on Uncle Emil. But we took this to mean that these stupid dogs do everything they can simply to 'put the wind up us'.[8]

The newspaper reported that *Rome* has been occupied by the Germans.[9] I don't know if that's true, but if it is, then the Italians are absolutely useless soldiers because they were unable to defend Rome; but on the other hand, the Allies could also have acted more quickly – but they either can't or they won't.

At supper, Grandmother kept saying that she was the only one here who was eating something warm, and [wondering] whether Uncle Emil – who knows if he is still alive? – has anything to eat in the forest, etc.

*Hela* was up there (in the Beskids)[10] and brought news that *Artur* had been interrogated in connection with the disappearance of Melcia (Emil).

1 The handwritten original could not be located. A typewritten copy made by Emil Urman is held in YVA, O-3/2730, fols. 8–10. Published in English translation in Jerzy Feliks Urman, *I'm Not Even a Grown-up: The Diary of Jerzy Feliks Urman*, ed. Antony Rudolf, trans. Antony Rudolf and Joanna Voit (London: Menard Press, 1991), pp. 28–29. This document has been newly translated from Polish.

2 Jerzy Feliks Urman (1932–1943); lived in the Stanisławów ghetto from Dec. 1941; from Oct. 1942 lived in hiding in Drohobych, at first alone, later with his parents; kept a diary from Sept. to Nov. 1943. When the apartment in which the family was hiding was searched by Criminal Police officers on 13 Nov. 1943, Jerzy swallowed potassium cyanide out of fear of being arrested and deported; his parents Izydor and Zofia escaped and survived.

3 Maria (Marysia) Mielnik was the tenant in the neighbouring apartment at 10 Górna Brama, the building in which Jerzy Urman lived. She is thought to have revealed the Urman family's hiding place to the Criminal Police in Nov. 1943.

4 Hela, whose surname is not known, was the former housekeeper of Jerzy's uncle, Artur Urman; Artur's mother, his brothers Emil and Izydor Urman, and his wife Zofia lived in her apartment from March 1942.

5 Hermina Urman, née Vogel (1874–1950), mother of Emil, Izydor, and Artur Urman; died in Bytom.

6 Dr Emil Urman (1899–1956), lawyer; worked at the University of Lwów; attempted to escape over the border into Hungary in Sept. 1943; initially lived in Katowice after the war, then in Israel.

7 Presumably: 'the Urman family'.

8 The Polish original uses an uncommon idiom, literally 'to put a rat in our belly'.

9 Mussolini had been deposed on 25 July 1943, and a new government had been installed, which agreed an armistice with the Allies on 8 Sept. 1943. The Wehrmacht subsequently occupied Italy.

10 A reference to the oil refinery at Drohobych; Jerzy's uncle Artur Urman (1897–1944), engineer, worked there as a senior manager; he died in Jelenia Góra. The words in brackets here and below were presumably added by Emil Urman when he copied the diary.

Sunday, 12 September 1943
Today, Mama[11] went to church with Hela. When Mama returned, she said first that Hela had gone to the *Tiersts*,[12] and then that in church they had met Mrs *Urbanowicz*,[13] who confirmed that in Borysław eight Jews had been arrested and loaded into a car belonging to the 'Galicja'[14] […].[15] All the Jews are said to be in court (prison) already.

Hela is already back from the Tiersts – and says nothing.

Not until a few hours after lunch, as we sat at the table with Papa,[16] did Hela emerge from her room with a stupid smile on her face and say, 'Well, news has come from Mr Emil that he has crossed the border, and Mr Tierst said it is a pity that you did not go with him.' Having said this, she went into the kitchen and we did not manage to ask her anything else. But after a while her talkative nature won through. She returned and, with the same stupid smile, said, 'Mr Tierst said that they attacked, robbed, and beat up Mr Emil and handed him over to the Gestapo, and that it appears he is no longer alive.' Just like the first time, this time too I did not doubt that she was 'taking us for fools'; but while up until now I had thought that she was accommodating us out of kindness, this time her tone and the way she communicated such important or sad news suggested either a very simple mind or 'Schadenfreude'.[17]

Hitler has delivered a speech.[18] His speech was quoted in the papers. The person who has broken so many agreements, promises, and treaties is now complaining that his allies have betrayed their loyalty – well, excuse me! For Hitler I used the term … person, though in fact he is the devil incarnate. But it is precisely because he has waged war with empty promises; because he promised safety to women and children among the civilian population but has now covered Europe with thousands of mass graves containing millions of victims of the Gestapo, an institution created by him in order to terrorize the peaceful population and massacre certain groups within society, mainly the *most valuable* – it is because of this that his closest and most long-standing ally has deserted him so that he may slowly pay the penalty for the sea of blood – that of his own people and other peoples – that he has spilled.

11 Zofia Urman, née Arbeit, nurse; her memoirs are published in Urman, *I'm Not Even a Grown-Up*, pp. 17–25.
12 Tierst was employed as a chauffeur at the oil refinery.
13 Mrs Urbanowicz's husband worked for Artur Urman.
14 Polish for Galicia; a reference to the oil refinery Raffinerie Galicja, Towarzystwo Naftowe.
15 The rest of the sentence is incomprehensible.
16 Izydor Urman (1904–1992), physician; studied in Lwów and Vienna; lived in Tel Aviv after the war.
17 German in the original: 'malicious pleasure in another's misfortune'.
18 In response to Italy's capitulation, a speech by Hitler was recorded during the afternoon of 10 Sept. 1943 and broadcast by the German radio stations shortly after 8 p.m. In the speech Hitler stated among other things that the Badoglio government formed after Mussolini's deposition had broken the commitments Italy had made under its alliance with the German Reich.

## DOC. 271

## Prior to 28 September 1943 an escapee from Treblinka describes conditions in the camp and how he got out during the prisoners' uprising[1]

Eyewitness report on Treblinka extermination camp[2] for the government delegation's Internal Affairs Department, Warsaw, recorded before 28 September 1943 (carbon copy)[3]

*Report by a Jew who escaped from Treblinka*

I was picked up on 22 August 1942 during a street raid in the Warsaw ghetto. Our transport was destined for work in the East, or so we were told. We travelled packed together in wagons, under guard. The Lithuanians who escorted us took our money and our jewellery. I don't quite understand how we could have believed the story about work then, as there were women and children among us. But no one foresaw the reality. Only when we arrived at the destination were our eyes opened. There were literally piles of corpses lying around in the camp. We were split up: 'Women and children to the left, men to the right.' We had to surrender our money, papers, and valuables. We were ordered to sort piles of clothes, suitcases, and bundles. A transport from Międzyrzecz arrived a few hours later.[4] We were then made to remove the corpses from the wagons (this was largely a transport of corpses)[5] and were beaten in an inhuman way. When we had finished this work, they sat us down in a semicircle and pointed machine guns at us. We had to change places on command, move to the right or to the left. Finally 100 were 'pardoned' on the basis of some arbitrary grouping, and the remainder (a few hundred) were shot. This ended around midnight. Work from early morning – sorting clothes, packages, etc. and burying corpses in pits excavated by machines. The corpses were partly decomposed, and there were cases when an arm or a leg came off in a worker's hand. I worked with corpses for two days, after which, as a trained carpenter, I was employed in constructing gas chambers under Ukrainian command. There were already three – ten were built [in total]. The procedure was as follows: upon arrival the people from a transport were ordered to undress for a bath and were led to the chambers. A Ukrainian standing at the door encouraged those who hesitated by goading them with a bayonet, and killed anyone who resisted.[6] After roughly fifteen minutes, the corpses were removed through the other door. The daily 'baths' continued more or less until February. Apart from the chambers, the 'field hospital' was also used,

1 AAN, 1325/202/II-29, fol. 72. Published in *Kraj*, no. 9/10, 28 Sept. 1943, pp. 30–31. *Kraj*: *Agencja Informacyjna* was the government delegation's bulletin and appeared once or twice a week from July 1943, with a circulation of 750 copies; its editor was Kirył Sosnowski (1910–1966). This document has been translated from Polish.

2 The author is thought to be Jankiel Wiernik (1889–1972), carpenter and building contractor; joined the Bund in 1904; exiled to Siberia; military service in the Russian army; subsequently lived in Warsaw; deported to Treblinka in late August 1942; fought in the uprising; survived by hiding in a rural area, 1943–1944, thanks to the help of the writer Stefan Krzywoszewski (1866–1950).

3 There is a note at the top left-hand corner of the document: 'Żyd.' (Polish: Żydowski; 'Jewish'). This document is taken from a file entitled 'Reports on the situation of Jews outside Warsaw'.

4 On 25 and 26 August 1942 approximately 11,000 Jews from Międzyrzec Podlaski were deported to Treblinka.

5 See Doc. 169.

6 This is thought to have been Ivan Marčenko, one of the auxiliaries from the SS training camp at Trawniki.

especially for the elderly and the sick. Its director walked around in a white coat bearing a red cross. Those sent to the 'field hospital' were seated on a bench in front of a long ditch and pushed into it with a shot. There were also transports from abroad. I reckon there were about 3,000,000 corpses in the camp.[7] The average life of a worker was 3–4 days, sometimes one week. About forty people from my transport, skilled workers, were left. Many committed suicide. At times there would be a spate of hangings, because the guards' sadism was also inhuman. There was a Ukrainian who cut off ears and noses, and drove nails into anuses … One can't imagine the reality of this camp. I'm not even attempting to describe it; only a film could illustrate it all. Our compatriots, the Kapos, also tormented us. There were rumours that Himmler visited the camp in February.[8] A clean-up operation began. The corpses were exhumed and burned, and lupins were planted on the sites of the graves. The mass liquidations also ceased during this period. We built watchtowers, and the camp commandant[9] even 'honoured' me with the task of building a house in the 'Zakopane style'.[10] During this period we were fed a little better and not tortured so much. The 'liquidation' of the corpses continued; three quarters of the graves had already been eliminated. We were under no illusions: we knew that the moment this work ended, it would be the end for us too. People began to conspire. The craftsmen who worked across the camp served as liaisons; sometimes the gravediggers 'removed a few things' when they cleared out the corpses. The Ukrainians were tempted with money and valuables buried in secret places. The guard was taken to do some 'business', which meant that his attention was diverted. In late May we were ready, but the date was cancelled. Groups of five were assigned various tasks (attacking the guardhouse, eliminating the guards after luring them from the watchtower, setting fires, cutting the barbed wire). Our 'uprising' broke out on 28 May at 5.30 a.m.[11] I don't know the details of the fighting because most of it took place in the grounds of Camp II,[12] where our groups of five attacked the barracks guards, seized weapons, and took up the fight. We had only tools. The fighting lasted about 15[13] minutes, and the camp went berserk. I used an axe to kill a Ukrainian who was chasing me and whose pistol had jammed, and ran after my comrades into the forest. In the forest we split up. I made my way to Warsaw thanks to the help and information I received from farmers. Personally my life is ruined, but I have two wishes that give me the strength to live:[14] that the truth about Treblinka may be preserved.[15]

7 According to current calculations, at least 750,000 people were murdered in Treblinka.

8 Himmler was in Warsaw at the beginning of the year. Nothing is known about him visiting Treblinka.

9 Franz Stangl.

10 A style of building and furnishing attributed to the Polish artist Stanislaw Witkiewicz (1851–1915) and inspired by the art and architecture of Poland's highland regions.

11 The uprising took place on 2 August 1943: see also Docs. 259 and 266.

12 The segregated section of the camp in which the gas chambers were located and the corpses were burned.

13 Corrected by hand from: '10'.

14 The version published in *Kraj* reads differently here: 'I have one wish, which gives me the strength to live.'

15 The report breaks off at this point with the first few words of an incomplete sentence, which have been crossed out: 'That after the war'. Wiernik wrote a detailed report, which was published in Polish with a print run of 2,000; one of the copies reached London by courier on 24 May 1944; in addition to a Yiddish edition, a more than 40-page English edition had appeared in New York by late 1944: Yankel Wiernik, *A Year in Treblinka: An Inmate Who Escaped Tells the Day-to-day Facts of One Year of his Torturous Experience* (New York: American Representation of the General Jewish Workers' Union of Poland, 1944).

## DOC. 272

## On 1 October 1943 the Jewish Aid Office reports on supplies for the last labour camps[1]

Report from the Jewish Aid Office[2] for the General Government, Cracow, signed Dr Weichert,[3] dated 1 October 1943[4]

*Activity report* no. III[5] for the months August–September 1943

In August and September of this year, the Jewish Aid Office's work was further expanded. The number of labour camps and factories supplied to date has increased to 47. The number of shipments dispatched has also risen significantly. While 81 shipments were sent out in the first 3 months after the work resumed,[6] 136 shipments were dispatched in the last two months: 68 of them contained medicine, bandages, and processed food; 67 contained food items; and 1 contained clothing and undergarments. In all, from 12 May to 30 September, 217 shipments were sent. With one exception, where a small part was lost, all shipments reached their destinations without any losses.

We are kept precisely informed at all times about the use of the donations delivered. We visit the nearby labour camps often and regularly, and we have the opportunity to receive requests from the bodies that provide care and assistance. Jewish physicians or members of the camp councils[7] visit us from other camps and keep us informed about supply needs. Upon arrival, the shipments we send are received by Jewish camp physicians, compared against the list of contents, and signed for using the carbon receipt that accompanies the list. In addition, individual recipients confirm receipt of processed foods such as condensed milk and the like on a list that the head of medical services sends to us.

We were able to continue the food aid that had been undertaken in July and August. Eight camps in and around Cracow received deliveries of additional bread every week, made in the bakery at the largest camp with flour from the Jewish Aid Office. Several factory kitchens received allocations of Avo and Maggi soup[8] from us, which, like the flour, came from the exchange of foreign alcohol and tobacco. Further expansion of the food aid programme is highly desirable, but it will only be feasible if we receive

1 BArch, R 52/III/1, fols. 69–71. This document has been translated from German.

2 The Jewish Aid Office (Jüdische Unterstützungsstelle, JUS) was the replacement for the Jewish Social Self-Help, which had ceased operating in summer 1942. The JUS was dissolved in 1943.

3 Michał Weichert (1890–1967), lawyer and theatre director; studied in Vienna and in Berlin under Max Reinhardt; co-founder of the Yiddish-language Yung Teater; head of the Jewish Social Self-Help (JSS) from May 1940 to 1942; head of the Jewish Aid Office (JUS) from Oct. 1942 and again from March 1943; in hiding on the 'Aryan side', 1944–1945; charged with collaboration in Cracow after the war, on account of his work in the JUS, and acquitted; emigrated to Israel in 1957.

4 This document is followed by enclosure 4, a report by the accountant Dr Bruno Siebert on the general audit undertaken at the JUS with regard to cash management, as well as the overall administration of funds and economic management (after 15 Feb. 1944).

5 Correctly: II. In his first activity report, dated 1 August 1943, Weichert had described developments from 12 May 1943 to July 1943: see BArch, R 52/III/1, fols. 67–68.

6 That is, from May to July 1943.

7 Various labour camps had Jewish Lagerräte, i.e. Jewish camp councils for the Jewish inmates.

8 Brands of instant soup.

foodstuffs such as flour, flour products, and pulses from the foreign charitable organizations.

An additional step has been taken concerning the milk supply. Following a suggestion from the Jewish Aid Office, some camps have gone over to supplying entire groups of people who perform heavy or hard labour with white sweetened coffee made from our condensed milk, although only twice a week in view of the scarce supplies on hand. However, this did not interfere with the daily distribution of milk to those who are ill and convalescing in the camps. The milk deliveries continue to be very popular.

In connection with this, permit me to quote a passage from a letter written by a Jewish camp physician in District Cracow, dated 19 August of this year: 'The medicines that you have sent us on several occasions have indeed worked wonders. The number of patients is decreasing by the day, and the amount of bandaging material now at my disposal enables me to quickly heal the various injuries that occur daily during work. I am especially grateful to you for the condensed milk. The enclosed list will allow you to work out for yourself exactly how extensive the aid has been and how successful the results have been in this regard as well.'

Apart from the charitable donations listed in Report I, the Jewish Aid Office recently received a portion of the general shipment for the non-German population of the General Government. This portion, the share that had been allocated to the Jews, includes 1,965 kg of Lactocao (sweetened cocoa with powdered milk), 3,716 tins of sweetened powdered milk, of which 3,365 tins are sweetened with glucose, 1,411 tins of sweetened condensed milk, 368 tins of Ovaltine, and 331 tins of other processed food. The total weight of the food is around 4,900 kg. In addition, the shipment contains valuable medicines such as Redoxon, Adovern, Larosan, Larostidin,[9] and others. By means of exchange, we were able to acquire caffeine and strychnine vials. The aforementioned food and medicine, along with instruments, clothing, and undergarments, are contained in Lists IV and V, which have now been made available.

We also took delivery of 23 packages of a shipment from the OSE in Geneva which had been sent to Warsaw last year but could not be delivered due to customs difficulties.[10] This shipment consists of 388 kg of medicine and 1,615 kg of chemicals and disinfectants. By using sizeable quantities of chlorinated lime and cresol solution, which also come from our inventory, some of which is old and some newly purchased, certain camps were able to carry out thorough disinfection and disinfestation operations.

Lastly, we received a shipment of typhus vaccine weighing almost 3 kg from the Bikur Cholim association in St Gallen,[11] which will be used primarily in the labour camps in districts Lublin and Galicia.

The approach of autumn and winter prompted the Jewish Aid Office to make arrangements for assistance with clothing. With the agreement of the relevant authorities,

9 Redoxon was a vitamin C supplement (ascorbic acid), Adovern was prescribed to treat cardiac insufficiency in cases of infectious disease, Larosan was given to young children as a protein substitute, and Larostidin was for gastric ulcers.

10 According to a correction in the next report, no. III, the Jewish Aid Office had received the shipment from the Jewish medical aid society Bikur Cholim (Hebrew: 'sickbed visit') in St Gallen and not from the aid organization Œuvre de secours aux enfants (OSE).

11 See previous footnote.

several hundred items of clothing and undergarments were purchased from the Polish Chief Social Welfare Council. This, however, is far from commensurate with the enormous need for clothing and undergarments. We therefore appealed to the organizations supporting us based in neutral foreign countries and asked them to undertake a drive for used clothes in those countries on our behalf.

The Jewish Aid Office's relief work, which is so greatly appreciated by the Jews in the labour camps, can only be successfully continued if the Jewish charitable organizations in neutral foreign countries send shipments of medicine, food, and clothing at regular intervals.

## DOC. 273

## On 19 October 1943 the GG government deems the labour camps for Jews a security threat[1]

Minutes of the security meeting in Cracow, dated 19 October 1943

*Security meeting in the Royal Hall*
[…][2]
The Polish nationalist resistance movement relies on England, while the communist one is receiving a steady stream of reinforcements from the East: armed individuals who are parachuted in as well as forces that trickle through the front.

In addition, there is the *Ukrainian resistance movement*, the so-called Bandera [organization],[3] which is an increasingly strong presence and is convinced that it must fight to create a Ukrainian state if German power in the East collapses. So far it has been supporting the rebels in Volhynia and Podolia, but it has already made all the arrangements to be able to fight in Ukraine too. According to reports received by the Security Police, its members have instructions to keep their weapons concealed for the time being.

In view of this situation, [SS-Oberführer Bierkamp] considered a more conciliatory policy on the part of the German administration to be misguided and recommended to the Governor General that more stringent measures be taken. This was how the *regulation of 10 October* came about.[4]

1 AIPN, GK 95, vol. 29. Copy in IfZ-Archives, Fb 105, vol. 33, fols. 8054–8067, 8074; here fols. 8057–8060, 8066. This document has been translated from German.

2 The document is twenty pages long. At the outset, Governor General Frank stated that the security situation was 'in complete disarray', but the General Government must 'remain firmly in German hands as the bulwark of the East'; the next to report was Walter Bierkamp (1901–1945), lawyer; joined the NSDAP in 1932 and the SS in 1939; public prosecutor in the 1930s, then Kriminaldirektor at Hamburg Regional Court and head of the Criminal Police head office; inspector of the Security Police and the SD in Düsseldorf, Feb. 1941 – June 1942; also Commander of the Security Police and the SD (KdS) in Belgium and Northern France, Sept. 1941 – April 1942, then head of Einsatzgruppe D; KdS in the General Government, June 1943 – Feb. 1945; committed suicide.

3 The part of the Organization of Ukrainian Nationalists (OUN) that was under the leadership of Stepan Bandera (1909–1959) after a split in 1940.

4 The Regulation for the Suppression of Attacks on the German Development Effort in the General Government, 2 Oct. 1943, authorized Security Police summary courts to try defendants and to execute sentences.

Some death sentences that were immediately carried out in public based on this regulation, specifically for people found guilty of belonging to the resistance movement, made an impression on the population. The practice of publicly declaring guilty prisoners to be hostages and saying they will be shot in retribution for any future murders of Germans has also brought some relief. In Warsaw, for example, the murders of Germans, which before the regulation of 10 October was issued had amounted to seven to eight every night, have thus decreased to two.

On the other hand, [SS-Oberführer Bierkamp noted that] the resistance movement has now moved its units to Warsaw and plans to answer terror with counterterror. But so far they have not dared to do so, although leaflets have been found containing these words: 'We will fight terror with terror. The German oppressors will be forced to give way.' To lead this fight, the nationalist units are seeking to unite with the communist movement.

Only a small part of the Warsaw population, made up of young people under the leadership of former officers and communist officials, is joining the resistance movement; 90 per cent or even more want to live in peace and quiet. In [Bierkamp's] opinion, the German forces presently deployed in the General Government are sufficient to suppress the resistance movement. In addition, the German forces are being reinforced by German troops being moved back. Unfortunately, Hungarian formations are also coming back into the General Government.

*Major General Haseloff*[5] stated that this has to do with a Hungarian corps. At the request of the Governor General, he will keep an eye on this situation.

In reply to a question from the Governor General, SS-Oberführer Bierkamp characterized the powers now given to the Security Police as sufficient. He noted that only in places known to the Security Police as meeting points for members of the resistance movement must more drastic methods be used.

*Police Generalmajor Grünwald*[6] concurred with SS-Oberführer Bierkamp's remarks concerning the security situation. Even in District Cracow, so far the quietest one, the situation is beginning to deteriorate; numerous attacks have been occurring in the Miechow area in particular. The transport trains, largely spared until now, have recently been attacked by bandits armed with grenade launchers. Nonetheless, he believed he could remain in control of the situation with the German forces available.

Since groups of bandits are constantly crossing the San river from the Lublin to the Cracow district, the police have been forced to stop all traffic across the river, which unfortunately creates certain difficulties in bringing in the harvest; however, he said he hopes to be able to lift the strict blockade again in a few days.

5 Kurt Haseloff (1894–1978), career officer; commander of the Wehrmacht's 5th Rifle Brigade; chief of staff for the commander of the replacement army in 1940; chief of the general staff in the General Government military district, March 1943 – May 1944; then head of the Army High Command's budget department; suspended from duty in connection with the 20 July 1944 plot to assassinate Hitler.

6 Hans Dietrich Grünwald (1898–1975), police officer; member of a Freikorps in 1918; joined the NSDAP in 1932 and the SS in 1938; in the gendarmerie from 1928; head of Office Group I in the Order Police Main Office in 1942; Commander of the Order Police (KdO) in the General Government from August 1943; sentenced by an SS court to eleven months in prison for disobedience in April 1944; lived in Munich after the war.

In September the number of robberies for the entire General Government averaged 223 per day; in the first third of October it already stood at 250. In January of last year, robberies numbered as low as six per day. Since the Regulation of 10 October was issued, there has been a slight decrease.

It was noted that *the camps for Jews in the General Government* also represent a significant threat, as a recent escape of Jews from such a camp had shown.[7]

The discussion turned to this question, and the *Governor General* tasked the head of the GG armaments inspectorate, General Schindler, SS-Oberführer Bierkamp, and Generalmajor Grünwald with examining the lists of camps for Jews in the General Government to determine exactly how many of the inmates are being deployed as workers. The others, he said, should be deported from the General Government.

Generalmajor *Grünwald* described *Organization Todt's agricultural estates*, the offices and guardhouses of the *Customs Border Guard* along with their *firearms* held there *as sources* that the bandits attack to supply themselves with weapons. [...][8]

The *security situation* [said Frank] is generally viewed as *very serious*, but in the event of an uprising, the forces on hand are sufficient to keep the situation under control. Security is most closely related to how much personnel from the security agencies is available in the country. *Reinforcement of the Security Police* appears to be particularly urgent; he said he will possibly make a personal appeal to the Reichsführer-SS to this effect.

The existence of *camps for Jews* has turned out to be an acute threat to the security of Germans. [...][9]

7 This presumably refers to the prisoner revolt in Sobibor on 14 Oct. 1943; the German police estimated that 300 Jews escaped. See Doc. 274.

8 In what followed, the discussion of individual security measures continued until Frank summed up the results of the meeting.

9 In conclusion, Frank announced that a further meeting about the security situation would be held four weeks later; it was discussed again on 8 Nov. 1943: see Präg und Jacobmeyer (eds.), *Das Diensttagebuch des deutschen Generalgouverneurs*, pp. 755–756. In addition to the speakers named, the following officials also took part in the meeting: Waldemar von Dazur, Otto Fischer, Karl Naumann, Schmid, Sommé, Albert Weh, and two other individuals.

## DOC. 274

## Around 24 October 1943 an Urban Police officer files a report on the pursuit of escapees from Sobibor by mounted police[1]

Report from the 1st Squadron of Mounted Police Division III (post at military mail postcode 16 107 B), signed Urban Police Oberleutnant and Deputy Squadron Commander H. Knaack,[2] for Mounted Police Division III (received 24 October 1943), undated

*Situation report* for the period 26 September – 25 October 1943
1. *General situation*:
a) *Political*: nothing to report.
b) *Economic*: nothing to report.
c) *Mood and behaviour of the population*: nothing to report.
[…][3]

6. *Activity report*:
a) *Mobile formations*:
Apart from securing the Bug border, the squadron was mainly deployed on large-scale operations during the month under review, such as on 11 October 1943 in the Hansk area (30 km north-west of Cholm), together with Wehrmacht and SD [units]. During this operation 36 members of the Pol[ish] r[esistance] m[ovement], including several leaders, were taken prisoner. On 14 October 1943 the squadron was deployed with the division for a large-scale operation in the wooded area north of Kaplonosy (56 km north-north-west of Cholm). Seventy bandits were shot dead and 17 carbines, 3 pistols, and 535 rounds of ammunition were captured, among other items. During the period from 14–18 October 1943 the squadron took part in the Jew operation carried out by the Sobibor SS special detachment (40 km north-east of Cholm). Of the 300 escaped Jews,[4] approximately 100 Jews were killed in cooperation with the Wehrmacht[5] and the Customs Border Guard. Together with the Wehrmacht and the Waffen-SS, the wooded area (4 km north of Cholm) was combed on 21 October. The last operation was unsuccessful.

Apart from these large-scale operations, the platoons' activities also continued to include taking surveillance positions and carrying out foot and mounted patrols. In addition to reconnaissance work to combat banditry, these platoons are tasked with monitoring traffic on the roads and in the towns and villages, preventing illicit trade, and ensuring that the delivery of supplies is duly carried out. The squadron also provided

1 APL, 514/38, fols. 130–132. Published in Wojciech Zyśko (ed.), 'Eksterminacyjna działalność Truppenpolizei w dystrykcie lubelskim w latach 1943–1944: Wybór źródeł', *Zeszyty Majdanka*, vol. 6 (1972), pp. 155–210, here p. 186. This document has been translated from German.

2 Heinz Knaack (1914–1980), police officer; joined the NSDAP in 1932 and the SS in 1940; Oberleutnant in the Urban Police; platoon commander in the 1st Squadron of Mounted Police Division III in District Lublin in 1943; lived near Salzgitter after the war; later police officer in Braunschweig.

3 The following section contains information on personnel, command posts, communications, and motor vehicles.

4 Around 320 of the 550 Jewish prisoners in Sobibor managed to escape during an uprising on 14 Oct. 1943. Only 53 of those who escaped survived the war.

5 Security Battalion 689.

personnel for the combined forces patrols (Troop Police,[6] Wehrmacht, Feldgendarmerie,[7] and SD) ordered by the Higher SS and Police Leader for the purpose of securing the thoroughfares. To date, these patrols in the security sector have been without success.

In the month under review the troop's platoons were deployed for rounding up cattle, as in previous months.[8]

g) *Results and status of pacification efforts*: nothing to report.

h) *Planned activities in the near future*:

In addition to the large-scale operations planned by the division, the squadron will continue to mainly take up lookout positions in the regions particularly threatened by bandits. The plan is to increasingly deploy patrols on horseback to monitor the roads. Reconnaissance patrols in small one-horse carts and on foot will be intensified. Since the grain harvest has been almost completely brought in, more forces will be available for these efforts in future.

7. *Ideological instruction and troop entertainment*:

Ideological instruction was carried out in the form of weekly training sessions using the daily newspapers and *SS Leithefte*.[9]

As part of the troop entertainment programme, the group 'Die 6 Spaßvögel'[10] played for the men and were very well received.

[…][11]

10. *Troop morale*:

Troop morale can still be characterized as good. Eagerness to serve, courage, and bravery are not diminishing in any way. Every NCO and enlisted man enthusiastically puts his heart into the operations.

6 In the original: Truppenpolizei. This is probably a reference to a reserve police battalion, the members of which were sometimes referred to as 'Troop Police', because such units were barracked like soldiers.

7 In Nazi Germany the Feldgendarmerie were a type of military police unit within the Wehrmacht. Members of the Feldgendarmerie underwent full infantry training and were given extensive policing powers, including the task of maintaining discipline in the Wehrmacht.

8 See Doc. 266. There is no information for items (b) to (f).

9 Literally: 'SS guide booklets'. This periodical was published by the SS Main Office and appeared monthly from 1935 to 1944.

10 'The Six Jokers'.

11 The following section contains information about the supply situation and loss of personnel.

## DOC. 275
## On 4 November 1943 Globocnik asks Himmler to decorate the SS men who participated in the murder of Jews in the General Government[1]

Letter from the Higher SS and Police Leader in the Operational Zone Adriatic Coast (Gl./Go. – log no. 225/43), signed SS-Gruppenführer and Police Generalleutnant Globocnik in Trieste, to Reichsführer-SS and Chief of the German Police Heinrich Himmler in Berlin (date of receipt illegible), dated 4 November 1943

Reichsführer,

Effective 19 October 1943 I concluded Operation Reinhardt, which I had conducted in the General Government, and closed down all the camps.

As a final account, I take the liberty of presenting the enclosed folder[2] to you, Reichsführer.

My assessments in Lublin indicated that the General Government and especially District Lublin were sites from which the affliction had emanated in particular, and I therefore sought to depict these potential dangers in graphic form.[3]

It will perhaps prove useful in future to be able to point to the elimination of this threat.

At the same time, however, I have attempted to give an account of labour deployment, which shows not only how much work is being done, but also how few Germans have been needed to make this large-scale operation possible. In any event, it has now expanded to such an extent that renowned industries are showing interest in it.

I have since handed over these labour camps to SS-Obergruppenführer *Pohl.*[4]

I would like to ask you, Reichsführer, to look through this folder.

During a visit, Reichsführer, you held out to me the prospect that, after the work had been concluded, several EKs[5] might be awarded to recognize special achievements associated with this difficult task. Reichsführer, I kindly ask whether I may submit suggestions for this purpose.

I take the liberty of pointing out that such decorations were granted to personnel of the local SS and Police Leader for the Warsaw operation,[6] which accounted for a relatively small portion of the overall work.[7]

1 BArch, NS 19/2234, fols. 30–31. Published as a facsimile in Stanisław Piotrowski, *Misja Odyla Globocnika: Sprawozdania o wynikach finansowych zagłady Żydów w Polsce* (Warsaw: Państwowy Instytut Wydawniczy, 1949), pp. 16–17. This document has been translated from German.

2 The folder is not part of the file.

3 Globocnik sought to veil the reference to the mass murder of Jews by employing euphemisms that are difficult to translate. For example, in the German original Globocnik called the General Government and District Lublin an 'Ausstrahlungsherd', which is a term usually used in a medical context to describe a point from which pain radiates.

4 See Docs. 249 and 268.

5 German abbreviation: Eiserne Kreuze, i.e. Iron Crosses; this military decoration was usually awarded for achievements in battle.

6 Officers and units under the command of the SS and Police Leader in Lublin had been deployed during the deportations from the Warsaw ghetto carried out between July and Sept. 1942, and one unit of men from the SS training camp for non-German auxiliary personnel in Trawniki was also deployed to suppress the Warsaw Ghetto Uprising in April/May 1943.

7 See Doc. 263.

I would be very grateful to you, Reichsführer, for a decision in the affirmative, as I would be glad to see the hard work of my men rewarded.

*Heil Hitler!*[8]

## DOC. 276

## On 14 November 1943 the Home Army reports on the number of victims killed during Operation Harvest Festival in Lublin and Poniatowa[1]

Handwritten message, signed Elżbieta[2] (received on 14 November 1943), dated 14 November 1943[3]

Figures on the liquidations of Jews in Majdanek.

1) Letter from Dr H. Wieliczański:[4] on 3 November approximately 20,000 Jews were shot here.
2) Letter from Jan Zaprawa:[5] together with new arrivals from outside[6] – approximately 17,000.
3) Statement by a worker based on a report by a German employed at a depot in Majdanek – 19,000.
4) At present there are still approximately 200 Jewish inmates in Majdanek. After 3 November there were 300. One hundred have been deported. There are also several dozen Jewish women (message from an eyewitness, an intel.[7] worker, received on 13 November).
5) I am enclosing a report from Joanna from Mełgiew about the Jews being finished off in Trawniki.[8]
6) Approximately 20,000 were liquidated in Poniatowa.

8 For the final report, see Doc. 281.

1 APMM, XII-10, fol. 249. Published as a facsimile in Tomasz Kranz, *Die Vernichtung der Juden im Konzentrationslager Majdanek*, trans. Christhardt Henschel (Lublin: Państwowe Muzeum na Majdanku, 2007 [Polish edn, 2007]), fig. 38. This document has been translated from Polish.

2 One of Wanda Szupenko's code names.

3 There are several additions at the top of the original document: 'Sachara' (another of Wanda Szupenko's code names); 'Serial number: 24/B, 14.11.1943, to Bürger Lodzia': code name of Aleksander Bienicki (d. 1944), career officer; lieutenant colonel and head of intelligence in the Home Army's Lublin area command in 1943; arrested by the communist secret police in Oct. 1944 and murdered shortly thereafter.

4 Presumably Dr Izrael Henryk Halpern-Wieliczański (b. 1903), physician; lived in Warsaw; in 1943 deported to Lublin-Majdanek concentration camp, where he became head of the Home Army's intelligence service; later lived in Denmark; honoured by the State of Israel as Righteous Among the Nations in 1981.

5 Dr Jan Zaprawa-Ostromecki (b. 1915), psychologist and lawyer; active in the Home Army in District Lublin from 1941; imprisoned in Lublin-Majdanek concentration camp from 1942; escaped to Britain in 1945; lived in the USA from 1952.

6 Jewish prisoners from other forced labour camps in Lublin were also murdered at the camp.

7 This abbreviation reflects the Polish original; presumably: intelligence.

8 This report could not be found in the archive compiled by the Central Underground Welfare (OPUS) organization. On the OPUS archive, see Doc 258, fn. 3. Almost all of the 6,000 Jewish prisoners in Trawniki forced labour camp were shot on 3 Nov. 1943.

## DOC. 277

## On 15 November 1943 the Jewish National Committee provides information about the ongoing murder of Jews in the Lublin area[1]

Letter from the Jewish National Committee, signed Dr A[dolf Abraham] Berman (Borowski), Icchak Cukierman, and D. Kaftor,[2] Warsaw, to Dr Szwarcbard,[3] London, dated 15 November 1943[4]

Dear Doctor,

We are writing to you with blood shed once again by tens of thousands of Jewish martyrs. We in Poland are currently experiencing the final act of our terrible tragedy. In the face of their defeat, the National Socialist barbarians are murdering the remnants of the Jewish population.

They began in the Lublin area, which the front is quickly approaching. The Germans had set up a number of camps in the area, in which approximately 40,000 Jews, mainly from Warsaw and District Lublin, were vegetating. The largest of the camps were Trawniki (10,000 [people]) and Poniatowa (15,000). We were in constant contact with both camps, helped in every way that we could, and supplied them with money and weapons.

On Wednesday, 3 November, at 6 a.m., all the men in Trawniki were ordered to dig trenches, allegedly for protection against air raids. Two hours later they were encircled, machine guns were set up around them, and they were all shot without exception. Meanwhile fifty vehicles had driven into the camp, and all the women and children were loaded into them. They were taken to the execution site. There they were ordered to strip naked and were annihilated in the same way.[5] After this massacre 3,000 Italian Jews were brought to the camp; a similar fate awaited them.[6]

The same slaughter took place in the camps in Lublin on Friday. Several thousand Jews were murdered there. At almost the same time, a bloody 'selection' took place in Poniatowa. The majority of the camp inmates, including almost every woman and child, were sent to their deaths.

In the first days of November, the Germans set about liquidating the camps for Jews in another area close to the front: Eastern Małopolska.[7] In the camp on Janowska Street, the only camp in Lwów, which held about 7,000 people, 2,000 were 'selected' and brutally murdered at the execution site at the Sands.[8]

1 AAN, 1325/202/XV-2, fols. 378–382. This document has been translated from Polish.
2 Daniel Dawid Guzik's code name.
3 Correctly: Dr Ignacy Schwarzbart (1888–1961), lawyer and journalist; chairman of the Zionist student fraternity Haschachar in Cracow in 1911; officer and field judge in the Austro-Hungarian army during the First World War; editor-in-chief of the Cracow daily newspaper *Nowy Dziennik*, 1921–1925; activist with the General Zionists; member of the Sejm, 1938–1939; member of the National Council (the parliament in exile) of the Republic of Poland in London, 1940–1945; lived in New York from 1946; director of the Jewish World Congress's Organizational Department.
4 The original document includes a handwritten note at the top: 'sent to L[ondon] 29 Nov.[1943]'.
5 All the victims were probably shot in the camp grounds.
6 No further evidence of this is known.
7 Eastern Galicia.
8 Piaski (meaning 'sands') in the original; a reference to the sandhills of the Piaski ravine in the immediate vicinity of the camp, where prisoners were shot. The penultimate murder operation at Janowska camp was carried out on 26–27 Oct. 1943; the remaining Jewish prisoners were murdered on 19 Nov. 1943.

We are in no doubt that the inhabitants of the remaining Jewish population centres, the camps, and the few remaining ghettos will also be murdered over the course of the days and weeks to come.

At present we are desperately trying to save our most valuable social and cultural activists from the camps at the last moment. But these efforts are exceedingly difficult and costly. We are convinced that out of the once 3.5 million Jews in Poland, there will soon be only a small handful left alive, a few tens of thousands of people in hiding outside the camps and the ghettos, in the Aryan districts, or the forests, literally as cave dwellers.

As recently as last month we calculated that there were between 250,000 and 300,000 Jews in the whole country. In a few weeks' time, no more than 50,000 of them will be left.

In the final moments before their death, the remains of Polish Jewry appealed to the whole world for rescue.

We know that you are with us with all your hearts and souls, and that you have deep compassion for our unprecedented martyrdom. We also know that you are powerless. But at the very least, those people with influence who could have helped us should know what we think of them.

The blood of three million Polish Jews will be avenged, not only on the National Socialist beasts, but also on the indifferent and half-hearted individuals who thought words were sufficient and did nothing to save the people whom the Nazi murderers have condemned to total annihilation. Not one of us, the last Mohicans of an extinct community, will forgive or forget this.

Let our most likely last words from the abyss be heard by the whole world.

We want the Jewish people and the whole world to know that our youth bravely defended our people's lives and dignity. In recent months, following the heroic epic of the Warsaw ghetto, we have witnessed the wonderful, glorious struggle of the Jews of Białystok. It took place at the end of August. On 17 August in Białystok, the liquidation of the only large ghetto in the eastern territories began. Approximately 40,000 Jews lived there. During the first three days of the operation, seven transports were sent to Treblinka death camp. In addition, a passenger train full of children left Białystok: there were two Jewish nurses in each carriage. The general conviction is that before their death these children were to have their blood drawn for wounded German soldiers. On the fourth day of the operation, the armed struggle began. There was heavy fighting in several streets. The Germans used tanks and field artillery, as in Warsaw.

They brought in approximately 1,000 gendarmes, SS men, and numerous Ukrainian units. The Jews mainly used grenades and incendiary shells, as well as a few machine guns. They fought with an extraordinary determination that astonished the entire city and the district. Several hundred Germans and Ukrainians were killed or wounded in the fighting.[9]

To overcome the armed resistance, the Germans set fire to the ghetto from all sides, just as in Warsaw. The fierce fighting lasted eight days.

9 No further evidence of this could be found.

Even after this, the Jews' armed resistance did not cease, but continued for almost a month, until mid September.[10] Just like the defence of the Warsaw ghetto, the heroic struggle in Białystok will go down in history.

Over the past few months the Jews have carried out two armed operations of great symbolic value. They destroyed two execution sites: the death camps in Treblinka (near Małkinia) and in Sobibór (in the vicinity of Chełm Lubelski). In both camps the remainder of the condemned Jews organized themselves into groups of five and commenced the struggle at an agreed time: in a heroic revolt, they fell upon the Germans and the Ukrainian camp personnel, disarmed them, massacred the majority of the camp personnel, burned down the gas chambers and the 'live crematoria',[11] and, having completed their task, fled into the surrounding forests.[12]

News of these wonderful deeds met with a resounding response throughout the country. The Jews put up active resistance not only in Warsaw, Białystok, Treblinka, and Sobibór; acts of armed resistance also took place in a number of other cities: in Częstochowa, Będzin, Vilna, Tarnów, and other, smaller centres.

The final liquidation of the Tarnów ghetto occurred on 1, 2, and 3 September of this year. In this case, 150 Jews were loaded into each goods wagon, which was strewn with carbide and quicklime. The wagons were then sealed, sprayed with water, and sent for execution.[13]

All the children in the ghetto were herded into a single building. The children were told that they were going to a children's home. The building was hermetically sealed and blown up. Over the course of the liquidation, the Jews began to defend themselves. The Germans used grenades and quelled the fighters' resistance.

In all of these places, fighters from virtually every ideological direction participated in the combat, united as brothers: Hehalutz, Hashomer youth, and members of Poale Zion and the Bund. They were united in the fight that was about death, not life – the fight for the honour and dignity of the Jewish people. Through our Jewish Combat Organization we endeavoured to organize, support, and encourage this struggle to the best of our ability.

Apart from armed operations, our efforts are focused on relief operations for the Jews who are still in the camps or are hiding in Aryan districts. We are doing all that we can to rescue prominent individuals from the camps, and we have already rescued a certain number of activists and academics. We maintain contact with the camps via our emissaries, through whom we send financial aid, documents, etc. to the camps. We provide considerable financial aid to the Jews hiding in Aryan districts; we obtain

10 During the preparations for the uprising in Białystok in 1942–1943, approximately 200 young people had been organized into two large combat groups, which included members of all the major youth organizations. Most of them died within a few hours after the fighting began on 16 August 1943; 71 retreated into the insurgents' bunker, were captured, and were shot on 19 August 1943; their leaders – Mordechaj Tenenbaum (b. 1916) and Daniel Moszkowicz (b. 1905) – took their own lives. See PMJ 10, Introduction.

11 Polish original: 'żywe krematoria'. It is not clear what is meant.

12 See Docs. 259, 261, 264, 266, and 274.

13 Almost all of the remaining 11,000 Jews were rounded up on 2 Sept. 1943; 7,000 of them were deported to Auschwitz, 2,000 to Plaszow concentration camp, and a few to Szebnie labour camp. No further evidence has been found of transports being doused with water.

documents, attempt to find housing for them (the biggest problem), etc. We provide a relatively large number of social and cultural activists with everything they need to survive.

We conduct both our defensive operations and our charitable work under the indescribable conditions of an existence that is conspiratorial on two fronts, against the backdrop of the raging German reign of terror, which is also directed at Poles when 'raids' – manhunts – take place in the streets of Warsaw every day, when the streets of Warsaw are flooded with the blood of Polish 'hostages' shot en masse.

We are a handful of activists who have managed to stay alive and have resolved to provide welfare services and to care for the remnants of the tormented Jewish population, despite the new dangers and difficulties that are constantly accumulating. We are determined to fulfil this duty until the very end, despite all the difficulties and obstacles.

For almost a year we have been carrying out our activities as the Jewish National Committee (ŻKN), which includes the following parties and organizations: the General Zionists, Poale Zion-Right, Poale Zion-Left, Hehalutz, Hashomer Hazair, Dror, Akiba, and Gordonia. At the head of the ŻKN is an executive committee of three people, which directs all of our activities. The executive committee comprises Dr A. Berman (Borowski), Icchak Cukierman, and D. Kaftor. In addition, the ŻKN includes representatives of the above-mentioned organizations. Among the closest collaborators are Dr Emanuel Ringelblum, Cywja Lubetkin, the lawyer Gotesman[14] from Cracow, Józef Sack,[15] Lejzor Lewin,[16] Szloma Grajek, Szymon Rathauzer,[17] Pola Elster,[18] Hersz Berliński,[19] and Basia Temkin-Bermanowa.[20] Unfortunately, many of them cannot go out (on account of their non-Aryan appearance), and most of the work, which is extremely diverse, difficult, and complex, rests on a few people. An atmosphere of harmonious, friendly cooperation reigns in the ŻKN. The ŻKN is in contact with the 'Bund', with which it coordinates its activities. The ŻKN and the Bund together constitute the Jewish Coordinating Committee (ŻKK). Like the ŻKN, the ŻKK is not an independent political entity, nor does it constitute a political representation. The ŻKK's task is to coordinate defence and relief

14 Dr Szymon Gotesman (Gottesman), lawyer; member of the Jewish National Council's executive committee in Warsaw, 1943–1944.

15 Józef Sack (Sak) (1899–1965), journalist; leading Poale Zion representative in the Warsaw ghetto; member of the Central Committee of Polish Jews and editor of the periodical *Dos naje lebn* after the war; Sejm member, 1947–1952. Emigrated to Israel.

16 Lejzor Lewin (1891–1967), member of Poale Zion; Jewish Social Self-Help (JSS) activist; in charge of the soup kitchens in the Warsaw ghetto; escaped from the ghetto to the 'Aryan side' in spring 1943.

17 Correctly: Szymon (Symcha) Ratajzer.

18 Pola Elster (1911–1944), seamstress; member of Hashomer Hatzair and Poale Zion-Left; worked for the underground press in the Warsaw ghetto; simultaneously manager of a soup kitchen; killed during the Warsaw Uprising.

19 Hersz Berliński (1908–1944), social activist; Poale Zion-Left representative on the High Command of the Jewish Combat Organization (ŻOB); escaped to the forests near Wysków in spring 1943; killed during the Warsaw Uprising.

20 Barbara (Basia) Temkin-Bermanowa (1907–1956), librarian; member of Poale Zion-Left; married to Adolf Berman; active in the Jewish resistance on the 'Aryan side' from 1943; lived in Israel after the war. Her wartime diary is published in English translation as *City within a City*, trans. Jerzy Michałowicz (New York: IPBooks and YIVO Institute for Jewish Research, 2013 [Polish edn, 2000]).

operations, and it fulfils this current mandate as the responsible representative of the surviving Jewish population.

The bulk of the ŻKK's practical work rests on our shoulders. The ŻKN cooperates closely with the Council to Aid Jews at the government delegation. The ŻKN representative is the secretary of the Council to Aid Jews.[21] Additionally, the ŻKN is in constant contact with the government delegation's National Minorities Department[22] and with the Polish Armed Forces Command's Jewish affairs section.[23] The ŻKN has close, cordial relations with representatives of the Fighting Polish Underground.[24]

Apart from its defence and relief operations, the ŻKN is engaged in gathering chronicles, materials, and documents which in the future will document our martyrdom, which is unprecedented in human history. Among our ranks, the historian Dr Ringelblum directs this work, along with Hersz Wasser, the writer Rachel Auerbach, and others.

In all of our activity, we have until recently been faced with enormous financial constraints. Until June of this year we had no financial resources at all and were unable to expand our work.

Throughout the year, the organizations under the banner of the ŻKN received two relatively small sums thanks to the Bund's mediation: 3,000 dollars for 'Poale Zion-Right', and later 1,500 dollars for both Poale Zion parties (1,000 for the Left and 500 for the Right).

Only in June of this year did we receive the first larger sum: 10,000 dollars for the General Zionists and Poale Zion-Right. Then in July, August, and September we received three successive instalments of 10,000 dollars each as an advance payment for the 10,000 pounds you sent. Thanks to these funds we were able to expand our work considerably in all areas. But in view of the enormous need for comprehensive defence, relief, and rescue operations, these sums are no more than a drop in the ocean. Only recently, in November of this year, did we receive larger sums as advances on the funds we have already received from you. We should receive the following amounts in the immediate future: the final instalment, 10,000 dollars (out of the total 10,000 pounds), plus 20,000 dollars (5,000 pounds), and 36,000 dollars (9,000 pounds), which the government delegation recently received from you, a total of 66,000 dollars.

We have also been told that another 15,000 pounds will arrive from you. On behalf of all our organizations, we wish to extend our sincere thanks for these funds. They will enable us to significantly expand our activities in the area of relief and rescue operations.

Unfortunately this important help came too late for many of our brothers. Nevertheless, we do hope that thanks to these funds we will be able to save many valuable individuals from extermination and to provide significant aid to support thousands of Jews in their difficult and dangerous lives. Further substantial financial aid from your side is indispensable for this purpose.

21 Adolf Abraham Berman.

22 This department was established in Oct. 1942 and was headed by Stanisław Piotrowski (1901–1972) until mid 1943; after it was disbanded, a Nationalities Council (Rada Narodowościowa) was established, chaired by Adam Bień.

23 A reference to the Home Army; Henryk Woliński headed this section.

24 Capitalized in the original: presumably a reference to the Polish resistance generally.

Consider that, under the present conditions, it costs 50,000 złoty to rescue a single person from the camp, and accommodating one person in the Aryan district costs 5,000–10,000 złoty.

Your telegrams and letters provide us all with rare moments of joy in our difficult lives. We do not feel alone. We received your letters sent on 21 July (Dr Swarzbard's letters to Warsaw and Cracow, Berel's[25] letter, and the letter from the Committee for the Rescue of Jews in Occupied Europe[26]), and noted their contents with satisfaction. We have not received the letter from Tabenkin[27] and Jaare.[28]

We also received your telegrams of 27 September and 4 October of this year. Let us know the concrete aims and prospects of your Stockholm children's operation, and whether it involves an exchange.[29] There are only a small handful of Jewish children left alive; [we ask you to] save them from certain death at the last moment.

This week we received alarming news from the camp for foreigners in Bergen,[30] near Hanover. There were about 4,000 Jews from Poland in this camp, including prominent figures such as the novelist J. Perle,[31] the social activist Antoni Buxbaum,[32] and many others.

The camp was reportedly under the protection of the International Red Cross. Apparently, it was recently dissolved,[33] just like the camps in the Lublin area. Arrange immediate intervention by the Red Cross and the Swiss embassy in Berlin!

South American citizens are held in this camp. Disturbing news is also reaching us from Vittel camp (in Alsace). Monitor both camps and tell us what has happened there.[34]

25 Probably Berl Locker (1887–1972), lawyer and journalist; Poale Zion politician; board member of the Zionist Executive and the Jewish Agency in London, 1931–1936; trade union official in Palestine, 1936–1938; thereafter representative of the Jewish Agency in London; chairman of the Jewish Agency in Jerusalem, 1948–1956; subsequently elected to the Knesset.

26 This is a reference to the Jewish Agency's Joint Rescue Committee, which operated from Jerusalem between 1943 and 1944.

27 Yitzhak (Isaac) Tabenkin (1887–1971), labour leader; lived in Palestine from 1911; co-founded the Histadrut (General Federation of Labour in Israel) trade union and the social-democratic Mapai (Workers' Party of the Land of Israel); elected to the Knesset.

28 Probably Meir Yaari (1897–1987), agronomist; officer in the Austro-Hungarian army, 1917–1918; lived in Palestine from 1920; co-founded the communist Mapam (United Workers' Party) in 1948; elected to the Knesset.

29 This presumably refers to efforts made by the vice chairman of the Swedish Red Cross, Folke Bernadotte (1895–1948), who negotiated prisoner exchanges with the German authorities on several occasions in autumn 1943 and autumn 1944.

30 Bergen-Belsen concentration camp, established in 1943, was initially used to house Jewish prisoners holding passports of neutral countries whom the Nazis hoped to exchange for Germans held abroad.

31 Jehoszua Perle (1888–1944), Yiddish-language writer; arrested by the Germans in 1943; held at Hotel Polski (see Doc. 248); imprisoned in Bergen-Belsen camp from summer 1943; deported in Oct. 1943 to Auschwitz, where he perished in spring 1944.

32 Correctly: Antoni (also Natan) Buksbaum (1890–1943), journalist and Poale Zion-Left activist; city councillor in Warsaw, 1928–1932; imprisoned from 1941 until 1942 or 1943 in Janowska camp in Lwów, from where he escaped; deported to Bergen-Belsen camp in mid 1943, and to Auschwitz in Oct. 1943.

33 In Oct. 1943 many of the Jews who had been taken from Hotel Polski to Bergen-Belsen in the summer were deported via Bergau camp, near Dresden, to Auschwitz, where they were murdered. Bergen-Belsen concentration camp was in fact in operation until April 1945.

We are enclosing with this letter a series of messages to individual organizations, responses to your questionnaires, reports on ŻOB activities, a list of the fallen defenders of the Warsaw ghetto,[35] and a brief financial report.

Convey our sincere thanks and greetings to the agency, the executive,[36] the Committee for the Rescue of the Jews, and the individual fraternal organizations of all orientations. Chaim and Eljasz[37] from Cracow send you warm greetings; they are in Płaszów camp, near Cracow. We are urging them to escape. They do not want to escape because the Germans practise collective punishment in the camps and shoot fifty people for every escapee.

Nearly 15,000 Jews are in camps and detention centres in the Cracow municipal area. Their fate is sealed.

The lawyer Gotesman from Cracow is in Warsaw and cooperating with us. He sends his warm greetings to you and to all Zionists.

Kaftor sends his greetings to you all and to the colleagues from the JDC. He wonders why they are not communicating.

We send our warmest greetings to Berl Locker and to all the activists cooperating with you.

The Jewish Combat Organization in Poland sends combat greetings to the Jews fighting against National Socialism and fascism and for freedom on all fronts around the world.

*Last-minute special report*

The ŻKN delegates whom we sent to the Lublin area due to alarming news about the camps have come back with terrible reports. The inmates of the two largest camps in Trawniki (10,000 [people]) and Poniatowa (15,000) have all been murdered, without exception.

The report on Trawniki corresponds to the description in our letter to Dr Szwarcbard. The massacre in Trawniki took place on Wednesday, 3 November. It started at 6 a.m. and by 4 p.m. not one of the 10,000 camp prisoners was still alive. The massacre in Lublin took place on Friday, 5 November. Jews from all the camps in the Lublin area were taken to the extermination camp in Majdanek, where they were shot. On Monday, 5 November, the murder operation in Poniatowa began.[38]

Early in the morning a large number of SS, SD, and gendarmerie cars arrived, and the entire camp was surrounded by a dense cordon of guards. When the Jews realized that the time of their extermination had come, the local branch of the Jewish Combat Organization set fire to all the depots and workshops where large quantities of clothing intended for the Wehrmacht were stored. The Jews tried to resist. A terrible massacre began, which lasted three days. On Wednesday, 10 November, it was all over – 15,000 people had been

34 A total of 300 Jews from Poland who had been interned in Vittel were deported in April 1944 to Auschwitz, where they were murdered.

35 The list of defenders of the Warsaw ghetto is not printed here.

36 These are references to the Jewish Agency and the Zionist Executive, the executive committee of the World Zionist Organization.

37 Probably Dr Chaim Hilfstein and Dr Eliasz (Elijahu) Tisch.

38 The murder operation at Poniatowa was carried out on Thursday, 4 Nov. 1943.

murdered. The corpses were burned on the spot. In the process, many people were burned alive. People's screams and groans and the non-stop gunfire could be heard throughout the entire area. The smell of the burned bodies hung in the air across the area for an entire week.

Both in Trawniki and in Poniatowa, the Jews tried to fight back with weapons. The Germans, aware that there were units of the Jewish Combat Organization in both camps, employed a new tactic. They deployed large numbers of gendarmerie and SS in the camps. Both in Trawniki and in Poniatowa, they simply flooded the whole site with them. Several thousand Germans carried out the massacre. Resistance was practically impossible.

In Poniatowa the Germans used encircling tactics several times: they herded the Jews into ever-narrower areas and slaughtered them non-stop.

Significantly, the Germans no longer employed Ukrainians in these operations. In Trawniki the training camp for Ukrainians was surrounded by SS men during the operation. In Poniatowa, too, the Ukrainian camp personnel were excluded from the operation. The Germans did not trust their vassals, the Ukrainians, to carry out the murderous work with the required precision.[39]

The massacre in the camps in the Lublin area signifies the end of Warsaw's Jewish population. There were tens of thousands of Jews in the camps who had been taken from Warsaw during the last liquidation operation in April of this year.

The murdered victims include a significant section of Warsaw's intellectuals, a comparatively large number of political activists of all persuasions, and especially many organized labourers and labour leaders (primarily skilled workers and craftsmen had been sent to these camps). We will mention by name those who, in both camps, constantly rendered self-sacrificing service to the community and were leaders of the local clandestine [Jewish] Social Self-Help and ŻOB sections.

In Poniatowa: Mełach Fajnkind, the commandant of the local ŻOB section (an activist for Poale Zion-Left), Etkin (Bund), Szmidt (Poale Zion-Right), Hofman (Bund), Przedecz (a former city councillor in Warsaw, Poale Zion-Left), Dr Dobrin (General Zionists), Tencer (a former city councillor in Kalisz, Poale Zion-Left).

In Trawniki: Dr Włodzimierz Szyfrys, the commandant of the local ŻOB section (not affiliated with any party), the lawyer Dawid Szulman (revisionist),[40] Malinowski (Bund, a former trade union official in Łódź), the lawyer Abraham Witelson (Zionist).[41]

In the numerous hermetically sealed camps in Lublin, the following were among those who were imprisoned and have now lost their lives: Dr Ignacy Schipper; Aleksander (Zysze) Frydman (a leading representative of Agudas [Yisroel] and an important social activist);[42] Dr Tulo Nussenblatt (a historian of the Zionist movement and a biog-

39 The non-German auxiliary personnel from the SS training camp in Trawniki, who guarded the nearby Trawniki forced labour camp and the camp in Poniatowa, were left in the barracks during the massacres.

40 Dawid Szulman, lawyer; one of the leaders of the Jewish Military Union (ŻZW).

41 Abraham Witelson, member of the Order Service in the Warsaw ghetto; worked in the Wilfried Hoffmann workshop at 51a Nowolipki Street.

42 Aleksander Frydman (1897–1943), journalist and rabbi; in the Warsaw ghetto a member of the clandestine advisory board of the American Jewish Joint Distribution Committee (JDC) and chairman of the Jewish Council's Religious Affairs Council.

rapher of Theodor Herzl);[43] Dr Edmund Stein (a prominent Jewish studies scholar);[44] A. Samberg (actor);[45] Remba (Zionist activist);[46] the wife of I. Giterman, the director of the 'Joint' [JDC] who was murdered in the January operation;[47] I. Kirman (poet);[48] Luzer Stolar-Rychter (an activist for Poale Zion-Left);[49] and many other social activists, intellectuals, and artists.

The liquidation of the camps in the Lublin area marks the beginning of massacres in all the remaining camps for Jews in Poland: the beginning of Polish Jewry's irrevocable end.

P.S. We will send the responses to the survey and the reports on the ŻOB's activities and on the course of the armed combat in the Warsaw ghetto with the next post.[50]

## DOC. 278

## Leon Feiner reports on the Bund's activities and the situation of the Jews in Poland from July to mid November 1943[1]

Report from the Central Directorate of the Movement of the Jewish Working Masses in Poland (CKRŻMP), signed Berezowski,[2] to the Bund's representation in London, for the attention of Dr Emanuel Szerer,[3] sometime after 15 November 1943[4]

*Report*

In June of this year I was told I had the opportunity to send you a brief report. I seized this opportunity and wrote a report, following up on my memorandum of 31 August 1942, which I sent to you last year.[5] The report covered the period from 1 September

43 Naftali Tulo Nussenblatt (Nussenblath) (1895–1943) was the author of *Zeitgenossen über Herzl* (Brno: Jüdischer Buch und Kunstverlag, 1929) and the editor of the *Theodor-Herzl-Jahrbuch* (Vienna: Dr Heinrich Glanz Verlag, 1937).

44 Dr Edmund Stein (1893–1943), director of a clandestine teacher training college in the Warsaw ghetto; Jewish Council employee.

45 Ajzyk Samberg (1889–1943); in the Warsaw ghetto worked for the Jewish Central Association for the Care of Orphans (CENTOS) and at the soup kitchen for artists.

46 Nachum Remba (1910–1943), Jewish Community employee; in the Warsaw ghetto worked for the Organization for Yiddish Culture (IKOR) and contributed to the newspaper *Gazeta Żydowska*.

47 Ester Giterman, née Sapożnikowa (b. 1895), married to Icchak (Isaak) Giterman (1889–1943), director of the JDC in Poland; member of the ŻOB's Civilian Committee.

48 Josef Kirman (1896–1943), factory worker; active in the provision of welfare for writers from 1940; contributed to the underground archive of the Warsaw ghetto.

49 Luzer Stolar Rychter (Eliezer Stoler-Richter), head of a construction workers' trade union.

50 What was presumably the next transmission was compiled between 15 and 20 May 1944; its contents included a report on the establishment of the ŻOB and eyewitness accounts of the fighting in the Warsaw ghetto in April and May 1943 by Ratajzer, Borzykowski, and Grajek.

1 AAN, 1325/202/XV-2, fols. 99–110. This document has been translated from Polish.

2 Leon Feiner's code name.

3 Dr Emanuel Scherer (1901–1977), lawyer and trade unionist; practised law and edited Bund periodicals in the 1930s; city councillor in Warsaw and member of the Bund's Central Committee from 1938; in the USA in 1941; member of the Polish National Council in Exile from 1943.

4 The original document contains a handwritten note at the top: 'sent to L[ondon] on 29 Nov. [1943]'.

5 See Doc. 126.

1942 to the end of June 1943. Unfortunately, it was not possible to forward it to you due to technical difficulties.[6] But I have now had the opportunity to write a general report with no restrictions in terms of length. Due to the lack of time and other very urgent matters, I shall limit myself to writing an activity report for the period covering 1 July to 15 November of this year. I enclose the aforementioned previous report, i.e. for the period from 1 September 1942 to the end of June 1943, and have marked it with the letter A. I have marked the present report with the letter B.

*B) Report for the period from 1 July 1943 to 15 November 1943*
When reporting on our work and our efforts, it is essential to mention the background and conditions which give rise to our work. The basic underlying factor determining virtually all our activity is National Socialism's persistent aim to eradicate all that is left of the Jewish population.

I. *The liquidation of the Jews continues*
The mass liquidations during the period covered by the last report, of which you are already aware, have resulted in the murder of the vast majority of the Jewish community. During the period covered by this report, extermination measures of varying intensity and following different procedures have taken place at the various assembly points for Jews. The insidious – and in any case bestial and barbaric – methods applied here were known from previous liquidation operations.

The ghettos in the territory of the GG, the Ostland, and the Reich, which had already been decimated in earlier operations against the population, were completely liquidated during this period (with what is probably the sole exception of Łódź, where there is still a ghetto with approximately 30,000 Jews from Łódź and 100,000 from abroad[7]). The liquidation took place according to the familiar pattern: some people were shot on the spot, while others were taken to the gas chambers in Treblinka, Bełżec, Sobibór, Oświęcim, and other death factories (then burned in the crematoria); primarily men in the prime of their lives were taken to existing labour camps for Jews or to new camps that are being built. Finally, the smallest percentage were left behind in the deserted and ruined ghettos to perform clean-up work and to collect and sort the Jews' belongings so that the Germans could seize them.

As a result of these liquidation operations, smaller groups of people and a few 'lucky' individuals escape[8] into the forests or to neighbouring cities, which at this point in time have been almost completely 'cleansed' of the Jewish element. During the period in question, the ghettos were liquidated in Będzin (30,000), Częstochowa, Tarnów, Rzeszów, Przemyśl, Mielec, Radom, Piotrków (a few thousand Jews in each), Białystok (30,000), Vilna (15,000), and in other places in Eastern Małopolska,[9] such as Stryj, Sambor, Kołomyja, Buczacz, Drohobycz, Borysław, and others (a few thousand Jews in each case, or 10,000–20,000 at most).

6 The report was not forwarded to the Polish government in exile until 29 Nov. 1943: see Doc. 250.
7 The number of foreign Jews given here is too high.
8 Change in tense as in the original.
9 Eastern Galicia.

During the liquidation of the ghettos, there was also an increased effort to track down, capture, and execute the Jews who had hidden in the forests or in Aryan districts before the catastrophe.

In addition, the Germans searched out groups that were still hiding in the catacombs of the burned-out Warsaw ghetto, today referred to as bunkers, and they liquidated these groups on the spot.

During the period covered by this report, Jews continued to be deported to Poland from abroad – from countries in Southern and Western Europe, as well as from the vassal states of Bulgaria, Romania, Greece, Yugoslavia, and, more recently, Italy. Some of them were taken to the gas chambers, and some to the labour camps for Jews.

A new period began just one week ago – surely in connection with German defeats and the Red Army's westward advance: *the dissolution of the camps.*

On 3 November of this year, the germans[10] liquidated the camp in Trawniki, which contained approximately 10,000 Jews, most of them from the Warsaw ghetto, who were brought from there during the armed struggle. The [liquidation] procedure was extremely insidious: the men were first led out of the camp under the pretext that they were to dig protective trenches. Then they had to strip naked and were shot dead with machine guns. After that the women and children were led out of the camp, and the German executioners handled them the same way. A similar procedure took place on 5 November of this year, partially in Poniatowa camp[11] (approximately 15,000 Jews from the Warsaw ghetto had been deported there during the fighting), the camps in Lublin,[12] and partially in Janowska camp near Lwów, where approximately 2,000 Jews were liquidated.

II. *The Jewish population's current situation and distribution*

Jews are thus currently living in four fundamentally different types of settings: in camps, in the forests, in Aryan districts, and in camps for foreigners.

1) *In labour camps*: located either within the former ghettos (the smallest number) or outside the cities (most common). In the vicinity or further away, there are enterprises which employ Jews and produce goods for the Germans. They have a strict regime: hunger, torture, shootings for the smallest offences and for escaping, for which a few dozen people are held collectively responsible. In addition, Jews are employed outside the camp grounds at so-called 'deployment sites', where they are quartered in barracks or to which they walk from the camps. At these sites outside the camps they work either alone or alongside Polish labourers. There are a few dozen such camps in GG territory, with varying numbers of inmates: two near Cracow (in Płaszów and in the Jewish cemetery on Jerozolimskie Street), which contain 10,000–20,000 Jews; Janowska camp in Lwów (with approximately 2,000 Jews left after the last liquidation); in Piotrków (approximately 2,000 [Jews]); in Częstochowa (approximately 2,000); in Trawniki (approximately 10,000), which has only just been dissolved; in Poniatowa (approximately 15,000), which has just been partially dissolved; in Bochnia (a few hundred); in Tarnów (approximately 200), some of whom have

10 This term is written in lower case in the original as an expression of contempt.

11 The massacre at Poniatowa took place on 4 Nov. 1943.

12 On the murders in Lublin-Majdanek camp, see Doc. 276 and Nikolaus Wachsmann, *KL: A History of the Nazi Concentration Camps* (New York: Farrar, Straus & Giroux, 2016), pp. 330–332.

been deported to Płaszów camp; in Rzeszów (a few hundred); in Szebnie, near Jasło (a few thousand); in Pustków, near Dębica (a few thousand); in Brody (approximately 10,000); in Złoczów (a few thousand); in Borysław (approximately 1,200); plus the camps in Budzyń (a few thousand), Bliżyn, and Kielce (2,000); in Radom, where the ghetto was recently converted into a camp (approximately 2,000); in Skarżysko-Kamienna; in Starachowice; in Annopol; in Św. Krzyż (1,000); and in other places.

During the recent liquidation of the ghetto in Białystok,[13] a small proportion [of the Jews] were sent to Trawniki. During the liquidation of the Vilna ghetto, many Jews were executed on the spot, while others were transported to the camp in Woronów,[14] and others to the area around Kaunas. Ultimately only the ghetto in Łódź was left – a large factory producing goods for the Germans.

2) *In the forests*: Several groups that were saved from the pogroms in the ghettos fled – armed or unarmed – by various means into the forests, where they are eking out an existence. Out of necessity, simply to survive, the vast majority join groups of bandits[15] that rob the surrounding areas of whatever they need to live. A fraction of them have joined the partisan groups that are active in the areas in question. The elemental force and circumstances of the German campaign of terror dictate all of this. These people lead a nomadic life, hounded from one place to another, persecuted and exterminated.
3) *In the Aryan districts*: The third group live as Aryans scattered in the Aryan districts of various larger cities. Some of them are hiding in apartments and houses, while others go to work (especially women, who work as housekeepers). Some are also engaged in clandestine work for underground organizations. They frequently live in great poverty, which is alleviated by the activities of the Council to Aid Jews and other Jewish organizations, i.e. the Bund and the ŻKN. This miserable existence is interrupted from time to time, mostly due to denunciations, or occasionally by blackmail or Gestapo raids and liquidation.
4) *In camps for foreigners*: the fourth and final group is held in camps for foreigners in Vittel (Alsace), Salzburg,[16] and Bergen,[17] near Hanover. This group consists of between 10,000 and 20,000 people. These Jews have received citizenship of Paraguay and of other countries.[18] According to our information, living conditions in these camps vary. Conditions in one camp – Vittel, for example – are reportedly good, but in another – Bergen, for example – they are allegedly very difficult. Rumours have recently reached us that this camp in Bergen is to be dissolved.[19] However, this news has not been confirmed.

The survivors are distributed among the above-mentioned centres in various proportions. Due to the high fluctuation in the most recent period, it is difficult to determine the exact numbers across these various settings. In any case, the highest per-

13 The Białystok ghetto was liquidated during the second half of August 1943.
14 A small town in the Grodno region in Byelorussia.
15 Polish original: 'dzikie grupy', 'wild groups'.
16 Nothing more is known about a camp with this name.
17 This is a reference to Bergen-Belsen concentration camp.
18 In fact, most of these people were not foreign citizens, but the promise of citizenship had been held out to them with pledges issued by the consulates of Latin American countries in Switzerland.
19 Bergen-Belsen concentration camp was in fact not liquidated; it was liberated by British troops in April 1945.

centage of Jews is probably in the camps, and the next largest percentage in the Aryan districts. A much smaller percentage is in the camps for foreigners, and the groups in the woods make up the smallest proportion.

III. *Our tasks:*
The unprecedented situation and extraordinary circumstances created by the occupiers' acts of terror against the Jewish community – or rather, what is left of it – have given rise to equally unprecedented requirements and tasks. We are faced with a huge plethora of tasks that even organizations in larger and stronger nations could not manage. These are nations that not only have governmental organizations, complex administrative bodies, and considerably greater material, physical, and spiritual resources than we have, but – and this is the most important thing – are not compelled to operate under the immensely difficult conditions with which we are forced to contend. In any case, it is true that in those nations bound by the iron band of the occupation, especially Poland, the lifeblood of the best among them is shed day after day, on a mass scale and incessantly.

Nation after nation, one more powerful than the next, has fallen under the iron fist of the Huns of our times, yet they each had a government administration and, above all, an army that had been trained for decades, even centuries. And not one of them could halt this raging tide, which was weaker than the flood that has overwhelmed us. How should we, who are so much weaker than the others, with no state instruments of power, unprepared, and with few opportunities, a lost minority of whom only a few remain – how should we, under such extraordinary circumstances, have the strength to cope with the plethora of urgent tasks and requirements that arise from our tragic situation, as briefly outlined here? And how can we continuously devote ourselves to work and to a struggle that ultimate prove to be absolutely hopeless, a Sisyphean task, because the murder programme is carried out with steely consistency until the very last member of the community as a whole is murdered! Even in semi-normal times, such enormous tasks would require equally enormous amounts of human resources, which no longer exist here because unfortunately almost everyone has perished. Of the many activists who supported us in various ways before the war, and to a certain extent even during the first years of the occupation, only a small fraction remain, and they are completely absorbed in the Bund's work and the underground struggle.

And yet we are not discouraged or deterred by anything: neither by the plethora of diverse, completely new, extraordinarily difficult tasks, nor by the hopelessness of our efforts, nor by the dangers lurking at every turn; nor finally by the fact that there are so few of us undertaking this work, or that death snatches one or another from our ranks from time to time.

Just like a physician who treats a terminally ill patient until the very end, like the captain of a sinking ship who does everything he can to save those who are drowning and steadfastly shoulders the responsibilities his position entails – so we too continue to work tirelessly. We do so because we are animated by the will to fulfil our duty, with which we may yet salvage something for the future from this terrible deluge – a duty dictated by the stubborn will to fight the enemy, a duty that fittingly crowns our glorious socialist past, steeped in a rich tradition of combat.

At present our work is focused on keeping alive those who are still left – and this of course not only from a purely organizational perspective, but in a general sense, so that at least a remnant will remain for the future, and so that there will be witnesses to this crime. Furthermore, alongside other adversaries, we continue to fight the perpetrators of these crimes and to carry out organizational and ideological work.

Our current tasks therefore include:

1) exhaustive material and moral assistance,

2) active resistance activities against the common enemy,

3) organizational and ideological work, with everything that these tasks entail.

It is not possible to list or to describe precisely everything that pertains to the above-mentioned areas of responsibility. These involve housing issues, the distribution of material aid, certification (of documents, reports, etc.), the complicated consequences of extortion, preparations for active struggle, arrests, parcels, clothing, medication, various contacts locally and in the camps, letters, correspondence, trips, meetings, and so on – all of this takes a toll on us; it costs us time, nerves, and our health.

IV. *The Coordinating Committee and the ŻOB*

As you already know, after the liquidation operations in July of last year, a committee was set up in the territory of the Warsaw ghetto, as a centre of active resistance, to coordinate our organization's efforts with the similar activities undertaken by the ŻKN. This work has yielded positive results (the armed struggles in January and in April and May 1943). Following the complete liquidation of the Warsaw ghetto, this coordination, which already existed de facto in the Aryan sphere, was made official as of July. The committee's activities and scope of action were expanded, i.e. to include material aid, and extended to the whole of Poland. It was not and is not a political entity, even less a political-social representation of the Jewish community, but merely a body that coordinates the efforts of both sides in their common spheres of activity and areas of combat, thereby keeping in mind their objectives and priorities. Neither side intended to give this body a political orientation. As paragraph 2 of the Coordinating Committee's charter states: 'Political matters, which each coordinating party handles independently, according to its own political perspective, are not part of the coordination.'

On the basis of these joint resolutions, we have carried out coordinated work here in Warsaw and in the provinces – in the field of self-help in the camps and in preparations for armed resistance. As far as the former is concerned, as the CC [Coordinating Committee] we have come to the aid of various people in the Warsaw municipality who were not members of our organization or of the ŻKN, and who did not receive adequate support from the Council to Aid Jews either, because there was no money available. In addition, in our role as the CC, we have also spent considerable sums on rescuing people after they were arrested – not only Jews, but also non-Jews who are active in the area of self-help activities on the Council's behalf.

As far as the provinces are concerned, as the CC we sent fairly large sums of up to several hundred thousand złoty to various camps and similar facilities. Incidentally, you will find the financial details below.

All that remains is to point out at this juncture that the CC has neither its own funds nor its own treasurer. The corresponding payments are made on a case-by-case basis, according to a joint resolution. Some of our comrades are also active in performing the tasks that fall within the CC's area of responsibility (carrying out various often difficult and dangerous assignments). In preparation for the armed resistance, two representatives of the CC, more specifically the ŻOB, contacted an official military representative of the Polish underground. Furthermore, a number of the CC's typical activities will be discussed in the relevant parts of the sections that follow.

V. *The armed struggle*

A. During the period covered by this report – surely as a result of a series of *armed resistance operations* which triggered the fighting in the Warsaw ghetto and as a result of the general atmosphere this struggle has generated in the country – a series of armed *operations undertaken by Jews occurred in various locations.* These operations are part of a whole chain of activities that began with and are comparable to the heroic struggle in Warsaw.

1. First and foremost *Białystok*, one of the many Jewish centres of productive labour which remained under the Bund's strong influence before the war, actively resisted the German executioners when they began liquidating the ghetto there in mid August of this year. The armed resistance lasted about a month and was a significant act of determination and heroism. The Germans, who employed similar methods and means as in Warsaw, suffered considerable losses.[20] The Białystok ghetto was liquidated, many of the 30,000 inhabitants perished there, and a small proportion were transported to Trawniki.
2. In addition, Treblinka, a gas-chamber camp in which the Nazis have executed hundreds of thousands of Jews, was destroyed in early August of this year by the Jews who were assigned to work there. The Jews revolted and overpowered the 30-strong German-Ukrainian camp guard force, took their weapons, burned down the buildings at the execution site, destroyed the barbed wire fence, and organized the escape of approximately 2,000 Jews into the surrounding forests.[21]
3. Other considerably smaller resistance operations took place during the period covered by this report in *Tarnów*, *Będzin*, *Częstochowa*, and *Borysław*, in connection with the dissolutions of the ghettos in these cities.
4. A similarly defiant and heroic act of resistance as that in Treblinka took place in October of this year in *Sobibór*, another place where hundreds of thousands of Jews have been executed. Here, too, a considerable number of Jews managed to escape.[22]
5. Moreover, as early as February of this year, the Jews in the *Łódź* ghetto carried out an unarmed but important act of resistance. They staged a *general strike* when the Germans commenced mass executions, which were then called off as a result of this struggle.[23]
6. Last but not least, armed resistance operations were organized in a few other Jewish population centres, especially in *Poniatowa* and *Trawniki*, with assistance from the CC and the ŻOB, which supplied money, weapons, and instructions via

20 The SS and the police quashed the armed resistance within a short period of time.

21 According to eyewitness estimates, there were in fact around 850 Jews in the camp on that day. Approximately 400 of them managed to escape from the camp, but many of the escapees were killed almost immediately afterwards.

22 On the uprising at Sobibor, see Introduction, pp. 57–58.

23 There were several strikes at individual factories in the Lodz ghetto to support demands for better food provision, but these did not succeed in influencing the actions of the occupation authorities.

intermediaries. Inside the camps, coordinating committees similar to ours directed the preparations for the resistance as well as the self-help activities; our comrades, who constituted the largest groups or percentages in these camps, were very active and played a leading role.

B. *The partisan movement.* As I mentioned above in connection with the liquidations in the ghettos, and then their dissolution, and the cruel regime in the camps for Jews, groups of Jews (especially the more active groups and those with a so-called unfavourable appearance[24]) escape from the execution sites and into the forests from time to time. They form 'requisitioning' groups[25] or (much more rarely) join the partisan groups already active there. The intention was to integrate these Jewish groups into the existing organizational structures. To this end, talks took place between the CC, specifically a ŻOB delegation, and the responsible military representative of the Polish underground, who initially criticized this solution to the issue as well as the idea of arming the camps for Jews in general. However, this position was later changed to the affirmative, which should logically lead to a similar development with regard to the partisan movement. For if arming the camps leads to their destruction and to Jews making their way into the forests, then this must therefore mean that those who have fled into the forests with weapons should be allowed to continue their existence as partisans.

C. *The Uprising Division in Warsaw.* This has already been formally organized; it includes several dozen Jews under the leadership of a Polish army officer. As the name suggests, once this division has been de facto mobilized, it will play an active role in the general uprising against the occupiers as an integral part of the other units. This is also the result of talks between a CC and ŻOB delegation and the relevant official underground circles concerning military issues.

VI. *The provinces*

One of our biggest concerns and efforts during the period covered by this report was to establish and maintain contacts with the provinces, or rather with the camps for Jews scattered throughout Poland. Of course this concern also mainly weighed on the CC. With the help of existing contacts, or contacts that the CC had established via its own delegates or thanks to the mediation of the Council [to Aid Jews] (particularly with the help of the comrades from the WRN and the [Polish] Democracy Party), letters with instructions and words of encouragement were sent to the camps, along with money and weapons. Bodies similar to our CC, with a similar character and scope, were set up everywhere. We sought and maintained constant contact primarily with Cracow, Poniatowa, Trawniki, Piotrków, Lwów, Ostrowiec, Radom, Kielce, Częstochowa, Budzyń, and a series of smaller localities such as Skarżysko-Kamienna, Starachowice, Bliżyn, and others. Sometimes the camps themselves set up contacts with neighbouring ones, pass on the news they have received from us, and also share the funds we send. Furthermore, we managed to establish contact with Białystok (Ostland)[26] immediately after the armed operation in the ghetto there. The letters that arrived from these centres of suffering, humiliation, and

24 In other words, a 'non-Aryan' appearance, which made it more difficult to go underground on the 'Aryan side'.

25 The Jewish escapees attempted to obtain what they needed to survive from farmers.

death are moving. For instance, we were deeply moved by a letter we received in response to our letter to the comrades in Białystok: 'Dream or reality – a call for help from the comrades in Warsaw …', wrote Comrade Kosower, deeply shocked and in tears, just after he had managed to save himself from the German-Jewish war in Białystok. He is now staying with a Polish comrade, who took him in along with another of our comrades. The letters from our comrades in Płaszów camp, near Cracow, are similar; they were in contact with one of our comrades in Tarnów and gave them part of the financial assistance we had sent. From Trawniki (already dissolved) we again received a message from our comrades, saying that even there, naturally in a very unusual manner, they had celebrated the forty-sixth anniversary of our party's foundation. In short: we are trying to get through everywhere, in order to provide moral and material aid. As you have already observed, a letter that reaches someone who lives far away or funds are often an incentive and an impetus to continue and to persevere in the struggle. For example, we sent 20,000 złoty to our comrades in the camp in Piotrków. If only you could read the letter from there! The words moved us to tears. The comrade writes that it was the most wonderful moment of his life. Under the most terrible conditions, he contacted the surviving political comrades, sought out other work sites, and brought them money and the news he had received from us. He even miraculously sent money to Skarżysko and Bliżyn, where there were comrades from his town, from Piotrków, whose names he gave to us so that we now have addresses in Skarżysko and Bliżyn as well. A plan for how to get people out of the camps was formulated there and is still being developed. It is the same in Częstochowa. Kuśnierz,[27] Brenner,[28] and others are there. We may receive news from them about comrades in other towns who are collaborating with them. In this way we are expanding our contacts once again, and with them our work also increases. Full of gratitude and a sense of duty, we face the necessity of satisfying ever-growing needs. Thus we sent hundreds of thousands of złoty to the camps; we send and will continue to send hundreds of thousands more. Incidentally, further details about this work can be found in the financial section of this report. But the most important thing is that the entire cause is not entirely hopeless, that at least a few small groups escape from the hell of the camps and are rescued for the future. Nevertheless, these are such extraordinarily difficult tasks that they break one's heart, especially now that the phase of liquidating the camps has begun.

VII. *The Council to Aid Jews*

The work of our CC and that of the Council are becoming increasingly integrated in terms of joint activity in the field of material assistance. For example, the certification[29] which the Council arranges for all Jews free of charge is extremely valuable and useful. This also applies to aid for the camps, which we are able to reach via the Council. On

26 The city of Białystok was the main urban centre in Bezirk Bialystok, which was annexed to East Prussia and was not located in the Reich Commissariat Ostland.

27 Presumably Motek Mordechaj Kusznir.

28 Correctly: Liber Brener (b. 1901), teacher and Bund activist; head of the Society for the Protection of the Health of the Jewish Population in Poland (TOZ) in Częstochowa, 1934–1939; then active in the underground movement and the resistance against the German occupation; emigrated to Israel in the late 1960s; editor of *Resistance and Death in the Czenstochower Ghetto*, trans. Gloria Berkenstat Freund (New York: JewishGen, 2018 [Yiddish edn, 1950]).

29 'Certification' involved procuring forged 'Aryan' papers.

the other hand, since we have been receiving significant sums from abroad, we have been transferring larger sums to the Council's coffers, as has the ŻKN. Our contribution for the period from August to the end of November of this year was 300,000 złoty; further details about this are to be found in the financial section of this report. Last but not least, among other things, social matters, such as the matter with the JUS and the Council's attitude towards this institution – more on this below – are expressed in a statement formulated by the CC and also adopted by the Council.

VIII. *Camps for foreign Jews*

Unfortunately, despite everything, the Jews continue to suffer from a delusion of strength – even after the mass Jewish tragedies. The camps for foreign Jews in Vittel and near Hanover[30] are glaring proof of this. A large number of the letters sent to the Paraguayan consulate in Switzerland to Jews living in the ghettos under German occupation – letters with the assurance that they would receive Paraguayan citizenship – never reached their addressees because they had been killed during the liquidation of the Warsaw ghetto. Subsequently these letters became valuable commodities. Scoundrels in the form of Jewish agents working for the Gestapo took the matter into their own hands and repeatedly extorted huge sums for these letters. In some incorrigible Jewish circles, such a letter was seen as a passport to freedom, an opportunity to save a life under threat, a powerful letter of protection. This sentiment spread further and further, and soon the word 'Vittel' was heard everywhere. The desperate Jews, condemned to extermination, developed a mass psychosis that was deliberately fuelled by the Gestapo's Jewish agents. This mood also spread to some of our otherwise completely rational comrades, who even resented our central leadership for some time because we were critical of this whole matter. We considered it a new German tactic against the Jews. Moreover, we ourselves were unable to take action in the matter for reasons of principle, because this would have meant, albeit indirectly, cooperating with Jewish Gestapo agents.

In our capacity as the CC, we sent you a telegram on this subject, asking you to clarify whether these camps were under the official protection of the International Red Cross. Anyway, we did not receive a reply. Nevertheless, it was not long before this new delusion came to a tragic end. During one of the transports – probably the third – which was due to depart for the 'paradise camp' for foreigners near Hanover, more than 300 Jews destined for the aforementioned camp were arrested and shot in Pawiak. Recently we received unconfirmed reports of the liquidation of the Bergen camp near Hanover, according to the well-known German pattern. Following these shootings, the grumbling voices have gone completely silent.

IX. *The JUS*

After the liquidation operation in the ghettos in Cracow and elsewhere, the Germans established an institution in Cracow called the Jüdische Unterstützunges-Stelle (JUS).[31] It was led by Dr Weichert, in unofficial cooperation with two important members of

30 Bergen-Belsen concentration camp was located near Hanover.

31 German in the original; correctly: 'Unterstützungsstelle'. See the directive issued by the deputy head of the Population and Welfare Division in the General Government, Richard Türk, on 16 Oct. 1942: published in Tyszkowa, 'Eksterminacja Żydów w latach 1941–1943', part 1, pp. 317–318.

the Zionist organization in Cracow.[32] This organization (the JUS) allegedly aimed to distribute medicine and other items that had been sent by Jews from abroad via the International Red Cross to the camps for Jews in the GG. In reality, however, this is an act of subversion on the part of the occupiers, who still maliciously seek to deceive the public abroad about their attitudes towards the Jews, and what is more, get their hands on the medicine they need for themselves. In response to our proposal, to which the other party[33] agreed, the CC decided to refuse the cooperation indirectly suggested by the head of the JUS. At the CC's request, the Council took a similar position and notified the government delegation about it. The CC sent a telegram on this matter to you and to Dr Szwarcbard, in order to warn the public abroad about the JUS and the whole affair, and to demand that the shipment of medicine and other items to the JUS be stopped.

The CC upheld this decision a second time, after the gentlemen from the JUS had asked us to reconsider.

After some time, the gentlemen declared that they would comply with the CC's decision and hand over the remaining JUS items. But as we have now foreseen, they are stalling. We on the CC will draw the obvious conclusions, on the basis of the CC's decision in principle.

X. *Our organizational work in other areas*

1. During the period covered by this report we remained in contact with the government delegation. The subject of the consultations, which took place via the section for Jewish affairs within the government delegation's Department for Minorities,[34] was the distribution of the funds you sent as well as communication with you.
2. The question of armed resistance – especially that of arming the camps for Jews, Jewish participation in partisan groups, and a Jewish Uprising Division in Warsaw and possibly throughout the country – was the subject of talks between a representative of the CC, more specifically the ŻOB as one of its bodies, and an official military representative of the underground, as already mentioned above. We advocated mixed units in both cases.
3. During the current period, contacts were also maintained with the Polish socialist camp, especially with the WRN and the [Polish] Democracy Party, with whom we met mainly during work relating to the Council to Aid Jews.
4. Our internal work is based on the executive committee, as the governing body at the top, and a technical-logistical apparatus, with the help of which – as well as others – we contact our groups in Warsaw and in the provinces and provide them with a variety of assistance by informing them about our work, either verbally or in writing, and by listening to their wishes etc. Newsletters (an internal one and an anniversary issue) and a questionnaire on the Jewish problem and other issues have been prepared.
5. Relations with [organizations] abroad, i.e. with you, are a sore point. When Comrade Artur[35] was still in office, you contacted us occasionally. But since his tragic death there has been complete silence, despite the entire series of telegrams we sent you – either as

32 Chaim Hilfstein and Eliasz (Elijahu) Tisch.
33 The ŻKN.
34 The Section for Jewish Affairs was headed by Witold Bieńkowski.
35 Szmul Zygielbojm's code name.

a Bund organization or sometimes via the CC; in some of them we informed you about general matters, and in others we raised the question of outstanding remittances, which caused us to run out of steam and threatened our people with a genuine catastrophe. I hope that we will finally see a lasting improvement in this respect, and that after this interruption of several months you will send us regular telegrams and letters, and also publications, from yourselves and from others, informing us what you are doing, what you think about the issues concerning us and other, more general issues, and what others are saying and doing about this.

6. More detail next time about the basic problems of Jewish 'life' here in Poland and abroad, as well as about important general matters and our stance on them. Despite the disastrous situation and our constant concern with quite concrete and difficult matters, the matter is close to our hearts, and as a community we are very concerned.
7. I am quoting a resolution by our Central Leadership, dated 9 May 1943 and briefly mentioned in the previous report, on the subject of the executions of comrades Henryk and Wiktor.

The protest reads:

> We are shocked to the core by the news of the executions of comrades Henryk Erlich[36] and Wiktor Alter by Soviet authorities, which reached us during the most critical phase of the fighting in the Warsaw ghetto, and by the official justification of the sentence on the grounds of alleged 'propaganda promoting an immediate, separate peace with Hitler' within the Red Army. Before the whole world, which is bound to socialism and freedom, and in the strongest terms, we condemn this act as a crime and vigorously protest against the attempt to tarnish their innocent names. Our best comrades have become victims because they stood up for the ideals of freedom and revolutionary socialism and remained steadfastly true to their convictions. This crime against them inflicts irreparable damage not only on the Jewish socialist movement and the workers' movement in Poland, but on the entire international socialist movement as well, especially in this historically decisive situation, in which the entire working class must be consolidated first and foremost in order to smash fascism and immediately begin the struggle for the socialist reconstruction of the world. Henryk Erlich and Wiktor Alter will forever live on in the Bund's history and in all progressive Polish society, in the history of Poland's struggle and the history of international socialism as outstanding leaders, as the standard-bearers of an uncompromising struggle against fascism, as revolutionaries in deed and in spirit – as luminaries who died tragic martyrs' deaths and serve as shining examples. Central Leadership, [CK]RZMP in Poland.

This protest was circulated in the socialist underground press in Poland and published in the *Materials and Documents of the Movement of the Jewish Working Masses in Poland*, a WRN publication.

XI. *Financial report*

I now come to the financial report. First, I consider it necessary to explain to you the following, which you will no doubt appreciate. Our political organization is known within Jewish society for its reliability in all respects. We have remained faithful to this good tradition of solidarity in financial matters, which has been so characteristic of our move-

36 Correctly: 'Ehrlich'.

ment in the past. Under covert conditions, which are unimaginable to the elders who are not active here with us in the underground, we conduct all of our financial affairs on the basis of the original accounting records, invoices, and receipts from the entities and people concerned. These are entered in the accounting ledgers, which we keep as concise as possible, according to the principles of rational accounting. Even more than the formal side of accounting, we are concerned with substantive verification. The central leadership has set up an audit committee, which carefully checks the receipts and the disbursements every month, settles them, and records them. This committee, which we and you hold in high esteem, from both an organizational and a moral perspective, always determines that our accounting is managed in a rational and exemplary manner. Its basic requirements are: strict economy wherever possible, ample financial aid where necessary, the waiver of all privileges, and at the same time an understanding of the needs of all of our 'charges': whether individuals for whom we alone are directly responsible, in other words our party comrades and their families, or people who are not associated with us organizationally, but who suffer and are persecuted because of the fascist decrees; or even Aryans to whom we deem it appropriate to render services on the grounds of their merits; or generally Jews who must be helped regardless of their political affiliation.

For technical reasons, it is not possible to provide details of our financial activities over such a long period. However, the general figures given below will give you an overall picture of our financial management and will allow you to draw your own conclusions about our activities, tasks, and needs.

Here are the figures:

I. *Revenue*

We received from you, via the government delegation, [the following amounts] in dollar banknotes, and paid out in the same currency:

A.

| | |
|---|---|
| In October 1942 | 5,000 |
| In December 1942 | 5,000 |
| In February 1943 | 10,000 |
| In April 1943 | 13,000 |
| In total | 33,000 dollars |

B. Thereafter we received [the following amounts] from the government delegation, in Polish złoty:

| | |
|---|---|
| On 1 September 1943 | 300,000 |
| On 2 September 1943 | 345,000 |
| On 3 September 1943 | 150,000 |
| In total | 795,000 zł. |

This is equivalent to 10,000 dollars.

C. We received [the following amounts] from the government delegation, also in Polish złoty:

| | |
|---|---|
| On 7 October 1943 | 500,000 |
| On 13 October 1943 | 700,000 |
| On 19 October 1943 | 194,000 |
| On 27 October 1943 | 456,000 |
| In total | 1,850,000 zł. |

This is equivalent to 15,000 dollars.

II. *Expenditure*

Out of the revenue listed under A, we repaid to the government delegation a loan we had previously received (we were completely without funds) in the amount of 15,000 złoty, which according to the exchange rate at the time corresponded to a sum of approximately 300 dollars. We spent, in dollars:

A. *Repayments. Your disbursement orders, and our subsidies:*

a) 5,000 dollars to repay the sum borrowed by our comrades in the former Warsaw ghetto for organizational work (preparation of self-defence, publishing, press activities, and other [tasks]).

b) 2,000 dollars as our subsidy to the 'Joint' [JDC] administration

c) 500 dollars paid to Poale Zion-Right, on your instructions

d) 1,000 dollars paid to Poale Zion-Left, on your instructions

e) 3,000 dollars paid to Poale Zion-Right, on your instructions

f) 400 dollars paid in early May 1943 to the CC, more specifically to the ŻOB, according to the mandate given by our comrades in the Warsaw ghetto.

g) 300 dollars repaid, as mentioned, to the government delegation (15,000 złoty).

In total: 12,200 dollars.

B. Our *budgetary expenditure*

From mid October 1942 to 1 July 1943, i.e. over a period of 8.5 months, our budget expenditure averaged 2,500 dollars per month, which for 8.5 months means:

the sum of 21,250 dollars,
plus the 12,200 dollars mentioned under A,
a total of 33,450 dollars.

This means that as of 1 July, our debt to private individuals amounted to 450 dollars.

Our expenditure included: living expenses for several hundred comrades and their families; housing; providing clothing, undergarments, shoes, and medicine; shelters (if necessary); ransoms for release from prison (we spent a total of 2,000 dollars for this purpose); payments to extortionists (for example, our comrade Rozowski, commander of a frontline ŻOB battalion, whom we mentioned in our activity report, was twice the victim of extortion, which cost us 20,000 złoty, and yet he perished after the second time); and support for people hiding in Aryan districts in the provinces or for comrades' surviving family members. The months of June, July, and August of this year were the most dramatic for us in financial terms because the increased liquidation operations and the expansion of our operations generated the highest demand. We incurred debts and were constantly short of money. Disaster loomed, especially for the children, women, and men who had to remain at home all the time. At the same time, along with the ŻKN, we launched a major relief operation for the camps (Poniatowa, Trawniki, Piotrków, Częstochowa, Cracow, Lwów, Kielce, Radom, Lublin, and many other places), to which we sent hundreds of thousands of złoty. We were indebted to the ŻKN in the amount of 125,000 zł. at that time, and in the amount of 292,000 złoty in the previous period. Only when we received the funds from you via the government delegation in September/October were we able to pay off all the debts and thus had the funds necessary to cover our current expenses. The accounting for this period is as follows:

*From 1 July 1943 to 30 November 1943*

Revenue (as listed above)

| | |
|---|---|
| 1 September 1943 | 300,000 zł. |
| 2 September 1943 | 345,000 zł. |
| 3 September 1943 | 150,000 zł. |
| In total | 795,000 złoty |
| 7 October 1943 | 500,000 zł. |
| 13 October 1943 | 700,000 zł. |
| 19 October 1943 | 194,000 zł. |
| 27 October 1943 | 456,000 zł. |
| In total | 1,850,000 złoty. |
| Altogether: | 2,645,000 złoty, or 8,000 dollars. |

The remainder is only just coming in.

*Expenditure*

| | |
|---|---|
| 1) Covering the shortfall of 450 dollars for the period ending 1 July 1943 | 40,000 zł |
| 2) Repaying the loan from the ŻKN in the amount of | 125,000 zł. |
| 3) Our contribution to the total expenses of the Coordinating Committee of the Bund and the ŻKN (for the camps, the ŻOB, etc.), and the ŻKN's outlay as of 15 October 1943, for the period from May 1943 | 292,000 zł. |
| 4) Living expenses and supplies for people (charges) and budgetary expenditure averaging 450,000 [złoty] per month, from 1 July 1943 to 30 November 1943,[37] i.e. for 5 months: 5 times 450,000 | 2,250,000 zł. |
| In total | 2,606,500 zł. |
| Since revenue during this period totalled | 2,645,000 zł. |
| the cash balance as of 30 November is | 38,500 złoty |
| plus | 8,000 dollars. |

The above-mentioned expenditure includes our regular disbursements to the government delegation. These amounted to 275,000 złoty from 1 August up until the present. In October we made a one-off payment of 25,000 złoty specifically for the children's welfare section of the Council to Aid Jews. We would like to point out here once again that our comrades and their families, for whose care we are solely responsible, have not received and do not receive any funds from the Council [to Aid Jews]. The sums disbursed by our Council representative[38] via his liaison cells among several hundred welfare recipients (this month the Council has more than 400), which come out of the Council's funds, go to people who are not associated with our organization but who fall within our sphere of influence due to personal acquaintances, contacts with associated organizations, or other circumstances. It goes without saying that these sums are not included in our report. They fall under separate accounting records, like the amounts from representatives of other

37 The original gives the year as 1944, which is incorrect.

38 Leon Feiner was one of the founders of the Council to Aid Jews and served as its deputy chairman from Jan. 1943 to July 1944.

parties and groups, which are under the Council's control and which the Council distributes. But we mention this here for the sake of order and clarity.

Finally, one more remark about the Coordinating Committee of the ŻKN and the Bund (I will write about our activities in this sector elsewhere). Its financial situation is as follows. *The Coordinating Committee has neither its own funds nor its own treasury.* As I said above, its expenditure is approved unanimously on a case-by-case basis and earmarked for concrete, jointly determined self-help and ŻOB purposes. Both parties contribute corresponding sums from their own organization's coffers, which are covered by the Bund and the ŻKN at a ratio of 40–60, or recently 50–50. Expenditure is planned within the framework of matters that are agreed upon jointly. We manage our own financial affairs in compliance with our own organizational budgets, according to current capacities and requirements.

You will find the following explanation useful: it may seem paradoxical that our financial resources are increasing at a time when the extermination of the Jews is proceeding rapidly and on a large scale. However, this is no coincidence. The enormous burden of responsibility for the fate of the last Jews who have escaped extermination forces us to make extraordinary efforts. Every individual, to say nothing of entire groups who still live in [certain] population centres (camps, bunkers), is valuable to our society and must be taken into our care. The situation is therefore only seemingly paradoxical. It merely reflects the extraordinary conditions under which we must operate.

In conclusion to this section of my report – and to my report as a whole – I would like to draw your attention to the fact that we are in constant need of new financial resources and that, as you well know, we as an organization depend *entirely* on your help, as we neither want to nor should accept help from any sources other than our party representation. Always bear this in mind, so that the recent situation in which we were devoid of funds for several months, and hundreds of families were threatened with disaster as a result, does not happen again. You should also draw up an accurate account of the sums you have been sending to us all this time, and send us information on how you envision the future and what your plans are.

Please tell us at long last whether you once sent us a certain sum of money intended for both the ŻKN and for us, because we know nothing about it and have never received such joint funds.

In addition, I ask for clarification as to whether any funds were ever sent here intended for all the Jews in Poland – and if so, by whom.

We send you heartfelt party greetings, and ask that you immediately confirm receipt of this activity report.

## DOC. 279

### On 17 December 1943 a Polish informer writes to the Security Police in Tomaschow (Tomaszów Mazowiecki) asking that three people who had allegedly distinguished themselves in the persecution of Jews be released from custody[1]

Letter from a Polish informer, member of the NSZ,[2] signed LAS,[3] sent from Opoczno to the head of the Security Police and the SD in Tomaschow,[4] dated 17 December 1943 (copy)

NSZ
Polish sabotage unit
LAS 17 December 1943
To the Chief of the Security Police and the SD *in Tomaschow*:

On the 14th of this month, the following persons were arrested in the village of Stuzno:[5] Mieczyslaw *Gil*, Jan *Pluta*, and Raczynski. We hereby wish to inform you that Pluta and *Raczynski* were directly involved in the liquidation of two Jews in Adamow[6] and two in Krzyzowka[7] near Gielnow.[8] All three men have always been helpful to us in uncovering Jews and communists. We hope that you will recognize this operation to liquidate Jewish-communist bandit groups and will allow the three men named above to continue this operation in freedom.
signed *LAS*

1 BArch, R 70 Polen/194, fol. 2 (copy of the German translation). This document has been translated from the German translation of the lost Polish original.
2 See Doc. 218, fn. 2.
3 The code name is possibly derived from the Polish word *las*: 'woods, forest'.
4 Karl Macher (b. 1911), insurance salesman; joined the NSDAP in 1932, the SA in 1933, and the SS in 1940; served with the Criminal Police in Vienna in 1938; worked for the Gestapo in Vienna in 1940; later head of the Security Police field office in Tomaszów Mazowiecki; sentenced to prison terms of several years' duration by Vienna People's Court in 1949 and by Graz Regional Court in 1970.
5 Village south-west of Gielniów in Kreis Opoczno in District Radom.
6 Village south-west of Gielniów.
7 This may be a reference to the intersection (Polish: *krzyżówka*) of two roads 2 km west of Gielniów.
8 Correctly: Gielniów. The remaining Jews in Gielniów had been ghettoized there on 21 Sept. 1942 and transported to Opoczno on 24 Oct. 1942; they were deported to Treblinka on 27 Oct. 1942.

## DOC. 280

## In late 1943 Halina Nelken writes a poem about Plaszow camp[1]

Poem (copy)

*Plaszow 1943*[2]
They trudge through mud, the army of the wooden-shoed.
The shouts are vulgar, the conversation crude.
The searchlights' glare illuminates barbed wire.
Shoes sink in the red soil's slippery mire.
Step after step, this trudging is tough.
This road, like life, is rocky and rough.
Beatings and hoarse cries resound all the way.
The army of captives trudges on, all in grey.
Like dim shadows, swallowed by the black night,
they succumb to the power without a fight.
It has stripped the remnants of their humanity,
locked them in a hell of death and insanity.
Like a nightmare: they come from night and vanish into it
What terrible crime did they commit,
these people the world detests and eschews?
The condemned, all of them nameless,
are Jews …

## DOC. 281

## On 5 January 1944 Globocnik reports on the volume and value of the possessions stolen from murdered Jews[1]

Letter (marked 'secret Reich matter') from the Higher SS and Police Leader in the Operational Zone Adriatic Coast (Gl./Go. – log no. 1/44 secret Reich matter PK), signed Globocnik, Trieste, to Reichsführer-SS (log no. 1851/44 secret) and Reich Minister of the Interior Heinrich Himmler, Berlin (received on 10 January 1944), dated 5 January 1944[2]

Reichsführer,

I take the liberty of submitting the enclosed report on the economic process of winding up Operation Reinhardt, since you, Reichsführer, ordered in your letter of 22 Sep-

1 The original has not been preserved. The copy the author made after the war is in the Nelken family's possession. Copy in IfZ-Archives, F 601. An abridged version is published in Michał Borwicz (ed.), *Pieśń ujdzie cało … Antologia wierszy o Żydach pod okupacją niemiecką* (Warsaw: Centralna Żydowska Komisja Historyczna w Polsce, 1947), p. 263. This document has been translated from Polish.

2 Halina Nelken is thought to have been imprisoned from Dec. 1943 at Plaszow concentration camp, where her parents had previously been held. She wrote her poems on loose slips of paper.

1 BArch, NS 19/2234, fols. 33–55, here fols. 33–43. Published in *Trial of the Major War Criminals before the International Military Tribunal*, vol. 34 (Nuremberg: Secretariat of the Tribunal, 1947), pp. 70–76, 82–85. This document has been translated from German.

tember 1943[3] that I need to have finished winding it up and handing it over by 31 December 1943.

Yet the recognition given to me for the operation[4] also compels me to give you, Reichsführer, an account of the economic side, so that you, Reichsführer, can see that this aspect of the work was in good order as well.

If SS-Obergruppenführer Pohl has not yet had time to complete the handover, I still hope that the basic information provided here will lead to my being released from any liability.[5]

A proper conclusion and my discharge from any liability are necessary because I carried out this activity within the framework of the SS, and it must therefore be brought to an unambiguous close with respect to the relevant Reich authorities. Operation Reinhardt was too dangerous not to do this.

Furthermore, I have laboured under persistent allegations against me of financial irregularities.[6] and I therefore have to furnish impeccable proof that this is not the case here.

The whole account contains two parts:

1. The economic part of Operation Reinhardt, divided into
   a) accounting and delivery of the assets seized and
   b) accounting of the assets generated through labour.
2. The Siedlerwirtschaftsgemeinschaft,[7] whose economic management was also based on my work and which is now being transferred into civilian hands.

When it comes to the exact accounting [of Operation] Reinhardt, there is an additional factor: its receipts must be destroyed as soon as possible, after the records for all other work on this matter have already been destroyed.

Regarding the SWG, it is a matter not just of the financial order itself, but also of a transfer, so that this institution will be preserved for the settlers.

My role in both matters will only have been completed after I have been discharged from liability for both matters. I request, Reichsführer, that you set a deadline by which, on the basis of my documents, all will have been brought to a definitive close right there and then.

I have taken the liberty of sending a copy to SS-Obergruppenführer Pohl.

Heil Hitler!

Respectfully

2 In the original, incorrectly: 1943. At the top of each of the following reports is a stamp stating 'secret Reich matter'.

3 This was not found.

4 Himmler had thanked Globocnik on 30 Nov. 1943 for the 'great and unparalleled services that you rendered to the whole German nation during the conduct of Operation Reinhard': see BArch, NS 19/2234, fol. 32.

5 An audit of Operation Reinhard by the Reich Audit Office had revealed substantial irregularities: 'Bericht über Unregelmäßigkeiten in der Verwaltung öffentlicher Mittel', no date; BArch, R 2301/2073/2, fol. 30.

6 Globocnik had been replaced as Gauleiter of Vienna on 1 Feb. 1939 due to financial irregularities; see the audit report from 1941: BArch, BDC, SSO, 16A (personnel file of Odilo Globocnik), fr. 1250.

7 The Siedlerwirtschaftsgemeinschaft GmbH ('Settlers' Economic Aid Association', SWG), founded in late 1942, was an SS enterprise; it was intended to support ethnic Germans from outside the Reich who were resettled in the Zamość area using the stolen property of murdered Jews.

*4 copies*
*Copy 1*
*The economic part of Operation Reinhardt*
Grouped together in the SS Business and Administration Main Office – Special Tasks 'G', of which I am in charge and for which I have not been discharged from liability.

The entire Operation Reinhardt is divided into four areas:

A) the resettlement itself

B) the exploitation of labour

C) the exploitation of material assets

D) the recovery of hidden assets and real estate.

*A. The resettlement*
It is done and completed.

The necessary objective here was to gather the people by using the proper method with the little manpower available and to do as little economic damage as possible to production for the war effort.

By and large this was successful. Significant damage occurred only in Warsaw, where, owing to a misjudgement of the situation on the ground, the method used to carry out this process was flawed.[8]

I was no longer able to carry out the operation in Litzmannstadt because I had been transferred.[9]

The facilities created for this operation from accumulated funds, which are nonetheless to be regarded as Reich assets, have been entirely dismantled. For surveillance reasons a small farm has been established in each of the camps, which is occupied by an expert. A regular income must be paid to him in order to maintain the farm.[10]

*B. Exploitation of labour*
All workers were gathered together in closed-off camps[11] to which manufacturing operations essential to the war effort had been relocated.
To achieve this, the following steps had to be taken:
1) Construction of all residential camps.
2) Construction of production areas with all operational requirements, such as procurement of machinery, power supply, etc.
3) Ensuring basic provisions, on the one hand by drawing on the contents of the Wehrmacht's troop supply depots and on the other by establishing farms in the vicinity of the camps.
4) Facilities for creating proper sanitary and hygienic conditions.
5) Security measures
a. by ensuring appropriate security precautions,
b. by providing a security setup within the camp,
c. by providing an appropriate guard force.

8 This is a reference to the Warsaw Ghetto Uprising.

9 The remaining Jewish inhabitants of the Litzmannstadt (Lodz) ghetto were deported in July and August 1944.

10 After the Operation Reinhard extermination camps were closed down, the buildings were demolished, the grounds were planted, and a farmhouse was erected at each site in order to cover the traces of the crimes.

11 Forced labour camps for Jews in District Lublin.

For this purpose, the SS guard squads were formed; commanded by Germans, the vast majority of them performed their duties flawlessly.[12]

Mixing these guard squads with Reich German guard squads from the concentration camps was intended to increase their reliability.

d. Transferring the camps to the concentration camp division of the SS Business and Administration Main Office created the basis for a sound security situation.

6) The German command staff received extensive training to ensure the proper leadership and methodological approach.

It became apparent that the productivity of the Jews in the camps was steadily increasing.

7) The technical and commercial sides were safeguarded by introducing operational and financial structures.

'Osti'[13] was established for this purpose, with Deutsche Ausrüstungswerke as the second operational organization.

In total, 18 operations were established, and plans called for more. Around 52,000 workers were available. This labour force made it possible to quickly take over production from both the GG armaments inspectorate and the Speer Reich Ministry[14] in order to compensate for plants that had been bombed.

The demand from these agencies was very high.

'Osti' and Deutsche Ausrüstungswerke were operations I ran myself,[15] while others, such as the Heinkel aircraft manufacturing plant, were only under my supervision.[16]

Operating reports and sales figures are to be found in Enclosure 1.[17]

The backlog of orders was so large that the DAW was at full capacity until March, and the other factories were snowed under with work for two to three months.

*C. Exploitation of material assets*

The exploitation of material assets carried out in the course of Reinhardt I is documented in Enclosure 2 and has been concluded.[18]

*D. Recovery of hidden assets*

The recovery of hidden assets and exploitation of real estate is subdivided into:

1) Assets such as machines, raw materials, etc. transferred to Aryan ownership through 'Osti'.

The amount realized so far is 6.3 million Reichsmarks; 7–8 million have yet to be recovered.

12 The SS training camp for non-German auxiliary personnel had been established as early as autumn 1941.

13 See Doc. 268, fn. 3.

14 The Reich Ministry of Armaments and War Production.

15 Deutsche Ausrüstungswerke (DAW) was in fact under the control of the Berlin headquarters of the SS Business and Administration Main Office.

16 In autumn 1942 the SS had converted the factory in Budzyń into a labour camp for Jews. In Nov. 1943 it became a concentration camp.

17 Enclosure 1, with four appendixes, is not included here; it provides information about the orders on hand as of 3 Nov. 1943 at the factories in the SS labour camps in the District, the Osti facilities, the DAW facilities, the Poniatowa textile factory, and the Trawniki fur-processing operation: BArch, NS 19/2234, fols. 44–49.

18 Enclosure 2, 'Preliminary Final Report for the Operation Reinhardt Lublin Cash Office, as of 15 December 1943', is not included here: see BArch, NS 19/2234, fols. 50–54.

The additional advantage of this method was that it would include all those who built up businesses in this way at no cost, with the help of the Jews, and had become rich without any effort.

2) Registration of Jewish receivables both domestically and abroad by requiring the camp inmates to transfer these receivables to 'Osti', which then recovered them.

The first attempt yielded a sum of 11,000,000 zloty for transfer, at least half of which appeared to be recoverable. As, however, this procedure was also able to identify funds that had been moved abroad, it would have been able to recover valuable foreign currency for the Reich.

3) Real estate was assigned to the property management division of the General Government for appraisal and exploitation.

All the organizations described above were running without issue upon my departure. Because I had received indications from the Reichsführer-SS as early as July 1943 that I might potentially be transferred in the course of the year, I immediately began to work on the final arrangements for and consolidation of the setup I had created and handed over all the organizations to the SS Business and Administration Main Office to this end.

The measures undertaken were as follows:

1) On 13 August 1943 the SS training camp in Trawniki was handed over by SS-Obergruppenführer Pohl (see letter dated 13 August 1943 – Chef A/Fr./S – Appendix 3).[19]

2) In a meeting with SS-Obergruppenführer Pohl on 7 September 1943, the takeover of ten SS labour camps in District Lublin as subcamps of Lublin concentration camp[20] was agreed upon, as well as the further handover of other labour camps in the General Government. The head of Lublin concentration camp was given orders to this effect. This meeting was prompted by a visit of SS-Obergruppenführer Krüger and SS-Standartenführer Schellin (see memo from the head of the SS Business and Administration Main Office dated 7 September 1943 – D II/L, file ref.: 29 Ma./F., Enclosure 4).[21]

3) Following the meeting, the SS labour camps were informed by the commandant of Lublin concentration camp in a letter dated 14 September 1943 that they had become subcamps of Lublin concentration camp.[22]

The process of mixing the non-German auxiliary security squads with Reich German concentration camp guard personnel was also set in motion.

4) On 22 October 1943 SS-Obergruppenführer Pohl announced that he had ordered the takeover of the following labour camps by Office Group D:[23]

1. Old Airfield, Lublin
2. SS labour camp in Trawniki
3. " in Poniatowa

19 Enclosure 3 is the copy of a letter from the SS Business and Administration Main Office, signed Pohl, dated 13 August 1943. The SS Business and Administration Main Office took over the SS training camp in Trawniki. The commandant of Lublin-Majdanek concentration camp, who was also subordinate to Globocnik, was put in charge of operations: see BArch, NS 19/2234, fol. 55.

20 This is a reference to Majdanek camp.

21 This is not included in the file. See Doc. 268.

22 No such letter has been found.

23 No details have been found.

4. Forced labour camp and SS workshops in Radom
5. " " Budzyn
6. Cracow-Plaszow main camp
7. Deutsche Ausrüstungswerke facility, Lublin
8. Armaments camps in Lemberg.

5) During the meeting on 22 October 1943, SS-Obergruppenführer Pohl let it be known that I was to be replaced as director of 'Osti' by the deputy director, and that a new deputy director would be appointed.[24]

I was also assured that I would be discharged from liability.

I fully briefed my successor[25] as well and reminded him of his supervisory duty. I thereby fulfilled all the necessary prerequisites for operations to continue.

Fundamental security precautions were in place and guaranteed by their management through the concentration camps.

To date, discharge from liability has not been granted.[26]

On 3 November 1943 the workers were withdrawn from the labour camps and the factories were shut down.[27]

The senior camp officials were not informed of this operation even though responsibility rested with them; I was therefore hindered in carrying out my duty of supervision.

I instructed the senior camp officials to carry out the closures and to continue assessing orders or transferring them.

On the day before the camps were evacuated, General Schindler from the GG armaments inspectorate, based on an assurance from SS-Obergruppenführer Krüger, had agreed with the senior camp officials that

a) the labour camps will in future receive only armaments orders,

b) he had been assured on 2 November that 10,000 additional Jews would be assigned to armaments production.

This agreement could no longer be fulfilled.

*Report on the administrative wind-up of Operation Reinhardt*

I. All assets resulting from this operation were registered centrally in an administrative system I set up, sorted accordingly, and posted. The registration covers the entire General Government. The manpower came from the SS Business and Administration Main Office.

The assets were used and liquidated in accordance with guidelines issued by the Reichsführer-SS, which were summarized in the course of the operation in instructions dated 26 September 1942 and 9 December 1943; the SS Business and Administration Main Office was entrusted with the [assets'] handling in relation to the Reich agencies.

24 Osti's deputy manager was Max Horn. Oswald Pohl had already picked a new deputy manager, although his name is not known; he was never installed, because all Jewish prisoners were murdered.

25 Globocnik's successor as SS and Police Leader in Lublin was Jakob Sporrenberg (1902–1952).

26 On 16 Feb. 1944 Pohl discharged Globocnik from liability for the period audited by then, i.e. from 25 Oct. 1942 to 31 March 1943: see BArch, NS 19/2234, fol. 67.

27 This is a reference to the murder of almost all the remaining Jews in District Lublin in the Majdanek, Poniatowa, and Trawniki camps: see Docs. 276 and 277.

The assets collected by me were regularly handed over to the SS Business and Administration Main Office in return for confirmation, and the latter passed the assets on to the Reichsbank, the Reich Ministry of Finance, textile factories, etc.

On the order of the Reichsführer-SS, necessary [items or funds] were allowed to be taken out to supply ethnic Germans, but the Reichsführer-SS prohibited any such use for the SS's own purposes.

The distinctive feature of the accounting is that there was no regular, established procedure for the seizure of assets, as they were collected in response to an order, and only the SS men's decency and unimpeachable character, as well as their supervision, meant that absolutely everything was handed in. But that which was seized and collected and then transferred to the Reinhardt Dept. was indeed accounted for and delivered with the greatest accuracy and without any misconduct. A preliminary audit up to 1 April 1943 conducted by SS-Obersturmbannführer Vogt from the SS Business and Administration Main Office[28] has already been carried out and revealed everything to be in perfect order. The preliminary audit has yet to be performed for the remainder.

Based on an agreement with the Reich Ministry of Finance, this preliminary audit is final, and, without involving the Reich Audit Office, the records and documents will be destroyed in accordance with secrecy regulations.

II. The assets accounted for break down as follows:

1) *Reichsmark and zloty amounts*

These [cash] receipts were used to cover all material expenses, transport expenses, fees, etc. resulting from this operation. By far the largest part was made available to the SS business officer in the General Government.[29] The amounts were then adjusted by the SS Business and Administration Main Office and credited to Operation Reinhardt in Reichsmarks and forwarded to the Reichsbank.

For foreign-exchange reasons, a small part was used as credit for various business operations and then also adjusted and credited by the SS Business and Administration Main Office. In addition, excess price differences were covered so that urgently needed materials could be procured. All these transactions took place with the authorization of the SS Business and Administration Main Office.

An additional amount was made available to the concentration camp[30] on an ongoing basis to fund expansions, to further develop the business enterprises, and to procure the necessary agricultural machinery etc. Exact records were kept of these purchases, which I approved on an ongoing basis; these documents are also enclosed with the final accounting. The books were kept by the concentration camp's chief of administration, and it was kept separately from my administration, since the concentration camp administration was independent of the SS administration for Lublin, as instructed by the SS Business and Administration Main Office. For these expenditures there still has to be a payment to [Operation] Reinhardt from the agency that ultimately takes over the operation.

28 Joseph Vogt (b. 1884), military official and auditor; member of far-right organizations from 1920; joined the SA in 1933, the SS in 1936, and the NSDAP in 1937; head of Office A IV (auditing) at the SS Business and Administration Main Office; in 1947 tried alongside other Business and Administration Main Office personnel by a US military tribunal as part of the Subsequent Nuremberg Proceedings ('Pohl trial'); was acquitted.

29 Erich Schellin.

30 This is a reference to Lublin-Majdanek concentration camp.

2) *Foreign currency* in banknotes or gold coins was collected, sorted, and also handed over to the Reichsbank via the SS Business and Administration Main Office.
3) *Jewels*, pieces of jewellery, watches, and the like were sorted according to value and delivered to the SS Business and Administration Main Office. At its direction, watches made of base metals were delivered to the Wehrmacht; eyeglasses were made available after repair to invalids; and everyday objects of no value were mainly provided to Wehrmacht agencies where they were urgently needed. The receipt slips for these transactions have been retained.
4) *Textiles*, clothing, linen, feather beds, and rags were collected and sorted according to quality.

The sorted items had to be searched for hidden assets and then fumigated.

More than 1,900 wagons were then made available to the agencies specified by the Reich Ministry of Economics, as instructed by the SS Business and Administration Main Office. Not only were these stocks used to supply non-German workers with clothing, but a large part was also respun.

No case of illness was reported, although the clothing often came primarily from persons who were sick, mainly with typhus. This means that the disinfection process was adequate.

The best garments were separated out and used to supply ethnic Germans by order of the Reichsführer-SS. Shoes were also sorted on the basis of serviceability, and then given either to ethnic Germans or to the concentration camps for use by prisoners, or they were taken apart and [the leather was] used in the manufacture of wooden clogs for prisoner uniforms.
5) *Individual assets* of a special nature, such as stamps, coins, and the like, were sorted and delivered to the SS Business and Administration Main Office; worthless things were destroyed.
6) Other items collected, such as soap, detergent, dishes, and the like, were used in the camps for Jews; glass, scrap metal objects, etc. were taken to the utilization centres to be re-processed.
7) The food brought along on the transports was added to the provisions for the Jew camps.
8) Valuable furnishings and household goods were repaired and mostly given to the ethnic German settlers for use. However, both German authorities and Wehrmacht agencies were also lent furnishings in exchange for pro forma receipts.

Inferior items were either destroyed or given to the population as rewards for good harvest performances etc.

Efforts were made to remove parts such as locks, hinges, and the like from objects that were no longer serviceable and to reuse them.

The receipts for the objects on loan were passed on to the Higher SS and Police Leader East every month.

In accordance with the Reichsführer-SS's order of 22 September, the total yield was processed, realized, and transferred, so that scarcely anything remains.

There is still equipment that was needed to carry out the operation, such as barracks, storage racks, conveyances, and the like, and that was purchased with the accrued funds.

These items have been collected, but a decision still has to be made as to what purpose they are to serve.

According to the enclosed breakdown, the total value of the items accrued is approximately 180,000,000 Reichsmarks. However, this estimate is based on minimum values, which means the total value is probably twice that, aside from the [use] value of the collected items that are in short supply, such as textiles, of which more than 1,900 wagonloads alone were supplied to German industry.

## DOC. 282

### On 15 January 1944 the SS Business and Administration Main Office informs Himmler about the use of formerly Jewish-owned real estate in the General Government[1]

Letter (marked 'secret') from the head of the SS Business and Administration Main Office, SS-Obergruppenführer and General of the Waffen-SS Oswald Pohl (file ref.: A II/3 Reinh[ard] secret, log no. 18/44), Berlin, to the Reichsführer-SS (received on 21 January 1944, log no. 40/10/44g), Berlin, dated 15 January 1944[2]

*Re*: utilization of the Jews' immovable assets
*Subject*: decree issued by the Reichsführer-SS, field command post, dated 19 September 1942[3]
General Directive no. 18/c[4] issued by the Reichsführer-SS and Reich Commissioner for the Strengthening of Germandom
File ref.: C – 6/10/19.9.42 log no. 38/42 s[ecret]
*Enclosure*: – –

Reichsführer,

There are still some difficulties that need to be resolved in relation to the utilization of immovable assets owned by the Jews in the General Government.

By your order of 19 September 1942, I was tasked with administering all Jewish assets.

By a subsequent decree of 15 December 1942, you, Reichsführer, in your capacity as Reich Commissioner for the Strengthening of Germandom, tasked the Higher SS and Police Leader in Cracow[5] with the administration and utilization of the immovable assets.

In a telex dated 27 January 1943, the Governor General informed us that negotiations between the Governor General and you, Reichsführer, concerning the administration of the immovable assets were currently ongoing.[6]

I have not been informed about the outcome of these negotiations; it is certain, however, that the question of responsibilities has so far not been clarified.

1 BArch, NS 19/2648, fol. 158r–v. This document has been translated from German.
2 The original contains handwritten annotations and underlining.
3 This has not been found.
4 See Doc. 190.
5 At the time, this post was held by Friedrich-Wilhelm Krüger.
6 On 26 Jan. 1943 Governor General Frank had declared Himmler's decree of 15 Dec. 1942 to be invalid and had instructed State Secretary Bühler to reach an understanding with State Secretary Krüger regarding the 'control of Jewish property': Präg and Jacobmeyer (eds.), *Das Diensttagebuch des deutschen Generalgouverneurs*, p. 613.

The situation is now such that the buildings and real estate are still being managed by the district governors' trustee offices, and both the Jews' securities and their bank deposits are being held back by the banks without being turned to account for the benefit of the Reich.

I do not know to what extent Jewish real estate has now been utilized, but I do know that in some cases properties have been sold at giveaway prices instead of being made available to the Reich Commissioner's agencies for resettlement purposes as planned.

The assets invested in securities and, in part, the bank deposits have apparently been seized by an official I appointed; their worth has already been assigned to him by the previous owners. However, the banks decline to pay out the equivalent value, noting that it is not clear who is responsible for the assets' release.

I request that this matter be raised in a meeting with the Governor General, and that it be clarified who is responsible for the utilization of the confiscated Jewish real estate, securities, and bank deposits for the benefit of the Reich and has sole charge and is authorized to issue orders for this purpose.[7]

Heil *Hitler*!

## DOC. 283

## On 31 January 1944 an SS-Hauptscharführer reports damage to his firearm during the Harvest Festival murder operation in Trawniki[1]

Report by SS-Hauptscharführer Miller[2] to Department II C b,[3] in-house, Lublin, dated 31 January 1944

*Re*: damage to firearm – rifle no. 6682

On 3 November 1943 I was physically attacked and slightly injured by a Jewess who struck me in the face during the resettlement of Jews[4] taking place in Trawnicki.[5] Because the individual was getting ready to strike me again, I felt compelled to defend myself and hit her on the head with my rifle butt, thereby slightly damaging the butt. The damage itself is insignificant (a small crack in the butt) and does not impair the weapon's firing power and safety in the least, as was proven when it was used following this incident.

7 Himmler replied to Pohl that he and Higher SS and Police Leader Koppe should arrange with Frank for Jewish assets to be allocated to a 'Damage Fund for Settlement Purposes'. On 12 Feb. 1944 Himmler and Frank agreed that the real estate should continue to be administered by the General Government, but that 'the movable Jewish assets still on hand' would be put at the Governor General's disposal, and the sales proceeds used for settlement projects: BArch, NS 19/2648, fols. 160, 163r–v.

1 BArch, R 70 Polen/113. Published as a facsimile in Grabitz and Scheffler, *Letzte Spuren*, p. 266. This document has been translated from German.

2 Probably Georg Miller (b. 1911), SS-Hauptscharführer; worked for the Senior Commander of the Security Police and the SD (BdS) in Prague; worked for the Commander of the Security Police and the SD (KdS) in Lublin as head of the filing department from June 1943.

3 The department for supply and material expenses at the office of the KdS.

4 See Docs. 277 and 278.

5 Correctly: Trawniki.

## DOC. 284
## On 4 February 1944 Ukrainian police accuse the Balicki family from Siemianówka of having sheltered Jews[1]

Report by the Ukrainian police officer and head of the Ukrainian police unit in Lemberg (log no. 32/44), unsigned, Lemberg, dated 4 February 1944[2]

*Final report*
1. *Crime*: sheltering Jews
2. *Time of the crime*: from 17 December 1942 to 1 February 1944
3. *Scene of the crime*: Siemianowka, Kreis Lemberg-Land
4. *The accused*:
   1) Josef Balicki,[3] b. 15 February 1893, resident in Siemianowka, house no. 272
   2) Kateryna Balicka, née Bezronk,[4] b. 10 June 1896, resident in Siemianowka
   3) Wladyslaw Balicki, son of Josef, age 17
   4) Stanislaw Balicki,[5] son of Josef, age 21
   5) Wanda Balicki, daughter of Josef, age 23
5. *The witnesses (evidence)*: Rubin Pasternak and Moses Pasternak, Jews
6. *Seized*: four 20-dollar gold pieces in gold, four quilts, two pillows, one detector with one set of earphones, the Jews' identity cards
7. *Arrested*: the aforementioned Jews and Josef Balicki with his wife Kateryna Balicka

*Brief statement of the facts*
When searching the residence[6] of Josef Balicki in Siemianowka, Kreis Lemberg-Land, house no. 272, the Ukrainian policemen Andrij Kubaj and Hryhorij Prystasz[7] arrested two Jews who had been in hiding.

During the Jews' interrogation, it was ascertained that Josef Balicki as well as his wife Kateryna had kept the Jews concealed in the basement of their house since 17 December 1942.[8] Balicki and his wife admitted this. Balicki received 2,000 zl. per month from the Jews for supporting them.

Balicki's adult children were also aware that the Jews were being sheltered. Balicki's sons brought the hidden Jews newspapers from Lemberg and frequently spoke with

1 DALO, R-16/1/28, fol. 2. Copy in USHMM, Acc. 1995.A.1086, reel 4. This document has been translated from German.
2 The original contains handwritten corrections and insertions, and the year is incorrectly given as 1943.
3 Józef Balicki was a native of Siemianówka; he was a pointsman on the railway prior to Sept. 1939, then a casual labourer.
4 Correctly: Katarzyna Balicka, née Bezrąk. Katarzyna Balicka was relocated to Lower Silesia after the war and lived near Wrocław; she, her sons, and her deceased husband were honoured as Righteous Among the Nations by the State of Israel in 1987.
5 Stanisław Balicki had been conscripted for forced labour in construction and worked in a quarry before escaping from the German forced labour camp; his hiding places included the home of Rubin (Bernard) Pasternak in Lwów (see fn. 8).
6 Władysław Balicki stated in 1984 that a neighbour had informed on the family: see Jarosław Syrnyk, 'Historia Józefa Balickiego', in Aleksandra Namysło (ed.), *'Kto w takich czasach Żydów przechowuje?' Polacy niosący pomoc ludności żydowskiej w okresie okupacji niemieckiej* (Warsaw: Instytut Pamięci Narodowej, 2009), pp. 145–156, here p. 147.
7 The original indicates that Kubaj had a higher rank than Prystasz did.

them. It was not possible to arrest them, however, as they were not found at home when the residence was searched. Their whereabouts are unknown.

Josef Balicki and his wife Frau Kateryna, as well as the Jews, were arrested, but after breaking open the door of the police holding cell in Szczerzec, the Jews fled and to date have not been arrested.[9]

The married couple under arrest, J. B. and his [wife] Kateryna, were taken to the gendarmerie station in Lemberg, along with the confiscated items.[10]

## DOC. 285

## On 19 February 1944 the Security Police report on Jewish inmates who had made preparations to escape from the labour camp in Kraśnik[1]

Report from the Krasnik field office of the Commander of the Security Police and the SD for District Lublin (IV P 4-273/44), unsigned,[2] to the Commander of the Security Police and the SD for District Lublin (IV B 4) in Lublin,[3] dated 19 February 1944 (copy)[4]

*Re*: Jews making preparations to escape from the labour camp in Krasnik[5]
*Dossier*: none
*Enclosures*:[6] 1 envelope with 12 fake Polish identity cards
Through various confidential informants, it was made known to the office here that a number of Jews in the Krasnik labour camp were planning to escape from the camp in the near future, as the dissolution of the concentration camps in Lublin and Poniatowa,[7]

8 In their home Mr and Mrs Balicki hid the brothers Rubin (1919–1944) and Mojżesz Pasternak (1922–1944), who had escaped from the ghetto in Lwów. According to another source, the Pasternak brothers had left the ghetto wearing railway workers' uniforms given to them by Józef Balicki: see Syrnyk, 'Historia Józefa Balickiego', p. 146.

9 The Pasternaks were betrayed shortly before the Red Army arrived in Siemianówka. They were taken by the Gestapo to Lwów, where they were murdered.

10 Józef Balicki and his wife, Katarzyna, were later taken to Cracow and sentenced to death by the German special court on 25 July 1944. Józef Balicki's death sentence was carried out in Breslau; Katarzyna Balicka's punishment was commuted to life imprisonment.

1 APL, 510/2, fols. 121–124. Copy in BArch, R 70 Polen/179, fols. 4–7. This document has been translated from German.

2 The head of the field office of the Commander of the Security Police and the SD (KdS) in Krasnik was Erich Augustin (1900–1945), officer with the Criminal Police; as Kriminalsekretär affiliated with the Security Police and the SD in Lublin; died in Soviet captivity.

3 From Oct. 1943 to July 1944, the KdS in Lublin was Dr Karl Pütz (1911–1945), lawyer; member of the ethnic German movement in Eupen and Malmedy from 1929; joined the NSDAP and the SA in 1933, and the SS in 1938; KdS in Rowno from Feb. 1942 to Oct. 1943, and in Posen from August 1944; committed suicide at the end of the war.

4 Stamp: The Commander of the Security Police and the SD for District Lublin, Office 3.

5 Kraśnik forced labour camp still held 200 to 300 prisoners in Feb. 1944, and approximately 100 people were confined in the labour camp for Jews that was run by Wirtschaftliche Forschungsgesellschaft mbH [Wifo]; on Wifo, see fn. 28.

6 These are not included in the file.

7 This is a reference to the murder of the Jewish prisoners in Lublin-Majdanek concentration camp and in Poniatowa camp on 3 and 4 Nov. 1943. Both camps continued to exist, however.

as well as the relocation of the Budzyn[8] labour camp to a concentration camp, caused them to feel uncertainty and unease regarding their fate.

After some clues to the planned escape became known here – it was to take place right away, and fake identity cards had already been acquired – the camp commandant, SS-Unterscharführer *Gröger*,[9] was informed. After he had been consulted, initially eight Jews were arrested on 13 February 1944 and brought here to shed light on the matter. In the process it became clear that the information from the informant was entirely accurate. During a search of the quarters of the Jews in question, twelve Polish identity cards (fake) and cash totalling 21,490 zloty were found. The money was handed in to the camp commandant, SS-Unterscharführer *Gröger*.

The Jews who were in possession of the Polish identity cards in question were led by the Jewish camp commandant[10] Peisach *Kawa* and family; also involved were members of the Order Service, supervisors, a [prisoner] physician, and medical orderlies.

In the course of the questioning to gather information, it became clear that an unidentified Jew had appeared in Krasnik from Warsaw when the camp in Poniatowa was liquidated, and had given the fake Polish identity cards to the holders for 5,000 zloty apiece. Despite the most thorough and rigorous interrogation, it was not possible to ascertain the name and origin of this Jew, so that further inquiries into this matter have proven unsuccessful. However, further efforts will be made to identify the middlemen as well as the producers of the fake identity cards. But it seems advisable to have the issuing authorities concerned carry out checks on the stamps, signatures, and file cards that were used in order to find out who the perpetrators are.

On 14 and 18 February 1944, the final solution was applied to the Jews listed below, who were connected with the planned escape attempt:

1. *Kawa*, Peisach, b. 13 February 1892 in Belzyce[11]
2. *Kawa*, Berek, b. 18 July 1916 in Krasnik[12]
3. *Kawa*, Bela, née Hoffert, b. 17 August 1917 in Krasnik
4. *Fiterman*, Fryda, née Kawa, b. 3 January 1920 in Krasnik[13]
5. *Hoffert*, Israel, b. 15 May 1914 in Krasnik[14]
6. *Hoffert*, Moschek, b. 17 April 1894 in Lublin
7. *Grünwald*, Schama, b. 1923 in Krasnik
8. *Herschsohn*, Crana, b. 16 May 1924 in Krasnik
9. *Schmukler*, Leiba, b. 1925 in Krasnik[15]

8 The labour camp for Jews at the Ernst Heinkel aircraft factory in Budzyń, near Kraśnik was converted into a concentration camp subcamp in Nov. 1943.

9 Alois Josef Gröger (1905–1980), joiner; originally from Bohemia; joined the NSDAP and probably also the SS in 1938; worked in Breslau, 1938–1939; in Radom, 1939–1940; then in Lublin; worked in Minsk in 1941; worked for the SS and Police Leader in Lublin, 1941–1942, and in Kraśnik, Nov. 1942 – April 1944; oversaw Wifo's labour camp, 1943–1944; sentenced to life imprisonment by Hamburg Regional Court in 1974.

10 Correctly: camp elder.

11 Peisach (Pesach, Jechiel) Kawa, merchant from Bełżyce. Many of the Yiddish names in this list are given in a Germanized form.

12 Berek Kawa, merchant; he was the son of Pesach Kawa and married to Bela, née Hupert.

13 Fryda (Fraida) Fiterman, née Kawa; she was the daughter of Pesach Kawa and wife of Szyja (Jehoszua) Fiterman.

14 Israel Hupert, merchant.

15 Leiba or Lajb Szmukler.

10. *Schmukler*, Josef, b. 15 July 1918 in Krasnik
11. *Süsberg*, Schlama-Leib, b. 1 July 1906 in Krasnik
12. *Weissbrot*, Jankiel, b. 2 March 1903 in Krasnik[16]
13. *Weissbrot*, Chana, née Pasch, b. 3 February 1903 in Wzodowa[17]
14. *Weissbrot*, Mendel, b. 30 April 1924 in Krasnik[18]
15. *Perlsohn*, Aron, b. 1 February 1909 in Krasnik
16. *Fiterman*, Schija, b. 20 October 1920 in Wysokie
17. *Erlich*, Schol, b. 28 March 1906 in Krasnik
18. *Erlich*, Berek, b. 1916 in Krasnik[19]
19. *Rosenbusch*, Süskind, b. 3 April 1910 in Krasnik
20. *Beck*, Icek, b. 8 September 1900 in Krasnik[20]
21. *Beck*, Chaja, née Rosenbusch, b. 10 January 1903 in Krasnik
22. *Beck*, Aron, b. 25 March 1906 in Krasnik
23. *Sapiro*, Josef, b. 11 September 1906 in Vilna[21]
24. *Schuldberg*, Zdzislaw, b. 7 December 1919 in Litzmannstadt
25. *Kaminer*, Max, b. 19 September 1890 in Bilgoraj[22]
26. *Kaminer*, Berek, b. 23 September 1899 in "
27. *Kaminer*, Leon, b. 14 March 1893 in "
28. *Kaminer*, David, b. 25 September 1913 in "
29. *Kaminer*, Josef, b. 12 February 1926 in "
30. *Kaminer*, Schmerjohn, b. 3 July 1925 in "
31. *Kaminer*, Aron, b. 27 April 1901 in Bilgoraj[23]
32. *Kaminer*, Hersch, b. 3 October 1915 in Bilgoraj
33. *Berman*, Hersch, b. 13 June 1919 in Krasnik
34. *Steingos*, Luzer, b. 30 November 1912 in Krasnik[24]
35. *Münzberg*, Schlomo, b. 22 December 1911 in Ostrowiec
36. *Fein*, Mendel, b. 28 February 1915 in Lublin[25]
37. *Kohen*, Abraham-Symcha, b. 17 April 1899 in Krasnik
38. *Kohen*, Chaskiel, b. 16 February 1922 in Lublin
39. *Nordman*, Schija, b. 5 July 1910 in Krasnik[26]
40. *Erlichsohn*, Jankiel, b. 14 January 1904 in Krasnik
41. *Grünapel*, Sara, b. 6 April 1925 in Turobin, Kreis Krasnystaw[27]
42. *Brener*, Chaim, b. 5 May 1922 in Krasnik
43. *Reinstein*, Abraham, b. 15 September 1898 in Chodel
44. *Altwark*, Froim, b. 1 October 1917 in Drohizin.

16 Jankiel Weisbrot (Jakob Wajsbrot), merchant from Kraśnik.
17 Chana Weisbrot, née Bash, is thought to have been born in Włodawa.
18 Mendel Weisbrot (Pesach Mendel Wajsbrot) is thought to have been the son of Jankiel and Chana.
19 Berek Erlich was the younger brother of Schol (Shaul) Erlich.
20 Icchak (Icek) Bek, merchant, was the husband of Chaja Bek, née Rozenbusz.
21 Dr Josef Sapiro (Szapira) (1906–1944) was the physician at the camp.
22 Maks Kaminer was the owner of a printing shop in Biłgoraj prior to Sept. 1939.
23 Aron Kaminer was a dentist in Biłgoraj prior to Sept. 1939.
24 Eliezer Steingos (Luzer Sztajngos), house painter from Kraśnik.
25 Mendl Fajn lived in Kraśnik prior to Sept. 1939.
26 Jehoszua (Szyja) Hirsz Nordman, merchant from Kraśnik.
27 Sara Grunapel lived in Kraśnik prior to Sept. 1939.

The Jews listed under 18, 42, 43, and 44 were employed at the fuel depot (Wifo)[28] and housed in a camp.

During the investigations here, the following Jews escaped from Krasnik labour camp: On 14 February 1944, the Jew Jankiel *Erlich*, b. 16 April 1920 in Krasnik,[29]
on 16 February 1944, the Jew Chil *Rolnik*, b. 24 July 1911 in Krasnik.

So far, no trace of these Jews has been found.

On 17 February 1944 the Jews listed below ran away from the fuel depot in Krasnik:

1. *Brener*, Lejba, b. 8 August 1925 in Krasnik[30]
2. *Brener*, Schmul-Leiser, b. 1924 in Krasnik[31]
3. *Brukierer*, Ascher,[32] b. 3 December 1922 in Annopol
4. *Dorn*, Moses, b. 1926 in Litzmannstadt
5. *Diament*, Adam, b. 7 March 1916 in Krasnik[33]
6. *Datum*, Daniel, b. 1919 in Krasnik
7. *Datum*, Hersch, b. 1922 in Krasnik
8. *Datum*, Schija, b. 10 June 1926 in Bychawa
9. *Feder*, Daniel, b. 26 June 1905 in Jozefow
10. *Himelblau*, Schlomo-Zudik, b. 2 February 1916 in Krasnik[34]
11. *Hecht*, Leiba, b. 1913 in Litzmannstadt
12. *Kuchcik*, Lemel, b. 15 January 1914 in Litzmannstadt[35]
13. *Powroznik*, Hercko, b. 8 January 1920 in Krasnik[36]
14. *Reinstein*, Gabriel, b. 1 January 1925 in Chodel
15. *Schor*, Israel-Moschek, b. 3 June 1916 in Krasnik[37]
16. *Stalhammer*, Moschek, b. 16 October 1923 in Krasnik
17. *Sukmann*, Israel-Jeskiel, b. 9 January 1918 in Krasnik
18. *Schwarzbard*, Jeskiel, b. 1920 in Krasnik.

By order of the camp commandant, SS-Unterscharführer *Gröger*, the closest relatives of the Jews listed were immediately resettled that very same day. This pertained to twenty Jews.[38] Of those who escaped, the Jews listed under 4 and 12 have been captured.[39] Once further investigations have been concluded, the final solution will also be applied to them.

28 Wirtschaftliche Forschungsgesellschaft was a company that built fuel depots.
29 Jankiel Erlich survived.
30 Lejba Brener (b. 1926) survived.
31 Szmuel Eliezer Brener (1923–1944) lived in Kraśnik prior to Sept. 1939.
32 Aszer Bruchirer (Brukierer), escaped successfully; in the United Nations Relief and Rehabilitation Administration (UNRRA) camp in Berlin-Schlachtensee until mid 1948, then lived in Berlin-Wilmersdorf until July 1951; emigrated in 1951 to the USA; subsequently used the name Oscar Brooks.
33 Mojżesz Dorn and Adam Diament (Djament), survived.
34 Szlomo Caduk Himlbloj was caught and murdered.
35 Leon (Lejba) Hecht and Lemel Kuchcik lived in Łódź prior to Sept. 1939, later in Kraśnik; according to their brother-in-law/brother Max Kuchcik, they were captured half frozen in the woods and hanged in Feb. 1944.
36 Herc (Hercko) Powrożnik, labourer, was caught and murdered.
37 Moszek Szor, clerk, was shot dead by the SS in 1944, according to his cousin Leon Schor.
38 According to the report dated 19 Feb. 1944 submitted by Urban Police Officer Menzel, who was in charge of the operation, '21 relatives of the escapees were shot': BArch, R 70 Polen/179, fol. 3.
39 Himlbloj and Powrożnik were also caught. Fourteen persons initially managed to escape: Lejba and Szmuel Eliezer Brener; Daniel, Hersz, and Szyja Datum; Diament; Szor; Sztolhamer; Sukman; Szwarcbard; Rajnsztajn; Bruchirer; Feder; and Hecht.

## DOC. 286

## On 28 February 1944 the Polish government's representation in occupied Poland submits a detailed report on Treblinka extermination camp[1]

Report by the government delegation's intelligence service (S I – MO 4), dated 28 February 1944[2] (copy)

*TREBLINKA*

*The place*

On the Siedlce–Ostrołęka railway line, on the left bank of the Bug (powiat Sokołów, Warsaw voivodeship), 4 km from Małkinia, is the small station Treblinka; 3 km south of Małkinia there is an estate called 'Milewko', which is known for its very poor soil. A large plot of partially wooded wasteland stretches behind Milewko. The main resource and source of income at Milewko are the large and rich gravel deposits, to which a track was laid specially from Treblinka station.

*The construction of the camp*

In 1939–1940 the Germans began to amass troops on the border of the territory occupied by the Bolsheviks. For this reason, a large number of barracks were built in powiat Sokołów, a border district, to house troops, equipment, and materials. After the German-Bolshevik War began in 1941, these barracks were emptied and stood unused. Just a few weeks after the war began, parts of the abandoned barracks began to be brought to the site at Milewko. At the same time, a Gestapo unit took over the local buildings and the whole estate and began to bring in workers and craftsmen – mainly Jewish – from nearby towns. An extensive area was fenced off and the construction of a penal camp began, later named 'Treblinka No. 1'. In autumn of that year [1941] the camp was ready, and people arrested for so-called sabotage, that is, for smuggling food, committing other misdemeanours, or refusing to obey orders issued by the German authorities, began to be sent there. Only Poles were sent to this camp, where they were held for a specific period. Jews were taken there only as specialist workers, craftsmen, and labourers; they were kept in separate barracks, and none of them were released. 'Von Eupen'[3] became the camp commander – some German aristocrat, a degenerate and sadist, who tortured the Jews in horrible ways, hunting them as if they were ducks. One night, while drunk, he shot thirty-two Jews in one of the barracks. When this camp was up and running, construction began on the second one adjacent to it. A large area was fenced off with barbed wire and surrounded with a trench and an embankment; a railway track was extended to run through the middle of the camp; a makeshift station with signalling equipment was built; and an electric power plant and a whole series of barracks and other structures were erected. This camp was divided into two sections; the second was screened off by a high wooden fence, barbed wire, a trench, and an embankment. The

1 AAN, 1325/202/III-21, fols. 8–12. This document has been translated from Polish.

2 Above the date stamp (28 February 1944) is a handwritten note: 'Mr Klemens'; this is a reference to W. P. Klemens, who wrote accounts of the situation in occupied Poland; his full name is not known.

3 Correctly: Theodor van Eupen.

materials needed to complete this camp – including tableware – had to be procured by the Jewish communities in Kosów Lacki, Sokołów, and other towns in the area. To everyone's astonishment, the order also called for 1,000 kg of chloride of lime, which was supplied in bulk.

In spring 1942 various machines and excavators used for earthworks were brought to Treblinka railway station. Rumours circulated that the Bug was to be deepened, and that Jews would be used for this work. These rumours did not come to anything; all the machines were sent to the second section of what was already being called Camp No. 2. For the first half of July, the mysterious Camp No. 2 stood ready and empty, awaiting its destiny, as it were. The personnel in both camps consisted mainly of Ukrainians, with a smaller proportion of Germans. Approximately 600 Jewish labourers were specially selected for Camp No. 2. There were also Jewish personnel on the makeshift train platform, and between ten and twenty well-fed, well-dressed Jewish militiamen awaited unknown passengers, as it were, on the train platform.

*Camp operations and transports*

The first transports of Jews arrived in Treblinka on 22 July 1942, that is, with the start of the liquidation of the ghetto in Warsaw. Several railway transports arrived every day. Each transport consisted of between forty and sixty goods wagons with sealed doors and bars across the window hatches. At the front and the rear of these transports were two passenger coaches for the guards, most of whom were Ukrainian.[4] Guards with machine guns stood on the brakesman's cabin and watched carefully to ensure that no one escaped from the transport. Between 120 and 150 people were crammed into each wagon, pressed up against each other. The floorboards in the wagons were sprinkled with chloride of lime. Incidentally, summer and autumn 1942 were very hot, with the thermometer reaching 30–40 degrees [Celsius]. Overcrowding, the lack of air and lavatories, the chloride of lime, a train journey that sometimes lasted several days, and especially the lack of water led to conditions on the transports that are difficult to describe and would hardly seem credible to anyone who had not seen them with their own eyes. When such a transport approached Małkinia or Treblinka station, an unbearable stench emanated from the wagons, and terrified faces looked out of the window hatches, shouting, 'Water! Water!' Giving water to the supplicants was difficult because the guards would not let anyone near the transport and would shoot anyone who handed out water. Many Poles, primarily railway workers, were killed when they tried to distribute bottles of water. Later people came up with the idea of wetting rags and throwing them through the window hatches.

Upon the arrival of such a transport at Treblinka station, a locomotive would take twenty wagons and shunt them in the direction of Camp No. 2. The locomotive was uncoupled at the gate, and the gate was immediately closed. The wagons were then shunted to the makeshift train station and platform, where the Jewish militiamen stood. After the people had been unloaded from the transport, one of the Gestapo men gave a speech in which he said that nothing would happen to them there [in the camp], that they were being sent to work in the East on Hitler's orders, and that before their depar-

4 See Doc. 111.

ture they would have to undergo quarantine, wash in a bathhouse, and have their clothes disinfected to rid them of germs and disease. Suitcases and good-quality outerwear (both light and heavy coats) were to be handed in immediately for safekeeping, but they were to keep their jewellery and cash with them. Men, women, children, the elderly, and the infirm were immediately separated from one another. The presence of Jewish militiamen on the platform and the fact that it was also Jews who were issuing receipts to the Jews who handed in their belongings meant that the Jews continued to believe they would be sent to work in the East until the war ended. After handing in their better-quality belongings, they were taken deeper into the camp, near to the mysterious place where an engine roared incessantly. In a designated barracks they had to take off their remaining clothes, fold them separately, and hold on to their receipts, jewellery, gold, and foreign currency. Those who had gradually begun to realize what was going on and refused to undress voluntarily were stripped by members of a special group of Jewish workers who collected the jewellery and cash at the same time. Those who had undressed were then led to another barracks – the bathhouse – and in the passageway, two Gestapo cashiers[5] collected the jewellery and the cash at counters, this time without issuing a receipt. The bathhouse had a low ceiling and could hold up to 1,000 people. Those who resisted were pushed inside with force. There they fully grasped the situation and uttered terrible screams, but these were drowned out by the noise of the engines. There were two such [bathhouse] barracks, and they were movable; they could be shifted on rollers and had movable floors. They were situated above a deep ditch that had been dug with the special machines, the excavators. The barracks, packed with people, were tightly sealed. It was difficult to determine whether the air was pumped out or some kind of gas was pumped in, but the whole procedure took no longer than twenty minutes, and the entire barracks went completely silent. Two Gestapo men were involved in this final act, pressing some secret buttons, one of which made the floor of the death barracks split in two as it rose into the air, letting the bodies of those who had been gassed fall into this deep ditch.[6] Some were still alive; groans arose from the depths, and the bodies writhed as if in an anthill. The barracks was pushed aside, and the excavator covered up the knot of people. Thus group followed group – men, women, and children. When it came to the elderly, the infirm, and the little children, they did not even bother with the bathhouse; they simply transported them to the pits and shot them with machine guns. Between 7,000 and 15,000 people passed through the bathhouse in this way daily. The transports were emptied quickly; they arrived mainly at night and left empty in the morning.

Only certain guards had access to this section of the camp with the death chambers, so not everyone knew exactly what was going on. One could see that the transports were constantly arriving and that a line of people was constantly moving into the mysterious section of the camp, but no one ever saw anyone returning.

The transports from Warsaw arrived between the end of July and the middle of August. In mid August the liquidation of the Warsaw ghetto was suspended for seven days; however, all the ghettos along the Warsaw–Otwock and the Warsaw–Siedlce routes were

5 In fact, no Gestapo personnel were assigned to the camp.

6 In fact, Jewish work details opened and emptied the gas chambers and had to carry the bodies to the mass graves.

liquidated.[7] The liquidation operation in Warsaw was completed between the second half of August and 15 September.[8] Next, the liquidation of the ghettos in all the areas of Warsaw voivodeship on the right bank of the Vistula, in some of the neighbouring powiats of Lublin voivodeship, throughout the entire Kielce voivodeship, and in Białystok voivodeship proceeded at an accelerated pace. The second half of September and October was when the number of transports escalated the most and the deportees were a truly frightening sight to behold. That is why in some of the transports, especially from Kielce voivodeship, the number of dead and decomposing corpses would reach 25 per cent [of the total number of people]. Sometimes people broke open the sides or doors of the wagons during the transport and jumped out [while the train was moving] at full speed. These [escapees] were fired upon with machine guns; some fell under the wheels of the train, with the result that the railway tracks to Treblinka were littered with corpses. Usually a certain number managed to escape. Some of the camp personnel, Ukrainians as well as Germans, suffered nervous breakdowns and committed suicide.[9] They drank copious amounts of vodka and took cocaine and morphine. Transports left Treblinka carrying clothes, shoes, and closely guarded crates containing gold, precious stones, foreign currency, and młynarki.[10]

In November the number of transports declined. At the same time, new facilities were installed in the secret section of the camp, mainly underground, where they began to burn the bodies of those who had been gassed.[11] A crematorium had already been operating previously, but its capacity was small. Burying the bodies in mass graves was stopped altogether. In late 1942 and early 1943, transports began to arrive from the Balkan states, especially from Greece, Slovakia, France, the Netherlands, and Belgium. Some of these transports consisted of passenger coaches with luggage wagons, and some were even unguarded. The passengers were so firmly convinced that they were going to a recreational or industrial location called Treblinka that they did not believe it when they asked at the next-to-last stations, in Małkinia or Kosów Lacki,[12] how much further it was to Treblinka, and were given to understand what was there and what awaited them. It was only when they were surrounded by an armed convoy at Treblinka station and the locomotive shunted the wagons into the camp that the truth dawned on them, and they began to utter terrible screams. The luggage was immediately taken from the luggage wagons to the depots. Some of the rich Jews had previously sent letters and transferred cash to their acquaintances in Warsaw, requesting to buy or rent a villa in the resort known as Treblinka, which – as they emphasized – must be equipped with all the modern conveniences.

*Covering the tracks*

Around the time when the Germans began reporting on the Katyń affair,[13] they began opening the mass graves at the camp and burning the bodies. For this task a special unit

7 From 19 to 21 August 1942 the transports from Warsaw were suspended and the residents of the ghettos in the vicinity of Warsaw were taken to Treblinka.

8 The transports from Warsaw to Treblinka were suspended again from 28 August until 2 September 1942, and then continued until 21 September 1942.

9 Nothing is known about suicides among the camp personnel.

10 A popular name for the currency in the General Government.

11 Jewish work details took the corpses from the mass graves and burned them on pyres: see below.

12 Kosów Lacki was the first stop on the railway line between Treblinka and Siedlce.

of Ukrainians and groups of Jewish workers were used – they were brought in for this purpose (approximately 1,000 people). The bodies were burned not only in the crematorium, but also in the deep, open graves, using a white chemical compound that looked like powdered lime. From the early spring until August, thick clouds of smoke hung over the camp for Jews, rising from the depths of the ground, and an unbearable stench spread throughout the surrounding area over a radius of more than 20 km. During this time, a few transports arrived from liquidated ghettos in the GG, from the eastern regions, and mainly from Greece.[14] By early August, all traces of this massive crime had been erased, the bodies had been dug up and burned, and even the ashes left over from the cremation had been scattered on the fields of grain and the root vegetables growing on the Milewko estate.

*The revolt*

On 3 August, when some of the Germans and Ukrainians from the camp had gone to the beach on the Bug river or to the shops in Kosów or Małkinia, a revolt broke out in the camp for Jews.[15] A group of Jewish workers took advantage of the fact that only a small number of guards were present, seized the arms depot, and attacked the remaining guards with the weapons, killing or wounding dozens of Germans and Ukrainians. They did not manage to take the main gate, but they destroyed the wooden screen fence; they threw blankets, straw sacks, and other objects over the barbed wire in their attempt to get out of the camp. At the same time, in the first section of the camp, they set all the buildings on fire and burned them to the ground; the temporary railway station, the full storage depots, and the other barracks burned down [as well]. The Jews did not manage to take control of the second section of the camp, where the gas chambers and crematorium were located, so it remained intact. At the sound of the shots and sight of the fire, they [the personnel] from Camp No. 1 rushed to help, followed by those from the Bug and from Treblinka and Małkinia stations. Several hundred Jews were killed on the spot, mostly while trying to cross the barbed wire, but over 600 ran into the surrounding forests. Some of them were killed in the immediate pursuit and in subsequent search operations, but some managed to escape. The Jewish craftsmen who worked in the workshops in Camp No. 1 did not take part in the revolt.

*Liquidation of the camp*

The buildings that had burned down were not rebuilt. In September the final transports from Vilna and Białystok arrived.[16] In October the remaining buildings and the gas chambers in the second section of the camp, which had escaped the fire, were demolished. Some of the equipment was taken to Majdanek. The wooden screen fence was demolished, the barbed wire was rolled up, the trenches and ditches were filled in, and the entire area was ploughed up and sown with winter grain or planted with groves of pine trees.

13 German news sources first reported on the discovery of mass graves in Katyń on 13 April 1943. See also Doc. 228, fn. 6.

14 In February and March 1943 transports arrived from Bezirk Bialystok, and in March and April 1943 from the formerly Greek regions of Macedonia and Thrace, which were at that time occupied by Bulgaria.

15 The prisoners' uprising in Treblinka took place on 2 August 1943.

16 On 21 August 1943, after the prisoner uprising, two transports arrived from Białystok, and the SS murdered the prisoners from these transports in the gas chambers.

Camp No. 1, the penal labour camp, continued to operate, and a small number of Jewish craftsmen remained there, working in the workshops as well as for the medical and sanitation services which served the remainder of the camp.[17]

*Losses among the Jewish population*

How many of the Jewish population were put to death in Treblinka? This question will be difficult to answer definitively. There is no data on this[18] and there probably never will be. One can only provide provisional, approximate figures based on the number of Jewish people in all the areas from which transports were sent to Treblinka. Let us begin with the 1931 census.

| | |
|---|---|
| Jewish population of Mosaic faith: | 352,000 in the city of Warsaw |
| | 220,000 in Warsaw voivodeship |
| | 317,000 in Kielce voivodeship |
| | 197,000 in Białystok voivodeship |
| Total | 1,086,000 |
| Jews of other denominations and population growth over eight years: | 114,000 |
| Grand total | 1,200,000 |

Of these, a certain number emigrated abroad in 1939, and a significant number made their way to Bolshevik-occupied territory after the Germans annexed Poland. Altogether, however, no more than 100,000–150,000 people went abroad.

Starting in late 1939, the Germans had begun to purge the cities and towns in western Poland and even on Reich territory by sending the Jewish population to eastern Poland, especially to the above-mentioned regions (with the exception of Białystok voivodeship) and to the city of Warsaw. In 1942 the Jewish population in all the cities, towns, and villages was at least 50 per cent larger than it had been before the war. One can assume that when the liquidation began and Treblinka was in operation, there were at least 1.5 million Jews living in the above-mentioned localities. About 35 per cent of these escaped during the liquidation of the ghettos or were killed on the spot or deported to the workshops for craftsmen in Trawniki and Poniatowa (mainly from Warsaw), which means that approximately 1 million people passed through Treblinka.

| | |
|---|---|
| One must add to this number: | 100,000 foreign Jews |
| | 50,000 from powiats in Lublin voivodeship |
| | 50,000 from Vilna and Polesia voivodeship |

This gives a total of approximately 1.2 million people.[19] The figure is not based on sources; there are none and never will be. But one thing is certain: there are no Jews left in the above-mentioned regions – neither in the ghettos nor in the work details – except for those who are hiding in the cities with the help of Polish identity cards, or in the forests with various gangs or in hiding places.

17 The penal labour camp remained in operation until July 1944.

18 As of 31 December 1942 the SS put the number of people murdered at Treblinka at 713,555: see Doc. 204. Tens of thousands more victims – possibly as many as 200,000 – had been murdered by August 1943, when the camp was shut down after the prisoner uprising.

19 According to recent calculations, at least 750,000 people were murdered in Treblinka.

## DOC. 287

## From 16 December 1943 to February 1944 Fryderyk Winnykamień describes life in hiding in Warsaw[1]

Handwritten diary of Fryderyk Winnykamień, entries for 16 December 1943 – February 1944[2]

*16 December 1943*. Purtowa, Anka, and Helena come by and knock on the door.[3] The postman comes. It's cold, we shiver. Straight after dinner we go to bed. Shots in our building at 7.30 p.m. We immediately jump up and get ready to go downstairs.[4] Mama[5] goes first and finds out that a Polish policeman has been shot at the gate to our building. He is lying wounded at the caretaker's. As we expect the gendarmerie to surround the building, we go down to our hole and stay there overnight.

*17 December*. We crawl out of our hole. Mama learns the details of the incident: three men tried to take away the policeman's weapon, they had followed him from the street, etc., [he was] taken to hospital – there is no investigation. In the morning Piotr[6] brings us a letter from Marek[7] and the rest of Przeradowska's things – she was upset because Mama asked for her wool headscarf back. At 10 p.m. an exact description of the entire incident with the Gestapo at Krystyna Gryniewicz's: Heniek killed, his mother wounded and dead. The police guard the neighbourhood all night long.

*18 December*. The whole building is bustling, especially the cellar. Discussions about the incident.

*19 December*. Mrs Gryniewicz's funeral. No one comes to visit us: the Przeradowskis do not want to. Jadzia[8] is preparing everything for Christmas – she has no time. Łaszewski and Władek[9] are selling Christmas trees on Jasna Street. They earn several thousand daily.

1 USHMM, Collections Division, gift from Frederick Weinstein (formerly Fryderyk Winnykamień), fol. 254. This document has been translated from Polish.
2 This diary fragment is part of Winnykamień's chronicle, which he composed from Dec. 1943 to August 1944, following his escape from the Warsaw ghetto, when he was hiding in a room in a cellar at 54 Wolska Street in the city's Wola district.
3 Barbara Purtowa, Anka Jakubiak, and Helena Maryniak were neighbours of Fryderyk's mother who was renting a small room at 54 Wolska Street under an assumed Polish identity; only a few people knew she was hiding her husband and son in her apartment, which was why they had to hide when visitors knocked at the door.
4 A hiding place for Fryderyk and his father had been dug under a cupboard.
5 Isabella (Izabella) Winnykamień, née Gerszange (1899–2000), Leopold Winnykamień's wife; emigrated to Israel in 1948; emigrated to the USA in the mid 1950s.
6 Piotr Przeradowski, lathe operator at the Ursus factory in Warsaw; helped the Winnykamień family and passed on post from Marek Mydlarz; did not live in the building at 54 Wolska Street.
7 Marek Mydlarz (Midlasch) (1919–1989), businessman; engaged to Fryderyk's older sister, Apolonia (1920–1943), who was killed in the Warsaw Ghetto Uprising; forced labourer in Starachowice camp; joined a partisan group after escaping the camp in 1944; lived in Berlin from the late 1940s.
8 Jadwiga (Jadzia) Łazarowicz, a neighbour in the building at 54 Wolska Street who helped the Winnykamień family.
9 Łaszewski was Jadzia Łazarowicz's boyfriend; Władek, actually Władysław Łazarowicz, was her son.

*Christmas Eve*. The Maryniaks[10] invite Mama to a joint dinner. Mama declines. On Christmas Day, Mama goes to the Maryniaks for breakfast. Jadzia brings us a food parcel, but I don't want to try it, and I don't try it. I look out the window: I listen to and watch the Poles enjoying themselves, but I can't go out. The New Year 1944 is coming. What will it bring us? Our people are going on the offensive from Žitomir.[11] We'll see what comes of it. We don't get any visits at all. Władek came once, just to show us how he eats an apple.

*New Year 1944*. The Maryniaks have left for the entire day. It is quiet, empty, cold, the food is counted in spoonfuls. Dry bread with onions. I look out the window – it's snowing and snowing … And young Poles are having fun, walking around, singing, throwing snowballs. And I am freezing.

*3 January 1944*. Jadzia comes to visit [with news that] Sarny[12] has been captured. Joy – it won't be long now. Now we wait, from one day to the next. Równe and Łuck are captured.[13] Otherwise nothing. We are hungry, freezing. A letter comes from B[erlin] with an address for registered mail. I send my Kennkarte and Ausweis.[14] They send us 100 RM per month.[15] None of the Przerad[owskis] comes to visit. Jadzia comes very rarely – she can't stay longer than five minutes – her feet freeze! They are to take away apartments from newcomers; we are afraid for ours! Nice letters from Rysia:[16] she's getting a little help from Berlin.[17] The Poles are denouncing Jews – a policeman's story about Miłosna,[18] about a cave and fifteen Jews. Jews have been hauled out of 53 Wolska.

Zofia[19] sends packets: noodles, blancmange, wheat flour, semolina. We shiver terribly in the cold, from morning till night. Meanwhile the Bolsheviks have come to a halt. Rather good letters from Rysia. Not from Marek because Przeradowski doesn't come to see us. Germans are being killed in the streets. The Poles talk about the Jews. They say the Bolsheviks won't come here! We will fight them! Anka Jakubiak and Ewiakowa.[20] We await the invasion.[21] At the same time we must be on our guard on all sides. Jadzia hardly visits us any more, neither does Władek – they have things to eat at home. We

10 Jan and Helena Maryniak.

11 The Red Army began its winter offensive on 24 Dec. 1943 and crossed the pre-war Polish-Soviet border in early Jan. 1944.

12 The Red Army captured the fortified town of Sarny in what had been eastern Poland (now Ukraine) on 4 Jan. 1944.

13 In fact, the Red Army captured the cities of Rovno and Lutsk (now part of Ukraine) on 2 Feb. 1944.

14 German in the original: 'identity card'; '[work] permit'.

15 The Winnykamień family was in contact (probably from Dec. 1942) with the sisters Karola Woop, Tania Pakman, and Pela Rozen in Berlin, who sent them money and food. Fryderyk sent them a blank identity card by post; the intention was for this card to be filled out using a German typewriter.

16 Ryszarda (Rysia) Winnykamień (1927–1945), the author's younger sister; lived under an 'Aryan' identity as a forced labourer in Bötzow, north-west of Berlin, from Nov. 1942; died in an air raid on Berlin.

17 In other words, from the Woop-Pakman-Rozen family.

18 A small town east of Warsaw, which is today part of the city of Warsaw.

19 Zofia is a code name for the sisters Karola Woop, Tania Pakman, and Pela Rozen in Berlin.

20 A neighbour in the building at 54 Wolska Street.

21 This could be a reference to the Red Army or to the Allied landings.

count the remaining money and the last bites [of food]. Mum sells her dress to Purtowa – Jadzia receives 40 złoty as a percentage [of the sale], although they have so much money that they don't even know how much. Raids […][22] Karol[23] and the Mongols.[24]

*February 1944*. We are freezing. None of the Przerad[owskis] comes over. A fire. An incident with Jews on Płocka (nine Jews in the underground). Letters from Berlin and from Rysia – [everything is] normal. The *Kennk[arte]* arrives from B[erlin]. I produce stamps.[25] Władek comes by more and more often with arithmetic problems, lately every day. Jadzia comes by now and then.

Several times we stay down in the hole, because according to Jadzia, the gendarmes have surrounded our building.[26] Meanwhile all of Wolska is surrounded – Frank is driving through the city.[27] Every day since 19 January we have been receiving the previous day's *Kurier*.[28] Quiet on all fronts and the days pass. The Poles are having fun, living life, while we sit in a prison, and in such a prison as this! I read books and newspapers, and I learn (review) English.

On 14 February I turned 22 years old. Jadzia ran into Piotr in the street: 'They should thank God they're alive and that bread is cheap with coupons!' Franto Tuna's account of some Jews in Skierniewicka [Street] who hanged themselves.

22 Preposition missing in the original: presumably 'by' or 'on'.
23 Presumably a reference to the German occupiers.
24 Presumably a reference to auxiliary troops fighting for the Germans.
25 In the weeks that followed, Fryderyk used the completed identity card to forge a work permit, which he used from August 1944.
26 On 1 Feb. 1944 Polish resistance fighters from the Home Army mounted an attack on the SS and Police Leader in Warsaw, Franz Kutschera, in which he and several of his companions were killed. In response, the Germans searched countless buildings in the city's Wola district during the night of 2–3 Feb. 1944; the Security Police shot several hundred Polish prisoners in retaliation – including a group at 79/81 Wolska Street on 10 Feb. 1944.
27 This may be a reference to the funeral ceremonies for Kutschera and his companions, during which vehicle convoys drove through the city; Governor General Frank did not travel to Warsaw on this occasion.
28 The *Nowy Kurier Warszawki* was the official Warsaw daily newspaper in Polish and was published from 1939 to 1944.

## DOC. 288

## On 1 March 1944 Emanuel Ringelblum and Adolf Berman look back on the cultural and political work done in the Warsaw ghetto[1]

Typewritten letter[2] from Emanuel Ringelblum and Adolf Berman in Warsaw to YIVO, the Jewish PEN Club,[3] Szalom Asz,[4] Lejwik,[5] Opatoszu,[6] and Dr Rafał Mahler[7] in New York, dated 1 March 1944

Dear friends,

We are writing to you at a time when 95 per cent of Polish Jews have already been murdered in terrible agony in the gas chambers at the execution sites in Treblinka, Sobibór, Chełmno, and Oświęcim, or during countless 'liquidation operations' in the ghettos and the camps. The fate of the few Jews who continue to vegetate and suffer in a number of concentration camps has already been sealed. Perhaps a small handful of Jews will remain alive, [those now] leading an illegal existence in the 'Aryan districts' under the constant threat of death, or roaming the forests like hunted animals. We doubt that any of us, the social activists working under the conditions necessitated by our double lives,[8] will survive the war. Therefore, in this way we wish to inform you briefly about the work that connects us most closely to you.

When the Polish Jews fell under the monstrous National Socialist yoke, an independent Jewish social activist group immediately commenced a broad range of activities under the motto of self-help and struggle. With active and generous help from the 'Joint' [JDC], a vast network of welfare institutions was established in Warsaw and in the countryside, led by 'ŻTOS' (the Jewish Social Welfare Association), 'CENTOS' (the Jewish Central Association for the Care of Orphans), and 'TOZ' (the Society for the Protection of the Health of the Jewish Population). 'ORT' was also very active. Tens of thousands

1 BLHG, no. 5672, fols. 26–28. Published in Meylekh Nayshtadt, *Khurbm un oyfshtand fun di yidn in varshe: Eydes-bleter un azkores*, vol. 1: *Eydes-bleter* (Tel Aviv: Algemeyner yidisher arbeter-organizatsye in yisroel and Yidish-natsionaler arbeter-farband in amerike, 1948), pp. 307–315. This document has been translated from Polish.

2 The letter is based on Berman's handwritten draft, dated 25 Jan. 1944, with numerous deletions and some reordering of the text: BLHG, no. 5672, fols. 13–19. After it had been typed out, the letter was sent to London as part of a consolidated mailing on 25 May 1944: SPP, MSW, Teka 46, L.p. 6, Z/6.

3 In addition to the PEN Club for writers working in Polish, since 1927 there had also been a PEN Club in Poland for writers working in Yiddish. From 1936 its chairman was Yekhiel Yeshaye Trunk (1887–1961), who arrived in New York in March 1941 after fleeing Poland.

4 Szalom Asz (Schalom or Sholem Asch) (1880–1957), Yiddish-language writer from Poland, lived in the USA, 1914–1923; worked for the *Jewish Daily Forward* in New York; became a US citizen in 1920; from 1932 honorary president of the PEN Club for writers working in Yiddish.

5 Halper Leivick, né Levi Halpern (1888–1962), poet and dramatist who wrote in Yiddish; Bund activist; exiled to Siberia for his work with the Bund; fled to the USA in 1913.

6 Josef Opatoszu, né Josef Meir Opatowski (1886–1954), writer; lived in New York from 1907; wrote historical novels about the life of Jews in Poland.

7 Dr Rafał (Raphael) Mahler (1899–1977), historian; member of Poale Zion-Left; studied in Vienna; thereafter employed as a teacher in Warsaw; researcher and editor in the Historical Section of YIVO (the Yiddish Scientific Institute) from 1935; worked in the USA from 1937; emigrated to Israel in 1950; worked with Yad Vashem; professor in Tel Aviv from 1961.

8 The term 'double life' was true of Adolf Berman, who lived under an 'Aryan' identity in Warsaw and worked for both the Jewish ('national') underground and the Polish ('political') underground; Ringelblum was living in hiding at this time.

of people, adults and children, were able to survive over a longer period of time thanks to the help of these institutions and the extensive network of building committees[9] that cooperated with them. These organizations carried on their self-sacrificing work until the very last moment, as long as the faintest spark of life still glimmered within the Jewish community. All the political parties and groups of every ideological persuasion conducted their clandestine activities under the cover of these organizations. Almost all cultural work was organized under their umbrella.

The motto of Jewish social activism was: 'To live and die with dignity!' We made an effort to implement this motto in the ghettos and the camps. Our wide-ranging cultural activities, which defied the indescribable terror, hunger, and misery and spread in all directions until the martyrdom of Polish Jewry, were an expression of this.

When the Warsaw ghetto was hermetically sealed, a clandestine cultural organization was established under the name 'IKOR' (Organization for Yiddish Culture), which carried out extensive cultural activities and organized a series of academic lectures, jubilee celebrations (in honour of Perec, Sholem Aleichem, Mendełe [Moicher Sforim], Borochov, and others), and literary and artistic events.[10] The soul of 'IKOR' was a young economist, Menachem Linder,[11] murdered by the Germans back in April 1942.

Under the guise of the children's kitchens and 'CENTOS' branches, a network of clandestine schools of various orientations (Ciszo,[12] Tarbut, Szuł-Kult, Jabne, Chorew, Bajs-Jakow, and others) was created.[13] The secular schools in which Yiddish was the language [of instruction] were particularly active. They were set up by the unforgettable activists Szachne Sagan and Sonia Nowogródzka; both were deported to Treblinka to their deaths.

9 See Doc. 29, fn. 3.

10 IKOR had been established in Dec. 1941. The other main organization in this field was the Yiddish-Hebrew Tekumah cultural institution, which was led by the historian Menachem (Edmund) Stein.

11 Menachem Linder (1911–1942), economist; employed by YIVO in the 1930s; activist in the political underground in the Warsaw ghetto and member of Oyneg Shabes; organized soup kitchens; murdered during the night of 17–18 April 1942. The document uses the title Mgr. (magister), which indicates he held a master's degree.

12 The Central Yiddish School Organization (Tsentrale Yidishe Shul Organizatsye) was the Bund's educational organization from 1921 to 1942 and provided instruction in Yiddish. More than 15,000 pupils attended 169 CISzO schools in Poland in 1935.

13 Tarbut (Hebrew: 'culture') was a Zionist network of secular educational institutions founded in 1922; in 1939 the organization was running 270 schools and colleges attended by 45,000 people, which corresponded to about 9 per cent of Jewish schoolchildren and students in Poland. The School and Cultural Society (Szuł- un Kulturfarband), founded in 1928 under the influence of Poale Zion-Left and the Jewish People's Party, ran schools where Yiddish and Hebrew were the languages of instruction; 2,135 children attended its 17 schools and kindergartens in 1934–1935; it also ran night schools, libraries, and adult education centres. The Zionist Mizrachi party's cultural and educational association Jabne (Jawne), founded in 1922, combined a focus on religious and Zionist education with teaching in Hebrew; in the 1930s it ran 65 schools attended by 5,686 students. The Khorev Central Educational Organization ('Chorew') was an association of boys' schools founded by Agudas Yisroel in 1929; during the 1934–1935 academic year it ran 469 institutions, with 18,300 children in cheder schools and 43,000 in Talmud Torah schools (both are religious primary schools); 18,758 students attended yeshivas (Jewish religious schools) for students aged 13 or older. Bajs-Jakow (Bejs Jakow or Bejt Jaakow) was an association of girls' schools affiliated with Agudas Yisroel; in the 1930s it ran 110 schools attended by 31,000 students. In addition to primary schools, there were a number of illegal or semi-legal secondary education institutions.

A clandestine Jewish central archive was set up under the innocent name of the 'Oneg Szabes' association. Under the leadership of Dr Emanuel Ringelblum, the founder of the archive, and with the active assistance of H. Wasser, Gutkowski,[14] Rabbi Sz. Huberband,[15] Sz. Winter,[16] Menachem Kon, Abram Lewin,[17] and others, materials and documents on the martyrdom of the Jews in Poland were collected. Thanks to the intensive efforts of the entire staff, a dozen boxes of extraordinarily valuable documents, chronicles, diaries, reports, illustrations, etc. have been collected. All of these materials are buried in the territory of the ghetto;[18] we have no access to them. Most of the material sent abroad came from our archive. With this detailed information we have alerted the world to the greatest crime in history. We continue to archive documents as before. Despite the terrible conditions, we are gathering diaries and documents about the martyrdom, the struggle, and the current living conditions of the remaining Polish Jews. In 1941 and 1942 we were in contact with Z. Kalmanowicz[19] in Vilna, who collated the YIVO's materials under German supervision and hid a considerable amount of them. Now there are no Jews left in Vilna. A major centre of Jewish culture and modern scholarly activity has been completely destroyed.

Virtually all parties and political organizations, especially those for young people, were actively engaged in clandestine cultural activities. For almost the entire duration of the ghetto's existence there was an underground press, and magazines and periodicals appeared. The following organizations were particularly active in the press: the 'Bund' (*Biuletin*,[20] *Cajt-Fragn*,[21] *Jugnt-Sztime*, *Za naszą i waszą wolność*, *Nowa Młodzież*), 'Poale Zion-Left' (*Proletarisher Gedank*, *Jugnt-ruf*, *Avangard*,[22] *Nasze Hasło*), 'Haszomer Hacair' (*Przedwiośnie*, *Jutrznia*, *Ojfbrojz*, a series of anthologies), 'Dror' (*Dror*, *Idies*, *Cama-*

14 Eliasz Gutkowski (1900–1943), teacher; member of the Poale Zion party; worked at the Dror school in the Warsaw ghetto; simultaneously worked as an editor for the underground publication *Wiadomości*; escaped from a transport to Treblinka and returned to the ghetto in August 1942; perished during the Warsaw Ghetto Uprising. The document uses the title Mgr. (magister), which indicates he held a master's degree.

15 Szymon (Shimon) Huberband (1909–1942), rabbi; expelled from Piotrków; thereafter worked as a Jewish affairs official for ŻTOS (later the Social Welfare Department of the Jewish Social Self-Help (JSS)) in Warsaw; deported to Treblinka in August 1942.

16 Szmul (Samuel) Winter (1891–1943), businessman; grain merchant from Włocławek; co-founder of YIVO; worked in the Warsaw Jewish Council's Supply Office and as a liaison to the Jewish Social Self-Help (JSS); shot and killed by Germans during the Warsaw Ghetto Uprising.

17 Abram Lewin (1893–1943), teacher; provided welfare services in the Warsaw ghetto from 1940; deported to Treblinka in Jan. 1943. His diary, covering the period 26 March 1942 to 16 Jan. 1943, is published in English as *A Cup of Tears: A Diary of the Warsaw Ghetto*, ed. Antony Polonsky, trans. from Hebrew and Yiddish Christopher Hutton (Oxford: Basil Blackwell, 1988 [Yiddish edn, 1952 and 1954]).

18 See Doc. 106.

19 Dr Zelig Kalmanovič (1885–1944), linguist and translator; studied in Berlin and Königsberg; completed his doctorate in St Petersburg in 1919; co-founder of YIVO in Vilna; deported to Estonia in Sept. 1943; murdered in Narva forced labour camp.

20 At least eighteen issues of this underground newspaper appeared under the name *Biuletin* in 1940–1941, after which it was published under constantly changing titles until the end of 1942: *Dos Fraye Vort*, *Der Glok*, *Der Shturm*, and *Oyf der vakh*.

21 Correctly: *Tsayt-Fragn*, a theory-based Bund publication; at least two issues came out in 1941.

22 At least two issues of this publication appeared in Yiddish in 1942; four issues were published in Polish under the title *Awangarda Młodzieży*.

*darich, Gwure un Pajn*[23]), 'Poale Zion-Right' (*Bafrajung*), the anti-fascist block (*Der Ruf*), the communists (*Morgn-Frajhajt*[24]), and others.[25] Some of these publications, which appeared in Warsaw, were distributed in almost every ghetto, despite the severe obstacles to transport and communications.

The Jewish Central Association for the Care of Orphans, 'CENTOS', carried out a broad range of cultural activities that reached the majority of children and young people. Under the leadership of Dr A. Berman and the unforgettable Róża Symchowicz[26] (she died of typhus, which she contracted while working with street children), and supported by a team of Jewish teachers, educators, and artists, they organized hundreds of events for children in boarding schools, centres, and common rooms.

A central children's library was set up under the direction of Basia Temkin-Bermanowa; a theatre was founded under the direction of Bluma Fuswerk,[27] with the cooperation of A. Samberg, Chana Braz,[28] A. Kurc,[29] Michał Znicz,[30] and others; and courses in Yiddish language and literature were offered. In particular, impressive cultural and artistic events took place, especially within the framework of the major community initiatives for 'Children's Month', which thousands of listeners attended in order to escape the nightmare of their real lives for a few hours and to spend some carefree time with their children. Hundreds of children from 'CENTOS' institutions and schools participated in these events, which were of a high artistic standard. Today there are no longer any Jewish children left in Poland! The National Socialist criminals have murdered 99[31] per cent of the children.

In the ghetto there was a symphony orchestra, led by the famous conductor Szymon Pullman.[32] Wonderful symphony and chamber music concerts provided listeners with rare moments to pause and forget. Pullman and almost every member of the orchestra,

23 Correctly: *Payn un gvure.*
24 Correctly: *Morgn-fray.*
25 Other publications were also produced, such as Hashomer Hatzair's programmatic periodical *Neged Hazerem*. The titles of some of these publications are known, but no copies have survived.
26 Dr Róża Symchowicz (1890–1942?), psychologist and educator from Slutsk; worked for YIVO and lived in Warsaw prior to Sept. 1939.
27 Bluma (Klima) Fuswerk, teacher; ran the children's events programme for CENTOS as well as a puppet theatre in the Warsaw ghetto; lived on the 'Aryan side' from 1943 at the latest; worked with the Council to Aid Jews on behalf of the Jewish National Committee (ŻKN); director of the Polish Children's Theatre after the war.
28 Chana Braz (Bras(s)), Yiddish-speaking actor; member of the Vilner trupe (Vilna Troupe); performed at a puppet theatre in the Warsaw ghetto; simultaneously worked for IKOR; deported to Treblinka in Sept. 1942.
29 Abram (Abraham) Kurc (1892–1942), actor and comedian; ran the artists' canteen in the Warsaw ghetto; member of the theatre group that worked for CENTOS; deported to Treblinka in 1942.
30 Michał Znicz, né Michał Feiertag (1888?–1943), actor; master of ceremonies at the Quid pro Quo revue in Warsaw; performed at cabaret theatres in the Warsaw ghetto; admitted to Zofiówka sanatorium due to depression; thereafter lived on the 'Aryan side'; died in Pruszków on 24 Dec. 1943 (thought to have taken his own life).
31 Instead of this figure, the typewritten original reads: '!!'; the number is supplied here on the basis of the handwritten draft: BLHG, no. 5672, fol. 15.
32 Szymon Pullman (1887–1942), violinist; appointed violin teacher at the Vienna Conservatory in 1927; lived in Paris, 1938–1939; returned to Poland in summer 1939. In addition to Pullman, Marian Neuteich, Adam Furmański, and Izrael Hamerman also conducted the Warsaw Symphony Orchestra between 1940 and 1942.

including the violinist Ludwik Holcman,[33] perished in Treblinka. The young musical director Marian Neuteich perished in Trawniki camp.[34] New young talent sprang up in the ghetto. The phenomenal young singer Marysia Ajzensztadt – the 'ghetto nightingale', daughter of the conductor of the Warsaw Synagogue Choir – was a shining star. She was murdered by SS men during the liquidation operation.[35] Choirs were founded. The children's choirs under the direction of I. Fajwiszyc were of a particularly high standard. Fajwiszyc[36] perished in Poniatowa camp. Other choirmasters, including Gladstein[37] and Zaks,[38] perished in Treblinka. Jewish painters and sculptors, who lived in extreme poverty, organized exhibitions sporadically. Feliks Fryfman was one of them.[39] All the Jewish visual artists were taken away to Treblinka to their deaths.

Even in the SS concentration camps, to which a certain portion of the Jews from Warsaw and other cities were taken, our social and cultural activists continued their work. They did not succumb, but continued to serve the community. In Poniatowa, in Trawniki, and in other camps, clandestine social self-help [groups] emerged. From time to time there were even illegal cultural events, celebrations, etc. The wellspring of social and cultural activity bubbled as long as life pulsed in the Jewish communities. You should know that the last surviving activists remained true to the ideals of our culture until the very end. Until their deaths, they never let the banner of culture and the struggle against barbarism fall from their hands.

When the phase of murderous 'resettlement operations' began, the idea of self-help receded into the background and gave way to the idea of combat. At the forefront were our heroic young people of all stripes, as well as labour activists, headed by pro-Palestine organizations. The glorious epic of the Jewish armed struggle in Poland commenced: the heroic defence of the Warsaw ghetto, the magnificent struggle in Białystok, the destruction of the execution sites in Treblinka and Sobibór, the battles in Tarnów, Będzin, Częstochowa, and other centres. The Jews showed the world that they are capable of fighting with weapons in their hands, that they know how to die with dignity in the struggle against the mortal enemy of the Jewish people and of all humankind.

That is all we wanted to share with you, dear friends. There are not many of us left alive. Of the writers, Rachela Auerbach lives, writes, and collaborates with us; the young

33 Ludwik Holcman (1889–1942), violinist; soloist with the Warsaw Symphony Orchestra until 1939.

34 Marian Neuteich (1906–1943), musical director and composer from Łódź; cellist and co-founder of the Warsaw String Quartet; returned to Warsaw after a European tour in August 1939.

35 Miriam (Marysia) Ajzensztadt (1922–1942), singer; daughter of the synagogue choir leader Dawid Ajzensztadt.

36 Correctly: Izrael Fajwiszys (1887–1943), singer and conductor from Yampil (Ukraine); studied in Cracow and Vienna; lived in Łódź prior to Sept. 1939; engaged in musical activities including the role of synagogue choir leader; children's choir leader in the Warsaw ghetto.

37 Israel Gladstein (Glatsztajn, Gladsztejn) (1887–1942), composer and conductor from Gostynin; later lived in Łódź and Berlin; expelled from Berlin in summer 1939; children's choir leader in the Warsaw ghetto.

38 Icchak Zaks (1887–1942?), music teacher and conductor from Radomsko; lived in Łódź prior to Sept. 1939.

39 Correctly: Feliks Frydman (Friedman) (1897–1942), painter; chairman of the Association of Jewish Visual Artists in Poland prior to 1939; member of the Jewish Council's Cultural Council in the Warsaw ghetto; probably perished during the deportations in late August 1942.

poet Nachman Blic[40] is alive; a number of Jewish-Polish literary figures are alive – Rudnicki,[41] Jastrun,[42] Lec,[43] Maksymilian Boruchowicz,[44] and others. The artists Jonas Turkow[45] and Diana Blumfeld,[46] along with her daughter, are alive and under our care. The painter Nacht is alive.[47] As you probably know, Icchak Kacenelson is in the camp for foreigners in Vittel.[48] J. Perle, N. Buksbaum, and a few other activists were taken to the camp for foreigners in Bergen, near Celle and Hanover. We do not know whether they are alive. Look after them via the International Red Cross. We enclose a list of the murdered cultural activists.[49]

We doubt that we will see each other again. Convey our heartfelt greetings to all Jewish cultural activists, writers, journalists, musicians, sculptors, everyone who has contributed to Jewish culture, and to fighters for national liberation and the liberation of all humankind.

Warsaw, 1 March
Dr A. Berman
Dr E. Ringelblum

40 Nachman Rosenberg, nom de plume Nachman Blic (b. 1906), Yiddish-language writer from Lwów; later lived in Warsaw and Kazimierz Dolny; returned to live in Lwów, 1939–1941; survived the war on the 'Aryan side'.

41 Adolf Rudnicki, né Aron Hirschhorn (1909/1912–1990), bank employee and writer; member of the Jewish National Committee (ŻKN) in Lwów, 1940–1941; lived in Warsaw from 1942; member of the Home Army from 1944; fought in the Warsaw Uprising in 1944; frequently addressed the persecution and murder of the Jews in his literary works.

42 Dr Mieczysław Jastrun, né Mojsze Agatstajn (1903–1983), teacher, poet, and translator; converted to Christianity in 1920; fled to Lwów in 1939; returned to Warsaw in 1941; contributed to the underground press; lived in Międzylesie from July 1944; received various honours, including a prize in 1969 for his translations from German.

43 Stanisław Jerzy Lec (1909–1966), lawyer, poet, and aphorist; fled from Warsaw to Lwów in 1939; held in a forced labour camp in Tarnopol, 1941–1943; escaped and fought with the partisans; joined the Polish Workers' Party (PPR) and the People's Guard; worked in a Polish army propaganda unit; press attaché in Vienna, 1949–1950.

44 Dr Michał Borwicz, né Michał Maksymilian Boruchowicz (1911–1987), writer and sociologist; member of the Polish Socialist Party (PPS); fled from Cracow to Lwów in 1939; held in Janowska camp, 1942–1943; escaped and joined the partisans; head of the Jewish Historical Commission in Cracow voivodeship, 1945–1947; thereafter lived in Paris.

45 Jonas Turkow (1898–1982), actor and director of the Yiddish theatre in Poland; began his career with the Vilner trupe; contributed to the underground archive of the Warsaw ghetto, 1940–1942; thereafter lived on the 'Aryan side'; emigrated to the USA in 1946; worked for YIVO in New York; lived in Israel from 1966; author of *C'était ainsi 1939–1943: La vie dans le ghetto de Varsovie*, trans. from Yiddish by Maurice Pfeffer (Paris: Austral, 1995).

46 Correctly: Diana (Dina) Blumenfeld (1903–1961), actor and singer; Jonas Turkow's wife; lived in the Warsaw ghetto, 1940–1942; then on the 'Aryan side'; emigrated to the USA in 1946.

47 Artur (Stefan) Nacht-Samborski (1898–1974), artist known for his colourist works; lived in Berlin and Vienna, 1921–1924; lived in Paris, 1924–1938, and in Lwów, 1939–1941; subsequently lived on the 'Aryan side' in Warsaw under a false name; professor at the Academy of Fine Arts in Warsaw from 1949.

48 Icchak Kacenelson (Yitzhak Katsenelson) (1886–1944), Yiddish-language writer; worked for Dror in the Warsaw ghetto; held a Honduran passport and was interned in Vittel camp from May 1943; deported in April 1944 to Auschwitz, where he was murdered.

49 The list Ringelblum compiled, which included the names of 320 people who had been murdered by the Germans, is not published here.

*Note*

Letter written on 1 March 1944. A week later, on 7 March 1944, the Gestapo discovered the underground shelter in the Jewish quarter[50] where Dr E. Ringelblum was hiding. Dr Ringelblum, his wife and son, and thirty-five [other] people, mainly from intellectual circles, were tortured dreadfully by the Germans and shot in the ruins of the ghetto.[51] Through this martyrdom the life of this outstanding historian, passionate social activist, and enthusiastic champion of modern Jewish culture came to an end.

20 May 1944

## DOC. 289
## On 7 March 1944 a Polish underground chronicle records the arrest of Jews who had been living in hiding in the 'Krysia' bunker on Grójecka Street in Warsaw[1]

Report in a chronicle of events for the city of Warsaw, unsigned, Warsaw, dated 7 March 1944 or later[2]

March 1944

[…][3]

7 [March]

Thirty-eight Jews hiding on gardener Wolski's[4] premises at 81 Grójecka Street were arrested. Among them was a child who was only a few days old. These Jews had been hiding in a comfortably furnished shelter underneath the greenhouse, where they had running water, a bathroom, and electricity.[5] Gardener Wolski supplied them with food. The Jews had been staying in this shelter since 5 March 1943.[6] They were rich people well known in the area of the 23rd commissariat[7] (baker Gitter,[8] restaurateur Rawicz, Dr Cendrowicz, and others[9]). The German gendarmerie found them thanks to a denun-

50 The context suggests this should read: 'in the "Aryan" part of the city'.

51 See Doc. 289.

1 AAN, 1325/202/II-44, fol. 284. This document has been translated from Polish.

2 The chronicle covers the period from 1 August 1942 to 30 April 1944 (with a gap between April and Oct. 1943).

3 The previous sections of the chronicle record events up to 7 March 1944.

4 Mieczysław Wolski (1912–1944), gardener; provided refuge to nearly 40 Jewish men and women in an underground hiding place on his property at 81 Grójecka Street, for which the Gestapo murdered him in March 1944. The State of Israel honoured him; his mother, Małgorzata Wolska; and his sisters, Wanda and Halina, as Righteous Among the Nations in 1989.

5 This hiding place was known as the 'Krysia' bunker. It measured just under 30 square metres in size and was located beneath a greenhouse in an extensive garden on the Wolski property, which covered a hectare of land in Warsaw's Ochota district. Although the original Polish document refers to 'cellars' in the plural, the hideout comprised a single room.

6 Józef Grodziński and his wife, Irena, née Klinger (later Orna Jagur), hid there from June 1943 until about the turn of the year 1943/1944, before moving to an apartment belonging to Halina Michałecka, née Wolska: see Orna Jagur (Irena Grodzińska), *The Hiding Place* (Łódź: Oficyna Bibliofilów, 2000 [Polish edn, 1997]).

7 This is a reference to the local Polish police precinct.

8 Possibly Mejer Gyter (b. 1903), baker from Warsaw.

9 Among the murdered were Emanuel Ringelblum, his son, Uri (1930–1944), and his wife, Jehudis (Józia, Judyta), née Herman (1904?–1944), teacher; member of Poale Zion-Left; managed the CENTOS warehouses in the Warsaw ghetto; escaped to the 'Aryan side' in Jan. 1943.

ciation. The police from the 23rd commissariat were also present during the liquidation of this shelter. The Jews were removed and deported, along with their belongings (fur coats, jewellery, 4 kg of gold, etc.).[10] The greenhouse with all its equipment and fittings was destroyed with grenades and burned down. Wolski, his sister, and nephew[11] were arrested, and his private apartment was sealed.[12]
[…][13]

## DOC. 290

## On 26 March 1944 Franciszka Reizer notes that the Ulma family in Markowa were murdered because they had hidden Jews[1]

Diary of Franciszka Reizer, entry for 26 March 1944

*26 March*
In Markowa[2] the Gestapo[3] shot the entire Ulma family[4] for harbouring Jews.[5] They then set fire to the Ulmas' farm and threw the corpses into the fire.[6] Everyone is shocked by

10 One of the men hidden there had taken his own life with cyanide by the time the German police officers forced their way into the shelter: Tadeusz Klinger (1898–1944), lawyer; practised law in Łódź prior to Sept. 1939; in the Warsaw ghetto from 1940/1941; escaped to the 'Aryan side' in 1942.
11 This is probably a reference to the then 18-year-old son of one of Mieczysław Wolski's sisters, Janusz Wysocki, who was also murdered by the Gestapo in March 1944; honoured by the State of Israel as one of the Righteous Among the Nations in 1989.
12 Wolski's sisters, Wanda Szandurska and Halina Michałecka, survived.
13 The following sections contain further entries for 7 March 1944 and the remaining days of the month.

1 On the preservation of this diary, see Doc. 183, fn. 1. Published in Franciszka Reizer, *Dzienniki 1939–1944* (Warsaw: Ludowa Spółdzielnia Wydawnicza, 1984), p. 98. This document has been translated from Polish.
2 A rural community in powiat Łańcut, between Rzeszów and Jarosław.
3 The individuals who participated in the murder included the head of the gendarmerie in Łańcut, Eilert Dieken (1898–1960) from East Friesland; Josef Kokott (1921–1980) from the Sudetenland, who was extradited from Czechoslovakia to Poland in 1958 and sentenced to 25 years in prison in Rzeszów; and the gendarmes Erich Wilde (1921–1944) and Michael Dziewulski, both ethnic Germans from Poland. The four to six Polish police officers included Eustachy Kolman and Włodzimierz Leś, who was acquainted with the Szall family (see fn. 5) and was later killed by Polish resistance fighters: see Mateusz Szpytma, *The Risk of Survival: The Rescue of the Jews by the Poles and the Tragic Consequences for the Ulma Family from Markowa*, trans. from Polish Aleksandra Rodzińska-Chojnowska (Warsaw: Instytut Pamięci Narodowej – Komisja Ścigania Zbrodni przeciwko Narodowi Polskiemu, 2009), pp. 78–79, 97–101.
4 Józef Ulma (1900–1944), farmer, and his wife, Wiktoria, née Niemczak (1912–1944), who was pregnant in March 1944; they had been married since 1935 and had six children: Stanisława (1936–1944), Barbara (1937–1944), Władysław (1938–1944), Franciszek (1940–1944), Antoni (1941–1944), and Maria (1942–1944). Józef and Wiktoria Ulma were honoured by the State of Israel as Righteous Among the Nations in 1995.
5 In addition to the Ulma family, eight other people were murdered: the Szall family from Łańcut, who comprised a roughly 70-year-old father and his four sons; two of Chaim and Estera Goldman's daughters from Markowa, Gołda and Lajka; and a small child, presumably Lajka's daughter.
6 In fact, the perpetrators looted the farm and, at the request of the Poles who were present, the victims were buried in separate graves for Jews and Catholics; local residents reburied the Catholics in the cemetery shortly thereafter: Szpytma, *The Risk of Survival*, p. 79.

this tragedy. They talk and look at each other questioningly, as if asking: Maybe at your place? Maybe at mine? Maybe you, maybe me? No one knows anything. Is the commandment to 'love thy neighbour', repeated daily, meant to be just a hollow phrase? What does the motto 'Gott mit uns'[7] on their belts therefore mean?

## DOC. 291

## On 23 and 24 July 1944 Kazimiera Poraj describes an attempt to hand over Jews in hiding to the police in Lwów immediately prior to liberation[1]

Diary of Kazimiera Poraj, entries for 23 and 24 July 1944[2]

23 July 1944
The streets were somehow strangely empty in the morning; only a few civilians and not that many from the military either. Here and there a soldier walking around, armed and nervous.

I got to Halicki Square and saw people in front of the Polish police building on the corner of Akademicka Street and Halicki Square. I found out that it was locked and already deserted. In the crowd I saw a man and a woman with a 4-year-old girl. And what had happened? The man had brought the woman and the child here because she was a Jew. She had hidden in the apartment of a postal worker who had left along with the Germans.[3] When the man broke into the apartment to loot it, he encountered the woman and the child. She is the wife of a plumber, and her name is Münz. Her husband died shortly after the Germans entered Lwów.[4] Policemen who had evidently not managed to escape sent the woman back to where she came from and berated the man; he left with his tail between his legs. He made it only as far as the corner of Batory Street, then a shot rang out from somewhere and hit him in the head, killing him on the spot. I took the woman and the child to my place for today and tonight.

24 July 1944
Today, before evening, Red Army troops marched into the city. Mrs Frage and her daughters showered me with kisses.

7 German in the original: 'God with us'. This inscription was engraved on the belt buckles worn by Wehrmacht soldiers.

1 AŻIH, 302/217, fols. 117–118. Published in Kazimiera Poraj, 'Dziennik Lwowski', *BŻIH*, no. 52 (1964), pp. 79–106, here p. 106. This document has been translated from Polish.

2 On the preservation of this diary, see Doc. 112, fn. 1.

3 In July 1944, during the Red Army's summer offensive, occupation and auxiliary personnel began evacuating from Lwów.

4 Possibly Wilhelm Münz (1907/1908–1942), who was imprisoned in Janowska camp and died in Lwów in Jan. 1942, at the age of 35.

This is the happiest day of my life. First, my beloved husband[5] is alive, and second, I have saved the lives of three women: Mrs Frage and her daughters.[6]

Nevertheless, I am now broken and sick. The Germans have destroyed my health, but at least I have achieved what I've been fighting for.

## DOC. 292

## *Warszawianka*, 3 August 1944: the Jewish Combat Organization calls on surviving Jews to support the Warsaw Uprising[1]

*To the defenders of the Warsaw ghetto! To the Jews who are still alive!*

The people of Warsaw have been waging an armed struggle against the German occupier for three days.[2]

This battle is also our battle.

A year has passed since the glorious resistance in the ghettos and the 'labour camps', since we defended our lives and our honour; today we stand together with the entire Polish *nation* in the fight for freedom.

Hundreds of Jewish young people and ŻOB fighters are standing shoulder to shoulder with their Polish comrades at the barricades. We send our defiant greetings to the combatants.

We call upon all surviving ŻOB members as well as all able-bodied Jewish youth to continue the resistance and the struggle, from which no one may stand aside.

Join the resistance!

Fight for victory, for a free, independent, strong, and just Poland!

Jewish Combat Organization

Commander

*Antek*[3]

Warsaw, 3 August 1944

5 On the rescue of Kazimiera Poraj's husband, see Doc. 112, fn. 9.

6 In April 1943 the author had confided to her diary that, in addition to her husband, three women with the surname Frage – a mother and her two daughters – were living in hiding in her home; they had had to leave their previous place of refuge. Mr Frage died of typhus a few days later and was then secretly transported to the Jewish cemetery, covered with a sack; thereafter the three women found another hiding place: Poraj, 'Dziennik Lwowski', p. 101.

1 *Warszawianka: Wydawnictwo Warszawskiego O[kręgowego] K[omitetu] R[obotniczego] P.P.S.*, no. 4, 1 August 1944; AAN, 1583/1051, fol. 5. *Warszawianka* was the official publication of the Workers' Committee of the Polish Socialist Party (PPS) in Warsaw and appeared during the Warsaw Uprising. This document has been translated from Polish.

2 The Home Army began its long-prepared uprising against the German occupation in Warsaw on 1 August 1944.

3 Icchak Cukierman's code name.

## DOC. 293

## On 4 August 1944 Tadeusz Pełczyński, a leader of the insurgents in Warsaw, proposes that liberated Jews be placed in a camp[1]

Report from Grzegorz[2] to Prom[3] – Nurt,[4] Warsaw, dated 4 August 1944[5]

I inform you that an issue has arisen in Wola territory with regard to interned Jews from Yugoslavia, Greece, etc.[6] Our units liberated some of these Jews from German hands. Prepare to set up a temporary camp to which all the liberated Jews and other undesirable elements can be directed. The units should be given instructions to prevent any potential excesses against the Jews.[7]

## DOC. 294

## *Głos Starego Miasta*, 17 August 1944: the Jewish National Committee in Warsaw reports to the World Jewish Congress on the Home Army's liberation of Jews[1]

Report from Józef[2] in Warsaw to Anzelm[3] in London, dated 17 August 1944

*Telegram from the Jews of Warsaw to London*
The Jews who were liberated in Warsaw have sent the following telegram to the Jewish organization in London:[4]

*For Anzelm*
We are taking part in the fight. The Home Army has recovered several hundred Hungarian, Czech, Greek, and French Jews from captivity,[5] set them free, and given them the

1 WCEO-WBBH, Armia Krajowa, KG, Sztab – Oddział II, III/40/12, fol. 25. This document has been translated from Polish.
2 Code name for Tadeusz Pełczyński (1892–1985), career officer; Lublin area commander of the Union of Armed Struggle (ZWZ), 1940–1941; chief of staff at Home Army High Command, July 1941 – Oct. 1944; simultaneously deputy commander-in-chief and army general from July 1943; prisoner of war; thereafter emigrated to London.
3 Polish: 'ferry'; this was the Home Army's code name for the Warsaw area (comprising the municipal Kreis and Warschau-Land).
4 Polish: 'current'; code name for Antoni Chruściel (1895–1960), career officer; chief of staff of the ZWZ for the Warsaw city area from Oct. 1940; Warsaw area commander from May 1941; de facto commander of the insurgents in Warsaw, August–Oct. 1944; held as a prisoner of war; thereafter emigrated to Britain, and then to the USA.
5 The original features partly illegible handwritten annotations: '4.8.1944, 13.30 hrs … Heller' (code name for Kazimierz Iranek-Osmecki (1897–1984), career officer; head of intelligence for the Home Army High Command from Jan. 1944).
6 The Jewish prisoners were liberated from Warsaw concentration camp.
7 See also Doc. 294.

1 *Głos Starego Miasta*, no. 6, 17 August 1944, p. 2; AAN, 1583/267, fol. 2. Published in Halina Czarnocka et al. (eds.), *Armia Krajowa w dokumentach*, vol. 6: *Uzupełnienia* (London: Studium Polski Podziemnej, 1989), p. 413. *Głos Starego Miasta* was one of the newsletters published by the insurgents during the Warsaw Uprising. This document has been translated from Polish.
2 Szymon Gotesman's code name.
3 Anzelm (Ansh(e)l) Reiss.
4 The World Jewish Congress.

opportunity to work and to fight for the common cause. Greetings from the fighting front in Warsaw. We expect immediate aid.

*Józef*

## DOC. 295

## On 10 December 1944 the Council to Aid Jews in Cracow reports on its activities from August to October 1944[1]

Activity report from the Council to Aid Jews in Cracow, signed Chairman Staniewski[2] and Secretary Czerski,[3] Cracow, dated 10 December 1944 (copy)[4]

*Report* for the period August, September, October

During the period covered by this report, despite various obstacles, work continued within the established framework, maintaining all existing contacts in and beyond Cracow, while at the same time establishing cells and support points in the surrounding areas. In this way Council branches were set up in the powiats of Miechów, Brzesko, Tarnów, and Nowy Sącz.[5] In the process, the existing organizational channels of the PPS were often used to maintain links. Outside District Cracow itself, contact is being maintained with Radom, the Dąbrowa Basin, Upper Silesia, and the camp in Oświęcim. Based on the experience gained, several sections have been established to implement the tasks, covering all areas of the Council's activities. The following sections should be mentioned: (1) camps, (2) welfare, (3) documentation and propaganda, (4) legalization, (5) finance, (6) technical and organizational matters, and (7) the secretariat. In order to be able to perform all the tasks reasonably well, with such an expanded range of activities, a large number of people who support the Council's aims and activities were engaged. Apart from the board members, who were personally involved in all areas, technical work, liaison services, and the distribution of welfare payments was carried out by twenty-five people (four [from the] SPD[6] and twenty-one [from the] PPS), either by persons under our protection selected to perform these tasks, or by Aryans.

5 These were prisoners from Warsaw concentration camp, which was located on Gęsia Street in the former ghetto; the prisoners had been deported there from other concentration camps.

1 YVA, O-6/493. This document has been translated from Polish.

2 Code name for Dr Stanisław Wincenty Dobrowolski (1915–1993), lawyer; member of the underground Polish Socialist Party (PPS-WRN); chairman of the Council to Aid Jews in Cracow; co-founded the Polish Anti-Racist League in 1945; editor-in-chief of the journal *Świat i Polska*; later a member of the Sejm and Polish ambassador to Denmark and Greece.

3 Code name for Władyslaw Wójcik (1917–1974), tax official; member of the PPS-WRN; secretary of the Council to Aid Jews in Cracow, 1943–1944; first secretary of the PPS in Cracow from 1945; member of the State National Council.

4 The original features handwritten underlining and one illegible handwritten note.

5 These are powiats in the western part of District Cracow.

6 Stronnictwo Polskiej Demokracji: Polish Democracy Party (SPD); emerged out of a left-wing split within the clandestine Alliance of Democrats (SD) in July 1943; its leading politicians established ties with the Polish Workers' Party (PPR) and sent their representatives to the communist-dominated State National Council in 1944.

Special mention should be made of the documentation section (previously located at the secretariat) in view of the great importance that the collected materials could have in the future, such as the compilation of letters from the camps written by people of various professions and from various social groups, camp memoirs, various reports, site plans of camps, etc. These materials are being collated and prepared for publication. The legalization section[7] is exploiting existing opportunities, and now that a Council member has joined the PPS legalization cell, all legalization work is supported by this cell. As a result, the opportunities are now much greater than they were before.

The distribution of monthly welfare payments continued as in previous months, with the monthly amount set at 1,000 złoty. During the period from July to October of this year, the expenditure for this purpose amounted to 1,200,000 złoty. On average 400 people received welfare payments. Certain upward and downward adjustments of the monthly amount took place, depending on the recipient's requirements and circumstances. During the same period, the expenditure on additional payments to recipients for housing costs, living expenses, clothing, and other purposes amounted to 86,000 złoty.

After the welfare section, the camps section was the most active. Regarding this section, mention should be made of the fact that towards the end of July of this year, we received a letter from the RPŻ[8] in Warsaw, stating that the RPŻ in Cracow would receive a grant in the amount of 1 million złoty, with appropriate instructions on how this should be distributed to the recipients and the various camps – i.e. Płaszów, Mielec, Wieliczka,[9] and Stalowa Wola.[10] The Council complied with these instructions when distributing the received amount, as far as was possible under the prevailing conditions at the time, which resulted from the political situation and caused a sudden, fundamental change in the configuration of the camps in District Cracow.

Up until July of this year, the following camps were under the Council's authority:

| | | |
|---|---|---|
| 1) Mielec | approx. | 2,000 people |
| 2) Pustków[11] | approx. | 1,000 people |
| 3) Rzeszów[12] | approx. | 500 people |
| 4) Stalowa Wola | approx. | 500 people |

7 This section produced forged 'Aryan' papers.

8 Abbreviation for the Council to Aid Jews (Rada Pomocy Żydom, ŻPZ).

9 The prisoners from Mielec camp were taken to Wieliczka on 22 July 1944: see also Doc. 51. This forced labour camp for Jews had existed since spring 1944 and held Jews from Poland and other countries who were to be deployed in an underground aircraft factory; the 3,000–4,000 prisoners who remained there in late August 1944 were sent to Plaszow concentration camp.

10 In early August 1944 the remaining 300 prisoners were to be transferred to Plaszow camp from the forced labour camp for Jews in Stalowa Wola, which had been set up around the turn of the year 1939/1940. However, 90 of the prisoners managed to escape; the remainder were transported to Groß-Rosen.

11 The labour camp for Jews in Pustków, which was part of Heidelager SS training camp, was in operation from 1940 to 23 July 1944; when the camp was closed down, the prisoners were taken to Auschwitz concentration camp, and later to Sachsenhausen and Ravensbrück.

12 The labour camp for Jews in Łysa Góra, near Rzeszów, which operated from 1942, was located in the vicinity of an aircraft engine plant that had been taken over by the Heinkel aircraft company. When the camp was closed down in August 1944, approximately 100 prisoners managed to escape, including Soviet prisoners of war. Some of the remaining prisoners were shot on the spot, while 340 (or 520, according to other sources) were taken to Plaszow camp, and from there further west; very few survived.

5) Wieliczka approx. 1,000 people; from June until 31 July, up to 4,000 people
6) Cracow
a) Płaszów approx. 15,000 people
b) Zabłocie[13] approx. 1,500 people
c) Kabel[14] approx. 500 people
Altogether approx. 22,000 people

However, the circumstances changed in July of this year when, as a result of the Russian offensive, the Germans began to liquidate the camps in the eastern parts of District Cracow, transferring the people to the camps in Cracow.[15] In August all attention was therefore focused on Plaszów camp, where the numbers during this period exceeded 20,000.[16] All existing contacts with the camp were exploited in an attempt to provide aid to as many people as possible. Between August and October, 1 million złoty were delivered to the camp premises via organized channels. Approximately 1,000 of the people most in need benefited from this aid. The money sent was used to buy food and clothing. Apart from the allocation of material aid, constant efforts were made to organize resistance in the camp. In the end, it was possible to organize a combat group consisting of 300 people. Its task was to carry out a combat operation against the camp personnel and then to help as many people as possible to escape. For this purpose, money was sent to buy weapons from several of the camp personnel with whom the combat group had established contact. An automatic weapon and pistols were purchased. The date for the operation was set for 7 August.

There is no doubt that the operation would have stood a chance of success were it not for certain incidents that occurred and circumstances that prevented the fighters from taking action at that precise time. On 6 August raids and roundups took place on a large scale throughout Cracow and the surrounding area, as a result of which approximately 7,000 people were brought to the camp.[17] Dense cordons of police were stationed around the entire camp, and the camp personnel were heavily reinforced with the deployment of SS men inside the camp. This state of affairs continued over the next few weeks. The Gestapo conducted daily on-the-spot inquiries and investigations of the people arrested during the raids. These circumstances ruled out any chance of an armed operation, and the transports carried out in the meantime resulted in the dissolution of the [combat] group, as its members were sent in different directions. Contacts and aid

13 From April 1943 there was a labour camp in Zabłocie, on the premises of Oskar Schindler's Deutsche Emailwarenfabrik (enamelware factory) at 4 Lipowa Street; on average it held 1,000–1,200 Jews from Poland.

14 This is a reference to the camp at the cable factory on Prokocimska Street.

15 In July 1944 transports arrived at Plaszow concentration camp with Jewish forced labourers from Stalowa Wola, Rzeszów, Pustków, and Mielec.

16 Three large transports left Plaszow camp shortly after this date: one went to Flossenbürg concentration camp in late July/early August 1944 (with 2,700 people); one to Auschwitz on 6 August 1944 (with 7,500 people), and one to Mauthausen on 6/7 August 1944 (with 4,589 people). On 1 Sept. 1944 there were still 4,952 prisoners registered at Plaszow camp, and on 1 Oct. 1944 there were 4,595. Following further transports to the west in Oct. 1944, the last remaining 625 prisoners were sent on a death march to Auschwitz on 14 Jan. 1945. This was to evade the Soviet troops, which were at the gates of Cracow.

17 These people were Poles.

to Płaszów camp were maintained throughout the liquidation period and continue to this day.

The Council's budget over two months was based solely on the July grant from the RPŻ in Warsaw, which amounted to 489,000 złoty (in one consignment of 190,000 złoty, 1,000 złoty were missing) and 2,000 dollars, which were sent to us on 25 July. Because the dollars were sold at a considerably higher exchange rate, giving a total sum of 841,000 złoty, benefits to the recipients could be paid out for the months of July and August and the camp's needs as well as other expenditure covered.

In September the Council was confronted with the fact that there was a lack of funds and consequently all activities had to cease. Therefore, at the Council meeting on 12 September 1944, the decision was taken to turn to the District representation[18] for financial support in order to continue the work. When the District representation's delegate at the meeting[19] refused and explained that the District representation was in an identical situation and had no funds at its disposal, another request was made: to requisition and take over certain stocks of goods belonging to the 'Jus',[20] which had been privately deposited in a secret location and not included in any of the official accounting records. This request was justified on the grounds that the 'Jus' is no longer in operation because the director of this institution[21] has fled, and the Ge[sta]po has sealed its offices and depots. The aforementioned storage depots are therefore communal assets intended for the Jewish population, and cannot be wasted or used for any other purpose. At present the Council is the only representative body duly authorized to secure, take over, and use this inventory for the purpose of providing assistance to the Jewish population. The delegate from the District representation approved this request on the representation's behalf and instructed the Council to take possession of the inventory and dispose of the items. Upon receiving this instruction from the District representation, the Council instructed Chairman Staniewski to take over the 'Jus' stock.

The aforementioned hidden 'Jus' depots contained the following food items: (1) 139.8 kg of tea, (2) 20.5 kg of coffee, (3) 315 kg of almonds, (4) 6,351 tins of sardines between 50 and 200 g each, and (5) 150 bottles of juice (some of them spoiled due to leakage), with a total estimated value of 1,700,000 złoty. A person hired specifically for this purpose, under the Council chairman's continuous supervision, gradually sold off these items according to what the market could absorb. By 31 October this year, sales of these goods had generated 1,363,500 złoty for the Council's coffers. The remaining stock of 3,600 tins of sardines was estimated to be worth 400,000 złoty. Almost all of this stock has now been sold. Once sales are complete, a detailed report based on the goods and inventory records and the sales ledger will follow.

Apart from these foodstuffs, another depot contains nine cases of medicine that are part of the 'Jus' inventory and were not included in the official accounting records. At

18 This is a reference to the Polish government in exile's representation in District Cracow, which was under the authority of Dr Jan Jakóbiec (1876–1955).

19 Presumably Dr Tadeusz Seweryn (1894–1975), ethnographer; member of the Peasants' Party (SL); head of the Polish underground movement's Directorate of Civil Combat (KWC) in District Cracow from late 1941; head of the Directorate of Underground Combat (KWP) from June 1943; from March 1943 KWP representative on the Council to Aid Jews in District Cracow.

20 The Jewish Aid Office (Jüdische Unterstützungsstelle, JUS).

21 Michał Weichert.

present we are endeavouring to acquire these medicines in order to use them for the sick among our recipients and to send them to the camps. With regard to taking over these two secret 'Jus' depots, it must be noted that they represent but a fraction of the enormous assets of the 'Jus', most of which the Germans have already appropriated. The 'Jus' obtained the goods via the regular official deliveries from abroad addressed specifically to the 'Jus', as well as via deliveries from the International Red Cross, which the RGO[22] distributed to Polish, Ukrainian, and Jewish organizations, and of which the 'Jus' received an 8 per cent share. The assets of the 'Jus' were thus vast compared to those of other organizations of this kind in the territory of the GG. One need only consider the medicines, the amount of which in the 'Jus' depots exceeds one third of the total inventory of the PCK[23] and the RGO.

For almost a year, efforts were made to explain to the 'Jus' director how urgent it was to move 'Jus' supplies from the official depots to secret locations in order to salvage these communal assets and to use them illegally for the benefit of the Jewish population, and it was also made clear that he and his whole family should go into hiding in order to dissolve this German institution, which operates at the expense of the Jewish community. Unfortunately all of this urging merely resulted in constant avoidance and procrastination on the part of the 'Jus' director, Mr Weichert. When he fled in early August of this year, the depots at 2 Jozefińska Street contained enormous quantities of clothing and textiles, food, pharmaceutical goods, bandages, and disinfectant. Moreover, the PCK and RGO depots contained considerable supplies of medicine and food items, which had been carefully recorded.

The SS and German authorities immediately stole almost 80 per cent of the inventory in the central depots at 2 Jozefińska Street. On 10 August, on instructions from the German authorities, the RGO took over the temporary administration of the 'Jus' inventory – in other words, after the assets had already been destroyed. However, the administrator sold the food items acquired by the RGO for a total of 187,850 złoty. This money was used to buy flour and buckwheat, which were sent to Płaszów camp.

The foodstuffs taken over and sold by the Council enabled it to continue its work during a difficult period, and particularly to support the refugees from Warsaw, who are pouring into the Cracow region in ever-increasing numbers. A total of 400,000 złoty was spent for this purpose during the period covered by this report. The number of recipients from Warsaw is constantly increasing. At the same time, individual welfare payments had to be increased considerably on account of the rising cost of living, which averages 3,000 złoty, as well as higher housing costs. The refugees from Warsaw are arriving here without the most essential clothing, and even local recipients of aid lack the necessary clothing due to the long war. Therefore, at its meeting on 24 November, the Council resolved to earmark a sum of 400,000–500,000 złoty as additional winter aid, which will be paid out as individual sums in the amount of 1,000–5,000 złoty.

In an effort to expand its assistance and to act where this assistance is currently needed, the Cracow Council has focused its attention on the Kielce–Częstochowa region

22 Rada Główna Opiekuńcza: Polish Central Welfare Council. From May 1940 this was the central welfare organization for the Polish (non-Jewish) population in the General Government. Its central office was in Cracow.

23 Polski Czerwony Krzyż: 'Polish Red Cross'.

where the large camp at Częstochowa[24] is located, as well as on individual groups or settlements of refugees from Warsaw in Suchedniów, Kielce, and Koniecpol, consisting of several to a few dozen people.

The camp at Częstochowa initially held 3,000 people, but this number has gradually increased, especially with the arrival of larger transports from Skarżysko, Ostrowiec, and other places. At present the camp holds 17,000 people. Due to overcrowding, living conditions in the camp are terrible, and hunger is the worst aspect of all the suffering endured in the camp. So far the Council has spent 250,000 złoty on aid for Częstochowa, Koniecpol, Suchedniów, and Kielce. Further aid must be mobilized without delay. The task at present is to increase the number of contacts and to expand existing communication channels.

At the same time, constant efforts have been made to establish contact with people deported from Płaszów to other camps in the Reich. The first news we received was from people who had been deported to near Vienna in Austria.[25] Further information came from the Czech region, from Brünnlitz (Sudetenland). Contacts were established, and the letters that arrived from these places confirm our expectations. The armaments department of the enamelware factory in Zabłocie (Cracow) has been transferred to Brünnlitz, where there are 1,000 people who had previously been in Oświęcim.[26] They had been robbed of everything and were clothed only in thin, old canvas overalls. They are in a state of total exhaustion, half-naked, and above all hungry; dying of exhaustion, they await immediate aid. At the moment there is a unique opportunity to provide extensive aid by delivering entire wagonloads organized by the factory management. The German involved in this aid[27] was previously our liaison with the Szewski-Stern distribution point in Płaszów and is currently our liaison with Stern.[28] Since this is a unique opportunity and a secure channel, the Council decided to participate in this aid to the greatest extent possible and has earmarked a sum of 200,000–300,000 złoty for this purpose. The aid will be provided in the form of cash in Reichsmarks as well as food, clothing, and medicine. The transport is in the final stages of preparation.

After a long break, contact was also re-established with the centres in Upper Silesia and in the Dąbrowa Basin. In Dziedzice a group of 3,000 people are working in a factory,[29] and in Heidebreck (Gliwice) a similarly large group of people are employed at the synthetic petrol plant.[30] There is a smaller group at the Radocha chemical plant near

24 Towards the end of 1944 the HASAG company was running the largest forced labour camp in the General Government at Częstochowa: see Doc. 205, fn. 9.

25 On around 7 August 1944 prisoners were deported to Mauthausen concentration camp and distributed among its subcamps.

26 Most of the prisoners were brought to the main Plaszow camp on 6 August 1944. Those who stayed behind as a 'clean-up squad' (*Aufräumungskommando*) were deported on 15 Oct. 1944 and the subcamp at Schindler's enamelware factory was thereby closed down.

27 Presumably Oskar Schindler.

28 Presumably Itzhak Stern (1901–1969), accountant; studied in Vienna and elsewhere; later deputy chairman of the Jewish Agency in western Poland; worked at a shop in the Cracow ghetto, 1941–1943; subsequently held at Plaszow camp, where he distributed among the prisoners aid money that the Jewish Agency had donated to Oskar Schindler; died in Israel.

29 This is presumably a reference to Tschechowitz, a subcamp of Auschwitz concentration camp located in Czechowice-Dziedzice, where 500–600 Jewish men had to undertake forced labour in a factory run by the Vacuum Oil Company.

Sosnowiec.[31] Dr Liebermann[32] is also there. Additionally, numerous groups in various locations in the territory of the Reich are engaged in repairing bomb damage. Links with the centres nearby are being strengthened and activated, with the aim of increasing aid.

The broad range of activity, the numerous tasks, and continuously emerging new problems require constant vigilance and ongoing cooperation on the part of as many active group members as possible. The RPŻ therefore held a two-day board meeting to address the growing demand and handle current issues.

At a time when the Nazi occupation is being cast off, it is necessary to summon all available strength in order to overcome difficulties, to extend the aid operations, and to proceed undaunted through the present phase – which, on account of the Polish–Russian problem, is somewhat unfavourable to the development of the RPŻ's work, since anti-semitism is on the rise in Polish society.

## DOC. 296

## On 23 February 1945 Hugo Steinhaus writes about Jewish Auschwitz survivors and the new communist press[1]

Diary of Hugo Steinhaus,[2] entry for 23 February 1945

23 February 1945. The day before yesterday, Dolek[3] went to 'mother'[4] to fetch butter, where he met some Jews who had returned from Oświęcim.[5] We sent them a dozen eggs. They told us about the gas chamber, and how an SS man had pulled out one of them, a

30 This is presumably a reference to Blechhammer, a subcamp of Auschwitz concentration camp located near Kędzierzyn (Heydebreck) in Upper Silesia (today part of the town of Kędzierzyn-Koźle), where 3,000–4,000 Jewish men and 100–200 Jewish women were deployed to construct a synthetic petrol factory for Oberschlesische Hydrierwerke AG in Jan. 1945.

31 Radocha is a neighbourhood in Sosnowiec; this is possibly a reference to Sosnowitz II, a subcamp of Auschwitz concentration camp, where approximately 900 Jewish prisoners were deployed to work for the company Oberschlesische Maschinen- und Waggonfabrik AG (OSMAG) in a former metal-rolling mill.

32 Presumably Dr Henryk Liebermann (Liberman) (1896–1945), physician from Sosnowiec; perished in Bergen-Belsen camp in May 1945.

1 Zakład Narodowy im. Ossolińskich, Rękopis 16 189, tom III (20.12.1944–22.11.1953), fols. 303–304. Published in Hugo Steinhaus, *Wspomnienia i zapiski*, ed. Aleksandra Zgorzelska (London: Aneks, 1992). An abridged English version of the diary has been published: Hugo Steinhaus, *Mathematician for All Seasons: Recollections and Notes*, vol. 1: *1887–1945*, ed. Robert G. Burns, Irena Syzmaniec, and Aleksander Weron, trans. Abe Shenitzer (Cham: Birkhäuser, 2015). This document has been translated from Polish.

2 Hugo Dionizy Steinhaus (1887–1972), mathematician; studied in Göttingen, 1906–1911; completed his postdoctoral degree in Lwów in 1917; co-founder of the Lwów School of Mathematics; lived under a false name from summer 1941, initially in Osiczyna, then in Berdechów, near Bobowa (District Cracow); worked as a teacher in the clandestine school system; professor of mathematics in Wrocław after the war.

3 The author's brother-in-law: Adolf (Dolek) Szmosz (b. 1900), engineer; worked at the Zgoda steelworks in Świętochłowice, near Katowice, prior to Sept. 1939.

4 In the original 'Matusiczka', diminutive for 'mother'; likely to have referred to an elderly woman in the neighbourhood.

5 This is a reference to Auschwitz camp.

15-year-old boy, at the very last moment. They were on their way to Slovakia. They escaped from a transport of 80,000 people, the first to be herded to Gliwice.[6] They stayed in the forest until the Soviet offensive caught up with them. They saw Gestapo men being transported to Siberia. A Jew jumped onto the wagon and slapped the scoundrel. To that he cried: 'You hit me when I'm unarmed?' The Jew replied: 'Was I armed when you hit me?' This scene is priceless: it reveals the mentality of an Adolphite,[7] who sees the revolver as an extension of himself – others have no right to it and are designated as targets from the outset, as it were. The Adolphite was astonished when he was punched in the face – just as a marksman at a shooting range would be if the dummy, with a target in place of the heart, had slapped him in the face.

We occasionally receive newspapers; apart from *Dziennik Polski*,[8] which is published in Cracow, the newspapers are all vehicles of Lublin propaganda.[9] They remind me of the wolf disguised as grandmother in 'Little Red Riding Hood'. There is much talk there of the 'ancient lands of the Piasts'[10] and of 'democracy'. *Nowa Epoka* writes sensational things about Poles who used to be Austrian civil servants and transferred over to Polish service in 1918.[11] Kozłowski[12] and Łoś,[13] Skrzyński Aleksander,[14] and the Habsburg man[15] from Żywiec are all mentioned in a single breath, so the best Poles find themselves in the company of Kozłowski the traitor. (The Habsburg man did not let himself be turned into a Reichsdeutscher[16] or a Volksdeutscher.[17]) Not a word about communism,

6 Between 17 and 21 Jan. 1945, the SS took approximately 56,000 prisoners from Auschwitz and drove them westward on what came to be known as 'death marches': see PMJ 16.

7 Polish: 'adolfita', here meaning 'Nazi'.

8 *Dziennik Polski* appeared from 4 Feb. 1945.

9 This is a reference to the official publications of the ruling Polish Committee for National Liberation, which had been installed by the Soviet authorities on 22 July 1944 and initially governed from Lublin.

10 The eastern German territories that were transferred to Poland based on the decisions taken at the Potsdam conference in 1945 were referred to in contemporary Polish propaganda as the 'reclaimed territories', since parts of them had been ruled by the Piast dynasty for a period during the Middle Ages.

11 This refers to an unsigned and untitled article that appeared in the first issue, published on 21 Jan. 1945, p. 6. It attacked the governments that were in power in the years immediately preceding the war. The weekly newspaper *Nowa Epoka* was published from Jan. 1945 to Sept. 1946 as the main official publication of the Democracy Party (SPD). Henryk Lukrec (1884–1952) was its editor.

12 Dr Leon Kozłowski (1892–1944), archaeologist; studied in Germany; thereafter professor in Lwów; prime minister, 1934–1935; in Soviet custody, Sept. 1939–1941; then served with the newly established Polish forces in the Soviet Union ('Anders Army'), defected to the German forces in autumn 1941; died of injuries sustained during an Allied air raid on Berlin.

13 Dr Stanisław Łoś (1890–1974), lawyer; studied in Vienna, 1908–1913; worked in the Polish Ministry of Foreign Affairs, 1919–1929; imprisoned by the Polish security service, 1944–1945; subsequently taught ancient history at the Catholic University of Lublin.

14 Dr Aleksander Skrzyński (1882–1931), lawyer; studied in Vienna, 1900–1904; in the Austro-Hungarian diplomatic service from 1909; Polish foreign minister, 1922–1923 and 1924–1925; simultaneously prime minister, 1925–1926; died in a car accident.

15 Karl Albrecht von Habsburg-Altenburg (1888–1951), career officer; regarded as a pretender to the throne in the Regency Kingdom of Poland, 1916–1917; Polish citizen from 1919 after taking the name Karol Olbracht Habsburg-Lotaryński; served in the Polish-Soviet War, 1919–1921, and the Second World War in 1939; then imprisoned in Cracow; lived in Sweden from 1946.

16 German in the original: 'Reich German'.

17 German in the original: 'ethnic German'.

not a word about godlessness, not a word about the history of the 'great party of the Bolsheviks',[18] not a word about the deportations, not a word about the NKVD. But Katyń is mentioned: 'German propaganda.'[19] Anyone who does not recognize the wolf might think it is the grandmother. Under Crimea's influence,[20] this music has been muffled. However, it is only a step from *Nowa Epoka* to [Poland's] incorporation into the USSR.

18 The Polish edition of the official *History of the Communist Party of the Soviet Union (Bolsheviks): Short Course*, first published in 1939, played a significant role in indoctrinating intellectuals under Soviet rule.

19 See Doc. 237.

20 A reference to the Yalta Conference in Crimea, 4–11 Feb. 1945.

# Glossary

Agudas Yisroel ('Union of Israel')

An Orthodox, anti-Zionist (non-Zionist from 1937), conservative political party founded in Kattowitz (Katowice) in 1912. As the largest religiously oriented Jewish party, it played a key role in representing the interests of a significant portion of the Jewish population during the Second Polish Republic. Today it is part of the United Torah Judaism party in Israel.

American Jewish Joint Distribution Committee (AJDC, JDC, Joint)

Committee founded in the United States in 1914 to coordinate the relief efforts of American Jewish aid organizations. It provided funding and aid to Jews and Jewish organizations, especially in Eastern Europe. Before the outbreak of the Second World War, the JDC provided extensive aid to German and Austrian Jews for vocational training, emigration and more. During the war, its efforts extended to Nazi-occupied and Nazi-controlled territories, including the ghettos, where it supported schools, orphanages, cultural institutions, and other important areas of Jewish life.

Aryan (*Arier*)

Term used in nineteenth-century European racist thought to describe peoples supposedly descended from the Indo-Europeans. It was used in Nazi Germany to support the idea of the inequality of human races and the superiority of 'Aryans', particularly of those with 'German and related blood', over 'non-Aryan races', above all Jews.

Bezirk

An administrative subdivision within a geographical region. In the annexed Polish territories, the term was used as shorthand for Regierungsbezirk, an administrative area that consisted of a number of Kreise.

Blue Police

Officially: Polish Police in the General Government (Policja Polska Generalnego Gubernatorstwa); this was a police force made up of Poles, also known as the Blue Police (Policja Granatowa) because of their dark blue uniforms. It was subordinate to the German Order Police and had to carry out tasks related to public order and discipline and to control the Polish population. It was also involved in enforcing anti-Jewish measures. It consisted mainly of police officers from the pre-war State Police (Policja Państwowa); in early 1940 it comprised 8,700 people, by late 1942 approximately 12,000, and in 1943 approximately 16,000.

Building committee

Autonomous administrative bodies established in the Warsaw ghetto among the residents of larger apartment buildings. Their purpose was to organize and distribute food, clothing, and other daily necessities, particularly to those in greatest need, and to organize childcare and social activities. The committees were placed under the guidance of the Jewish Social Self-Help (JSS).

Bund (short for Algemeyner Yidisher Arbeter-bund in Lite, Poyln un Rusland; General Jewish Labour Bund in Lithuania, Poland, and Russia)

Jewish socialist party formed in 1897 in the Russian Empire. Its Polish section was active until the German invasion in 1939, when it went underground. The Bund was Yiddishist, anti-Zionist, and anti-religious, and it was the only Jewish underground resistance group that was not affiliated with any strand of Zionism. Members of the Bund played an important role in the Warsaw Ghetto Uprising.

CENTOS (Centralne Towarzystwo Opieki nad Sierotami i Dziećmi Opuszczonymi; Jewish Central Association for the Care of Orphans)

Polish-Jewish children's aid agency formed in 1924 to coordinate the activities of local children's aid organizations and orphanages. It was funded by the American Jewish Joint Distribution Committee and through individual donations, and continued its activities after the German invasion of Poland. CENTOS was very active in the Warsaw ghetto, where it ran around twenty day care facilities and orphanages, and also supported the resistance.

Chief Social Welfare Council (Naczelna Rada Opiekuńcza, NRO)

Umbrella organization consisting of the welfare organizations for the Polish population ([Polish] Central Welfare Council, RGO), the Ukrainian population (Ukrainian Central Welfare Council), and the Jewish population (Jewish Social Self-Help, JSS).

Council to Aid Jews (Rada Pomocy Żydom, RPŻ)

Code-named Żegota, a resistance organization affiliated with the Polish underground state and government in exile. It existed from 1942 to 1945 and its aim was explicitly to help Jews in German-occupied Poland. Żegota helped Jews in the ghettos by helping them escape. Later, its main work became helping Jews who had escaped to stay in hiding.

Criminal Police (Kriminalpolizei)

German criminal investigation force that, together with the Gestapo, from 1936 onwards constituted the Security Police (Sicherheitspolizei or Sipo). Absorbed into the Reich Security Main Office in 1939.

District (of the General Government)

Administrative region in the General Government which comprised several smaller administrative subdivisions from the Second Polish Republic. There were initially four such districts (*Distrikte*): District Warsaw, District Radom, District Cracow, and District Lublin. A fifth district, District Galicia, was added after the German invasion of the Soviet Union in summer 1941.

District Governor (Gouverneur des Distrikts or Distriktchef)

Head of a district in the General Government.

Dror/Frayheyt (Hebrew/Yiddish for 'freedom')

Left-wing Zionist youth organization with a strong educational programme modelled on principles of the scouting movement. It formed part of the Hehalutz organization.

Eastern Railway (Ostbahn)

The General Government's state railway company. It was established in November 1939 as an independent company, taking over materials and rolling stock from the Polish State Railway. Although the Eastern Railway coordinated closely with the Reich Railway, the two organizations were never merged.

Einsatzgruppe

Special task force of the Security Police first deployed during the occupation of Austria and the Sudetenland in 1938. The Einsatzgruppen were instructed to monitor political activity and to identify and arrest political opponents and other targeted groups. Following the invasion of Poland (1939) and the Soviet Union (1941), they were tasked with eliminating 'racial and political enemies', and operated as mobile killing units as the German armed forces advanced into Eastern Europe. Additional Einsatzgruppen were formed and deployed as the Germans occupied more countries.

Einsatzkommando

A subunit of an Einsatzgruppe deployed locally in parts of occupied Europe.

Emissionsbank in Polen (Bank Emisyjny w Polsce)

The central bank in the General Government established by the Germans in 1940. The majority of its staff was transferred from the Deutsche Reichsbank. The bank issued its own złoty notes between 1940 and 1944. It was the only Nazi institution to ever include Poland in its name or make reference to Poland as a territory.

Endecja (contracted form of ND for Narodowa Demokracja; National Democracy)

A right-wing nationalist and antisemitic political movement founded by Roman Dmowski in 1897 and active during the Second Polish Republic. In the 1930s, its aims were mostly represented by the National Party (Stronnictwo Narodowe, SN). The movement ceased to exist in 1947.

'Euthanasia' programme

National Socialist programme to murder patients with psychiatric illnesses or mental or physical disabilities, led by the head of the Chancellery of the Führer, Philipp Bouhler, and Hitler's personal physician, Karl Brandt. The murders were initiated by Hitler's 'mercy killing decree' of autumn 1939, which authorized doctors to terminate the lives of people deemed 'unworthy of life'. Between January 1940 and August 1941, over 70,000 patients were murdered in six killing centres in Germany and Austria. Hitler stopped the programme in August 1941 as a result of protests, especially from the churches. However, the 'euthanasia' killings continued in a more decentralized way until the end of the war, both in the German Reich and in German-occupied territories. Between 1939 and 1945 some 200,000 people were murdered in Germany and Austria, and around 100,000 others were killed elsewhere in occupied Europe.

Freikorps

Nationalist and anti-revolutionary paramilitary groups formed in the wake of Germany's defeat in the First World War. The Reich government used the Freikorps to suppress domestic left-wing revolts and patrol the Reich's eastern borders. In 1919 approximately 200,000 men were members of a Freikorps. Many prominent representatives of the Nazi state came from the Freikorps ranks.

Gau (Nazi Party term for 'region')

The largest NSDAP territorial subdivision below the level of the Reich. After the Nazis came to power in 1933, the Gaue increasingly replaced the individual states (Länder) as the regional administrative unit of the Third Reich.

Gauleiter ('Gau leader(s)')

Head of an NSDAP Gau.

Gendarmerie

German rural police force in charge of keeping order in rural areas and smaller municipalities. The gendarmerie was part of the Order Police (Ordnungspolizei).

General Government

German administrative region in occupied central and southern Poland. The General Government was initially divided into four districts: Cracow, Warsaw, Lublin, and Radom. A fifth district, District Galicia, was added in August 1941 after the German invasion of the Soviet Union. The position of governor general was held by Hans Frank from October 1939 to January 1945.

Gestapo (contracted form of Geheime Staatspolizei; Secret State Police)
Political police, first established as an autonomous force by Hermann Göring in Prussia in 1933 with the aim of combating internal 'enemies of the state'. From 1934 the political police forces in Germany were led by Himmler. In 1936, when Himmler was appointed as chief of the centralized German police, the Gestapo became part of Heydrich's Security Police. In 1939 the Security Police merged with the SD to form the Reich Security Main Office (RSHA). Thereafter it became known as RSHA Amt IV (Office IV) and was headed by Heinrich Müller. It was divided into five departments: (a) Political Opponents, (b) Sects and Churches, (c) Administration and Party Affairs, (d) Occupied Territories, and (e) Security and Counter-intelligence.

Ghetto
A common term for a poor, densely populated Jewish neighbourhood; originally the name of the restricted Jewish quarter of sixteenth-century Venice. After the German invasion of Poland in 1939, it was used for sections of towns and cities in Nazi-dominated Europe where the Jewish population was concentrated and segregated prior to its deportation. The German administration officially referred to these areas as 'Jewish residential districts' and imposed a Jewish self-administration.

Government delegation in Poland (Delegatura Rządu na Kraj)
Representative body of the Polish underground state based in the General Government. It represented the Polish government in exile in both the General Government and the annexed territories. The government delegation was headed by the delegate, who was officially the deputy prime minister of the Polish state, and it comprised all departments necessary for a shadow government, such as a justice department, an agricultural department, and, from December 1942, the Council to Aid Jews.

Hehalutz (Hebrew for 'the pioneer')
International umbrella organization, dating from before the First World War, for Zionist youth movements seeking to prepare *halutzim* (pioneers) for agricultural settlement in Palestine.

Higher SS and Police Leaders (Höhere SS- und Polizeiführer, HSSPF)
Officials appointed by Himmler from 1937 to act as his deputies, responsible for ensuring police control and coordinating the activities of the Security Police, the SD, and the Order Police in all occupied territories and, to a more limited extent, in the Reich.

Home Army (Armia Krajowa, AK)
Polish underground army under the control of the Polish government in exile in London. It was formed in February 1942 from its precursor organization, the Union of Armed Struggle (Związek Walki Zbrojnej, ZWZ), and absorbed most other Polish armed resistance groups. The Polish Home Army was one of the most significant resistance organizations in German-occupied Europe.

Hotel Polski
Former hotel in Warsaw commandeered by the German authorities. In 1943 it was used to intern Jews who held citizenships of neutral, mostly South American coun-

tries. Most of the 3,000 Jews interned there were deported either to Bergen-Belsen concentration camp or to the German internment camp in the French town of Vittel. From these camps, nearly all the internees were taken to Auschwitz, where most of them were murdered.

Jewish Combat Organization (Żydowska Organizacja Bojowa, ŻOB; Yidishe Kamf Organizatsye)
Jewish armed underground resistance group formed in the Warsaw ghetto on 28 July 1942 with cells in several other ghettos. The ŻOB recruited its members mostly from among the younger left-wing inhabitants of the ghettos. It was one of the driving forces behind the Warsaw Ghetto Uprising in spring 1943.

Jewish Community (Kehilla)
Body representing the Jewish inhabitants of a municipality.

Jewish Coordinating Committee (Żydowski Komitet Koordynacyjny, ŻKK)
Committee set up in the Warsaw ghetto in October 1942 to coordinate the activities of the different Jewish resistance groups and establish contacts with the Polish resistance.

Jewish Council (Judenrat) / Jewish Council of Elders (Jüdischer Ältestenrat)
Administrative agency established on German orders in Jewish communities in Nazi-occupied Europe. The first councils were set up in Poland only days after the German invasion in early September 1939. Their tasks were described on 21 September in instructions from Heydrich to the commanders of the Einsatzgruppen. The councils' main function was to ensure the implementation of anti-Jewish orders and regulations. They were also in charge of providing services to the Jewish population inside and outside the ghettos (housing, medical supplies, food distribution) and organized cultural events. From 1940 they were ordered to provide workers for forced labour and they were later also required to prepare lists with names of Jews to be deported to extermination camps.

Jewish elder (Judenältester)
A Jewish representative appointed by the German authorities to head a Jewish Council in the Jewish communities of the occupied territories.

Jewish Military Union (Żydowski Związek Wojskowy, ŻZW)
Jewish armed resistance group associated with the more right-wing branches of Zionism and led by former officers in the Polish army. The ŻZW played a major part in the Warsaw Ghetto Uprising and maintained contacts with the Polish Home Army.

Jewish National Committee (Żydowski Komitet Narodowy, ŻKN)
Committee founded in the Warsaw ghetto in 1942 which brought together representatives of most strands of Zionism in the ghetto.

Jewish Order Service (Jüdischer Ordnungsdienst)
Public order service made up of Jews and formed by many Jewish councils in autumn 1940 on German orders. Its units were deployed by the Jewish councils inside the ghettos and residential districts in occupied Poland and charged with maintaining order as well as enforcing the councils' orders. The service was officially subordinate to the Jewish Council, but in fact it was also under the control of the German police authorities. It was colloquially referred to as the 'ghetto police'.

Jewish Social Self-Help (Jüdische Soziale Selbsthife, JSS; Żydowska Samopomoc Społeczna, ŻSS; Yidishe Sotsyale Aleynhilf)

Jewish relief organization in the General Government founded shortly after the German invasion of Poland under the chairmanship of Michał Weichert. It had its headquarters in Cracow and local branches in a number of ghettos. The JSS was supported by the American Jewish Joint Distribution Committee and coordinated the efforts of welfare organizations across Poland to provide material relief to Jews. It was initially independent of the Jewish councils and under strict German control. On 20 Jan. 1942 the German authorities put the Jewish councils in charge of the local JSS committees. Following mass deportations of ghetto inhabitants as part of Operation Reinhard, the work of the JSS ended in summer 1942. It was replaced by the Jewish Aid Office (Jüdische Unterstützungsstelle, JUS). The JUS continued parts of the JSS's work until it was dissolved in 1943.

Junak (plural: junacy)

Polish term used in the General Government for members of non-German auxiliary units working for the German occupiers. The junacy were mostly recruited among Ukrainians, Latvians, or Lithuanians.

Kapo

Term used in concentration camps for prisoners supervising other prisoners, on the authority of the SS.

Kreis (plural: Kreise)

German administrative subdivision above the local/municipal level; also used to refer to the subdivision of a Nazi Party Gau.

Kreishauptmann (plural: Kreishauptmänner, Kreishauptleute)

Head of a German Kreis administration in the General Government. The Kreishauptleute were in charge of rural administrative subdivisions, while the Stadthauptleute were in charge of larger towns and cities.

Kreishauptmannschaft

German Kreis administration in the General Government.

Kreisleiter

Head of an NSDAP Kreis, a Nazi Party regional subdivision.

Kreisleitung

Head office of an NSDAP Kreis.

Landkommissar

Official appointed in a rural area at the level below the Kreis in the General Government, subordinate to the Kreishauptmann.

Landrat (plural: Landräte)

Head of a Kreis administration within the German Reich and the annexed territories.

Ministerialdirektor

Senior civil servant in the administration of the German Reich, typically within a ministry.

Ministerialdirigent

High-ranking civil servant in the Reich administration, typically within a ministry. The rank of Ministerialdirigent was above Ministerialrat and below Ministerialdirektor.

Ministerialrat
High-ranking civil servant in the Reich administration, typically within a ministry.

National Party (Stronnictwo Narodowe, SN)
Conservative-nationalist and antisemitic party founded in 1928 during the Second Polish Republic. It constituted the main right-wing opposition to Józef Piłsudski's Sanacja regime. The SN was dissolved in 1947.

Oberfeldkommandantur (OFK)
Headquarters of the German military administration for larger regions.

Oberregierungsrat
Civil service rank in a German ministry or other government agency, senior to Regierungsrat.

Old Reich (Altreich)
Germany within its 1937 borders, prior to the annexation of Austria in March 1938 and of the Sudetenland in October 1938.

Operation Harvest Festival (German: 'Aktion Erntefest')
Code name for the concerted operation on 3 and 4 November 1943 to kill the remaining Jewish forced labourers in District Lublin. The massacre was ordered by Himmler following a series of uprisings in ghettos and extermination camps and carried out at the Majdanek, Trawniki, and Poniatowa camps by German police units, SS and Waffen-SS units, and so-called Trawniki men, Eastern European Nazi collaborators. Approximately 43,000 Jews were murdered in the course of the two-day operation, one of the biggest single shooting massacres during the Holocaust.

Operation Reinhard (Aktion Reinhard/Reinhardt)
Code name for the deportation of Jews from the General Government and Bezirk Bialystok, as well as other German-occupied regions, and their murder in the Belzec, Sobibor, and Treblinka extermination camps between spring 1942 and summer/autumn 1943. The operation was overseen by Odilo Globocnik and was named after Reinhard Heydrich, Chief of the Security Police and the SD. Heydrich had died on 4 June 1942 of injuries sustained during an assassination attempt in Prague.

Order Police (Ordnungspolizei, Orpo)
German uniformed police force. From 1936 it constituted one of the two branches of the German police, the other one being the Security Police, and it was made up of the Urban Police (Schutzpolizei), Municipal Police (Gemeindepolizei), the gendarmerie, and their respective subdivisions. The Order Police was incorporated into the SS and police apparatus in 1936. During the war, its tasks extended to policing the civilian population in Nazi-occupied territories, and it was also directly involved in killing operations.

Organization Todt (OT)
German military and civil engineering organization established in 1938 and led by Fritz Todt until his death in 1942; Todt was succeeded by Albert Speer, minister of armaments and munitions. During the war, the organization used large numbers of forced labourers and sometimes concentration camp prisoners for its large-scale construction projects both inside the Reich and in the occupied territories.

Ortskommandantur
Local (town-level) headquarters of the German military administration in the occupied territories.

Ostindustrie GmbH (Osti)

SS-owned company established to exploit the labour of Jewish camp and ghetto inmates in the General Government for the German war effort. It was founded in February 1943 and operated several production facilities. The company was disbanded in November 1943 after most of the Jewish forced labourers it used were murdered in the murder campaign codenamed 'Operation Harvest Festival'.

*Ostjuden* ('Eastern Jews')

Yiddish-speaking, mainly non-assimilated Jews who had migrated from Eastern Europe, mainly Poland, to Western Europe, North and South America, and Palestine from the nineteenth century onwards. The term initially emerged as a result of the division between these Jews and the emancipated Jews in the countries to which they migrated. *Ostjuden* were early targets of the Nazi regime, and the negative stereotype associated with them played a central role in Nazi propaganda.

Pawiak

Prison located between Dzielna Street and Pawia Street in Warsaw operated by the German Security Police. It became the central Gestapo prison for Warsaw. It was used to imprison and execute Jews arrested outside the ghetto and later, during the liquidation of the ghetto, as a transit point for Jews on the way to the extermination camps.

Poale Zion (Hebrew: 'Workers of Zion')

Left-wing party established by Marxist-Zionist circles around the turn of the twentieth century in several Russian cities. Its principles were based on Ber Borochov's concepts of proletarian Zionism. In 1920 the World Union of Poale Zion split into two independent parties, of which Poale Zion-Left (Polish: Poalej Syjon Lewica) was the dominant force in Poland. It sympathized with the Bolshevik revolution in Russia, boosted the use of Yiddish, and influenced many leading Jewish intellectuals in Poland. Poale Zion-Right was supported by the majority of Poale Zion members in Palestine, the UK, and the USA and became part of the Second International. In Poland, it organized the small school association Shul-Kult and merged with the Dror/Frayheyt youth association. It founded its own World Union in Gdańsk in 1932.

Polish Workers' Party (Polska Partia Robotnicza, PPR)

Underground Polish communist party founded in early 1942 in Warsaw. The PPR was the successor organization to the Communist Party of Poland (KPP), which had been dissolved by the Comintern in 1938. It merged with the Polish Socialist Party (PPS) after the war to form the Polish United Workers' Party (PZPR).

Powiat

Administrative and local government unit in Poland above the local (gmina) and below the regional (voivodeship) level, roughly equivalent to a German Kreis.

Regierungsrat

Senior civil service rank in a German ministry or other government agency, subordinate to an Oberregierungsrat.

Reich Commissariat for the Strengthening of Germandom (Reichskommissariat für die Festigung deutschen Volkstums)

Office created by a decree issued by Hitler on 7 October 1939 which put Himmler in charge of the Reich's overall Germanization policy. Himmler's agenda involved 'retrieving' those allegedly of 'German blood' from among the resident population of the occupied territories, displacing and deporting persons classified as 'of alien race' from the annexed eastern territories, and resettling ethnic Germans from different parts of Eastern Europe there. Beyond these immediate resettlement operations, the Reich Commissariat drew up extensive plans and strategies for 'ethnically reordering' the territories occupied by the Reich.

Reich Commissariat Ostland

The German civil administration of the occupied territories of Estonia, Latvia, Lithuania and Western Byelorussia. It was established in 1941 after the German invasion of the Soviet Union and a transitional period of military administration. The Reich Commissariat Ostland was the site of large-scale massacres of the local Jewish population by the Einsatzgruppen.

Reich Commissariat Ukraine

The German civil administration of the occupied Ukrainian territories. It was established in 1941 after the German invasion of the Soviet Union and a transitional period of military administration. Like the Reich Commissariat Ostland, the Ukrainian lands were sites of large-scale massacres of the local Jewish population by the Einsatzgruppen.

Reich Germans (Reichsdeutsche)

Designation commonly used by the Nazi regime to distinguish Reich citizens who lived inside the German Reich from Reich citizens who were resident abroad (Auslandsdeutsche) and from foreign citizens with German ethnicity (Volksdeutsche, ethnic Germans).

Reich Security Main Office (Reichssicherheitshauptamt, RSHA)

Office headed by Reinhard Heydrich and created by Heinrich Himmler on 27 September 1939 by merging the SD and the Security Police (Gestapo and Criminal Police). This meant combining institutions of the Nazi Party and of the state within a single organization. The RSHA played an important role in the Nazi regime's policies of persecution and extermination. It was tasked with intelligence gathering and criminal investigation. Through the work of Section IV D 4 (later IV B 4), run by Adolf Eichmann, the RSHA was instrumental in the implementation of the 'final solution'.

Reichsamtsleiter

High-ranking Nazi Party official, head of an NSDAP office or section at Reich level.

Reichsgau

Administrative subdivision in some of the territories annexed to the German Reich between 1938 and 1945, including Austria and western and northern Poland.

*Reichsgesetzblatt* (Reich Law Gazette, *RGBl*)

Official gazette in the German Reich that published laws and regulations between 1871 and 1945.

Reichsleiter (Reich leader)

The most senior political rank in the NSDAP, second only to the Führer. Hitler appointed these individuals to oversee a range of portfolios (i.e. propaganda, law, finance, foreign policy). The different Reichsleiter were collectively designated as the Reichsleitung ('Reich leadership').

Reichsstatthalter (Reich governor)

One of the officials appointed to head the German states (Länder) and implement Hitler's political orders. The Gauleiter frequently also held the post of

Reichsstatthalter. After the German invasion of Poland in September 1939, two new Reichsstatthalter posts were created for the Reichsgaue Posen (later Wartheland) and Danzig-West Prussia.

Sanacja ('healing')
: Authoritarian-centrist political movement concerned with 'national healing' in interwar Poland. Its name has become synonymous with the authoritarian regime in power between 1926 and the German invasion in 1939. The movement was led by Jozef Piłsudski, who remained the driving force behind the regime until his death in 1935. Marshal Edward Rydz-Śmigły succeeded him as the movement's leader.

SD (abbreviation for Sicherheitsdienst; SS Security Service)
: The intelligence service of the SS and NSDAP, founded in 1931 by Heinrich Himmler and headed by Reinhard Heydrich. Its tasks included the detection and surveillance of those classed as political and ideological enemies, especially Jews, communists, Social Democrats, and Freemasons. In 1939 the SD was incorporated into the Reich Security Main Office (RSHA) along with the Security Police (Gestapo and Criminal Police). The SD played an instrumental role in the planning and implementation of the 'final solution'.

Security Police (Sicherheitspolizei, Sipo)
: One of the two police branches created by Himmler's reorganization of the entire German police apparatus in 1936 (the other being the Order Police or Orpo). The Security Police was headed by Reinhard Heydrich between 1936 and 1942 and was made up of the Gestapo and the Criminal Police. It was incorporated into the Reich Security Main Office in 1939.

Sejm
: The Polish parliament: the lower of the two houses in the two-chamber parliamentary system.

Selbstschutz ('self-protection')
: Term used for several ethnic German militias formed with the support of the Nazi regime in the late 1930s in areas of Central and Eastern Europe which had a sizeable ethnic German population, particularly Czechoslovakia, Poland, and Transnistria. Selbstschutz units were involved in many crimes against Poles and Jews in Poland, Transnistria, and elsewhere. The units were dissolved in 1940 and many of their members joined the Sonderdienst auxiliary units, the SS, and police forces.

Shaulis men
: Term for mostly Lithuanian members of volunteer units serving the German occupiers. The name is derived from the Lithuanian word for 'marksman'.

Shtetl
: Yiddish-language term for a small town inhabited mostly by Jews in Eastern Europe.

Sołtys
: Head of a rural community in Poland.

Special court (Sondergericht)
: Nazi court which dealt with transgressions and crimes supposedly committed against the German people. In Nazi-occupied Poland, their aim was to quell internal resistance to the German occupation.

SS (abbreviation for Schutzstaffel; 'protection squadron')
Paramilitary force established in 1925 by the NSDAP and led by Heinrich Himmler from 1929. From 1934 the SS ran the concentration camps. Other branches of the SS included the Waffen-SS and the Allgemeine-SS (membership organization).

SS Business and Administration Main Office (WVHA)
SS main office formed in 1942 by Oswald Pohl through a merger of the SS Administration and Business Main Office and the SS Budget and Construction Main Office. It was in charge of the SS's business ventures, finances, and material supply questions and administered the entire concentration camp system and the systematic exploitation of its prisoners for the German war economy.

Stadthauptmann (plural: Stadthauptmänner, Stadthauptleute)
Head of a German municipal Kreis in the General Government, analogous to Kreishauptmann.

Stadtkommandant
Head of the military administration for a city (Stadtkommandantur).

Stadtkommissar
Official appointed in an urban area at the level below the Kreis in the General Government, subordinate to the Kreishauptmann.

Stadtpräsident
Term used for the German head of the city administration in occupied Warsaw.

Stalag (contraction of Kriegsgefangenen-Mannschafts-Stammlager).
German name for prisoner-of-war camps for enlisted personnel. Commissioned officers were held in Oflags (short for 'Offizierslager').

Starosta (plural: starostowie)
Head of a Polish regional authority.

Szop (plural: szopy)
Polish term for the workshops and factories in the Warsaw ghetto where German companies exploited the labour of Jewish inhabitants to produce goods for the German market.

Transfer Bureau (Transferstelle)
German administrative office responsible for controlling the flow of goods and services in and out of the Warsaw ghetto from December 1940. Effectively, the Transfer Bureau became the German agency in charge of the official ghetto economy.

Trawniki
Name of a village in eastern Poland where the Trawniki labour camp was located. From 1941 the camp was also used as a training centre for non-German auxiliary troops that the Germans recruited mostly in their POW camps. The so-called Trawniki men were then deployed as auxiliary guards in the labour and concentration camps, to guard deportation trains, or to liquidate ghettos. The majority of the Trawniki men were Ukrainians, but their numbers also included Latvians, Lithuanians, Estonians, and Poles.

Umschlagplatz
Originally a German logistics term for a transport hub or a reloading point. The German ghetto administration used the term for the area outside the Danzig railway station immediately adjacent to the Warsaw ghetto, from where goods entered and left the ghetto. From summer 1942 it served as the holding area for Jews who were

forced to assemble here prior to their deportation to Treblinka extermination camp in the course of Operation Reinhard.

Underground archive of the Warsaw ghetto (Oyneg Shabes / Oneg Shabbat or Ringelblum archive)

Secret collection of accounts, notes, and documents compiled by the Oyneg Shabes ('Joy of the Sabbath') group led by historian Dr Emanuel Ringelblum, which used to meet on the Sabbath. The archive was intended to document conditions in the ghetto and form the basis of future books about it. Its collection was buried in 1943, and most of it has been recovered. The surviving roughly 25,000 sheets today form one of the most important resources for first-hand accounts of the Holocaust in occupied Poland from a Jewish perspective.

Union of Armed Struggle (Związek Walki Zbrojnej, ZWZ)

Armed underground resistance organization affiliated with the Polish government-in-exile. It was established in late 1939 and tasked with coordinating the activities of different armed resistance groups in Poland. In February 1942 it was renamed the Armia Krajowa (Home Army).

*Verordnungsblatt* (*VOBl*)

Gazette that published legislation, regulations, and decrees, including anti-Jewish ones, issued by the German authorities in the different occupied territories.

Wachtmeister

Lower to NCO rank in the various subdivisions of the Order Police (Urban police, Gendarmerie etc.). The lowest uniformed rank in the German police was the Unterwachtmeister, followed by the non-commissioned ranks of Wachtmeister and Hauptwachtmeister.

Waffen-SS

Military branch of the SS, established in 1939.

Warsaw Ghetto Uprising

The largest concerted Jewish resistance operation in German-occupied Poland. After the first armed conflicts in January 1943, the armed insurgency against the deportations to Treblinka began on 19 April 1943 and ended on 16 May with the complete liquidation of the Warsaw ghetto and the deportation of its remaining inhabitants. The revolt was led by the two most important Jewish underground resistance groups, the Jewish Combat Organization (ŻOB) and the Jewish Military Union (ŻZW). The German forces, after initially having to withdraw, responded by razing the Warsaw ghetto. The Warsaw Ghetto Uprising served as a model for many subsequent resistance operations in occupied Poland.

Warsaw Uprising

Armed insurgency by the population of Warsaw from early August to early October 1944 led by the Polish Home Army. It was prompted by Wehrmacht retreats and Red Army advances in eastern Poland (during the Uprising, the Red Army then halted at the Vistula and did not intervene) and was the largest organized insurgency against German occupation anywhere in occupied Europe. The Germans managed to quell the uprising after nine weeks and responded by razing the city of Warsaw to the ground and deporting large numbers of insurgents and civilians to the concentration camps.

Wehrmacht

Collective term for the German armed forces – army (Heer), air force (Luftwaffe), and navy (Kriegsmarine) – from 1935 to 1945. The Wehrmacht was the successor organization to the Reichswehr (1919–1935). The Wehrmacht High Command (Oberkommando der Wehrmacht, OKW) under Wilhelm Keitel coordinated military activities, while each of the three military branches had its respective high command: OKH (army), OKM (navy), and OKL (air force).

Wójt (plural: wojtowie)

Polish local administrative official.

World Jewish Congress (WJC)

International organization founded in Geneva in August 1936 with the backing of the American Jewish Congress (AJC). Its aim was to represent Jews around the world, promote Jewish unity, support the establishment of a Jewish national home in Palestine, campaign for political and economic equality for Jews across Europe, and combat Nazism and antisemitism. The organization still exists today.

Yeshiva

Traditional Jewish learning institution in which boys study the Talmud and Halacha, but also the Torah and other rabbinic literature.

Zionism

Jewish nationalist movement that originated in Central and Eastern Europe in the late nineteenth century and advocated the re-establishment of a Jewish state in Eretz-Israel (Land of Israel – Palestine).

# Institutional Ranks and Hierarchies

| SS | Wehrmacht | British Army | US Army |
|---|---|---|---|
| Reichsführer-SS | Reichsmarschall | – | – |
| – | Generalfeldmarschall | Field Marshal | General of the Army |
| SS-Oberstgruppenführer | Generaloberst | – | General |
| SS-Obergruppenführer | General der Waffengattung (Infanterie, Artillerie, etc.) | General | Lieutenant General |
| SS-Gruppenführer | Generalleutnant | Lieutenant General | Major General |
| SS-Brigadeführer | Generalmajor | Major General | Brigadier General |
| SS-Oberführer | – | Brigadier | – |
| SS-Standartenführer | Oberst | Colonel | Colonel |
| SS-Obersturmbannführer | Oberstleutnant | Lieutenant Colonel | Lieutenant Colonel |
| SS-Sturmbannführer | Major | Major | Major |
| SS-Hauptsturmführer | Hauptmann | Captain | Captain |
| SS-Obersturmführer | Oberleutnant | First Lieutenant | First Lieutenant |
| SS-Untersturmführer | Leutnant | Second Lieutenant | Second Lieutenant |
| SS-Sturmscharführer | Stabsoberfeldwebel | Regimental Sergeant Major (Warrant Officer Class 1) | Sergeant Major |
| – | Oberfähnrich | – | Senior Officer Candidate |
| SS-Hauptscharführer | Oberfeldwebel | Staff Sergeant Major (Warrant Officer Class 1) | Master Sergeant |
| SS-Oberscharführer | Feldwebel | Warrant Officer Class 2 | Technical Sergeant |
| – | Fähnrich | Ensign | Officer Candidate |
| SS-Scharführer | Unterfeldwebel | Staff Sergeant | Staff Sergeant |
| SS-Unterscharführer | Unteroffizier | Sergeant | Sergeant |
| – | Stabsgefreiter | Corporal (senior) | – |
| – | Obergefreiter | Corporal | Corporal |
| SS-Rottenführer | Gefreiter | Lance Corporal | Acting Corporal |

| SS | Wehrmacht | British Army | US Army |
|---|---|---|---|
| SS-Sturmmann | Obersoldat | Private (senior) | Private First Class |
| SS-Mann | Soldat | Private | Private |
| SS-Anwärter | – | – | – |

Each column shows the hierarchy within the respective institution.

| Sicherheitspolizei (SIPO) Ranks |
|---|
| Reichsführer-SS und Chef der deutschen Polizei |
| Chef der SIPO |
| Kriminaldirigent |
| Reichskriminaldirektor |
| Regierungs- und Kriminaldirektor |
| Kriminalrat |
| Kriminalkommissar |
| Kriminalinspektor |
| Kriminalobersekretär |
| Kriminalsekretär |
| Kriminaloberassistent |
| Kriminalassistent |
| Kriminalassistentenanwärter |

| NSDAP Ranks |
|---|
| Reichsleiter |
| Gauleiter |
| Hauptbefehlsleiter |
| Oberbefehlsleiter |
| Befehlsleiter |
| Hauptdienstleiter |
| Oberdienstleiter |
| Hauptbereichsleiter |
| Kreisleiter |
| Oberbereichsleiter |
| Bereichsleiter |
| Hauptgemeinschaftsleiter |
| Ortsgruppenleiter |
| Obergemeinschaftsleiter |
| Gemeinschaftsleiter |
| Haupteinsatzleiter |
| Einsatzleiter |
| Hauptbereitschaftsleiter |
| Oberbereitschaftsleiter |
| Bereitschaftsleiter |
| Hauptarbeitsleiter |
| Oberarbeitsleiter |
| Arbeitsleiter |
| Oberhelfer |
| Helfer |
| Polit. Leiter-Anwärter |

| Civil Service Ranks |
|---|
| Staatssekretär |
| Oberpräsident (only in Prussia) |
| Unterstaatssekretär |
| Ministerialdirektor |
| Regierungspräsident |
| Ministerialdirigent |
| Ministerialrat |
| Regierungsdirektor |
| Amtsrat |
| Oberinspektor |
| Inspektor |
| Obersekretär |
| Sekretär |
| Verwaltungsassistent |
| Assistent |
| Amtsgehilfe |

# Abbreviations

| | |
|---|---|
| § | section (of a German law, code, or regulation) |
| §§ | sections (of a German law, code, or regulation) |
| AA | Auswärtiges Amt (German Foreign Office) |
| AAN | Archiwum Akt Nowych (Central Archives of Modern Records), Warsaw |
| AG | Aktiengesellschaft (public limited company) |
| AIP | Archiwum Instytutu Polskiego (Archives of the Polish Institute), London |
| AIPN | Archiwum Instytutu Pamięci Narodowej (Archive of the Institute of National Remembrance), Warsaw |
| AIZ | Archiwum Instytutu Zachodniego (Archives of the Institute for Western Affairs), Poznań |
| AMV | Archiv Ministerstva vnitra České Republiky (Archives of the Ministry of the Interior of the Czech Republic) |
| APL | Archiwum Państwowe w Lublinie (State Archive in Lublin) |
| APMM | Archiwum Państwowego Muzeum na Majdanku (Majdanek State Museum) |
| APW | Archiwum Państwowe w Warszawie (State Archive in Warsaw) |
| ARG | Archiwum Getta (ghetto archive) |
| AŻIH | Archiwum Żydowskiego Instytutu Historycznego (Archives of the Jewish Historical Institute), Warsaw |
| BArch | Bundesarchiv (German Federal Archives) |
| BdO | Befehlshaber der Ordnungspolizei (Senior Commander of the Order Police) |
| BdS | Befehlshaber der Sicherheitspolizei und des SD (Senior Commander of the Security Police and the SD) |
| BHE | Bund der Heimatvertriebenen und Entrechteten (League of Expellees and Persons Deprived of Rights) |
| BLHG | Beit Lohamei Hagetaot (Ghetto Fighters' House), Israel |
| *BŻIH* | *Biuletyn Żydowskiego Instytutu Historycznego* (Bulletin of the Jewish Historical Institute), Warsaw |
| CE | Common Era |
| CENTOS | Centralne Towarzystwo Opieki nad Sierotami i Dziećmi Opuszczonymi (Jewish Central Association for the Care of Orphans) |
| CISzO (also Tsysho) | Tsentrale Yidishe Shul Organizatsye (Central Yiddish School Organization) |
| CKRŻMP | Centralne Kierownictwo Ruchu Żydowskich Mas Pracujących (Central Directorate of the Movement of the Jewish Working Masses in Poland) |
| CKŻP | Centralny Komitet Żydów Polskich (Central Committee of Polish Jews) |
| CKZZ | Centralna Komisja Związków Zawodowych (Central Committee of Trade Unions) |
| Comintern | Communist International |
| CSU | Christlich-Soziale Union (Christian Social Union) |
| CZA | Central Zionist Archives, Jerusalem |
| DAF | Deutsche Arbeitsfront (German Labour Front) |
| DALO | Derzhavnyy arkhiv L'vivs'koyi oblasti (State Archives of the Lviv Region), Lviv |
| DAW | Deutsche Ausrüstungswerke (German Military Equipment Works) |

| | |
|---|---|
| DGAP | Deutsche Gesellschaft für Auswärtige Politik (German Council on Foreign Relations) |
| DÖW | Dokumentationsarchiv des österreichischen Widerstands (Documentation Centre of Austrian Resistance), Vienna |
| FDP | Freie Demokratische Partei (Free Democratic Party) |
| fol. | folio (of an archival source) |
| FOP | Front Odrodzenia Polski (Front for Poland's Rebirth) |
| Gestapa | Geheimes Staatspolizeiamt (Gestapo Central Office) |
| Gestapo | Geheime Staatspolizei (Secret State Police) |
| GG | General Government |
| GmbH | Gesellschaft mit beschränkter Haftung (limited company) |
| GPU | Gosudarstvennoye politicheskoye upravleniye (State Political Directorate, also translated as the State Political Administration) |
| gr. | grosz (Polish currency) |
| GVP | Gesamtdeutsche Volkspartei (All-German People's Party) |
| HHStA | Hessisches Hauptstaatsarchiv (Hessian Main State Archives), Wiesbaden |
| ICRC | International Committee of the Red Cross |
| IDO | Institut für Deutsche Ostarbeit (Institute for German Eastern Research) |
| IfZ-Archives | Archiv des Instituts für Zeitgeschichte München – Berlin (Archives of the Leibniz Institute for Contemporary History), Munich |
| IKOR | Yidishe Kultur Organizatsye (Organization for Yiddish Culture) |
| IMT | International Military Tribunal, Nuremberg |
| JDC | American Jewish Joint Distribution Committee |
| JPS | Jewish Publication Society |
| JSS (also ŻSS) | Jüdische Soziale Selbsthilfe, Żydowska Samopomoc Społeczna (Jewish Social Self-Help) |
| JUS | Jüdische Unterstützungsstelle (Jewish Aid Office) |
| KdO | Kommandeur der Ordnungspolizei (Commander of the Order Police) |
| KdS | Kommandeur der Sicherheitspolizei und des SD (Commander of the Security Police and the SD) |
| KJV | King James Version (Bible) |
| KPD | Kommunistische Partei Deutschlands (Communist Party of Germany) |
| KPP | Komunistyczna Partia Polski (Communist Party of Poland) |
| KTB | Kriegstagebuch (military log) |
| KWC | Kierownictwo Walki Cywilnej (Directorate of Civil Combat) |
| KWK | Kierownictwo Walki Konspiracyjnej (Directorate of Covert Combat) |
| KWP | Kierownictwo Walki Podziemnej (Directorate of Underground Combat) |
| KZMP | Komunistyczny Związek Młodzieży Polskiej (Communist Union of Polish Youth) |
| mbH | mit beschränkter Haftung (limited liability company) |
| MHK | Muzeum Historyczne Miasta Krakowa (Historical Museum of the City of Cracow) |
| NARA | National Archives and Records Administration, College Park, MD |
| NCO | non-commissioned officer |
| ND ('Endecja') | Narodowa Demokracja (National Democracy) |
| NKJV | New King James Version (Bible) |
| NKVD | Narodnyy komissariat vnutrennikh del (People's Commissariat for Internal Affairs) |

| | |
|---|---|
| NRO | Naczelna Rada Opiekuńcza (Chief Social Welfare Council) |
| NSDAP | Nationalsozialistische Deutsche Arbeiterpartei (National Socialist German Workers' Party) |
| NSZ | Narodowe Siły Zbrojne (National Armed Forces) |
| NZO | New Zionist Organization |
| OFK | Oberfeldkommandantur (regional headquarters of the German military administration) |
| Oflag | Offizierslager (prisoner-of-war camp for officers) |
| ÖGfZ | Österreichische Gesellschaft für Zeitgeschichte (Austrian Society for Contemporary History) |
| OKW | Oberkommando der Wehrmacht (Wehrmacht High Command) |
| OPUS | Centralna Opieka Podziemia (Central Underground Welfare) |
| ORT | Russian acronym for the 'Association for the Promotion of Skilled Trades and Agriculture among Jews' |
| OS | Oyneg Shabes (also Oneg Shabbat, 'Joy of the Sabbath'; underground archive) |
| OSE | Œuvre de secours aux enfants (Children's Aid Society) |
| OUN | Orhanizatsiya ukrayins'kykh natsionalistiv (Organization of Ukrainian Nationalists) |
| OZN | Obóz Zjednoczenia Narodowego (Camp of National Unity) |
| PA AA | Politisches Archiv des Auswärtigen Amts (Political Archives of the German Foreign Office), Berlin |
| PCK | Polski Czerwony Krzyż (Polish Red Cross) |
| PISM | Instytut Polski i Muzeum im. Gen. Sikorskiego (Polish Institute and Sikorski Museum) |
| PMJ | *The Persecution and Murder of the European Jews by Nazi Germany, 1933–1945* |
| POW | Polska Organizacja Wojskowa (Polish Military Organization) |
| p.p. | *per procurationem* (by proxy) |
| PPR | Polska Partia Robotnicza (Polish Workers' Party) |
| PPS | Polska Partia Socjalistyczna (Polish Socialist Party) |
| PSL | Polskie Stronnictwo Ludowe (Polish Peasants' Party) |
| r–v | recto and verso (front and reverse side of a page) |
| RELICO | Relief Committee for the War-Stricken Jewish Population |
| RF | Reichsführer |
| RGO | Rada Główna Opiekuńcza (Polish Central Welfare Council) |
| RGVA | Rossiyskiy gosudarstvennyy voyennyy arkhiv (Russian State Military Archives) |
| RM | Reichsmark |
| RPŻ | Rada Pomocy Żydom (Council to Aid Jews, codenamed Żegota) |
| RSHA | Reichssicherheitshauptamt (Reich Security Main Office) |
| SA | Sturmabteilung (Storm Troopers) |
| SD | Sicherheitsdienst (SS Security Service) |
| SD | Stronnictwo Demokratyczne (Alliance of Democrats) |
| SdP | Sudetendeutsche Partei (Sudeten German Party) |
| SL | Stronnictwo Ludowe (Peasants' Party) |
| SPD | Sozialdemokratische Partei Deutschlands (Social Democratic Party of Germany) |
| SPD | Stronnictwo Polskiej Demokracji (Polish Democracy Party) |
| SPP | Studium Polski Podziemnej (Polish Underground Movement Study Trust), London |

| | |
|---|---|
| SS | Schutzstaffel (Protection Squadron) |
| SSPF | SS- und Polizeiführer (SS and Police Leader) |
| TOZ | Towarzystwo Ochrony Zdrowia Ludności Żydowskiej (Society for the Protection of the Health of the Jewish Population in Poland) |
| TSKŻ | Towarzystwo Społeczno-Kulturalne Żydów w Polsce (Social and Cultural Society of Jews in Poland) |
| USHMM | United States Holocaust Memorial Museum, Washington, DC |
| USSR | Union of Soviet Socialist Republics |
| v. | verso (reverse side of a page) |
| VEJ | *Die Verfolgung und Ermordung der europäischen Juden durch das nationalsozialistische Deutschland 1933–1945* |
| *VOBl* | *Verordnungsblatt* (law gazette) |
| *VOBl-GG* | *Verordnungsblatt für das Generalgouvernement* (law gazette for the General Government) |
| WCEO-WBBH | Wojskowe Centrum Edukacji Obywatelskiej – Wojskowe Biuro Badań Historycznych, Warsaw (Military Archive and Centre for Citizenship Training) |
| WFSt | Wehrmachtführungsstab (Wehrmacht High Command, operations staff) |
| WiG | Wehrkreisbefehlshaber im Generalgouvernement (military district commander in the General Government) |
| WIZO | Women's International Zionist Organization |
| WJC | World Jewish Congress |
| WRN | Centralne Kierownictwo Ruchu Mas Pracujących Polski – Wolność, Rowność, Niepodległość (Central Directorate of the Movement of the Polish Working Masses – Freedom, Equality, Independence) |
| WVHA | SS-Wirtschafts-Verwaltungshauptamt (SS Business and Administration Main Office) |
| WZO | World Zionist Organization |
| YIVO | Yidisher Visnshaftlekher Institut (Institute for Jewish Research, formerly known as Yiddish Scientific Institute), New York |
| YVA | Yad Vashem Archives, Jerusalem |
| ŻKK | Żydowski Komitet Koordynacyjny (Jewish Coordinating Committee) |
| ŻKN | Żydowski Komitet Narodowy (Jewish National Committee) |
| ŻKOM | Żydowski Komitet Opiekuńczy Miejski (Jewish Municipal Welfare Committee) |
| zł. | złoty (Polish currency) |
| ZNP | Związek Nauczycielstwa Polskiego (Polish Teachers' Union) |
| ŻOB | Żydowska Organizacja Bojowa (Jewish Combat Organization) |
| ŻOS | Żydowska Opieka Społeczna (Jewish Welfare Service) |
| ŻPS | Żydowska Partia Socjalno-Demokratyczna (Jewish Social Democratic Party) |
| ŻSS | Żydowska Samopomoc Społeczna (Jewish Social Self-Help) |
| ŻTOS | Żydowskie Towarzystwo Opieki Społecznej (Jewish Social Welfare Association) |
| ZUS | Zakład Ubezpieczeń Społecznych (Social Insurance Institution) |
| ZWM | Związek Walki Młodych (Union of Fighting Youth) |
| ZWZ | Związek Walki Zbrojnej (Union of Armed Struggle) |
| ZWZ-AK | Związek Walki Zbrojnej-Armia Krajowa (Home Army) |
| ŻZW | Żydowski Związek Wojskowy (Jewish Military Union) |

# List of Archives, Sources, and Literature Cited

*Archives*

Archiv des Instituts für Zeitgeschichte München – Berlin (IfZ-Archives, Archives of the Leibniz Institute for Contemporary History), Munich
Archiv Ministerstva vnitra Česke Republiky (AMV, Archives of the Ministry of the Interior of the Czech Republic), Prague
Archiwum Akt Nowych (AAN, Central Archives of Modern Records), Warsaw
Archiwum Instytutu Pamięci Narodowej (AIPN, Archive of the Institute of National Remembrance), Warsaw
Archiwum Instytutu Polskiego (AIP, Archives of the Polish Institute), London
Archiwum Instytutu Zachodniego (AIZ, Archives of the Institute for Western Affairs), Poznań
Archiwum Państwowe w Lublinie (APL, State Archive in Lublin)
Archiwum Państwowe w Warszawie (APW, State Archive in Warsaw)
Archiwum Państwowego Muzeum na Majdanku (APMM, Majdanek State Museum)
Archiwum Uniwersytetu Jagiellońskiego (Jagiellonian University Archives), Cracow
Archiwum Żydowskiego Instytutu Historycznego (AŻIH, Archives of the Jewish Historical Institute), Warsaw
Beit Lohamei Hagetaot (BLHG, Ghetto Fighter's House), Israel
Biblioteka Narodowa (National Library), Warsaw
Biblioteka Uniwersytecka Katolickiego Uniwersytetu Lubelskiego
Bundesarchiv (BArch, German Federal Archives)
Central Zionist Archives (CZA), Jerusalem
Derzhavnyy arkhiv L'vivs'koyi oblasti (DALO, State Archives of the Lviv Region), Lviv
Dokumentationsarchiv des österreichischen Widerstands (DÖW, Documentation Centre of Austrian Resistance), Vienna
Herinnerungscentrum Kamp Westerbork (Camp Westerbork Memorial Centre)
Hessisches Hauptstaatsarchiv (HHStA, Hessian Main State Archives), Wiesbaden
Historisches Archiv des Max-Planck-Instituts für Psychiatrie (Historical Archive of the Max Planck Institute of Psychiatry), Munich
Landeskirchliches Archiv der Evangelischen Kirche von Westfalen (Regional Archive of the Protestant Church in Westfalia), Bielefeld
Moreshet Mordechai Anielevich Memorial Holocaust Study and Research Center (Moreshet Archive) Givat Haviva
Muzeum Historyczne Miasta Krakowa (MHK, Historical Museum of the City of Cracow)
Muzeum im. prof. Stanisława Fischera w Bochni (Museum in Bochnia)
Muzeum Regionalny w Kozienicach (Kozienice Regional Museum)
The National Archives, Kew
Ośrodek Dokumentacji i Badań Korczakianum, Archiwum Korczakowskie (Korczak Documentation and Research Centre, Korczak Archives), Warsaw
Ośrodek Karta (Karta Center), Warsaw
Österreichische Gesellschaft für Zeitgeschichte (ÖGfZ, Austrian Society for Contemporary History)
Polish Institute and Sikorski Museum (PISM), London
Politisches Archiv des Auswärtigen Amtes (PA AA, Political Archives of the German Foreign Office), Berlin
Rossiyskiy gosudarstvennyy voennyy arkhiv (RGVA, Russian State Military Archives), Moscow
Staatsanwaltschaft Hamburg (Hamburg Public Prosecutor's Office)
Studium Polski Podziemnej (SPP, Polish Underground Movement Study Trust), London

Tsentralnyi derzhavnyi istorychnyi arkhiv, m. Lviv (TSDIAL, Central State Historical Archives of Ukraine, Lviv)
United States Holocaust Memorial Museum (USHMM), Washington, DC
Uniwersytet Warszawski, Biblioteka Uniwersytecka (Warsaw University Library)
US National Archives and Records Administration (NARA), College Park, MD
Wojskowe Centrum Edukacji Obywatelskiej – Wojskowe Biuro Badań Historycznych (WCEO-WBBH, Military Archive and Centre for Citizenship Training), Warsaw
Yad Vashem Archives (YVA), Jerusalem
Yidisher Visnshaftlekher Institut (YIVO, Institute for Jewish Research, formerly known as Yiddish Scientific Institute), New York
Zakład Narodowy im. Ossolińskich (Ossileum, Ossoliński National Institute), Wrocław
Żydowski Instytut Historyczny (Jewish Historical Institute), Warsaw

*Newspapers, Magazines, and Official Bulletins*

*Agencja Prasowa*
*Amtlicher Anzeiger für das Generalgouvernement*
*Amtliches Mitteilungsblatt des Kreishauptmanns von Grojec*
*Amtsblatt des Chefs des Distrikts Warschau*
*Avangard*
*Biuletin*
*Biuletyn Informacyjny*
*Biuletyn Radiowy*
*Dagens Nyheter*
*Daily Telegraph*
*Das Reich*
*Department of State Bulletin*
*Der Mittag*
*Der Ruf*
*Deutsche Forschung im Osten: Mitteilungen des Instituts für deutsche Ostarbeit Krakau*
*Dziennik Polski* (after 1945)
*Dziennik Polski: Organ Demokratyczny*
*Echo Żyrardowskie*
*Gazeta Lwowska*
*Gazeta Żydowska*
*Głos Starego Miasta*
*Głos Warszawy*
*Hechaluc Halochem: Pismo Bojowej Organizacji Żydowskiej Młodzieży Chalucowej*
*Informacja Bieżąca*
*Jewish Chronicle*
*Kennst Du die Wahrheit? Mitteilungsblatt für Deutsche in Polen. Ausgabe für Volksdeutsche*
*Kraj: Agencja Informacyjna*
*Krakauer Zeitung*
*Mitteilungsblatt der Stadt Warschau*
*Neue Zürcher Zeitung*
*New York Times*
*Nowa Epoka*
*Nowy Dzień*
*Nowy Głos Lubelski*
*Nowy Kurier Warszawki*
*Oyf der vakh*
*Polish Fortnightly Review*
*Polska Informacja Prasowa*
*Pravda*
*Prawda: Pismo Frontu Odrodzenia Polski*
*Pressedienst des Generalgouvernements*
*Reichsgesetzblatt*
*Rzeczpospolita Polska*
*Sierp i Młot*
*Słowo Młodych*
*Tagespost*
*Toronto Globe*
*Tsayt-Fragn*
*Verordnungsblatt für das Generalgouvernement (VOBl-GG)*
*Völkischer Beobachter*
*Walka Młodych*
*Warschauer Zeitung*
*Warszawianka: Wydawnictwo Warszawskiego O[kręgowego] K[omitetu] R[obotniczego] P.P.S.*
*Wiadomości*
*WRN*
*Za naszą i waszą wolność*

*Diaries, Letters, and Memoirs*

Berg, Mary, *The Diary of Mary Berg: Growing up in the Warsaw Ghetto* (Oxford: Oneworld Publications, 2007).
Birenbaum, Halina, *Hope Is the Last to Die: A Coming of Age under Nazi Terror*, trans.

David Welch (London and New York: Routledge, 1996 [Polish edn, 1982]).

Blatt, Thomas Toivi, *From the Ashes of Sobibor: A Story of Survival* (Evanston, IL: Northwestern University Press, 1997).

Borzykowski, Tuvia (Tuvye Bozhikovski), *Between Tumbling Walls*, trans. from Yiddish Mendel Kohansky (Tel Aviv: Ghetto Fighters' House, 1972).

Bozhikovski, Tuvye (Tuvia Borzykowski), *Tsvishn falndike vent* (Warsaw: Merkaz Hehalutz, 1949).

Celemeński, Jakub, *Elegy for My People: Memoirs of an Underground Courier of the Jewish Labor Bund in Nazi-occupied Poland 1939–1945*, ed. Sandra Goldblum Zerbo, trans. Gershon Freidlin (Melbourne: Jacob Celemenski Memorial Trust, 2000 [Yiddish edn, 1963]).

Czerniaków, Adam, *Dziennik getta warszawskiego 6 IX 1939 – 23 VII 1942*, ed. Marian Fuks (Warsaw: Państwowe Wydawnictwo Naukowe, 1983).

Czerniaków, Adam, *The Warsaw Diary of Adam Czerniakow: Prelude to Doom*, ed. Raul Hilberg, Stanislaw Staron, and Joseph Kermish, trans. Stanislaw Staron and the Staff of Yad Vashem (Chicago, IL: Ivan R. Dee, 1999).

Ernest, Stefan, *O wojnie wielkich Niemiec z Żydami Warszawy 1939–1943*, ed. Marta Młodkowska (Warsaw: Czytelnik, 2003).

Gelbart, Josef, *'Ach, es ist alles ohne Ufer …': Briefe aus dem Warschauer Ghetto*, ed. Konrad Plieninger and Karl-Heinz Rueß, 2nd edn (Göppingen: Jüdisches Museum Göppingen, 2002).

Glazar, Richard, *Trap with a Green Fence: Survival in Treblinka*, trans. Roslyn Theobold (Evanston, IL: Northwestern University Press, 1995 [German edn, 1992]).

Goebbels, Joseph, *Die Tagebücher von Joseph Goebbels*, part 2, *Diktate 1941–1945*, vol. 3: *Januar – März 1942*, ed. Elke Frohlich (Munich: Saur, 1994).

Goetzel-Leviathan, Sophie, *The War from Within*, ed. Rebecca Fromer, trans. from German Geoffrey A. M. Block (Berkeley, CA: Judah L. Magnes Museum, 1987).

Hosenfeld, Wilm, *'Ich versuche jeden zu retten.' Das Leben eines deutschen Offiziers in Briefen und Tagebüchern*, ed. Thomas Vogel (Munich: DVA, 2004).

Jagur, Orna (Irena Grodzińska), *The Hiding Place* (Łódź: Oficyna Bibliofilów, 2000).

Kaplan, Chaim, *Megillat yissurin: Yoman getto varshah* (Tel Aviv: Am Oved, 1966).

Kaplan, Chaim, *Scroll of Agony: The Warsaw Diary of Chaim A. Kaplan*, ed. and trans. from Hebrew Abraham I. Katsh (New York: Macmillan, 1965).

Kast, Jochen, Bernd Ziegler, and Peter Zinke (eds.), *Das Tagebuch der Partisanin Justyna: Jüdischer Widerstand in Krakau*, trans. Victor Mika (Berlin: Elefanten Press, 1999 [Polish edn, 1946]).

Kazik (Simha Rotem), *Memoirs of a Warsaw Ghetto Fighter*, ed. and trans. from Hebrew Barbara Harshav (New Haven, CT, and London: Yale University Press, 1994).

Klukowski, Zygmunt, *Diary from the Years of Occupation 1939–44*, ed. Andrew Klukowski and Helen Klukowski May, trans. George Klukowski (Urbana, IL: University of Illinois Press, 1993 [Polish edn, 1958]).

Klukowski, Zygmunt, *Zamojszczyzna*, vol. 1: *1918–1943*, ed. Agnieszka Knyt (Warsaw: Ośrodek Karta, 2007 [1958]).

Korczak, Janusz, *Ghetto Diary*, trans. Jerzy Bachrach and Barbara Krzywicka (New Haven, CT, and London: Yale University Press, 2003 [Polish edn, 1958]).

Kramer, Clara (with Stephen Glantz), *Clara's War: A Miraculous Story of One Girl's Survival under the Nazis* (London: Ebury Press, 2009).

Krzepicki, Abraham (Jakub), 'Treblinka', *Bleter far geszichte*, no. 11 (1956), pp. 71–141.

Lewin, Abraham, *A Cup of Tears: A Diary of the Warsaw Ghetto*, ed. Antony Polonsky, trans. from Yiddish and Hebrew Christopher Hutton (Oxford: Basil Blackwell, 1988 [Yiddish edn, 1952, 1954]).

Liempt, Ad van, *Selma: De vrouw die Sobibor overleefde* (Laren: Verbum, 2010).

Ligocka, Roma, *The Girl in the Red Coat: A Memoir*, trans. Margot Bettauer Dembo (New

York: Random House, 2003 [German edn, 2002]).
*Listy z Majdanka: KL Lublin w świetle grypsów – katalog wystawy* (Lublin: Państwowe Muzeum na Majdanku, 2008).
Lubetkin, Zivia, *In the Days of Destruction and Revolt*, ed. Yehiel Yanay, trans. Ishai Tabbai (Tel Aviv: Hakibbutz Hameuchad, 1981 [based on the 3rd Hebrew edn, 1960]).
Mannheimer, Max, *A Diary Delayed: Theresienstadt, Auschwitz, Warsaw, Dachau*, trans. Kathryn Woodard (Munich: Oettingen Press, 2017 [German edn, 2010]).
Margolis-Edelman, Alina, *Ala z elementarza* (Aneks: London, 1994).
Margolis-Edelman, Alina, 'Ala from the Primer', *Polin: Studies in Polish Jewry*, vol. 11, *Focusing on Aspects and Experiences of Religion*, ed. Antony Polonsky (Liverpool: Liverpool University Press; London: Littmann Library of Jewish Civilization, 1998), pp. 94–111.
Nelken, Halina, *And Yet, I Am Here!*, trans. Halina Nelken with Alicia Nitecki (Amherst, MA: University of Massachusetts Press, 1999 [Polish edn, 1987]).
Nelken, Halina, *Pamiętnik z getta w Krakowie*, ed. Stanisław Wcisło (Toronto: Polski Fundusz Wydawniczy w Kanadzie, 1987).
Perechodnik, Calek, *Am I a Murderer? Testament of a Jewish Ghetto Policeman*, ed. and trans. from Polish Frank Fox (Boulder, CO: Westview, 1996).
Perechodnik, Calek, *Spowiedź: Dzieje rodziny żydowskiej podczas okupacji hitlerowskiej w Polsce*, ed. David Engel (Warsaw: Ośrodek Karta, 2004).
Poraj, Kazimiera, 'Dziennik Lwowski', *BZIH*, no. 52 (1964), pp. 79–106.
Rajchman, Chil, *The Last Jew of Treblinka: A Survivor's Memory, 1942–1943*, trans. Solon Beinfeld (New York: Pegasus, 2011 [German edn, 2009]).
Reich-Ranicki, Marcel, *The Author of Himself: The Life of Marcel Reich-Ranicki*, trans. Ewald Osers (London: Phoenix, 2002 [German edn, 1999]).
Reizer, Franciszka, *Dzienniki 1939–1944* (Warsaw: Ludowa Spółdzielnia Wydawnicza, 1984).
Rembek, Stanisław, *Dziennik okupacyjny* (Warsaw: Agawa, 2000).
Ringelblum, Emanuel, *Ksovim fun geto*, vol. 1: *Togbukh fun varshever geto, 1939–1942*, ed. Tatiana Berenstein et al. (Warsaw: Yidish bukh, 1961).
Ringelblum, Emanuel, *Notes from the Warsaw Ghetto: The Journal of Emanuel Ringelblum*, ed. and trans. Jacob Sloan (n.p.: Normanby Press, 2015 [1958]).
Rosenfeld, Else, and Gertrud Luckner (eds.), *Lebenszeichen aus Piaski: Briefe Deportierter aus dem Distrikt Lublin 1940–1943* (Munich: Biederstein, 1968).
Rubinowicz, Dawid, *The Diary of Dawid Rubinowicz*, trans. Derek Bowman (Edinburgh: William Blackwood, 1981 [Polish edn, 1960]).
Sheinkinder, S., 'The Diary of S. Sheinkinder', *Yad Vashem Studies*, no. 5 (1963), pp. 255–269.
Steinhaus, Hugo, *Mathematician for All Seasons: Recollections and Notes*, vol. 1: *1887–1945*, ed. Robert G. Burns, Irena Syzmaniec, and Aleksander Weron, trans. Abe Shenitzer (Cham: Birkhauser, 2015).
Steinhaus, Hugo, *Wspomnienia i zapiski*, ed. Aleksandra Zgorzelska (London: Aneks, 1992).
Szajn Lewin, Eugenia, *W getcie warszawskim: Lipiec 1942 – kwiecień 1943*, ed. Maria Line and Anna Grupińska (Poznań: a5, 1989).
Szpilman, Władysław, *The Pianist: The Extraordinary Story of One Man's Survival in Warsaw, 1939–45*, trans. Anthea Bell (London: Gollancz, 1999 [Polish edn, 1946]).
Szwajgier, Adina Blady, *I Remember Nothing More: The Warsaw Children's Hospital and the Jewish Resistance*, trans. Tasja Darowska and Danusia Stok (London: Collins Harvill, 1990 [Polish edn, 1988]).
Temkin-Berman, Basia, *City within a City*, trans. Jerzy Michałowicz (New York: IPBooks and YIVO Institute for Jewish Research, 2013 [Polish edn, 2000]).
Tomaszewski, Tadeusz, *Lwów: Pejsaż psychologiczny*, ed. Zofia Ratajczak (Warsaw: WIP, 1996).

Turkow, Jonas, *C'était ainsi 1939–1943: La vie dans le ghetto de Varsovie*, trans. from Yiddish Maurice Pfeffer (Paris: Austral, 1995).

Urman, Jerzy Feliks, *I'm Not Even a Grown-up: The Diary of Jerzy Feliks Urman*, ed. Antony Rudolf, trans. from Polish Antony Rudolf and Joanna Voit (London: Menard Press, 1991).

Weinstein, Frederick, *Aufzeichnungen aus dem Versteck: Erlebnisse eines polnischen Juden 1939–1946* (Berlin: Lukas Verlag für Kunst- und Geistesgeschichte, 2006).

Weiser, Piotr (ed.), *Patrzyłam na usta … Dziennik z warszawskiego getta* (Cracow: Homini, 2008).

Wewryk, Kalmen, *To Sobibor and Back: An Eyewitness Account*, ed. and trans. from Yiddish Howard Roiter (Montreal: Montreal Institute for Genocide and Human Rights, 1999).

Wiernik, Yankel, *A Year in Treblinka: An Inmate Who Escaped Tells the Day-to-Day Facts of One Year of his Torturous Experience* (New York: American Representation of the General Jewish Workers' Union of Poland, 1944).

Willenberg, Samuel, *Revolt in Treblinka* (Warsaw: Żydowski Inst. Historyczny, 2008 [Polish edn, 1991]).

Zapruder, Alexandra (ed.), *Salvaged Pages: Young Writers' Diaries of the Holocaust* (New Haven: Yale University Press, 2002).

Zylberberg, Michael, *A Warsaw Diary 1939–1945* (London: Vallentine Mitchell, 1969).

*Works Published before 1945*

Apenszlak, Jacob et al. (eds.), *The Black Book of Polish Jewry: An Account of the Martyrdom of Polish Jewry under the Nazi Occupation* (New York: Roy, 1943).

Fuhrmann, Ernst et al. (eds.), *Strafrecht und Strafverfahren: Eine Sammlung der wichtigsten Gesetze des Strafrechts und des Strafverfahrens mit Erläuterungen*, 33rd edn (Berlin: Schweitzer, 1942).

'German Policy of Extermination of the Jewish Race', *Department of State Bulletin*, vol. VII, no. 182, 19 Dec. 1942.

Gollert, Friedrich, *Zwei Jahre Aufbau im Distrikt Warschau* (Warsaw: Buchverlag Deutscher Osten, 1941).

Kann, Maria, *Na oczach świata* (Warsaw: Wydawnictwo K.O.P.R. Komisji Propagandy Biura Informacji in Propagandy KG AK, 1943).

Karski, Jan, *Story of a Secret State: My Report to the World*, trans. Krystyna Sokołowska (Washington, DC: Georgetown University Press, 2013 [1944]).

Katzenelson, Yitzhak, *The Song of the Massacred Jewish People*, trans. Jack Hirschmann (Berkeley, CA: Regent Press, 2021 [Yiddish edn, 1945]).

Lehnert, Reinhold, and Karl Schafer, *Kleines Strafrechts-Lehrbuch (Strafrecht und Strafprozeß) für Polizei und Gendarmerie: Mit einer Übersicht über die Grundgedanken des kommenden Deutschen Strafrechts*, 28th edn (Berlin: Kameradschaft Verlagsgesellschaft Gersbach & Co., 1941).

*Na oczach świata* (Zamość [Warsaw]: Wydawnictwo 'GLOB' [Wydawnictwo K.O.P.R.], 1932 [1943]).

Pecherskiy, Aleksandr A., *Vosstaniye v Sobiburovskom lagere* (Rostov-on-Don: Rostizdat, 1945).

Polish Ministry of Information, *The German New Order in Poland* (London: Hutchinson, 1941).

Republic of Poland, Ministry of Foreign Affairs, *The Mass Extermination of Jews in German Occupied Poland: Note Addressed to the Governments of the United Nations on December 10th, 1942, and other Documents* (London: Hutchinson & Co., 1942).

Taffet, Gerszon (ed.), *Extermination of Polish Jews: Album of Pictures* (Łodź: Wydawnictwa Centralnej Żydowskiej Komisji Historycznej przy C. K. Żydow Polskich, 1945).

*Published Primary Sources*

Arad, Yitzhal, Israel Gutman, and Abraham Margaliot (eds.), *Documents on the Holocaust: Selected Sources on the Destruction of the Jews of Germany and Austria, Poland, and the*

*Soviet Union*, 8th edn, trans. Lea Ben Dor (Lincoln, NE: University of Nebraska Press; Jerusalem: Yad Vashem, 1999), pp. 315–316.

Beer, Frank, Wolfgang Benz, and Barbara Distel (eds.), *Nach dem Untergang: Die ersten Zeugnisse der Shoah in Polen 1944–1947. Berichte der Zentralen Jüdischen Historischen Kommission* (Berlin: Metropol, 2014).

Berenstein, Tatiana, 'Dokument o ruchu oporu w Warszawie', *BŻIH*, nos. 19 and 20 (1956), pp. 162–168.

Berenstein, Tatiana (ed.), 'Materiały i dokumenty z drugiej części podziemnego archiwum getta warszawskiego, tzw. Archiwum Ringelbluma II', *BŻIH*, nos. 71 and 72 (1969), pp. 137, 140–144.

Berenstein, Tatiana, Artur Eisenbach, and Adam Rutkowski (eds.), *Eksterminacja Żydów na ziemiach polskich w okresie okupacji hitlerowskiej: Zbiór dokumentów* (Warsaw: Żydowski Instytut Historyczny, 1957).

Berenstein, Tatiana et al. (eds.), *Faschismus – Getto – Massenmord: Dokumentation über Ausrottung und Widerstand der Juden in Polen während des 2. Weltkrieges* (Berlin: Rütten & Loening, 1961).

Bialik, Hayim Nahman, *Songs from Bialik: Selected Poems of Hayim Nahman Bialik*, trans. from Hebrew Atar Hadari (Syracuse, NY: Syracuse University Press, 2000).

Bildungswerk Stanisław Hantz e.V. / Forschungsstelle Ludwigsburg der Universität Stuttgart, *Fotos aus Sobibor: Die Niemann-Sammlung zu Holocaust und Nationalsozialismus* (Berlin: Dietz, 2020).

Blumental, Nachman (ed.), *Te'udot mi-geto lublin – yudenrat le-lo derekh* [Documents from Lublin Ghetto: Judenrat without Direction] (Jerusalem: Yad Vashem, 1967).

Borwicz, Michał (ed.), *Pieśń ujdzie cało ... Antologia wierszy o Żydach pod okupacją niemiecką* (Warsaw: Centralna Żydowska Komisja Historyczna w Polsce, 1947).

Brener, Liber (ed.), *Resistance and Death in the Czenstochower Ghetto,* trans. Gloria Berkenstat Freund (New York: JewishGen, 2018 [Yiddish edn, 1950]).

Büchler, Yehoshua, 'A Preparatory Document for the Wannsee "Conference"', *Holocaust and Genocide Studies*, vol. 9, no. 1 (1995), pp. 121–129.

Chodakiewicz, Marek Jan, Piotr Gontarczyk, and Leszek Żebrowski (eds.), *Tajne oblicze GL-AL i PPR: Dokumenty*, vol. 2 (Warsaw: Burchard Edition, 1997).

Churchill, Winston S., *Winston S. Churchill: His Complete Speeches, 1897–1963*, ed. Robert Rhodes James, vol. 6: *1935–1942* (New York: Chelsea House, 1983 [1974]).

Czarnocka, Halina, and Jozef Żmigrodzki (eds.), *Armia Krajowa w dokumentach: 1939–1945*, vol. 3: *Kwiecień 1943–lipiec 1944* (London: Studium Polski Podziemnej, 1976).

Czarnocka, Halina et al. (eds.), *Armia Krajowa w dokumentach*, vol. 6: *Uzupełnienia* (London: Studium Polski Podziemnej, 1989).

Długołęcki, Piotr (ed.), *Confronting the Holocaust. Documents on the Polish Government-in-Exile Concerning Jews 1939–1945* (Warsaw: Polski Instytut Spraw Miedynarodowych, 2022).

Domarus, Max (ed.), *Hitler: Speeches and Proclamations, 1932–1945, and Commentary by a Contemporary. The Chronicle of a Dictatorship*, vol. 4: *The Years 1941 to 1945*, trans. Mary Fran Gilbert (Wauconda, IL: Bolchazy-Carducci, 2004 [German edn, 1965]).

Dunin-Wąsowicz, Krzysztof et al. (eds.), *Raporty Ludwiga Fischera gubernatora Dystryktu Warszawskiego 1939–1944* (Warsaw: Książka i Wiedza, 1987).

Fatal-Knaani, Tikva (ed.), *The Jewish Underground Press in Warsaw*, vols. 1–3, trans. from Yiddish, Polish, and Hebrew Shulamit Berman et al. (Jerusalem: Yad Vashem, 2017–2021).

Grabitz, Helge, and Wolfgang Scheffler, *Der Ghetto-Aufstand Warschau 1943 aus der Sicht der Täter und Opfer in Aussagen vor deutschen Gerichten* (Munich: Goldmann, 1993).

Grabitz, Helge, and Wolfgang Scheffler, *Letzte Spuren: Ghetto Warschau – SS-Arbeitslager Trawniki – Aktion Erntefest. Fotos und*

*Dokumente über Opfer des Endlösungswahns im Spiegel der historischen Ereignisse* (Berlin: Hentrich, 1988).

Hochberg-Mariańska, Maria, and Grüss, Noe (eds.), *The Children Accuse*, trans. Bill Johnston (London and Portland: Vallentine Mitchell, 1996 [Polish edn, 1993]).

Hoffenberg, Sam H., with Patrick Girard, *Le Camp de Poniatowa: la liquidation des derniers Juifs de Varsovie* (Paris: Éditions Bibliophanes, 1988).

Huberband, Shimon, *Kiddush Hashem: Jewish Religious and Cultural Life in Poland during the Holocaust*, ed. Jeffrey Gurock and Robert Hirt, trans. from Yiddish David Fishman (Hoboken, NJ: Ktav, 1987).

Jackiewicz, Danuta, and Eugeniusz Cezary Król (eds.), *W obiektywie wroga: Niemieccy fotoreporterzy w okupowanej Warszawie (1939–1945)* (Warsaw: Oficyna Wydawnicza RYTM, 2008).

Jockusch, Laura (ed.), *Khurbn-Forshung: Documents on Early Holocaust Research in Postwar Poland* (Göttingen: Vandenhoeck & Ruprecht, 2021).

Kermish, Joseph (ed.), *Dokumenty i materiały do dziejów okupacji niemieckiej*, vol. 2: *'Akcje' i 'wysiedlenia'* (Warsaw: Centralna Żydowska Komisja Historyczna w Polsce, 1946).

Kermish, Joseph (ed.), *To Live with Honor and Die with Honor! Selected Documents from the Warsaw Ghetto Underground Archives 'O.S.' ('Oneg Shabbath')*, trans. M. Z. Prives et al. (Jerusalem: Yad Vashem, 1986).

Kermish, Joseph et al. (eds.), *Ittonut ha-mahteret ha-yedhudit be-Warsha*, 6 vols. (Jerusalem: Yad Vashem, 1979–1997).

Klee, Ernst, Willi Dresen, and Volker Ries (eds.), *'Schöne Zeiten': Judenmord aus der Sicht der Täter und Gaffer* (Frankfurt am Main: Fischer, 1988).

Moll, Martin (ed.), *Führer-Erlasse 1939–1945: Edition sämtlicher überlieferter, nicht im Reichsgesetzblatt abgedruckter, von Hitler während des Zweiten Weltkriegs schriftlich erteilter Direktiven aus den Bereichen Staat, Partei, Wirtschaft, Besatzungspolitik und Militärverwaltung* (Stuttgart: Steiner, 1997).

Mussolini, Benito, *Opera omnia*, ed. Edoardo and Duilio Susmel, vol. 30, *Dall'intervento dell'Italia nella Seconda guerra mondiale al discorso al direttorio nazionale del P.N.F. del 7 gennaio 1942 (11 giugno 1940 – 3 gennaio 1942)* (Florence: La Fenice, 1960).

Nayshtadt, Meylekh, *Khurbn un oyfshtand fun di yidn in varshe: Eydes-bleter un askores*, vol. 1: *Eydes-bleter* (Tel Aviv: Algemeyner yidisher arbeter-organizatsye in erets-yisroel and Yidish-natsionaler arbeter-farband in amerike, 1948).

Nayshtadt, Meylekh, *Khurbm un oyfshtand fun di yidn in varshe: Eydes-bleter un askores*, vol. 2: *Di gefalene oyf der vakh* (Tel Aviv: Algemeyner yidisher arbeter-organizatsye in erets-yisroel and yidish-natsionaler arbeter-farband in amerike, 1948).

Pełczyński, Tadeusz, and Jan Tokarski (eds.), *Armia Krajowa w dokumentach 1939–1945*, vol. 2: *Czerwiec 1941 – kwiecień 1943* (London: Studium Polski Podziemnej, 1973).

Präg, Werner, and Wolfgang Jacobmeyer (eds.), *Das Diensttagebuch des deutschen Generalgouverneurs in Polen 1939–1945* (Stuttgart: DVA, 1975).

*The Ringelblum Archive: Underground Archive of the Warsaw Ghetto* (Warsaw: Emanuel Ringelblum Historical Institute, 2017–present).

Sakowska, Ruta (ed.), *Archiwum Ringelbluma: Getto warszawskie lipiec 1942 – styczeń 1943* (Warsaw: Państwowe Wydawnictwo Naukowe, 1980).

Sakowska, Ruta et al. (eds.), *Archiwum Ringelbluma: Konspiracyjne Archiwum Getta Warszawy* (Warsaw: Żydowski Instytut Historyczny, 1997–2020).

Sakowska, Ruta et al. (eds.), *Archiwum Ringelbluma: Konspiracyjne Archiwum Getta Warszawy*, vol. 1: *Listy o Zagładzie*, ed. Ruta Sakowska (Warsaw: Wydawnictwo Naukowe PWN, 1997).

Sakowska, Ruta et al. (eds.), *Archiwum Ringelbluma: Konspiracyjne Archiwum Getta Warszawy*, vol. 2: *Dzieci – tajne nauczanie w getcie warszawskim*, ed. Ruta Sakowska

(Warsaw: Żydowski Instytut Historyczny, 2000).

Sakowska, Ruta et al. (eds.), *Archiwum Ringelbluma: Konspiracyjne Archiwum Getta Warszawy*, vol. 4: *Życie i twórczość Geli Seksztajn*, ed. Magdalena Tarnowska (Warsaw: Żydowski Instytut Historyczny, 2011).

Sakowska, Ruta et al. (eds.), *Archiwum Ringelbluma: Konspiracyjne Archiwum Getta Warszawy*, vol. 5: *Getto warszawskie: Życie codzienne*, ed. Katarzyna Person (Warsaw: Żydowski Instytut Historyczny, 2011).

Sakowska, Ruta et al. (eds.), *Archiwum Ringelbluma: Konspiracyjne Archiwum Getta Warszawy*, vol. 6: *Generalne Gubernatorstwo: Relacje i dokumenty*, ed. Aleksandra Bańkowska (Warsaw: Żydowski Instytut Historyczny, 2011).

Schubert, Kurt, and Jonny Moser, *Der gelbe Stern in Österreich: Katalog und Einführung zu einer Dokumentation* (Eisenstadt: Edition Roetzer, 1977).

Smith, Bradley F., and Agnes Peterson (eds.), *Heinrich Himmler: Geheimreden 1933 bis 1945 und andere Ansprachen* (Frankfurt am Main: Propylaen, 1974).

*The Stroop Report: The Jewish Quarter of Warsaw Is No More! A Facsimile Edition and Translation of the Official Nazi Report on the Destruction of the Warsaw Ghetto*, trans. from German Sybil Milton (New York: Pantheon, 1979).

*Trial of the Major War Criminals before the International Military Tribunal*, vols. 34 and 37 (Nuremberg: Secretariat of the Tribunal, 1949).

Tyszkowa, Maria, 'Eksterminacja Żydów w latach 1941–1943: Dokumenty Biura Informacji i Propagandy Komendy Głównej Armii Krajowej ze zbiorów Oddziału Rękopisów Biblioteki Uniwersytetu Warszawskiego', *BŻIH*, nos. 162 and 163 (1992), pp. 35–61 (part 1), and no. 164 (1992), pp. 47–60 (part 2).

Wirth, Andrzej (ed.), *'Es gibt keinen jüdischen Wohnbezirk in Warschau mehr': Stroop-Bericht* (Neuwied: H. Luchterhand, 1960).

Witte, Peter et al. (eds.), *Der Dienstkalender Heinrich Himmlers 1941/42* (Hamburg: Christians, 1999).

*Secondary Literature*

Ainsztein, Reuben, *Jewish Resistance in Nazi-occupied Eastern Europe: With a Historical Survey of the Jew as Fighter and Soldier in the Diaspora* (London: Paul Elek, 1974).

Aly, Götz, *'Final Solution': Nazi Population Policy and the Murder of the European Jews*, trans. Allison Brown and Belinda Cooper (London: Arnold; New York: Oxford University Press, 1999 [German edn, 1995]).

Arad, Yitzhak, *The Operation Reinhard Death Camps: Belzec, Sobibor, Treblinka*, 2nd edn (Bloomington: Indiana University Press; Jerusalem: Yad Vashem, 2018).

Arczyński, Marek, and Wiesław Balcerak, *Kryptonim 'Żegota': Z dziejów pomocy Żydom w Polsce 1939–1945* (Warsaw: Czytelnik, 1979).

Bajohr, Frank, and Dieter Pohl (eds.), *Der Holocaust als offenes Geheimnis: Die Deutschen, die NS-Führung und die Alliierten* (Munich: Beck, 2006).

Bartoszewski, Władysław, and Zofia Lewinowna, *Ten jest z ojczyzny mojej: Polacy z pomocą Żydom 1939–1945* (Cracow: Znak, 1969).

Bauer, Yehuda, 'When Did They Know?, *Midstream*, vol. 14, no. 4 (1968), pp. 61–69.

Bem, Marek (ed.), *Sobibór: Bunt wobec wyroku* (Warsaw: Ośrodek Karta, 2012).

Bem, Marek, *Sobibor Extermination Camp, 1942–1943*, trans. Tomasz Karpiński and Natalia Sarzyńska-Wójtowicz (Amsterdam: Stichting Sobibor, 2015 [Polish edn, 2011]).

Benz, Angelika, *Handlanger der SS: Die Rolle der Trawniki-Männer im Holocaust* (Berlin: Metropol, 2015).

Benz, Wolfgang, and Barbara Distel (eds.), *Der Ort des Terrors*, vol. 8: *Riga-Kaiserwswald, Warschau, Vaivara, Kauen (Kaunas), Płaszów, Kulmhof/Chełmno, Belzec, Sobibor, Treblinka* (Munich: Beck, 2008).

Berendt, Grzegorz, *Żydzi zbiegli z gett i obozów śmierci*, in Adam Sitarek, Michał Trębacz, and

Ewa Wiatr (eds.), *Zagłada Żydów na polskiej prowincji* (Łódź: Instytut Pamięci Narodowej, 2012), pp. 121–158.

Bereś, Witold, and Krzysztof Burnetko, *Marek Edelman: Being on the Right Side*, trans. William R. Brand (Redwood City and Cracow: Bereś Media, 2016 [Polish edn, 2013]).

Berger, Sara, *Experten der Vernichtung: Das T4-Reinhardt-Netzwerk in den Lagern Belzec, Sobibor und Treblinka* (Hamburg: Hamburger Edition, 2013).

Biberstein, Aleksander, *Zagłada Żydów w Krakowie* (Cracow: Wydawnictwo Literackie, 2001).

Black, Peter R., 'Foot Soldiers of the Final Solution: The Trawniki Training Camp and Operation Reinhard', *Holocaust and Genocide Studies*, vol. 25, no. 1 (2011), pp. 1–99.

Black, Peter R., 'Odilo Globocnik: Himmlers Vorposten im Osten', in Ronald Smelser, Enrico Syring, and Rainer Zitelmann (eds.), *Die Braune Elite II* (Darmstadt: WBG, 1993), pp. 103–115.

Blank, Manfred, 'Zum Beispiel: Die Ermordung der Juden im "Generalgouvernement" Polen', in Adalbert Rückerl (ed.), *NS-Prozesse: Nach 25 Jahren Strafverfolgung. Möglichkeiten – Grenzen – Ergebnisse* (Karlsruhe: C. F. Müller, 1971), pp. 35–64.

Blatman, Daniel, *En direct du ghetto: La presse clandestine juive dans le ghetto de Varsovie 1940–1943*, trans. Nelly Hansson (Paris: Cerf, 2005 [Hebrew edn, 2002]).

Blatman, Daniel, *For Our Freedom and Yours: The Jewish Labour Bund in Poland, 1939–1949*, trans. Naftali Greenwood (London: Vallentine Mitchell, 2003 [Hebrew edn, 1996]).

Blatman, Daniel (ed.), *Geṭo Varshah: Sipur itonai – mivḥar me itonut ha-maḥteret, 1940–1943* (Jerusalem: Yad Vashem, 2002).

Borwicz, Michał, *Arishe Papirn* (Buenos Aires: Unión central israelita polaca en la Argentina, 1955).

Browning, Christopher R., 'Genocide and Public Health: German Doctors and Polish Jews, 1939-1941', *Holocaust and Genocide Studies* vol. 3, no. 1 (1988), pp. 21-36.

Browning, Christopher R., 'Mehr als Warschau und Lodz: Der Holocaust in Polen', in *Der Weg zur 'Endlösung': Entscheidungen und Täter* (Bonn: Dietz, 1998), pp. 127–148.

Browning, Christopher R., *Ordinary Men: Reserve Police Battalion 101 and the Final Solution in Poland* (New York: Harper Collins, 1992).

Browning, Christopher R., *Remembering Survival: Inside a Nazi Slave-Labor Camp* (New York: Norton & Co., 2010).

Bruder, Franziska, *Das eigene Schicksal selbst bestimmen: Fluchten aus den Deportationszügen in die Vernichtungslager der 'Aktion Reinhardt' in Polen* (Mainz: Unrast, 2019).

Bruder, Franziska, *Hunderte solcher Helden: Der Aufstand jüdischer Gefangener im NS-Vernichtungslager Sobibór. Berichte, Recherchen und Analysen* (Hamburg and Münster: Unrast, 2013).

Brustin-Berenstein, Tatiana, 'Akta i zeznania w drugiej części Archiwum Podziemnego Getta warszawskiego', *BŻIH*, no. 1 (1951), pp. 51–126.

Büchler, Yehoshua R., 'The Deportation of Slovakian Jews to the Lublin District of Poland in 1942', *Holocaust and Genocide Studies*, vol. 6, no. 2 (1991), pp. 151–166.

Budz, Kateryna, and Andrew Kloes, 'Ethnonationalism as a Theological Crisis: Metropolitan Andrey Sheptytsky and the Greek Catholic Church in Western Ukraine, 1923-1944', in Kevin Spicer and Rebecca Carter-Chand (eds.), *Religion, Ethnonationalism and Antisemitism in the Era of the Two World Wars* (Montreal: McGill-Queen's University Press, 2022), pp. 274-304.

Caban, Ireneusz and Zygmunt Mańkowski (eds.), *Związek Walki Zbrojnej i Armia Krajowa w Okręgu Lubelskim 1939–1944* (Lublin: Wydawnictwo Lubelskie, 1971).

Chrostowski, Witold, *Extermination Camp Treblinka* (London: Vallentine Mitchell, 2004).

Cohen, Raya, 'Against the Current: Hashomer Hatzair in the Warsaw Ghetto', *Jewish Social Studies*, vol. 7, no. 1 (2000), pp. 63–80.

Cohen, Raya, 'The Lost Honour of Bystanders? The Case of Jewish Emissaries in Switzerland', *Journal of Holocaust Education*, vol. 9, nos. 2/3 (2000), pp. 146–170.

Corni, Gustavo, *Hitler's Ghettos: Voices from a Beleaguered Society, 1939–1945*, trans. Nicola Rudge Iannelli (London: Arnold, 2002 [Italian edn, 2001]).

Curilla, Wolfgang, *Der Judenmord in Polen und die deutsche Ordnungspolizei 1939–1945* (Paderborn: Schöningh, 2011).

Datner, Szymon, '"Wiadomości": Podziemny organ prasowy w getcie warszawskim z okresu po wielkim "wysiedleniu"', *BŻIH*, no. 76 (1970), pp. 49–79.

Dieckmann, Christoph, and Babette Quinkert (eds.), *Im Ghetto 1939–1945: Neue Forschungen zu Alltag und Umfeld* (Göttingen: Wallstein, 2009).

Dreifuss, Havi (Ben Sasson), 'Changing Perspectives on Polish-Jewish Relations during the Holocaust', *Search and Research*, vol. 18 (2012), pp. 32–69.

Dreifuss, Havi (Ben Sasson), *Geto Varsha HaSof* (Jerusalem: Yad Vashem, 2017).

Dreifuss, Havi (Ben-Sasson), *Relations between Jews and Poles: The Jewish Perspective*, trans. from Hebrew Ora Cummings (Jerusalem: Yad Vashem, 2017).

Dreßen, Willi, and Volker Rieß, 'Ausbeutung und Vernichtung: Gesundheitspolitik im Generalgouvernement', in Norbert Frei (ed.), *Medizin und Gesundheitspolitik in der NS-Zeit* (Munich: Oldenbourg, 1991), pp. 157–171.

Edelman, Marek, *The Ghetto Fights* (New York: American Representation of the General Jewish Workers' Union of Poland, 1946 [Polish edn, 1945]).

Eisenbach, Artur, *Hitlerowska polityka zagłady Żydów* (Warsaw: Książa i Wiedza, 1961).

Eisenblätter, Gerhard, 'Grundlinien der Politik des Reichs gegenüber dem Generalgouvernement 1939–1945' (doctoral thesis, Johann-Wolfgang-Goethe Universität, Frankfurt am Main, 1969).

Engel, David, *Facing a Holocaust: The Polish Government-in-Exile and the Jews, 1943–1945* (Chapel Hill, NC: University of North Carolina Press, 1993).

Engel, David, *In the Shadow of Auschwitz: The Polish Government-in-Exile and the Jews, 1939–1942* (Chapel Hill, NC: University of North Carolina Press, 1987).

Engelking, Barbara, *Such a Beautiful Sunny Day... Jews Seeking Refuge in the Polish Countryside, 1942–1945*, trans. Jerzy Michalowicz (Jerusalem: Yad Vashem, 2016 [Polish edn, 2011]).

Engelking, Barbara, *'Szanowny panie gistapo': Donosy do władz niemieckich w Warszawie i okolicach w latach 1940–1941* (Warsaw: Instytut Filozofii i Socjologii PAN, 2003).

Engelking, Barbara, and Jacek Leociak, *The Warsaw Ghetto: A Guide to the Perished City*, trans. Emma Harris (New Haven: Yale University Press, 2009 [Polish edn, 2001]).

Ferenc, Maria, *'Każdy pyta, co z nami będzie': Mieszkańcy getta warszawskiego wobec wiadomości o wojnie i Zagładzie* (Warsaw: Żydowski Instytut Historyczny, 2021).

Fijałkowski, Zenon, *Kościół katolicki na ziemiach polskich w latach okupacji hitlerowskiej* (Warsaw: Książka i Wiedza, 1983).

Finder, Gabriel, 'Jewish Prisoner Labour in Warsaw after the Ghetto Uprising, 1943–1944', *Polin: Studies in Polish Jewry*, vol. 17 (2004), pp. 325–352.

Fleming, Michael, *Auschwitz, the Allies and Censorship of the Holocaust* (Cambridge: Cambridge University Press, 2014).

Friedrich, Klaus-Peter, *Der nationalsozialistische Judenmord und das polnisch-jüdische Verhältnis im Diskurs der polnischen Untergrundpresse (1942–1944)* (Marburg: Herder-Institut, 2006) (unabridged dissertation version available at http://kups.ub.uni-koeln.de/id/eprint/952).

Friedrich, Klaus-Peter, 'Die polnische Regierungsdelegatur und ihr "jüdisches Problem" 1940–1945', *Jahrbücher für Geschichte Osteuropas*, vol. 57, no. 1 (2009), pp. 23–53.

Friszke, Andrzej, 'Attitudes toward the Jews in the Polish Underground Press', in David Bankier and Israel Gutman (eds.), *Nazi Europe and the Final Solution* (Jerusalem: Yad Vashem, 2003), pp. 163–174.

Frydel, Tomasz, '"Judenjagd": Reassessing the Role of Ordinary Poles as Perpetrators in the Holocaust', in Timothy Williams and Susanne Buckley-Zistel (eds), *Perpetrators and Perpetration of Mass Violence: Action, Motivation and Dynamics* (London: Routledge, 2020).

Geldmacher, Thomas, *'Wir als Wiener waren ja bei der Bevölkerung beliebt': Österreichische Schutzpolizisten und die Judenvernichtung in Ostgalizien 1941–1944* (Vienna: Mandelbaum, 2002).

Gerlach, Christian, 'Die Bedeutung der deutschen Ernährungspolitik für die Beschleunigung des Mordes an den Juden 1942', in Christian Gerlach, *Krieg, Ernährung, Völkermord: Forschungen zur deutschen Vernichtungspolitik im Zweiten Weltkrieg* (Hamburg: Hamburger Edition, 1998), pp. 167–257.

Gerlach, Christian, *The Extermination of the European Jews* (Cambridge: Cambridge University Press, 2016).

Geshuri, Meir Shimon (ed.), *Sefer Podhaytse* (Tel Aviv: Farlag fun der podhaytser landsmanshaft in yisroel, 1972).

Gicewicz, Ryszard, 'Obóz pracy w Poniatowej (1941–1943)', *Zeszyty Majdanka*, vol. 10 (1980), pp. 88–104.

Gilbert, Martin, *The Holocaust: The Jewish Tragedy* (New York: HarperCollins, 1989).

Golczewski, Frank, 'Polen', in Wolfgang Benz (ed.), *Dimension des Völkermords: Die Zahl der jüdischen Opfer des Nationalsozialismus* (Munich: Oldenbourg, 1991), pp. 411–497.

Goldberg, Amos, 'Rumor Culture among Warsaw Jews under Nazi Occupation: A World of Catastrophe Reenchanted', *Jewish Social Studies*, vol. 21, no. 3 (2016), pp. 81–125.

Gondek, Leszek, *Polska karząca 1939–1945: Polski podziemny wymiar sprawiedliwości w okresie okupacji niemieckiej* (Warsaw: Pax, 1988).

Gottwaldt, Alfred B., and Diana Schulle, *Die 'Judendeportationen' aus dem Deutschen Reich von 1941–1945: Eine kommentierte Chronologie* (Wiesbaden: Marix, 2005).

Grabowski, Jan, *Hunt for the Jews: Betrayal and Murder in German-Occupied Poland* (Bloomington: Indiana University Press, 2014).

Grabowski, Jan, *'Ja tego Żyda znam!' Szantażowanie Żydów w Warszawie 1939–1943* (Warsaw: Instytut Filozofii i Socjologii PAN, 2004).

Grabowski, Jan, *Na posterunku: Udział polskiej policji granatowej i kryminalnej w zagładzie Żydów* (Wołowiec: Czarne, 2020).

Grabowski, Jan, *Rescue for Money: Paid Helpers in Poland, 1939–1945* (Jerusalem: Yad Vashem, 2008).

Grabowski, Jan, 'Strażacy, wiejska straż nocna i granatowa policja a zagłada Żydów na obszarach wiejskich w dystrykcie krakowskim', in Adam Sitarek, Michał Trębacz, and Ewa Wiatr (eds.), *Zagłada Żydów na polskiej prowincji* (Łódź: Instytut Pamięci Narodowej, 2012), pp. 245–264.

Grabowski, Jan, and Barbara Engelking (eds.), *Night without End: The Fate of Jews in German-Occupied Poland*, trans. Anna Brzostowska et al. (Bloomington: Indiana University Press; Jerusalem: Yad Vashem, 2022 [Polish exp. edn, 2018]).

Grabowski, Jan, and Dariusz Libionka (eds.), *Klucze i kasa: O mieniu żydowskim w Polsce pod okupacją niemiecką i we wczesnych latach powojennych 1939–1950* (Warsaw: Stowarzyszenie Centrum Badań nad Zagładą Żydów, 2014).

Grądzka, Martyna, *Przerwane dzieciństwo: Losy dzieci Żydowskiego Domu Sierot przy ul. Dietla 64 w Krakowie podczas okupacji niemieckiej* (Cracow: Wysoki Zamek, 2012).

Gross, Jan Tomasz (ed.), *The Holocaust in Occupied Poland: New Findings and New Interpretations* (Frankfurt am Main: Peter Lang, 2012).

Gross, Jan Tomasz, with Irena Gudzinska Gross, *Golden Harvest: Events at the Periphery of the*

*Holocaust* (New York: Oxford University Press, 2012).

Gruner, Wolf, *Jewish Forced Labor under the Nazis: Economic Needs and Racial Aims, 1938–1944*, trans. from German Kathleen M. Dell'Orto (Cambridge: Cambridge University Press, 2006).

Gryglewski, Elke, Hans-Christian Jasch, and David Zolldan (eds.), *The Meeting at Wannsee and the Murder of the European Jews: Exhibition Catalogue*, trans. Caroline Pearce (Berlin: House of the Wannsee Conference, 2020 [German edn, 2020]).

Gutman, Israel (ed.), *Emanuel Ringelblum: The Man and the Historian* (Jerusalem: Yad Vashem), 2006.

Gutman, Israel, *Resistance: The Warsaw Ghetto Uprising* (Boston: Houghton Mifflin, 1994).

Gutman, Israel, 'Some Issues in Jewish–Polish Relations during the Second World War', in Joshua D. Zimmerman (ed.), *Contested Memories: Poles and Jews during the Holocaust and its Aftermath* (New Brunswick: Rutgers University Press, 2003), pp. 212–217.

Gutman, Yisrael, *The Jews of Warsaw, 1939–1943: Ghetto, Underground, Revolt*, trans. Ina Friedman (Bloomington: Indiana University Press, 1982 [Hebrew edn, 1977]).

Gutman, Yisrael (ed.), *Rescuers of Jews during the Holocaust: Europe (Part I) and Other Countries* (Jerusalem: Yad Vashem, 2007).

Haas, Carlos Alberto, *Das Private im Ghetto: Jüdisches Leben im deutsch besetzten Polen 1939 bis 1944* (Göttingen: Wallstein, 2020).

Haimi, Yoram, and Wojciech Mazurek, 'Uncovering the Remains of a Nazi Death Camp: Archaeological Research in Sobibór', *Yad Vashem Studies*, vol. 41, no. 2 (2013), pp. 55–94.

Hänschen, Steffen, *Das Transitghetto Izbica im System des Holocaust* (Berlin: Metropol, 2018).

Hartman, John J., and Jacek Krochmal (eds.), *Pamiętam każdy dzień … Losy Żydów przemyskich podczas II wojny światowej* (Przemyśl: Towarzystwa Przyjaciół, 2001).

Haska, Agnieszka, *'Jestem Żydem, chcę wejść': Hotel Polski w Warszawie, 1943* (Warsaw: Instytut Filozofii i Socjologii PAN, 2006).

Hembera, Melanie, *Die Shoah im Distrikt Krakau: Jüdisches Leben und deutsche Besatzung in Tarnów 1939–1945* (Darmstadt: WBG, 2016).

Hensel, Jürgen, and Stephan Lehnstaedt (eds.), *Arbeit in den nationalsozialistischen Ghettos* (Osnabrück: fibre, 2013).

Hilberg, Raul, *Sonderzüge nach Auschwitz* (Frankfurt am Main: Ullstein, 1987).

Hirszfeld, Ludwik, *Historia jednego życia* (Warsaw: Pax, 2000 [1946]).

Janczewska, Marta, 'Obozy pracy przymusowej dla Żydów na terenie dystryktu warszawskiego', in Barbara Engelking, Jacek Leociak, and Dariusz Libionka (eds.), *Prowincja noc: Życie i zagłada Żydów w dystrykcie warszawskim* (Warsaw: Wydawnictwo Instytutu Filozofii i Socjologii PAN, 2007), pp. 271–320.

Joniec, Jarosław, *Niemiecki obóz zagłady w Bełżcu: Zarys historii* (Lublin: Państwowe Muzeum na Majdanku, 2016).

Kaczmarski, Krzysztof, *Podziemie narodowe na Rzeszowszczyźnie 1939–1944* (Rzeszów: Instytut Pamięci Narodowej, 2003).

Kadosh, Sara, *We Think of You as an Angel: Shaul Weingort and the Rescue of Jews during the Holocaust* (Jerusalem: Yad Vashem, 2019).

Kampe, Norbert, and Peter Klein (eds.), *Die Wannseekonferenz am 20. Januar 1942: Dokumente, Forschungsstand, Kontroversen* (Vienna and Cologne: Böhlau, 2013).

Karay, Felicja, *Death Comes in Yellow: Skarzysko-Kamienna Slave Labor Camp*, trans. from Hebrew Sara Kitai (Amsterdam: Harwood, 1996).

Kassow, Samuel D., 'Polish-Jewish Relations in the Writings of Emmanuel Ringelblum', in Joshua D. Zimmerman (ed.), *Contested Memories: Poles and Jews during the Holocaust and its Aftermath* (New Brunswick: Rutgers University Press, 2003), pp. 142–157.

Kassow, Samuel D., *Who Will Write Our History? Rediscovering a Hidden Archive from the Warsaw Ghetto* (Bloomington: Indiana University Press, 2007).

Kiełkowski, Roman, *Zlikwidować na miejscu: Z dziejów okupacji hitlerowskiej w Krakowie* (Cracow: Wydawnictwo Literackie, 1981).

Klein, Peter, *Die 'Wannsee-Konferenz' am 20. Januar 1942: Eine Einführung* (Berlin: Metropol, 2017).

Klemp, Stefan, *Freispruch für das 'Mord-Bataillon': Die NS-Ordnungspolizei und die Nachkriegsjustiz* (Münster: LIT, 1998).

Kogon, Eugen, Hermann Langbein, and Adalbert Rückerl (eds.), *Nazi Mass Murder: A Documentary History of the Use of Poison Gas,* trans. Mary Scott and Caroline Lloyd-Morris (New Haven, CT, and London: Yale University Press, 1993 [German edn, 1986]).

Kopka, Bogusław, *Konzentrationslager Warschau: Historia i następstwa* (Warsaw: Instytut Pamięci Narodowej, 2007).

Kopówka, Edward, *Stalag 366 Siedlce* (Siedlce: Stowarzyszenie Kreatorów Unikalnej Niebanalnej Kultury Studenckiej-SKUNKS w Siedlcach, 2004).

Kosmala, Beate, 'Ungleiche Opfer in extremer Situation: Die Schwierigkeiten der Solidarität im okkupierten Polen', in Wolfgang Benz and Juliane Wetzel (eds.), *Solidarität und Hilfe für Juden während der NS-Zeit: Regionalstudien 1. Polen, Rumänien, Griechenland, Luxemburg, Norwegen, Schweiz* (Berlin: Metropol, 1996), pp. 19–98.

Kotula, Franciszek, *Losy Żydów rzeszowskich 1939–1944: Kronika tamtych dni* (Rzeszów: Mitel, 1999).

Krakowski, Shmuel, 'The Attitude of the Polish Underground to the Jewish Question during the Second World War', in Joshua D. Zimmerman (ed.), *Contested Memories: Poles and Jews during the Holocaust and its Aftermath* (New Brunswick: Rutgers University Press, 2003), pp. 97–106.

Krakowski, Shmuel, 'The Polish Underground and the Jews in the Years of the Second World War', in David Bankier and Israel Gutman (eds.), *Nazi Europe and the Final Solution* (Jerusalem: Yad Vashem, 2003), pp. 215–230.

Krakowski, Shmuel, *The War of the Doomed: Jewish Armed Resistance in Poland, 1942–1944* (New York: Holmes and Meier, 1984).

Kranz, Tomasz, 'Between Planning and Implementation: The Lublin District and Majdanek Camp in Nazi Policy', in Larry V. Thompson (ed.), *Lessons and Legacies IV: Reflections on Religion, Justice, Sexuality, and Genocide* (Evanston, IL: Northwestern University Press, 2003), pp. 215–235.

Kranz, Tomasz, *Die Vernichtung der Juden im Konzentrationslager Majdanek*, trans. Christhardt Henschel (Lublin: Państwowe Muzeum na Majdanku, 2007 [Polish edn, 2007]).

Kranz, Tomasz, *Extermination of Jews at the Majdanek Concentration Camp* (Lublin: Państwowe Muzeum na Majdanku, 2010).

Kroll, Bogdan, *Rada Główna Opiekuńcza 1939–1945* (Warsaw: Książka i Wiedza, 1985).

Krugłow, Aleksander, 'Deportacja ludności żydowskiej z dystryktu Galicja do obozu zagłady w Bełżcu w 1942 r.', *BŻIH*, no. 151 (1989), pp. 101–118, here pp. 117–118.

Kuwałek, Robert, *Das Vernichtungslager Bełżec* (Berlin: Metropol, 2013).

Kuwałek, Robert, 'Die Durchgangsghettos im Distrikt Lublin (u. a. Izbica, Piaski, Rejowiec und Trawniki)', in Bogdan Musiał (ed.), *Die 'Aktion Reinhardt': Der Völkermord an den Juden im Generalgouvernement 1941–1944* (Osnabrück: fibre, 2004), pp. 197–232.

Kuwałek, Robert, 'Obóz zagłady w Sobiborze w historiografii polskiej i obcej', *Zeszyty Majdanka*, vol. 21 (2001), pp. 115–160.

Lehnstaedt, Stephan, 'Die deutsche Arbeitsverwaltung im Generalgouvernement und die Juden', *Vierteljahrshefte für Zeitgeschichte*, vol. 60 (2012), pp. 409–440.

Lenarczyk, Wojciech, and Dariusz Libionka, *Erntefest 3–4 listopada 1943: Zapomniany epizod Zagłady* (Lublin: Państwowe Muzeum na Majdanku, 2009).

Leydesdorff, Selma, *Sasha Pechersky: Holocaust Hero, Sobibor Resistance Leader, and Hostage of History* (New York: Routledge, 2017).

Libionka, Darius, 'Antisemitism, Anti-Judaism, and the Polish Catholic Clergy during the Second World War, 1939–1945', in Robert Blobaum (ed.), *Antisemitism and its Opponents in Modern Poland* (Ithaca, NY, and London: Cornell University Press, 2005), pp. 233–264.

Libionka, Dariusz, *Die Ermordung der Juden im Generalgouvernement*, trans. Steffen Hänschen (Berlin: Metropol, 2021 [Polish edn, 2017]).

Libionka, Dariusz, 'Głową w mur: Interwencje Kazimierza Papee, polskiego ambasadora przy Stolicy Apostolskiej, w sprawie zbrodni niemieckich w Polsce, listopad 1942 – styczeń 1943', *Zagłada Żydów*, vol. 2 (2006), pp. 307–308.

Libionka, Dariusz (ed.), *Obóz zagłady w Bełżcu w relacjach ocalonych i zeznaniach polskich świadków* (Lublin: Państwowe Muzeum na Majdanku, 2013).

Libionka, Dariusz, 'Polska ludność chrześcijańska wobec eksterminacji Żydów – dystrykt lubelski', in Dariusz Libionka (ed.), *Akcja Reinhardt: Zagłada Żydów w Generalnym Gubernatorstwie* (Warsaw: Instytut Pamięci Narodowej, 2004), pp. 306–333.

Libionka, Dariusz, 'ZWZ-AK i Delegatura Rządu RP wobec eksterminacji Żydów polskich', in Andrzej Żbikowski (ed.), *Polacy i Żydzi pod okupacją niemiecką 1939–1945: Studia i materiały* (Warsaw: Instytut Pamięci Narodowej, 2006), pp. 15–207.

Libionka, Dariusz, and Laurence Weinbaum, *Bohaterowie, hochsztaplerzy, opisywacze: Wokół Żydowskiego Związku Wojskowego* (Warsaw: Stowarzyszenie Centrum Badań nad Zagładą Żydów, 2011).

Libionka, Dariusz, and Laurence Weinbaum, 'Deconstructing Memory and History: The Jewish Military Union (ŻZW) and the Warsaw Ghetto Uprising', *Jewish Political Studies Review*, vol. 18, no. 1/2 (2006), pp. 86–194.

Lichtheim, Richard, *Die Geschichte des deutschen Zionismus* (Jerusalem: Rubin Mass, 1954).

Longerich, Peter, *Holocaust: The Nazi Persecution and Murder of the Jews*, trans. Shaun Whiteside (Oxford: Oxford University Press, 2010 [German edn, 1998]).

Longerich, Peter, *Wannsee: The Road to the Final Solution*, trans. Lesley Sharpe and Jeremy Noakes (Oxford: Oxford University Press, 2021 [German edn, 2016]).

Longerich, Peter, and Dieter Pohl (eds.), *Die Ermordung der europäischen Juden: Eine umfassende Dokumentation des Holocaust 1941–1945* (Munich: Piper, 1989).

Loose, Ingo, 'Die Bedeutung der Ghettoarbeit für die nationalsozialistische Kriegswirtschaft', in Jürgen Hensel and Stephan Lehnstaedt (eds.), *Arbeit in den nationalsozialistischen Ghettos* (Osnabrück: fibre, 2013), pp. 71–90.

Loose, Ingo, 'Eastern European Shoah Victims and the Problem of Group Identity', in Randall Hansen et al. (eds.), *Authenticity and Victimhood after the Second World War: Narratives from Europe and East Asia* (Toronto: University of Toronto Press, 2021), pp. 79–93.

Loose, Ingo, 'Joseph Bühler, State Secretary for the General Government: A Behind-the-Scenes Perpetrator', in Hans-Christian Jasch and Christoph Kreutzmüller (eds.), *The Participants: The Men of the Wannsee Conference*, trans. Charlotte Kreutzmüller-Hughes and Jane Paulick (New York and Oxford: Berghahn, 2017 [German edn, 2017]), pp. 152–170.

Löw, Andrea, and Markus Roth, *Juden in Krakau unter deutscher Besatzung 1939–1945* (Göttingen: Wallstein, 2011).

Madajczyk, Czesław, *Polityka III Rzeszy w okupowanej Polsce*, 2 vols. (Warsaw: Państwowe Wydawnictwo Naukowe, 1970).

Madajczyk, Czesław (ed.), *Zamojszczyzna – Sonderlaboratorium SS: Zbiór dokumentów polskich i niemieckich z okresu okupacji hitlerowskiej*, 2 vols. (Warsaw: Ludowa Spółdzielnia, 1977).

Magocsi, Paul (ed.), *Morality and Reality: The Life and Times of Andrei Sheptyts'kyi* (Edmonton: Canadian Institute of Ukrainian Studies, 1989).

Majewski, Tomasz, and Anna Zeidler-Janiszewska (eds.), *Pamięć Shoah: Kulturowe reprezentacje i praktyki upamiętnienia* (Łódź: Officyna, 2009).

Marczewska, Krystyna, and Władysław Ważniewski, 'Treblinka w świetle akt Delegatury Rządu RP na Kraj', *Biuletyn Głównej Komisji Badania Zbrodni Hitlerowskich w Polsce*, vol. 19 (1968), pp. 129–164.

Marczyk, Wiesław, *Jeńcy radzieccy w niewoli Wehrmachtu na ziemiach polskich w latach 1941–1945* (Opole: Centralne Muzeum Jeńców Wojennych w Łambinowicach-Opolu, 1987).

Markowska, Marta (ed.), *Archiwum Ringelbluma: Dzień po dniu Zagłady* (Warsaw: Karta, 2008).

Marrus, Michael R. (ed.), *The Nazi Holocaust*, part 8, *Bystanders to the Holocaust*, vol. 2 (Westport: Meckler, 1989).

Marszałek, Józef, *Obozy pracy w Generalnym Gubernatorstwie w latach 1939–1945* (Lublin: Państwowe Muzeum na Majdanku, 1998).

Maurer, Trude, *Ostjuden in Deutschland 1918–1933* (Hamburg: Christians, 1986).

Mędykowski, Witold Wojciech, *Macht Arbeit frei? German Economic Policy and Forced Labor of Jews in the General Government, 1939–1943* (Boston: Academic Studies Press, 2018), pp. 221–245.

Megargee, Geoffrey P. (ed.), *The United States Holocaust Memorial Encyclopedia of Camps and Ghettos, 1933–1945*, vol. 2: *Ghettos in German-Occupied Eastern Europe*, ed. Martin Dean (Bloomington, IN: Indiana University Press, 2012).

Melchior, Małgorzata, *Zagłada a tożsamość: Polscy Żydzi ocaleni 'na aryjskich papierach'. Analiza doświadczenia biograficznego* (Warsaw: Instytutu Filozofii i Socjologii PAN, 2004).

Mencel, Tadeusz (ed.), *Majdanek 1941–1944* (Lublin: Wydawnictwo Lubelskie, 1991).

Michman, Dan, *The Emergence of Jewish Ghettos during the Holocaust*, trans. from Hebrew Lenn J. Schramm (Cambridge: Cambridge University Press; Jerusalem: Yad Vashem, 2001).

Miron, Guy, and Shlomit Shulhani (eds.), *The Yad Vashem Encyclopedia of the Ghettos during the Holocaust* (Jerusalem: Yad Vashem, 2009).

Młynarczyk, Jacek Andrzej, '"Akcja Reinhard" w gettach prowincjonalnych dystryktu warszawskiego 1942–1943', in Barbara Engelking, Jacek Leociak, and Dariusz Libionka (eds.), *Prowincja noc: Życie i zagłada Żydów w dystrykcie warszawskim* (Warsaw: Wydawnictwo Instytutu Filozofii i Socjologii PAN, 2007), pp. 39–74.

Młynarczyk, Jacek Andrzej, *Judenmord in Zentralpolen: Der Distrikt Radom im Generalgouvernement 1939–1945* (Darmstadt: WBG, 2007).

Młynarczyk, Jacek Andrzej et al., 'Eastern Europe: Belarusian auxiliaries, Ukrainian Waffen-SS soldiers and the special case of the Polish "Blue Police"', in Jochen Böhler and Robert Gerwarth (eds.), *The Waffen-SS: A European History* (Oxford: Oxford University Press, 2017), pp. 169–179.

Morsch, Günter, and Bertrand Perz (eds.), *Neue Studien zu nationalsozialistischen Massentötungen durch Giftgas: Historische Bedeutung, technische Entwicklung, revisionistische Leugnung* (Berlin: Metropol, 2011).

Musiał, Bogdan, *Deutsche Zivilverwaltung und Judenverfolgung im Generalgouvernement: Eine Fallstudie zum Distrikt Lublin 1939–1944* (Wiesbaden: Harrassowitz, 1999).

Musiał, Bogdan, 'The Origins of "Operation Reinhard": The Decision-making Process for the Mass Murder of the Jews in the Generalgouvernement', trans. William Templer, *Yad Vashem Studies*, vol. 28 (2000), pp. 113–153.

Mychalejko, Andrij, *Metropolit Andrey Graf Sheptytskyi und das NS-Regime: Zwischen christlichem Ideal und politischer Realität* (Paderborn: Brill Schöningh, 2020).

Offer, Miriam, *White Coats in the Ghetto: Jewish Medicine in Poland during the Holocaust* (Jerusalem: Yad Vashem, 2020).

Pankiewicz, Tadeusz, *The Krakow Ghetto Pharmacy*, trans. Garry Malloy (Cracow: Wydawnictwo Literackie, 2013 [Polish edn, 1947]).

Pätzold, Kurt, and Erika Schwarz (eds.), *Tagesordnung, Judenmord: Die Wannsee-*

*Konferenz am 20. Januar 1942. Eine Dokumentation zur Organisation der 'Endlösung'* (Berlin: Metropol, 1992).

Paulsson, Gunnar, *Secret City: The Hidden Jews of Warsaw, 1940–1945* (New Haven, CT: Yale University Press, 2002).

Peled, Yael (Margolin), *Krakov ha-yehudit 1939–1943: Amidah, Mahteret, Ma'avak* (Tel Aviv: Hakibbutz Hame'uhad, 1993).

Person, Katarzyna, *Warsaw Ghetto Police: The Jewish Order Service during the Nazi Occupation*, trans. Zygmunt Nowak-Soliński (Ithaca, NY, and London: Cornell University Press, 2021 [Polish edn, 2018]).

Perz, Bertrand, 'The Austrian Connection: SS and Police Leader Globocnik and His Staff in the Lublin District', *Holocaust and Genocide Studies*, vol. 29, no. 3 (2015), pp. 400–430.

Piętrzykowski, Jan, *Stalag 367: Obóz jeńców radzieckich w Częstochowie* (Katowice: Śląsk, 1976).

Pilichowski, Czesław, 'Verbrauch von Nahrungsmitteln durch jüdische Bevölkerung und Häftlinge der Okkupationslager im besetzten Polen', *Studia Historiae Oeconomicae*, vol. 17 (1982), pp. 205–215.

Piotrowski, Stanisław, *Misja Odyla Globocnika: Sprawozdania o wynikach finansowych zagłady Żydów w Polsce* (Warsaw: Państwowy Instytut Wydawniczy, 1949).

Podolska, Aldona, *Służba porządkowa w getcie warszawskim w latach 1940–1943* (Warsaw: Fundacji 'Historia Pro Futuro', 1996).

Pohl, Dieter, 'Die "Aktion Reinhard" im Licht der Historiographie', in Bogdan Musiał (ed.), *Die 'Aktion Reinhardt': Der Völkermord an den Juden im Generalgouvernement 1941–1944* (Osnabrück: fibre, 2004), pp. 15–47.

Pohl, Dieter, 'Die Rolle des Distrikts Lublin im Völkermord an den Juden', in Bogdan Musiał (ed.), *Die 'Aktion Reinhardt': Der Völkermord an den Juden im Generalgouvernement 1941–1944* (Osnabrück: fibre, 2004), pp. 87–107.

Pohl, Dieter, 'Die Trawniki-Männer im Vernichtungslager Belzec', in Alfred Gottwaldt, Norbert Kampe, and Peter Klein (eds.), *NS-Gewaltherrschaft: Beiträge zur historischen Forschung und juristischen Aufarbeitung*, vol. 11 (Berlin: Edition Hentrich, 2005), pp. 278–289.

Pohl, Dieter, 'The Killing of the Jews in the General Government', in Ulrich Herbert (ed.), *National Socialist Extermination Policies: Contemporary German Perspectives and Controversies* (Oxford and New York: Berghahn, 2000), pp. 83–103.

Pohl, Dieter, *Nationalsozialistische Judenverfolgung in Ostgalizien 1941–1944: Organisation und Durchführung eines staatlichen Massenverbrechens* (Munich: Oldenbourg, 1996).

Pohl, Dieter, *Von der 'Judenpolitik' zum Judenmord: Der Distrikt Lublin des Generalgouvernements 1939–1944* (Frankfurt am Main: Peter Lang, 1993).

Poliakov, Léon, and Joseph Wulf, *Das Dritte Reich und die Juden* (Berlin: arani, 1955).

Polonsky, Antony, Hanna Węgrzynek, and Andrzej Żbikowski (eds.), *New Directions in the History of the Jews in the Polish Lands* (Boston: Academic Studies Press, 2018).

Poraj, Kazimiera, 'Dziennik Lwowski', *BŻIH*, no. 52 (1964), pp. 79–106.

Porat, Dina, 'The November 23, 1942, Communiqué by the Jewish Agency Executive: A Renewed Examination', in Dina Porat and Dan Michman (eds.), *The End of 1942: A Turning Point in WWII and in the Comprehension of the Final Solution?* (Jerusalem: Yad Vashem 2017), pp. 317–338.

Prais, Lea, *Displaced Persons at Home: Refugees in the Fabric of Jewish Life in Warsaw, September 1939 – July 1942*, trans. from Hebrew Naftali Greenwood (Jerusalem: Yad Vashem, 2015).

Prekerowa, Teresa, *Konspiracyjna Rada Pomocy Żydom w Warszawie 1942–1945* (Warsaw: Państwowy Instytut Wydawniczy, 1982).

Prekerowa, Teresa, 'Wojna i okupacja', in Jerzy Tomaszewski (ed.), *Najnowsze dzieje Żydów w Polsce w zarysie (do 1950 roku)* (Warsaw: Państwowy Instytut Wydawniczy, 1993), pp. 273–384.

Puławski, Adam, *W obliczu zagłady: Rząd RP na Uchodźstwie, Delegatura Rządu RP na*

*Kraj, ZWZ-AK wobec deportacji Żydow do obozów zagłady (1941–1942)* (Lublin: Instytut Pamięci Narodowej, 2009).

Puławski, Adam, *Wobec 'niespotykanego w dziejach mordu': Rząd RP na uchodźstwie, Delegatura Rządu RP na Kraj, AK a eksterminacja ludności żydowskiej od wielkiej akcji do powstania w getci warszawskim* (Chełm: Biblioteka Rocznika Chełmskiego, 2018).

Rączy, Elżbieta, and Igor Witowicz (eds.), *Zagłada Żydów na Rzeszowszczyźnie: Album pamięci / Extermination of Jews in the Rzeszów Region: Album of Remembrance*, bilingual Polish-English edn (Rzeszów and Warsaw: Instytut Pamięci Narodowej, 2004).

Radzik, Tadeusz, *Lubelska dzielnica zamknięta* (Lublin: Wydawnictwo Uniwersytetu Marii Curie-Skłodowskiej, 1999).

Rajca, Czesław, 'Lubelska filia Niemieckich Zakładów Zbrojeniowych', *Zeszyty Majdanka*, vol. 4 (1969), pp. 237–299.

Reder, Rudolf, *I Survived a Secret Nazi Extermination Camp*, ed. Mark Forstater, trans. from Polish Feliks Pastusiak (Hove: Psychology News Press, 2015).

Reder, Rudolf, 'Testimony of the Camp in Bełżec', in Rudolf Reder, *Bełżec*, trans. from Polish Michael Jacobs (Cracow: Fundacja Judaica, 1999 [1946]), pp. 115–143.

'Relacje dwóch zbiegów z Treblinki II', *BŻIH*, no. 40 (1961), pp. 78–88.

Ringelblum, Emanuel, *Polish-Jewish Relations during the Second World War*, ed. Joseph Kermish and Shmuel Krakowski, trans. Dafna Allon, Danuta Dabrowska, and Dana Keren (Jerusalem: Yad Vashem, 1992 [1974] [Polish edn, 1958–1959]).

Roland, Charles G., *Courage under Siege: Disease, Starvation and Death in the Warsaw Ghetto* (New York: Oxford University Press, 1992).

Roseman, Mark, *The Past in Hiding: Memory and Survival in Nazi Germany* (London: Penguin, 2000).

Roseman, Mark, *The Villa, the Lake, the Meeting: Wannsee and the Final Solution* (London: Penguin, 2002).

Roth, Markus, *Herrenmenschen: Die deutschen Kreishauptleute im besetzten Polen – Karrierewege, Herrschaftspraxis und Nachgeschichte* (Göttingen: Wallstein, 2009).

Roth, Markus, and Andrea Löw, *Das Warschauer Getto: Alltag und Widerstand im Angesicht der Vernichtung* (Munich: Beck, 2013).

Rothfels, Hans, 'Zur "Umsiedlung" der Juden im Generalgouvernement', *Vierteljahrshefte für Zeitgeschichte*, vol. 7, no. 3 (1959), pp. 333–336.

Rowiński, Aleksander, *Zygielbojms Reise: Eine Spurensuche*, trans. Agnieszka Karaś (Osnabrück: fibre, 2004 [Polish edn, 2000]).

Różycki, Sebastian, Marek Michalski, and Edward Kopówka, *Obóz pracy Treblinka I: Metodyka integracji danych wieloźródłowych* (Warsaw and Treblinka: Ministerstwo Kultury i Dziedzictwa Narodowego, 2017).

Rückerl, Adalbert (ed.), *NS-Vernichtungslager im Spiegel deutscher Strafprozesse: Belzec, Sobibor, Treblinka, Chelmno* (Munich: DTV, 1977).

Rutkowski, Adam, *Męczeństwo, walka, zagłada Żydów w Polsce 1939–1945* (Warsaw: Wydawnictwo Ministerstwa Obrony Narodowej, 1960).

Rutkowski, Adam, 'Ruch oporu w hitlerowskim obozie straceń Sobibór', *BŻIH*, nos. 65 and 66 (1968), pp. 3–49.

Sabrin, B. F. (ed.), *Alliance for Murder: The Nazi–Ukrainian Nationalist Partnership in Genocide* (New York: Sarpedon, in association with Shapolsky, 1991).

Sakowska, Ruta, *Die zweite Etappe ist der Tod: NS-Ausrottungspolitik gegen die polnischen Juden, gesehen mit den Augen der Opfer. Ein historischer Essay und ausgewählte Dokumente aus dem Ringelblum-Archiv 1941–1943* (Berlin: Edition Hentrich, 1993).

Sakowska, Ruta, *Menschen im Ghetto: Die jüdische Bevölkerung im besetzten Warschau 1939–1943* (Osnabrück: fibre, 1999).

Sandkühler, Thomas, *'Endlösung' in Galizien: Der Judenmord in Ostpolen und die Rettungsinitiativen von Berthold Beitz 1941–1944* (Bonn: Dietz, 1996).

Schäfer, Torsten, *'Jedenfalls habe ich auch mitgeschossen': Das NSG-Verfahren gegen Johann Josef Kuhr und andere ehemalige Angehörige des Polizeibataillons 306, der Polizeireiterabteilung 2 und der SD-Dienststelle von Pinsk beim Landgericht Frankfurt am Main 1962–1973. Eine textanalytische Fallstudie zur Mentalitätsgeschichte* (Münster: LIT, 2007).

Schelvis, Jules, *Sobibor: A History of a Nazi Death Camp*, trans. Karin Dixon (London: Bloomsbury, 2014 [Dutch edn, 1993]).

Schmidt, Annalena, '(Selbst-)Hilfe in Zeiten der Hilfslosigkeit? Die "Jüdische Soziale Selbsthilfe" und die "Jüdische Unterstützungsstelle" im Generalgouvernement, 1939–1944/45' (doctoral thesis, Justus-Liebig-Universität Gießen, 2015).

Schnepf-Kołacz, Zuzanna, 'Pomoc Polaków dla Żydów na wsi w czasie okupacji niemieckiej: Próba opisu na przykładzie Sprawiedliwych wśród Narodów Świata', in Barbara Engelking and Jan Grabowski (eds.), *Zarys krajobrazu: Wieś polska wobec zagłady Żydów 1942–1945* (Warsaw: Stowarzyszenie Centrum Badań nad Zagładą Żydów, 2011), pp. 195–258.

Schulte, Jan Erik, 'Initiative der Peripherie: Globocniks Siedlungsstützpunkte und die Entscheidung zum Bau des Vernichtungslagers Belzec', in Jan Erik Schulte (ed.), *Die SS, Himmler und die Wewelsburg* (Paderborn: Schöningh, 2009), pp. 118–137.

Schulte, Jans Erik, 'Zwangsarbeit für die SS: Juden in der Ostindustrie GmbH', in Norbert Frei et al. (eds.), *Ausbeutung, Vernichtung, Öffentlichkeit: Neue Studien zur nationalsozialistischen Lagerpolitik*, vol. 4: *Darstellungen und Quellen zur Geschichte von Auschwitz* (Munich: Saur, 2000), pp. 43–74.

Schulte, Jan-Erik, *Zwangsarbeit und Vernichtung: Das Wirtschaftsimperium der SS. Oswald Pohl und das SS-Wirtschafts-Verwaltungshauptamt 1933–1945* (Paderborn: Schöningh, 2001).

Schwindt, Barbara, *Das Konzentrations- und Vernichtungslager Majdanek: Funktionswandel im Kontext der 'Endlösung'* (Würzburg: Königshausen & Neumann, 2005).

Sereny, Gitta, *Into That Darkness: From Mercy Killing to Mass Murder* (London: Pimlico, 1995 [1974]).

Shapiro, Robert Moses, and Tadeusz Epsztein (eds.), *The Warsaw Ghetto: Oyneg Shabes-Ringelblum Archive. Catalog and Guide*, trans. Robert Moses Shapiro (Bloomington, IN: Indiana University Press, 2009).

Shneiderman, S. L., *Between Fear and Hope*, trans. Norbert Guterman (New York: Arco, 1947 [Yiddish edn, 1947]).

Silberklang, David, *Gates of Tears: The Holocaust in the Lublin District* (Jerusalem: Yad Vashem, 2013).

Skibińska, Alina, 'The Return of Jewish Holocaust Survivors and the Reaction of the Polish Population', in Feliks Tych and Monika Adamczyk-Garbowska (eds.), *Jewish Presence in Absence: The Aftermath of the Holocaust in Poland, 1944–2010*, trans. Grzegorz Dąbskowski and Jessica Taylor-Kucia (Jerusalem: Yad Vashem, 2014 [Polish edn, 2011]), pp. 25–66.

Skibińska, Alina, 'Życie codzienne Żydów v Kozienicach pod okupacją niemiecką', *Zagłada Żydów*, vol. 3 (2007), pp. 64–85.

Skibińska, Alina, and Jakub Petelewicz, 'The Participation of Poles in Crimes against Jews', *Yad Vashem Studies*, vol. 35, no. 1 (2007), pp. 5–48.

Stola, Dariusz, *Nadzieja i zagłada: Ignacy Schwarzbart. Żydowski przedstawiciel w Radzie Narodowej RP, 1940–1945* (Warsaw: Oficyna Naukowa, 1995).

Sturdy Colls, Caroline, *Holocaust Archaeologies: Approaches and Future Directions* (Heidelberg: Springer, 2015).

Syrnyk, Jarosław, 'Historia Jozefa Balickiego', in Aleksandra Namysło (ed.), *'Kto w takich czasach Żydów przechowuje?' Polacy niosący pomoc ludności żydowskiej w okresie okupacji niemieckiej* (Warsaw: Instytut Pamięci Narodowej, 2009), pp. 145–156.

Szapiro, Pawel (ed.), *Wojna żydowsko-niemiecka: Polska prasa konspiracyjna 1943–1944 o powstaniu w getcie Warszawy* (London: Aneks, 1992).

Szpytma, Mateusz, *The Risk of Survival: The Rescue of the Jews by the Poles and the Tragic Consequences for the Ulma Family from Markowa*, trans. from Polish Aleksandra Rodzińska-Chojnowska (Warsaw: Instytut Pamięci Narodowej – Komisja Ścigania Zbrodni przeciwko Narodowi Polskiemu, 2009).

Taffet, Gerszon, *The Holocaust of the Jews of Zolkiew*, trans. Piotr J. Drozdowski (Łódź: Centralnej Żydowskiej Komisji Historycznej, 1996 [Polish edn, 1946]).

Tec, Nechama, *When Light Pierced the Darkness: Christian Rescue of Jews in Nazi-occupied Poland* (New York: Oxford University Press, 1986).

Trunk, Isaiah, *Judenrat: The Jewish Councils in Eastern Europe under Nazi Occupation* (Lincoln, NE: University of Nebraska Press, 1996 [1972]).

Tych, Feliks, 'Polish Society's Attitudes towards the Holocaust', in Beate Kosmala and Feliks Tych (eds.), *Facing the Nazi Genocide: Non-Jews and Jews in Europe* (Berlin: Metropol, 2004), pp. 87–105.

Tych, Feliks, 'Witnessing the Holocaust: Polish Diaries, Memoirs and Reminiscences', in David Bankier and Israel Gutman (eds.), *Nazi Europe and the Final Solution* (Jerusalem: Yad Vashem, 2003), pp. 175–198.

Tych, Feliks, and Monika Adamczyk-Garbowska (eds.), *Jewish Presence in Absence: The Aftermath of the Holocaust in Poland, 1944–2010*, trans. Grzegorz Dąbskowski and Jessica Taylor-Kucia (Jerusalem: Yad Vashem, 2014 [Polish edn, 2011]).

Urbański, Krzysztof, *Zagłada Żydów w dystrykcie radomskim* (Cracow: Wydawnictwo Naukowe Akademii Pedagogicznej, 2004).

Urynowicz, Marcin, *Adam Czerniaków 1880–1942: Prezes getta Warszawskiego* (Warsaw: Instytut Pamięci Narodowej, 2009).

Urynowicz, Marcin, *Epilogue: Refractions of Jewish Self-Government under German Occupation in the Second World War*, in François Guesnet and Jerzy Tomaszewski (eds.), *Sources on Jewish Self-Government in the Polish Lands from Its Inception to the Present* (Leiden: Brill, 2021), pp. 627–680.

Urynowicz, Marcin, 'Stosunki polsko-żydowskie w Warszawie w okresie okupacji hitlerowskiej', in Andrzej Żbikowski (ed.), *Polacy i Żydzi pod okupacją niemiecką 1939–1945: Studia i materiały* (Warsaw: Instytut Pamięci Narodowej, 2006), pp. 537–626.

Vilenskiy, Semen S., Grigoriy B. Gorbovitskiy, and Leonid A. Terushkin, *Sobibor: Vosstaniye v lagere smerti. Sostaviteli* (Moscow: Vozvrashcheniye, 2008).

Wachsmann, Nikolaus, *KL: A History of the Nazi Concentration Camps* (New York: Farrar, Straus & Giroux, 2016).

Webb, Chris, *The Belzec Death Camp: History, Biographies, Remembrance* (Stuttgart: ibidem, 2016).

Webb, Chris, and Michal Chocholatý, *The Treblinka Death Camp: History, Biographies, Remembrance* (Stuttgart: ibidem, 2014).

Weiss, Aharon, 'Jewish Leadership in Occupied Poland – Postures and Attitudes', *Yad Vashem Studies*, vol. 12 (1977), pp. 335–365.

Wenzel, Mario, *Arbeitszwang und Judenmord: Die Arbeitslager für Juden im Distrikt Krakau des Generalgouvernements 1939–1944* (Berlin: Metropol, 2017).

Wenzel, Mario, 'Zwangsarbeitslager für Juden in den besetzten polnischen und sowjetischen Gebieten', in Wolfgang Benz and Barbara Distel (eds.), *Der Ort des Terrors*, vol. 9: *Arbeitserziehungslager, Ghettos, Jugendschutzlager, Polizeihaftlager, Sonderlager, Zigeunerlager, Zwangsarbeiterlager* (Munich: Beck, 2009), pp. 125–154.

Wetzel, Juliane, and Wolfgang Benz (eds.), *Solidarität und Hilfe für Juden während der NS-Zeit: Regionalstudien 1. Polen, Rumänien, Griechenland, Luxemburg, Norwegen, Schweiz* (Berlin: Metropol, 1996).

Winstone, Martin, *The Dark Heart of Hitler's Europe: Nazi Rule in Poland under the General Government* (London and New York: I. B. Tauris, 2015).

Witte, Peter, and Stephen Tyas, 'A New Document on the Deportation and Murder of Jews during "Einsatz Reinhardt" 1942', *Holocaust and Genocide Studies*, vol. 15, no. 3 (2001), pp. 468–486.

Wolny, Jerzy, 'Biogram Kardynała Adama Stefana Sapiehy', in Roman Bogacz (ed.), *Książę Niezłomny: Kardynał Adam Stefan Sapieha* (Cracow: UNUM, 2001), pp. 7–72.

Wóycicka, Zofia, *Arrested Mourning: Memory of the Nazi Camps in Poland, 1944–1950*, trans. Jasper Tilbury (Frankfurt am Main: Peter Lang, 2013 [Polish edn, 2009]).

Wroński, Stanisław, and Maria Zwolakowa (eds.), *Polacy-Żydzi 1939–1945* (Warsaw: Książkę i Wiedza, 1971).

Wyleżyńska, Aurelia, 'Z notatek pamiętnikarskich (1942–1943)', *BŻIH*, nos. 45 and 46 (1963), pp. 212–231.

Yones, Eliyahu, *Die Straße nach Lemberg: Zwangsarbeit und Widerstand in Ostgalizien 1941–1944*, ed. Susanne Heim (Frankfurt am Main: Fischer, 1999 [Hebrew edn, 1960]).

Yones, Eliyahu, *Smoke in the Sand: The Jews of Lvov in the War Years, 1939–1944* (Jerusalem and New York: Gefen, 2004).

Ząbecki, Franciszek, *Wspomnienia dawne i nowe* (Warsaw: Instytut Pax, 1977).

Zawadzka, Halina, *Ucieczka z getta* (Warszawa: Karta, 2001).

Żbikowski, Andrzej (ed.), *Friedrich Katzmann: Rozwiązanie kwestii żydowskiej w dystrykcie Galicja* (Warsaw: Instytut Pamięci Narodowej, 2001).

Żbikowski, Andrzej (ed.), *Polacy i Żydzi pod okupacją niemiecką 1939–1945: Studia i materiały* (Warsaw: Instytut Pamięci Narodowej, 2006).

Zimmerer, Katarzyna, *Zamordowany świat: Losy Żydów w Krakowie 1939–1945* (Cracow: Wydawnictwo Literackie, 2004).

Zimmerman, Joshua D., *The Polish Underground and the Jews, 1939–1945* (Cambridge: Cambridge University Press, 2015).

Zisenwine, Joel, 'The Intelligence Community and the Holocaust: Was December 1942 a Turning Point?', in Dina Porat and Dan Michman (eds.), *The End of 1942: A Turning Point in World War II and in the Comprehension of the Final Solution?* (Jerusalem: Yad Vashem, 2017).

Zuckerman, Yitzhak, *A Surplus of Memory: Chronicle of the Warsaw Ghetto Uprising*, ed. and trans. Barbara Harshav (Berkeley: University of California Press, 1993 [Hebrew edn, 1990]).

Zyśko, Wojciech (ed.), 'Eksterminacyjna działalność Truppenpolizei w dystrykcie lubelskim w latach 1943–1944: Wybór źródeł', *Zeszyty Majdanka*, vol. 6 (1972), pp. 155–210.

# Index

Newspapers and periodicals are included in the index only if the text contains information about them (e.g. publication period, editors), and not if they are merely mentioned or cited as a source.

T



U

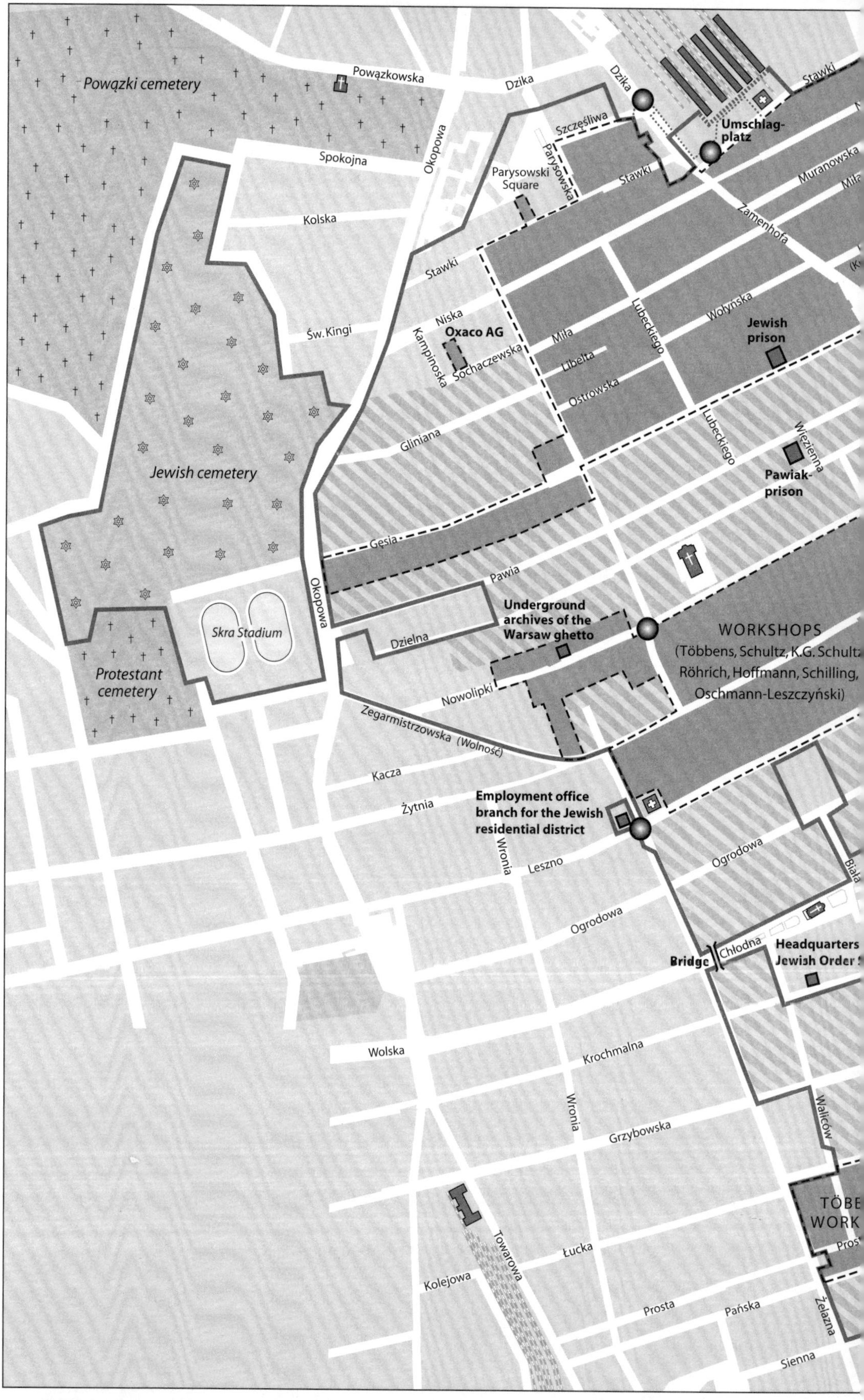

Powązki cemetery
Powązkowska
Dzika
Dzika
Stawki
Umschlag-
platz
Szczęśliwa
Parysowska
Parysowski
Square
Okopowa
Spokojna
Kolska
Stawki
Stawki
Muranowska
Zamenhofa
Jewish cemetery
Św. Kingi
Niska
Kampinoska
Oxaco AG
Sochaczewska
Miła
Libelta
Ostrowska
Lubeckiego
Wołyńska
Jewish
prison
Gliniana
Lubeckiego
Więzienna
Pawiak-
prison
Gęsia
Pawia
Okopowa
Skra Stadium
Protestant
cemetery
Underground
archives of the
Warsaw ghetto
Dzielna
WORKSHOPS
(Többens, Schultz, K.G. Schultz
Röhrich, Hoffmann, Schilling,
Oschmann-Leszczyński)
Nowolipki
Zegarmistrzowska (Wolność)
Kacza
Żytnia
Employment office
branch for the Jewish
residential district
Wronia
Leszno
Ogrodowa
Ogrodowa
Biała
Chłodna
Bridge
Headquarters
Jewish Order
Wolska
Krochmalna
Wronia
Grzybowska
Walicków
Towarowa
Łucka
Kolejowa
Prosta
Pańska
Żelazna
Sienna